Thailand's Islands & Beaches

Joe Cummings

LONELY PLANET PUBLICATIONS
Melbourne • Oakland • London • Paris

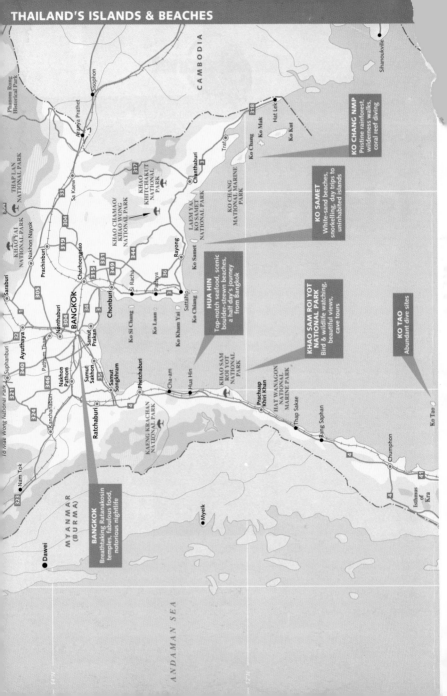

THAILAND'S ISLANDS & BEACHES

KO CHANG NMP
Pristine rainforest, wilderness walks, coral reef diving

KO SAMET
White-sand beaches, snorkelling, day trips to uninhabited islands

HUA HIN
Top-notch seafood, scenic boulder-strewn beaches, a half day's journey from Bangkok

KHAO SAM ROI YOT NATIONAL PARK
Bird & wildlife watching, beautiful views, cave tours

KO TAO
Abundant dive sites

BANGKOK
Breathtaking Ratanakosin temples, fabulous food, notorious nightlife

CAMBODIA

MYANMAR (BURMA)

ANDAMAN SEA

BANGKOK

To Wae Wong National Park

KHAO YAI NATIONAL PARK

KHAO CHAMAO/ KHAO WONG NATIONAL PARK

KHAO KHITCHAKUT NATIONAL PARK

THAP LAN NATIONAL PARK

LAEM YA/ KO SAMET NATIONAL PARK

KO CHANG NATIONAL MARINE PARK

KHAO SAM ROI YOT NATIONAL PARK

HAT WANAGON NATIONAL MARINE PARK

KAENG KRACHAN NATIONAL PARK

Phanom Rung Historical Park

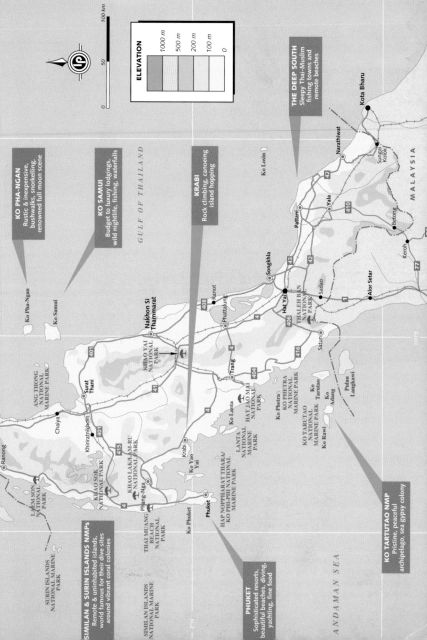

THAILAND'S ISLANDS & BEACHES

ELEVATION
- 1000 m
- 500 m
- 200 m
- 100 m
- 0

0   50   100 km

THE DEEP SOUTH
Sleepy Thai-Muslim fishing towns and remote beaches

KO PHA-NGAN
Rustic & inexpensive, bushwalks, snorkelling, renowned full moon scene

KO SAMUI
Budget to luxury lodgings, wild nightlife, fishing, waterfalls

KRABI
Rock climbing, canoeing, island hopping

SIMILAN & SURIN ISLANDS NMPs
Remote & uninhabited islands, world famous for their dive sites around vibrant coral colonies

PHUKET
Sophisticated resorts, beautiful beaches, diving, yachting, fine food

KO TARTUTAO NMP
Pristine, peaceful archipelago, sea gypsy colony

GULF OF THAILAND

ANDAMAN SEA

MALAYSIA

Kota Bharu, Narathiwat, Sungai Kolok, Yala, Betong, Keroh, Pattani, Alor Setar, Sadao, Hat Yai, Songkhla, Pulau Langkawi, Satun, Ko Adang, Ko Rawi, Ko Tarutao, Trang, Ko Lanta, Ko Phetra, Krabi, Ko Yao Yai, Phang-Nga, Phuket, Ko Phuket, Khao Lak, Khiri Ratnikhom, Surat Thani, Chaiya, Ranong, Nakhon Si Thammarat, Phattalung, Ranot, Ko Losin, Ko Samui, Ko Pha-Ngan

Thailand's Islands & Beaches
2nd edition – February 2000
First published – January 1998

Published by
Lonely Planet Publications Pty Ltd A.C.N. 005 607 983
192 Burwood Rd, Hawthorn, Victoria 3122, Australia

Lonely Planet Offices
Australia PO Box 617, Hawthorn, Victoria 3122
USA 150 Linden St, Oakland, CA 94607
UK 10a Spring Place, London NW5 3BH
France 1 rue du Dahomey, 75011 Paris

Photographs
Many of the images in this guide are available for licensing from
Lonely Planet Images.
email: lpi@lonelyplanet.com.au

Front cover photograph
Ko Chang (Sara-Jane Cleland)

ISBN 0 86442 728 X

Contents – Text

Contents – Maps

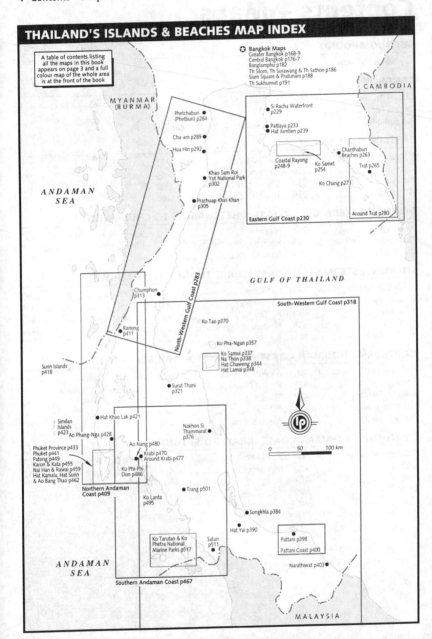

THAILAND'S ISLANDS & BEACHES MAP INDEX

A table of contents listing all the maps in this book appears on page 3 and a full colour map of the whole area is at the front of the book

Bangkok Maps
Greater Bangkok p168-9
Central Bangkok p176-7
Banglamphu p182
Th Silom, Th Surawang & Th Sathon p186
Siam Square & Pratunam p188
Th Sukhumvit p191

MYANMAR (BURMA)

CAMBODIA

Phetchaburi (Phetburi) p284

Cha-am p289

Hua Hin p292

Khao Sam Roi Yot National Park p302

Prachuap Khiri Khan p305

Si Racha Waterfront p229

Pattaya p233
Hat Jomtien p239

Coastal Rayong p248-9

Ko Samet p254

Chanthaburi Beaches p263

Trat p265

Ko Chang p273

Around Trat p280

Eastern Gulf Coast p230

ANDAMAN SEA

GULF OF THAILAND

Chumphon p313

Ranong p411

North-Western Gulf Coast p283

Ko Tao p370

South-Western Gulf Coast p318

Ko Pha-Ngan p357

Ko Samui p337
Na Thon p338
Hat Chaweng p344
Hat Lamai p348

Surin Islands p418

Surat Thani p321

Nakhon Si Thammarat p376

Similan Islands p423

Hat Khao Lak p421

Ao Phang-Nga p428

Ao Nang p480

Krabi p470
Around Krabi p477

Phuket Province p433
Phuket p441
Patong p449
Karon & Kata p455
Nai Han & Rawai p459
Hat Kamala, Hat Surin & Ao Bang Thao p462

Ko Phi-Phi Don p486

Northern Andaman Coast p409

Ko Lanta p495

Trang p501

Songkhla p384

Hat Yai p390

Pattani p398
Pattani Coast p400

Ko Tarutao & Ko Phetra National Marine Parks p517

Satun p511

Narathiwat p403

ANDAMAN SEA

Southern Andaman Coast p467

MALAYSIA

0   50   100 km

The Authors

Joe Cummings

Joe began travelling in South-East Asia shortly after finishing university. Before writing became a full-time job, he was a Peace Corps volunteer in Thailand, a movie extra in *The Deer Hunter*, a graduate student of Thai language and Asian art history at the University of California in Berkeley, an East-West Center scholar in Hawaii, a university lecturer in Malaysia and a Lao bilingual studies consultant in the USA.

For Lonely Planet and other publishers he has written over 30 original guidebooks, photographic books, phrasebooks and atlases for countries in Asia and North America. For Lonely Planet he has authored the *Thai* and *Lao* phrasebooks as well as guides to *Thailand*, *Laos* and *Myanmar (Burma)*, plus *World Food Thailand*, part of Lonely Planet's new culinary guide series. Joe has also published articles on culture, politics and travel in many print and online periodicals, including *Ambassador*, *Asia Magazine*, *Asian Wall Street Journal*, *Bangkok Post*, *Expedia*, *Fables*, *Geographical*, *Mexico Connect*, *The Nation*, *Outside*, *San Francisco Examiner* and *South China Morning Post*.

Joe has been covering South-East Asia for over 20 years and is fluent in Thai and Lao. He has twice been a finalist for London's Thomas Cook Guidebook of the Year Award for Lonely Planet's *Thailand* (1984) and *Vietnam, Laos & Cambodia* (1991). In 1995 he earned the Lowell Thomas Travel Journalism Gold Award for Lonely Planet's *Thailand*, an honour he also shared as a contributor and anonymous editor for *Travelers Tales Thailand* in 1993.

Nicko Goncharoff

Escaping from New York at age 17, Nicko headed for the mountains (and university) in Colorado. After graduating he moved to Taiwan for a brief stint that ended up lasting eight years, including four years covering financial news in Hong Kong. In 1995 Nicko joined Lonely Planet to work on the 5th edition of *China*. He has since contributed to four other guides in Asia and the USA, including the 1st edition of *Thailand's Islands & Beaches*.

FROM JOE CUMMINGS

Thanks to the following people in Thailand who assisted along the way: André Barguirdjian and Mau Travel Service, Jennifer Bartlett, the Chandler girls – Nancy, Nima and Siri, Kaneungnit Chotikakul, Ian Crawshaw, Lynne Cummings, John Demodena, Oliver Hargreave, Steve Martin, Richard Sandler and Tara Sauvage.

The Tourism Authority of Thailand (TAT) and its employees throughout Thailand, as usual, were of considerable assistance.

5

This Book

The 1st edition of *Thailand's Islands & Beaches* was researched and written by Joe Cummings and Nicko Goncharoff. This 2nd edition has been researched and updated by Joe Cummings.

FROM THE PUBLISHER

This edition of *Thailand's Islands & Beaches* was edited in Lonely Planet's Melbourne office by Tony Davidson and proofed by Sarah Mathers. Jakov Gavran coordinated the mapping, design and layout. Illustrations were provided by Simon Borg, Jenny Bowman, Martin Harris, Simon de la Loubère, Kate Nolan and Mick Weldon. Quentin Frayne compiled the Language chapter and Lindsay Brown wrote the Marine Environment special section. Guillaume Roux designed the cover. Images were supplied by Lonely Planet Images. Thanks to Richard Gregg, world cyclist extraordinaire, for providing information about cycling in southern Thailand.

ACKNOWLEDGMENTS

Many thanks to the travellers who used the last edition and wrote to us with helpful hints, useful advice and interesting anecdotes:

Martin Ade-Hall, Ingrid Berg, G Boer, Donna Clarke, Jayne Coombes, Robin Crompton, James Dillon, Jed Doherty, Patrick Dumon, Tracy Elofson, Tor Evensen, Patrick Fuller, Scott Goebl, Lorne Goldman, Ole Gadegaard, Laura Grace, David Keeble, Tom Lally, Edward Nicholson, John Ogilvie, Simon Palmer, Malinda Quartel, Bob Radke, Carmen Riley, Will Robert, G Saunders, Claire Swallow, Anna Tryc, Kevin Withers, Michael Wuest, Richard Yorke.

Foreword

ABOUT LONELY PLANET GUIDEBOOKS

The story begins with a classic travel adventure: Tony and Maureen Wheeler's 1972 journey across Europe and Asia to Australia. Useful information about the overland trail did not exist at that time, so Tony and Maureen published the first Lonely Planet guidebook to meet a growing need.

From a kitchen table, then from a tiny office in Melbourne (Australia), Lonely Planet has become the largest independent travel publisher in the world, an international company with offices in Melbourne, Oakland (USA), London (UK) and Paris (France).

Today Lonely Planet guidebooks cover the globe. There is an ever-growing list of books and there's information in a variety of forms and media. Some things haven't changed. The main aim is still to help make it possible for adventurous travellers to get out there – to explore and better understand the world.

At Lonely Planet we believe travellers can make a positive contribution to the countries they visit – if they respect their host communities and spend their money wisely. Since 1986 a percentage of the income from each book has been donated to aid projects and human rights campaigns.

Updates Lonely Planet thoroughly updates each guidebook as often as possible. This usually means there are around two years between editions, although for more unusual or more stable destinations the gap can be longer. Check the imprint page (following the colour map at the beginning of the book) for publication dates.

Between editions up-to-date information is available in two free newsletters – the paper *Planet Talk* and email *Comet* (to subscribe, contact any Lonely Planet office) – and on our Web site at www.lonelyplanet.com. The *Upgrades* section of the Web site covers a number of important and volatile destinations and is regularly updated by Lonely Planet authors. *Scoop* covers news and current affairs relevant to travellers. And, lastly, the *Thorn Tree* bulletin board and *Postcards* section of the site carry unverified, but fascinating, reports from travellers.

Correspondence The process of creating new editions begins with the letters, postcards and emails received from travellers. This correspondence often includes suggestions, criticisms and comments about the current editions. Interesting excerpts are immediately passed on via newsletters and the Web site, and everything goes to our authors to be verified when they're researching on the road. We're keen to get more feedback from organisations or individuals who represent communities visited by travellers.

Lonely Planet gathers information for everyone who's curious about the planet – and especially for those who explore it first-hand. Through guidebooks, phrasebooks, activity guides, maps, literature, newsletters, image library, TV series and Web site we act as an information exchange for a worldwide community of travellers.

Research Authors aim to gather sufficient practical information to enable travellers to make informed choices and to make the mechanics of a journey run smoothly. They also research historical and cultural background to help enrich the travel experience and allow travellers to understand and respond appropriately to cultural and environmental issues.

Authors don't stay in every hotel because that would mean spending a couple of months in each medium-sized city and, no, they don't eat at every restaurant because that would mean stretching belts beyond capacity. They do visit hotels and restaurants to check standards and prices, but feedback based on readers' direct experiences can be very helpful.

Many of our authors work undercover, others aren't so secretive. None of them accept freebies in exchange for positive write-ups. And none of our guidebooks contain any advertising.

Production Authors submit their raw manuscripts and maps to offices in Australia, USA, UK or France. Editors and cartographers – all experienced travellers themselves – then begin the process of assembling the pieces. When the book finally hits the shops, some things are already out of date, we start getting feedback from readers and the process begins again ...

WARNING & REQUEST

Things change – prices go up, schedules change, good places go bad and bad places go bankrupt – nothing stays the same. So, if you find things better or worse, recently opened or long since closed, please tell us and help make the next edition even more accurate and useful. We genuinely value all the feedback we receive. Julie Young coordinates a well travelled team that reads and acknowledges every letter, postcard and email and ensures that every morsel of information finds its way to the appropriate authors, editors and cartographers for verification.

Everyone who writes to us will find their name in the next edition of the appropriate guidebook. They will also receive the latest issue of *Planet Talk*, our quarterly printed newsletter, or *Comet*, our monthly email newsletter. Subscriptions to both newsletters are free. The very best contributions will be rewarded with a free guidebook.

Excerpts from your correspondence may appear in new editions of Lonely Planet guidebooks, the Lonely Planet Web site, *Planet Talk* or *Comet*, so please let us know if you *don't* want your letter published or your name acknowledged.

Send all correspondence to the Lonely Planet office closest to you:

Australia: PO Box 617, Hawthorn, Victoria 3122
USA: 150 Linden St, Oakland, CA 94607
UK: 10A Spring Place, London NW5 3BH
France: 1 rue du Dahomey, 75011 Paris

Or email us at: talk2us@lonelyplanet.com.au

For news, views and updates see our Web site: www.lonelyplanet.com

HOW TO USE A LONELY PLANET GUIDEBOOK

The best way to use a Lonely Planet guidebook is any way you choose. At Lonely Planet we believe the most memorable travel experiences are often those that are unexpected, and the finest discoveries are those you make yourself. Guidebooks are not intended to be used as if they provide a detailed set of infallible instructions!

Contents All Lonely Planet guidebooks follow roughly the same format. The Facts about the Destination chapters or sections give background information ranging from history to weather. Facts for the Visitor gives practical information on issues like visas and health. Getting There & Away gives a brief starting point for researching travel to and from the destination. Getting Around gives an overview of the transport options when you arrive.

The peculiar demands of each destination determine how subsequent chapters are broken up, but some things remain constant. We always start with background, then proceed to sights, places to stay, places to eat, entertainment, getting there and away, and getting around information – in that order.

Heading Hierarchy Lonely Planet headings are used in a strict hierarchical structure that can be visualised as a set of Russian dolls. Each heading (and its following text) is encompassed by any preceding heading that is higher on the hierarchical ladder.

Entry Points We do not assume guidebooks will be read from beginning to end, but that people will dip into them. The traditional entry points are the list of contents and the index. In addition, however, some books have a complete list of maps and an index map illustrating map coverage.

There may also be a colour map that shows highlights. These highlights are dealt with in greater detail in the Facts for the Visitor chapter, along with planning questions and suggested itineraries. Each chapter covering a geographical region usually begins with a locator map and another list of highlights. Once you find something of interest in a list of highlights, turn to the index.

Maps Maps play a crucial role in Lonely Planet guidebooks and include a huge amount of information. A legend is printed on the back page. We seek to have complete consistency between maps and text, and to have every important place in the text captured on a map. Map key numbers usually start in the top left corner.

Although inclusion in a guidebook usually implies a recommendation we cannot list every good place. Exclusion does not necessarily imply criticism. In fact there are a number of reasons why we might exclude a place – sometimes it is simply inappropriate to encourage an influx of travellers.

Introduction

Once known only to a trickle of backpacking hedonists plying the beach circuit between Crete and Bali, the beauty and bargains of Thailand's seaside resorts are now enjoyed by visitors of every ilk. In terms of variety and sheer attractiveness, and in many cases, cost, Thailand's islands and beaches more than hold their own against sun-and-sand offerings anywhere in the world.

Tropical Thailand offers the gentlest introduction to the Orient, combining images of the exotic – sparkling temple spires, sarong-clad farmers bending over rice shoots – with high standards of hygiene (including the best medical facilities in mainland South-East Asia) and most of the comforts of home. The country's 2710km dual coastline, rimming the Andaman Sea and Gulf of Thailand, includes many of Asia's finest stretches of sand and marine recreation spots. The friendly and relaxed nature of the Thai people is also infectious: it doesn't take long for most visitors to slow their pace and move to the calmer rhythms of tropical Thai life.

Only a relatively small portion of coastline has been seriously developed for tourism. Travellers to these areas can choose from a variety of environments, from very casual palm-thatch and bamboo beach huts to luxurious Mediterranean-style idylls perched on sea cliffs. Seafood feasts, prepared as only the Thais know how, form a major part of coastal Thai culture and are available for every budget. Away from the tourist resorts and beach huts, a lesser known world of sand, rock, palm and salt water awaits discovery. Among the country's

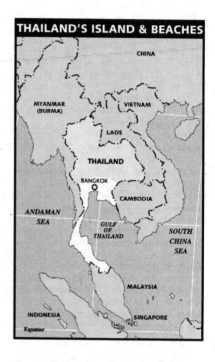

innumerable oceanic islands are many that few foreigners have yet stepped upon. Other beaches and islands – including several marine areas that enjoy national park status – receive only the occasional beachcomber, scuba diver, rock-climber or kayaker. Whatever your style, whatever type of marine experience you may enjoy, Thailand's islands and beaches should fit the bill.

Facts about Thailand

HISTORY
Prehistory

The Mekong River Valley and Khorat Plateau areas of what today encompasses much of Thailand were inhabited as far back as 10,000 years ago. Modern linguistic theory and recent archaeological finds in Thailand show a culture that was among the world's earliest agrarian societies.

The ancestors of today's Thais were scattered amid a vast, non-unified zone of Austro-Thai influence that involved periodic migrations along several geographic lines. The early Thais proliferated over all South-East Asia, including the islands of Indonesia, and some later settled in south and south-west China, later to 're-migrate' to northern Thailand to establish the first Thai kingdom in the 13th century.

Early Kingdoms

With no surviving written records or chronologies, it is difficult to say with certainty what kind of cultures lived in Thailand before the middle of the first millennium AD. However, by the 6th century an important network of agricultural communities was thriving as far south as modern-day Pattani and Yala, and as far north and north-east as Lamphun and Muang Fa Daet (near Khon Kaen).

Khmer conquests of the 7th to 11th centuries brought their cultural influence in the form of art, language and religion. A number of Thais became mercenaries for the Khmer armies in the early 12th century, as depicted on the walls of Angkor Wat. The Khmer called the Thais 'Syam', possibly from the Sanskrit *shyama* meaning 'golden' or 'swarthy', because of their relatively deeper skin colour at the time. Another theory claims the word means 'free'. Whatever the meaning, this was how the Thai kingdom came to be called Sayam or Syam. In north-western Thailand and Myanmar (Burma) the pronunciation of Syam became 'Shan'. English trader James Lancaster penned the first known English transliteration of the name as 'Siam' in 1592.

Meanwhile southern Thailand – the upper Malay peninsula – was under the control of the Srivijaya empire, the headquarters of

A view of 19th century Bangkok

which may have been in Palembang, Sumatra, between the 8th and 13th centuries. The regional centre for Srivijaya was Chaiya, near the modern town of Surat Thani. Srivijaya art remains can still be seen in Chaiya and its environs.

Several Thai principalities in the Mekong Valley united in the 13th and 14th centuries, when Thai princes wrested the lower north from the Khmer – whose Angkor government was fast declining – and created Sukhothai or 'Rising of Happiness'. They later took Hariphunchai from the Mon to form Lan Na Thai (literally, 'million Thai rice fields').

The Sukhothai kingdom declared its independence in 1238 under King Si Intharathit and quickly expanded its sphere of influence, taking advantage not only of the declining Khmer power but the weakening Srivijaya domain in the south. Thais consider Sukhothai the first true Thai kingdom. Although it was annexed by Ayuthaya in 1376, a national identity of sorts had already been forged. Many Thais today view the Sukhothai period sentimentally, seeing it as a golden age of politics, religion and culture – an egalitarian, noble period when everyone had enough to eat and the kingdom was unconquerable.

Among other accomplishments, the third Sukhothai king, Ram Khamhaeng, sponsored a fledgling Thai writing system that became the basis for modern Thai; he also codified the Thai form of Theravada Buddhism, as borrowed from the Sinhalese. Under Ram Khamhaeng, the Sukhothai kingdom extended as far as Nakhon Si Thammarat in the south, to the upper Mekong River Valley in Laos and to Bago (Pegu) in southern Myanmar. For a short time (1448-86), the Sukhothai capital was moved to Phitsanulok.

The Thai kings of Ayuthaya grew very powerful in the 14th and 15th centuries, taking over U Thong and Lopburi, former Khmer strongholds, and moving east until Angkor was defeated in 1431. Even though the Khmer were their adversaries in battle, the Ayuthaya kings incorporated large portions of Khmer court customs and language.

Ayuthaya was one of the greatest and wealthiest cities in Asia, a thriving seaport envied not only by the Burmese but by the Europeans who were in great awe of the city. It has been said that London, at the time, was a mere village in comparison. The kingdom sustained an unbroken monarchical succession through 34 reigns, from King U Thong (1350-69) to King Ekathat (1758-67), over a period of 400 years.

By the early 16th century Ayuthaya was receiving European visitors, and a Portuguese embassy was established in 1511. The Portuguese were followed by the Dutch in 1605, the English in 1612, the Danes in 1621 and the French in 1662. In the mid-16th century Ayuthaya and the independent kingdom of Lanna came under the control of the Burmese, but the Thais regained rule of both by the end of the century. In 1690 Londoner Engelbert Campfer proclaimed, 'Among the Asian nations, the Kingdom of Siam is the greatest. The magnificence of the Ayuthaya Court is incomparable'.

The Burmese again invaded Ayuthaya in 1765 and the capital fell after two years of fierce battle. This time the Burmese destroyed everything sacred to the Thais, including manuscripts, temples and religious sculpture. The Burmese, despite their effectiveness in sacking Ayuthaya, could not maintain a foothold in the kingdom, and Phaya Taksin, a half-Chinese, half-Thai general, made himself king in 1769. He ruled from the new capital of Thonburi on the banks of the Chao Phraya River, opposite present-day Bangkok. The Thais regained control of their country and further united the disparate provinces to the north with central Siam.

Taksin eventually came to regard himself as the next Buddha; his ministers, who did not approve of his religious fantasies, deposed and then executed him in the custom reserved for royalty – by beating him to death in a velvet sack so that no royal blood touched the ground.

Bangkok Rule

Another general, Chao Phaya Chakri, came to power and was crowned in 1782 under the title Phraphutthayotfa Chulalok. He moved the royal capital across the river to Bangkok and ruled as the first king of the Chakri dynasty. He and his heir, Loet La (1809-24), assumed the task of restoring the culture so severely damaged decades earlier by the Burmese.

The third Chakri king, Phra Nang Klao (1824-51), went beyond reviving tradition and developed trade with China while increasing domestic agricultural production. He also established a new royal title system, posthumously conferring 'Rama I' and 'Rama II' upon his predecessors and taking the title 'Rama III' for himself.

Rama IV, commonly known as King Mongkut (Phra Chom Klao to the Thais), was one of the more colourful and innovative of the early Chakri kings. He originally missed out on the throne in deference to his half-brother Rama III and lived as a Buddhist monk for 27 years. During his long

Rama V (1868-1910). Considered a champion of the common person, and now venerated as a demi-god within contemporary Thai culture.

monastic term he became adept in Sanskrit, Pali, Latin and English, studied western sciences and adopted the strict discipline of local Mon monks. He kept an eye on the outside world and when he took the throne in 1851 he immediately courted diplomatic relations with European nations, while avoiding colonialisation.

Thai trade restrictions were loosened and many western powers signed trade agreements with the monarch. He also established Siam's first printing press and instituted educational reforms, developing a school system along European lines. Although the king courted the west, he did so with caution and warned his subjects: 'Whatever they have invented or done which we should know of and do, we can imitate and learn from them, but do not wholeheartedly believe in them'. Mongkut was the first monarch to show Thai commoners his face in public; he died of malaria in 1868.

His son, King Chulalongkorn (known to the Thais as Chulachomklao or Rama V, 1868-1910), continued Mongkut's tradition of reform, especially in the legal and administrative realm. Educated by European tutors, Chula abolished prostration before the king as well as slavery and corvée (state labour). Thailand further benefited from relations with European nations and the USA: railways were built, a civil service established and the legal code restructured. Though Siam still managed to avoid colonialisation, the king was compelled to concede territory to French Indochina (Laos in 1893, Cambodia in 1907) and British Burma (three Malayan states in 1909) during his reign.

In 1912 a group of Thai military officers unsuccessfully attempted to overthrow the monarchy – the first in a series of 20th century coup attempts that continues to the present day.

Revolution & Succession

While King Prajadhipok (Pokklao or Rama VII, 1925-35) ruled, a group of Thai students living in Paris became so enamoured of democratic ideology that they mounted a successful coup d'état against absolute monarchy in Siam. This bloodless revolution led to the development of a constitutional monarchy along British lines, with a mixed military-civilian group in power.

In 1935 the king abdicated without naming a successor and retired to Britain. The cabinet named his nephew, 10-year-old Ananda Mahidol, to the throne as Rama VIII, though Ananda didn't return to Thailand from school in Switzerland until 1945. Phibul (Phibun) Songkhram, a key military leader in the 1932 coup, maintained an effective position of power from 1938 until the end of WWII.

Under the influence of Phibul's government, the country's name was officially changed in 1939 from 'Siam' to 'Thailand' – rendered in Thai as 'Prathêht Thai'. 'Prathêht' is derived from the Sanskrit *pradesha* or 'country'. 'Thai' is considered to have the connotation of 'free', though in actual usage it simply refers to the Thai, Tai or T'ai peoples, who are found as far east as Tonkin, as far west as Assam, as far north as south China and as far south as north Malaysia.

Ananda Mahidol ascended the throne in 1945, but was shot dead in his bedroom under mysterious circumstances in 1946. His brother, Bhumibol Adulyadej, succeeded him as Rama IX. Nowadays no one ever speaks or writes publicly about Ananda's death. Even as recently as 1993, a chapter in David Wyatt's *A Short History of Thailand* chronicling the known circumstances surrounding the event had to be excised before the Thai publisher would print and distribute the title in Thailand.

WWII & Postwar Periods

During their invasion of South-East Asia in 1941, the Japanese outflanked Allied troops in Malaya and Myanmar. The Phibul government complied with the Japanese in this action by allowing them into the Gulf of Thailand; consequently the Japanese troops occupied a portion of Thailand itself. Phibul declared war on the USA and Great Britain in 1942 but Seni Pramoj, the Thai ambassador in Washington, refused to deliver the declaration. Phibul resigned in 1944 under pressure from the Thai underground resistance (Thai Seri), and, after V-J Day in 1945, Seni became premier.

In 1946, the year King Ananda was shot dead, Seni and his brother Kukrit were unseated in a general election and a democratic civilian group took power under Pridi Phanomyong, a law professor who had been instrumental in the 1932 revolution. Pridi's civilian government, which changed the country's name back to Siam, ruled for a short time, only to be overthrown by Phibul in 1947. Two years later Phibul suspended the constitution and reinstated 'Thailand' as the country's official name. Under Phibul the government took an extreme anticommunist stance, refused to recognise the People's Republic of China and became a loyal supporter of French and US foreign policy in South-East Asia.

In 1951 power was wrested from Phibul by General Sarit Thanarat, who continued the tradition of military dictatorship. However, Phibul somehow retained the actual title of premier until 1957 when Sarit finally had him exiled. Elections that same year forced Sarit to resign and go abroad for 'medical treatment'; he returned in 1958 to launch another coup. This time he abolished the constitution, dissolved the parliament and banned all political parties, maintaining effective power until he died of cirrhosis in 1963. From 1964 to 1973 the Thai nation was ruled by army officers Thanom Kittikachorn and Praphat Charusathien, during which time Thailand allowed the USA to develop several military bases within its borders in support of the US campaign in Vietnam.

Reacting to political repression, 10,000 students publicly demanded a real constitution in June 1973. In October that year the military brutally suppressed a large demonstration at Thammasat University in Bangkok, but General Krit Sivara and King Bhumibol refused to support further bloodshed, forcing Thanom and Praphat to leave Thailand. Oxford-educated Kukrit Pramoj took charge of a 14 party coalition government and steered a leftist agenda past a conservative parliament. Among his lasting successes were a national minimum wage, the repeal of anticommunist laws and the ejection of US forces from Thailand.

Polarisation & Stabilisation

Kukrit's elected, constitutional government ruled until October 1976 when students demonstrated again, this time protesting Thanom's return to Thailand as a monk. Thammasat University again became a battlefield as border patrol police, along with right-wing, paramilitary civilian groups, assaulted a group of 2000 students holding a sit-in. Hundreds of students were killed and injured; more than a thousand were arrested. Using public disorder as an excuse, the military stepped in and installed a new right-wing government with Thanin Kraivichien as premier.

This bloody incident disillusioned many Thai students and older intellectuals not directly involved with the demonstrations, the result being that numerous idealists 'dropped out' of Thai society and joined the People's Liberation Army of Thailand (PLAT) – armed communist insurgents, based in the hills of northern and southern Thailand, who had been active since the 1930s.

In October 1977 the military replaced Thanin with the more moderate General Kriangsak Chomanand in an effort to conciliate anti-government factions. When this failed, the military-backed position changed hands again in 1980, leaving Prem Tinsulanonda at the helm. By this time the PLAT had reached a peak force of around 10,000.

Prem served as prime minister until 1988 and is credited with the political and economic stabilisation of Thailand in the post-Indochina War years (only one coup attempt in the 1980s). The major accomplishment of the Prem years was a complete dismantling of the Communist Party of Thailand and PLAT through an effective combination of amnesty programs (which brought the students back from the forests) and military action. His administration is also considered responsible for the gradual democratisation of Thailand, culminating in the 1988 election of his successor, Chatichai Choonhavan.

Approximately 60% of Chatichai's cabinet were former business executives rather than ex-military officers, as compared to 38% in the previous cabinet. Thailand seemed to be entering a new era in which the country's double-digit economic boom coincided with democratisation. Critics praised the political maturation of Thailand, even if they grumbled that corruption seemed as rife as ever. By the end of the 1980s, however, certain high-ranking military officers had become increasingly dissatisfied with this *coup d'argent*, complaining that Thailand was being governed by a plutocracy.

February 1991 Coup

On 23 February 1991, in a move that shocked Thailand observers around the world, the military overthrew the Chatichai administration in a bloodless coup *(pàtìwát)* and handed power to the newly formed National Peace-Keeping Council (NPKC), led by General Suchinda Kraprayoon. It was Thailand's 19th coup attempt and one of 10 successful coups since 1932; however, it was only the second coup to overthrow a democratically elected civilian government. Charging Chatichai's civilian government with corruption and vote-buying, the NPKC abolished the 1978 constitution and dissolved the parliament. Rights of public assembly were curtailed but the press was closed down for only one day.

Following the coup, the NPKC handpicked the civilian prime minister, Anand Panyarachun, a former ambassador to the USA, Germany, Canada and the UN, to dispel public fears that the junta was planning a return to 100% military rule. Anand claimed to be his own man, but like his predecessors – elected or not – he was allowed the freedom to make his own decisions only insofar as they didn't affect the military. In spite of obvious constraints, many observers felt Anand's temporary premiership and cabinet were the best Thailand had ever had.

In December 1991 Thailand's national assembly passed a new constitution that guaranteed an NPKC-biased parliament. Under this constitution, regardless of who was chosen as the next prime minister or which political parties filled the lower house, the government would remain largely in the hands of the military. The new charter included a provisional clause allowing for a 'four year transitional period' to full democracy.

Elections & Demonstrations

A general election in March 1992 ushered in a five party coalition government with Narong Wongwan, whose Samakkhitham (Justice Unity) Party received the most votes, as premier. But amid allegations that Narong was involved in Thailand's drug trade, the military exercised its constitutional prerogative and immediately replaced Narong with (surprise, surprise) General Suchinda in April.

Back in power again, the NPKC promised to eradicate corruption and build democracy, a claim that was difficult to accept since they had previously done little on either score. In many ways, it was like letting the proverbial fox guard the henhouse, as the military is perhaps the most corrupt institution in the country – always claiming to be free of politics and yet forever meddling in it. Thailand's independent political pundits agreed there was more oppression under the NPKC than under any administration since 1980.

In May 1992 several huge demonstrations demanding Suchinda's resignation – led by charismatic Bangkok governor Chamlong Srimuang – rocked Bangkok and larger provincial capitals. Chamlong won the 1992 Magsaysay Award (a humanitarian service award issued by a foundation in the Philippines) for his role in galvanising the public to reject Suchinda. After street confrontations between protesters and the military near Bangkok's Democracy Monument resulted in nearly 50 deaths and hundreds of injuries, Suchinda resigned after less than six weeks as premier. The military-backed government also agreed to institute a constitutional amendment requiring that Thailand's prime minister come from the ranks of elected MPs. Anand Panyarachun was reinstated as interim premier for a four month term, once again winning praise from several circles for his even-handed and efficient administration.

The September 1992 elections squeezed in veteran Democrat Party leader Chuan Leekpai with a five seat majority. Chuan led a coalition government consisting of the Democrat, New Aspiration, Palang Dharma and Solidarity parties. A food vendor's son and native of Trang Province, the new premier didn't fit the usual Thai prime minister mould since he was neither general nor tycoon nor academic. Though well regarded for his honesty and high morals, Chuan accomplished little in the areas of concern to the majority of Thais – most pointedly Bangkok traffic, national infrastructure and the undemocratic NPKC constitution. By the end of 1993 the opposition was calling for parliamentary dissolution and a royal command appointed a new cabinet for Chuan in December 1994.

Chuan never completed his four year term, and a new general election ushered in a seven party coalition led by the Chart Thai (Thai Nationality) Party. At the helm was 63-year-old billionaire Banharn Silapaarcha, whom the Thai press called a 'walking ATM (automatic teller machine)'. Two of the largest partners in the coalition, the Palang Dharma and New Aspiration parties, were former participants from the Chuan coalition. Barnharn wasn't very popular with the Thai media, who immediately attacked his tendency to fill senior government positions from a pool of rural politicians known to be heavily involved in money politics. In September 1996 the Barnharn government collapsed amid a spate of corruption scandals and a crisis of confidence. The November national election, marked by violence and accusations of vote-buying, saw former deputy prime minister and army commander Chavalit Yongchaiyudh of the New Aspiration Party secure the premiership with a dubious mix of coalition parties.

In July 1997, following several months of warning signs that almost everyone in Thailand and in the international community chose to ignore (see the Economy section of this chapter for details), the Thai currency fell into a deflationary tailspin and the national economy crashed to a virtual halt. In September 1997 Thai parliament voted in a new constitution that guaranteed – at least on paper – more human and civil rights than had hitherto been codified in Thailand. As the first national charter to be prepared under civilian auspices, the 'people's constitution' fostered great hope in a people emotionally battered by the ongoing economic crisis.

Hope faded as Chavalit, living up to everyone's low expectations, failed to deal effectively with the economy and was forced to resign in November 1997. An election brought Chuan Leekpai back into office, where he seems to be doing a reasonable job as an international PR man for the crisis. Chuan's team of 'young Turk' economists are working round the clock to right the listing economy. Another election is expected soon.

Despite the economic downturn, which is predicted to last well into 2000, Thai cynics will tell you that things *never* change and that the democratic Chatichai, Banharn, Chavalit and Chuan governments may merely be short-lived deviations from the norm of military rule. Hardened cynics might hold the view that Thailand's 20th century coups and counter-coups are a mere extension of the warlordism of early Thai *jâo meuangs*.

Optimists, on the other hand, see Suchinda's hasty resignation as a sign that the military coup was an instrument of change in Thailand was only a minor detour on the country's road towards a more responsive and democratic national government. Corruption remains a problem, though the Berlin-based watchdog Transparency International recently dropped Thailand from its top 10 list in the annual Corruption Percep-

tion Index. Without question, Thailand's revised and amended constitution strengthens the nation's future claim to democratic status and political stability, even while the economy remains shaky.

GEOGRAPHY

Thailand has an area of 517,000 sq km, making it slightly smaller than the US state of Texas, or about the size of France. Its shape on the map has been compared to the head of an elephant, with its trunk extending down the Malay peninsula. The centre of Thailand, Bangkok, is at about 14° north latitude, putting it on a level with Madras, Manila, Guatemala and Khartoum.

The country's longest north-to-south distance is about 1860km, but its shape makes distances in any other direction 1000km or less. Because the north-south reach spans roughly 16 latitudinal degrees, Thailand has perhaps the most diverse climate in South-East Asia. The topography varies from high mountains in the north – the southern-most extreme of a series of ranges that extends across northern Myanmar and south-west China to the south-eastern edges of the Tibetan Plateau – to the limestone-encrusted tropical islands in the South that are part of the Malay archipelago. The rivers and tributaries of northern and central Thailand drain into the Gulf of Thailand via the Chao Phraya Delta near Bangkok; those of the Mun River and other north-eastern waterways exit into the South China Sea via the Mekong River.

These broad geographic characteristics divide the country into four main zones: the fertile centre region, dominated by the Chao Phraya River; the north-east plateau, the kingdom's poorest region (thanks to 'thin' soil plus occasional droughts and floods), rising some 300m above the central plain; northern Thailand, a region of mountains and fertile valleys; and the southern peninsular region, which extends to the Malaysian frontier and is predominantly rainforest. The southern region receives the most annual rainfall and the north-east least, although the north is less humid.

Seacoasts & Islands

Extending from the east coast of Peninsular Malaysia to Vietnam, the Sunda Shelf separates the Gulf of Thailand from the South China Sea. The Gulf is relatively shallow, with an average depth of 30m, up to 85m at its deepest points. Most of Thailand's major rivers drain into the Gulf, tempering the water's surface salinity significantly.

On the opposite side of the Thai-Malay peninsula, the much deeper Andaman Sea – over 100m deep in offshore areas – encompasses that part of the Indian Ocean east of India's Andaman and Nicobar islands. Together Thailand's Andaman Sea and Gulf of Thailand coastlines form 2710km of beaches, hard shores and wetlands.

Hundreds of oceanic and continental islands are found on both sides. Those with tourist facilities constitute only a fraction. The two broad types of island geography in Thai waters are gently sloped, granitic islands, such as those of the Surin and Similan groups, and the more dramatic limestone islands which characterise marine karst topography, often with steep cliffs, overhangs, and caverns above and below the tideline. Abundant examples of such limestone islands can be found in Ao Phang-Nga (Phang-Nga Bay, also known as the Sea of Phuket).

CLIMATE
Rainfall

Thailand's climate is ruled by monsoons which produce three seasons in northern, north-eastern and central Thailand, and two in southern Thailand. The three season zone, which extends roughly from the country's northern-most reaches to Phetchaburi Province on the southern peninsula, experiences a 'dry and wet' monsoon climate, with the south-west monsoon arriving between May and July and lasting into November. This is followed by a dry period from November to May, a period that begins with lower relative temperatures until mid-February (because of the influences of the north-east monsoon, which bypasses this part of Thailand but results in cool

breezes), followed by much higher relative temperatures from March to May.

It rains more and longer along the Thai-Malay peninsula south of Phetchaburi, an area subject to the north-east monsoon from November to January, as well as the countrywide south-west monsoon. Because of this dual monsoon pattern, and because it is located closer to the equator, most of southern Thailand has only two seasons, a wet and a dry, with smaller temperature differences between the two.

Although the rains officially begin in July (according to the Thai agricultural calendar), they actually depend on the monsoons in any given year. As a rule of thumb, the dry season is shorter the farther south you go. From Chiang Mai north, the dry season may last six months (mid-November to May); in most of central and north-east Thailand five months (December to May); on the upper peninsula three months (February to May); and below Surat Thani only two months (March and April). Occasional rains in the dry season are known as 'mango showers' (as they arrive with the onset of the mango season).

In central Thailand it rains most during August and September, though there may be floods in October since the ground has reached full saturation by then. If you are in Bangkok in early October don't be surprised if you find yourself in hip-deep water in certain parts of the city. Along the Andaman coast it rains most in May and October, as this area undergoes both monsoons.

Coastal Conditions

Having two curving coastlines to choose from means you can usually find good beach or island weather somewhere in Thailand virtually any month of the year. Hence, which coast you choose – the Gulf of Thailand or the Andaman Sea – might best be determined by the time of year. Both sides are mostly rain-free from January to April, both are more or less equally rainy from June to November, while the Gulf is drier than the Andaman coast from November to January, and in May and June. The south-west monsoon affects

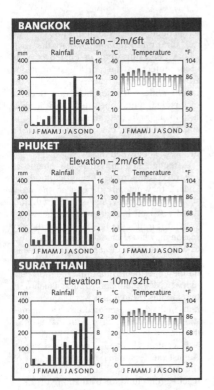

though some generated along the Vietnamese coast may produce heavier than usual wind and rain conditions in the Gulf of Thailand from time to time. For climate detail as it affects divers, see Dive Seasons in the Activities section of the Facts for the Visitor chapter. See also When to Go in the Planning section of ,the same chapter for more climate information.

Temperature

Most of Thailand is very humid, with an overall average humidity of 66 to 82%, depending on the season and time of day. The dry season reaches its hottest along the north-east plain, and temperatures easily soar to 39°C in the daytime, dropping only a few degrees at night.

Temperatures south of Phetchaburi are more stable year-round. When it is 35°C in Bangkok, it may be only 30 to 32°C on Phuket or Ko Samui.

The Eastern Gulf Coast, stretching from Bangkok to Trat, can be uncomfortably warm (over 35°C) during the months of March, April and May, although sea breezes tend to moderate inland temperatures.

ECOLOGY & ENVIRONMENT
Environmental Policy

Like all densely populated countries, Thailand has put enormous pressure on its fragile ecosystems. Fifty years ago forests covered approximately 70% of the countryside; as of 1997 an estimated 25% of the natural forest cover remained. The loss of forest cover has been accompanied by a similar reduction in wildlife populations. Logging and agriculture are mainly to blame for the decline.

In response to environmental degradation, the Thai government has created a large number of protected lands since the 1970s, and has enacted legislation to protect specific plant and animal species. The government hopes to raise total forest cover to 40% by the middle of the 21st century. Thailand has also become a signatory to the UN Convention on International Trade in Endangered Species (CITES).

the Andaman Sea coast the most, while only the southern Gulf coast – south of Phetchaburi – generally receives rain from the north-east monsoon. There is some rain year-round in the south, while it's very dry along the northern and eastern Gulf coast areas from November to May.

In general, monsoon rains in southern Thailand last only a couple of hours a day, occasionally longer. Travelling in the rainy season is usually not unpleasant, but unpaved roads may become impassable. 'Monsoon' comes from the Arabic *mausim*, which means 'season', and is not a reference to any type of tropical storm as is mistakenly believed by many outside tropical Asia. In the last half-century only one typhoon has entered the Gulf of Thailand,

In 1989 logging was banned following a 1988 disaster in which hundreds of tonnes of cut timber washed down deforested slopes in Surat Thani Province, killing more than a hundred people and burying a number of villages. It is now illegal to sell timber felled in the country, and all imported timber is theoretically accounted for before going on the market. The illegal timber trade further diminished with Cambodia's ban on all timber exports, along with the termination of all Thai contracts by the Burmese. Laos is now the number one source for imported timber in Thailand, both legal and illegal.

These days builders even need government permission to use timber salvaged from old houses. This has helped curb illegal logging in the interior (unfortunately, Thai timber brokers are now turning their attention to Laos and Myanmar), but corruption remains a problem.

Corruption also impedes government attempts to shelter 'exotic' species from the illicit global wildlife trade and to preserve Thailand's sensitive coastal areas. The Forestry Department is currently under pressure to take immediate action where preservation laws have gone unenforced, including coastal zones where illegal tourist accommodation has flourished. There has also been a crackdown on restaurants serving 'jungle food' (aahãan pàa), which consists of exotic and often endangered wildlife species like barking deer, bear, pangolin, civet and gaur.

The tiger is one of the most endangered of Thailand's large mammals. Although tiger hunting or trapping is illegal, poachers continue to kill them for the lucrative Chinese pharmaceutical market; among the Chinese, the ingestion of tiger penis and bone is thought to have curative effects. In Taipei, the world centre for Thai tiger consumption, at least two-thirds of the pharmacies deal in tiger parts (in spite of the fact that such trade is forbidden by Taiwanese law). Around 200 to 300 wild tigers are thought to be hanging on in the national parks of Khao Yai, Kaeng Krachan and Khao Sok.

Forestry Department efforts are limited by lack of personnel and funds. The average ranger is paid only 75B a day – some aren't paid at all but receive food and lodging – to face down armed poachers backed by the rich and powerful godfathers who control illicit timber and wildlife businesses. Increasing unemployment since the economic crisis of 1997 has also made wildlife poaching more attractive to those with dwindling livelihood options. This may be balanced by the countrywide decrease in land development and construction, as habitat loss is far more threatening to wildlife than hunting or poaching.

Marine resources are also threatened by a lack of long-term conservation goals. The upper portion of the Gulf of Thailand between Rayong and Prachuap Khiri Khan was once one of the most fertile marine areas in the world. Now it is virtually dead due to overfishing and pollution.

Experts say it's not too late to rehabilitate the upper Gulf by reducing pollution and the number of trawlers, and by restricting commercial fishing to certain zones. A ban on the harvest of plaa tuu (mackerel) at the spawning stage has brought this fish back from the brink of total depletion. The Bangkok Metropolitan Administration (BMA) is currently developing a system of sewage treatment plants in the Chao Phraya Delta area, with the intention of halting all large-scale dumping of sewage into Gulf waters. Similar action needs to be taken along the entire eastern seaboard, which is rapidly becoming Thailand's new industrial centre.

Over-development on Ko Phi-Phi Don is starving the surrounding coral reefs by blocking nutrient-rich run-off from the islands' interiors, as well as smothering the reefs with pollutants. Ko Samui and Ko Samet face a similar fate if growth isn't controlled and waste-disposal standards aren't improved.

One encouraging sign was the passing of the 1992 Environmental Act, which sets environmental quality standards and designates conservation and pollution control areas. Pattaya and Phuket were the first locales decreed pollution control areas, making them eligible for government cleanup funds. With such assistance, officials in Pattaya claim they'll be able to restore Ao Pattaya – exposed to improper waste disposal for at least the past 20 years – to its original state by the year 2000.

A large number of Thais remain ignorant of the value of taking a pro-environment stance in everyday life or in encouraging ecologically sound tourism. The director of a certain regional Tourism Authority of Thailand (TAT) office was recently heard to complain that eco-tourism was *lambàak* (inconvenient or bothersome) for Thai people but there was little she could do about it because 'that's national policy'. Fortunately such attitudes are steadily changing, especially among the young, who have grown up in relative affluence but who have begun to perceive the dangers of environmental neglect.

Even though environmentalism is national policy, only with strong popular support can protective laws, which are already plentiful but often ignored, be enforced. Current examples of 'people power' include the hundreds of forest monasteries that voluntarily protect chunks of forest. When one such *wát* (temple) was forcibly removed by the military in Buriram Province, thousands of Thais around the country rallied behind the abbot, Phra Prachak, and the wát's protectorship was re-established. On the other hand, wáts with less ecologically minded trustees have sold off virgin land to developers.

Non-government organisations play a large role surveying and designating threatened areas and educating the public about the environment. In 1983 Wildlife Fund Thailand (WFT) was created under Queen Sirikit's patronage as an affiliate of the World Wide Fund for Nature (WWF). The main function of the WFT is to raise consciousness about the illegal trade in endangered wildlife. A list of several other groups is included in the following section. Citing the country's free press as a major incentive, the international watchdog organisation Greenpeace – known for its campaigns against whale hunting and nuclear weapons testing – may soon be opening a regional office in Thailand.

Tourism & the Environment

In some instances tourism has had positive effects on conservation in Thailand. Conscious that the country's natural beauty is a major tourist attraction for both residents and foreigners, and that tourism is a major revenue earner, the government has stepped up efforts to protect wilderness areas and to add more acreage to the park system. In Khao Yai National Park, for example, all hotel and golf-course facilities were removed to reduce damage to the park environment and upgrade the wilderness. Under government and private sector pressure, the fishing industry has all but eliminated coral dynamiting in the Similan and Surin islands, to preserve the area for tourist visitation.

According to *National Parks of Thailand* by Denis Gray, Colin Piprell & Mark Graham:

A growing number of conservationists, development experts and government officials believe that boundary markers and even guns do little to halt encroachment. The surrounding communities must somehow be allowed to share in whatever economic benefits a park can offer. Some sanctuaries, like Huay Kha Khaeng, recruit employees from local villages. In Thaleh Noi Wildlife Preserve, local fishermen are hired to take visitors around the lake in their boats to view the rich bird life. Rangers at Laem Son National Park encourage local fishermen to take visitors to outlying islands rather than over-fish the sea. Phu Kradung National Park takes on several hundred locals as porters to carry hikers' gear up the mountain. Some have become so protective of their park that they report violations of regulations to the rangers.

Of course, tourism has also caused environmental damage. Eager to make fistfuls of cash, hotel developers and tour operators have rushed to provide ecologically inappropriate services in areas that are unable to sustain high-profile tourism. Concerns about this have prompted the government to look more closely at Ko Phi-Phi and Ko Samet – two national park islands notorious for overdevelopment. Part of the problem is that it's not always clear which lands are protected and which are privately owned.

Common problems in marine areas include the anchoring of tour boats on coral reefs and the dumping of rubbish into the sea. Coral and seashells are also illegally collected and sold in tourist shops. 'Jungle food' restaurants – with endangered species on the menu – flourish near inland national parks. Perhaps the most visible abuses occur in areas without basic garbage and sewage services, where there are piles of rotting garbage, mountains of plastic and open sewage run-off.

One of the saddest sights is the piles of discarded plastic water bottles on popular beaches. Those floating in waterways are sometimes swallowed by aquatic wildlife with fatal results. Many of these bottles started out on a beach only to be washed into the sea during the monsoon season.

What can the average visitor to Thailand do to minimise the impact of tourism on the environment? First off, avoid all restaurants serving wildlife (eg barking deer, pangolin, bear). Visitors should also consider taking down the names of any restaurants serving or advertising such fare and filing a letter of complaint with the TAT, the WFT and the Forestry Department (addresses are listed later in this section). The main patrons of this type of cuisine are the Thais themselves, along with visiting Chinese from Hong Kong and Taiwan; fortunately such restaurants are becoming increasingly rare as the Thais come to understand the importance of preserving biological diversity.

When using hired boats near coral reefs, urge boat operators not to lower anchors onto coral formations. This is becoming less of a problem with established boating outfits – some of whom mark off sensitive areas with blue-flagged buoys – but is common among small-time pilots. Perhaps volunteer to collect (and later dispose of) rubbish if it's obvious that the usual mode is to throw everything overboard.

Obviously, you shouldn't buy coral or shell products. Thai law forbids the collection of coral or seashells anywhere in the country – report any observed violations in tourist or marine park areas to the TAT and

Forestry Department, or in other places to the WFT.

One of the difficulties in dealing with rubbish and sewage problems in tourist areas is that many Thais don't understand why tourists should expect different methods of disposal than are used elsewhere in the country. In urban areas or populated rural areas, piles of rotting rubbish and open sewage lines are frequently the norm – after all, Thailand is still a 'developing' country. Thais sensitive to western paternalism are quick to point out that on a global scale the so-called 'developed' countries cause far more environmental damage than Thailand does (eg per capita greenhouse emissions for Australia, Canada or the USA average over 5 tonnes each, while ASEAN countries contribute less than half a tonne per capita).

Hence, when making environmental complaints or suggestions to Thais in the tourist industry, it's important to emphasise that you want to work *with* them rather than against them in improving environmental standards.

Whether on land or at sea, refrain from purchasing or accepting drinking water offered in plastic bottles wherever possible; when there's a choice, request glass bottles, which are recyclable in Thailand. The 5B deposit is refundable when you return the bottle to any vendor who sells drinking water in glass bottles. When only plastic-bottled water is available, consider transferring the water to your own reusable container and leave the plastic bottle with the vendor or dispose of it yourself later at a dumpster or other legitimate collection site.

A few guesthouses now offer drinking water from large, reusable plastic containers as an alternative to the individual disposable containers. This service is available in most areas of Thailand (even relatively remote areas like Ko Chang). Encourage hotel and guesthouse staff to switch from disposable plastic to either glass or reusable plastic.

In outdoor areas where rubbish has accumulated, consider organising an impromptu cleanup crew to collect plastic, styrofoam and other non-biodegradables for delivery to a regular rubbish pick-up point. If there isn't a pick-up nearby, inquire about the nearest collection point and deliver the refuse yourself.

By expressing your desire to use environmentally friendly materials – and by taking direct action to avoid the use and indiscriminate disposal of plastic – you can provide an example of environmental consciousness not only for the Thais but for other international visitors.

Visitors should consider filing letters of complaint regarding any questionable environmental practices with TAT, the WFT and the Forestry Department (addresses follow). Any municipal markets where endangered species are on sale should also be duly noted – consider enclosing photographs to support your complaints. For a list of endangered species in Thailand, contact the WFT.

Write to the following organisations to offer your support for stricter environmental policies or to air specific complaints or suggestions:

Asian Society for Environmental Protection
    c/o CDG-SEAPO, Asian Institute of Technology, GPO 2754, Bangkok 10501
Bird Conservation Society of Thailand
    PO Box 13, Ratchathewi Post Office, Bangkok 10401
Community Ecological Development Programme
    PO Box 140, Chiang Rai 57000
Friends of Nature
    670/437 Th Charansavatwong, Bangkok 10700
Magic Eyes
    15th floor, Bangkok Bank Bldg, 333 Th Silom, Bangkok 10400
Office of the National Environment Board
    60/1 Soi Prachasumphan 4, Th Rama IV, Bangkok 10400
Project for Ecological Recovery
    77/3 Soi Nomjit, Th Naret, Bangkok 10500
Raindrop Association
    105-7 Th Ban Pho, Thapthiang, Trang 92000
Royal Forestry Department
    61 Th Phahonyothin, Bangkhen, Bangkok 10900
Siam Environmental Club
    Chulalongkorn University, Th Phayathai, Bangkok 10330
The Siam Society
    131 Soi Asoke, Th Sukhumvit, Bangkok 10110

Thailand Information Centre of Environmental Foundation
    58/1 Sakol Land, Th Chaeng Wattana, Pak Kret, Nonthaburi
Tourism Authority of Thailand (TAT)
    372 Th Bamrung Meuang, Bangkok 10100
Wildlife Fund Thailand
    (☎ 02-521 3435, fax 552 6083)
    251/88-90 Th Phahonyothin, Bangkhen, Bangkok 10220; 255 Soi Asoke, Sukhumvit 21, Bangkok 10110
World Wildlife Fund (Thailand)
    (☎ 02-524 6128)
    WWF Project Office, Asian Institute of Technology, 104 Outreach Bldg, PO Box 2754, Bangkok 10501

FLORA & FAUNA
Flora

Unique in South-East Asia because its north-south axis extends some 1800km from mainland to peninsular South-East Asia, Thailand provides potential habitats for an astounding variety of flora and fauna. As in the rest of tropical Asia, most indigenous vegetation in Thailand is associated with two basic types of tropical forest: monsoon forest (with a distinctive dry season of three months or more) and rainforest (where rain falls during more than nine months of each year). Natural forest area – defined as having crowns of trees covering over 20% of the land – covers about 25% of Thailand's land mass. According to the UN World Development Report, Thailand ranks 44th in the amount natural forest cover worldwide, ahead of Cambodia but behind Laos regionally, and equivalent to Mexico globally.

Monsoon forests constitute about a quarter of all the remaining natural forest cover in the country; they are characterised by deciduous tree varieties that shed their leaves during the dry season in order to conserve water. Rainforests constitute about half of all forest cover in Thailand; they are typically evergreen. The central, northern, eastern and north-eastern regions of Thailand mainly contain monsoon forests, while southern Thailand is predominantly a rainforest zone. There is much overlap – some forest zones support a mix of monsoon forest and rainforest vegetation.

The country's most famous flora includes an incredible array of fruit trees, bamboo (more species than any country outside China), tropical hardwoods and over 27,000 flowering species, including Thailand's national floral symbol, the orchid.

Fauna

As with plant life, the variation in the animal kingdom is closely affiliated with geographic and climatic differences. Hence the indigenous animals of Thailand's northern half are mostly of Indochinese origin, while those of the south are generally Sundaic (ie typical of Malaysia, Sumatra, Borneo and Java). The invisible dividing line between the two zoogeographical zones runs across the Isthmus of Kra, about halfway down the southern peninsula. The large overlap area between zoogeographical and vegetative zones – extending from Uthai Thani in the lower north to around Prachuap Khiri Khan on the southern peninsula – means that much of Thailand is a potential habitat for plants and animals from both zones.

Thailand is particularly rich in bird life, with more than 1000 recorded resident and migratory species – approximately 10% of all bird species. Coastal and inland waterways of the southern peninsula are especially important habitats for South-East Asian waterfowl.

Loss of habitat due to human intervention remains the greatest threat to birdlife; shrimp farms along the coast are robbing waterfowl of their rich intertidal diets, while in the south the over harvesting of swiftlet nests for bird's nest soup may threaten the continued survival of the nests' creators.

Marine Life

Thailand's marine world falls within two major oceanic spheres. The Gulf of Thailand is itself an extension of the South China Sea, which is part of the Pacific Ocean, while the Andaman Sea is the section of the Indian Ocean east of the Andaman-Nicobar Ridge. Coelenterates – a class of marine fauna characterised by the presence of a tentacle-rimmed mouth – are among the most exotic of Thailand's underwater life. They include jellyfish, sea anemones and the colourful corals appreciated by divers from all over the world. Among the most commonly seen are gorgonians, sea fans and sea whips.

Coral reefs may contain hundreds of thousands of species of flora and fauna; after tropical rainforests they are the most productive life habitat on the planet. A true coral reef develops on a substratum made up of the calcified 'skeletons' of hard coral. Most coral formations in Thai waters have established themselves on clusters of rock or on artificial structures such as shipwrecks. Over 200 hard coral species have been identified in the Andaman Sea, and around 60 in the Gulf. Coral generally isn't found below 30m, as its survival requires sufficient sunlight for photosynthesis.

Although they have yet to be properly catalogued, there are hundreds of species of fish in Thailand, from tiny gobies, the world's smallest fish (only around 20mm), to gargantuan whale sharks, the world's largest fish (up to 18m and 3600kg). Reef fish, camouflaged among the colourful corals, provide endless hours of underwater entertainment for human observers. They include clownfish, parrotfish, wrasses, angelfish, soldierfish, rabbitfish, sweetlip, cardinalfish, triggerfish, tang, butterflyfish and lionfish. Deeper waters are home to larger species like snapper, jack, grouper, barracuda, mackerel, shark, marlin, sailfish, tuna and wahoo.

Four of the world's six species of sea turtle can be found in the Andaman Sea and the Gulf of Thailand: the Pacific ridley, green turtle, leatherback turtle and hawksbill turtle. All are endangered because their eggs, meat and shells are highly valued among coastal Thais. The loggerhead turtle once brought the list to five but has now been hunted to extinction in Thai waters. Turtle hunting and turtle egg collecting are now illegal and the destruction of the turtles has slowed considerably, but has not yet stopped. The main culprit in recent times has been Japan, the world's largest importer of sea turtles (including the endangered ridley and hawksbill). The Japanese use both of these for meat, leather and turtle-shell fashion accessories.

Thailand's warm waters attract whales and dolphins, around 25 species of which are known to frequent either or both the Andaman Sea and the Gulf of Thailand. Another marine mammal of note, the endangered dugong (also called manatee or sea cow), is occasionally spotted off the coast of Trang Province in southern Thailand. The dugong is sacred to *pàk tâi* (southern Thais) and is now protected by law from all molestation.

National Parks & Wildlife Sanctuaries

Despite Thailand's rich diversity of flora and fauna, only in recent years have most of the 79 national parks (only 50 of which receive an annual budget), 89 'non-hunting areas' and wildlife sanctuaries, and 35 forest reserves been established.

Eighteen of the national parks are marine parks that protect coastal, insular and open-sea areas. The majority of these are well maintained by the Forestry Department, but a few have allowed rampant tourism to threaten the natural environment, most notably on the islands of Ko Samet and Ko Phi-Phi. Poaching, illegal logging and shifting cultivation have also taken their toll on protected lands, but since 1990 the government has cracked down with some success.

Marine national parks offer very basic visitor facilities. There is usually somewhere to stay for a reasonable fee, and sometimes meals are provided, but it's a good idea to take your own sleeping bag or mat; basic camping gear is useful for parks without fixed accommodation. You should also take a torch (flashlight), rain gear, insect repellent, a water container and a small medical kit.

Most of the national parks are easily accessible, yet only around 5% of visitors are from outside Thailand. Most parks charge a small entry fee (typically 3B to 5B for Thais, 15B to 25B for foreigners) and there is usually somewhere to stay for a reasonable fee. For more information about staying in national parks, see Accommodation in the Facts for the Visitor chapter.

If you are interested in a more in-depth description of Thailand's protected areas the well researched *National Parks of Thailand* by Denis Gray, Colin Piprell & Mark Graham is highly recommended reading.

For a true appreciation of Thailand's geography and natural history, a visit to at least one national park is a must. In Bangkok the reservations office is at the national parks division of the Forestry Department (☎ 02-579 4842, 579 0529), Th Phahonyothin, Bangkhen (north Bangkok). Bookings from Bangkok must be paid in advance.

GOVERNMENT & POLITICS

The Kingdom of Thailand (to use its official English name) has been an independent nation since 1238 AD, the only country in South or South-East Asia never colonised by a foreign power.

Since 1932, the government of Thailand has nominally been a constitutional monarchy inspired by the bicameral British model but with myriad subtle differences. National polls elect the 393 member lower house (Saphaa Phuu Thaen Ratsadon or House of Representatives, with four-year terms) and prime minister, but the 270 senators of the upper house (Wuthisaphaa or Senate, six-year terms) are appointed by the prime minister. In Thailand the Senate is not as powerful as the House of Representatives; the latter writes and approves legislation, while the Senate votes on constitutional changes.

Eleven political parties field candidates in national elections, of which five receive the bulk of the votes: Thai Nation Party, Democrat Party, New Aspiration Party, National Development Party and Palang Dharma Party.

The 1997 Constitution

Thailand's 15th constitution, enacted on 9 December 1991 by the military-controlled and now-defunct National Peace-Keeping Council (NPKC), replaced that promulgated in December 1978 and limited public participation in the choosing of government officials.

On 27 September 1997, the Thai parliament voted in a new charter, Thailand's 16th such document since 1932 and the first to be promulgated by a civilian government. Known as the *rátthamnuun pràchaachon* or 'people's constitution', it puts new mechanisms in place to monitor the conduct of elected officials and political candidates and to protect civil rights. In many ways the new charter constitutes a bloodless popular revolution, as pro-democracy groups had been fighting for more than 10 years to reform the constitution. These groups were initially opposed by many in power, including the king, whose birthday speech in 1991 suggested leaving the military constitution in place. Such opposition to amendment of the military constitution led directly to the violence of May 1992 (see the History section earlier in this chapter).

The new document makes voting in elections compulsory, allows public access to information from state agencies, establishes free public education for 12 years, permits local communities to manage, maintain, and use natural resources in their areas and forces Parliament to consider new laws upon receipt of 50,000 or more signatures in public referendum. It also establishes several watchdog entities, including a constitution court, administrative court, national anti-corruption commission, national election commission, human rights commission and parliamentary ombudsmen to support constitutional enforcement. Other amendments include requirements for election candidates to hold at least a bachelor's degree, and for legislators who become prime minister or members of the premier's cabinet to relinquish MP status.

As the pro-democracy newspaper *The Nation* pointed out when the new charter was passed, the document is not a panacea, but merely the start of a political reform process. Much depends on the will of Thailand's politicians to see that the charter guides new legislation and that such legislation is enforced.

Administrative Divisions

For administrative purposes, Thailand is divided into 76 *jangwàat* (provinces). Each province is subdivided into *amphoe* (districts), which are subdivided at a further five levels. Urban areas with more than 50,000 inhabitants and a population density of over 3000 per square kilometre are designated *nákhon*; those with populations of 10,000 to 50,000 with not less than 3000 per square kilometre are *meuang* (usually spelt 'muang' on roman-script highway signs). The term 'meuang' is also used loosely to mean metropolitan area (as opposed to an area within strict municipal limits).

A provincial capital is an *amphoe meuang*. An amphoe meuang takes the same name as the province of which it is capital, eg amphoe meuang Surat Thani (often abbreviated as 'meuang Surat Thani') means the city of Surat Thani, capital of Surat Thani Province.

Provincial governors *(phûu wâa râatchakaan)* are appointed to their four year terms by the Ministry of the Interior – a system that leaves much room for corruption. Bangkok's governor and provincial assembly were elected for the first time in November 1985, when Chamlong Srimuang, a strict Buddhist and a former major general, won by a landslide. The mid-1996 elections saw independent Dr Pichit Ruttakul take over as Bangkok governor.

District officers *(nai amphoe)* are also appointed by the Ministry of the Interior but are responsible to their provincial governors. The cities are headed by elected mayors *(naiyók thêtsàmontrii)*, tambons by elected commune heads *(kamnan)* and villages by elected village chiefs *(phûu yài bâan)*.

The Monarchy

His Majesty Bhumibol Adulyadej (pronounced 'Phumíphon Adunyádèt') is the ninth king of the Chakri Dynasty (founded in 1782) and, since 1988, the longest reigning king in Thai history. His Majesty is also the world's longest reigning, living monarch.

Born in the USA in 1927 and schooled in Bangkok and Switzerland, King Bhumibol was a nephew of King Rama VII (King Prajadhipok, 1925-35) as well as the younger brother of King Rama VIII (King Ananda Mahidol). His full name – including royal title – is Phrabaatsomdet Boramintarama-haphumiphonadunyadet.

His Majesty ascended the throne in 1946 following the death of Rama VIII, who had reigned as king for only one year (Ananda served as regent for 10 years after his uncle's abdication in 1935 – see the History section earlier). In 1996 Thailand celebrated the 50th year of the king's reign. A jazz composer and saxophonist, King Bhumibol wrote the royal anthem, which accompanies photos of the royal family shown before every film at cinemas across the country. He is fluent in English, French, German and Thai. His royal motorcade is occasionally seen passing along Thanon (Th) Ratchadamnoen (Royal Promenade) in Bangkok's Banglamphu district; the king is usually seated in a vintage yellow Rolls Royce or a 1950s Cadillac.

The king has his own privy council composed of up to 14 royal appointees who assist with his formal duties; the president of the privy council serves as interim regent until an heir is throned.

The king and his wife, Queen Sirikit, have four children: Princess Ubol Ratana (born 1951), Crown Prince Maha Vajiralongkorn (1952), Princess Mahachakri Sirindhorn (1955) and Princess Chulabhorn (1957). A royal decree issued by King Trailok (1448-88) to standardise succession in a polygamous dynasty makes the king's senior son or full brother his *uparaja* or heir apparent. Thus Prince Maha Vajiralongkorn was officially designated as crown prince and heir when he reached 20 years of age in 1972; if

The current king, His Majesty Bhumibol Adulyadej (Rama IX), the longest reigning monarch in Thai history.

he were to decline the crown or be unable to ascend the throne due to incurable illness or death, Ubol Ratana would be next in line.

Princess Ubol Ratana married American Peter Jensen in 1972 against palace wishes, thus forfeiting her royal rank, but was reinstated as Princess a few years ago. The Crown Prince has married twice, most recently to an ex-actress. His son Prince Juthavachara is the eldest male of the next Chakri generation.

Though Thailand's political system is officially classified as a constitutional monarchy, the constitution stipulates that the king be 'enthroned in a position of revered worship' and not be exposed 'to any sort of accusation or action'. With or without legal writ, the vast majority of Thai citizens regard King Bhumibol as a sort of demigod, partly in deference to tradition but also because of his impressive public works record.

Neither the constitution nor the monarchy's high status prevent Thai people from gossiping about the royal family in private, however. Gathered together, the various whisperings and speculations with regard to royal intrigue would make a fine medieval fable. Many Thais, for example, favour the Princess Sirindhorn for succession to the Thai throne, though none would say this publicly, nor would this popular sentiment appear in the Thai media. Among the nation's soothsayers, it has long been prophesied that the Chakri dynasty will end with Rama IX; current political conditions, however, suggest the contrary.

It is often repeated that the Thai king has no political power (by law his position is strictly titular and ceremonial) but in times of national political crisis, Thais have often looked to the king for leadership. Two attempted coups d'état in the 1980s may have failed because they received tacit royal disapproval. By implication, the successful military coup of February 1991 must have had palace approval, whether *post facto* or *a priori*.

Along with nation and religion, the monarchy is very highly regarded in Thai society – negative comment about the king or any member of the royal family is a social as well as legal taboo. See the Society & Conduct section in this chapter for details.

ECONOMY

During the 1980s, Thailand maintained a steady GNP growth rate that by 1988 had reached 13% per annum. Thailand in the early and mid 1990s found itself on the threshold of attaining the exclusive rank of NIC or 'newly industrialised country'. Soon, economic experts said, Thailand would be joining Asia's 'little dragons', also known as the Four Tigers – South Korea, Taiwan, Hong Kong and Singapore – in becoming a leader in the Pacific Rim economic boom.

The Bubble Bursts

In mid 1997 the 20-year boom went bust throughout South-East and East Asia, with Thailand leading the way. The economies worst affected by the financial turmoil – Thailand, Indonesia, Malaysia, the Philippines and South Korea – displayed certain common pre-crisis characteristics, including wide current account deficits, little government transparency, high levels of external debt and relatively low foreign exchange reserves. For the most part, the crisis stemmed from investor panic, with the rush to buy dollars to pay off debts creating a self-fulfilling collapse. Between 30 June and 31 October the baht depreciated roughly 40% against the US dollar, and dollar-backed external debt rose to 52.4% of the country's GDP. Such currency problems echoed the European currency crisis of 1992-93 when sudden, unforeseen drops in the pound, lira and other currencies sounded the death knell for a long period of steady growth and economic stability.

By January 1998 the Bank of Thailand stated that worsening economic conditions in the latter half of 1997 resulted in a doubling in the number of bad loans in the banking sector – about 18% of the total. Many banks and finance companies were forced to close in 1998, as the government made valiant efforts to restructure the economy and most especially the financial and property sectors. The International Monetary Fund (IMF) has promised huge loans, with the stipulation that the Thai government follow the IMF's prescriptions for recapitalisation and restructuring.

With or without the IMF bailout, Thailand is in for a period of self-imposed austerity, increasing unemployment, negative growth and plain old hard times. How long the hard times will last before Thailand begins bouncing back – and all experts agree the economy will boom again eventually – is anyone's guess, though the common refrain is that things will be back on track by 2000 (unless of course the 'Asian economic flu' spreads to the world's healthier economies). Some observers have concluded that this forced cooling off is the best thing that could have happened to the overheated economy, giving the nation time to focus on infrastructure priorities and offering the Thai citizenry an opportunity to re-assess cultural change.

What tends to get lost in discussions of current economic conditions in Thailand is a long-term assessment of the journey the nation has travelled over the last three decades. Except for Malaysia and South Korea, no other country in the world has produced more rapid economic growth or seen such a dramatic reduction in poverty during that period. Per capita income in Thailand increased 19-fold between 1963 and 1997. Even accounting for the recent baht devaluation, this means most Thais today are economically better off than they were in the 1960s. Per capita income figures measured by the purchasing power parity method – which allows for inflation and considers the varying prices of necessary goods on a global scale – in fact demonstrate a 1% increase between 1997 and 1998, even in the midst of the recession (raw GDP figures show a 6% contraction). See Money in the Facts for the Visitor chapter for an account of the opportunities the baht devaluation has created for many foreign visitors.

The Big Picture

Around 60% of Thailand's exports are agricultural; the country ranks first in the world for rice (followed by the USA and Vietnam), second in tapioca (after Brazil) and fifth in coconut (following Indonesia, the Philippines, India and Sri Lanka). Since 1991 Thailand has been the world's largest producer of natural rubber, although it still ranks behind Malaysia in total rubber exports. Other important agricultural exports include sugar, maize, pineapple, cotton, jute, green bean, soybean and palm oil. Processed food and beverages – especially canned shrimp, tuna and pineapple – also account for significant export earnings. Thailand's top export markets are the USA, Japan and Singapore.

About 57% of the Thai labour force is engaged in agriculture, 17% in industry (including manufacturing), 15% in services and 11% in commerce. Manufactured goods have become an increasingly important source of foreign exchange revenue and now account for at least 30% of Thailand's exports. Cement, textiles and electronics lead the way, with car and truck manufacture coming up fast. The country also has substantial natural resources, including tin, petroleum and natural gas.

Since 1987 tourism has become a leading earner of foreign exchange, occasionally outdistancing Thailand's largest single export, textiles, with receipts as high as US$6 billion per annum. The government's economic strategy remains focused, however, on export-led growth through the continued development of textiles and other light industries such as electronics, backed by rich reserves of natural resources and a large, inexpensive labour force. Observers predict that such a broad-based economy will continue to make Thailand a major economic competitor in Asia in the long-term.

Raw average per capita income by 1998 was US$2450 per year; if measured using the 'purchasing power parity' method (which takes into account price differences between countries), the Thais average US$6940 per capita annually. With an average net escalation of 11.2% per annum between 1985 and 1995, Thailand has ranked highest in Asia in terms of real GDP growth per employee over the last decade. Regional inequities, however, mean that annual income averages range from US$400 in the north-east to US$3000 in Bangkok. An estimated 20% of Thai citizens – most of them in Bangkok or Phuket – control 63% of the wealth. The minimum wage in Bangkok and surrounding provinces is 162B (US$4.37) per day; it can be as low as 140B a day in the outer provinces.

By October 1998, the inflation rate had risen to 7.6% per annum; travellers should keep this in mind when referring to prices in this edition. As in most other countries, prices continue to rise. Unemployment has risen to nearly 6%, over double what it was two years ago but still less than in many so-called industrialised countries.

Regional Economies

Southern Thailand is the richest region outside Bangkok, due to abundant agricultural (fruit, rubber, rice), fishing and mineral (tin and oil) resources along with burgeoning beach tourism. Central Thailand, including the eastern Gulf coast, grows fruit (especially pineapples), sugar cane and rice for export, and supports most of the ever-growing industry (textiles, food processing and cement).

North-eastern Thailand has the lowest inflation rate and cost of living. Hand-woven textiles and farming remain the primary means of livelihood, though Nakhon Ratchasima (Khorat) is an emerging centre for metals and automotive industry. Northern Thailand produces mountain or dry rice (as opposed to water rice, the bulk of the crop produced in Thailand) for domestic use, maize, tea, various fruits and flowers, and is very dependent on tourism.

Tourism

According to figures from the TAT, the country averages over seven million tourists per year, a 64-fold increase since 1960 when the government first began keeping statistics. In 1997 – the most recent year for which full statistics are available – 62.6% of all visitors (4.5 million total) came from East and South-East Asia, with Malaysians leading the way at 1.04 million, followed by Japanese (965,000). Europeans as a whole made up approximately 1.6 million of the total, with Germans at the top (342,000), followed by Britons (288,000). US visitors accounted for 311,000 of the total, and Australians 234,000. Other major markets include China (439,000), Taiwan (448,000) and South Korea (411,000). Thailand's fastest-growing tourist segments in 1997 were overseas Thais (up 39%), Argentina (up 34%), Hong Kong (up 19%) and Singapore (up 12.5%). With regard to per-day expenditures, Asians spent the most, Europeans the least.

Tourist revenue amounts to between US$5 billion and US$6 billion a year. A recent study carried out by the Thailand Development Research Institute confirms that:

'although the average daily expenditure of typical guesthouse tourists may not be as high as that of hotel dwellers, they … normally spend more because they usually stay in the country much longer. Income generated by these tourists is thought to penetrate more deeply and widely to the poorer segments of the industry'.

The biggest growth in tourism since 1990 has been among the Thais themselves. Spurred by steady economic growth earlier this decade, and by the general lack of funds for international travel in the present economic situation, an estimated 40 million Thais per year are now taking domestic leisure trips. Ten or 15 years ago western tourists often outnumbered Thais at some of the nation's most famous tourist attractions. Now the opposite is true; except at major international beach destinations like Phuket and Ko Samui, Thai tourists tend to outnumber foreign tourists in most places at a rate of more than five to one.

POPULATION & PEOPLE

The population of Thailand is about 61.4 million and currently growing at a rate of 1 to 1.5% per annum (as opposed to 2.5% in 1979), thanks to a vigorous nationwide family-planning campaign.

Over a third of all Thais live in urban areas. Bangkok is by far the largest city in the kingdom, with a population of over six million (more than 10% of the total population) – too many for the scope of its public services and what little 'city planning' exists. Ranking the nation's other cities by population depends on whether you look at *thêtsàbaan* (municipal district) limits or at *meuang* (metropolitan district) limits. By the former measure, the four most populated cities in descending order (not counting the densely populated 'suburb' provinces of Samut Prakan and Nonthaburi, which would rank second and third if considered separately from Bangkok) are Nakhon Ratchasima (Khorat), Chiang Mai, Hat Yai and Khon Kaen. Using the rather misleading meuang measure, the ranking runs Udon Thani, Lopburi, Nakhon

Faràngs Forever?

Visitors of European descent travelling in Thailand may sometimes hear themselves referred to as *faràng*. Although there's some debate as to the true historical derivation of the term, most linguists who understand Thai orthography agree it comes from the Thai word for 'French', *faràng-sèht*, which is the Thai pronunciation of the French word *français*. A few amateur linguists argue that the Thais derived faràng from the Arabic 'ferringi' or other term used by Middle Eastern traders in South-East Asia, but this seems unlikely since the Thai spelling – not the romanised version, but the way the word is written in Thai script – makes it obvious it's simply the shortened version of the Thai word for 'French', and furthermore historical Thai phonology would not naturally transfigure 'ferringi' as 'farang'. At any rate the argument is somewhat of a moot point since 'ferringi' comes from the northern Indo-European 'frank', which simply means 'French'! It has even been suggested that the English word 'foreign' originally meant 'French'.

Wherever the word originated, nowadays faràng is used more broadly to refer to any and all foreigners who appear to have European features. Most Thais would say the term has a neutral, non-pejorative connotation, but there is recognition in some quarters that some faràng take offence at being racially identified. Thus the more polite and well educated Thai will instead say *khon dàang châat* (person of a different birth), which is of course equally racial! A very, very few will say *khon dàang prathêht* (person of a different country). However most Thais will only use either of the latter two terms in front of faràng or on radio or television. In private conversation it's back to faràng.

Most faràng living in Thailand do not take umbrage at the term. Like the word 'gringo' in Latin America and perhaps 'gaijin' in Japan, much depends on how the word is used. I've heard Thais mutter under their breath 'faràng' after a particularly unpleasant encounter with some boorish tourist, in such a way as to leave little doubt as to the intended pejorative sense.

Joe Cummings

Rachasima and Khon Kaen. Most of the other towns in Thailand have populations of well below 100,000.

The average life expectancy in Thailand is 69, the highest in mainland South-East Asia. Yet only an estimated 59% of people have access to local health services; in this the nation ranks 75th worldwide, behind countries with lower national incomes such as Sudan and Guatemala. There is only one doctor per 4316 people, and infant mortality figures are 26 per 1000 births (figures for neighbouring countries vary from 110 per 1000 in Cambodia to 12 in Malaysia). Thailand has a relatively youthful population; only about 12% are older than 50, 6% over 65.

The Thai Majority

About 75% of the citizenry are ethnic Thais, who can be divided into the central Thais or Siamese of the Chao Phraya Delta (the most densely populated region of the country); the Thai Lao of north-eastern Thailand; the Thai Pak Tai of southern Thailand; and the northern Thais. Each of these groups speak their own Thai dialect and to a certain extent practise customs unique to their region. Politically and economically the central Thais are the dominant group, although they barely outnumber the Thai Lao of north-eastern Thailand.

continued on page 49

THAILAND'S
MARINE
ENVIRONMENT

Thailand's underwater wonders can be conveniently accessed from island and beach resorts – there is easy snorkelling and, for those who wish to venture deeper, scuba courses and beginner dives, as well as adventurous live-aboard charters for the hardcore diver. Even the relatively shallow and busy Gulf of Thailand offers coral gardens around its offshore islands, but across the Isthmus of Kra the Andaman Sea beckons divers from around the world with its first class diving. The Similan and Surin Islands, the Burma Banks and numerous deserted limestone islands can be accessed from popular resort centres such as Phuket and Krabi.

Soft corals and their relatives the gorgonians and sea whips do not develop the limestone skeleton of the reef-building, and more familiar, hard corals. Also unlike their hard cousins, soft corals do not contain light-dependent algae within their tissues and so are free to grow at greater depths away from sunlight. These graceful corals develop an amazing variety of form in order to strain their microscopic food from the currents, and because the individual polyps of soft corals are not encased in a limestone cup, they are more visible, giving the colony its vivid colour.

Title page: A seahorse perches among the coral, sponges and weed using its prehensile tail – a rare and rewarding sight in Thailand's famous coral reefs. (photograph: Mark Strickland/Oceanic Impressions).

Top Left & Left: Delicate soft corals and sea whips dominatre the reef bottom at the Similan Islands. A diver must exercise buoyancy control and great care not to damage these habitats. (photographs: Mark Strickland/Oceanic Impressions).

Molluscs, in their immense variety of form, inhabit all parts of the coral reef; among the most dramatic are the nudibranchs, or sea-slugs, unrivalled in the animal kingdom for elaborate shape and vibrant colour. Other molluscs of the reef include the snails, which encompass cowries and cone shells; bivalves, such as clams and oysters; and perhaps the most interesting of all, the cephalopods – octopus, squid and cuttlefish. The octopus is the master of stealth and camouflage, squeezing and contorting its colour-coded body and arms through impossible crevices to pounce on unwary crustaceans, particularly crabs. Squid and cuttlefish are superb swimming carnivores and can often be seen swimming in schools. Along with the octopus, they possess unrivalled intelligence in the invertebrate world.

Top Right: Many species of nudibranch are bad tasting or poisonous – concentrating in their own tissues the stinging cells from their coral prey – and it pays to advertise such traits with vibrant colours (Similan Islands).

Bottom Right: Rapid colour changes enable the cuttlefish to blend with its immediate surroundings and to communicate mood swings or alarm. The diver may be left watching a pool of ink and a rapidly retreating cuttlefish.

MARK STRICKLAND/OCEANIC IMPRESSIONS

MARK STRICKLAND/OCEANIC IMPRESSIONS

Crabs, shrimps and other crustaceans abound on the coral reef, but it will take more than a cursory glance to spot them. Many are minute, spindly, almost transparent, others are masters of disguise – some crabs paste weeds and reef debris onto their carapace. Many of the small shrimps and crabs play a vital role in the reef ecosystem, removing detritus, dead tissue and parasites from their hosts, which may be a coral, sponge, fish or other reef creature.

MARK STRICKLAND/OCEANIC IMPRESSIONS

MARK STRICKLAND/OCEANIC IMPRESSIONS

Top Left: The tiny imperial shrimp explores the lumpy surface of a sea cucumber in search of food. The shrimp will probably spend most of its life on the one host (Andaman Sea).

Bottom Left: A twin-pronged spider crab, a slow-moving scavenger, crawls over a brilliant red gorgonian coral (Similan Islands).

Looking more like a plant than an animal, the featherstar, or crinoid, is a primitive echinoderm, a group which also includes starfish, brittlestars, sea urchins and sea cucumbers. Featherstars, sometimes seen in 'rainbow' clusters of different species, grip onto coral outcrops with their claw-like cirri, and wave their brightly coloured arms in the current to trap water-borne food. Of the many starfish species, the most easy to recognise is the crown-of-thorns. Notorious for destroying large areas of reef when their populations periodically boom, the crown-of-thorns is, nevertheless, an integral part of the reef ecosystem.

Top Right: A featherstar nestles among soft coral in the Andaman Sea. Although appearing to have numerous arms, these are actually branches of just five arms – the five part body plan is common to all echinoderms.

Bottom Right: The crown-of-thorns starfish feeds at night, everting its stomach over a hard coral, digesting the polyps to leave behind a bleached white coral skeleton (Burma Banks, Andaman Sea).

Shark encounters in Thailand are usually limited to the passive leopard and nurse shark, which shelter during the day in gutters and crevices, and the white-tip reef shark – easily excited predators, often baited to 'perform' for visiting divers. Along with the leopard shark, stingrays inhabit the sand and mud bottom adjacent to the reefs, feeding on molluscs and echinoderms which they find with acute senses of touch and taste. Stingrays mostly rest during the day, partially burying themselves in the substrate, and therefore posing a potential danger to unwary divers. Should a stingray be stepped on, its reflex action is to strike upwards with its poison-barbed tail. (See Marine Hazards later in this section for more information about sharks, stingrays and other scary things.)

MARK STRICKLAND/OCEANIC IMPRESSIONS

Top Left: A marbled stingray glides to the reef floor where it will partially bury its mottled form and all but disappear.

MICHAEL AW

Bottom Left: The leopard shark is large (up to 3m) and docile, living on the sea floor. Its sluggish nature and size has made it a target for harassment by divers. Such behaviour is now actively discouraged by conscientious dive operators (Ko Tachai, Andaman Sea).

MARK STRICKLAND/OCEANIC IMPRESSIONS

Morays and other eels usually hunt at night, when they can be seen sliding in and around coral cavities and crevices searching for food which, for them, is virtually any animal, dead or alive. Morays must swallow their food quickly to re-establish sufficient water flow through the mouth and over the gills for breathing. During the day, morays retire to a coral grotto, their large heads and fang-filled mouths all that is visible as they gape and 'pant' water. At a few popular dive sites in the Andaman Sea, morays have been accustomed to hand feeding to the point where they will leave their protective lairs at the first sign of an approaching diver and beg for hand-outs.

Top Right: A gaping moray eel in its coral cave – a comon sight on day trips from Phuket. Lacking a swim-bladder, and thus much in the way of buoyancy control, morays must rest among the reef crevices during the day after spending the night hunting and scavenging.

Bottom Right: Growing to over 1m long, though more usually seen at half that size, the blue ribbon eel starts life as a mostly black male, changing later into the blue-and-yellow female form (Similan Islands).

MARK STRICKLAND/OCEANIC IMPRESSIONS

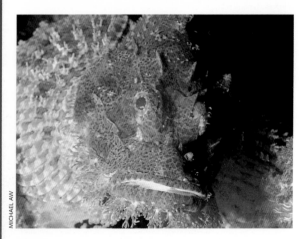

MICHAEL AW

To live among the riot of colour and shapes of the coral reef, many animals have evolved elaborate camouflage for protection and to aid hunting. Scorpionfish, stonefish and lionfish are related masters of camouflage, hunting by stealth and ambush. The scorpionfish lies motionless in the coral and reef rubble awaiting the approach of small fish; after a few small adjustments in position the strike will be a lightening-swift gulp. The lionfish uses a different tactic, slowly sneaking up on its prey before rapidly opening a cavernous mouth, sucking in a great volume of water and, if successful, a meal.

MARK STRICKLAND/OCEANIC IMPRESSIONS

Top Left: Festooned with fleshy fringes, protrusions and mottled skin, the scorpionfish ingeniously blends into its surroundings (Richelieu Rock, Andaman Sea).

Bottom Left: Spotfin lionfish (also known as firefish) hunt by stealth. Their elaborate, elongate spines and contrasting markings confuse their prey; the familiar body shape of a predator does not register – until it is too late (Similan Islands).

Relentless competition for food and a place to shelter has led to the amazing variety of shape, size, colour and behaviour of coral reef fish. There are algal grazers, coral grinders and large-mouthed gulpers and sievers. There are countless ecological niches in the reef ecosystem, and often when a species rests, either during the day or night, another species will start its shift in that same niche.

Top Right: This splendid coral grouper, normally a voracious and opportunistic feeder, patiently allows a cleaner wrasse to clean its gills.

Middle Right: Facial markings are common among angelfish species. The yellow mask angelfish is a rare but memorable sight on Thai reefs (Similan Islands).

Bottom Right: This ember parrotfish retreats to a small cave at night, after a day of scraping and grazing coral surfaces. Occasionally parrotfish secrete a clear mucous membrane in which they become encased while sleeping – perhaps as protection against predators that hunt using smell.

MARK STRICKLAND/OCEANIC IMPRESSIONS

MARK STRICKLAND/OCEANIC IMPRESSIONS

MARK STRICKLAND/OCEANIC IMPRESSIONS

MARK STRICKLAND/OCEANIC IMPRESSIONS

In Thailand and all over the tropics, certain fish species have evolved a close relationship with sea anemones. These fish are able to move freely among the stinging tentacles that would quickly paralyse other fish on contact. Although the anemone fish gains protection, and indeed is always found in proximity to an anemone, the anemone does not need the anemone fish and probably gains very little out of the deal.

MARK STRICKLAND/OCEANIC IMPRESSIONS

Top Left: Clown anemone fish never venture far from their host anemone. A typical group consists of a large dominant female, a single mature male and several immature males. When the female dies, the largest male will change sex and one of the smaller males will mature (Phuket).

Bottom Left: Anemone fish, such as this saddle back anemone fish at the Similan Islands, are not born immune to the anemone's stinging tentacles. The fish acquire immunity by gradually covering themselves in the anemone's own mucous. Chemicals in the mucous stop the anemone from stinging itself and this feature is put to use by the anemone fish.

Many fish choose to feed at the edge of the reef where the plankton-rich waters of the open sea meet the reef. But away from the confines of the reef there is the increased danger of being eaten, so often fish will feed in tightly packed schools for protection. Along with common reef sharks and the occasional visit from larger oceanic sharks, other predators of the reef edge include turtles. Not great migrators like other turtles, hawksbill turtles are usually seen close to their feeding and breeding grounds, the coral reefs and tropical islands.

MARK STRICKLAND/OCEANIC IMPRESSIONS

Top Right: Fusiliers are among the most common schooling fish in Thailand's tropical waters. At night they disband and individuals find shelter in the nooks and crannies of the reef (Similan Islands).

Bottom Right: The hawksbill turtle is losing the battle for survival in South-East Asia. Not only is it still hunted for its 'tortoiseshell', but the quiet, sandy beaches it requires for nesting are disappearing under human encroachment (Ko Surin National Park).

MARK STRICKLAND/OCEANIC IMPRESSIONS

The largest animals likely to be encountered at Thailand's off-shore dive locations are the magnificent whale shark, which is the largest living fish, and the manta ray, probably one of the most graceful and majestic of fishes. These docile plankton feeders are both entirely harmless and amazingly patient in the presence of over-friendly divers, but their true wonder is best appreciated from a respectful distance.

MARK STRICKLAND/OCEANIC IMPRESSIONS

MARK STRICKLAND/OCEANIC IMPRESSIONS

Top Left: Dwarfing a diver, the immense bulk of a whale shark is an unforgettable sight. Such encounters, though rare, can be had on day trips from Phuket.

Bottom Left: Manta rays are relatively common in the reef waters of Thailand. This manta at Ko Tachai is using its 'horns', modified from part of the pectoral fins, to feed by directing plankton-carrying water through its cavernous mouth.

Hazardous Marine Life

Several marine organisms can cause physical pain to humans who come into contact with them. Although such occurrences are largely a matter of bad luck, it helps if you're aware of the hazards and ways to avoid contact. Don't touch anything underwater except rocks or sand, and never reach beneath rocks or into holes or crevices where marine life may be.

Jellyfish stings are the most common source of marine mishaps after sunburn. The presence of jellyfish at a beach is largely seasonal or storm related; a beach may be jellyfish free one day and seemingly full of them the next. Small ones without dangling tentacles (some may be almost invisible) usually cause only transitory discomfort. Larger jellyfish, especially those with long tentacles, can cause more severe and lasting pain.

For the latter, treat by removing any tentacles that may have become detached from the jellyfish. Don't use your bare hands but rather paper, leaves or some other object. Smaller more clinging tentacles or tentacle particles may require removal with soap and razor. Once all the stinging bits have been removed, wash the affected area with salt water, then rinse thoroughly with vinegar to deactivate any stingers that have not 'fired'. When vinegar isn't available, urine reputedly has the same effect. Calamine lotion, antihistamines and analgesics may reduce the reaction and relieve the pain.

Fire coral, found among reefs and other coral sites, is a branching hydroid (not actually a coral) that looks harmlessly fernlike but

Top Right: Schooling bannerfish patrol reef outcrops where these conspicuous reef dwellers actively feed on plankton during the daylight hours.

Far Right: Fire coral is often found encrusting the skeletons of dead coral. Contact with the stinging white hairs that protrude from its mustard-coloured surface will cause painful irritation that can last several days.

Right: Large conspicuous jellyfish pose little danger to divers and swimmers but the long trailing arms that carry innumerable stinging cells can be dislodged in rough seas and these almost invisible tentacles can still cause harm.

packs a distinctly uncomfortable – sometimes quite intense – prickle if exposed skin brushes against it. Treat as for jellyfish.

Coral cuts acquired by brushing against dead coral can easily become infected as tiny pieces of bacteria-infested coral can work themselves deep into the cuts. Wash thoroughly with soap and hot water, disinfect with alcohol or hydrogen peroxide, apply antibiotic ointment and bandage.

Sea urchins are found in sandy spots near rocks and coral, often in popular snorkelling areas. They are easily spotted – look for dark spheres radiating thin spines. Take care when wading or snorkelling not to be knocked over by waves or tidal surges. Contact with sea urchins may leave their spines embedded in your skin. Larger spines can sometimes be removed with tweezers, but some are too fine to be plucked out; locals break them up using a blunt instrument such as a smooth stone or knife handle. Once the spines have been dealt with, the painful venom can be neutralised by immersing the infected area in very hot water (recommended 43°C to 45°C, or as hot as you can stand) for 30 to 90 minutes. The venoms of marine organisms are protein based and are broken down by intense heat.

Scorpionfish, **lionfish** and **zebrafish** are very colourful and interesting but their dorsal spines can pack a painful wallop – don't touch! Stings from these bizarre beauties are uncommon, but they can be treated with hot water as described for sea urchins.

MICHAEL AW

MICHAEL AW

Top Left: Sea urchins often gather in large numbers – the sea floor a mass of spiny balls. In some species light-sensitive cells scattered over the body help the urchin direct the thin, hollow spines towards any potential attacker.

Bottom Left: The elaborately decorated zebra lionfish seems to forewarn would-be predators and divers of its painfully poisonous spines, which it will raise while manoeuvring into a defensive posture.

Cone shells are cone shaped sea snails with a venomous proboscis that darts from the narrow end of the shell to ward off aggressors. Never touch or even get close to a cone shaped shell in the sea. For emergency treatment, immobilise the affected limb if possible and keep it at a lower level than the victim's heart. Dress the wound with an elastic bandage to prevent the spread of venom and seek medical help. If help is unavailable, apply the hot water method described for sea urchins.

Stonefish, which as their name suggests may resemble stones lying in the sand, also have a rather potent venom. If approached by unwary divers or a carelessly placed foot of a reef fossicker it will maintain its stand among the reef rubble or mud bottom and simply raise its lethal dorsal spines. Treat as for cone shell stings.

MICHAEL AW

MICHAEL AW

Top Right: The various species of beautiful cone shells are sought after by collectors, although their bite is potentially lethal. The poison is injected by a highly modified radula or mouthpart.

Bottom Right: Expertly camouflaged, the potentially deadly stonefish lies in wait for its next meal to swim by.

MICHAEL AW

Sea snakes, all of which produce some venom, are common but tend to avoid humans. At any rate their mouths are so small that it's very difficult for them to bite humans except between the fingers and toes. In the highly unlikely event of a bite, wrap the site with an elastic bandage, immobilise the affected limb and seek medical help for an injection of commonly available antivenin.

Sting rays have barbed tail spines that can inflict painful wounds. Experienced beachgoers perform the 'stingray shuffle' when walking on sandy bottoms. If you bump into a ray resting on the bottom, it will usually swim away; if you step on one, it's likely to give you a flick of the barb. Treat with very hot water as previously described, but first be sure to remove the barb sac from the wound, or it will continue to release venom. Remember that all protein-based venoms break down when heated.

Sharks have a bad reputation, but are not a significant danger in Thailand. In fact, there has never been a single report of a shark attack on humans in Thai waters, which favours the propagation of smaller species such as the leopard shark, nurse shark and whitetip or blacktip reef shark – all of which tend to be quite timid. One exception to the 'small sharks' rule is the Burma Banks area of the Andaman Sea (and possibly other as yet unexplored areas far west of the mainland), where there are some large hammerheads and tiger sharks with the potential to inflict serious bites on humans.

Nevertheless, handing food to sharks underwater – an activity practised and promoted by a few recreational dive operations in Thailand – is never a good idea. Besides the potential risk it poses (long-term studies suggest hand-feeding makes sharks more aggressive around humans), such practices habituate wildlife to getting human handouts. This interrupts the natural marine food chain and disrupts the undersea ecological balance.

Top Left: Sea snakes are reptiles that have evolved from land-dwelling ancestors to live a totally aquatic life. They can hold their breath for up to an hour while hunting for small eels and other fish before replenishing their lungs at the surface.

Far Left: The white tip reef shark is a territorial, bottom-dwelling shark sometimes seen resting under ledges or in caves. Its curiosity aroused, this shark will approach divers but it is rarely aggressive and is not considered dangerous.

Left: Gregarious and inquisitive, grey reef sharks investigate the slightest disturbance or unusual object in their territory. These skittish sharks can be aggressive if approached and are easily excited by baiting.

MICHAEL AW

MICHAEL AW

continued from page 32

Smaller groups with their own Thai dialects include the Shan (Mae Hong Son), the Thai Lü (Nan, Chiang Rai), the Lao Song (Phetchaburi and Ratchaburi), the Phuan (Chaiyaphum, Phetchaburi, Prachinburi), the Thai Khorat or Sawoei (Nakhon Ratchasima), the Phu Thai (Mukdahan, Sakon Nakhon), the Yaw (Nakhon Phanom, Sakon Nakhon) and the Thai-Malay (Satun, Trang, Krabi).

The Chinese

People of Chinese ancestry make up 11% of the population, most of whom are second or third-generation Hokkien (Hakka), Tae Jiu (Chao Zhou/Chiu Chao) or Cantonese.

Ethnic Chinese probably enjoy better relations with the majority population here than in any other country in South-East Asia, due partly to historical reasons and partly to traditional Thai tolerance of other cultures (although there was a brief spell of anti-Chinese sentiment during the reign of Rama VI). King Rama V used Chinese businesspeople to infiltrate European trading houses, a manoeuvre that helped defeat European colonial designs on Siam. Wealthy Chinese also introduced their daughters to the royal court as consorts, developing royal connections and adding a Chinese bloodline that extends to the current king.

Minorities

The second largest ethnic minority group living in Thailand are the Malays (3.5%), most of whom reside in the southern Thai provinces of Songkhla, Yala, Pattani and Narathiwat. The remaining 10.5% of the population are divided among smaller non-Thai-speaking groups like the Vietnamese, Khmer, Mon, Semang (Sakai), Moken (*chao leh* or 'sea gypsies'), Htin, Mabri, Khamu and a variety of hill tribes in the north. There are also a small number of Europeans and other non-Asians living in Bangkok and the provinces.

EDUCATION

The literacy rate in Thailand runs at 93.8%, one of the highest rates in mainland South-East Asia. In 1993 the government raised compulsory schooling from six to nine years, and in 1997 it decreed that all citizens were entitled to free public schooling for 12 years. Although a high social value is placed on education as a way to achieve material success, the system itself favours rote learning over independent thinking at most levels.

Thailand's public school system is organised around six years at the *pràthŏm* (primary) level beginning at age six, followed by three years of *mátháyom* (middle) and three years of *udom* (high) school. In reality less than nine years of formal education is the national norm. These statistics don't take into account the education provided by Buddhist *wáts* in remote rural areas, where monastic schooling may be the only formal education available.

Private and international schools for the foreign and local elite are found in Bangkok and Chiang Mai, and to a lesser extent in other larger cities. The country boasts 12 public and five private universities, plus numerous trade schools and technical colleges. A teaching certificate may be obtained after attending a two year, post-mátháyom programme at one of the many teachers' colleges scattered throughout the country. Two of Thailand's universities, Thammasat and Chulalongkorn, rank among Asia's top 50 institutes of higher learning.

ARTS
Theatre & Dance

Traditional Thai theatre consists of six dramatic forms: *khŏn*, formal masked dance-drama depicting scenes from the *Ramakian* (the Thai version of India's *Ramayana*) and originally performed only for the royal court; *lákhon*, a general term covering several types of dance-dramas (usually for non-royal occasions) as well as western theatre; *lí-khe* (likay), a partly improvised, often bawdy folk play featuring dancing, comedy, melodrama and music; and *hùn lŭang* or *lákhon lék* – puppet theatre.

Manohra Also known simply as *nora*, this is southern Thailand's equivalent to líkhe and the oldest surviving Thai dance-drama. The basic story line bears some similarities to the 2000-year-old *Ramayana*. In this case the protagonist, Prince Suthon (Sudhana in Pali), sets off to rescue the kidnapped Manohra, a *kinnari* or woman-bird princess. As in lí-khe, performers add extemporaneous comic rhymed commentary – famed nora masters sometimes compete at local festivals to determine who's the best rapper.

Nang Shadow-puppet theatre – in which two-dimensional figures are manipulated between a cloth screen and light source at night-time performances – has been a South-East Asian tradition for perhaps five centuries. Originally brought to the Malay peninsula by Middle Eastern traders, the technique eventually spread to all parts of mainland and peninsular South-East Asia; in Thailand it is mostly found only in the south. As in Malaysia and Indonesia, shadow puppets in Thailand are carved from dried buffalo or cow hides (*nǎng* in Thai).

Two distinct shadow-play traditions survive in Thailand. The most common, *nǎng thálung*, is named after Phattalung Province, where it developed from Malay models. Like their Malay-Indonesian counterparts, the Thai shadow puppets represent an array of characters from classical and folk drama, principally the *Ramakian* and *Phra Aphaimani* in Thailand. A single puppet master manipulates the cutouts, which are bound to the ends of buffalo-horn handles. Nǎng thálung is still occasionally seen at temple fairs in the south, mostly in Songkhla and Nakhon Si Thammarat provinces. Performances are also held periodically for tour groups or visiting dignitaries from Bangkok.

The second tradition, *nǎng yài* (literally, 'big hide'), uses much larger cutouts, each bound to two wooden poles held by a puppet master; several masters (almost always male) may participate in a single performance. Nǎng yài is rarely performed nowadays because of the lack of trained nǎng masters and the expense of the shadow puppets. Most nǎng yài made today are sold to interior decorators or tourists – a well-crafted hide puppet may cost as much as 5000B.

In 1994, in order to celebrate the King's 50th year on the throne, the Fine Arts Department initiated a project to restore the original 180-year-old set of nǎng yài figures used by the Thai royal court. The project required the refurbishing of 352 puppets along with the creation of 100 new ones to complete the royal set, known as Phra Nakhon Wai ('City-Shaking') – a tribute to the impact they had on audiences nearly two centuries ago. In addition to the occasional performance in Nakhon Si Thammarat or Bangkok, nǎng yài can be seen at Wát Khanon in Ratburi Province, where nǎng yài master Khru Chalat is passing the art on to younger men.

Music
Traditional Music The classical, central Thai music is spicy, like Thai food, and features an incredible array of textures and subtleties, hair-raising tempos and pastoral melodies. The classical orchestra is called the *pìi-phâat* and can include as few as five players or more than 20. Among the more common instruments is the *pìi*, a woodwind instrument that has a reed mouthpiece; it is heard prominently at Thai boxing matches. The pìi is a relative of a similar Indian instrument, while the *phin*, a banjo-like stringed instrument whose name comes from the Indian *vina*, is considered to be native to Thailand. A bowed instrument similar to ones played in China and Japan is aptly called the *saw*. The *ranâat èk* is a bamboo-keyed

SIMON BORG

The phin is distinctly Thai but its name has Indian origins.

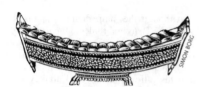

The ranâat èk, a type of xylophone with bamboo keys.

percussion instrument resembling the western xylophone, while the *khlui* is a wooden flute.

One of the more amazing Thai instruments is the *kháwng wong yài*, tuned gongs arranged in a semicircle. There are also several different kinds of drums, some played with the hands, some with sticks. The most important Thai percussion instrument is the *tà-phon* (or *thon*), a double-headed hand drum that sets the tempo for the ensemble. Prior to a performance, the players make

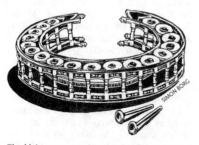

The kháwng wong yài consists of tuned gongs arranged in a circular shape.

offerings of incense and flowers to the tà-phon, which is considered to be the 'conductor' of the music's spiritual content.

The pìi-phâat ensemble was originally developed to accompany classical dance-drama and shadow theatre but can be heard in straightforward performance these days, in temple fairs as well as concerts. One reason classical Thai music may sound strange to the western ear is that it does not use the

tempered scale we have been accustomed to hearing since Bach's time. The standard Thai scale does feature an eight note octave but it is arranged in seven full-tone intervals, with no semi-tones. Thai scales were first transcribed by Thai-German composer Phra Chen Duriyanga (Peter Feit), who also composed Thailand's national anthem in 1932.

Recommended books on the subject are *The Traditional Music of Thailand* by David Morton and *Thai Music* by Phra Chen Duriyanga (Peter Feit).

Modern Music Popular Thai music has borrowed much from western music, particularly its instruments, but still retains a distinct flavour of its own. Although Bangkok bar bands can play fair imitations of everything from Hank Williams to Madonna, there is a growing preference among Thais for a blend of Thai and international styles.

The best example of this is Thailand's famous rock group Carabao. Recording and performing for nearly 20 years now, Carabao is by far the most popular musical group in Thailand, and has even scored hits in Malaysia, Singapore, Indonesia and the Philippines with songs like 'Made in Thailand' (the chorus is in English). This band and others have crafted an exciting fusion of Thai classical and *lûuk thûng* (very rhythmic popular music from north-east Thailand) forms with heavy metal. These days almost every other Thai pop group sounds like a Carabao clone, and members of the original band are putting out solo albums using the now classic Carabao sound.

Another major influence on Thai pop was a 1970s group called Caravan, which created a modern Thai folk style known as *phleng phêua chii-wít* or 'songs for life'. Songs of this nature have political and environmental topics rather than the usual moonstruck love themes; during the authoritarian dictatorships of the 1970s many of Caravan's songs were banned by the government. Though they dissolved in the early 1980s, Caravan re-form for the occasional live concert. The group's most gifted songwriter, Surachai, continues to record and release solo efforts.

Yet another inspiring movement in modern Thai music is the fusion of international jazz with Thai classical and folk motifs. The leading exponent of this newer genre is the composer and instrumentalist Tewan Sapsanyakorn (also known as Tong Tewan), whose performances mix western and Thai instruments. The melodies of his compositions are often Thai-based but the improvisations and rhythms are drawn from such heady sources as Sonny Rollins and Jean-Luc Ponty. Tewan plays soprano and alto sax, violin and khlui with equal virtuosity.

Other notable groups fusing international jazz and indigenous Thai music include Kangsadarn and Boy Thai; the latter adds Brazilian *samba* to the mix. Thai instrumentation in world music settings are specialities of Todd Lavelle and Nupap Savantrachas, each of whom has had a steady flow of recent hits. Fong Nam, a Thai orchestra led by American composer Bruce Gaston, performs an inspiring blend of western and Thai classical motifs.

Cassette tapes of Thai music are readily available in department stores, cassette shops and from street vendors. The average price for a Thai music cassette is 55B to 75B. Western tapes are cheaper (about 30B each) if bootlegged, but the days of pirate tapes in Thailand are numbered now that the US music industry is enforcing international copyright laws. Licensed western music tapes cost 90B to 110B, still a good deal by the pricing standards of most western nations.

Literature

Of all classical Thai literature, the *Ramakian* is the most pervasive and influential in Thai culture. The Indian source – the *Ramayana* – came to Thailand with the Khmer 900 years ago, first appearing as stone reliefs on Prasat Hin Phimai and other Angkor-period temples in the north-east. Oral and written versions may also have been available; eventually, though, the Thais developed their own version of the epic, first written down during the reign of Rama I (1782-1809). This version contained 60,000 stanzas, about 25% longer than the Sanskrit original.

Although the main theme remains the same, the Thais embroidered the *Ramayana* by providing much more biographical detail on arch-villain Ravana (Dasakantha, called Thótsàkan or '10-necked' in the *Ramakian*) and his wife Montho. The monkey-god, Hanuman, differs substantially in the Thai version insofar as he is very flirtatious with females (in the Hindu version he follows a strict vow of chastity). One of the classic *Ramakian* reliefs at Bangkok's Wát Pho depicts Hanuman clasping a maiden's bared breast as if it were an apple.

Also passed on from Indian tradition are the many *jatakas* or life stories of the Buddha (*chaa-tòk* in Thai). Of the 547 jataka tales in the Pali *tripitaka* (Buddhist canon) – each one chronicling a different past life – most appear in Thailand almost word-for-word as they were first written down in Sri Lanka. A group of 50 'extra' stories, based on Thai folk tales of the time, were added by Pali scholars in Chiang Mai 300 to 400 years ago. The most popular jataka in Thailand is one of the Pali originals known as the *Mahajati* or *Mahavessandara* (Mahaa-Wetsandon in Thai), the story of the Buddha's penultimate life. Interior murals in the *bòt* (ordination chapel) of Thai wáts typically depict this jataka and nine others: *Temiya*, *Mahaachanaka*, *Suwannasama*, *Nemiraja*, *Mahaasotha*, *Bhuritat*, *Chantakumara*, *Nartha* and *Vithura*.

The 30,000 line *Phra Aphaimani*, composed by poet Sunthorn Phu in the late 18th century and set on the island of Ko Samet, is Thailand's most famous classical literary work. Like many of its epic predecessors around the world, it tells the story of an exiled prince who must complete an odyssey of love and war before returning to his kingdom in victory.

Architecture & Sculpture

The scheme outlined in the 'Thai Art Styles' boxed table is the latest one used by Thai art historians to categorise historical styles of Thai art, principally sculpture and architecture (since very little painting prior to the 19th century has survived).

Thai Art Styles

Mon Art (formerly Dvaravati, 6th to 11th century & Hariphunchai, 11th to 13th century)
Originating in Central, North and North-Eastern Thailand, Mon Art is an adaptation of Indian styles, principally Gupta.

Khmer Art (7th to 13th century)
Centred in the Central and North-Eastern areas of Thailand, this style is characterised by post-classic Khmer styles accompanying the spread of Khmer empires.

Peninsular Art (formerly Srivijaya, 3rd to 14th century)
Centred in Chaiya and Nakhon Si Thammarat, this style exhibits Indian influences from the 3rd to 5th century, Mon; 5th to 13th century local influences; and Khmer influences from the 11th to 14th century.

Lanna (formerly Chiang Saen, 13th to 15th century)
Centred in Chiang Mai, Chiang Rai, Phayao, Lamphun and Lampang, Lanna is influenced by Shan/Burmese and Lao traditions, mixed with local styles.

Sukhothai (13th to 15th century)
Centred in Sukhothai, Si Satchanalai, Kamphaeng Phet and Phitsanulok, this style is unique to Thailand.

Lopburi (10th to 13th century)
This Central Thailand style is characterised by a mixture of Khmer, Pali and local styles.

Suphanburi-Sangkhlaburi (formerly U Thong,13th to 15th century)
A central Thailand style combining Mon, Khmer and local styles. A prototype for the later Ayuthaya style.

Ayuthaya A (1350 to 1488)
Central Thailand style characterised by Khmer influences and gradually replaced by revived Sukhothai influences.

Ayuthaya B (1488 to 1630)
Central Thailand style with characteristic ornamentation distinctive of Ayuthaya style, eg crowns and jewels on Buddhas.

Ayuthaya C (1630 to 1767)
This Central Thailand style heralded a baroque stage followed by a decline.

Ratanakosin (19th century to the present)
This is a Bangkok style which heralds a return to simpler designs and marks the beginning of European influences.

A good way to acquaint yourself with these styles is to visit Bangkok's National Museum, in Banglamphu, where works from each of these periods are on display. Then, as you travel and view old monuments and sculpture, you'll know what you're seeing, as well as what to look for.

Areas in coastal Thailand of historical interest for art and architecture include Thonburi, Phetchaburi, Chaiya and Nakhon Si Thammarat. Some of the monuments at these sites have been restored by the Fine Arts Department and/or by local interests. For more detail on historical sites, see the relevant regional sections in this book.

Recommended books on Thai art and architecture include AB Griswold's classic *Arts of Thailand* (Indiana University Press, 1960); the similarly titled *The Arts of Thailand* (Thames & Hudson, 1991) by Steve Van Beek; *A Concise History of Buddhist Art in Siam* (Tokyo, 1963) by Reginald Le May; and *Naga: Cultural Origins in Siam and the West Pacific* (Bangkok, 1998) by Sumet Jumsai. There are several decent English-language books on various aspects of Thai art for sale at the national museums around Thailand (particularly at the Bangkok National Museum) and at the Ancient City (Muang Boran) office on Th Ratchadamnoen Klang in Bangkok.

For information about the export of antiques or objects of art from Thailand see Antiques & Art in the Customs section of the Facts for the Visitor chapter.

Traditional Architecture Traditional home and temple architecture followed relatively strict rules of design that dictated proportion, placement, materials and ornamentation. With the modernisation of Thailand in the 19th and 20th centuries, stylistic codification gave way first to European functionalism and then to stylistic innovation in more recent times.

Traditional Thai residential architecture consists either of single-room wood houses raised on stilts, or more elaborate structures of interlocking rooms with both indoor and shaded outdoor spaces, all supported at least two metres above the ground on stilts. Since originally all Thai settlements were founded along river or canal banks, the use of stilts protected the house and its inhabitants from flooding during the annual monsoon. Even in areas where flooding wasn't common, the Thais continued to raise their houses on stilts until relatively recently, using the space beneath the house as a cooking area, for tethering animals, or for parking their bicycles and motor vehicles. Teak has always been the material of choice for wood structures, although with the shortage of teak in Thailand nowadays few houses less than 50 years old are constructed of it.

Rooflines in central Thailand are steeply pitched and often decorated at the corners or along the gables with motifs related to the *naga* or mythical sea serpent, long believed to be a spiritual protector of Tai cultures throughout Asia. In southern Thailand, bamboo and palm thatch have always been more common building materials than wood, and even today these renewable plant sources remain important construction elements. In certain areas of the South you'll also see thick-walled structures of stuccoed brick, architecture introduced by Chinese, Portuguese, French and British settlements along the Malay Peninsula.

In Thailand's four southern-most provinces, it's not unusual to come upon houses of entirely Malay design in which high masonry pediments or foundations, rather than wood stilts, lift the living areas well above the surrounding ground. Roofs of tile or thatch tend to be less steeply pitched, and hipped gables – almost entirely absent in traditional Thai architecture further north – are common in these Malay-influenced buildings.

Contemporary Architecture Modern Thai architects are among the most daring in South-East Asia, as even a short visit to Bangkok will confirm. Thais began mixing traditional Thai with European forms in the late 19th and early 20th centuries, as exemplified by Bangkok's Vimanmek

Teak Mansion, the Author's Wing of the Oriental Hotel, the Chakri Mahaprasat (part of the Grand Palace) next to Wat Phra Kaew, the Thai-Chinese Chamber of Commerce on Th Sathon Tai and any number of older residences and shophouses in Bangkok or provincial capitals throughout Thailand. This style is usually referred to as 'old Bangkok' or 'Ratanakosin'. The Old Siam Plaza shopping centre, adjacent to Bangkok's Chalermkrung Royal Theatre, is an attempt to revive the old Bangkok school.

Buildings of mixed heritage in the south typically show Portuguese influence. Shophouses throughout the country, whether 100 years or 100 days old, share the basic Chinese shophouse (*hâwng tháew* in Thai) design in which the ground floor is reserved for trading purposes while the upper floors contain offices or residences.

During most of the post-WWII era, the trend in modern Thai architecture – inspired by the European Bauhaus movement – was towards a boring functionalism in which the average building looked like a giant egg carton turned on its side. The Thai aesthetic, so vibrant in prewar eras, almost entirely disappeared in this characterless style of architecture.

When Thai architects finally began experimenting again during the building boom of the mid-1980s, it was to provide high-tech designs like Sumet Jumsai's famous robot-shaped Bank of Asia on Th Sathon Tai in Bangkok. Few people seemed to find the space-age look endearing, but at least it was different. Another trend affixed gaudy Roman and Greek-style columns to rectangular Art Deco boxes in what was almost a parody of western classical architecture. One of the outcomes of this fashion has been the widespread use of curvilinear banisters on the balconies of almost every new shophouse, apartment or condominium throughout Thailand, often with visually disturbing results.

A good book on Thai residential design, interior or exterior, is William Warren's *Thai Style* (Asia Books), a coffee-table tome with excellent photography by Luca Invernizzi Tettoni.

Painting

Except for prehistoric and historic cave or rock-wall murals found throughout the country, not much formal painting predating the 18th century exists in Thailand. Presumably there were a great number of temple murals in Ayuthaya that were destroyed by the Burmese invasion of 1767. The earliest surviving temple examples are found at Ayuthaya's Wat Ratburana (1424), Wat Chong Nonsii near the river in southern Bangkok (1657-1707) and Phetchaburi's Wat Yai Suwannaram (late 17th century).

Nineteenth century religious painting has fared better. Ratanakosin-style temple art is in fact more highly esteemed for painting than for sculpture or architecture. Typical temple murals feature rich colours and lively detail. Some of the finest are found in Wát Phra Kaew's Wihan Buddhaisawan (Phutthaisawan) Chapel in Bangkok and at Wát Suwannaram in Thonburi.

SOCIETY & CONDUCT

Citizens of the only South-East Asian country never to be colonised by a foreign power, the Thais are independent-minded yet steeped in a tradition of friendliness towards visitors. Although the pressures of modern development (Thailand enjoyed double-digit growth throughout the 80s) have brought a changing set of national values – not always for the better – the travel-poster epithet 'Land of Smiles' still applies to the treatment most visitors receive. The influence of Buddhism, arguably the most tolerant of the world's major religions, is said to be largely responsible for the Thais' easy friendliness.

Traditional Culture

When outsiders speak of 'Thai culture' they're referring to a complex of behavioural modes rooted in the history of Thai migration throughout South-East Asia, with many commonalities shared by the Lao of neighbouring Laos, the Shan of north-eastern Myanmar and the numerous tribal

Thais found in isolated pockets from Dien Bien Phu in Vietnam all the way to Assam in India. Nowhere are such norms more generalised than in Thailand, the largest of the Thai homelands.

Practically every ethnicity represented in Thailand, whether of Thai ancestry or not, has to a greater or lesser degree been assimilated into the Thai mainstream. Although Thailand is the most 'modernised' of the existing Thai (more precisely, Austro-Thai) societies, the cultural underpinnings are evident in virtually every facet of everyday life. Those aspects that might be deemed 'westernisation' – eg the wearing of trousers instead of *phâkhamāa*, the presence of cars, cinema and 7-eleven stores – show how Thailand has adopted and adapted tools invented elsewhere.

Such adaptations do not necessarily represent cultural loss. Ekawit Na Talang, a scholar of Thai culture and head of the government's National Culture Commission, defines culture as 'the system of thought and behaviour of a particular society – something which is dynamic and never static'. Talang and other world culture experts agree that it's paradoxical to try to protect a culture from foreign influences as cultures cannot exist in a vacuum. Culture evolves naturally as outside influences undergo processes of naturalisation. From this perspective, cultures that don't change, die. As Talang has said, 'Anything obsolete, people will reject and anything that has a relevant role in life, people will adopt and make it part of their culture'.

Nevertheless there are certain aspects of Thai society that virtually everyone recognises as 'Thai' cultural markers. The Thais themselves don't really have a word that corresponds to the English term 'culture'. The nearest equivalent, *wátánátham*, emphasises fine arts and ceremonies over other aspects usually covered by the concept. So if you ask Thais to define their culture, they'll often talk about architecture, food, dance, festivals and the like. Religion – obviously a big influence on culture as defined in the western sense – is considered more or less separate from wátánátham.

Sanùk

The Thai word *sanùk* means 'fun'. In Thailand anything worth doing – even work – should have an element of sanùk, otherwise it becomes drudgery. This doesn't mean Thais don't want to work or strive, they just tend to approach tasks with a sense of playfulness. Nothing condemns an activity more than the description *mâi sanùk*, 'not fun'. Sit down beside a rice field and watch workers planting, transplanting or harvesting rice; it's obviously back-breaking work, but participants generally inject the activity with lots of sanùk – flirtation, singing, trading insults and cracking jokes. The same goes in an office or a bank, or other white-collar work – at least when the office is predominantly Thai (businesses run by non-Thais don't necessarily exhibit sanùk). The famous Thai smile comes partially out of this desire to make sanùk.

Face

Thais believe strongly in the concept of 'saving face', that is, avoiding confrontation and trying not to embarrass themselves or other people (except when it's sanùk to do so!). The ideal face-saver doesn't bring up negative topics in everyday conversation, and when they notice stress in another's life, they usually won't say anything unless that person complains or asks for help. Laughing at minor accidents – like when someone trips and falls – may seem callous to outsiders but it's really just an attempt to save face on behalf of the person suffering the mishap. This is another source of the Thai smile – it's the best possible face to put on in almost any situation.

Status & Obligation

All relationships in traditional Thai society – and virtually all relationships in the modern milieu as well – are governed by connections between *phûu yài* (big person) and *phûu náwy* (little person). Phûu náwy are supposed to defer to phûu yài following simple lines of social rank defined by age, wealth, status, and personal and political power. Examples of 'automatic' phûu yài status include adults (vs children), bosses (vs employees), elder classmates (vs younger classmates), elder siblings (vs younger siblings), teachers (vs pupils), military (vs civilian), Thai (vs non-Thai) and so on.

While this tendency towards social ranking is to some degree shared by many societies around the world, the Thai twist lies in the set of mutual obligations linking phûu yài to phûu náwy. Sociologists have referred to this phenomenon as the 'patron-client relationship'. Phûu náwy are supposed to show a degree of obedience and respect (together these concepts are covered by the term *kreng jai*) towards phûu yài, but in return phûu yài are obligated to care for or 'sponsor' the phûu náwy they have frequent contact with. In such relationships phûu náwy can, for example, ask phûu yài for favours involving money or job opportunities. Phûu yài reaffirm their rank by granting such requests when possible; to refuse would be to risk loss of face and status.

Age is a large determinant where other factors are absent or weak. In such cases the terms *phîi* (elder sibling) and *náwng* (younger sibling) apply more than phûu yài/phûu náwy, although the intertwined obligations remain the same. Even people unrelated by blood quickly establish who's phîi and who's náwng; this is why one of the first questions Thais ask new acquaintances is 'How old are you?'.

When dining, touring or entertaining, the phûu yài always picks up the tab; if a group is involved, the person with most social rank pays the check for everyone, even if it empties his or her wallet. For a phûu náwy to try and pay would risk loss of face. Money plays a large role in defining phûu yài status in most situations. A person who turned out to be successful in his or her post-school career would never think of allowing an ex-classmate of lesser success – even if they were once on an equal social footing – to pay the bill. Likewise a young, successful executive will pay an older person's way in spite of the age difference.

The implication is that whatever wealth you come into is to be shared – at least partially – with those who have been less fortunate. This doesn't apply to strangers – the average Thai isn't big on charity – but always comes into play with friends and relatives.

Foreigners often feel offended when they encounter such phenomena as two tiered pricing for hotels or sightseeing attractions – one price for Thais, a higher price for foreigners. But this is simply just another expression of the traditional patron-client relationship. On the one hand foreigners who can afford to travel to Thailand from abroad are seen to have more wealth than Thai citizens (on average this is true), hence they're expected to help subsidise Thai enjoyment of these commodities; and at the same time, paradoxically, the Thais feel they are due certain special privileges as locals – what might be termed the 'hometown discount'. Another example: in a post office line, Thais get served first as part of their national privilege.

Comportment

Personal power (*baará-mii*, sometimes mistranslated as 'charisma') also has a bearing on one's social status, and can be gained by cleaving as close as possible to the ideal 'Thai' behaviour. 'Thai-ness' is first and foremost defined, as might be expected, by the ability to speak Thai. It doesn't matter which dialect, although southern Thai – with its Malay/Yawi influences – is slightly suspect, mainly due to the region's association with the 'foreign' religion of Islam.

Other hallmarks of the Thai ideal – heavily influenced by Thai Buddhism – include discretion towards the opposite sex, modest dress, a neat and clean appearance, and modes of expression and comportment that value the quiet, subtle and indirect rather than the loud, obvious and direct.

The degree to which Thais conform to these ideals matches the degree of respect they receive from most of their associates. Although high rank – age-related, civil, military or clerical – will exempt certain individuals from chastisement by their social 'inferiors', it doesn't exempt them from the way they are perceived by other Thais. This goes for foreigners as well, even though most first-time visitors can hardly be expected to speak idiomatic Thai. But if you do learn some Thai, and you make an effort to respect Thai social ideals, you'll come closer to enjoying some of the perks awarded for Thai-ness.

Dos & Don'ts

Monarchy and religion are the two sacred cows in Thailand. Thais are tolerant of most kinds of behaviour as long as it doesn't insult one of these.

King & Country The monarchy is held in considerable respect in Thailand and visitors should be respectful too – avoid making disparaging remarks about the king, queen or anyone in the royal family. One of Thailand's leading intellectuals, Sulak Sivaraksa, was arrested in the 1980s for lese-majesty because of a passing reference to the king's fondness for yachting (Sulak referred to His Majesty as 'the skipper') and again in 1991 when he referred to the royal family as 'ordinary people'. Although on the first occasion he received a royal pardon, in 1991 Sulak had to flee the country to avoid prosecution again for alleged remarks made at Thammasat University about the ruling military junta, with reference to the king (Sulak has since returned under a suspended sentence). The penalty for lese-majesty is seven years imprisonment.

While it's OK to criticise the Thai government and even Thai culture openly, it's considered a grave insult to Thai nationhood, as well as to the monarchy, not to stand when you hear the national or royal anthems. Radio and TV stations in Thailand broadcast the national anthem daily at 8 am and 6 pm. In towns and villages (and even in some Bangkok neighbourhoods) the anthem is broadcast over public loudspeakers in the streets. The Thais stop whatever they're doing to stand during the anthem (except in Bangkok where nobody can hear above the din of the street) and visitors are expected to do likewise. The royal anthem is played just before films are shown in cinemas; again, the audience always stands until it's over.

Religion Correct behaviour in temples entails several considerations, the most important of which is to dress neatly and take your shoes off when you enter any building that contains a Buddha image. Buddha images are sacred, so don't pose in front of them for pictures and definitely do not clamber upon them.

Shorts or sleeveless shirts are considered improper for both men and women when visiting temples. Locals wearing either would be turned away by monastic authorities, but except for the most sacred temples in the country (eg Wát Phra Kaew in Bangkok), Thais are often too polite to refuse entry to improperly clad foreigners. Some wáts hire trousers or long sarongs so that shorts-wearing tourists can enter the compound.

Monks are not supposed to touch or be touched by women. If a woman wants to hand something to a monk, the object should be placed within reach of the monk, not handed directly to him.

When sitting in a religious edifice, keep your feet pointed away from any Buddha images. The usual way to do this is to sit in the 'mermaid' pose in which your legs are folded to the side, with the feet pointing backwards.

A few of the larger wáts in Bangkok charge small entry fees. In other temples, offering a small donation before leaving the compound is appropriate but not mandatory. Usually there are donation boxes near the entry of the *bòt* (central sanctuary) or next to the central Buddha image at the rear. In rural wáts, there may be no donation box available; in these places, it's OK to leave money on the floor next to the central image or even by the doorway, where temple attendants will collect it later.

Show respect for religious symbols and rituals. Avoid touching spirit houses, household altars, village totems and other religious symbols, as this often 'pollutes' them spiritually and may force the villagers to perform purification rituals after you have

moved on. Keep your distance from ceremonies being performed unless you're
asked to participate.

Social Gestures & Attitudes Traditionally, Thais greet each other not with a handshake but with a prayer-like palms-together
gesture known as a *wâi*. If someone wâis
you, you should wâi back (unless wâi-ed by
a child). Most urban Thais are familiar with
the western-style handshake and will offer
the same to a foreigner, although a wâi is always appreciated.

Thais are often addressed by their first
name with the honorific *khun* or other title
preceding it. Other formal terms of address
include *Nai* (Mr) and *Naang* (Miss or Mrs).
Friends often use nicknames or kinship
terms like *phîi* (elder sibling), *náwng*
(younger sibling), *mâe* (mother) or *lung*
(uncle), depending on the age difference.

A smile and *sawàt-dii khráp/khâ* (the all-
purpose Thai greeting) goes a long way towards calming the trepidation locals may
initially feel upon seeing a foreigner,
whether in the city or the countryside.

When handing things to other people you
should use both hands or your right hand
only, never the left hand (reserved for toilet
ablutions). Books and other written material are given a special status over other sec-
ular objects. Hence you shouldn't slide
books or documents across a table or
counter-top, and never place them on the
floor – use a chair instead if table space
isn't available.

When encounters take a turn for the
worse, don't get angry – losing one's temper means loss of face for everyone present.
Remember that this is Asia, where keeping
your cool is paramount. Talking loudly is
seen as rude by cultured Thais, whatever the
situation. Remember, the pushy foreigner
often gets served last.

Feet & Head The feet are the lowest part
of the body (spiritually as well as physically) so don't point them at people or at
things. Even when sitting crossed-legged,
for example, it's good to make sure you're

not inadvertently aiming your lowliest body
part at your neighbour. Don't prop your feet
on chairs or tables while sitting. Never
touch any part of someone else's body with
your foot.

In the same context, the head is regarded
as the highest part of the body, so don't
touch Thais on the head – or ruffle their hair
– either. If you touch someone's head acci-
dentally, offer an immediate apology or
you'll be perceived as very rude. Don't sit
on pillows meant for sleeping, even your
own, as this represents a variant of the taboo
against head-touching.

Never step over someone, even on a
crowded 3rd class train where people are
sitting or lying on the floor. Instead squeeze
around them or ask them to move.

Dress & Nudity Shorts (except knee-length
walking shorts), sleeveless shirts, tank tops
(singlets) and other beach-style attire are not
considered appropriate dress in Thailand for
anything other than sporting events. Such
dress is especially counter-productive if
worn to government offices (eg when applying for a visa extension). Having an attitude
of 'This is how I dress at home and no-one
is going to stop me' gains nothing but con-
tempt or disrespect from the Thais.

Sandals or slip-on shoes are OK for all
but the most formal occasions. Short-
sleeved shirts and blouses with capped
sleeves are quite acceptable.

Thais would never dream of wearing
dirty clothes while abroad, so they are often
shocked to see westerners travelling around
Thailand in clothes that apparently haven't
been washed in weeks. Keep up with your
laundry and you'll receive far more respect
everywhere you go.

Regardless of what the Thais may (or
may not) have been accustomed to centuries
ago, they are quite offended by public nudity today. According to Thailand's National Parks Act, any woman who goes
topless on a national park beach (eg Ko
Chang, Ko Phi-Phi, Ko Samet) is breaking
the law. If you are at a truly deserted beach
and are sure no Thais may come along,

there's nothing stopping you; however, at most beaches travellers should wear suitable attire. Topless bathing for females is frowned upon in most places except on heavily-touristed islands like Phuket, Samui, Samet and Pha-Ngan. Likewise, except when on the beach, men should keep a shirt on; entering a shop or (particularly) a restaurant half naked looks barbaric to the Thais. Many Thais say nudity on the beach is what bothers them most about foreign travellers. Thais often take nudity as a sign of disrespect for the locals, rather than as a libertarian symbol or modern custom. Thais are extremely modest in this respect (Patpong-style go-go bars are cultural aberrations, hidden from public view and designed for foreign consumption) and visitors who have any respect for their hosts won't try to 'reform' them.

Shoes As in temples, shoes are not worn inside people's homes, nor in some guesthouses and shops. If you see a pile of shoes at or near the entrance, you should respect the house custom and remove your shoes before entry. Several Thais have confided to the author that they can't believe how oblivious some foreigners appear to be of this simple and obvious custom. For them the wearing of shoes indoors is disgusting and the behaviour of those who ignore the custom is nothing short of boorish.

Visiting Homes Thais can be very hospitable and it's not unusual to be invited home for a meal or a sociable drink. Even if your visit is very brief, you will be offered something to eat or drink, probably both – a glass of water, a cup of tea, a piece of fruit, a shot of rice liquor, or whatever they have on hand. You are expected to partake of whatever is offered; whether you've already eaten or not, whether you're thirsty or not, to refuse at least a taste is considered impolite.

Message from a Reader As a final comment on avoiding offence, here is a plea from a reader who wrote following an extended visit to Thailand:

Please do whatever you can to impress on travellers the importance of treating the Thai people, who are so generous and unassuming, with the respect they deserve. If people sunbathe topless, take snapshots of the people like animals in a zoo, and demand western standards then they are both offending the Thai people and contributing to the opinion many of them have of us as being rich, demanding and promiscuous.

Treatment of Animals

Thailand is a signatory to the UN Convention on International Trade in Endangered Species (CITES). Educational levels have risen to the point that many international watchdog groups, such as the World Wildlife Fund and Wildlife Conservation Society, receive much local support. An illicit trade in endangered and threatened wildlife continues but appears to be much smaller than even 10 years ago.

In less developed rural regions of the country, particularly in the north and north-east, and among Thailand's hill tribes, hunting remains a norm for obtaining animal protein. Over-fishing of lakes, rivers and oceans poses a danger to certain fish species.

Harder to understand, at least for some of us, is the taking of monkeys, birds and other animals from the jungle to be kept as pets – usually tied by a rope or chain to a tree, or confined to cages. Several Non Government Organisations (NGOs) such as the Phuket Gibbon Rehabilitation Centre are working to educate the public about the cruelty of such practices, and have initiated wildlife rescue and rehabilitation projects.

In any case wildlife experts agree that the greatest threat to Thai fauna is neither hunting nor the illegal wildlife trade, but rather habitat loss – as is true for most of the rest of the world. Protect the forests, mangroves, marshes and grasslands, and they will protect the animals.

For further comment on this topic, see the Ecology & Environment section earlier in this chapter.

Prostitution

As throughout most of south and South-East Asia, men in Thailand have greater freedom in their sexual activities than women, who are expected to arrive at the marriage altar as virgins and to refrain from extramarital affairs. This attitude creates a sexual imbalance in which large numbers of males are seeking casual sexual contact, but few females are available. The resulting commercial sex industry, catering largely to indigenous demand, thus maintains an ongoing reservoir of sex workers and clients. In Bangkok (and to a much lesser degree in other large urban centres), the imbalance is righting itself as premarital/extramarital sex between non-paying consenting Thais becomes more common.

Among foreigners it's a common perception that Thai women become sex workers because they don't have recourse to similar or better-paying employment in other fields. But employment statistics don't support this notion. Thailand's work force is 44% female, ranking it 27th on a world scale, just ahead of China and the USA. On a purely economic level there is no compelling reason to choose prostitution over weaving, rice-milling or office work. Thai women who participate in prostitution either do so unwillingly – in the case of bonded or forced service – or willingly in hopes of obtaining luxuries in excess of mere livelihood. In either case it's the demand side of the equation – caused by the lack of available female sex partners – that appears to drive the industry.

RELIGION
Buddhism

Approximately 95% of Thais are Theravada Buddhists. The Theravada school (literally, 'teaching of the elders') is an earlier and, according to its followers, less corrupted form of Buddhism than the Mahayana schools found in East Asia or in the Himalayan lands. Also called the 'southern' school, it took a southern route from India, its place of origin, through South-East Asia (Myanmar, Thailand, Laos and Cambodia), while the 'northern' school proceeded north into Nepal, Tibet, China, Korea, Mongolia, Vietnam and Japan. Because the Theravada school tried to preserve or limit the Buddhist doctrines to only those canons codified in the early Buddhist era, the Mahayana school gave Theravada Buddhism the name Hinayana, or the 'lesser vehicle'. The Mahayana school was the 'great vehicle', because it built upon the earlier teachings, 'expanding' the doctrine in such a way as to respond more to the needs of lay people, or so it is claimed.

The ultimate end of Theravada Buddhism is *nibbana* (Sanskrit: *nirvana*), which literally means the 'blowing out' or extinction of all desire and thus of all suffering (dukkha). Effectively, it is also an end to the cycle of rebirths (both moment to moment and life to life) that is existence. In reality, most Thai Buddhists aim for rebirth in a 'better' existence rather than the supramundane goal of nibbana, which is highly misunderstood by Asians as well as westerners.

Many Thais express the feeling that they are somehow unworthy of nibbana. By feeding monks, giving donations to temples and performing regular worship at the local wát they hope to improve their lot, acquiring enough merit (Pali: *puñña*; Thai: *bun*) to prevent or at least lessen the number of rebirths. The making of merit *(tham bun)* is an important social and religious activity in Thailand. The concept of reincarnation is almost universally accepted, even by non-Buddhists, and the Buddhist theory of karma is well expressed in the Thai proverb *tham dii, dâi dii; tham chûa, dâi chûa* – 'do good and receive good; do evil and receive evil'.

Thai Buddhism has no particular 'sabbath' or day of the week to make temple visits. Nor is there anything corresponding to a liturgy or mass over which a priest presides. Instead Thai Buddhists visit the wát whenever they feel like it, most often on *wan phrá* (literally, 'excellent days'), which occur every full and new moon, ie every 15 days. On such a visit lotus buds, incense and candles are offered at various altars, and bone reliquaries are placed around the

wát compound. Other activities include offering food to the temple Sangha (monks,
nuns and lay residents – monks always eat
first), meditating (individually or in
groups), listening to monks chanting *suttas*
or Buddhist discourse, and attending a *thêt*
or *dhamma* talk by the abbot or other respected teacher. Visitors may also seek
counsel from monks or nuns regarding new
or ongoing life problems.

Monks & Nuns Socially, every Thai male
is expected to become a monk for a short
period, optimally between the time he finishes school and the time he starts a career or
marries. Men or boys under 20 may enter the
Sangha as novices – this is not unusual since
a family earns great merit when one of its
sons takes robe and bowl. Traditionally,
three months is spent in the wát during the
Buddhist lent *(phansāa)*, which begins in
July and coincides with the rainy season.
However, nowadays men may spend as little
as a week or 15 days to accrue merit as a
monk. There are about 32,000 monasteries in
Thailand and 200,000 monks; many of them
ordain for life. Of these a large percentage
become scholars and teachers, while some
specialise in healing and/or folk magic.

At one time the Theravada Buddhist
world had a separate monastic lineage for
females, who called themselves *bhikkhuni*
and observed more vows than monks did –
311 precepts as opposed to the 227 followed by monks. Started in Sri Lanka
around two centuries after the Buddha's
lifetime by the daughter of King Asoka (a
Buddhist king in India), the bhikkhuni tradition in Sri Lanka eventually died out and
was unfortunately never restored.

In Thailand, the modern equivalent is the
mâe chii (Thai for 'nun'; literally, 'mother
priest') – women who live the monastic life
as *atthasila* or 'Eight-Precept' nuns. Thai
nuns shave their heads, wear white robes
and take vows in an ordination procedure
similar to that undergone by monks. Generally speaking, nunhood in Thailand isn't
considered as 'prestigious' as monkhood.
The average Thai Buddhist makes a great

show of offering new robes and household
items to the monks at their local wát but pay
much less attention to the nuns. This is
mainly due to the fact that nuns generally
don't perform ceremonies on behalf of
laypeople, so there is less incentive to make
offerings to them. Furthermore, many Thais
equate the number of precepts observed
with the total Buddhist merit achieved,
hence nunhood is seen as less 'meritorious'
than monkhood since mâe chiis keep only
eight precepts.

This difference in prestige represents social Buddhism, however, and is not how
those with a serious interest regard the mâe
chii. Nuns engage in the same fundamental
activities – meditation and dhamma study –
as monks do. In fact wáts that have sizeable
contingents of mâe chiis are highly respected, since women don't choose temples
for reasons of clerical status. When more
than a few nuns reside at one temple, it's
usually a sign that the teachings there are
particularly strong.

An increasing number of foreigners are
coming to Thailand to ordain as Buddhist
monks or nuns, especially to study with the
famed meditation masters of the forest wáts
in southern and north-eastern Thailand.

Further Information If you wish to
find out more about Buddhism you can
contact the World Fellowship of Buddhists
(☎ 02-251 1188), 33 Th Sukhumvit (between sois 1 and 3), Bangkok. Senior
faràng monks hold English-language
dhamma/meditation classes there on the
first Sunday of each month from 2 to 6 pm;
all are welcome.

A Buddhist bookshop opposite the north
entrance to Wát Bovornives (Bowonniwet)
in the Banglamphu district of Bangkok
sells a variety of English-language books
on Buddhism. Asia Books and DK Book
House also stock Buddhist literature. (See
the Bookshops section in the Bangkok
chapter for locations.)

For more information on meditation
study in southern Thailand see the sections
on Chaiya's Wát Suan Mokkhaphalaram

and also Wát Khao Tham on Ko Pha-Ngan. Both are in the South-Western Gulf Coast chapter.

Recommended books about Buddhism include:

Buddhism Explained by Phra Khantipalo
Heartwood of the Bodhi Tree by Buddhadasa Bhikku
In This Very Life: The Liberation Teachings of the Buddha by Sayadaw U Pandita
Living Dharma: Teachings of Twelve Buddhist Masters edited by Jack Kornfield
The Long View: An Excursion into Buddhist Perspectives by Suratano Bhikku (T Magness)
The Mind and the Way by Ajaan Sumedho
Phra Faràng: An English Monk in Thailand by Phra Peter Pannapadipo
A Still Forest Pool: the Teaching of Ajaan Chaa at Wát Paa Pong compiled by Jack Kornfield & Paul Breiter
Thai Women in Buddhism by Chatsumarn Kabilsingh
What the Buddha Taught by Walpola Rahula

Two good sources of publications on Theravada Buddhism are the Buddhist Publication Society, PO Box 61 54, Sangharaja Mawatha, Kandy, Sri Lanka, and the Barre Center for Buddhist Studies, Lockwood Rd, Barre, MA 01005 USA.

On the Internet, an excellent source from which you can freely download many publications, including the complete English version of the Pali canon, is the Access to Insight: Readings in Theravada Buddhism Web site (world.std.com/~metta/index .html) The site is cross-indexed by subject, title, author, proper names and even Buddhist similes. Two other recommended Internet sites with lots of material on Theravada Buddhism, as well as links to other sites, include DharmaNet Electronic Files Archive (sunsite .unc.edu/pub/academic/religious_studies/ Buddhism/DEFA/Theravada/) and Buddha Net (www.buddhanet.net/).

Other Religions

A small percentage of Thais and most of the Malays in the south, amounting to about 4% of the population, are followers of Islam. Half a percent of the population – primarily missionised hill tribes and Vietnamese immigrants – profess Christianity, while the remaining half percent are Confucianists, Taoists, Mahayana Buddhists and Hindus. Mosques (in the south) and Chinese temples are both common enough that you will probably come across some in your travels in Thailand. Before entering *any* temple, sanctuary or mosque you must remove your shoes, and in a mosque your head must be covered.

Facts for the Visitor

HIGHLIGHTS

Thailand's unique geography offers three starkly different coastal settings.

The eastern Gulf coast, stretching southeast from Bangkok to the Cambodian border, is a succession of beaches and offshore islands which face south-west and thus escape one of the two major monsoons that sweep across mainland South-East Asia each year. The oldest and most well established of the resorts along this coast is densely developed Pattaya, although Gulf alternatives nearby are expanding with each passing season. The main advantage of the eastern Gulf resorts is their proximity to Bangkok; except for some of the islands, such as Ko Samet and Ko Chang (in Thai, 'ko' means 'island'), the beaches aren't all that spectacular.

The Malay peninsula extends 1600km south-east from Bangkok, creating a slender land barrier between the South China Sea and the Indian Ocean. Lined on either side by sandy bays, lagoons, mangroves, islands and islets, over half the length of this peninsula falls within Thailand's borders.

The west side of this peninsula, referred to in this book as the Andaman coast, faces the Andaman Sea (the part of the Indian Ocean that lies between the Andaman islands and Thailand's west coast). This coastline is characterised by craggy cliffs and islands composed of a chalky limestone that dissolves to impart a deep turquoise hue to coastal shallows. Diving among the coral reefs in this area can be superb.

Phuket, Thailand's largest island, is the Andaman coast's most popular resort, followed by Ko Phi-Phi and a number of up-and-coming beaches and islands, including Ko Lanta to the south and Hat Khao Lak to the north. Travel to the more remote island groups is seasonal, since during the height of the south-west monsoon (May to October) the Andaman Sea becomes too rough for offshore navigation.

Waters along the gulf coast of the Malay peninsula are calmer year-round. This coast remains the most undeveloped, with the bulk of the tourist activity focused on Ko Samui, Thailand's third largest island. The opening of Samui's airport in the late 1980s spurred the island's already rapid development, while other islands nearby remain favoured destinations for those with more time than money.

Which side of the peninsula you choose – the Gulf of Thailand (for Prachuap Khiri Khan, Ko Samui, Songkhla) or the Andaman Sea (Phuket, Krabi, Trang) – might be determined by the time of year. See When to Go earlier in this chapter and Climate in the previous chapter for more information on seasonal considerations.

If time is an issue, check out the beaches and islands along the eastern Gulf coast of central Thailand (Pattaya, Ko Samet, Ko Chang) or upper peninsular Gulf (Cha-am, Hua Hin) for shorter beach excursions. Head to southern Thailand if you have a week or more and will be using ground transport. Or fly to one of the airports in the southern beach resort areas (eg Ko Samui, Phuket, Krabi).

One of the main highlights of Thai travel is soaking up the general cultural ambience, which can be done just about anywhere away from the resorts. You won't experience much if you spend most of your time sitting around in guesthouse cafes, hanging out on the beach or diving with your own kind. At least once during your trip, try going to a small to medium-sized town well off the main tourist circuit, staying at a local hotel, and eating in Thai curry shops and noodle stands. It's not as easy as going with the crowd but you'll learn a lot more about Thailand, and the experiences you have will likely be the ones you remember best years later.

Resorts & Convenient Escapes

Ko Samet Off the eastern Gulf coast, and only three hours from Bangkok by road and boat, this island can be quite over-run on weekends and holidays. The fine white sand and clear waters attract a cross-section of expats, Thais and tourists. There's some decent snorkelling at nearby islets. Prices: inexpensive to moderate. Accessible by boat only.

Hua Hin & Prachuap Khiri Khan The upper peninsula province of Prachuap Khiri Khan, facing the Gulf, offers sandy beaches of medium quality along much of its length, from the well-touristed Hua Hin in the north to little known Thai resorts near Ao Manao and Bang Saphan. Most accommodation is in medium-priced hotels. Not much in the way of diving, but seafood is superb and economical. Crowded on holidays. Prices: inexpensive to moderate. Accessible by air (Hua Hin only), rail and road.

Ko Samui In the Gulf of Thailand, off the coast of Surat Thani, this is the third largest island in the country and quite heavily developed. Once a haven for backpackers on the Asia Trail, it is for the most part now given over to middle-class hotels and guesthouses, though dirt-cheap digs can still be found. Snorkelling and diving are fair, beaches superb. Prices: inexpensive to moderate, with a few luxury resorts. Accessible by ferry from Surat Thani, air from Bangkok or by train/bus/ferry combo from Bangkok.

Phuket In the Andaman Sea, Thailand's largest and most geographically varied island was the first to develop a tourist industry. Phuket has become a fairly sophisticated international resort, albeit one with the highest number of 'green' hotel developments as well as two well-respected national parks. Good diving at nearby islands and reefs of the Andaman Sea and Ao Phang-Nga (Sea of Phuket). Best Thai cuisine of any of the islands. Prices: moderate to expensive. Accessible by air and road (via a causeway).

More Remote Beach & Island Areas

Ko Chang & Ko Kut In the Gulf of Thailand, near the Cambodian border, these islands are relatively untouristed. Though part of a national park, both islands have coastal zones where development is permitted, but so far high-profile development has been kept at bay by their distance from Bangkok and mountainous geography. Attracts those looking for quiet, economical beach stays, with some spillover from Ko Pha-Ngan. Waterfalls and hiking trails on Ko Chang add to the attraction. Prices: inexpensive, save for a couple of moderate to expensive beach resorts. Accessible by boat only from Trat.

Songkhla, Pattani & Narathiwat These deep south, Gulf of Thailand, provinces near Malaysia offer hundreds of kilometres of deserted beach. During the north-east monsoon (November to March), the water tends to be murky due to cross-currents. Culturally these are some of the most interesting coastal areas in the country due to Islamic Malay influences. Good for regional handicrafts, including cotton prints, sarongs and batik. Very little is available in the way of beach accommodation, though village housing is a possibility for those with initiative and who can speak some Thai. Prices: inexpensive. Accessible by rail (parts of Narathiwat and Songkhla only) and road. Hat Yai is the nearest air hub.

Ko Similan, Ko Surin & Ko Tarutao National Marine Parks These Andaman island groups enjoy some of the best park protection in Thailand. There is fantastic diving and snorkelling at all three; Similan and Surin are rated among the world's top 10 dive destinations. Accommodation is limited to park bungalows and camping, except for one private island in Tarutao. Prices: inexpensive. Accessible by boat only, and only during the non-monsoon months (November to April), from Phuket and the mainland.

Krabi This province facing Ao Phang-Nga, opposite Phuket, offers a range of beaches and islands ringed with striking limestone formations. Rock climbing, snorkelling, diving, boating and fishing provide opportunities for active holidays. Generally quiet, though accommodation tends to book out from December to February, while during May, June, September and October it can be nearly deserted. Prices: inexpensive to moderate (or luxurious at the Dusit Rayavadee Resort). Provincial capital accessible by half-day boat or bus trip from Phuket; overnight bus from Bangkok. Islands, and some beaches, accessible by boat only.

Ko Lanta Actually part of Krabi Province, this slender island is a perennial winter favourite among low-budget travellers; it's practically deserted from April to November when lashed by south-west monsoon rains. Some snorkelling and diving; good seafood. Crowded on holidays. Prices: inexpensive. Accessible by boat from Krabi and Ko Phi-Phi, by road and ferry from nearby coastal towns.

Trang The next province south of Krabi, facing the Andaman Sea, Trang is largely undiscovered, but the beaches and islands aren't as pretty as Krabi's. Good diving but you'll have to bring your own gear. Prices: inexpensive to moderate. Islands accessible by boat only, mainland by road and air.

National Parks in Coastal Areas

Thailand boasts nearly 80 national parks. See the National Parks & Wildlife Sanctuaries section under Flora & Fauna in the Facts about Thailand chapter for general information about the country's protected areas, and the destination chapters for complete details on each of the parks covered in this book. The book *National Parks of Thailand* by Denis Gray, Collin Piprell & Mark Graham is the most comprehensive source of English-language material on the parklands.

Ko Chang National Marine Park, Trat Province The mountainous Ko Chang archipelago encompasses around 50 islands, all but three of which are almost completely undeveloped. Beaches and interiors tend to be pristine, though transport among them can be problematic (except for Ko Chang, where boat transport is regular). Good any

time of year, although the June to October south-west monsoon strikes here with more force than elsewhere on the Gulf coast.

Khao Sam Roi Yot National Park, Prachuap Khiri Khan Province This 98 sq km park on the coast near Hua Hin is one of the country's most scenic due to a blend of mountains and coast. Good trails and camping. Best visited November to July, though it's relatively protected from the south-west monsoon so don't rule out other months.

Khao Sok National Park, Surat Thani Province Limestone crags, rainforests and jungle streams provide the perfect environment for the remnants of Thailand's threatened tiger and clouded leopard populations, as well as two species of *Rafflesia*. Treehouse accommodation protects the forest floor and gives visitors an opportunity to experience one of the country's most important ecosystems. Best visited December to February.

Khao Lak/Lam Ru National Park, Phang-Nga Province This 125 sq km park combines sea cliffs and beaches with 1000m peaks, original rainforest and mangroves. Good hiking and the chance to see wildlife, including gibbons and (less likely) the Asiatic black bear. Bungalow accommodation at the visitor centre and private resorts nearby. Best visited November to April.

Ao Phang-Nga National Marine Park, Phang-Nga Province The coastline is marked by stunning karst topography, with steep-sided, verdant limestone islets dropping straight into deep, turquoise waters. Over 40 islands are included in this park near Phuket. Best visited November to April.

Hat Noppharat Thara/Ko Phi-Phi National Marine Park, Krabi Province Although this huge marine park in the southern half of Ao Phang-Nga is unevenly protected, many designated park islands are still pristine. Ko Phi-Phi is the glaring exception as it is crowded with illegal beach accommodation and is probably a lost cause (as a parkland). Great kayaking, diving and snorkelling. No park accommodation, though there is private accommodation on Ko Phi-Phi. Typical marine karst topography as elsewhere in Ao Phang-Nga. Best visited November to April.

Sirinat National Marine Park, Phuket Province This new park in the north-west corner of Phuket, comprising two smaller, formerly separate national parks and Thailand's longest beach, now covers a total of 22km of shoreline. Sea turtles nest here, and there is a coral reef offshore. A visitor centre, toilets and picnic tables are the only facilities provided. Best visited from November to April.

Cultural Pursuits
Those who would like to temper beach time with cultural and spiritual diversions can do so in southern Thailand, though less so along the eastern Gulf coast. Below are a few recommended sights; greater detail can be found in the relevant destination chapters.

Historic Temples Although the eastern Gulf coast is predominantly Buddhist, there are virtually no temples of particular historic value in the region. southern Thailand, despite its heavily Muslim character (predominantly so in the deep south), does have several Buddhist centres with significant temple sites.

The provincial capital of Phetchaburi on the north-western Gulf coast contains numerous older wáts, including a few with some of the best preserved Ayuthaya-period temple murals in the country.

In Chaiya, Surat Thani Province, a highly venerated stupa at Wat Phra Boromathat dates from the Srivijaya era (8th to 13th centuries).

Nakhon Si Thammarat boasts Wat Phra Mahathat, one of the oldest Buddhist temples in Thailand, in a large 13th century compound which also contains an exhibit of antique religious objects.

Museums Coastal Thailand isn't known for the outstanding quality of its museums, but there are a few worth looking out for. Nakhon Si Thammarat's national museum features a room dedicated to works of religious art and handicrafts that originated in southern Thailand.

The Songkhla National Museum is a work of art in itself, an old Sino-Portuguese mansion converted into exhibition space for historic artefacts from around the south and beyond.

The Southern Thai Folklore Museum on Ko Yo, near Songkhla, contains an impressive array of southern Thai religious and folk art, while Nakhon Si Thammarat National Museum features the country's best collection of southern Thai religious art, plus Dong-Son bronze drums, Dvaravati Buddha images and Pallava (south Indian) Hindu sculpture.

If you're coming through Bangkok, a visit to the National Museum, Vimanmek Teak Mansion and Jim Thompson's House can be recommended for their displays of art and artefacts from centuries past.

SUGGESTED ITINERARIES
Most visitors to Thailand's beaches pick one beach or one island and spend their entire holiday there, whether it's one week or one month. Those with more ambitious beach-hopping talents might sample one or more of the following coastal routes.

One Week
Temples & Gulf Beaches For a short Thailand sampler, start with a two day taste of Bangkok's heavily gilded temples and urban intensity, then flee towards the former royal capital of Ayuthaya to take in the 400-year-old temple and palace ruins, right in the centre of the city. A day in Ayuthaya is enough for most people in a hurry. Transit back through Bangkok and head southeast to Ko Samet off the eastern Gulf of Thailand coast for two or three nights on this all-season island before saying farewell to Thailand. Substitute Hat Jomtien near Pattaya for Samet if your tastes run towards

international-class hotels rather than simpler beach bungalows.

Two Weeks
Bangkok to Ko Chang Start with Bangkok as above, then hopscotch along the north-eastern Gulf to coastal Rayong, Ko Samet and the islands in the Ko Chang archipelago, spending more or less time at each according to your tastes.

Bangkok to the Malaysian Border After you've had enough of Bangkok – three or four days does the trick for most people who have only two weeks in the country – start rolling down the Malay peninsula with a day and two nights in Phetchaburi, a city of venerable late Ayuthaya-period temples and a hill-top royal palace.

After Phetchaburi, take your pick among the beaches at Cha-am, Hua Hin or in the vicinity of Prachuap Khiri Khan – all places where middle-class Thais like to vacation. And/or visit Khao Sam Roi Yot National Park, good for coastal and hillside hiking.

For some serious beach time, zero in on one or more of the three major islands off the coast of Chumphon and Surat Thani provinces – Ko Tao, Ko Pha-Ngan and Ko Samui – depending on your tastes (see Islands & Beaches in the earlier Highlights section for descriptive summaries).

If you're ready for a little culture, sail back to the mainland and visit Chaiya (Srivijaya-era ruins and a world-famous meditation monastery) or Songkhla (Sino-Portuguese architecture and a national museum).

Follow with a night or two in Hat Yai to sample some of Thailand's best Chinese food outside Bangkok and to shop for southern Thai or Malay textiles. For your entry into Malaysia, take the east coast route via Narathiwat for the best natural scenery, the west coast if you're in a rush to reach Penang or Kuala Lumpur.

Three Weeks
Choose one of the two week itineraries outlined previously, and tack on a week roaming the northern Andaman coast from Ranong to Phang-Nga. Consider taking at least a day for a sea canoe trip in Ao Phang-Nga or a jungle walk at Khao Sok National Park.

One Month
With a month of beach- and island-hopping you can easily add the southern Andaman coast, sampling Krabi's rugged sea karst topography as well as the virtually untouched Surin, Similan, Phetra or Tarutao archipelagos.

PLANNING
When to Go
The best time to visit coastal Thailand vis-à-vis climate is between November and March – during these months it rains least and is not so hot. Temperatures are more steady in the south, making it a good refuge when the heat peaks in the rest of Thailand (April to June).

Both the Gulf of Thailand and Andaman Sea coastlines are mostly rain-free from March to May, both are somewhat rainy from June to November, while the Gulf side is drier than the Andaman side from November to January. See Climate in the Facts about Thailand chapter for more detail on seasons, which can vary significantly from one part of the country to another.

The peak tourist months are November, December, February, March and August, with secondary peaks in January and July. Consider travelling during the least crowded months of April, May, June, September and October if you want to avoid crowds to take advantage of discounted rooms and other low season rates.

Who Goes Where
These days in Thailand you're liable to meet people from all walks of life and from just about any country in the world, but when it comes to beaches and islands, certain types of visitors tend to favour certain areas. Phuket and nearby Hat Khao Lak attract a well-heeled, middle-aged singles and couples crowd of Australians and Europeans who are most numerous in August,

December and January. They tend to stay for a week or less.

Older Europeans, Russians and families on short-stay budget packages tend to frequent Pattaya and increasingly, Hua Hin and Cha-am. Since these areas are within an easy afternoon's drive of Bangkok, both resort areas tend to be more crowded on weekends and holidays than at other times.

Despite the gentrification of tourist facilities in recent years, Ko Samui continues to attract a younger, if slightly more wealthy, group of international beachgoers who like to party. Peak seasons on Ko Samui are July to August and November to February.

Krabi, Ko Lanta and other Ao Phang-Nga beach areas draw a younger, more adventurous bunch, who are typically on a more long-term search for low-cost, less discovered Asian beaches. The winter tourist season is a bit longer here, extending from mid-November to early March.

Rustic Ko Pha-Ngan and Ko Chang are favoured by backpackers who spend less but stay longer than any of the aforementioned groups. The high season on these islands more or less corresponds with that in Ao Phang-Nga.

Maps

In May 2000 Lonely Planet will publish the completely redisigned and updated, 112 page *Thailand, Vietnam, Laos & Cambodia Travel Atlas*. It has full colour maps at a scale of 1:1,000,000, a full index of all features and is compact and sturdy. The atlas will be available at many Bangkok bookshops, as well as overseas. The comprehensive information in the atlas has been fully cross referenced with Lonely Planet's guide books.

Lonely Planet also publishes the handy *Bankok City Map*.

Nelles Maps and Bartholomew Maps each publish decent 1:500,000 scale maps of Thailand with general topographic shading. The Bartholomew map tends to be a bit more up-to-date and accurate than the Nelles.

Periplus Travel Maps publishes a series of five folding sheet maps covering Thai-

land: one each on Thailand, Bangkok, Chiang Mai, Phuket and Ko Samui. The 1:2,000,000 Thailand map is quite useful, as are the Phuket and Ko Samui maps. Several Thai map publishers issue various regional maps of Thailand, but none of them can be recommended except for Window Group/Book Athens *Thailand Highway Map* series.

The Roads Association of Thailand annually publishes a large format, 48 page, bilingual road atlas called *Thailand Highway Map* (same name as the Window Group/Book Athens publications, but not the same maps). The atlas has cut the Highway Department maps to a more manageable size and includes dozens of city maps, driving distances and lots of travel and sightseeing information. It costs 120B, but beware of inferior knock-offs. A big advantage of the Thailand Highway Maps is that the town and city names are printed in Thai as well as roman script.

The Lonely Planet atlas, or the maps from either the Highway Department or Periplus, are more than adequate for most people.

Regional Maps Several companies in Thailand publish 'guide maps' to Phuket, Krabi and the Samui archipelago. Most accurate and current are those published by V Hongsombud, such as the *Guide Map of Koh Samui, Koh Pha-Ngan & Koh Tao*. Periplus Editions' *Ko Samui Southern Thailand Travel Map* contains maps of the Samui archipelago, southern Thailand, the Tarutao archipelago and a city plan for Hat Yai.

The beaches and islands of the eastern Gulf coast, save for the area around Pattaya, have so far been neglected by regional map publishers.

Prannok Witthaya publishes individual maps of most of the provinces along the coast. These include English and Thai script, and can be found in most bookshops in Thailand. The maps are often a little out of date and therefore are not always accurate, but are of a larger scale than the regional and country maps.

What to Bring

Pack light, tropical-weight clothes, along with a light parka or windbreaker for occasional breezy or rainy evenings. Natural fibres can be cool and comfortable, except when they get soaked with sweat or rain, in which case they quickly become heavy and block air flow. Some of the newer, lightweight synthetics breathe much better than natural fibres, wick sweat away rather than holding it in, and may be more suitable for the beach and the rainy season. Sunglasses are important, and slip-on shoes or sandals are highly recommended – besides being cooler than lace-up shoes, they are easily removed before entering a Thai home or temple.

You might also think about picking up a *phâakhamā* (short Thai-style sarong for men) or a *phâasîn* (a longer sarong for women) to wear in your room, on the beach or when bathing outdoors. These can be bought at any local market (different patterns/colours in different parts of the country) and the vendors will show you how to tie them.

The sarong is a very handy item; it can be used to sleep on or as a light bedspread, as a makeshift 'shopping bag', as a turban/scarf to keep off the sun and absorb perspiration, as a towel, as a small hammock and as a device with which to climb coconut palms – to name just a few of its many functions. It is not considered proper street attire, however.

A small torch (flashlight) is a good idea, as it makes it easier to find your way back to your bungalow at night if you are staying at the beach or at a remote guesthouse. Other handy items include a compass, a plastic lighter for lighting candles and mosquito coils, and foam ear plugs for noisy nights.

Toothpaste, soap and most other toiletries can be purchased anywhere in Thailand. Sun block and mosquito repellent are now widely available in beach areas. If you want to wash your own clothes, bring a universal sink plug, a few plastic pegs and 3m of plastic cord or plastic hangers for hanging wet clothes out to dry.

If you're a keen snorkeller, you might want to bring your own equipment (see Diving & Snorkelling in the Activities section of this chapter). This would save you having to rent gear and would also assure a proper fit. Shoes designed for water sports, eg aquasocks, are great for wearing in the water whether you're diving or not. They protect your feet from coral cuts, which easily become infected.

If you require computer modem communications in Thailand, see the Email & Internet Access section later in this chapter for items you might need to bring with you.

TOURIST OFFICES

The Tourism Authority of Thailand (TAT), a government-operated tourist information/promotion service, attached to the prime minister's office, maintains 22 offices within the country and 16 overseas. TAT has regulatory powers to monitor tourism-related businesses throughout Thailand, including hotels, tour operators, travel agencies and transport companies, in an effort to improve these services and prosecute unscrupulous operators.

The quality of the printed information that TAT produces is second to none among South-East Asian countries, including copious pamphlets describing sightseeing, accommodation and transport options for each province. The staff is huge; the main office in Bangkok occupies 10 floors of a new office building in the Ratchada area of Huay Khwang.

You can dial 1155 from any phone in Thailand, then ask for extension 2, to receive tourist information in English, French, German, Japanese, Chinese or Thai from 8.30 am to 4.30 pm daily.

In addition to the following offices, you'll also find TAT Information Counters in the international and domestic terminals of Bangkok's Don Muang airport.

Local TAT Offices

Bangkok
(☎ 02-694 1222, hotline 1155, ext 2, fax 694 1220/1, email center@tat.or.th)

Le Concorde Bldg, 202 Th Ratchadapisek,
Huay Khwang, Bangkok 10310;
(☎ 02-282 9773)
4 Th Ratchadamnoen Nok, Bangkok 10100
Cha-am
(☎ 032-471005/8, fax 471502)
500/51 Thang Luang Phetkasem, Amphoe
Cha-am, Phetchaburi 76
Hat Yai
(☎ 074-243747, fax 245986, email
tathatyai@hatyai.inet.co.th)
1/1 Soi 2, Th Niphat Uthit 3, Hat Yai,
Songkhla 90110
Nakhon Si Thammarat
(☎ 075-346515/6, fax 346517, email
tatnakhon@nst.a-net.net.th)
Sanam Na Meuang, Th Ratchadamnoen
Klang, Nakhon Si Thammarat 80000
Narathiwat (Sungai Kolok)
(☎ 073-612126, fax 615230, email
tatnarat@cscoms.com)
Asia Hwy 18 (temporary office), Sungai
Kolok, Narathiwat 96120
Pattaya
(☎ 038-427667, fax 429113, email
tatpty@chonburi.ksc.co.th)
382/1 Th Chaihat, Hat Pattaya, South Pattaya
21000
Phuket
(☎ 076-212213, 211036, fax 213582, email
tathkt@phuket.ksc.co.th)
73-75 Th Phuket, Phuket 83000
Rayong
(☎/fax 038-655420/1, fax 655422, email
tatry@infonews.co.th)
153/4 Th Sukhumvit, Rayong 21000
Surat Thani
(☎ 077-288818/9, fax 282828, email
tatsurat@cscoms.com)
5 Th Talaat Mai, Ban Don, Surat Thani 84000
Trat (Laem Ngop)
(☎/fax 038-597255)
100 Muu 1, Th Trat-Laem Ngop, Laem Ngop,
Trat 23120

TAT Offices Abroad
Australia
(☎ 02-9247 7549, fax 9251 2465, email
info@thailand.net.au)
Level 2, 75 Pitt Street, Sydney, NSW 2000
France
(☎ 01-53 53 47 00, fax 45 63 78 88, email
tatpar@wanadoo.fr)
90 Avenue des Champs Elysées, 75008 Paris
Germany
(☎ 069-138 1390, email tatfra@t-online.de)
Bethmannstrasse 58, 60311 Frankfurt/Main

Hong Kong
(☎ 02-2868 0732, fax 2868 4585, email
tathkg@hk.super.net)
Room 401, Fairmont House, 8 Cotton Tree
Drive, Central
Japan
(☎ 03-3218 0337, fax 3218 0655, email
tattky@crisscross.com)
Room 259, 2nd floor, South Tower, Yurakucho Denki Bldg, 1-7-1 Yurakucho, Chiyoda-
ku, Tokyo 100
Laos
(☎ 21-217157, fax 217158)
79/9 Th Lan Xang, Vientiane, Lao PDR or PO
Box 12, Nong Khai 43000
Malaysia
(☎ 093-262 3480, fax 262 3486, email
sawatdi@po.jaring.my)
c/o Royal Thai embassy, Suite 22.01, Level 22,
Menara Lion, 165, Jalan Ampang, 50450,
Kuala Lumpur
Singapore
(☎ 65-235 7694, fax 733 5653)
c/o Royal Thai embassy, 370 Orchard Road,
238870
UK
(☎ 020-7499 7679, fax 7629 5519)
49 Albemarle St, London W1X 3FE
USA
(☎ 212-432 0433, toll-free ☎ 1-800 THAI-
LAND, fax 912 0920)
Suite 3443, 5 World Trade Center, New York,
NY 10048
(☎ 213-461 9814, fax 461 9834, email
tatla@aol.com)
1st floor, 611 North Larchmont Blvd, LA, CA
90004

VISAS & DOCUMENTS
Passport
Entry into Thailand requires a passport
valid for at least six months from the time
of entry. If you anticipate your passport
may expire while you're in Thailand, you
should obtain a new one before arrival or
inquire from your government whether
your embassy in Thailand (if one exists –
see the Embassies & Consulates section in
this chapter) can issue a new one after arrival.

Visas
Whichever type of visa you have, be sure to
check your passport immediately after

stamping. Overworked officials sometimes stamp 30 days on arrival even when you hold a longer visa; if you point out the error before you've left the immigration area at your port of entry, officials will make the necessary corrections. If you don't notice this until you've left the port of entry, go to Bangkok and plead your case at the central immigration office.

Similarly, if you plan to come back to Thailand at some point, make sure your visa is stamped when you leave the country. One poor fellow, who had last left Thailand via an unmanned checkpoint at the Malaysian border, flew in from London for a return visit only to be refused entry and put on the next flight back home! All because he didn't have the proper exit stamp.

Once a visa is issued, it must be used (ie you must enter Thailand) within 90 days.

Transit & Tourist Visas The Thai government allows 56 different nationalities to enter the country without a visa for 30 days at no charge. Seventy-eight other nationalities – those from smaller European countries like Andorra or Liechtenstein, or from West Africa, South Asia or Latin America – can obtain a 15 day Transit Visa on arrival for a 300B fee. Some visitors, such as those from eastern European countries, have found that on-arrival visas can only be obtained if they fly into Bangkok, and can't be arranged at land border crossings.

A few nationalities, eg Hungarians, must obtain a visa before arriving or they'll be turned back. Check with a Thai embassy or consulate to be sure if you plan to try arriving without a visa.

Without proof of an onward ticket and sufficient funds for one's projected stay any visitor can be denied entry, but in practice your ticket and funds are rarely checked if you're dressed neatly for the immigration check. See Exchange Control in the Money section in this chapter for officially required amounts for each visa type.

Next in its length of validity is the Tourist Visa, which is good for 60 days and costs US$15. Three passport photos must accompany all applications.

Non-Immigrant Visas You must apply for a Non-Immigrant Visa in your home country. It is good for 90 days, costs US$20 and is not difficult to obtain if you can offer a good reason for your visit. Business, study, retirement and extended family visits are among the purposes considered valid. If you want to stay longer than six months, this is the one to get as it is the only type that can be extended for such periods.

A new type of Non-Immigrant Business Visa (usually abbreviated by Thai immigration officials as 'non-B') allows unlimited entries in and out of Thailand for one year. The only hitch is that you must leave the country at least once every 90 days to keep the visa valid.

Re-Entry & Multiple-Entry Visas If you need to leave and re-enter the kingdom before your visa expires, say for a return trip to Laos or the like, you may need to apply for a Re-Entry Permit at a Thai immigration office. The cost is 500B; you'll need to supply one passport photo. There is no limit to the number of Re-Entry Permits you can apply for and use during the validity of your visa. Thailand's Interior Ministry recently proposed that the fee for Re-Entry Permits be raised from 500B to 2000B. Under the same proposal, a new 'Multiple Re-Entry Permit' valid for unlimited re-entries for one year would cost 5000B.

Other than the new Non-Immigrant Business Visa, Thailand does not issue multiple-entry visas. If you want a visa that enables you to leave the country and then return, the best you can do is to obtain a visa permitting two entries; this will cost double the single-entry visa. For example, a two entry, 90 day Non-Immigrant Visa will cost US$40 and will allow you six months in the country, as long as you cross a border with immigration facilities by the end of your first three months. The second half of your visa is validated as soon as you recross the Thai border, so there is no need to go to a

Thai embassy/consulate abroad. An alternative is to apply for a Re-Entry Permit (or the Multiple Re-Entry Permit, if established as proposed by Thai immigration) after you're already in Thailand, as described in the previous paragraph.

See Non-Immigrant Visas earlier in this section for a description of the multiple-entry Non-Immigrant Business Visa.

Visa Extensions Sixty-day Tourist Visas may be extended for up to 30 days at the discretion of Thai immigration authorities. The Bangkok office (☎ 02-287 3101) is on Soi Suan Phlu, Thanon (Th) Sathon Tai, but you can apply at any immigration office in the country – every province bordering a neighbouring country has at least one. The usual fee for extension of a Tourist Visa is 500B. Bring along one photo and one copy each of the photo and visa pages of your passport. Normally only one 30 day extension is granted.

The 30 day, no-visa stay can be extended by seven to 10 days (depending on the immigration office) for 500B. You can also leave the country and return immediately to obtain another 30 day stay. There is no limit on the number of times you can do this, nor is there a minimum interval you must spend outside the country.

Extension of the 15 day, on-arrival Transit Visa is only allowed if you hold a passport from a country that has no Thai embassy.

If you overstay your visa, the usual penalty is a fine of 200B per day of your overstay, with a 20,000B limit; fines can be paid at the airport or in advance at the Investigation Unit (☎ 02-287 3129, ext 2204), Immigration Bureau, Room 416, 4th floor, Old Building, Soi Suan Phlu, Th Sathon Tai in Bangkok.

Extending a Non-Immigrant Visa very much depends on how the officials feel about you – if they like you then they will extend it. Other than the 500B extension fee, money doesn't usually come into it; neat appearance and polite behaviour count for more. Typically, you must collect various signatures and go through various

interviews which result in a 'provisional' extension. You may then have to report to a local immigration office every 10 to 14 days for the next three months until the actual extension comes through. Becoming a monk doesn't necessarily mean you'll get a longer visa either – again, it depends on whom you see and how they feel about you.

Retirees 55 years of age or older can actually extend the 90 day Non-Immigrant Visa to a yearly visa. To do this you will need to bring the following documents to the Immigration Bureau: a copy of your passport's personal details pages, one photo, 500B extension fee, proof of financial status or pension. The requirement for the latter is that foreigners aged 60 or older must show proof of an income of not less than 200,000B per year (or 20,000B per month for extensions of less than a year); for those aged 55 to 59 the minimum is raised to 500,000B/50,000B. According to immigration regulations, however, 'If the alien is ill, or has weak health and is sensitive to colder climates, or has resided in Thailand for a long period, and is 55-59 years of age, special considerations will be granted'.

Foreigners with Non-Immigrant Visas who have resided in Thailand continuously for three years – on one-year extensions – may apply for permanent residency at Section 1, Subdivision 1, Immigration Division 1, Room 301, 3rd floor, Immigration Bureau, Soi Suan Phlu (☎ 02-287 3117/01). Foreigners who receive permanent residence must carry an 'alien identification card' at all times.

The Thai government recently established the new One-Stop Visa Centre (☎ 02-693 9333, fax 693 9340) at Krisda Plaza, 207 Th Ratchadaphisek, where Non-Immigrant Visas for investors, businesspeople and foreign correspondents – only – can be renewed in less than three hours.

Various law offices in Thailand, especially in Bangkok, Chiang Mai and Hat Yai, can assist with visa extensions, renewals and applications – for a fee of course. Two in Bangkok that have been around a while are Siam Visa (☎ 02-238 2989, fax 238 2987, email siamvisa@loxinfo.co.th), Kasemkit Building, 7th floor, Th Silom, and Express Visa Service (☎ 02-617 7258, ext 418, fax 272 3764, email thaivisa@usa.net), Sirida Place, 278 Th Viphavadi Rangsit, Soi 3 Yak 10, Latyao, Chatuchak. These mentions do not constitute an endorsement of either agency – be cautious and ask plenty of questions before plunking down your money.

Residence Permits These are reserved for foreign nationals married to Thai citizens and residing in Thailand long-term, or for certain other categories certified by the Interior Ministry. At present a Residence Permit costs 50,000B, but a current ministerial proposal is asking for an increase to a steep 200,000B.

Tax Clearance

Anyone who receives income while in Thailand must obtain a tax clearance certificate from the Revenue Department before they'll be permitted to leave the country. The Bangkok office (☎ 02-281 5777, 282 9899) of the Revenue Department is on Th Chakkapong not far from the Democracy Monument. There are also Revenue Department offices in every provincial capital.

Old Thai hands note: the tax clearance requirement no longer applies to those who have simply stayed in Thailand beyond a cumulative 90 days within one calendar year – this regulation was abolished in 1991. This makes it much easier for expats or other long-termers who live in Thailand on Non-Immigrant Visas – as long as they don't receive income. Hence there's no more hustling for tax clearance every time you make a visa trip to Penang or Vientiane.

Onward Tickets

Thai immigration does not seem very concerned with whether or not you arrive with proof of onward travel. Legally speaking all holders of Tourist Visas or the no-visa 30 day stay permit are *supposed* to carry such proof. In many years of frequent travel in and out of the kingdom, the author's documents haven't been checked a single time.

Travel Insurance

A travel insurance policy to cover theft, loss and medical problems is strongly recommended. Though Thailand is generally a safe country to travel in, sickness, accidents and theft do happen. There are a wide variety of policies and travel agents can advise you. Check the small print to see if the policy covers any potentially dangerous sporting activities you may do, such as diving or trekking, and make sure that it adequately covers your valuables. You may prefer a policy that pays doctors or hospitals directly rather than having to pay on the spot and claim later. If you have to claim later, make sure you keep all documentation. Some policies ask you to call back (reverse charges) to a centre in your home country, where an immediate assessment of your problem is made.

Check that the policy covers ambulances or an emergency flight home.

A few credit cards offer limited, sometimes full, travel insurance to the holder.

Driving Licence & Permits

An international driving permit is necessary for any visitor who intends to drive a motorised vehicle while in Thailand. These are usually available from motoring organisations, such as AAA (USA) or BAA (UK), in your home country. If you'd like to obtain a Thai driving licence, see the Driving Permits section of the Getting Around chapter for details.

Hostel Cards

Hostelling International (HI; formerly International Youth Hostel Federation) issues a membership card that will allow you to stay at Thailand's member hostels, which are in Bangkok and some other inland locations. There are no hostels at the beaches and islands covered by this book. Without such a card or the purchase of a temporary membership you won't be admitted. Since 1992, only HI card holders have been accepted as guests in Thai hostels; membership costs 300B per year or 50B for a temporary (one night) membership.

For further information, check HI's Web site at www.iyhf.org/iyhf/ehome.html.

Student Cards

The International Student Identity Card (ISIC), issued by the International Student Travel Confederation (☎ 3393 9303, fax 3393 7377), Box 9048, DK1000, Copenhagen, Denmark, can be used as identification to qualify for the rare student discount at some museums in Thailand. It's probably not worth getting just for a visit to Thailand, but if you already have one, or plan to use one elsewhere in Asia, then bring it along.

Photocopies

It's a good idea to keep photocopies of all vital documents – passport data page, all credit card numbers, airline tickets, travellers cheque serial numbers and so on – in a separate place from the originals. Replacement will be much easier to arrange if you can provide issuing agencies with copies. You might consider leaving extra copies of these documents with someone at home or in a safe place in Bangkok or other entry point.

It's also a good idea to store details of your vital travel documents in Lonely Planet's free online Travel Vault in case you lose the photocopies or can't be bothered with them. Your password-protected Travel Vault is accessible online anywhere in the world. You can create it at www.ekno.lonelyplanet.com.

EMBASSIES & CONSULATES
Thai Embassies & Consulates

To apply for a visa, contact the Royal Thai Embassy (or consulate) in any of the following countries. In many cases, if you apply in person you may receive a tourist or Non-Immigrant Visa on the day of application; by mail it generally takes anywhere from two to six weeks.

Australia
(☎ 02-6273 1149, 6273 2937) 111 Empire Circuit, Yarralumla, Canberra, ACT 2600
Canada
(☎ 613-722 4444)

180 Island Park Drive, Ottawa, Ontario K1Y 0A2
China
(☎ 010-532 1903)
40 Guanghua Lu, Beijing 100600
France
(☎ 01-47 27 80 79, 47 24 32 22)
8 Rue Greuze, 75116 Paris
Germany
(☎ 0228-35 5065, 35 5068)
Ubierstrasse 65, 53173 Bonn
Hong Kong
(☎ 02-2521 6481, 2521 6482)
8th floor, Fairmont House, 8 Cotton Tree Drive, Central
India
(☎ 11-60 5679, 60 7289)
56-N Nyaya Marg, Chanakyapuri, New Delhi, 110021
Indonesia
(☎ 021-390 4052, 390 4053, 390 4054)
Jalan Imam Bonjol 74, Jakarta
Japan
(☎ 03-3441 1386, 3341 1387)
3-14-6 Kami-Osaki, Shinagawa-ku, Tokyo 141
Laos
(☎ 21-21 4582, 21 4583)
Th Phonkheng, Vientiane Poste 128
Malaysia
(☎ 03-248 8222, 248 8350)
206 Jalan Ampang, Kuala Lumpur
Myanmar (Burma)
(☎ 01-28 2471, 27 6555)
91 Th Pyi, Yangon
Nepal
(☎ 01-21 3910, 21 3912)
Jyoti Kendra Bldg, Thapathali, Kathmandu
Netherlands
(☎ 070-345 2088, 345 9703)
Buitenrustweg 1, 2517 KD The Hague
New Zealand
(☎ 04-476 8618, 476 8619)
2 Cook St, Karori, Wellington 5
Philippines
(☎ 02-810 3833, 815 4219)
107B Rada St, Legaspi Village, Makati, Metro Manila
Singapore
(☎ 65-235 4175, 737 2158, 737 3372)
370 Orchard Rd
Sweden
(☎ 08-791 7340)
Floragatan 3, 5-11431, Stockholm
UK
(☎ 020-7589 0173, 589 2944, 7589 2944)
29-30 Queen's Gate, London SW7 5JB
USA
(☎ 202-944 3600)

1024 Wisconsin Ave NW, Washington, DC
20007
Vietnam
(☎ 04-235 092, 235 094)
63-65 Hoang Dieu St, Hanoi

Embassies & Consulates in Thailand

Bangkok is a good place to collect visas for onward travel, and most countries have diplomatic representation in Bangkok. The visa sections of most embassies and consulates are open from around 8.30 to 11.30 am, Monday to Friday only (but call first to be sure).

Countries with diplomatic representation in Bangkok include:

Australia
(☎ 02-287 2680)
37 Th Sathon Tai
Cambodia
(☎ 02-254 6630)
185 Th Ratchadamri, Lumphini
Canada
(☎ 02-636 0540)
15th floor, Abdulrahim Bldg, 990 Th Rama IV
China
(☎ 02-245 7032)
57 Th Ratchadaphisek
France
(☎ 02-266 8250)
35 Soi Customs House, Th Charoen Krung
(☎ 02-287 2585)
consular section (visas), 29 Th Sathon Tai
Germany
(☎ 02-287 9000)
9 Th Sathon Tai
India
(☎ 02-258 0300)
46 Soi Prasanmit (Soi 23), Th Sukhumvit
Indonesia
(☎ 02-252 3135)
600-602 Th Phetchaburi
Ireland
(☎ 02-223 0876)
205 United Flour Mill Bldg, Th Ratchawong
Japan
(☎ 02-252 6151)
1674 Th Phetchaburi Tat Mai
Laos
(☎ 02-538 3696)
520/1-3 Soi 39, Th Ramkhamhaeng
Malaysia
(☎ 02-254 1700)

15th floor, Regent House Bldg, 183 Th Ratchadamri
Myanmar (Burma)
(☎ 02-233 2237, 234 4698)
132 Th Sathon Neua
Nepal
(☎ 02-391 7240)
189 Soi Phuengsuk (Soi 71), Th Sukhumvit
Netherlands
(☎ 02-254 7701, 252 6103)
106 Th Withayu
New Zealand
(☎ 02-254 2530)
93 Th Withayu
Philippines
(☎ 02-259 0139)
760 Th Sukhumvit
Singapore
(☎ 02-286 2111)
129 Th Sathon Tai
Sweden
(☎ 02-254 4954)
20th floor, Pacific Place, 140 Th Sukhumvit
Taiwan
(☎ 02-251 9274)
Far East Trade Office, 10th floor, Kian Gwan Bldg, 140 Th Withayu
UK
(☎ 02-253 0191)
1031 Th Withayu
USA
(☎ 02-205 4000)
120-122 Th Withayu
Vietnam
(☎ 02-251 5835)
83/1 Th Withayu

CUSTOMS

Like most countries, Thailand prohibits the import of illegal drugs, firearms and ammunition (unless registered in advance with the Police Department) and pornographic media. A reasonable amount of clothing for personal use, toiletries and professional instruments are allowed in duty free, as are one still or one movie/video camera with five rolls of still film or three rolls of movie film or videotape. Up to 200 cigarettes can be brought into the country without paying duty, or for other smoking materials a total of up to 250g. One litre of wine or spirits is allowed in duty-free.

Electronic goods like stereos, calculators and computers can be a problem if the

Your Own Embassy

It's important to realise what your own embassy – the embassy of the country of which you are a citizen – can and can't do to help if you get into trouble.

Generally speaking, it won't be much help in emergencies if the trouble you're in is remotely your own fault. Remember that you are bound by the laws of the country you are in. Your embassy will not be sympathetic if you end up in jail after committing a crime locally, even if such actions are legal in your own country.

In genuine emergencies you might get some assistance, but only if other channels have been exhausted. For example, if you need to get home urgently, a free ticket home is exceedingly unlikely – the embassy would expect you to have insurance. If you have all your money and documents stolen, it might assist with getting a new passport, but a loan for onward travel is out of the question.

Some embassies used to keep letters for travellers or have a small reading room with home newspapers, but these days the mail holding service has usually been stopped and even newspapers tend to be out of date.

customs officials have reason to believe you're bringing them in for resale. As long as you don't carry more than one of each, you should be OK. Occasionally, customs will require you to leave a hefty deposit for big-ticket items (eg a lap-top computer or midi-component stereo) which is refunded when you leave the country with the item in question. Don't say that you're just passing through and don't plan to use the item in Thailand, or they may ask you to leave it with customs until you leave the country.

For information on currency import or export, see Exchange Control in the Money section of this chapter.

Antiques & Art

Upon leaving Thailand, you must obtain an export licence for any antiques or objects of art you want to take with you. An antique is any 'archaic movable property, whether produced by man or by nature, any part of ancient structure, human skeleton or animal carcass, which by its age or characteristic of production or historical evidence is useful in the field of art, history or archaeology'. An art object is a 'thing produced by craftsmanship and appreciated as being valuable in the field of art'. Obviously these are very sweeping definitions, so if in doubt go to the Fine Arts Department for inspection and licensing.

Applications can be made by submitting two front-view photos of the object(s) (no more than five objects to a photo) and a photocopy of your passport, along with the object(s) in question, to one of three national museums: Bangkok, Chiang Mai or Songkhla. Allow three to five days for the process to be completed.

Thailand has special regulations for taking a Buddha or other deity image (or any part thereof) out of the country. These require not only a licence from the Fine Arts Department but a permit from the Ministry of Commerce as well. The one exception to this are the small Buddha images (phrá phim or phrá khreûang) that are meant to be worn on a chain around the neck; these may be exported without a licence as long as the reported purpose is religious.

Temporary Vehicle Importation

A passenger vehicle (car, van, truck or motorcycle) can be brought into Thailand for tourist purposes for up to six months. Documents needed are a valid international driving permit, passport vehicle registration papers (in the case of a borrowed or hired vehicle, authorisation from the owner) and a cash or bank guarantee equal to the value of the vehicle plus 20%. (For entry through Khlong Toey port or Bangkok international airport, this means a letter of bank credit; a 'self-guarantee' filled in at the border is sufficient for overland crossings via Malaysia.)

Home Country Customs

Be sure to check the import regulations in your home country before bringing in or sending back a large quantity of (or high value) Thai goods. The limit varies from country to country; the USA, for example, allows US$400 worth of foreign-purchased goods to enter without duty (with no limit on handicrafts and unset gems), while in Australia the total value is limited to A$400.

MONEY
Currency

The basic unit of Thai currency is the *baht*. There are 100 *satang* in one baht; coin denominations include 25 satang and 50 satang and 1B, 5B and 10B. Older coins exhibit Thai numerals only, while newer coins have Thai and Arabic numerals. Twenty-five satang equals one *saleng* in colloquial Thai, so if you're quoted a price of six saleng in the market, say, for a banana or a bag of peanuts, this means 1.50B. The term is becoming increasingly rare as inflation makes purchases of less than 1B or 2B almost extinct.

Paper currency comes in denominations of 10B (brown), 20B (green), 50B (blue), 100B (red), 500B (purple) and 1000B (beige). A 10,000B bill is on the way. The 10B bills are being phased out in favour of the 10B coin and have become rather uncommon. Fortunately for newcomers to Thailand, numerals are printed in their western as well as Thai forms. Notes are also scaled according to the amount; the larger the denomination, the larger the note. Large denominations – 500B and especially 1000B bills – can be hard to change in small towns, but banks will always change them.

Exchange Rates

Exchange rates at the time of writing include:

country	unit		baht
Australia	A$1	=	26.23B
Cambodia	100r	=	1.13B
Canada	C$1	=	26.25B
Euro	€1	=	43.23B
France	FF1	=	6.37B
Germany	DM1	=	20.41B
Japan	¥100	=	30.87B
Malaysia	M$1	=	10.49B
New Zealand	NZ$1	=	20.58B
Singapore	S$1	=	23.69B
UK	UK£1	=	66.08B
USA	US$1	=	39.77B

Prior to June 1997 the baht was pegged to a basket of currencies heavily weighted towards the US dollar, and for over 20 years it hardly varied beyond 20B to 26B to the dollar. A year after flotation, in June 1998, the baht had slipped approximately 30% against the dollar.

Lately exchange rates seem to have stabilised, but there's always the chance the Thai currency will go for another roller coaster ride. Hence it's a good idea to stay abreast of exchange rates during your stay in Thailand – changing currencies at the right time could extend your budget significantly. Exchange rates are printed in the *Bangkok Post* and *The Nation* every day, or you can walk into any Thai bank and ask to see their daily rate sheet. Thai Farmers Bank also posts a daily rate sheet on the Internet at www.tfb.co.th/cgiehg2.nsf/exchange?openagent.

Exchanging Money

There is no black market for baht. Banks or legal moneychangers offer the best exchange rate within the country. US dollars are the most readily acceptable currency and travellers cheques get better exchange rates than cash. Since banks charge up to 23B commission and duty for each travellers cheque cashed, you will save on commissions if you use larger cheque denominations (eg a US$50 cheque will only cost 23B while five US$10 cheques will cost 115B). British pounds are second to the US dollar in general acceptability, and during the 1997-98 baht devaluation the UK currency appreciated very well against the baht – in some periods better than the US dollar.

Note that you can't exchange Malaysian ringgit, Indonesian rupiah, Nepali rupees,

Cambodian riel, Lao kip, Vietnamese dong or Myanmar kyat into Thai currency at banks, though some Bangkok moneychangers along Th Charoen Krung and Th Silom in Bangkok carry these currencies. The latter can in fact be good places to buy these currencies if you're going to any of these countries. Rates are comparable with black-market rates in countries with discrepancies between the 'official' and free market currency values.

Visa and MasterCard credit-card holders can get cash advances of up to US$500 (in baht only) per day through some branches of the Thai Farmers Bank, Bangkok Bank and Siam Commercial Bank (and also at the night-time exchange windows in well touristed spots like Banglamphu, Chiang Mai, Ko Samui and so on).

American Express card holders can also get advances, but only in travellers cheques, and no more than US$500 in any one 30-day period. The Amex agent is SEA Tours (☎ 02-216 5759), Suite 88-92, Payathai Plaza, 8th floor, 128 Th Phayathai, Bangkok.

See the Business Hours section later in this chapter for information on bank opening hours.

Exchange Control Legally, any traveller arriving in Thailand must have at least the following amounts of money in cash, travellers cheques, bank draft or letter of credit, according to visa category: Non-Immigrant Visa, US$500 per person or US$1000 per family; Tourist Visa, US$250 per person or US$500 per family; Transit Visa or no visa, US$125 per person or US$250 per family. Your funds may be checked by authorities if you arrive on a one way ticket or if you look as if you're at 'the end of the road'.

According to 1991 regulations, there are no limits to the amounts of Thai or foreign currency you may bring into the country. Upon leaving Thailand, you're permitted to take no more than 50,000B per person without special authorisation; exportation of foreign currencies is unrestricted.

It's legal to open a foreign currency account at any commercial bank in Thailand.

As long as the funds originate from abroad, there are no restrictions on their maintenance or withdrawal.

International Transfers If you have a reliable place to receive mail in Thailand, one of the safest and cheapest ways to receive money from overseas is to have an international cashier's cheque (or international money order) sent by courier. It usually takes no more than four days for courier mail to reach Thailand from anywhere in the world.

If you have a bank account in Thailand or your home bank has a branch in Bangkok, you can have money wired direct via a telegraphic transfer. This costs a bit more than having a cheque sent; telegraphic transfers take anywhere from two days to a week to arrive. International banks with branches in Bangkok include HongkongBank, Standard Chartered Bank, Sakura Bank, Bank of America, Banque Indosuez, Citibank, Banque Nationale de Paris, Chase Manhattan Bank, Bank of Tokyo, Deutsche Bank, Merrill Lynch International Bank, United Malayan Bank and many others.

Western Union (☎ 02-254 9121), justifiably claiming to be 'the fastest way to send money worldwide', has an office in Central department store at 1027 Th Ploenchit, as well as in other branches of Central around the city and in Hat Yai and Chiang Mai.

ATM & Credit/Debit Cards An alternative to carrying around large amounts of cash or travellers cheques is to open an account at a Thai bank and request an automatic teller machine (ATM) card. Major banks in Thailand now have ATMs in provincial capitals, and in many smaller towns as well, open 24 hours. Once you have a card you'll be able to withdraw cash at machines throughout Thailand, whether those machines belong to your bank or another Thai bank. ATM cards issued by Thai Farmers Bank or Bangkok Bank can be used with the ATMs of 14 major banks – there are over 3000 machines nationwide. A 10B transaction charge is usually deducted for using an ATM belonging to a bank with whom you don't have an account.

Debit cards (also known as cash cards or check cards) issued by a bank in your own country can also be used at several Thai banks to withdraw cash (in Thai baht only) directly from your cheque or savings account back home, thus avoiding all commissions and finance charges. You can use MasterCard debit cards to buy baht at foreign exchange booths or desks at either Bangkok Bank or Siam Commercial Bank. Visa debit cards can buy cash through Thai Farmers Bank exchange services.

These cards can also be used at many Thai ATMs, though a surcharge of around US$1 is usually subtracted from your home account each time you complete a machine transaction. Some travellers now use debit or ATM cards in lieu of travellers cheques because they're quicker and more convenient, although it's a good idea to bring along an emergency travellers cheque fund in case you lose your card. One disadvantage of debit card accounts, as opposed to credit card accounts, is that you can't arrange a 'charge back' for unsatisfactory purchases after the transaction is completed – once the money's drawn from your account it's gone.

Plastic money is becoming increasingly popular in Thailand and many shops, hotels and restaurants now accept credit as well as debit cards. The most commonly accepted cards are Visa and MasterCard, followed by American Express and Japan Card Bureau (JCB). Diner's Club and Carte Blanche are of much more limited use.

Card Problems Occasionally when you try to use a Visa or MasterCard at rural hotels or shops, the staff may try to tell you that only cards issued by Thai Farmers Bank or Siam Commercial Bank are acceptable. With a little patience, you should be able to make them understand that the Thai Farmers Bank will pay the merchant and that your bank will pay the Thai Farmers Bank – and that any Visa or MasterCard issued anywhere in the world is indeed acceptable.

Another problem concerns illegal surcharges on credit-card purchases. It's against Thai law to pass on to the customer the 3% merchant fee charged by banks, but almost all merchants in Thailand do it anyway. Some even ask 4% or 5%! The only exception seems to be hotels (although even a few hotels will hit you with a credit card surcharge). If you don't agree to the surcharge they'll simply refuse to accept your card. Begging and pleading or pointing out the law doesn't seem to help. The best way to get around the illegal surcharge is to politely ask that the credit card receipt be itemised with cost of product or service and the surcharge listed separately. Then when you pay your bill, photocopy all receipts showing the surcharge and request a 'charge back'. If a hotel or shop refuses to itemise the surcharge, take down the vendor's name and address and report them to TAT's Tourist Police – they may be able to arrange a refund. Not all banks in all countries will offer refunds – banks in the UK, for example, refuse to issue such refunds, while banks in the USA usually will.

To report a lost or stolen credit/debit card, call the following telephone hotlines in Bangkok: American Express (☎ 02-273 0022/44), Diners Club (☎ 02-238 3660), MasterCard (☎ 02-260 8572), Visa (☎ 02-273 1199/7449). See Dangers & Annoyances in this chapter for important warnings on credit-card theft and fraud.

Security

Give some thought in advance to how you're going to carry your financial media – whether travellers cheques, cash, credit and debit cards, or some combination of these. Many travellers favour hidden pouches that can be worn beneath clothing. Hip-pocket wallets are easy marks for thieves. Pickpockets work markets and crowded buses throughout the country, so it pays to keep your money concealed. See Dangers & Annoyances in this chapter for more on petty crime.

It's a good idea not to keep all your money in one place; keep an 'emergency' stash well concealed in a piece of luggage separate from other money. Long-term travellers might even consider renting a safety deposit box at a bank in Bangkok or other major cities. Keep your onward tickets, a copy of your passport, a list of all credit card numbers and some money in the box just in case all your belongings are stolen while you're on the road. It's not common, but it does happen.

Costs

For most visitors the major expense of a Thai beach holiday is getting there. Comfortable beach or island accommodation is inexpensive by international standards, and a full day's worth of world-class Thai cuisine usually costs less than a standard lunch back home. Since the baht devaluation, prices have dropped even lower, at least vis-à-vis hard currencies. If measured against the US dollar, for example, the cost of the average hotel room dropped 24% between June 1997 and June 1998, the price of the average hotel buffet came down 32%, a bowl of rice noodles cost 19% less and the air fare between Bangkok and Phuket fell 32%. With current inflation of baht prices running just over 7% per year, some of these savings will evaporate over the life of this guidebook edition, of course.

Outside major beach resorts, budget-squeezers should be able to get by on 200B per day if they really keep watch on their expenses, especially if they share rooms with other travellers. This estimate includes basic guesthouse accommodation, food, nonalcoholic beverages and local transport, but not film, souvenirs, tours, long-distance transport or vehicle hire. Add another 60B to 80B per day for every large beer (30B to 40B for small bottles) you drink.

Expenses vary, of course, from place to place; where there are high concentrations of budget travellers, for example, accommodation tends to be cheaper and food more expensive. With experience, you can travel in Thailand for even less if you live like a Thai of modest means and learn to speak the language.

Someone with more money to spend will find that for around 400B to 500B per day, life can be quite comfortable; cleaner and quieter accommodation is easier to find once you pass the 250B-a-night zone in room rates. Of course, a 70B guesthouse room with a mattress on the floor and responsive management is better than a poorly-maintained 400B room with air-con that won't turn off and a noisy all-night card game next door.

In Bangkok, Phuket and Ko Samui there's almost no limit to the amount you *could* spend, but if you live frugally, avoid the tourist ghettos and ride the public bus system you can get by on only slightly more than you would spend in more remote areas. Where you stay at the resort beaches or in Bangkok is of primary concern, as accommodation can cost more than 300B per day when it includes air-con (in a twin room).

Those seeking international-class accommodation and food will spend at least 1000B to 1600B a day for a room with all the modern amenities – IDD phone, 24 hour hot water and air-con, carpeting, fitness centre and all-night room service. Such hotels are found only in the major cities and resort areas.

Food, likewise, is somewhat more expensive in Bangkok and resort beaches than elsewhere. Western food (especially beef) costs significantly more than Thai and Chinese food. Seafood – particularly shrimp and lobster – also increases the tab. Still, when you consider that Thailand has possibly the best seafood cuisine in the world, it's often a bargain.

Tipping & Bargaining

Tipping is not normal practice in Thailand, although they're getting used to it in expensive hotels and restaurants. Elsewhere don't bother. The exception is loose change left from a large Thai restaurant bill; for example if a meal costs 288B and you pay with a 500B note, some Thais and foreign residents will leave the 13B coin change on the change tray. It's not so much a tip as a way of saying 'I'm not so money-grubbing

Sample Prices

1L petrol	13B
average meter taxi ride, central Bangkok	75B
average bus fare, Bangkok	3.50B
songthaew ride in a provincial city	10B per person, or 40B to 50B charter
3rd class train fare, Bangkok to Surat Thani	107B
one day's 100cc motorcycle rental, Hua Hin	150B
dorm bed in a guesthouse or youth hostel	50B to 80B
mid-range hotel double, Bangkok	1600B
beach hut single, Ko Pha-Ngan	80B to 150B
budget beach hotel single, Phuket	500B
bowl of *kŭaytĭaw*, Prachuap Khiri Khan	20B
10 eggs from a market	19B
can of Campbell's Vegetarian Vegetable soup	45B
substantial lunch for two at an average Thai vegetarian restaurant	50B
five-dish dinner for three at an ordinary Thai-Chinese khâo tôm restaurant, no booze	245B
small New Orleans BBQ Chicken pizza, Pizza Hut	145B
large dinner for four at a good non-hotel Thai restaurant, including two large bottles of beer	1000B
dinner for two, with wine, at Lord Jim's, Oriental Hotel	3000B
one copy of the *Bangkok Post* or *The Nation*	20B
monthly rent for an economical two-bedroom apartment or house, Rayong Province	4000B to 10,000B

as to grab every last baht'. On the other hand change from a 50B note for a 44B bill will usually not be left behind.

Good bargaining, which takes practice, is another way to cut costs. Anything bought in a market should be bargained for; prices in department stores and most non-tourist shops are fixed. Sometimes accommodation rates can be bargained down. One may need to bargain hard in heavily touristed areas since the one week, all air-con type of visitor often pays whatever's asked, creating an artificial price zone between the local and tourist market that the budgeter must deal with.

On the other hand the Thais aren't *always* trying to rip you off, so use some discretion when going for the bone on a price. There's a fine line between bargaining and niggling

– getting hot under the collar over 5B makes both seller and buyer lose face. Likewise a frown is a poor bargaining tool. Some more specific suggestions concerning costs can be found in the Accommodation and Shopping sections later on in this chapter.

Taxes

In 1997 Thailand's value-added tax (VAT) was raised from 7 to 10%. The tax applies only to certain goods and services, but unfortunately no one seems to know what's subject to VAT and what's not, so the whole situation can be rather confusing. Legally, the tax is supposed to be applied to a retailer's cost for the product. For example, if a merchant's wholesale price is 100B for an item that retails at 200B, the maximum adjusted retail including VAT should be 210B, not 220B. But this doesn't always stop Thai merchants from trying to add 'VAT' surcharges to their sales. Like the credit-card surcharge, a direct VAT surcharge is illegal; if you're charged a full 10% on retail, you can try reporting it to the TAT Tourist Police. So far we've heard of no refunds for VAT however, such attempts would probably be a waste of time.

Tourist hotels will usually add a 10% hotel tax, and sometimes an 8 to 10% service charge as well, to your room bill.

POST & COMMUNICATIONS

Thailand has an efficient postal service and, within the country, postage is very cheap.

Bangkok's main post office on Th Charoen Krung (New Rd) is open from 8 am to 8 pm Monday to Friday, and until 1 pm weekends and holidays. A 24 hour international telecommunications service (including telephone, fax, telex and telegram) is in a separate building behind and to the right of the main post office building.

Outside Bangkok the typical main provincial post office is open from 8.30 am to 4.30 pm Monday to Friday, and from 9 am to noon Saturday. Larger main post offices in provincial capitals may also be open for a half day on Sunday.

Postal Rates

Air mail letters weighing 10g or less cost 14B to anywhere in Asia (Zone 1 in Thai postal parlance), 17B to Europe, Africa, Australia and New Zealand (Zone 2), and 19B to the Americas (Zone 3). Aerograms cost 15B regardless of the destination, while postcards are 12B to 15B depending on size.

Letters sent by registered mail cost 25B in addition to regular air mail postage. International express mail (EMS) fees vary according to 15 zones of destination radiating out from Thailand, ranging from 310B for a document sent to zone 1 to 2050B for a document sent to zone 15. EMS packages range from 460B to 2400B. Within Thailand, this service costs only 25B (100 to 250g) in addition to regular postage.

Sample air rates include: Singapore, 500B for the first kilogram, then 100B for each additional kilogram; Europe 1100B and 350B; USA 700B and 300B. A new service called Economy Air SAL (for Sea, Air, Land) uses a combination of surface and air mail modes with rates beginning at 250B for the first kilogram, plus 180B for each kilogram after that. As a comparison, a 2kg parcel sent to the US by regular airmail would cost 1000B, while the same parcel sent via Economy Air SAL would cost only 430B. There are a few other wrinkles to all this depending on what's in the package. Printed matter, for example, can travel by air more cheaply than other goods.

Parcels sent domestically cost 15B for the first kilogram, then 10B for each additional kilogram.

You can insure a package's contents for 50B per each 5380B of the goods' value.

Sending Mail

Couriers The following companies will pick up mail or parcels anywhere in Bangkok for overnight delivery to other towns in Thailand, or to most places in the world within three to four days. DHL has the best reputation for punctuality and efficiency. Be sure to allow plenty of time between your call and the expected pick-up time for traffic jams.

DHL Worldwide
   (☎ 02-207 0600) 22nd floor, Grand Amarin Tower, Th Phetchaburi Tat Mai
Federal Express
   (☎ 02-367 3222) 8th floor, Green Tower, Th Rama IV
UPS
   (☎ 02-712 3300) 16/1 Soi 44/1, Th Sukhumvit

Two international courier services also have offices in Phuket:

DHL Worldwide
   (☎ 076-219005) 145 Th Phang-Nga
UPS
   (☎ 076-218719) Phuket Business Service, 9/44 Th Chao Fa

Packaging In Bangkok there's an efficient and inexpensive packaging service at the main post office where you can have parcels wrapped, or you can simply buy the materials at the counter and do it yourself. The packaging counter is open weekdays from 8 am to 4.30 pm and Saturday from 9 am to noon. When the parcel counter is closed (weekday evenings and Sunday mornings) an informal packing service (using recycled materials) is open behind the service windows at the centre rear of the building. Branch post offices throughout the city also offer parcel services.

Most provincial post offices sell do-it-yourself packing boxes (11 sizes) costing 5B to 35B; tape and string are provided free. Some offices even have packing services, which cost 4B to 10B per parcel depending on size. Private packing services may also be available near large provincial post offices.

Receiving Mail

Thailand's poste restante service is reliable, though during high tourist months (December to February, July, August) you may have to wait in line at post offices in Bangkok and on Ko Samui. There is a fee of 1B for every piece of mail collected, 2B for each parcel. As with many Asian countries, confusion at poste restante offices is most likely to arise over given names and surnames. Ask people writing to you to print your surname clearly and to underline it. If you're certain a letter should be waiting for you and it cannot be found, it's always wise to check if it has been filed under your given name. You can collect poste restante at almost any post office in Thailand.

The American Express office (☎ 02-216 5757), Suite 88-92, Payathai Plaza, 8th floor, 128 Th Phayathai, will also take mail on behalf of Amex card holders. The hours are from 8.30 am to noon and 1 to 4.30 pm Monday to Friday, and 8.30 to 11.30 am on Saturday. Amex won't accept courier packets that require your signature. The mail window staff have a reputation for being less than helpful.

Telephone

The telephone system in Thailand, operated by the government-subsidised Telephone Organization of Thailand (TOT) under the Communications Authority of Thailand (CAT), is quite efficient and from Bangkok you can usually direct dial most major centres with little difficulty.

The country code for Thailand is ☎ 66. See the Thai Area Codes table opposite for listings of domestic area codes.

Telephone Office Hours Main post office phone centres in most provincial capitals are open daily from 7 am to 11 pm; smaller provincial phone offices may be open from 8 am to 8 or 10 pm. Bangkok's international CAT phone office at the Th Charoen Krung main post office is open 24 hours.

Domestic Calls In most places in Thailand there are two kinds of public pay phones: red phones for local city calls and blue for both local and long-distance calls (within Thailand). Local calls from pay phones cost 1B for three minutes (add more coins for more time). Local calls from private phones cost 3B, no time limit. Some hotels and guesthouses feature private pay phones that cost 5B per call.

Card phones can be found at most Thai airports as well as major shopping centres and other public areas throughout urban Thailand. Phonecards come in 25B, 50B, 100B, 200B and 240B denominations, all roughly the same size as a credit card; they can be purchased at any TOT office. In airports you can usually buy them at the airport information counter or at one of the gift shops.

Another way to pay for domestic calls is to use the Pin Phone 108 system, which allows you to dial '108' from any phone – including cellular phones and public pay phones, then enter a PIN code to call any number in Thailand. To use this system, however, you must have your own phone number in Thailand.

Another phone booth service – found mostly in Bangkok – is called Telepoint, a system that uses a one way mobile phone network operated by TOT. Such mobile

Thai Area Codes

The area codes for Thailand's major cities are presented below. See the relevant destination chapters for the area codes of smaller towns not listed here. Note that zeros aren't needed in area codes when dialling from overseas but they must be included when dialling domestically. To dial a long-distance, domestic phone number use the full area code (eg to call the THAI office in Bangkok from Chiang Mai) dial ☎ 02-513 0121. The country code for Thailand is ☎ 66, but omit the 0 from the domestic area code if calling from outside Thailand. To call Bangkok from overseas, dial ☎ 66 2-513 0121.

Mobile phone numbers begin with 01, and the zero should always be dialled.

Bangkok, Nonthaburi, Pathum Thani, Samut Prakan, Thonburi	☎ 02
Cha-am, Phetchaburi, Prachuap Khiri Khan, Pranburi, Ratchaburi	☎ 032
Kanchanaburi, Nakhon Pathom, Samut Sakhon, Samut Songkhram	☎ 034
Ang Thong, Ayuthaya, Suphanburi	☎ 035
Lopburi, Saraburi, Singburi	☎ 036
Aranya Prathet, Nakhon Nayok, Prachinburi	☎ 037
Chachoengsao, Chonburi, Pattaya, Rayong, Si Racha	☎ 038
Chanthaburi, Trat	☎ 039
Chiang Khan, Loei, Mukdahan, Nakhon Phanom, Nong Khai, Sakon Nakhon, Udon Thani	☎ 042
Kalasin, Khon Kaen, Mahasarakham, Roi Et	☎ 043
Buriram, Chaiyaphum, Nakhon Ratchasima (Khorat)	☎ 044
Si Saket, Surin, Ubon Ratchathani, Yasothon	☎ 045
Chiang Mai, Chiang Rai, Lamphun, Mae Hong Son	☎ 053
Lampang, Nan, Phayao, Phrae	☎ 054
Kamphaeng Phet, Mae Sot, Phitsanulok, Sukhothai, Tak, Utaradit	☎ 055
Nakhon Sawan, Phetchabun, Phichit, Uthai Thani	☎ 056
Narathiwat, Pattani, Sungai Kolok, Yala	☎ 073
Hat Yai, Phattalung, Satun, Songkhla	☎ 074
Krabi, Nakhon Si Thammarat, Trang	☎ 075
Phang-Nga, Phuket	☎ 076
Chaiya, Chumphon, Ko Samui, Ranong, Surat Thani	☎ 077

phones can be used within 100m to 200m of a Telepoint location to communicate with other mobile phones and pagers. For a Telepoint account TOT charges a monthly service fee of 350B plus 1B per minute (three minute minimum) in Bangkok, or normal TOT rates for upcountry and overseas calls, plus registration fees.

Mobile Phones TOT authorises use of private mobile phones using two systems, NMT 900MHz (Cellular 900) and the older NMT 470MHz. The former system is becoming more common.

It costs 1000B to register a phone and 700B per month for 'number rental' with the 900MHz or 450B per month for 470MHz. Rates are 3B per minute within the same area code, 8B per minute to adjacent area codes and 12B per minute to other area codes. Mobile phone users must pay for incoming as well as outgoing calls. Keep this in mind whenever you consider calling a number that begins with the code ☎ 01 – this means you're calling a mobile phone number and will be charged accordingly. Note also that the zero in '01' needs to be dialled.

In Bangkok and Chiang Mai we've seen sidewalk tables where you can make pirate mobile phone calls anywhere in Thailand for 3B to 5B per minute. In the inimitable Thai scofflaw fashion, these vendors are illegally tapping signals from registered phones; such pirated services will probably die out as cellular system providers devise more secure systems.

Directory Assistance If you're trying to find a phone number within Thailand, you can try ringing English-language directory assistance: ☎ 13 for the Bangkok area and ☎ 183 for provincial locations. The operators aren't always exactly fluent, so be patient and speak clearly.

International Calls To direct dial an international number (except those in Malaysia and Laos, see later this section) from a private phone, simply dial ☎ 001 before the number. For operator-assisted international calls, dial ☎ 100.

A service called Home Direct is available at Bangkok's main post office (Th Charoen Krung), at airports in Bangkok, Phuket, Hat Yai and Surat Thani, and at post office CAT centres in Bangkok, Hat Yai, Phuket, Surat Thani, Pattaya and Hua Hin. Home Direct phones offer easy one button connection with international operators in 20-odd countries around the world. You can also direct dial Home Direct access numbers from any private phone (but not most hotel phones) in Thailand.

For Home Direct service, dial ☎ 001-999 followed by:

Australia	☎ 61-1000
Canada	☎ 15-1000
Denmark	☎ 45-1000
Germany	☎ 49-1000
Hong Kong	☎ 852-1086
Japan	☎ 81-0051
Korea	☎ 82-1000
Netherlands	☎ 31-1035
New Zealand	☎ 64-1066
Philippines	☎ 63-1000
Singapore	☎ 351-1000
UK	☎ 44-1066
USA (AT&T)	☎ 1111
USA (MCI)	☎ 12001
USA (Sprint)	☎ 13877

Hotels generally add surcharges (sometimes as much as 30% over and above the CAT rate) for international calls; it's always cheaper to call abroad from a CAT telephone office. These offices are almost always attached to a city's main post office, often on the building's 2nd floor, around the side or just behind the main post office. There may also be a separate TOT office down the road, used only for residential or business services (eg billing or installation), not public calls. Even when public phone services are offered, TOT offices accept only cash payments – reverse-charge and credit card calls aren't permitted. Hence the CAT office is generally your best choice.

To make an international call *(thorásàp ráwàang pràthêt)* at a CAT office you must fill out a bilingual form with your name and details of the call's destination. Except for reverse-charge calls *(kèp plai-thaang)*, you must estimate in advance the time you'll be on the phone and pay a deposit equal to the time/distance rate. There is always a minimum three minute charge, refunded if your call doesn't go through.

Usually, only cash or international phone credit cards are acceptable for payment at CAT offices; some provincial CAT offices also accept Amex and a few take Visa or MasterCard.

If the call doesn't go through you must pay a 30B service charge anyway – except for reverse-charge calls, for which you pay the 30B charge only if the call goes through. Depending on where you're calling, reimbursing someone later for a reverse-charge call to your home country may be less expensive than paying CAT/TOT rates – it pays to compare at source and destination. For calls between the USA and Thailand, for example, AT&T collect rates are less than TOT's direct rates.

Private long-distance telephone offices operate in most towns, but sometimes these are only for calls within Thailand. Often they're just a desk or a couple of booths in the rear of a shop. These private offices typically collect a 10B surcharge for long-distance domestic calls, 50B for international calls. The vast majority accept only cash.

Whichever type of phone service you use, the least expensive time of day to make calls is from 10 pm to 7 am (66% discount), followed by 6 to 10 pm (50% discount). You pay full price from 7 am to 6 pm. Some sample rates for a three minute call during the daytime: Africa 55B, Asia 40B, Australia 40B, Europe 46B.

Phonecards There's a wide range of local and international phonecards. Lonely Planet's eKno Communication Card (see the insert at the back of this book) is aimed specifically at travellers and provides cheap international calls, a range of messaging services and free email – for local calls, you're usually better off with a local card. You can join by phone from Thailand by dialling ☎ 001-800-13-288-7648, or online at www.ekno.lonelyplanet.com. Once you have joined, to use eKno from Thailand, dial ☎ 001-800-13-286-9029.

A new CAT-issued international calling card, called Thai Card, comes in 300B and 500B denominations and allows calls to the USA, UK, Hong Kong, Japan, Macau, Korea, New Zealand, Belgium, Singapore, Philippines, Indonesia, Australia, Taiwan and Italy.

Malaysia & Laos CAT does not offer long-distance service to Malaysia or Laos. To call these countries you must go through TOT. For Laos, you can direct dial ☎ 007 and country code 856, followed by the area code and number you want to reach. Malaysia can be dialled direct by prefixing the Malaysian number (including area code) with the code ☎ 09.

Fax

Major post office telephone offices throughout the country offer fax service. There's no need to bring your own paper, as the post offices supply their own forms. A few TOT offices also offer fax services. International faxes typically cost a steep 90B to 120B for the first page, and 65B to 110B

per page for the remaining pages, depending on the size of the paper and destination.

Larger hotels with business centres offer the same services but always at higher rates.

Email & Internet Access

The Internet is rapidly gaining in popularity in Thailand, especially as an increasing number of local, Thai-language pages go online and folks get their Internet software installed for Thai language. The scene is changing rapidly. When the last edition of this guide came out, the few Internet services providers (ISPs) in business had nodes only in Bangkok, and there were only a handful of Internet cafes in Bangkok and upcountry. Nowadays Thailand's better ISPs offer nodes in a dozen or more towns and cities around the country, which means if you are travelling with a laptop you won't necessarily have to pay long-distance charges to Bangkok. Some nodes work better than others, however, and for some ISPs only the Bangkok node seems stable.

Local ISPs – of which there were 16 at last count – typically charge around 900B per month for 20 hours of Internet access (or 500B for 10 hours) with 33.5Kbps modem connections and bandwidths of around 2.5Mbps. Low-grade, text-only services are available for as low as 300B a month. With any of these accounts additional per-hour charges are incurred if you max out on your online time.

The major limitation in email and Internet access continues to be CAT, which connects all ISPs via the Thailand Internet Exchange (THIX) at a local speed of 512Kbps. CAT also collects a hefty access charge from local ISPs, which keeps rates high relative to the local economy.

Nevertheless Thailand is more advanced in the cybernautic world than any other country in South-East Asia at the moment and rates have dropped as much as 75% over the last two or three years. Many guesthouses and bars/cafes in Bangkok, Chiang Mai, Ko Samui and Phuket now offer email and Internet log-ons at house terminals. For the visitor who only needs to log on once in a while, these are a less expensive alternative to getting your own account – and it certainly beats lugging around a laptop. The going rate is 1B or 2B per on- and offline minute. As these services become more popular, other places around the country where wireheads congregate will surely follow suit.

Plugging in Your Own Machine In older hotels and guesthouses the phones may still be hard-wired, but RJ11 phone jacks are the standard in new hotels. A pocketknife and pair of alligator clips are useful for stripping and attaching wires, or bring along an acoustic coupler.

Loxinfo, one of the better ISPs in Thailand, offers prepaid NetAccess cards with special uses for modem communications. These cards come in denominations of two hours (150B), four hours (250B), 10 hours (500B) and 20 hours (900B). Purchasers are provided with a sealed envelope containing a user name, password, local phone access numbers and log-on procedures. Follow the latter and you'll be able to navigate the Internet, check email at your online home address, and access any online services you subscribe to, such as CompuServe or America Online. Complete details about the Net-Access Card, including a list of authorised agents, can be obtained through Loxinfo's home page at www.loxinfo.co.th.

INTERNET RESOURCES

A growing number of online entities offer information on Thailand. Many of these Web sites are commercial ones established by tour operators or hotels; the ratio of commercial to non-commercial sites is liable to increase over time if current Internet trends continue. Remember that all URL's (universal resource locators) mentioned are subject to change without notice. There's a lot of information out there: a quick search on Yahoo in mid 1999 yielded a list of 170,000 Web pages devoted to Thailand!

Consider starting with the Lonely Planet Web site (www.lonelyplanet.com). Here you'll find succinct summaries on travelling to most places on earth, postcards from other travellers and the Thorn Tree bulletin board, where you can ask questions before you go or dispense advice when you get back. You can also find travel news and upgrades to this edition, and the subWWWay section links you to the most useful travel resources elsewhere on the Web. For a direct link to Thailand-related material, go for www.lonelyplanet.com.au/dest /sea/thai.htm.

TAT maintains a well designed Web site (www.tat.or.th) containing a province guide, numerous and up-to-date press releases, tourism statistics, TAT contact info and trip planning hints. The well tuned National Electronics and Computer Technology Center (NECTEC, www.nectec.or.th) site exhibits great depth and breadth and contains links on everything from a list of all Thai embassies and consulates abroad and details of visa requirements to weather updates. Another Web site sourced from Thailand is ThaiIndex (www.thaiindex.com). Pages include general information, government office listings, travel listings, a hotel directory and other links. Most hotel lists on the Internet appear to be sorely incomplete, whether oriented towards budget or luxury properties.

Mahidol University in Bangkok maintains a very useful site (www.mahidol.ac.th/Thai land) that's searchable by keyword.

The *Bangkok Post* Web site (www.bang kokpost.net) runs around 60 pages of stories as well as photos. Aside from the Web, another Internet resource is the ftp usenet group soc.culture.thai. – it's very uneven as it's basically a chat outlet for anyone who thinks they have something to say about Thailand – but it's not a bad place to start if you have a burning question that you haven't found an answer to elsewhere.

BOOKS

Most books are published in different editions by different publishers in different countries. As a result, a book might be a hardcover rarity in one country while it's readily available in paperback in another.

Fortunately, bookshops and libraries search by title or author, so your local bookshop or library is best placed to advise you on the availability of the following recommendations.

For books on Buddhism and Buddhism in Thailand, see the Religion section of the Facts about Thailand chapter.

Lonely Planet

Lonely Planet publishes several other books to Thailand: the *Thailand* guidebook; *Bangkok* city guide; *Thailand, Vietnam, Laos & Cambodia travel atlas*; *Thai phrasebook;* and *Thai Hill Tribes phrasebook*. For diving books, see Diving & Snorkelling in the 'Activities' boxed text in this chapter.

Finally there's Lonely Planet's new *World Food Thailand*, an intimate guide to exploring the country, and its cuisine. This full colour book covers every food and drink situation the traveller could encounter and plots the evolution of what we know as Thai cuisine. It also includes an extremely useful language section.

Description & Travel

The earliest western literature of note on Thailand, Guy Tachard's *A Relation of the Voyage to Siam*, recounts a 1680s French expedition through parts of the country with little literary flair. Shortly thereafter, Simon de la Loubére's 1693 *New Historical Relation of the Kingdom of Siam* chronicled the French mission to the Ayuthaya court in great detail. Maurice Collis novelised this period with a focus on the unusual political relationship between King Narai and his Greek minister, Constantin Phaulkon, in *Siamese White*.

Joseph Conrad evoked Thailand in several of his pre-WWII novels and short stories, most notably in his 1920s *The Secret Sharer* and *Falk: A Reminiscence*.

Pico Iyer, Robert Anson Hall and several other well known and not-so-well known authors have contributed travel essays of varying styles to *Travelers' Tales Thailand* (edited by James O'Reilly & Larry Habegger, 1994). It was the first title in a series

that assembles travel articles and chapters from various sources into a single anthology devoted to a particular country. Savvy travel tips are sprinkled through the text.

A more serious collection of literature is available in *Traveller's Literary Companion: South-East Asia*, edited by Alastair Dingwall. The Thailand chapter, edited by scholar Thomas John Hudak, is packed with information on the history of literature in Thailand and includes extracts from various works by Thai as well as foreign authors.

Culture & Society

Naga: Cultural Origins in Siam & the Western Pacific by Sumet Jumsai (Chalermnit Press/DD Books, 1997) is an inspired theory on the supposed oceanic origins of Thai people and culture. With direct inspiration from the late R Buckminster Fuller, who collaborated with author/architect/Cambridge lecturer Sumet to a limited degree, the book outlines in prose and carefully collected illustrations how the myths, symbols and architecture common to Thailand and other mainland South-East Asian civilisations – in particular the *naga* or sea dragon motif – stem from an earlier phase in Asian-Western Pacific history, when most of the peoples of the region inhabited islands and lived largely seafaring lives.

Culture Shock! Thailand by Robert & Nanthapa Cooper is an interesting book about adapting to the Thai way of life, although it's heavily oriented towards Bangkok life. *Letters from Thailand* by Botan (translated by Susan Fulop Kepner), and Carol Hollinger's *Mai Pen Rai Means Never Mind* can also be recommended for their insights into traditional Thai culture. *Bangkok Post* reporter Denis Segaller's *Thai Ways* and *More Thai Ways* present further expat insights into Thai culture.

Behind the Smile: Voices of Thailand (1990) by Sanitsuda Ekachai is a very enlightening collection of interviews with Thai peasants from all over the country. *In the Mirror* (1985) is an excellent collection of translated modern Thai short stories from the 1960s and 70s. The Siam Society's *Culture*

& Environment in Thailand is a collection of scholarly papers by Thai and foreign authors delivered at a 1988 symposium that examined the relationship between Thai culture and the natural world; topics range from the oceanic origins of the Thai race and nature motifs in Thai art to evolving Thai attitudes towards the environment.

Siam in Crisis by Sulak Sivaraksa, one of Thailand's leading intellectuals, analyses modern Thai politics from his Buddhist-nationalist perspective. Sivaraksa has written several other worthwhile titles on Thai culture that have been translated into English. Essays by this contrary and contradictory character posit an ideal that neither Thailand nor any other country will likely ever achieve, and his attempts to use western-style academic argument to discredit western thinking can be exasperating and inspiring.

History & Politics

George Coedes' classic prewar work on South-East Asian history, *The Indianised States of South-East Asia*, contains ground-breaking historical material on early Thai history, as does WAR Wood's *A History of Siam*, published in the same era. One of the more readable general histories written in the latter half of the 20th century is David Wyatt's *Thailand: A Short History* (Trasvin Publications, Chiang Mai).

Concentrating on post-revolutionary Thailand, *The Balancing Act: A History of Modern Thailand* (Asia Books, 1991) by Joseph Wright Jr, starts with the 1932 revolution and ends with the February 1991 Coup. Wright's semi-academic chronicle concludes that Thai history demonstrates a continuous circulation of elites governed by certain 'natural laws' and that, despite the 1932 revolution, democracy has never gained a firm foothold in Thai society.

Axel Aylwen's novel *The Falcon of Siam* and its sequel *The Falcon Takes Wing* capture the feel and historical detail of 17th century Siam, including several locales in southern Thailand; Aylwen obviously read Collis, Loubére and Tachard closely (see the earlier Description & Travel entry in this section).

Fiction

The Lioness in Bloom, translated by Susan Fulop Kepner, is an eye-opening collection of 11 short stories written by or about Thai women. Jack Reynolds' 1950s *A Woman of Bangkok* (republished in 1985), a well-written and poignant story of a young Englishman's descent into the world of Thai brothels, remains the best novel yet published with this theme. Expat writer Christopher G Moore covers the Thai underworld in his 1990s novels *A Killing Smile, Spirit House, A Bewitching Smile,* and a raft of others, with an anchor firmly hooked into the go-go bar scene. His description of Bangkok's meta-sleazy Thermae Coffee House (called 'Zeno' in *A Killing Smile*) is the closest literature comes to evoking the perpetual male adolescence such places cater to.

Natural History

Complete with sketches, photos and maps, *The Mammals of Thailand* (Association for the Conservation of Wildlife, 1988), by Boonsong Lekagul & Jeffrey McNeely, remains the classic on Thai wildlife in spite of a few out-of-date references (it was first published in 1977). Bird lovers should seek out the *Bird Guide of Thailand* (Association for the Conservation of Wildlife, 1972) by Boonsong Lekagul & EW Cronin for comprehensive descriptions of Thailand's birdlife.

Detailed summaries of 77 of Thailand's national parks, along with an objective assessment of current park conditions, are available in *National Parks of Thailand* (Communication Resources, Bangkok, 1994) by Gray, Piprell & Graham.

FILMS

A number of classic international films have used Thailand either as a subject or as a location – more often the latter. In fact nowadays location shooting in Thailand has become something of a boom industry as Thailand's jungles, rice fields and islands find themselves backdrops for all manner of scripts set in 'exotic' tropical countries.

The first film to come out of Thailand was *Chang*, a 1927 silent picture shot entirely in Nan Province (then still a semi-independent principality with Siamese protection). Produced by American film impresarios Copper and Schoedsack – who later produced several major Hollywood hits – *Chang* contains some of the best jungle and wildlife sequences filmed in Asia to date. *Chang* is available on film or video from speciality houses. Around 1930 a movie called *I Am from Siam*, produced and narrated by *Bangkok Post* founder Don Gardner and starring none other than King Rama VII, emerged. It's virtually impossible to find this film today outside Thailand's National Film Archives.

Next came *Anna & the King of Siam*, a 1946 American production (filmed on Hollywood sets) starring Rex Harrison and based on the book *The English Governess at the Siamese Court* by Anna Leonowens, who cared for Rama IV's children in the 19th century. *The King & I*, grew from a very successful Broadway stage production starring Yul Brynner (who earned an Oscar for the film). Both films, as well as the musical, are banned in Thailand because they are seen to compromise the dignity of the monarchy.

Probably the most famous movie associated with Thailand is *The Bridge on the River Kwai*, a 1957 Academy Award-winning production stemming from Pierre Boulle's book of the same name and starring Alec Guinness. Although based on WWII events in Thailand, much of the film was shot on location in Sri Lanka (then Ceylon).

The Man with the Golden Gun, a pedestrian 1974 James Bond vehicle starring Roger Moore and Christopher Lee, brought the karst islands of Ao Phang-Nga to international attention for the first time. A year later the French soft-porn movie *Emmanuelle* ('Much hazy, soft-focus coupling in downtown Bangkok', wrote *The Illustrated London News)* added to the myth of Thailand as sexual idyll and set an all-time box office record in France.

Virtually every film produced with a Vietnam War theme has been shot either in the Philippines or in Thailand, with the latter ahead by a long shot as the location of choice due to relative logistical ease. The first Vietnam-themed movie to use Thailand as a location was *The Deer Hunter*, which won the 1978 Academy Award for best picture. The dramatic Russian-roulette scene was shot in an old neighbourhood on Th Charoen Krung, while the Saigon bar scenes were shot in Bangkok's Patpong district. Oliver Stone's *Heaven and Earth* (1993), is one of the more recent pictures to paint Vietnam on a Thai canvas.

The Killing Fields (1984) skilfully used Thailand as a stand-in for Cambodia. In a 1987 spin-off of this movie, *Swimming to Cambodia*, monologist Spalding Gray recounts behind-the-scenes anecdotes of the Thailand shooting of the film.

Jean-Claude Van Damme's *The Kickboxer* brought muay thai (Thai boxing) to the big screen with a bit more class than the average martial arts flick; more than a few foreign pugilists have packed their bags for Bangkok after viewing the movie's exotic mix of ring violence and Thai Buddhist atmospherics. Sly Stallone's 1980s *Rambo* movies (Rambos II and III used Thailand locations) did little for Thailand, but the success of *Good Morning Vietnam* (1988), a Robin Williams comedy widely publicised as having been shot in Bangkok and Phuket, helped generate a tourism boom for the country.

Trainspotting's Danny Boyle directed teenage heart-throb Leonardo DiCaprio in a film adaptation of Alex Garland's novel *The Beach* in early 1999. The shooting of this film on Ko Phi-Phi caused some controversy, see the 'Notes on *The Beach*' boxed text in the South-West Gulf Coast chapter for more.

Thailand now maintains a substantial contingent of trained production assistants and casting advisers who work continuously with foreign companies on location shoots – many of them from Japan, Hong Kong and Singapore.

NEWSPAPERS & MAGAZINES

Thailand's 1997 constitution guarantees freedom of the press, though the National Police Department reserves power to suspend publishing licences for national security reasons. Editors nevertheless exercise self-censorship in certain realms, particularly with regard to the monarchy. Monarchical issues aside, Thailand is widely considered to have the freest print media in South-East Asia. In a survey conducted by the Singapore-based Political and Economic Risk Consultancy, 180 expatriate managers in 10 Asian countries ranked Thailand's English-language press the highest in Asia. Surprisingly, these expats cited the *Bangkok Post* and *The Nation* more frequently as their source of regional and global news than either the *Asian Wall Street Journal* or the *Far Eastern Economic Review*.

These two English-language newspapers are published daily in Thailand and distributed in most provincial capitals throughout the country – the *Bangkok Post* in the morning and *The Nation* in the afternoon. *The Nation* is almost entirely staffed by Thais and presents, obviously, a Thai perspective, while the *Post*, which was Thailand's first English language daily (established 1946), has a mixed Thai and international staff and represents a more international view. For international news, the *Post* is the better of the two papers and is in fact regarded by many journalists as the best English daily in the region. *The Nation*, on the other hand, has better regional coverage – particularly with regard to Myanmar and former Indochina, and the paper is to be commended for taking a harder anti-NPKC stance during the 1991 coup.

The Singapore edition of the *International Herald Tribune* is widely available in Bangkok, Chiang Mai and heavily touristed areas like Pattaya and Phuket.

The most popular Thai-language newspapers are *Thai Rath* and *Daily News*, but they're mostly full of blood-and-guts stories. The best Thai journalism is found in the somewhat less popular *Matichon* and *Siam Rath* dailies. Many Thais read the English-language dailies as they consider them better news sources. The *Bangkok Post* also publishes a Thai-language version.

Magazines

English-language magazine publishing has faltered with the economic slowdown in Thailand, and several mags failed after 1996. Now Thailand's biggest selling Enlish-language magazine, *Bangkok Metro* continues to inject urban sophistication into the publishing scene with extensive listings concerned with art, culture, cuisine, film and music in Bangkok, along with less extensive Pattaya, Phuket and Chiang Mai pages.

Le Gavroche offers monthly news and features on Thailand for the francophone community.

Many popular magazines from the UK, USA, Australia and Europe – particularly those concerned with computer technology, cars, fashion, music and business – are available in bookshops that specialise in English-language publications (see Bookshops under Shopping later in this chapter).

RADIO & TV
Radio

Thailand has more than 400 radio stations, with 41 FM and 35 AM stations in Bangkok alone. Radio station 107 FM, affiliated with Radio Thailand and Channel 9 on Thai public television, broadcasts CNN news coverage of the Asia region almost every hour between 5 pm and 2 am daily, and features some surprisingly good music programmes with British, Thai and American DJs. Bilingual DJs at Star FM 102.5 present R&B, pop, rock and alternative music 24 hours a day. Another station with international pop and English-speaking DJs is Radio Bangkok (Gold FMX), 95.5 FM, which plays contemporary hits as well as oldies 24 hours a day.

If you're looking for Thai music, Station 87.5 FM broadcasts classic Thai pop, including old *lûuk thûng* (very rhythmic popular music from north-east Thailand) styles played on accordion.

Chulalongkorn University broadcasts classical music at 101.5 FM from 10.30 pm to 1 am nightly, and 'light classical, popular golden oldies and jazz' from 4 to 6.30 pm. A schedule of the evening's programmes can be found in *The Nation* and *Bangkok Post* newspapers.

The Voice of America, BBC World Service, Radio Canada, Radio New Zealand, Singapore Broadcasting Company, Radio New Zealand, Radio Japan and Radio Australia all have English and Thai-language broadcasts over short-wave radio. The radio frequencies and schedules, which change hourly, also appear in the *Post* and *The Nation*. BBC, Radio Australia and VOA are the most easily received by the average short-wave radio.

Radio France Internationale and Deutsche Welle carry short-wave programmes in French and German respectively. Deutsche Welle also broadcasts 50 minutes of English programming three times daily.

TV

Thailand has five VHF TV networks based in Bangkok. Following the 1991 coup the Thai government authorised an extension of telecast time to 24 hours and networks have been scrambling to fill air time ever since. As a result, there has been a substantial increase in English-language telecasts – mostly in the morning hours when Thais aren't used to watching TV.

Upcountry cities will generally receive only two networks – Channel 9 and a local private network with restricted hours.

Satellite & Cable TV As elsewhere in Asia, satellite and cable television services are swiftly multiplying in Thailand, and competition for the largely untapped market is keen. The most successful cable company in Thailand is UBC (a recent merger of two companies, UTV and IBC), available via CaTV, MMDS and DTH systems. Among the many satellite transmissions carried by UBC are six English-language movie channels (including HBO and Cinemax, both censored in Asia for language, nudity and violence), two to four international sports

channels, imported TV series, MTV Asia, Channel V (a Hong Kong-based music video telecast), CNN International, CNBC, NHK, BBC World Service Television, the Discovery Channel and all the standard Thai networks. For further information see UBC's Web site (www.ubctv.com) or obtain a copy of their free monthly *UBC Magazine*.

Thailand has its own ThaiCom 1 and 2 as uplinks for AsiaSat and as carriers for the standard Thai networks and Thai Sky (TST). The latter includes five channels offering news and documentaries, Thai music videos and Thai variety programmes. Other satellites tracked by dishes in Thailand include China's Apstar 1 and Apstar 2. Additional transmissions from these and from Vietnam, Myanmar and Malaysia are available with a satellite dish.

VIDEO SYSTEMS

The predominant video format in Thailand is PAL, a system compatible with that used in most of Europe (France's SECAM format is a notable exception) as well as in Australia. This means if you're bringing video tapes from the USA or Japan, which use the NTSC format, you'll have to bring your own VCR to play them. Some video shops (especially those that carry pirated or unlicensed tapes) sell NTSC as well as PAL and SECAM tapes. A 'multisystem' VCR has the capacity to play both NTSC and PAL, but not SECAM (except in black and white).

PHOTOGRAPHY & VIDEO
Film & Equipment

Print film is fairly inexpensive and widely available throughout Thailand. Japanese print film costs around 100B per 36 exposures, US print film a bit more. Fujichrome Velvia and Provia slide films cost around 225B per roll, Kodak Ektachrome Elite is 200B and Ektachrome 200 about 280B. Slide film, especially Kodachrome, can be hard to find outside Bangkok and Chiang Mai, so be sure to stock up before heading upcountry.

VHS video cassettes of all sizes are readily available in Bangkok, Chiang Mai, Hat Yai and Phuket.

Processing

Film processing is generally quite good in the larger cities and also quite inexpensive. Dependable E6 processing is available at several labs in Bangkok and Chiang Mai. Kodachrome must be sent out of the country for processing, so it can take up to two weeks to get it back.

Pros will find a number of labs in Bangkok that offer same-day pickup and delivery at no extra cost within the city. IQ Lab offers the widest range of services, including all types of processing (except Kodachrome), slide duping, scanning, digital prints, OutPut slides, photo CDs and custom printing.

Technical Tips

Pack some silica gel with your camera to prevent mould growing on the inside of your lenses. A polarising filter could be useful to cut down on tropical glare at certain times of day, particularly around water or highly polished glazed-tile work. Tripods are a must for shooting interiors in natural light.

Video

Properly used, a video camera can give a fascinating record of your holiday. As well as videoing the obvious things – sunsets, spectacular views – remember to record some of the ordinary everyday details of life in the country. Often the most interesting things occur when you're actually intent on filming something else. Remember too that, unlike still photography, video 'flows' – so, for example, you can shoot scenes of countryside rolling past the train window to give an overall impression that isn't possible with still photos.

Video cameras these days have amazingly sensitive microphones, and you might be surprised how much sound will be picked up. This can also be a problem if there is a lot of ambient noise – filming by the side of a busy road might seem OK when you do it, but viewing it back home might simply give you a deafening cacophony of traffic noise. One good rule to follow for beginners is to try to film in long takes, and don't move the camera around too much. Otherwise, your video could well make your viewers seasick! If your camera has a stabiliser, you can use it to obtain good footage while travelling on various means of transport, even on bumpy roads. And remember, you're on holiday – don't let the video take over your life and turn your trip into a Cecil B de Mille production.

Make sure you keep the batteries charged, and have the necessary charger, plugs and transformer.

Finally, remember to follow the same rules regarding people's sensitivities as for still photography – having a video camera shoved in their face is probably even more annoying and offensive for locals than a still camera. Always ask permission first.

Airport Security

The X-ray baggage inspection machines at Thailand's airports are all deemed film safe. Nevertheless if you're travelling with high-speed film (ISO 400 or above), you may want to have your film hand-inspected rather than X-rayed. Security inspectors are usually happy to comply. Packing your film in see-through plastic bags generally speeds up the hand inspection process. Some photographers pack their film in lead-lined bags to ward off potentially harmful rays.

TIME
Time Zone

Thailand's time zone is seven hours ahead of GMT/UTC (London). Thus, noon in Bangkok is 10 pm the previous day in Los Angeles, 1 am in New York, 5 am in London, 6 am in Paris, 1 pm in Perth and 3 pm in Sydney.

Thai Calendar

The official year in Thailand is reckoned from 543 BC, the beginning of the Buddhist Era, so 1999 AD is 2542 BE.

ELECTRICITY

Electric current is 220V, 50 cycles. Electrical wall outlets are usually of the round, two pole type; some outlets also accept flat, two bladed terminals, and some will accept either flat or round terminals. Any electrical supply shop in Thailand will carry adapters for any international plug shape as well as voltage converters.

WEIGHTS & MEASURES

Dimensions and weight are usually expressed using the metric system in Thailand. The exception is land measure, which is often quoted using the traditional Thai system of *waa*, *ngaan* and *râi*. Old-timers in the provinces will occasionally use the traditional Thai system of weights and measures in speech, as will boat-builders, carpenters and other craftspeople when talking about their work. Here are some conversions to use for such occasions:

thai units		metric conversion
1 sq *waa*	=	4 sq m
1 *ngaan*	=	400 sq m
		(100 sq waa)
1 *râi* (4 ngaan)	=	1600 sq m
1 *bàht*	=	15g
1 *taleung* or *tamleung*		
(4 bàht)	=	60g
1 *châng* (20 taleung)	=	1.2kg
1 *hàap* (50 châng)	=	60kg
1 *níu*	=	about 2cm
1 *khêup* (12 níu)	=	25cm
1 *sàwk* (2 khêup)	=	50cm
1 *waa* (4 sàwk)	=	2m
1 *sén* (20 waa)	=	40m
1 *yôht* (400 sén)	=	16km

LAUNDRY

Virtually every hotel and guesthouse in Thailand offers a laundry service. Rates are generally geared to room rates; the cheaper the accommodation, the cheaper the washing and ironing. Cheapest of all are public laundries, where you pay by the kilogram.

Many Thai hotels and guesthouses also have laundry areas where you can wash your clothes at no charge; sometimes there's even a hanging area for drying. Laundry detergent is readily available in general mercantile shops and supermarkets.

For dry-cleaning, be aware that laundries advertising dry-cleaning often don't really dry-clean (they just boil everything!) or do it badly. Luxury hotels usually have dependable dry-cleaning services.

TOILETS & BATHING

In Thailand, as in many other Asian countries, the 'squat toilet' is the norm, except in hotels and guesthouses geared towards tourists and international business travellers. Instead of trying to approximate a chair or stool like a western sit-down toilet, a traditional Asian toilet sits more or less flush with the surface of the floor, with a footpad on either side of the porcelain abyss. For travellers who have never used a squat toilet it takes a bit of getting used to. If you find yourself feeling awkward the first couple of times you use one, you can console yourself with the knowledge that, according to those who study such matters, people who use squat toilets are much less likely to develop haemorrhoids than people who use sit toilets.

Next to the typical squat toilet is a bucket or cement reservoir filled with water. A plastic bowl usually floats on the water's surface or sits nearby. This water supply has a two-fold function; toilet-goers scoop water from the reservoir with the plastic bowl and use it to clean their nether regions while still squatting over the toilet. Since there is usually no mechanical flushing device attached to a squat toilet, a few extra scoops must be poured into the toilet basin to flush waste into the septic system. In larger towns, mechanical flushing systems are becoming increasingly common, even with squat toilets. More rustic toilets in rural areas may simply consist of a few planks over a hole in the ground.

Even in places where sit-down toilets are installed, the plumbing may not be designed to take toilet paper. In such cases the usual washing bucket will be standing nearby or there will be a waste basket where you're supposed to place used toilet paper.

Public toilets are common in cinema houses, department stores, bus and train stations, larger hotel lobbies and airports.

While on the road between towns and villages it is perfectly acceptable to go behind a tree or bush or even to use the roadside when nature calls.

Some hotels and most guesthouses in the country do not have hot water, though places in the larger cities will usually offer small electric shower heaters in their more expensive rooms. Very few boiler-style water heaters are available outside larger international-style hotels.

Many rural Thais bathe in rivers or streams. Those living in towns or cities may have washrooms where a large jar or cement trough is filled with water for bathing. A plastic or metal bowl is used to sluice water from the jar or trough over the body. Even in homes where showers are installed, heated water is uncommon. Most Thais bathe at least twice a day, and never use hot water.

If ever you find yourself having to bathe in a public place you should wear a *phâakhamāa* or *phâasîn* (the cotton wraparounds); nude bathing is not the norm.

HEALTH

Travel health depends on your predeparture preparations, your daily health care while travelling and how you handle any medical problem that does develop. While the potential dangers can seem quite frightening, in reality few travellers experience anything more than an upset stomach.

Predeparture Planning

Health Insurance Make sure that you have adequate health insurance. See Travel Insurance under Visas & Documents in this chapter for details.

Travel Health Guides If you are planning to be away or travelling in remote areas for a long period of time, you may like to consider taking a more detailed health guide.

Healthy Travel Asia & India, Dr Isabelle Young, Lonely Planet Publications, 2000. Designed as a companion to Lonely Planet's guide books, it is detailed, practical and easy to use.

CDC's Complete Guide to Healthy Travel, Open Road Publishing, 1997. The US Centers for Disease Control & Prevention recommendations for international travel.

Staying Healthy in Asia Africa & Latin America, Dirk Shroeder, Moon Publications, 1994. One of the best all round guides to carry; it's detailed and well organised.

Travellers' Health, Dr Richard Dawood, Oxford University Press, 1995. Comprehensive, easy to read, authoritative and highly recommended, although it's rather large to lug around.

Travel with Children, Maureen Wheeler, Lonely Planet Publications, 1995. Includes advice on travel health for younger children.

There are also a number of excellent travel health sites on the Internet. From the Lonely Planet home page there are links at www.lonelyplanet.com/weblinks/wlprep .htm#heal to the World Health Organization and the US Centers for Disease Control & Prevention.

Other Preparations Make sure you're healthy before you start travelling. If you are going on a long trip make sure your

Everyday Health

Normal body temperature is up to 37°C or 98.6°F; more than 2°C (4°F) higher indicates a high fever. The normal adult pulse rate is 60 to 100 per minute (children 80 to 100, babies 100 to 140). As a general rule the pulse increases about 20 beats per minute for each 1°C (2°F) rise in fever.

Respiration (breathing) rate is also an indicator of illness. Count the number of breaths per minute: between 12 and 20 is normal for adults and older children (up to 30 for younger children, 40 for babies). People with a high fever or serious respiratory illness breathe more quickly than normal. More than 40 shallow breaths a minute may indicate pneumonia.

teeth are OK. If you wear glasses take a spare pair and your prescription.

If you require a particular medication take an adequate supply, as it may not be available locally. Take part of the packaging showing the generic name rather than the brand, which will make getting replacements easier. It's a good idea to have a legible prescription or letter from your doctor to show that you legally use the medication to avoid any problems with customs on arrival.

Immunisations

Plan ahead for getting your vaccinations: some of them require more than one injection, while some vaccinations should not be given together. Note that some vaccinations should not be given during pregnancy or to people with allergies – discuss with your doctor.

It is recommended that you seek medical advice at least six weeks before travel. Be aware that there is often a greater risk of disease with children and during pregnancy.

There are currently no immunisation requirements for entry into Thailand except for yellow fever if you come from an infected zone. Discuss your requirements with your doctor, but vaccinations you should consider for this trip include the following (for more details about the diseases themselves, see the individual disease entries later in this section).

Diphtheria & Tetanus Vaccinations for these two diseases are usually combined and are recommended for everyone. After an initial course of three injections (usually given in childhood), boosters are necessary every 10 years.

Polio Everyone should keep up to date with this vaccination, which is normally given in childhood. A booster every 10 years maintains immunity.

Hepatitis A Hepatitis A vaccine (eg Avaxim, Havrix 1440 or VAQTA) provides long-term immunity (possibly more than 10 years) after an initial injection and a booster at six to 12 months.

Alternatively, an injection of gamma globulin can provide short-term protection against hepatitis A – two to six months, depending on the dose given. It is not a vaccine, but a ready-made antibody collected from blood donations. It is reasonably effective and, unlike the vaccine, it is protective immediately, but because it is a blood product, there are current concerns about its long-term safety.

Hepatitis A vaccine is also available in a combined form, Twinrix, with hepatitis B vaccine. Three injections over a six-month period are required, the first two providing substantial protection against hepatitis A.

Typhoid Vaccination against typhoid may be required if you are travelling for more than a couple of weeks in most parts of Asia, Africa, Central and South America and Central and Eastern Europe. It is now available either as an injection or as capsules to be taken orally.

Cholera The current injectable vaccine against cholera is poorly protective and has many side effects, so it is not generally recommended for travellers. However, in some situations it may be necessary to have a certificate as travellers are very occasionally asked by immigration officials to present one, even though all countries and the World Health Organisation (WHO) have dropped cholera immunisation as a health requirement for entry.

Hepatitis B Travellers who should consider vaccination against hepatitis B include those undertaking a long trip, as well as those visiting countries where there are high levels of hepatitis B infection, where blood transfusions may not be adequately screened or where sexual contact or needle sharing is a possibility. Vaccination involves three injections, with a booster at 12 months. More rapid courses are available if necessary.

Rabies Vaccination should be considered by those who will spend a month or longer in a country where rabies is common, especially if they are cycling, handling animals, caving or travelling to remote areas, and for children (who may not report a bite). Pre-travel rabies vaccination involves having three injections over 21 to 28 days. If someone who has been vaccinated is bitten or scratched by an animal, they will require two booster injections of vaccine; those not vaccinated require more.

Japanese B Encephalitis Consider vaccination against this disease if spending a month or longer in a high risk area (parts of Asia), making repeated trips to a risk area or visiting during an epidemic. It involves three injections over 30 days.

Tuberculosis The risk of TB to travellers is usually very low, unless you will be living with or closely associated with local people in high risk areas such as Asia, Africa and some parts of the Americas and Pacific. Vaccination against TB (BCG) is recommended for children and young adults living in these areas for three months or more.

Malaria Medication
Antimalarial drugs do not prevent you from being infected, but kill the malaria parasites during their development and significantly reduce the risk of becoming very ill or dying. Expert advice on medication should be sought, as there are many factors to consider, including the area to be visited, the risk of exposure to malaria-carrying mosquitoes, the side effects of medication, your medical history and whether you are a child or an adult or pregnant. Travellers to isolated areas in high risk countries may like to carry a treatment dose of medication for use if symptoms occur.

Basic Rules
Food There is an old colonial adage that says: 'If you can cook it, boil it or peel it you can eat it ... otherwise forget it'. Vegetables and fruit should be washed with purified water, or peeled where possible. Beware of ice cream that is sold in the street or anywhere it might have been melted and re-frozen; if there's any doubt (eg a power cut in the last day or two), steer well clear. Shellfish, such as mussels, oysters and clams, should be avoided, as well as under-cooked meat, particularly in the form of mince. Steaming does not make shellfish safe for eating.

If a place looks clean and well run and the vendor also looks clean and healthy, then the food is probably safe. In general, places that are packed with travellers or locals will be fine, while empty restaurants are questionable. The food in busy restaurants is cooked and eaten quite quickly with little standing around and is probably not reheated.

Water If you don't know for certain that the water is safe always assume the worst. Reputable brands of Thai bottled water or soft drinks are generally fine, although in some places bottles refilled with tap water are not unknown. Only use water from containers with a serrated seal – not tops or corks. Tea or coffee should be OK, since the water should have been boiled.

Ice is produced from purified water under hygienic conditions and is therefore theoretically safe in Thailand. During transit to the local restaurant, however, conditions are not so hygienic (you may see blocks of ice being dragged along the street), but it's very difficult to resist in the hot season. The rule of thumb is that if it's chipped ice, it probably came from an ice block (which may not have been handled well) but if it's ice cubes or 'tubes', it was delivered from the ice factory in sealed plastic. In rural areas, villagers mostly drink collected rainwater. Most travellers can drink this without problems, but some people can't tolerate it.

In Thailand, virtually no-one bothers with filters, tablets or iodine since bottled water is so cheap and readily available. Try to purchase glass water bottles, however, as these are recyclable (unlike the plastic disposable ones), or bring your own refillable bottle. Water served in restaurants by the glass always comes from a purified source.

Medical Problems & Treatment

Self-diagnosis and treatment can be risky, so you should always seek medical help. Although we do give drug dosages in this section, they are for emergency use only. Correct diagnosis is vital. An embassy, consulate or five-star hotel can usually recommend a local doctor or clinic.

Antibiotics should ideally be administered only under medical supervision. Take only the recommended dose at the prescribed intervals and use the whole course, even if the illness seems to be cured earlier. Stop immediately if there are any serious reactions and don't use the antibiotic at all if you are unsure that you have the correct one. Some people are allergic to commonly prescribed antibiotics such as penicillin; carry this information (eg on a bracelet) when travelling.

Environmental Hazards

Heat Exhaustion Dehydration and salt deficiency can cause heat exhaustion. Take time to acclimatise to high temperatures, drink sufficient liquids and do not do anything too physically demanding.

Salt deficiency is characterised by fatigue, lethargy, headaches, giddiness and muscle cramps; salt tablets may help, but adding extra salt to your food is better.

Anhidrotic heat exhaustion is a rare form of heat exhaustion that is caused by an inability to sweat. It tends to affect people who have been in a hot climate for some time, rather than newcomers. It can progress to heatstroke. Treatment involves removal to a cooler climate.

Heatstroke This serious, occasionally fatal, condition can occur if the body's heat-regulating mechanism breaks down and the body temperature rises to dangerous levels. Long, continuous periods of exposure to high temperatures and insufficient fluids can leave you vulnerable to heatstroke. The symptoms are feeling unwell, not sweating very much (or at all) and a high body temperature (39° to 41°C or 102° to 106°F). Where sweating has ceased, the skin becomes flushed and red. Severe, throbbing headaches and lack of coordination will also occur, and the sufferer may be confused or aggressive. Eventually the victim will become delirious or convulse. Hospitalisation is essential, but in the interim get victims out of the sun, remove their clothing, cover them with a wet sheet or towel and fan continually. Give fluids if they are conscious.

Jet Lag Jet lag is experienced when a person travels by air across more than three time zones (each time zone usually represents a one-hour time difference). It occurs because many of the functions of the human body (such as temperature, pulse rate and emptying of the bladder and bowels) are regulated by internal 24-hour cycles. When we travel long distances rapidly, our bodies take time to adjust to the 'new time' of our destination, and we may experience fatigue, disorientation, insomnia, anxiety, impaired concentration and loss of appetite. These effects will usually be gone within three days of arrival, but to minimise the impact of jet lag:

- Rest for a couple of days prior to departure.
- Try to select flight schedules that minimise sleep deprivation; arriving late in the day means you can go to sleep soon after you arrive. For very long flights, try to organise a stopover.
- Avoid excessive eating (which bloats the stomach), alcohol (which causes dehydration) and caffeine (which also causes dehydration and interferes with natural sleep patterns) during the flight. Instead, drink plenty of non-carbonated, nonalcoholic drinks such as fruit juice or water.
- Avoid smoking.
- Make yourself comfortable by wearing loose-fitting clothes and perhaps bringing an eye mask and ear plugs to help you sleep.
- Try to sleep at the appropriate time for the time zone you are travelling to.

Motion Sickness Eating lightly before and during a trip will reduce the chances of motion sickness. If you are prone to motion sickness try to find a place that minimises movement – near the wing on aircraft, close to midships on boats, near the centre on buses. Fresh air usually helps; reading and cigarette smoke don't. Commercial motion-sickness preparations, which can cause drowsiness, have to be taken before the trip commences. Ginger (available in capsule form) and peppermint (including mint-flavoured sweets) are natural preventatives.

Prickly Heat Prickly heat is an itchy rash caused by excessive perspiration trapped under the skin. It usually strikes people who have just arrived in a hot climate. Keeping cool, bathing often, drying the skin and using a mild talcum or prickly heat powder or resorting to air-con may help.

Sunburn In the tropics, the desert or at high altitude you can get sunburnt surprisingly quickly, even through cloud. Use a sunscreen, a hat, and a barrier cream for your nose and lips. Calamine lotion or Stingose are good for mild sunburn. Protect your eyes with good quality sunglasses, particularly if you will be near water, sand or snow.

Infectious Diseases

Diarrhoea Simple things like a change of water, food or climate can all cause a mild bout of diarrhoea, but a few rushed toilet trips with no other symptoms is not indicative of a major problem.

Dehydration is the main danger with any diarrhoea, particularly in children or the elderly as dehydration can occur quite quickly. Under all circumstances *fluid replacement* (at least equal to the volume being lost) is the most important thing to remember.

Weak black tea with a little sugar, soda water, or soft drinks allowed to go flat and diluted 50% with clean water are all good. With severe diarrhoea a rehydrating solution is preferable to replace minerals and salts lost. Commercially available oral rehydration salts (ORS) are very useful; add them to boiled or bottled water. In an emergency you can make up a solution of six teaspoons of sugar and a half teaspoon of

salt to a litre of boiled or bottled water. Urine is the best guide to the adequacy of replacement – if you have small amounts of concentrated urine, you need to drink more. Keep drinking small amounts often. Stick to a bland diet as you recover.

Gut-paralysing drugs such as diphenoxylate or loperamide can be used to bring relief from the symptoms, although they do not actually cure the problem. Only use these drugs if you do not have access to toilets, eg if you *must* travel. For children under 12 years these drugs are not recommended. Do not use these drugs if the person has a high fever or is severely dehydrated.

In certain situations antibiotics may be required: diarrhoea with blood or mucus (dysentery), any diarrhoea with fever, profuse watery diarrhoea, persistent diarrhoea not improving after 48 hours and severe diarrhoea. These suggest a more serious cause of diarrhoea and in these situations gut-paralysing drugs should be avoided.

In these situations, a stool test may be necessary to diagnose what bug is causing your diarrhoea, so you should seek medical help urgently. Where this is not possible the recommended drugs for bacterial diarrhoea (the most likely cause of severe diarrhoea in travellers) are norfloxacin 400mg twice daily for three days or ciprofloxacin 500mg twice daily for five days. These are not recommended for children or pregnant women. The drug of choice for children would be co-trimoxazole with dosage dependent on weight. A five day course is given. Ampicillin or amoxycillin may be given in pregnancy, but medical care is necessary.

Two other causes of persistent diarrhoea in travellers are giardiasis and amoebic dysentery.

Giardiasis is caused by a common parasite, *Giardia lamblia*. Symptoms include stomach cramps, nausea, a bloated stomach, watery, foul-smelling diarrhoea and frequent gas. Giardiasis can appear several weeks after you have been exposed to the parasite. The symptoms may disappear for a few days and then return; this can go on for several weeks.

Amoebic dysentery, caused by the proto-zoan *Entamoeba histolytica*, is charac-terised by a gradual onset of low-grade diarrhoea, often with blood and mucus. Cramping abdominal pain and vomiting are less likely than in other types of diarrhoea, and fever may not be present. It will persist until treated and can recur and cause other health problems.

You should seek medical advice if you think you have giardiasis or amoebic dysen-tery, but where this is not possible, tinida-zole or metronidazole are the recommended drugs. Treatment is a 2g single dose of tinidazole or 250mg of metronidazole three times daily for five to 10 days.

Fungal Infections Fungal infections occur more commonly in hot weather and are usually found on the scalp, between the toes (athlete's foot) or fingers, in the groin and on the body (ringworm). You get ring-worm (which is a fungal infection, not a worm) from infected animals or other peo-ple. Moisture encourages these infections.

To prevent fungal infections wear loose, comfortable clothes, avoid artificial fibres, wash frequently and dry yourself carefully. If you do get an infection, wash the infected area at least daily with a disinfectant or medicated soap and water, and rinse and dry well. Apply an antifungal cream or powder like tolnaftate. Try to expose the in-fected area to air or sunlight as much as possible and wash all towels and underwear in hot water, change them often and let them dry in the sun.

Hepatitis Hepatitis is a general term for in-flammation of the liver. It is a common dis-ease worldwide. There are several different viruses that cause hepatitis, and they differ in the way that they are transmitted. The symptoms are similar in all forms of the ill-ness, and include fever, chills, headache, fatigue, feelings of weakness and aches and pains, followed by loss of appetite, nausea, vomiting, abdominal pain, dark urine, light-coloured faeces, jaundiced (yellow) skin and yellowing of the whites of the eyes.

People who have had hepatitis should avoid alcohol for some time after the illness, as the liver needs time to recover.

Hepatitis A is transmitted by contami-nated food and drinking water. You should seek medical advice, but there is not much you can do apart from resting, drinking lots of fluids, eating lightly and avoiding fatty foods. Hepatitis E is transmitted in the same way as hepatitis A; it can be particularly se-rious in pregnant women.

There are almost 300 million chronic car-riers of **Hepatitis B** in the world. It is spread through contact with infected blood, blood products or body fluids, for example through sexual contact, unsterilised needles and blood transfusions, or contact with blood via small breaks in the skin. Other risk situations include having a shave, tattoo or body piercing with contaminated equip-ment. The symptoms of hepatitis B may be more severe than type A and the disease can lead to long term problems such as chronic liver damage, liver cancer or a long term carrier state. Hepatitis C and D are spread in the same way as hepatitis B and can also lead to long term complications.

There are vaccines against hepatitis A and B, but there are currently no vaccines against the other types of hepatitis. Follow-ing the basic rules about food and water (hepatitis A and E) and avoiding risk situa-tions (hepatitis B, C and D) are important preventative measures.

HIV & AIDS Infection with the human im-munodeficiency virus (HIV) may lead to acquired immune deficiency syndrome (AIDS), which is a fatal disease. Any expo-sure to blood, blood products or body fluids may put the individual at risk. HIV is a major health problem in Thailand although the overall incidence of infection has slowed recently. In Thailand transmission is predominantly through heterosexual sexual activity (81%); the second most common source of HIV infection is intravenous in-jection with used needles (6.32%). The dis-ease is often transmitted through sexual contact or dirty needles – vaccinations, acupuncture, tattooing and body piercing can be as dangerous as intravenous drug use. HIV/AIDS can also be spread through infected blood transfusions, although in Thailand this risk minimal due to vigorous blood-screening procedures.

The Thai phrase for 'condom' is *thũng anaamai*. Latex condoms are more effective than animal-membrane condoms in preventing disease transmission; to specify latex ask for *thũng yaang anaamai* – actually the latter are the only kinds we've ever seen in Thailand. Since the 1970s, when Thai health educator Mechai Viravaidya initiated a vigorous national programme aimed at educating the public about contraception, the most common Thai nickname for 'condom' has been 'Mechai'. Good-quality latex condoms are distributed free by offices of the Ministry of Public Health throughout the country. Better yet, bring your own: a public health ministry survey found that around 11% of commercial Thai condoms were damaged, mostly due to improper storage. One of the better commercial brands available in Thailand is Durex.

If you do need an injection, ask to see the syringe unwrapped in front of you, or take a needle and syringe pack with you.

Fear of HIV infection should never preclude treatment for serious medical conditions.

Intestinal Worms These parasites are most common in rural, tropical areas. The different worms have different ways of infecting people. Some may be ingested on food such as undercooked meat (eg tapeworms) and some enter through your skin (eg hookworms). Infestations may not show up for some time, and although they are generally not serious, if left untreated some can cause severe health problems later. Consider having a stool test when you return home to check for these and determine the appropriate treatment.

Sexually Transmitted Diseases Gonorrhoea, herpes and syphilis are among these diseases; sores, blisters or rashes around the genitals and discharges or pain when urinating are common symptoms. In Thailand gonorrhoea, nonspecific urethritis (NSU) and syphilis are the most common of these diseases. In some STDs, such as wart virus or chlamydia, symptoms may be less marked or not observed at all, especially in women. Syphilis symptoms eventually disappear completely but the disease continues and can cause severe problems in later years. While abstinence from sexual contact is the only 100% effective prevention, using condoms is also effective. The treatment of gonorrhoea and syphilis is with antibiotics. The different sexually transmitted diseases each require specific antibiotics. There is no cure for herpes or AIDS.

Typhoid Typhoid fever is a dangerous gut infection caused by contaminated water and food. Medical help must be sought.

In its early stages sufferers may feel they have a bad cold or flu on the way, as early symptoms are a headache, body aches and a fever that rises a little each day until it is around 40°C (104°F) or more. The victim's pulse is often slow relative to the degree of fever present – unlike a normal fever where the pulse increases. There may also be vomiting, abdominal pain, diarrhoea or constipation.

In the second week the high fever and slow pulse continue and a few pink spots may appear on the body; trembling, delirium, weakness, weight loss and dehydration may occur. Complications such as pneumonia, perforated bowel or meningitis may present.

Insect-Borne Diseases

Filariasis, Lyme disease and typhus are also insect-borne diseases, but they do not pose a great risk to travellers. For more information on them see Less Common Diseases later in this section.

Malaria This serious and potentially fatal disease is spread by mosquitoes. If you are travelling in endemic areas it is extremely important to avoid mosquito bites and to take tablets to prevent this disease. Symptoms range from fever, chills and sweating, headache, diarrhoea and abdominal pains to a vague feeling of ill-health. Seek medical help immediately if malaria is suspected. Without treatment malaria can rapidly become more serious and can be fatal.

There are a number of different types of malaria. The one of most concern is falciparum malaria, which is responsible for the very serious cerebral malaria. Malaria risk exists throughout the year in rural Thailand, especially in forested and hilly areas. Among Thais it's the 11th leading cause of death, well behind heart disease, stroke, diarrhoea and traffic accidents. At the moment Thailand's high-risk areas include northern Kanchanaburi Province (especially Thung Yai Naresuan National Park) and parts of Trat Province along the Cambodian border (including Ko Chang). According to the CDC and to Thailand's Ministry of Public Health, there is virtually no risk of malaria in urban areas or the main tourist areas (eg Bangkok, Phuket and Pattaya).

The problem in recent years has been the emergence of increasing resistance to commonly used antimalarials like chloroquine, mefloquine, maloprim and proguanil. Doxycycline (Vibramycin, Doryx) is often recommended for chloroquine, mefloquine and multi-drug resistant areas, which includes most of Thailand. Doxycycline is particularly recommended by the WHO for travel to areas near the Cambodian and Myanmar borders. According to the Journal of the American Medical Association, Thailand has shown widespread resistance to mefloquine since 1982.

If medical care is not available, malaria tablets can be used for treatment. You need to use a malaria tablet that is different from the one you were taking when you contracted malaria. The standard treatment dose of mefloquine is two 250mg tablets and a further two six hours later. For Fansidar, it's a single dose of three tablets. If you were previously taking mefloquine and cannot obtain Fansidar, then other alternatives are Malarone (atovaquone-proguanil; four tablets once daily for three days),

halofantrine (three doses of two 250mg tablets every six hours) or quinine sulphate (600mg every six hours). There is a greater risk of side effects with these dosages than in normal use if used with mefloquine, so medical advice is preferable. Be aware also that halofantrine is no longer recommended by the WHO as emergency standby treatment, because of side effects, and should only be used if no other drugs are available.

In Thailand, where malaria tends to be resistant to most if not all the previously mentioned prophylactics, the Chinese herb *qinghao* – or its chemical derivative artemether – has proven to be very effective. Its use in Thailand (and other mainland South-East Asian countries) has been endorsed by the UN Tropical Disease Programme as well as the WHO director-general.

Travellers are advised to prevent mosquito bites at all times. The main messages are:

- wear light-coloured clothing
- wear long trousers and long-sleeved shirts
- use mosquito repellents containing the compound DEET on exposed areas (prolonged overuse of DEET may be harmful, especially to children, but its use is considered preferable to being bitten by disease-transmitting mosquitoes)
- avoid perfumes or aftershave
- use a mosquito net impregnated with mosquito repellent (permethrin) – it may be worth taking your own
- impregnating clothes with permethrin effectively deters mosquitoes and other insects

For those with an allergy or aversion to synthetic repellents, citronella makes a good substitute. Mosquito coils *(yaa kan yung bàep jùt)* do an excellent job of repelling mosquitoes in your room and are readily available in Thailand. Day mosquitoes do not carry malaria, so it is only in the night that you have to worry – peak biting hours are a few hours after dusk and a few hours before dawn.

Dengue Fever This viral disease is also transmitted by mosquitoes, and occurs mainly in tropical and subtropical areas of the world. Generally, there is only a small risk to travellers except during epidemics, which are usually seasonal (during and just after the rainy season). With unstable weather patterns thought to be responsible for large outbreaks in the Pacific, South-East Asia and Brazil, travellers to these areas may be especially at risk of infection.

The *Aedes aegypti* mosquito, which transmits the dengue virus, is most active during the day, unlike the malaria mosquito, and is found mainly in urban areas, in and around human dwellings.

Signs and symptoms of dengue fever include sudden onset of high fever, headache, joint and muscle pains (hence its old name, 'breakbone fever') and nausea and vomiting. A rash of small red spots appears three to four days after the onset of fever. Dengue is commonly mistaken for other infectious diseases, including influenza.

You should seek medical attention if you think you may be infected. Infection can be diagnosed by a blood test. There is no specific treatment for dengue. Aspirin should be avoided, as it increases the risk of haemorrhaging. Recovery may be prolonged, with tiredness lasting for several weeks. Severe complications are rare in travellers but include dengue haemorrhagic fever (DHF), which can be fatal without prompt medical treatment. DHF is thought to be a result of second infection due to a different strain (there are four major strains) and usually affects residents of the country rather than travellers.

There is no vaccine against dengue fever. The best prevention is to avoid mosquito bites at all times – see the malaria section earlier for more details.

Japanese B Encephalitis This viral infection of the brain is transmitted by mosquitoes. Most cases occur in rural areas as the virus exists in pigs and wading birds. Symptoms include fever, headache and alteration in consciousness. Hospitalisation is needed for correct diagnosis and treatment. There is a high mortality rate among those

who have symptoms; of those who survive many are intellectually disabled.

Persons who may be at risk in Thailand are those spending long periods of time in rural areas during the rainy season (July to October). If you belong to this group, you may want to get a Japanese encephalitis vaccination. As the vaccine itself can occasionally have serious side effects it is only recommended for people going to high exposure areas for long periods. People vaccinated should be accessible to urgent medical care for 10 days after each injection as breathing difficulties and facial swelling may occur during this time. Vaccination consists of three injections at zero, one and four weeks.

Immunity lasts about a year, at which point it's necessary to get a booster shot; then it's every three years after that.

Cuts, Bites & Stings

See Less Common Diseases for details of rabies, which is passed through animal bites.

Cuts & Scratches Wash well and treat any cut with an antiseptic such as povidone-iodine. Where possible avoid bandages and Band-Aids, which can keep wounds wet. Coral cuts are notoriously slow to heal and if they are not adequately cleaned, small pieces of coral can become embedded in the wound.

Bedbugs & Lice Bedbugs live in various places, but particularly in dirty mattresses and bedding, evidenced by spots of blood on bedclothes or on the wall. Bedbugs leave itchy bites in neat rows. Calamine lotion or Stingose spray may help.

All lice cause itching and discomfort. They make themselves at home in your hair (head lice), your clothing (body lice) or in your pubic hair (crabs). You catch lice through direct contact with infected people or by sharing combs, clothing and the like. Powder or shampoo treatment will kill the lice and infected clothing should then be washed in very hot, soapy water and left in the sun to dry.

Bites & Stings Bee and wasp stings are usually painful rather than dangerous. However, in people who are allergic to them, severe breathing difficulties may occur and require urgent medical care. Calamine lotion or Stingose spray will give relief and ice packs will reduce the pain and swelling. There are some spiders with dangerous bites but antivenins are usually available. Scorpion stings are notoriously painful and in some parts of Asia, the Middle East and Central America can actually be fatal. Scorpions often shelter in shoes or clothing.

There are various fish and other sea creatures that can sting or bite dangerously or which are dangerous to eat – seek local advice. See the 'Hazardous Marine Life' boxed text in this chapter for information about dealing with their bites and stings.

Leeches & Ticks Leeches may be present in damp rainforest conditions; they attach themselves to your skin to suck your blood. Trekkers often get them on their legs or in their boots. Salt or a lighted match or cigarette end will make them fall off. Do not pull them off, as the bite is then more likely to become infected. Clean and apply pressure if the point of attachment is bleeding. An insect repellent may keep them away.

You should always check all over your body if you have been walking through a potentially tick-infested area as ticks can cause skin infections and other more serious diseases. If a tick is found attached, press down around the tick's head with tweezers, grab the head and gently pull upwards. Avoid pulling the rear of the body as this may squeeze the tick's gut contents through the attached mouth parts into the skin, increasing the risk of infection and disease. Smearing chemicals on the tick will not make it let go and is not recommended.

Snakes To minimise your chances of being bitten always wear boots, socks and long trousers when walking through undergrowth where snakes may be present. Don't put your hands into holes and crevices, and be careful when collecting firewood.

Snake bites do not cause instantaneous death and antivenin is available at hospitals throughout Thailand and in pharmacies in larger towns and cities. Immediately wrap the bitten limb tightly, as you would for a sprained ankle, and then attach a splint to immobilise it. Keep the victim still and seek medical help, if possible with the dead snake for identification. Don't attempt to catch the snake if there is a possibility of being bitten again. Tourniquets and sucking out the poison are now comprehensively discredited.

Women's Health

Gynaecological Problems Antibiotic use, synthetic underwear, sweating and contraceptive pills can lead to fungal vaginal infections, especially when travelling in hot climates. Fungal infections are characterised by a rash, itch and discharge and can be treated with a vinegar or lemon-juice douche, or with yoghurt. Nystatin, miconazole or clotrimazole pessaries or vaginal cream are the usual treatment. Maintaining good personal hygiene and wearing loose-fitting clothes and cotton underwear may help prevent these infections.

Sexually transmitted diseases are a major cause of vaginal problems. Symptoms include a smelly discharge, painful intercourse and sometimes a burning sensation when urinating. Medical attention should be sought and male sexual partners must also be treated. Remember that in addition to these diseases, HIV or hepatitis B may also be acquired during exposure. Besides abstinence, the best thing is to practise safe sex using condoms.

Pregnancy It is not advisable to travel to some places while pregnant as some vaccinations normally used to prevent serious diseases are not advisable during pregnancy (eg yellow fever). In addition, some diseases are much more serious for the mother (and may increase the risk of a stillborn child) in pregnancy (eg malaria).

Most miscarriages occur during the first three months of pregnancy. Miscarriage is not uncommon and can occasionally lead to severe bleeding. The last three months should also be spent within reasonable distance of good medical care. A baby born as early as 24 weeks stands a chance of survival, but only in a good modern hospital. Pregnant women should avoid all unnecessary medication, vaccinations and malarial prophylactics should still be taken where needed. Additional care should be taken to prevent illness and particular attention should be paid to diet and nutrition. Alcohol and nicotine, for example, should be avoided.

Less Common Diseases

The following diseases pose a small risk to travellers, and so are only mentioned in passing. Seek medical advice if you think you may have any of these diseases.

Cholera This is the worst of the watery diarrhoeas and medical help should be sought. Outbreaks of cholera are generally widely reported, so you can avoid such problem areas. *Fluid replacement is the most vital treatment* – the risk of dehydration is severe as you may lose up to 20L a day. If there is a delay in getting to hospital, then begin taking tetracycline. The adult dose is 250mg four times daily. It is not recommended for children under nine years nor for pregnant women. Tetracycline may help shorten the illness, but adequate fluids are required to save lives.

Filariasis This is a mosquito-transmitted parasitic infection found in many parts of Africa, Asia, Central and South America and the Pacific. Possible symptoms include fever, pain and swelling of the lymph glands; inflammation of lymph drainage areas; swelling of a limb or the scrotum; skin rashes; and blindness. Treatment is available to eliminate the parasites from the body, but some of the damage already caused may not be reversible. Medical advice should be obtained promptly if the infection is suspected.

Lyme Disease This is a tick-transmitted infection which may be acquired throughout North America, Europe and Asia. The

Medical Kit Check List

Following is a list of items you should consider including in your medical kit – consult your pharmacist for brands available in your country.

☐ **Aspirin** or **paracetamol** (acetaminophen in the USA) – for pain or fever

☐ **Antihistamine** – for allergies, eg hay fever; to ease the itch from insect bites or stings; and to prevent motion sickness

☐ **Antibiotics** – consider including these if you're travelling well off the beaten track; see your doctor, as they must be prescribed, and carry the prescription with you

☐ **Loperamide** or **diphenoxylate** –'blockers' for diarrhoea; **prochlorperazine** or **metaclopramide** for nausea and vomiting

☐ **Rehydration mixture** – to prevent dehydration, eg due to severe diarrhoea; particularly important when travelling with children

☐ **Insect repellent, sunscreen, lip balm** and **eye drops**

☐ **Calamine lotion, sting relief spray** or **aloe vera** – to ease irritation from sunburn and insect bites or stings

☐ **Antifungal cream** or **powder** – for fungal skin infections and thrush

☐ **Antiseptic** (such as povidone-iodine) – for cuts and grazes

☐ **Bandages, Band-Aids (plasters)** and other wound dressings

☐ **Water purification tablets** or **iodine**

☐ **Scissors, tweezers** and a **thermometer** (note that mercury thermometers are prohibited by airlines)

☐ **Syringes** and **needles** – in case you need injections in a country with medical hygiene problems. Ask your doctor for a note explaining why you have them.

☐ **Cold** and **flu tablets, throat lozenges** and **nasal decongestant**

☐ **Multivitamins** – consider for long trips, when dietary vitamin intake may be inadequate

illness usually begins with a spreading rash at the site of the tick bite and is accompanied by fever, headache, extreme fatigue, aching joints and muscles and mild neck stiffness. If untreated, these symptoms usually resolve over several weeks but over subsequent weeks or months disorders of the nervous system, heart and joints may develop. Treatment works best early in the illness. Medical help should be sought.

Rabies This fatal viral infection is found in many countries. Many animals can be infected (such as dogs, cats, bats and monkeys) and it is their saliva that is infectious. Any bite, scratch or even lick from an animal should be cleaned immediately and thoroughly. Scrub with soap and running water, and then apply alcohol or iodine solution. Medical help should be sought promptly to receive a course of injections to prevent the onset of symptoms and death.

Tetanus This disease is caused by a germ that lives in soil and in the faeces of horses and other animals. It enters the body via breaks in the skin. The first symptom may be discomfort in swallowing, or stiffening of the jaw and neck; this is followed by painful convulsions of the jaw and whole body. The disease can be fatal. It can be prevented by vaccination.

Tuberculosis (TB) TB is a bacterial infection usually transmitted from person to person by coughing but which may be transmitted through consumption of unpasteurised milk. Milk that has been boiled is safe to drink, and the souring of milk to make yoghurt or cheese also kills the bacilli. Travellers are usually not at great risk as close household contact with the infected person is usually required before the disease is passed on. You may need to have a TB test before you travel as this can help diagnose the disease later if you become ill.

Typhus This disease is spread by ticks, mites or lice. It begins with fever, chills, headache and muscle pains followed a few days later by a body rash. There is often a large painful sore at the site of the bite and nearby lymph nodes are swollen and painful. Typhus can be treated under medical supervision. Seek local advice on areas where ticks pose a danger and always check your skin carefully for ticks after walking in a danger area such as a tropical forest. An insect repellent can help, and walkers in tick-infested areas should consider having their boots and trousers impregnated with benzyl benzoate and dibutylphthalate.

Hospitals & Clinics

Thailand's most technically advanced hospitals are in Bangkok. In the south, Phuket and Hat Yai have the best medical care. Elsewhere in the country, every provincial capital has at least one hospital of varying quality as well as several public and private clinics. The best emergency health care, however, can usually be found at military hospitals *(rohng phayaabaan tha-hǎan)*; they will usually treat foreigners in an emergency. See the respective destination chapters for information on specific health-care facilities.

WOMEN TRAVELLERS
Attitudes towards Women

Chinese trader Ma Huan noted in 1433 that among the Thais 'All affairs are managed by their wives, all trading transactions large or small'. In rural areas females typically inherit land and, throughout the country they tend to control family finances.

A recent UNDP Human Development Report noted that on the Gender-Related Development Index (GDI) Thailand ranked 31st of 130 countries, thus falling into the 'progressive' category. The nation's GDI increase was greater than that of any country in the world over the past 20 years. According to the report, Thailand 'has succeeded in building the basic human capabilities of both women and men, without substantial gender imparity'. Noted Thai feminist and Thammasat University professor Dr Chatsumarn Kabilsingh has written that 'In economics, academia and health services, women hold a majority of the administrative positions and manifest a strong sense of self-confidence in dealing independently with the challenges presented by their careers.'

Thailand's work force is 44% female, ranking it 27th on a world scale, just ahead of China and the USA. So much for the good news. The bad news is that although women generally fare well in the labour force and in rural land inheritance, their cultural standing is a bit further from parity. An oft-repeated Thai saying reminds us that men form the front legs of the elephant, women the hind legs (at least they're pulling equal weight).

Thai Buddhism commonly holds that women must be reborn as men before they can attain nirvana, though many Thai *dharma* teachers point out that this presumption isn't supported by the *suttas* (discourses of the Buddha) or by the commentaries. But it is a common belief, supported by the availability of a fully ordained Buddhist monastic status for men and a less prestigious eight precept ordination for women.

On a legal level, men enjoy more privilege. Men may divorce their wives for committing adultery, but not vice versa, for example. Men who take a foreign spouse continue to have the right to purchase and own land, while Thai women who marry foreign men lose this right. However, Article 30 of the 1997-ratified Thai constitution states 'Men and women hold equal rights'. Few so-called 'developed' countries in the western world have charters containing such equal rights clauses; we can expect to see a reformation of such discriminatory laws as 'organic' legislation is put in place.

Safety Precautions

Around 38% of foreign visitors to Thailand are women, a figure equal to the worldwide average as measured by the World Tourism Organisation, and on a par with Singapore and Hong Kong. For all other Asian countries the proportion of female visitors runs lower than 35%. The ratio of women travellers is growing year by year; the overall visitor increase between 1993 and 1994, for example, was 2.3%, while the number of women visitors jumped 13.8%.

Everyday incidents of sexual harassment are much less common in Thailand than in India, Indonesia, Malaysia or Nepal, and this may lull women who have recently travelled in these countries into thinking that Thailand travel is safer than it is. Over the past seven years, several foreign women have been attacked while travelling alone in remote areas.

Solo women travellers should take special care on arrival at Bangkok international airport, particularly at night. Don't take one of Bangkok's very unofficial taxis (black and white licence tags) by yourself – better a licensed taxi (yellow and black tags) or even the public bus. If you're a woman travelling alone, try to pair up with other travellers when travelling at night or in remote areas. Urban areas seem relatively safe; one exception is Ko Pha-Ngan, where there have been several reports of harassment (oddly, we've had no reports from Bangkok). Make sure hotel and guesthouse rooms are secure at night – if they're not, demand another room or move to another hotel/guesthouse.

In social situations, especially in bars or at beach resorts, it's also good to bear in mind that Thai women are very modest in their behaviour. This makes it that much easier for Thai men to misinterpret even platonic friendly gestures from western women. There are Thai males who already view western women as 'easy': exercising discreet behaviour is the best way not to encourage such attitudes.

From a reader:

Thailand is easy to travel alone in as a woman. Virtually no slimy approaches or whistling by males. It's a real joy compared with Kuta Beach in Bali (bad) or India (horror!).

What to Wear Unlike in neighbouring countries to the south, women travelling in Thailand can dress pretty much the way they do back home without raising too much of a fuss. The exceptions include places of worship – whether Buddhist, Hindu, Muslim or Taoist/Confucianist – and government offices. For any place of worship, including all wáts, sleeveless tops (capped sleeves will do), shorts of any kind or short skirts are taboo. The same goes for government offices; it's not unusual to see English signs in Thai immigration offices admonishing visitors to 'Please Dress Politely'. In general people dress more conservatively in rural areas of Thailand, so if you want to be treated with respect in these areas, don't wear clothing that reveals your breasts or thighs.

For more on dress, including what to wear at the beach, see Society & Conduct in the Facts about Thailand chapter. In cases or rape or other assault, the Thai police will investigate and prosecute the crime, but offer little in the way of counselling. If you need to talk with someone, try Community Services of Bangkok (☎ 02-258 4998), 15 Soi 33, Th Sukhumvit, which offers a range of counselling services to foreign residents and newcomers to Thailand.

Tampons

Most Thai women don't use tampons, and thus they can be difficult to find in Thailand. In general only the o.b. brand is available, usually in middle-class pharmacies or minimarts that carry toiletries. In Bangkok more upmarket pharmacies may also carry Tampax brand tampons. If you're coming for a relatively short interval, it's best to bring your own. Sanitary napkins are widely available from minimarts and supermarkets throughout Thailand.

Many women have found that the Keeper menstrual cap – a re-usable natural rubber device that may be vaginally inserted to catch menstrual flow – is a very good alternative to disposable tampons or pads. For information on this product, contact Health Keeper (☎ 519-896 8032, 800-663 0427, fax 519-896 8031, email orderinfo@keeper.com), 83 Stonegate Drive, Kitchener, Ontario, Canada N2A 2Y8 or check its Web site at www.keeper.com.

GAY & LESBIAN TRAVELLERS

Thai culture is very tolerant of homosexuality, both male and female. The nation has no laws that discriminate against homosexuals and there is a fairly prominent gay/lesbian scene around the country. Since there's no anti-gay establishment to move against, there is no 'gay movement' in Thailand as such. Whether speaking of dress or mannerisms, lesbians and gays are generally accepted without comment.

Public displays of affection – whether heterosexual or homosexual – are frowned upon. As the guide *Thai Scene* (Gay Men's Press, Box 247, London N6 4AT, England) has written, 'For many gay travellers, Thailand is a nirvana with a long-established gay bar scene, which, whilst often very Thai in culture, is particularly welcoming to tourists. There is little, if any, social approbation towards gay people, providing Thai cultural mores are respected. What people do in bed, whether straight or gay, is not expected to be a topic of general conversation nor bragged about'.

According to *Pink Ink*, a relatively new newspaper published by and for Bangkok's English-speaking gay/lesbian community, "Thai lesbians prefer to call themselves *tom* (for tomboy) or *dee* (for lady). The term 'lesbian', in Thailand, suggests pornographic videos produced for straight men. Tom and dee, by contrast, are reasonably accepted and integrated categories for Thai women, roughly corresponding to the western terms 'butch' and 'femme'".

Organisations & Publications

Utopia (☎ 02-259 1619, fax 258 3250, email utopia@ksc9.th), at 116/1 Soi 23, Th Sukhumvit, is a gay and lesbian multipurpose Bangkok centre consisting of a guesthouse, bar, cafe, gallery and gift shop. Utopia maintains a very well organised Internet site called the Southeast Asia Gay and Lesbian Resources ('Utopia Homo Page') at www.utopia-asia.com/tipsthai.htm. Another good page for information on gay/lesbian venues in Bangkok is Information

Thailand's at www.ithailand.com/living /entertainment/bangkok/gay/index.htm.

Pink Ink is yet another useful resource. It's distributed monthly at gay/lesbian venues around Bangkok, or you can check their Web site at www.khsnet.com/pinkink.

Anjaree Group (☎/fax 02-477 1776), PO Box 322, Ratchadamnoen, Bangkok 10200, is Thailand's premier (and only) lesbian society. Anjaree sponsors various group activities and produces a Thai-only newsletter.

Gay men may be interested in the services of the Long Yang Club (☎/fax 02-679 7727) at PO Box 1077, Silom Post Office, Bangkok 10504 – a 'multicultural social group for male-oriented men who want to meet outside the gay scene' with branches in London, Amsterdam, Toronto, Canberra, Ottawa and Vancouver.

DISABLED TRAVELLERS

Thailand presents one large, ongoing obstacle course for the mobility-impaired. With its high curbs, uneven sidewalks and nonstop traffic, Bangkok can be particularly difficult – many streets must be crossed via pedestrian bridges flanked by steep stairways, while buses and boats don't stop long enough for even the mildly handicapped. Rarely are there any ramps or other access points for wheelchairs.

Hyatt International (Bangkok, Pattaya), Novotel (Bangkok, Phuket), Sheraton (Bangkok, Phuket) and Holiday Inn (Bangkok, Phuket) are the only hotel chains in coastal Thailand that make consistent design efforts to provide handicapped access for each of their properties. Because of their high employee-to-guest ratios, home-grown luxury hotel chains such as those managed by Dusit, Amari and Royal Garden Resorts are usually very good in accommodating the mobility-impaired by providing staff help where architecture fails. For the rest, you're pretty much left to your own resources.

For wheelchair travellers, any trip to Thailand will require a good deal of advance planning; fortunately a growing network of information sources can put you in touch with those who have wheeled through

Thailand before. There is no better source of information than someone who's done it.

A reader recently wrote with the following tips:

- The difficulties you mention in your book are all there. However, travel in the streets is still possible, and enjoyable, providing you have a strong, ambulatory companion. Some obstacles may require two carriers; Thais are by nature helpful and could generally be counted on for assistance.
- Don't feel you have to rely on organised tours to see the sights – these often leave early in the morning at times inconvenient to disabled people. It is far more convenient (and often cheaper) to take a taxi or hired car. It's also far more enjoyable as there is no feeling of holding others up.
- Many taxis have an LPG tank in the boot (trunk) which may make it impossible to get a wheelchair in and close it. You might do better to hire a private car and driver (this usually costs no more – and sometimes less – than a taxi).
- A tuk-tuk is far easier to get in and out of and to carry two people and a wheelchair than a taxi. Even the pedicabs can hang a wheelchair on the back of the carriage.
- Be ready to try anything – in spite of my worries, riding an elephant proved quite easy.

Organisations

Three international organisations that act as clearing houses for information on world travel for the mobility-impaired are: Mobility International USA (☎ 541-343 1284), PO Box 10767, Eugene, OR 97440, USA; Access Foundation (☎ 516-887 5798), PO Box 356, Malverne, NY 11565, USA; and Society for the Advancement of Travel for the Handicapped (SATH; ☎ 718-858 5483), 26 Court St, Brooklyn, NY 11242, USA.

Abilities magazine (☎ 416-766 9188, fax 762 8716), PO Box 527, Station P, Toronto, ON, Canada M5S 2T1, carries a new column called 'Accessible Planet' which offers tips on foreign travel for people with disabilities. One story described how two French wheelchair travellers trekked around northern Thailand. The book *Exotic Destinations for Wheelchair Travelers* by Ed Hansen and Bruce Gordon (Full Data Ltd, San Francisco) contains a useful chapter on seven locations in Thailand. Other books of value include *Holidays and Travel Abroad – A Guide for Disabled People* (RADAR, London) and *Able to Travel* (Rough Guides, London).

Accessible Journeys (☎ 610-521 0339), 35 West Sellers Ave, Ridley Park, Pennsylvania, USA, specialises in organising group travel for the mobility-impaired. Occasionally the agency offers Thailand trips.

In Thailand you can also contact:

Association of the Physically Handicapped of Thailand
 (☎ 02-951 0569, fax 580 1098, ext 7)
 73/7-8 Soi 8 (Soi Thepprasan), Th Tivanon, Talaat Kawan, Nonthaburi 11000
Disabled Peoples International (Thailand)
 (☎ 02-583 3021, fax 583 6518)
 78/2 Th Tivanon, Pak Kret, Nonthaburi 11120
Handicapped International
 87/2 Soi 15 Th Sukhumvit, Bangkok 10110

SENIOR TRAVELLERS

Senior discounts aren't generally available in Thailand, but the Thais more than make up for this in the respect they typically show for the elderly. In traditional Thai culture, status comes with age; there isn't as heavy an emphasis on youth as in the western world. Deference for age manifests itself in the way Thais go out of their way to help older persons in and out of taxis or with luggage, and – usually but not always – in waiting on them first in shops and post offices.

Nonetheless, some cultural spheres are reserved for youth. Cross-generational entertainment in particular is less common than in western countries. There is strict stratification among discos and nightclubs, for example, according to age group. One place will cater to teenagers, another to people in their early 20s, one for late 20s and 30s, yet another for those in their 40s and 50s, and once you've reached 60 you're considered to old to go clubbing! Exceptions to this rule include the more traditional entertainment venues, such as rural temple fairs and other wát-centred events, where young and old will dance and eat together. For men, massage parlours are another place where old and young clientele mix.

TRAVEL WITH CHILDREN

Like many places in South-East Asia, travelling with children in Thailand can be a lot of fun as long as you come well prepared with the right attitudes, physical requirements and the usual parental patience. Lonely Planet's *Travel with Children* by Maureen Wheeler and others contains useful advice on how to cope with kids on the road and what to bring along to make things go more smoothly, with special attention paid to travel in developing countries.

Thais love children and in many instances will shower attention on your offspring, who will find ready playmates among their Thai counterparts and a temporary nanny service at practically every stop.

For the most part parents needn't worry too much about health concerns, though it pays to lay down a few ground rules – such as regular hand-washing – to head off potential problems. All the usual health precautions apply (see the Health section earlier for details); children should especially be warned not to play with animals as rabies is relatively common in Thailand.

DANGERS & ANNOYANCES
Precautions

Although Thailand is in no way a dangerous country to visit, it's wise to be a little cautious, particularly if you're travelling alone. Both men and women should ensure their rooms are securely locked and bolted at night. Inspect cheap rooms with thin walls for strategic peepholes. Take caution when leaving your valuables in hotel safes.

Many travellers have reported unpleasant experiences at Ko Samui guesthouses (particularly on Chaweng beach). Make sure you obtain an itemised receipt for property left with hotels or guesthouses – note the exact quantity of travellers cheques and all other valuables. On the road, keep zippered luggage secured with small locks, especially while travelling on buses and trains. Several reader letters have recounted tales of thefts from their bags or backpacks during long overnight bus trips, particularly on routes between Bangkok and Surat Thani/Ko Samui.

Credit Cards

After returning home, some visitors have received huge credit card bills for purchases (usually jewellery) charged to their cards while the cards had, supposedly, been secure in the hotel or guesthouse safe. It's said that over the two peak months that this was first noticed, credit card companies lost over US$20 million in Thailand – one major company had 40% of their worldwide losses here! You might consider taking your credit cards with you if you go trekking – if they're stolen on the trail at least the bandits won't be able to use them. Organised gangs in Bangkok specialise in arranging stolen credit card purchases – in some cases they pay 'down and out' foreigners to fake the signatures.

When making credit card purchases, don't let vendors take your credit card out of your sight to run it through the machine. Unscrupulous merchants have been known to rub off three or four or more receipts with one credit card purchase; after the customer leaves the shop, they use the one legitimate receipt as a model to forge your signature on the blanks, then fill in astronomical 'purchases'. Sometimes they wait several weeks – even months – between submitting each charge receipt to the bank, so that you can't remember whether you'd been billed at the same vendor more than once.

Druggings

On trains and buses beware of friendly strangers offering cigarettes, drinks or sweets (candy). Several travellers have reported waking up with a headache sometime later to find that their valuables have disappeared. One traveller was offered what looked like a machine-wrapped, made-in-England Cadbury's chocolate. His girlfriend spat it out immediately, while he woke up nine hours later in hospital having required emergency resuscitation after his breathing nearly stopped. This happened on the Surat Thani to Phuket bus. We have not had any reports of bus druggings in the last six years, so apparently it's a practice that is thankfully on the wane.

Travellers have also encountered drugged food or drink from friendly strangers in bars and from prostitutes in their own hotel rooms. Thais are also occasional victims, especially at the Northern (Moh Chit) bus terminal and Chatuchak Park in Bangkok, where young girls are sometimes drugged and sold to brothels. Conclusion – don't accept gifts from strangers.

Assault

Robbery of travellers by force is very rare in Thailand, but it does happen. Isolated incidents of armed robbery have tended to occur along the Thai-Myanmar and Thai-Cambodian borders and on remote islands.

The safest practice in remote areas is not to go out alone at night and, if trekking, always walk in groups.

Touts

Touting – grabbing newcomers in the street or in train stations, bus terminals or airports to sell them a service – is a long-time tradition in Asia, and while Thailand doesn't have as many touts as, say, India, it has its share. In the popular tourist spots it seems like everyone – young boys waving flyers, tuk-tuk drivers, *samlor* drivers, schoolgirls – is touting something, usually hotels or guesthouses.

For the most part they're completely harmless and sometimes they can be very informative. But take anything a tout says with two large grains of salt. Since touts work on commission and get paid just for delivering you to a guesthouse or hotel (whether you check in or not), they'll say anything to get you to the door.

Often the best (most honest and reliable) hotels and guesthouses refuse to pay tout commissions – so the average tout will try to steer you away from such places. Hence don't believe them if they tell you the hotel or guesthouse you're looking for is 'closed', 'full', 'dirty' or 'bad'.

Sometimes (rarely) they're right, but most times it's just a ruse to get you to a place that pays more commission. Always have a careful look yourself before checking into a place recommended by a tout. Tuk-tuk and samlor drivers often offer free or low-cost rides to the place they're touting; if you have another place you're interested in, you might agree to go with a driver only if he or she promises to deliver you to your first choice after you've had a look at the place being touted. If drivers refuse, chances are it's because they know your first choice is a better one.

This type of commission work isn't limited to low-budget guesthouses. Taxi drivers and even airline employees at Thailand's major airports – including Bangkok and Ko Samui – reap commissions from the big hotels as well. At either end of the budget spectrum, the customer ends up paying the commission indirectly through raised room rates. Bangkok international airport employees are notorious for talking newly arrived tourists into staying at badly located, overpriced hotels.

Bus Touts Watch out for touts wearing (presumably fake) TAT badges at Hualamphong train station. They have been known to coerce travellers into buying tickets for private bus rides, saying the train is 'full' or 'takes too long'. Often the promised bus service turns out to be sub-standard and may take longer that the equivalent train ride due to the frequent changing of vehicles. You may be offered a 24-seat VIP 'sleeper' bus to Penang, for example, and end up stuffed into a minivan all the way. Such touts are 'bounty hunters' who receive a set fee for every tourist they deliver to the bus companies.

From a recent reader:

After reading your book's general chapters I was expecting a much worse situation. Compared to travelling in countries like Morocco, Tunisia, Turkey etc I think travelling in Thailand is relatively easy and hassle-free. When people in Thailand tout something, usually saying 'No' once – or rarely twice – persuades them that you are not interested. In some countries you have to invest much more energy to get rid of people trying to sell.

Insurgent Activity

Since the 1920s and 30s several insurgent groups have operated in Thailand: the Communist Party of Thailand (CPT), with its tactical force the People's Liberation Army of Thailand (PLAT) in rural areas throughout the country; Hmong guerrillas in the north hoping to overthrow the Communist regime in Laos; and Malay separatists and Muslim revolutionaries in the extreme south.

These groups have been mainly involved in propaganda activity, village infiltration and occasional clashes with Thai government troops. Very rarely have they had encounters with foreign travellers. Aside from sporadic terrorist bombings – mostly at train stations in the south and sometimes at upcountry festivals – 'innocent' people have not been involved in the insurgent activity. In the south, traditionally a hot spot, Communist forces have been all but limited to Camp 508 in a relatively inaccessible area along the Surat Thani-Nakhon Si Thammarat provincial border.

The Betong area of Yala Province on the Thai-Malaysian border was once the tactical headquarters for the armed Communist Party of Malaya (CPM). But it appears that this area is now safe for travel following an agreement by the CPM in December 1989 'to terminate all armed activities' and to respect the laws of Thailand and Malaysia in exchange for an amnesty.

PULO One continuing thorn in the side of the Thai government is the very small but militant Malay-Muslim movement in the south. The Pattani United Liberation Organisation (PULO) was formed in 1957, trained in Libya and reached its peak in 1981 with a guerrilla strength of around 1800. The PULO refers to Thailand's three predominantly Muslim, Malay-speaking provinces of Pattani, Yala and Narathiwat collectively as 'Pattani'; their objective is to create a separate, sovereign state or, at the very least, to obtain annexation to Malaysia. Intelligence sources claim the rebels have been supported by PAS, Malaysia's main opposition party, which is dedicated to making Malaysia a more Islamic state than it already is. UMNO, Malaysia's current ruling party, is clearly against supporting the PULO in any way, and have recently extradited several captured members back to Thailand for trial.

PULO's former Muslim separatist allies, Barisan Revolusi Nasional (BRN, or National Revolutionary Front) and Barisan Nasional Pembebasan Pattani (BNPP, or National Front for the Freedom of Pattani), surrendered in late 1991, along with a number of PULO members. PULO remnants persist in southern Thailand's villages and jungles, but only a few dozen guerrillas are still active, mainly involved in propaganda and extortion activities, plus the occasional attack on Thai government vehicles. PULO members collect regular 'protection' payments, for example, from rubber plantations. Occasional PULO bombings rock the deep south, the most heinous of which killed three people and injured 73 at the Hat Yai train station in 1992. In August 1993 a coordinated terrorist effort set fire to 35 government schools in Pattani, Yala and Narathiwat. Since the fire incident, law enforcement efforts in the south have intensified and the area has stayed relatively quiet, save for one bombing of a railway bridge between Hat Yai and Chana in 1994, which injured no-one.

Drugs

Opium, heroin and marijuana are widely used in Thailand, but it is illegal to buy, sell or possess these drugs in any quantity. A lesser known narcotic, *kràtom* (a leaf of the *Mitragyna speciosa* tree), is used by workers and students as a stimulant – similar to Yemen's *qat*. A hundred kràtom leaves sell for around 60B, and are sold for 3B to 5B each; the leaf is illegal and is said to be addictive.

In the south, especially on the rainy Gulf islands, hallucinogenic mushrooms (*hèt khîi khwai*, 'buffalo-shit mushrooms', or *hèt mao*, 'drunk mushrooms'), containing psilocybin, are sometimes sold to or gathered by foreigners. The legal status of mushroom use or possession is questionable; police have been

known to hassle Thais who sell them. Using such mushrooms is a risky proposition as the dosage is always uncertain; there is one confirmed story of a foreigner who swam to his death off Ko Pha-Ngan after a 'special' mushroom omelette. Another recently fell to his death from a cliff.

Although in certain areas of the country drugs seem to be used with some impunity, enforcement is arbitrary – the only way not to risk getting caught is to avoid the scene entirely. Every year perhaps dozens of visiting foreigners are arrested in Thailand for drug use or trafficking and end up doing hard time. A smaller but significant number die of a heroin overdose. Th Khao San has recently become a target of infrequent drug enforcement sweeps.

Ko Pha-Ngan is also one of Thailand's leading centres for recreational drug use, and the Thai police have begun to take notice there as well. Particularly on days leading up to Hat Rin's famous monthly full moon rave, police often set up inspection points on the road between Thong Sala and Hat Rin. Every vehicle, including bicycles and motorcycles, is stopped and the passengers thoroughly searched.

The legal penalties for drug offences are stiff; if you're caught using marijuana, you face a fine (the going rate for escaping a small pot bust – or 'fine' if you wish – is 50,000B) and/or up to five years in prison, while for heroin the penalty for use can be anywhere from six months to 10 years imprisonment. Smuggling – defined as attempting to cross a border – carries higher penalties.

LEGAL MATTERS

In general Thai police don't hassle foreigners, especially tourists. If anything they generally go out of their way not to arrest a foreigner breaking minor traffic laws, rather taking the approach that a friendly warning will suffice.

One major exception is the drug laws (see the previous Dangers & Annoyances section for a general discussion of this topic), which most Thai police view as either a social scourge about which it's their duty to enforce the letter of the law, or an opportunity to make untaxed income via bribes. The approach they take often depends on dope quantities; small-time offenders are sometimes offered the chance to pay their way out of an arrest, while traffickers usually go to jail.

A strong anti-littering law was passed in Bangkok in 1997 and there were rumours that foreigners were being singled out for enforcement. We have received no firsthand accounts of such cases, so can only note that these remain unconfirmed reports. However it won't hurt to be extra vigilant about where you dispose of cigarette butts and other refuse when in Bangkok.

If you are arrested for any offence, the police will allow you the opportunity to make a phone call to your embassy or consulate in Thailand if you have one, or to a friend or relative if not. There's a whole set of legal codes governing the length of time and manner in which you can be detained by the police before being charged or put on trial, but a lot of discretion is left to the police. With foreigners the police are more likely to bend these codes in your favour than the reverse. However, as with police worldwide if you don't show respect to the men in brown you will only make matters worse.

Thai law does not presume an indicted detainee to be either 'guilty' or 'innocent' but rather a 'suspect' whose guilt or innocence will be decided in court. Trials are usually speedy.

Thailand has its share of attorneys, and if you think you're a high arrest risk for whatever reason, it might be a good idea to get out the Bangkok yellow pages, copy down a few phone numbers and carry them with you.

Tourist Police Hotline

The best way to deal with most serious hassles regarding rip-offs or thefts is to contact the Tourist Police, who are used to dealing with foreigners, rather than the regular Thai police. The Tourist Police maintain a hotline – dial 1155 from any phone in Thailand, and ask for extension 1.

The Tourist Police can also be very helpful in cases of arrest. Although they typically have no jurisdiction over the kinds of cases handled by regular cops, they may be able to help with translation or with contacting your embassy.

BUSINESS HOURS

Most government offices are open from 8.30 am to 4.30 pm Monday to Friday, but closed from noon to 1 pm for lunch. Banks are open from 9.30 am to 3.30 pm Monday to Friday, but in Bangkok in particular several banks have special foreign-exchange offices that are open longer hours (generally until 8 pm) and every day of the week. Note that all government offices and banks are closed on public holidays (see Public Holidays & Special Events for details).

Businesses usually operate between 8.30 am and 5 pm Monday to Friday, and sometimes Saturday morning as well. Larger shops usually open from 10 am to 6.30 or 7 pm but smaller shops may open earlier and close later.

PUBLIC HOLIDAYS & SPECIAL EVENTS

The number and frequency of festivals and fairs in Thailand is incredible – there always seems to be something going on, especially during the cool season between November and February. Exact dates for festivals vary from year to year, either because of the lunar calendar – which isn't quite in sync with our solar calendar – or because local authorities decide to change festival dates.

The TAT publishes an up-to-date *Major Events & Festivals* calendar each year.

January
New Year's Day
> A rather recent public holiday in deference to the western calendar.

February
Magha Puja (Makkha Buchaa)
> This national public holiday is held on the full moon of the third lunar month to commemorate the preaching of the Buddha to 1250 enlightened monks who came to hear him

'without prior summons'. It culminates in a candle-lit walk around the main chapel at every wát.

Chinese New Year

Chinese populations all over Thailand celebrate their lunar new year *(trùt jiin)* with a week of house-cleaning, lion dances and fireworks. The date shifts from year to year between late February and early March.

March

ASEAN Barred Ground Dove Fair

This large dove-singing contest in Yala attracts dove-lovers from all over Thailand, Malaysia, Singapore and Indonesia.

Bangkok International Jewellery Fair

During the third week of March in several large Bangkok hotels, this is Thailand's most important annual gem and jewellery trade show. Runs concurrently with the Department of Export Promotion's Bangkok Gems & Jewellery Fair.

April

Chakri Day

A public holiday on 6 April commemorates the founder of the Chakri dynasty, Rama I.

Songkhran Festival

The celebration of the lunar year New Year in Thailand is celebrated from 13 to 15 April. Buddha images are 'bathed', monks and elders receive the respect of younger Thais who sprinkle water over their hands, and a lot of water is tossed about for fun. Songkhran generally gives everyone a chance to release their frustrations and literally cool off during the peak of the hot season. Hide out in your room or expect to be soaked; the latter is a lot more fun.

May

Visakha Puja (Wisakha Buchaa)

This public holiday, which falls on the 15th day of the waxing moon in the 6th lunar month, commemorates the Buddha's birth, enlightenment and *parinibbana*, or passing away. Activities are centred around the wát, with candle-lit processions, much chanting and sermonising.

Coronation Day

The king and queen preside at a ceremony at Wat Phra Kaew in Bangkok on this public holiday on 5 May, commemorating their 1946 coronation.

Royal Ploughing Ceremony

The king participates in this ancient Brahman ritual – the kick off for the official rice-planting season – at Sanam Luang (the large field across from Wat Phra Kaew) in Bangkok in the second week of the month. Thousands of Thais gather to watch, and traffic in this part of the city comes to a standstill.

July

Asanha Puja

Commemorates the first sermon preached by the Buddha.

Khao Phansaa

A public holiday and the beginning of Buddhist 'lent' *(phansãa)* in mid to late July, this is the traditional time of year for young men to enter the monkhood for the rainy season and for monks to station themselves in a single monastery for three months. It's a good time to observe a Buddhist ordination.

August

Queen's Birthday

This Public holiday is celebrated on 12 August. In Bangkok, Th Ratchadamnoen Klang and the Grand Palace are festooned with coloured lights.

September

Thailand International Swan-Boat Races

These take place in the middle of the month on the Chao Phraya River in Bangkok, near the Rama IX Bridge.

Narathiwat Fair

This annual festival celebrates local culture with boat races, dove-singing contests, handicraft displays, traditional southern Thai music and dance. The king and queen almost always attend.

Vegetarian Festival

During this nine day celebration, at the beginning of the ninth lunar month of the Chinese calendar (usually late September or early October), in Trang and Phuket devout Chinese Buddhists eat only vegetarian food. There are also various ceremonies at Chinese temples and merit-making processions that bring to mind Hindu Thaipusam in its exhibition of self-mortification. Smaller towns in the south such as Krabi and Phang-Nga also celebrate on a smaller scale.

October

Chulalongkorn Day

A public holiday in commemoration of King Chulalongkorn (Rama V). It is celebrated on 23 October.

Thawt Kathin

This is a one month period at the end of the Buddhist 'lent' – usually starting around mid

October – during which new monastic robes and requisites are offered to the Sangha.

November
Loi Krathong
On the proper full-moon night small lotus-shaped baskets or boats made of banana leaves containing flowers, incense, candles and a coin are floated on Thai rivers, lakes and canals. This is a peculiarly Thai festival that probably originated in Sukhothai and is best celebrated in the north.

December
King's Birthday
A public holiday (5 December) celebrated with some fervour in Bangkok. As with the queen's birthday, it features lots of lights along Th Ratchadamnoen Klang. Some people erect temporary shrines to the king outside their homes or businesses.
Constitution Day
Celebrated 10 December – public holiday.

ACTIVITIES
Diving & Snorkelling
Thailand's two coastlines and countless islands are popular among divers from all over the globe for their mild waters and colourful marine life. Sandy coves, coral reefs, limestone outcrops, rock reefs, seamounts and pinnacles, undersea caverns and tunnels, and sunken ships provide a wide variety of dive sites. Water temperature hovers at 27 to 29°C year-round, ideal for recreational divers, not to mention coral and tropical fish.

Guided dives and diving instruction have become sizeable industries in Thailand, especially during the high tourist season, November to April. The biggest diving centre – in terms of the number of participants, – is still Pattaya, simply because it's less than two hours drive from Bangkok and has a year-round dive season. There are several islands with reefs within a short boat ride from Pattaya and the little town is packed with dive shops.

Phuket is the second biggest jumping-off point, or largest if you count dive operations. It has the advantage of offering the largest variety of dive sites to choose from, including small offshore islands less than an hour away, Ao Phang-Nga (a one to two hour boat ride) with its unusual rock formations and clear green waters, and the world-famous Similan and Surin islands in the Andaman Sea (about four hours away by fast boat). Reef dives in the Andaman are particularly rewarding – some 210 hard corals and 108 reef fish have so far been catalogued in this under-studied marine zone, where probably thousands more species of reef organisms live.

In recent years dive operations have proliferated on the palmy islands of Ko Samui, Ko Pha-Ngan and Ko Tao in the Gulf of Thailand off Surat Thani. Chumphon Province, just north of Surat Thani, is another up-and-coming area where there are a dozen or so islands with undisturbed reefs. Newer frontiers include the so-called Burma Banks (north-west of the Surin archipelago), Hat Khao Lak (on the mainland north of Phuket), Ko Chang and islands off the coast of Krabi and Trang provinces. All of these places, with the possible exception of the Burma Banks, have areas that are suitable for snorkelling as well as scuba diving, since many reefs are no deeper than 2m.

Dive Centres Most dive centres rent equipment at reasonable rates and offer instruction and NAUI or PADI qualification for first-timers – PADI is by far the most prevalent. The average four day, full-certification course costs around 6000B to 8000B (up to 15,000B at luxury resorts), including instruction, equipment and several open-water dives. Shorter, less expensive 'resort' courses are also available, including half-day 'introductory' dives. Speciality courses may include dive master certification and underwater photography. It's a good idea to shop around for courses, not just to compare prices but to suss out the types of instruction, the condition of the equipment and the personalities of the instructors.

The minimum age for PADI or NAUI certification is 12 years; children aged between 12 and 15 are classified 'junior divers' and must be accompanied by an adult. There are no maximum age limits.

Considerations for Responsible Diving

The popularity of diving is placing immense pressure on many sites. Please consider the following tips when diving and help preserve the ecology and beauty of reefs:

Do not use anchors on the reef, and take care not to ground boats on coral. Encourage dive operators and regulatory bodies to establish permanent moorings at popular dive sites.

Avoid touching living marine organisms with your body, or dragging computer consoles and gauges across the reef. Polyps can be damaged by even the gentlest contact. Never stand on coral, even if they look solid and robust. If you must secure yourself to the reef, only hold fast to exposed rock or dead coral.

Be conscious of your fins. Even without contact the surge from heavy fin strokes near the reef can damage delicate organisms. When treading water in shallow reef areas, take care not to kick up clouds of sand. Settling sand can easily smother the delicate organisms of the reef.

Practise and maintain proper buoyancy control. Major damage can be done by divers descending too fast and colliding with the reef. Make sure you are correctly weighted and that your weight belt is positioned so that you stay horizontal. If you have not dived for a while, have a practice dive in a pool before taking to the reef. Be aware that buoyancy can change over the period of an extended trip; initially you may breath harder and need more weighting, a few days later you may breath more easily and need less weight.

Take great care in underwater caves. Spend as little time in them as possible as your air bubbles may be caught within the roof and thereby leave previously submerged organisms high and dry. Taking turns to inspect the interior of a small cave will lessen the chances of damaging contact.

Respect the integrity of marine archaeological sites (mainly shipwrecks); they may even be protected by law from looting.

Ensure that you take home all your rubbish, and any litter you may find as well. Plastics are a particularly serious threat to marine life. Turtles will mistake plastic for jelly fish and eat it.

Resist the temptation to feed fish. You may disturb their normal eating habits, encourage aggressive behaviour or feed them food that is detrimental to their health.

Minimise your disturbance of marine animals. In particular, do not ride on the backs of turtles as this causes them great anxiety.

Beginners should note that courses are usually only available at the larger centres: for example, you can't take an open water course at the remote Similan Islands.

German and English are the most common languages of instruction, but French and Italian courses are also available at a few places. See the relevant destination sections of this book for names and locations of established diving centres.

Equipment Virtually every dive operation rents gear and air compressors. The better ones provide high-quality equipment, while cheaper places may offer sub-standard gear – inspect carefully before renting. Tanks, regulators and Buoyancy Compensation Devices (BCDs) are especially critical.

Masks, fins and snorkels are readily available not only at dive centres but also at guesthouses in beach areas. If you're fussy about the quality and condition of the equipment you use, you might be better off bringing your own mask and snorkel – some of the stuff for rent is second-rate. And people with large heads may have difficulty finding masks that fit since most of the masks are made or imported for Thai heads.

Wetsuits are not usually required except for deeper Andaman Sea dives where cold water upwellings and/or thermoclines occur, but a lycra suit or 'skin' does serve as protection against scrapes and jellyfish. These are available from most dive shops, but if you're unusually tall or large they may have trouble fitting you – in which case bring your own.

Because divers and anglers occasionally frequent the same areas, a good diving knife is essential for dealing with a wayward fishing line or net. Bring two knives so you'll have a spare. Include extra O-rings, CO_2 cartridges for flotation vests and a wetsuit patching kit if you plan to dive away from resort areas.

Dependable air for scuba tanks is available in Pattaya, Ko Chang, Ko Samui, Ko Tao, Hat Khao Lak and Phuket. Always check the compressor first to make sure it's well maintained and running clean. Divers with extensive experience usually carry a portable compressor, not only to avoid contaminated air but to use in areas where tank refills aren't available.

Dive Seasons Generally speaking, the Gulf of Thailand has a year-round dive season, although tropical storms sometimes blow out visibility temporarily. The south-western monsoon seems to affect the Ko Chang archipelago more than other eastern Gulf coast dive sites, hence November to May is the ideal season for these islands.

On the Andaman coast the best diving conditions – calm surf and good visibility – fall between December and April; from May to November monsoon conditions prevail. However, there are still many calm days even during the south-west monsoon season – it's largely a matter of luck. Whale sharks and manta rays in the offshore Andaman Sea (eg Similan and Surin Islands) can be spotted during the March and April planktonic blooms.

Dive Medicine Due to the overall lack of medical facilities oriented toward diving injuries, great caution should be exercised when diving anywhere in Thailand. Recompression chambers are located at three permanent facilities:

Bangkok
  (☎ 02-460 0000, 460 0019, ext 341, 460-1105)
  Department of Underwater & Aviation Medicine, Somdej Phra Pinklao Naval Hospital, Th Taksin, Thonburi; open 24 hours
Chonburi
  (☎ 038-601185)
  Apakorn Kiatiwong Naval Hospital Sattahip; 26km east of Pattaya; urgent care available 24 hours
Phuket
  (☎ 076-342518, fax 342519, mobile 01-606 1869)
  Sub-aquatic Safety Service (SSS), Hat Patong

Guidebooks *Diving in Thailand* (Asia Books, 1994), by Collin Piprell & Ashley J Boyd, contains well-researched and well-organised information on diving throughout the country. *ScubaGuide Thailand* (1994), published by *Asian Diver* magazine, is also helpful. Both guides are illustrated with colour photos; *Diving in Thailand* has many more maps, plus a detailed section on underwater photography.

Environmental Issues To preserve Thailand's impressive marine environment for the future, it is imperative that divers take care not to disrupt the fragile ecosystems beneath the seas. This means, first and foremost, not touching corals, fish or other marine life. It includes refraining from hitching rides on fish, dolphins or turtles by grabbing onto their fins or shells, practices that are thought to frighten them and cause undue stress. Such contact can also adversely affect the health of marine life by scraping away mucous coverings that protect the creatures against infection.

Spearfishing is not appropriate on a recreational dive as it reduces the number of larger fish necessary to the marine ecosystem. Errant spears also often damage coral. It is also absolutely illegal in national marine parks.

Resist the temptation to collect or buy corals or shells. Aside from the ecological damage, taking home marine souvenirs depletes the beauty of a site and spoils the site for others.

See the Tourism & the Environment entry in the Facts about Thailand chapter for important recommendations on boat anchoring and waste disposal. See also Considerations for Responsible Diving in this chapter for more tips.

Windsurfing

The best combination of rental facilities and wind conditions are found on Pattaya and Jomtien beaches in Chonburi Province, on Ko Samet, on the west coast of Phuket and on Chaweng beach on Ko Samui. To a lesser extent you'll also find rental equipment on Hat Khao Lak (north of Phuket), Ko Pha-Ngan, Ko Tao and Ko Chang.

Windsurfing gear rented at Thai resorts is generally not the most complete and up-to-date. Original parts may be missing, or may have been replaced by improvised Thai-made parts. For the novice windsurfer this probably won't matter, but hot-doggers may be disappointed by the selection. Bring your own if you have it. In Thailand's year-round tropical climate, wetsuits aren't necessary.

If you have your own equipment you can set out anywhere you find a coastal breeze. If you're looking for something 'undiscovered', you might check out the cape running north from Narathiwat's provincial capital in southern Thailand. In general, the windier months on the Gulf of Thailand are mid-February to April. On the Andaman Sea side of the Thai-Malay peninsula, winds are strongest from September to December.

Sea Canoeing & Kayaking

Paddling your own watercraft is one of the best ways to experience Thailand's magnificent coastline, yet as a recreational pastime it has barely begun. Touring the islands and coastal limestone formations around Phuket and Ao Phang-Nga by inflatable canoe or kayak, however, has become an increasingly popular activity over the past five years. The typical sea canoe tour seeks out half-submerged caves called 'hongs' (*hâwng*, Thai for 'room'), timing the trips so they can paddle into and out of caverns at low tide. Several outfits in Phuket and Krabi hire equipment and guides – see the relevant destination sections for details. Faràng outfitters claim to have 'discovered' the hongs, but local fishermen have known about them for hundreds of years. Several islands with partially submerged caves in Ao Phang-Nga have carried the name Ko Hong (Room Island) for at least the last half century.

You might also consider bringing your own craft. Inflatable or folding kayaks make the most sense for travellers, though hardshell kayaks track better. In Thailand's tropical waters an open-top or open-deck kayak – whether hardshell, folding or inflatable – is more comfortable and practical than the closed-deck type with spray skirt and other sealing paraphernalia, which only transforms your kayak into a floating sauna. As the paddler sits on top of the deck rather than beneath it, the open-top is much easier to exit and thus a bit safer overall. Open-cockpit kayaks are also easier to paddle and more stable than traditional kayaks – almost anyone can paddle one with little or no practice. But they do manoeuvre a bit more slowly due to a wider beam and higher centre of gravity.

Surfing

This sport has never really taken off in Thailand, mainly as there don't seem to be any sizeable, annually dependable breaks (tell us if you find any). Phuket's west coast occasionally kicks up some surfable waves during the south-west monsoon from May to November, as does the west coast of Ko Chang. Ko Samet's east coast gets some

MARTIN HARRIS

National Park; see the Health section of this chapter.

Cycling

Cycling is a great way to get around Thailand: it's cheap, non-polluting and allows you to travel at a speed that permits interaction with your surroundings. It is possible to hire bikes at various places throughout Thailand, especially in centres that attract backpackers, put if you plan to do more than the occassional jaunt it might be advisable to bring to your own. See Cycling in the Getting Around chapter for more information.

The sapping heat and humidity are the main adversaries to cyclists in southern Thailand but there's often a strong cross wind which cools you down, though it also drains you of fluids because it makes your sweat disappear fast. So drink plenty and try to get on the road early in the day when its cooler and there are fewer motorists.

Main roads are smooth and wide with plenty of space at the side for cyclists to avoid larger vehicles. Roads near the coast are more variable in quality, and on the islands can be extremely steep and rough, but there are some high quality roads on the better known and more touristed ones like Phuket. Often these carry little traffic.

Expect to pay for your bike on ferries, though locals may not be required to.

It is normal for motorists to alert cyclists when approaching from behind, so try not to get too wound up at people hooting at you all the time. They will usually give you a respectfully wide berth, especially if you look sufficiently non-local or weird.

There are plenty of places where cold drinks can be bought and food replenished. Some very good sports-type drinks are available. But water is most essential and it's usually easy to get boiled water wherever you buy something else, like the thick, high-carbohydrate, good-for-cycling noodles.

Cycling will often land you in places with little or no accommodation, so try what you can; often wáts will provide sleeping space for a small contribution or occasionally for free. Police stations are sometimes an option

waves during the dry season (November to February).

Low-quality boards can be rented in Pattaya and on Phuket's Patong beach (but bigger surf is usually found on nearby Laem Singh and Hat Surin). Coastal Trang is reputed to receive large waves during the south-west monsoon, but there aren't many tales of surfers hitting the breaks out there.

Hiking

You can hike in southern Thailand's larger national parks – Khao Sam Roi Yot, Khao Sok and Khao Lak – where park rangers may be hired as guides/cooks for a few days. Rates are reasonable; see the respective park descriptions later in this book.

Parks suitable for hiking without guide – because they contain marked trails – include Khao Sam Roi Yot and Ko Tarutao. Inter-village footpaths on southern Ko Chang can also easily be hiked without guides, though paths in the island's hilly interior can be challenging due to steep grades and undergrowth.

When hiking without a guide, it is recommended that you always hike with at least one other person and that you let someone in the local community know where you're headed and for how long. Always take plenty of water and insect repellent.

Leeches can be a hindrance during the monsoon seasons, particularly in Khao Sok too. At some petrol stations you can wash and possibly even stay the night in fairly modern surroundings. Camping is an option if you feel confident of the safety of the locality, and if there are two or more of you. (Check for snakes when camping.) It's a good idea to carry a mat for those more innovative stops, or for the many occasions when people will take you into their homes and make you feel like one of the family. They may even try to make that a reality.

COURSES
Language
Several language schools in Bangkok and other places where foreigners congregate offer courses in Thai language. Tuition fees average around 250B per hour. Some places will let you trade English lessons for Thai lessons; if not, you can usually teach English on the side to offset tuition costs.

If you have an opportunity to 'shop around' it's best to enrol in programmes that offer plenty of opportunity for linguistic interaction rather than rote learning or the passé 'natural method', which has been almost universally discredited for the over-attention paid to teacher input.

Schools in Bangkok with the best reputations include:

AUA Language Center
(☎ 02-252 8170) 179 Th Ratchadamri. American University Alumni (AUA) runs one of the largest English-language teaching institutes in the world, so this is a good place to meet Thai students. AUA-produced books are stodgy and outdated, but many teachers make their own – better – instructional materials. Some foreigners who study Thai here complain that there's not enough interaction in class because of an emphasis on the so-called 'natural method', which focuses on teacher input rather than student practice and has been thoroughly discredited in most western countries. Others find the approach useful. Baw Hok courses are available. AUA also has branches in Songkhla and Phuket. Not all AUAs offer regularly scheduled Thai classes, but study can usually be arranged on an ad hoc basis.
Nisa Thai Language School
(☎ 02-286 9323) YMCA Collins House, 27 Th Sathon Tai. This school has a fairly good reputation, though teachers may be less qualified than at Union or AUA language schools. In addition to all the usual levels, Nisa offers a course in preparing for the Baw Hok or Grade 6 examination, a must for anyone wishing to work in the public school system.
Siri Pattana Thai Language School
(☎ 02-286 1936) YWCA, 13 Th Sathon Tai, Bangkok. Offers Thai language lessons as well as preparation for the Baw Hok exam. Siri Pattana has a second branch at 806 Soi 38, Th Sukhumvit.
Union Language School
(☎ 02-233 4482) CCT Bldg, 109 Th Surawong. Generally recognised as the best and most rigorous course (many missionaries study here). Employs a balance of structure-oriented and communication-oriented methodologies in 80 hour, four week modules. Private tuition is also available.

Meditation
Thailand has long been a popular place for western students of Buddhism, particularly those interested in Buddhist meditation. Two basic systems of meditation are taught, *samatha* and *vipassana*. Samatha aims towards the calming of the mind and development of refined states of concentration, and as such is similar to other traditions of meditation or contemplation found in most of the world's religions. Unique to Buddhism, particularly Theravada and to a lesser extent Tibetan Buddhism, is a system of meditation known as *vipassana (wípàtsanãa)*, a Pali word which roughly translated means 'insight'.

Foreigners who come to Thailand to study vipassana can choose among dozens of temples and meditation centres *(sãmnák wípàtsanãa)* that specialise in these teachings. Teaching methods vary from place to place but the general emphasis is on learning to observe mind-body processes from moment to moment. Thai language is usually the medium of instruction but several places also provide instruction in English. Some centres and monasteries teach both vipassana and samatha, others specialise in one or the other.

Details on some of the more popular meditation-oriented temples and centres are given in the relevant sections. Instruction and accommodation are free of charge at temples, though donations are expected.

The two month Tourist Visa is ample for most courses of study, but long-term students may want to consider a three or six month Non-Immigrant Visa. A few westerners are ordained as monks or nuns in order to take full advantage of the monastic environment. Monks and nuns are generally (but not always) allowed to stay in Thailand as long as they remain in robes.

Places where English-language instruction is usually available include:

Boonkanjanaram Meditation Centre
(☎ 038-231865)
    Hat Jomtien, Pattaya, Chonburi
International Buddhist Meditation Centre
(☎ 02-222 6011, 623 6325)
    Wat Mahathat, Th Maharat, Tha Phra Chan, Bangkok
Thailand Vipassana Centre
(☎ 02-216 4772, fax 215 3408)
    Patumwan, Bangkok
Wat Khao Tham
(no phone)
    Ko Pha-Ngan, Surat Thani
Wat Suan Mokkhaphalaram-Chaiya,
(fax 076-391851, attn SMI)
    Surat Thani

Before visiting one of these centres, it's a good idea to call or write to make sure space and instruction are available. Some places require that lay persons staying overnight wear white clothes. For even a brief visit, wear clean and neat clothing (ie long trousers or skirt and sleeves that cover the shoulder).

For a detailed look at vipassana study in Thailand, including visa and ordination procedures, read *The Meditation Temples of Thailand: A Guide* (Spirit Rock Center, PO Box 909, Woodacre, CA 94973, USA, or Silkworm Publications, Chiang Mai); or *A Guide to Buddhist Monasteries & Meditation Centres in Thailand* (available from the World Federation of Buddhists in Bangkok).

Useful pre-meditation course reading includes Jack Kornfield's *Living Dharma* and *The Path of Purification (Visuddhi Magga)*, available at bookshops in Bangkok. (See Shopping.)

Martial Arts

Many westerners have trained in Thailand, but few last more than a week or two in a Thai camp – and fewer still have gone on to compete on Thailand's pro circuit.

Muay Thai (Thai Boxing) Training in muay thai takes place at dozens, perhaps as many as a hundred, camps around the country. Most would be relatively reluctant to take on foreign trainees, except in special cases where the applicant can prove a willingness to conform *totally* to the training system, the diet, the rustic accommodations and most of all an ability to learn the Thai language. Newcomers interested in training at a traditional muay thai camp can try the Sityodthong-Payakarun Boxing Camp in Naklua (north of Pattaya) or Fairtex Boxing Camp outside Bangkok (c/o Bunjong Busarakamwongs, Fairtex Garments Factory, 734-742 Trok Kai, Th Anuwong, Bangkok), both of which have been known to accept foreign students.

A relatively new place that specialises in international training is the Muay Thai Institute, associated with the respected World Muay Thai Council. The Institute is located inside the Rangsit Muay Thai Stadium north of Bangkok international airport.

The Pramote Gym (☎ 02-215 8848) at 210-212 Th Phetchaburi, Ratthewi, in Bangkok, offers training in muay thai as well as other martial arts (judo, karate, tae kwon do, krabi-krabong) to foreigners as well as locals.

Patong Boxing Club (☎ 01-978 9352, fax 076-292189) at 59/4 Muu 4, Th Na Nai, Hat Patong, Phuket, specialise in training for foreigners.

Be forewarned: muay thai training is gruelling and features full-contact sparring, unlike tae kwon do, kenpo, kung fu and other East Asian martial arts.

In Thailand look for copies of *Muay Thai World*, a biannual periodical published by Bangkok's World Muay Thai Council. Although it's basically a cheap martial arts flick, Jean-Claude Van Damme's *The Kickboxer*, filmed on location in Thailand, gives a more comprehensive, if rather exaggerated, notion of muay thai than most films on the subject.

For more information about muay thai, see the Spectator Sports section later in this chapter.

Thai Massage

Described by some as a 'brutally pleasant experience', this ancient form of healing was first documented in the west by the French liaison to the Thai Royal Court in Ayuthaya in 1690, who wrote: 'When any person is sick in Siam he causes his whole body to be moulded by one who is skilful herein, who gets upon the body of the sick person and tramples him under his feet'.

Unlike in most western massage methodologies, such as popular Swedish and Californian techniques, Thai massage does not directly seek to relax the body through a kneading of the body with palms and fingers. Instead a multipronged approach, using hands, thumbs, fingers, elbows, forearms, knees and feet, is applied to traditional pressure points along various *sên* or meridians (the human body is thought to have 72,000 of these, of which 10 are crucial). The client's body is also pulled, twisted and manipulated in ways that have been compared to a 'passive yoga'. The objective is to distribute energies evenly throughout the nervous system so as to create a harmony of physical energy flows. The muscular-skeletal system is also manipulated in ways that can be compared to modern physiotherapy and chiropractic.

Thailand offers ample opportunities to study its unique tradition of massage therapy. Wat Pho in Bangkok is considered the master source for all Thai massage pedagogy. For details see the Wat Pho section in the Bangkok chapter.

Cooking

More and more travellers are coming to Thailand just to learn how to cook. It's not unusual to meet foreign chefs in Thailand seeking out recipe inspirations for the east-west fusion cuisine that seems to be taking the world by storm. You, too, can amaze your friends back home after attending a course in Thai cuisine at one of the following places:

The Boathouse
(☎ 076-330557, fax 330561, ☎ 02-438 1123 in Bangkok)
Hat Kata Yai, Phuket; the chefs at this outstanding Phuket beach restaurant offer occasional weekend workshops.
Modern Housewife Centre
(☎ 02-279 2834)
45/6-7 Th Sethsiri, Bangkok
Oriental Hotel Cooking School
(☎ 02-236 0400, 236 0439)
Soi Oriental, Th Charoen Krung, Bangkok; features a plush five day course under the direction of well known star chef Chali (Charlie) Amatyakul.
UFM Food Centre
(☎ 02-259 0620, 259 0633)
593/29-39 Soi 33/1, Th Sukhumvit, Bangkok; the most serious and thorough cooking school in Thailand, with a multi-layered curriculum; most classes offered in Thai – you need at least four people for an English-language class.

WORK

Thailand's steady economic growth has provided a variety of work opportunities for foreigners, although in general it's not as easy to find a job as in the more developed countries. The one exception is English teaching; as in the rest of East and South-East Asia, there is a high demand for English speakers to provide instruction to Thai citizens. This is not due to a shortage of qualified Thai teachers with a good grasp of English grammar, but rather to the desire to have native speaker models in the classroom.

Work Permits

All work in Thailand requires a Thai work permit. Thai law defines work as 'exerting one's physical energy or employing one's knowledge, whether or not for wages or other benefits', hence theoretically even volunteer work requires a permit. A 1979 royal decree closed 39 occupations to foreigners, including civil engineering, architecture, legal services and clerical or secretarial services.

However, in 1998 several jobs on this list were re-opened to foreigners.

Work permits should be obtained through an employer, who may file for the permit before the foreigner enters Thailand. The permit itself is not issued until the employee enters Thailand on a valid Non-Immigrant Visa.

Substantial supporting documents must be submitted with work permit applications. They must be translated into Thai and accompanied by a certificate of their authenticity issued by a Thai embassy/consulate or the Ministry of Foreign Affairs and range from a valid passport with visa and references from past employers to lists of shareholders and foreign employees of the prospective employer. The application and supporting documents should be submitted to the Labour Department of the Ministry of the Interior, Aliens Occupation Division (☎ 02-221 5140, 223 4912), Th Fuang Nakhon, Bangkok 10200, which will also tell you exactly what documents are required.

Teaching English

Those with academic credentials such as teaching certificates or degrees in English as a second language get first crack at the better-paying jobs, ie at universities and international schools. But there are perhaps hundreds of private language teaching establishments that hire non-credentialed teachers by the hour throughout the country. Private tutoring is also a possibility in the larger, wealthier cities such as Bangkok, Phuket, Hat Yai and Songkhla. International oil companies pay the highest salaries for English instructors but are also quite picky.

If you're interested in looking for such teaching work, start with the English-language *Yellow Pages of the Greater Bangkok Metropolitan Telephone Directory*. Check all the usual headings – Schools, Universities, Language Schools and so on. Organisations such as Teachers of English to Speakers of Other Languages (TESOL; 1600 Cameron St, Suite 300, Alexandria, Virginia 22314, USA) and International Association of Teachers of English as a Foreign Lan-

guage (IATEFL; 3 Kingsdown Chamber, Kingsdown Park, Whitstable, Kent CT52DJ, UK) publish newsletters with lists of jobs in foreign countries, including Thailand.

Other Work

Voluntary and paid positions with organisations that provide charitable services in education, development or public health are available for those with the right educational backgrounds and/or experience. Contact the usual prospects such as: Voluntary Service Overseas (☎ 020-8780 2266) in London; Volunteers in Overseas Cooperative Assistance (VOCA; ☎ 202-383 4961) in Washington; Overseas Service Bureau (OSB; ☎ 03-9279 1788) in Melbourne; or Volunteer Service Abroad (☎ 04-472 5759) in Wellington.

The United Nations supports a number of ongoing projects in the country. In Bangkok interested people can try contacting: United Nations Development Programme (☎ 02-282 9619); UN World Food Programme (☎ 02-280 0427); World Health Organisation (☎ 02-282 9700); Food & Agriculture Organisation (☎ 02-281 7844); UNICEF (☎ 02-280 5931); or UNESCO (☎ 02-391 0577).

Busking is illegal in Thailand, where it is legally lumped together with begging.

ACCOMMODATION

Places to stay are abundant, varied and reasonably priced in coastal Thailand.

A word of warning though: don't believe touts who say a place is closed, full, dirty or crooked. Sometimes they're right but most times they just want to get you to a place that pays them more commission. (See the Touts entry in the Dangers & Annoyances section.)

National Park Accommodation/Camping

All but 10 of Thailand's national parks have bungalows for rent that sleep as many as 10 people for 500B to 1500B, depending on the park and the size of the bungalow. During the low season you can often get a room in one of these park bungalows for 100B per person. A few parks also have *reuan tháew* or long houses, where rooms are around 150B to 200B for two, or tents on platforms for 50B to 60B a night.

Camping is allowed in all but four of the national parks (Chanthaburi Province's Nam Tok Phliu; Doi Suthep-Pui in Chiang Mai Province; Hat Chao Mai in Trang Province; and Thap Laan in Prachinburi Province) for only 5B to 10B per person per night if you bring your own tent. Some parks have tents for rent at 50B to 60B a night, but always check the condition of the tents before agreeing to rent one. It's a good idea to take your own sleeping bag or mat and other basic camping gear. You should also take a torch (flashlight), rain gear, insect repellent, a water container and a small medical kit.

On weekends and holidays, reservations for bungalows are recommended. In Bangkok the reservations office is at the National Parks Division of the Forestry Department (☎ 02-579 4842, 579 0529), Th Phahonyothin, Bangkhen (north Bangkok). Bookings from Bangkok must be paid in advance.

Beach Huts

Simple palm-thatch and bamboo beach huts are generally the cheapest beach and island accommodation in Thailand. Often referred to as 'bungalows', beach huts vary quite a bit in facilities and are particularly popular in the Samui archipelago and on Ko Chang.

Nightly rates vary according to the popularity of the beach, from a low of 40B per night for a simple hut with shared bathroom on the north-western beaches of Ko Pha-Ngan to around 600B for a high-season beach hut with private facilities on Ko Samui's Hat Chaweng. Competition keeps rates low on Ko Pha-Ngan and Ko Chang, while Ko Tao's emphasis on dive instruction has driven prices well above the average despite its relatively small size.

Some beach huts are especially good value, while others are mere flophouses. Many serve food, although there tends to be a bland sameness to meals at beach huts wherever you are in Thailand.

In Phuket – and on many parts of Ko Samui – beach huts have given way to more luxurious beach cottages made of wood, brick and tile costing 500B to 1500B a night. These same islands also now feature highrise hotels and international-quality beach resorts that offer much more in terms of amenities and recreational options – and charge accordingly.

Guesthouses

Cheap urban guesthouses so prevalent in Bangkok and Chiang Mai, as well as in a few other towns in northern and north-eastern Thailand, for the most part don't exist in the coastal areas. Beach huts replace guesthouses on the beaches, while cheap Chinese-Thai hotels for the most part fill the bill in the inland cities. Exceptions include the provincial capitals of Trat, where there are three or four guesthouses, and Krabi, which has over a dozen guesthouses, and the beach resorts of Hua Hin and Pattaya, which have guesthouses in neighbourhoods back from the beach.

The typical Thai guesthouse features simple rooms with very little furniture – at their most basic no more than a mattress on the floor. The cheaper places have shared bathrooms for 50B to 100B per night; some places have private facilities for 100B to 300B a night.

Chinese-Thai Hotels

In inland cities such as Hat Yai, Trat or Surat Thani, standard Thai hotels – often run by Chinese-Thai families – are the most economical accommodation and generally have very reasonable rates (average 100B for rooms without bath or air-con, 120B to 250B with fan and bath, 250B to 500B with air-con). They may be located on the main street of town and/or near bus and train stations.

The cheapest hotels are those without air-con; typical rooms are clean and include a double bed and a ceiling fan. Some have attached Thai-style bathrooms (this will cost a little more). Rates may or may not be posted; if not, they may be increased for foreigners, so it is worth bargaining. It's best to have a look around before agreeing to check in, to make sure the room *is* clean, the fan and lights work and so on. If there is a problem, request another room or a good discount. If possible, always choose a room off the street and away from the front lounge to cut down on ambient noise.

For a room without air-con, ask for a *hâwng thamádaa* (ordinary room) or *hâwng phát lom* (room with fan). A room with air-con is *hâwng ae*. Sometimes travellers asking for air-con are automatically offered a 'VIP' room, which usually comes with air-con, hot water, fridge and TV and is about twice the price of a regular air-con room. The cheapest hotels may have their names posted in Thai and Chinese only, but you will learn how to find and identify them with experience. Many of these hotels have restaurants downstairs; if they don't, there are usually restaurants and noodle shops nearby.

Some Chinese-Thai hotels may double as brothels; the perpetual traffic in and out can be a bit noisy but is generally bearable. Unaccompanied males are often asked if they want female companionship when checking into inexpensive hotels. Even certain middle-class (by Thai standards) hotels are reserved for the 'salesman' crowd, meaning travelling Thai businessmen who frequently expect extra night-time services. Foreign women are usually left alone.

Tourist-Class, Business & Luxury Hotels

These are found only in the main tourist and business destinations: Bangkok, Pattaya, Cha-am, Hua Hin, Ko Pha-Ngan, Ko Samui, Phuket, Songkhla, Hat Yai, and a sprinkling of large provincial capitals such as Chumphon and Surat Thani. Prices start at around 600B outside Bangkok and proceed to 2000B or more – genuine tourist-class hotels in Bangkok start at 1000B or so and go to 2500B for standard rooms, and up to 5000B or 10,000B for a suite. These will all have air-con, TV, western-style toilets and restaurants.

Hotels in the provinces tend to cost around 30% less than Bangkok hotels, even

in Pattaya and Phuket. Tariffs of around 800B to 1500B usually buy the above-mentioned amenities, plus a pool, while anything over 1500B might incslude additional restaurants and recreational facilities. The most exclusive places, such as Phuket's Amanpuri, charge as much as 15,000B for their more luxurious quarters. Virtually all beach and island destinations apply high season surcharges – anywhere from 15 to 50% – from around mid-December to mid-March. Added to this is an 11% government tax on hotels, and most establishments will include an extra service charge of 8 to 10%.

In addition to the reputable international hotel chains of Hyatt, Sheraton, Accor, Hilton and Westin, Thailand has several respectable home-grown chains, including Dusit, Amari and Royal Garden. Of the internationals, Accor is expanding the most rapidly, introducing moderately priced tourist/business hotels in provincial capitals under the Ibis and Mercure brands to complement their more upmarket Sofitel/Novotel properties. Amari is the most active in terms of managing new or newly acquired hotels, while Royal Garden is for the moment focusing on further developing its existing properties.

Resorts

In most countries 'resort' refers to hotels that offer substantial recreational facilities (eg tennis, golf, swimming, sailing etc) in addition to high-class accommodation and dining. In Thai hotel lingo, however, the term simply refers to any hotel that isn't located in an urban area. Hence a few thatched beach huts or a cluster of bungalows in a forest may be called a 'resort'. Several places in Thailand fully deserve the name under any definition – but it pays to look into the facilities before making a reservation.

Discounts Discounts of 30 to 50% for hotels costing 1000B or more per night can easily be obtained through many Thai travel agencies. In Bangkok international airport, in the arrival halls of both the international and domestic terminals, the Thai Hotels Association (THA) desk can also arrange discounts. If you are holding Thai International Airways tickets, or flew in with THAI, the airlines can also arrange substantial discounts. A reader wrote that THAI arranged a double room at the Mandarin Hotel in Bangkok for 1000B the first night, 380B for subsequent nights.

Temple Lodgings

If you are a Buddhist or can behave like one, you may be able to stay overnight in some temples for a small donation. Facilities are very basic, though, and early rising is expected. Temple lodgings are usually for men only, unless the wát has a place for lay women to stay. Neat, clean dress and a basic knowledge of Thai etiquette are mandatory.

FOOD

In a survey that polled 1450 travel agencies in 26 countries, Thailand ranked fourth after France, Italy and Hong Kong in the perceived excellence of cuisine. Still, some people take to the food in Thailand immediately while others don't; Thai dishes can be pungent and spicy. Lots of garlic and chillies are used, especially *phrík khîi nǔu* (literally, 'mouse-shit peppers' – these are the small torpedo-shaped devils which can be pushed aside if you are timid about red-hot curries). Almost all Thai food is cooked with fresh ingredients, including vegetables, fish, poultry, pork and some beef. Of course, in coastal Thailand seafood predominates. Plenty of lime juice, lemon grass and fresh coriander leaf are added to give the food its characteristic tang, and fish sauce *(náam plaa,* generally made from anchovies) or shrimp paste *(kà-pì)* to make it salty.

Other common seasonings include 'laos' or galanga root *(khàa),* black pepper, three kinds of basil, ground peanuts (more often a condiment), tamarind juice *(náam makhǎam),* ginger *(khǐng)* and coconut milk *(kà-tí).* The Thais eat a lot of what could be called Chinese food, which is generally, but not always, less spicy.

Fresh from the Sea

Thailand has a well-deserved reputation for its seafood cuisine, which many gourmets rank among the world's best. The Thais consume more protein via fish than from any other single source. With two lengthy seacoasts from which to harvest marine food products, plus an intricate spice pantry that draws from indigenous, Indian and Chinese cooking traditions, the menu possibilities are virtually limitless.

Thai chefs are masters at employing quick-cooking techniques to maintain the delicate flavours of fresh seafood. Shrimp and crab are year-round favourites no matter how far inland one wanders; spiny lobster is abundant along the Andaman Coast. Other common fruits of the sea include cuttlefish, oysters, cockles, sea perch, kingfish, shark and pompano.

Thais seem to have a particular genius for preparing molluscs such as shrimp, lobster, mussels and squid so that they remain tender and succulent – no easy task when the difference between undercooking and overcooking is often only a matter of seconds. The liberal use of lime juice, fresh coriander leaf and preserved Chinese plums eliminates or tempers the 'fishy' taste many westerners object to.

Dipping sauces *(náam jîm)* served in small saucers with Thai seafood can be very simple or very intricate. One of the most typical sauces combines salty *náam plaa* (a thin sauce made from anchovies), tangy *náam mánao* (lime juice), plenty of fresh minced *kràtiam* (garlic), a little *náam -taan* (sugar) and a healthy portion of fresh sliced *phrìk* (chillies).

See the Language chapter at the end of this book for a glossary of seafood terms.
Joe Cummings

Rice *(khâo)* is eaten with most meals; 'to eat' in Thai is literally 'eat rice' or *kin khâo*. Thais can be very picky about their rice, insisting on the right temperature and cooking times. Ordinary white rice is called *khâo jâo* and there are many varieties and grades. The finest quality Thai rice is known as *khâo hǎwm máli* or 'jasmine fragrant rice' for its sweet, inviting smell when cooked. 'Sticky' or glutinous rice *(khâo nǐaw)*, a staple in northern and north-eastern Thailand, is sometimes found in other regions. A very few vegetarian or health-oriented restaurants will also offer *khâo kâwng*, semi-polished brown rice.

What to Eat
Thai food is served with a variety of condiments and sauces, including ground red pepper *(phrík bon)*, ground peanuts *(thùa bon)*, vinegar with sliced chillies *(náam sôm phrík)*, fish sauce with chillies *(náam plaa phrík)*, a spicy orange-red sauce called *náam phrík sǐi raachaa* (from coastal Si Racha, of course) and any number of dipping sauces *(náam jîm)* for particular dishes. Soy sauce *(náam sǐi-yú)* can be requested, though this is normally used as a condiment for Chinese food only.

Except for the 'rice plates' and noodle dishes, Thai meals are usually ordered family style, ie two or more people order together and share the different dishes. Traditionally, the party orders one of each kind of dish, eg one chicken, one fish, one soup etc. One dish is generally large enough for two people. One or two extras may be ordered for a large party. If you come to eat at a Thai restaurant alone and order one of these 'entrees', you had better be hungry or know enough Thai to order a small portion. This latter alternative is not really acceptable socially; Thais generally consider eating alone in a restaurant unusual – but then as a faràng you're an exception anyway.

A cheaper alternative is to order dishes 'over rice' or *râat khâo*. Curry *(kaeng)* over rice is called *khâo kaeng*; in a standard curry shop khâo kaeng is only 10B to 15B a plate. Another category of Thai food is called *kàp*

klâem – dishes meant to be eaten while drinking alcoholic beverages. On some menus these are translated as 'snacks' or 'appetisers'. Typical *kàp klâem* include *thùa thâwt* (fried peanuts), *kài sǎam yàang* (literally 'three kinds of chicken', a plate of chopped ginger, peanuts, mouse-shit peppers and bits of lime – to be mixed and eaten by hand) and various kinds of *yam*, Thai-style salads made with lots of chillies and lime juice.

To end a meal with something sweet, the Thais overwhelmingly prefer to nibble from the country's seemingly infinite variety of tropical fruits. Thai pineapples, available year-round, are among the world's sweetest and juiciest. Bananas come in over 20 varieties, from the tiny, slender 'princess fingernail' bananas (eaten by the bunch) to the pendulous 'fragrant' bananas more familiar in the west. Rambutan – a succulent grape-like orb surrounded by a thick, soft hull with bright red tendrils poking in all directions – quickly becomes a favourite with many visitors. Definitely an acquired taste is the large, spiky durian fruit that is in season only a couple of months a year. Protected by a formidable, mace-like exterior, the slippery yellow segments inside the fruit exude a musky odour that has been described as a cross between peaches and onions. Aficionados claim that if you can get past the smell, you're more than amply rewarded by a rich, toothsome flavour that has earned the durian its 'king of fruits' reputation in Asia.

Where to Eat
Many smaller restaurants and food stalls do not have menus, so it is worthwhile memorising a standard 'repertoire' of dishes. Most provinces have their own local specialities in addition to the standards, and you might try asking for 'whatever is good', allowing the proprietors to choose for you. Of course, you might get stuck with a large bill this way, but with a little practice in Thai social relations you may get some very pleasing results.

The most economical places to eat – and the most dependable – are noodle shops *(ráan kǔaytǐaw)*, curry-and-rice shops *(ráan khâo kaeng)* and night markets *(talàat tôh*

The Green Bowl

Sponsored by the famous oil company, Thai food critic Thanad Sri bestows his favourite dishes at restaurants around the country with the 'Shell Chuan Chim' (Shell's Invitation to Taste) designation. Look for a sign bearing the outline of a green bowl next to the familiar Shell symbol posted somewhere on the outside of the restaurant. Though such a designation usually means the food is good at such places, it's not a foolproof guarantee; some restaurants hang onto their Chuan Chim signs long after the kitchen has lowered its standards.

Joe Cummings

rûng). Most towns and villages have at least one night market and a few noodle and/or curry shops. Curry shops are generally open for breakfast and lunch only, and are a cheap source of nutritious food.

Another common eatery in larger cities is the *ráan khâo tôm*, literally 'boiled rice shop', a type of Chinese-Thai restaurant that offers not just boiled rice soups *(khâo tôm)* but an assortment of *aahāan taam sàng*, 'food according to order'. In the better places cooks pride themselves in being able to fix any Thai or Chinese dish you name. One attraction of the *ráan khâo tôm* is that they tend to stay open late – some are even open 24 hours.

In larger cities you may also come across 'food centres' where hawkers serve their specialities from rented stalls in a large room. These are often attached to department stores. You typically purchase a meal via a coupon system – you buy, say, 50B worth of paper coupons printed in denominations of 5B, 10B, 20B etc, and then exchange these coupons for dishes you select.

Vegetarian

Visitors who wish to avoid eating meat while in Thailand can be accommodated with some effort. Vegetarian restaurants are increasing in number throughout the country, thanks largely to Bangkok's ex-Governor Chamlong Srimuang, whose strict vegetarianism has inspired a nonprofit chain of vegetarian restaurants *(ráan aahāan mangsàwírát)* in Bangkok and several provincial capitals. Many of these are sponsored by the Asoke Foundation, an ascetic (some would say heretic) Theravada Buddhist sect that finds justification for vegetarianism in the Buddhist *suttas*. Look for the green sign out the front featuring large Thai numerals – each restaurant is numbered according to the order in which it was established. The food at these restaurants is usually served buffet style and is very inexpensive – typically 5B to 10B per dish. Most are open only from 7 or 8 am until noon.

Other easy, though less widespread, sources of vegetarian meals are Indian restaurants, which usually feature a vegetarian section on the menu. Currently Indian restaurants are most prevalent in Bangkok, Pattaya and Phuket's Patong beach. Chinese restaurants are also a good bet since many Chinese Buddhists eat vegetarian food during Buddhist festivals, especially in southern Thailand.

More often than not, however, vegetarians are left to their own devices at the average Thai restaurant. In Thai the magic words are *phŏm kin jeh* (for men) or *dii-chān kin jeh* (women). Like other Thai phrases, getting the tones right makes all the difference – the key word, *jeh*, should rhyme with the English 'jay' without the 'y'. Loosely translated this phrase means 'I eat only vegetarian food'. It might also be necessary to follow with the explanation *phŏm/dii-chān kin tàe phàk*, 'I eat only vegetables'. Don't worry – this won't be interpreted to mean no rice, herbs or fruit. For other useful food phrases, see the Food Glossary in the Language chapter. In Thai culture, 'brown' (unpolished) rice *(khâo kâwng)* is said to be reserved for pigs and prisoners! Look for it at the local feed store or in the less common natural food shops.

Those interested in tapping into the Thai vegetarian movement can phone the Vegetarian Society of Bangkok (☎ 2-254-5444, 254-3502) for information. The society usually meets monthly to share a vegetarian feast, swap recipes and discuss the whys and wherefores of vegetarianism.

DRINKS
Nonalcoholic Drinks
Fruit Juices & Shakes The incredible variety of fruits in Thailand means an abundance of nutritious juices and shakes. The all-purpose term for fruit juice is *náam phõn-lá-mái*. Put *náam* (water or juice) together with the name of any fruit and you can get anything from *náam sôm* (orange juice) to *náam taeng moh* (watermelon juice). When a blender or extractor is used, fruit juices may be called *náam khán* or 'squeezed juice' (eg *náam sàppàrót khán*, pineapple juice). When mixed in a blender with ice the result is *náam pon* (literally, 'mixed juice') as in *náam málákaw pon*, a papaya 'smoothie' or 'shake'. Night markets will often have vendors specialising in juices and shakes.

Thais prefer to drink most fruit juices with a little salt mixed in. Unless a vendor is used to serving faràngs, your fruit juice or shake will come slightly salted. If you prefer unsalted fruit juices, specify *mâi sài kleua* (without salt). Sugar cane juice *(náam âwy)* is a Thai favourite and a very refreshing accompaniment to curry and rice plates. Many small restaurants or food stalls that don't offer any other juices will have a supply of freshly squeezed náam âwy on hand.

Coffee Over the past 10 years or so, Nescafé and other instant coffee producers have sadly made deep inroads into Thai coffee culture at the expense of freshly ground coffee. The typical Thai restaurant – especially those in hotels, guesthouses and other tourist-oriented establishments – serves instant coffee with packets of artificial, non-dairy creamer on the side. Upmarket hotels and coffee shops sometimes

also offer filtered and espresso coffees at premium prices.

Traditionally, coffee in Thailand is locally grown (mostly in hilly areas of northern and southern Thailand), roasted by wholesalers, ground by vendors and filtered just before serving. Thai-grown coffee may not be as full and rich-tasting as gourmet Sumatran, Jamaican or Kona beans but it's still considerably tastier than Nescafé or other instant coffees. To get real Thai coffee ask for *kafae thũng* (literally, 'bag coffee'), which refers to the traditional method of preparing a cup of coffee by filtering hot water through a bag-shaped cloth filter. Thailand's best coffee of this sort is served in Hokkien-style cafes in the southern provinces. Elsewhere in Thailand outdoor morning markets are the best place to find kafae thũng. The usual kafae thũng is served mixed with sugar and sweetened condensed milk – if you don't want either ask for *kafae dam* (black coffee) followed with *mâi sài náam-taan* (without sugar). Kafae thŭng is often served in a glass instead of a ceramic cup – to pick up a glass of hot coffee, grasp it along the top rim.

Tea Both Indian-style (black) and Chinese-style (green or semi-cured) teas are commonly served in Thailand. The latter predominates in Chinese restaurants and is the usual ingredient in *náam chaa*, the weak, often lukewarm tea-water traditionally served free in Thai restaurants. The aluminium teapots seen on every table in the average restaurant are filled with náam chaa; ask for a plain glass *(kâew plào)* and you can drink as much as you like at no charge. For iced náam chaa ask for a glass of ice (usually 1B) and pour your own; for fresh, undiluted Chinese tea request *chaa jiin*.

Black tea, both imported and Thai-grown, is usually available in the same restaurants or food stalls that serve real coffee. An order of *chaa ráwn* (hot tea) almost always results in a cup (or glass) of black tea with sugar and condensed milk. As with coffee you must specify as you order if you want black tea without milk and/or sugar.

A favourite thirst quencher, especially for those adventuring among the more chilli-laden dishes, is Thai iced tea. This frothy orange potion – a blend of Thai-grown tea seasoned with ground tamarind seed and mixed with a healthy dollop of palm sugar and condensed milk over ice – is extremely refreshing.

Water Purified water is simply called *náam dèum* (drinking water), whether boiled or filtered. *All* water offered to customers in restaurants or to guests in an office or home will be purified, so you needn't fret about the safety of taking a sip (for more information on water safety, see the Health section earlier in this chapter). In restaurants you can ask for *náam plào* (plain water), which is always either boiled or taken from a purified source; it's served by the glass at no charge or you can order by the bottle. A bottle of carbonated water (soda) costs about the same as a bottle of plain purified water, but the bottles are smaller.

Alcoholic Drinks
Drinking in Thailand can be expensive in relation to the cost of other consumer activities. The Thai government has placed increasingly heavy taxes on liquor and beer, so that it accounts for about 30B out of the 60B to 80B that you pay for a large beer. One large bottle (630ml) of Singha beer costs more than half the minimum daily wage of a Bangkok worker.

Beer Three brands of beer are brewed in Thailand by Thai-owned breweries: Singha, Kloster and Leo. Singha (pronounced 'Sĭng' by the Thais) is by far the most common beer in Thailand. Singha is a strong, hoppy-tasting brew thought by some to be the best beer produced in South or South-East Asia. Singha is sometimes available on tap in pubs and restaurants.

Kloster is quite a bit smoother and lighter than Singha and generally costs about 5B more per bottle, but it is a good-tasting brew often favoured by western visitors, expats and upwardly mobile Thais who view it as somewhat of a status symbol. Boon Rawd Breweries, makers of Singha, also produce a lighter beer called Singha Gold which comes only in small bottles; most people seem to prefer either Kloster or regular Singha to Singha Gold, which is a little on the bland side. Better is Singha's canned 'draft beer' – if you like cans.

Carlsberg, jointly owned by Danish and Thai interests, is a strong newcomer to Thailand. As elsewhere in South-East Asia, Carlsberg has used an aggressive promotion campaign (backed by the makers of Mekong whisky) to grab around 25% of the Thai market in only a relatively few years. The company adjusted its recipe to come closer to Singha's 6% alcohol content. It has a smoother finish than Singha, and is preferred by some drinkers during spells of hot weather.

Singha retaliated with advertisements suggesting that drinking Carlsberg was unpatriotic! Carlsberg responded by creating 'Beer Chang' (Elephant Beer), which matches the hoppy taste of Singha but ratchets the alcohol content up to 7%. Beer Chang has managed to gain an impressive market share – mainly because it costs significantly less than Singha. Predictably, the next skirmish in the beer war has been set off by the arrival of Boon Rawd's cheaper brand, Leo. Sporting a leopard label, Leo costs only slightly more than Chang but is similarly high in alcohol, with a slightly sweet, malty flavour.

Dutch giant Heineken opened a plant in Nonthaburi in 1995, but so far the green bottles have failed to inundate the market.

The Thai word for beer is bia. Draught beer is bia sòt (literally, 'fresh beer').

Spirits The more adventurous can tipple the Thai workingman's drink, Mekong brand whisky. Distilled from rice at a strength of around 70 proof (35% alcohol), Mekong goes well mixed with any number of fruit juices, with Coke or served in the manner preferred by traditionally minded Thai whisky drinkers – swirled with soda water (one measure of Mekong to two measures of soda) and a wedge of lime over ice. Mekong is pronounced 'Mâe-khõng', not 'Meekong'. It costs around 120B for a large bottle (klom) or 60B for the flask-sized bottle (baen).

More expensive Thai spirits appealing to the pre-Johnnie Walker set include Blue Eagle whisky and Spey Royal whisky, scotch-style whiskies with 40% alcohol. One company in Thailand produces a true rum, that is, a distilled liquor made from sugar cane, called Sang Thip (formerly Sang Som). Alcohol content is 40% and the stock is supposedly aged. Sang Thip costs several baht more than the rice whiskies, but for those who find Mekong and the like unpalatable, it is an alternative worth trying.

Other Liquor A cheaper alternative to whisky is lâo khão, or 'white liquor', of which there are two broad categories: legal and contraband. The legal kind is generally made from sticky rice and is produced for

regional consumption. Like Mekong and its competitors, it is 35% alcohol, but sells for 50B to 60B per klom, or roughly half the price. It tastes sweet and raw and is much more aromatic than the amber stuff – no amount of mixer will disguise the distinctive taste.

The illegal kinds are made from various agricultural products, including sugar palm sap, coconut milk, sugar cane, taro and rice. Alcohol content may vary from as little as 10 or 12% to as much as 95%. Generally this lâo thèuan (jungle liquor) is weaker in the south and stronger in the north and north-east. This is the choice of the many Thais who can't afford to pay the heavy government liquor taxes; prices vary but 20B worth of the stronger concoctions will intoxicate three or four people.

These types of home-brew or moonshine are generally taken straight with water as a chaser. In smaller towns, almost every garage-type restaurant (except, of course, Muslim restaurants) keeps some under the counter for sale. Sometimes roots and herbs are added to jungle liquor to enhance the flavour and colour.

Herbal liquors are somewhat fashionable throughout the country and can be found at roadside vendors, small pubs and in a few guesthouses. These liquors are made by soaking various herbs, roots, seeds, fruit and bark in lâo khão to produce a range of concoctions called yàa dawng. Many of the yàa dawng preparations are purported to have specific health-enhancing qualities. Some of them taste fabulous while others are rank.

Wine Thais are becoming increasingly interested in wine drinking, but still manage to average a minuscule one glass per capita per year. Various enterprises have attempted to produce wine in Thailand, most often with disastrous results. The latest is a winery called Chateau de Loei, near Phu Reua in Loei Province. Dr Chaiyut Karnasuta, the owner, spent a lot of money and time studying western wine-making methods, and his first vintage, a Chenin Blanc, is

Thai Whisky

As dusk falls on the beaches of Thailand, orange-labelled flat bottles filled with amber fluid start popping up everywhere: it's whisky time. Especially in the more Thai-style resorts, the beaches sport rows of open-air and thatched hut drinking places. Here, Thai rice whisky is more often than not the drink of choice.

As in the rest of Thailand, whisky is usually served with several bottles of soda water, a few slices of lime and a dripping bucket of ice. Often there's a waiter or waitress hovering nearby to regularly replenish the glasses, taking care to ensure that the mixture retains a consistent light amber colour. With self-serve groups (usually male), the drinks get darker and stronger over time as the ratio of whisky to soda gradually increases.

The most popular (and cheapest) brand of rice whisky is Mekong, though Sang Thip 'rum', which actually tastes quite similar, can also be seen gracing seaside bamboo tables. Turn a Mekong bottle over and you'll see a purple date, stamped in Thai, on the back of the label. Rarely is the stuff more than a few weeks or months old, though some proprietors keep a pricier 'aged' stock behind the counter for special customers. Still, it's a working class drink and many well-to-do young urban Thais prefer beer or imported whisky, foregoing what some see as a cultural birthright.

Mekong has a very mild sweet taste, and although some drinkers mix it with Coke or other flavoured drinks, the only way to really appreciate it is to drink it with water – either plain or carbonated. Foreign opinion on Mekong is quite mixed; some visitors can't stand it, while others find it almost dangerously appealing. With its mild taste, Mekong and soda can go down all too easily.

You may hear people saying that because you drink whisky with so much water, you rarely get a hangover from Mekong or Sang Thip. But years of research have shown us that, in excess, Mekong is just as capable as any other whisky of making the morning after a living hell.

One other note: if you find yourself making drinking buddies with the locals, be alert for signs of an impending whisky-chugging contest. Thais are just as susceptible to drunkenness and hangovers as foreigners, but some will gladly take the pain if they know they can bring you along for the ride. In the end, you may have to choose between pride and a quiet exit out the back door.

Nicko Goncharoff

a quite drinkable wine and a new cabernet shows promise. It's available at many of the finer restaurants in Bangkok and Phuket. Imported wines from France, Australia and the USA are also widely available in western restaurants and supermarkets. If you're a wine connoisseur, note that Thailand's best restaurant wine collection can be found at The Boathouse Wine & Grill on Phuket (see Hat Kata in the Phuket Beaches

& Nearby Islands section of the Northern Andaman Coast chapter for details).

ENTERTAINMENT
Bars & Member Clubs
Urban Thais are night people and every town of any size has a selection of nightspots. For the most part they are male-dominated, though the situation is changing rapidly in the larger cities, where young couples are increasingly seen in bars. Of the many types of bars, probably the most popular continues to be the 'old west' style, patterned after Thai fantasies of the 19th century American west – lots of wood and cowboy paraphernalia.

Another favoured style is the 'Thai classic' pub, which is typically decorated with old black and white photos of Thai kings Rama VI and Rama VII, along with Thai antiques from northern and central Thailand. The old west and Thai-classic nightspots are cosy, friendly and popular with couples as well as singles. In beach areas, 'reggae bars', with lots of recorded Marley and Tosh, continue to multiply.

The 'go-go' bars seen in lurid photos published by the western media are limited to a few areas in Bangkok, Pattaya and Phuket's Patong beach. These are bars in which girls typically wear swimsuits or other scant apparel. In some bars they dance to recorded music on a narrow raised stage. To some visitors it's pathetic, to others paradise. 'Member clubs,' similar to old-style Playboy clubs, provide a slinky, James Bond atmosphere of feigned elegance and savoir faire in which women clad in long gowns or tight skirts entertain suited men in softly lit sofa groups. Private rooms are also available. A couple of drinks and a chat with the hostesses typically costs around US$50, including membership. These clubs are thinly scattered across the Soi Lang Suan and Th Sukhumvit areas in Bangkok.

Under a law passed in 1995, all bars and clubs that don't feature live music or dancing are required to close by 1 am. Many get around the law by bribing local police.

Discos & Beach Clubs
Discotheques are popular in larger cities; outside Bangkok they're mostly attached to tourist or luxury hotels. The main disco clientele is Thai, though foreigners are welcome. Some provincial discos retain female staff as professional dance partners for men, but for the most part discos are considered fairly respectable nightspots for couples.

Beach clubs on Ko Samui and Phuket – mostly open-air ones – take the place of discos. Here the ratio of foreigners to Thais is reversed, with the former usually outnumbering the latter. The most numerous and popular beach clubs nowadays are those found on Ko Samui's Chaweng beach.

Thai law permits discotheques and beach clubs to stay open till 2 am. But many beach clubs stay open till 3 or 4 am – something to be aware of if you're looking at a hotel or beach bungalow sitting next to one. During the full moon parties on Hat Rin, Ko Pha-Ngan, beach clubs stay open all night and till around 11 am the following day.

Cinema
Movie theatres are found in towns and cities across the country. Typical programmes include US and European shoot-em-ups mixed with Thai comedies and romances. Violent action pictures are always a big draw; as a rule of thumb, the smaller the town, the more violent the film offerings. English-language films are only shown with their original soundtracks in a handful of theatres in Bangkok, Phuket and Hat Yai; elsewhere all foreign films are dubbed in Thai. Tickets range from 20B to 80B. Every film in Thailand begins with the playing of the royal anthem, accompanied by projected pictures of the royal family. Viewers are expected to stand during the anthem.

Coffee Houses
Aside from the western-style cafe, which is becoming increasingly popular in Bangkok, there are two other kinds of cafes or coffee shops in Thailand. One is the traditional Hokkien-style coffee shop (*ráan kaa-fae*), where thick, black, filtered coffee is served

in simple, casual surroundings. These coffee shops are mostly found in the Chinese quarters of southern Thai provincial capitals. Frequented mostly by older Thai and Chinese men, they offer a place to read the newspaper, sip coffee and gossip about neighbours and politics. The other type, called *kaa-feh* (cafe) or 'coffee house', is more akin to a nightclub, where Thai men consort with a variety of Thai female hostesses. This is the Thai counterpart to faràng go-go bars, except girls wear dresses instead of swimsuits.

A variation on this theme is the 'singsong' cafe in which a succession of female singers front a live band. Small groups of men sit at tables ogling the girls while putting away prodigious amounts of Johnnie Walker, J&B or Mekong whisky. For the price of a few house drinks, the men can invite one of the singers to sit at their table for a while. Some of the singers work double shifts as part-time mistresses, others limit their services to singing and pouring drinks.

Cafes that feature live music are permitted to stay open till 2 am.

SPECTATOR SPORTS
Muay Thai (Thai Boxing)
Almost anything goes in this martial sport, both in the ring and in the stands. If you don't mind the violence (in the ring), a *muay thai* match is worth attending for the pure spectacle – the wild musical accompaniment, the ceremonial beginning of each match and the frenzied betting around the stadium. Thai boxing is also telecast on Thai TV every Sunday afternoon; if you're wondering where everyone is, they're probably inside watching the national sport.

History Most of what is known about the history of muay thai comes from Burmese accounts of warfare between Myanmar and Thailand during the 15th and 16th centuries. The earliest reference (1411 AD) mentions a ferocious style of unarmed combat that decided the fate of Thai kings. A later description tells how Nai Khanom

Tom, Thailand's first famous boxer and a prisoner of war in Myanmar, gained his freedom by roundly defeating a dozen Burmese warriors before the Burmese court. To this day, many martial art aficionados consider the Thai style the ultimate in hand-to-hand fighting. Hong Kong, China, Singapore, Taiwan, Korea, Japan, the USA, Netherlands, Germany and France have all sent their best challengers and none have been able to defeat top-ranked Thai boxers. On one famous occasion, Hong Kong's top five Kung Fu masters were all dispatched in less than 6½ minutes, all knock outs.

Modern Muay Thai The high incidence of death and physical injury led the Thai government to institute a ban on muay thai in the 1920s, but in the 30s the sport was revived under a modern set of regulations based on the international Queensberry rules. Bouts were limited to five three-minute rounds separated by two-minute breaks. Contestants had to wear international-style gloves and trunks (always either red or blue), and their feet were taped – to this day no shoes are worn.

In spite of these concessions to safety, today all surfaces of the body are still considered fair targets and any part of the body except the head may be used to strike an opponent. Common blows include high kicks to the neck, elbow thrusts to the face and head, knee hooks to the ribs and low crescent kicks to the calf. A contestant may even grasp an opponent's head between his hands and pull it down to meet an upward knee thrust. Punching is considered the weakest of all blows and kicking merely a way to 'soften up' one's opponent; knee and elbow strikes are decisive in most matches.

The woven headbands and armbands worn into the ring by fighters are sacred ornaments that bestow blessings and divine protection; the headband is removed but the armband, which actually contains a small Buddha image, is worn throughout the match.

Thai boxing is telecast on Channel 7 every Sunday afternoon – just in case you're wondering where everyone is, they're probably glued to the TV watching the national sport

Musicians play throughout the match and the volume and tempo of the music rises and falls with the events in the ring. As muay thai has become more popular among westerners (both spectators and participants), an increasing number of bouts are staged for tourists in places like Pattaya, Phuket and Ko Samui. In these matches, the action may be genuine but the judging below par. Dozens of authentic matches are held every day of the year at the major Bangkok stadiums and in the provinces.

Meanwhile in some areas of the country a pre-1920s version of muay thai still exists. In pockets of southern Thailand, fighters practising *muay katchii* still bind their hands in hemp, and a more localised southern style in Chaiya known as *muay chaiya* uses the elbows and forearms to good advantage.

International Muay Thai The World Muay Thai Council (WMTC), a relatively new organisation sanctioned by Thailand's Sports Authority and headquartered at the Thai Army Officers Club in Bangkok, has begun organising international muay thai bouts in Bangkok stadiums and elsewhere. The WMTC tracks training facilities as well as ranked fighters, and is the first entity to match champs from all muay thai camps. So far the largest number of WMTC-affiliated muay thai training facilities is found in the USA, followed by Australia, the Netherlands, Canada, Japan, France and the UK.

International participation portends a new era for muay thai; some observers think it will upgrade the martial art by shifting the emphasis from ringside betting to fighting techniques.

Tàkrâw

Sometimes called Siamese football in old English texts, *tàkrâw* refers to a game in which a woven rattan ball about 12cm in diameter is kicked around. The rattan (or sometimes plastic) ball itself is called a *lûuk tàkrâw*. Tàkrâw is also popular in several neighbouring countries; it was originally introduced to the SEA Games by Thailand, and international championships tend to alternate between the Thais and Malays. The traditional way to play tàkrâw in Thailand is for players to stand in a circle (the size of the circle depends on the number of players) and simply try to keep the ball airborne by kicking it soccer style. Points are scored for style, difficulty and variety of kicking manoeuvres.

A popular variation on tàkrâw – and the one used in intramural or international competitions – is played with a volleyball net, using all the same rules as volleyball except only the feet and head are permitted to touch the ball. It's amazing to see the players perform aerial pirouettes, spiking the ball over the net with their feet. Another variation has players kicking the ball into a hoop 4.5m above the ground – basketball with feet, but without a backboard! It can be seen in smaller towns and rural areas.

SHOPPING

Many bargains await you in Thailand if you can carry them home. Always haggle to get the best price, except in department stores. And don't go shopping in the company of touts, tour guides or friendly strangers as they will inevitably – no matter what they say – take a commission on anything you buy, thus driving prices up.

Antiques

Real antiques cannot be taken out of Thailand without a permit from the Fine Arts Department. No Buddha image, new or old, may be exported without permission – again, refer to the Fine Arts Department, or, in some cases, the Department of Religious Affairs, under the Ministry of Education. Too many private collectors smuggling and hoarding Siamese art (Buddhas in particular) around the world have led to strict controls. See the Customs section earlier in this chapter for more information on the export of art objects and antiques.

Chinese and Thai antiques are sold in Bangkok's Chinatown in two areas: Wang Burapha (the streets that have Chinese 'gates' over their entrance) and Nakhon Kasem. Some antiques (and many fakes) are sold at the Weekend Market in Chatuchak Park. At the tourist antique shops art objects are fantastically overpriced, as would be expected.

Ceramics

Many kinds of hand-thrown pottery, old and new, are available throughout the kingdom.

Most well known are the greenish Sangkhalok or Thai celadon products from the Sukhothai-Si Satchanalai area and central Thailand's *bencharong* or 'five-colour' style. The latter is based on Chinese patterns, while the former is a Thai original that has been imitated throughout China and South-East Asia. Rough, unglazed pottery from the north and north-east can also be very appealing.

Clothing

Tailor-made and ready-made clothes are relatively inexpensive. If you're not particular about style you could pick up an entire wardrobe of travelling clothes at one of Bangkok's many street markets (eg Pratunam) for what you'd pay for one designer shirt in New York or Paris. You're more likely to get a good fit if you resort to a tailor but be wary of the quickie 24 hour tailor shops; the clothing is often made of inferior fabric or the poor tailoring means the arms start falling off after three weeks wear. It's best to ask Thai or long-time foreign residents for a tailor recommendation and then go for two or three fittings.

Hill-Tribe Crafts

Interesting embroidery, clothing, bags and jewellery from the north can be bought in Bangkok at Narayan Phand, Th Lan Luang, at branches of the Queen's Hillcrafts Foundation, at Chatuchak Weekend Market and at various tourist shops around town. See the Shopping section in the Bangkok chapter for more suggestions. Hill-tribe crafts are almost impossible to find in the south.

Jewellery

Thailand is one of the world's largest exporters of gems and ornaments, rivalled only by India and Sri Lanka. The International Colorstones Association (ICA) relocated from Los Angeles to Bangkok's Charn Issara Tower a few years ago, and the World Federation of Diamond Bourses (WFDB) has established a bourse in Bangkok – both events recognise that Thailand has become the world trade and production centre for precious stones. The biggest importers of

Thai jewellery are the USA, Japan and Switzerland. Although rough stone sources in Thailand have decreased dramatically, stones are now imported from Australia, Sri Lanka and other countries to be cut, polished and traded here.

There are over 30 diamond-cutting houses in Bangkok alone. One of the results of this remarkable growth of the gem industry – in Thailand the gem trade has increased nearly 10% every year for the past 15 years – is that the prices are rising rapidly. If you know what you are doing you can make some really good buys in both unset gems and finished jewellery. Gold ornaments are sold at a good rate as labour costs are low. The best bargains in gems are jade, rubies and sapphires. Buy from reputable dealers only, unless you're a gemologist.

Warning Be wary of special 'deals' that are offered for one day only or that set you up as a 'courier' in which you're promised big money. Many travellers end up losing big. Shop around and *don't be hasty*. Remember: there's no such thing as a 'government sale' or a 'factory price' at a gem or jewellery shop; the Thai government does not own or manage any gem or jewellery shops.

Lacquerware

Thailand produces some good lacquerware, much of it made and sold along the northern Burmese border. It's available in Bangkok at the shops named in the earlier Hill-Tribe Crafts entry, and at some tourist shops in Phuket.

Styles available today originated in 11th century Chiang Mai; in 1558 Myanmar's King Bayinnaung captured a number of Chiang Mai lacquer artisans and brought them to Bago in central Myanmar to establish the incised lacquerware tradition. Lacquer comes from the *Melanorrhea usitata* tree (not to be confused with 'lac', which comes from an insect), and in its most basic form is mixed with paddy-husk ash to form a light, flexible, waterproof coating over bamboo frames.

From start to finish it can take five or six months to produce a high-quality piece of lacquerware, which may have as many as five colours. Flexibility is one characteristic of good lacquerware. A top-quality bowl can have its rim squeezed together until the sides meet without suffering damage. The quality and precision of the engraving is another thing to look for.

Textiles

Fabric is possibly the best all-round buy in Thailand. Thai silk is considered the best in the world – its coarse weave and soft texture means it is more easily dyed than harder, smoother silks, resulting in brighter colours and a unique lustre. Silk can be purchased in Bangkok and in provincial capitals throughout Thailand. Excellent and reasonably priced tailor shops can make your choice of fabric into almost any garment. A Thai silk suit should cost around 4000B to 6500B. Chinese silk is about half the price – 'washed' Chinese silk makes inexpensive, comfortable shirts or blouses. Cottons are also a good deal – common items like the phâakhamáa (short Thai-style sarong for men – reputed in Thailand to have over a hundred uses) and the phâasîn (the slightly larger female equivalent) make great tablecloths and curtains. Good ready-made cotton shirts are available, such as the *máw hâwm* (Thai work shirt) and the *kúay hâeng* (Chinese-style shirt) – see Ko Yo in the South-western Gulf Coast chapter for places to see cotton-weaving.

Hat Yai is a big centre for trade in Thai cotton fabrics. Fairly nice batik *(pa-té)* is available in the south in patterns that are similar to batik found in Malaysia and Indonesia. Textiles from northern and north-eastern Thailand, including *mát-mìi* cloth, a thick cotton or silk fabric woven from tie-dyed threads, can often be found in larger markets throughout Thailand, including the south.

Nielloware

This art came from Europe via Nakhon Si Thammarat and has been cultivated in Thailand for more than 700 years. Engraved silver is inlaid with niello – an alloy of lead, silver, copper and sulphur – to form striking black-and-silver jewellery designs. Niel-loware is one of Thailand's best buys.

Other Crafts

Under Queen Sirikit's Supplementary Occu-pations & Related Techniques (SUPPORT) foundation, a number of regional crafts from around Thailand have been successfully re-vived. *Málaeng tháp* collages and sculptures are made by the artful cutting and assem-bling of the metallic, multicoloured wings and carapaces of female wood-boring beetles *(Sternocera aequisignata)*, harvested after they die at the end of their reproductive cycle between July and September each year. Hail-ing mostly from the north and north-east, they can nonetheless be found in craft shops all over Thailand. For 'Damascene ware' *(kràm)*, gold and silver wire is hammered into a cross-hatched steel surface to create exquisitely patterned bowls and boxes. Look for them in more upmarket Bangkok depart-ment stores and craft shops.

Yaan lipao is a type of intricately woven basket made from a hardy grass in southern Thailand. Ever since the queen and other female members of the royal family began carrying delicate yaan lipao purses, they've been a Thai fashion staple. Basketry of this type is most easily found in the southern provincial capitals, or in Bangkok shops specialising in regional handicrafts.

Bookshops

Bangkok probably has the largest selection of English-language books and bookshops in South-East Asia. The principal chains are Asia Books (headquarters on Th Sukhumvit near Soi 15) and DK Book House (Siam Square); each has branches in half a dozen locations around Bangkok as well as in Hat Yai and Phuket. Asia and DK offer a wide variety of fiction and periodicals as well as books on Asia. The Books in Phuket, Krabi and Phang-Nga also stock English language reading material. See the Bookshop entries under the relevant cities for further details.

Some of Thailand's larger tourist hotels also have bookshops with English-language books and periodicals.

Fake or Pirated Goods

In Bangkok, Phuket and other tourist cen-tres, there is black-market street trade in fake designer goods; particularly Benneton pants and sweaters, Lacoste (crocodile-logo) and Ralph Lauren polo shirts, Levi's jeans, and Rolex, Dunhill and Cartier watches. Tin-Tin T-shirts are also big. No-one pretends they're the real thing, at least not the vendors themselves. The European and American manufacturers are applying heavy pressure on the Asian governments involved to get this stuff off the street, but so far have met with little success. Members of the International Trademark Association claim that 24% of trademarked goods sold in Thailand are counterfeited or pirated and that they lose 25B for every 100B spent on their products in this country.

In some cases foreign name brands are legally produced under licence in Thailand and are still good value. A pair of legally produced Levi's 501s, for example, typi-cally costs US$10 from a Thai street ven-dor, and US$35 to US$45 in Levi's home town of San Francisco! Careful examina-tion of the product usually reveals telltale characteristics that confirm or deny the item's authenticity.

Pre-recorded cassette tapes are another illegal bargain in Thailand. The tapes are 'pirated', that is, no royalties are paid to the copyright owners. Prices average 35B per cassette for amazingly up-to-date music. Word has it that these will disappear from the streets, too, under pressure from the US music industry.

At the time of writing it was becoming quite difficult to find pirated tapes anywhere in the country except on Bangkok's Th Khao San. Licensed western-music tapes, when available, cost 88B to 110B each (average price 99B); Thai music tapes cost the same.

Getting There & Away

AIR

The expense of getting to Thailand per air kilometre varies quite a bit depending on your point of departure. However, you can take heart in the fact that Bangkok is one of the cheapest cities in the world to fly out of, due to the Thai government's loose restrictions on airfares and the close competition between airlines and travel agencies. The result is that with a little shopping around you can come up with some real bargains. If you can find a cheap one-way ticket to Bangkok, take it, because you are virtually guaranteed to find one of equal or lesser cost for the return trip once you get there.

From most places around the world your best bet will be budget, excursion or promotional fares – when speaking to airlines ask for the various fares in that order. Each carries its own set of restrictions and it's up to you to decide which works best in your case. Fares fluctuate, but in general they are cheaper from September to April (northern hemisphere) and from March to November (southern hemisphere).

Fares listed in this section should serve as a guideline – don't count on them staying this way (they may go down).

Airports & Airlines

Thailand has four international airports – in Bangkok, Chiang Mai, Phuket and Hat Yai. Chiang Rai and Sukhothai are both designated 'international', but at the time of writing they did not actually field any international flights.

Don Muang, directly north of the city, is home to Bangkok international airport, the busiest airport in South-East Asia in terms of scheduled arrivals and departures. A second, larger airport was intended to replace Don Muang around 2000 at Nong Ngu Hao, an area 20km east of Bangkok. Following the economic crisis of 97/98, the Thai government cancelled the Nong Ngu Hao

project despite having already spent US$200 million on its development.

Thai Airways International (commonly known as THAI) dominates air traffic, but 80 other international airlines also fly in and out of Bangkok – more than at any other Asian capital. Thailand's Angel Airways, which for the most part serves only domestic routes, also flies internationally between Singapore and Phuket.

See the Getting Around chapter for the locations of Thai and domestic airlines' offices and the Getting There & Away section of the Bangkok chapter for the Bangkok offices of all the international airlines.

For information on getting to/from the airport, see the Air section of the Getting Around chapter. THAI operates a free shuttle bus between the international and domestic terminals every 15 minutes between 6 am and 11.20 pm.

Buying Tickets

Although other Asian centres are now competitive with Bangkok for buying discounted airline tickets, it's still a good place for shopping around, especially with the baht at an all-time low vis à vis most hard currencies. Phuket flights are less flexible, but in general fares also run lower than average for international travel in Asia.

Travellers should note that some Bangkok travel agencies have a shocking reputation. Taking money and then delaying or not coming through with the tickets, or providing tickets with limited validity periods or severe restrictions are all part of the racket. There are a large number of perfectly honest agents, but beware of the rogues. Travel agents at Phuket are generally more reliable.

Some typical discount one-way fares being quoted from Bangkok include (an agency may quote a fare in baht, but in this time of fluctuating Thai currency it's always keyed to US dollars – hence a dollar

Air Travel Glossary

Baggage Allowance This will be written on your ticket and usually includes one 20kg item to go in the hold, plus one item of hand luggage.

Bucket Shops These are unbonded travel agencies specialising in discounted airline tickets.

Bumped Just because you have a confirmed seat doesn't mean you're going to get on the plane (see Overbooking).

Cancellation Penalties If you have to cancel or change a discounted ticket, there are often heavy penalties involved; insurance can sometimes be taken out against these penalties. Some airlines impose penalties on regular tickets as well, particularly against 'no-show' passengers.

Check-In Airlines ask you to check in a certain time ahead of the flight departure (usually one to two hours on international flights). If you fail to check in on time and the flight is overbooked, the airline can cancel your booking and give your seat to somebody else.

Confirmation Having a ticket written out with the flight and date you want doesn't mean you have a seat until the agent has checked with the airline that your status is 'OK' or confirmed. Meanwhile you could just be 'on request'.

Courier Fares Businesses often need to send urgent documents or freight securely and quickly. Courier companies hire people to accompany the package through customs and, in return, offer a discount ticket which is sometimes a phenomenal bargain. In effect, what the companies do is ship their freight as your luggage on regular commercial flights. This is a legitimate operation, but there are two shortcomings – the short turnaround time of the ticket (usually not longer than a month) and the limitation on your luggage allowance. You may have to surrender all your allowance and take only carry-on luggage.

Full Fares Airlines traditionally offer 1st class (coded F), business class (coded J) and economy class (coded Y) tickets. These days there are so many promotional and discounted fares available that few passengers pay full economy fare.

ITX An ITX, or 'independent inclusive tour excursion', is often available on tickets to popular holiday destinations. Officially it's a package deal combined with hotel accommodation, but many agents will sell you one of these for the flight only and give you phoney hotel vouchers in the unlikely event that you're challenged at the airport.

Lost Tickets If you lose your airline ticket an airline will usually treat it like a travellers cheque and, after inquiries, issue you with another one. Legally, however, an airline is entitled to treat it like cash and if you lose it then it's gone forever. Take good care of your tickets.

MCO An MCO, or 'miscellaneous charge order', is a voucher that looks like an airline ticket but carries no destination or date. It can be exchanged through any International Association of Travel Agents (IATA) airline for a ticket on a specific flight. It's a useful alternative to an onward ticket in those countries that demand one, and is more flexible than an ordinary ticket if you're unsure of your route.

No-Shows No-shows are passengers who fail to show up for their flight. Full-fare passengers who fail to turn up are sometimes entitled to travel on a later flight. The rest are penalised (see Cancellation Penalties).

Air Travel Glossary

On Request This is an unconfirmed booking for a flight.

Onward Tickets An entry requirement for many countries is that you have a ticket out of the country. If you're unsure of your next move, the easiest solution is to buy the cheapest onward ticket to a neighbouring country or a ticket from a reliable airline which can later be refunded if you do not use it.

Open Jaw Tickets These are return tickets where you fly out to one place but return from another. If available, this can save you backtracking to your arrival point.

Overbooking Airlines hate to fly empty seats and since every flight has some passengers who fail to show up, airlines often book more passengers than they have seats. Usually excess passengers make up for the no-shows, but occasionally somebody gets 'bumped' onto the next available flight. Guess who it is most likely to be? The passengers who check in late.

Point-to-Point Tickets These are discount tickets that can be bought on some routes in return for passengers waiving their rights to a stopover.

Promotional Fares These are officially discounted fares, available from travel agencies or direct from the airline.

Reconfirmation If you don't reconfirm your flight at least 72 hours prior to departure, the airline may delete your name from the passenger list. Ring to find out if your airline requires reconfirmation.

Restrictions Discounted tickets often have various restrictions on them – such as needing to be paid for in advance and incurring a penalty to be altered. Others are restrictions on the minimum and maximum period you must be away, such as a minimum of 14 days or a maximum of one year.

Round-the-World Tickets RTW tickets give you a limited period (usually a year) in which to circumnavigate the globe. You can go anywhere the carrying airlines go, as long as you don't backtrack. The number of stopovers or total number of separate flights is decided before you set off and they usually cost a bit more than a basic return flight.

Stand-by This is a discounted ticket where you only fly if there is a seat free at the last moment. Stand-by fares are usually available only on domestic routes.

Transferred Tickets Airline tickets cannot be transferred from one person to another. Travellers sometimes try to sell the return half of their ticket, but officials can ask you to prove that you are the person named on the ticket. This is less likely to happen on domestic flights, but on an international flight tickets are compared with passports.

Travel Agencies Travel agencies vary widely and you should choose one that suits your needs. Some simply handle tours, while full-service agencies handle everything from tours and tickets to car rental and hotel bookings. If all you want is a ticket at the lowest possible price, then go to an agency specialising in discounted fares.

Travel Periods Ticket prices vary with the time of year. There is a low (off-peak) season and a high (peak) season, and often a low-shoulder season and a high-shoulder season as well. Usually the fare depends on your outward flight – if you depart in the high season and return in the low season, you pay the high-season fare.

quote is more reliable here; special return prices appear in parentheses):

destination	fare (US$)
Asia	
Calcutta	130
Colombo	210
Delhi	189
Hong Kong	100
Jakarta	190
Kathmandu	131 (207 to 242)
Kuala Lumpur	115
Penang	90
Singapore	110 (160)
Yangon (Rangoon)	120 (162)
Tokyo	260
Australia & New Zealand	
Sydney, Brisbane, Melbourne	350
Darwin, Perth	250
Auckland	400
Europe	
Athens, Amsterdam, Frankfurt, London, Paris, Rome or Zurich	380 to 400
USA	
San Francisco, Los Angeles	390
New York	430

Booking Problems Bookings for flights to and from Bangkok during the high season (December to March) can be difficult. For travel during this time you should book as early as possible. Be sure to reconfirm return or ongoing tickets when you arrive in Thailand (though THAI claims this isn't necessary with their tickets). Failure to reconfirm can mean losing your reservation.

Departure Tax

All passengers departing Thailand on international flights are charged an international departure tax (officially called 'airport service charge') of 500B. The tax is not included in the price of the ticket, but rather is paid at the checkout counter. Only baht is accepted. Be sure to have enough baht left over at the end of your trip to pay this tax – otherwise you'll have to re-visit one of the currency exchange booths.

As of 1 October 1998 international passengers in transit/transfer at the airport were eligible for an airport service charge exemption should they return to the airport within a 12-hour period. The new regulation waives the 500B fee for transit/transfer passengers who temporarily depart the airport. Passengers only need to fill out a request form upon their arrival.

The USA

The *New York Times*, *LA Times*, *Chicago Tribune* and *San Francisco Examiner* all produce weekly travel sections in which you'll find any number of travel agents' ads. Council Travel and STA Travel have offices in major cities nationwide. The magazine Travel Unlimited (PO Box 1058, Allston, MA 02134) publishes details of the cheapest air fares and courier possibilities for destinations all over the world from the USA.

It is cheapest to fly to Bangkok via West Coast cities rather than from the East Coast. You can get some great deals through the many bucket shops (which discount tickets by taking a cut in commissions) and consolidators (agencies that buy airline seats in bulk) operating in Los Angeles and San Francisco. Through agencies such as these a return (round trip) airfare to Bangkok from any of 10 different West Coast cities starts at around US$750, with occasional specials (especially in May and September) of just US$525. If you're flying from the East Coast, add US$150 to US$200 to these fares.

One of the most reliable discounters is Avia Travel (☎ 800-950 AVIA toll-free, 415-536 4155, fax 536 4158) at 717 Market St, Suite 514, San Francisco, CA 94103. Avia specialises in customised around-the-world fares, and 'Circle Pacific' fares such as San Francisco to Hong Kong, Bangkok, Singapore, Jakarta, Denpasar and Los Angeles for US$1230. The agency sets aside a portion of its profits for Volunteers in Asia, a nonprofit organisation that sends grassroots volunteers to work in South-East Asia.

Another agency that works hard to get the cheapest deals is Ticket Planet (☎ 800-799 8888 toll-free, 415-288 9999, fax 288 9839, email trips@ticketplanet.com) at 59 Grant Ave, 3rd floor, San Francisco, CA 94108. One of their 'Circle Pacific' fares, for example, offers a San Francisco-Hong Kong-Bangkok-Kuala Lumpur-Denpasar-San Francisco ticket for US$975 plus tax during low season. You can add Honolulu, Singapore, Jakarta or Yogyakarta to this route for US$50 each stop. They also offer round-the-world airfares starting at $1299 for New York-Hong Kong-Bangkok-Delhi/Bombay-Europe-London-New York.

While the airlines themselves can rarely match the prices of the discounters, they are worth checking if only to get benchmark prices to use for comparison. Tickets bought directly from the airlines may also have fewer restrictions and/or less strict cancellation policies than those bought from discounters (though this is not always true).

Cheapest from the USA are: THAI, China Airlines, Korean Air, EVA Airways and CP Air. Each of these has a budget and/or 'super Apex' fare that costs around US$800 to US$1200 return from Los Angeles, San Francisco or Seattle (add US$150 to US$200 from the East Coast). THAI is the most overbooked of these airlines from December to March and June to August and hence their flights during these months may entail schedule delays (if you're lucky enough to get a seat at all). Korean Air was running specials in 1998 that included return airfare between San Francisco or Los Angeles and Bangkok for only US$575. Several of these airlines also fly out of New York, Dallas, Chicago and Atlanta – add another US$150 to US$250 to their lowest fares.

EVA's 'Evergreen Deluxe' class between the USA and Bangkok, via Taipei, offers business-class sized seats and per-sonal movie screens for about the same cost as regular economy fares on most other airlines.

Direct to Phuket If you want to fly straight through to Phuket without staying overnight in Bangkok, expect discount fares of US$850 to 900 (China Airlines) and US$950 to 1150 (Singapore Airlines). Singapore Airlines requires a layover of a few hours in Singapore on the way; for China Airlines it's in Bangkok. If you don't mind overnighting in Bangkok, you have the option of many different daily connections the day after your international flight.

Canada
Travel CUTS has offices in all major cities. The Toronto *Globe & Mail* and the *Vancouver Sun* carry travel agents' ads. The magazine *Great Expeditions* (PO Box 8000-411, Abbotsford BC V2S 6H1) is useful.

Canadian Pacific flies from Vancouver to Bangkok at fares beginning at around C$950 return for advance purchase excursion fares. Travellers living in eastern Canada will usually find the best deals out of New York or San Francisco, adding fares from Toronto or Montreal (see the USA section).

Australia
Some travel agents, particularly smaller ones, advertise cheap air fares in the travel sections of weekend newspapers, such as the *Age* in Melbourne and the *Sydney Morning Herald*.

Two well known agents for cheap fares are STA Travel and Flight Centre. STA Travel (☎ 03-9349 2411) has its main office at 224 Faraday St, Carlton, Vic 3053, and offices in all major cities and on many university campuses. Call 131 776 Australia-wide for the location of your nearest branch or visit its Web site at www.statravel.com .au. Flight Centre (☎ 131 600 Australia-wide) has a central office at 82 Elizabeth St, Sydney, and there are dozens of offices throughout Australia. Its Web address is www.flightcentre.com.au.

The full economy fare from Australia to Bangkok is around A$4000 from Sydney, Melbourne or Brisbane and A$3330 from Perth; however, tickets discounted either by travel agents or airlines are much cheaper. None of these are advance purchase nowadays, but they tend to sell out early – the airlines only allocate a limited number of these super-cheap seats to each flight. Prices start at about A$609 (one way) and A$849 (return) from Melbourne or Sydney on the cheaper carriers (eg Olympic and Alitalia), and get more expensive the better the airline's 'reputation'.

From Australia to most Asian destinations, including Bangkok, the airlines have recently introduced new seasons: the peak is December to 15 January; school holiday periods are 'shoulder' seasons; and the rest of the year is low season. Fares now also vary depending on how long you want to stay away – a fare valid for 35 days travel is about A$50 to A$60 cheaper than one valid for 90 days. This rule varies, so check with individual airlines for the best deal.

At the time of writing, fares available through agents specialising in discount fares on the better known airlines (eg THAI, Qantas and British Airways) are: A$1045/1155/1279 (low/shoulder/peak season) from Sydney, Melbourne or Brisbane and A$949/1025/1165 from Perth. Garuda Indonesia has cheap fares to Bangkok via Bali (Denpasar) or Jakarta (these flights continue on to London) for around A$1055 one way, A$1535 return.

New Zealand
THAI flies from Auckland to Bangkok daily. Fares start at NZ$1239 return for advance purchase and excursion fares.

The UK & Continental Europe
London to Bangkok is arguably the most competitive air route in the world. At least two dozen airlines will transport you between the two capitals, though only three of them – British Airways, Qantas and

THAI – fly non-stop. If you insist on a non-stop flight, you will probably have to pay between UK£500 and UK£800 return for the privilege (or around UK£100 less if you are a student or under 26). One-way tickets are only slightly cheaper than return tickets.

For lower fares, more flexibility or flights from regional airports in the UK, you will have to be prepared to change planes. Almost every carrier in Europe and Asia, from Aeroflot to Bangladesh Biman to Czech Airlines, will offer you a competitive fare to Bangkok. On airlines from the former Soviet bloc, such as Uzbekistan Airways and Turkmenistan Airlines, you could pay as little as £200 single or £320 return, including tax. Many of these air routes can also be picked up in the Continental Europe capitals such as Paris, Brussels, Prague, etc. One of the cheapest deals going is on Tarom (Romanian Air Transport), which has Brussels to Bangkok return fares that are valid for a year. Uzbekistan Airways offers a London to Bangkok flight via Tashkent. Other cheapies are Lauda Air from London (via Vienna) and Czechoslovak Airlines from Prague (via London, Frankfurt and Zurich).

European carriers such as Air France, KLM and Lufthansa, which offer good connections from UK airports and enhanced inflight service, charge £400 to £700 return depending on demand. At busy times around Christmas and in July/August, you may end up paying a lot for a flight on a carrier such as Tarom of Romania or Turkish Airlines.

There is nothing to be gained, and quite a bit to be lost, by contacting the airlines directly. Instead, go through a discount agent. For students and young people, the best bets are STA Travel (☎ 020-7361 6262) and Campus Travel (☎ 020-7730 8111). Discount agents in the UK who offer good deals for all travellers include Airline Network (☎ 0800 747000), Bridge The World (☎ 020-7911 0900), Flightbookers (☎ 020-7757 3000), Quest Worldwide (☎ 020-8547 3322) and Trailfinders (☎ 020-7938 3366).

Some of these agents may also offer good deals to Thai cities outside Bangkok, such as Phuket and Chiang Mai.

Alternatively, you could check with mainstream travel agents for last-minute deals on charter flights to Thailand. These can be sold for £300 or less, but are available only sporadically.

If you are planning to travel further than Thailand, note that several airlines offer good deals using Bangkok as a stopover for longer journeys, especially to Australia and New Zealand. In the lowest season for Australasia, from April to June, you could pay £500 return or less on airlines such as Royal Brunei.

For discounted flights out of Manchester or Gatwick, check with Airbreak Leisure (☎ 020-7712 0303) at South Quay Plaza 2, 193 Marsh Wall, London, E14 92H. Look in the Sunday papers and *Exchange & Mart* for ads. Also look out for the free magazines widely available in London – start by looking outside the main train stations. The Globetrotters Club (BCM Roving, London WC1N 3XX) publishes a newsletter called *Globe*, which covers obscure destinations and can help in finding travelling companions.

Asia
Bangkok There are regular flights to Bangkok international airport from every major city in Asia and, conveniently, most airlines offer about the same fares. Note that these same routes booked out of Bangkok may be less expensive. Here is a sample of current estimated one way fares in US dollars:

from	fare (US$)
Calcutta	150
Colombo	245
Hong Kong	140 to 200
Kathmandu	210
Kuala Lumpur	110 to 165
Kunming	150
Manila	200 to 250
New Delhi	255
Phnom Penh	150
Siem Reap	125
Singapore	125 to 175
Taipei	250 to 375
Vientiane	100
Yangon	130

Travellers heading for southern Thailand can skip Bangkok altogether by flying directly to several cities. THAI has regular flights to Phuket and Hat Yai from Singapore, and to Phuket from Perth, Australia. During the winter, German carrier LTU offers direct flights to Phuket from Düsseldorf and Munich.

You can also arrange same-day connections via Bangkok to Phuket from other departure points, depending on your Bangkok arrival time – only international flights arriving during the day will leave you enough time to make afternoon or evening connections to Phuket.

Bangkok Airways now also offers daily flights between Singapore and Ko Samui.

Regional Carriers Thailand allows several international carriers to provide regional air services from Myanmar (Burma), Vietnam, Laos and Cambodia. Routes to/from Thailand include China Yunnan Airways flights from Kunming to Bangkok; Silk Air between Singapore and Phuket; Dragonair between Hong Kong and Phuket; Malaysia Airlines between Ipoh, Malaysia, and Hat Yai; Royal Air Cambodge between Bangkok and Phnom Penh; Lao Aviation between Bangkok and Vientiane; and Vietnam Airlines between Bangkok and Ho Chi Minh City.

LAND
Malaysia
Hat Yai is the major transport hub in southern Thailand. See the South-Western Gulf Coast chapter for more details on land transport to Malaysia.

You can cross the west coast border between Malaysia and Thailand by taking a bus to one side and another bus from the other side, the most obvious direct route being between Hat Yai and Alor Setar. This is the route used by taxis and buses but

Thailand's International Border Crossings

These are border crossings where all nationalities are permitted to cross and where there are Thai customs and immigration posts.

Thailand	Malaysia
Betong	Keroh
Padang Besar	Kaki Bukit
Sadao	Changlun
Sungai Kolok	Pasir Mas

Thailand	Laos
Chiang Khong	Huay Xai
Chong Mek	Pakse
Mukdahan	Savannakhet
Nakhon Phanom	Tha Khaek
Nong Khai	Vientiane

Thailand	Cambodia
Aranya Prathet	Poi Pet

Thailand	Myanmar
Mae Sai	Tachilek
Three Pagodas Pass	Payathonzu*
Ranong	Kawthaung (Victoria Point)

*Entry to Payathonzu permitted for day trips only.

there's a 1km-long stretch of no-man's land between the Thai border control at Sadao (also known as Dan Nok) and the Malaysian one at Changlun.

It's much easier to go to Padang Besar, where the train line crosses the border. Here you can get a bus right to the border, walk across and take another bus or taxi on the other side. On either side you'll most likely be mobbed by taxi and motorcycle drivers wanting to take you to immigration. It's better to walk over the railway bridge into Thailand, and ignore the touts until you get to 'official' Thai taxis which will take you all the way to Hat Yai, with a stop at the immigration office (2.5km from the border), for 40B. A new immigration/customs office and bus/train station complex has been con-

structed on the Thai side, making the whole transition smoother.

A daily bus runs between Alor Setar, Hat Yai and Kota Baru and reverse.

There's also a border crossing at Keroh (Betong on the Thai side), mid-way between the east and west coasts. Few people other than Thais and Malaysians use this crossing as it puts you in the middle of nowhere along the Penang to Kota Bharu road.

See the Sungai Kolok and Ban Taba entries in the South-Western Gulf Coast chapter for information about crossing the border on the east coast.

Riding the rails between Singapore and Bangkok via Butterworth, Malaysia, is a great way to travel to Thailand – as long as you don't count on making a smooth change between the Kereta Api Tanah Melayu (KTM) and State Railway of Thailand (SRT) trains. The Malaysian train rarely arrives on time, and the Thai train almost always leaves Padang Besar on time, even if the Malaysian express from Kuala Lumpur (or the 2nd class connection from Butterworth) is late. It's best to purchase the Malaysian and Thai portions of your ticket with departures on consecutive days and plan a Butterworth/Penang stopover.

Laos

Lonely Planet's *Laos* and *Thailand* guides contain complete details on how and where to cross the border between these two countries by land or river. Following is a summary of the possibilities.

Road A 1174m Australian-financed bridge across the Mekong river near Nong Khai, the Thai-Lao Friendship Bridge (Saphan Mittaphap Thai-Lao), spans the river between Ban Jommani on the Thai side and Tha Na Leng on the Lao side – very near the old vehicle ferry. The next step in the plan is to build a parallel rail bridge in order to extend the Bangkok-Nong Khai railway into Vientiane. A similar plan for Nakhon Phanom (opposite Laos' Tha Khaek) is currently under consideration.

A land crossing from Pakse (Champasak Province) in Laos to Chong Mek in Thailand's Ubon Ratchathani Province is open to foreign visitors. You now need only a normal Lao visa if crossing from Thailand to Laos. Going from Laos to Thailand, you can obtain a visa on arrival, although you will probably have to go to Phibun Mangsahan, near Ubon, to get it. The immigration officers at Chong Mek will allow you to cross the border into Thailand and proceed to Phibun for this purpose.

Train A joint venture agreement between the Lao government and a new company, Lao Railways Transportation, was signed in 1998 to establish a railway line along the middle of the Friendship Bridge. After a two-year feasibility study is completed the line, which will reportedly extend to Vientiane and Luang Prabang, is supposed to become operational in four years. Like most other transport projects in Laos, however, it will probably take much longer – if it ever happens at all.

Another rail link under consideration is a spur eastward from Udon Thani, and across Laos to connect with the Ho Chi Minh City-Hanoi railway in Vietnam.

Myanmar

Several land border crossings between Thailand and Myanmar are open to daytrippers or short excursions in the vicinity. As yet none of these link up with routes to Yangon or Mandalay or other cities of any size. The only place you are permitted to enter Thailand from Myanmar is via boat from Kawthoung (Myanmar) to Ranong (Thailand); see the Sea section further on. For more detail, see Lonely Planet's *Thailand* and *Myanmar* guides.

Cambodia

As of early 1998, it has been legal to cross between Cambodia and Thailand at Aranya Prathet, opposite Poi Pet in Cambodia. If you're coming from Cambodia by rail or road, you don't need a Thai visa (or rather you will be granted a free 30-day tourist visa on arrival), but in the reverse direction you will need a Cambodian visa, which is available from the Cambodian embassy in Bangkok.

Other areas along the border won't be safe for land crossings until mines and booby traps left over from the conflict between the Khmer Rouge and the Vietnamese are removed or detonated.

Travellers can sometimes cross to Cambodia by sea via Hat Lek, but it's very much an on and off situation. See the Hat Lek to Cambodia section in the Eastern Gulf Coast chapter for details.

SEA
Malaysia

There are several ways of travelling between Thailand's southern peninsula and Malaysia by sea. Simplest is to take a longtail boat between Satun, in the south-west corner of Thailand, and Kuala Perlis. The cost is about M$5, or 50B, and boats cross over fairly regularly.

You can also take a ferry to the Malaysian island of Langkawi from Satun. There are immigration posts at both ports.

From Satun you can take a bus to Hat Yai and then arrange transport to other points in the south or further north. It's possible to bypass Hat Yai altogether by heading directly for Phuket or Krabi via Trang.

You can also take a ferry to Ban Taba on the east coast of Thailand from near Kota Bharu – see the Sungai Kolok and Ban Taba sections in the South-Western Gulf chapter.

Passenger ferry services also sometimes run between Pulau Langkawi and Phuket. Such services never seem to last longer than nine months or so; your best bet is to make inquiries through local travel agents to find out the latest on sea transport to/from Langkawi.

See the Yachting entry in the Phuket Province section of the Northern Andaman Coast chapter for information on yachts to Penang and other places.

Myanmar

You can travel by boat between Kawthoung (Victoria Point) in Myanmar's southernmost Tanintharyi Division and the port of Ranong in Thailand's Ranong Province via the Gulf of Martaban/Pakchan Estuary. Leaving Myanmar from Kawthoung is now legal, and you don't need a visa to enter Thailand for 30 days or less. In the reverse direction you won't need a Myanmar visa for a day trip, but if you plan to stay overnight or to continue farther north, you'll need to arrive with a valid Myanmar visa in your passport. For further details see the Ranong section in the North Andaman Coast chapter.

RIVER
Malaysia

You can take a ferry to Ban Taba on the South-Western Gulf of Thailand from near Kota Bharu – see the Sungai Kolok and Ban Taba sections in the South-Western Gulf Coast chapter.

Laos

It's legal for non-Thai foreigners to cross the Mekong River by ferry between Thailand and Laos at: Nakhon Phanom (opposite Tha Khaek), Chiang Khong (opposite Huay Xai) and Mukdahan (opposite Savannakhet).

Thais may cross at all of the above checkpoints and a half-dozen or so others in Thailand's Loei and Nong Khai provinces. In the future one or more of these may open to foreign visitors as well.

WARNING

The information in this chapter is particularly vulnerable to change: prices for international travel are volatile, routes are introduced and cancelled, schedules change, special deals come and go, and rules and visa requirements are amended. Airlines and governments seem to take a perverse pleasure in making price structures and regulations as complicated as possible. You should check directly with the airline or a travel agent to make sure you understand how a fare (and ticket you may buy) works. In addition, the travel industry is highly competitive and there are many lurks and perks.

The upshot of this is that you should get opinions, quotes and advice from as many airlines and travel agents as possible before you part with your hard-earned cash. The details given in this chapter should be regarded as pointers and are not a substitute for your own careful, up-to-date research.

Getting Around

AIR
Domestic Air Services

Three domestic carriers, Thai Airways International (THAI), Bangkok Airways and Angel Airways make use of domestic airports in 26 cities around the country.

Most domestic air services in Thailand are operated by THAI, which covers 20 airports throughout the kingdom. THAI operates Boeing 737 or Airbus 300 series aircraft on its main domestic routes.

The accompanying Airfares & Railways map shows some of the fares on routes to coastal Thailand. Note that through fares generally cost less than combination fares. This does not always apply to international fares, however. It's much cheaper to fly from Bangkok to Penang via Phuket or Hat Yai than direct, for example.

Bangkok Airways Owned by Sahakol Air, Bangkok Airways flies four main routes: Bangkok-Ranong; Bangkok-Ko Samui-Phuket; Bangkok-Sukhothai-Chiang Mai; and U Taphao (Pattaya)-Ko Samui. The mainstay of the Bangkok Airways fleet is the Franco-Italian ATR-72, and the most profitable route, by far, is the one between Bangkok and Ko Samui.

Bangkok Airways' fares are competitive with THAI's but the company is small and it remains to be seen whether or not it will grow to become a serious contender.

The airline's head office (☎ 02-229 3456, fax 229-3454) is at Queen Sirikit National Convention Centre, Thanon (Th) Ratchadaphisek Mai, Khlong Toey, Bangkok 10110. There are also offices in Hua Hin, Pattaya, Phuket and Ko Samui.

Angel Airways This new domestic airline began operations in 1998 and fills a couple of former gaps in domestic air routes, most notably the Chiang Mai to Udon Thani route vacated by the demise of Orient Express Air. Other routes include Bangkok to Chiang Mai and Bangkok to Phuket. Angel also flies internationally between Singapore and Phuket.

At the moment Angel Airways is headquartered at Bangkok international airport (☎ 02-535 6287), with branch offices in Chiang Mai, Phuket, Udon Thani and Singapore.

THAI Offices Offices for THAI's domestic services can be found throughout coastal Thailand:

Bangkok
  Head Office
  (☎ 02-513 0121, reservations ☎ 280 0060)
  89 Th Vibhavadi Rangsit;
  (☎ 02-234 3100/19)
  485 Th Silom;
  (☎ 02-280 0060, 628 2000)
  6 Th Lan Luang;
  (☎ 02-215 2020/1)
  Asia Hotel, 296 Th Phayathai;
  (☎ 02-223 9746/50)
  Grand China Tower, 3rd floor, 215 Th Yaowarat;
  (☎ 02-535 2081/2, 523 6121)
  Bangkok international airport, Don Muang
Hat Yai
  (☎ 074-245851, 246165, reservations ☎ 233433)
  166/4 Th Niphat Uthit 2
Nakhon Si Thammarat
  (☎ 075-342491)
  1612 Th Ratchadamnoen
Narathiwat
  (☎ 073-511161, 513090/2)
  322-4 Th Phupa Phakdi
Pattani
  (☎ 073-349149)
  9 Th Prida
Pattaya
  (☎ 038-250286/7, 250804)
  Royal Cliff Beach Resort, Th Cliff
Phuket
  (☎ 076-211195, 212499/946)
  78 Th Ranong;
  (☎ 076-212400/644/ 880)
  41/33 Th Montri
Songkhla
  (☎ 074-311012)
  2 Soi 4, Th Saiburi

Surat Thani
(☎ 077-273710/ 355)
3/27-8 Th Karunarat
Trang
(☎ 075-218066)
199/2 Th Visetkul

Air Passes

THAI occasionally offers special four-coupon passes – available only outside Thailand for foreign currency – in which you can book any four domestic flights for one fare of around US$260 as long as you don't repeat the same leg. Unless you plan carefully this isn't much of a saving, since it's hard to avoid repeating the same leg in and out of Bangkok.

For information on the four coupon deal, known as the 'Discover Thailand fare', inquire at any THAI office outside Thailand.

Also, the baht is so low these days it's often cheaper to make arrangements for domestic flights in Thailand rather than from abroad.

Domestic Departure Tax

A departure tax of 30B is now included in all domestic fares, ie it is no longer collected separately at airline check-in counters.

BUS
Government Bus

Several types of buses ply the roads of Thailand. The cheapest and slowest are the ordinary government-run buses (rót thamádaa) that stop in every little town and for every waving hand along the highway. For some destinations – smaller towns – these orange-painted buses are your only choice, but at least they leave frequently. The government also runs faster, more comfortable, but less frequent, air-conditioned buses called rót ae or rót pràp aakàat; these are painted with blue markings. If these are available to your destination, they are your best choice since they don't cost that much more than the ordinary stop-in-every-town buses. The government bus company is called Baw Khaw Saw, an abbreviation of Borisàt Khŏn Sòng (literally, 'the transportation company').

Every city and town in Thailand linked by bus has a Baw Khaw Saw terminal, even if it's just a patch of dirt by the roadside.

The service on the government air-con buses is usually quite good, and includes drinks service and video. On longer routes (eg Bangkok to Ko Samui, Bangkok to Phuket), the air-con buses even distribute claim checks (receipt dockets) for your baggage. Longer routes may also offer two classes of air-con buses, regular and 1st class; the latter buses have toilets. 'VIP' buses have fewer seats (30 to 34 instead of 44; some routes have Super VIP, with only 24 seats) so that each seat reclines more. Sometimes these are called rót nawn or sleepers. For small-to-medium-sized people they are more comfortable, but if you're big in girth you may find yourself squashed on the 34-seaters when the person in front of you leans back.

Occasionally you'll get a government air-con bus in which the air-con is broken or the seats are not up to standard, but in general they are more reliable than the private tour buses.

Private Bus

Private buses are available between major tourist and business destinations: Surat Thani, Ko Samui, Phuket, Hat Yai, Pattaya, Hua Hin and others. To Phuket, for example, several companies run daily buses from Bangkok. These can be booked through most hotels or any travel agency, although it's best to book directly through a bus office to be sure you get what you pay for.

Fares may vary from company to company, but usually not by more than a few baht. However, fare differences between the government and private bus companies can be substantial. Using Surat Thani as an example, the state-run buses from Bangkok's Southern bus terminal are 158B for ordinary bus, 285B (1st class) air-con, while the private companies charge up to 385B. On the other hand, to Phuket the private buses often cost less than the government buses, although those that charge less offer inferior service. Departures from some private

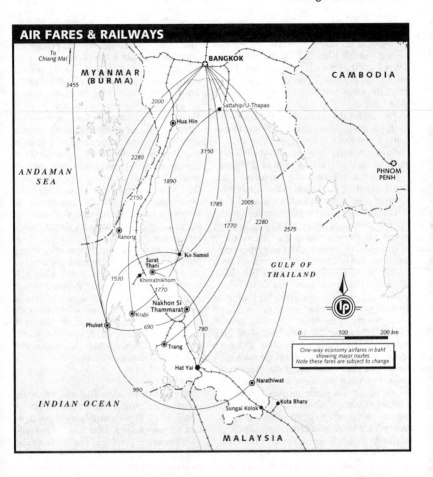

AIR FARES & RAILWAYS

To Chiang Mai

MYANMAR (BURMA)

3455

BANGKOK

CAMBODIA

2000

Sattahip/U-Thapao

Hua Hin

2280

3150

ANDAMAN SEA

1890

PHNOM PENH

2150

1785 2005

Ranong

1770 2280

2575

1530

Ko Samui

Surat Thani

GULF OF THAILAND

Khiriratnikhom

1770

Nakhon Si Thammarat

Krabi

Phuket

690

780

Trang

Hat Yai

0   100   200 km

One-way economy airfares in baht showing major routes.
Note these fares are subject to change.

INDIAN OCEAN

990

Narathiwat

Kota Bharu

Sungai Kolok

MALAYSIA

companies are more frequent than for the equivalent Baw Khaw Saw route.

There are also private buses running between major destinations within the various regions, eg Nakhon Si Thammarat to Hat Yai in the south. New companies are cropping up all the time. Their number seemed to reach a peak in the 1980s, but they have now stabilised because of a crackdown on licensing. Minibuses are used on some routes, eg Surat Thani to Krabi and Ranong to Takua Pa.

The private air-con buses are usually no more comfortable than the government air-con buses and feature similarly narrow seats and a hair-raising ride. On overnight journeys the buses usually stop somewhere en route and passengers are woken to get off the bus for a free meal of fried rice or rice soup. A few companies even treat you to a meal before a long overnight trip.

Like their state-run equivalents, the private companies offer VIP (sleeper) buses on long hauls. In general, private bus companies that deal mostly with Thais are good, while tourist-oriented ones – especially those connected with Th Khao San (Khao San Rd) – are the worst as the agents know they don't need to deliver good service because very few customers will be returning. In recent years, the service on many private lines has in fact declined, especially on the Bangkok to Ko Samui, Surat Thani to Phuket and Surat Thani to Krabi routes.

Sometimes the cheaper lines – especially those booked on Th Khao San in Bangkok – will switch vehicles at the last moment so that instead of the roomy air-con bus advertised, you're stuck with a cramped van with broken air-con. Another problem with the private companies is that they generally spend more time cruising the city for passengers before getting under way, meaning that they rarely leave at the advertised departure time. To avoid situations like this, it's always better to book bus tickets directly at a bus office – or at the government Baw Khaw Saw station – rather than through a travel agency.

For destinations outside of Bangkok, the safest, most reliable private bus services are the ones that operate from the three official Baw Khaw Saw terminals rather than from hotels or guesthouses. Picking up passengers from any points except these official terminals is actually illegal, and services promised by companies who flout the law are often not delivered. Although it can be a hassle getting out to the Baw Khaw Saw terminals, you're generally rewarded with safer, more reliable and punctual service.

Safety

Statistically, private tour buses have more accidents than government air-con buses. Turnovers on tight corners and head-on collisions with trucks are probably due to the inexperience of the drivers on a particular route. This in turn is probably a result of companies opening and folding so frequently, and because of the high priority given to making good time – Thais buy tickets on a company's reputation for speed.

As private bus fares are typically higher than government bus fares, the private bus companies attract a better-heeled clientele among Thais, as well as among foreign tourists. One result of this is that a tour bus loaded with money or the promise of money is a temptation for upcountry bandits. Hence, private tour buses occasionally get robbed by bands of thieves, but these incidents are diminishing due to increased security under provincial administration.

In an effort to prevent druggings and robbery in Southern Thailand, which peaked in the 1980s, Thai police now board tour buses plying the southern roads at unannounced intervals, taking photos and videotapes of the passengers and asking for IDs. Reported incidents are now on the decrease.

Keep an eye on your bags when riding buses – stealth is still the most popular tactic for robbery in Thailand (it's eminently preferable to the forceful variety), though again the risks are not that great – just be aware. Most pilfering seems to take place on the private bus runs between Bangkok and Chiang Mai, especially on buses booked on Th Khao San. Keep zippered bags locked and well secured.

TRAIN

The railway network in Thailand, run by the government-subsidised State Railway of Thailand (SRT), is surprisingly good. In fact, in many ways it's the best form of public transport in the kingdom. If you travel 3rd class, it is often the cheapest way to cover a long distance; by 2nd class it's about the same as a 'tour bus' but much safer and more comfortable. Trains take a bit longer than chartered buses on the same journey but, on overnight trips especially, are worth the extra travel time.

The trains have many advantages; there is more space and more room to breathe and stretch out (even in 3rd class) than there is on the best buses. The windows are big and usually open, so that there is no glass between you and the scenery (good for taking photos) and more to see. The scenery itself is always better along the train routes than the scenery along Thai highways – the trains regularly pass small villages, farmland, old temples etc. The pitch-and-roll of the railway cars is much easier on the bones, muscles and nervous system than the quick stops and starts, the harrowing turns and the pothole jolts endured on buses. The train is safer in terms of both accidents and robberies.

Rail Routes
Four main rail lines cover 4500km along the northern, southern, north-eastern and eastern routes. There are several side routes, notably between Nakhon Pathom and Nam Tok (stopping in Kanchanaburi) in the west central region, and between Tung Song and Kantang (stopping in Trang) in the south. The southern line splits at Hat Yai, one route going to Sungai Kolok on the Malaysian east coast border, via Yala, and the other route going to Padang Besar in the west, also on the Malaysian border.

A Bangkok to Pattaya spur has not been as popular as expected. Within the next few years, a southern spur may be extended from Khiriratnikhom to Phuket, establishing a rail link between Surat Thani and Phuket.

Bangkok Terminals Most long-distance trains originate from Bangkok's Hualamphong station. Before a railway bridge was constructed across the Chao Phraya River in 1932, all southbound trains left from Thonburi's Bangkok Noi station. Today Bangkok Noi station services commuter and short-line trains to Kanchanaburi/Nam Tok, Suphanburi, Ratchaburi and Nakhon Pathom (Ratchaburi and Nakhon Pathom can also be reached by train from Hualamphong). A slow night train to Chumphon and Lang Suan, both in Southern Thailand, leaves nightly from the Bangkok Noi station but it's rarely used by long-distance travellers.

Train Passes
The SRT issues a couple of rail passes that may save on fares if you plan to ride Thai trains extensively within a relatively short

interval. These passes are available in Thailand only, and may be purchased at Hualamphong train station.

The cost for 20 days of unlimited 2nd class rail travel ('blue pass') is 1100B, or for 1st class 2000B. These passes include all rapid or express surcharges but do not include sleeping berths or air-conditioning charges, which cost extra according to the standard SRT schedule. Passes must be validated at a local station before boarding the first train. The price of the pass includes seat reservations which, if required, can be made at any SRT ticket office. The pass is valid until midnight on the last day of the pass. However, if the journey is commenced before midnight on the last day of validity, the passenger can use the pass until that train reaches its destination.

The passes represent a savings over buying individual train tickets only if you can average more than 110km by rail per day for 20 days. If you travel at these levels (or less), then you'll be paying the same amount (or more) as you would if you bought ordinary train tickets directly. On less crowded routes where there are plenty of available 2nd class seats they save time that might otherwise be spent at ticket windows, but for high-demand routes (eg from Bangkok to Hat Yai) you'll still need to make reservations.

Classes
The SRT operates passenger trains in 1st, 2nd and 3rd class – but each varies considerably depending on whether you're on an ordinary, rapid or express train.

Third Class A typical 3rd class car consists of two rows of bench seats divided into facing pairs. Each bench seat is designed to seat two or three passengers, but on a crowded upcountry line nobody seems to care about design considerations. On a rapid train (which carries 2nd and 3rd class cars only), 3rd class seats are padded and reasonably comfortable for shorter trips. On ordinary, 3rd class-only trains in the east and north-east, seats are sometimes made of hard wooden slats, and are not recommended for more than a couple of hours. Express trains do not carry 3rd class cars at all. Commuter trains in the Bangkok area are all 3rd class, and the cars resemble modern subway or rapid transit trains, with plastic seats and ceiling loops for standing passengers.

Second Class In a 2nd class car, seating is similar to those on a bus, with pairs of padded seats all facing the front of the train. Usually the seats can be adjusted to recline, and for some people this is good enough for overnight trips. In a 2nd class sleeper, you'll find rows of facing seat pairs; each pair is separated from the next by a dividing wall. A table folds down between each pair and at night the seats convert into two fold-down berths, one over the other. Curtains provide a modicum of privacy and the berths are fairly comfortable, with fresh linen for every trip. A toilet stall is located at one end of the car and washbasins at the other. Second class cars are found only on rapid and express trains; some routes offer air-con 2nd class as well as ordinary 2nd class.

First Class First class cars provide private double cabins with individually controlled air-conditioning, an electric fan, a fold-down washbasin and mirror, a small table and two long bench seats that convert into beds. Drinking water and towels are provided free. First class cars are available only on express and special express trains.

Reservations

The disadvantage of travelling by rail, in addition to the time factor mentioned earlier, is that trains can be difficult to book. This is especially true around holiday time, eg the middle of April approaching the Songkhran Festival, since many Thais prefer the train. Trains out of Bangkok should be booked as far in advance as possible – a minimum of a week for a popular route such as the southern line to Hat Yai, especially if you want a sleeper. For the north-eastern and eastern lines a few days will suffice.

Advance bookings may be made one to 60 days before your intended date of departure. To book tickets in advance, go to Hualamphong station in Bangkok, walk through the front of the station house and go straight to the back right-hand corner where a sign says 'Advance Booking' (open 8.30 am to 4 pm Monday to Friday, to noon on weekends and holidays). The other ticket windows, on the left-hand side of the station, are for same-day purchases, mostly 3rd class.

Reservations are now computerised in the Advance Booking office, and you simply take a queue number, wait until your number appears on one of the electronic marquees, report to the desk above which your number appears and make your ticket arrangements. Only cash baht is acceptable here.

Note that buying a return ticket does not necessarily guarantee you a seat on the way back, it only means you do not have to buy a ticket for the return. If you want a guaranteed seat reservation it's best to make that reservation for the return immediately upon arrival at your destination.

Booking trains back to Bangkok is generally not as difficult as booking trains out of Bangkok; however, at some stations this can be quite difficult (eg buying a ticket from Surat Thani to Bangkok).

Tickets between any stations in Thailand can be purchased at Hualamphong station (☎ 02-223 3762, 225 6964, 224 7788, fax 225 6068). You can also make advance bookings at Don Muang station (across from Bangkok international airport) and at the Advance Booking offices at train stations in the larger cities. Advance reservations can be made by phone from anywhere in Thailand. Throughout Thailand SRT ticket offices are *generally* open from 8.30 am to 6 pm on weekdays and to noon on weekends and public holidays. Train tickets can also be purchased at certain travel agencies in Bangkok (see the Travel Agencies entry in the Information section of the Bangkok chapter). It is much simpler to book trains through these agencies than to book them at the station; however, many add a surcharge of 50B to 100B to the ticket price.

Costs

There is a 60B surcharge for express trains *(rót dùan)* and 40B for rapid trains *(rót raew)*. These trains are faster than ordinary trains, as they make fewer stops. For special express trains *(rót dùan phísèt)* there is an 80B surcharge. The special express trains are faster yet and some use newer, quieter passenger cars.

The charge for 2nd class sleeping berths is 100B for an upper berth and 150B for a lower berth (or 130B and 200B respectively on a special express). The difference between upper and lower is that there is a window next to the lower berth and a little more headroom. The upper berth is still quite comfortable. For 2nd class sleepers with air-con add 220/270B per upper/lower ticket (or 250/320 for special express trains). No sleepers are available in 3rd class.

All 1st class cabins have individually controlled air-conditioning and two beds, and costs 520B per person.

Eating Facilities

Meals are available in dining cars and at your seat in 2nd and 1st class cars. Menus change as frequently as the SRT changes catering services. The food is usually not all that great, and seems a bit overpriced (75B to 200B on average) by Thai standards – if you're concerned with saving baht, bring your own.

Train staff sometimes hand out face wipes, then come by later to collect 10B each for them – a racket since there's no indication to passengers that they're not complimentary. (On government buses they're free, and they're available in the station for 1B.) Drinking water is provided, albeit in plastic bottles; sometimes it's free, sometimes it costs 5B to 10B per bottle.

Several readers have written to complain about being overcharged by meal servers on trains. If you do purchase food on board, be sure to check prices on the menu rather than trusting server quotes. Also, check the bill carefully to make sure you haven't been overcharged.

Station Services

Accurate, up-to-date information on train travel is available at the Rail Travel Aids counter at Hualamphong station. You can pick up timetables or ask about fares and scheduling – one person behind the counter usually speaks a little English. There are two types of timetable available: four condensed English timetables with fares, schedules and routes for rapid, express and special express trains on the four trunk lines; and four Thai timetables for each trunk line, with side lines as well. These latter timetables give fares and schedules for all trains – ordinary, rapid and express. The English timetables only display a couple of the ordinary routes.

All train stations in Thailand have baggage storage services (sometimes called the 'cloak room'). The rates and hours of operation vary from station to station. At Hualamphong station the hours are from 4.30 am to 10.30 pm, and left luggage costs 30B per day per small bag, 40B for larger bags. Hualamphong station also has a 5B shower service in the rest rooms.

All stations in provincial capitals have restaurants or cafeterias as well as various snack vendors. These stations also offer an advance-booking service for rail travel anywhere in Thailand. Hat Yai station is the only one with a hotel attached, but there are usually hotels within walking distance of other major stations.

Hualamphong station has a travel agency where other kinds of transport can be booked, but beware of touts who try and drag you there saying the trains are fully booked when they aren't. This station also has a post office that's open from 7.30 am to 5.30 pm from Monday to Friday, 9 am to noon on Saturday and holidays; it's closed on Sunday.

CAR & MOTORCYCLE
Roads

Thailand has more than 170,000km of roads. Around 16,000km are classified 'national highways' (both two lane and four lane), which means they're generally well maintained. Route numbering is fairly consistent; some of the major highways have two numbers, one under the national system and another under the optimistic 'Asia Highway' system which indicates highway links with neighbouring countries. Route 105 to Mae Sot on the Burmese border, for example, is also called 'Asia 1', while Hwy 2 from Bangkok to Nong Khai is 'Asia 12'. For the time being, the only border regularly crossed by non-commercial vehicles is the Thai-Malaysian border.

Kilometre stones are placed at regular intervals along most larger roads, but place names are usually printed on them in Thai script only. Highway signs in both Thai and roman script showing destinations and distances are becoming increasingly common.

Road Rules

Thais drive on the left-hand side of the road – most of the time. Other than that just about anything goes, in spite of road signs and speed limits – Thais are notorious scofflaws when it comes to driving. Like many places in Asia, every two lane road has an invisible third lane in the middle that all drivers feel free to use at any time. Passing on hills and curves is common – as long as you've got the proper Buddhist altar on the dashboard, what could happen?

The main rule to be aware of is that the right of way belongs to the bigger vehicle; this is not what it says in the Thai traffic law, but it's the reality. Maximum speed limits are 60km/h within city limits, 80km/h on most highways (90km/h on dual carriageways) – but on any given stretch of highway you'll see vehicles travelling as slowly as 30km/h or as fast as 150km/h. Speed traps are becoming more common; they seem especially common along Hwy 4 in the south and Hwy 2 in the north-east.

Turn signals are often used to warn passing drivers about oncoming traffic. A left-turn signal means it's okay to pass, while a right-turn signal means someone's approaching from the other direction.

The principal hazard to driving in Thailand, besides the general disregard for traffic laws, is having to contend with so many different types of vehicles on the same road – bullock carts, 18-wheelers, bicycles, túk-túks and customised racing bikes. In village areas the vehicular traffic is lighter but you have to contend with stray chickens, dogs, water buffaloes, pigs, cats and goats. Once you get used to the challenge, driving in Thailand is very entertaining, but first-timers tend to get a bit unnerved.

Checkpoints Military checkpoints are common along highways throughout Northern and North-Eastern Thailand, especially in border areas. Always slow down for a checkpoint – often the sentries will wave you through without an inspection, but occasionally you'll be stopped and briefly questioned. Use common sense and don't be belligerent or you're likely to be detained longer than you'd like.

Rental

Cars, jeeps and vans can be easily rented in Bangkok, Pattaya, Phuket, Ko Samui and Hat Yai. A Japanese sedan (eg Toyota Corolla) typically costs 1000B to 1500B per day; minivans (eg Toyota Hi-Ace, Nissan Urvan) go for around 1800B to 2500B a day. International rental companies tend to charge a bit more; Avis, for example, rents Nissan 1.4 Sentras for 1500B a day (9000B weekly), slightly larger Mitsubishi 1.5 Lancers for 2000B a day (10,200B weekly) and Mitsubishi 4WD Pajeros for 2200B per day (13,200B weekly).

The best deals are usually on 4WD Suzuki Caribians (sic) or Daihatsu Miras, which can be rented for as low as 800B per day with no per-kilometre fees for long-term rentals or during low seasons. Unless you absolutely need the cheapest vehicle, you might be better off with a larger vehicle (eg the Mitsubishi 4WD Strada, if you absolutely need 4WD); Caribians are notoriously hard to handle at speeds above 90km/h and tend to crumple dangerously in collisions. Cars with automatic transmissions are uncommon. Drivers can usually be hired with a rental for an additional 300B to 400B per day.

Check with travel agencies or large hotels for rental locations. It is advisable always to verify that a vehicle is insured for liability before signing a rental contract; you should also ask to see the dated insurance documents. If you have an accident while driving an uninsured vehicle you're in for some major hassles.

Motorcycles can be rented in major towns as well as many smaller tourist centres like Krabi, Ko Samui, Ko Pha-Ngan, Ko Chang etc (see Motorcycle Touring in this section). Rental rates vary considerably from one agency to another and from city to city. Since there is a glut of motorcycles for rent on Ko Samui and Phuket, they can be rented on these islands for as little as 100B per day. A substantial deposit is usually required to rent a car; motorcycle rental usually requires that you leave your passport.

Driving Permits

Foreigners who wish to drive motor vehicles (including motorcycles) in Thailand need a valid international driving permit. If you don't have one, you can apply for a Thai driver's licence at the Police Registration Division (PRD; ☎ 02-513 0051/5) on Th Phahonyothin in Bangkok. Provincial capitals also have PRDs. If you present a valid foreign driver's licence at the PRD you'll probably only have to take a written test; other requirements include a medical certificate and two passport-sized colour photos. The forms are in Thai only, so you'll also need an interpreter. Some PRDs request an affidavit of residence, obtainable from your country's embassy in Thailand upon presentation of proof that you reside in Thailand (eg a utility bill in your name).

Fuel & Oil

Modern petrol (gasoline) stations with electric pumps are plentiful in Thailand where there are paved roads. In more remote off-road areas, petrol (ben-sin or náam-man rót yon) is usually available at small roadside or village stands – typically just a couple of ancient hand-operated pumps fastened to petrol barrels. As this book went to press,

regular (thamádaa, usually 91 octane) petrol cost about 12B per litre, super (phísèt, 94 to 95 octane) a bit more. Diesel (dii-soen) fuel is available at most pumps for around 10B.

The Thai phrase for 'motor oil' is náam-man khrêuang.

Motorcycle Touring

Motorcycle travel is becoming a popular way to get around Thailand, especially in the north. In the south there is more round-island touring and less long-distance motorcycling. Dozens of places in tourist areas, including many beach huts and guesthouses, have set up shop with no more than a couple of motorbikes for rent. It is also possible to buy a new or used motorbike and sell it before you leave the country – a good used 125cc bike costs around 20,000B to 25,000B (up to 50,000B for a good Honda AX-1).

Daily rental ranges from 100B a day for a 100cc step-through (eg Honda Dream, Suzuki Crystal) to 400B a day for a good 250cc dirt bike. The motorcycle industry in Thailand has stopped assembling dirt bikes, so many of those for rent are getting on in years; when they're well maintained they're fine, when they're not they can leave you stranded if not worse. The latest trend in Thailand is for small, heavy racing bikes that couldn't be less suitable for the typical faràng body.

The legal maximum size for motorcycle manufacture in Thailand is 150cc, though in reality few bikes on the road exceed 125cc. Anything over 150cc must be imported, which means an extra 600% in import duties. The odd rental shop specialises in bigger motorbikes (average 200 to 500cc) – some were imported by foreign residents and later sold on the local market, but most came into the country as 'parts' and were discreetly assembled, and licensed under the table.

While motorcycle touring is undoubtedly one of the best ways to see Thailand, it is also undoubtedly one of the easiest ways to cut your travels short, permanently. You can also run up very large repair and/or hospital bills in the blink of an eye. However, with proper safety precautions and driving conduct adapted to local conditions, you can see parts of Thailand inaccessible by other modes of transport and still make it home in one piece. Some guidelines to keep in mind:

- If you've never driven a motorcycle before, stick to the smaller 100cc step-through bikes with automatic clutches. If you're an experienced rider but have never done off-the-road driving, take it slowly the first few days.
- Always check a machine over thoroughly before you take it out. Look at the tyres to see if they still have tread, look for oil leaks, test the brakes. You may be held liable for any problems that weren't duly noted before your departure. Newer bikes cost more than clunkers, but are generally safer and more reliable. Street bikes are more comfortable and ride more smoothly on paved roads than dirt bikes; it's silly to rent an expensive dirt bike if most of your riding is going to be along decent roads. A two-stroke bike suitable for off-road riding generally uses twice the fuel of a four stroke bike with the same size engine, thus lowering your cruising range in areas where roadside pumps are scarce.
- Wear protective clothing and a helmet (the latter is now legally required in Thailand, though enforcement varies from place to place – most rental places will provide a helmet with the bike if asked). Without a helmet, a minor slide on gravel can leave you with concussion, cuts or bruises. Long pants, long-sleeved shirts and shoes are highly recommended as protection against sunburn and as a second skin if you fall. If your helmet doesn't have a visor, then wear goggles, glasses or sunglasses to keep bugs, dust and other debris out of your eyes. Gloves are also a good idea, to prevent blisters caused by holding on to the twist-grips for long periods of time. It is practically suicidal to ride on Thailand's highways without taking these minimum precautions.
- For distances of over 100km or so, take along an extra supply of motor oil, and if riding a two-stroke machine carry two-stroke engine oil. On long trips, oil burns fast.
- You should never ride alone in remote areas, especially at night. There have been incidents where faràng bikers have been shot or harassed while riding alone, mostly in remote rural areas. When riding in pairs or groups, spread out so you'll have room to manoeuvre or brake suddenly if necessary.
- In Thailand, the de facto right of way is determined by the size of the vehicle, which puts the motorcycle pretty low in the pecking order. Don't fight it and keep clear of trucks and buses.
- Distribute whatever weight you're carrying on the bike as evenly as possible across the frame. Too much weight at the back of the bike makes the front end less easy to control and prone to rising up suddenly on bumps and inclines.
- Get insurance with the motorcycle if at all possible. The more reputable motorcycle rental places insure all their bikes; some will do it for an extra charge. Without insurance you're responsible for anything that happens to the bike. If an accident results in the bike being 'totalled', or if the bike is lost or stolen, you can be out 25,000B plus. To be absolutely clear about your liability, ask for a written estimate of the replacement cost for a similar bike – take photos as a guarantee. Some agencies will only accept the replacement cost of a new bike. Health insurance is also a good idea – get it before you leave home and check the conditions in regard to motorcycle riding.

BICYCLE

Bicycles can be hired in many locations; guesthouses often have a few for rent at only 30B to 50B per day. Just about anywhere outside Bangkok, bikes are the ideal form of local transport because they're cheap, non-polluting and keep you moving slowly enough to see everything. Carefully note the condition of the bike before hiring; if it breaks down you are responsible and parts can be very expensive.

Many visitors are bringing their own touring bikes to Thailand these days. For the most part, drivers are courteous and move over for bicycles. Most roads are sealed, with roomy shoulders. Grades in most parts of the country are moderate; exceptions include the far north. There is plenty of opportunity for dirt-road and off-road pedalling, so a sturdy mountain bike would make a good alternative to a touring rig. Good potential touring routes include the back roads of Yala, Pattani and Narathiwat provinces in the deep south – the terrain is mostly flat and the village scenery is inspiring.

One note of caution: before you leave home, go over your bike with a fine-toothed comb and fill your repair kit with every imaginable spare part. As with cars and motorbikes, you won't necessarily be able to buy that crucial gismo for your machine when it breaks down somewhere in the back of beyond as the sun sets.

No special permits are needed for bringing a bicycle into the country, although bikes may be registered by Customs – which means if you don't leave the country with your bike you'll have to pay a huge Customs duty. Most larger cities have bike shops but they often stock only a few Japanese or locally made parts. All the usual bike trip precautions apply – bring a repair kit and helmet, reflective clothing and plenty of insurance.

You can take bicycles on the train for a little less than the equivalent of one 3rd class fare. Buses often don't charge (if they do it will be something nominal); on the ordinary buses they'll place your bike on the roof, and on air-con buses it will be put in the cargo hold.

Thailand Cycling Club, established in 1959, serves as an information clearinghouse on biking tours and cycle clubs around the country; call ☎ 02-243 5139 or ☎ 241 2023 in Bangkok. One of the best shops for cycling gear in Thailand is the Bike Shop in Bangkok, which has branches on Th Phetchaburi Mai opposite Wat Mai Chonglom (☎ 02-314 6317), at Soi 62, Th Sukhumvit (☎ 02-332 3538) and on Th Si Ayuthaya (☎ 02-247 7220) near Th Phayathai.

HITCHING

Hitching is never entirely safe in any country in the world, and we don't recommend it. Travellers who decide to hitch should understand that they are taking a small but serious risk. You may not be able to identify the local rapist/murderer before you get into his vehicle. However, many people do choose to hitch, and the advice that follows should help to make the journeys as fast and safe as possible.

It's safer to hitch in pairs and let someone know where you are planning to go.

People have mixed success with hitchhiking in Thailand; sometimes it's great and other times no one will pick you up. It seems easiest in the more touristed areas of the north and south, most difficult in the central and north-eastern regions where foreigners are a relatively rare sight. To stand on a road and try to flag every vehicle that passes by is, to the Thais, something only an uneducated villager would do.

If you're prepared to face this perception, the first step is to use the correct gesture used for flagging a ride – the thumb-out gesture isn't recognised by the average Thai. When Thais want a ride they stretch one arm out with the hand open, palm facing down, and move the hand up and down. This is the same gesture used to flag a taxi or bus, which is why some drivers will stop and point to a bus stop if one is nearby.

In general, hitching isn't worth the hassle as ordinary non-air-con buses are frequent and fares are cheap. There's no need to stand at a bus terminal – all you have to do is stand on any road going in your direction and flag down a passing bus or songthaew (see the Songthaew entry later in this chapter).

The exception is in areas where there isn't any bus service, though in such places there's not likely to be very much private vehicle traffic either. If you do manage to get a ride it's customary to offer food or cigarettes to the driver if you have any.

BOAT

As any flight over Thailand will reveal, there is plenty of water to get out on during your trip. The true Thai river and bay transport is the longtail boat (reua hang yao), so called because the propeller is mounted at the end of a long drive shaft extending from the engine. The engine, which varies from a small marine engine to a large car engine, is mounted on gimbals and the whole unit is swivelled to steer the boat. Longtail boats can travel at phenomenal speeds.

Between the mainland and islands in the Gulf of Thailand or Andaman Sea, all sorts of larger ocean-going craft are used. The standard is an all-purpose wooden boat, 8 to 10m long with a large inboard engine, a wheelhouse and a simple roof to shelter passengers and cargo. Faster, more expensive hovercraft or jetfoils are sometimes available in tourist areas.

LOCAL TRANSPORT

The Getting Around section in the Bangkok chapter has more information on various forms of local transport.

Bus

In most larger provincial capitals, there are extensive local bus services, generally operating with very low fares (4B to 8B). For the rest, you must rely on songthaews, tuk-tuks or samlors.

Taxi

Many regional centres have taxi services, but while there may well be meters, they're never used. Establishing the fare before departure is essential. Try to get an idea of the fare from a third party and be prepared to bargain. In general, fares are reasonably low.

Samlor/Tuk-Tuk

Samlor means 'three' (*sǎam*) 'wheels' (*láw*), and that's just what they are – three-wheeled

vehicles. There are two types of samlor, motorised and non-motorised. You'll find motorised samlors throughout the country. They're small utility vehicles, powered by a horrendously noisy two-stroke engine (usually LPG-powered) – if the noise and vibration doesn't get you, the fumes will. These samlors are more commonly known as *túk-túks* from the noise they make. On the other hand, the non-motorised versions are bicycle rickshaws, similar to those seen all over Asia. There are no bicycle samlors in Bangkok but you will find them elsewhere in the country. For both types of samlor the fare must be established, by bargaining if necessary, before departure.

Songthaew

A *songthaew* (*sǎwng tháew*, literally 'two rows') is a small pick-up truck with two rows of bench seats down the sides, very similar to an Indonesian *bemo* or a Filipino *jeepney*. Songthaews sometimes operate fixed routes, just like buses, but they may also run a share-taxi type of service or even be booked individually like a regular taxi.

ORGANISED TOURS

Many tour operators around the world can arrange guided tours of Thailand. Most of them simply serve as brokers for tour companies based in Thailand; they buy their trips from a wholesaler and resell them under various names in travel markets overseas. Hence, one is much like another and you might as well arrange a tour in Thailand at a lower cost. Two of Thailand's largest tour wholesalers in Bangkok are: World Travel Service (☎ 02-233 5900, fax 236 7169) at 1053 Th Charoen Krung; and Deithelm Travel (☎ 02-255 9150, fax 256 0248) at Kian Gwan Building II, 140/1 Th Withayu.

Several Bangkok-based companies specialise in ecologically oriented tours, including: Eco-Life (☎ 02-542 4085, fax 642 5885), 133/2 Th Ratchaprarop, Ratthewi; and Khiri Travel (☎ 02-629 0491, fax 629 0493), Viengtai Hotel, 42 Th Thani, Banglamphu.

Overseas Companies

The better overseas tour companies build their own Thailand itineraries from scratch and choose their local suppliers based on which ones best serve these itineraries. Of these, several specialise in adventure and/or ecological tours, including those in the following list. Asia Transpacific Journeys, for example, offers trips across a broad spectrum of Thai destinations and activities, from trekking in Northern Thailand to sea canoeing in the Phuket Sea. The average trip duration is around 14 to 17 days.

Ms Kasma Loha-Unchit (☎ 510-655 8900), 4119 Howe St, Oakland, California 94611, USA, a Thai native living in California, offers highly personalised, 26-day 'cultural immersion' tours of Thailand.

Asia Transpacific Journeys
(☎ 800-642 2742, 303-443 6789, fax 303-443 7078, email info@southeastasia.com)
3055 Center Green Dr, Boulder, CO 80301 USA

Club Aventure Voyages
(☎ 514-272 9919, fax 699 8756,
www.clubaventure.com)
1218 Bernard, Outremont, Québec H2V 1V6, Canada.

Exodus
(☎ 020-8673 5550, fax 8673 0779, email sales@exodustravels.co.uk)
9 Weir Rd, London SW12 OLT, UK

Intrepid Travel
(☎ 03-9416 2655, fax 9419 4426, email info@intrepidtravel.com.au)
246 Brunswick St, Fitzroy, Victoria 3065, Australia

Mountain Travel Sobek
(☎ 800-227 2384, 510-527 8100, fax 510-525 7710, email info@mtsobek.com)
6420 Fairmount Ave, Berkeley, CA 94530,USA

Bangkok

The very epitome of the modern, steamy Asian metropolis, Bangkok (560 sq km; population six million plus) has a surplus of attractions if you can tolerate the traffic, noise, heat (in the hot season), floods (in the rainy season) and pollution. The city is incredibly urbanised, but beneath its modern veneer lies an unmistakable Thai-ness.

The capital of Thailand was established at Bangkok in 1782 by the first king of the Chakri Dynasty, Rama I. The name Bangkok comes from *bang makok*, meaning 'place of olive plums' and refers to the original site, which is only a very small part of what is today called Bangkok by foreigners. The official Thai name is quite a tongue twister:

Krungthep mahanakhon bowon rattanakosin mahintara ayuthaya mahadilok popnopparat ratchathani burirom udomratchaniwet – mahasathan amonpiman avatansathir sakkathatitya visnukamprasit.

Fortunately, this is shortened to Krung Thep (City of Angels) in everyday usage. Metropolitan Krung Thep includes Thonburi, the older part of the city (and predecessor to Bangkok as the capital), which is across the Chao Phraya River to the west.

Those anxious to get to Thailand's sand and surf may just want to skip this massive urban sprawl and head directly south or east. But there is plenty to see in Bangkok, should you decide to stop over for a few days. Even if you're just in town for the afternoon, say waiting for the overnight train to Surat Thani, it's worth taking in a few sights and absorbing the frenetic energy that makes this one of Asia's most fascinating cities.

Bangkok caters to diverse interests: there are temples, museums and other historic sites for those interested in traditional Thai culture; an impressive variety of good restaurants, clubs, international cultural and social events; movies in several languages; and discos, heavy metal pubs and folk

HIGHLIGHTS

- Wat Phra Kaew, home of the diminutive, mysterious Emerald Buddha, is spectacular with its colourful mosaics, gold leaf and breathtaking spires.

- Jim Thompson's House is a beautifully maintained example of authentic Thai residential architecture, displaying the American silk entrepreneur's extensive Asian art collection.

- Vimanmek Teak Mansion is one of the world's largest golden teak buildings.

- River or canal trips on a Chao Phraya River Express boat provide an opportunity to observe Thai river life, or you could go for a dinner cruise.

- Eating in Bangkok's incredible restaurants. Try at least one riverside place to soak up the languid ambience of old Bangkok.

- Traditional dance drama at the National Theatre and shrine dancing at various wáts are highly recommended.

BANGKOK

GULF OF THAILAND

ANDAMAN
SEA

BANGKOK

cafes, even modern art galleries for those seeking contemporary Krung Thep. As the dean of expat authors in Thailand, William Warren, has said, 'The gift Bangkok offers me is the assurance I will never be bored'.

Following is a fairly selective guide to Bangkok's sights, accommodation, eateries and entertainment. For a more detailed look at the city, see Lonely Planet's *Bangkok* city and *Thailand* country guides.

ORIENTATION

The east side of the Chao Phraya River, Bangkok proper, can be divided in two by the main north-south train line. The portion between the river and the railway is old Bangkok (often called Ko Ratanakosin), where most of the older temples and the original palace are located, as well as the Chinese and Indian districts. The part of the city east of the railway, which covers many times more area than the old districts, is 'new' Bangkok. It can be divided again into the business/tourist district wedged between Thanŏn (Th) Charoen Krung (New Rd) and Th Rama IV, and the sprawling business/residential/tourist district stretching along Th Sukhumvit and Th Phetchaburi Tat Mai.

This leaves the hard-to-classify areas below Th Sathon Tai (South Sathon Rd, which includes Khlong Toey, Bangkok's main port), and the area above Th Rama IV between the train line and Th Withayu (Wireless Rd – where there are scores of office blocks, several cinemas, civil service buildings, the shopping area of Siam Square, Chulalongkorn University and the National Stadium). The areas along the east bank of the Chao Phraya River are undergoing a surge of redevelopment and many new buildings, particularly apartments, are going up.

On the opposite (west) side of the Chao Phraya River is Thonburi, which was Thailand's capital for 15 years before Bangkok was founded. Few tourists ever set foot on the Thonburi side except to visit Wat Arun, the Temple of Dawn. Fang Thon (Thon Bank), as it's often called by Thais, seems

an age away from the glittering high-rises on the east bank, although it is an up-and-coming area for apartment development.

Finding Addresses

Any city as large and unplanned as Bangkok can be tough to get around. Street names often seem unpronounceable to begin with, compounded by the inconsistency of romanised Thai spellings. For example, the street often spelt as Rajadamri is pronounced Ratchadamri (with the appropriate tones), or in abbreviated form Rat'-damri. The 'v' in Sukhumvit should be pronounced like a 'w'. The most popular location for foreign embassies is known both as Wireless Rd and Th Withayu (*wítháyú* is Thai for 'radio').

Many street addresses show a string of numbers divided by slashes and hyphens; for example, 48/3-5 Soi 1, Th Sukhumvit. This is because undeveloped property in Bangkok was originally bought and sold in lots. The number before the slash refers to the original lot number; the numbers following the slash indicate buildings (or entrances to buildings) constructed within that lot. The pre-slash numbers appear in the order in which they were added to city plans, while the post-slash numbers are arbitrarily assigned by developers. As a result, numbers along a given street don't always run consecutively.

The Thai word *thanŏn* means road, street or avenue (it's shortened to Th in this book). Hence Ratchadamnoen Rd (sometimes referred to as Ratchadamnoen Ave) is always called Thanŏn (Th) Ratchadamnoen in Thai.

A *soi* is a small street or lane that runs off a larger street. In our example, the address referred to as 48/3-5 Soi 1, Th Sukhumvit will be located off Th Sukhumvit on Soi 1. Alternative ways of writing the same address include 48/3-5 Th Sukhumvit Soi 1, or even just 48/3-5 Sukhumvit 1. Some Bangkok sois have become so large that they can be referred to both as thanŏn and soi, eg Soi Sarasin/Th Sarasin and Soi Asoke/Th Asoke.

Smaller than a soi is a *tràwk* (usually spelt 'trok') or alley. Well known alleys in Bangkok include Chinatown's Trok Itsanuraphap and Banglamphu's Trok Rong Mai.

MAPS

A map is essential for finding your way around Bangkok, and there are lots of maps competing for your attention. Lonely Planet publishes an easy to use, durable, full colour Bangkok City Map with an index of streeets and sites of interest.

A bus map is necessary if you intend to spend a lot of time in Bangkok and want to use the very economical bus system. One of the most popular, because it clearly shows all the bus routes (and some walking tours), and is cheap, is the *Tour 'n Guide Map to Bangkok Thailand*, often referred to by travellers as the 'blue map' because of its monotonous aqua colour. The map costs 35B to 40B and although it's regularly updated, some bus routes will inevitably be wrong, so take care. The coated paper, which resists stains, is a plus.

For more detail on bus routes you'll have to get the *Bus Guide*, a booklet published by Bangkok Guide for 35B. It contains maps and a listing of all the public bus routes in Bangkok as well as a Bangkok train schedule but it takes some patience to use since much of the guide is in Thai, and the English is horrendous.

The Tourism Authority of Thailand (TAT) publishes and distributes the free *City Map of Bangkok*, a folded sheet map on coated stock with bus routes, all major hotels, the latest expressways, sightseeing, hospitals, embassies and more – very useful if a bit hard to read due to small print. Separate inset maps of significant areas of the city are very helpful. You can pick it up at the airport TAT desk or at any Bangkok TAT office.

The long-running, oft-imitated and never equalled *Nancy Chandler's Map of Bangkok* costs 120B and contains a whole host of information on out-of-the-way places, including lots of stuff on where to buy unusual things around the city. The six different water-coloured panels (Greater Bangkok, Sampeng Lane, Th Sukhumvit, Chatuchak Weekend Market, Central Shopping Area and Markets of Central Bangkok) are all hand-drawn, hand-lettered and laid out by hand. The 18th edition, published in 1998, adds a handy categorised index.

A new contender on the market, *Litehart's Groovy Bangkok by Night Map & Guide* combines the usual sightseeing features with restaurant, bar and night-time entertainment recommendations, all on decent coated stock. It covers a smaller area (only central Bangkok) and lacks detail in wát and street naming – the main avenues are labelled, the rest (most of the streets on the map) are not, and few wáts are labelled at all. It is not a map to Bangkok sleaze, but rather a well rounded survey of many different entertainment venues.

Periplus Editions has recently issued a revised Bangkok map that is the most detailed sheet map of the city commercially available. It is especially good in terms of finding hotels (but not necessarily guesthouses), residential and office buildings by name (eg Sindhorn Bldg) and government offices, so is a good choice for anyone doing business in the city or staying long-term. All the major areas of Bangkok east of the river are covered, including Th Sukhumvit as far as the Eastern bus terminal.

Similarly detailed but covering a much larger portion of the city is *BangkokMap*, a 188-page hardcover street atlas put out by the Agency for Real Estate Affairs, a private company specialising in real estate surveys of the city.

INFORMATION
Guidebooks

Lonely Planet's *Bangkok* city guide covers all of the information in this chapter along with extra details concerning business services in the city as well as excursions to nearby provinces. *Vivre à Bangkok*, published by Une Équipe de Bénévoles Bangkok Accueil for La Commuanutée Francophone en Thaïlande, is a thick spiralbound book that covers all the usual territory with special attention to French speakers – including, for example, a list of French speaking travel agents. It's available in Bangkok bookshops where foreign language books are sold, such as Asia Books.

Tourist Offices

The TAT has a desk in the arrivals area of both Terminal 1 (☎ 02-523 8972) and Terminal 2 (☎ 02-535 2669) at Bangkok international airport, both open from 8 am to midnight. The TAT's main office (☎ 02-694 1222, fax 694 1220) occupies 10 floors of Le Concorde Bldg, 202 Th Ratchadaphisek, a location in northern Bangkok inconvenient for most visitors. TAT may move into a building near Ko Ratanakosin in the near future. Open daily 8.30 am to 4.30 pm.

An information office (☎ 02-282 9773, fax 280 1744) can also be found on Th Ratchadamnoen Nok near the Ratchadamnoen Boxing Stadium. It's open daily from 8.30 am to 4.30 pm. The TAT produces the usual selection of colourful brochures, but they're also one of the best tourist offices in Asia for putting out useful hard facts – on plain but invaluable duplicated sheets. Many of the staff speak English.

The TAT also maintains a Tourist Assistance Centre (TAC; ☎ 1155 or 02-282 8129, 281 5051) in the main compound for matters relating to theft and other mishaps; it's open 24 hours. The paramilitary arm of the TAT, the Tourist Police, can be quite effective in dealing with such matters, particularly 'unethical' business practices – which sometimes turn out to be cultural misunderstandings. Note that if you think you've been overcharged for gems (or any other purchase), there's very little the TAC can do.

Tourist Police can also be found at the corner of Th Rama IV and Th Ratchadamri, near the statue of Rama VI by Lumphini Park – this one specialises in investigating Patpong ripoffs.

A smaller TAT office with fewer materials can be found at Chatuchak Market, open daily from 9 am to 5 pm.

Immigration Department

For visa extensions or applications, you'll need to visit the Immigration Department office (☎ 02-287 1774) on Soi Suan Phlu, off Th Sathon Tai. It's open Monday to Friday from 8.30 am to 4.30 pm (with limited staff from noon to 1 pm), and Saturday until noon. Most applications/extensions require two photos and a photocopy of the photo page of your passport.

Money

Regular bank hours in Bangkok are now 10 am to 4 pm – this schedule was instituted in 1995 in an effort to relieve traffic congestion. ATMs are common in all areas of the city. Many Thai banks also have currency exchange offices in tourist-oriented areas of Bangkok which are open from 8.30 am to 8 pm (some even later) every day of the year. You'll find them in several places along the following thanōns: Sukhumvit, Nana Neua, Khao San, Patpong, Surawong, Ratchadamri, Rama IV, Rama I, Silom and Charoen Krung. If you're after currency for other countries in Asia, check with the moneychangers along Th Charoen Krung (New Rd) near the central post office.

Post

The central post office is on Th Charoen Krung. The easiest way to get there is via the Chao Phraya River Express, which stops at Tha Meuang Khae (Meuang Khae pier) at the river end of Soi Charoen Krung 34, next to Wat Meuang Khae, just south of the central post office. The poste restante counter is open Monday to Friday from 8 am to 8 pm, and on weekends until 1 pm. Each letter you collect costs 1B, parcels 2B. The staff are very efficient.

There's also a packaging service at the central post office where parcels can be wrapped for 5B to 12B plus the cost of materials (up to 40B). Or you can simply buy the materials at the counter and do it yourself. The packaging counter is open Monday to Friday from 8 am to 4.30 pm, and Saturday from 9 am to noon. At other times (weekday evenings and Sunday mornings)

GREATER BANGKOK

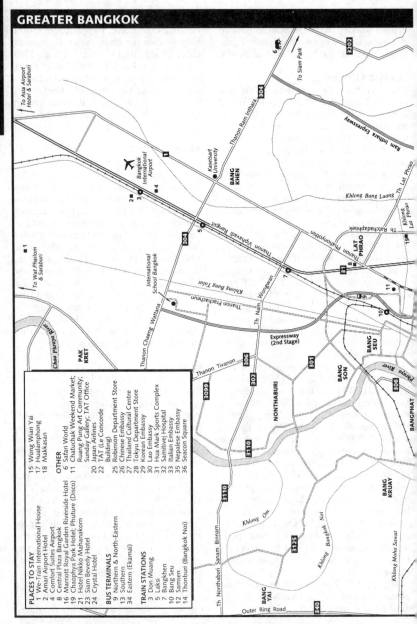

PLACES TO STAY
1 We-Train International House
2 Amari Airport Hotel
4 Comfort Suites Airport
8 Central Plaza Bangkok
16 Marriott Royal Garden Riverside Hotel
19 Chaophya Park Hotel; Phuture (Disco)
21 Hotel Nikko Mahanakorn
23 Siam Beverly Hotel
24 Crystal Hotel

BUS TERMINALS
9 Northern & North-Eastern
13 Southern
34 Eastern (Ekamai)

TRAIN STATIONS
3 Don Muang
5 Laksi
7 Bangkhen
10 Bang Seu
12 Samsen
14 Thonburi (Bangkok Noi)

15 Wong Wian Yai
17 Hualamphong
18 Makkasan

OTHER
6 Safari World
11 Chatuchak Weekend Market;
    Ruang Pung Art Community;
    Sunday Gallery; TAT Office
20 Japan Airlines
22 TAT (Le Concorde
    Building)
25 Robinson Department Store
26 Chinese Embassy
27 Thailand Cultural Centre
28 Tokyu Department Store
29 Korean Embassy
30 Lao Embassy
31 Hua Mark Sports Complex
32 Samitivej Hospital
33 Italian Embassy
35 Nepalese Embassy
36 Seacon Square

GREATER BANGKOK

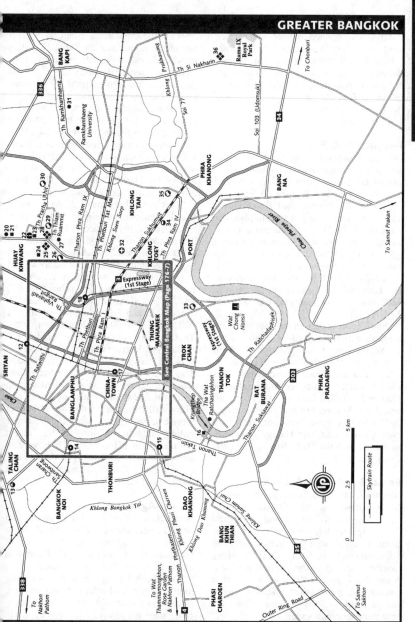

BANG KAPI

Th Ramkhamhaeng

336

Th Pracha Uthit

Ramkhamhaeng University

31

30

36

Rama IX Royal Park

Th Si Nakharin

Khlong Prakhanong

Soi 77

To Chonburi

Soi 103 (Udomsuk)

34

PHRA KHANONG

BANG NA

To Samut Prakan

Chao Phraya River

20
21
22
29
23
24
25
26
27
28

HUAY KHWANG

Th Pracha Uthit

Th Thiam Ruammit

Thanon Phra Ram IX

Th Phetburi Tat Mai

Khlong Saen Saep

32

35

34

KHLONG TAN

Thanon Sukhumvit

Th Phra Ram IV

KHLONG TOEY

PORT

Expressway (1st Stage)

18

Th Viphawadi Rangsit

Th Phetburi

Th Phra Ram I

THUNG MAHAMEK

33

Wat Chong Nonsi

Th Ratchadaphisek

Expressway (1st Stage)

12

SRIYAN

Th Ratwithi

Khlong

BANGLAMPHU

CHINA-TOWN

17

TROK CHAN

THANON TOK

Krungthep Bridge

Tha Wat Ratchasingkhon

16

RAT BURANA

Thanon Suksawat

PHRA PRADAENG

303

See Central Bangkok Map (Page 176-7)

13

TALING CHAN

Chan Thon Sanwong

14

THONBURI

15

BANGKOK NOI

Khlong Bangkok Yai

DAO KHANONG

Thanon Taksin

Khlong Dao Khanong

BANG KHUN THIAN

Khlong Samae Chai

5 km

2.5

0

— — — Skytrain Route

338

To Nakhon Pathom

To Wat Thammamongkhon, Rose Garden & Nakhon Pathom

Thanon Phetkasem

Thanon Phasi Charoen

PHASI CHAROEN

Outer Ring Road

35

To Samut Sakhon

an informal packing service (using recycled materials) is opened behind the service windows at the centre rear of the building.

Branch post offices throughout the city also offer poste restante and parcel services. In Banglamphu, the post office at the east end of Th Trok Mayom near Sweety Guest House was recently razed. It's reconstruction is planned.

Telephone & Fax
The Communications Authority of Thailand (CAT) international telephone office, around the corner from the main central post office building, is open 24 hours. At last count, 16 countries had Home Direct service, which means you can simply enter a vacant Home Direct booth and get one-button connection to an international operator in any of these countries (see the Telephone section in the Facts for the Visitor chapter for a list). Other countries (except Laos and Malaysia) can be reached via IDD phones. Faxes can also be sent from the CAT office.

Other Home Direct phones can be found at Queen Sirikit National Convention Centre, World Trade Centre, Sogo department store and the Hualamphong post office.

You can also make long-distance calls and faxes at the Telephone Organisation of Thailand (TOT) office on Th Ploenchit near Siam Square, but this office accepts cash only, no reverse charge or credit card calls. Calls to Laos and Malaysia can only be dialled from the TOT office or from private phones.

Email & Internet Access
Wireheads can check their email or skim the Net at dozens of Internet cafes, bars and centres throughout the city. Possibly the best deal going is the Internet/email service at the British Council Library at Siam Square, 254 Soi Chulalongkorn 64 Th Rama I, where members can log on for just 60B per hour. A membership costs 500B but it's worth it considering most other places in town charge 240B to 300B per hour. There are only three terminals so far.

The CyberPub (☎ 02-236 0450, ext 2971) in the Dusit Thani Hotel on the corner of Th Silom and Th Rama IV offers booze and food, along with a bank of 10 up-to-date computer stations. Charges are 5B per online minute plus 100B for a 'smart card' issued by CyberPub.

Cyberia Internet Cafe (☎ 02-259 3356, email kulthep@cyberia.co.th), 654-8 Th Sukhumvit on the corner of Soi 24, offers international cuisine along with their Internet service, open Sunday to Wednesday 11 am to 11 pm, Thursday and Saturday to 2 am, Friday 11 am to midnight. This is the hippest Internet spot in town, so far.

The CAT Telecommunications Center at Bangkok international airport, 2nd floor, terminal 2, offers Internet access 24 hours daily. To use their terminals you must purchase a 300B CATnet card, which gives you up to five hours on the Net and is good for a year.

Another reliable outlet, Cyber Cafe, has two Bangkok locations: Ploenchit (☎ 02-656 8472), 2nd floor, Ploenchit Center, Th Sukhumvit; and Silom Imagine (☎ 02-631 2022, fax 631 2028), 3rd floor, Liberty Bldg, Th Silom, open daily 10 am to midnight.

Bangkok Internet Cafe (☎ 02-629 3013), between Prakorp's House & Restaurant and Thai Guest House on Th Khao San (Khao San Rd), has an air-con restaurant section up on the 2nd floor, divided by a door and glass wall from the 14-computer Internet service section. Rates are a cheap 2B per online minute. This is the nicest Internet/email place in the Th Khao San area to date. Several other guesthouses and cafes in the Th Khao San area provide email and Internet service.

Travel Agencies
Bangkok is packed with travel agencies of every manner and description, but if you're looking for cheap airline tickets it's wise to be cautious. On and near Th Khao San alone, there are over a dozen places where you can book bus and air tickets; some are highly reliable and offer unbelievably low prices, but you should exercise caution because there are always a few bad apples in

the bunch. In the past five years at least two agencies on Th Khao San closed up shop and absconded with payments from dozens of tourists who never received their tickets. The bad agencies change their names frequently, so ask other travellers for advice. Wherever possible, try to see the tickets before you hand over the money.

STA Travel maintains reliable offices specialising in discounted yet flexible air tickets at Wall Street Tower (☎ 02-233 2582), 33 Th Surawong, and in the Thai Hotel (☎ 02-281 5314), 78 Th Prachatipatai, Banglamphu. Another reliable, long-running agency is Vieng Travel (☎ 02-280 3537), Trang Hotel, 99/8 Th Wisut Kasat, in Banglamphu.

Some agencies will make Thai train bookings and pick tickets up by courier – a service for which there's usually a 100B surcharge. Four agencies permitted to arrange direct train bookings (without surcharge) are:

Airland
  (☎ 02-255 5432)
  866 Th Ploenchit
SEA Tours
  (☎ 02-251 4862, 255 2080)
  Suite 414, 4th floor, Siam Center, Th Rama I
Songserm Travel Center
  (☎ 02-255 8790)
  121/7 Soi Chalermla, Th Phayathai
  (☎ 02-282 8080)
  172 Th Khao San
Thai Overland Travel & Tour
  (☎ 02-635 0500, fax 635 0504)
  407 Th Sukhumvit, between sois 21 and 23

If you are heading onto Europe and need a Eurail Pass, Dits Travel Ltd (☎ 02-255 9205) at Kian Gwan House, 140 Th Withayu, is one agency authorised to issue them.

Magazines & Newspapers

Several ad-laden free magazines and papers contain tourist information, but the best source for no frills info is the *Bangkok Metro* magazine. A lifestyle monthly, it is packed with listings on health, entertainment, events, social services, travel tips and consumer-oriented articles. The *Nation* and the *Bangkok Post* also contain useful articles and event listings.

Bookshops

Bangkok has many good bookshops, possibly the best selection in South-East Asia. For new books and magazines the two best chains are Asia Books and Duang Kamol (DK) Book House. Asia Books lives up to its name by having one of the largest selections of English-language titles on Asia in Bangkok. Its main branch (☎ 02-252 7277) is at 221 Th Sukhumvit at Soi 15. Other large branches are scattered around Bangkok in the larger shopping centres. Smaller Asia Books' stalls can be found in several larger hotels and at Thai airports.

DK Book House (☎ 02-251 6335, 250 1262), based in Siam Square at 244-6 Soi 2, Th Rama I, is good for textbooks. There's also a branch on Th Sukhumvit across from the Ambassador Hotel (excellent for fiction titles), and branches in other large shopping centres. There are two other bookshops with English-language books in the Siam Square complex: the Book Chest (Soi 2) and Odeon Store (Soi 1). Kinokuniya in The Emporium shopping centre, Soi 24, Th Sukhumvit, is also quite good, not only for Japanese language materials but for English.

Teck Heng Bookstore (☎ 02-630 8532), 1326 Th Charoen Krung between the Shangri-La and Oriental hotels, is one of the better independent bookshops in this neighbourhood.

Suksit Siam, opposite Wat Ratchabophit on Th Fuang Nakhon, specialises in books on Thai politics. The shop also has a number of mainstream titles on Thailand and Asia, both in English and Thai.

Used and rare books are available at a few shops, including Shaman Books (☎ 02-629 0418) at 71 Th Khao San, and Merman Books (☎ 02-231 3155), Silom Complex, 191 Th Silom. The Chatuchak Weekend Market in Chatuchak Park is also a source of used, often out-of-print books in several languages. On Th Khao San in Banglamphu, at least three streetside vendors specialise in used paperback novels and guidebooks, including many Lonely Planet titles.

Medical Services

Bangkok is Thailand's leading health care centre, with three university research hospitals, 12 public and private hospitals, and hundreds of medical clinics. Australian, US and UK embassies usually keep up-to-date lists of doctors who speak English; for doctors who speak other languages, contact the relevant embassy or consulate.

Several shop-front clinics in the Th Ploenchit area specialise in lab tests for sexually transmitted diseases. According to *Bangkok Metro* magazine, Bangkok General Hospital has the most sophisticated HIV blood testing programme. Bangkok's better hospitals include:

Bangkok Adventist (Mission) Hospital
  (☎ 02-281 1422, 282-1100)
  430 Th Phitsanulok
Bangkok Christian Hospital
  (☎ 02-233 6981/9, 235 1000)
  124 Th Silom
Bangkok General Hospital
  (☎ 02-318 0066)
  Soi 47, Th Phetchaburi Tat Mai
Bangkok Nursing Home
  (☎ 02-233 2610/9)
  9 Th Convent
Bumrumgrad Hospital
  (☎ 02-253 0250)
  33 Soi 3, Th Sukhumvit
Samitivej Hospital
  (☎ 02-392 0010/9)
  133 Soi 49, Th Sukhumvit
St Louis Hospital
  (☎ 02-212 0033/48)
  215 Th Sathon Tai

Emergency

All of the hospitals listed offer 24 hour service. Bangkok does not have an emergency phone system staffed by English-speaking operators. Between 8 am and midnight, your best bet for English-speaking assistance is the Tourist Assistance Centre (☎ 02-281 5051, 282 8129) or the Tourist Police (☎ 1155). After midnight, you'll have to rely on your own resources or on English-speaking hotel staff.

If you can find a Thai to call on your behalf, here are the city's main emergency numbers:

Police	☎ 191 or 123
Fire	☎ 199
Ambulance	☎ 252 2171/5

Dangers & Annoyances

Bangkok's most heavily touristed areas, especially around Wat Phra Kaew and Th Khao San, are favourite hunting grounds for Thai con artists of every ilk. There are also some who prowl the areas near Soi Kasem San 1 and Soi Kasem San 2, opposite Mahboonkrong shopping centre and near Jim Thompson's House, and typically dress in Thai business suits and carry mobile phones. The Chao Phraya River Express piers between Tha Tien and Tha Phra Athit also attract cons who may try to intercept tourists as they get off the boats – the favourite line is 'Wat Pho (or Wat Phra Kaew, or Wat Arun) is closed today for repairs, government holiday etc'.

Don't believe anyone on the street who tells you Wat Pho, Jim Thompson's House or some other attraction is closed for a holiday; check for yourself. More obvious are the tuk-tuk drivers who are out to make a commission by dragging you to a local silk or jewellery shop – even though you've requested an entirely different destination. In either case if you accept an invitation for 'free' sightseeing or shopping, you're quite likely to end up wasting an afternoon or – as happens all too often – losing a lot of money. Lonely Planet has also received letters from female travellers who have been scammed by Thai women con artists.

For details on common scams, see the Dangers & Annoyances section in the Facts for the Visitor chapter.

Tourist Police

The Tourist Police are a separate force established to deal with tourist problems under the Crime Suppression Division of the National Police Department. In Bangkok, some 500 English-speaking officers are stationed in tourist areas – their kiosks, cars and uniforms are clearly marked. If you have any problems relating to criminal activity, contact the Tourist Police. If they can't solve the problem, or if it's out of their jurisdiction, they can act as a bilingual liaison with the regular police. The head Tourist Police office (☎ 02-255 2964) at 29/1 Soi Lang Suan, Th Ploenchit, deals with tourism-related crime, particularly gem fraud and can be reached by dialling ☎ 1155. The Tourist Police also have a branch at the TAT compound on Th Ratchadamnoen Nok.

WAT PHRA KAEW & GRAND PALACE

Also called the Temple of the Emerald Buddha (Wat Phra Si Ratana Satsadaram), Wat Phra Kaew adjoins the Grand Palace (Phra Borom Maharatchawong) on common ground which was consecrated in 1782, the first year of Bangkok rule. The grounds encompass over a hundred buildings that represent over 200 years of royal history and architectural experimentation. (See the 'Emerald Buddha' boxed text in this chapter.)

The wát structures are extremely colourful, being comprised of gleaming, gilded *chedis* (stupas), polished orange and green roof tiles, mosaic-encrusted pillars and rich marble pediments. Extensive murals depicting scenes from the *Ramakian* (the Thai version of the Indian epic the *Ramayana*) line the inside walls of the compound.

Except for an anteroom here and there, the Grand Palace is closed to the public. The exteriors of the four buildings are worth a swift perusal, however, for their royal bombast.

Admission to the Wat Phra Kaew/Grand Palace compound is 125B, and opening hours are from 8.30 am to 3.30 pm. The admission fee includes entry to the Royal Thai Decorations & Coins Pavilion (on the same grounds) and to both Vimanmek and Abhisek Dusit Throne Hall, near the Dusit Zoo.

Since wáts are sacred to Thai Buddhists – this one particularly so because of its royal associations – visitors should dress and behave decently when they visit. If you wear shorts or a sleeveless shirt you may be refused admission; a sarong or baggy pants are sometimes available on loan at the entry area. For walking in the courtyard areas you must wear shoes with closed heels and toes – 'thongs' aren't permitted. As in any temple compound, shoes should be removed before entering the main chapel *(bòt)* or sanctuaries *(wihāan)* of Wat Phra Kaew.

The most economical way to reach Wat Phra Kaew and the Grand Palace is by aircon bus No 8 or 12. You can also take the Chao Phraya River Express, disembarking at Tha Chang.

WAT PHO (WAT PHRA CHETUPHON)

This is the oldest and largest wát in Bangkok, featuring the longest reclining Buddha and the largest collection of Buddha images in Thailand, and was the earliest centre for public education. As a temple site Wat Pho dates back to the 16th century, but its current history really begins in 1781 with the complete rebuilding of the original monastery.

Narrow Th Chetuphon divides the grounds in two, with each section surrounded by huge whitewashed walls. The most interesting part is the northern compound. It includes a very large bòt enclosed by a gallery of Buddha images and four wihāan (the counterpart to the bòt), four large chedis commemorating the first three Chakri kings (Rama III has two chedis), 91 smaller chedis, an old *tripitaka* (Buddhist scriptures) library, a sermon hall, the large wihāan housing the reclining Buddha, and a school building for classes in Abhidhamma (Buddhist philosophy), plus several less important structures.

Wat Pho is the national headquarters for the teaching and preservation of traditional Thai medicine, including Thai massage. A massage school convenes in the afternoons

Emerald Buddha

The so-called Emerald Buddha or Phra Kaew is actually made of a type of jasper or perhaps nephrite (a type of jade), depending on whom you believe. It's 60 to 75cm high (depending on how it is measured) and a definite aura of mystery surrounds it – enhanced by the fact that it cannot be examined closely (it sits in a glass case, on a pedestal high above the heads of worshippers) and photography within the *bòt* is forbidden. Its mystery further adds to the occult significance of the image, which is considered the 'talisman' of the Thai kingdom, the legitimator of Thai sovereignty.

It is not known for certain where the image originated or who sculpted it, but it first appeared on record in 15th century Chiang Rai. Legend says it was sculpted in India and brought to Siam by way of Ceylon, but stylistically it seems to belong to the Chiang Saen or Lanna period (13th to 14th centuries). Sometime in the 15th century, the image is said to have been covered with plaster and gold leaf and placed in Chiang Rai's own Wat Phra Kaew (literally 'Temple of the Jewel Holy Image'). While being transported elsewhere after a storm had damaged the chedi in which the image had been kept, it supposedly lost its plaster covering in a fall. It next appeared in Lampang where it enjoyed a 32 year stay (again at a Wat Phra Kaew) until it was brought to Wat Chedi Luang in Chiang Mai.

Laotian invaders took the image from Chiang Mai in the mid-16th century and brought it to Luang Prabang in Laos. Later it was moved to Wiang Chan (Vientiane). When Thailand's King Taksin waged war against Laos 200 years later, the image was taken back to the Thai capital of Thonburi by General Chakri, who later succeeded Taksin as Rama I, the founder of the Chakri dynasty. Rama I had the Emerald Buddha moved to the new Thai capital in Bangkok and had two royal robes made for it, one to be worn in the hot season and one for the rainy season. Rama III added another to the wardrobe to be worn in the cool season. The three robes are still solemnly changed at the beginning of each season by the king himself. The huge bòt at Wat Phra Kaew in which it is displayed was built expressly for the purpose of housing the diminutive image.

Joe Cummings

at the eastern end of the compound; a massage costs 200B per hour, 120B for a half hour. You can also study massage here in seven to 10-day courses.

You can hire English, French, German or Japanese-speaking guides for 150B for one visitor, 200B for two, 300B for three. Also on the premises are a few astrologers and palm readers.

The temple is open to the public from 8 am to 5 pm daily; admission is 20B. The ticket booth is closed from noon to 1 pm. Air-con bus Nos 6, 8 and 12 stop near Wat Pho. The nearest Chao Phraya Express pier is Tha Tien.

WAT MAHATHAT

Founded in the late 18th century, Wat Mahathat is a national centre for the Mahanikai monastic sect and houses one of Bangkok's two Buddhist universities, Mahathat Rajavidyalaya. The university is the most important place of Buddhist learning in mainland South-East Asia; the Lao, Vietnamese and Cambodian governments send selected monks to further their studies here.

Mahathat and its surrounding area have developed into an informal Thai cultural centre of sorts, though this may not be obvious at first glance. A daily open-air market features traditional Thai herbal medicine, and

Bangkok – Things to See & Do 175

BANGKOK

out on the street you'll find a string of shops selling herbal cures and Thai massage. On weekends, a large produce market held on the temple grounds attracts people from all over Bangkok and beyond.

The temple complex is open from 9 am to 5 pm every day and on *wan phrá* – Buddhist holy days (the full and new moons every fortnight). Admission is free.

Wat Mahathat is right across the street from Wat Phra Kaew, on the west side of Sanam Luang. Air-con bus Nos 8 and 12 both pass by it, and the nearest Chao Phraya Express pier is Tha Maharat.

OTHER WATS

Wat Traimit is also known as the Temple of the Golden Buddha. The main attraction here is, of course, the impressively gleaming, solid-gold Buddha image. It can be seen every day from 8 am to 5 pm, and admission is 20B. It pays to arrive in the early morning if you want avoid the tour groups. Wat Traimit is near the intersection of Th Yaowarat and Th Charoen Krung, near Hualamphong station.

Wat Arun, the striking 'Temple of Dawn', named after the Indian god of dawn, Aruna, appears in all the tourist brochures and is on the Thonburi side of the Chao Phraya River. The unique design of the 82m *prang* (Khmer-style tower) elongates the typical Khmer prang into a distinctly Thai shape. It's open daily from 8.30 am to 5.30 pm; admission is 10B. To reach Wat Arun from the Bangkok side, catch a cross-river ferry from Tha Tien at Th Thai Wang. Crossings are frequent and cost only 1B.

Wat Benchamabophit is made of white Carrara marble (hence its tourist name, 'Marble Temple') and was built at the end of the 19th century under King Chulalongkorn (Rama V). It is on the corner of Th Si Ayuthaya and Th Rama V, diagonally opposite the south-west corner of Chitlada Palace. It's open daily from 9 am to 5 pm, and admission is 10B. Bus Nos 2 (air-con) and 72 (non air-con) stop nearby.

Wat Bovornives (Bowonniwet), on Th Phra Sumen in Banglamphu, is the national

headquarters for the Thammayut monastic sect, a minority in Thai Buddhism. King Mongkut lived here as a monk – in fact, he was the abbot of Wat Bowon for several years. King Bhumibol, Crown Prince Vajiralongkorn and several other males in the royal family, have been temporarily ordained here as monks. Bangkok's second Buddhist university, Mahamakut University, is housed at Wat Bowon. India, Nepal and Sri Lanka all send monks to study here. Across the street from the main entrance to the wát are an English-language Buddhist bookshop and a Thai herbal clinic. Because of its royal status, be particularly careful to dress properly when visiting this wát – no shorts or sleeveless shirts. Entry is free and opening hours are unrestricted.

NATIONAL MUSEUM

On Th Na Phra That, west of Sanam Luang in Banglamphu, the National Museum is the largest in South-East Asia and an excellent place to learn something about Thai art.

Excellent free English-language tours of the museum are given on Wednesday (Buddhism) and Thursday (Thai art, religion and culture), starting from the ticket pavilion at 9.30 am. The tours are also conducted in French (Wednesday), German (Thursday) and Japanese (Wednesday). For more information on the tours, contact the museum at ☎ 02-215 8173. The museum is open from 9 am to 4 pm Wednesday to Sunday; admission is 20B.

JIM THOMPSON'S HOUSE

This is a great spot to see authentic Thai residential architecture and South-East Asian art. Located at the end of an undistinguished soi next to Khlong Saen Saep, the premises once belonged to American silk entrepreneur Jim Thompson, who deserves most of the credit for the worldwide popularity of Thai silk.

Thompson was a New York architect who briefly served in the Office of Strategic Services (OSS, the forerunner of the CIA) in Thailand during WWII. After the

BANGKOK

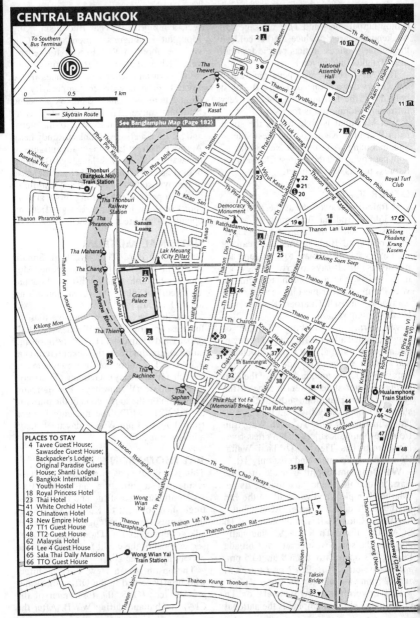

CENTRAL BANGKOK

To Southern
Bus Terminal

Skytrain Route

0   0.5   1 km

See Banglamphu Map (Page 182)

To Southern
Bus Terminal

Tha
Thewet

National
Assembly
Hall

Royal Turf
Club

Thonburi
(Bangkok Noi)
Train Station

Tha Thonburi
Railway
Station

Tha
Phrannok

Sanam
Luang

Democracy
Monument

Khlong
Bangkok Noi

Tha Maharat

Tha Chang

Lak Meuang
(City Pillar)

Khlong
Phadung
Krung
Kasem

Khlong Saen Saep

Grand
Palace

Tha Thien

Khlong Mon

Tha
Rachinee

Tha
Saphan
Phut

Phra Phut Yot Fa
(Memorial) Bridge

Tha Ratchawong

Hualamphong
Train Station

Wong
Wian
Yai

Wong Wian Yai
Train Station

Taksin
Bridge

PLACES TO STAY

4   Tavee Guest House;
    Sawasdee Guest House;
    Backpacker's Lodge;
    Original Paradise Guest
    House; Shanti Lodge
6   Bangkok International
    Youth Hostel
18 Royal Princess Hotel
23 Thai Hotel
41 White Orchid Hotel
42 Chinatown Hotel
43 New Empire Hotel
47 TT1 Guest House
48 TT2 Guest House
62 Malaysia Hotel
64 Lee 4 Guest House
65 Sala Thai Daily Mansion
66 TTO Guest House

CENTRAL BANGKOK

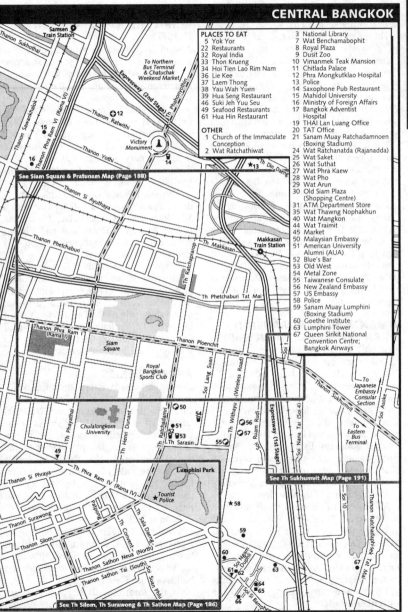

PLACES TO EAT
5 Yok Yor
22 Restaurants
32 Royal India
33 Thon Krueng
34 Hoi Tien Lao Rim Nam
36 Lie Kee
37 Laem Thong
38 Yau Wah Yuen
39 Hua Seng Restaurant
46 Suki Jeh Yuu Seu
49 Seafood Restaurants
61 Hua Hin Restaurant

OTHER
1 Church of the Immaculate Conception
2 Wat Ratchathiwat
3 National Library
7 Wat Benchamabophit
8 Royal Plaza
9 Dusit Zoo
10 Vimanmek Teak Mansion
11 Chitlada Palace
12 Phra Mongkutklao Hospital
13 Police
14 Saxophone Pub Restaurant
15 Mahidol University
16 Ministry of Foreign Affairs
17 Bangkok Adventist Hospital
19 THAI Lan Luang Office
20 TAT Office
21 Sanam Muay Ratchadamnoen (Boxing Stadium)
24 Wat Ratchanatda (Rajanadda)
25 Wat Saket
26 Wat Suthat
27 Wat Phra Kaew
28 Wat Pho
29 Wat Arun
30 Old Siam Plaza (Shopping Centre)
31 ATM Department Store
35 Wat Thawng Nophakhun
40 Wat Mangkon
44 Wat Traimit
45 Market
50 Malaysian Embassy
51 American University Alumni (AUA)
52 Blue's Bar
53 Old West
54 Metal Zone
55 Taiwanese Consulate
56 New Zealand Embassy
57 US Embassy
58 Police
59 Sanam Muay Lumphini (Boxing Stadium)
60 Goethe Institute
63 Lumphini Tower
67 Queen Sirikit National Convention Centre; Bangkok Airways

war he moved to Bangkok and developed an export market for Thai silk.

Thompson, who disappeared under quite mysterious circumstances in the Cameron Highlands of west Malaysia in 1967, collected parts of various derelict Thai homes in central Thailand and reassembled them in the current location in 1959. On display in the main house is his small but splendid Asian art collection as well as his personal belongings.

The house, on Soi Kasem San 2, off Th Rama I, is open from 9 am to 5 pm Monday to Saturday. When few people are around, it sometimes closes as early as 4.30 pm, so be sure to arrive earlier. Admission is 100B (proceeds go to Bangkok's School for the Blind) but you can wander around the grounds for free. Students under 25 years get in for 40B. The rather sleazy *khlong* at the end of the soi is one of Bangkok's most lively. Beware of well dressed touts in the soi who will tell you Thompson's house is closed – it's just a ruse to take you on a buying spree.

VIMANMEK TEAK MANSION (PHRA THII NANG WIMANMEK)

First built on Ko Si Chang in 1868 and moved to the present site in the Chitlada Palace grounds in 1910, this beautiful L-shaped, three storey mansion is said to be the world's largest golden teak building.

English-language tours leave every half hour beginning at 9.45 am. The tour covers around 30 rooms and lasts an hour. Smaller adjacent buildings display historic photography documenting the Chakri Dynasty. Thai classical and folk dances are performed at 10.30 am and 2 pm in a pavilion on the canal side of the mansion.

Admission is free if you've already been to the Grand Palace/Wat Phra Kaew and still have the entry ticket for Vimanmek/Abhisek. Otherwise it's 50B for adults, 20B for children. Vimanmek is open from 9.30 am to 3 pm daily. As this is royal property, visitors wearing shorts or sleeveless shirts will be refused entry. Call ☎ 02-281 4715 for further details.

ABHISEK DUSIT THRONE HALL (PHRA THII NANG APHISEK DUSIT)

Also in Chitlada Palace grounds, this hall is a smaller wood, brick and stucco structure completed in 1904 for Rama V. Typical of fine architecture of this era, the Victorian-influenced gingerbread- and Moorish-style porticoes blend to create a striking and distinctly Thai exterior. The hall houses an excellent display of regional handiwork crafted by members of the Promotion of Supplementary Occupations & Related Techniques (SUPPORT) foundation, an organisation sponsored by the queen.

Abhisek is open from 10 am to 4 pm daily, and admission is 50B (or free with a Wat Phra Kaew/Grand Palace/Vimanmek ticket). As at Wat Phra Kaew and Vimanmek, visitors must be properly dressed – no sleeveless shirts or shorts.

Vimanmek and Abhisek lie towards the northern end of the Chitlada Palace grounds, off Th U-Thong Nai (between Th Si Ayuthaya and Th Ratwithi), across from the western side of the Dusit Zoo. Air-con bus No 3 (Th Ayuthaya), air-con bus No 10 (Th Ratwithi) or red micro-bus No 4 (Th Ratwithi) will drop you nearby.

ART GALLERIES

Housed in an early Ratanakosin Era building opposite the National Theatre on Th Chao Fa in Banglamphu, the **National Gallery** (☎ 02-281 2224) displays traditional and contemporary art, mostly by artists who receive government support; the general consensus is that it's not Thailand's best, but the gallery is worth a visit for die-hard art fans or if you're in the vicinity. The gallery is closed Monday and Tuesday, and open from 9 am to 4 pm on other days. Admission is 30B.

Silpakorn University (near Wat Phra Kaew) is Bangkok's fine arts university and has a gallery of student works; it's open weekdays from 8 am to 7 pm, weekends and holidays from 8 am to 4 pm.

At the forefront of the contemporary Buddhist art movement is the **Visual**

Dhamma Art Gallery (☎ 02-258 5879) at 44/28 Soi Asoke (Soi 21), Th Sukhumvit. It's open Monday to Friday from 1 to 6 pm, Saturday from 10 am to 5 pm, or at other times by appointment. Although the address is Soi Asoke, the gallery is actually off Asoke – coming from Th Sukhumvit, take the second right into a small lane opposite Singha Bier Haus.

Bangkok's latest trend in public art consumption is the 'gallery pub', an effort to place art in a social context rather than leaving it to sterile galleries and museums. About Studio/About Cafe (☎ 02-623 1742), 402-408 Th Maitrichit, is the best of several venues that attempt to combine gallery with social space. The place that actually initiated this trend, Ruang Pung Art Community, opposite section 13 in Chatuchak Weekend Market, has been in business around 12 years. It's open weekends from 11 am to 6 pm and features rotating exhibits. Also in Chatuchak Market is the very active Sunday Gallery (Sunday Plaza), which contrary to its name is open Monday, Wednesday and Friday from 10 am to 5 pm, Saturday and Sunday from 7 am to 7 pm.

CHINATOWN (SAMPENG)

Bangkok's Chinatown, off Th Yaowarat and Th Ratchawong, comprises a confusing and crowded array of jewellery, hardware, wholesale food, automotive and fabric shops, as well as dozens of other small businesses. It's a good place to shop since goods here are cheaper than almost anywhere else in Bangkok, and the Chinese proprietors like to bargain, especially along Soi Wanit 1 (Sampeng Lane). Chinese and Thai antiques of various vintages, some authentic some less so are available in the so-called Thieves' Market (Nakhon Kasem), but it's better for browsing than buying these days.

PAHURAT

At the edge of Chinatown, around the intersection of Th Pahurat (Phahurat) and Th Chakraphet (Chakkaphet), is a small but thriving Indian district, generally called Pahurat. Here dozens of Indian vendors sell all kinds of fabric and clothes. This is the best place in the city to bargain for such items, especially silk.

Behind the more obvious shopfronts along these streets is a seemingly endless Indian bazaar selling not only fabric, but household items, food and other necessities. There are also some good, reasonably priced Indian restaurants in this area.

DUSIT ZOO (SUAN SAT DUSIT)

The collection of animals at Bangkok's 19-hectare zoo includes relatively rare indigenous species such as banteng, gaur, serow and rhinoceros, and is one of the best zoological facilities in South-East Asia.

A couple of lakeside restaurants serve good, inexpensive Thai food. Entry to the zoo is 20B for adults, 5B for children, 10B for those over 60; it's open from 9 am to 6 pm daily. Sunday can be a bit crowded.

The zoo is in the Dusit district between Chitlada Palace and the National Assembly Hall; the main entrance is off Th Ratwithi. Buses that pass the entrance include the ordinary Nos 18 and 28 and the air-con No 10.

LUMPHINI PARK

Named after Buddha's birthplace in Nepal, this is Bangkok's largest and most popular park. It is bordered by Th Rama IV to the south, Th Sarasin to the north, Th Withayu to the east and Th Ratchadamri to the west, with entrance gates on all sides. A large artificial lake (with boats for rent) in the centre is surrounded by broad, well tended lawns, wooded areas and walking paths.

In the early morning before 7 am legions of Chinese practise t'ai chi here. Also in the morning, vendors set up tables to dispense fresh snake blood and bile, considered health tonics by many Thais and Chinese.

From mid-February to April, Lumphini is a favoured kite flying zone; kites *(wâo)* can be purchased in the park during these months.

RIVER & CANAL TRIPS

The wheeled motor vehicle has long been Bangkok's conveyance of choice, but fortunately it hasn't yet become universal. A vast

BANGKOK

network of canals and river tributaries surrounding Bangkok still carry a motley fleet of watercraft, from canoes to rice barges. In these areas many homes, trading houses and temples remain oriented towards water life and provide a fascinating glimpse into the past, when Thais still considered themselves *jâo nâam* or 'water lords'.

Chao Phraya River Express

You can observe urban river life for 1½ hours for only 9B (or 10B on certain special express craft) by climbing aboard a Chao Phraya River Express boat at Tha Wat Ratchasingkhon, just north of Krungthep Bridge. If you want to ride the entire length of the express route all the way to Nonthaburi, this is where you must begin. Ordinary bus Nos 1, 17 and 75 and air-con bus No 4 pass Tha Ratchasingkhon. Or you could board at any other express boat pier in Bangkok for a shorter ride to Nonthaburi. Express boats run about every 15 minutes from 5.30 am to 6 pm daily. See the 'Know Your Boats' boxed text in the Getting Around section later in this chapter for more information on the Chao Phraya River Express service.

Other Canal Taxis

Another good boat trip is the **Bangkok Noi canal taxi** route which leaves from Tha Maharat. You can sometimes also catch taxis from nearby Tha Chang. The fare is reasonable, and the farther up Khlong Bangkok Noi you go, the better the scenery becomes, with teak houses on stilts, old wáts and plenty of greenery.

From Tha Tien pier near Wat Pho, you can get a canal taxi along **Khlong Mon** (leaving every half hour from 6.30 am to 6 pm, 4B) for more typical canal scenery, including orchid farms. A longer excursion could be made by making a loop along the khlongs Bangkok Noi, Chak Phra and then Mon, an all day trip. An outfit called Chao Phraya Charters (☎ 02-433 5453) runs a tour boat to Khlong Mon from Tha Tien each afternoon from 3 to 5 pm for 300B per person, including refreshments.

Boats from Tha Chang to **Bang Yai** (10B) leave every half hour from 6.15 am to 10 pm – this is the same trip that passes the Bang Khu Wiang Floating Market. Though this touristy market itself is over by 7 am, this trip is worthwhile later in the day as it passes a number of interesting wáts, traditional wooden homes and the Royal Barges, ornate long former war vessels now only used for high royal occasions.

Boat Charters

If you want to see the Thonburi canals at your own pace, the best thing to do is charter a longtail boat – it needn't be expensive if you can get a small group together to share the costs. The usual price is 300B to 400B per hour and you can choose from among eight canals in Thonburi alone. Beware of 'agents' who try to put you on the boat and rake off an extra commission. Before travelling by boat, establish the price – you can't bargain when you're in the middle of the river!

The best piers for hiring a boat are **Tha Chang**, **Tha Saphaan Phut** and **Tha Si Phraya**. Close to the latter, to the rear of the River City complex, the Boat Tour Centre charges the same basic hourly price (400B) and there are no hassles with touts. Of these four piers, Tha Chang usually has the largest selection of boats.

Dinner Cruises

A dozen or more companies run regular cruises along the Chao Phraya River for rates ranging from 70B to 700B per person, depending on how far they go and whether dinner is included. Most require advance bookings.

The less expensive, more casual cruise operators allow you to order as little or as much as you want from moderately priced menus; a modest charge of 40B to 70B per person is added to the bill for the cruise. It's a fine way to dine outdoors when the weather is hot, away from city traffic and cooled by a river breeze. Those dinner cruises offering the a la carte menu plus surcharge include:

Khanap Nam Restaurant
(☎ 02-433 6611) Krungthon Bridge to Sathon Bridge; twice daily

Loy Nava Co
(☎ 02-437 4932) Offers a more swanky weekend dinner cruise, from Krungthon Bridge to Rama IX Bridge, for a set price of 880B for the cruise and dinner; beer and liquor cost extra.

Riverside Company
(☎ 02-434 0090) Krungthon Bridge to Rama IX Bridge; daily

Yok Yor Restaurant
(☎ 02-281 1829) Yok Yor Restaurant (Tha Wisut Kasat) to Rama IX Bridge; daily

Sunset Cruise
Two hours before its regular 2½ hour 7.30 pm dinner cruise, the *Manohra* sails from the Marriott Royal Garden Riverside Hotel for an hour-long sunset cocktail cruise. Boarding is free; passengers are only charged for drinks purchased from the well-stocked on-board bar. A free river taxi operates between the River City pier and the Royal Garden pier at 5 pm, just in time for the 5.30 pm cruise departure. Call ☎ 02-476 0021 for more information.

FLOATING MARKETS
Among the most heavily published photo images of Thailand are those of wooden canoes laden with multicoloured fruits and vegetables, paddled by Thai women wearing indigo-hued clothes and wide-brimmed straw hats. Such floating markets *(talàat náam)* do exist scattered throughout the huge canal system surrounding Bangkok – but if you don't know where to go you may end up at a very unauthentic tourist-show scene.

There is a large if somewhat commercial floating market on **Khlong Damnoen Saduak** in Ratchaburi Province, 104km south-west of Bangkok, between Nakhon Pathom and Samut Songkhram. You can catch a bus from the Southern bus terminal on Th Charan Sanitwong in Thonburi to Damnoen Saduak starting at 6 am. Get there as early in the morning as possible to avoid the hordes.

PLACES TO STAY – BUDGET
Bangkok has perhaps the best variety and quality of budget places to stay of any Asian

capital, which is one of the reasons it's such a popular destination for roving world travellers. Because of the wide distribution of places, you might first narrow your choices by deciding what part of the city you want to be in – the tourist shopping ghettos of Th Sukhumvit and Th Silom-Surawong, the backpackers' ghetto of Banglamphu, the centrally located Siam Square area, boisterous Chinatown or the old travellers' centre around Soi Ngam Duphli, off Th Rama IV.

Chinatown (around Hualamphong station) and Banglamphu are the best all-round areas for seeing the real Bangkok, and are the cheapest districts for eating and sleeping. The Siam Square area is also well located, in that it's more or less in the centre of Bangkok – this, coupled with the good selection of city buses that pass through the Rama I and Th Phayathai intersection, makes even more of the city accessible. In addition, this area has good bookshops, several banks, shopping centres, excellent mid-range restaurants, travel agencies and eight movie theatres within a 10 to 15 minute walk.

In Bangkok, budget accommodation will be taken to mean places costing from 80B to 550B per night.

Banglamphu
If you're really on a tight budget head for the Th Khao San area, near the Democracy Monument, parallel to Th Ratchadamnoen Klang – ordinary bus Nos 2, 15, 17, 44, 56 and 59 will get you there, also air-con bus Nos 11 and 12. This is still very much the main travellers' centre and new guesthouses are continually springing up.

Rates in Banglamphu are the lowest in Bangkok and although some of the places are barely adequate (bedbugs are sometimes a problem), a few are excellent value if you can afford just a bit more. At the budget end, rooms are quite small and the walls dividing them are thin – in fact most are indistinguishable from one another. Some places have small attached cafes with limited menus. Bathrooms are usually down the hall or out the back somewhere; mattresses may be on the floor.

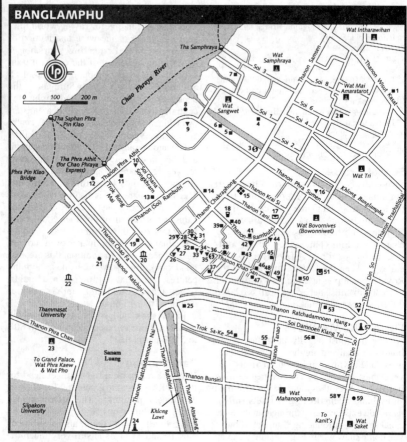

BANGLAMPHU

The least expensive rooms are 80/120B (60/100B with haggling in the low season) for singles/doubles, though these are hard to come by due to the hordes of people seeking them out. More common are the 100/140B rooms. Occasionally, triple rooms are available for as low as 160B and dorm beds for 50B. During most of the year, it pays to visit several guesthouses before making a decision, but in the high season (December to February), when Th Khao San is bursting with life), you'd better take

the first vacant bed you come across. The best time of day to find a vacancy is from around 9 to 10 am.

There are now close to 100 guesthouses in the immediate vicinity of Th Khao San, too many to list here. If you haven't already arrived with a recommendation in hand, you might best use the Banglamphu and Th Khao San area maps and simply pick a place at random for your first night. If you're not satisfied you can stow your gear and explore the area till something better turns up. The

BANGLAMPHU

PLACES TO STAY
1 Trang Hotel; Vieng Travel
2 AP Guest House
4 Villa Guest House
5 Gipsy Guest House
6 PS Guest House
7 River House
11 Phra Athit Mansion
13 Mango
14 Sawasdee House
19 Chai's House
25 Royal Hotel
32 Prakorp's House & Restaurant
37 Sawasdee Bangkok Inn
38 Orm; Wally House
39 Green House
40 Viengtai Hotel
41 Orchid House
43 Marco Polo Hostel
45 VS Guest House
46 Classic Place
47 Siri Guest House
50 Central Guest House

53 Sweety Guest House
54 Palace Hotel
55 Smile Guest House
56 Rajdamnoen Hotel

PLACES TO EAT
9 Roti-Mataba
10 Raan Kin Duem
16 Yod Kum
26 Chinese Noodle & Wonton Shop
27 No-Name Food Shop; Padung Chiip Mask Shop
28 Gulliver's Traveler's Tavern
29 Gaylord Indian Restaurant
30 Chochana
33 Hello Restaurant
34 Bangkok Center Restaurant
35 Royal Indian Restaurant
42 Chabad House
44 Pizza Hut
48 Buddy Beer Garden, Restaurant & Swimming Pool

49 Arawy Det
52 McDonald's
58 Arawy

OTHER
3 Siam Commercial Bank
8 Phra Sumen Fort
12 UNICEF
15 Banglamphu Department Store
17 Post Office
18 Salvador Dali
20 National Gallery; National Film Archives
21 National Theatre
22 National Museum
23 Wat Mahathat
24 City Pillar
31 Chana Songkhram Police Station
36 Krung Thai Bank
51 Mosque
57 Democracy Monument
59 City Hall

guesthouses along Th Khao San tend to be cubicles in modern shophouses, while those in Banglamphu's quieter lanes and alleys are often housed in old homes, some of them with a lot of character.

At the cheaper places it's not worth calling ahead, since the staff usually won't hold a room for you unless you pay in advance. For places that *may* take phone reservations phone numbers are included.

There are innumerable simple, adequate places on or just off Th Khao San. One that is highly recommended is *Prakorp's House & Restaurant,* where singles/doubles in a teak house cost 90/200B, and they serve good coffee.

A newcomer in the hotel category is *Sawasdee Bangkok Inn (☎ 02-280 1251, fax 281 7818, email sawasdee@sawasdee-hotels.com, 126/2 Th Khao San),* with three floors around a courtyard designed to look like early Ratanakosin but somehow coming off more like Creole New Orleans. A bed in a dorm room costs 100B, while a fan room with shared toilet is 200B. For 250B you can get an air-con room with shared facilities. Rooms with private bath cost 300B

to 350B with fan or 400B to 450B with air-con. All rooms have cable TV, hot showers and towels.

Two narrow alleys between Th Khao San and Th Rambutri feature a string of cramped places that nonetheless manage to fill up. All feature small, luggage-crammed lobbies with staircases leading to rooms layered on several floors and which cost around 80B to 150B. *Green House (☎ 02-281 0323),* in the more westerly of the two alleys is a bit more expansive than the rest, with a restaurant downstairs and rooms with fan and private bath for 150B to 280B, 380B for air-con doubles.

Moving just slightly upscale, friendly *Orchid House (☎ 02-280 2691),* near the Viengtai Hotel on Th Rambutri (north of Th Khao San, and sometimes called Soi Rambutri), offers quiet, clean apartment-style rooms for 350B single with fan and hot water, 380/430B single/double with air-con or 480B for larger air-con rooms.

There are several guesthouses clustered in the alleys east of Th Tanao. In general, rooms are bigger and quieter here than at places around Th Khao San. *Central Guest*

House (☎ 02-282 0667) is just off Th Tanao on Trok Bowonrangsi – look for the rather inconspicuous signs. Clean, simple rooms go for 80/150B single/double.

Farther south, on a small road parallel to Ratchadamnoen Klang is *Sweety Guest House* with small windowless rooms for 80B to 100B single, larger doubles for 120B to 200B and air-con rooms for 350B. Sweety has a roof terrace for lounging and for hanging laundry.

On the other side of Ratchadamnoen Klang, south of the Th Khao San area, are a couple of independent hotels and at least one guesthouse worth investigating. If you walk south along Th Tanao from Ratchadamnoen Klang, then left at the first soi, you'll come to *Rajdamnoen Hotel* (☎ 02-224 1012). Formerly known as Hotel 90, it's now a bit more respectable; large, clean singles/doubles with fan and private bath are 200/250B, 400B with air-con and TV.

Return west on this soi to Th Tanao, turn left and then take the right at Trok Sa-Ke towards the upper mid-range Royal Hotel, and after 50m or so you'll come to the relatively new *Smile Guest House* (☎ 02-622 1590, fax 622 0730), which offers quiet, very clean rooms with private toilet and cold shower in a four storey building for 250B with fan, 350B with air-con. There's a cafe downstairs. Another 50m or so farther west stands the *Palace Hotel* (☎ 02-224 1876), an all air-con version of the Rajdamnoen Hotel with rooms at 330/400B.

Several long-running guesthouses are on sois between Th Chakraphong and the Chao Phraya River, putting them within walking distance of Tha Phra Athit where you can catch express boats. This area is also close to the Thonburi (Bangkok Noi) station across the river, the National Museum and the National Theatre.

West of Chakraphong on Th Rambutri, *Sawasdee House* (☎ 02-281 8138, fax 629 0994) follows the trend towards hotel-style accommodation in the Th Khao San area, with a large restaurant downstairs and small to medium-sized rooms on several floors

upstairs. Fan rooms with shared facilities are 146B to 214B single, 257B to 300B double. Rooms with private bath and fan cost 265B to 335B, while air-con rooms go for 510B.

Mango, in a tin-roofed wooden house set back from Th Rambutri, is the cheapest in the area at 80/140B, though the ambience is rather seedy.

Also in this vicinity, off the southern end of Th Rambutri, the family run *Chai's House* offers clean rooms for 100/200/300B single/double/triple, or 300B single/double with air-con, all with shared bathroom. It's a quiet, security-conscious place with a sitting area out the front. The food must be cheap and good, as it's a favourite gathering spot for local Thai college students on weekends.

At 11/1 Soi Surao, off Th Chakraphong towards the Banglamphu department store and market, the friendly *BK Guest House* (☎ 02-281 3048) offers clean rooms with shared bath for 120/150B with fan, 300/ 350B with air-con. *PS Guest House* (☎ 02-282 3932), a Peace Corps favourite, is near the river end of Th Phra Sumen, off the south side of Khlong Banglamphu; well kept rooms go for 130B to 190B. Next door is the similar *Gipsy Guest House*, 110B to 180B streetside, 150B to 230B canalside (the latter have more windows). On the opposite side of Phra Sumen in this area is an alley with a couple of cheapies.

Off Th Samsen, north of Khlong Banglamphu, is a small cluster of guesthouses in convenient proximity to the Tha Samphraya river express landing. On Soi 1 Samsen, *Villa Guest House* (☎ 02-281 7009) is a quiet, leafy, private old teak house with 10 rooms from 200B to 450B; it's often full. Up on Soi 3 Samsen (also known as Soi Wat Samphraya), is the *River House* (☎ 02-280 0876), with small but clean rooms with shared bathroom for 100B to 150B. There are two other similar places here, but this is the best one. Note that Soi 3 zigs left, then zags right before reaching these three guesthouses, a good 10 minute walk from Th Samsen.

East of Th Samsen, near Wat Mai Amaratarot is *AP Guest House*, at 50/80B single/double probably the cheapest guest-house in Banglamphu.

Thewet & National Library Area

The district north of Banglamphu near the National Library is another little travellers' enclave. Heading north up Th Samsen from Th Wisut Kasat, you'll come to *TV Guest House* (*7 Soi Phra Sawat*), just off Th Samsen to the east. It's clean, modern and good value at 50B for a dorm bed, 100B a double.

Half a kilometre or so farther north across the canal is the intersection of Th Si Ayuthaya and Th Samsen. Just beyond this junction is the National Library. On two parallel sois that run off Th Si Ayuthaya towards the river (west from Samsen) are four guesthouses all run by various members of the same extended family: *Tavee Guest House* (☎ 02-282 5983), *Sawasdee Guest House* (☎ 02-282 5349), *Backpacker's Lodge* (☎ 02-282 3231), and *Original Paradise Guest House* (☎ 02-282 8673). All except the Paradise are clean, well kept and fairly quiet. Prices at all of them start at 150/200B for singles/doubles. The Sawasdee also offers dorm beds for just 50B. *Shanti Lodge* (☎ 02-281 2497) on the corner of this soi costs a bit more – 230/250B for fan rooms, 400/450B with air-con, or 100B for a dorm bed. Some visitors reckon it's worth the extra cost, others don't.

There's a good market across the road from these sois, and a few small noodle and rice shops along Th Krung Kasem, south of and parallel to Si Ayuthaya (and west of Th Samsen). Ordinary bus Nos 16, 30 and 53, and air-con bus Nos 56 and 6 pass Th Si Ayuthaya while going up and down Th Samsen; ordinary bus No 72 terminates on the corner of Th Phitsanulok and Th Samsen, a short walk from Th Si Ayuthaya. Air-con bus No 10 from the airport also passes close to the area along Th Ratwithi to the north, before crossing Krungthon Bridge.

East of Th Samsen you'll find the *Bangkok International Youth Hostel* (☎ 02-282 0950, fax 628 7416, 25/2 Th Phitsanulok). A bed in the eight-bed fan dorm costs 70B a night, while in the air-con dorm it's 90B.

Rooms with fan, air-con and private hot bath cost 250/300B single/double. There's a cafeteria downstairs. The hostel won't accept non-members as guests. Annual Hostelling International (formerly IYHF) membership costs 300B, or you can purchase a temporary membership for 50B.

Chinatown & Hualamphong Station

This area is central and colourful although rather noisy. There are numerous cheap hotels but it's not a travellers' centre like Soi Ngam Duphli or Banglamphu. Watch your pockets and bags around the Hualamphong area, both on the street and on the bus. The cream of the razor artists operate here as the train passengers make good pickings.

The *New Empire Hotel* (☎ 02-234 6990/6, fax 234 6997, 572 Th Yaowarat) is near the Th Charoen Krung intersection, a short walk from Wat Traimit. Air-con rooms with hot water are 444B to 500B, with a few more expensive rooms for up to 800B – a bit noisy but a great location if you like Chinatown. The New Empire is a favourite among Chinese Thais from Thailand's southern regions.

Other Chinatown hotels of this calibre, most without English signs, can be found along Th Yaowarat, Th Chakraphet and Th Ratchawong.

Straddling the budget and mid-range is the *River View Guest House* (☎ 02-234 5429, 235 8501, fax 237 5428, 768 Soi Pha-nurangsi, Th Songwat) in the Talaat Noi area south of Chinatown – wedged between Bangrak (Silom) and Chinatown (see the Th Silom, Th Surawong & Th Sathon map). The building is behind the Jao Seu Kong Chinese shrine, about 400m from the Royal Orchid Sheraton, in a neighbourhood filled with small machine shops. To get there, turn right from the corner of Th Si Phraya (facing the River City shopping complex), take the fourth left, then the first right. Large rooms are 450B with fan and private bath, 690B with air-con and hot water. As the name suggests, many rooms have a Chao Phraya River view; the view from the 8th

TH SILOM, TH SURAWONG & TH SATHON

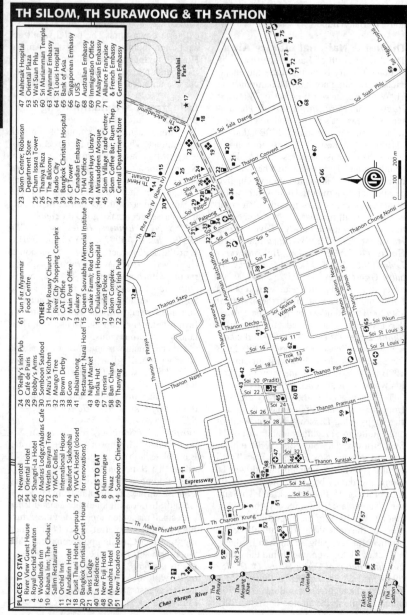

PLACES TO STAY
1 River View Guest House
4 Royal Orchid Sheraton
6 Woodlands Inn
10 Kabana Inn; The Cholas;
    Sallim Restaurant
11 Orchid Inn
12 Mandarin Hotel
18 Dusit Thani Hotel; Cyberpub
20 Bangkok Christian Guest House
21 Swiss Lodge
40 La Residence
48 New Fuji Hotel
50 Manohra Hotel
51 New Trocadero Hotel
52 Newrotel
54 Oriental Hotel
56 Shangri-La Hotel
62 Madras Lodge;Madras Cafe
72 Westin Banyan Tree
73 YMCA Collins
    International House
74 Beaufort Sukhothai
75 YWCA Hostel (closed
    for renovations)

PLACES TO EAT
8 Harmonique
9 Naaz
14 Somboon Chinese

24 O'Reilly's Irish Pub
28 Café de Paris
29 Bobby's Arms
30 Somboon Seafood
31 Mizu's Kitchen
32 Mango Tree
33 Brown Derby
38 Goro
41 Rabianthong
    Restaurant; Narai Hotel
43 Night Market
49 India Hut
57 Tiensin
58 Ban Chiang
59 Thanying

61 Sun Far Myanmar
    Food Centre

OTHER
2 Holy Rosary Church
3 River City Shopping Complex
5 CAT Office
7 Main Post Office
13 Galaxy
15 Queen Saovabha Memorial Institute
    (Snake Farm); Red Cross
16 Chulalongkorn Hospital
17 Tourist Police
19 Silom Complex
22 Delaney's Irish Pub

23 Silom Centre; Robinson
    Department Store
25 Charn Issara Tower
26 Thaniya Plaza
27 The Balcony
34 Radio City
35 Bangkok Christian Hospital
36 CP Tower
37 Canadian Embassy
39 THAI Office
42 Neilson Hays Library
44 Mirasaddeen Mosque
45 Silom Village Trade Centre;
    Silom Coffee Bar; Ruen Thep
46 Central Department Store

47 Mahesak Hospital
53 Oriental Plaza
55 Wat Suan Phlu
60 Sri Mariamman Temple
63 Myanmar Embassy
64 St Louis Hospital
65 Bank of Asia
66 Singaporean Embassy
67 USIS
68 Australian Embassy
69 Immigration Office
70 Malaysian Embassy
71 Alliance Française
    & French Embassy
76 German Embassy

floor restaurant is superb, even if you have
to wake up the staff to get a meal. If you call
from the River City complex, someone from
the guesthouse will pick you up. It's not far
from the Tha Ratchawong pier.

At least four cheap Chinese hotels can be
found west of the station along Th Maitrichit, all in the 120B to 200B range.

Also convenient to Hualamphong station,
and more suitable for stays of more than a
night or two, are the TT guesthouses. The
somewhat easier-to-find *TT 2 Guest House*
(☎ 02-236 2946, 516-518 Soi Sawang, Th Si
Phraya) is near the Th Mahanakhon intersection. Rooms here are 180B. To find the
TT 2 from the train station, turn left onto
Rama IV, right on Mahanakhon, left on Soi
Kaew Fa and then right on Soi Sawang. Or
from Si Phraya turn directly onto Soi
Sawang. To find the more hidden *TT 1
Guest House* (☎ 02-236 3053, 138 Soi Wat
Mahaphuttharam, Th Mahanakhon) from
the station, cross Th Rama IV, walk left
down Rama IV, then right on Mahanakhon
and follow the signs for TT 1. It's only
about a 10 minute walk from the station.
Dorm beds are just 50B; singles/doubles go
for 160B. Baggage storage and laundry service are available; both TTs enforce a strict
midnight curfew.

Th Silom & Th Surawong
Several cheaper mid-range guesthouses and
hotels can be found in and around the Silom
and Surawong area.

Opposite the central post office, on
Charoen Krung, are a couple of guesthouses
catering mostly to middle-class north Indians, Pakistanis and Bangladeshis – *Naaz* and
Kabana Inn, each charging a reasonable
400B to 500B for air-con rooms. Just a bit
more expensive but offering better service is
the *Woodlands Inn* (☎ 02-235 3894), on the
soi running along the northern side of the
central post office. Smaller air-con rooms
without refrigerators and no lift access are
available for 350B to 450B. Clean, air-con
rooms with hot water, phone, TV and fridge
are 600/700B single/double. Downstairs is
an air-con Indian restaurant, The Cholas.

Madras Lodge (☎ 02-235 6761), in Trok
Vaithi off Th Silom, not far from the Sri
Mariamman (Maha Uma Devi) Temple, has
somewhat unkempt rooms with fan starting
at 220B. The proprietor is a friendly retired
gem dealer from Madras and his kitchen
serves delicious south Indian food.

Soi Ngam Duphli
This area off Th Rama IV is where most
budget travellers used to come in the 70s
and early 80s. With a couple of notable exceptions, most places here are not especially
cheap or even good value any more, and the
area has become slightly seedy. Overall,
Banglamphu has better-value accommodation, although some travellers still prefer
less-crowded Soi Ngam Duphli, which has
less of a 'scene', and some places are good
value indeed. Several countries (Canada,
Australia, Germany, Singapore, Korea,
Laos, Myanmar) maintain embassies on
nearby Th Sathon, so it's also a convenient
location for those with visa/passport business at these embassies.

The entrance to the soi is on Th Rama
IV, near the Th Sathon Tai intersection,
and within walking distance of verdant
Lumphini Park and the Th Silom business
district. Ordinary bus Nos 4, 13, 14, 22, 45,
47, 74, 109 and 115, and air-con bus No 7
all pass by the entrance to Soi Ngam
Duphli along Th Rama IV.

Turn east from Ngam Duphli into Soi Si
Bamphen and before you reach the Boston
Inn take the alley to the right. Near the end
of the alley, *TTO Guest House* (☎ 02-286
6783, fax 287 1571) offers clean air-con
rooms for 350B, plus a few fan rooms for
250B, all with private bath and TV. Though
it isn't cheap, it's well managed with spacious rooms and reasonably friendly staff.

If you continue east along Soi Si Bamphen and turn left at the next soi, then take
the first right, you'll end up in a cul-de-sac
with four guesthouses of varying quality.
The best two are at either end; first on the
right as you enter the soi is the clean, secure
and well managed *Lee 4 Guest House* (the
best of the three Lees) with fan rooms for

BANGKOK

SIAM SQUARE & PRATUNAM

PLACES TO STAY
1 Siam City Hotel
3 Indra Regent Hotel
4 Classic Inn
5 Indra Regent Hotel
6 Borarn House
8 Amari Watergate
11 Opera Hotel
15 A-One Inn
17 Wendy House
18 Muangphol Mansion
31 Novotel Bangkok on Siam Square
37 Siam Orchid Inn
38 Le Meridien President
43 Hilton International Bangkok
45 Golden Palace Hotel
46 Holiday Mansion Hotel
49 Grand Hyatt Erawan
51 Regent Bangkok
55 Chateau de Bangkok
56 Jim's Lodge

PLACES TO EAT
16 Curry and Rice Vendors
19 Thai Sa Nyuan
22 Hard Rock Cafe
23 S & P Restaurant & Bakery
25 Scala; Penang; Bangkok
32 Coca Garden
40 Santa Barbara Grill

OTHER
2 Post Office
7 Pratunam Market
9 Nailert Market
10 Pantip Plaza
12 Indonesian Embassy
13 Tha Ratchathewi (Canal Taxis)
14 Jim Thompson's House
20 National Stadium
21 Mahboonkrong Shopping Centre
24 Scala Cinema
26 Siam Discovery Center
27 Siam Center
28 Lido Cinema
29 Siam Cinama
30 Post Office
33 Wat Patum
34 World Trade Centre
35 Narayana Phand
36 Robinson Department Store
39 Gaysorn Plaza; Planet Hollywood
41 TOT Office
42 Central Department Store
44 Post Office
47 UK Embassy
48 Erawan Shrine (Saan Phra Phrom)
50 Peninsula Plaza
52 Sogo Department Store
53 Maneeya Center
54 Tourist Police
57 Vietnam Embassy
58 US Embassy
59 US Visa Section

100/120B with shared bathroom, or 160/200B with private bath. Air-con rooms go for 350B. The friendly *Sala Thai Daily Mansion* (☎ 02-287 1436) is at the end of the alley and has large, very clean rooms for 150B to 200B, all with shared bathroom. A sitting area with TV on the 3rd floor makes for a pleasant gathering place, and there is a breezy rooftop terrace. The owner speaks English and her design background is evident in the tasteful furnishings. Many repeat or long-term guests fill the rooms here.

Th Sukhumvit

Staying in this area puts you in the newest part of Bangkok and the farthest from old Bangkok near the river. Taxis take longer to get here because of the one way street system. The majority of the hotels in this area are priced in the mid-range.

The oldest and most centrally located hostelry in the Sukhumvit area is the historic *Atlanta Hotel* (☎ 02-252 1650/6069, fax 255 2151, 78 Soi 2 (Soi Phasak), Th Sukhumvit). Owned since its construction in the 1950s by Dr Max Henn, a former secretary to the maharajah of Bikaner and owner of Bangkok's first international pharmacy, the Atlanta is a simple but reliable stand-by with clean, comfortable rooms in several price categories. Prices start at 300/400/ 500B for single/double/triple rooms with private shower, fan and balcony, and peak at 1200B for a large two-bedroom, air-con suite. Tax isn't included, but monthly stays paid in advance receive a 10% discount.

The Atlanta also has a swimming pool, coffee shop with a selection of international newspapers and evening videos which include film classics with Thailand themes (eg *Chang, Bridge on the River Kwai*). A map room and letter-writing lounge round out the offerings.

The L-shaped, aquamarine coloured *Golden Palace Hotel* (☎ 02-252 5115/ 5169, fax 254 1538, 15 Soi 1, Th Sukhumvit; see the Siam Square – Pratunam map) has a swimming pool, is well situated and costs 500B for a double with air-con and private bath. The clientele here are mostly middle-class tourists 'on a budget', but the Golden Palace has seen better days.

Moving farther out on Sukhumvit, the *Miami Hotel* (☎ 02-253 5611/3, 253 0369, fax 253 1266, 2 Soi 13, Th Sukhumvit) dates back to the 1960s and 1970s R&R period. The room and service quality seems to seesaw every three years or so but by all accounts it's decent value at 450/500B single/double for clean air-con rooms with hot water and TV, plus a small swimming pool and coffee shop; discounts for long-term stays.

Siam Square

Several good places can be found in this central area, which has the additional advantage of being on the Khlong Saen Saep canal taxi route.

There are several lower to mid-range places on or near Soi Kasem San 1, off Th Rama I near Jim Thompson's House and the National Stadium. *Muangphol (Muangphon) Mansion* (☎ 02-215 0033, fax 216 8053, 931/8 Th Rama I) on the corner of Soi

Kasem San 1 and Th Rama I has rooms from 500B. It's good value, with air-con, hot water, a 24 hour restaurant and good service.

On Soi Kasem San 1 is *Wendy House* (☎ 02-216 2436, fax 216 8053), where small but clean singles/doubles with air-con, hot shower and TV go for 350/450B. If you're carrying unusually heavy bags, note there's no lift. A small restaurant is on the ground floor.

Farther up the soi is *A-One Inn* (☎ 02-215 3029, fax 216 4771, 25/13-15 Soi Kasem San 1), a friendly and pleasant place that gets a lot of return business. Fair-sized air-con doubles with private bath, hot water and TV are 450B; spacious triples are 650B (rates may drop 100B in low season).

PLACES TO STAY – MID-RANGE

Bangkok is saturated with small and medium-sized hotels in this category (from roughly 500B to 1800B per night). The clientele are a very mixed bunch of Asian business travellers, western journalists on slim expense accounts, economy-class tour groups and a smattering of independent tourists who seem to have chosen their hotels at random. Not quite 'international class', these places often offer guests a better sense of being in Thailand than the luxury hotels.

In the off-season (March to November) you may be able to get a low-occupancy discount at these places.

Banglamphu

Before Th Khao San was 'discovered', the *Viengtai Hotel* (☎ 02-280 5434, fax 281 8153, 42 Th Rambutri) was the most popular in Banglamphu. Over the last decade or so the Viengtai has continually raised its prices (not always concomitant with an upgrading of facilities) until it now sits solidly in the middle-price range of Bangkok hotels. Standard singles/doubles/triples in the six storey old wing are 1225/1575/1750B while deluxe rooms in the remodelled nine storey new wing are 1575/1750/2275B; breakfast is included. A swimming pool is on the 3rd floor.

Close to the Tha Phra Athit riverboat stop, the apartment-style *Phra Athit Mansion* (☎ 02-280 0744, fax 280 0742, 22 Th Phra Athit) offers modern clean rooms with air-con, TV, hot showers and fridge for 650B single/double, 850B triple.

Besides the Oriental and the Atlanta, the oldest continually operating hotel in the city is the *Royal Hotel* (☎ 02-222 9111/26, fax 224 2083), still going strong on the corner of Ratchadamnoen Klang and Atsadang about 500m from the Democracy Monument. The Royal's 24 hour coffee shop is a favourite local rendezvous. Singles/doubles start at 960/1300B. One wing is currently being renovated and this may result in a price increase when finished. Most taxi drivers know this hotel as the 'Ratanakosin' (as the Thai sign on top of the building reads), not as the Royal.

Chinatown

Mid-range hotels in Chinatown are tough to find. The best bet is the *Chinatown Hotel* (☎ 02-225 0230, fax 226 1295, email malaysia@comnet3.ksc.net.th, 526 Th Yaowarat), with rooms for 700B to 1200B. *White Orchid Hotel* (☎ 02-226 0026, fax 255 6403, 409-421 Th Yaowarat), diagonally opposite the Chinatown Hotel, offers nicer accommodation beginning at 850B.

Th Silom & Th Surawong

This area is packed with upper mid-range places; discounts are often available between April and October. Bangkok's YMCA and YWCA are both in this area. The *YMCA Collins International House* (☎ 02-287 1900/2727, fax 287 1996, 27 Th Sathon Tai) has air-con rooms with TV, fridge, telephone, in-room safe and private bath for 1200B to 2200B, suites 2600B. Credit cards are accepted. Guests may use the Y's massage room, gym, track and swimming pool, and there's a coffee shop on the premises. The *YWCA Hostel* (☎ 02-237 6900, fax 287 3016, 13 Th Sathon Tai) was temporarily closed for re-modelling at the time of writing. It is expected to reopen in the near future with

cheaper air-con rooms, probably starting at around 1000B.

Bangkok Christian Guest House (☎ 02-233 6303, fax 237 1742, 123 Sala Daeng Soi 2, Th Convent) off Th Silom, has very nice air-con rooms for 640/910/1190B single/double/triple (plus 10% service), including breakfast. Lunch and dinner are also available at very low prices.

Classic mid-range hotels on Surawong include the *New Fuji* (☎ 02-234 5364, fax 233 4336), at No 299-310, with rooms from 1124B to 1338B, and the *New Trocadero Hotel* (☎ 02-234 8920/8, fax 234 8929) at No 343, where singles/doubles cost from 980B to 1190B, including breakfast. Because both hotels offer good service and amenities for under 1500B, they are favourites among journalists. A fair number of package tours stop here as well. A newer entry at No 173/8-9, *La Résidence* (☎ 02-233 3301, fax 237 9322, email residence@loxinfo.co.th), is an intimate 29 room place with a restaurant downstairs and daily rates of 950/1400B single/double (1200/1800B during the high season). Monthly rates are 650B to 950B per day, depending on room size.

A decent lower mid-range choice near the central post office and the river is the six storey *Newrotel* (☎ 02-237 1094, fax 237 1102, 1216/1 Th Charoen Krung). Clean air-con singles/doubles with TV cost 600B to 850B.

Near the Royal Orchid Sheraton, the River City complex and the river (Tha Si Phraya landing), the *Orchid Inn* (☎ 02-234 8934, fax 234 4159, 719/1-3 Th Si Phraya) provides decent mid-range value at 500/600B for tidy air-con single/doubles with TV and mini-fridge. Another advantage here is that the ordinary No 36 bus terminates almost directly opposite the hotel. The downside is the high number of touts and big-spending tourists in the neighbourhood.

Soi Ngam Duphli & Th Sathon

Near the southern end of Soi Ngam Duphli, *Malaysia Hotel* (☎ 02-679 7127/36, fax 287

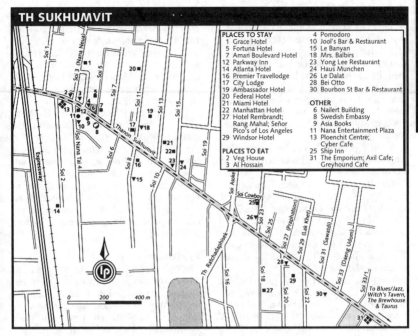

TH SUKHUMVIT

PLACES TO STAY		
1	Grace Hotel	
5	Fortuna Hotel	
7	Amari Boulevard Hotel	
12	Parkway Inn	
14	Atlanta Hotel	
16	Premier Travellodge	
17	City Lodge	
19	Ambassador Hotel	
20	Federal Hotel	
21	Miami Hotel	
22	Manhattan Hotel	
27	Hotel Rembrandt; Rang Mahal; Señor Pico's of Los Angeles	
29	Windsor Hotel	

4 Pomodoro
10 Jool's Bar & Restaurant
15 Le Banyan
18 Mrs. Balbirs
23 Yong Lee Restaurant
24 Haus Munchen
26 Le Dalat
28 Bei Otto
30 Bourbon St Bar & Restaurant

OTHER
6 Nailert Building
8 Swedish Embassy
9 Asia Books
11 Nana Entertainment Plaza
13 Ploenchit Centre; Cyber Cafe
25 Ship Inn
31 The Emporium; Axil Cafe; Greyhound Cafe

PLACES TO EAT
2 Veg House
3 Al Hossain

1457, 54 Soi Ngam Duphli) was once Bangkok's most famous budget travellers' hotel. Nowadays its air-con rooms with hot water cost from 548/636B for a standard single/double, 598/696B with a TV and small fridge and 740/790B with a TV, larger fridge and carpet. The Malaysia has a small swimming pool which may be used by visitors for 50B per day (it's free for guests). There's a small desk in the lobby where you can hook up your computer to check email, or use the house terminals. There seem to be fewer prostitutes around the lobby than in the old days – at least before midnight. After the Patpong bars close, bar girls who haven't already picked up a customer tend to congregate in the hotel coffee shop.

Well run *Charlie House* (☎ 02-679 8330, fax 679 7308), on a soi running north off Soi Si Bamphen, aims for a slightly more upscale market with carpeted rooms with

air-con, phone and TV starting at 750B (lower rates can be negotiated in off-season months like June and September). Smoking is prohibited; a sign in the reception area reads 'Decently dressed ladies, gentlemen and their children are welcome'.

Aquarius Guest House (*243 Soi Hutayan, Soi Suan Phlu, Th Sathon Tai)* is a quiet Thai-style place that courts a gay male clientele. It has satellite TV, a shady courtyard and rooms costing 750B per night.

Th Sukhumvit

This area is choked with hotels costing 800B to 1500B. Stick to the lower numbered sois to save cross-town travel time. Many of the Sukhumvit hotels in this price class were built as R&R hotels for soldiers on leave from Vietnam during the Indochina War era, 1962-74. Some made the transition from the soldiers-on-leave clientele to a traditional tourist base with style and grace, while others continue to have a slightly rough image.

A cluster of high-rise hotels on sois 3 and 4 for the most part cater to male tourists focused on the Nana Entertainment Plaza (NEP) girlie bar scene on Soi 4 (Soi Nana Tai). The well run *Parkway Inn*, on Sukhumvit at Soi 4, near the Landmark Hotel is better value than these at 700B to 800B a night; amenities include a rooftop pool.

A block over on Soi 5, but seemingly a world away from the NEP crowd, the older *Fortuna Hotel* (☎ 02-251 5121, fax 253 6282) offers 110 decent rooms with all the mod-cons for 900B to 1100B. Small, friendly *Premier Travelodge* (☎ 02-251 3031, 253-3201, fax 253 3195, 170-170/1 Soi 8 (Soi Prida), Th Sukhumvit) has rooms with air-con, carpet, safe deposit box, cable TV and video, refrigerator, hot water, phone and fax for 700B.

The *Federal Hotel* (☎ 02-253 0175, fax 253 5332, 27 Soi 11, Th Sukhumvit) is a favourite among Indochina War and Peace Corps vets with rooms for 800B to 1050B. The added-on rooms at ground level, which occasionally floods in the rainy season, aren't worth the price, so be sure to get one of the larger, older upstairs rooms. The small pool and large, plain coffee shop are the main attractions.

Dating back to the Indochina War era, the *Manhattan* (☎ 02-255 0166, fax 255 3481, 13 Soi 15, Th Sukhumvit) has good-sized and fairly well kept rooms starting at 1413B.

A bit nicer are the two *City Lodges* on sois 9 (☎ 02-253 7680, fax 255 4667) and 19 (☎ 02-254 4783, fax 255 7340). Rooms at either location are 1016B for a single or double, and include air-con, telephone, TV/video and mini-bar.

Siam Square, Th Ploenchit & Hualamphong

This area tends to offer either upper-end budget or top-end luxury hotels, with little in the middle.

Jim's Lodge (☎ 02-255 3100, fax 255 0190), on Soi Ruam Rudi off Th Ploenchit,

provides clean rooms with TV, fridge, air-con and carpeting in a six storey building for 1126B a night single/double.

The *Siam Orchid Inn* (☎ 02-255 3140/3, fax 255 3144), off Soi Gaysorn (Keson) close to Le Meridien President Hotel, offers well appointed rooms with all the amenities for around 1500B.

Opposite the UK embassy on Th Withayu, a little north of Th Ploenchit, the *Holiday Mansion Hotel* (☎ 02-255 009, fax 253 0130, 53 Th Withayu) is a simple but well-run mid-range place where good-sized rooms come with air-con, IDD phone and TV for a negotiated rate of around 1000B single/double per night, breakfast included. Other amenities include a pool, business centre and 24 hour coffee shop.

Pratunam

The *Opera Hotel* (☎ 02-252 4031, fax 253 5360, 16 Soi Somprasong 1, Th Phetchaburi) is very near the heart of Pratunam and features air-con doubles with hot water from 550B to 800B. The Opera also has a swimming pool and coffee shop.

Near the Indra Regent Hotel, the *Classic Inn* (☎ 02-208 0491, fax 208 0497) off Th Ratchaprarop costs 500B to 700B for simple but decent air-con rooms. A long walk east along the soi opposite the Indra (off Ratchaprarop) leads eventually to *Borarn House* (☎ 02-253 2252, fax 253 3639, 487/48 Soi Wattanasin), a Thai-style apartment building with singles/doubles for 850/950B with air-con and TV.

Airport Area

Finding decent, moderately priced accommodation in the airport area is difficult. Most of the hotels in this area charge nearly twice as much as comparable hotels in the city. Typical of these is *Don Muang Mansion* (☎ 02-566 3064, 118/7 Th Soranakom, Don Muang) which looks classy on the outside, but asks 1000B to 1200B for a small, stuffy room that in Bangkok would cost 500B to 750B. It's possible to negotiate a lower rate of 800B with some discussion.

If you can spend a bit more, a better choice is *Comfort Suites Airport* (☎ 02-552 8921/9, fax 552-8920, 88/117 Vibhavadi (Wiphaawadi) Rangsit Hwy), about five minutes south of the airport by car. Large rooms with all the amenities (satellite TV, air-con, private hot bath/shower) cost 1500B to 1800B if you book through a Bangkok travel agent, 2500B to 2800B for walk-ins. Best of all, the hotel provides a free shuttle to and from the airport every hour. Other facilities include a coffee shop, pool, sauna and health club. About the only drawback is that you can hear planes landing and taking off until around midnight.

The well run *We-Train International House* (☎ 02-929 2222, 929 2301, fax 929 2300, 501/1 Muu 3, Th Dechatungkha, Sikan, Don Muang) is quite a bit cheaper. Simple but very clean fan rooms with two beds, private hot bath, fridge and phone cost 550B single/double or 770B with air-con (extra beds cost 150B). You can also get a bed in a fan-cooled dorm for 165B. To these rates add the usual 10% service charge but no tax since it's operated by the nonprofit Association for the Promotion of the Status of Women (but male guests are welcome). Facilities include a pool, Thai massage, laundry service, coffee shop and beauty salon. One major drawback is its distance from the airport – you must get a taxi to cross the highway and railway, then go about 3km west along Dechatungkha to the Thung Sikan school (*rohng rian thûng sii-kan*). If you don't have much luggage, walk across the airport pedestrian bridge to reach Don Muang, then get a taxi – it's much cheaper that way because you avoid the high taxi-desk fees. From the guesthouse there are usually no taxis in the area when you're ready to return to the airport or continue on to Bangkok, but transportation to and from the airport can be arranged on request for 200B one way, or 70B one way to/from the Amari Airport Hotel.

PLACES TO STAY – TOP END

Bangkok has all sorts of international-class tourist hotels, from the straightforward package places to some of Asia's classic hotels. Three of Bangkok's luxury hotels, in fact, consistently make *Condé Nast Traveler*'s annual worldwide top 25 list: the Oriental, the Regent and the Shangri-La.

Although there's no single area for top-end hotels you'll find quite a few around the Siam Square area, along the parallel Th Surawong and Th Silom, and along the river, while many of the slightly less expensive 'international standard' places are scattered along Sukhumvit.

Since the 1997 devaluation of the baht, a few top-end places have begun quoting their prices in US dollars, while others raised their baht prices to bring exchange levels back in line with 1996 prices. Since many hotels in this category rely on imported goods (and imported management staff), prices had to be adjusted or the hotels would have risked massive losses.

Despite this rate shuffling, on average rates quoted in 1998 were lower than those from 1996 if measured against most western currencies. Even when they aren't, you should still be able to negotiate discounts of up to 40% on the rates listed during low season (April to June and July to August). Booking through a travel agency almost always means lower rates, or try asking for a hotel's 'corporate' discount. THAI can also arrange substantial discounts if you hold THAI air tickets.

A welcome trend in Bangkok hotels in the past few years has been the appearance of several European-style 'boutique' hotels – small, business-oriented places of around 100 rooms or less with rates in the 2000B to 3000B range, eg the Swiss Lodge (see the Th Silom Th Surawong & Th Sathon entry later in this section for details).

All hotels in this category will add a 10% service charge plus 10% tax to hotel bills.

Central Bangkok

Although there are as yet no top-end hotels in the Banglamphu area itself, a little bit east of the district are a couple of highly recommended places in this general price category. *Royal Princess Hotel* (☎ 02-281 3088, *fax 280 1314, 269 Th Lan Luang)* features rooms priced from 3800B, but discounts down to about half that are often available through travel agents. It's close to the main central THAI office and a short taxi ride from Banglamphu and the river.

Even nicer is the independently owned and operated *Siam City Hotel (☎ 02-247 0130, fax 247 0178, 477 Th Si Ayuthaya).* Large, well maintained rooms with all the amenities list for 4237B, but again, good discounts are often available through Thai travel agents. The restaurants at the Siam City are highly regarded by Thai businesspeople.

On the River

The 122-year-old *Oriental Hotel (☎ 02-236 0400, 236 0420, fax 236 1937, 48 Th Oriental)* on the Chao Phraya River, is one of the most famous hotels in Asia, right up there with the Raffles in Singapore or the Peninsula in Hong Kong. What's more it's also rated as one of the best hotels in the world, as well as being just about the most expensive in Bangkok. The hotel management prides itself on providing highly personalised service.

Nowadays the Oriental is looking more modern and less classic – the original Author's Wing is dwarfed by the Tower (built in 1958) and River (1976) wings. Room rates start at 6800B, suites are as much as 10 times that. It's worth wandering in, if only to see the lobby (no shorts, sleeveless shirts or thongs allowed). Ten restaurants and bars offer a variety of cuisines; the legendary Bamboo Bar is one of the city's best jazz venues and there's a sports centre and cooking school.

Another luxury gem along the river is the *Shangri-La Hotel (☎ 02-236 7777, fax 236 8579, 89 Soi Wat Suan Phlu, Th Charoen Krung).* The Shangri-La has rooms and suites starting from US$264, all with minibar, hair dryer, coffeemaker and security box. Facilities and services include helicopter transport from the airport (at extra cost), swimming pools, tennis courts, squash courts, a fully-equipped gymnasium overlooking the river, sauna, steam bath,

hydropool, outdoor jacuzzis and nine restaurants (including Angelini's, one of the best Italian eateries in the city). Service is of a very high standard. The capacious lounge areas off the main lobby have a less formal, more relaxed feel than those at the Oriental, and are a favourite rendezvous spot even for non-guests.

On the Thonburi bank of the Chao Phraya River, a bit south of central Bangkok, the tastefully appointed *Marriott Royal Garden Riverside Hotel (☎ 02-476 0021, fax 476 1120, 257/1-3 Th Charoen Nakhon),* near Krungthep Bridge, is highly valued for its serene atmosphere and expansive, airy public areas. The grounds encompass a large swimming pool, lush gardens, tennis courts and a health club. There are six restaurants and the *Manohra,* a luxury rice-barge dinner cruiser, is also moored here. A free water taxi service shuttles guests back and forth to the Oriental and River City piers every hour from 7 am to 11 pm. Rack rates for very spacious rooms are 4200B, or 4800B with a river view.

Th Silom, Th Surawong & Th Sathon

Another entry in the luxury/executive market is the 226 room *Beaufort Sukhothai (☎ 02-287 0222, fax 287 4980, reservation fax 285 0303, email beaufort@ksc11.th.com, 13/3 Th Sathon Tai).* The Sukhothai features an Asian minimalist decor, including an inner courtyard with lily ponds; the same architect created Phuket's landmark Amanpuri. Superior rooms cost US$220, deluxe rooms US$264; there are also more expensive suites. Upon request the staff will provide a fax machine for your room at no charge.

The ultra-modern *Westin Banyan Tree (☎ 02-679 1200, fax 679 1199)* towers over Th Sathon Tai with 216 business suites. The hotel is ensconced on the lower two and top 28 floors of the 60 storey Thai Wah Tower II; its huge rooms feature separate work and sleep areas, two-line speaker phones with data ports and two TV sets along with all the other amenities expected of lodgings that start at 5700B a night. The spa/fitness centre – the biggest such hotel facility in Bangkok – spans four floors.

At **Dusit Thani Hotel** (☎ 02-236 0450, fax 236 6400, 946 Th Rama IV), one of the top hotels in the busy financial and shopping district along Th Silom and Th Surawong, rooms start at 5200B.

There are many hotels with similar amenities, but which are a step down in price because of their smaller staff-to-guest ratios or location. With only 57 rooms, the management at the **Swiss Lodge** (☎ 02-233 5345, fax 236 9425, 3 Th Convent) is able to pay close attention to service details such as cold towels whenever you enter the lobby from outside. Data-ports and soundproof windows further enhance the attraction for people doing business in Bangkok. Facilities include a restaurant, pool and business centre. Rates run 3850B to 4300B (1999B to 2499B in low season).

Th Sukhumvit

The tastefully decorated **Hotel Rembrandt** (☎ 02-261 7100, fax 261 7014, 19 Soi 18, Th Sukhumvit) has 406 large rooms. Prices at the time of writing were 2700B, though rack rates were listed at over 3000B. Facilities include a swimming pool and the best Mexican restaurant in Bangkok, Señor Pico's of Los Angeles. Another advantage is the Rembrandt's proximity to Queen Sirikit National Convention Centre, off Soi 16.

Windsor Hotel (☎ 02-258 0160, fax 258 1491, 8-10 Soi 20 (Soi Nam Phung), Th Sukhumvit), is a fairly deluxe place with standard rooms for 2200/2400B single/double, superior rooms 2400/2600B; these rates include a cooked-to-order breakfast. Each of the 116 rooms and suites have aircon, phone, TV, video and refrigerator. On the premises is a 24 hour coffee shop. Guests of the Windsor have use of all amenities at the **Embassy Suites Windsor Palace** (☎ 02-262 1221, fax 262 1212) next door, which features 463 spacious suites (each with two TVs!). Amenities include a bakery, cafe, restaurant, fitness club, shopping arcade, swimming pool and jacuzzi. Rates start at 6000B single, 7000B double;

a complimentary buffet breakfast is included.

Siam Square, Th Ploenchit & Pratunam

People accustomed to heady hotels claim the plush **Regent Bangkok** (☎ 02-251 6127, fax 253 9195, 155 Th Ratchadamri) in some respects tops the Oriental in overall quality for the money. This is particularly true for business travellers because of the Regent's efficient business centre and central location (and local calls are free at the Regent, probably the only luxury hotel in the city to offer this courtesy). The hotel also offers (for around 2000B an hour) an 'office on wheels', a high-tech van equipped with computers, mobile phones, fax machines, TVs/VCRs and swivelling leather seats so that small conferences can be held while crossing town in Bangkok's turgid traffic. The Regent's rooms start at 5885B.

The **Grand Hyatt Erawan** (☎ 02-254 1234, fax 253 5856), at the intersection of Ratchadamri and Ploenchit, was raised on the site of the original Erawan Hotel (built at the same time as the Royal Hotel) with obvious ambitions to become one of the city's top-ranked hotels. The neo-Thai architecture has been well executed; inside is the largest collection of contemporary Thai art in the world. Adding to the elite atmosphere, rooms in the rear of the hotel overlook the prestigious Bangkok Royal Sports Club racetrack. For most visitors – whether for business or leisure – it vies with the Regent or the Novotel Bangkok on Siam Square for having the best location of all the city's luxury hotels vis-à-vis transport and proximity to shopping. Huge rooms start at 5000B.

Thailand's own Amari Hotels & Resorts opened the **Amari Watergate** (☎ 02-653 9000, fax 653 9045) at the end of 1994 right in the centre of Bangkok's busiest district, Pratunam. It boasts large rooms and impressive sports and entertainment facilities. The hotel is on Th Phetchaburi near the Th Ratchaprarop intersection. Tour groups check in via a separate floor and lobby while individually booked guests use the main lobby. Spacious rooms cost 4680B; the top three floors contain more luxuriously appointed executive rooms for another 1000B or so. Amari also has other hotels in central Bangkok and at the airport – see Airport Area later in this section.

Dropping down a notch or two in price is the *Chateau de Bangkok* (☎ 02-651 4400, fax 651 4500, 29 Soi Ruam Rudi, Th Ploenchit). Owned by the French hotel group Accor, it offers serviced apartments with one or two bedrooms, each with walk-in closet, IDD phone and fax for 2800B a night.

The tallest hotel in the world, the 93 story *Baiyoke Sky Hotel* (☎ 02-656 3000, fax 656 3555, email baiyoke@mozart.inet.co.th), stands right behind the Indra Hotel off Th Ratchaprarop in Pratunam. Spacious rooms and suites with all the amenities – though not quite as luxurious as one might expect cost 2800/3200B single/double and 3600/4000B respectively (plus tax and service), not a bad deal considering the altitude.

Ratchada

This newish entertainment and business district in the Huay Khwang neighbourhood of north-east Bangkok features several flash hotels along Th Ratchadaphisek. One of the least expensive places in the area, right next to Le Concorde building (home to TAT) and a stone's throw from several upscale 'entertainment centres', is the *Siam Beverly Hotel* (☎ 02-275 4046, 275 4397, fax 275 4049, 188 Th Ratchadapisek), where rates range from 1800B for a superior single to 2200B for deluxe double, including breakfast. It's nothing spectacular but service is friendly and the rooms have all the amenities; the 3rd floor coffee shop is well priced.

The best hotel in the area, the *Hotel Nikko Mahanakorn* (☎ 02-274 1515, fax 274 1510, 238 Th Ratchadaphisek), features 600 very well appointed rooms starting at 5200B.

Airport Area

Amari Airport Hotel (☎ 02-566 1020, fax 566 1941), directly across from the airport,

has undergone recent renovations and is quite well appointed. The executive floor features huge suites and 24 hour butler service. Rates start at 4200B for a standard double. Or stay five minutes from the airport at the less expensive *Comfort Suites Airport* (see Places to Stay – Mid-Range).

A new top-end project, the *Asia Airport Hotel* (☎ 02-992 6999, fax 531 2599), has recently opened north of the airport at Km 28. Rates for the 550 rooms start at 1500B.

PLACES TO EAT

Wherever you go in Bangkok, you're almost never more than 50m away from a restaurant or sidewalk food vendor. The variety of places to eat is simply astounding. You can find food in every price range in most districts – with a few obvious exceptions. Chinatown is naturally a good area for Chinese food, while Bangrak and Pahurat are good for Indian and Muslim cuisine. Some parts of the city tend to have higher priced restaurants (eg Siam Square, and Silom, Surawong and Sukhumvit) while other areas are full of cheap eats (eg Banglamphu and the river area around Tha Maharat).

As transport can be such a hassle in Bangkok, most visitors choose to eat in a district most convenient to reach (rather than seeking out a specific restaurant); this section has therefore been organised by area, rather than cuisine.

Banglamphu & Thewet

This area near the river and old part of the city is one of the best for cheap food. Many of the guesthouses on Th Khao San have open-air cafes, which are packed with travellers from November to March and July to August. The typical cafe menu has a few Thai and Chinese standards plus traveller favourites like fruit salads, muesli and yoghurt. None of them are particular standouts, though the side-by-side *Orm* and *Wally House* produce fair Thai, western and vegetarian meals at low prices, while *Prakorp's House & Restaurant* makes good coffee. *Hello Restaurant* (not to be confused with the guesthouse of the same name opposite) and **Bangkok Center Restaurant** on Khao San are both quite popular, but the food's nothing special. **Arawy Det**, an old Hokkien-style noodle shop on the corner of Khao San and Tanao, has somehow managed to stay authentic.

Up at the intersection of Th Khao San and Th Chakraphong, relatively new and air-conditioned **Gulliver's Traveler's Tavern** serves cocktails, shots, beers and has an international menu bearing such culinary arcana as Belgian fries, Australian 'dinkum chili', fried calamari, cottage pie and fish and chips. Prices run from around 80B to 100B a dish; the music is loud. **Buddy Beer Garden, Restaurant & Swimming Pool**, down towards the south-east end of Khao San, is a large place with low-key bamboo furnishings, good Thai and faràng food at reasonable prices, and a pool and barbecue out the back.

Gaylord Indian Restaurant, hidden away in the rear upstairs of a building on Th Chakraphong opposite the west entrance to Th Khao San, has decent Indian food in a slightly musty atmosphere. **Chabad House**, a Jewish place of worship on Th Rambutri, serves Israeli-style kosher food downstairs; open Sunday through Thursday noon to 9 pm, Friday noon to 4.30 pm. Cheaper felafel and hummus can be found at **Chochana**, down a trok off Th Chakraphong around the corner from Th Khao San.

For more authentic (and cheaper) Thai food check out other places on Th Rambutri. At the western end are several open-air restaurants serving excellent Thai food at low prices. A good spot for Southern Thai food is a **no-name food shop** at 8-10 Chakraphong, south of Th Khao San and two doors south of the Padung Chiip mask shop. In the mornings it serves *khâo mòk kài* (Thai chicken biryani) as well as *khâo yam*, a kind of rice salad which is a traditional breakfast in Southern Thailand. Nearby at No 22 is a cheap and efficient **Chinese noodle *(bàmìi)* and wonton *(kíaw)* shop**; **No 28** offers tasty Thai curries. A small shop called **Roti-Mataba** (no roman-script sign) on the corner of Phra

Athit and Phra Sumen near the river offers delicious *kaeng mátsàman* (Thai Muslim curry), chicken korma, chicken or vegetable *mátàbà* (a sort of stuffed crepe) and a bilingual menu; look for a white sign with red letters.

Along Th Phra Athit north of the New Merry V guesthouse are several small but up-and-coming Thai places with chic but casual decor and good food at prices local university students can afford. The **Raan Kin Deum** (no roman-script sign), a few doors down from New Merry V, is a nice two storey cafe with wooden tables and chairs, traditional Thai food and live folk music nightly; the laid-back atmosphere reaches its acme in the evenings when Thais and faràngs crowd the place. Bright and cheery **Saffron Bakery**, opposite the Food & Agriculture Organization on Th Phra Athit, has good pastries but only a few tables.

For an all-vegie menu at low prices, seek out the **Vegetarian Restaurant** at 117/1 Soi Wat Bowon, south of the wát. To find this out-of-the-way spot, turn left on Tanao at the eastern end of Th Khao San, then cross the street and turn right down the first narrow alley, then left at Soi Wat Bowon – an English sign reads 'Vegetarian'. The fare is basically western vegie, with wholemeal breads, salads and sandwiches; it's open from 8 am until around 10 pm. A very good Thai vegetarian place is **Arawy** *(152 Th Din So; the roman-script sign reads 'Alloy')*, south of Th Khao San, across Th Ratchadamnoen Klang (opposite the Municipal Hall) near a 7-eleven shop. This was one of Bangkok's first Thai vegetarian restaurants, inspired by ex-Bangkok Governor Chamlong Srimuang. It's open daily from 7 am to 7 pm.

Good curry-and-rice is available for around 20B at the outdoor dining hall at **Thammasat University** near the river; it's open for lunch only. Opposite the southern entrance of the university there are several good **noodle and rice shops**. For North-Eastern Thai food, try the **restaurants** next to the boxing stadium on Th Ratchadamnoen Nok, near the TAT office.

For authentic, sit-down Thai cuisine, try the long-running *Yod Kum* (Yawt Kham) opposite Wat Bowon on Th Phra Sumen. Specialities include *phàt phèt plaa dùk* (catfish stir-fried in basil and curry paste), *kaeng khĩaw-wāan* (green curry) and seafood.

For those in the mood for continental food, *Kanit's (68 Th Tee Thong)* is just south of Wat Suthat and is another worthwhile semi-splurge. The lasagne and pizza are probably the best you can find in this part of Bangkok.

At Tha Wisut Kasat in north-western Banglamphu, there's a very good floating seafood restaurant called *Yok Yor*. Especially good at Yok Yor is the *hàw mòk* (fish curry). Yok Yor also offers inexpensive evening dining cruises – you order from the regular menu and pay a nominal 50B charge for the boat service.

Chinatown, Hualamphong & Pahurat

Some of Bangkok's best Chinese and Indian food is found in these adjacent districts, but because few tourists stay in this part of town (for good reason – it's simply too congested) they rarely make any eating forays into the area. A few old Chinese restaurants have moved from Chinatown to locations with less traffic, the most famous being Hoi Tien Lao, now the excellent *Hoi Tien Lao Rim Nam* and located adjacent to River House Condominium on the Thonburi bank of the Chao Phraya River, more or less opposite the Portuguese embassy and River City shopping complex. But many places are still hanging on to their venerable Chinatown addresses, where the atmosphere is still part of the eating experience.

Most specialise in southern Chinese cuisine, particularly that of coastal Guangdong and Fujian provinces. This means seafood, rice noodles and dumplings are often the best choices. The large, banquet-style Chinese places are mostly found along Th Yaowarat and Th Charoen Krung, and include *Laem Thong* (on Soi Bamrungrat just off Th Charoen Krung) and *Yau Wah Yuen* (near the Yaowarat and Ratchawong

intersection). Each has an extensive menu, including dim sum before lunchtime. *Lie Kee* (☎ 02-224 3587, 360-362 Th Charoen Krung) is an excellent and inexpensive Chinese food centre on the third floor of a building at the corner of Charoen Krung and Bamrungrat, a block west of Th Ratchawong. It's air-conditioned, yet it's difficult to spend more than 50B for lunch.

The best noodle and dumpling shops are hidden away on smaller sois and alleys. At 54 Soi Bamrungrat is the funky *Chiang Kii*, where the 100B *khâo tôm plaa* (rice soup with fish) belies the casual surroundings – no place does it better.

All-night *food hawkers* set up along Th Yaowarat and along Th Ratchawong near where the two streets intersect; this is the least expensive place to dine in Chinatown. On weekends parts of these two streets are closed to vehicular traffic, turning the area into a pedestrian mall.

Over in Pahurat, the Indian fabric district, most places serve north Indian cuisine, which is heavily influenced by Moghul or Persian flavours and spices. For many people, the best north Indian restaurant in town is the *Royal India (392/1 Th Chakraphet)* in Pahurat. It can be very crowded at lunchtime, almost exclusively with Indian residents. The place has very good food at quite reasonable prices. Royal India also has a branch on Th Khao San but it's not as good.

The ATM department store on Th Chakraphet near the pedestrian bridge has a *food centre* on the top floor that features several Indian vendors – the food is cheap and tasty and there's quite a good selection. Running alongside the ATM building on Soi ATM are several small *teahouses* with very inexpensive Indian and Nepali food, including lots of fresh *chapatis* and strong milktea. In the afternoons, a Sikh man sets up a pushcart on the corner of Soi ATM and Th Chakraphet and sells *vegetarian samosas* often cited as the best in Bangkok.

Wedged between the western edge of Chinatown and the northern edge of Pahurat, the three storey Old Siam Plaza shopping centre houses a number of Thai,

Chinese and Japanese *restaurants*. The most economical places are on the 3rd floor, where a *food centre* serves inexpensive Thai and Chinese meals from 10 am to 5 pm. The 3rd floor also has several reasonably priced, *Thai-style coffee shops*.

During the annual Vegetarian Festival (centred around Wat Mangkon Kamalawat on Th Charoen Krung in September or October), Bangkok's Chinatown becomes a virtual orgy of vegetarian Thai and Chinese food. Restaurants and noodle shops in the area offer hundreds of different dishes. One of the best spreads is at *Hua Seng Restaurant*, a few doors west of Wat Mangkon on Th Charoen Krung.

Suki Jeh Yuu Seu (the English sign reads 'Health Food'), a Chinese vegetarian restaurant just 70m down Th Rama IV from Hualamphong station, serves excellent if a bit pricey vegetarian food in a clean, air-con atmosphere. The fruit shakes are particularly refreshing; this is a great place to fortify yourself with food and drink while waiting for a train at Hualamphong.

Th Silom, Th Surawong & Th Sathon

This area is in the heart of the financial district so it features a lot of pricey restaurants, along with cheaper ones that attract both office workers and the more flush. Many restaurants are found along the main avenues, but there's an even greater number tucked away in sois and alleys. The river end of Silom and Surawong towards Charoen Krung (the Bangrak district) is a good hunting ground for Indian food.

The *Soi Pracheun (Soi 20) Night Market*, which assembles each evening off Th Silom in front of the municipal market pavilion, is good for cheap eats. During the day there are also a few *food vendors* in this soi. At lunchtime and early evening a batch of *food vendors* – everything from noodles to raw oysters – set up on Soi 5 next to Bangkok Bank's main branch.

The area to the east of Silom off Th Convent and Soi Sala Daeng is a Thai gourmets' enclave. Most of the restaurants

tucked away here are very good, but a meal for two will cost 600B to 800B.

Ban Chiang (☎ 02-236 7045, 14 Soi Si Wiang, Th Pramuan), a restored wooden house in a verdant setting off Silom, west of Wat Khaek is a great place for traditional Thai and Isaan at moderate prices. Owned by a Thai movie star, *Thanying* (☎ 02-236 4361, 235 0371, 10 Soi Pramuan, Th Silom) features elegant decor and very good, moderately expensive royal Thai cuisine, ie, recipes that were created for the royal court in days past. It's open daily from 11 am to 11 pm; there's another branch at the World Trade Centre on Th Ploenchit (☎ 02-255 9838), open daily 11.30 am to 10.30 pm.

Mango Tree (☎ 02-236 2820, 37 Soi Anuman Ratchathon), opposite the Tawana Ramada Hotel between Silom and Surawong, offers classic Thai cuisine and live traditional Thai music amid a decor of historical photos and antiques. Prices are moderate and it's open daily for lunch and dinner.

A good one-stop eating place with a lot of variety is the Silom Village Trade Centre, an outdoor shopping complex at Soi 24. Though it's basically a tourist spot with higher than average prices, the restaurants are of high quality and plenty of Thais dine here as well.

Popular and clean *Thon Krueng (Ton Khreuang;* ☎ 02-234 9663, 235 8691) on Th Sathon Neua, on the Thonburi side of the Taksin Bridge, serves excellent Thai, Chinese and seafood at moderate prices in a large, no-nonsense dining room. The name means 'Spice Tree' in Thai, a tribute to the kitchen's solid command of Thai cuisine.

Towards the eastern end of Th Surawong, about a 10 minute walk west of Montien Hotel, is the famous *Somboon Seafood* (open from 4 pm to midnight), a good, reasonably priced seafood restaurant known for having the best crab curry in town. Soy-steamed seabass (*plaa kràphong nêung sii-yíu*) is also a speciality. Somboon has a second branch, called *Somboon Chinese (711-717 Chula Soi 8, Th Ban That Thong)*, farther north, across Th Rama IV near Chulalongkorn University.

Mizu's Kitchen on Th Patpong 1 has a loyal Japanese and Thai following for its inexpensive but good Japanese food, including Japanese-style steak. Another very good Japanese place, especially for sushi and sashimi, is *Goro* (399/1 Soi Siri Chulasewok, Th Silom); prices are reasonable.

Towards the western end of Silom and Surawong, Indian eateries begin making an appearance. Unlike at Indian restaurants elsewhere in Bangkok, the menus in Bangrak don't necessarily exhibit the usual, boring predilection towards north Indian Moghul-style cuisine. For authentic south Indian food (*dosa, idli, vada* etc), try the *Madras Cafe* (☎ 02-235 6761, 31/10-11 Trok Vaithi (Trok 13), Th Silom) in the Madras Lodge near the Narai Hotel (open daily 9 am to 10 pm). Across from the Narai Hotel, near the Sri Mariamman Temple, *street vendors* sometimes sell various Indian snacks.

India Hut (☎ 02-237 8812), a new place on Surawong opposite the Manohra Hotel, specialises in Nawabi (Lucknow) cuisine; it's quite good, friendly and moderate to high in prices (50B to 100B per dish). The vegetarian samosas and fresh prawns cooked with ginger are particularly good. It's three flights of steps off the street, with a modern Indian decor.

The Cholas, a small air-con place downstairs in the Woodlands Inn on Soi Charoen Krung 32 just north of the central post office, serves decent, no-fuss north Indian food for 50B to 80B a dish. The open-air *Sallim Restaurant*, next door to the Woodlands, is a cheaper place with north Indian, Malay and Thai-Muslim dishes – it's usually packed.

Around the corner on Soi Phuttha Osot is the very popular but basic-looking *Naaz* (Naat in Thai), often cited as having the richest *khâo mòk kài* (chicken biryani) in the city. Naaz is open from 7.30 am to 10.30 pm daily. There are several other Arab/Indian restaurants in this area.

On Soi Pracheun (Soi 20) off Silom there's a mosque, Masjid Mirasuddeen, so Muslim *food vendors* are common.

Sun Far Myanmar Food Centre (107/1 Th Pan), between Silom and Sathon near the Myanmar embassy, is an inexpensive place to sample authentic Burmese curries and *thok* (spicy Burmese-style salads). It's open daily 8 am to 10 pm.

Rabianthong Restaurant, in the Narai Hotel on Th Silom, offers a very good vegetarian section in its luncheon buffet, on wan phrá (full moon days) only, for 260B.

Tiensin (1345 Th Charoen Krung) opposite the entrance of the soi that leads to the Shangri-La Hotel, serves very good Chinese vegetarian food, including many mock meat dishes. It's open 7 am to 9 pm daily.

If you crave German or Japanese food, there are plenty of outlets on and around Th Patpong. *Bobby's Arms*, an Aussie-British pub on the 1st floor of a multi-storey carpark off Patpong 2, has good fish and chips. The *Brown Derby*, also on Patpong 1, is recommended for American-style deli sandwiches.

Authentically decorated *O'Reilly's Irish Pub* (☎ 02-235 1572, 62/1-2 Th Silom), at the entrance to Thaniya Plaza (corner of Th Silom and Soi Thaniya) opens at 8 am, stays open till 1 or 2 am, and features a good menu of reasonably priced pub grub.

Wedged between the go-go bars on Patpong 2 are several fast-food chicken joints. Probably the best Patpong find is the *Café de Paris* (☎ 02-237 2776) on Patpong 2, an air-con spot popular with French expats for its decent approximations of Parisian-style bistro fare; it's open daily from 11 am to 1 am.

In the CP Tower building on Silom are a cluster of air-con American and Japanese-style fast-food places.

The tiny *Harmonique* (☎ 02-237 8175) on Soi Charoen Krung 34, around the corner from the central post office, is a refreshing oasis in this extremely busy, smog-filled section of Charoen Krung. The little European-managed and unobtrusive shop serves a variety of teas, fruit shakes and coffee on Hokkien-style marble-topped tables – a pleasant spot to read poste restante mail while quenching your thirst. Well prepared if pricey (60B to 150B per dish) Thai food is also available. The shop discreetly sells silk, silverware and antiques. It's open daily from 11 am to 10 pm.

Soi Ngam Duphli

Hua Hin Restaurant, on Soi Atakanprasit (off Soi Ngam Duphli south-west of the Malaysia Hotel), serves decent western breakfasts, including fresh brewed coffee, for 35B to 50B; open daily from 7.30 am. Beside the Malaysia Hotel, an outdoor Thai place called *Station Just One* is a popular lunch spot.

On the 11th floor of Lumphini Tower on busy Th Rama IV is a cafeteria-style *food centre* open from 7 am to 2 pm. Opposite Lumphini Tower on the same road is a warren of *food vendors* with cheap eats.

Another restaurant in the Soi Ngam Duphli area worth mentioning is *Ratsstube* (☎ 02-287 2822) in the Thai-German Cultural Centre (Goethe Institute), also on Soi Atakanprasit. Home-made sausages and set meals from 120B attract a large and steady clientele; open daily from 10 am to 10 pm.

Th Sukhumvit

This avenue stretching east all the way to the city limits has hundreds of Thai, Chinese and western restaurants to choose from.

The *Mandalay* (☎ 02-255 2893, 23/7 Soi Ruam Rudi) along with a second branch on Th Surawong, is one of the only Burmese restaurants in town; it's good but not cheap.

The *Yong Lee Restaurant* at Soi 15, near Asia Books, has excellent Thai and Chinese food at reasonable prices and is a longtime favourite among Thai and faràng residents alike. There is a second Yong Lee between sois 35 and 37.

For nouvelle Thai cuisine, you can try the *Lemongrass* (☎ 02-258 8637, 5/1 Soi 24, Th Sukhumvit) which has an atmospheric setting in an old Thai house decorated with antiques. The food is exceptional; try the *yam pèt* (Thai-style duck salad). It is open from 11 am to 2 pm and 6 to 11 pm.

There are many restaurants around the major hotels on Th Sukhumvit with mixed Thai, Chinese, European and American

menus – most of average quality and slightly above-average prices.

The upscale *Le Dalat* (☎ 02-258 4192, 260 1849, 47/1 Soi 23, Th Sukhumvit) has the most celebrated Vietnamese cuisine in the city. Open daily 11 am to 2.30 pm and 5.30 to 10 pm. There are two other branches at 14 Soi 23, Th Sukhumvit (same hours) and at Premier Shopping Village, Th Chaeng Wattana (☎ 02-573 7017), open Friday to Sunday 11 am to 10 pm.

The Emporium shopping centre, Soi 24, Th Sukhumvit, has several *restaurants* on its 4th, 5th and 6th floors, including a wood-panelled *food centre* with upmarket Thai vendors.

If you go for the metal and blond wood, LA cafe-bar look, try *Axil Cafe* on Soi 39 (Soi Phromphong), Th Sukhumvit; *Kuppa* on Soi 16, Th Sukhumvit; or *Greyhound Cafe* in The Emporium on Soi 24, Th Sukhumvit. All specialise in a good Thai/Mediterranean cuisine.

A restaurant with a good variety of moderately priced vegetarian and meaty Indian food (mostly north Indian) is *Mrs Balbir's* (☎ 02-253 2281, 155/18 Soi 11), behind the Siam Commercial Bank and close to the Ambassador Hotel. A 150B buffet lunch is served daily. Mrs Balbir has been teaching Indian cooking for many years and has her own Indian grocery shop as well.

The splurge-worthy *Rang Mahal* (☎ 02-261 7100), a rooftop restaurant in the Rembrandt Hotel on Soi 18, offers very good north and south Indian 'royal cuisine' with cityscape views. On Sundays the restaurant puts on a sumptuous Indian buffet from 11.30 am to 3 pm.

A few medium to expensive restaurants serving Pakistani and Middle Eastern food can be found in the 'Little Arabia' area of Soi 3 (Soi Nana Neua). The best value in the whole area is *Al Hossain*, a roofed outdoor cafe on the corner of a lane (Soi 3/5) off the east side of Soi Nana Neua.

The *Veg House* (☎ 02-254 7357), in an alley off the west side of Soi Nana Neua, serves meatless Indian, Thai and Italian dishes in a 2nd floor walkup; open from noon to 11 pm.

Homesick Brits need look no farther than *Jool's Bar & Restaurant* at Soi 4 (Soi Nana Tai), past Nana Plaza on the left walking from Th Sukhumvit. The British-style bar downstairs is a favourite expat hangout while the dining room upstairs serves decent English food.

Several rather expensive European restaurants (Swiss, French, German etc) are also found on Sukhumvit. *Bei Otto* (☎ 02-260 0869, 1 Soi 20 (Soi Nam Phung), Th Sukhumvit), is one of the most popular German restaurants in town and has a comfortable bar. Attached are a bakery, deli and butcher shop.

Nostalgic visitors from the USA, especially those from southern USA, will appreciate the well run *Bourbon St Bar & Restaurant* (☎ 02-259 0328), on Soi 22 (behind the Washington Theatre). The menu here emphasises Cajun and Creole cooking, but there are also some Mexican dishes on the menu; some nights there is also free live music. A large dinner special for two costs 400B. Also open for breakfast.

One of the top French restaurants in the city, and probably the best outside the luxury hotels, is *Le Banyan* (☎ 02-253 5556, 59 Soi 8 (Soi Prida), Th Sukhumvit) in a charming early Ratanakosin-style house. This is definitely a splurge experience, although the prices are moderate when compared with other elegant French restaurants in the city.

Pomodoro (☎ 02-252 9090), with floor-to-ceiling windows on the ground floor of the Nai Lert Building on Sukhumvit (between sois 3 and 5), specialises in Sardinian cuisine. Special set lunch menus are available for 180B to 250B.

Señor Pico's of Los Angeles (☎ 02-261 7100, 2nd floor, Rembrandt Hotel, Soi 18, Th Sukhumvit) has the city's best Mexican food. This brightly decorated, festive restaurant offers reasonably authentic Tex-Mex cuisine, including *fajitas*, *carnitas*, *nachos* and combination platters. Expect to spend around 500B for two.

Siam Square, Th Ploenchit & Th Withayu

This shopping area is interspersed with several low and medium-priced restaurants as well as American fast-food franchises. Chinese food seems to predominate, probably because it's the well-off Chinese Thais who most frequent Siam Square. The square's Soi 1 has three shark-fin places: *Scala, Penang* and *Bangkok*. At the other end of Siam Square, on Th Henri Dunant, the big noodle restaurant called *Coca Garden* (open from 10.30 am to 10.30 pm) is good for Chinese-style sukiyaki.

S&P Restaurant & Bakery on Soi 11 has an extensive menu featuring mostly Thai specialities, with a few Chinese, Japanese, European and vegetarian dishes – all high-quality fare at low to moderate prices (dishes are 45B to 75B, or 35B to 65B at breakfast). It also has a bakery.

Just to the right (west) of the Siam Square's Scala cinema, plunge into the alley that curves behind the Th Phayathai shops to find a row of cheap, good *food stalls*. A shorter alley with food stalls also leads off the north end of Siam Square's Soi 2.

On both sides of Th Rama I in Siam Square and Siam Center you'll find a battery of American fast-food franchises. Prices are close to what you would pay in the USA. Siam Center also contains a bevy of good *Thai coffee shops* on its upper floors.

If you're staying on or near Soi Kasem San 1, there are two very good, inexpensive *curry-and-rice vendors* with tables along the east side of the soi. No need to be fluent in Thai – they're used to the 'point-and-serve' system. Two outdoor cafes on either side of the White Lodge serve more expensive Thai and European food, burgers, pastries, coffees and breakfast. Right around the corner on Rama I, next to the liquor dealer with the vintage British and US motorcycles out the front, is *Thai Sa Nguan* (no roman-script sign), a fairly clean shop with *khâo kaeng* (curry-and-rice) for 12B (two toppings 17B), *kŭaytĭaw pèt yâang* (fried duck with noodles) and *khâo man kài* (Hainanese-style chicken and rice).

Thai classic **Djit Pochana** has a branch on the third floor of Ploenchit Center, on Th Ploenchit. Very good value for generally high-quality Thai food, in an informal but comfortable setting.

Santa Barbara Grill (☎ 02-656 0035, 873 Th Ploenchit), in the basement of the President Tower adjacent to Le Meridien President Hotel, serves California fusion cuisine in a blond-wood interior. Most dishes cost 175B to 345B, not including tax and service.

Despite its faràng name, **Sarah-Jane's** (☎ 02-650 9992, Sindhorn Bldg, 130-132 Th Withayu), serves very good Isaan food in an air-con dining room.

Mahboonkrong Shopping Centre (MBK), another building studded with restaurants, is directly across from Siam Square at the intersection of Phayathai and Rama I. Among other amenities there are two **food centres** with vendors serving tasty dishes from all over Thailand, including vegetarian, at prices averaging 20B to 25B per plate. Hours are 10 am to 10 pm, but the more popular vendors run out of food as early as 8.30 or 9 pm – come earlier for the best selection.

East of Siam Square and off Th Ploenchit, Soi Lang Suan offers a number of popular medium-price eateries.

Dinner Cruises
There are a number of companies that run cruises during which you eat dinner. Prices range from 40B to 700B per person depending on how far they go and whether dinner is included in the fare. For more information, see Dinner Cruises under River & Canal Trips earlier in this chapter.

Hotel Restaurants
For splurge-level food, many of Bangkok's grand luxury hotels provide memorable – if expensive – eating experiences. With western cuisine, particularly, the quality usually far exceeds anything found in Bangkok's independent restaurants. Some of the city's best Chinese restaurants are also located in hotels. If you're on a budget, check to see if a lunchtime buffet is available on weekdays;

usually these are the best deals, ranging from 150B to 300B per person (up to 500B at the Oriental). Also check the *Bangkok Post* and *The Nation* for weekly specials presented by visiting chefs from far-flung corners of the globe.

The Oriental Hotel has six restaurants, all managed by world-class chefs, and buffet lunches are offered at several. The hotel's **China House** (☎ 02-236 0400, ext 3378), set in a charming restored private residence opposite the hotel's main wing, has one of the best Chinese kitchens in Bangkok, with an emphasis on Cantonese cooking. The lunchtime dim sum is superb and is a bargain by luxury hotel standards at 60B or less per plate, or all you can eat for 280B. Reservations are recommended.

For hotel dim sum almost as good as that at the Dusit or Oriental – but at less than a third the price – try the **Jade Garden** (☎ 02-233 7060) at the Montien Hotel. Though not quite as fancy in presentation, the food is nonetheless impressive.

For French food, the leading hotel contenders are **Ma Maison** (☎ 02-253 0123) at the Hilton International, *Normandie* (☎ 02-236 0400, ext 3380) at the Oriental and **Regent Grill** (☎ 02-251 6127) at the Regent Bangkok. All are expensive but the meals and service are virtually guaranteed to be of top quality.

One of the best Italian dining experiences in the city can be found at the very posh and formal **Grappino Italian Restaurant** (☎ 02-653 9000) in the Amari Watergate Hotel, on Th Phetchaburi in the busy Pratunam district. All pasta and breads are prepared fresh on the premises daily, and the small but high-tech wine cellar is one of Bangkok's best – the grappa selection is, of course, unmatched. Grappino is open daily for lunch and dinner; reservations are recommended.

Finally, if eating at one of these restaurants would mean spending your life savings, try this pauper's version of dining amid the bright hotel lights of Bangkok. Go to the end of the soi in front of the Shangri-La Hotel and take a ferry (2B) across the river to the wooden pier immediately opposite on the Thonburi shore. Wind your way through the narrow lanes opposite till you come to a main road (Th Charoen Nakhon), then turn left. The large, open-air *Thon Krueng (Ton Khreuang; ☎ 02-437 9671, 723 Th Charoen Nakhon)* is about 200m down on the left, back towards the river. Here you can enjoy a moderately priced Thai seafood meal outdoors with impressive night-time views of the Shangri-La and Oriental hotels opposite. The ferry runs till around 2 am.

Other Vegetarian Options

One of the oldest *Thai vegetarian restaurants* is operated by the Buddhist ascetic Asoke Foundation at Chatuchak Weekend Market off Th Kamphaeng Phet (near the main local bus stop, a pedestrian bridge and a Chinese shrine – look for a sign reading 'Vegetarian' in green letters). It's open only on weekends from 8 am to noon. Prices are almost ridiculously low – around 7B to 12B per dish. The *cafeteria* at the Bangkok Adventist Hospital at 430 Th Phitsanulok, a couple of kilometres east of Banglamphu, also serves inexpensive vegetarian fare. All the Indian restaurants in town also have vegetarian selections on their menus.

ENTERTAINMENT

In their round-the-clock search for *khwaam sa-nùk* (fun), Bangkokians have made their metropolis one that literally never sleeps. To get an idea of what's available, check out the entertainment listings in the daily *Bangkok Post* and *The Nation* or the monthly *Bangkok Metro*. The latter maintains a good Web page (www.bkkmetro.com) listing current happenings in the city. Possibilities include classical music performances, rock concerts, pubs, videotheque dancing, Asian music/theatre ensembles on tour, art shows and dinner theatre. Boredom should not be a problem in Bangkok, at least not for a short-term visit. But save some energy and money for your islands and beaches trip!

Bangkok's evening entertainment scene goes way beyond its over publicised naughty nightlife image, offering a heady assortment of entertainment venues, nightclubs, bars, cafes and discos appealing to every proclivity. Many specialise in live music – rock, country and western, Thai pop music and jazz – while you'll hear the latest recorded music in the mega-discos as well as in the smaller neighbourhood bars. Hotels catering to tourists and businesspeople often contain up-to-date discos as well.

All bars and clubs are supposed to close at 1 or 2 am (the latter closing time is for places with dance floors and/or live music), but in reality very few do.

Bars

Bangkok has long outgrown the days when the only bars around catered to male go-go oglers. Trendy among Bangkok Thais these days are bars that strive for a sophisticated but casual atmosphere, with good service, good drinks and choice music. The Thais often call them pubs but they bear little resemblance to any traditional English pub. Some are 'theme' bars, conceived around a particular aesthetic. All the city's major hotels feature western-style bars as well.

Salvador Dali, a block north of Th Khao San, on Th Rambutri (towards the west end) and tucked away amid a row of noodle stands, is a comfortable, two storey air-con bar with a more intimate feel.

Down an alley off Banglamphu's Th Phra Athit (just around the corner from Khrua Nopparat), you can down a few beers at *Underground* while watching alternative films like *Trainspotting* on Wednesday evening, music videos from Thursday to Sunday.

Delaney's Irish Pub (☎ 02-266 7160, 1-4 Sivadon Bldg, Th Convent), also in the Silom district, is one of only two places in Bangkok that serves Guinness on tap. Bands – some of them not very good – play on Tuesday to Saturday, and the place is often packed from 6 pm till closing.

Three low-key, British-style taverns include *Jool's* on Soi 4 near Nana Plaza, the *Ship Inn*, just around the corner from Soi Cowboy on the west side of Soi 23, and

Bull's Head on Soi 33/1, Th Sukhumvit, on the ground floor of Angus Steak House.

Henry J Bean's Bar & Grill in the basement of the Amari Watergate Hotel (there's a separate entrance so that you don't have to walk through the hotel) on Th Phetchaburi in Pratunam is a relaxed spot, where performing bartenders flip bottles and glasses while serving and there's an early evening happy hour daily. A house band plays roots rock and reggae most nights; other live bands occasionally appear.

Wong's Place (27/3 Soi Si Bamphen) is a low-key hangout with a good collection of music videos for local residents and visitors staying in the Soi Ngam Duphli area. Nicer is the low-key *Susie Pub* next to the Marco Polo Hostel, off Th Khao San.

For slick aerial city views, the place to go is the Baiyoke Sky Hotel on Th Ratchaprarop. On the 77th floor there's an observation deck, open 24 hours, or you can view the cityscape while dining in one of the *restaurants* on the 78th and 79th floors. The *Compass Rose*, a bar on the 59th floor of the Westin Banyan Tree is also sky high but is only open 11.30 am to 1 am. TV sports fans can keep up with their favourite teams via big-screen satellite TV at a huge American- style sports bar, *Champs* (☎ 02-252 7651), in the Nai Lert Building on Th Sukhumvit, near Soi 5.

Brewpubs
The Brewhouse (☎ 02-661 3535, 61/2 Soi 26, Th Sukhumvit), associated with the Taurus dance club opposite, features four brews (including low-alcohol 'Dynamite Lite' and high-test 'Naked Killer Ale'), in a split-level interior beneath a metallic dome.

In Siam Discovery Center, *Hartmanns-dorfer Brau Haus* (☎ 02-658 0229) does fresh beer, sausages, cheeses and other stout German fare in a polished but pleasant atmosphere.

Londoner Brew House (☎ 02-261 0238, basement, UBC II Bldg, Soi 33, Th Sukhumvit) has recently begun serving its own beers and ales but the ambience is limp.

If you find yourself stuck at Bangkok international airport, you could do a lot worse than the *Royal Hofbräuhaus*, towards the south end of Terminal 2 on the 4th floor, not far from the indoor carpark. This is a German-style pub, said to be the world's first airport micro-brewery. Fresh, doughy pretzels are served with every beer ordered and it's open 24 hours a day.

Discos & Dance Clubs
All the major hotels have international-style discotheques but only a small number – those at the Dusit Thani, the Shangri-La, the Grand Hyatt and the Regent – can really be recommended as attractions in themselves. Cover charges are pretty uniform: around 300B on weekday nights and around 400B on weekends, including two drinks. Most places don't begin filling up till after 11 pm.

Bangkok is famous for its huge high-tech discos that hold up to 5000 people and feature mega-watt sound systems, a giant-screen video and the latest in light-show technology. The clientele for these dance palaces is mostly young moneyed Thais experimenting with lifestyles of conspicuous affluence, plus the occasional Bangkok celebrity and a sprinkling of bloodshot-eyed expats. Cover charges typically run 400B to 500B per person and include three drinks on weeknights, two drinks on weekends.

The most 'in' disco of this nature at the time of writing was *Phuture* on Th Ratchadapisek, attached to the north side of the Chaophya Park Hotel. Other biggies include *Paradise* (☎ 02-433 7151, 451/3 Th Arun Amarin) in Thonburi and the *Palace* on Vibhavadi Rangsit Hwy towards the airport. A mega-disco that gets older as well as younger Thais is *Galaxy* on Th Rama IV, from which WBA world boxing champions Khaosai Galaxy and his brother Khaokor have taken their surname. Galaxy is also popular with some Japanese visitors who patronise the 'no-hands' section of the club, where hostesses feed the customers so they never have to lift their hands.

A string of small dance clubs on Soi 2 and Soi 4 (Soi Jaruwan), both parallel to

Patpong 1 and 2, off Th Silom, attracts a more mixed crowd in terms of age, gender, nationality and sexual orientation than either the hotel discos or the mega discos. The norm for recorded music here includes techno, trance, hip-hop and other current dance trends. Main venues – some of which are small and narrow – include on Soi 2 *Disco Disco (DD)*, *JJ Park* and *DJ Station*, and on Soi 4 *Hyper*, *Deeper*, *Kool Spot*, *Speed*, *Rome Club*, *Film Mix* and *Sphinx*. The larger places collect cover charges of around 100B to 300B depending on the night of the week; the smaller ones are free. The clientele at these clubs was once predominantly gay but has become more mixed as word got around about the great dance scene. Things don't get started here till relatively late – around midnight; in fact on most nights the Soi 2/Soi 4 dance clubs serve more as 'after hours' hangouts since they usually stay open past the official 2 am closing time.

Go-Go Bars

By and large these throwbacks are seedy, expensive and cater to men only, whether straight or gay. These are concentrated along Th Sukhumvit (between sois 21 and 23), off Th Sukhumvit on Soi Nana Tai and in the world-famous Patpong area, between Th Silom and Th Surawong.

Patpong has calmed down a lot over the years and become a general tourist attraction in itself. These days it has more of an open-air market feel as several of the newer bars are literally on the street, and vendors set up shop in the evening hawking everything from roast squid to fake designer watches. On Patpong's two parallel lanes there are around 35 to 40 go-go bars, plus a sprinkling of restaurants, cocktail bars, discos and live music venues. The downstairs clubs, with names like *King's Castle* and *Pussy Galore*, feature go-go dancing while upstairs the real raunch is kept behind closed doors. Women and couples are welcome. Avoid bars touting 'free' sex shows as there are usually hidden charges and when you try to ditch the outrageous bill the

doors are suddenly blocked by muscled bouncers. An exception is *Supergirls*, famous for its sex-on-a-flying motorcycle show, as covered by *Rolling Stone*. The 1 am closing law is strictly enforced on Patpong 1 and 2.

The gay men's equivalent can be found on nearby Soi Tantawan and Sao Anuman Ratchathon, where go-go bars feature in-your-face names like *Golden Cock* as well as the more cryptic *Super Lex Matsuda*.

A more direct legacy of the R&R days is *Soi Cowboy*, a single lane strip of 25 to 30 bars off Th Sukhumvit between sois 21 and 23. By and large it's seedier than Patpong, and you will see far fewer women and couples in the crowd.

Nana Entertainment Plaza, off Soi 4 (Soi Nana Tai) Th Sukhumvit, is a three storey complex which has surged in popularity among resident and visiting oglers. Nana Plaza comes complete with its own guesthouses in the same complex, used almost exclusively by Nana Plaza's female bar workers for illicit assignations. The 'female' staff at *Casanova* consists entirely of Thai transvestites and transsexuals – this is a favourite stop for foreigners visiting Bangkok for sex re-assignment surgery. There are 18 bars in the whole complex.

Gay & Lesbian Venues

See the information on Soi 2 and Soi 4, Th Silom dance club scene under Discos & Dance Clubs for places that attract mixed gay/straight/bi clientele. In general the Soi 2 clubs are more gay than the Soi 4 bars, though Soi 4's *Telephone* and *The Balcony* are more exclusively gay than other bars on this street. *DJ Station* still boasts Soi 2's hottest gay dance scene, plus *ká-toey* (transvestite) cabaret at midnight. *Khrua Silom*, in Silom Alley off Soi 2, attracts a young Thai gay and lesbian crowd; it's a 'kitchen disco', where you stand and dance next to your table. There's a cluster of seedier gay bars around Soi Anuman Ratchathon, off Soi Tantawan, which joins Th Surawong opposite the Tawana Ramada Hotel – more or less the gay equivalent of Patpong. *TG*

Studio is a club on Soi Anuman Ratchathon that's less sleazy than the others, more of an after hours dance scene.

City Men Pub, 45 Th Sukhumvit, is a long-running gay men's bar that's popular with expats. Monday night at *Discovery* (see Discos & Dance Clubs) is promoted as gay and lesbian night.

Utopia (☎ 02-259 9619, 116/1 Soi 23, Th Sukhumvit) is a combination bar, gallery, cafe and information clearing house for the local gay and lesbian community – the only such facility in South-East Asia. Friday nights are designated women's night, and there are regular film nights as well as Thai lessons. Special events, such as Valentine's Day candlelit dinners, are held from time to time. Utopia is open daily from noon to 2 am. Nearby on Soi 23 is the *Turning Point Men's Club*.

Kitchenette (☎ 02-3810861, 1st floor, Dutchess Plaza, 289 Soi 55 (Soi Thong Lor), Th Sukhumvit) is a lesbian/mixed cafe with live music on weekends. Other lesbian venues include: *By Heart Pub* (☎ 02-570 1841, 117/697 Soi Sena Nikhom 1, Th Phahonyothin, Bang Kapi)*; Be My Guest* (mixed crowd), around the corner from Utopia on Soi 31.

Babylon Bangkok (☎ 02-213 2108, 50 Soi Atakanprasit, Th Sathon Tai) is a four storey gay sauna which has been called one of the top 10 gay men's saunas in the world. Facilities include a bar, roof garden, gym, massage room, steam and dry saunas and jacuzzi baths. It's open daily from 5 to 11 pm. (See Gay & Lesbian Travellers in the Facts for the Visitor chapter for more detail on gay and lesbian resources in Bangkok.)

Ká-Toey Cabaret

Transvestite *(ká-toey)* cabarets are big in Bangkok. *Calypso Cabaret* (☎ 02-261 6355, 216 8937, 296 Th Phayathai), in the Asia Hotel, has the largest regularly performing transvestite troupe in town, with nightly shows at 8.15 and 9.45 pm. Tickets cost 600B and include one drink. Although the audience is almost 100% tourists, the show is very good and includes plenty of Thai and Asian themes as well as the usual Broadway camp. Several of the gay bars on sois 2 and 4 off Th Silom also feature short drag shows during intermissions between dance sets.

Live Music

Bangkok's live music scene has expanded rapidly over the past decade or so, with a multiplicity of new, extremely competent bands and new clubs. The three storey *Saxophone Pub Restaurant* (☎ 02-246 5472, 3/8 Victory Monument, Th Phayathai), south-east of the Victory Monument circle, has become a Bangkok institution for musicians of several genres. On the ground floor is a bar/restaurant featuring jazz from 9 pm to 1.30 am; the next floor up has a billiards hall with taped music or CDs playing in the background; the top floor has live bands playing reggae, R&B, jazz or blues from 10.30 pm to 4 am, and on Sundays there's an open jam session. There's never a cover charge at Saxophone and you don't need to dress up.

Another very casual spot to hear music is the open-air bar operated by *Ruang Pung Art Community* next to Chatuchak Weekend Market. Thai rock, folk, blues and jam sessions attract an artsy Thai crowd. Open only Saturday and Sunday afternoons.

Not to be overlooked on Th Sarasin, the *Old West* (Thailand's original old-west-style pub) books good Thai folk and blues groups – look for a rockin' outfit called D-Train here.

Concept CM2, a multi-themed complex in the basement of the Novotel on Siam Square, hosts a rotation of live western bands and Thai recording artists – generally focusing on what passes for alternative these days – interspersed with DJ dance music. Look for V4, a locally based but multi-ethnic outfit that does good reggae, funk and acid jazz covers.

Dance Fever (☎ 02-247 4295), a new large club at 71 Th Ratchadaphisek in the burgeoning 'Ratchada' entertainment district, features a state-of-the-art sound and lighting system, giant video screens, a bar and restaurant. International touring bands like Bush, Blur and others have played here.

The relatively new *Metal Zone* (☎ 02-255 1913), around the corner from Th Sarasin on Soi Lang Suan, just north of Lumphini Park, is the best of the city's heavy metal clubs. Along with the dragons-and-dungeons decor is a regular line-up of bands producing everything from thrash to gothic to speed metal, Ozzie squeal to Axel rasp, even a few convoluted Helmet tunes.

Bangkok's better-than-average *Hard Rock Cafe*, Siam Square, Soi 11, features live rock music most evenings from around 10 pm to 12.30 am, including the occasional big name act (an incendiary performance by the usually mellow Chris Isaak left bootnail dents in the bar top).

Many top-end hotels have bars or lounges with imported pop bands of varying talent who play mostly covers. *Angelini's* in the Shangri-La usually has one of the better cover bands, as does the elegant *Spasso* in the Grand Hyatt Erawan.

The only non-hotel bar with regular live jazz is *Blues/Jazz* (☎ 02-258 7747, Soi 53, Th Sukhumvit). The Oriental's famous *Bamboo Bar* has good live jazz nightly in an elegant but relaxed atmosphere. Bars at the Grand Hyatt and Beaufort Sukhothai Hotel also have live jazz from Tuesday to Sunday.

Cinema

Dozens of movie theatres around town show Thai, Chinese, Indian and western movies. The majority of films shown are comedies and shoot-em-ups, with the occasional drama slipping through. These theatres are air-con and quite comfortable, with reasonable rates (40B to 100B). All movies in Thai theatres are preceded by the Thai royal anthem. Everyone in the theatre is expected to stand quietly and respectfully for the duration of the anthem.

Movie ads appear daily in both *The Nation* and the *Bangkok Post*; listings in *The Nation* include addresses and programme times.

Foreign films are often altered before distribution by Thailand's board of censors; usually this involves obscuring nude sequences, although gunplay is also sometimes edited.

Film buffs may prefer the weekly or twice weekly offerings at Bangkok's foreign cultural clubs; French and German films screened at the cultural clubs are almost always subtitled in English. Admission is sometimes free, sometimes 30B to 40B. Addresses and contact details for the cultural centres can be found in *Bangkok Metro* magazine, which also publishes details of film festivals and other special film events.

The most state-of-the-art sound and projection facilities are found at *Ploenchit Cineplace*, Ploenchit Plaza Th Ploenchit, and *United Artists*, 7th and 8th floors, Central Plaza Th Ratchada-Rama III. Check the listings in the *Nation* for addresses of other cinemas.

Video

Video rentals are very popular in Bangkok; not only are videos cheaper than film admissions, but many films are available on video that aren't approved for theatre distribution by Thailand's board of censors. For those with access to a TV and VCR, the average rental is around 20B to 50B. Th Sukhumvit has the highest concentration of video shops; the better ones are found in the residential area between sois 39 and 55.

TVs and VCRs (both PAL and NTSC) can be rented at *Silver Bell* (☎ 02-236 2845, 113/1-2 Surawong Centre, Th Surawong).

Thai Dance-Drama

Thailand's most traditional *lákhon* and *khŏn* performances are held at the *National Theatre* (☎ 02-224 1342) on Th Chao Fa, Banglamphu, near Phra Pinklao Bridge. The theatre's regular public roster schedules six or seven performances per month, usually on weekends. Admission fees are very reasonable at around 20B to 200B depending on the seating. Attendance at a khŏn performance (masked dance-drama based on stories from the *Ramakian*) is highly recommended.

Occasionally, classical dance performances are also held at the *Thailand*

medium at the Vegetarian Festival, Phuket.

HERMANN MOLL

An old man and his rooster, central Thailand.

JOHN HAY

monk helps a layman prepare for ordination.

JOE CUMMINGS

A cooling drink – *máphráo àwn*.

JOHN HAY

A tuk-tuk driver in Bangkok.

RICHARD I'ANSON

Fresh seafood is abundant in Bangkok.

Hawker's stalls along Thanon Silom, Bangkok.

Damnoen Saduak floating market, near Bangkok.

Thanon Silom is a 'shopping ghetto'.

A basket of durians (a tropical fruit).

Early evening at a night market in Bangkok.

Cultural Centre (☎ 02-245 7711) on Th Ratchadaphisek and at the **College of Dramatic Arts** (☎ 02-224 1391), near the National Theatre.

For more information on Thai classical dance see the Arts section in the Facts about Thailand chapter.

Shrine Dancing

Free performances of traditional *lákhon kae bon* can be seen daily at the **Lak Meuang** and *Erawan* shrines if you happen to arrive when a performance troupe has been commissioned by a worshipper. Although many of the dance movements are the same as those seen in classical lákhon, these relatively crude performances are specially choreographed for ritual purposes and don't represent true classical dance forms. But the dancing is colourful – the dancers wear full costume and are accompanied by live music – so it's worth stopping by to watch a performance if you're in the vicinity.

Dinner Theatres

Most tourists view performances put on solely for their benefit at one of the several Thai classical dance/dinner theatres in the city. Admission prices at these evening venues average 200B to 500B per person and include a 'typical' Thai dinner (often toned down for faràng palates), a couple of selected dance performances and a martial arts display.

The historic Oriental Hotel has its own dinner theatre the **Sala Rim Nam** (☎ 02-437 2918, 437 3080) on the Thonburi side of the Chao Phraya River opposite the hotel. The admission is well above average but so is the food, the performance and the Thai pavilion decor (teak, marble and bronze); the river ferry between the hotel and restaurant is free. Dinner begins at 7 pm, the dance performance at 8.30 pm. The much less expensive dinner performance at Silom Village's **Ruen Thep** restaurant on Th Silom is recommended because of the relaxed, semi-outdoor setting. Some other dinner theatre venues include:

Maneeya Lotus Room
(☎ 02-251 0382) 518/5 Th Ploenchit
Phiman Restaurant
(☎ 02-258 7866) 46 Soi 49, Th Sukhumvit
Ruen Thep
(☎ 02-233 9447) Silom Village, Th Silom
Sala Rim Nam
(☎ 02-437 6221/3080) opposite the Oriental Hotel, Th Charoen Nakhon
Suwannahong Restaurant
(☎ 02-245 4448/3747) Th Si Ayuthaya

Cigar Bars

One half of the lobby in **Regent Hotel** is devoted to the smoker, with Dominican and Cuban brands (including Montecristo and Cohiba) available from the hotel's humidor; The Regent claims the largest selection of single-malt whiskies in Asia – 64 of them, dating back to a 1940 Glenlivet.

La Casa del Habano, in The Oriental Hotel, has 25 brands of Cuban cigars ranging in price from US$3 to US$120 per cigar, with a tiny lounge equipped with a select list of fine cognacs, port and single-malt whiskies. Not to be out-done, the Beaufort Sukhothai has its own **Lotus Arts de Vivre Cigar and Wine Lounge**.

Massage Parlours

Massage parlours have been a Bangkok attraction for many years now, though the TAT tries to play down the city's reputation in this respect. Massage as a healing art is a centuries-old tradition in Thailand, and it is easy to find a legitimate massage in Bangkok, despite the commercialisation of recent years (see the following Traditional Massage entry). That many of the city's modern massage parlours (*àap òp nûat* or 'bathe-steam-massage', sometimes referred to as 'Turkish bath') also deal in prostitution is well known; less well known is the fact that many (but by no means all) of the girls working in the parlours are bonded labour – they are not necessarily there by choice. There is a definite AIDS presence in Thailand (see the information on this and other sexually transmitted diseases under Health in the Facts for the Visitor chapter).

All but the most insensitive males will be saddened by the sight of 50 girls/women behind a glass wall with numbers pinned to their dresses. Often the bank of masseuses is divided into sections according to skill and/or appearance. Most expensive is the 'superstar' section, in which the women try to approximate the look of fashion models or actresses. A smaller section is reserved for women who are actually good at giving massages, and who offer nothing extra. (See the Prostitution entry in the Society and Conduct section of the Facts about Thailand chapter.)

Traditional Massage

Traditional Thai massage, also called 'ancient' massage, is now widely available in Bangkok as an alternative to the red-light massage parlours. One of the best places to experience a traditional massage is at *Wat Pho*, Bangkok's oldest temple. Massage here costs 200B per hour or 120B for half an hour. For those interested in studying massage, the temple also offers two 30-hour courses – one on general Thai massage, the other on massage therapy. Call the Wat Pho Thai Traditional Medical & Massage School, ☎ 02-221 2974, for further information.

Next door to Wat Mahathat (towards Thammasat University at the south-east corner of Th Maharat and Th Phra Chan) is a strip of Thai herbal medicine shops offering good massage for a mere 80B to 100B an hour.

A more commercial area for traditional Thai massage, as well as Thai herbal saunas, is Th Surawong near infamous Patpong. Here you'll find *Marble House* (☎ 02-235 3519, 37/18-19 Soi Surawong Plaza, Th Surawong)* and *Eve House* (☎ 02-266 3846, 18/1 Th Surawong)*, opposite Thaniya Plaza, among others. Eve House charges 150B per hour and accepts women only. The others charge 200B to 300B per hour and offer Thai herbal sauna as well as massage. *Arima Onsen* (☎ 02-235 2142, 37/10-11 Soi Surawong Plaza)* specialises in Japanese-style massage and reflexology.

Out on Th Sukhumvit you can find traditional Thai massage at *Buathip Thai Massage* (☎ 02-255 1045, 4/13 Soi 5, Th Sukhumvit)* and at *Winwan* (☎ 02-251 7467)* between sois 1 and 3, Th Sukhumvit.

Fees for traditional Thai massage should be no more than 300B per hour, though some places have a 1½ hour minimum. Be aware that not every place advertising traditional or ancient massage offers a really good one; sometimes the only thing 'ancient' about the pummelling is the age of the masseuse or masseur. Thai massage aficionados say that the best massages are given by blind masseurs (available at Marble House).

Most hotels also provide a legitimate massage service either through their health clubs or as part of room service.

SPECTATOR SPORTS
Muay Thai (Thai Boxing)

Muay thai can be seen at two boxing stadiums, *Sanam Muay Lumphini* (on Th Rama IV near Th Sathon Tai) and *Sanam Muay Ratchadamnoen* (on Th Ratchadamnoen Nok, next to the old TAT office). Admission fees vary according to seating: around 150B for the outer circle or 500B ringside, for eight fights of five rounds each. The outer circle seats are quite OK. Monday, Wednesday, Thursday and Sunday the boxing is at Ratchadamnoen, while Tuesday, Friday and Saturday it's at Lumphini. The Ratchadamnoen matches begin at 6 pm, except for the Sunday shows which start at 5 pm, and the Lumphini matches all begin at 6.20 pm. Aficionados say the best-matched bouts are reserved for Tuesday nights at Lumphini, and Thursday nights at Ratchadamnoen. The restaurants on the north side of Ratchadamnoen stadium are well known for their delicious *kài yâang* and other North-Eastern dishes.

Warning Avoid the special 2 pm shows on Sunday at Ratchadamnoen which are really just practice bouts put on for tourists. At some programmes (especially the 2 pm tourist show) a ticket mafia try to steer every tourist into buying a 500B ringside seat, often claiming all other seats are sold out. It's a pretence; if you walk around the touts you'll find a window selling seats as cheap as 50B. The same thing happens at the night matches, only the cheap seats are 150B – ignore the touts and look for windows marked at that price. Don't believe anyone who says seats are sold out, unless you hear it directly from a window ticket vendor.

Tàkrâw

This peculiarly Thai ball sport can be seen at schools and universities around Bangkok, and occasionally at the National Stadium.

SHOPPING

Regular visitors to Asia know that, in many ways, Bangkok beats Hong Kong and Singapore for deals on handicrafts, textiles, gems, jewellery, art and antiques – nowhere else will you find the same combination of range, quality and prices. The trouble is finding the good spots, as the city's intense urban tangle makes orientation sometimes difficult. *Nancy Chandler's Map of Bangkok* makes a very good buying companion, with annotations on all sorts of small, out-of-the-way shopping venues and markets (called *tàlàat* in Thai).

Be sure to read the introductory Shopping section in the Facts for the Visitor chapter before setting out on a buying spree. Amid all the bargains are a number of cleverly disguised rip-off schemes – caveat emptor!

Chatuchak Weekend Market

Known in Thai as Talaat Jatujak, this is the Disneyland of Thai markets; on weekends 8672 vendor stalls cater to an estimated 200,000 visitors a day. Everything is sold here, from live chickens and snakes to opium pipes and herbal remedies. Thai clothing such as the *phâakhamãa* (sarong for males) and the *phâasîn* (sarong for females), *kaang keng jiin* (Chinese pants) and *sêua mâw hâwm* (blue cotton farmer's shirt) are good buys. You'll also find musical instruments, hill-tribe crafts, religious amulets, antiques, flowers, clothes imported from India and Nepal, camping gear and

military surplus. The best bargains of all are household goods like pots and pans, dishes, drinking glasses etc. Don't forget to try out your bargaining skills.

The main part of the Weekend Market is open on Saturday and Sunday from around 8 am to 6 pm, though some places may stay open as late as 8 pm. There are a few vendors out on weekday mornings and there's a daily market for vegetables, plants and flowers opposite the market's south side. One section of the latter, known as the Aw Taw Kaw Market, sells organically grown (no chemical sprays or fertilisers) fruit and vegetables.

The Weekend Market lies at the southern end of Chatuchak Park, off Th Phahonyothin, south of the Northern bus terminal. Air-con bus Nos 2, 3, 9, 10 and 13, and a dozen other ordinary city buses (including No 3 from Th Phra Athit in Banglamphu), all pass the market – get off before the Northern bus terminal. The air-con bus No 12 and ordinary bus No 77 conveniently terminate right next to the market.

Nailert (Nai Loet) Market

This new market complex opposite the Amari Watergate Hotel, on Th Phetchaburi in Pratunam, was recently opened as an alternative to Chatuchak Market nearer the city centre. The array of goods for sale is similar; it remains to be seen whether the market will succeed, although it's definitely a more convenient location than Chatuchak for most visitors.

Other Thai Markets

Under the expressway at the intersection of Rama IV and Th At Narong in the Khlong Toey district is the Khlong Toey Market, possibly the cheapest general market in Bangkok (best on Wednesday). South of the Khlong Toey Market, closer to the port, is the similar Penang Market, so called because a lot of the goods 'drop off' cargo boats from Penang (and Singapore, Hong Kong etc). Both markets may be demolished under current urban renewal plans.

Pratunam Market, at the intersection of Phetchaburi and Ratchaprarop, runs every day and is very crowded, but has great deals in new, cheap clothing. You won't see it from the street; you must look for one of the unmarked entrances that lead back behind the main shopfronts. While browsing Pratunam you can easily visit Nailert Market also (see earlier entry).

The huge Banglamphu Market spreads several blocks over Th Chakraphong, Th Phra Sumen, Th Tanao and Th Rambutri, a short walk from the Th Khao San guesthouse area. The Banglamphu Market area is probably the most comprehensive shopping district in the city as it encompasses everything from street vendors to up-market department stores. Also in this part of Bangkok you'll find the Thewet flower market near Tha Thewet, on Th Krung Kasem.

The Pahurat and Chinatown districts have interconnected markets selling tonnes of well priced fabrics, clothes and household wares, as well as a few places selling gems and jewellery. The Wong Wian Yai Market in Thonburi, next to the large roundabout directly south-west of Phra Phut Yot Fa (Memorial) Bridge, is another general market, though gets few tourists.

Tourist Markets

Th Khao San has itself become a shopping bazaar offering cheap audio tapes, used books, jewellery, beads, clothing, Thai axe pillows, T-shirts, tattoos, body piercing and just about any other product or service you might wish for.

At night Patong sois 1 and 2 fill up with vendors selling cheap tourist junk, inexpensive clothing, fake watches, you name it. Along both sides of Th Sukhumvit between Soi 1 and Soi 5 there are also lots of street vendors selling similar items.

Shopping Centres & Department Stores

The growth of large and small shopping centres has accelerated over the last few years into a virtual boom. Central and Robinson department stores, the original stand-bys, have around a dozen branches apiece, with all the usual stuff (designer

clothes, western cosmetics etc) plus supermarkets and Thai delis, cassette tapes, fabrics and other local products that might be of interest to some travellers. Typical opening hours are 10 am to 8 pm.

Oriental Plaza (Soi Oriental, Th Charoen Krung) and River City shopping complex (near the Royal Orchid Sheraton, off Th Charoen Krung and Th Si Phraya) are centres for high-end consumer goods. They're expensive but do have some unique merchandise; River City has good quality art and antique shops on the 3rd and 4th floors.

The much smaller Silom Village Trade Centre on Th Silom has a few antique and handicraft shops with merchandise several rungs lower in price. Anchored by Central department store, the six storey Silom Complex nearby remains one of the city's busiest shopping centres. Also on Th Silom is the posh Thaniya Plaza, a newer arcade housing clothing boutiques, bookshops, jewellery shops and more.

Along Ploenchit and Sukhumvit you'll find many newer department stores and shopping centres.

The eight floors of the World Trade Centre, near the intersection of Ploenchit and Ratchaprarop, seem to go on and on. The main focus is the Zen department store, which has clothing shops reminiscent of Hong Kong's high-end boutiques.

Siam Square, on Th Rama I near Phayathai, is a network of some 12 sois lined with shops selling mid-price designer clothes, books, sporting goods and antiques. On the opposite side of Rama I stands Thailand's first shopping centre, built in 1976, the four storey Siam Center. Recently renovated, it still features designer clothing shops, as well as cafes, travel agencies, banks and airline offices. Next to Siam Center, and connected by an enclosed pedestrian bridge, Siam Discovery Center contains yet more designer shops, plus Asia Books (books and magazines), Habitat (furniture) and several large restaurants.

One of the most varied and affordable shopping centres to wander around in is the MBK shopping centre near Siam Square.

It's all air-con, but there are many small, inexpensive vendors and shops in addition to the middle-class Tokyu department store. Bargains can be found here if you look. The Travel Mart on MBK's 3rd floor stocks a reasonable supply of travel gear and camping equipment – not the highest quality but useful in a pinch.

Seacon Square is South-East Asia's largest shopping centre/mall, out on Th Si Nakharin, in the south-east. It encompasses practically every type of shop mentioned in this section, including huge branches of DK Books and Asia Books, plus a cinema multiplex and a number of cafes.

Antiques & Decorative Items
Real Thai antiques are rare and costly. Most Bangkok antique shops keep a few antiques around for collectors, along with lots of pseudo-antiques or traditionally crafted items that look like antiques. The majority of shop operators are quite candid about what's really old and what isn't. As Thai design becomes more popular abroad, many shops are now specialising in Thai home decorative items.

Reliable antique shops (using the word 'antique' loosely) include Elephant House (☎ 02-233 6973), Soi Phattana, Th Silom and 67/12 Soi Phra Phinit (☎ 02-679 3122), off Soi Suan Phlu; Peng Seng, on the corner of Th Rama IV and Th Surawong; Asian Heritage (☎ 02-259 9593) 245/14 Sukhumvit Soi 31; Thai House (☎ 02-258 6287), 720/6 Th Sukhumvit, near Soi 28; and Artisan's in the Silom Village Trade Centre, Th Silom.

River City complex, on the river and attached by a tunnel to the Royal Orchid Sheraton Hotel off Th Yotha, contains a number of high quality art and antique shops on the 3rd and 4th floors. The Oriental Plaza shopping complex, adjacent to the Oriental Hotel, also has several good, if pricey, antique shops.

Gems & Jewellery
Recommending specific shops is tricky, since to the average eye one coloured stone looks as good as another, so the risk of a

rip-off is much greater than for most other popular shopping items. One shop that's been a longtime favourite with Bangkok expats for service and value in set jewellery is Johnny's Gems (☎ 02-224 4065) at 199 Th Fuang Nakhon (off Th Charoen Krung). Another reputable jewellery place is Merlin et Delauney (☎ 02-234 3884), with a large showroom and gem-cutting workshop at 1 Soi Pradit, Th Surawong and a smaller shop at the Novotel Bangkok, Soi 6, Siam Square. Both have unset stones as well as jewellery. Also dependable and specialising in unset stones is Lambert Holding (☎ 02-236 4343) at 807 Th Silom.

Bronzeware
Thailand has the oldest bronze-working tradition in the world and there are several factories in Bangkok producing bronze sculpture and cutlery. Two factories that sell direct to the public (and where you may also be able to observe the bronze-working process) are Siam Bronze Factory (☎ 02-234 9436), at 1250 Th Charoen Krung, and Somkij Bronze (☎ 02-251 0891), at 1194 Th Phetchaburi Tat Mai (New Phetburi). Make sure any items you buy are silicon-coated, otherwise they'll tarnish. To see the casting process for Buddha images, go to the Buddha Casting Foundry next to Wat Wiset Khan on Th Phrannok, Thonburi (take a river ferry from Tha Phra Chan or Tha Maharat on the Bangkok side to reach the foot of Th Phrannok).

Many vendors at Wat Mahathat's Sunday market sell old and new bronzeware – haggling is imperative.

Handicrafts
Bangkok has excellent buys in Thai handicrafts, though for Northern hill-tribe materials you might be able to do better in Chiang Mai. Narayana Phand (☎ 02-252 4670) on Th Ratchadamri is a bit on the touristy side but has a large selection and good marked prices – no haggling is necessary. Central department store on Th Ploenchit has a Thai handicrafts section with marked prices.

The International School Bangkok (ISB; ☎ 02-583 5401/28) puts on a large charity sale of Thai handicrafts every sixth Saturday or so (except during ISB's summer holiday, June to August). Sometimes you can find pieces at the ISB craft sales that are practically unavailable elsewhere. At other times it's not very interesting; it all depends on what the sales managers are able to collect during the year. Call for the latest sale schedule. ISB is north of the city proper, towards the airport, off Route 304 (Th Chaeng Wattana), inside the Nichada Thani condo/townhouse complex; the address is 39/7 Soi Nichadathani Samakhi.

Perhaps the most interesting places to shop for handicrafts are the smaller, independent handicraft shops, each of which has its own style and character. Quality is high at Rasi Sayam (☎ 02-258 4195), 32 Soi 23, Th Sukhumvit; many of the items it stocks, including wall-hangings and pottery, are made specifically for this shop. Another good one for pottery as well as lacquerware and especially fabrics is Vilai's (☎ 02-391 6106) at 731/1 Soi 55 (Thong Lor), Th Sukhumvit.

Khŏn masks of intricately formed wire and papier mâché can be purchased at Padung Chiip (no roman-script sign) on Th Chakraphong just south of the Th Khao San intersection.

For quality Thai celadon (a type of green or blue-glazed porcelain), check out Thai Celadon (☎ 02-229 4383) at 8/6-8 Th Ratchadaphisek Tat Mai. Inexpensive places to pick up new Thai pottery of all shapes and sizes at wholesale prices include two places on Soi On Nut, off Soi 77, Th Sukhumvit: United Siam Overseas (☎ 02-721 6320) and Siamese Merchandise (☎ 02-333 0680). Overseas shipping can be arranged.

Tailor Shops

Bangkok abounds in places where you can have shirts, trousers, suits and just about any other article of clothing designed, cut and sewn by hand. Workmanship ranges from shoddy to excellent, so it pays to ask

around before committing yourself. Shirts and trousers can be turned around in 48 hours or less with only one fitting. But no matter what a tailor may tell you, it takes more than one or two fittings to create a good suit, and most reputable tailors will ask for two to five sittings. A custom-made suit, no matter what the material is, should cost less than US$200. An all-cashmere suit can be had for as little as US$150 to US$175 with a little bargaining; bring your own fabric and it will cost even less.

Bangkok tailors can be particularly good at copying your favourite piece of clothing. If possible, bring your own personally selected fabric from home or abroad, especially if it's 100% cotton you want. Most of the so-called 'cotton' offered by Bangkok tailors is actually a blend of cotton and a synthetic; more than a few tailors will actually try to pass off full polyester or dacron as cotton. Good quality silk, on the other hand, is plentiful. Tailor-made silk shirts should cost no more than US$12 to US$20, depending on the type of silk (Chinese silk is cheaper than Thai).

Generally speaking the best shops are those found along the outer reaches of Th Sukhumvit (out beyond Soi 20 or so) and on or off Th Charoen Krung. Th Silom also has some good tailors. The worst tailor shops tend to be those in tourist-oriented shopping areas in inner Th Sukhumvit, Th Khao San, the River City Shopping Complex and other shopping malls. 'Great deals' like four shirts, two suits, a kimono and a safari suit all in one package almost always turn out to be of inferior materials and workmanship.

Recommended tailor shops include: Marzotto at 3 Soi Wat Suan Phlu, off Th Charoen Krung; Julie at 1279 Th Charoen, near Silom Centre; Marco Tailor on Soi 7, Siam Square; and Macway's Exporters at 975/3 Soi Gaysorn (Keson), near Le Meridien President Hotel. In Siam Center on the 3rd floor, Siam Emporium (☎ 02-251 9617) can also be recommended. The latter has a second branch in the Mandarin Hotel on Th Rama IV.

Camera Supplies, Film & Processing

For a selection of camera supplies across a wide range of models and brand names, two of the best shops are Sunny Camera at 1267/1 Th Charoen Krung (☎ 02-233 8378), 134/5-6 Soi 8, Th Silom (☎ 02-237 2054) and on the 3rd floor of the Mahboonkrong shopping centre (☎ 02-217 9293), and Niks (☎ 02-235 2929) at 166 Th Silom.

Film prices in Bangkok are generally lower than anywhere else in Asia, including Hong Kong. The highest concentration of photo shops can be found along Th Silom and Th Surawong. In Mahboonkrong shopping centre, FotoFile on the ground floor has the best selection of slide films, including refrigerated pro films.

Quick, professional quality processing of most film types is available at: E6 Processing Centre (☎ 02-259 9573), 46 Soi 51, Th Sukhumvit; Image Quality Lab (IQ Lab) at 60 Th Silom (☎ 02-238 4001) or at 9/33 Thana Arcade, Soi 63, Th Sukhumvit (☎ 02-714 0644); Eastbourne Professional Color Laboratories (☎ 02-235 5234), 134/4 Th Silom; and Hollywood Film (☎ 02-692 2330, 692 0690, fax 692 0689) where they offer a pick-up and delivery service (ask for John).

Scuba Supplies

Larry's Dive Center, Bar & Grill (☎ 02-663 4563, email larrybkk@larrysdive.com), 8/3 Soi 22, Th Sukhumvit, stocks all manner of diving and snorkelling gear. There's a restaurant and bar attached, so you can fill both your air tanks and your stomach.

GETTING THERE & AWAY
Air

Bangkok is a major centre for international flights throughout Asia, and its international airport is a busy one. Bangkok is also a major centre for buying discounted airline tickets (see the Getting There & Away chapter for details), but be warned that the Bangkok travel agency business has more than a few crooked operators. Domestic flights operated by THAI, Bangkok Airways

and Angel Airlines also fan out from Bangkok all over the country (see the Getting Around chapter). Addresses of airline offices in Bangkok are:

Air India
(☎ 02-256-9620, reservations ☎ 256 9614/8)
16th floor, Amarin Tower, Th Ploenchit
Air New Zealand
(☎ 02-233 5900/9, 237 1560/2)
1053 Th Charoen Krung
Alitalia
(☎ 02-233 4000/4)
8th floor, Boonmitr Bldg, 138 Th Silom
Angel Airways
(☎ 02-535 6287)
Bangkok international airport
Bangkok Airways
(☎ 02-229 3434/56, 253 4014)
Queen Sirikit National Convention Centre, Th Ratchadaphisek Tat Mai, Khlong Toey
(☎ 02-254 2903)
1111 Th Ploenchit
British Airways
(☎ 02-236 0038)
Abdulrahim Place, 14th fl, 990 Th Rama IV
Cathay Pacific Airways
(☎ 02-263 0606)
11th floor, Ploenchit Tower, Th Ploenchit
Garuda Indonesia
(☎ 02-285 6470/3)
27th floor, Lumphini Tower, 1168 Th Rama IV
Japan Airlines
(☎ 02-274 1400, 274 1435)
254/1 Th Ratchadaphisek
Lao Aviation
(☎ 02-236 9821/3)
Silom Plaza, 491/17 Th Silom
Lufthansa
(☎ 02-255 0385)
Bank of America Bldg, 2/2 Th Withayu
(☎ 02-264 2400)
Asoke Bldg, Soi 21, Th Sukhumvit
Malaysia Airlines
(☎ 02-236 5871; reservations ☎ 236 4705/9)
98-102 Th Surawong
(☎ 02-263 0565)
20th floor, Ploenchit Tower, Th Ploenchit
Myanmar Airways International
(☎ 02-267 5078)
Charn Issara Tower, Th Rama IV
Qantas
(☎ 02-267 5188, 236 0307)
Charn Issara Tower, 942/51 Th Rama IV

Royal Air Cambodge
  see Malaysia Airlines
Silk Air
  (☎ 02-236 0303, reservations ☎ 236-0440)
  12th floor, Silom Centre Bldg, Th Silom
Singapore Airlines
  (☎ 02-236 0303, reservations ☎ 236 0440)
  12th floor, Silom Centre Bldg, 2 Th Silom
Thai Airways International (THAI)
  (head office ☎ 02-513 0121)
  89 Th Vibhavadi Rangsit
  (☎ 02-234 3100/19)
  485 Th Silom
  (☎ 02-288 0060, 628 2000)
  6 Th Lan Luang
  (☎ 02-215 2020/1)
  Asia Hotel, 296 Th Phayathai
  (☎ 02-535 2081/2, 523 6121)
  Bangkok international airport, Don Muang
United Airlines
  (☎ 02-253 0558)
  9th floor, Regent House, 183 Th Ratchadamri
Vietnam Airlines (Hang Khong Vietnam)
  (☎ 02-251 4242)
  3rd floor, 572 Th Ploenchit

Airport Facilities During the past decade, the airport facilities at Bangkok international airport have undergone a US$200 million redevelopment, including the construction of an international terminal that is one of the most modern and convenient in Asia. However, the very slow immigration lines in the upstairs arrival hall in Terminal 1 are still a problem. Despite a long row of impressive-looking immigration counters, there never seem to be enough clerks on duty, even at peak arrival times. Even when the booths are fully staffed, waits of 45 minutes to an hour are not unusual. On the other hand, baggage claim is usually quick and efficient (of course, they have lots of time to get it right while you're inching along through immigration).

The Customs area has a green lane for passengers with nothing to declare – just walk through if you're one of these and hand your Customs form to one of the clerks by the exit. Baggage trolleys are free for use inside the terminal.

The Thai government has planned for some time to open another international airport about 20km east of Bangkok at Nong Ngu Hao. In theory, the new facility is supposed to be open by 2004, but the project's future is murky at best; it's already three years behind schedule, and some government officials have said construction will be suspended for 10 years. At the time of writing, local media reported that the government was instead planning to concentrate on further expansion at the existing international airport.

In the meantime Terminal 2, a second international terminal adjacent to Terminal 1, has opened to accommodate increasing air traffic. Terminal 2 has few facilities other than currency exchange booths, a public taxi desk and some restaurants on the 4th floor.

Foreign currency booths on the ground floor of the arrival hall and in the departure lounge of both terminals which give a good rate of exchange, so there's no need to wait till you're in the city centre to change money. There are also ATMs in the arrival and departure halls.

There is a 24 hour post/telephone office with a Home Direct phone service in the departure hall (3rd floor) of Terminal 1. Another 24 hour post office is located in the departure lounge; a third one in the arrival hall is open Monday to Friday from 9 am to 5 pm.

Left-luggage facilities (20B per piece per day, three months maximum) are available in the departure halls in both terminals. In the transit lounge of Terminal 1, clean day rooms with washing and toilet facilities can be rented for 900B per six hours.

On the 4th floor of Terminal 1 is a small, reasonably priced 24 hour cafeteria area, a larger THAI restaurant with more expensive fare and on the 2nd level, above the arrival area, is a coffee shop which is open from 6 am to 11 pm. There is also a small snack bar in the waiting area on the ground floor. The departure lounge has two snack bars which serve beer and liquor.

On the 4th floor of Terminal 2 is a cluster of new fast-food-style places. Opposite these is a posh Chinese restaurant and on the arrival floor of this terminal is a KFC.

The Airbridge Cafe, a European-style coffee shop on the enclosed bridge between Terminal 1 and the Amari Airport Hotel, provides a quiet alternative to the airport places.

There are several newsstands and souvenir shops in the arrival and departure areas of Terminal 1. Duty-free shopping is available in the departure lounge as well. The book and magazine selection at the newsstands is spotty; if you have enough time to walk across the enclosed footbridge from Terminal 1 to the Amari Airport Hotel, you'll find a much better bookshop in the hotel's shopping arcade (south of reception).

If you leave the airport building area and cross the expressway on the pedestrian bridge (just north of the passenger terminal), you'll find yourself in Don Muang town where there are all sorts of shops, a market, lots of small restaurants and food stalls, even a wát, all within 100m or so of the airport.

The modern and luxurious Amari Airport Hotel (☎ 02-566-1020/1) has its own air-conditioned, enclosed footbridge from Terminal 1 and 'special mini-stay' daytime rates (8 am to 6 pm) for stays of up to a maximum of three hours for around 500B for singles/doubles, including tax and service. Longer daytime rates are available on request. For additional information on overnight accommodation in the Don Muang area, see Places to Stay in the Bangkok chapter.

The Amari also has a selection of decent restaurants serving Italian, Japanese and Thai food.

Bus

Bangkok is the centre for bus services that fan out all over the kingdom. There are basically three types of long-distance bus. First there is the ordinary public bus, then the air-con public bus. The third choice is the many private air-con services which leave from various offices and hotels all over the city and provide a deluxe service for those people for whom simple air-con isn't enough!

Public Bus There are three main public bus (Baw Khaw Saw) terminals. The Northern & North-Eastern bus terminal (☎ 02-272 5255, 279 4484/7, 271 2961 for Northern routes, 272 0390, 272 5242 for North-Eastern routes) is on Th Phahonyothin on the way out to the airport. It's also commonly called the Moh Chit station (*sathǎanii mǎw chít*), or, since it moved to a brand new air-con building on the other side of the highway a little farther north, it's sometimes referred to as 'New' Moh Chit (*mǎw chít mài*). Air-con city bus Nos 2, 3, 9, 10, 12, 29 and 39, along with a dozen or more airconning city buses will take you there.

The Eastern bus terminal (☎ 02-391 2504 ordinary, ☎ 391 9829 air-con), the departure point for buses to Pattaya, Rayong, Chanthaburi and other points east, is a long way out along Th Sukhumvit, at Soi 40 (Soi Ekamai) opposite Soi 63. Most folks call it Ekamai station (*sathǎanii èk-amai*). Air-con city bus Nos 1, 8, 11 and 13 all pass this station.

The Southern bus terminal (☎ 02-434 5558 ordinary, ☎ 434 7192 air-con) for buses south to Phuket, Surat Thani and closer centres to the west like Nakhon Pathom and Kanchanaburi, has one Thonburi location for both ordinary and air-con buses at the intersection of Hwy 338 (Th Nakhon Chaisi) and Th Phra Pinklao. A convenient way to reach the station is by air-con city bus No 7, which terminates here.

When travelling on night buses take care of your belongings. Some long-distance buses that leave from Bangkok now issue claim checks for luggage stored under the bus, but valuables are still best kept on your person or within reach.

Allow an hour to reach the Northern bus terminal from Banglamphu or anywhere along the river, over an hour to reach the Southern bus terminal. The Eastern bus terminal takes 30 to 45 minutes under most traffic conditions. During occasional gridlock, eg Friday afternoons before a holiday, it can take up to three hours to get across town to the terminals by public transport.

Private Bus The more reputable and licensed private tour buses leave from the public terminals listed previously. Some private bus companies arrange pick-ups at Th Khao San and other guesthouse areas – these pickups are illegal since it's against municipal law to carry passengers within the city limits except en route to or from an official terminal. This is why the curtains on these buses are sometimes closed when picking up passengers.

Although fares can be lower on private buses, the incidence of reported theft is far greater than on the Baw Khaw Saw buses. They are also generally – but not always – less reliable, promising services (such as air-con or VIP seats) that they don't deliver. For safer, more reliable, and more punctual service, stick to buses that leave from the official Baw Khaw Saw terminals.

See the Getting Around chapter for more information about bus travel in Thailand. Also, for details on bus fares to/from other towns and cities in Thailand, see the Getting There & Away sections under each place.

Train

Bangkok is the terminus for main trunk rail services to the South, North, North-East and East. There are two principal train stations. The big Hualamphong station on Th Rama IV handles services to the North, North-East and some of the Southern services. The Thonburi (Bangkok Noi) station handles a few services to the South. If you're heading down to Southern Thailand, make sure you know which station your train departs from. See the Train section in the Getting Around chapter for further details.

GETTING AROUND

Getting around in Bangkok may be difficult for the uninitiated but once you're familiar with the transport system the whole city is accessible. The main obstacle is traffic, which moves at a snail's pace during much of the day. This means advance planning is a must when you are attending scheduled events or making appointments.

Travelling by river or canal from one point to another is always the best choice.

To/From the Airport

There is a choice of transport from the international airport, in Don Muang district, 25km north of Bangkok, to the city; prices range from 3.50B to 300B.

Airport Bus Since mid-1996 a new airport express bus service has been operating from Bangkok international airport to three different Bangkok districts for 70B per person. Buses run every 15 minutes from 5 am to midnight. A map showing the designated stops is available at the airport; each route makes approximately six stops in each direction. A great boon to travellers on a budget, these new buses mean you can avoid hassling with taxi drivers to get a reasonable fare as well as forgo the slow pace of the regular bus routes.

The Airport Bus counter stands around 200m to the left (with your back to Terminal 1) of the left-most terminal exit.

A-1 – To the Silom business district via Pratunam and Th Ratchadamri, stopping at big hotels like the Indra, Grand Hyatt Erawan, Regent Bangkok and Dusit Thani.
A-2 – To Sanam Luang via Th Phayathai, Th Lan Luang, Th Ratchadamnoen Klang and Th Tanao; this is the one you want if you're going to the Victory Monument, Siam Square or Banglamphu areas. In Banglamphu, it stops opposite the FAO (Food & Agriculture Organization) headquarters on Th Phra Athit.
A-3 – To the Phrakhanong district via Th Sukhumvit, including Eastern (Ekamai) bus terminal (for buses east to Si Racha (for Ko Samet), Pattaya and Trat) and Soi 55 (Soi Thong Lor).

To catch an Airport bus to the airport, just wait at one of the stops listed above and buy a ticket on board the bus.

Public Bus Cheapest of all are the public buses to Bangkok which stop on the highway in front of the airport. There are two non air-con (ordinary) bus routes and four air-con routes that visitors find particularly useful for getting into the city. The ordinary buses, however, no longer accept passengers carrying luggage.

Air-con bus No 29 costs 16B and plies one of the most useful, all-purpose routes from the airport into the city as it goes to the Siam Square and Hualamphong areas. After entering the city limits via Th Phahonyothin (which turns into Th Phayathai), the bus passes Th Phetchaburi (where you'll want to get off to change buses for Banglamphu), then Th Rama I at the Siam Square/Mahboonkrong intersection (for buses out to Th Sukhumvit, or to walk to Soi Kasem San 1 for various lodgings) and finally turns right on Th Rama IV to go to the Hualamphong district (where the main train station is located). You'll want to go the opposite way on Th Rama IV for the Soi Ngam Duphli lodging area. No 29 runs only from 5.45 am to 8 pm, so if you're arriving on a late-night flight you'll miss it.

Air-con bus No 13 (16B; 5.45 am to 8 pm) also goes to Bangkok from the airport, coming down Th Phahonyothin (like No 29), turning left at the Victory Monument to Th Ratchaprarop, then south to Th Ploenchit, where it goes east out Th Sukhumvit all the way to Bang Na. This is definitely the one to catch if you're heading for the Th Sukhumvit area.

Air-con bus No 4 (16B; 5.45 am to 8 pm) begins with a route parallel to that of the No 29 bus – down Th Vibhavadi Rangsit to Th Ratchaprarop and Th Ratchadamri (Pratunam district), crossing Phetchaburi, Rama I, Ploenchit and Rama IV, then down Silom, left on Charoen Krung, and across the river to Thonburi.

No large pieces of luggage are allowed onto the ordinary buses. Ordinary bus No 59 costs 3.50B (5B between 11 pm to 5 am) and operates 24 hours – it zigzags through the city to Banglamphu (the Democracy Monument area) from the airport, it can take up to 1½ hours or more in heavy traffic.

Ordinary bus No 29 (3.50B or 5B; from 11 pm to 5 am; 24 hours) plies much the same route as air-con bus No 29. Green bus No 2 (16B; 5.30 am to 8 pm) has a similar route to the air-con No 4; first it goes through Pratunam, then to Th Ratchadamri, Th Silom and Th Charoen Krung.

To catch a bus to the airport, just wait at one of the circular bus stop signs along these routes.

It's worth the extra 12.50B for the air-con and almost guaranteed seating, especially in the hot season, since the trip to central Bangkok usually takes an hour or more. Even better is the 70B Airport Bus.

Train You can also get into Bangkok from the airport by train. Just after leaving Terminal 1, turn right (north), cross the highway via the pedestrian bridge, turn left and walk about 100m towards Bangkok. Opposite the big Amari Airport Hotel is the small Don Muang station from where trains depart regularly to Bangkok. The 3rd class fare from Don Muang is only 5B on the ordinary and commuter trains if you buy your ticket on the platform, 10B if purchased on the train. First and 2nd class fares are 21B and 11B (plus any rapid/express charges that may apply).

There are trains every 15 to 30 minutes between 3.23 am and 10.56 pm and it takes about 50 minutes to reach Hualamphong, the main station in central Bangkok. In the opposite direction trains run frequently between 4.20 am and 9.10 pm. From Hualamphong station you can walk to the bus stop almost opposite Wat Traimit for bus No 23 to Banglamphu, if that's your destination.

Taxi The Dept of Land Transport has stepped in to police the airport taxi service, and for the moment at least there seem to be substantially fewer hassles with airport taxi drivers than in previous years. We've had no problems at all during the last year getting regular metered taxis.

Taxis waiting near the arrival area of the airport are supposed to be airport-regulated. Ignore all the touts waiting in the arrival hall and buy a taxi ticket from the public taxi booth at the kerbside outside the hall. Fares differ according to city destination; most destinations in central Bangkok are around 200B to 250B by the meter.

On top of the meter fare, airport taxis are permitted to collect a 50B airport surcharge.

Future Traffic Alternatives

At times, Bangkok's traffic situation seems quite hopeless. An estimated three million vehicles crawl through the streets at an average of 13km/h during commuter hours, and nearly half the municipal traffic police are undergoing treatment for respiratory ailments! It's estimated that the typical Bangkok motorist spends a cumulative 44 days per year in traffic; petrol stations throughout the capital sell the Comfort 100, a portable potty that allows motorists to relieve themselves in their own vehicles during traffic jams. Mobile phones, TVs and food warmers are other commonplace auto accessories among wealthier drivers.

The main culprit, in addition to the influx of motor vehicles, is the lack of road surface, which represents only 8.5% of Bangkok's mass; to reach international standards the road surface needs to be increased to at least 20%. Private cars aren't causing the problem; only 25% of the city's population use them. Motorcycles, buses, trucks and taxis make up the bulk of Bangkok traffic. In 1996 the government established an excise tax on products and services that harm the environment, beginning with two-stroke motorcycles, a major polluter. The buses are in dire need of attention, as they make up less than 1% of the vehicles on city roads but account for as much as half the pollutants found in the air.

Several mass transit systems (which are either in the planning or very early construction phases) promise much needed 'decongestion'. In the meantime the Bangkok Metropolitan Authority (BMA) has completed several elevated expressways. Although sceptics warned more roadways would simply encourage Bangkok residents to buy more cars, the latest crop of expressways has had a visible positive effect on traffic. An even bigger boon to Bangkok traffic was the economic meltdown of 1997-98, during which tens of thousands of cars were repossessed in Bangkok and new car buying declined from nearly a thousand a day in early 1997 to only around 300 a day in late 1998. Bus patronage is up, taxi fares down. Traffic is estimated to be around 25 to 30% lighter today than it was two years ago.

Skytrain

The mass transit system most likely to be completed first is the much ballyhooed Skytrain network, which is an extensive elevated rail project that was proposed in 1986 and went from contractor to contractor until construction finally began in 1994. The US$3.2 billion Hopewell Bangkok Elevated Road and Train System (BERTS) was supposed to offer 60km of light rail and 48km of expressways; the project was designed so that the railways would be stacked on top of the expressways, both of which would in turn be stacked atop existing roadways. Five thousand piles for BERTS have already been driven throughout Bangkok, but the plan fell victim to interdepartmental squabbles and problems with the Hong Kong contractor.

In 1996 BERTS was taken over by the optimistically named Metropolitan Rapid Transit Authority (MRTA) and, at the time of writing, the Skytrain was around 45% complete. Initially there will be two lines, a blue line from Taksin Bridge to the National Stadium on Th Rama I,

Future Traffic Alternatives

and a longer red line from Moh Chit Northern bus terminal to Awn Nut in Phrakhanong (Soi 81, Th Sukhumvit). Estimates say the longer rail route can be done in under 30 minutes (a journey currently taking up to 80 minutes by road), the shorter one in 15 minutes. The two lines will intersect at the double-height Central Station at Siam Square. The first trains were tested in October 1998, and the first fully operational train is supposed to be online by January 2000. It will reportedly be the first all-private mass transit system since the advent of the London Underground in the 19th century. Just to add to the confusion, the project has been re-named the Bangkok Mass Transit System (BMTS)!

Subway

Finally there's the MRTA's US$3.2 billion subway, which will consist of one 42km north-east to south-west main line, with a separate loop around central Bangkok. This one has also begun construction, and a 2003 completion is projected. As if all these plans weren't enough, there has also been serious talk of a monorail loop around outer Bangkok, with a feeder line for the Skytrain.

The problem with every one of these projects is the lack of coherent coordination. With separate contracts and separate supervision, it's doubtful any can remain on schedule. The main villains in all this appear to be BMA principals, who want inflexible control over every project brought to the table even where there are clear conflicts of interest. In 1993 the BMA shot down a reasonable proposal put before the Interior Ministry to split the 560 sq km city into five to eight separate townships for ease of traffic administration.

The investments involved in these rail and road projects are enormous, but as current traffic congestion costs the nation over 14 billion baht per year in fuel bills, the potential savings far exceed the outlay. Bangkok lost out to Singapore in a 1995 bid to be named the site of the new Asia-Pacific Economic Cooperation (APEC) secretariat largely because of the city's appalling traffic congestion. And it won a 1997 bid to become the new home of the Pacific Area Travel Association (PATA) because it looked like at least one of the promised mass transit systems was actually going to become operational.

Traffic Controls

One cheaper alternative that the government is seriously considering is a toll zone or traffic control zone within the central business district. City planners from the Massachusetts Institute of Technology, hired as consultants by BMA, concur that this would be the best approach for quick and lasting traffic congestion relief. This sort of plan has worked very well in nearby Singapore but it remains to be seen whether such a system would work in Bangkok, where even enforcement of traffic lights, parking and one way streets is shaky.

While you're stuck in a Bangkok traffic jam you can take comfort in knowing that the average rush-hour traffic flows are worse in Hong Kong, Taipei, Bombay and Manila. Dirty air? Bangkok doesn't even make UNEP/WHO's list of Asia's five worst cities for air pollution – honours were captured by Delhi, Xian, Beijing, Calcutta and Shenyang. Ambient noise ratios are equal to those measured in Seoul, Chongqing and Saigon.

Joe Cummings

You must also reimburse drivers for any toll charges paid if they take the tollway into the city (20B to 50B) depending on where you get off the tollway. Taking the tollway almost always saves time. During heavy traffic you can save money by staying on the surface (non-tollway) streets – which are just as speedy as (if not speedier than) the expressway during heavy commuter hours. Drivers will usually ask if you want to take the tollway and you'll know which is best by the number of cars on the road; if it's heavy you might as well save the toll and take the surface streets.

If you end up taking a flat-rate taxi, the driver should pay all toll charges. Two, three, or even four passengers (if they don't have much luggage) can split the fare.

Sometimes unscrupulous drivers will approach you before you reach the kerbside and try to sell you a ticket for 350B or 400B – ignore them and head straight for the kerb queue. A few touts from the old taxi mafia that used to prowl the arrival area are still around and may approach you with fares of around 200B. Their taxis have white-and-black plates and are not licensed to carry passengers, hence you have less legal recourse in the event of an incident than if you take a licensed taxi (yellow-and-black plates).

A few drivers still try to renegotiate the fare once you're inside a metered cab. The occasional driver will refuse to use his meter and quote a flat rate of 300B to 400B – though this is a less frequent occurrence than it used to be. Passengers now receive a bilingual Taxi-Meter Information sheet, issued by the Dept of Land Transport, on which is written the name of the driver, the cab licence number, the date and the time. A phone number for registering complaints against the driver is listed on this sheet.

Metered taxis flagged down on the highway in front of the airport (turn left from the arrival hall) are even cheaper since they don't have to pay the 50B airport surcharge. When the queue at the public taxi desk is particularly long, it's sometimes faster to go upstairs or walk out to the highway and flag one down.

THAI Services THAI offers an airport limousine, which is really just a glorified aircon taxi service, for 400B to central Bangkok, 300B to the Northern bus terminal or 500B to the Southern bus terminal, and direct air-con buses to Pattaya from the airport thrice daily at 9 and 11 am, and 7 pm; the fare is 200B one way. Private sedans cost 1500B per trip.

THAI also operates a free shuttle bus between the international and domestic terminals every 15 minutes between 6 am and 11.20 pm.

Helicopter The Shangri-La Hotel (☎ 02-236 7777) can arrange helicopter service – introduced for the World Bank/IMF meeting in 1991 – from Bangkok international airport to the hotel rooftop for around 3000B per person, minimum three passengers. The flight takes only 10 minutes but is reserved for Shangri-La guests only. If you can afford the copter flight you can certainly afford this hotel, which has one of Bangkok's best river locations.

Hiller Helicopter Services (☎ 02-661 6841, 688 3433) can arrange airport transfers to any helipad in the city for 9000B per trip.

City Bus

You can save a lot of money in Bangkok by sticking to the public buses, which are 3.50B for any journey under 10km on the ordinary blue or smaller green buses, 3.50B on the red buses or 6B for the first 8km on the air-con lines. Longer trips cost more. The fare on ordinary buses is 4B for longer trips (eg from Chulalongkorn University to King Mongkut's Institute of Technology in Thonburi on bus No 21) or as high as 16B for air-con buses (eg from Th Silom to Bangkok airport on air-con bus No 4). The air-con buses are not only cooler, but are usually less crowded (all bets are off during rush hours).

Maps To do any serious bus riding you'll need a Bangkok bus map – the easiest to read is the *Bangkok Bus Map (Walking Tours)* published by Bangkok Guide, or Thaveepholcharoen's *Bangkok Thailand Tour'n Guide Map*. If you plan to do a lot of bus riding, the Bangkok Bus Map is the more accurate, but the Tour'n Guide Map (travellers often call it 'the blue map' due to its predominating aqua hue) also has a decent map of the whole country on the flip side. The bus numbers are clearly marked in red, with air-con buses in larger type. Don't expect the routes to be 100% correct, a few will have changed since the maps last came out, but they'll get you where you're going most of the time. These maps usually retail for around 35B to 40B.

A more complete 113-page *Bus Guide* is available in some bookshops and newsstands for 35B, but it's not as easy to use as the bus maps.

Safety Be careful with your belongings while riding Bangkok buses. The place you are most likely to be 'razored' is on the crowded ordinary buses. Razor artists are common, particularly on buses in the Hualamphong train station area. These dexterous thieves specialise in slashing your backpack, shoulder bag or even your trouser pockets with a sharp razor and slipping your valuables out unnoticed. Hold your bag in front of you, under close attention, and carry money in a front shirt pocket, preferably (as the Thais do) maintaining a tactile and visual sensitivity to these areas if the bus is packed shoulder to shoulder. Seasoned travellers don't need this advice, as the same precautions are useful all over the world – the trick is to be relaxed but aware.

Skytrain

See the boxed text 'Future Traffic Alternatives' for information on the new Bangkok Transit System (BTS), also known as the 'Skytrain'.

Car & Motorcycle

Cars and motorbikes are easily rented in Bangkok, if you can afford it and have steel nerves. Rates start at around 1200B per day

for a small car, much less for a motorcycle, excluding insurance. For long-term rentals you can usually arrange a discount of up to 35% off the daily rate. An International Driving Permit and passport are required for all rentals.

For long, cross-country trips, you might consider buying a new or used motorcycle and reselling it when you leave – this can end up being cheaper than renting, especially if you buy a good used bike. See the Getting Around chapter for more details.

A few car-rental companies are:

Avis Rent-A-Car
    (☎ 02-255 5300/4, fax 253 3734)
    2/12 Th Withayu
    (☎ 02-535 4052)
    Bangkok international airport, terminal 1
    (☎ 02-535 4032)
    Bangkok international airport, terminal 2
    (☎ 02-254 1234)
    Grand Hyatt Erawan Hotel, Cnr Th
    Ratchadamri and Th Ploenchit
Central Car Rent
    (☎ 02-251 2778)
    24 Soi Tonson, Th Ploenchit
Hertz
    (☎ 02-535 3004)
    Don Muang airport
    (☎ 02-251 7575)
    1620 Th Phetchaburi Tat Mai
Highway Car Rent
    (☎ 02-266 9393)
    1018/5 Th Rama IV
Inter Car Rent
    (☎ 02-252 9223)
    45 Th Sukhumvit, near Soi 3
Lumpinee Car Rent
    (☎ 02-255 1966/3482)
    167/4 Th Withayu
Sathorn Car Rent
    (☎ 02-633 8888)
    6/8-9 Th Sathon Neua
SMT Rent-A-Car
    (☎ 02-216 8020)
    931/11 Th Rama I
Toyota Rental & Leasing
    (☎ 02-637 5050)
    Vibultnani Bldg, 3199 Th Rama IV

There are more car-rental agencies along Th Withayu and Th Phetchaburi Tat Mai.

Some also rent motorcycles, but you're better off renting or leasing a bike at a place that specialises in motorcycles, such as:

Chusak Yont Shop
(☎ 02-251 9225) 1400 Th Phetchaburi Tat Mai
SSK Co
(☎ 02-514 1290) 35/33 Th Lat Phrao
Visit Laochaiwat
(☎ 02-278 1348) 1 Soi Prommit, Th Suthisan

Taxi

Metered taxis *(tháeksii miitôe)* were finally introduced in Bangkok in 1993 and now outnumber the old non-meter taxis. The ones with meters have signs on top reading 'Taxi Meter', the others 'Taxi Thai' or just 'Taxi'. Fares for metered taxis are always lower than for non-metered, the only problem being that they can be a little harder to flag down during peak commuter hours. Demand often outstrips supply from 8 to 9 am and 6 to 7 pm, also late at night when the bars are closing (1 to 2 am). Because metered-taxi drivers use rented vehicles and must return them at the end of their shifts, they sometimes won't take longer fares as quitting time nears.

Metered taxis charge 35B at flagfall for the first 2km, then 4.50B for the next 10km, 5B for 13 to 20km and 5.50B for any distance over 20km, but only when the cab travels at 6km/h or more; at speeds under 6km/h, a surcharge of 1.25B per minute kicks in. Freeway tolls – 20B to 40B depending where you start – must be paid by the passenger. A 24 hour 'phone-a-cab' service (☎ 02-319 9911) is available for an extra 20B over the regular metered fare. This is only really necessary if you're in an area where there aren't a lot of taxis; residents who live down long sois are the main clientele. Previously such residents had to catch a motorcycle taxi or 'baht bus' to the *pàak soi* ('soi mouth', where a soi meets a larger street) to hail a taxi.

For certain routes it can be very difficult to find a taxi driver who's willing to use the meter. One such instance is going from the Southern bus terminal across the river to Bangkok proper – most drivers will ask for a flat 350B but settle for 250B. In the reverse direction you can usually get them to use the meter.

You can hire a taxi all day for 1000B to 1500B depending on how much driving is involved. A better option – in terms of the quality of both car and driver – would be to hire through J&J Car Rent (☎ 02-531 2262), an agency that specialises in car/driver combos at competitive rates.

A useful *Taxi Guide* brochure distributed by TAT to both tourists and taxi drivers lists Thai and English addresses of hotels, guesthouses, embassies, airlines, shopping centres, temples and various tourist attractions. The guide can be of considerable help in communication between non-English-speaking drivers and non-Thai-speaking passengers.

Tuk-Tuk

In heavy traffic, tuk-tuks are usually faster than taxis since they're able to weave in and out between cars and trucks. This is the main advantage to taking a tuk-tuk for short hops. On the down side, tuk-tuks are not air-conditioned, so you have to breathe in all that lead-soaked air (at its thickest in the middle of Bangkok's wide avenues), and they're also more dangerous since they easily flip when braking into a fast curve. The typical tuk-tuk fare nowadays offers no savings over a metered taxi – around 40B for a short hop (eg Siam Square to Soi 2, Th Sukhumvit).

Tuk-tuk drivers tend to speak less English than taxi drivers, so many new arrivals have a hard time communicating their destination. Although some travellers have complained about tuk-tuk drivers deliberately taking them to the wrong destination (to collect commissions from certain restaurants, gem or silk shops), others never seem to have a problem with tuk-tuks, and swear by them. Beware tuk-tuk drivers who offer to take you on a sightseeing or factory tour for 10 or 20B – it's a touting scheme designed to pressure you into purchasing overpriced goods.

Know Your Boats

Chao Phraya River Express The main boats that you'll want to use are the rapid Chao Phraya River Express boats *(reua dùan)*, a sort of river bus service. These cost 4B to 10B (depending on the distance) and follow a regular

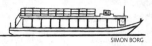
SIMON BORG

route up and down the river; a trip from Banglamphu to the main post office, for example, costs 6B. They may not necessarily stop at each pier if there are no people waiting, or if no-one wants to get off. You buy your tickets on the boat. Chao Phraya River Express boats are big, long boats with numbers on their roofs; the last boat from either end of the route departs at 6 pm.

Chao Phraya River Express has a competitor called Laemthong Express that for the most part serves outlying areas to the north and south of central Bangkok. Hence it stops at some of the same piers but not necessarily all. It also runs less frequently than Chao Phraya River Express. The latter boats usually feature white bodies with red stripes, while Laemthong have blue or red bodies; if you're heading for one of the Chao Phraya River Express piers listed in this book, be sure not to get on the wrong boat.

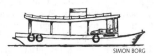
SIMON BORG

Cross-River Ferry From the main Chao Phraya stops and also from almost every other jetty, there are slower cross-river ferries *(reua khâam fâak)* that simply shuttle back and forth across the river. The standard fares are 1B and you usually pay this at the entrance to the jetty. Be careful – there will probably be a pay window at the jetty and also a straight-through aisle for people taking other boats.

Longtail Taxi Finally there are the longtail boats *(reua hang yao)* that operate a share taxi system off the main river and up the smaller khlongs. Fares usually start from 5B or 10B – you've really got to know where you're going on these. There are also river charter taxis where you take the whole boat – you'll find them at certain jetties (primarily Tha Chang and Tha Si Phraya), and you can charter them for trips around the river-canal system for a standard 400B per hour.

One of the most useful canal services for most visitors runs along Khlong Saen Saep. This one provides a quicker alternative to road transport between the river and eastern Bangkok (ie outer Sukhumvit and Bang Kapi). The boat from Banglamphu to the Ramkhamhaeng University area, for example, costs 10B and takes only 40 minutes. A bus would take at least an hour under Bangkok's normal traffic conditions. The main detraction from this route is the seriously polluted canal – passengers typically hold newspapers over their clothes and faces to prevent being splashed by the stinking black water. Not the best choice of transport if you're dressed for a formal occasion.

A handy little run along this route is by longtail boat (5B) from the Siam Square area (from Tha Ratchathewi by the bridge next to the Asia Hotel) to Tha Banglamphu near Wat Saket and the Democracy Monument. At its western end, this route intersects a north-south boat route along Khlong Banglamphu and Khlong Phadung Krung Kasem. Along this route you can catch a boat from the Khlong Banglamphu pier near the corner of Th Phra Sumen and Th Chakraphong (north side of the canal) all the way to Hualamphong station in 15 minutes for 5B.

SIMON BORG

Joe Cummings

When in doubt, use a metered taxi rather than a tuk-tuk.

Motorcycle Taxi

As passengers become more desperate in their attempts to beat rush-hour gridlocks, motorcycle taxis have moved from the sois to the main avenues. Fares for a motorcycle taxi are about the same as tuk-tuks except during heavy traffic, when they may cost a bit more.

Riding on the back of a speeding motorcycle taxi is even more of a kamikaze experience than riding in a tuk-tuk. Keep your legs tucked in – the drivers are used to carrying passengers with shorter legs than those of the average faràng and they pass perilously close to other vehicles while weaving in and out of traffic.

Boat

Although many of Bangkok's khlongs (canals) have been paved over, there is still plenty of transport along and across the Chao Phraya River and up adjoining canals. River transport is one of the best ways of getting around Bangkok as well as, quite often, being much faster than any road-based alternatives. For a start you get quite a different view of the city; also, it's much less of a hassle than tangling with the polluted, noisy, traffic-crowded streets. (Just try getting from Banglamphu to the central post office as quickly by road).

Along the Chao Phraya River the main transport consists of the Chao Phraya River Express (☎ 02-222 5330), which runs between the Wat Ratchasingkhon pier in south central Bangkok and Nonthaburi Province from 5.30 am to 6 pm daily. Fares range from 4B to 9B, except for a special express boat (denoted by a red and orange striped flag) which runs only between the hours of 6 to 9 am and 3 to 6 pm, costs 10B and stops at fewer piers along the way.

Over the last five years the Bangkok Metropolitan Authority has revived four lengthy and very useful canal routes: Khlong Saen Saep (Banglamphu to Bang Kapi), Khlong Phrakhanong (Sukhumvit to Sinakarin campus), Khlong Bang Luang/Khlong Lat Phrao (Th Phetchaburi Tat Mai to Phahonyothin Bridge) and Khlong Phasi Charoen in Thonburi (Kaset Bang Khae port to Rama I Bridge). Although the canal boats can be crowded, the service is generally much faster than either an auto taxi or bus.

See the longtail taxi entry in the 'Know Your Boats' boxed text for more details.

Eastern Gulf Coast

To the south-east of Bangkok, along the fast-developing east coast of the Gulf of Thailand, is a broken string of beaches and islands that range from the country's most heavily touristed to some of its quietest. A major plus for this section of the Gulf is that the waters tend to be calmer – during both monsoon seasons – than anywhere else in coastal Thailand, hence most of it can be considered a year-round destination. Another is that scuba divers and would-be divers will find in Pattaya some of Thailand's highest quality dive operations. And despite the negative aspects of Ao Pattaya (Pattaya Bay) itself, there are some decent dive sites nearby. The eastern Gulf coast's third asset is its proximity to Bangkok – the farthest coastal capital, Trat (the jumping-off point for Ko Chang National Marine Park), is only five to six hours away by bus. Ban Phe, where boats depart for the beautiful island of Ko Samet, is only a three hour ride away.

The downside is that this section of coastline – often termed the 'eastern seaboard' by the English-language press – is the country's most industrialised and developed. Some stretches of the coast, especially in Chonburi and Rayong provinces, are lined with factories, condo developments and fishing or shipping ports. But it's also a region of fruit plantations, saltwater estuaries and beaches hardly anyone outside Thailand has heard of.

SI RACHA
• pop 23,700

About 105km from Bangkok on the east coast of the Gulf of Thailand is the small town of Si Racha, home of the famous spicy sauce *náam phrík sii raachaa*. Some of Thailand's best seafood, especially the local oysters, is served here accompanied by this sauce.

Si Racha itself is not that interesting, but it's the departure point for boats to nearby Ko Si Chang, a small island flanked by two smaller islands – Kham Yai to the north and

HIGHLIGHTS

• Ko Chang archipelago is a remote national marine park with forest tracts, waterfalls, coastal walks, diving and coral reefs.

• Ko Samet boasts some of the whitest, squeakiest sand in the kingdom, delectable seafood and boat trips to uninhabited islands.

• Popular Pattaya is Thailand's busiest beach resort, with palm-fringed beaches, diving at nearby islets, water-skiing, go-karting and exciting nightlife.

• Watch the money change hands in gem trading markets in Chanthaburi and Trat, and on the Cambodian border.

Khang Kao to the south. As this provides a natural shelter from the wind and sea, the lee of the island is used as a harbour by large incoming freighters. Smaller boats transport goods to the Chao Phraya delta some 50km away.

On **Ko Loi**, a small rocky island which is connected to the mainland by a long jetty, there is a Thai-Chinese Buddhist temple.

Si Racha Tiger Farm

This relatively new attraction covers 250 *rai* (around 40 hectares) off Route 3241 about 9km east-south-east of town. The unique vision of Khun Suradon Chommongkol, the zoo combines a world famous tiger breeding facility with a crocodile farm, 'herbivores zone', scorpion farm and circus-like performances. The tiger farm – said to be the largest and most successful such facility in the world – contains over 130 Bengal tigers. At the unusual 'kinship to the different families complex' you'll see tiger cubs, pigs and dogs living together; don't be too surprised to see sows nursing tiger cubs. Other animals on hand include camels, deer, wallabies, elephants and iguanas.

The park is open daily from 8 am to 6 pm. Admission is 250B for adults, 150B children (60B/30B for Thais). There's a separate charge of 30B (20B children) for the circus, which takes place at 11 am and 1.30 and 4 pm. For further information call ☎ 038-296571.

Places to Stay

For most people, Si Racha is more of a transit point than an overnight stop. The best places to stay in Si Racha are the rambling wooden hotels built on piers over the waterfront – this is the part of town with the most character. The *Siriwatana Hotel* (☎ 038-311037, 35 Th Jermjompol), across from Thanon (Th) Tessaban 1 and the Bangkok Bank, is the cleanest of the lot and has the best service. There are rustic sitting areas with tables outside the 31 rooms along the piers. The basic fan-cooled rooms with private shower cost 140B (up to 260B for multibed rooms), while rooms with shared shower are 120B. Simple, inexpensive meals can be prepared on request, or you're free to bring your own food and use the tables provided.

Siwichai Hotel, next to the Siriwatana, has similar rooms for 200B, plus its own pier restaurant. *Samchai Hotel*, on Soi 10, across from Th Surasakdi 1, has reasonable rooms for 180B and some air-con rooms (350B) as well. All three are open and breezy, with outdoor tables where you can bring food in the evening from nearby markets.

On Soi 18, *Grand Bungalows* (☎ 038-311079) has bungalows of various sizes, built off the pier, for 400B to 1100B. Each one sleeps several people and they are very popular among holidaying Thais and Chinese.

There are several newish top-end hotels in town, including the 20 storey *Laemthong Residence Hotel* (☎/fax 038-322888) in the centre of town, just off Th Sukhumvit (Hwy 3). Comfortable rooms with all the amenities cost 700B to 1000B; there's also a swimming pool and tennis courts.

The classy *City Hotel* (☎ 038-322700, fax 322739, 6/126 Th Sukhumvit) offers capacious rooms for 2300B. An escalator leads from the pavement to 2nd floor reception; facilities include a pub, coffee shop, fitness centre and business centre.

Places to Eat

There is plenty of good seafood in Si Racha, but you have to watch the prices. Best known is the Chinese-owned *Chua Lee* on Th Jermjompol (Joemjomphon) next to Soi 10, across from the Krung Thai Bank. The seafood is great but probably the most expensive in town. Next door and across the street are several seafood places with similar fare at much more reasonable prices, such as the *Fast Food Seafood Restaurant* just south of Th Tessaban 1.

Jarin, on the Soi 14 pier (the pier with boats to Ko Si Chang), has very good one-plate seafood dishes, especially seafood curry steamed with rice (*khâo hàw mòk tha-leh*) and Thai-style rice noodles with fresh shrimp (*kũaytĩaw phàt thai kûng sòt*). It's a great place to kill time while waiting for the next boat to Ko Si Chang; prices are low to moderate.

SI RACHA WATERFRONT

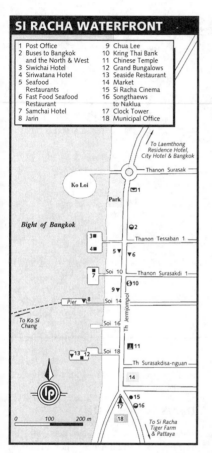

1 Post Office	9 Chua Lee
2 Buses to Bangkok and the North & West	10 Kring Thai Bank
3 Siwichai Hotel	11 Chinese Temple
4 Siriwatana Hotel	12 Grand Bungalows
5 Seafood Restaurants	13 Seaside Restaurant
6 Fast Food Seafood Restaurant	14 Market
	15 Si Racha Cinema
7 Samchai Hotel	16 Songthaews to Naklua
8 Jarin	17 Clock Tower
	18 Municipal Office

Labels on map: To Laemthong Residence Hotel, City Hotel & Bangkok; Thanon Surasak; Ko Loi; Park; Bight of Bangkok; Thanon Tessaban 1; Soi 10; Thanon Surasakdi 1; Pier; Soi 14; To Ko Si Chang; Th Jermjompol; Soi 16; Soi 18; Th Surasakdisa-nguan; To Si Racha Tiger Farm & Pattaya; 0 100 200 m

At the end of the pier at Soi 18 is the large **Seaside Restaurant** – just about the best all-round seafood place in town for atmosphere, service and value. Try the tasty grilled seafood platter stacked with squid, mussels, shrimp and cockles. Häagen-Dazs ice cream is also available.

The most economical place to eat is in the **market** near the clock tower at the southern end of town. In the evening the market offers everything from noodles to fresh seafood, while in the day-

time it's mostly an ordinary food and clothing market with some noodle and snack stands.

Outside town, off Th Sukhumvit (Hwy 3) on the way to Pattaya, there are a couple of cheap, but good, fresh seafood places. Closer to town is Ao Udom, a small fishing bay where there are several open-air seafood places.

Getting There & Away

Buses to Si Racha leave the Eastern bus terminal in Bangkok every 30 minutes or so from 5 am to 7 pm. The ordinary bus is 35B, air-con is 61B; it takes around 1¾ hours. Ordinary direct buses stop near the pier for Ko Si Chang, but through buses and air-con buses stop on Th Sukhumvit (Hwy 3), near the Laemthong Department Store, from where tuk-tuks are available to the pier.

You can also reach Si Racha by 3rd class train, though not many people do. Train No 365/283 leaves Hualamphong station at 6.55 am and arrives at Si Racha at 10.11 am (about an hour slower – but a good deal more scenic – than the bus). The fare is 28B.

White songthaews go to Naklua (North Pattaya) from near the clock tower in Si Racha frequently throughout the day. The fare is 12B per person and the ride takes about half an hour. Once you're in Naklua you can easily catch another songthaew on to central Pattaya.

Boats to Ko Si Chang leave from the Soi 14 pier.

Getting Around

In Si Racha and on Ko Si Chang there are fleets of huge motorcycle taxis, many powered by Nissan engines, that will take you anywhere in town or on the island for 20B.

KO SI CHANG
• pop 4100

Ko Si Chang makes a nifty one or two day getaway from Bangkok. There is only one town on the island, facing the mainland; the rest of the island is practically deserted and fun to explore. Don't come here looking for perfect white sand and turquoise

EASTERN GULF COAST

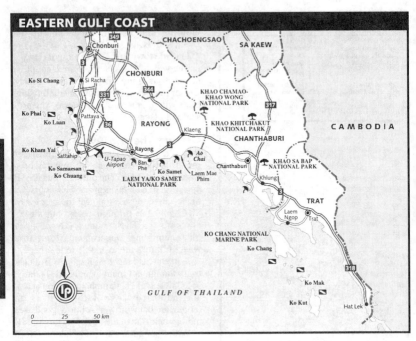

EASTERN GULF COAST

waters though: the island's proximity to shipping lanes and fishing grounds means its shores are less than tidy. Depending on sea currents and time of year, the shoreline can be relatively clean or cluttered with flotsam. If you're going mainly for beaches, you're better off heading farther south-east to Ko Samet.

Ko Si Chang's small population is made up of fisherfolk, mariners and government workers stationed with the Customs office or with one of the aquaculture projects on the island. Tourism fills a relatively small portion of local coffers, and the island has a very real, working-class feel to it. Although there has been talk of building a deep-water port, so far Ko Si Chang has remained free of industry.

Information

Money A branch of Thai Farmer's Bank in town – on the main road to the right as you walk up from the pier – does foreign exchange on weekdays.

Things to See & Do

The main points of interest on the island are the ruins of a royal palace, a splendid Chinese temple, a Buddhist cave hermitage and a couple of so-so beaches.

On the opposite side of the island, facing out to sea, are some sandy areas with decent swimming – take care with the tide and the sea urchins.

Secluded **Hat Tham** (also called Hat Sai), can be reached by following a branch of the ring road on foot to the back of the island. During low tide there's a strip of sand here; when the tide comes in it disappears. A partially submerged cave can be visited at the east end of the little bay. There is also a more public – and generally less clean – beach at the western end of the island

EASTERN GULF COAST

JENNY BOWMAN

(about 2km from the pier) near the old palace grounds, called **Hat Tha Wang**. Thai locals and visitors from the mainland come here for picnics.

The palace was once used by King Chulalongkorn (Rama V) in the summer, but was abandoned when the French briefly occupied the island in 1893. Little remains of the various palace buildings, but there are a few ruins to see. The main throne hall – a magnificent golden teak structure called Vimanmek – was moved to Bangkok in 1910, but the stairs leading up to it are still there. If you follow these stairs to the crest of the hill overlooking Tha Wang, you'll come to a stone outcrop wrapped in holy cloth. The locals call it 'Bell Rock' because if struck with a rock or heavy stick it rings like a bell. Flanking the rock are what appear to be two ruined *chedi*. The large chedi on the left actually contains **Wat Atsadangnimit**, a small consecrated chamber where King Chulalongkorn used to meditate. The unique Buddha image inside was fashioned over 50 years ago by a local monk who now lives in the cave hermitage. Attempts to rebuild this palace were abandoned following the 1997 economic downturn.

Not far from Wat Atsadangnimit is a large limestone cave called **Tham Saowapha**, which appears to plunge deep into the island – over a kilometre according to the locals. If you have a torch, the cave might be worth exploring.

To the east of town, high on a hill overlooking the sea, is a large Chinese temple called **San Jao Phaw Khao Yai**. During Chinese New Year in February, the island is overrun with Chinese visitors from the mainland. This is one of Thailand's most interesting Chinese temples, with shrine-caves, several different temple levels and a good view of Si Chang and the ocean. It's a long and steep climb from the road below.

Yai Phrik Vipassana Centre, a meditation hermitage, is ensconced in limestone caves and palm huts along the island's centre ridge. The hermit caves make an interesting visit but should be approached with respect – monks and nuns from all over Thailand come here to take advantage of the peaceful environment for meditation. Be careful that you don't fall down a limestone shaft; some are almost completely covered with vines.

Like most islands along Thailand's eastern seaboard, Ko Si Chang is best visited on weekdays; on weekends and holidays the island can get crowded.

Places to Stay

The cheapest place to stay is the rather bland *Tiewpai (Thiu Phai) Guest House* (☎ 038-216084) in town, not far from the main piers. They have one basic room that costs 120B; the remaining nine rooms, arranged around a courtyard behind the restaurant and reception area, range from 190B for a simple double with shared bathroom to nicer rooms with private shower for 250B and air-con rooms for 500B. Perhaps because they have the lowest prices on the island and send touts to the pier to meet arrivals, the place is often full and the staff can be rather cold.

Out near the gate to Hat Tha Wang, *Benz Bungalow* (☎ 038-216091) offers clean rooms facing the sea in a basic hotel-style building, or in one of its unique stone bungalows for 300B to 500B with fan and bath, 600B to 700B with air-con.

Si Phitsanu Bungalow (☎ 038-216034) is near Hat Tham towards the south side of the island. Rooms in a row house here cost 300B to 500B per night, or you can get a one/two bedroom bungalow overlooking the small bay for 800/1200B. *Top Bungalow* (☎ 038-216001), off the road on the way to Si Phitsanu, is similar in price but has no sea view and the buildings are decaying badly. To reach this area from town, take the first right past the Tiewpai Guest House, then follow the road straight past the Yai Phrik Vipassana Centre. Or take a motorcycle samlor for 25B one-way.

At *Green House* (☎ 038-216024), off the ring road towards the Chinese temple, somewhat dark and dingy singles/doubles in a 10 room row house cost 150/300B. Also in the vicinity of the Chinese temple is the newer *Sichang View Resort* (☎ 038-216210), with 10 tidy apartment-style bungalows on nicely landscaped grounds for 800B to 1100B, or as low as 500B in quiet months, such as June and September.

Sichang Palace (☎ 038-216276), a relatively new hotel in the middle of town on Th Atsadang, has clean, comfortable rooms facing the swimming pool for 1000/1200B single/double. Rooms with sea views are 1500/1700B. During the week the staff may knock 100B to 200B off these prices.

You can camp anywhere on the island without any hassle, including in Rama V's abandoned palace at Hat Tha Wang.

Places to Eat

There are several small restaurants, but nothing special, with all the Thai and Chinese standard dishes. Along the road that leads to the public beach are a couple of rustic *seafood places*.

Sichang Palace and *Sichang View Resort* each have their own restaurants serving good seafood at medium-high prices. *Tiewpai Guest House* offers reasonably priced Thai and western food.

Getting There & Away

Boats to Ko Si Chang leave hourly from a pier in Si Racha at the end of Soi 14, Th Jermjompol. The fare is 30B one way; the first boat leaves at about 5 am and the last at 7 pm. The last boat back to Si Racha from Ko Si Chang is at 5 pm.

As you approach Ko Si Chang by boat, check out the dozens of barges anchored in the island's lee. Their numbers have multiplied from year to year as shipping demand from Thailand's booming import and export business have increased.

Getting Around

There are fleets of motorcycle taxis that will take you anywhere in town for 20B to 30B. You can also get a complete tour of the island for 150B per hour. Asking prices for any ride tend to be outrageous; the supply of taxis is plentiful, however, and you can usually get the local price after talking to several drivers.

PATTAYA
• pop 56,700

Pattaya, 147km south-east of Bangkok, is Thailand's busiest beach resort with over 12,000 rooms available in hotels, bungalows and guesthouses spread along Hat Pattaya and adjoining Hat Naklua and Hat Jomtien. Pattaya is the most active of the three, a crowded crescent of sand where jetskis and powerboats slice the surf and parasails billow over the palms all day long. Sunburned visitors jam the beachfront road in rented jeeps and motorbikes.

According to recent Tourist Authority of Thailand (TAT) statistics, an average one-third of foreign tourists in Thailand visit Pattaya; in a typical November to March season Pattaya receives around a million visitors. Most of them are package tourists from Europe, Russia and the Middle East. Depending on their tastes, some visitors may find Pattaya lacking in culture, since much of the place seems designed to attract tourists interested in a prefabricated, western-style beach vacation with almost no 'Thai' ingredients. Hat Pattaya is also not that great (although it must have been at one time) and the town's biggest businesses – water sports and street sex – have driven prices for food and accommodation beyond Bangkok levels. Compared with

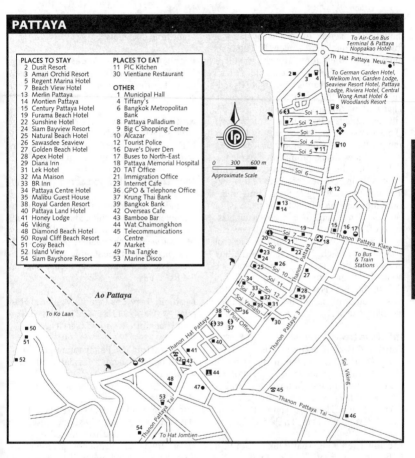

PATTAYA

PLACES TO STAY
2 Dusit Resort
3 Amari Orchid Resort
5 Regent Marina Hotel
7 Beach View Hotel
13 Merlin Pattaya
14 Montien Pattaya
15 Century Pattaya Hotel
19 Furama Beach Hotel
22 Sunshine Hotel
24 Siam Bayview Resort
25 Natural Beach Hotel
26 Sawasdee Seaview
28 Golden Beach Hotel
28 Apex Hotel
29 Diana Inn
31 Lek Hotel
32 Ma Maison
33 BR Inn
34 Pattaya Centre Hotel
35 Malibu Guest House
38 Royal Garden Resort
40 Pattaya Land Hotel
41 Honey Lodge
46 Viking
48 Diamond Beach Hotel
50 Royal Cliff Beach Resort
51 Cosy Beach
52 Island View
54 Siam Bayshore Resort

PLACES TO EAT
11 PIC Kitchen
30 Vientiane Restaurant

OTHER
1 Municipal Hall
4 Tiffany's
6 Bangkok Metropolitan Bank
8 Pattaya Palladium
9 Big C Shopping Centre
10 Alcazar
12 Tourist Police
16 Dave's Diver Den
17 Buses to North-East
18 Pattaya Memorial Hospital
20 TAT Office
21 Immigration Office
23 Internet Cafe
36 GPO & Telephone Office
37 Krung Thai Bank
39 Bangkok Bank
42 Overseas Cafe
43 Bamboo Bar
44 Wat Chaimongkhon
45 Telecommunications Centre
47 Market
49 Tha Tangke
53 Marine Disco

Ao Pattaya

To Ko Laan

To Hat Jomtien

EASTERN GULF COAST

many other Thai resort areas, it's more mercenary and less friendly in our experience.

Still, it continues to attract a loyal following of Bangkok oil company expats, *faràng* (European) retirees, conventioneers and package tourists. Local authorities and travel suppliers have been trying to upgrade Pattaya's image and clean the place up. Consequently the South Pattaya sex scene has diminished and families are returning.

Pattaya got its start as a resort when American GIs from a base in Nakhon Rat-chasima began visiting the one-time fishing village in 1959. US navy men from nearby Sattahip added to the military influx during the Indochina War years. There are still plenty of sailors around, but of many nationalities. National and international conventioneers make up another large segment of the current market, along with Asian golfers seeking out the 12 local golf courses, including those designed by names such as Robert Trent Jones and Jack Nicklaus.

Pattaya is acclaimed for its seafood, though it's generally overpriced by national (but not international) standards. Pattaya's lingering notoriety for sex tourism revolves around a collection of discos, outdoor bars and transvestite cabarets comprising its red-light district at the south end of the beach. That part of South Pattaya known as 'the village' attracts a large number of *ka-toeys* (Thai transvestites), who pose as hookers and ply their trade among the droves of sex tourists, as well as a prominent gay scene.

The one thing the Pattaya area has going for it is diving centres (see later in this section and under Diving & Snorkelling in the Activities section of Facts for the Visitor chapter). There are over a dozen nice islands off Pattaya's shore, although they can be expensive (compared with the rest of Thailand) to reach. If you're a snorkelling or scuba enthusiast, equipment can be booked at any of the several diving shops/schools at Hat Pattaya. Ko Laan, the most popular of the offshore islands, even has places to stay.

Information

Tourist Office The TAT office (☎ 038-427667) in Pattaya, at the midpoint of Th Hat Pattaya, keeps an up-to-date list of accommodation in the Pattaya area, and is very helpful. They're open daily from 8.30 am to 7.30 pm. There is a Tourist Police office (☎ 038-429371) on Th Pattaya 2.

Money The Krung Thai Bank on Soi Post Office is open from 10 am to 9 pm.

Post The main post office in South Pattaya is on Soi 15 (Soi Post Office). Hours are 8.30 am to 4.30 pm Monday to Friday, 9 am to noon on public holidays.

Telephone The international telephone office is located at the main post office. There are also several private long-distance phone offices in town: the best one is the Overseas Cafe, near the intersection of Th Hat Pattaya and Th Pattaya Tai. Rates are among the lowest in town, and it's open from 9 am

to 4 am, allowing you to take advantage of night-time discounts.

Email & Internet Access Next to the Siam Bayshore on Th Pattaya Tai, the Internet Cafe offers several terminals for online communications.

Radio Pattaya has an English-language radio station which broadcasts at FM 107.7 MHz. American and British announcers offer a mix of local news and music.

Magazines & Newspapers *Explore Pattaya*, a free monthly magazine distributed around town, contains information on current events, sightseeing and advertisements for hotel and restaurant specials. *Pattaya Mail*, a weekly newspaper, publishes articles on political, economic and environmental developments in the area, as well as the usual ads.

Medical Services Pattaya Memorial Hospital (☎ 038-429422/4, 422741) on Th Pattaya Klang offers 24 hour service.

Immigration The Pattaya immigration office is open Monday to Friday 8.30 am to 4.30 pm.

Beaches

Curving around Ao Pattaya (Pattaya Bay), **Hat Pattaya** is a relatively scenic crescent of sand backed by a narrow thread of palms and a very dense layer of hotels, restaurants, dive shops, car and motorbike rental agencies and other commercial establishments.

A better beach in the immediate Pattaya area is 6km-long **Hat Jomtien** (Jawmthian), a couple of kilometres south of Pattaya. Here the water is cleaner and you're well away from the noisy Pattaya bar scene. The hotels and restaurants are more spread out here as well, so there's a better sense of space and relaxation.

Hat Naklua, a smaller beach north of Pattaya, is also quiet and fairly tastefully developed. As Pattaya/South Pattaya is pretty much given over to single male tourists or

Changing the Image

In many ways Pattaya serves as the prime example of what can happen to a beach resort area if no controls are applied to the quality and quantity of tourism development. After garnering a long streak of bad press in both the domestic and international media, Pattaya began experiencing a steady decline in tourism in the early 1990s. In 1992 Pattaya lost the privilege of hosting the annual Siam World Cup – one of Asia's biggest windsurfing competitions – to Phuket. The two principal complaints have been the sidewalk sex scene and Pattaya Bay's water quality. Powerboats zooming in and out of the beach swimming areas have been a nuisance as well as a hazard.

Local authorities and travel suppliers continue to struggle to upgrade Pattaya's image as well as clean the place up. You can actually begin to feel sorry for Pattaya in spite of the fact that local developers and authorities have only themselves to blame for creating the reality on which the image is based. It's too late to turn Pattaya back into the fishing village it once was, but it's not too late to re-create a clean, safe tourist destination if all concerned cooperate.

Positive signs that things are changing for the better include a waste water treatment plant and a new pier where powerboats must moor.

couples on package tours, Jomtien and Naklua are where families tend to stay. **Hat Cliff** is a small cove just south of Hat Pattaya, over which looms a set of cliffs that are home to Pattaya's glitziest hotels.

Water Sports

Pattaya and Jomtien have some of the best water sports facilities in Thailand. Waterskiing costs around 1000B per hour, including equipment, a boat and driver. Parasailing is 200B to 300B a shot (about

10 to 15 minutes) and windsurfing costs 500B an hour. Game-fishing is also a possibility; rental rates for boats, fishing guides and tackle are quite reasonable.

Hat Jomtien is the best spot for windsurfing, not least because you're a little less likely to run into parasailors or jet-skiers. Surf House on Th Hat Jomtien rents equipment and offers instruction.

Diving & Snorkelling Pattaya is the most convenient dive location to Bangkok, but it is far from being the best Thailand has to offer. In recent years the fish population has dwindled considerably and visibility is often poor due to heavy boat traffic. Although nearby Ko Laan, Ko Sak and Ko Krok are fine for beginners, accomplished divers may prefer the 'outer islands' of Ko Man Wichai and Ko Rin which have more visibility. In most places expect 3 to 9m of visibility under good conditions, or in more remote sites 5 to 12m. Farther south-east, shipwrecks *Petchburi Bremen* and *Hardeep* off Sattahip and Samae have created artificial reefs which remain the most interesting dive sites.

Diving costs are quite reasonable: a two dive excursion averages 1300B to 1800B for boat, equipment, underwater guide and lunch. Snorkellers may join such day trips for 500B to 800B. For shipwrecks, the price goes up to 2000B, and for an overnight trip with five to seven dives, figure up to 6000B per person. Full NAUI or PADI certification, which takes three to four days, costs 9000B to 12,000B for all instruction and equipment.

Some shops do half-day group trips to nearby islands for as low as 500B to 800B per person, and to islands a bit farther out for 650B; these prices include lunch, beverages, transport and dive master but not equipment rental beyond mask, fins and snorkel.

Average rental rates are: mask, fins and snorkel 150B to 250B (depending on quality); regulator w/SPG 300B to 400B; buoyancy compensation device 250B to 400B; weightbelt 150B; tank 150B; wetsuit 200B; or full scuba outfit 1000B. Airfills typically cost 100B to 150B. To protect themselves from steep baht fluctuations, some dive operators quote only in US dollars these days – a reasonable strategy considering virtually all equipment must be imported, not to mention the increasing price of imported fuel for boats.

Shops along Th Hat Pattaya advertise trips, and several Pattaya hotels also arrange excursions and equipment.

Dave's Diver Den
  (☎ 038-429387, 420411, fax 360095, email drd@loxinfo.co.th)
  190/11 Muu 9, Th Pattaya Klang
Discovery Divers
  (☎ 038-427185, fax 427158)
  183/29 Muu 10, Soi Post Office (Praisani)
Diver's World
  (☎ 038-426517)
  Soi Yamato, South Pattaya
Fun 'n' Sun Divers
  (☎ 038-251310, fax 251209)
  Pattaya Park Beach Resort, Hat Jomtien
Paradise Scuba Divers
  (☎ 038-710587)
  Siam Bayview Resort
Scuba Professionals
  (☎ 038-221860, fax 221618)
  3 Th Pattaya-Naklua
Scuba Tek Dive Center
  (☎ 038-361616, email rickr@loxinfo.co.th)
  Weekender Hotel, Th Pattaya 2
Seafari Sports Center
  (☎ 038-429253, fax 424708)
  Soi 5, North Pattaya
Steve's Dive Shop
  (☎ 038-428392)
  Soi 4, North Pattaya

Dive Medicine Apakorn Kiatiwong Naval Hospital (☎ 038-601185), 26km south-east of Pattaya in Sattahip, has a fully operative recompression chamber; urgent care is available 24 hours.

Karting

One of the legacies left behind by American GIs in Pattaya is karting, the racing of miniature cars (go-karts) powered by 5 to 15hp engines. Karting has since turned into an international sport often described as the closest approximation to Formula One racing available to the average driver.

Water Quality

One of Pattaya's main problems during recent years has been the emptying of raw sewage into the bay, a practice that poses serious health risks for swimmers. Local officials have finally begun to take notice and are now taking regular bacteria counts along the shoreline, and fining hotels and other businesses found to be releasing untreated sewage.

The Thai government allocated US$60 million for pollution clean-up and prevention at Pattaya. By 1998, water treatment plants in Pattaya, Naklua and Jomtien were in operation; authorities claim the coastal waters will be pollution-free by the end of the century.

In the meantime, according to a TAT pamphlet entitled *Striving to Resolve Pattaya's Problems*, beach areas considered safe for swimming (with a coliform count of less than 1000 MPN (Most Probable Number) per 100ml) include those facing Wong Amat Hotel, Dusit Resort Hotel, Yot Sak shopping centre and the Royal Cliff Hotel. Shoreline areas found to exceed the coliform standard extend from Siam Commercial Bank in South Pattaya to where Khlong Pattaya empties into the sea. Coliform counts here have exceeded 1700 MPN per 100ml.

Joe Cummings

MICK WELDON

Pattaya Kart Speedway (☎ 038-423062), at 248/2 Th Thepprasit, boasts Asia's only track sanctioned by the Commission Internationale de Karting (CIK). It's a 1080m loop that meets all CIK safety and sporting standards, plus a beginners track and an 'off-road' (unpaved) track. It's open daily 9.30 am to 9.30 pm (except when international kart races are hosted). Prices range from 180B for 10 minutes of racing in a 5hp kart (oriented towards children) to 300B for a 10 to 15hp kart.

Other Sports
Out of the water, other recreational activities available in the area include golf, bowling, snooker, archery, target-shooting, horse riding and tennis. Among the several gyms and fitness centres is Gold's Gym in South Pattaya's Julie Complex. Gold's has a second branch in North Pattaya just past Soi 1 on Th Naklua-Pattaya.

Places to Stay – Budget
The number of places to stay in Naklua, Pattaya and Jomtien is mind-boggling, with close to 200 hotels, guesthouses and bungalows offering over 13,000 rooms. Because of low occupancy rates, some hotels offer special deals, especially mid-week; bargaining for a room may also get a lower rate. On weekends and holidays the cheaper rooms tend to book out.

In Pattaya itself, North Pattaya and Naklua are quieter and better places to stay if you want to avoid the full-on nightlife of South Pattaya. Overall Hat Jomtien is much better, with clean water and beach, and no obvious sex scene. No place in the area is entirely immune from sex tourism, however; almost every place from Naklua to Jomtien comes with a significant clientele of fat European men and their tiny rent-by-the-day-or-week Thai girlfriends.

The average hotel price ranges from 350B to 2000B, and for guesthouses the range is 200B to 450B.

North Pattaya & Hat Naklua
Wedged between North and Central Pattaya on Th Hat Pattaya Neua, three storey *BJ Guest*

House (☎ 038-421147) sits right across from the beach and rents air-con rooms for 350B, fan rooms from 200B. BJ's restaurant serves Thai and German dishes.

German Garden Hotel (☎ 038-225612, fax 225932, 535/25 Soi 12, Th Naklua) in Naklua, is a bit far from the beach, but it's quiet and rooms cost from 500B. All menus and signs are in German. Another German-oriented place is *Welkom Inn* (☎ 038-422589, fax 361193, Soi 3, Th Hat Pattaya) where fan doubles cost 300B, air-con 450B; a large pool, Thai garden-restaurant and Franco-Belgian restaurant are pluses.

Pattaya Noppakao Hotel (☎/fax 038-370582, 10/17 Muu 6, Th Hat Pattaya Neua), next to the terminal for air-con buses to Bangkok, offers spacious, clean rooms with air-con, hot shower and satellite TV for 450B – good value for Pattaya.

Central & South Pattaya You'll find the cheapest places in town are the guesthouses in South Pattaya along Th Pattaya 2, the street parallel to Th Hat Pattaya. Most are clustered near sois 6, 10, 11 and 12. On Th Pattaya 2, at 216/2 opposite Soi 11, the modern four storey *Apex Hotel* (☎ 038-429233, fax 421184), has rooms with air-con, hot water, TV, fully stocked mini-bar and fridge for 350B in the front of the building, 300B in the back – great value. There's also a pool on the premises. Almost next door, *Diana Inn* (☎ 038-429675, fax 424566) has large rooms with air-con and hot bath for 600B, plus a restaurant and a pool with bar service.

Honey Lodge (☎ 038-429133, fax 710185, 597/8 Muu 10, Th Pattaya Tai), has air-con rooms with hot water, mini-bar and phone for 500B; with restaurant and pool. Another bargain, for Pattaya, is the *Sawasdee Seaview* (☎ 038-720264, Soi 10, Central Pattaya), a four storey lilac-coloured hotel with air-con rooms with TV and hot water for 400B.

In a lane south of Soi 12 *BR Inn* (☎ 038-428229) offers reasonably clean rooms for 300B with fan, 400B air-con. Many Japanese budget travellers stay here. On Soi 13,

Malibu Guest House (☎ 038-428422) has 350B air-con rooms that include breakfast. The rest of the many guesthouses on Soi 13 are in the 200B to 350B range, but rooms are usually cramped and without windows. An exception is *Ma Maison* (☎ 038-429318, fax 426060), which offers chalet-style air-con rooms around a swimming pool for 600B; as the name suggests, it's French-managed and there's a French restaurant on the premises. Advance reservations are highly recommended as it's often booked out.

Down in South Pattaya on Soi Viking, the *Viking* (☎ 038-423164, fax 425964) has been a long-time favourite for its quiet 250B to 350B rooms and pool. *Pattaya Land Hotel* (☎ 038-429569, fax 421945, 325/42-45 Soi 1, Th Pattaya Land), sits right smack in the middle of 'Boys Town' and has some of the cheapest rooms in South Pattaya – fan with cold shower for 200B, air-con a bit more.

Hat Jomtien At Hat Jomtien, the budget end consists of several places around the mid-range Surf House International Hotel towards the north end of the beach. *AA Guest House* (☎ 038-231183) has 500B rooms with air-con and TV – and some rather unfriendly staff. Right behind AA is the friendlier *Moonshine Place Guest House* (☎ 038-231956, fax 232162) at 480B. There is a popular old-west-style bar/restaurant downstairs which could make it noisy at night. Next to Surf House is *Sunlight Seafood & Hotel* (☎ 038-231835) with similar 400B air-con rooms and fan rooms ranging from 250B to 300B; most have private balconies.

Ran Nong Sam Guest House, Restaurant & Beer Garden (☎ 01-835-6587, 114/6 Th Hat Jomtien), located between the burnt remains of the Royal Jomtien Resort and the 7-Eleven store, has rooms for 300B with cold shower and air-con, plus one larger room for 400B.

DD Inn (☎ 038-232995, 410/50 Th Hat Jomtien) is also at the north end of the beach (sometimes referred to separately as

Hat Dong Tan or 'Sugar Palm Beach'), where the road turns towards Pattaya; very clean air-con rooms cost 500B daily, 9000B monthly; showers for beach-going non-guests are available for 10B. Almost next door, the *Sugar Palm Beach Hotel* (☎ 038-231386, fax 231713) offers rooms with air-con, TV and refrigerator for 630B in a small but well kept beachfront property.

Nearby *JB Guest House* (☎ 038-231581) takes the prize, with very decent fan rooms with private cold bath for 250B, simple air-con rooms for 350B, air-con rooms with sea view for 400B and larger rooms for 500B. *Seaview Villa* (☎ 038-231070) has seven fan-cooled bungalows for 300B to 400B. The French-owned *Maisonette Guest House* (☎ 038-231835, fax 232676) has 450B rooms with air-con, fridge and hot water; attached is a French restaurant.

At the friendly four storey *Villa Navin* (☎ 038-231066, fax 231318, 350 Muu 12, Th Hat Jomtien) doubles start at 500B and three-bedroom air-con bungalows start at 1900B; cabins can be rented by the week for 1200B per night. An outdoor restaurant specialises in seafood.

One of the cheapest places to stay is the tidy *RS Guest House* (☎ 038-231867), at the southern end of the beach, near Th Chaiyapreuk. Reasonable smallish rooms cost 300B with fan or 400B with air-con; all with private cold showers.

You can also find unnamed *rooms for rent* in 'condotels' along Hat Jomtien for about 200B to 400B a night with fan, 400B to 600B with air-con. Most are little more than concrete cubes filled with box-like rooms, often lacking in ventilation and plumbing efficiency.

Jomtien Hotel (☎ 038-251606, fax 251097, 403/74 Muu 12, Th Hat Jomtien), at the north end of Jomtien off the road leading to South Pattaya, stands well away from the beach. It's basically a low-end tourist hotel with clean rooms with TV and fan for 250B, or air-con rooms for up to 726B. There is a small rectangular pool on the roof. It's OK value if you don't mind staying in a cement box.

HAT JOMTIEN

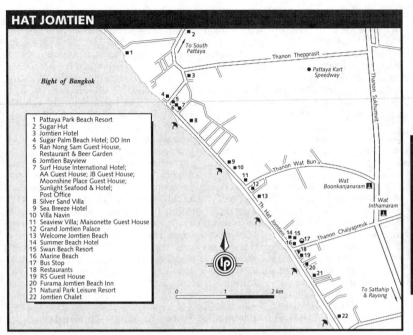

1 Pattaya Park Beach Resort
2 Sugar Hut
3 Jomtien Hotel
4 Sugar Palm Beach Hotel; DD Inn
5 Ran Nong Sam Guest House,
  Restaurant & Beer Garden
6 Jomtien Bayview
7 Surf House International Hotel;
  AA Guest House; JB Guest House;
  Moonshine Place Guest House;
  Sunlight Seafood & Hotel;
  Post Office
8 Silver Sand Villa
9 Sea Breeze Hotel
10 Villa Navin
11 Seaview Villa; Maisonette Guest House
12 Grand Jomtien Palace
13 Welcome Jomtien Beach
14 Summer Beach Hotel
15 Swan Beach Resort
16 Marine Beach
17 Bus Stop
18 Restaurants
19 RS Guest House
20 Furama Jomtien Beach Inn
21 Natural Park Leisure Resort
22 Jomtien Chalet

EASTERN GULF COAST

Places to Stay – Mid-Range

Good mid-range places can be found in Naklua, North Pattaya and Jomtien. In Pattaya the quiet *Sunshine Hotel* (☎ 038-429247, fax 421302) is tucked away at 217/1 Soi 8, where all rooms come with aircon, TV and mini-fridge for a well-priced 550B. The hotel also has two pools and a 24 hour restaurant. On Soi 11 *Natural Beach Hotel* (☎ 038-710121, fax 429650) overlooks the beach with good air-con rooms for 1100B. This modern breezy two storey hotel also contains a small restaurant. Farther south, on the corner of Th Pattaya 2 and Soi 13, is the high-rise *Lek Hotel* (☎ 038-425550/2, fax 426629) with decent air-con rooms with TV for 650B.

The two storey *Garden Lodge* (☎ 038-429109, fax 421221), built around a circular drive just off Th Naklua, features air-con rooms for 650B, a clean pool, good service

and an open-air breakfast buffet. *Seaview Resort Hotel* (☎ 038-429317, fax 423668, Soi 18, Th Pattaya-Naklua), on a quiet soi off of Th Naklua, is an L-shaped four storey hotel with decent air-con rooms for 1000B per night. Families and small groups may like *Pattaya Lodge* (☎ 038-225464, Bangkok ☎ 02-238 0230), which is farther off Th Naklua, right on the beach and far from the pollution and bars. Two-storey, air-con bungalows cost 2700B (two bedrooms, sleeps six), 3300B (three bedrooms, sleeps nine) and 3800B (four bedrooms, sleeps 12). The *Riviera Hotel Pattaya* (☎ 038-225230, fax 225764, Bangkok ☎ 02-252 5068, 157/1 Soi Wat Pa Samphan, Th Naklua) stands between the road and the beach and has cosy, quiet air-con rooms with fridge and TV from 380B in the hotel, up to 2000B in a bungalow. The Riviera also boasts a large garden and pool.

In North Pattaya, *Regent Marina Hotel* (☎ 038-428015, fax 423296, Bangkok ☎ 02-390 2511, 463/31 Th Pattaya Neua), bridges the mid-range to top-end gap with rooms from 1000B, including air-con, TV, phone and mini-fridge.

Furama Beach Hotel (☎ 038-428580, fax 428580, 164 Muu 9, Th Pattaya Klang), a couple of blocks back from the beach, is a worn but clean hotel with all the basic resort amenities. Rooms cost 800B per night or 700B if you stay more than three days. On the premises are a 24 hour coffee shop, seafood restaurant and pool.

In South Pattaya, *Diamond Beach Hotel* (☎ 038-428071, fax 424888, Bangkok ☎ 02-314 4133, 499 Th Hat Pattaya) stands on a busy soi filled with faràng restaurants and bars. Standard air-con rooms go for 500B. On the premises are two swimming pools, a sauna and a large women-behind-glass massage parlour. The Diamond Beach's location and amenities means it effectively caters primarily to male tourists.

Peaceful Hat Jomtien has mostly mid-range condotel places ranging from 500B to 800B. Set back from the main drag, the *Silver Sand Villa* (☎ 038-231288/9, fax 232491) has spacious double air-con hotel rooms and single/double bungalows for 700/800B, including breakfast. There's also a large swimming pool on the premises. The *Jomtien Bayview* (☎ 038-251889) has air-con rooms for 350B to 650B.

The friendly *Surf House International Hotel* (☎ 038-231025/6), next to the Thai Farmer's Bank, has air-con rooms for 600B, 700B with sea view; all rooms come with TV and fridge. The Surf House restaurant serves fresh seafood and offers a good wine selection. The *Marine Beach Hotel* (☎ 038-231129/31, 131/62 Th Hat Jomtien) and the well run *Sea Breeze Hotel* (☎ 038-231056/8, fax 231059) cost 550B to 1200B per air-con room; the latter is very good value at this rate. Another good-value place is the friendly five storey *Summer Beach Inn* (☎ 038-231777, fax 231778), near the Marine Beach Hotel, where fairly new air-con rooms cost 650B to 750B, including

satellite TV and mini-bar in all rooms. Next door is the eight storey *Swan Beach Resort* (☎/fax 038-231266, 132/3 Muu 12, Th Hat Jomtien) with 126 somewhat shabby rooms from 600B, and a tiny pool out front.

Another good deal is the pink-walled *Furama Jomtien Beach Inn* (☎ 038-231545), where standard rooms with TV and air-con cost 500B to 600B a day, deluxe rooms 1200B. The Furama caters especially to Japanese, Chinese and Korean package tourists.

Jomtien Chalet (57/1 Muu 1, Th Hat Jomtien) offers simple, clean air-con bungalows for 1650B to 2200B. Two rooms in an old refurbished railway car go for 1200B to 2000B, depending on number of people and season; a restaurant on the property serves Thai and western food.

Jomtien also has several more expensive places that rent bungalows in the 2000B to 3000B range (see Places to Stay – Top End). The high-rise development of Pattaya and Hat Cliff is spreading fast to Jomtien.

Places to Stay – Top End
Pattaya is really a resort for package tourists and conventioneers so the vast majority of its accommodation is in this bracket. All of the hotels mentioned below have air-con rooms and swimming pools (unless otherwise noted). In most cases the higher prices quoted are for suites, while the lower ones are for standard doubles. Many of the top-end hotels have lowered rates on standard singles and doubles so it's worth asking if anything cheaper is available when requesting a rate quote. Rooms are also often cheaper when booked through a Bangkok travel agency.

Luxury Among the reigning monarchs of Pattaya luxury hotels is *Dusit Resort Pattaya* (☎ 038-425611, fax 428239, Bangkok ☎ 02-236 0450, 240/2 Th Hat Pattaya) at the northern end of Hat Pattaya, with two pools, tennis and squash courts, a health centre, a semi-private beachfront and exceptional dim sum in the rooftop restaurant. Rates: 5700B to 11,398B.

A traditional wooden boat at Ko Chang's Hat Kaibae, Ranong Province.

RICHARD NEBESKY

RICHARD NEBESKY

shrine on Thanon Sukhumvit in Trat.

A palm-fringed white sand beach on Ko Chang.

KRAIG LIEB

The port at Ko Si Chang, Eastern Gulf Coast.

RICHARD NEBESKY

Dried salted fish for sale, Ban Phe, Rayong Province.

Dried star and puffer fish look like macabre mobiles, Ban Phe, Rayong Province.

Another excellent choice in this category is the *Amari Orchid Resort (☎ 038-428161, fax 428165, Bangkok ☎ 02-267 9708, email amorchid@loxinfo.co.th)* set on four lush hectares in North Pattaya, with an Olympic-size swimming pool, two illuminated tennis courts, children's playground, minigolf, garden chess and one of the best Italian restaurants in Pattaya. The Amari quotes only in dollars: US$84 to US$191.

Royal Garden Resort Pattaya (☎ 038-412120, fax 429926, Bangkok ☎ 02-476 0021, 218/2-4 Muu 10, Th Hat Pattaya), one of Pattaya's most well established resorts, sits on 3.5 hecares of palms in central Pattaya and has lotus ponds and Thai-style pavilions. It's attached to a four storey shopping centre as well as a Ripley's Believe It or Not Museum; also on the premises are a fitness centre, two tennis courts, two cinemas and a pool. Rooms start at US$118 a night.

Another older luxury property is the *Royal Cliff Beach Resort (☎ 038-250421/30, fax 250522, Bangkok ☎ 02-282 0999, Th Cliff)* at the southern end of Pattaya, which is really three hotels in one: a central section for package tours and conventions, a family wing and the very up-market Royal Wing; rooms start at 3600B.

Hat Naklua & North Pattaya On Hat Naklua, *Central Wong Amat Hotel (☎ 038-426990, fax 428599, Bangkok ☎ 02-547 1234, email cghsales@samart.co.th, 277-8 Muu 5, Th Naklua)* is a very quiet 25 acre resort with rooms starting at 4114B. *Woodlands Resort (☎ 038-421707, fax 425663, Bangkok ☎ 02-392 2159, 164/1 Th Pattaya-Naklua)* is a smaller place oriented towards families – with a children's pool, playground, babysitting services and lots of 'bear' logos to make the little ones feel at home – starting at 1584B.

In North Pattaya the multistorey *Beach View Hotel (☎ 038-422660, fax 422664, 389 Soi 2, Th Hat Pattaya)* offers discounted rates of 590B to 850B (850B to 1290B walk-in). Once one of Pattaya's finest hotels, the *Merlin Pattaya (☎ 038-428755/9, fax 421673, Bangkok ☎ 02-253 2140, Th Hat Pattaya)*, now seems rather plain beside more elegant properties, but caters to the new and growing wave of Russian tourists with rooms for 2900B a night. *Montien Pattaya (☎ 038-428155/6, fax 423155, Bangkok ☎ 02-233 7060, email monpat@chonburi.ksc.co.th, Th Hat Pattaya)* is a bit better with rooms costing 3146B to 4598B.

Central & South Pattaya Moving south, the top-enders drop in price a bit. Several offer comfortable air-con rooms with phone, TV and mini-fridge, plus other amenities on the premises such as a coffee shop or restaurant, travel agent and swimming pool. One such place is *Pattaya Centre Hotel (☎ 038-425877, fax 420491, Soi 12, Th Hat Pattaya)*, 1400B single/double including breakfast for two, across the road from the beach.

Right in the thick of Central Pattaya, *Siam Bayview Resort (☎ 038-423871, fax 423879, email siamcity@siamhotels.com, 310/2 Th Hat Pattaya)* features rooms from 2904B plus a lovely pool, garden and terrace cafe.

Set at South Pattaya's quieter edge, The labyrinthine *Siam Bayshore Resort (☎ 038-428678/81, fax 428730, Bangkok ☎ 02-221 1004, Th Pattaya Tai)*, costs 2299B for a cut above the standard.

Hat Cliff or Cliff Beach, named for the Royal Cliff Resort, bears a few other places, including the *Cosy Beach (☎ 038-428818, fax 422818, Th Cliff)*, from 1600B to 1800B, and *Island View (☎ 038-250813, fax 250818, Bangkok ☎ 02-249 8941, Th Cliff)*, 1200B to 1452B, among others of a similar standard.

Hat Jomtien This beach, which is around the corner from South Pattaya, is lined with hotels, resorts and guesthouses, several of which qualify as top end. One of the best places to stay in the entire Pattaya area, *Sugar Hut (☎ 038-251686, fax 251689, 391/18)*, is not even on the beach, but off the road that runs between Pattaya and Hat Jomtien. There are 33 Thai-style bungalows on stilts thoughtfully scattered among 15 rai (approximately 2.4 hectares) of tropical

EASTERN GULF COAST

gardens, complete with rabbits and birds, three swimming pools, a restaurant, a modern fitness centre and jogging track. The bungalows feature partially open bathrooms inspired perhaps by upscale Balinese resorts. A single/double bungalow costs 2750B plus tax and service, while a double bungalow housing three or more people is 6820B.

Pattaya Park Beach Resort (☎ 038-251201, fax 251209, Bangkok ☎ 02-511 0717, 345 Th Hat Jomtien) is a huge cement entertainment/hotel complex oriented towards package tourists or families, with such attractions as a tailor shop, huge 'fun complex', beer garden, dive shop and water park. Rooms cost 2662B to 4840B.

The **Grand Jomtien Palace** (☎ 038-231405, fax 231404, Bangkok ☎ 02-271 3613, 356 Th Hat Jomtien) has rooms for 2420B to 5445B; it's popular with German and Russian package tourists. **Welcome Jomtien Beach** (☎ 038-232701/15, fax 232716, Bangkok ☎ 02-252 0594) nearby also caters to package tourists (especially Russians) with rooms from 1600B. The much nicer **Natural Park Leisure Resort** (☎ 038-231561, fax 231567, Bangkok ☎ 02-247 2825, fax 247 1676, 412 Th Hat Jomtien) is a low-rise hotel with rooms starting at 1950B and an attractive free-form swimming pool.

Places to Eat

Most food in Pattaya is expensive. The signs outside the many snack bars and restaurants in town reveal that *bratwurst mit brot* is far more readily available than *khâo phàt*. Arabs and South Asians have been coming to Pattaya for many years now, so there are also plenty of Indian, Pakistani and Middle Eastern restaurants in town, some with fairly moderate prices. The recent influx of Russians has inspired several restaurants to add Russian translations to their menus; more recently a few Russian cafes have been added to the scene.

Decent Thai food is available in shops along Pattaya's back street (Th Pattaya 2), away from the beach. The best seafood restaurants are in South Pattaya, where you pick out the sea creatures yourself and are charged by weight. Prices tend to be sky-high by Thai standards. **Savoey Seafood** (☎ 038-428580/1), part of the Furama Beach Hotel in Central Pattaya, is one of the better places for fresh seafood without breaking the bank.

One moderately priced yet well appointed Pattaya restaurant is the **PIC Kitchen** on Soi 5 (second entrance on Soi 4). The Thai-style *salas* (open sided rooms) have low wooden tables and cushions for dining and the emphasis is on Thai food with a limited selection of western dishes; prices average 70B to 140B per dish. The upstairs bar area features live jazz nightly. Open 8 am to midnight. Another interesting place to eat is **Vientiane Restaurant** (☎ 038-411298, 485/18 Th Pattaya 2), opposite Soi Yamato. The 503-item menu includes mostly Thai and Lao dishes ranging from 60B to 120B, plus lunch specials for 30B to 50B; open 11 am to midnight.

San Domenico's (☎ 038-426871), Th Hat Jomtien between South Pattaya and Hat Jomtien, is operated by the same Italian family that started Pan Pan in Bangkok. The Italian menu is superb and, though regular meals are pricey, there is also an excellent buffet for just under 200B stocked with antipasti, pasta, seafood and Luciano Pantieri's famous desserts.

Moonshine Place on Th Hat Jomtien specialises in Mexican and southern Thai food; you can also buy a picnic lunch here.

Alt Heidelberg (273 Th Hat Pattaya), in South Pattaya, is one of the more established German restaurants. It opens at 9 am for breakfast and stays open till 2 am. The Royal Garden Plaza shopping centre, attached to Royal Garden Resort, contains several fast-food franchise restaurants. The Big C shopping centre on Th Pattaya 2 contains **KFC, Burger King, Baskin Robbins** and **Mister Donut**.

Opposite the bus station on the corner of Th Hat Jomtien and Th Chaiyapreuk are a few basic and cheap **restaurants** serving the usual Thai/Chinese dishes.

Entertainment

Eating, drinking and making merry are the big pastimes once the sun goes down. Making merry in Pattaya, aside from the professional sex scene, means everything from hanging out in a video bar to dancing all night at one of the discos in South Pattaya. Two transvestite palaces, *Alcazar* (☎ 038-428746, 78/14 Th Pattaya 2) and *Tiffany's* (☎ 038-421700), offer complete drag-queen shows; the Alcazar is the best and puts on three shows nightly at 6.30, 8 and 11 pm. Tickets for the shows range from 400B to 600B.

Among the several discos in town, the very glitzy *Pattaya Palladium* (☎ 038-424922, 78/33-35 Th Pattaya 2) is a large entertainment complex featuring 12 snooker tables, a 200-bed massage parlour, a Chinese restaurant, karaoke bar, cocktail lounge and a 360 degree Panorama Cinema. The disco has a capacity of 6000 customers, reportedly the largest disco in Thailand; open from 9.30 pm till 2 am. The older *Marine Disco* is still popular.

Actually, one of the best things to do in the evening is just to stroll down Th Hat Pattaya and check out the amazing variety of bars – there's one for every proclivity, including a couple of outdoor Thai boxing bars featuring local talent. Truly the Garden of Earthly Delights, in the most Boschean sense. 'Pattaya Land', encompassing sois 1, 2 and 3 in South Pattaya, is one of the most concentrated bar areas. The many gay bars on Soi 3 are announced by a sign over the soi reading 'Boys Town'.

Pattaya's civic leaders are now attempting to clean up the town's seamy nightlife image. Though the bars and discos are still tolerated, public soliciting is discouraged outside that part of South Pattaya known as 'the village', which attracts a large number of Thai prostitutes as well as ka-toeys (Thai transvestites). There is also a prominent gay scene. Incidentally, the easiest way to tell a ka-toey is by the Adam's apple – a scarf covering the neck is a dead give-away. Nowadays, though, some ka-toeys have their Adam's apples surgically removed.

With all the emphasis on girlie bars, there's precious little in the way of live music in Pattaya. One of the few places you can find it is at one of the town's original nightspots, the *Bamboo Bar*, on Th Pattaya Tai near the intersection with Th Hat Pattaya. There are two bands each night (the second act, starting around midnight, is usually better). There are of course plenty of hostesses happy to keep you company, but no-one minds if you just want to knock back a few drinks and take in the music. A smaller place with live tunes is *Orn's Beer Bar*, next to the Apex Hotel. The quality of the musicians varies, but the place has a good vibe to it, and if you feel you can do justice to a song, you might be able to take to the stage yourself.

Delaney's Pattaya (☎ 038-710641, Th Pattaya 2) brings Bangkok's popular Irish pub to Pattaya with all the usual trimmings, including Guinness on tap.

A *cinema* in the Big C shopping centre on Th Pattaya 2 shows first-run English-language movies.

Getting There & Away

Air Bangkok Airways flies four times per week between Ko Samui and U-Taphao airfield (about 30km south of Pattaya). The one-way fare is 1890B, half that for children.

Direct road transport from the international airport at Bangkok is available to Pattaya; see the Bus entry later in this section.

Bangkok International Airport
If you've just flown into Bangkok and need to get to Pattaya right away, there are airport minibuses that go directly to Pattaya at 9 and 11 am and 7 pm daily for 200B one way. In the opposite direction, the THAI minibus leaves from the Royal Cliff Resort in Pattaya at 9 and 11 am and 1, 3 and 5 pm. It takes around 2½ hours to reach the airport; the fare is 150B. Some hotels in Pattaya also run their own buses to Bangkok for fares ranging from 160B to 300B one way.

Bus Ordinary buses from Bangkok's Eastern bus terminal cost 45B one way and leave at 30 minute intervals from 5.20 am to

9 pm daily. In Pattaya they leave from the depot on Th Sukhumvit, where it meets Th Pattaya Klang. Count on around three hours for this trip.

Air-con buses from the same station in Bangkok leave at similar intervals between 6.30 am and 8 pm for 70B. Air-con buses to Pattaya are also available from Bangkok's Northern bus terminal for the same fare. In Pattaya the air-con bus stop is on Th Pattaya Neua, near the intersection with Th Sukhumvit. The air-con route takes around 2½ hours. Several hotels and travel agencies in Bangkok also run thrice-daily air-con tour buses to Pattaya for around 100B to 150B. Cramped minivans from Th Khao San (Khao San Rd) typically cost 170B per person. These buses take around two hours in either direction. Once you reach the main Pattaya bus terminal, waiting red songthaews will take you to the main beach road for 20B per person.

From Si Racha you can grab a public bus on Th Sukhumvit to Pattaya for 12B.

Pattaya has a separate bus stop for buses to the north-east on Th Pattaya Klang, a couple of blocks east of Th Pattaya 2.

Train The No 365/283 train goes from Hualamphong station to Pattaya via Chachoengsao daily at 6.55 am, arriving at 10.37 am. In the opposite direction train No 284 departs Pattaya at 2.50 pm and arrives at Hualamphong at 6.35 pm. The trip costs 31B one way. Although this is an hour longer than the typical bus ride from Bangkok, it beats biting your nails in traffic jams along the highway from Bang Na to Trat. The Pattaya train station is just north of the T-junction of Th Pattaya Klang and Th Sukhumvit.

Getting Around
Songthaew Songthaews cruise up and down Th Hat Pattaya and Th Pattaya 2 frequently – just hop on and when you get out pay 10B anywhere between Naklua and South Pattaya, 20B as far as Jomtien. Don't ask the fare first as the driver may interpret this to mean you want to charter the vehicle.

A chartered songthaew to Jomtien should be 40B. It's usually easier to get a share songthaew from Jomtien to Central Pattaya rather than vice versa.

Many, many readers have complained about riding the 10B songthaews with local passengers and then being charged a high 'charter' price of 20B to 50B or more when they get off. In some instances drivers have threatened to beat faràng passengers when they wouldn't pay the exorbitant fare. It's little use complaining to the Tourist Police unless you can give them the licence plate number of the offending driver's vehicle. A refund is highly unlikely but perhaps if the Tourist Police receive enough complaints, they'll take some action to reduce or eliminate the rip-offs. So far, however, they have done absolutely nothing to remove this black spot on Pattaya's already tarnished reputation.

Car & Jeep Jeeps can be hired for around 2000B per day, and cars start at 1200B (as low as 800B for a 4WD Suzuki in the low season) depending on size and model; insurance and tax cost up to 160B more. All rentals in Pattaya are on a 24 hour basis. Avis Rent-A-Car (☎ 038-361627/8) has an office at the Dusit Resort, and is by far the most expensive option. Budget (☎ 038-726185) has better rates, and has the same advantage as Avis: if something goes wrong you don't have to worry about any hassles (like a formerly unseen disclaimer popping up in your insurance policy). Both companies also offer pickup and drop off service at your hotel.

SIE (☎ 038-410629), located near the Diana Inn on Th Pattaya 2, is pretty good and has competitive rates. Although SIE has signs claiming it's 'European managed' don't expect smooth sailing if anything goes wrong with the car, or you decide to return it early. There are no refunds, no matter what.

Motorcycle Motorbikes cost 150B to 200B per day for an 80 or 100cc; a 125 to 150cc will cost 300B, and you'll even see a few 750 to 1000cc machines for 500B to 1000B. There are several motorcycle hire places along Th Hat Pattaya and a couple on Th Pattaya 2. Pattaya is a good place to purchase a used motorcycle – check the rental shops.

Boat The ferry to Ko Laan leaves from Tha Tangke in South Pattaya, takes 40 minutes and costs 100B. For 250B the ferry company will throw in lunch. The boat departs in the morning around 9 am and returns at 4 pm. Boat charters cost around 1000B to 1500B per day depending on the size of the boat.

AROUND PATTAYA

Farther south and east from Pattaya are more beaches and more resorts.

In quiet Bang Saray, *Khum Det (☎ 038-437304, 472 Th Ban Na)* offers simple rooms with private cold shower for 100B to 400B. *Bang Saray Villa (☎ 038-436070)* has air-con bungalows for a reasonable 350B to 700B, while the *Bang Saray Fishing Inn (☎ 038-436095)* is a small hotel with air-con rooms for 550B to 850B. *Sea Sand Club (☎ 038-435163, fax 435166)* has air-con bungalows for 750B from Sunday to Thursday, and 900B on Friday and Saturday. All of these have competitors of similar style, quality and price.

There are still some good seafood restaurants for local Thais in Bang Saray – something Pattaya hasn't seen for years.

Still farther south is Sattahip, a vacation spot for the Thai military – some of the best beaches in the area are reserved for their use. There are several Thai navy and air force bases in the vicinity.

Ko Laan

This is the only nearby island with tourist accommodation and regular transport. The beach becomes quite crowded during the day in high season (November to April) and is crowded on weekends year-round. At night, though, you and the other guests at the resort will have it all to yourselves.

Ko Laan Resort (☎ 038-428422, fax 426229) offers OK fan rooms for 800B, air-con rooms for 1000B and up.

RAYONG

• pop 46,400

Rayong municipality lies on the Gulf coast 220km from Bangkok by the old highway (Hwy 3) or 185km on Hwy 36. The general topography surrounding the provincial capital consists of a series of mountains interspersed by plains, large tracts of forest and rubber and fruit plantations. The province produces fine fruit (especially durian, rambutan and mangosteen) and *náam plaa* (fish sauce). Rayong itself is not really worth visiting, but nearby beaches are fair and Ko Samet is a favourite island getaway for Bangkokians. Except for Ko Samet, this area has not received many foreign visitors yet, although it has been popular with Thai tourists for several years.

Estuarial beaches at **Laem Charoen**, 2km south of the provincial capital of Rayong, aren't that great but there are some reasonable seafood restaurants. Better are the beaches near **Ban Phe**, a seaside town around 25km south-east of Rayong (this is also the departure point for Ko Samet). If sun and sand are what you've come for, head straight for Ban Phe. Then pick out a beach or board a boat bound for Samet.

Another much smaller island near Rayong is **Ko Saket**, which is a 20 minute boat ride from the beach of Hat Sai Thong, south-west of Rayong (turn south off Hwy 3 at Km 208).

Suan Son (Pine Park), 5km farther down the highway from Ban Phe, is a popular place with Thai picnickers and has white sand beaches as well.

Suan Wang Kaew is 11km east of Ban Phe and has more beaches and rather expensive bungalows. **Ko Thalu**, across from Wang Kaew, is said to be a good diving area – the proprietors of Suan Wang Kaew, a private park, can arrange boats and gear. A few kilometres north-east of Wang Kaew, the white sand beach of **Hat Ban Sang** has recently become a new area for residential and resort development. Other resort areas along the Rayong coast include **Laem Mae Phim**, to the east, and **Hat Sai Thong**, to the west. **Hat Mae Ramphung**, a

10km strip of sand between Ban Taphong and Ban Kon Ao (11km east of Rayong), is part of Laem Ya-Ko Samet National Park. See the Ko Samet section for more information on the park.

Khao Chamao-Khao Wong National Park is inland, about 17km north of Km 274 off Hwy 3. Though less than 85 sq km, the park is famous for limestone mountains, caves, high cliffs, dense forest, waterfalls and freshwater swimming and fishing. The park service here rents bungalows, longhouses and tents. To get here from Ban Phe take a songthaew to Km 274 for 24B, and another songthaew to the park.

Many more resort-type places are popping up along Rayong's coastline. Bangkok developers envisage a string of Thai resorts all the way to Trat along the eastern seaboard, banking on the increasing income and leisure time of Bangkok Thais.

One non-resort development along the coast is the new deep-water port at **Maptaphut**, west of Rayong which, along with Chonburi's Laem Chabang Port, catches the large shipping overflow from Bangkok's Khlong Toey Port.

Information

Tourist Office The TAT (☎ 038-655420) has a rather inconveniently located office 7km east of Rayong town on the north side of Hwy 3. They can provide maps and fairly up-to-date lists of accommodation and sights in Rayong and Chanthaburi provinces, but unless you're in dire need of this info, it's probably not worth the trip.

Money Several banks along Rayong's main drag, Th Sukhumvit, have exchange services, including Bangkok Bank, Thai Farmers Bank and Bank of Ayudhuya. Opening hours are 8.30 am to 3.30 pm weekdays, 8.30 am to noon on Saturday.

Things to See & Do

The **King Taksin Shrine**, on the grounds of Wat Lum Mahachai Chumpon, commemorates King Taksin's brief sojourn in Rayong. According to legend, Taksin tethered his elephant mount to the large tree in front of the shrine, which is highly revered by Thais of Chinese ancestry. Thai-Chinese flock to the shrine during Chinese New Year.

Wat Pa Pratu, constructed during the Ayuthaya period, boasts a highly stylised Buddha measuring 11.95m long by 3.60m high. Unlike most reclining Buddhas throughout Asia, this one is lying on its left side rather than its right. No one today seems to know whether this was intentional (a Tantric explanation is possible) or an artisan error. A large *wihăan* (chapel) was built in 1981 to enshrine the Buddha, which previously was uncovered. There's also a large European-pose Buddha in a wihăan nearby, as well as an exquisite 500-year-old wihăan that's kept locked most of the time.

A very old, 10m-tall stupa known as **Phra Chedi Klang Nam** stands about 2km from the town centre on an islet at the mouth of the Rayong River. An annual festival at the islet every November features boat races in the estuarial bay.

Laem Charoen is a long, narrow cape lined with the homes of local fisherfolk and seafarers. On the inside of the cape facing an estuary are numerous *rohng ngaan năam plaa*, small factory warehouses where Rayong's famous fish sauce is produced and stored. The aromas in this neighbourhood, as might be expected, can be a little overwhelming. A small garden at the end of Laem Charoen contains sculpted figures of Phra Aphaimani, one of Thailand's most famous heroes of classical myth, along with a pond and a Chinese shrine where locals often bring picnics.

Places to Stay

Should you somehow get caught overnight in Rayong, there are a few inexpensive hotels near the bus station off Th Sukhumvit. The relatively old, **Rayong Otani** (☎ 038-611112, 69 Th Sukhumvit) has OK fan rooms for 230B, air-con from 400B. To reach it, walk south from the bus station out to Th Sukhumvit, turn left and proceed past Rayong hospital, soon after which you'll see the hotel sign.

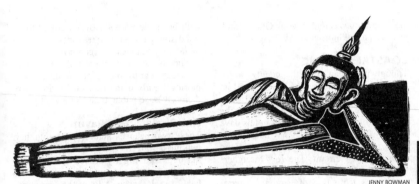

JENNY BOWMAN

Reclining Buddha at Wat Pa Pratu – Rayong

Rayong President Hotel (☎ 038-611307, fax 612570, 168 Th Phochanakon) is more upmarket, with relatively new air-con rooms from 450B. The hotel is down a small side street, so it's probably quiet at night. From the bus station, cross to the other side of Th Sukhumvit, turn right and after about three minutes you'll see a sign pointing down the side street to the hotel. The fairly new *Rayong Palace* (☎ 038-616438, 01-942 4632, fax 038-617204, 109 Th Ratbamrung) offers rooms costing a moderate 400B to 500B a night. There are plenty of other places strung out along Sukhumvit with rooms ranging from 150B for simple fan rooms to around 700B for air-con and hot water.

Top-end lodgings include the *Rayong Orchid* (☎ 038-614340, fax 614780, Bangkok ☎ 02-392 0143, fax 381 3984, 011 Th Ratbamrung), with rooms costing from 1800B.

PMY Beach Resort (☎ 038-614855, fax 614887, Bangkok ☎ 02-321 8875, fax 321 8878), at the west end of Laem Charoen, is a huge place with rates starting at 1883B for a large double to 6120B for a two-bedroom suite. The narrow strip of beach here isn't very good, however, so it's really only visitors with business at the Maptaphut industrial estate who stay here.

Places to Eat

For cheap food, check out the *market* near the Thetsabanteung cinema, or there's a string of *restaurants* and *noodle shops* on Th Taksin Maharat just south of Wat Lum Mahachaichumphon.

The *Samakhom Pramong* (Fishing Co-operative) on the harbour in Laem Charoen has re-opened in a clean new sala and does fantastic Thai seafood. If you have plenty of time, take a songthaew (3B) south from Th Sukhumvit to the mouth of the Rayong River at Laem Charoen, where the well established indoor-outdoor *Laem Charoen*, *Saeng Chan* and *Ocharos (Ocha Rot)* serve very good, moderately priced seafood. Songthaews (8B) from the bus station take you to a small wooden bridge that crosses the Rayong River onto a long spit of land. After crossing the bridge you can catch a motorcycle taxi (10B) to the restaurants.

Getting There & Away

Regular buses (63B) to Rayong leave about every 15 minutes between 4.30 am and 10 pm from Bangkok's Eastern (Ekamai) bus terminal. The trip usually takes more than four hours. First class air-con buses leave hourly from 5 am to 10 pm, cost 101B and take about three hours, 2nd class air-con is 88B. Songthaews from Rayong bus station to Ban Phe cost 10B.

Ordinary buses to Chanthaburi or Pattaya from Rayong cost 30B and take about 1½ hours in either direction. These buses, as well as buses to Bangkok, depart form near the central market and Rayong Otani Hotel, just off Th Sukhumvit (Hwy 3).

COASTAL RAYONG

Though none can rival the beauty of Ko Samet, there are numerous beaches and islands along Rayong's 100km coast. The tourists here are almost all Thai. Even the stretches of beach with strips of hotels have a sleepy feel that, for some, may make a nice change from doing the standard Thailand foreign tourist circuit. The few foreigners here are likely to be local residents, mostly employees from one of Rayong's major joint-venture industrial operations, like the enormous petrochemical-refinery complex at Maptaphut west of Rayong town.

Though not outstanding, some of the beaches, such as Mae Ramphung, Ban Sang and Laem Mae Phim, are quite nice. One downside to this area for budget travellers is that it's often difficult to find accommodation for under 500B per night. Unlike foreign travellers, vacationing Thais are usually out to spend cash, and want air-con, a swimming pool and TV, not simple thatched bungalows

with bugs and no bath. Beaches tend to be lined not with palm trees but rather *sŏn tháleh* or 'sea pines' (casuarina).

The best way to visit most of these places is to rent a car from Pattaya, and then go exploring. Nearly all the Thai tourists drive here themselves, so public transport is spotty.

Hat Phala & Hat Payun

These two beaches actually link together, making a 5km strip of yellow sand, casuarina trees and slightly cloudy surf. There's not a lot going on around here, even in the heat of high season. A lot of the accommodation is aimed at long-term visitors, with numerous apartment buildings and homes going for 15,000B to 25,000B per month.

Of the shorter term options, none are cheap. Starting at the bottom, the ***Pala Resort*** (*☎/fax 038-630358*) is about five minutes walk from Hat Phala, and has a small complex of air-con bungalows for 700B to 1500B. Moving towards Hat Payun is the ***Banchang Cliff Beach*** (*☎ 038-630316*), a towering hotel with swimming pool, tennis courts and air-con rooms from 700B.

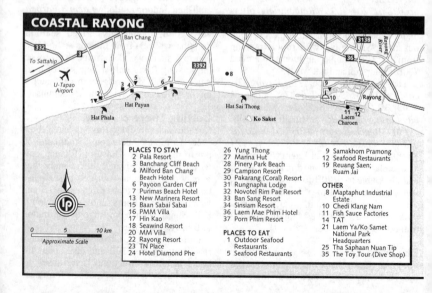

COASTAL RAYONG

PLACES TO STAY	26 Yung Thong	9 Samakhom Pramong
2 Pala Resort	27 Marina Hut	12 Seafood Restaurants
3 Banchang Cliff Beach	28 Pinery Park Beach	19 Reuang Saen;
4 Milford Ban Chang	29 Campson Resort	Ruam Jai
Beach Hotel	30 Pakarang (Coral) Resort	
6 Payoon Garden Cliff	31 Rungnapha Lodge	OTHER
7 Purimas Beach Hotel	32 Novotel Rim Pae Resort	8 Maptaphut Industrial
13 New Marinera Resort	33 Ban Sang Resort	Estate
15 Baan Sabai Sabai	34 Sinsiam Resort	10 Chedi Klang Nam
16 PMM Villa	36 Laem Mae Phim Hotel	11 Fish Sauce Factories
17 Hin Kao	37 Porn Phim Resort	14 TAT
18 Seawind Resort		21 Laem Ya/Ko Samet
20 MM Villa	PLACES TO EAT	National Park
22 Rayong Resort	1 Outdoor Seafood	Headquarters
23 TN Place	Restaurants	25 Tha Saphaan Nuan Tip
24 Hotel Diamond Phe	5 Seafood Restaurants	35 The Toy Tour (Dive Shop)

However, it's not on the beach. Another kilometre east, and on the beach side of the road, the *Milford Ban Chang Beach Hotel* (☎ 038-630019, fax 630024, Bangkok 02-261 4271) is a palatial resort hotel where rates start at 2340B, excluding tax and service charges. It has a nice stretch of beach in front of it and it's quiet: the only sound you're likely to hear will be your own steps echoing down the vast hallways.

Towards the end of Hat Payun is another luxury spot, *Purimas Beach Hotel* (☎ 038-630382, fax 630380, Bangkok ☎ 02-392 6900), an elegantly designed resort complex with pool, health club and business centre. Rooms start at around 2800B per night.

Aside from the hotels, there are numerous open-air *seafood restaurants* along the beaches, particularly at Hat Phala and at Hat Payun where the road from Ban Chang ends.

Getting There & Away To get there by public transport, take a bus to Rayong and get off at the town of Ban Chang. From there you can catch a songthaew to Payun (5B). Most of them stop where the road from Ban

Chang meets the beach, so you may have to pay a bit extra if you want them to take you to your hotel, (although the more expensive places should have pickup service). There is no regular songthaew service to Hat Phala: a charter should cost around 20B.

If you're driving, just after entering Ban Chang, look for a sign indicating the turn-off for Hat Phala, soon after Km 194 and opposite Route 3376. The beach is 6km south along this road. When you get to the intersection before the beach, turn right for Hat Phala, and left for Hat Payun.

Hat Sai Thong & Ko Saket

Forget what the TAT brochures tell you, there's no reason to come to these places. The beach of Hat Sai Thong has been replaced with a concrete breakwater, and the entire area is in spitting distance of the Map-taphut industrial park, home to massive petrochemical plants. Tiny Ko Saket, a 15 minute boat ride from Hat Sai Thong, used to have accommodation, but it has been razed as the island is now being adapted for industrial purposes.

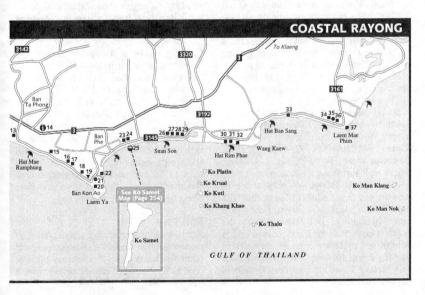

COASTAL RAYONG

EASTERN GULF COAST

Hat Mae Ramphung

This 10km stretch of beach is part of the Khao Laem Ya/Ko Samet National Park, though you'd never know it by the dozens of resort hotels and bungalows lining the road. Although it's very narrow, even at low tide, it has fairly soft, whitish sand, not much litter, and plenty of space for those long morning or evening walks. The western and middle sections of the beach are the best. The eastern part is a bit more cluttered as the fishing village of Ban Kon Ao is at this end.

The headquarters of Khao Laem Ya/Ko Samet National Park is on the headland behind the eastern end of Mae Ramphung. The office has very basic English info and maps of the park, and there are some trails to hike around the headland. However, the military occupies the very top portion and thus has kept the best views for itself. Entry to the park is 20B.

Again, most accommodation in this area is up-market. Budget travellers could try the *New Marinera Resort* (☎ *038-655101*) which has rooms and bungalows from 600 to 1500B. The place is a bit run-down, and is off the beach, but does have the unique feature of having several fruit-shaped concrete bungalows, including an apple, a melon and a durian! At the other end of the beach, hidden among a small cluster of bungalows, *MM Villa* (☎ *038-651559*) has simple air-con rooms and bungalows from 700B, a better deal.

Along the beach there are at least a dozen places to choose from. In terms of value for money, one of the better places is *Seawind Resort* (☎ *038-651562, fax 652735, Bangkok* ☎ *02-234 6195, fax 233 2158)*, where well-furnished air-con rooms go for 750B to 1500B, though you may be able to bargain this down a bit if it's not full. The hotel has a pleasant courtyard around a large swimming pool (even though the beach is just across the road). Less palatable but OK in a pinch are condotel-style places like the *Royal Rayong*, *VIP Condo Chain* and *Victory View*, all with rates similar to the Seawind Resort.

Hin Kao (☎ *038-664471, Bangkok* ☎ *02-451 9389)* has small but pleasant fan and air-con bungalows from 800B to 5000B – the price goes up on weekends. The grounds are well kept and there is a friendly manager who speaks English, a bit of a rarity in these parts. Nearby, the *PMM Villa* (☎/*fax 038-664647)* has more luxurious bungalows from 1000B to 2500B. Higher end travellers should skip all the high-rise hotels and head straight for *Baan Sabai Sabai* (☎ *038-898911, 01-982 3163)*, an immaculate, tastefully landscaped warren of cottages and small homes. Nightly rates range from 2850B for a double to 6500B for a suite, and luxury apartments are available for monthly rental from 25,000B.

Rayong Resort (☎ *038-651000, fax 651007, Bangkok* ☎ *02-255 2392, fax 255 2391)*, near the turnoff for the park headquarters coming from Ban Phe, offers rooms in cottages spread over the hills of Laem Ya. Rates start at 3205B for spacious units with all the amenities and views of the bay between Laem Ya and Ko Samet.

Of the several simple seaside restaurants strung out along the beach (particularly toward Ban Kon Ao), the best are *Reuang Saen* and *Ruam Jai*.

Getting There & Away The easiest way to get here by public transport is to get a bus to Rayong, and then from the bus station catch a songthaew (12B) to Mae Ramphung. The latter run erratically, and you may have to wait for a while if you're going later in the afternoon. If you're driving, take Hwy 3 about 5km west past Rayong to the small town of Ban Ta Phong where you'll see a sign indicating the turn-off for the road to Mae Ramphung. Rayong-bound songthaews can be flagged down anywhere along the road to Mae Ramphung.

Ban Phe

After Hat Mae Ramphung, the coastal road passes through Ban Phe, the jumping-off point for Ko Samet. If you miss the last boat to Ko Samet, there are several hotels near the pier.

Information There is an immigration office at Ban Phe, opposite the Nuanthip pier. Visa extensions are available here, but the office is only open on Monday, Wednesday and Friday.

Money Thai Farmers Bank and Bangkok Bank both have branches with ATMs on the main waterfront street in Ban Phe.

Places to Stay & Eat There are several hotels in Ban Phe near the central market and within walking distance of the Seri pier. *TN Place*, about 100m from the pier, has decent rooms with fan for 250B or with air-con for 300B to 500B. The owners are friendly and provide plenty of information, but the hotel can get a bit noisy. The *Queen Hotel* (☎ 038-651018, 651679) is across and up the road from the pier, on a soi next to a 7-Eleven store (near the central market), and has rooms for 150B (shared bathroom), 250B with private bath, or 350/400B for singles/doubles with air-con; painted ladies on hand testify to its mainly short-time clientele though it's basically an OK place. Also close to the pier is the midrange, six storey *Hotel Diamond Phe* (☎ 038-651826, fax 651757, Bangkok ☎ 02-314 4133), with air-con rooms for 500B to 700B. A German restaurant is on the 1st floor.

The *restaurant* in front of which the tour bus from Bangkok stops, opposite Nuanthip pier, has OK Thai food. The *market* next to the pier is a good place to stock up on food, mosquito coils and the like to take to Ko Samet. You'll most likely be spending some time in this spot, waiting either for the boat to leave the nearby pier for Ko Samet or for the bus to arrive from Bangkok.

Getting There & Away Air-con buses to Ban Phe leave Bangkok's Eastern bus terminal 12 times per day between 4 am and 6.30 pm. The fare is 108B and the trip takes 3½ to four hours, more if traffic between Si Racha and Bangkok is bad. Cheaper still is the 60B ordinary bus with eight departures per day. Buses from Bangkok stop in Ban Phe in front of the restaurant opposite Tha Saphaan Nuanthip.

Taxis wait along the main waterfront street linking Ban Phe's piers, and will be happy to drive you just about anywhere in the province for around 500B per half day. Minivans to Pattaya leave from Tha Saphaan Nuanthip thrice daily for 150B per person, or you can take a taxi for 500B. There's also one daily minivan departure from the pier to Ko Chang (or rather to the pier at Laem Ngop, sailing point for Ko Chang) for 250B per person.

For information on boat travel between Ban Phe and Ko Samet, see the Ko Samet section later in this chapter.

Suan Son & Hat Rim Phae
East of Ban Phe, the road is enveloped by a grove of casuarina pine trees that stretches along the beach for 4km. This area is known as Suan Son, and while the beach is no great shakes, the overall atmosphere is pleasant. It's also a popular spot for Thai picnickers, and you'll find dozens of food vendors servicing sling chairs and beach umbrellas along the beach.

Suan Son is also one of the few places where you can find more reasonably priced accommodation. As the trees thin out, one of the first places you'll come to is *Yung Thong* (☎ 038-648463, fax 648465), which has decent fan-cooled or air-con bungalows for 400B to 2000B. There's no English sign: the resort is opposite a beachfront cafe with tables shaded by thatched umbrella 'roofs'.

A few hundred metres down the road, there are good bungalows with fan and private bath for 400B to 800B at *Marina Hut* (☎ 038-648468, Bangkok ☎ 02-424 0668). It's conveniently near a row of beachfront restaurants and Thai-style beach bars.

Pinery Park Beach (☎ 038-648460 advance reservations, Bangkok ☎ 02-917 0380) is a gleaming white condo resort on spacious grounds on the highway side of Suan Son with comfortable rooms starting at 800B a night. East of Pinery Park, *Campson Resort* (☎ 038-648313, Bangkok ☎ 02-433 4739) offers rooms in tidy cottages costing 400B to 4000B a night depending on size.

After turning inland and crossing a small river, the road leads back towards the seashore and Hat Rim Phae. The beach gets quite nice around here, and although there are plenty of hotels and bungalows, there's more than enough room for everyone.

Among the best value in accommodation is *Pakarang (Coral) Resort* (☎ *038-648412, 01-213 3174, Bangkok* ☎ *02-224 8901, fax 221 7207)*. It looks over a beautiful stretch of clean beach, has plenty of casuarina trees for shade, and has well kept red-tile roofed cottages for 500B with fan, 600B with air-con. Next door, *Rungnapha Lodge* (☎ *038-648297, Bangkok* ☎ *02-277 0288, fax 275 6471)* enjoys the same fine beach, but is a bit more upscale, at least in price, with rooms/bungalows ranging from 1000B to 5000B.

For top-of-the-line luxury, you probably won't do better than the *Novotel Rim Pae Resort* (☎ *038-648008, fax 648002, Bangkok* ☎ *02-237 1305, fax 236 4353, email novotel@loxinfo.co.th)*. This place is sheer elegance, with graceful architecture, five-star facilities, including two restaurants, two swimming pools, two children's pools, a playground, lighted tennis courts, a fitness centre, Thai massage, sailing and canoeing, and a complimentary tuk-tuk to Ban Phe. Rooms range from 3507B for a standard double to 6400B for a family villa. A 30% discount is available Sunday to Thursday.

Beyond Rim Pae lies the headland of **Wang Kaew**. Though trumpeted in tourist literature as one of coastal Rayong's most scenic spots, this place is actually fairly run-down, and the beach is definitely shabbier than others in the area. **Ko Thalu**, across from Wang Kaew, is said to be a good diving and snorkelling area, with beautiful, relatively intact coral. You can arrange trips there at The Toy Tour, in Laem Mae Phim (see later in this section).

Getting There & Away Songthaews from Rayong and Ban Phe run past Suan Son and Rim Phae on their way to Laem Mae Phim.

The fare should range from 10B to 15B depending on how far you're going.

Laem Mae Phim

This long stretch of beach outdoes Mae Ramphung for beauty and cleanliness, and also benefits from shade trees along the entire beachfront. Unfortunately, this idyllic scene evaporates at the eastern end of the beach, where all the accommodation is concentrated. This may explain why the rest of Laem Mae Phim – especially Hat Ban Sang – is so pleasant; in any event you need only walk west about 10 minutes to get away from the ugly buildings, jet-skis and speedboats.

Laem Mae Phim village has the area's only dive operation, The Toy Tour (☎ 038-638146). The shop has a fleet of speedboats, and rents snorkelling gear for 50B and full scuba sets for 950B. Boat charters range from 2500B to 6000B per day. The Toy Tour also operates daily trips out to **Ko Man Nai** and **Ko Thalu** for 300 and 400B per person respectively. The trips last about two hours and include snorkelling and the chance to see sea turtles. All-day fishing charters are 4000B.

More low-key activities similar to those found at Suan Son include picnicking and lounging about under beach umbrellas, or floating on the calm seas using large inner tubes available for rent from beach vendors. All in all the water is much cleaner here than at Suan Son, though the beach can become just as crowded on weekends.

At the east end, one of the few places to stay actually on the beach is, sadly, the *Porn Phim Resort* (☎ *038-638027)*, a dump of a place with tiny rooms in bungalows starting at 500B. This place also doubles as a karaoke parlour at night.

Options in the village include the *Laem Mae Phim Hotel* (☎ *038-638147, 01-321 1887)*, a white hulk with pseudo Greco-Italian columns and balconies. Air-con rooms are 700B. Nearby, the pseudo-Thai style *Sinsiam Resort* (☎ *038-638114, 01-211 7026, fax 038-638153, Bangkok* ☎ *02-439 135, fax 439 1388)* is decaying and a bit pricey at 1200B for an air-con room.

Much better options are the newer and quieter accommodations along Hat Bang San to the west toward Rayong town. Best of the bunch is **Ban Sang Resort** (☎ 038-638158, Bangkok ☎ 02-392 2146), which features two-room bungalows with rates of 2500B to 3500B. The restaurant is one of the best in the area, and the beach is very clean. The much larger **Hin Suay Nam Sai Resort** (☎ 038-638260, 638035, fax 638034, Bangkok ☎ 02-243 0095, fax 243 5188) nearby starts at 2600B for large two-room units. Less expensive places on or near Hat Bang San include **Siri Home-On-Sea**, **Seabreeze** and **Morakot Hotel**, all off the highway near Km 17.

The long string of **seafood restaurants** along the east end of Laem Mae Phim all have aquariums where you can pick out live rock lobster (*kâng kràdaan*), spiny lobster (*kûng mangkon*), zebra crab (*puu máa laai*) and more. **Sinsiam Seafood,** across from the resort of the same name, was one of the first restaurants to open here and is still one of the best.

Getting There & Away Songthaews from Rayong and Ban Phe occasionally make their way down to Laem Mae Phim. Expect to pay around 15B to Ban Phe and up to 30B to get to Rayong. By car, you can either take Hwy 3 to the intersection with Route 3192, which heads south to the coastal road or drive to Ban Phe and then follow the pleasant route east along the coast for about 15km.

Ko Man Klang & Ko Man Nok

Ko Man Klang and Ko Man Nok, lying 7 to 10km off of Laem Mae Phim, along with Ko Man Nai to their immediate west, are part of Khao Laem Ya/Ko Samet National Park. As with Ko Samet, this official designation has not prevented development, only moderated it. The islands are in fair ecological condition, the main threat to the surrounding corals being the arrival of jet-skis.

Resorts on Ko Man Klang and Ko Man Nok offer accommodation packages that include boat transport from the nearest pier as well as three meals a day. These are best

arranged by phone in advance through Bangkok reservation numbers. Just showing up isn't really practical: chartering a boat could easily cost several thousand baht, and the resorts may not have the food and other supplies needed to accommodate you. But book, and the resort operators should help arrange transport to the pier departure points, which can change depending on the season.

Ko Nok Resort (☎ 038-661136, 01-987 8600, Bangkok ☎ 02-255 0836, 255 0836) on Ko Man Nok charges 1990B to 3990B per person for a one night, two day package in a bungalow room. On Ko Man Klang, the **Raya Island Resort** (Bangkok ☎ 02-316 6717) offers bungalows for 1100B each (two nights and three days costs 2000B per person); boat transport and meals included.

KO SAMET

Though relatively close to Bangkok and quite developed, this island still boasts some of Thailand's nicest beaches featuring the whitest, squeakiest sand in the kingdom. It is equally popular with Thais and foreigners, giving it a different feel than other established spots like Ko Samui or Ko Phi-Phi, which currently cater almost exclusively to faràng tastes.

The northern end of the island is where most of the development is. Though there's nowhere near the kind of bar and entertainment scene you'd find on Ko Samui, there are some opportunities for more social travellers with a few late night bars and restaurants. As you move south, things get progressively quieter, with the exception of the heavily built-up Ao Wong Deuan. Below there, it really tones down: those seeking solitude will find several beaches and bungalows that should fit the bill.

The T-shaped island earned a permanent place in Thai literature when classical Thai poet Sunthorn Phu set part of his epic *Phra Aphaimani* on its shores. The story follows the travails of a prince exiled to an undersea kingdom ruled by a lovesick female giant. A mermaid aids the prince in his escape to Samet where he defeats the giant by playing a magic flute. Formerly called Ko

KO SAMET

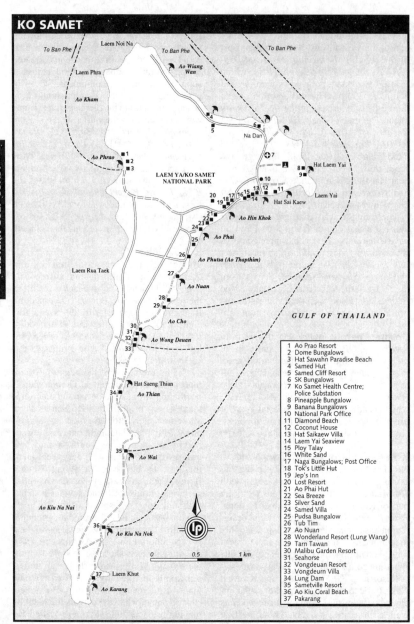

To Ban Phe
Laem Noi Na
To Ban Phe
To Ban Phe

Laem Phra
Ao Wiang Wan

Ao Kham

Na Dan

Ao Phrao
LAEM YA/KO SAMET NATIONAL PARK

Hat Laem Yai

Laem Yai

Hat Sai Kaew

Ao Hin Khok

Ao Phai

Laem Rua Taek
Ao Phutsa (Ao Thapthim)

Ao Nuan

Ao Cho
GULF OF THAILAND

Ao Wong Deuan

Hat Saeng Thian
Ao Thian

Ao Wai

Ao Kiu Na Nai

Ao Kiu Na Nok

Laem Khut
Ao Karang

0   0.5   1 km

1   Ao Prao Resort
2   Dome Bungalows
3   Hat Sawahn Paradise Beach
4   Samed Hut
5   Samed Cliff Resort
6   SK Bungalows
7   Ko Samet Health Centre;
    Police Substation
8   Pineapple Bungalow
9   Banana Bungalows
10 National Park Office
11 Diamond Beach
12 Coconut House
13 Hat Saikaew Villa
14 Laem Yai Seaview
15 Ploy Talay
16 White Sand
17 Naga Bungalows; Post Office
18 Tok's Little Hut
19 Jep's Inn
20 Lost Resort
21 Ao Phai Hut
22 Sea Breeze
23 Silver Sand
24 Samed Villa
25 Pudsa Bungalow
26 Tub Tim
27 Ao Nuan
28 Wonderland Resort (Lung Wang)
29 Tarn Tawan
30 Malibu Garden Resort
31 Seahorse
32 Vongdeuan Resort
33 Vongdeurn Villa
34 Lung Dam
35 Sametville Resort
36 Ao Kiu Coral Beach
37 Pakarang

Ko Samet: Environment or Economics?

Beneath all the resorts, restaurants and jet-skis, Ko Samet is actually part of Khao Laem Ya/Mu Ko Samet Marine National Park. For years the National Parks Division of the Royal Forest Department has been trying to keep developers at bay, obviously with little success. But now there is a chance the tourist industry may be booted off the island in favour of the flora and fauna.

The park was established in 1981, around the same time that the 13.1 sq km island began receiving its first tourists – young Thais in search of a retreat from city life. They arrived to find only about 40 houses on the island, built by fisherfolk and Ban Phe locals. But Rayong and Bangkok speculators saw the sudden interest in Ko Samet as a chance to cash in on an 'up-and-coming Phuket' and began buying land along the beaches. No-one bothered about Ko Samet's national park status. When the flow of tourists started picking up, the National Parks Division stepped in and built a visitor office on the island, ordered that all bungalows be moved back behind the tree line and started charging admission to the park. In later years, the Royal Forest Department temporarily closed the park to all visitors a couple of times in an effort to halt encroachment, but always reopened the island within a month or less in response to protests by resort operators.

However, in late 1996 the Thai courts sided with the Forestry Department and, on a case by case basis, began ordering bungalow operations on Ko Samet to shut down. Resort owners say that no-one will have to really do anything until the court has waded through all the bungalow outfits. Even then they should have one year to pack up and move out. And of course there's always the chance of a 'political solution'. So although the judicial die has been cast, resort owners are still confident they'll be on Ko Samet through 2000, and perhaps far longer. At the same time, some are looking into business opportunities on the mainland or other islands. 'The closure may not happen, but I'm not investing any more here. This time there's really a chance we'll all have to leave', said one Ko Samet bungalow operator.

Court hearings continue; until a decision is reached, a permanent moratorium on new developments remains in place in order to preserve the island's forested interior.

Joe Cummings

Kaew Phitsadan or 'Vast Jewel Isle', a reference to the abundant white sand, this island became known as Ko Samet or 'Cajeput Isle' after the cajeput tree which grows in abundance here and which is very highly valued as firewood throughout South-East Asia. Locally, the *samet* tree has also been used in boat building.

Ko Samet can be very crowded during Thai public holidays: early November (Loi Krathong Festival); 5 December (King's Birthday); 31 December to 1 January (New Year); mid-to-late February (Chinese New Year); and mid-April (Songkran Festival).

During these times there may be people sleeping on the floors of beach restaurants, on the beach, everywhere. September gets the lowest number of visitors (average 2500), March the most (around 40,000 – approximately 36,000 of them Thai). Thais are more prevalent than foreigners, but many are day visitors; most stay at Hat Sai Kaew or Ao Wong Deuan in the more up-market accommodation.

In spite of being supposedly under the protection of the National Parks Division, recently the runaway growth in the Na Dan and Hat Sai Kaew areas has been appalling. Piles of rubbish and construction materials spoil the island's charm at the northern end. Once you get away from this end of the island, however, things start looking a bit better.

Ko Samet is very dry. While this makes it a good place to visit during the rainy season, it also means that fresh water can sometimes be scarce. Please try to conserve water and help ease the strain on an already overtaxed ecosystem. A very new reservoir has been constructed next to the main cross-island road which may alleviate the traditional water shortage. (See the 'Ko Samet: Environment or Economics' boxed text for more.)

Information

National Park Office Ko Samet is part of a marine national park, and there is an entry fee of 20B for adults, 10B for children ages three to 14. The park has a main office near Hat Sai Kaew, and smaller units at each of the other beaches. An excellent guide to the history, flora and fauna of Ko Samet is Alan A Alan's 94 page *Samet*, published by Asia Books. Instead of writing a straightforward guidebook, Alan has woven the information into an amusing fictional travelogue involving a pair of Swedish twins on their first trip to the island.

Post & Telephone A small post office next to Naga Bungalows offers a poste restante service. It's open weekdays from 9 am to noon and from 1 to 4 pm, Saturday from 9 am to noon. An international satellite phone can be found outside the visitor centre at the main park office; cards cost 1500B and are available at the park office. There's also an ordinary phone booth for domestic calls within Thailand.

Travel Agencies Near Na Dan and on Hat Sai Kaew and Ao Wong Deuan are several small travel agencies that can arrange long-distance phone calls as well as bus and train reservations – they even do air ticketing.

Medical Services The Ko Samet Health Centre, a small public clinic, is located mid-

way between the village harbour and Hat Sai Kaew. English-speaking doctors are on hand to help with problems like heat rash, or bites from poisonous sea creatures or snakes.

Malaria A few years ago, if you entered the park from the northern end near the village, you'd see a large English-language sign warning visitors that Ko Samet was highly malarial. The sign is gone now, but the island still has a bit of malaria. If you're taking malarial prophylactics you have little to worry about. If not, take a little extra care to avoid being bitten by mosquitoes at night. Malaria is not that easy to contract, even in malarial areas, unless you allow the mosquitoes open season on your flesh. It's largely a numbers game – you're not likely to get malaria from just a couple of bites (that's what the experts say anyway), so make sure you use repellent and mosquito nets at night. (See the Health section in the Facts for the Visitor chapter for information about precautions against malaria.)

Activities

Several bungalows on the island can arrange boat trips to nearby reefs and uninhabited islands. Ao Phutsa, Naga Beach (Ao Hin Khok), Hat Sai Kaew and Ao Wong Deuan each have sailboard rental places that do boat trips as well. Typical day trips to Ko Thalu, Ko Kuti etc cost 300B per person, including food and beverages (minimum of 10 people). Sailboards rent for around 150B per hour or 600B to 700B per day. Jaray Windsurfing School on Hat Sai Kaew offers one-hour lessons for 80B. Parasailing is also available on Hat Sai Kaew for 400B per flight.

Ao Prao Divers at Ao Prao Resort (see the following Places to Stay section) on the west side of the island offers a full range of dive options, including entry level open water PADI certification (four days, 15,000B) and advanced open water course (five dives, two to three days, 13,000B).

Places to Stay

The two most developed areas are Hat Sai Kaew and Ao Wong Deuan. All of the other

A Request

The Rayong tourist police request that visitors refrain from hiring jet-skis on Samet beaches because they are harmful to coral and dangerous to swimmers. They're hard on the aural environment, too.

The local police won't do anything about them even though they're illegal – either because they're afraid of beach developers or are in their pockets. You'll be doing Ko Samet a big favour by avoiding the use of these polluters.

Joe Cummings

spots are still rather peaceful. Every bungalow operation on the island has at least one restaurant and most now have running water and electricity. Most places have electric power from 5 or 6 pm till 6 am; the more up-market places have 24 hour power.

On less popular beaches you may come across abandoned bungalow sites, and some of the most expensive places even during the high season offer discounts for accommodation to attract customers. Very basic small huts with a hard mattress on the floor cost in the 50B to 80B range, similar huts with bath start from 80B to 120B, and those including a bed and a fan average 150B to 200B. Bungalows with furniture and aircon start at 600B. Most places offer discounts for stays of four or more days, while on weekends and public holidays most will raise their rates to meet the demand – sometimes dramatically.

Some resorts, mostly around the Hat Sai Kaew area, have also been known to boot out foreigners without warning to make room for free-spending Thai tour groups. You won't need to worry about this at the more reputable spots, like Naga and Samed Villa. But even so, if possible avoid Ko Samet during the peak times, especially public holidays.

Since this is a national park, camping is allowed on any of the beaches. In fact, this is a great island to camp on because it

hardly ever rains. There is plenty of room; most of the island is uninhabited and, so far, tourism is pretty much restricted to the north-eastern and north-western beaches.

Places to Stay – East Coast

Hat Sai Kaew Samet's prettiest beach, 'Diamond Sand', is 800m long and 25 to 30m wide. The bungalows here are the most commercial on the island, with video in the restaurants at night and lots of lights. They're all very similar and offer a range of accommodation from 120B (in the low season) for simple huts without fan or bath, to 200B to 600B for one with fan, mosquito net and private bath, or as high as 2500B with air-con. All face the beach and most have outdoor restaurants serving a variety of seafood. Like elsewhere in Thailand, the daily rate for accommodation can soar suddenly with demand. The more scrupulous places don't hike rates by much, though.

Coconut House (☎ 038-651661, 01-943 2134) has bungalows ranging from 300B with fan up to 1500B with air-con. *Diamond Beach* (☎ 01-239 0208) offers fan bungalows for 350B, 900B with air-con (or up to 2000B on holidays). Another option is *Ploy Talay* (☎ 01-218 6109) with rooms for 300B to 800B, along with a disco and snooker.

Just beyond Ploy Talay, *Laem Yai Seaview* (☎ 01-943 2134, 321 0814) features well spaced wood huts, all with decks, set in a quieter location among trees; rates run 350B to 400B (up to 1000B on holidays). Prices at *White Sand* (☎ 038-651598, 01-218 6734) start at 500B – they also have a disco.

Hat Saikaew Villa (☎ 038-651535, 01-318 6618, 321 1696, fax 038-652548) is a huge complex, off the beach, with fan rooms ranging from 600B to 800B, 1500B and up for air-con – it's the top-end place near the prettiest part of the beach. They boast 24 hour power – try to get a room away from the noisy generators.

Ao Hin Khok The beach here is about half the size of Sai Kaew but just as pretty – the rocks that give the beach its name add a certain character. Hin Khok is separated from

Sai Kaew by a rocky point surmounted by a mermaid statue, a representation of the mermaid that carried the mythical Phra Aphaimani to Ko Samet in the Thai epic of the same name. Ao Hin Khok and Ao Phai, the next inlet south, offer the advantage of having among the least expensive huts on the island along with reasonably priced restaurants serving good food.

Two of Samet's original bungalow operations still reign here – *Tok's Little Hut* (☎ 01-218 5195) and *Naga* (☎ 01-218 5372, 353 2575). Naga offers simple bungalows set on a hill overlooking the sea for 100B, and decent ones with a good mattress and fan from 120B. The restaurant here sells great bread (it is distributed to several other bungalows on the island), cookies, cakes, pizzas and other pastries. While Naga's owners are dead-set against video entertainment, there are billiards, darts, various board games and some interesting drinking bargains to keep guests amused. However, these can make for some noisy evenings: light sleepers beware. The bungalows at Tok's Little Hut are a little more solid and go for 100B to 200B.

A bit farther down the road is *Jep's Inn*, with 14 nicely designed, clean bungalows with bath and fan for 350B and up. The restaurant here is also quite good, and there's a nice shaded dining area right at the edge of the beach.

Lost Resort, on a hill behind Hin Khok (and best accessed from the interior road rather than the beach), features a two storey building with well ventilated rooms, good mattresses, ceiling fans and private cold shower for 250B a night, with a three-night minimum stay.

Ao Phai Around the next headland is another shallow bay with a nice wide beach, though it can get fairly crowded. The friendly *Ao Phai Hut* (☎ 01-353 2644, 213 6392) is at the northern end, with screened bungalows with private bath and fan for 200B double, 400B double with air-con; weekends and holidays add 200B. Electricity is available from 5 pm to 6 am. They or-

ganise tours around the island and have an international telephone service, as well as basic postal services. The next place is *Sea Breeze* (☎/fax 01-239 4780, ☎ 321 0195), with a variety of rather closely spaced bungalows from 150B to 500B. Adjacent is a small shop and a bookshop/library that also has international phone and fax service. Next is *Silver Sand* (☎ 01-218 5195), with 30 good basic bungalows for 100B to 300B; there's a disco of sorts on Saturdays.

Swiss-run *Samed Villa* (☎ 01-494 8090) has very clean, screened, well maintained tree-shaded bungalows with large verandahs from 450B for smaller units with private bath and up to 900B for family accommodation. They offer 24 hour electricity. The food here is quite good, and some of the bungalows have great sea views. This is also one of the few places in the area that doesn't screen videos at night.

Near Sea Breeze, the main road south to Ao Wong Deuan turns inland and heads down the middle of the island. A little farther along the road from here is where the cross-island road to Ao Phrao on the west coast starts.

Ao Phutsa On Ao Phutsa, also known as Ao Thapthim, you'll find *Pudsa Bungalow* (☎ 01-438 0098), where basic well-worn huts cost 300B and newer ones 500B to 800B. Some of the smaller huts are quite close to the water, making them pretty good value for money. At the south end of the beach *Tub Tim* (☎/fax 01-218 7759, ☎ 218 6425) has older, smaller bungalows on a shady hillside for 200B to 300B, while newer, more spacious wooden bungalows with sea views cost from 400B up to 1200B with air-con. At both places, the more expensive huts have private showers.

After Ao Phutsa, the remaining beaches south are separated from one another by fairly steep headlands. To get from one to the next, you have a choice of negotiating rocky paths over the hilly points or walking west to the main road, which goes along the centre of the island, then cutting back on side roads to each beach.

Ao Nuan If you blink, you'll miss this beach. It's one of the quieter, more secluded places to stay without having to go to the far south of the island. The six rustic huts at *Ao Nuan* have neither running water nor electricity. This certainly adds to the *thammachâat* (natural) ambience, but the rent's a bit steep (compared to other places along this coast) at 250B to 400B. The food is said to be quite good here. It's a five minute walk over the headland from Ao Phutsa.

Ao Cho (Chaw) A five minute walk across the next headland from Ao Nuan, this bay has its own pier and can be reached directly from Ban Phe on the boat *White Shark* or aboard the supply boat. Though just north of crowded Ao Wong Deuan, it's fairly quiet here, though the beach is not among Samet's best.

At the north end of the beach *Wonderland Resort (Lung Wang; ☎ 038-653167, 01-218 5682)* has basic, rather unkempt bungalows with private shower and toilet for 100B to 350B, more on weekends and holidays. Tin-roofed cement and bamboo-thatch huts at *Tarn Tawan* cost 150B to 200B; the kitchen here specialises in Isaan food.

Ao Wong Deuan This once gorgeous bay is now filled with speedboats and jet-skis, and there's a lot of accommodation packed into a small area, making things a bit cramped. The crescent shaped beach is still nice, but it is noisy and often crowded. The best of the lot is *Vongdeuan Resort (☎/fax 038-651819, ☎ 651777, Bangkok ☎ 02-391 9065)* with bungalows for 600B to 900B, complete with running water, flush toilet and fan. The air-con ones cost 1100B to 1200B. *Vongduern Villa (☎ 038-652300, 651741, 01-945 9954)* is similar in amenities but all air-con, ranging from 600B to 2500B.

Malibu Garden Resort (☎ 038-651292, 01-218 5345, fax 038-426229) has well built brick or wooden bungalows with fan for 400B to 700B or air-con for 1000B to 1200B; the more expensive rooms have TVs. *Seahorse (☎ 01-440 7003, Bangkok ☎ 02-969 2091)* has practically taken over the beachfront with two restaurants, a travel agency and fan-equipped rooms and bungalows for 250B to 500B.

Three boats – the *Malibu, Seahorse* and *Vongduern* – go back and forth between Ao Wong Deuan and Ban Phe.

Ao Thian From this point south things start to get much quieter. Better known by its English name, 'Candlelight Beach', the bay is quite scenic, and rocky outcrops break up the beach, though there's plenty of sand to stretch out upon. Unfortunately the bungalow operation here is no great shakes.

At the southern end of the beach *Lung Dam (☎ 01-452 9472)* charges 100B for quite roughly built huts with shared bathroom and 200B to 400B for ones with private bath. There is also an interesting treehouse you can rent for 150B per night. Keep in mind you're a captive of guesthouse kitchen choices here; you may want to bring some of your own food from the village on the northern tip of the island.

Other Bays You really have to be determined to get away from it all to go farther south on the east coast of Ko Samet, but it can be well worth the effort. Lovely **Ao Wai** is about a kilometre from Ao Thian but can be reached by the boat *Phra Aphai* from Ban Phe, which sails once a day and charges 50B per person. There's only one bungalow operation here, the very private *Sametville Resort (☎ 038-652561, Bangkok ☎ 02-246 3196, 247 1090)* which offers a fine combination of upscale accommodation and isolation. Two-bed bungalows with private bath cost 500B to 900B with fan, or 1300B to 3500B with air-con. Most bookings are done by phone, but you could try your luck by contacting someone on the *Phra Aphai* at the Ban Phe pier.

A 20 minute walk over the rocky shore from Ao Wai, **Ao Kiu Na Nok** also still had only one place to stay at the time of writing – the friendly and clean *Ao Kiu Coral Beach (☎ 038-652561, 01-218 6231, 812 2046, Bangkok ☎ 02-579 6237, 241 0058)*. Bamboo huts are 400B while unattractive but better equipped cement huts cost 600B to 3000B. Tents may be rented for 100B a night. The beach here is gorgeous, one of the nicest on the island. Another plus is that it's a mere five minute walk to the western side of the island and a view of the sunset.

Just a bit farther is rocky **Ao Karang**. The very rustic *Pakarang* (☎ *02-517 7620)* has 12 wooden huts (no electricity, no running water – just rainwater from ceramic jars) for 150B to 300B, but it's often booked out by park officials who reside there.

Places to Stay – West Coast

Hat Ao Phrao This is the only beach on the west side of the island, and it has nice sunset views. In Thai the name means 'Coconut Bay Beach' but for marketing reasons bungalow operators tend to use the cliched 'Paradise Beach' moniker. So far there are no jet-skis on this side of the island, so it tends to be quieter than the island's east coast. Local bungalow operators also do a good job of keeping the beach clean.

At the northern end of the beach is *Ao Prao Resort* (☎ *038-651814, fax 651816, ☎/fax 01-278 5977, 213 3533, Bangkok office* ☎ *02-438 9771, fax 439 0352, 367 Th Krung Thonburi)*, where attractive air-con bungalows with large verandas are surrounded by lush landscaping. Amenities include cable TV, private hot showers and perhaps the best restaurant on the island. Rates range from 2000B to 2800B. Ao Prao Divers at the resort offers diving, windsurfing, kayaking and boat trips. Ao Prao Resort offers free boat service to and from Saphaan Seree in Ban Phe for all guests.

In the middle of the beach is *Dome Bungalows* (☎ *038-651377, 01-321 0786)*, which has nice huts built with private bathroom on the hillside for 100B to 500B, or 1200B for four in a 'VIP' bungalow; the more expensive huts have insect-screened windows. A pleasant restaurant on the premises features a menu of Thai and western dishes; the service can be a bit slow. At the southern end near the cross-island trail is the friendly *Hat Sawahn Paradise Beach* (☎ *01-401 4807)*, where rustic bamboo huts

with fan and bath cost 250B to 350B (up to 500B weekends and holidays). There's also a large 15 bed bungalow that goes for 1500B. An attached restaurant serves Thai and western food.

There is a daily boat between Saphaan Nuanthip in Ban Phe and Ao Phrao for 50B per person, or you can charter a boat for 1000B.

Places to Stay – North Coast

To the north-west of Ko Samet's main pier in Na Dan is a long beach called Ao Wiang Wan, where several rather characterless bungalows are set up in straight lines facing the mainland. Here you get neither sunrise (maybe a little) nor sunset. The cheapest place here is *SK Bungalows* at 100B to 350B, but it only seems to open during Thai holidays when every other place is full, which is just as well since the rooms are very shabby.

Further north-west from Na Dan, *Samed Hut* (☎ *01-211 4029, 929 5537, Bangkok 02-678 4645)* has Santa Fe/Mexican style cottages on the beach and on a hillside across the road. The owner is a Thai man who lived in the US for over 20 years. Terracotta-coloured stuccoed cottages cost 700B (1400B with air-con), while more simple thatched bungalows are 300B (500B with a better view). There's a small cafe on the beach. It's quite a pleasant place and a good alternative if the more popular beach accommodations elsewhere on the island are booked out. Also in this area, the *Samed Cliff Resort* (☎ *01-911 9034, Bangkok* ☎ *02-235 3383)* offers 24 white-painted, well-maintained masonry cottages built on a hillside opposite the beach for 1500B to 2500B. There's a small pool on the nicely landscaped grounds.

South-east of Na Dan toward Hat Sai Kaew, along the north-east corner of the island, are a couple of small beach bays with bungalow operations. Hardly anyone seems to stay here. *Pineapple Bungalow* (☎ *038-651508, 01-218 8265)* at Hat Laem Yai (also known as Ao Yon) charges an overpriced 400B to 500B per bungalow. Nearby, *Banana Bungalows* charges 150B for a room in a big brick duplex unit or 100B for an individual small cement hut.

Places to Eat

All bungalows except Pakarang at Ao Karang have restaurants offering mixed menus of Thai and traveller food; prices are typically 30B to 50B per dish. Fresh seafood is almost always available and costs around 60B to 150B per dish. The pleasant *Bamboo Restaurant* at Ao Cho, behind Tarn Tawan, offers inexpensive but tasty food and good service. It's open for breakfast, lunch and dinner.

Naga on Ao Hin Khok has a very good bakery with all kinds of breads and cakes. Ao Wong Deuan has a cluster of restaurants serving western and Thai food: *Tom's, Coconut, Sea Horse, Bay Watch, Oasis* and *Nice & Easy*. At the southern tip of the beach the *Vongduern Villa* restaurant is a bit more expensive, but both the food and the location are quite nice.

On Hat Sai Kaew, the *White Sands Restaurant* has good seafood in the 100B range. For cheaper fare on this beach, try the popular *Toy Restaurant*, next to Saikaew Villa. *Samet Beach Restaurant* next to Diamond Beach has also been recommended for good food at reasonable prices and friendly staff.

Probably the best eatery on the island is the fancy open-air terrace *restaurant* at Ao Prao Resort.

Getting There & Away

Bus Many Th Khao San agencies in Bangkok offer return transport to Ko Samet, including the boat trip, for 170B (300B return). This is more expensive than doing it on your own, but for travellers who don't plan to go anywhere else on the east coast it's convenient. For information on getting to and from Ban Phe by bus, see the Ban Phe section.

Boat There are various ways to get to and from the island by boat.

To Ko Samet In Ban Phe four piers service Ko Samet: Saphaan Nuanthip for the regularly scheduled passenger boats, Saphaan Mai (or Saphaan Phe) and Saphaan Seree for supply boats and Saphaan Si Ban Phe

for tour groups. Nuanthip is usually the only one you'll need, but if you arrive between passenger boat departure times you can try for a ride aboard one of the cargo boats from Saphaan Mai (you must still pay the regular passenger fare). Nuanthip is also where buses from Bangkok arrive and depart. It's best to avoid the Saphaan Si Ban Phe pier: without a doubt there are more sharks at the ticket booths here than in the surrounding waters.

Passenger boats to Ko Samet leave at regular intervals throughout the day starting at around 8 am and ending around 5 pm. How frequently they depart depends mostly on whether they have enough passengers and/or cargo to make the trip profitable, so there are more frequent boats in the high season (December to March). Still, there are always at least three or four boats a day going to Na Dan and Ao Wong Deuan.

It can be difficult to find the boat you need, as agents and boat owners want you to go with them rather than with their competitors. In most cases they'll be reluctant to tell you about another boat if they will not be making any money from you. Some travellers have reported being hassled by 'agents' who present photo albums of bungalows on Samet, claiming that they must book a bungalow for several days in order to get onto the island. This is false; ignore these touts and head straight for the boats. Report any problems to the TAT office in Rayong.

Probably the best place to head is the Nuanthip pier ticket office, behind all the food and souvenir stalls. They sell tickets for a number of different boat operators, and also are willing to tell you about private resort boats.

For Hat Sai Kaew, Ao Hin Khok, Ao Phai and Ao Phutsa, catch a boat to Na Dan. These generally leave as soon as there are at least 20 passengers: the round trip costs 80B. Ignore touts or ticket agents who claim the fare is 100B or more; simply climb into one of these boats and wait to pay the ticket collector directly. From Na Dan you can either walk to these beaches (10 to 15 minutes) or take one of the trucks that go round the island. See the Getting Around section for standard fares.

The Nuanthip pier ticket office also has boats to Ao Wong Deuan (60B one way), Ao Phrao (50B) and Ao Wai (100B). All boats need at least seven people before they'll depart.

The boat *White Shark* also goes directly to Ao Cho from Ban Phe for 40B – have a look around the Ban Phe pier to see if it's available, or ask the staff at the Nuanthip pier ticket office.

The *Seahorse*, *Malibu* and *Vongduern* all go to Ao Wong Deuan for 30B. There's no jetty here, so passengers are pulled to shore on a raft or in longtail boats. You can also get a truck-taxi here from Na Dan, but the fare could be as high as 250B if you're alone. For Ao Thian, you should get either the *White Shark* to Ao Cho or one of the Ao Wong Deuan boats.

The *Phra Aphai* makes direct trips to Ao Wai for 60B. For Ao Kiu Na Nok or Ao Karang, get the *Thep Chonthaleh* (60B).

For Ao Phrao, you can take a taxi from Na Dan or possibly get a direct boat from Ban Phe for 50B.

If you want to charter a powerboat from Ban Phe to Samet (at night this would be your only choice), the rates are:

Ao Phrao	1000B
Hat Sai Kaew	1100B
Ao Phai	1200B
Ao Phutsa (Thapthim)	1200B
Ao Cho	1300B
Ao Wong Deuan	1400B
Ao Thian	1400B
Ao Wai or Ao Kui Na Nok	1500B

From Ko Samet Samet Tour seems to have the monopoly on return trips from Na Dan and they leave only when they're full – a minimum of 18 people for some boats, 25 for others – unless someone contributes more to the passage. The usual fare is 40B.

These days it is so easy to get boats back from the main beaches to Ban Phe that few tourists go to Na Dan to get a boat. There are four daily boats from Ao Wong Deuan,

and at least one daily boat from Ao Wai, Ao Kiu and Ao Phrao.

While waiting for a boat back to the mainland from Na Dan, you may notice a shrine not far from the pier. This *sãan jâo phâw* is a spirit shrine to Puu Dam (Grandfather Black), a sage who once lived on the island. Worshippers offer statues of *reusĩi* (hermit sages), flowers, incense and fruit.

Getting Around

If you take the boat from Ban Phe to the village harbour (Na Dan), you can walk to Hat Sai Kaew, Ao Phai or Ao Phutsa: to the latter it's about 1.5km. Don't believe the taxi operators who say these beaches are a long distance away. If you're going farther down the island, or have a lot of luggage, you can take the taxi truck as far as Ao Wong Deuan.

Set fares for transport around the island from Na Dan are posted on a tree in the middle of a square in front of the Na Dan harbour: 15B per person to Hat Sai Kaew (or 100B charter); 20B to Ao Phai or Ao Phutsa (150B to charter); 30B to Ao Wong Deuan or Ao Phrao (200B to charter); 40B to Ao Thian or Ao Wai (300B and 400B charter); 50B to Ao Kiu Na Nok (500B charter). Exactly how many people it takes to constitute 'public service' rather than a 'charter' is not a hard and fast number. Figure on 20B per person for six to eight people to anywhere between Na Dan and Ao Cho. If they don't have enough people to fill the vehicle, they either won't go, or passengers will have to pay up to 200B to charter the vehicle.

There are trails from Ao Wong Deuan all the way to the southern tip of the island, and a few cross-island trails as well. All are heavily rutted and the ones toward the southern tip of the island may be overgrown from disuse. Taxis will make trips to Ao Phrao when the road isn't too muddy.

Honda Nova trail bike motorcycles can be rented in Na Dan or near Ao Phutsa for 400B per day.

Toy Speed Boat (☎ 01-626 7749) on Hat Sai Kaew offers a half-day trip around the island, stopping for snorkelling etc, for 1000B for up to four people.

COASTAL CHANTHABURI

Pickings are a bit more sparse here than in Rayong, with the best beaches pretty much confined to the western section of the province. While not spectacular, they feel even more remote than the beach areas of coastal Rayong. Adding to the sense of isolation is the fact that getting to these places can be quite difficult and time consuming, unless you have your own vehicle. Even then, unless you speak Thai, finding your destination could still prove to be a bit of an adventure.

Chanthaburi's most promising beaches are located about 25km south of Hwy 3, and about 14km west of the border with Rayong Province. Probably the quietest spot around the area is **Hat Khung Wiman**, a 500m strip of golden sand interspersed with rocky outcrops. There is one bungalow operation here, *Khung Wiman Resort* (☎ 01-213 0406), which has well-constructed slate and plaster bungalows ranging from 1200B (two-person units) to 1500B (four-person). Discounts should be no problem for longer-term stays and during the off-season. Along the beach are about a dozen small thatched-roof open-air *restaurant/bars*. There's a scenic, undeveloped bay along the road following the shore to the south-east.

A bit farther east are the beaches of **Laem Sadet** and **Hat Chao Lao**. Together they form an 8km stretch of uninterrupted sand and surf. As with many other Thai resorts, litter is allowed to pile up on some parts of the beach, but it's not enough to ruin the scenery.

Laem Sadet ends in a small peninsula. There's no accommodation at this end, aside from some corporate and long-term facilities. But there are plenty of open-air *restaurants*, and scores of casuarina pines provide good shade for picnicking.

Hat Chao Lao is a bit more developed, with several bungalow outfits and a few faded resort hotels. The beach seems to get a bit whiter as you move south, and even with the hotels nearby, a short walk either north or south will soon reward you with your own private patch of sand.

Despite it's name, *Laem Sadet Resort* (☎ 039-369194, 01-212 4960) actually

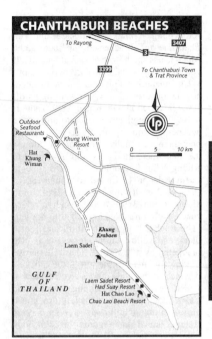

CHANTHABURI BEACHES

overlooks Hat Chao Lao. It's one of the nicest bungalow outfits in the area, with nine spacious cottages, a grassy yard and scattered palm trees. But it's not cheap; rates range from 1200B to 1500B, depending on the size of the bungalow, though discounts are probably available. *Had Suay Resort* (☎ 039-351078, 01-327 1152), a few hundred metres east, is a bit more haphazard an operation, and has fan and air-con rooms starting at 600B, and six bungalows from 1000 to 1500B.

Down near the end of Hat Chao Lao is the *Chao Lao Beach Resort* (☎ 039-321630). Though still the fanciest spot in the area, it looks a bit like its glory days have passed. You wouldn't know it from the rates, though: rooms in the multi-storey hotel block are 1700B per night, and family-size two-storey bungalows are 4500B.

EASTERN GULF COAST

Getting There & Away

Hat Khung Wiman, Laem Sadet and Hat Chao Lao are all accessed via Route 3399, which heads south from Hwy 3 at Km 302. If you're taking public transport, hop on a bus to Chanthaburi or Trat: you'll have to somehow let the driver know you want to get off at the intersection with Route 3399. There is no regular songthaew service to any of the beaches, so you'll probably have to charter one: there are usually a few hanging around the area where the buses stop. A charter to Khung Wiman should cost 150B, one to Laem Sadet or Hat Chao Lao around 180B.

If you're driving, about 12km south along Route 3399 you'll reach a sharp curve, with a road leading off it to the left. (The road is between the third and fourth black and yellow curve signs, and is also bracketed by a few small Thai billboards.) Taking this road to the left is the quickest way to the beaches, and as you follow it you'll see signs for Khung Wiman and Laem Sadet. If you miss the left turn, you'll almost immediately see a sign saying 'Laem Sadet 15km': ignore this sign, look behind you and you'll see the road leading off to the left.

Heading to Laem Sadet you'll eventually reach a T-intersection near the beach; turning right takes you to Laem Sadet, left to Hat Chao Lao and accommodation. Laem Sadet Resort is 1.4km from the intersection, Had Suay 1.7km and Chao Lao Beach Resort 4.5km.

TRAT

• pop 14,400

About 400km from Bangkok, Trat Province borders Cambodia and, as in Chanthaburi, gem mining and gem trading are important occupations. Gem markets *(talàat phloi)* are open intermittently at the **Hua Thung** and **Khlong Yaw** markets in the Bo Rai district, about 40km north of Trat on Route 3389. A smaller market is sometimes open all day in **Khao Saming** district only 20km north-west of Trat. There has been a drop in activity in the gem markets due to the dwindling supply of local gem stock. A sad by-product of

gem mining has been the destruction of vast tracts of land – the topsoil is stripped away, leaving acres of red-orange mud.

If the gem business doesn't interest you, another attraction Bo Rai district offers is **Salak Tai Falls**, 15km north-west of Bo Rai. The other big industry in Trat is the smuggling of consumer goods between Cambodia and Trat. For this reason, travelling alone along the border, or around the offshore islands which serve as conduits for sea smuggling, requires caution. More and more people have discovered the beaches and islands of Trat, however, and as the nearby Khmer Rouge conflict appears to be diminishing, security has improved. A good spot for observing the border trade is at the Thai-Cambodian market in **Khlong Yai**, near the end of Route 318/Hwy 3 south of Trat. As much as 10 million baht changes hands in these markets daily.

South-east of Trat along Route 318 towards Khlong Yai district, the province thins to a narrow sliver between the Gulf of Thailand and Cambodia. Along this sliver are a number of little-known beaches, including **Hat Sai Si Ngoen**, **Hat Sai Kaew**, **Hat Thap Thim** and **Hat Ban Cheun**. Ban Cheun has a few bungalows, but there is still no accommodation at the other beaches.

At Km 70, off Route 318, is **Jut Chom Wiw** (View-Admiring Point), where you can get a panorama of the surrounding area, including Cambodia. Trat Province's southeasternmost point is at **Hat Lek**, which is also a semi-legal jumping-off point for boat trips to the Cambodian coast. Although there are Thai military checkpoints between Trat and Hat Lek (two at last count), they seem to be getting less strict about allowing foreigners through. From time to time the Trat provincial government and its counterpart on the Cambodian side of the border allows foreigners to cross by boat to Cambodia's Ko Kong.

Information

Tourist Office TAT (☎ 039-597255, 597259) maintains an office at 100 Muu 1, Th Trat-Laem Ngop, in Laem Ngop district.

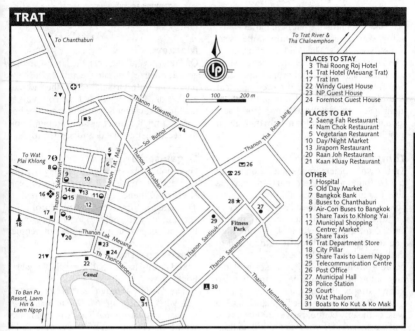

TRAT

To Chanthaburi

To Trat River &
Tha Chaloemphon

0   100   200 m

To Wat
Plai Khlong

To Ban Pu
Resort, Laem
Hin &
Laem Ngop

Fitness
Park

Canal

PLACES TO STAY
3 Thai Roong Roj Hotel
14 Trat Hotel (Meuang Trat)
17 Trat Inn
22 Windy Guest House
23 NP Guest House
24 Foremost Guest House

PLACES TO EAT
2 Saeng Fah Restaurant
4 Nam Chok Restaurant
5 Vegetarian Restaurant
10 Day/Night Market
13 Jiraporn Restaurant
20 Raan Joh Restaurant
21 Kaan Kluay Restaurant

OTHER
1 Hospital
6 Old Day Market
7 Bangkok Bank
8 Buses to Chanthaburi
9 Air-Con Buses to Bangkok
11 Share Taxis to Khlong Yai
12 Municipal Shopping
Centre; Market
15 Share Taxis
16 Trat Department Store
18 City Pillar
19 Share Taxis to Laem Ngop
25 Telecommunication Centre
26 Post Office
27 Municipal Hall
28 Police Station
29 Court
30 Wat Phailom
31 Boats to Ko Kut & Ko Mak

EASTERN GULF COAST

Ko Chang National Marine Park Information on Ko Chang National Marine Park is available at the park headquarters in Laem Ngop, a small town 20km south-west of Trat town. This is also where you get boats to Ko Chang.

Immigration There is no immigration office in Trat – you must go to the provincial offices in Khlong Yai or Laem Ngop for visa extensions or other immigration matters. If Cambodian border crossings from Trat by land or sea are officially permitted in the future, Khlong Yai is where you'll have to come to have your passport stamped upon return from Cambodia.

Money Bangkok Bank and Krung Thai Bank on Th Sukhumvit have foreign exchange windows open daily from 8.30 am to 5 pm. In Laem Ngop, a Thai Farmers Bank (between Chut Kaew Guest House and the pier) has an exchange counter open Monday to Friday from 8.30 am to 3.30 pm.

Post & Telephone The main post office is a long walk from the city centre on Th Tha Reua Jang. It's open from 8.30 am to 4.30 pm weekdays, 9 am to noon Saturday and Sunday. The telecommunications office is located on the corner a few doors down from the post office and offers international phone and fax service daily from 7 am till 10 pm.

Malaria Rates of infection for malaria are significantly higher for rural Trat (including Ko Chang) than for much of the rest of Thailand, so take the usual precautions. There is a malaria centre on the main road through Laem Ngop (20km south-west of Trat); here you can get the latest information on the disease. This office can also assist with testing and/or treatment for malaria. Malaria is not that easy to contract, even in malarial areas, unless you allow the mosquitoes open season on your flesh. That said, there are travellers who have contracted the disease while on Ko Chang, so malarial prophylactics are probably worth taking. But more important is use of a repellent and mosquito nets at night. (See the Health section in the Facts for the Visitor chapter for information about avoiding malaria.)

Things to See & Do

Trat town's older homes and shophouses can be found along the canal. You may be able to rent a canoe through Windy Guest House or Foremost Guest House (see Places to Stay later in this section) to paddle around for a water-level look. During high tide it's possible to boat from the canal to the Trat estuary on the Gulf. This can also be done from the Trat River, north of the city; inquire at Tha Chaloemphon (also known simply as *thâa reua* or 'boat pier').

Wat Plai Khlong (Wat Bupharam), 2km west of the city centre, is over 200 years old and worth a visit if you want to kill an hour or so. Several of the wooden buildings date to the late Ayuthaya period, including the wihǎan, bell tower and *kutis* (monk quarters). The wihǎan contains a variety of sacred relics and Buddha images dating from the Ayuthaya period and earlier.

Trat is famous for 'yellow oil' *(náam-man lěuang)*, a herb-infused liquid touted as a remedy for everything from arthritis to stomach upsets. It's produced by a local resident, Mae Ang-kii (Somthawin Pasananon), using a secret pharmaceutical recipe that has been handed down through her Chinese-Thai family for generations. Among Thais it is said that if you visit Trat and don't leave with a couple bottles of Mae Ang-kii's yellow oil, then you really haven't been to Trat. The stuff is available direct from her house at No 5 Th Rat Uthit (☎ 039-511935).

Farther afield, **Ban Nam Chiaw** – about 8km from Trat – is a mostly Muslim village where one of the main industries is the handweaving of hemispherical straw hats

called *ngôp*, the traditional Khmer rice farmer's hat.

Markets

Of Trat's several markets, the largest are the new day market beneath the municipal shopping centre off Th Sukhumvit, the old day market off Th Tat Mai and the day market next to the air-con bus office; the latter becomes a night market in the evening. Look for eccentricities like deep-fried lizards.

Organised Trips

Guesthouses can arrange local day trips to gem markets, the Trat River estuary or even Ko Chang, if enough people are interested. The estuary trips leave by boat from the canal in town to gather clams (in season) – the price depends on the number of people.

Places to Stay

Trat The city has a small but reliable guesthouse scene.

The friendly **Windy Guest House** (☎ 01-455 9605, 633 0059, 64 Th Thoncharoen) consists of a traditional Thai wooden house with a porch built beneath the canal and a cosy outdoor lounge area with a small library, travel info and games. Prices are 60/80B single/double. Bicycles for cruising the town are offered free to guests and motorcycles are also available for rent. Ask about borrowing canoes for exploring the canal (no charge to guests) – depending on availability and who's managing the guesthouse at the time.

Foremost Guest House (☎ 039-511923, 49 Th Thoncharoen) also near the canal, offers rooms upstairs in an old shophouse; bathrooms are shared but clean, and a hot shower is available. Dorm rooms are 50B and single/double rooms are 80/120B (110B for one person in a double room). The staff are a good source of current info on travel to Cambodia from Trat.

Kudos goes to both Windy and Foremost for encouraging guests to tap drinking water from refillable, recyclable containers for a charge of only 1B per litre – a considerable savings over the cost of a typical plastic bottle of drinking water, not to mention the environmental merit.

NP Guest House (☎ *039-512270*) is down a quiet lane at 1-3 Soi Luang Aet (a soi which is a south-west continuation of Th Tat Mai), Th Lak Meuang; it's a short walk from the main day and night markets as well as local bus stops. It's basically an old wooden shophouse with a glassed-in downstairs; a bed in the clean three bed dorm costs 70B or you can get a single/double private room for 90/120B with shared bathroom. Those just passing through can take a shower here for 20B and bag storage for 10B per piece per day is also offered. The guesthouse rents motorcycles for 50B per hour, or 300B for the day. Thai and western food is available.

Kaan Kluay restaurant on Th Sukhumvit (see Places to Eat) plans to open a guesthouse behind the restaurant sometime in 1999.

Most of the hotels in Trat are along or just off Th Sukhumvit. The *Trat Inn* (☎ *039-511208, 1-5 Th Sukhumvit*), though housed in a run-down concrete shell, has friendly staff and rooms from 110B to 190B. The *Thai Roong Roj (Rung Rot;* ☎ *039-511141)* in a soi off Th Sukhumvit, is a decaying, mould-ridden place with fan rooms from 200B or with air-con from 330B. *Sukhumvit Inn* (☎ *039-512151, 234 Th Sukhumvit*) has rooms for 140B to 180B.

More comfortable than any of the previous options, and the only hotel in town with a lift, the renovated *Trat Hotel (Meuang Trat;* ☎ *039-511091*), off Th Sukhumvit next to the main market, has standard fan rooms for 220B to 300B, air-con from 370B.

Eleven kilometres south-east of town at Laem Sok, the *Ban Pu Resort (*☎*/fax 039-512400)* stands adjacent to Suan Puu, a famous seafood restaurant/crab farm. Large, well appointed wooden bungalows connected by a boardwalk surrounding a large crab pond start at 1200B for a one bedroom unit with two double beds or one king-size bed; a larger one bedroom unit with six beds costs 2600B. All of these come with air-con, TV and a fridge. There are also deluxe VIP two-bedroom bungalows with

TV, VCR and private karaoke room for 3400B, and there's a health club on the premises. It's a 20B, 15 minute songthaew ride from town. Ban Pu can arrange speedboat transport to Ko Chang and other Trat islands for 6000B to 8000B, including lifejackets and snorkelling gear.

Laem Ngop There's usually no reason to stay here since most boats to Ko Chang leave in the morning and early afternoon and it's only 20km from Trat. However, there are a couple of good accommodation choices. A five minute walk from the harbour on the right is the *Chut Kaew Guest House* (☎ *039-597088*), which is run by a nurse, teacher and university student – local, somewhat dated information (including hiking info for Ko Chang) is available in thick notebooks compiled by guests. Fan rooms with bamboo-thatch walls cost 80B per person and are relatively clean; facilities are shared. Food and laundry services are available as are bike rentals for just 10B a day.

The next place on the right, about 100m from the road, is *PI Guest House*, a clean place with large rooms in a Thai house; it's usually closed during the June to November rainy season. All rooms have one double bed for 70/120B single/double. The *Laem Ngop Inn* (☎ *039-597044, fax 597144*) is farther up again, but down a side lane 300m from the road. The clean, concrete bungalows (each with separate garage) come with fan, phone and TV for 300B, with air-con for 450B. For 600B add a refrigerator, bathtub and hot water. The *Paradise Inn* (☎ *039-512831*) near the police station has similarly priced rooms.

Places to Eat

With all the markets in Trat, you're hardly ever more than 50m away from something good to eat. The *indoor municipal market* beneath the shopping centre has a food section with cheap, good noodle and rice dishes from early morning to early evening. Another good spot for a cheap breakfast is the ancient *coffee stand* in the old day market on Th Tat Mai.

In the evenings, there's a good *night market* next to the air-con bus station. On the Trat River in the northern part of town is a small but atmospheric *night market* – a good choice for long, leisurely meals. Trat is a good city for seafood, which is cheaper here than in Bangkok or in more touristed cities around the country (it's not the international tourists who drive up the seafood prices but the Thais, who spend huge sums of money eating out).

One of the longest running Thai-Chinese restaurants in town is the *Jiraporn*, a small cafe-style place a few doors up from the Trat Hotel where a small crowd of older regulars hang out over tea and coffee every morning. As it's mostly a breakfast place, the main menu offerings are toast and eggs with ham, *jók* and *khâo tôm*, but they can also do fried rice or noodles.

The *Nam Chok*, a tin-roofed, Christmas light-trimmed open-air restaurant on the corner of Soi Butnoi and Th Wiwatthana is another local institution. Around lunchtime a good find is *Raan Joh (no roman-script sign; 90 Th Lak Meuang)*. The number is next to impossible to see, just look for the only place making *khanŏm beûang*, a Khmer vegie crepe prepared in a wok. They also do other local specialities – it's very inexpensive but open lunchtime only.

A good mid-range restaurant, the air-con *Saeng Fah (☎ 039-511222, 157-9 Th Sukhumvit)* has a large menu with Thai specialities between 30B and 100B. The food is good, and there are plenty of seafood dishes. Try the 'jally fish soup' or 'bloody clam salad'. They also serve breakfast, when you might (or might not) want to try the house speciality – 'rice with curdled pig's blood'.

A *Thai vegetarian restaurant* down a lane behind the area where the night market is held offers seven or eight pots of fresh vegie dishes daily from around 6 am to 2 pm, or when the food runs out. A plate of rice with your choice of toppings costs only 20B.

Kaan Kluay (no roman-script sign) on Th Sukhumvit, opposite the mouth of Th Thoncharoen, is an outdoor garden restaurant full of tropical plants and ceramic figurines of frogs, lizards and elephants. The Thai menu includes several vegetarian options, and prices range from a modest 25B to 70B per dish.

The best place in the whole province for seafood is *Suan Puu* (Crab Farm) in Ban Laem Hin, on the way to Laem Sok, 11km south-east of town (a 20B songthaew ride each way). Tables are atmospherically arranged on wooden piers over Ao Meuang Trat (Trat Bay). All seafood is served fresh; crab, raised on the premises, is of course the house speciality and prices are moderate to medium high (but still considerably cheaper than Bangkok). The menu is in Thai only, so bring along a Thai friend to translate.

Laem Ngop At the Laem Ngop pier there are two good seafood restaurants. The *Saengchan Restaurant*, on the right in front of the pier, doesn't have great food but many travellers wait here for minibuses to Trat which connect with air-con buses to Bangkok.

Nearby are several rustic seafood places with views of the sea and islands. One of the more popular spots with local Thais and Thai tourists is the inexpensive *Ruan Talay*, a wooden place on stilts over the water. Also good are *Kung Ruang Seafood, Tamnak Chang* and *Krua Rim Nam*, all moderately priced.

Getting There & Away

Bangkok Buses between Trat and Bangkok cost 169B air-con (132B 2nd class, without toilet) or 113B ordinary and use Bangkok's Eastern bus terminal. The trip takes five to six hours one way by air-con bus, or about eight hours by ordinary bus. Three bus companies operate a Trat to Bangkok service; Sahamit-Cherdchai, on Th Sukhumvit near the Trat Hotel and night market, has the best and most frequent (14 a day) air-con buses to Bangkok.

Chanthaburi Ordinary buses between Chanthaburi and Trat are 26B, depart every 30 minutes between 5.50 am and 2.30 pm and at 3.45, 4.20 and 5.30 pm. The 66km trip takes about 1½ hours.

You can also take the quicker share taxis between Trat and Chanthaburi for 60B per person – these take around 45 minutes. During the middle of the day, however, it may take up to an hour to gather the seven passengers necessary for a departure; try to schedule your departure between 7 and 9 am or 4 and 6 pm for the shortest wait.

Laem Ngop Share taxis to Laem Ngop leave Trat from a stand along Th Sukhumvit next to the municipal market; these cost 15B per person shared or 100B to charter. They depart regularly throughout the day, but after dark you will have to charter. Travel agents at the Laem Ngop pier arrange daily minibuses to Th Khao San in Bangkok (11 am departure, 250B, five to six hours); Pattaya (1 pm departure, 400B, three hours); and Ban Pae (11 am departure, 200B, two hours).

Khlong Yai, Hat Lek & Bo Rai Songthaews and share taxis to Khlong Yai cost 35B per person (400B charter) and take about 45 minutes. The songthaew fare from Khlong Yai to Hat Lek is 30B (180B charter) for the 16km trip; these taxis leave from the back of the municipal market. Motorcycle taxis are also available between Hat Lek and Khlong Yai for 60B. A door-to-door minibus to Bo Rai is 40B.

Getting Around

Samlors around town should cost 10B per person. Small songthaews cost 5B per person on a share basis or 20B to 40B for the whole vehicle.

KO CHANG NATIONAL MARINE PARK

Forty-seven of the islands off Trat's coastline belong to a national park named after **Ko Chang** (Elephant Island), which at 492 sq km is Thailand's second largest island after Phuket. The entire park officially encompasses 192 sq km of land surface, and 458 sq km of sea. Ko Chang itself is about 70% undisturbed island rainforest – the best preserved in Thailand, perhaps in all South-East Asia – with steep hills and cliffs rising to the 744m Khao Jom Prasat. Beach forest and mangrove are also found in abundance. Notable wildlife includes the stump-tailed macaque, small Indian civet, Javan mongoose, monitor lizard, water monitor, Burmese and reticulated pythons, king cobra, barking deer and wild pig. Avian species include Pacific reef egret, nightjar, green imperial pigeon, white-winged tern, blue-winged pitta, hooded pitta and three hornbill species. An endemic amphibian, the Ko Chang frog *(Rana kohchang)* is also found here.

Other major islands in the park include Ko Kut and Ko Mak. Ko Chang is ringed with small bays and beaches, among them Ao Khlong Son, Hat Sai Khao, Ao Khlong Phrao, Hat Kaibae, Ao Bang Bao and Ao Salak Phet. Near each of these beaches are small villages.

Until rather recently there wasn't a single paved road on Ko Chang, only red dirt roads between Khlong Son and Hat Kaibae on the west coast of the island, and between Khlong Son and Ban Salak Phet on the east side, plus walking trails passable by motorcycle from Kaibae to Bang Bao and Salak Kok to Salak Phet. Road crews are working to extend the road along the west side. A paved section now exists between Khlong Son/Ao Sapparot and Khlong Phrao, and Trat authorities say the island will have a paved ring road – or at least the beginnings of one – within the next two or three years. Electricity now comes from the mainland to the northern part of the island via a submarine cable, and power lines will probably continue to follow the sealing of the roads around the island.

Ko Chang receives around 75,000, mostly Thai, visitors a year who tend to arrive on weekends and holidays only, stay for 24 hours or less, and stay in the more expensive accommodation. The average stay for non-Thai visitors is around five days; a small number of visitors take up residence for weeks on end.

A combination of steep terrain and permanent streams creates several scenic waterfalls. A series of three falls along the stream of Khlong Mayom in the interior of the island, **Than Mayom Falls**, can be reached via Tha Than Mayom on the east coast. The waterfall closest to the shore can be climbed in about 45 minutes via a well marked footpath. The view from the top is quite good and there are two inscribed stones bearing the initials of Rama VI and Rama VII nearby. The second waterfall is about 500m farther east along Khlong Mayom and the third is about 3km from the first. At the third waterfall is another inscribed stone, this one with the initials of Rama V. At the lower levels are public picnic areas.

A smaller waterfall on the west coast, **Khlong Phu Falls**, can be visited from Ao Khlong Phrao (45 minutes on foot) or from Hat Kaibae (one hour) by following Khlong Phrao 2km inland. Or pedal a bicycle along the main dirt road until you see the sign on the eastern side of the road. Ride up to the restaurant near the falls, from where it is only a 15 minute walk to the falls themselves. A pool beneath the falls is a good spot for a refreshing swim, and it is possible to stay in the bungalows or camp here.

On **Ko Kut** you'll find beaches mostly along the west side, at Hat Khlong Chao, Hat Khlong Yai Kii and Hat Tapho. A dirt road runs between Ban Khlong Hin Dam, the island's main village on the west coast, and Ao Salat along the north-east shore. Other villages on the island include Ban Ta Poi, Bang Ao Salat, Ban Laem Kluai, Bang Khlong Phrao and Ban Lak Uan. Tan Sanuk Falls and Khlong Chao offer inland water diversions. The nearby small islands of Ko Rang and Ko Rayang have good coral in spots. Ko Kut can be reached from Khlong Yai on the mainland or from Ko Mak.

Ko Mak, the smallest of the three main islands, has a beach along the north-west bay and possibly others as yet undiscovered. Monsoon forest covers 30% of the island while coconut plantations take up another 60%. A few tractors or jeeps travel along the single paved road which leads from the pier to the main village. It is possible to rent motorbikes and organise diving trips from the resorts on the island.

Ko Wai has some of the best coral and is excellent for snorkelling and diving. The island has one bungalow operation. **Ko Kham** is also recommended for underwater explorations; accommodation is available. **Ko Laoya** has natural attributes similar to those at Ko Wai, with one rather expensive place to stay. The tiny **Ko Rang** archipelago, south-west of Ko Chang, is a primary nesting ground for the endangered hawksbill sea turtle.

As with other national marine parks in Thailand, park status versus resort development is a hot issue. On Ko Chang, so far, everyone seems to be in agreement about what is park land and what isn't. Any land that was planted before the conferral of park status in 1982 can be privately deeded, bought, sold and developed – this includes many beach areas used for coconut plantations, or about 15% of the island. The Forestry Department makes regular flights over the island to check for encroachment on the 85% belonging to the national park – mostly in the interior – and they are said to be very strict with interlopers.

Information

Park Information The park headquarters are divided into four units, found at Than Mayom, Khlong Son, Tha Khlong Plu and Salak Phet. All offer roughly the equivalent information, but the Than Mayom visitors' centre features informative displays on park flora and fauna.

Money There is no bank on Ko Chang, but moneychangers will change US dollars and travellers cheques at very unfavourable rates. The only post office is near the pier at Khlong Son, where there is a telegram service but no international phones. On Hat Sai Khao and Hat Kaibae, a few places offer international telephone service at very high rates.

Medical Services There is a health clinic at Khlong Son; the nearest hospital is in Laem Ngop on the mainland.

Dangers & Annoyances The local police headquarters is located in Ban Dan Mai where they have a jail that detains an average of three visitors each month caught smoking dope on the island.

Nudity and topless sunbathing are forbidden by law in Ko Chang National Marine Park; this includes all beaches on Ko Chang, Ko Kut, Ko Mak, Ko Kradat etc.

Walking on Ko Chang

In general the more interesting hikes can be found in the southern half of the island where there are fewer roads. At the northern end you can walk from **Khlong Son to Hat Sai Khao** in about 1½ to two hours, from Hat Sai Khao to Hat Khlong Phrao in about two hours, and from Hat Khlong Phrao to Hat Kaibae in about two hours. All three are straightforward walks along the main road. If you're looking for more grunt, just head into the interior – the steep, forested hills will have you sweating in no time. A footpath connects Khlong Phrao on the west coast with Khlong Mayom on the east, but this all-day cross-island route shouldn't be undertaken without a local guide. Hedi at the White House Bakery at Hat Sai Khao has information on local guides.

Down south a challenging walk is to hike from **Kaibae to Ao Bang Bao** through coconut and rubber plantations – this takes three to four hours and is a bit more involved. You may have to ask directions from villagers along the way as there are several interconnecting trails.

Don't try the walk from **Bang Bao to Salak Phet** unless you're an experienced tropical hiker with moderate orienteering skills – there's a lot of up-and-down and many interconnecting trails. A Swede who hiked the entire perimeter of the island suggested that for this part of the island you carry a note in Thai reading 'I would like to go to Salak Phet. I like very much to walk in the jungle and have done it before. Please show me the start of this trail'. If you don't get lost, this hike will take four to six hours; should you decide to attempt it, carry enough food and water for an overnight, just

in case. If you do get lost, climb the nearest hilltop and try to locate the sea or a stream to get a bearing. Following any stream will usually take you either to a village or to the sea. Then you can either follow the coast or ask directions. This advice is also good for hiking anywhere across the island, as it is very easy to get lost on the many intersecting, unmarked trails. At the south-east end of Ao Bang Bao, around a headland that leads to Ao Salak Phet, is a beautiful and secluded beach, **Hat Wai Chek**.

On the east side of the island it's a one hour walk between Dan Mai and Than Mayom, two hours between Dan Mai and Sai Thong (or between Khlong Son and Sai Thong). Salak Kok to Salak Phet is straightforward and takes around three hours. The **estuary** at Ao Salak Kok's western end boasts one of the best mangrove systems in Thailand, though like other coastal wetlands it's threatened by increased shrimp farming.

A hike around the entire island can be done at a comfortable pace in a week to 10 days. Remember to carry plenty of water and watch out for snakes – a few poisonous varieties live on the island.

Diving & Snorkelling

Ko Chang and its vicinity is a new frontier relative to other marine locales in Thailand. With regard to climate and visibility, November to April is the main diving season. The better dive sites are at islets and seamounts off the south-western tip of the island. **Hin Luuk Bat** and **Hin Laap** are both coral-encrusted seamounts with depths of around 18 to 20m. Nearby **Ko Rang Yai** gets scenic at 10 to 25m, while **Hin Phrai Nam** has whitetip and reef sharks to around 20m. A small islet near Ko Rang Yai's northern tip, **Ko Kra**, has good snorkelling in depths of 4 or 5m near the islet's south end. The islets around Ko Rang are favoured nesting grounds for sea turtles – this is one of your better opportunities to see them in Thailand.

South-west of Ao Salak Phet, reef-fringed **Ko Wai** features a good variety of colourful hard and soft corals at depths of 6 to 15m.

Near the mouth of Ao Salak Phet, at the south-eastern tip of the island, lies the wreck of a Thai warship at a depth of 15m; the ship was supposedly sunk by the French in 1941 during a dispute over whether these islands belonged to Thailand or to French-colonised Cambodia. According to Thai history there should be a second wreck nearby but divers have yet to report on it.

Dive Services Ko Chang Divers at Haad Sai Khao Bungalows on Hat Sai Khao specialises in PADI certification for novice divers. Dive trips typically include two dives with all guiding, transport and equipment for 1500B; snorkellers are welcome to join for 400B per day. Ko Chang Divers offers a free half hour, one tank introduction at beachside, or a full PADI course for 8000B; instructors speak German, English, French and Thai. The only other full-time dive guiding/instruction centre on the island so far is Sea-Horse Dive Centre at Hat Kaibae, between Nangnuan Bungalows and Porn's.

You can also hire your own boats from Ko Chang's western beaches for around 1000B a day, but there's no guarantee the boat pilots will be able to locate the dive sites described above. They may know the islands but not necessarily the best places for coral, or the best way to moor the boats near the coral.

Other Activities

Some of the guesthouses at Hat Sai Khao and to a lesser extent Hat Kaibae rent kayaks, sailboards, masks and snorkels and boogie boards. Mountain bikes can be rented for 100B per day at several places on the island, including Muk Hut Restaurant and Ban Nuna's Restaurant at Hat Sai Khao and Coral Resort at Hat Kaibae.

Several bungalow operations along Ko Chang's west coast beaches (as well as Bang Bao Blue Wave Bungalow on Ao Bang Bao) offer day trips to nearby islands; eg 150B per person to Ko Yuak or Ko Man; 300B to Ko Rang, Ko Wai, Ko Khlam or Ko Mak; and 1000B to Ko Kut.

Island Hopper Tours at Arunee's Resort at Hat Sai Khao offers one day boat trips to

Ko Wai and Ko Mak for 450B per person, including lunch and snorkel gear. Island Hopper also does a 'black market Cambodian border tour' for 450B.

Places to Stay – Ko Chang

Many beach huts on the island have only been open about eight years and standards vary quite a bit. Some of the older simpler bungalow complexes are in the process of being upgraded. A few close down during the rainy season (June to October) but as the island has become more popular, most places stay open and offer low season prices, sometimes as low as 40% of the normal rate. During the rainy season, boats usually only go as far as Ao Sapparot (Pineapple Bay), Dan Mai and Than Mayom – the surf farther south along the west coast can be impassable during heavy rains.

Even during dry months, the trend now is for all boats to drop off at Ao Sapparot so that visitors can continue on to the beaches by songthaew.

West Coast As the island's better beaches are along the west coast, this is where most of the beach accommodation is. Most huts and bungalows have one double mattress on the floor or on a raised platform plus a mosquito net. If you are staying longer than a few days all places will discount their rates, even in peak season. Most of the island now has electricity; if your bungalow isn't on the grid yet, kerosene or gas lanterns are usually provided. Only a few places have music and, blessedly, even fewer have TVs and videos.

At the northern tip of the island is the largest village, Khlong Son, which has a network of piers at the mouth of the khlong, a wat, a school, several noodle shops and a health clinic. On the northern cape of Ao Khlong Son, *Manee Guest House* (☎ 01-945 1930) offers thatched huts for 150B (some with private bath, but no electricity). Farther south is *Premvadee Resort* (☎ 01-933 5455) where simple bungalows with electricity and shared bathroom go for 500B, while large two-room houses with private bath and fan are 1500B.

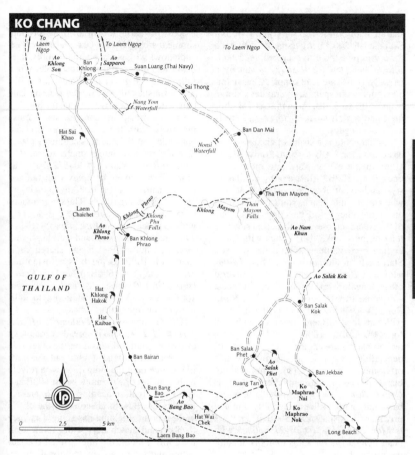

KO CHANG

To Laem Ngop
To Laem Ngop
To Laem Ngop

Ao Khlong Son
Ban Khlong Son
Ao Sapparot
Suan Luang (Thai Navy)

Sai Thong

Nang Yom Waterfall

Hat Sai Khao

Ban Dan Mai

Nonsi Waterfall

Tha Than Mayom

Laem Chaichet
Khlong Phrao
Khlong Phu Falls
Khlong Mayom
Than Mayom Falls

Ao Khlong Phrao
Ban Khlong Phrao

Ao Nam Khun

GULF OF THAILAND

Hat Khlong Hakok

Ao Salak Kok

Hat Kaibae

Ban Salak Kok

Ban Bairan

Ban Salak Phet
Ao Salak Phet
Ban Jekbae

Ban Bang Bao
Ao Bang Bao
Ruang Tan
Ko Maphrao Nai

Hat Wai Chek
Ko Maphrao Nok

0   2.5   5 km

Laem Bang Bao
Long Beach

It's 5km from Khlong Son to Hat Sai Khao (White Sand Beach). At the lower end of the beach, well off the road and separated from other Hat Sai Khao bungalow developments by a couple of small rocky points, is the nicely landscaped *White Sand Beach Resort* (☎ 01-218 7526) where a long row of simple thatched huts along the beach (no electricity, shared bathroom) are 150B. Behind these are wooden bungalows (no electricity, private bath) for 250B and

more up-market tiled-roof bungalows with private bath, electricity and fan for 600B.

Next south are a couple of less isolated spots beginning with the *Rock Sand Bungalow*, which has a few rustic wooden huts on a rocky outcrop surrounded by beach on both sides for 100B per hut and better ones up to 500B. There's a nice two storey restaurant/bar with hammocks on the premises. Rock Sand is usually closed during the rainy season. *KC* (☎ 01-211 5607) has bamboo-thatch huts located behind a row of palms for 200B (no electricity, shared bathroom). KC's Pyramid Herbal Sauna costs 200B per person or 150B each for a group of three to four people. *Yakah Bungalows* (☎ 01-219 3897) is run by a friendly Thai/American couple. Clean bamboo huts with spacious verandahs range from 150B to 350B. A swing set for children and a well stocked library are made available to guests.

Farther south is a string of cheapies with basic huts for 100B to 200B (only 40B to 100B in the off season), and more solid ones from 300B. All are very similar in style and layout; if you get off the boat anywhere along this beach, you can walk from one to the other before deciding. This is one of the island's more 'social' beaches, where long-termers stoke their bongs with Cambodian herb while watching the sun set. Starting from the north you'll find *Tantawan* and *Bamboo*, which – like several other bungalow operations along this coast – organise trips to other islands. *Ban Rung Rong* (☎ 039-597184) offers flashier huts with fans for 100B and nicer ones with bath for 300B (50B to 100B in the low season); techno parties are another draw or turn-off, depending on your disposition. They also offer money exchange (5% commission), boat trips and mountain bike rental. Next is *Cookie Bungalow* (☎ 01-219 3859), where basic huts with 24 hour electricity, fan and private bath cost 300B to 500B. Then there is *Mac Bungalow* (☎ 01-219 3056) with nicer bungalows for 250B to 400B, including private bath.

Opposite Cookie, *Arunee's Resort* (☎ 01-219 3869) offers rooms with private bath and fan in a wooden hotel-style building for 250B. Arunee's offers copy and fax services.

South of Cookie on the beach again, the *Sabai Beach Bungalow* (☎ 01-949 3256) features three rows of cottages that descend in price as you back away from the sand: 450/800B low season/high season in the first row, 350/600B in the second and 250/450B in the third. The accompanying Sabay Bar is the local full moon party headquarters.

The well run *Haad Sai Khao* is in the process of tearing down all of its original simple thatched huts to be replaced by flash bungalows with private bath for 900B; telephone and mail service are available. When full, Haad Sai Khao rents tents for 100B. *Apple* finishes off this stretch with upscale huts with fan and private baths for 850B.

Cross a stream and continue south, moving away from the more densely packed huts, and you'll come to a couple of places favoured by those into a quieter scene. *Best Garden Beach Resort* (☎ 01-212 7493) has rooms in a wooden complex with fan and private bath for 150B to 300B, plus larger air-con cabins for 1000B. The semi-outdoor restaurant is huge. Set above a rocky area with no beach, *Sunsai Bungalow* (☎ 01-211 4488) has friendly staff and well kept, well separated huts with fan and shared bathrooms for 100B. Better huts with fan and private bath go for 600B. *Moonlight Resort* (☎ 01-936 1703) prices its huts by row, from 100B in the back (shared bathroom) to 500B in front (private bath).

The German-owned *Plaloma Cliff Resort* (☎ 01-219 3880) is spread over a rocky cliff a bit south of Sunsai on the other side of a rocky headland. Quiet and spacious tile-and-cement fan bungalows with private bath – shades of Ko Samui – cost 600B and 900B per night, depending on size and location, 1500B with air-con. On the cliff's highest point, Plaloma has some very nice bamboo-and-thatch huts with private bath for 250B a night; the interspersed coconut palms and sea views are additional pluses.

Around 500m or so farther south, then 200m west down a dirt road, high on a hill over the sea and encircled by garden, stands *Ban Nuna Tropical Garden Seaview*. The two-storey modern Thai-style house contains 10 rooms, each with large picture windows. Rooms start at 1000B and include private hot showers, fans and western-style toilets, plus complimentary use of a motorcycle.

About 4km south of Hat Sai Khao (9km from Khlong Son) is Ao Khlong Phrao (Coconut Bay). It stretches south of Laem Chaichet and encompasses the canal Khlong

Phrao as well as its namesake village Ban Khlong Phrao (12km from Khlong Son). On the north side of the canal is *Chaichet Bungalows* (☎ 01-219 3458) starting at 100B to 250B for A-frame wooden huts facing north-west and reaching 200B to 500B for concrete bungalows with private baths. The bungalows are strung out along Laem Chaichet, a gently curving cape, though there's no beach here. Also on the north bank of Khlong Phrao, *Klong Plow (Phrao) Resort* (☎ 01-219 3899) has fan-cooled wooden bungalows in a semicircle around a lagoon for 600B to 700B, air-con for 1400B. A two storey house that can accommodate 20 people goes for 4000B. Near Ban Chaichet south of Ao Khlong Phrao is *Coconut Beach Bungalows* (☎ 01-219 3432), where new wooden bungalows cost 150B to 200B for singles/doubles or you can pay 400B to 500B for concrete bungalows with private bath. The bungalows are well kept, though somewhat close together.

About a 10 minute walk farther south along the beach is the pricey *Rooks Ko Chang Resort* (☎ 039-538055, 01-923 4867). Up-market bungalows here cost from 1500B to 1900B and include all the usual comforts with air-con, hot water and satellite TV. The majority of the guests are Thai businesspeople on vacation, many on incentive travel packages. The resort owns the Centrepoint pier in Laem Ngop; private boats between that pier and the resort are available for 200B per person.

It is possible to cross the river in a long-tail boat but you need to call for one on the southern bank. If you are staying at the PSS huts the service is only 5B but if you're staying anywhere else it's 10B. The *PSS Bungalow* charges 100B for simple grass huts; it's closed in the rainy season. About a 10 minute walk farther south, near Wat Ban Khlong Phrao, is *KP Bungalows* (01-219 1225) where well spaced basic thatched huts cost 80B, nicer ones with private bath cost 200B, and a large wooden bungalow is available for 2000B. The food here is good, but the restaurant closes at 8 pm and the lights are out by 9 pm. The service could be

a little friendlier. It is closed during the rainy season.

About 700m past the turn-off for Khlong Phu Falls, off the main road in Ban Khlong Phrao, is the secluded *Hobby Hut* (☎ 01-213 7668). A favourite with Thais associated with the music/art business, Hobby Hut has only four simple huts (more are under construction). Rates depend on length of stay and number of guests. It's 300m to the nearest beach; a small inland lagoon offers canoeing. There's live music on Wednesday to Friday evenings.

Around another headland to the south are two beach areas separated by a canal – Hat Khlong Makok and Hat Kaibae (15km south of Khlong Son). These beaches tend to disappear during high tide but they're OK – lots of coconut palms. *Magic* (☎ 01-219 3408) and *Erawan* have bungalows with fans for 80B to 100B, but they're none too clean, while the better bungalows with bath cost from 150B to 300B. New log-cabin-style bungalows go for 700B at Magic. Magic has a pier, telephone service and scuba diving. The owner has a private boat service from Laem Ngop so is able to funnel many passengers directly to this beach. Magic's best feature is its restaurant built over the bay. Next door is *Pikanade Resort* (☎ 01-219 3814), formerly Chokdee Bungalow (set amid coconut palms but with no beach to speak of) has cleaner, nicer thatched huts for 150B or concrete bungalows with bath for 800B.

Next south on Hat Kaibae proper (15km south of Khlong Son) is an area that has become quite developed, with a pier and bungalows with generator-powered electricity (yes, this means more videos of Arnold firing large weapons or Van Damme kicking snot from people's faces). Starting in the north, the first place you come to is the *Palm Beach-Comfortable Bar Resort*, a German-run place where funky painted wooden huts are 150B each with fan and private bath. The food here is reputedly good; mountain bikes cost 150B per day.

Coral Resort (☎ 01-219 3815) is set amid a bumper crop of coconut palms and

EASTERN GULF COAST

costs 350B to 600B for bungalows with fan and private bath. They also have an international telephone service and mountain bikes can be rented for 100B per day. A khlong separates the *Nang Nual Resort*, where new natural-looking bungalows start at 200B. The resort restaurant serves Thai and French dishes. Canoes are available for rent. This area is a bit trashed out in places and the adjacent shrimp farm is a definite detraction.

Kaibae Hut, on the south side of the khlong, has a nicely laid-out restaurant and fair bungalows, plus a bit of a beach even at high tide; rates are the usual 200B for nice clean bungalows with private bath, and a large deluxe air-con bungalow (with TV, fridge and fan) which can fit up to eight people is available for 2500B. It's quiet, too, and has a security gate that's locked at night. SeaHorse Dive Centre offers dive trips and instruction during the dry season.

There is more of a beach down towards the southern end of Hat Kaibae. *KaiBae Beach Bungalow* (☎ 039-529022, 01-218 5055) has clean, well separated huts that range from very simple ones costing 100B to 150B up to four or six-person huts at 1500B, all with fan and private bath. Walk another 100m to *Porn's*, with basic 150B huts, followed by the large *Siam View Resort* (☎ 039-529022, 01-218 5055) with deluxe bungalows costing 750B to 1200B with fan, 1200B to 1700B air-con, or 3500B for a 10 person bungalow. The last place on the beach is the secluded and friendly *Siam Bay Resort* (☎ 01-452 7061) with huts for 150B and bungalows with private bath from 400B, fancier concrete bungalows up to 600B. At low tide you can walk out to Ko Man Nai opposite (not to be confused with the Ko Man Nai off the Rayong Coast).

A 30 minute walk along the path to Ao Bang Bao, behind the Siam Bay Resort, will take you to *Tree House Lodge* in a rocky area near a secluded white sand beach. Simple thatched huts on stilts in a coconut grove start at just 60B. During high season the Lodge operates a taxi boat from Laem Ngop that costs 50B per person.

South Coast None of the following south coast places is normally open during the rainy season, from May to November, when regular transport is difficult. Nevertheless, this is the place to go if you want to get a feel for the life of Thai fisherfolk or to explore beautiful jungle paths and nearby islets.

Ao Bang Bao has the friendly *Bang Bao Blue Wave* (☎ 01-4390349) with thatched huts in the back with shared bathroom for 80B, or 150B for huts in the front with private bath. Electricity is on from 6 to 10 pm. You may also be able to rent rooms cheaply in the village (Ban Bang Bao). At the moment you can walk between Bang Bao and Hat Kaibae in about three hours; eventually a road will connect the two. Or you can hop the once-daily boat from Laem Ngop, in the high season only, for 130B to the beach, 100B back to Laem Ngop. During the rainy season the only way here is on foot from Kaibae.

The next bay along the coast, Ao Salak Phet, features several possibilities. About 300m from the Ban Salak Phet, *Diamond Hill Resort* tries to rent filthy wooden huts for 150B to 200B. Up the road past the Salak Phet National Park unit, the *Ko Chang Marina Resort* (☎ 038-237374, 01-213 0323) is still under construction, but claims it will have air-con rooms for 1000B.

At the head of the road near the pier, *Salakpet Seafood Restaurant & Resort* has clean rooms built over the water for 300B with fan and private bath, plus some air-con rooms across the road that house four persons for 1200B.

Nearby *Sang Aroon Restaurant* (☎ 01-650 2658) has rooms for 200B. The same family owns *Sang Aroon Bungalows* at Ban Jaekbae, a 20 minute boat ride across the bay (provided free by the restaurant). Rooms at the latter cost 200B to 500B.

Long Beach Bungalows (☎ 039-511145, email longbeachcoralresort@aol.com), is very secluded near the end of the long cape to the south-east of Ao Salak Phet; it has well-made huts with electricity for 150B a night. It's closed between July and December. Farther on, right at the tip of the cape, is the friendly **Tantawan House** on a rocky outcrop with only seven huts costing 100/200B per single/double. The beach is only a two minute swim away. To get here take a boat from Ao Salak Phet for 30B.

A partially sealed road leads from Ao Sapparot all the way to Ban Salak Phet; songthaews meet the Ao Sapparot and Than Mayom boats. The village itself is very spread out; the main road terminates at the Salakpet Seafood Restaurant, from where there are smaller paths along the southern coast. Power lines also terminate in Ban Salak Phet.

East Coast There are a couple of mediocre places to stay near the nicely landscaped national park headquarters at Than Mayom. Privately managed, **Than Mayom Bungalows** (no sign), opposite the park offices, charges 500B for a large, white two room house and 2200B for a house that can accommodate 30 people. A couple of kilometres north, **Thanmayom Resort** rents A-frame huts for 100B a night; there is a pier but no beach to speak of, and since the huts are on the other side of a dusty road from the sea, it's not very inviting. **Koh Chang Cabana** (☎ 01-219 3428) nearby rents rooms in a long rowhouse for 600B with fan, or separate air-con bungalows for 1200B. Tour groups are the main clientele here.

If you have camping gear, it might be better to hike up and camp near Than Mayom Falls.

The visitor centre contains faded photo displays with English labels and useful info. At the end of a small pier is a very casual *restaurant* with rice and noodle dishes.

Places to Stay – Other Islands

Ko Kut, Ko Mak, Ko Kradat and Ko Kham all now feature beach bungalow accommodation. In general these places are quieter and obviously more secluded than their Ko Chang counterparts. The drawbacks are that transport can be a little tricky – though during months of high visitation (December to April) there are daily boats – and the fact that you can't just pick up and walk down

the beach to another bungalow if you don't like the one you landed at. Except at the package places, room rates overall are less expensive than on Ko Chang.

From May to November, it's a good idea to call in advance to make sure boat transportation is available. Most close down completely from June to September.

Ko Kut As on Ko Chang, the best beaches are along the west coast, particularly at Hat Tapho. The five bungalow operations on this island are open only from November to May. Three cater to visitors coming on prearranged packages that include boat transport, accommodation and meals: **Ko Kut Sai Khao Resort** (☎ 039-511824, 511429), 1300B; **Kut Island Resort** (Bangkok ☎ 02-374 3004, 375 6188), 1600B; and **Khlong Hin Hut** (☎ 039-530236, 01-947 1760), 1000B to 1800B.

Two others, **Ko Kut Cabana** (Bangkok ☎ 02-923 2456) and **Khlong Jaow Resort** (☎ 039-520337, 520318), offer a range of accommodation from 150B for basic huts to nicer bungalows up to 1000B. You can also try village homes in nearby Ban Hin Dam.

Ko Mak On the west bay, amid a coconut and rubber plantation, the friendly **Ko Mak Resort & Cabana** (☎ 01-219 1220, Bangkok ☎ 02-319 6714/5) has bungalows with fan and private bath starting at 300B. In the same area, **TK Huts** (☎ 039-521133/631) has bungalows with 'natural air' (no fans) for 300B. **Ao Kok Resort** (☎ 039-425263) offers comfortable bungalows with fan and private bath for 500B a night in the low season, 700B high season. Diving equipment and instruction are available from Ao Kok Resort.

Ko Mak Guest House (☎ 01-444 2796) rents basic huts with verandahs for 100B a night, shared bathroom, while nicer ones with private bath at **Fantasia** (☎ 01-219 1220, Bangkok ☎ 02-219 3290) are 250B. A scuba centre operates out of Fantasia in the high season. Fantasia also rents bikes for exploring the plantations and fishing villages around the island.

Over on the east side of Ko Mak, *Sunshine* (☎ 01-916 5585) offers solid bungalows for 650B a night.

As on Ko Kut, all of the above tend to close during the rainy season.

Ko Kradat The *Ko Kradat* has air-con bungalows for 600B. Mr Chumpon in Bangkok (☎ 02-311 3668) can arrange accommodation at Ko Kradat and transport to the island in advance.

Ko Kham *Ko Kham Resort*, run by a friendly ex-cop, offers bamboo bungalows for 100B to 120B. More upscale huts are available for up to 700B. A boat, sponsored by the resort, leaves the main Laem Ngop pier daily at 3 pm, November to April only.

Places to Eat

Menus at all the bungalows on Ko Chang are pretty similar. On Hat Sai Khao, highest marks this time around go to the kitchens at *Sunsai* and *Tantawan*. Several small eateries offer ex-bungalow options along the east side of the main road in Hat Sai Khao. *Ban Nuna Restaurant-Cafe*, an upstairs place where you sit on cushions, is good for Thai lunches and dinners, pizza and western breakfasts, while the *Muk House* next door does huge western breakfasts, homemade bread and a daily changing menu of Thai and faràng food.

Swedish-managed *White House Bakery*, across the road from Sabai Beach Bungalow, offers a variety of baked goods, fruit shakes and plenty of info on island activities.

The *Salakpet Seafood Restaurant*, in the southern part of Ko Chang, at Ao Salak Phet, serves the very best seafood on the island; prices are moderate.

Getting There & Away

Ko Chang Take a songthaew (15B, 25 minutes) from Trat to Laem Ngop on the coast, then a ferry to Ko Chang. In Laem Ngop there are now three piers serving Ko Chang – the main one at the end of the road from Trat, Ko Chang Centrepoint (operated by Rooks Ko Chang Resort), 4km north-west of Laem Ngop, and a newer one called Tha Thammachat at Ao Thammachat, farther west of Laem Ngop.

From Tha Laem Ngop, the main pier at Laem Ngop, boats go to Ao Sapparot (Pineapple Bay) on Ko Chang year-round; this is still the boat most people take. During the high season – roughly December to April – boats depart hourly from 7 am to 5 pm. The remainder of the year the schedule is reduced to about every two hours, although departures ultimately depend on weather, number of passengers and any number of other factors. The trip takes one hour and costs 50B per person. You should check on fares in advance – some of the boat crews have been known to overcharge faràngs. At Ao Sapparot, songthaews will be waiting to take you to any of the various beaches along the west coast at a cost of 30B per person.

One boat leaves Tha Laem Ngop at 1 pm daily for the 45 minute trip to Than Mayom on Ko Chang's east coast. In the return direction it departs from Than Mayom at 6.30 am. The fare is 30B per person. This is the boat to take if you want to catch a songthaew south to Ao Salak Phet.

Another boat travels from Laem Ngop to Ao Bang Bao at 1 pm on Mondays and Fridays only, returning at 3 or 4 am the next morning. The trip takes two hours and costs 80B out, 100B back.

From the gleaming Ko Chang Centrepoint pier, at Km 4, Route 3156, Ko Chang Ferry (☎ 01-318 9789) runs four daily boat departures between 7 am and 4 pm. The trip takes 45 minutes and costs 70B per person, including the cost of a songthaew ride to one of the beaches. Centrepoint's vehicle ferry has an 18-car capacity; you'll pay 400B for vehicle and driver, plus 50B for each passenger.

A newer vehicle ferry service, Ferry Ko Chang (☎ 039-597143), leaves from a pier on Ao Thammachat at Km 10, Route 3156. This one leaves five times daily; because of the pier's position in relation to the island, and the craft's more powerful engines, the car ferry from Ao Thammachat reaches Ao

Sapparot in half an hour. It costs 500B for a vehicle and driver, plus 50B per passenger or pedestrian, to ride the Thammachat ferry. So far custom is for the most part restricted to people doing business on the island but in the future this service could very well supplant the Laem Ngop tourist ferry as well.

There are direct minivans from Th Khao San in Bangkok to Laem Ngop for 250B per person. Although it's no longer the case that the minivans necessarily miss the last boat to Ko Chang, it's better to take a regular bus, spend the night in Trat or Laem Ngop and take your time choosing a boat the next day. Or start out earlier in the day by government tour bus to Trat from Bangkok's Eastern bus terminal, then in Trat catch a songthaew to Laem Ngop in time for the afternoon boats.

Ko Mak During the November to May dry season, boats to Ko Mak leave daily from the Laem Ngop pier at 3 pm (8 am in the reverse direction); the fare is 170B per person and the trip takes around 3½ hours. During the rainy season the departure schedule is cut back to every other day – except in high surf when boats may be cancelled altogether for several days.

Coconut boats also go to Ko Mak from the pier near the slaughterhouse in Trat twice a month. The trip takes five hours and if you can get on (depends on whether they like you), the cost is around 125B per person.

Ko Kut Most people get to Ko Kut from Ko Mak, a 150B per person boat ride. There are regular boats to Ko Mak from Laem Ngop as previously mentioned.

Although it's a less dependable way to get there (but more adventurous for sure), two or three fishing boats a week go to Ko Kut from the pier of Tha Chaloemphon on the Trat River towards the east side of Trat. They'll take passengers for around 100B to 150B per person. Similar boats leave slightly less frequently (six to eight times a month) from Ban Nam Chiaw, a village about halfway between Trat and Laem Ngop. Departure frequency and times from either pier depend on the weather and the fishing season – it's best to inquire ahead of time. The boats take around six hours to reach Ko Kut.

Coconut boats go to Ko Kut once or twice a month from a pier next to the slaughterhouse in town – same fare and trip duration as the fishing boats.

If you want to charter a boat to Ko Kut from the mainland, the best place to do so is from Ban Ta Neuk, near Km 68 southeast of Trat, about 6km before Khlong Yai off Hwy 318. A longtail boat, capable of carrying up to 10 people, can be chartered here for 1200B. Travel time is about one hour. During the rainy season these boats may suspend service.

Other Islands Daily boats to **Ko Kham** depart from Laem Ngop around 3 pm (arriving at 6 pm) for 150B. A boat to **Ko Wai** leaves at 3 pm and arrives at 5.30 pm, costing 120B. Both boats return the next day at around 8 am.

Getting Around
To get from one part of Ko Chang to another you have a choice of songthaew, motorbike, mountain bike, boat and walking (see the earlier Walking on Ko Chang section).

Songthaew Songthaews meeting the boats at Ao Sapparot charge 30B per person to any beach along the west coast. Between Than Mayom and Ban Salak Phet, the local price is only 20B per person, though tourists may be charged more.

Motorcycle Bungalow operations along the west coast charge 60B per hour or 400B per day for motorbike hire; elsewhere on the island rental bikes are scarce. The owners claim they have to charge these rates because the island roads are so hard on the bikes.

Boat Charter trips to nearby islands average 500B to 800B for a half-day, 1000B to 2000B all day, depending on the boat and distances covered. Make sure that the charter includes all user 'fees' for the islands – sometimes the boatmen demand 200B on top of the charter fee for 'using' the beach.

On the southern end of the island, you can charter a longtail boat or fishing boat between Hat Kaibae and Ao Bang Bao for 1000B or around 150B per person shared by a boatful of passengers. Similar charters are available between Ao Bang Bao and Ao Salak Phet and Long Beach Bungalows for around 150B.

Boat rides up Khlong Phrao to the falls cost 50B per person and can be arranged through most bungalows.

AROUND TRAT PROVINCE
Trat Beaches

The sliver of Trat Province that extends south-eastward along the Cambodia border is fringed by several Gulf of Thailand beaches. Hat Sai Ngoen (Silver Sand Beach), lies just north of Km 41 off Hwy 3; a billboard says a resort will be constructed here, but so far there's no sign of development. Nearby at Km 42 is Hat Sai Kaew (Crystal Sand Beach) and at Km 48 Hat Thap Thim (Sapphire Beach); neither quite lives up to its fanciful name, though they're OK places to walk along the water's edge or picnic in the shade of casuarina and eucalyptus trees.

The most promising beach is Hat Ban Cheun, a very long stretch of clean sand near Km 63. The partially paved, 6km road (currently being upgraded) that leads to the beach passes the leftover foundation pillars from a defunct Cambodian refugee camp. There are the usual casuarina and eucalyptus trees, a small restaurant and four unattractive huts (200B) set on swampy land behind the beach. Camping on the beach would be a far better choice; you could also ask the restaurant owners to look after your valuables for you.

Khlong Yai

Khlong Yai consists of a cluster of older wooden buildings west of the highway, surrounded by modern structures on both sides of the highway. There's a large market in the centre of town, as well as the moderately

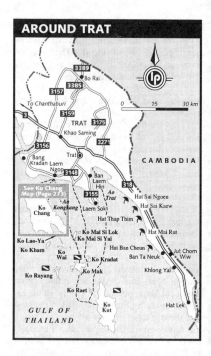

priced Suksamlan Hotel and two banks with foreign exchange services. Just south of town is a large shrimp farm.

An old-fashioned Thai-Chinese-style place, *Suksamlan Hotel* (☎ *039-581109, fax 581311)*, on a street between the market and the highway, offers rooms with fan from 120B, or 250/300B single/double with air-con. Out of town a bit off Hwy 3, *Bang In Villa (039-581401, fax 581403)* has nicer rooms, but with less character, for 150B to 250B.

See the Trat Getting There & Away section for information on public transport to Khlong Yai and Hat Lek.

Hat Lek to Cambodia

The small Thai border outpost of Hat Lek is the southern-most point on the Trat mainland. Untaxed goods ply back and forth between Cambodia and Thailand here; at the small market just before the border crossing itself, next to the pier for boats to Cambodia, American Budweiser beer and other untaxed contraband is often available. Opposite Hat Lek on Cambodian turf (Sao Thong) there's a cockfighting arena and casino, popular with residents from both sides of the border.

There are two military checkpoints along Hwy 3 between Trat town and Hat Lek. These are serious checkpoints where searches are common, especially since this area between Khlong Yai and Hat Lek was discovered to harbour a clandestine paramilitary force allegedly training to overthrow Vietnam's Communist government.

Small boats are available from Hat Lek to Pak Khlong on the island of Ko Kong (on the Cambodian side of the border) for 100B per person or 800B charter. If you plan to continue farther, you can take a passenger ferry from Pak Khlong to Sao Thong for 20B, then change to a speedboat for the three hour ride (500B per boat) to Sihanoukville. From there it's a three hour, 50B share taxi ride to Phnom Penh. You may also be able to catch the once-daily bus all the way to Phnom Penh. Baht are accepted for these fares.

A Cambodian visa is necessary, and obtainable in Bangkok, not at the border. As far as the Thai authorities are concerned

this is semi-illegal and while in Cambodia, you are technically in Thailand! You need to do the trip with a valid Thai visa on which you can return to Thailand. Some foreign expats in the Trat/Ko Chang area use the Trat-Cambodia route for Thai visa renewals – especially since most nationalities now automatically receive one month's visa on arrival in Thailand.

If this option is not available or you just feel like getting a taste of Cambodian border life, it's easy to visit Ko Kong, an island on the Cambodian side of the border, by boat as described above. Though not a particularly exciting destination in itself, Ko Kong is an important relay point for goods imported from Singapore into Cambodia, which is now Singapore's largest trade entrepôt in Indochina. Contact the Foremost or Windy guesthouses in Trat for the latest information about entering Cambodia.

Warning Travel into Cambodia is potentially dangerous and many embassies advise against it. You may like to check with your embassy in Thailand before making extensive plans for Cambodian travel. Although many Khmer Rouge have switched sides, the situation is still volatile with ongoing internal conflict as well as skirmishes between government and opposition forces.

North-Western Gulf Coast (Phetchaburi to Chumphon)

Heading south from Bangkok, the Gulf of Thailand's western coast undulates along the edges of four provinces (Samut Sakhon, Samut Songkhram, Phetchaburi and Prachuap Khiri Khan) in a south-westerly direction until it makes an abrupt turn to the north-east at the southern end of Chumphon Province, near Surat Thani. Just north of this point lies the Isthmus of Kra, the narrowest point, and official beginning of the Thai-Malay peninsula.

This coastal section has seen little exploration by foreign tourists. There isn't much in the way of beaches until you pass south of Phetchaburi to the low-key seaside resorts of Cha-am, Hua Hin and Chumphon. Away from these small but slowly growing areas, most of the countryside is agricultural and rural; pineapple-growing and fishing are the mainstays of the local population. In terms of everyday costs for food, lodging and public transport, this is one of Thailand's least expensive coastal areas to visit. But in many ways this stretch requires more initiative, since the most interesting shorelines aren't necessarily signposted. Nor do any guided tours or easy-to-book Bangkok minivans reach the majority of them.

PHETCHABURI (PHETBURI)
• pop 36,000
Phetchaburi (more commonly known by its short name Phet'buri, and sometimes Meuang Phet), 160km south of Bangkok, is worth a visit for its many old temples spanning several centuries; it's a nice cultural stopover on the way to beaches at Cha-am or Hua Hin a bit farther south. Six or seven temples can be seen while taking a circular walk of two or three hours through the city: Wat Yai Suwannaram, Wat Trailok, Wat Kamphaeng Laeng, Wat Phra Suang, Wat

BANGKOK

GULF OF THAILAND

ANDAMAN SEA

NORTH-WESTERN GULF COAST

RATCHABURI
Phetchaburi
To Bangkok
Hat Chao Samran
Hat Peuktian

PHETCHABURI
Phetchaburi Reservoir
KAENG KRACHAN NATIONAL PARK
Cha-am
GULF OF THAILAND
Hua Hin
Ko Singtoh
Khao Takiap
Khao Tao
Pranburi
Bang Pu
Pranburi Dam
PRACHUAP KHIRI KHAN
Kuiburi
Hat Laem Sala
KHAO SAM ROI YOT NATIONAL PARK
Ao Khan Kradai
Ao Noi
Prachuap Khiri Khan
Ao Prachuap
Ao Manao
Dan Singkhon
Huay Yang Falls
Ko Phing
Hat Wanakon
Ko Phang
Thap Sakae
Hat Laem Kum
Hat Sai Kaew
Ban Krut
Hat Baw Thawng Lang
Bang Saphan Yai
MYANMAR (BURMA)
Hat Sombun
Ao Bang Saphan
Ko Thalu
Bang Saphan Noi
Ko Sing
Ko Sang
Ko Wiang
GULF OF THAILAND
Tha Sae
Pathiu
Ao Baw Mao
Ao Thung Wua Laen
Ko Jarakhe
Ao Phanang Tak
Hat Pharadon Phap
Ko Ngam Yai & Ko Ngam Noi
Chumphon
Ko Samet
Ko Mattara
Pak Nam Chumphon
Ko Maphrao
CHUMPHON
Hat Sairi
Ao Sawi
Ko Rang Kachiu
To Ko Tao
Sawi
Tako Estuary
Hat Arunothai
RANONG
Lang Suan
ISTHMUS OF KRA
Hat Tawan Chai
Ranong
Hat Suan Son
To Phuket
Lamae
To Surat Thani

0   20   40 km

Ko Kaew Sutharam and Wat Mahathat. These temples have made very few concessions to the 20th century, let alone the 21st, and thus provide a glimpse of the traditional Siamese urban wát.

Also noteworthy is Khao Wang, just west of the city, which has the remains of a King Mongkut palace and several wáts, plus a good view of the city. The underground Buddhist shrine at the Khao Luang Caves is also worth seeing.

Orientation

If you arrive at the train station, follow the road along the south-eastern side of the tracks until you come to Thanon (Th) Ratchadamnoen, then turn right. Follow Th Ratchadamnoen south to the second major intersection, Th Chisa-in, and turn left towards central Phetchaburi to begin the walk. Or take a samlor from the train station to Chomrut Bridge (Saphaan Chomrut), for 20B. If you've come by bus, you'll be getting off very near Khao Wang, and will have to take a samlor into the centre of town.

Information

Money The Siam Commercial Bank has an exchange office at 2 Th Damnoen Kasem, just south of the post office. Several other banks in the vicinity have foreign exchange and ATMs.

Post & Telephone The post office, on the corner of Th Ratwithi and Th Damnoen Kasem is open from 8.30 am to 4.30 pm. Upstairs in the same building, an international telephone office is open daily from 7 am to 10 pm.

Khao Wang & Phra Nakhon Khiri Historical Park

Just west of the city, a short walk or samlor ride from the bus station, is Khao Wang. Cobblestone paths lead up and around the hill, which is studded with wáts and various components of King Mongkut's palace on Phra Nakhon Khiri (Holy City Hill). The views are great, especially

PHETCHABURI (PHETBURI)

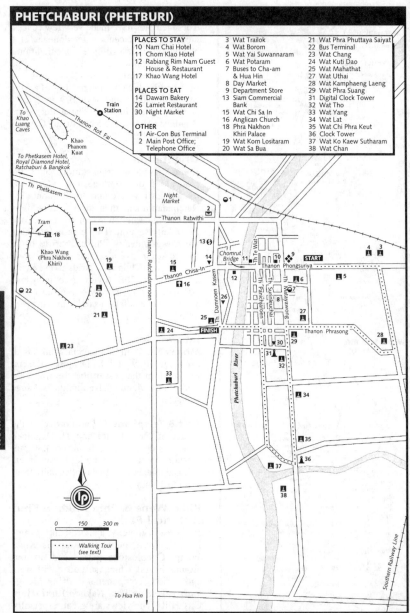

PLACES TO STAY
10 Nam Chai Hotel
11 Chom Klao Hotel
12 Rabiang Rim Nam Guest
      House & Restaurant
17 Khao Wang Hotel

PLACES TO EAT
14 Dawarn Bakery
26 Lamiet Restaurant
30 Night Market

OTHER
1 Air-Con Bus Terminal
2 Main Post Office;
    Telephone Office

3 Wat Trailok
4 Wat Borom
5 Wat Yai Suwannaram
6 Wat Potaram
7 Buses to Cha-am
    & Hua Hin
8 Day Market
9 Department Store
13 Siam Commercial
      Bank
15 Wat Chi Sa In
16 Anglican Church
18 Phra Nakhon
      Khiri Palace
19 Wat Kom Lositaram
20 Wat Sa Bua

21 Wat Phra Phuttaya Saiyat
22 Bus Terminal
23 Wat Chang
24 Wat Kuti Dao
25 Wat Mahathat
27 Wat Uthai
28 Wat Kamphaeng Laeng
29 Wat Phra Suang
31 Digital Clock Tower
32 Wat Tho
33 Wat Yang
34 Wat Lat
35 Wat Chi Phra Keut
36 Clock Tower
37 Wat Ko Kaew Sutharam
38 Wat Chan

Train Station

To Khao Luang Caves

Thanon Rot Fai

Khao Phanom Kuat

To Phetkasem Hotel, Royal Diamond Hotel, Ratchaburi & Bangkok

Th Phetkasem

Tram

■ 18

■ 17

Khao Wang (Phra Nakhon Khiri)

19

■ 20

● 22

21 ■

■ 23

Thanon Ratchadamnoen

Night Market

● 1

☎ 2

Thanon Ratwithi

13 ●

14

15 ■

Thanon Chisa-In

■ 16

Chomrut Bridge 11

12

Th Wat

10

9

START

Thanon Phongsuriya

Th Surindruchi

Th Panichanon

Th Matayawong

■ 5

6

27

26 ▼

8

■ 25

Th Damnoen Kasem

24

FINISH

Thanon Phrasong

29

30

28 ■

31 ■

32

33

Phetchaburi River

■ 34

■ 35

■ 36

37 ■

38

Southern Railway Line

0   150   300 m

······ Walking Tour (see text)

To Hua Hin

NORTH-WESTERN GULF COAST

Walking Tour – Phetchaburi Temples

Wat Yai Suwannaram

If you walk east from Chomrut Bridge along Th Phongsuriya about 300m past the Nam Chai Hotel on the left, you will see a big temple on the right. This is Wat Yai Suwannaram, originally built in the 17th century and renovated during the reign of King Chulalongkorn (1868-1910). The main *bòt* is surrounded by a cloister filled with sober Buddha images. The murals inside the *bòt* date to the 1730s and are in good condition. Next to the *bòt*, in the middle of a pond, is a beautifully designed old *haw trai*, or tripitaka library.

Wat Borom & Wat Trailok

These two *wáts* are next to one another on the opposite side of Th Phongsuriya from Wat Yai, a little to the east. They are distinctive for their monastic halls and long, graceful, wooden 'dormitories' on stilts.

Wat Kamphaeng Laeng

Turn right onto the road heading south from Wat Trailok and follow this road down, past a bamboo fence on the right, to the entrance of Wat Kamphaeng Laeng. This is a very old (13th century) Khmer site with five *prangs* and part of the original laterite wall (the literal meaning of *kamphaeng laeng*) still standing. The prang in front contains a Buddha footprint. Of the other four, two contain images dedicated to famous *lŭang phâw* (venerable elderly monks), one was in ruins (but is being restored) and the last has recently been uncovered from a mound of dirt. The Khmers built these as Hindu monuments, so the Buddhist symbols are late additions.

Wat Phra Suang & Wat Lat

Follow the road (Th Phrasong) beside Wat Kamphaeng Laeng, heading west back towards the river until you pass Wat Phra Suang on the left, undistinguished except for one very nice Ayuthaya-style *prasat*. Turn left immediately after this *wát*, heading south again until you come to the clock tower at the southern edge of town. You'll have passed Wat Lat on the left side of the street along the way, but it's not worth breaking your momentum for; this is a long walk.

Wat Ko Kaew Sutharam

Turn right at the clock tower and look for signs leading to the Ayuthaya-period Wat Ko. Two different sois on the left lead to the *wát*, which is behind the shops along the curving street. The *bòt* features early 18th century murals that are among the best conceived in Thailand. One mural panel depicts what appears to be a Jesuit priest wearing the robes of a Buddhist monk, while another shows other foreigners undergoing Buddhist conversions. There is also a large wooden monastic hall on stilts similar to the ones at Wat Borom and Wat Trailok, but in much better condition.

Wat Mahathat

Follow the street in front of Wat Ko north (back towards central Phetchaburi) and walk over the first bridge you come to on the left, which leads to Wat Mahathat. Alternatively, you can cross the river at Wat Ko, near the clock tower, and take the street on the other side of the river around to Wat Mahathat. The large white prang of this *wát* can be seen from a distance – a typical late Ayuthaya/early Ratanakosin adaptation of the Khmer prangs of Lopburi and Phimai. This is obviously an important temple in Phetchaburi, judging from all the activity here.

Joe Cummings

Phetchaburi Festival

The Phra Nakhon Khiri Fair takes place in early February and lasts about eight days. Centred around Khao Wang and the city's historic temples, the festivities include a sound-and-light show at the Phra Nakhon Khiri Palace, temples festooned with lights and performances of Thai classical dance-drama, *lákhon chatrii*, *lí-khe* and modern-style historical dramas. A twist on the usual beauty contest provides a showcase for Phetchaburi widows.

Joe Cummings

at sunset. The walk up looks easy but is fairly strenuous. Fat monkeys loll about in the trees and on top of the walls along the main paths. In 1988 Phra Nakhon Khiri was declared a national historical park, so there is now an entry fee of 40B. A tram has been installed to save you walking up to the peak (20B per person one way). The park is open Monday to Friday from 8 am to 5.30 pm and on weekends till 6 pm.

Khao Luang Caves

Five kilometres north of Phetchaburi is the cave sanctuary of Khao Luang (Great Hill). Concrete steps lead down into an anteroom, then into the main cavern, which is filled with old Buddha images, many of them put in place by King Mongkut (Rama IV). Two holes in the chamber ceiling spray sunlight on the images, which are a favourite subject for photographers. To the rear of the main cavern is an entrance to a third, smaller chamber. On the right of the entrance is Wat Bunthawi, with a *sala* (open-sided shelter) designed by the abbot and a *bòt* with impressively carved wooden door panels.

Admission to the caves is free (though donations are accepted). A samlor from the city centre to Khao Luang costs 50B, a motorcycle taxi 25B to 30B.

Places to Stay

On the eastern side of Chomrut Bridge, on the right bank of Phetchaburi River, is *Chom Klao Hotel* (☎ 032-425398), an ordinary, fairly clean Chinese hotel with friendly staff. It costs 120B for a room with fan and shared bathroom, or 150B with private bath.

The *Nam Chai Hotel* (no roman-script sign) is a block farther east from the Chom Klao Hotel, and has rooms for 120B with shared bathroom, 150B with private bath, but is not as good value as the Chom Klao.

Better still is the relatively new *Rabieng Rim Nam Guest House* (☎/fax 032-425707, 1 Th Chisa-In), attached to the restaurant of the same name. Cosy rooms with fan and clean shared bathroom cost 120B per person.

Khao Wang Hotel (☎ 032-425167), opposite Khao Wang, used to be a favourite in Phetchaburi, but the rooms have gone downhill a bit in recent years. A fairly clean room with fan and bath costs 210/310B for one/two beds. Air-con rooms are 310/550B. Most rooms have TV.

The best hotel value in town is the friendly and clean *Phetkasem Hotel* (☎ 032-425581, 86/1 Th Phetkasem), which is on Highway (Hwy) 4, on the western edge of town near the highway bus stop. Rooms cost 250B with fan and private bath, 300B with air-con and 450B with hot water. Nearby *Royal Diamond* (☎ 032-428272, 555 Muu 1, Th Phetkasem) is more upscale with 60 air-con rooms in the 700B to 1500B range.

Places to Eat

Local dishes for which Phetchaburi is famous include *khanõm jiin thawt man* (thin noodles with fried spicy fish cake), *khâo châe phêtburii* (moist chilled rice served with sweetmeats, a hot season speciality) and *khanõm mâw kaeng* (egg custard). You'll find these dishes, along with a range of standard Thai and Chinese dishes, at several good restaurants in the Khao Wang area. A variety of cheap eats is available at the *night market* at the southern end of Th Surinleuchai, under the digital clock tower. Another very good *night market* sets up along Th Rot Fai between the train station and the town centre.

Other good eating places can be found in the town centre along the main street to the clock tower. Across from Wat Mahathat, *Lamiet* sells really good khanŏm mâw kaeng and *fãwy thawng* (sweet shredded egg yolk) – which they also ship to Bangkok. This shop also has a branch near Khao Wang, where a whole group of *egg custard places* serve tourists.

The *Rabieng Rim Nam*, on the south side of Th Chisa-In near Chomrut Bridge, features a Thai and English menu of over 100 items, including seafood and 30 kinds of *yam*; most non-seafood dishes cost around 25B to 50B, seafood and some soups 70B or more.

Dawarn Bakery at the corner of Th Chisa-In and Th Damnoen Kasem offers a decent assortment of baked goods.

Getting There & Away

Bus From Bangkok, buses leave regularly from the Southern bus terminal in Thonburi for 50B (ordinary) on the new road, 46B on the old road (via Ratchaburi and Nakhon Pathom), 60B for 2nd class air-con and 75B for 1st class air-con. The bus takes about 2½ hours.

Buses to Phetchaburi from Cha-am and Hua Hin are 18B (25B air-con) and 22B (31 air-con) and take 60 and 90 minutes respectively. Other ordinary bus fares are: Ratchaburi 18B (45 minutes), Nakhon Pathom 29B (two hours), Prachuap Khiri Khan 40B (three hours) and Phuket 210B ordinary, 304B air-con (12 hours). The main bus terminal in Phetchaburi is just south-west of Khao Wang. The terminal for air-con buses is near the intersection of Th Damnoen Kasem and Th Rot Fai. Ordinary buses to and from Cha-am and Hua Hin stop on Th Matayawong.

Train Trains leave Bangkok's Hualamphong station at 12.20 pm (rapid), 2.15 and 2.35 pm (special express), 3.50, 5.35 and 6.20 pm (rapid), 7.15 pm (express), and 10.30 and 10.50 pm (express diesel railcar). All of these trains offer 1st, 2nd and 3rd class seat-

ing except for the 3.15 pm special express (1st and 2nd class only) and the 10.30 and 10.50 pm express diesel railcar (2nd class only), and take about three hours to reach Phetchaburi. Fares are 34B, 78B and 153B, not including rapid or express surcharges. The bus is faster, unless you count getting out to Bangkok's southern bus terminal.

There is no longer an ordinary train between Hualamphong and Phetchaburi, but there are still three ordinary 3rd class trains daily from Thonburi (Bangkok Noi) station at 7.45 am and 1.30 and 2 pm (34B, no surcharges).

Getting Around

Samlors go anywhere in the town centre for 20B; you can charter one for the whole day for 150B. Share mini-songthaews cost 6B around town, including to and from the train station.

CHA-AM
• pop 22,700

A tiny town 178km from Bangkok, 38km from Phetchaburi and 25km from Hua Hin, Cha-am is known for its long, casuarina-lined beach, good seafood and, on weekends and school holidays, its party atmosphere which attracts large numbers of Thai students; during the week the beach is virtually deserted.

Like Ko Samet in the Eastern Gulf, Cha-am tends to stay relatively dry during the south-west monsoon compared with almost any other beach destination in Thailand. It receives virtually no rain during the north-east monsoon and is a particularly popular retreat for Bangkokians during the hot, dry months of March, April and May.

Beach umbrellas and sling chairs are available for hire. The emergence of jet-skis is a definite detraction but they are not that common yet; if the local tourism promoters want to lure visitors away from fast-developing Hua Hin, the first thing they should do is get rid of the jet-skis. There are public bathhouses where you can bathe in fresh water for 5B to 7B.

Near the beach there's not much of a town to speak of – the old centre is on the opposite side of Phetkasem Hwy, where you'll find the post office, market, train station and government offices. Inland from the beach (follow the signs) at **Wat Neranchararama** is a fat, white, six-armed Buddha statue; the six hands cover the nine bodily orifices in a symbolic gesture denying the senses.

Information

Tourist Office On Phetkasem Hwy, just 500m south of town, a helpful TAT office (☎ 032-471502) distributes information on Cha-am, Phetchaburi and Hua Hin. The office is open daily from 8.30 am to 4.30 pm.

Money Several banks maintain foreign exchange booths along the beach strip, typically open 10 am to 8 pm. In the town centre, west of Hwy 4, are a number of banks with foreign exchange services and ATMs.

Post There is a post office on the main beach strip. It's open Monday to Friday from 8:30 am to 4:30 pm and on Saturday from 9 am to noon.

Telephone International telephone services are available at the post office.

Email & Internet Access Peggy's Pub (see Places to Eat) offers pay-as-you-go email and Internet services.

Places to Stay – Budget & Mid-Range

Hat Cha-am has three basic types of accommodation: charming, old-style, spacious wooden beach bungalows on stilts, set back from the road; tacky apartment-style hotels built from cheap materials with faulty plumbing, right on the beach road; and more expensive 'condotel' developments. New places are going up all the time at the northern and southern ends of town. Expect a 20 to 50% discount on posted rates on weekdays, except during Chinese New Year (February or March) and Thai New Year (mid-April).

Th Narathip is the main road leading to the beach area from the highway.

South of Th Narathip Near the air-con bus terminal a couple of *guesthouses* which change name from time to time can be found in a row of modern shophouses similar to the scourge of Pattaya, Hua Hin and Phuket's Hat Patong – they all look the same. Rooms run from 300B with fan and shared bathroom to 500B with air-con.

South of the air-con bus terminal, the *Anantachai Guest House* (☎ 032-471980) has nice rooms with a beach view, air-con, TV, private shower and toilet for 400B to 600B. They also provide information about the area and have a cheap Thai restaurant. *Savitree Resort* (☎ 032-434088, 01-931 3638), next door, offers rooms with air-con and TV in semi-detached brick bungalows for 500B.

Moving south, slightly cheaper rooms are available at *Cha-am Guest House* (☎ 032-433401), where clean air-con rooms with TV cost 350B to 450B.

A long-time favourite is *Santisuk Bungalows & Beach Resort* (☎ 032-471212, Bangkok ☎ 02-298 0532) with both early Cha-am-style wooden cottages and a newer, equally tasteful section. A room in a hotel-style section with private bath is 300B with fan, 400B air-con. Larger two-bedroom cottages with fan, bath and sitting area are 1500B, 2000B with air-con. It's 3000B for places with three bedrooms and two baths. The *Nirandorn Resort* (☎ 032-471893) has similar cottages for 300B with fan, 500B with air-con, TV and hot water.

Saeng Thong Condominiums (☎ 032-471466) costs 500B to 1100B per night, less in the rainy season. All rooms have TV and air-con. *Sea Pearl Hotel* (☎ 032-471118), formerly White Hotel, is an apartment-style place, with rates of 400B for a fan room with private bath, 500B to 600B with air-con, 700B for larger rooms with carpet, tub and TV.

JJ House (☎ 032-471231) and *Somkheat Villa* (☎ 032-471834, fax 471229) are adjacent apartment-style hotels with rooms

JOHN HAY

fisherman repairs his nets at Hua Hin, North-Western Gulf Coast.

CHRIS MELLOR

askets of fish harvested from the Gulf of Thailand, Hua Hin.

JOHN HAY

Football on the beach at Hua Hin, North-Western Gulf Coast.

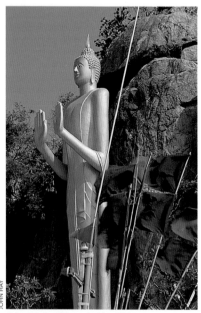

JOHN HAY

A temple by the sea in Hua Hin.

RICHARD NEBESKY

A colourfully decorated truck in Chumphon.

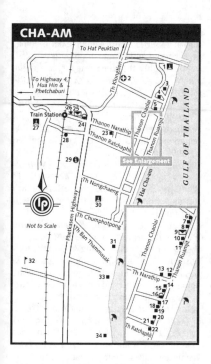

CHA-AM

PLACES TO STAY
3 Long Beach Cha-am Hotel
4 Cha-am Methavalai Hotel
5 Kaen-Chan Hotel
6 Rua Makam Villa
7 Jolly & Jumper
8 Thiptari Place
10 Cha-am Villa
11 Jitravee Resort
12 JJ Guesthouse
13 Somkheat Villa
14 Nirandorn Resort
15 Saeng Thong Condominiums
17 Savitree Resort
18 Anantachai Guest House
19 Cha-am Guest House
20 Sea Pearl Hotel
21 Viwathana Bungalows
22 Santisuk Bungalows & Beach Resort
23 Inthira Plaza
31 Springfield Beach Resort
33 Regent Cha-am Beach Resort
34 Dusit Resort & Polo Club

OTHER
1 Wat Neranchararama
2 Hospital
9 Post Office
16 Air-con Bus Terminal
24 Bus Station
25 Post Office
26 Police Station
27 Wat Cha-am Khiri
28 Market
29 TAT Office
30 Wat Nong Chaeng
32 Springfield Beach Resort Golf Course

from 300B to 600B at the former, and from 400B to 600B at the latter.

Naluman Bungalows (☎ 032-471440) is an old-style place with large bungalows that can sleep 10 to 12 people in three bedrooms. None have a sea view, but all have a big sink and shower outside as well as a toilet inside, TV and a large porch and carport. Fan-cooled bungalows cost 1200B while bungalows with air-con and a fridge cost 1700B.

Nipon Resort (☎ 032-433193) offers rooms in a main hotel-like building for 800B with TV, air and hot water. Bungalows with fan go for 300B or with air-con 800B, but these do not have TVs. The air-con bungalows can sleep up to four people.

Viwathana Bungalows (☎ 032-471289, Bangkok ☎ 02-243 3646) are more old-style, but not as well kept as some of the others; 500B with fan or 700B with air-con.

North of Th Narathip *Thiptari Place* (☎/fax 032-471879) is fairly reasonable, with air-con rooms from 800B to 1200B, about 40% less on weekdays. Farther up, *Rua Makam Villa* (☎ 032-471073) has old-style wood and concrete cottages, spacious and off the road, for 500/1000B single/double with fan, 1200/2400B air-con. The friendly *Kaen-Chan Hotel* (☎ 032-471314) has a variety of accommodation – bungalows are 200B with fan, 300B with air-con; air-con rooms in the hotel are 600B to 800B. There is a pool on the 6th floor, though it was closed when we visited.

The next cheapest places are the *Jitravee Resort* (☎ 032-471382) and the *Cha-am*

Villa (☎ *032-471124*); both offer rooms ranging from 300B to 600B. Better value yet is *Prathonchok House* (☎ *032-471215*), clean fan rooms with shared facilities are 150B to 200B (250B with private bath, 300B with TV), air-con rooms with private bath are 300B and fancier air-con rooms with TV and fridge are 400B.

Top House (☎ *032-433307*) is a big place with a sign downstairs that says 'International Beverage Mix Bar'. Rooms are 400B to 600B with fan and private bath, 800B to 1200B with air-con, TV and hot water. Discounts up to 50% are available during the week. *Jolly & Jumper* (☎ *032-433887, 274/3 Th Ruamjit*), operated by a Dutch couple, has fan rooms for 150B to 250B, plus air-con rooms for 300B to 500B.

Happy Home has older-style cement cottages from 300B with fan, and from 400B with air-con and TV. At the northern end of the beach are the closely clustered bungalows of *Paradise Bungalow*, which cost 600B with air-con and TV.

Inthira Plaza This complex off Th Narathip is striving to become a Pattaya-style bar centre ('entertainment centre' in the jargon of the moment). Apartment-style rooms upstairs at a couple of the bars are 250B to 300B with fan and private bath, 350B to 400B with air-con. They could be noisy at night.

Places to Stay – Top End
Many places in Cha-am call themselves 'resorts' but only two places in the central area come close to the term. First is *Cha-am Methavalai Hotel* (☎ *032-433250, fax 471590*), which has well kept, modern rooms with flowers spilling from every balcony, plus a pool (available to non-guests from 7 am to 7 pm for 50B) and a small private beach area. Walk-in rates (ie if you don't book in advance) are 2500B to 2950B including tax, but during the week an automatic 50% discount applies and you can sometimes get a 30% discount even on weekends unless it's a major holiday.

In the towering *Mark-Land Hotel* (☎ *032-433833, fax 433834*), next door to Happy Home on Th Ruamjit, large, luxurious rooms start at 2360B. Facilities include pool, sauna, fitness room and various food outlets.

For roughly the same price, *Gems Cha-am* (☎ *032-434060, fax 434002*) is a resort-style hotel in which all rooms have ocean views and all the amenities, from satellite TV to IDD phones. There's also a business centre on the premises. Rates start at 2700B per room, plus tax and service, discounted by 50% on weekdays.

Long Beach Cha-am Hotel (☎ *032-472442, fax 472287, Bangkok* ☎ *02241 3897, fax 241 3995*), nearby, offers luxury rooms starting at 1573B, though the 'official' rate is 3000B.

South of town a bit, *Regent Cha-am Beach Resort* (☎ *032-471480/91, fax 471491*) has rooms starting at 3000B; they advertise a 30 to 40% discount for weekdays. Facilities include a swimming pool, squash and tennis courts and a fitness centre.

Also on the beach, south of town, is the posh *Dusit Resort & Polo Club* (☎ *032-520009, fax 520296, email polo@dusit.com*), where rates start at 3872B. The Dusit has a fitness centre, mini-golf, horse riding, pool, tennis and squash courts and, of course, polo.

Springfield Beach Resort (☎ *032-451181, fax 451194, Bangkok* ☎ *02-231 2244, fax 231 2249*), south of town at Km 210 off Phetkasem Hwy, is a newer luxury hotel. All rooms and suites have sea views, balconies, phones, air-con, refrigerators, electronic safe boxes, long bathtubs and hair dryers. Rates start at 3000B and go up to 6000B for a family room. On the premises are a terrace coffee shop overlooking the ocean, swimming pool and jacuzzi, tennis court, putting green, exercise room, sauna, steam room and karaoke. Across the highway the resort has a 10-hole Jack Nicklaus-designed golf course.

Places to Eat
Opposite the beach are several good seafood restaurants, which, unlike the bungalows, are reasonably priced. Vendors on the beach sell all manner of barbecued and fried seafood.

Moderately priced **Khan Had Restaurant** has an extensive menu of Thai, Chinese and seafood dishes. **Anantachai Guest House** is a good place for inexpensive to moderately priced Thai and seafood dishes, while the **Jolly & Jumper** does reasonable western food. **Peggy's Pub** on the same soi leading down to the Long Beach Cha-am Hotel serves Thai and Scandinavian dishes.

The luxury hotels have generally fine Thai, seafood and western cuisine at the standard hotel prices. Seafood and Thai cuisine are especially good at the Methavalai Hotel's **Sorndaeng Restaurant**, a branch of the famous Bangkok restaurant of the same name.

Getting There & Away
Buses from Phetchaburi cost 20B. From Hua Hin, take a Phetchaburi-bound bus and ask to be let off at Hat Cha-am (Cha-am Beach); the fare is 10B.

Ordinary buses from Bangkok's Southern bus terminal (Thonburi) to Cha-am cost 55B (101B air-con). In Cha-am ordinary buses stop on Phetkasem Hwy, from where you can take a motorbike-taxi (10B) or a share-taxi (5B) out to the beach. A few hundred metres south of the corner of Th Narathip and Th Ruamjit, a private bus company operates six daily air-con buses to Bangkok for 83B.

The train station is on Th Narathip, west of Phetkasem Hwy and a 20B motorcycle ride to/from the beach. There's only one train from Hualamphong station, the rapid No 43 at 3.50 pm. The train is slower than the bus by one hour (taking about four hours) and costs 40B 3rd class. First and 2nd class seats are also available on the No 43 for 183B and 91B respectively. There is also one 3rd class departure from the Sam Saen station in Bangkok at 9.25 am, and three departures from Thonburi's Bangkok Noi station, at 7 am and 1.05 and 7.15 pm. Cha-am isn't even listed on the English language train schedule.

Getting Around
Standard prices for motorbike taxis and public songthaews are 20B and 10B (40B to

charter) respectively. You can also rent motorcycles yourself for 200B to 300B a day.

Avis Rent-A-Car (☎ 032-520008) operates out of the Dusit Resort & Polo Club Hotel.

AROUND CHA-AM
Hat Peuktian
This sandy beach between Cha-am and Phetchaburi has the usual casuarina trees and food vendors favoured by Thai beach-goers, and hardly in faràng in sight. Three rocky islets are within wading distance of shore, one with a sala for shade. Standing knee-deep just offshore is a 6m-high statue of Phi Seua Samut, the undersea female deity that terrorised the protagonist of the Thai classical epic *Phra Aphaimani*. A statue of the prince playing a flute sits on a nearby rock.

A tasteless two storey townhouse-style development has been built off the beach. Designed in the pseudo-classical style prevalent in modern city blocks all over Thailand, it looks rather incongruous with the natural beach surroundings.

HUA HIN
• pop 35,500
The beaches of Hua Hin first came to the country's attention in 1922, when King Rama VI's royal architect MJ Ithithepsan Kreudakon constructed Phra Ratchawong Klai Kangwon, a seafront summer palace of golden teak just north of what was then a small fishing village. Rama VII learned of Thailand's first coup d'état in 1932 while playing golf at the Royal Hua Hin Golf Course. Once endorsed by the royal family, Hua Hin remained a traditional favourite among the Thais long after the beaches of Pattaya and Phuket had been taken over by foreign tourists. The palace is still used by the royal family occasionally.

Hua Hin's 5km-long sand beach is studded with large, smooth boulders, enough to give the beach a scenic appeal but not enough to hinder swimming. The surf is safe for swimming year-round, although jellyfish are an occasional problem during

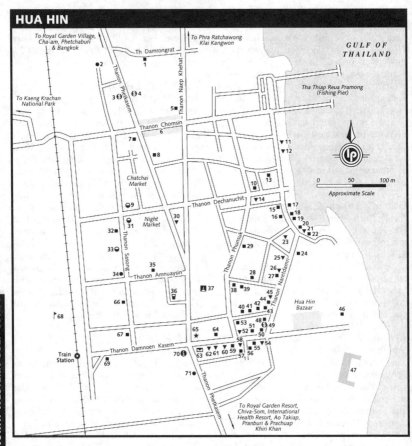

HUA HIN

To Royal Garden Village,
Cha-am, Phetchaburi
& Bangkok

To Phra Ratchawong
Klai Kangwon

GULF OF
THAILAND

Th Damrongrat

Thanon Naep Khehat

Thanon Phetkasem

To Kaeng Krachan
National Park

Tha Thiap Reua Pramong
(Fishing Pier)

Thanon Chomsin

Chatchai
Market

Thanon Dechanuchit

0   50   100 m
Approximate Scale

Night
Market

Thanon Sasong

Thanon Phunuk

Thanon Naretdamri

Thanon Amnuaysin

Hua Hin
Bazaar

Thanon Damnoen Kasem

Train
Station

Thanon Phetkasem

To Royal Garden Resort,
Chiva-Som, International
Health Resort, Ao Takiap,
Pranburi & Prachuap
Khiri Khan

the rainy season (May to October). Water sports are limited to sailing and jet-skiing. Overall Hua Hin is still a fairly quiet, economical place to get away from it all, and is less than four hours by train from Bangkok.

Hua Hin, like Cha-am, has traditionally been the domain of domestic beach tourism. The renovation of the colonial-style, 1923-vintage Hua Hin Railway Beach Hotel (now the Hotel Sofitel Central Hua Hin) by a major French hotel group in the late 80s attracted overseas attention. Now a number of

cafes and bistros offer Spanish, French, Italian and German cuisine to an older polyglot bunch enjoying two-week Thai beach holidays at bargain rates.

Perhaps the major sign that Hua Hin has arrived on the international beach scene was the arrival of a high-rise property belonging to Spain's Meliá hotel chain. Still, most visitors – Thai or foreign – stay at the numerous smaller hotels, inns and guesthouses located a couple of blocks east of the beach. There is accommodation for every budget,

HUA HIN

PLACES TO STAY

1	Thanachai Hotel
5	Phananchai Hotel
7	Damrong Hotel
8	Chaat Chai Hotel
10	All Nations; All Nations Bar
13	Pattana Guest House
15	Memory Guest House
16	Fulay Guest House
17	Rom Ruen Guest House; Piaf
18	Fulay on the Sea
19	Ketsarin Guest House & Restaurant
20	Seabreeze (Sirima); Mod (Mot) Guest House
22	Bird
24	Meliá Hua Hin
27	Fresh Inn
28	Relax Guest House
29	Sand Inn
32	Siripetchkasem (Siri Phetkasem) Hotel
35	Subhamitra (Suphamit) Hotel
38	Sukvilay Guest House
39	Ban Pak Hua Hin
40	Information Guest House
41	Maple Leaf

42	Usaah; MP
43	Som Waan Guest House
44	Europa; Sunee Guest House
46	Mercure Resort Hua Hin
47	Hotel Sofitel Central Hua Hin
48	Parichart Guest House; Khun Daeng's House
50	Thai Tae (Thae) Guest House
51	Sirin Hotel
53	Ban Boosarin
55	Puangpen Villa Hotel; PP Villa Guest House
56	Patchara House
57	Ban Somboon
59	Jed Pee Nong Hotel
64	City Beach Resort
66	Silapetch Hotel
67	Srichan Hua Hin Hotel
69	Golf Inn

PLACES TO EAT

6	Night Market
11	Seafood Restaurants
12	Le Chablis
14	Fa Mui
21	Taj Mahal
23	Nice Restaurant

25	Sunshine Restaurant & Bakery
26	Lo Stivale
30	Kuang Seng; Thara Jan
45	Headrock Cafe
52	La Villa
54	Lucky Restaurant
58	Gee Cuisine; Stone Town
60	Buffalo Bill's Steak & Grill
61	Capo's; Al Fresco
62	Italian Ice Cream

OTHER

2	Cinema
3	Thai Farmers Bank
4	Bank of Ayudhya
9	Bus Terminal
31	Songthaews to Ao Takiap
33	Pran Tour
34	Top Center Supermarket
36	Hurricane Pub
37	Wat Hua Hin
49	Bank of Ayudhya
63	Main Post Office; CAT Office
65	Police
68	Royal Hua Hin Golf Course
70	Municipal Office
71	Bangkok Airways

and the area now attracts a mix of Thais and older faràng tourists seeking a comfortable beach holiday close to Bangkok without the sleaziness of Pattaya.

Unfortunately, Hua Hin hasn't been totally spared Pattaya-style development. You'll see a lot of the same kind of cheap, unsightly shophouse-apartment buildings with bad plumbing as in Pattaya and Phuket's Hat Patong, as well as the relatively recent invasion of girlie bars. Hua Hin has for the most part lost its fishing-village atmosphere – the fishing fleet is being moved out and the town's infamous squid-drying piers have been replaced by hotels.

On the bright side, a sewage treatment plant and municipal sewer system are functioning and the beach is cleaner than ever. The main swimming beach still has thatched umbrellas and long chairs; vendors from the nearby food stalls will bring loungers steamed crab, mussels, beer etc and there are pony rides for the kids. The Hotel Sofitel Central Hua Hin has successfully campaigned to have the vendors removed from the beach fronting the hotel – a minus for atmosphere but a plus for cleanliness. Vendors are now restricted to a small area near the public entrance to the beach, and to another short string south of the Sofitel. Beer, soft drinks and seafood are reasonably cheap and umbrellas and sling chairs are free if you order food.

Information

Tourist Office Tourist information on Hua Hin and the surrounding area is available at the municipal office (☎ 032-511047, 532433) on the corner of Th Phetkasem and Th Damnoen Kasem, about 200m east of the train station. Its brochure *Welcome to Hua Hin* contains a lot of useful info on hotels, restaurants and transport. It's open daily from 8.30 am to 4.30 pm.

An expat-published newsletter, The *Hua Hin Observer*, contains snippets on food, culture and entertainment, as well as short features in English (and a few in German). Its distributed free at hotels, restaurants and bars frequented by tourists.

Money There are several banks around town. Most convenient to the beach is the Bank of Ayudhya's exchange booth on Th Naretdamri, near the corner of Th Damnoen Kasem.

Post The post office is on Th Damnoen Kasem near the corner of Th Phetkasem.

Telephone The CAT office, attached to the Th Damnoen Kasem post office, offers Home Direct international phone service daily from 8 am to midnight.

Email & Internet Access All Nations (email gary@infonews.co.th), see Places to Stay – Budget, has the only cyber cafe in town so far, though doubtless others will soon follow.

Beaches
Th Damnoen Kasem leads east directly from the train station to the main beach, which runs about 2km along the southern half of town. The nicest stretch of sand lies in front of the Sofitel. Smooth granite boulders – source of the town's name, which means 'Stone Head' – pierce the surfline.

Eight to 13km south of Hua Hin along Ao Takiap (Chopsticks Bay) are the beaches of **Hat Khao Takiap**, **Hat Suan Son** and **Hat Khao Tao**, all of which are undergoing resort development. Two hilltop temples can be visited here. **Wat Khao Thairalat** is well off the beach on a rocky hill and is nothing special. At the end of the bay is the more-well-endowed **Wat Khao Takiap**; climb the steps for a good bay view.

The southern end of Ao Takiap is now one big construction site as one high-rise after another goes up, blocking the sea view from all points inland. North along the bay, however, are several quiet, wooded spots with cabins and beach houses.

If you're driving, the turn-off for Ao Takiap is 4km south of Hua Hin. Regular songthaews go back and forth from town.

Places to Stay – Budget
Prices are moving up quickly for places near the beach. Hotels in town are still reasonably priced and it's only a five or 10 minute walk to the beach from most of them.

Guesthouses Near – but not on – the beach, the cheapest places are found along or just off Th Naretdamri. A room glut has kept rates low. Several small hotels and guesthouses in this area have rooms for 150B to 200B a night with fan and private bath, 300B to 500B with air-con. Next to the more top-end Sirin Hotel on Th Damnoen Kasem, the *Thai Tae (Thae) Guest House* offers rooms with fan and bath for 200B, air-con for 450B. Rooms at *Khun Daeng's House* on Th Naretdamri cost 100B with shared bathroom, 150B with private bath. *Parichart Guest House* (☎ 032-513863), next to Khun Daeng's, is a slightly more up-market, modern, multi-storey place with rooms for 150B with fan and private bath, 250B to 500B with air-con; rates increase in the high season.

Europa (☎ 032-513235) at No 158, on the next block north, has rooms over a clothing shop for 150B with private bath. *Sunee Guest House*, next door, is an old wooden building with rooms for 150B with shared bathroom.

Along Soi Kanjanomai, off Th Naretdamri just north of Th Damnoen Kasem, is the comfortable-looking *Information Guest House* (☎ 032-533757), which seems to change owners every year or two. Rooms cost 120B to 200B, some with private bath. On the same soi are the similar *Maple Leaf, Usaah* and *MP* guesthouses, all with small rooms in the 100B to 200B range. The Usaah has a bar downstairs which is open till 2 am so is likely to be noisy till then. *Som-Waan Guest House* on the same soi has basic but clean rooms upstairs, 100B with fan and private toilet during slow times, 250B in the high season; air-con rooms go for 250B to 450B depending on the season.

Along the next soi off Th Naretdamri to the north are a string of guesthouses in old wooden buildings with some charm. Unfortunately the soi has become something of a bar scene, complete with freelance Thai hookers, so can no longer be recommended for anyone wanting a good night's sleep. *Relax Guest House* (☎ 032-513585), down an alley just before Phuen, charges 150/200B single/double for four medium-size rooms with fan and bath in a private home. Farther along is the similar looking *Sukvilay Guest House*, where quiet fan rooms cost 150B to 200B, air-con rooms with hot showers 350B to 400B; it's a bit more respectable than others on this soi. A little to the east on this soi is the modern, apartment-style *Ban Pak Hua Hin* (☎ 032-511653, fax 533649); it's quiet, exceptionally clean, and costs 200B with fan and private bath, 300B with air-con.

Farther up Th Naretdamri, where the old squid piers used to be, are a string of wooden motel-like places built on piers over the edge of the sea. *Mod (Mot) Guest House* has rather small but otherwise OK fan rooms for 200B (up to 650B for a large room with a sea view), rooms with one bed, air-con and TV for 550B, and a three-bed room with TV and fridge for 1500B. Next-door, *Seabreeze (Sirima; ☎ 032-511060)* costs 200B for fan rooms, while air-con room rates range from 550B to 750B, depending on size and amenities. In the same area, *Rom Ruen Guest House* has small but clean rooms for 200B with fan, 400B air-con. A new place over the water, *Fulay on the Sea* is very clean and features a nicely constructed pier complete with Thai-style gazebos. Rooms with fan start at 200B, while air-con rooms cost 600B to 900B, or 750B to 950B in the high season. One problem here is that during low tide the exposed beach beneath the piers emits a terrible smell, probably arising from inadequate waste disposal.

A little south-east of here, up a soi that leads toward the beach, *Bird* (☎ 032-511630) is the best of the seaside guesthouses; it's well kept, well designed and charges 300B to 500B a double. In the op-

posite direction is the rather motel-like *Ketsarin Guest House* (☎ 032-511339), which combines the pier-style guesthouse business with a seafood restaurant, as do others nearby. Ketsarin offers fan or air-con rooms ranging from 250B to 700B.

Pattana Guest House (☎ 032-513393, fax 530081, email adrianus@prachuab1 .anet.net.th, 52 Th Naretdamri), farther north along an alley off Naretdamri, has comfortable fan rooms in two wooden houses from 200B. A bar and restaurant are on the premises.

Farther south along Th Naretdamri on the same side of the street, in a long two storey white building, is *Memory Guest House* (☎ 032-511816). It's super-clean and has a locked entrance gate; rates start at 200B. Nearby *Fulay Guest House* (same owners as Fulay on the Sea) offers large, comfortable rooms with air-con, cable TV, fridge and balcony for 750B.

West off Th Naretdamri on Th Dechanuchit (east of Th Phunsuk), over an expat-managed pub, is the friendly and clean *All Nations* (☎ 032-512747, fax 530474, email gary@infonews.co.th), where rooms cost 130B to 150B depending on the size. Each room in the tall, narrow building comes with its own balcony and fan; each floor has a bathroom shared by two or three rooms. This guesthouse features Hua Hin's first Internet cafe.

Hotels To find hotels under 300B, you'll have to go up to Th Phetkasem, the main north-south road through town. Starting at rock bottom, the decaying, Thai-Chinese-style *Chaat Chai Hotel (59/1 Th Phetkasem)* has rooms with fan and private bath for 150B to 220B. Just past the Chatchai Market is the *Damrong Hotel* (☎ 032-511574, 46 Th Phetkasem), where rooms with fan and private bath are 150B, 300B with air-con; like the Chaat Chai, this one's fading fast.

Just off Phetkasem, behind the bank, is the considerably nicer *Subhamitra (Suphamit) Hotel* (☎ 032-511208, fax 511508) where very clean rooms with fan and bath start at 250/300B single/double, 450B single/double to 800B triple with aircon; a little more with TV or fridge. There's a pool on the premises. Behind the Chatchai Market area on Th Sasong, the *Siripetchkasem (Siri Phetkasem) Hotel* (☎ 032-511394, fax 511464) is similar to the hotels along Th Phetkasem. Rooms with fan are 300B and air-con rooms with TV are 400B. South of here on the same side of Th Sasong, the *Silapetch Hotel* (☎ 032-530404, 01-452 0478) and *Srichan Hua Hin Hotel* (☎ 032-513130) charge 500B to 600B for rooms with carpet and air-con – a bit overpriced for this location.

Sand Inn (☎ 032-533667, fax 533669, 38-38/4 Th Phunsuk) stands along a stretch of Th Phunsuk, between Th Damnoen Kasem and Th Dechanuchit – look for lush plants hanging over the front wall. Spacious fan rooms with TV, phone and hot water rent for 400B, while the same with air-con cost 500B; attached are a restaurant and coffee shop.

Finally, north at 11 Th Damrongrat, is *Thanachai Hotel* (☎ 032-511755), an upper budget place for 250B with fan and bath, 450B for air-con. It's a bit far from the centre if you're on foot. The Thanachai accepts credit cards.

Places to Stay – Mid-Range

Hua Hin's mid-range places are typically small, sedate, modern hotels with air-con rooms and such luxuries as telephones. *Ban Boosarin* (☎ 032-512076), the forerunner of this trend, is near the corner of Th Phunsuk and Th Damnoen Kasem. It calls itself a 'mini-deluxe hotel' and although it's 950B a night (discounted to 800B in the low season), all rooms come with air-con, hot water, telephone, TV, fridge and private terrace. It's super-clean and rates don't rise on weekends. There's a 10% discount for stays of a week or more.

Along Soi Kasem Samphan near the Jed Pee Nong Hotel are a couple of Ban Boosarin clones. *Patchara House* (☎ 032-511787) costs 700B for rooms with air-con, TV/video, telephone, hot water and fridge.

Also on this soi is the similar *Ban Somboon* (☎ 032-511538), where nicely decorated rooms are 450B with fan, TV and hot showers, 550B with air-con, TV and fridge; all rates include breakfast and there is a pleasant garden on the premises. On the corner of Soi Kasem Samphan and Th Damnoen Kasem is *Puangpen Villa Hotel* and *PP Villa Guest House* (☎ 032-533785, fax 511216), which share a garden, pool and reception area. Clean, air-con rooms cost 780B with hot water, TV and fridge in the former, 600B with hot water in the latter. These hotels, as well as the Jed Pee Nong and City Beach described below, are only a couple of hundred metres from the beach.

The popular *Jed Pee Nong* (☎ 032-512381) is on Th Damnoen Kasem. Modern, clean but otherwise unimpressive rooms cost 450B with fan, TV and hot bath, 650B with air-con or 800B for air-con rooms by the swimming pool behind the hotel.

On Th Naretdamri, the modern *Fresh Inn* (☎ 032-511389, fax 532166) has all aircon rooms for 700B to 875B. This pleasant tourist-class hotel would have had a sea view if not for the construction of the highrise Meliá Hua Hin between it and the sea. Downstairs is an Italian restaurant called Lo Stivale.

Running north from Th Chomsin (the road leading to the main pier) is Th Naep Khehat. At No 73/5-7, the *Phananchai Hotel* (☎ 032-511707, fax 530157) has fan rooms for 380B to 520B, carpeted air-con rooms from 520B to 600B. It's a bit of a walk from the swimming beaches but all rooms come with hot water, TV and telephone. The hotel has an attached restaurant.

Places to Stay – Top End

At the air-con *Sirin Hotel* (☎ 032-511150, fax 513571), on Th Damnoen Kasem towards the beach, rooms are well kept and come with hot water and a fridge. The semi-outdoor restaurant area is pleasant. Double rooms are 890B during the week and 1200B on weekends and holidays; rates include breakfast.

Nearby, the *City Beach Resort* (☎ 032-512870/75, 16 Th Damnoen Kasem) offers

Hua Hin Railway Hotel

In 1922 the State Railway of Thailand (then the Royal Thai Railway) extended the national rail network to Hua Hin to allow easier access to the Hua Hin summer palace. The area proved to be a popular vacation spot among commoners too, so in the following year they built Hua Hin Railway Hotel, a graceful colonial-style inn by the sea, with sweeping teak stairways and high-ceilinged rooms. When I researched the first edition of this guide in 1981, a double room was still only 90B and the service was just as unhurried as it had been when I first stayed here in 1977. It probably hadn't changed much since 1923, except for the addition of electric lighting and screened doors and windows. Big-bladed ceiling fans stirred the humid sea air and in the dining room, one ate using weighty State Railway silverware and thick china from the 1920s. Unfortunately, when Bangkok's Central Department Store took over the management of the hotel they floundered in their attempt to upgrade the facilities, failing to take advantage of the hotel's original ambience.

In 1986 the French hotel chain Accor became part of a joint venture with Central and together they restored the hotel to most of its former glory. It now bears the awkward name *Hotel Sofitel Central Hua Hin*, but if you've been looking for a historic South-East Asian hotel to spend some money on, this might be it. All of the wood panelling and brass fixtures throughout the rooms and open hallways have been restored. While the old railway silverware and china have been retired to antique cabinet displays, the spacious, lazy ambience of a previous age remains. Even if you don't want to spend the money to stay here, it's worth a stroll through the grounds and open sitting areas for a little history. It's more interesting in terms of atmosphere than either the Raffles in Singapore or the Oriental in Bangkok (neither of which have eight hectare grounds), and somewhere in between in terms of luxury. Latest reports, however, say standards have slipped since the lay-off of all European management.

Incidentally, in 1983 this hotel was used as Hotel Le Phnom for the filming of *The Killing Fields*. Also, the State Railway of Thailand still owns the hotel; Sofitel/Central are just leasing it.

Joe Cummings

quiet, semi-luxurious rooms with the usual service and extras from 1331B (discounted from the 2662B rack rate).

Near the train station, off Th Damnoen Kasem near the Royal Hua Hin golf course, is the *Golf Inn* (☎ 032-512473), where aircon rooms are 600B to 700B weekdays, 700B to 800B weekends.

Hua Hin also has several super-luxury hotels. *Hotel Sofitel Central Hua Hin* (☎ 032-512021, fax 511014, Bangkok ☎ 02-541 1463, email sofitel_central@hotmail.com), formerly the Hua Hin Railway Hotel, is a magnificent two storey colonial-style place on the beach at the end of Th Damnoen Kasem. Rooms in the original L-shaped colonial wing cost 5100B; rooms in the new wing are more expensive. Discounts may be possible during the week and in low season.

Opposite is the old Railway Hotel's former Villa Wing, now the *Mercure Resort Hua Hin* (☎ 032-512036, fax 511014, email sofitel_central@hotmail.com), a collection of charming one and two bedroom wooden beach bungalows ranging from 4500B to 7300B. From 20 December to 20 February there's a 1300B peak-season supplement on all room charges at both the Mercure and the Sofitel.

The plush *Meliá Hua Hin* (☎ 032-512879, fax 511135, Bangkok ☎ 02-271 3435, fax 271 3689), off Th Naretdamri, is part of the Spanish-owned Meliá hotel chain and was the first high-rise to mar the

Hua Hin skyline. Rooms with all the amenities are listed at 4000B, though the actual everyday price runs 30 to 50% lower except during peak season. From 20 December to 10 January there's a 900B peak-season supplement on all room charges. There's not much of a beach in front of the hotel at high tide, but the adjacent free-form pool area is well designed to encompass sea views. Other facilities include two tennis courts, two air-con squash courts, a fitness centre, sauna and massage facilities.

Along Hua Hin's southern beach at 107/1 Th Hat Phetkasem, the *Royal Garden Resort* (☎ 032-511881, fax 512422) offers rooms and suites with sea views in a modern high-rise-style complex. Spacious rooms start at 3800B (usually discounted to 2400B, including breakfast) and go to 13,000B for penthouse suites with jacuzzis and private rooftop gardens. The more laid-back *Royal Garden Village* (☎ 032-520250, fax 520259, Bangkok ☎ 02-476 0021, fax 476 1120, email royalgardenvhh@minornet.com, 43/1 Th Hat Phetkasem) north of town features Thai-style villas on 14 landscaped acres from 9800B (often discounted to 4119B). Both Royal Garden resorts offer tennis courts and swimming pools, nearby golf course privileges, Thai massage services and water sport activities; the Royal Garden Resort also has a golf driving range.

The US$26 million *Chiva-Som International Health Resort* (☎ 032-536536, fax 511154, 74/4 Phetkasem Hwy) is a new concept featuring ocean-view rooms and Thai-style pavilions on seven beachside acres south of town (before Nong Khae and Ao Takiap). The name means 'Haven of Life' in Thai-Sanskrit. The staff of 200 fuses eastern and western approaches to health with planned nutrition, step and aqua aerobics, Thai, Swedish or underwater massage, t'ai chi, dance and the usual round of mudpacks, saunas (including a multi-level steam room), jacuzzis and hydrotherapy. Flotation tanks containing tepid salt water are on hand for sensory deprivation sessions. You can pick up a life membership with unlimited use of the facilities for

US$15,000, or pay US$420 single, US$630 double per day, a rate that includes three meals (with wine at dinner) along with health and fitness consultations, massage and all other activities. One week, 10 day and two-week packages are also available.

There are a few more top-end places on beaches just north and south of town. Some of these add peak-season supplements in December and January.

Places to Stay – Out of Town

Around Hat Takiap and Nong Khae south of Hua Hin you'll find a mixture of high-rise condo-style hotels and low-rise cottages. In Hat Takiap, the *Fangkhlun Guest House* (☎ 032-512402) has fan-cooled rooms for 600B, air-con for 700B. The *Khao Ta-kiap Resort* (☎ 032-512405) offers air-con cottages for 1500B a night, while *Ta-kiab Beach Resort* (☎ 032-512639, fax 515899), south of Khao Takiap, has air-con rooms and a pool from 900B a night per person.

In a forested area called Nong Khae at the north end of Ao Takiap is the quiet and comfortable low-rise *Nern Chalet* (☎ 032-513528), with air-con rooms with TV, hot water and phone for 800/900B single/double. Between Nong Khae and Takiap, *Hua Hin Bluewave Beach Resort* (☎ 032-511036) is a condotel-style place with rooms listed for 2178B, discounted to 1200B including breakfast; on the grounds are a pool and fitness centre.

In Hat Suan Son, the modern *Suan Son Padiphat* (☎ 032-511239) has fan-cooled rooms for 300B (600B on the sea) or air-con rooms for 500B to 1000B.

In low-key Pranburi, the *Pransiri Hotel* (☎ 032-621061, 283 Th Phetkasem) and *Pranburi Hotel* (☎ 032-622042, 30/9-10 Th Phetkasem) each have rooms starting at 150B.

At water-sports oriented *Club Aldiana* (☎ 032-611701, Bangkok ☎ 02-203 0601, fax 203 0600, email aldiana@mozart .inet.co.th) resort-style accommodation starts at 2100B (1900B weekdays), which includes three buffet meals, all sports activities and entertainment. Among the amenities on the grounds are eight quartz-sand tennis courts.

Places to Eat

One of Hua Hin's major attractions has always been the colourful and inexpensive Chatchai seafood market in the centre of town off Th Phetkasem on Th Dechanuchit, where vendors gather nightly to fry, steam, grill, parboil or bake fresh Gulf seafood for hordes of hungry Thais. During the day many of these same vendors prepare seafood snacks on the beach; cracked crab and cold Singha beer can be ordered without leaving one's sling chair.

The best seafood to eat in Hua Hin is *plaa sãmlii* (cotton fish or kingfish), *plaa kapõng* (perch), *plaa mèuk* (squid), *hãwy malaeng phùu* (mussels) and *puu* (crab). Fresh seafood is found in three main areas. Firstly, there are some medium-priced restaurants along Th Damnoen Kasem near the Jed Pee Nong and City Beach hotels, and off Th Damnoen Kasem, on Th Phunsuk and Th Naretdamri. Secondly, there's excellent and inexpensive food in nearby Chinese-Thai restaurants and in the Chatchai seafood market described earlier. The third area is next to Tha Thiap Reua Pramong, the big fishing pier at the end of Th Chomsin. The fish is, of course, fresh off the boats but not necessarily the cheapest in town.

Saeng Thai, near the pier, is the oldest seafood restaurant in Hua Hin and quite reliable if you know how to order. The best value for money can be found in the smaller eating places on and off Th Chomsin, and in the Chatchai night market. There is also a *night market* on Th Chomsin.

Two Chinese-Thai seafood places along Th Phetkasem, *Khuang Seng* and *Thara Jan*, neither bearing roman-script signs, are both fairly good value.

Chatchai Market is excellent for Thai breakfast – they sell very good *jók* and *khâo tôm* (rice soups). Fresh-fried *paa-thông-kõ* (in the Hua-Hin-style – small and crispy, not oily), are 2B for three. A few vendors also serve hot soy milk in bowls (5B) – break a few paa-thông-kõ into the soy milk

and drink free *náam chaa* – a very tasty and filling breakfast for 11B if you can eat nine paa-thông-kõ.

Gee Cuisine, next to the Jed Pee Nong, caters mostly to faràngs but the Thai food is generally good. *Lucky Restaurant*, next to PP Villa nearby, is very similar to Gee Cuisine.

Fa Mui, on Th Dechanuchit near All Nations, is a cosy, atmospheric place serving Thai and seafood cuisine to a hip crowd of local and visiting Thais; prices are low to moderate.

Relatively new *Taj Mahal* on Th Naretdamri next to Bird Guest House serves decent Indian food.

Th Phunsuk and Th Naretdamri are becoming centres for faràng-oriented eateries. There must be more Italian restaurants per capita here than anywhere else in Thailand. The popular *Lo Stivale* (☎ 032-513800, 132 Th Naretdamri) serves the usual Italian dishes as well as pizza. It's more of a drinking place, but *Headrock Cafe* (☎ 032-514002) also has Thai and western food; it's not a misspelling, but a pun on the name Hua Hin – head rock. Located just off Th Naretdamri at 7A Soi Selakam in a cosy wooden house, *Nice Restaurant* (☎ 032-530709) features seafood, western and Thai dishes at reasonable prices. Breakfast is their speciality – a simple meal of eggs, toast and coffee is only 25B. *Piaf* (23 Th Naretdamri) is a German/Austrian restaurant that also offers Thai cuisine. *Le Chablis* (88 Th Naretdamri) serves French food and wine (along with live piano music in the evenings). On the next street west, Th Phunsuk, the Italian *La Villa* (☎ 032-513435) has pizza, spaghetti, lasagne etc. *Sunshine Restaurant & Bakery* on Th Naretdamri serves German food and fresh baked goods.

Al Fresco (☎ 032-532678) and *Italian Ice Cream* (☎ 032-53753), both on Th Damnoen Kasem, offer homemade Italian-style ice cream. *Capo's*, in the same building as Al Fresco, specialises in steak and spare ribs. Meat lovers can also get their fill at *Buffalo Bill's Steak & Grill*, also on Th Damnoen Kasem, near the post office.

The British-run **Berny's Inn** (The Golfer's 19th Hole) at the Hua Hin Bazaar, a small shopping centre off Th Damnoen Kasem, specialises in steaks, pork chops, burgers, sandwiches and other hearty western fare from 2 pm to 2 am.

Entertainment
Several faràng bars under German, Swiss, Italian, French and New Zealand management can be found in and around Th Naretdamri and Th Phunsuk. Most offer the familiar Thai hostess atmosphere. One that dares to be different, **All Nations Bar** (10-10/1 Th Dechanuchit), successfully creates a pub atmosphere and has quite a collection of flags and other international memorabilia.

Stone Town, an old-west style pub next to Jed Pee Nong Hotel on Th Damnoen Kasem, features live folk and country music nightly. For rock 'n' roll, check out the semi-outdoor **Hurricane Pub** off Th Phetkasem, where a live Thai band plays Thai and western pop nightly. There's no cover charge and drinks are no more expensive than at any of the town's faràng bars.

Getting There & Away
Air Until a couple of years ago Bangkok Airways operated flights into Hua Hin, but the airport is now closed. City authorities claim it is being expanded to accommodate international air traffic.

Bus Buses from Bangkok's Southern bus terminal cost 110B for 1st class air-con, 85B 2nd class air-con, 61B ordinary. The trip takes 3½ to four hours. Various agencies on Th Khao San (Khao San Rd) in Bangkok operate minivans to Hua Hin for 150B per person – but why pay more for less leg and head room than you'd get on a 1st class air-con bus?

Ordinary buses for Hua Hin leave Phetchaburi regularly for 25B (30B air-con). The same bus can be picked up in Cha-am for 10B (20B air-con). Other ordinary buses from the main terminal in Hua Hin go to/from Prachuap Khiri Khan (30B, 42B air-con), Chumphon (77B, 108B air-con), Surat

Thani (136B, 190B air-con), Phuket (198B, 277B air-con), Krabi (177B, 248B air-con) and Hat Yai (251B, 392B air-con).

Pran Tour (☎ 032-511654) on Th Sasong near the Siripetchkasem Hotel in Hua Hin runs air-con buses to Bangkok about every two hours from 3 am to 9 pm, for 63B 2nd class air-con or 110B 1st class air-con. BJ Travel (☎ 032-530593), nearby, offers long-distance air-con VIP buses to the following points south: Surat Thani (530B), Ko Samui (bus/ferry combo, 650B), Ko Pha-Ngan (bus/ferry, 700B), Krabi (650B), Phuket (650B), Hat Yai (750B), Padang Besar (1050B), Butterworth (1050B), Penang (1150B), Kuala Lumpur (1450B) and Singapore (1600B). BJ also has minivans to Chumphon for a steep 350B, plus a minivan/ferry combo to Ko Tao (550B).

Train In 1922 the Royal Railway of Siam (now the State Railway of Thailand) extended a rail link to Hua Hin and today the restored, dollhouse-like train station is a minor attraction in itself. The southern trains described under Phetchaburi's Getting There & Away section also stop here. The train takes 3¾ hours from Bangkok; 1st class train fare is 202B (express only), 2nd class 102B (rapid and express only), 3rd class is 44B. Rapid and express surcharges apply.

You can also come by train from any other station on the southern railway line, including Phetchaburi (3rd class, 10B), Nakhon Pathom (2nd/3rd class, 71/30B), Prachuap Khiri Khan (3rd class, 14B), Surat Thani (2nd/3rd class, 146/63B) and Hat Yai (2nd/3rd class, 243/105B). The 1st and 2nd class fares do not include rapid or express surcharges.

Getting Around
Local buses/songthaews from Hua Hin to the beaches of Khao Takiap, Khao Tao and Suan Son cost 7B per person, though faràngs are sometimes charged 10B. These buses run from around 6 am until 5.50 pm; the ones to Hat Takiap leave from opposite the main bus terminal on Th Sasong, while the latter two leave from Th

Chomsin opposite the wát. Buses to Pranburi are 10B and leave from the same area on Th Chomsin.

Samlor fares in Hua Hin have been set by the municipal authorities so there shouldn't be any haggling. Here are some sample fares: the train station to the beach, 20B; the bus terminal to Th Naretdamri, 30B to 40B (depending on size of your bags); Chatchai Market to the fishing pier, 20B; the train station to the Royal Garden Resort, 40B.

Motorcycles and bicycles can be rented from a couple of places on Th Damnoen Kasem near the Jed Pee Nong Hotel. Motorcycle rates are reasonable: 150B to 200B per day for 100cc, 250B to 300B for 125cc. Occasionally larger bikes – 400 to 750cc – are available for 500B to 600B a day. Bicycles are 30B to 70B per day. Avis Rent-A-Car (☎ 032-512021/38) has an office at Hotel Sofitel Central Hua Hin. There are also cheaper places renting sedans for 1300B to 1500B a day, or Suzuki Caribians for 800B to 1000B.

You can hire boats out to Ko Singtoh for 800B a day at the fishing pier in Hua Hin, or for 700B on Hat Takiap if you haggle.

KHAO SAM ROI YOT NATIONAL PARK

This 98 sq km park's name means 'Three Hundred Peaks'. It has magnificent views of the Gulf coastline if you can stand a little climbing. Khao Daeng is only about half an hours walk from the park headquarters, and from here you can see the ocean as well as some brackish lagoons. If you have the time and energy, climb the 605m Khao Krachom for even better views. If you're lucky, you may come across a serow (Asian goat-antelope) while hiking. The lagoons and coastal marshes are great places for bird watching. Along the coast you may see an occasional pod of Irrawaddy dolphins *(plaa lohmaa hŭa bàat)*.

Be sure to bring insect repellent for any park visits. King Rama IV (King Mongkut) and a large entourage of Thai and European guests convened here on 18 August 1868 to observe a total solar eclipse – predicted, so

the story goes, by the monarch himself – and enjoy an elaborate feast prepared by a French chef. Two months later the king expired from malaria, contracted via mosquito bites inflicted here. The risk of malaria in the park is relatively low, but mosquitoes can be pesky.

Fauna

Notable wildlife around Khao Sam Roi Yot includes the crab-eating macaque, dusky langur, barking deer, slow loris, Malayan pangolin, fishing cat, palm civet, otter, serow, Javan mongoose and monitor lizard. However, park officials admit that it's fairly uncommon to actually spot any wild animals, possibly due to the rise of tourism!

Because the park lies at the intersection of the east Asian and Australian flyways, as many as 300 migratory and resident bird species have been recorded, including the yellow bittern, cinnamon bittern, purple swamp hen, water rail, ruddy-breasted crake, bronze-winged jacana, grey heron, painted stork, whistling duck, spotted eagle and black-headed ibis. The park protects Thailand's largest fresh water marsh (along with mangroves and mudflats), and is one of only three places in the country where the purple heron breeds.

Waterfowl are most commonly seen in the cool season. Encroachment by shrimp farmers in the vicinity has sadly destroyed a substantial portion of mangroves and other wetlands, thus depriving the birds of an important habitat.

Beaches, Canals & Marshes

A sandy beach flanked on three sides by dry limestone hills and casuarinas, **Hat Laem Sala** has a small visitor centre, restaurant, bungalows and camping area. Boats, which take up to 10 people, can be hired from Bang Pu to the beach for 150B return. You can also reach the beach from Bang Pu via a steep trail, about 20 minutes walk.

Hat Sam Phraya, 5km south of Hat Laem Sala, is a kilometre-long beach with a restaurant and washrooms. The park headquarters is just past the village of Khao

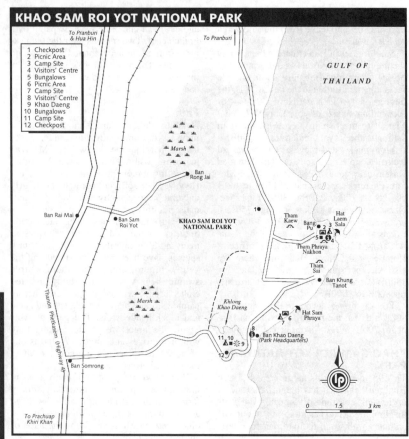

KHAO SAM ROI YOT NATIONAL PARK

1 Checkpost
2 Picnic Area
3 Camp Site
4 Visitors' Centre
5 Bungalows
6 Picnic Area
7 Camp Site
8 Visitors' Centre
9 Khao Daeng
10 Bungalows
11 Camp Site
12 Checkpost

GULF OF
THAILAND

To Pranburi
& Hua Hin

To Pranburi

Marsh

Ban
Rong Jai

Ban Rai Mai

Ban Sam
Roi Yot

KHAO SAM ROI YOT
NATIONAL PARK

Tham
Kaew

Bang
Pu

Hat
Laem
Sala

Tham Phraya
Nakhon

Tham
Sai

Ban Khung
Tanot

Thanon Phetkasem (Highway 4)

Marsh

Khlong
Khao Daeng

Hat Sam
Phraya

Ban Khao Daeng
(Park Headquarters)

Ban Somrong

To Prachuap
Khiri Khan

0   1.5   3 km

Daeng, about 4km south-west of Hat Sam
Phraya. A larger visitor centre at the headquarters features well curated exhibits;
there are also nature trails nearby. Binocu-
lars or telescopes can be rented for bird
watching; there are several bird blinds
nearby. September to March are the best
months to see waterfowl.

A 4km canal trip in a 10 person boat
along **Khlong Khao Daeng** can be arranged
in Ban Khao Daeng for 200B. The trip lasts
about 1½ hours and passes mangrove rem-

nants and waterfowl habitats. The birds are
most active in the early morning or late
afternoon. You might also spot monitor
lizards and monkeys. Before heading out,
however, you may want to have a chat with
your prospective guide:

After being offered a guide for a 20km canoe trip,
I failed to inquire further. Bad idea. We ended up
with a 'guide' who spoke no English and couldn't
canoe. He turned out to be just a local man to
whom we paid 300B to sit in the middle of our
boat – safely oarless – so he wouldn't dump us in

the river, as he repeatedly did early in the trip. I now advocate asking about the expertise of purported 'guides'.

Brad Berthal

Caves

The other big attraction at Sam Roi Yot are the caves of Tham Kaew, Tham Sai and Tham Phraya Nakhon. **Tham Phraya Nakhon** is the most visited and can be reached by boat or foot. The boat trip takes only about half an hour there and back, while it's half an hour each way on foot along a steep, rocky trail. There are actually two large caverns, both with sinkholes that allow light in. In one cave is a royal sala built for King Chulalongkorn, who would stop off here when travelling back and forth between Bangkok and Nakhon Si Thammarat.

Tham Kaew, 2km from the Bang Pu turn-off, features a series of chambers connected by narrow passageways; you enter the first cavern by means of a permanent ladder. Stalactites and other limestone formations – some of which glitter with calcite crystals

---

The Wrath of Rahu?

Despite many years as a highly disciplined Buddhist monk in the austere Thammayut sect prior to the death of his brother, Rama III, and his own ascension to the throne, King Mongkut (Rama IV) had a keen interest in science. He felt that one of his duties as Siam's monarch was to replace Thai superstition with logic and reason wherever possible.

One of the king's scientific passions was the study of astronomy, and in early 1868 his majesty calculated the timing of the upcoming 18 August solar eclipse, as well as its exact path over Siam. The king decided to make the event a public lesson in astronomy by organising a large expedition to a spot on the Thai coast where the eclipse could be viewed in totality. According to *Katya and the Prince of Siam* by Eileen Hunter and Narisa Chakrabongse, Rama IV chose 'a wild and uninhabitable spot about 140 miles south of Bangkok'. That translates to 228.4km, almost exactly where Khao Sam Roi Yot shows up in today's atlases, although other chronicles claim the spot was 50km to 60km further south at Wa Kaw, near Prachuap Khiri Khan.

At the king's invitation, a French expedition travelled all the way overland (the Suez Canal hadn't yet been dug) to Siam to join Rama IV in convincing his subjects that 'contrary to their belief, the eclipse would not be caused by the dragon Rahu making a meal of the sun and disgorging it only when frightened by beating of gongs and letting off fireworks, but could be predicted beforehand and explained by rather more rational methods.' According to the French expedition leader, 'The King of Siam with all his court, part of his army and a crowd of Europeans, arrived by sea on 8th August in twelve steamboats of the Royal Navy, while by land came troops of oxen, horses and fifty elephants'. Also in attendance were Mongkut's sons Damrong and Chulalongkorn, along with the court astrologers, 'who could hardly be blamed if they concealed a certain lack of enthusiasm'.

Although a thick layer of clouds threatened to spoil the event – much to the chagrin of the French who had travelled 10,000 miles and spent a fortune to support this royal endeavour – the sky cleared 20 minutes before totality and the event became a grand success.

Unaccounted for in the king's calculations was the fact that the chosen viewing spot was a low-lying swamp. Both Rama IV and 15 year old Prince Chulalongkorn contracted malaria during their 10-day astronomical sojourn; the king died shortly after his return to Bangkok, on the day he turned 64.

Joe Cummings

as if diamond-encrusted (hence the cave's name, 'Jewel Cave') – are plentiful. Lamps can be rented for 100B, but Tham Kaew is best visited in the company of a park guide because of the dangerous footing.

Tham Sai is in a hill near Ban Khrun Tanot, about 2.5km from the main road between Ale Sala and Sam Phraya beaches. Villagers rent lamps for around 30B at a shelter near the cave mouth. A 280m trail leads up the hillside to the cave, which features a large single cavern. Be careful of steep drop-offs in the cave.

Guides can be hired at the park office for 100B per hike; not much English is spoken but they're accustomed to leading non-Thai as well as Thai visitors.

Places to Stay & Eat

The Forestry Department hires out large *bungalows* near the park headquarters' visitor centre as well as at Hat Laem Sala for 400B to 1000B per night or 100B per person; they sleep four to 20 people. Three-person tents are 40B a night or you can pitch your own tent for 10B per person at campsites at the park headquarters, Hat Laem Sala or Hat Sam Phraya. There are restaurants at all three places. Bring insect repellent along as the park is rife with mosquitoes.

For accommodation reservations, contact the Royal Forest Department in Bangkok on ☎ 02-561 4292, ext 747.

Getting There & Away

The park is 37km south of Pranburi. Catch a bus or train to Pranburi (10B from Hua Hin) and then a songthaew to Bang Pu for 20B – these run between 6 am and 4 pm. From Bang Pu you must charter a vehicle, hitch or walk.

You can save the hassle of finding a ride in Bang Pu by chartering a songthaew for 280B or a motorcycle taxi for 150B from Pranburi all the way to the park. Be sure to mention you want to go the national park *(ùthayaan hàeng châat)* rather than the village of (Ban) Khao Sam Roi Yot.

Most convenient of all would be to rent a car or motorbike in Hua Hin. If you're coming by car or motorcycle from Hua Hin, it's about 25km to the park turn-off, then another 38km to park headquarters.

If you're coming straight from Bangkok, another option is to catch an air-con bus bound for Prachuap Khiri Khan, ask to get off at Ban Somrong (Km 286.5) and then hitch a ride 13km to the park headquarters at Ban Khao Daeng.

PRACHUAP KHIRI KHAN
• pop 14,900

Roughly 80km south of Hua Hin, Prachuap Khiri Khan serves as the capital of the province of the same name, though it is somewhat smaller than Hua Hin. There are no real swimming beaches in town, but the 8km-long bay of Ao Prachuap is pretty enough. Better beaches can be found north and south of town. The seafood here is fantastic, however, and cheaper than in Hua Hin. Fishing is still the mainstay of the local economy.

Prachuap (specifically Ao Manao) was one of seven points on the Gulf of Thailand coast where Japanese troops landed on 8 December 1941 during their invasion of Thailand. Several street names around town commemorate the ensuing skirmish: Phitak Chat – Defend Country; Salachip – Sacrifice Life; Suseuk – Fight Battle.

Information

Tourist Office Prachuap has its own city-run tourist office in the centre of town. The staff are very friendly and they have maps and photos of all the attractions in the area.

Things to See & Do

At the northern end of Ao Prachuap is **Khao Chong Krajok** (Mirror Tunnel Mountain – named after the hole through the side of the mountain which appears to reflect the sky). At the top is **Wat Thammikaram**, established by Rama VI. You can climb the hill for a view of the town and bay – and entertain the hordes of monkeys who live here. A metal ladder leads into the tunnel from the wát grounds.

If you continue north from Prachuap Khiri Khan around Ao Prachuap to the headland you'll come to a small boat-building village on **Ao Bang Nang Lom**, where they still make wooden fishing vessels using traditional Thai methods. It takes about two months to finish a 12m boat, which will sell for around 400,000B without an engine. The industrious folks at Bang Nang Lom also catch a fish called *plaa ching chang*, which they dry along the roadsides and then store for Sri Lankan traders who arrive by ship at certain times of the year specifically to buy up the catch.

West of the beach at Ao Bang Nang Lom is a canal, **Khlong Bang Nang Lom**, lined with picturesque mangroves. A few kilometres north of Ao Prachuap is another bay, **Ao Noi**, the site of a small fishing village with a few rooms to let.

Beaches South of Ao Prachuap, around a small headland, is the scenic **Ao Manao**, a bay ringed by a clean white-sand beach with small islands offshore. A Thai air force base guards access to the bay (a possible legacy of the 1941 Japanese invasion), and the beach was closed to the public until 1990, when the local authorities decided to open the area to day visitors. The beach is about 2.5km from the base entrance. There are several salas along the beach, a hotel, restaurant, toilets and a shower. Beach vendors offer chairs, umbrellas and inner tubes for rent at 10B each, plus seafood, North-Eastern Thai dishes and beverages. You must show your passport at the gate and sign in; the beach closes at 8 pm except for military and guests at the hotel (see the Ao Manao entry under Places to Stay later in this chapter).

Each year in September, on the air force base at Ao Manao, the Thai air force sponsors an impressive sound-and-light show commemorating Thai WWII heroes; it's open to the public and free.

Eight kilometres south of Ao Manao, **Hat Wa Kaw** is a pleasant, casuarina-lined beach that is even quieter and cleaner than Ao Manao. A small, recently built museum of astronomy (no English labels) and a Rama IV monument commemorate the 1868 solar eclipse which the king and his 15-year-old son Prince Chulalongkorn

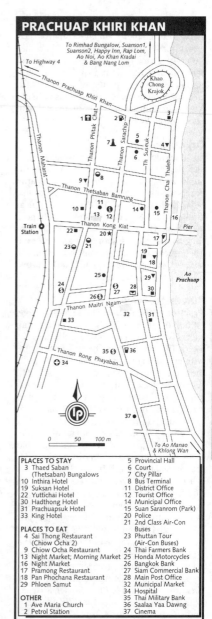

PRACHUAP KHIRI KHAN

PLACES TO STAY
3 Thaed Saban (Thetsaban) Bungalows
10 Inthira Hotel
19 Suksan Hotel
22 Yuttichai Hotel
30 Hadthong Hotel
31 Prachuapsuk Hotel
33 King Hotel

PLACES TO EAT
4 Sai Thong Restaurant (Chiow Ocha 2)
9 Chiow Ocha Restaurant
13 Night Market; Morning Market
16 Night Market
17 Pramong Restaurant
18 Pan Phochana Restaurant
29 Phloen Samut

OTHER
1 Ave Maria Church
2 Petrol Station
5 Provincial Hall
6 Court
7 City Pillar
8 Bus Terminal
11 District Office
12 Tourist Office
14 Municipal Office
15 Suan Saranrom (Park)
20 Police
21 2nd Class Air-Con Buses
23 Phuttan Tour (Air-Con Buses)
24 Thai Farmers Bank
25 Honda Motorcycles
26 Bangkok Bank
27 Siam Commercial Bank
28 Main Post Office
32 Municipal Market
34 Hospital
35 Thai Military Bank
36 Saalaa Yaa Dawng
37 Cinema

came south to witness. Both contracted malaria during their visit and Rama IV died soon after returning to Bangkok. (Whether the eclipse viewing event really happened here, or at Khao Sam Roi Yot as other chronicles say, is a matter of debate.) Also on display on the museum grounds is an old American-built steam locomotive (Baldwin Locomotive Works, 1925).

Organised Tours

Local resident Pinit Ounope arranges popular day tours to Khao Sam Roi Yot National Park, Dan Singkhon and to nearby beaches, other national parks and waterfalls. He lives at 144 Th Chai Thaleh near the beach in town and invites travellers to visit him. His house is rather difficult to find, so take a tuk-tuk or a motorcycle taxi. The typical day tour is 500B for person (on the back of a motorcycle) or 1000B for two people (in a pickup truck).

Places to Stay

Prachuap Khiri Khan The *Yuttichai Hotel* (☎ 032-611055, 115 Th Kong Kiat) has fair rooms with fan and shared bathroom for 120/170B one bed/two beds, or 180/240B with private bath; the latter are quieter since they're towards the back of the hotel. The proprietors lock the front door at 11 pm, after which you'll have to ring a doorbell to get in. Around the corner on Th Phitak Chat is the eight room *Inthira Hotel* (☎ 032-611418, 118-120 Th Phitak Chat) with similar rooms with private bath for 200B single/double. Both these hotels are quite near the night market and tourist office.

Prachuapsuk Hotel (☎ 032-601019, fax 601711, 63-5 Th Suseuk, no English sign), in a two storey shophouse near the market, is a friendly, family-run place; rooms cost 150B with fan and bath, 250B for air-con.

The three storey *King Hotel* (☎ 032-611170, 203 Th Phitak Chat, no English sign), farther south, has larger fan-cooled rooms for 200B. Facing Ao Prachuap is the *Suksan* (☎ 032-611145, 11 Th Suseuk), with fan-cooled rooms for 270B to 320B and air-con bungalows from 370B to 450B.

Also facing the bay are the plain but well kept *Thaed Saban Bungalows (Thetsaban Bungalows, meaning 'Municipal Bungalows' but also known as the 'Mirror Mountain Bungalows';* ☎ 032-611204), which are now privately owned. A one room bungalow for one or two persons costs 300B with fan and bath or 500B for air-con; a two room bungalow (sleeps four) is 600B; a three room (sleeps six) is 1200B; and a four room (sleeps eight) is 1500B. Extra persons may be crammed into rooms for 50B each.

The slightly up-market *Hadthong Hotel* (☎ 032-601050, fax 601057), also next to the bay near Th Maitri Ngam, has modern air-con rooms with TV, fridge and phone, starting at 400B for a basement single, 693B for a double with mountain view, 824B to 890B with sea view. Suites for up to 1386B are also available. Add 10% tax and 10% service charge plus a 200B surcharge from 20 December to 31 January. A pool and restaurant/coffee shop are on the premises.

North of the city, on the road to Ao Noi, *Rimhad Bungalow* (☎ 032-601626, 35 Th Suanson, a sign reads 'Rimhad Rest') offers tiny fan-cooled rooms for 300B to 400B depending on size, larger rooms with air-con for 600B single, or 800B for a double with TV. The bungalows face scenic Khlong Bang Nang Lom and mangroves. *Happy Inn* nearby has depressing concrete bungalows for 300B, air-con for 500B, and the staff can be surly – probably reserved for the quickie trade.

Along the same road are the *Suanson 1* (☎ 032-611204) and *Suanson 2 (same phone)*, with wooden two-bedroom bungalows and row houses on a treeless lot for 300B each. Each unit sleeps four and has its own parking space and private bath. Though a bit shabby, they're popular with Bangkok Thais.

Ao Manao *Ahkan Sawadii Khan Wing 53 (Manow Bay Beach Hotel;* ☎ 032-611087, no English sign) sits near the centre of the beach and is operated by the Thai air force. Rooms are supposedly reserved for Thai air force officers and their guests and only open to foreigners who make reservations through a Wing 53 officer – no 'walk-ins' accepted. All units have sea views; rooms with TV, phone and private shower cost 500B. Larger town houses in a separate wing cost 1000B and include bathtubs and hot water.

Seasand House Resort (☎ 032-661483, fax 661250, 409/1 Th Prachuap – Khlong Wan), a few kilometres south of Ao Manao at Khlong Wan, offers small, concrete bungalows with TV, fridge, air-con and hot water for 700/800B single/double. The Chao Reua Restaurant (see Places to Eat following) is on the premises.

Ban Forty (☎ 032-661437, 555 Th Prachuap – Khlong Wan), in the same area, offers four concrete bungalows located on 8 sq *rai* of land with a private coconut palm-lined beach. Owned by a friendly retired Thai air force officer of Thai/English descent, the simple but clean units cost 700B to 800B, depending on size. Meals can be arranged ahead of time and served in a sala near the beach.

Ao Noi In Ao Noi there are several rooms and small 'weekend inns', most catering to Thais. *Aow Noi Beach Bungalows (☎ 032-601350, 601354, 206 Tambon Ao Noi)* offers well kept cottages with private bath for 300B to 600B a night. Faràngs – particularly Germans – make up a large percentage of the clientele. Facilities include a small bar and restaurant with Thai and German food, plus a clean, secluded beach. This establishment was up for sale when we visited, so things could change.

Places to Eat

Because of its well deserved reputation for fine seafood, Prachuap has many restaurants. One of the seafood specialities of Prachuap Khiri Khan that you shouldn't miss is whole cottonfish that's sliced lengthways and left to dry in the sun for half a day, then fried quickly in a wok, called *plaa sãmlii tàet dìaw*. It's often served with mango salad on the side.

The least expensive place to dine in the evening is the *night market* that convenes

near the government offices in the middle of town. On Th Chai Thaleh, north of the pier, is a smaller *night market* with around 10 vendors selling good seafood at affordable prices; tables set up along the sea wall sometimes get a good breeze. Both night markets are open late; the first until midnight, the second till 2 am.

Of the many seafood restaurants, the best are the *Pan Phochana Restaurant (☎ 032-611195, 11 Th Suseuk)* behind Suksan Hotel and the *Sai Thong Restaurant (Chiow Ocha 2; ☎ 032-550868)* on Th Chai Thaleh, near the Thaed Saban Bungalows. Both serve great-tasting seafood at reasonable prices. Sai Thong serves Carlsberg draught beer and imported wine, and is a popular stop for tour buses. The Pan Phochana is famous for its *hàw mòk hãwy*, ground fish curry steamed in mussels on the half-shell. Just south of the Pan Phochana is a good *night market* with many seafood stalls.

Other good restaurants include the *Chiow Ocha (☎ 032-611118, 100 Th Phitak Chat, no roman-script sign)* and the *Pramong (☎ 032-611168, 36 Th Chai Thaleh, no roman-script sign)*. The *Phloen Samut Restaurant (☎ 032-611115, 44 Th Chai Thaleh)*, adjacent to Hadthong Hotel, is a good outdoor seafood place, though it doesn't have everything that's listed on the menu. The staff here don't speak English.

Off Th Suseuk, *Suan Krue (Khrua) Food & Drink (☎ 032-611672, 7 Soi Taampramuk)* calls itself a 'vegetarian food centre', but also serves meat. Most Thai standards, including curries, are available in vegetarian form. The amiable owner also sells organic products such as herbal shampoo and grain-based beverages. It's open 7 am to 4 pm.

Across from the Inthira Hotel is a small *morning market* with tea stalls that serve cheap curries and noodles. A small, no-name *duck noodle restaurant* in the same building as the Yuttichai Hotel has excellent *bàmìi pèt* (duck noodle soup) and is open from 11 am to 3.30 pm daily.

Several good seafood restaurants can be found along the road north of Ao Prachuap on the way to Ao Noi. *Rap Lom (literally, 'breeze-receiving';* ☎ *032-601677)* is the most popular. A house speciality is prawns in sour tamarind-leaf soup *(kaeng sôm yâwt mákhãam)* – look for the Beck's/Carlsberg Beer sign.

Chao Reua (☎ *032-661482),* located at the Seasand House Resort a few kilometres south of town at Khlong Wan (see Places to Stay), is also quite good for seafood; it's only open 10 am to 4 pm.

Entertainment

Saalaa Yaa Dawng (no roman-script sign), on Soi Phun Samakhi opposite the Thai Military Bank, is a low-key, open-air, old-west-style bar with live Thai folk music *(phleng phêua chiwít).* Although the place touts its namesake *yaa dawng* (herbal liquor), which can be bought by the bottle or by the shot, beer is also available. A small khâo tôm stall next door supplies the bar with eats.

Getting There & Away

Bus From Bangkok, ordinary buses cost 93B and leave the Southern bus terminal frequently between 3 am and 9.20 pm. Second class air-con buses cost 122B from the same terminal, operating between 7 am and 1 am. Phuttan Tour operates 15 first class air-con buses a day in both directions between 6.15am and 1 am for 155B a seat. In the opposite direction, Phuttan Tour air-con buses to Bangkok leave from 182 Th Phitak Chat at similar intervals. In either direction the trip takes four to five hours.

From Hua Hin buses are 25B and leave from the bus station on Th Sasong every 20 minutes from 7 am to 3 pm, taking 1½ to two hours.

From Prachuap you can catch ordinary buses or 2nd class air-con buses to Chumphon (55B/77B), Surat Thani (110/240B), Nakhon Si Thammarat (150/210B), Krabi (170/240B), Phang-Nga (150/210B), Don Sak (for Ko Samui, 128/193B) and Phuket (173/242B).

The air-con bus from Bangkok to Samui stops on the highway in Prachuap between midnight and 1 am – if seats are available you can buy a through ticket to Samui for 240B.

It's a five minute, 30B motorcycle taxi ride from the town centre to the highway bus stop.

Train For departure details from Bangkok, see the earlier Phetchaburi Getting There & Away section: the same services apply. Fares from Bangkok are 272B for 1st class, 135B 2nd class and 58B 3rd class; to these add the appropriate rapid or express charges. The ordinary train between Hua Hin and Prachuap costs 14B; from Hua Hin it leaves at 5.50 pm, arriving in Prachuap at 7.10 pm. There are also several rapid and express trains between the two towns, but the time saved is negligible. A 3rd class ticket on to Chumphon is 24B.

Getting Around

Prachuap is small enough to get around on foot, or you can hop on a tuk-tuk – actually more akin to the Isaan-style *sakailaep*, here called *sãaleng* – for 10B anywhere on the main roads.

A sãaleng to Ao Noi costs 30B to 40B. The Honda dealer on Th Sarachip rents 100cc motorcycles for 200B a day plus 20B for a helmet.

A motorbike taxi to Ao Manao costs 20B to 25B. They aren't permitted past the gate unless both driver and passenger are wearing helmets. Without a helmet you'll have to walk the 3km to the beach.

AROUND PRACHUAP KHIRI KHAN
Wat Khao Tham Khan Kradai

About 8km north of town, following the same road beyond Ao Noi, is this small cave wát at one end of **Ao Khan Kradai** (also known as Ao Khan Bandai – a long, beautiful bay).

A trail at the base of the limestone hill leads up and around the side to a small cavern and then to a larger one which contains a reclining Buddha. If you have a torch you can proceed to a larger second chamber also containing Buddha images. From this trail you get a good view of Ao Khan Kradai. The beach here is suitable for swimming and is virtually deserted. It's not far from

Ao Noi, so you could stay in Ao Noi and walk to the beach. Or you could stay in town, rent a motorcycle and make a day trip to Ao Khan Kradai.

Dan Singkhon

Just south of Prachuap is a road leading west to Dan Singkhon on the Myanmar border. This is the narrowest point in Thailand between the Gulf of Thailand and Myanmar – only 12km across. The Myanmar side changed from Karen to Yangon control following skirmishes in 1988-89. The border is open to Thai and Burmese citizens only. On the Thai side is a small frontier village and a Thai police camp with wooden semi-underground bunkers built in a circle.

Off the road on the way to Dan Singkhon are a couple of small cave hermitages. The more famous one at **Khao Hin Thoen**, surrounded by a park of the same name, has some interesting rock formations and sculptures – but watch out for the dogs. The road to Khao Hin Thoen starts where the paved road to Dan Singkhon breaks left. **Khao Khan Hawk** (also known as Phutthakan Bang Kao) is a less well known cave nearby where an elderly monk, Luang Phaw Buaphan Chatimetho, lives. Devotees from a local village bring him food each morning.

THAP SAKAE & BANG SAPHAN

These two districts lie south of Prachuap Khiri Khan and together they offer a string of fairly good beaches that receive hardly any tourists.

The town of Thap Sakae is set back from the coast and isn't much, but along the seashore there are a few places to stay (see the following Places to Stay & Eat section). The beach opposite Thap Sakae isn't anything special either, but north and south of town are the white-sand beaches of **Hat Wanakon** and **Hat Laem Kum**. There is no private accommodation at these beaches at the moment, but you could ask permission to camp at Wat Laem Kum, which is on a prime spot right in the middle of Hat Laem Kum. Laem Kum is only 3.5km from Thap Sakae and at the northern end is the fishing

village of Ban Don Sai, where you can buy food. Hat Wanakon is part of Hat Wanakon National Marine Park, which covers 22.6 sq km of coastline and 15.4 sq km of marine resources; it's primary use is as a training centre for park division staff.

Bang Saphan (Bang Saphan Yai) is no great shakes as a town either, but the long beaches here are beginning to attract some speculative development. In the vicinity of Bang Saphan you'll find the beaches of **Hat Sai Kaew, Hat Ban Krut, Hat Khiriwong, Hat Ban Nong Mongkon, Hat (Ao) Baw Thawng Lang, Hat Pha Daeng** and **Hat Bang Boet**. All are worth looking up. Getting around can be a problem; there isn't much public transport between these beaches.

There are also islands off the coast, including **Ko Thalu** and **Ko Sing**, where there is good snorkelling and diving from the end of January to mid-May. Coral Resort and Suan Luang Resort in Bang Saphan can arrange 9 am to 2 pm diving excursions to Ko Thalu for 600B per person or Ko Sing for 400B.

Places to Stay & Eat

Thap Sakae The *Chaowarit (Chawalit;* ☎ 032-671010), right off the highway near the south end of town, has simple but clean rooms for 170B with shared bathroom, 200B to 300B with fan and private bath – good value overall. Around the corner, less than 100m away from Chaowarit, the *Sukkasem* (☎ 032-671598) has very basic rooms for 100B to 120B.

Thap Sakae Hotel (☎ 032-546240, 546242), a relatively new place at the north end of town on the highway, offers clean fan rooms for 400/500B single/double or air-con bungalows for 1000B.

On the coast opposite Thap Sakae are a couple of concrete block-style bungalows for 200B to 450B, eg *Chan Reua* (☎ 032-671890, 671930, fax 671401).

Hat Ban Krut *Reun Chun Seaview* (☎/fax 032-695061) has single bedroom bungalows for 800B, two-bedroom, two-bath ones for 1800B, all air-con with TV and fridge – not bad for families. A seafood restaurant is on the premises. Nearby *Ban Rim Haad* (☎ *032-695205*) offers bungalows in a nicely landscaped garden adjacent to a large coconut grove. Rooms have air-con, TV and fridge, and the restaurant serves Isaan/seafood. Rates are 600/800B, double/triple, 2000B for a larger bungalow (sleeps ten).

Roong Samut (☎ *032-696045*), formerly Long Samut, rents air-con bungalows for 800B, or larger ones for 1500B.

Ban Klang Aow Beach Resort (☎ *032-695086, Bangkok 02-463 7908*) is an upmarket place on the beach with a nice pool. Standard bungalows costs 1000B, larger ones 2000B, all with air-con, TV and fridge. *Suan Ban Krut Resort* (☎ *032-695103, ☎/fax 695217*) is a similar affair with 21 bungalows (a bit smaller than the ones at Ban Klang Aow Beach Resort) for 1500B to 3000B, as well as a number of beach homes for sale or rent. Facilities include a pool, fitness centre and putting green.

Hat Khiriwong *Tawee Beach Resort* (also Tawees, Tawee Sea) has simple thatched bungalows with private scoop showers for 100B single/double, plus a few concrete bungalows with fans for 200/400B.

Sai-Eak Beach Resort (☎ *01-213 0317, Bangkok 02-321 4543*) opened in 1996 and is the nicest resort in the area. It's right on the beach, and features a swimming pool and a variety of bungalows with satellite TV and fridge ranging from 2000B to 4000B – depending on whether they face the pool or sea. Low season discounts of up to 50% are available from May to November.

Take a train or bus to the nearby town of Ban Krut, then a motorcycle taxi (30B daytime, 50B night) to Hat Khiriwong.

Bang Saphan Along the bay of Ao Bang Saphan are several beach hotels and bungalows. At Hat Sombun, the *Hat Somboon Sea View* (☎ *032-543344, fax 543345*) has single fan rooms for 250B, rooms with private hot bath, TV, fridge and air-con for 330/440B single/double; bungalows are 400B. The cheaper *Boonsom Guest House* (☎ *032-291273*) has wooden bungalows

with fan for 200B in the low season, 300B in the high season. Also in this area, *Van Veena Hotel* (☎ *032-691251*) has rooms with fan for 250B or air-con for 400B, including TV and fridge. The same management also handles the slightly run-down *Bangsaphan Resort* (☎ *032-691152/3*), which has fan rooms for 280B, air-con for 550B, and 'VIP' rooms for 750B.

Karol L's, operated by a Thai family, has 100B (shared bathroom) and 100B (private bath) bungalows in the old Samui-style 6km south of Bang Saphan Yai. Meals here are very reasonably priced as well, and they provide free maps for exploring the area.

Suan Luang Resort (☎ *01-212 5687, fax 032-548177*) at 13 Muu 1 is 600m from the beach, just up from Karol L's. They will also pick up customers from the train station if you call. The resort is run by a friendly and helpful Thai-French couple, a combination also reflected in their dining-room menu. Spacious bungalows with mosquito proofing cost 300B for wooden ones with fans, 500B for concrete ones with hot water, TV and air-con. There are discounts for longer stays. They have four motorbikes for rent (250B for guests, 300B for non-guests) as well as sailboarding, diving and sailing equipment. They can organise boat trips to nearby islands, or motorbike trips to surrounding areas, including Myanmar if the border is open.

The going rate for a half-day snorkel trip to Ko Sing is 300B, or full day to Ko Thalu 400B, including lunch. An overnight camping trip to Ko Thalu with meals included costs 1200B.

The French managed *Bang Saphan Coral Hotel* (☎ *01-215 1889, 171 Muu 9*) offers beautiful bungalows with terracotta-tiled roofs in a garden setting. All rooms have air-con, TV, fridge and hot water for 995/1350B double/triple and two-bedroom bungalows (sleeps four) with viewless verandas for 1735B. During holidays prices jump to 1290/1800/2190B, plus tax and service. The hotel restaurant serves pricey American and continental breakfasts. They also have a swimming pool and offer sailing, sailboarding, canoeing, diving and fishing equipment for rent, as well as 750B day trips to Ko Thalu.

The ***Krua Klang Ao*** restaurant, right near the centre of Ao Bang Saphan, is a good place for seafood. Because of an Italian-staffed development project nearby, many of the local hotel and restaurant staff speak a smattering of Italian.

Hat Bo Kaew Eight kilometres south of Hat Bang Saphan Yai (15km south of Bang Saphan town), this up and comer boasts two places to stay. ***Suan Annan Resort*** has 10 bungalows around 300m from the beach costing 400B a night with air-con, TV and fridge.

Getting There & Away
Buses from Prachuap Khiri Khan to Thap Sakae are 12B and from Thap Sakae to Bang Saphan Yai 8B. If you're coming from farther south, buses from Chumphon to Bang Saphan Yai are 25B.

You can also get 3rd class trains between Hua Hin, Prachuap Khiri Khan, Thap Sakae, Ban Koktahom, Ban Krut and Bang Saphan Yai for a few baht each leg, as all of them have train stations (the rapid and express lines do not stop in Thap Sakae, Ban Krut or Bang Saphan). Each of these train stations is around 4km from the beach, with motorcycle taxis the only form of public transport available. It's possible to rent 100cc motorbikes in Bang Saphan for 150B per day.

CHUMPHON
• **pop 15,500**
About 500km south of Bangkok and 184km from Prachuap Khiri Khan, Chumphon is the junction town where you turn west to Ranong and Phuket or continue south on the newer road to Surat Thani, Nakhon Si Thammarat and Songkhla. In reference to its function as a crossroads, the name derives from the Thai *chumnumphon*, which means 'meeting place'. This busy provincial capital is of no particular interest, except that this is where southern Thailand really begins in terms of ethnic markers like dialect and religion.

Pak Nam, Chumphon's port, is 10km from Chumphon, and in this area there are a few beaches and a handful of islands with good reefs for diving. The best local beach is 4km-long Hat Thung Wua Laen (12km north of town), also known locally as 'Hat Cabana' because the long-running Chumphon Cabana Resort & Diving Center is here.

Sometime in March or April the city hosts the Chumphon Marine Festival, which features cultural and folk art exhibits, a sailboarding competition at Hat Thung Wua Laen and a marathon. In October, the five day Lang Suan Buddha Image Parade & Boat Race Festival includes a procession of temple boats and a boat race on the Lang Suan River, about 60km south of the capital.

Pak Nam is a major departure point for boats to Ko Tao, a popular island north of Ko Samui and Ko Pha-Ngan. Hence many travellers bound for Ko Tao stop over for a night or two in Chumphon.

Nearer islands include Ko Samet (not to be confused with the island of the same name off the coast near Rayong), Ko Mattara, Ko Maphrao, Ko Rang Kachiu, Ko Ngam Yai and Ko Raet. Landing on Ko Rang Kachiu is restricted as this is where the precious swiftlet's nest is collected for the gourmet market. If you want to visit there, you can request permission from the Laem Thong Bird Nest Company in Chumphon. Contact Infinity Travel Service (☎ 077-501937) for more information. The other islands in the vicinity are uninhabited; the reefs around Ko Raet and Ko Mattara are the most colourful.

There are many other islands a bit farther out that are also suitable for diving – see Diving & Snorkelling under Around Chumphon later for details. Fishing is also popular around the islands – inquire at any of the hotels or guesthouses in town for information on organised fishing trips.

Information
Tourist Office Chumphon Tourist Services Center, in the provincial offices at the intersection of Th Poramin Mankha and Th Phisit Phayap, has some information on the area but the level of spoken English is not very high.

Money Several banks in town offer foreign exchange services and ATMs; most are located along Th Sala Daeng and are open weekdays from 8.30 am to 3.30 pm.

Post & Telephone The main post office on Th Poramin Mankha is open weekdays from 8.30 am to 4.30 pm, weekends 9 am to noon. The CAT office, about a kilometre south-east on the same road, is open for international telephone services daily from 8.30 am to 9 pm.

Books & Maps A DK Book Store has been established opposite the Jansom Chumphon Hotel but so far it's predominantly Thai-oriented and carries only a few titles in English. Maps of Chumphon may be purchased here, however.

Organised Tours

Several travel agencies and guesthouses organise outdoor tours to the surrounding areas. Infinity Travel Service (see Places to Stay following) is one of the best. Tri Star Adventure Tours offers a series of interesting jungle treks, local cave trips and island tours lasting from two to five days and starting at 1250B per person. A one day cave exploration costs 400B and up, depending on the number of people. Tri Star can be contacted through any travel service or guesthouse.

Club Paradise (☎ 077-503331, 570114, 01-476 7760) at 120 Th Tawee Sinka offers all-day boat trips around the islands for 450B, and camping and fishing tours for 600B to 700B. Again, any guesthouse or travel agency can hook you up with Club Paradise.

Places to Stay – Budget

Places continue to spring up as more people use Chumphon as a gateway to Ko Tao. North of the bus terminal, on the opposite side of the street, the *Infinity Travel Service* (☎ 077-501937, 68/2 Th Tha Taphao) has four basic but clean rooms with shared bathroom upstairs over their travel agency/restaurant for 100/150B single/double. They provide plenty of information on boats to Ko Tao and things to do in the area,

and also allow travellers to shower while waiting for boat or bus transfers.

Sooksamer Guest House (☎ 077-502430, 118/4 Th Suksamoe), also known as Pat's Place, has small rooms in a home-like atmosphere for 120B. The English-speaking owner, Pat, cooks both Thai and European food and is happy for you to use the shower if you drop by to eat a meal on your way to Pak Nam for a Ko Tao boat. Information on Chumphon Province and Ko Tao is plentiful.

(New) Chumphon Guest House (☎ 077-501242), also known as Miow House, is around the corner from Sooksamer on a soi off Th Krom Luang Chumphon and has basic, clean rooms in an old teak house for 140B to 180B with shared facilities. The friendly proprietors can arrange car and motorcycle rental as well as local tours.

Mayaze's Resthouse (☎ 077-504452, fax 502217), down a soi connecting Th Sala Daeng and Th Tha Taphao, offers five immaculate rooms for 200/250B single/double with fan, 280/350B single/double with aircon. The shared bathroom facilities are equally immaculate.

Other cheaper hotels can be found along Th Sala Daeng in the centre of town. *Si Taifa Hotel* is a clean, old Chinese hotel built over a restaurant, with large rooms for 140/180B single/double with shared bathroom, 260B with private shower and Thai-style toilet or 300/350B with air-con. Each floor has a terrace from which you can watch the sun set over the city. There's also the similar-looking *Thai Prasert (202-204 Th Sala Daeng, no roman-script sign)* with rooms from 100B to 150B; and the rather drab *Suriya* (☎ 077-511144, 125/24-26 Th Sala Daeng), 130/220B for rooms with fan and private bath – neither of them are particularly good.

Farther north on Th Sala Daeng, *Sri Chumphon Hotel* (☎ 077-511280, 127/22-24 Th Sala Daeng) is a clean and efficient Chinese hotel with rooms for 300B to 400B with fan and bath, 500B to 600B for air-con. The almost identical *Suriwong Chumphon Hotel* (☎ 077-511203, fax 502699, 125/27-29 Th Sala Daeng) is better value at

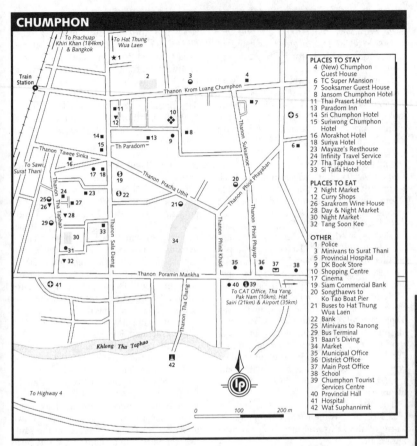

CHUMPHON

PLACES TO STAY
4 (New) Chumphon Guest House
6 TC Super Mansion
7 Sooksamer Guest House
8 Jansom Chumphon Hotel
11 Thai Prasert Hotel
13 Paradorn Inn
14 Sri Chumphon Hotel
15 Suriwong Chumphon Hotel
16 Morakhot Hotel
18 Suriya Hotel
23 Mayaze's Resthouse
24 Infinity Travel Service
27 Tha Taphao Hotel
33 Si Taifa Hotel

PLACES TO EAT
2 Night Market
12 Curry Shops
26 Sarakrom Wine House
28 Day & Night Market
30 Night Market
32 Tang Soon Kee

OTHER
1 Police
3 Minivans to Surat Thani
5 Provincial Hospital
9 DK Book Store
10 Shopping Centre
17 Cinema
19 Siam Commercial Bank
20 Songthaews to Ko Tao Boat Pier
21 Buses to Hat Thung Wua Laen
22 Bank
25 Minivans to Ranong
29 Bus Terminal
31 Baan's Diving
34 Market
35 Municipal Office
36 District Office
37 Main Post Office
38 School
39 Chumphon Tourist Services Centre
40 Provincial Hall
41 Hospital
42 Wat Suphannimit

200/260B for a single/double fan room with bath and just 280/360B for air-con.

The quiet, apartment-style *TC Super Mansion* on the east side of town near the provincial hospital offers decent rooms for 300B with fan, 350B to 400B with air-con. *Morakot Hotel* (☎ 077-503628, fax 570196) on Th Tawee Sinka has very clean, spacious rooms for 250B with fan, private shower, TV and phone. Air-con rooms with the same amenities start at 300B. Parking is available.

Tha Yang & Pak Nam Near the piers for boats to/from Ko Tao, *Tha Yang Hotel* (☎ 077-521953) has clean air-con rooms for 315 to 490B. *Tha Yang Guest House* offers rooms starting at 150B. At adjacent Pak Nam *Siriphet Hotel* (☎ 077-521304) has basic fan rooms with shared toilet for 150B.

Places to Stay – Mid-Range
At *Tha Taphao Hotel* (☎ 077-511479, 66/1 Th Tha Taphao) near the bus terminal, worn but comfortable rooms cost 400B

with air-con, TV, phone and balcony. The large *Paradorn Inn* (☎ *077-511500, fax 501112, 180/12 Th Paradorn*) as standard air-con rooms with TV for 300B or 500B to 600B with TV and fridge.

Though a bit newer, the *Jansom Chumphon Hotel* (☎ *077-502502, fax 502503, 118/138 Th Sala Daeng*) is already looking a bit run down. Standard air-con rooms start at 551B, deluxe rooms with complimentary breakfast are 708B.

Places to Eat

Food vendors line the south side of Th Krom Luang Chumphon between Th Sala Daeng and Th Suksamoe nightly from around 6 pm to 10 or 11 pm.

The several *curry shops* along Th Sala Daeng are proof that you are now in Southern Thailand. Over on Th Tha Taphao is a smaller *night market* and a very popular Chinese place called *Tang Soon Kee*. Several *Isaan-style places* can be found along Th Krom Luang Chumphon.

Sarakrom Wine House, opposite the Tha Taphao Hotel on Th Tha Taphao, is a clean, slightly upscale restaurant serving Thai food from a menu printed in Thai, English and German. The wine list is dominated by wines from South Africa, along with some from Chile, France and Australia. Open evenings only.

The disco at Jansom Chumphon Hotel is locally known as the *Khao Tom-teque* because of the *khâo tôm* meals served after midnight.

In Tha Yang, the indoor/outdoor *Reun Thai Restaurant*, next door to the Tha Yang Hotel and near the pier for boats to/from Ko Tao, has good seafood.

Chumphon Province is famous for *klûay lép meu naang*, 'princess fingernail bananas'. Very tasty and cheap – 25B would buy around a hundred of these small, slender bananas – they're available in any fresh market in town.

Getting There & Away

Chumphon can be difficult to get away from, especially if you want to head north to Bangkok during the high season (December to April). If you're planning to use this place as a transport junction, you may need to spend the night here: if you arrive in town late, trains and overnight buses to Bangkok may all be booked out.

Air Bangkok Airways used to fly to Chumphon airport, 35km from town, but at the time of writing all services had been cancelled.

Bus From Bangkok's Southern bus terminal ordinary buses cost 136B and depart at 3.30, 4, 6.05 and 6.50 am only. First class air-con buses are 245B and leave at 2, 9.40 and 10 pm; 2nd class costs 190B and leaves nightly at 9 pm. There are no government VIP departures for Chumphon, but Songserm Travel (next to the Tha Taphao Hotel) does one between 9 and 10 pm each evening for 450B.

Ordinary minivans run every two hours between Surat Thani and Chumphon for 60B (120B air-con, hourly departures, 3½ hours). The last van departs at 5 pm. To/from Bang Saphan is 35B (80B air-con), Prachuap Khiri Khan is 55B (2nd class air-con 76B). In Chumphon the main terminal for these buses is on the west side of Th Tha Taphao.

Air-con minivans run to/from Ranong daily every hour between 8 am and 5.30 pm for 80B from opposite Infinity Travel Service (ordinary minivans depart every two hours for 45B); other places do the same trip for 90B. There is also a minivan to Bangkok which meets the Ko Tao boat at the Pak Nam pier, and leaves from Infinity Travel Service at noon and 5 pm, costing 350B. Baan's Diving on Th Tha Taphao near the Tha Tapao Hotel also runs a minivan to/from Bangkok, departing at 1 pm and arriving in Bangkok at 8 pm; the fare is 350B. Others go to Surat Thani (150B, 2½ hours, 2.30 pm), Hat Yai and Phattalung (230B, four to five hours); these leave from the north side of Th Krom Luang Chumphon. There are no direct buses to Phuket, you must go to Surat Thani then transfer to a Phuket-bound bus.

Train Rapid and express trains from Bangkok take about 7½ hours to reach Chumphon and cost 190B for 2nd class, or 394B 1st class, not including rapid or express surcharges. There are no longer any ordinary trains between Bangkok and Chumphon.

There are four local 3rd class trains daily to Prachuap Khiri Khan (34B), Surat Thani (34B) and Hat Yai (99B). Southbound rapid and express trains – the only trains with 1st and 2nd class service – are much less frequent and can be difficult to book out of Chumphon.

Boat The small island of Ko Tao, north of Ko Samui and Ko Pha-Ngan (covered in the South-Western Gulf Coast chapter) can be reached by boat from Tha Reua Ko Tao (Ko Tao boat pier), 10km south-east of town in Pak Nam. The regular daily boat leaves at midnight, costs 200B and takes about six hours to reach Ko Tao. From Ko Tao the boat usually leaves at 10 am and arrives at Tha Reua Ko Tao around 3.30 pm.

More expensive but faster is the speed boat from the Tha Yang pier, which takes only 2½ hours and costs 400B. Depending on the weather, it usually departs at 7.30 am daily (8 am in the reverse direction).

Songthaews run to both piers frequently between 6 am and 6 pm for 10B. After 6 pm, Infinity and most other travel services and guesthouses can send a van to the pier around 10 pm for 50B per person. Going later by van means you won't have to wait at the pier for six hours before the boat departs. The only other alternative is a 60B motorcycle taxi ride to the pier.

Regular air-con minibuses to/from Bangkok's Th Khao San guesthouses and travel agencies also connect with the slow boat for 300B.

You can also charter a boat to Ko Tao from Pak Nam for around 2500B.

Getting Around
Motorcycle taxis around town cost a flat 10B per trip.

Songthaews to the port of Chumphon (Pak Nam Chumphon) are 13B per person.

To Hat Sairi and Hat Thung Wua Laem they cost 20B. Buses to Tako Estuary (for Hat Arunothai) are 40B. A motorcycle taxi out to Thung Wua Laem should be no more than 150B.

Infinity Travel Service can arrange rentals of motorcycles (200B per day) and cars (1000B per day).

AROUND CHUMPHON
Meditation Temple
Around 48km south of town in Sawi district, Wat Tham Phan Meuang is a Thammayut monastery offering instruction in *vipassana*. There is one Thai monk who can speak English and translate.

Beaches
The best beaches in Chumphon Province are north of Chumphon at **Ao Phanang Tak**, **Ao Thung Wua Laem** and **Ao Baw Mao**. Nearer to town, in the vicinity of Pak Nam Chumphon, are the lesser beaches of **Hat Pharadon Phap** and **Hat Sairi**. About 40km south of Chumphon, past the town of Sawi, is the Tako Estuary and the fair beach of Hat Arunothai. Most of these beaches have at least one set of resort bungalows.

Diving & Snorkelling
At Chumphon the Gulf of Thailand begins opening up more to the oceanic influences of the South China Sea and is less affected by fresh river water drainage than the upper gulf. This means more coral growth than at Pattaya, Ko Chang and other northern gulf dive sites. Because there is no operational airport nearby, only the more determined foreign divers seem to make it to Chumphon, which is an all-day bus ride from Bangkok, or 3½ hours from Surat Thani.

There are at least half a dozen small islands and seamounts off the Chumphon coast that are worth diving, most of them are 15 to 35km east of the mainland. Among the best are **Ko Ngam Yai** and **Ko Ngam Noi**, where there is abundant coral at depths of 5 to 20m and visibility of up to 15m or more in good conditions. Just off the north end of Ko Ngam Yai, **Hin Lak Ngam** (also known as Hin Phae) is also very good. All three spots are also suitable for snorkelling in good weather.

Diving conditions in this area tend to be best between May and November.

Baan's Diving has an office in town on Th Tha Taphao near the Tha Taphao Hotel. It offers dive trips, instruction and certification, equipment rental and repair, and airfills. Baan's also provides a taxi service to the harbour, speedboat tickets to Ko Tao and minivans to Bangkok. (see Getting There & Away in the Chumphon section).

Chumphon's original dive shop, at Chumphon Cabana Resort & Diving Center (☎ 077-501990, Bangkok 02-224 1994) on Hat Thung Wua Laen (see Places to Stay & Eat later), has rental diving equipment and offers instruction and airfills. It also has an office in town, next to Infinity Travel. Chumphon Cabana can organise dive trips to Ko Tao, an island which is technically located in Chumphon Province although it's geographically closer to Surat Thani's Ko Samui archipelago (it's covered in the following South-Western Gulf Coast chapter). For Ko Tao diving, however, you're better off staying on Ko Tao itself as the island is three hours away from Chumphon by the fastest boats.

Places to Stay & Eat

Hat Pharadon Phap & Hat Sairi The air-con *Porn Sawan Home Beach Resort* (☎ 077-521521) is at Pak Nam Chumphon and has standard air-con rooms for 450B, 750B with a sea view and 950B for a suite. The resort has a pool, but no restaurant. *Sai Ree Lodge* (☎ 077-521212) at nearby Hat Sairi has concrete bungalows with corrugated roofs for 950B with fan, 1150B with air-con. Farther north along Hat Pharadon Phap, *Sweet Guest House* (☎ 077-521324) offers air-con rooms for 400B to 500B.

Hat Thung Wua Laen Twelve kilometres north of Chumphon on Hat Thung Wua Laen – also known as Hat Cabana – the

well established *Chumphon Cabana Resort & Diving Center* (☎ 077-501990, Bangkok 02-224 1994) has well appointed and energy-efficient bungalows plus 36 new rooms in a three storey building, and they operate the oldest dive operation in the area. The nightly tariff for a standard room is 1200B, a superior room is 1400B and a suite goes for 2100B. They offer the best – and priciest – dive trips in the area.

Near the centre, *Cleanwave* (☎ 077-560151) is one of the cheapest places on the beach, with clean, wood and bamboo, A-frame bungalows with fan for 300B, 600B air-con. Next door, the *View Seafood Resort* (☎ 077-560214) rents wood and thatch A-frames for 300/400B single/double with fan and bath, or more solid concrete bungalows, across the road, with air-con and TV for 700B to 900B.

Seabeach Bungalow (☎ 077-560115) is the cheapest place in this area. Clean fan rooms are available for 250B, air-con for 550B; a restaurant is on the premises. *Khun Rim Lay* has three air-con rooms ranging from 600B to 800B, and are in the process of building more. The restaurant at View Seafood Resort is reasonably priced and quite good. There are several other casual seafood restaurants along Hat Thung Wua Laen where you can dine on the beach.

Hat Sapli A couple of kilometres north of Hat Thung Wua Laem is this newly developing beach area, where the friendly, well situated *Si Sanyalak* (☎ 01-477 6602) features four rooms in a longhouse-style building with fan for 350B each, plus two separate bungalows with air-con, TV and fridge for 750B.

Hat Arunothai *Chumphon Sunny Beach* (☎ 077-579148) is at the Tako Estuary on Hat Arunothai, about 50km south of Chumphon. Bungalows are a steep 750B with fan or 950B with air-con.

South-Western Gulf Coast (Surat Thani to Narathiwat)

South of Chumphon the Thai-Malay peninsula – the second longest peninsula in the world after the Kamchatka Peninsula in Russia – swells to its widest girth in Thailand. Beyond the well known islands of Ko Samui, Ko Pha-Ngan and Ko Tao, few tourists are seen along this extensive coastline. With relatively little agribusiness, aquaculture or manufacturing, there's less development here than anywhere else along either the Gulf or the Andaman Sea shores.

The overall lack of tourism south of the Samui archipelago can only be explained by the fact that the South-Western Gulf's best season climatically runs from April to October, the exact opposite of Thailand's 'natural' tourist season (which coincides with the European and North American winter). Ko Samui's natural assets as a beautiful, remote island – coupled with the fact that the original Hainanese inhabitants of the island were quite open to foreign visitation and tourism development – counter this seasonal aspect. The mostly Muslim residents of the coastal provinces farther south have historically been more indifferent to tourism, so they haven't built beach huts, guesthouses and restaurants catering to the foreign tourist trade. This is all the better for those global wanderers seeking less trodden sands.

SURAT THANI
• pop 41,800

There is little of particular historical interest at Surat Thani, a busy commercial centre and port dealing in rubber and coconut, but the town's busy waterfront lends character nonetheless. It's 651km from Bangkok and the first point in a southbound journey towards Malaysia that really feels and looks like southern Thailand. For most people Surat Thani (often called simply Surat) is only a stop on the way to Ko

HIGHLIGHTS

• Chaiya, near Surat Thani, is one of Thailand's oldest cities, with ancient *wát* ruins, a famous Buddhist meditation centre and peninsula rainforest.

• Khao Sok National Park's native rainforests, waterfalls, limestone cliffs and waterways are home to a plethora of wildlife, including the *Rafflesia*, the world's largest flower.

• Ko Pha-Ngan has diving on offshore reefs, hikes to stunning waterfalls, day-trips to Ang Thong National Marine Park and uncrowded beaches.

• Nakhon Si Thammarat is one of the few places where traditional life-size, buffalo-hide shadow puppets are still made.

• Soak up the traditional *pàk tâi* way of life in Pattani, Narathiwat, Songkhla and Hat Yai, where Buddhism and Islam meet.

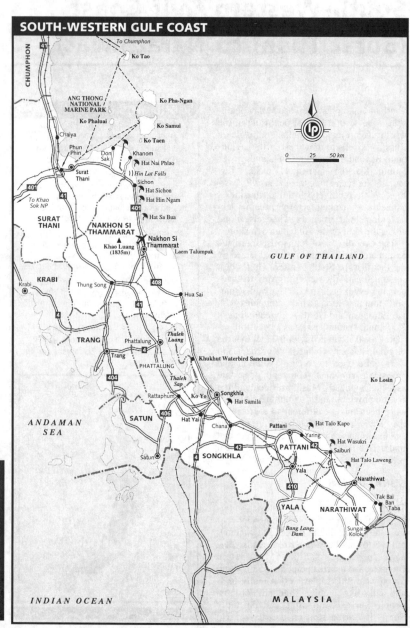

SOUTH-WESTERN GULF COAST

To Chumphon
CHUMPHON
Ko Tao
ANG THONG
NATIONAL
MARINE PARK
Ko Phaluai
Ko Pha-Ngan
Chaiya
Ko Samui
Phun
Phin
Ko Taen
Don
Sak
Khanom
Hat Nai Phlao
Surat
Thani
Hin Lat Falls
Sichon
To Khao
Sok NP
Hat Sichon
SURAT
THANI
Hat Hin Ngam
NAKHON SI
THAMMARAT
Hat Sa Bua
Khao Luang
(1835m)
Nakhon Si
Thammarat
Laem Talumpuk
GULF OF THAILAND
KRABI
Krabi
Thung Song
Hua Sai
TRANG
Phattalung
Thaleh
Luang
Trang
Khukhut Waterbird Sanctuary
Ko Losin
PHATTALUNG
Thaleh
Sap
Rattaphum
Ko Yo
Songkhla
SATUN
Hat Samila
ANDAMAN
SEA
Hat Yai
Chana
Hat Talo Kapo
Pattani
Yaring
Hat Wasukri
PATTANI
Hat Talo Laweng
Satun
SONGKHLA
Yala
Narathiwat
YALA
Tak Bai
Ban
Taba
NARATHIWAT
Bang Lang
Dam
Sungai
Kolok
INDIAN OCEAN
MALAYSIA

0   25   50 km

Samui or Ko Pha-Ngan, luscious islands 32km off the coast – so the Talaat Kaset bus stations in the Ban Don area of Surat and the ferry piers to the east become the centres of attention.

Information

Tourist Offices The friendly TAT office (☎ 077-288819), at 5 Thanon (Th) Talaat Mai near the south-western end of town, distributes plenty of useful brochures and maps. It's open daily from 8.30 am to 4.30 pm.

Several travel agencies in town, including Phantip Travel (☎ 077-272230) at 442/24-5 Th Talaat Mai and Songserm Travel (☎ 077-285124, fax 285127) at 30/2 Muu 3, Th Bang Kung, with another office opposite the pier, handle travel to the islands or elsewhere in southern Thailand. Phantip is the most reliable travel agent in town; Songserm's parent company has a near monopoly on all boat transport to the islands and it's notorious for a couldn't-care-less attitude.

Money There's a string of banks – one on every block for five blocks – along Th Na Meuang south-west of Th Chonkasem. All have ATMs and most offer foreign exchange. Bangkok Bank at 193 Th Na Meuang has an exchange booth open daily from 8.30 am to 5 pm.

Post & Telephone The main post office is on Th Talaat Mai; Ban Don has it's own post office on Th Na Meuang. The telecommunications centre on Th Don Nok, open daily from 7 am to 11 pm, is the place to make international calls.

Places to Stay – Budget

At some of Surat Thani's cheaper hotels, business consists largely of 'short-time' trade. This doesn't make them any less useful as regular hotels – it's just that there's likely to be rather more noise as guests arrive and depart with some frequency. In fact, if you're on a tight budget, it may be better to zip straight through Surat Thani via the night boat; you may even sleep better on the night boat than in a noisy hotel.

Surat Thani Festivals

In mid October Chak Phra and Thawt Phaa Paa celebrations occur on the same day (first day of the waning moon in the 11th lunar month) at the end of the Buddhist rains retreat and are major events in Surat Thani Province.

Thawt Phaa Paa, or 'Laying-Out of Forest Robes', begins at dawn with the offering of new monastic robes to the monks, while Chak Phra or 'Pulling of the Buddha Image' takes place during the day and evening. During Chak Phra local, lay devotees place sacred Buddha images on boats for a colourful procession along the Tapi River. A similar terrestrial procession uses trucks and hand-pulled carts. Lots of food-stalls are set up and musical performances, including *li-khe*, are staged for the occasion.

If you arrive in Surat by train or bus in the morning you'll have no problem making a connection with one of the day express boats. Another alternative is to stay near the train station in Phun Phin (see under Places to Stay & Eat – Phun Phin later in this section).

All of the following places are within walking (or samlor) distance of the Ban Don boat pier.

The best budget value in Surat continues to be the **Ban Don Hotel** (☎ 077-272167) on Th Na Meuang towards the morning market, with clean singles/doubles with fan and bath for 180/200B. You enter the hotel through a Chinese restaurant. **Surat Hotel** (☎ 077-272243, 496 Th Na Meuang), between the Grand City Hotel and the bus station, costs 150B to 300B for spacious rooms with fan and bath, 350B with air-con. At the rear are some quiet, renovated rooms. Across the street from the Surat, **Phanfa Hotel** (☎ 077-272287, 247/2-5 Th Na Meuang) has similar rooms with fan and private bath for 180B.

Grand City Hotel (☎ 077-272960, 428 *Th Na Meuang)* has been renovated and has plain but clean rooms with fan and bath for 230/280B one bed/two beds, and air-con rooms for 380/500B.

Off Th Ban Don, near the municipal pier, on a fairly quiet street off Th Si Chaiya, is *Seree (Seri) Hotel* (☎ 077-272279), where you'll find adequate but somewhat airless rooms with fan and private bath for 250/300B, air-con rooms are 320/400B. There's a coffee shop on the premises.

One block from the night boat pier on Th Si Chaiya is *Thai Hotel* (☎ 077-272932), where dingy but fairly quiet rooms with fan and bath cost 200B.

On Th Na Meuang near the Talaat Kaset 1 bus station is the scruffy, not-too-clean *Ratchathani (Rajthani) Hotel* (☎ 077-287638, fax 272972), which starts at 280B for rooms with fan and private bath, and from 360B for air-con.

Places to Stay – Mid-Range

Popular with travelling business people, the *Tapi Hotel* (☎ 077-272575, 100 *Th Chonkasem)* has fan-cooled rooms for 260B to 380B, air-con for 500B to 600B. The similar but older *Muang Tai* (☎ 077-272367, 390-392 *Th Talaat Mai)* has fan-cooled rooms from 250B and air-con rooms from 370B and has received good reviews from travellers. The recently renovated *Thai Rung Ruang Hotel* (☎ 077-273249, fax 286353, 191/199 *Th Mitkasem)*, off Th Na Meuang near Talaat Kaset 1 bus terminal, is also good, with rooms from 310/390B (fan) for one/two beds and 420/520B (air-con, TV, phone). Although these hotels don't cost much more than the budget places mentioned, the facilities are considerably better.

Places to Stay – Top End

Surat Thani also has a number of more up-scale hotels priced slightly lower than those in other large provincial capitals. *Wang Tai* (☎ 077-283020/39, fax 281007, 1 *Th Talaat Mai)* is a big place with nearly 300 rooms, a swimming pool and prices from 800B.

Siam Thani (☎ 077-273081, fax 282169, 180 *Th Surat Thani-Phun Phin)* costs 840B (as low as 630B in low season) and has a swimming pool. There's a coffee shop and a good restaurant on the premises. *Siam Thara*, on Th Don Nok near the Th Talaat Mai intersection, has air-con rooms ranging from 395B to 960B.

Southern Star Hotel (☎ 077-216414, fax 216427, 253 *Th Chonkasem)*, south of the Muang Tai Hotel, is home to the biggest discotheque in Southern Thailand, the Star Theque. All 150 rooms feature sitting areas that have inspired the hotel to call them 'suites'. A standard single/double costs 1110B, a superior 2690B. Other facilities include a coffee shop, restaurant, sky lounge and karaoke pub.

The newest top-end place in town, the 11 storey *Saowaluk Thani Hotel* (☎ 077-213700, fax 213735, 99/99 *Th Kanjana-withi)*, stands on the north-eastern city limits on the road to Don Sak. Rooms list for 1900/2100B single/double but are readily available for 820/940B with breakfast. Deluxe rooms cost 2900B rack and 1450B discounted. On the premises are a coffee shop, a lobby bar, a Chinese restaurant and several function rooms.

Places to Eat

The *Talaat Kaset market* area next to the Talaat Kaset 1 bus terminal (TK1) and the *morning market* (between Th Na Meuang and Th Si Chaiya) are good food-hunting places. Many stalls near TK1 specialise in *khâo kài òp*, a marinated baked chicken on rice which is very tasty. During mango season, a lot of street vendors sell incredible *khâo niāw má-mûang*, coconut-sweetened sticky rice with sliced ripe mango.

The best of Surat's several *night markets* is one that runs along both sides of Th Ton Pho, near the Seree Hotel.

There is an exemplary Southern-style *khanõm jiin place* in an old wooden building, just around the corner, south-west from Bangkok Bank, off Th Na Meuang.

NPA Cafe, an air-con place on Th Na Meuang between the Thai Military Bank

Homage cloth on traditional fishing boats placates sea spirits.

PAUL PIAIA

A fishing boat near Ko Samui.

PAUL PIAIA

Ko Nang Yuan off Ko Tao, South-Western Gulf Coast.

PAUL BEINSSEN

The big buddha on Ko Samui.

PAUL PIAIA

Early morning over Ao Chalok Ban Kao, Ko Tao.

RICHARD NEBESKY

A fishing boat wrecked on Hat Chaweng, Ko Samui, South-Western Gulf Coast.

Bronze mermaid, Hat Samila, Songkhla.

A Thai fisherman on Ko Samui.

A bathing beauty on Hat Chaweng, Ko Samui.

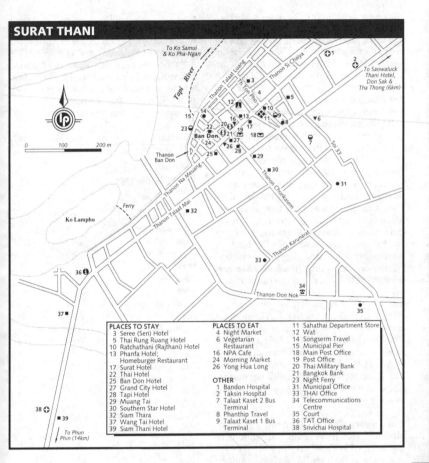

SURAT THANI

PLACES TO STAY
3 Seree (Seri) Hotel
5 Thai Rung Ruang Hotel
10 Ratchathani (Rajthani) Hotel
13 Phanfa Hotel;
   Homeburger Restaurant
17 Surat Hotel
22 Thai Hotel
25 Ban Don Hotel
27 Grand City Hotel
28 Tapi Hotel
29 Muang Tai
30 Southern Star Hotel
32 Siam Thara
37 Wang Tai Hotel
39 Siam Thani Hotel

PLACES TO EAT
4 Night Market
6 Vegetarian
   Restaurant
16 NPA Cafe
24 Morning Market
26 Yong Hua Long

OTHER
1 Bandon Hospital
2 Taksin Hospital
7 Talaat Kaset 2 Bus
   Terminal
8 Phanthip Travel
9 Talaat Kaset 1 Bus
   Terminal

11 Sahathai Department Store
12 Wat
14 Songserm Travel
15 Municipal Pier
18 Main Post Office
19 Post Office
20 Thai Military Bank
21 Bangkok Bank
23 Night Ferry
31 Municipal Office
33 THAI Office
34 Telecommunications
   Centre
35 Court
36 TAT Office
38 Srivichai Hospital

and the Phanfa Hotel, has western breakfasts, pizza, burgers, salads, macaroni, spaghetti, sandwiches, Thai and Chinese food – plus Corona beer, Bud's Ice Cream, Geno's Pizza and an extensive list of appetisers. *Homeburger Restaurant*, next to the Phanfa Hotel, does hamburgers, pizza, steak and some Thai dishes.

Around the corner from the Grand City Hotel is the inexpensive and popular *Yong Hua Long*, a decent Chinese restaurant with roast duck and a large buffet table.

Vegetarian Food, on the east side of Soi 33, Th Talaat Mai, serves good vegetarian *kŭaytĭaw* and some very hot Thai curries. It's a little more expensive than the average for Thai vegetarian.

Places to Stay & Eat – Phun Phin

You may find yourself needing accommodation in Phun Phin (where the Surat Thani train station is actually located), either because you're stranded due to booked-out trains or because you've come in from Ko Samui in the evening and plan to get an early morning train out of Surat before the Surat to Phun Phin bus service starts. If so, there are a couple of cheap, dilapidated hotels just across from the train station. The *Tai Fah* has rooms for 120B with shared bathroom, 150B with private bath.

If you can afford a few baht more, around the corner on the road to Surat, but still quite close to the train station, is the better *Queen* (☎ 077-311003), where rooms cost 180B to 250B with fan and 400B with air-con.

Across from the Queen is a good *night market* with cheap eats. The *Tai Fah* does Thai, Chinese and western food at reasonable prices. Opposite the north end of the train station, *Oum's Restaurant* has an English menu and serves good Thai coffee, western breakfasts and simple Thai dishes. Nearby are the similar *Wuts* and *Sincere*; the latter offers email and Internet services.

Getting There & Away
Air THAI flies to Surat Thani from Bangkok twice daily (70 minutes, 1785B). The THAI office (☎ 077-272610, 273710) in Surat is at 3/27-28 Th Karunarat.

A THAI shuttle van between Surat Thani and the airport costs 40B per person. THAI also runs a more expensive limo service for 150B.

Bus, Share Taxi & Minivan First class air-con buses leave Bangkok's Southern bus terminal in Thonburi twice in the morning, once in the evening, arriving in Surat 11 hours later; the fare is 315B. There is also one 2nd class air-con departure at 10 pm (250B) and one VIP departure at 8 pm (400B). Private companies also run 'Super VIP' buses with only 24 seats for 500B.

Ordinary buses leave the Southern bus terminal once in the morning and once in the evening for 180B.

Take care when booking private air-con and VIP buses out of Surat. Some companies have been known to sell tickets for VIP buses to Bangkok, then pile hapless travellers onto an ordinary air-con bus and then

refuse to refund the fare difference. If possible get a recommendation from another traveller or inquire at the TAT office.

Public buses and share taxis run from the Talaat Kaset 1 or 2 markets. Phantip Travel handles minivan and bus bookings (as well as air, train and boat bookings).

Other fares to/from Surat are:

destination	fare (B)	hours
Hat Yai	100	5
(air-con)	160	4
(share taxi or van)	160	3½
Krabi	70	4
(air-con)	90	3
(share taxi or van)	150	2
Nakhon Si Thammarat	36	2½
(air-con)	70	2
(share taxi)	80	2
Narathiwat	127	6
Phang-Nga	50	4
(air-con)	100	3
(share taxi)	70	2½
Phuket	90	6
(air-con)	150	5
(share taxi or van)	160	4
Ranong	70	5
(air-con)	120	4
(share taxi or van)	130	3½
Satun	85	4
Trang	60	3
(van)	120	3
Yala	120	6
(van)	160	6

Buses from Phun Phin If you're taking the train to Surat Thani, but going on to the Andaman Coast rather than Ko Samui or Pha-Ngan, there are bus services operating out of Phun Phin (where the Surat train station is actually located). This saves you having to go into Surat Thani proper.

The main destinations served are Takua Pa (where you can get buses north to Ranong), Phuket, and Phang-Nga on the Andaman Coast. Nearly all services are by ordinary bus, except for two air-con services to Phuket, which leave at 7.30 and 10.30 am.

Other buses leave every one to two hours from 6 am to 3.30 pm. The ordinary buses to Phuket run past Khao Sok National Park, Takua Pa and Hat Khao Lak; Takua Pa buses also pass Khao Sok. Buses leave from next to a white building, south of the train station: look for the bus schedule painted on the wall.

Train Trains for Surat, which don't really stop in Surat but in Phun Phin, 14km west of town, leave Bangkok's Hualamphong terminal at 12.20 pm (rapid), 2.15 and 2.35 pm (special express), 3.50 pm (rapid), 5.05 pm (express), 5.35 and 6.20 pm (rapid) and 7.15 pm (express), arriving 10½ to 11 hours later. There are also all 2nd class express diesel railcars (no sleeping berths) which leave Bangkok daily at 10.30 and 10.50 pm and arrive in Phun Phin at 7.10 and 7.47 am for 368B. The 6.20 pm train (rapid No 167) is the most convenient, arriving at 5.28 am and giving you plenty of time to catch a boat to Samui, if that's your destination. Fares are 519B in 1st class, 248B in 2nd class and 107B 3rd class, not including the surcharges for rapid/express/special express or berths.

The Phun Phin train station has a 24 hour left-luggage room that charges 5B a day for the first five days, 10B a day thereafter. The advance ticket office is open daily from 6 to 11 am and noon to 6 pm.

It is sometimes quite difficult to book long-distance trains out of Phun Phin – for long-distance travel, it may be easier to take a bus, especially if heading south. The trains are often full and it's a drag to take the bus 14km from town to the Phun Phin train station without a reservation and be turned away. However, you could buy a 'standing room only' 3rd class ticket and stand for an hour or two until someone vacates a seat down the line.

Advance reservations can be made, without going all the way out to Phun Phin station, at Phantip Travel on Th Talaat Mai near the market/bus station. You might try making an onward reservation *before* boarding a boat for Ko Samui. Songserm Travel on Ko Samui can also assist travellers with reservations.

Train/Bus/Boat Combinations These days many travellers are buying tickets, from the State Railway, that go straight through to Ko Samui or Ko Pha-Ngan from Bangkok on a train, bus and boat combination. The savings is typically little more than 50B. See the Getting There & Away sections under each island for more details.

Getting Around
Air-con vans from the airport to Surat Thani cost 80B per person. THAI also runs a more expensive limo service for 150B (280B all the way to Ko Samui).

Buses to Ban Don from Phun Phin train station leave every 10 minutes or so from 6 am to 8 pm for 10B per person. Some of the buses drive straight to the pier (if they have enough tourists on the bus), while others will terminate at the Talaat Kasem 1 bus terminal, from where you must get another bus to Tha Thong (or to Ban Don if you're taking the night ferry).

If you arrive in Phun Phin on one of the night trains, you might be able to get a free bus from the train station to the pier, courtesy of the boat service, for the morning boat departures. If your train arrives in Phun Phin when the courtesy and public buses aren't running, then you're out of luck and will have to hire a taxi to Surat for about 70B to 80B, or hang out in one of the Phun Phin street cafes until buses start running.

Orange buses run from Ban Don bus station to Phun Phin train station about every 10 minutes from 5 am to 7.30 pm for 8B per person. Buses also wait at Tha Thong for passengers arriving from Ko Samui on the express boat, ready to drive them directly to the train station or destinations farther afield.

Around town, share songthaews cost 6B to 10B depending on the distance, while samlor rides cost 20B.

AROUND SURAT THANI
Two inland places near Surat are worth visiting if you're looking for a break from sea and sand. Chaiya is an important footnote in Thai history, and boasts one of Thailand's most famous Buddhist meditation centres,

while Khao Sok National Park preserves a large chunk of peninsular rainforest.

Chaiya

Just north of Surat Thani and best visited as a day trip from there, Chaiya is one of the oldest cities in Thailand, dating back to the Srivijaya Empire. In fact, the name may be a contraction of Siwichaiya, the Thai pronunciation of the city that was a regional capital between the 8th and 10th centuries. Before this time the area was on the Indian trade route through South-East Asia. Many Srivijaya artefacts in the National Museum in Bangkok were found in Chaiya, including a famous Avalokitesvara Bodhisattva bronze that's considered a masterpiece of Buddhist art.

Wat Phra Boromathat, Wat Kaew & Chaiya National Museum

The restored Borom That Chaiya stupa at Wat Phra Boromathat, just outside of town, is a fine example of Srivijaya architecture. In the courtyard surrounding the revered *chedi* are several pieces of sculpture from the region, including an unusual two-sided *yoni* (the uterus-shaped pedestal that holds the *Shivalingam*), *rishis* (hermit sages) performing yoga and several Buddha images.

A ruined stupa at nearby Wat Kaew (also known as Wat Long), also from the Srivijaya period, shows the influence of central Javanese architecture (or perhaps vice versa) as well as Cham (9th century South Vietnam) characteristics.

The national museum near the entrance to Wat Phra Boromathat displays prehistoric and historic artefacts of local provenance, as well as local handicrafts and a shadow puppet exhibit. Admission to the museum is 30B; it's open Wednesday to Sunday from 9 am to 4 pm.

You can catch any songthaew heading west from the main intersection south of the train station to Wat Phra Boromathat for 5B. This same songthaew route passes the turn-off for Wat Kaew, which is about 500m before the turn-off for Boromathat. Wat Kaew is less than 500m from this junction, on the left, almost directly opposite Chaiya Witthaya School.

Wat Suan Mokkhaphalaram (Suanmok)

This is a modern forest *wát* founded to the west of Wat Kaew by Ajaan Buddhadasa Bhikku (Phutthathat), Thailand's most famous monk. Born in Chaiya in 1906, Buddhadasa ordained as a monk when he was 21, spent many years studying the Pali scriptures and then retired to the forest for six years of solitary meditation. Returning to ecclesiastical society, he was made abbot of Wat Phra Boromathat, a high distinction, but conceived of Suanmok as an alternative to orthodox Thai temples. His philosophy was ecumenical in nature, comprising Zen, Taoist and Christian elements as well as the traditional Theravada schemata. During Thailand's turbulent 1970s, he was branded a Communist because of his critiques of capitalism, which he saw as a catalyst for greed. Buddhadasa died in July 1993 after a long illness.

Wat Suanmok, which literally means 'Garden of Liberation', is spread over 120 hectares of wooded hillside and features huts for up to 70 monks, a museum/library and a 'spiritual theatre'. This latter building has bas-reliefs on the outer walls which are facsimiles of sculptures at Sanchi, Bharhut and Amaravati in India. The interior walls feature modern Buddhist painting – eclectic to say the least – executed by the resident monks.

At the affiliated International Dhamma Hermitage, across the highway 1.5km from Wat Suanmok, resident monks hold meditation retreats during the first 10 days of every month. Anyone is welcome to participate; a donation is requested to cover food and utilities costs. There is no advance registration or reservation for the retreats. Simply arrive in time to register on the final day of the month preceding the retreat. Registration takes place at the main monastery.

A 12 minute stroll south of IDH is Dawn Kiam (officially called Suan Atammayatarama), a monastic centre for training foreign *bhikkhus* under the direction of Phra Santikaro, an American monk who trained under Ajaan Buddhadasa. Men may study at Dawn Kiam for stays of a week or more, not less, and if they intend to ordain must stay three months first. Women who would like to practice at Dawn Kiam may arrange accommodation at IDH.

Places to Stay Travellers could stay in Surat Thani for visits to Chaiya or request permission from the monks to stay in the guest quarters at Wat Suanmok. *Udomlap Hotel* (☎ *077-431123, 431946*), a Chinese-Thai hotel in Chaiya, has clean rooms in an old wooden building for 150B, while rooms in a new modern multi-storey air-con wing go for 250B to 400B.

Getting There & Away If you're going to Surat Thani by train from Bangkok, you can get off at the small Chaiya train station, then catch another train to Phun Phin, Surat's train station.

From Surat you can either take a songthaew from Talaat Kaset 2 in Ban Don (18B to Wat Suanmok or 25B to Chaiya) or get a train going north from Phun Phin. The trains between Phun Phin and Chaiya may be full, but you can always stand or squat in a 3rd class car for the short trip. The ordinary train costs 10B in 3rd class to Chaiya and takes about an hour to get there. The songthaew takes around 45 minutes. Or you can take a share taxi from Surat for 30B per person; in Chaiya, Surat-bound taxis leave from opposite the train station.

Suanmok is about 7km outside town on the highway to Surat and Chumphon. Until late afternoon there are songthaews from the Chaiya train station to Wat Suanmok for 8B per passenger. From Chaiya you can also catch a Surat-bound bus from the front of the movie theatre on Chaiya's main street and ask to be let off at Wat Suanmok. (Turn right, east, on the road in front of the train station.) The fare to Wat Suanmok is 5B. If buses aren't running you can hire a motorcycle taxi for 20B anywhere along Chaiya's main street.

Khao Sok National Park

Established in 1980, this 646 sq km park lies in the western part of Surat Thani Province, off Route 401, about a third of the way from Takua Pa to Surat Thani. The park features 65,000 hectares of thick native rainforest with waterfalls, limestone cliffs, numerous streams, an island-studded lake, and many trails, mostly along rivers. According to Thom Henley, author of the highly informative *Waterfalls and Gibbon Calls*, the Khao Sok rainforest is a remnant of a 160-million-year-old forest ecosystem that is much older and richer than the forests of the Amazon or central Africa. Connected to two other national parks, Kaeng Krung National Park and Phang-Nga National Park, along with the Khlong Saen and Khlong Nakha wildlife sanctuaries (thus forming the largest contiguous nature preserve – around 4000 sq km – on the Thai peninsula), Khao Sok shelters a plethora of wildlife, including wild elephant, leopard, serow, banteng, gaur, dusky langur, tiger and Malayan sun bear as well as over 180 bird species. The tiger population – currently estimated by park staff at less than 10 individuals – is extremely threatened due to the high demand for tiger parts in Taiwan.

A major watershed for the south, the park is filled with lianas, bamboo, ferns and rattan, including the giant rattan or *wāai tào phráw*, with a stem over 10cm in diameter. One floral rarity found in the park is *Rafflesia kerri meyer*, known to the Thais as *bua phut* or wild lotus, the largest flower in the world. Found only in Khao Sok and an adjacent wildlife sanctuary (different varieties of the same species are found in Malaysia and Indonesia), mature specimens reach 80cm in diameter. The flower has no roots or leaves of its own; instead it lives parasitically inside the roots of the liana, a jungle vine. From October to December, buds burst forth from the liana root and swell to football size. When the bud blooms in January and February it emits a potent stench (said to resemble that of a rotting corpse) that attracts insects responsible for pollination.

SOUTH-WESTERN GULF COAST

A map of hiking trails within the park is available for 5B from park headquarters near the park entrance. Various trails lead to the waterfalls of **Mae Yai** (5.5km from park headquarters), **Than Sawan** (9km), **Sip-Et Chan** (4km) and **Than Kloy** (9km). Guesthouses near the park entrance can arrange guided hikes that include waterfalls, caves and river-running. Park rangers can lead jungle tours and/or rafting trips for 150B per day. Leeches are quite common in certain areas of the park, so take the usual precautions – wear closed shoes when hiking and apply plenty of repellent.

The 95m high, 700m long, shale-clay Ratchaprapha Dam (also referred to as Chiaw Lan Dam), erected across the Pasaeng River in 1982, creates the vast 165km-long **Chiaw Lan Lake**. Limestone outcrops protruding from the lake reach as high as 960m, over three times the height of similar formations in Ao Phang-Nga. A limestone cave known as **Tham Nam Thalu** contains striking cavern formations and subterranean streams, while **Tham Si Ru** features four converging passageways used as a hideout by Communist insurgents between 1975 and 1982. **Tham Khang Dao**, high on a limestone cliff face, is home to many bat species. All three caves can be reached on foot from the south-western shore of the lake. The dam is 65km from the visitors' centre via a well marked side road off Route 401 (back towards Surat Thani). You can rent boats from local fishermen to explore the coves, canals, caves and cul-de-sacs along the lakeshore. Two floating lodges belonging to the national park provide overnight accommodation. Park rangers offer a good two day tour to the Chiaw Lan for 1600B per person, including food, transport, guide service and an overnight stay at one of the lodges.

The best overall time of year to visit Khao Sok is December to May, when trails are less slippery, river crossings are easier and riverbank camping is safer due to the lower risk of flash flooding. During the June to November wet season, on the other hand, you're more likely to see Malayan and Asiatic black bear, civets, slow loris, wild boar, gaur, deer and wild elephants – and tiger if you're very, very lucky – along the trail system. During dry months the larger mammals tend to stay near the reservoir in areas without trails.

The park headquarters is 1.5km off Route 401 between Takua Pa and Surat Thani at Km 109. Besides the camping area and bungalows at the park headquarters, there are several private bungalow operations featuring 'tree house' style accommodation outside the park. Entrance to the park is 10B per person, 20B per vehicle.

Rainforest Safari (☎/fax 076-330852) in Phuket arranges treks and elephant rides in Khao Sok for 2500B to 4500B. At the visitors' centre, as well as various bookshops in Southern Thailand, you can purchase a copy of the well written and inspirational *Waterfalls and Gibbon Calls*, a wildlife guide to Khao Sok by Krabi resident Thom Henley. The author pulls no punches when it comes to his critiques of park management and national policy.

Places to Stay & Eat Khao Sok National Park offers a camping area and several places to stay. The park no longer offers tents for rent; pitching your own costs 10B. Two *bungalows* near the visitors' centre are available for 350B, and there's a *longhouse* sleeping up to 12 people on rice mats only, available for just 300B. Near the entrance, a small co-operative *restaurant* serves inexpensive meals – when it's open (infrequently it seems).

Private accommodation and food are also available at several places just outside the park. All places offer guides for jungle trips. Right next to the park entrance, 1.9km from the highway, *Treetop River Huts* (☎ 076-421155/613, both ext 107), offers six dilapidated thatched-roof rooms with private bath for 200/300B single/double, or a tree house with private bath for 400B, plus meals for 40B to 70B. The whole place is plagued with rubbish, though the family who run the show are friendly enough. They offer tyre inner tubes for tubing, and many of their bungalows are lined up along a stream.

Bamboo House, off the main road to the park, has seven primitive but clean rooms for 100/150B with shared bathroom, 170/250B with private bathroom, plus 120B extra for three meals a day. Several other establishments offering thatch-roofed huts for 150B can be found in the vicinity of the park entrance and on the road leading past Bamboo House.

Art's Riverview Jungle Lodge (☎ 01-421 2394), beyond the Bamboo House, about a kilometre from the park, has seven rooms for 200B to 300B, plus tree houses for 400B and two large houses with rooms with private bath and deck for 600B. Two of the newer tree houses are right on the Sok River and boast good views of nearby mountains. Meals cost 250B a day or you can order à la carte at breakfast and lunch, 80B for a set Thai dinner. Art's seems to be the best run of the bunch, and despite the operation's obvious success, the owner prefers a lamplit night-time ambience and thus has no plans to install electricity.

Past Art's and the Bamboo House is the somewhat pricier ***Our Jungle House*** (☎ 01-211 2564, fax 229 1337, Bangkok ☎/fax 02-863 1301, email sadler@mozart.inet.co.th), run by the owners of the Similana Resort near Takua Pa. Nicely designed tree houses with private bath, set along the river facing a huge limestone cliff (good gibbon viewing) cost 800B depending on the season, and there are also smaller, less expensive rooms in the main house where the dining room is. Full board costs another 400B per person per day, and an overnight lake trip is available for two for 6600B (including lots of animal-viewing on the jungle's edge), full-day rainforest hikes with a guide cost 800B for two people.

Under the same management as the ecologically oriented Dawn of Happiness in Krabi, ***Khao Sok Rainforest Resort*** (☎ 01-464 4362, 075-612730, ext 207, fax 612914) offers sturdy cottages raised on stilts with large verandahs overlooking the forest, with private showers and toilets, for

300B to 600B. All cottages have electricity, and thus fans.

Chiaw Lan Lake At Substation 3 near the dam, two large *floating raft houses* contain screened rooms with two to three beds each and good toilet/shower facilities. A smaller *raft house* at Substation 4 offers seven small bamboo huts with mattresses on the floor and communal facilities outside. The price at either is 500B per person including meals.

Getting There & Away

From Phun Phin or Surat Thani catch a bus bound for Takua Pa and get off at Km 109 (the park's entrance) on Hwy 401. If you're having trouble seeing the kilometre markers, just tell the bus driver or ticket attendants 'Khao Sok' and they'll let you off in the right place. The bus will cost you 82B air-con, 33B ordinary. You can also come from the Phuket side of the peninsula by bus, but you'll have to go to Takua Pa first; Surat-bound buses from Phuket don't use Hwy 401 anymore.

To reach Chiaw Lan Lake and the park's floating raft houses, you'll need your own transport – or you can try hitchhiking. The turnoff occurs between Km 52 and Km 53 on Route 401, at Ban Takum (see the North Andaman Coast map). From here it's 14km north-west to Substation 2.

KO SAMUI
• pop 35,000

Ko Samui is part of an island group that used to be called Muu Ko Samui (Samui Archipelago), though you rarely hear that term these days. The archipelago sits well off the coast of Surat Thani Province and consists of around 80 islands, of which seven – Samui, Pha-Ngan, Tao, Ta Loy, Taen, Ma Ko and Ta Pao – are inhabited. So far the bulk of the tourist interest has focused on the three largest islands, Ko Samui, Ko Pha-Ngan and Ko Tao.

At 247 sq km, Ko Samui is Thailand's third-largest island. Samui's first settlers were seafaring islanders from Hainan Island (now part of the People's Republic of

The Face of Peninsula Thailand

Although under Thai political domination for several centuries, the narrow pendant of land dangling between the Andaman Sea and Gulf of Thailand has always remained culturally apart from the other regions of Thailand. Historically, the peninsula has been linked to cultures in ancient Indonesia, particularly the Srivijaya empire, which ruled a string of principalities in what is today Southern Thailand, Malaysia and Indonesia. The Srivijaya dynasty is thought to have been based in Sumatra, with a major satellite in Chaiya. Srivijaya – Siwichai to the Thais – lasted nearly 500 years from the 8th to 13th centuries. The influence of Malay-Indonesian culture is still apparent in the ethnicity, religion, art and language of the *Thai pàk tâi*, the Southern Thais.

Geography & Economy

Bounded by water on two sides, the people of southern Thailand are by and large a seafaring lot. One consequence of this natural affinity with the ocean is the abundance of delectable seafood. Brightly painted fishing boats, hanging nets and neat thatched huts add to the *pàk tâi* setting; travellers who do a stint in southern Thailand are likely to come face to face with more than a few visions of 'tropical paradise', whatever their expectations might be.

Three of Thailand's most important exports – rubber, tin and coconut – are produced in the south so that the standard of living is a bit higher than in other provincial regions. However, southern Thais claim that most of the wealth is in the hands of ethnic Chinese. Throughout the peninsula – in Malaysia as well as Thailand – the Chinese are concentrated in the urban provincial capitals while the poorer Muslims live in the rural areas. This urban concentration of Chinese is a fact of life throughout South-East Asia, becoming more noticeable in southern Thailand and the Islamic state of Malaysia because of religious-cultural differences.

As in Malaysia, higher concentrations of Muslims live on the eastern side of the peninsula than on the western side – a legacy of non-Muslim immigration patterns during the 19th and early-20th century British colonial period when Phuket and Penang were important international trading centres. Although most Thais will vehemently deny that Britain ever ruled any part of the Thai half of the peninsula, the reality is that the British did claim dominion over parts Narathiwat, Satun and Yala provinces before the Anglo-Siamese Treaty of 1909.

Culture & Language

Officially, as well as ethnolinguistically, southern Thailand is made up of 14 provinces: Chumphon, Krabi, Nakhon Si Thammarat, Narathiwat, Pattani, Phang-Nga, Phattalung, Phuket, Ranong, Satun, Songkhla, Surat Thani, Trang and Yala. The Thai pàk tâi dress differently, build their houses differently and eat differently from Thais in the North. Due to a common history with Malaysia, many southern Thais are followers of Islam, and in many areas mosques outnumber Buddhist wáts. Local men often cover their heads with white-lace haji caps or black Nehru-style 'topis' and in rural areas they may favour the long sarong over ordinary western style trousers worn in the northern, central and north-eastern regions of Thailand. Muslim Thai women sport brightly coloured batik dresses and may wrap their hair in gauzy scarves.

These regional differences will become most visible to those who leave the coastal resort areas and explore inland towns and cities. In the larger southern cities a strong Chinese presence adds another element to the cultural mosaic, so that one can wander from Buddhist wát to Malay

The Face of Peninsula Thailand

tea shop to Chinese joss house in the space of a few blocks. The Chinese influence can also be seen in old urban architecture and in the baggy Chinese pants worn by rural non-Muslims.

All pàk tâi speak a dialect common among southern Thais that confounds even visitors from other Thai regions. Diction is short and fast: *pai nǎi* (Where are you going?) becomes *p'nái*, and *tham arai* (What are you doing?) becomes *rái*. The clipped tones fly into the outer regions of intelligibility, giving the aural impression of a tape played at the wrong speed. In the provinces nearest Malaysia – Yala, Pattani, Narathiwat and Satun – many Thai Muslims speak Yawi, an old Malay dialect with similarities to modern Bahasa Malaysia and Bahasa Indonesia.

You'll notice that 'Ao' 'Hat' and 'Ko' sometimes precede place names; ao means bay, hàt is beach and ko is island.

Southern Thais are stereotypically regarded as rebellious folk, considering themselves reluctant subjects of Bangkok rule and Thai (Central Thai) custom. Indeed, Thai Muslims (ethnic Malays) living in the provinces bordering Malaysia complain of persecution by the Thai government troops who police the area for insurgent activity. There has even been talk in some quarters of these provinces seceding from Thailand, an event that is unlikely to occur in the near future.

Joe Cummings

China) who took up coconut farming here around 150 years ago. You can still see a map of Hainan on the *sǎan jâo* or Chinese spirit shrine near Siam City Bank in Na Thon, the oldest town on the island. Muslim families of Thai-Malay descent live in a few of the villages scattered around the island as well. Beginning around 20 years ago, the island attained a somewhat legendary status among travellers in Asia, but it wasn't until the late 80s that its popularity escalated to the proportions of other similar getaways found between Goa and Bali.

Since the advent of the bus and ferry system and the opening of the airport, things have changed rapidly. During the high seasons, late December to February and July to August, it can be difficult to find a place to stay, even though most beaches are crowded with bungalows and resorts. The port town of Na Thon teems with foreign travellers getting on and off the ferry boats, booking tickets onward, and collecting mail at the post office. With nearly a dozen daily flights to Samui from

Bangkok, the island is rushing headlong into top-end development.

Airport or no airport, Samui is still an enjoyable place to spend some time, and more than a few people have been making regular visits for nearly 20 years. It still has some of the best accommodation values in Thailand and a casual, do-as-you-please atmosphere that makes it quite attractive. Even with an airport, it still has the advantage of being off the mainland and far away from Bangkok. Coconuts are still an important part of the local economy – up to two million are shipped to Bangkok each month.

But there's no going back to 1971, when the first two tourists arrived on a coconut boat from Bangkok, much to the surprise of a friend who had been living on the island for four years as a Peace Corps volunteer. The main difference is that there are now many more places to stay, most of them in the mid to high range by Thai standards. And of course, with this 'something for everyone' climate have come more people, more traffic, more noise and more rubbish,

SOUTH-WESTERN GULF COAST

but so far, not in intolerable proportions. Samui residents are beginning to formulate policies to deal with these social and environmental challenges and the prognosis is, tentatively, optimistic – only time will tell.

Perhaps due to the Hainanese influence, Samui culture differs from that of other islands in southern Thailand. Its inhabitants refer to themselves as *chao samūi* (Samui folk) rather than Thais. They can be even friendlier than the average rural Thai and have a great sense of humour, although those who are in constant contact with tourists are often more jaded. Nowadays many of the larger resorts, restaurants, bars and other tourist enterprises are owned or operated by Bangkok Thais or Europeans, so you have to get into the villages to meet true chao samūi.

The island has a distinctive cuisine, influenced by the omnipresent coconut, still the main source of income for chao samūi, who have disproportionately less ownership in beach property than outsiders. Coconut palms blanket the island, from the hillocks right up to the beaches. The durian, rambutan and langsat fruits are also cultivated.

The population of Ko Samui is for the most part concentrated in the port town of Na Thon, on the western side of the island facing the mainland, and in 10 or 11 small villages scattered around the island. One main road, which is now paved all the way around, encircles the island with several side roads poking into the interior. About 90% of the island is still uninhabited though you wouldn't know it from looking at the coastline. Retirement homes owned by foreigners as well as Thais are beginning to appear in the interior. Condos start at half a million baht, with 100% ownership possible (in condo developments only) even for non-Thais.

Ecology & Environment

Samui's visitors and inhabitants produce over 50 tonnes of garbage a day, much of it plastic. Not all is properly disposed of, and quite a few plastic bottles end up in the sea, where they wreak havoc on marine life.

Remember to request glass water bottles instead of plastic, or to try to fill your own water bottle from the guesthouse or hotel restaurant's large, reusable canisters. On Ko Tao the TAT arranges monthly volunteer rubbish collections with half a dozen dive agencies who offer discounts to customers who participate; ask your Samui dive shop if a beach cleanup is planned. A new incinerator is supposed to go on line soon to burn island rubbish.

Information

When to Go The best time to visit the Samui group of islands is during the hot and dry season, February to late June. From July to October (south-west monsoon) it can rain on and off, and from October to January (north-east monsoon) there are sometimes strong winds. However, many travellers have reported fine weather (and fewer crowds) in September and October. November tends to get some of the rain which also affects the east coast of Malaysia at this time. Prices tend to soar from December to July, whatever the weather.

Maps In Surat or on Ko Samui, you can pick up the TAT's helpful Surat Thani map, which has maps of Surat Thani Province, Ang Thong National Marine Park and Ko Samui, along with travel info. A couple of private companies now do good maps of Ko Samui, Pha-Ngan and Tao, which are available in tourist areas of Surat and on the islands for 50B. The most accurate and up-to-date is V Hongsombud's *Guide Map of Koh Samui, Koh Pha-Ngan & Koh Tao*.

If you fly into Samui airport, you may be handed the Bangkok Airways island map, which is quite good for a freebie.

Tourist Offices The friendly, helpful TAT office (☎ 077-420504) at the northern end of Na Thon, past the post office on the west side of the road, dispenses the usual handy brochures and maps. TAT claims this is a temporary office, though it has been there over three years now, and that it is looking for a new location elsewhere in town. The office is open daily 8.30 am to 4.30 pm.

Immigration Travellers have been able to extend their tourist visas for 500B at the Ko Samui immigration office (☎ 077-42106) about 3km south of Na Thon, at the intersection of the round island road (Route 4169) and the road that leads to the hospital (Route 4172). Hours are 8.30 am to noon and 1 pm to 4.30 pm weekdays (closed public holidays).

Money Changing money isn't a problem in Na Thon, Chaweng or Lamai, where several banks and exchange booths offer daily exchange services.

Post The island's main post office is in Na Thon, near the TAT office, but in other parts of the island there are privately run branches. The main office is open from 8.30 am to 4.30 pm Monday to Friday and 9 am to noon on Saturday. Many bungalow operations also sell stamps and mail letters, but most charge a commission.

Telephone International telephone service is available daily from 7 am to 10 pm on the 2nd floor of the CAT office, attached to the main post office. Many private phone offices around the island will make a connection for a surcharge over the usual TOT or CAT rates.

Email & Internet Access There are several places in Na Thon, Chaweng and Lamai that allow you to send and receive electronic mail and surf the Worldwide Web. Go Internet Cafe and Internet & Pub in Chaweng, and Island Tour in Na Thon across from the new pier all offer online access for around 60B per hour.

If you'd like to be seen live on the Internet, visit Poppies Beach Bar on Hat Chaweng, where a digital videocam dangles from the bar with views of the beach. Or visit www.sawadee.com/cam/ to watch the antics of tourists on the beach.

Internet Resources The Web site Koh Samui Thailand at www.sawadee.com contains lists of info on dive centres, accommodations and tours, plus timetables for Bangkok Airways, ferries, trains and VIP buses.

Travel Agencies Surat Thani travel agencies Phantip (☎ 077-421221/2) and Songserm (☎ 077-421316) have offices in Na Thon. The friendly staff at Asia Travel (☎ 077-236120, ☎/fax 421185) can handle travel arrangements and visas, and they have a photocopy machine.

Newspapers & Magazines *Samui Welcome*, a home-grown, tourist-oriented newspaper with articles in German, English and Thai, comes out a couple of times a year and is free. The much glossier, advertisement-packed *Samui* magazine, issued annually, contains lots of photos of topless Caucasians on the beach and is the kind of magazine in which only the advertisers are marked on the maps; the articles, however, show respect for the island's history and environment.

Medical Services Bandon International Hospital (☎ 077-245236, fax 425342), at Hat Chaweng, is a modern medical facility with staff and facilities adequate for most treatment; emergency ambulance service is available 24 hours and credit cards are accepted for treatment fees. Muang Thai Clinic (☎ 077-424219) on Hat Lamai is open Monday to Friday from 9 to 11 am and 5 to 7 pm, Saturday from 9 to 11 am and Sunday from 5 to 7 pm. House calls can be arranged if necessary.

Samui International Clinic (☎ 01-606 5833, 606 0235, 077-230186) on Th Ring in Chaweng is open daily from 11 am to 7 pm and they make house calls from 9 am to 9 pm. English and German are spoken.

Dangers & Annoyances Several travellers have written to warn others about local agents for train and bus bookings. Bookings sometimes aren't made at all, the bus turns out to be far inferior to what was expected or other hassles develop. In another scam involving air tickets, agents say economy class is booked and that only business class is available; the agent then sells the customer an air ticket – at business class prices of course – that turns out to be economy class after all.

Take care with local boat trips to nearby islands. Visitors have reported boats being swamped on windy days, and sometimes being forced to spend the night stranded on an uninhabited island.

Diving & Snorkelling

Reefs lie off many parts of the island but the better ones are found along the east side near the beaches of Chaweng and Lamai. These areas are OK for snorkelling but there is better diving to the north around Ko Pha-Ngan and especially Ko Tao.

Samui's many dive operators offer guided dives to the better underwater sites. Gear hired for beach dives costs around 500B per day. Beach dives cost around 750B per day. Dives from boats start at 2000B, and a four day certification course ranges from 7500B up to 9900B for the beach and boat option. An overnight dive trip to Ko Tao, including food and accommodation, costs around 5800B, plus 2000B for each additional day.

The highest concentration of dive shops is found on Hat Chaweng. Among the more established are:

Calypso Diving
  (☎ 077-422437)
  Hat Chaweng
Chang Divers
  (☎ 077-230891)
  Hat Chaweng and Hat Lamai
The Dive Shop
  (☎/fax 077-230232, email diveshop@samart.co.th)
  Hat Chaweng
Easy Divers
  (☎ 077-231190)
  Hat Chaweng and Hat Lamai
Samui International Diving School
  (☎/fax 077-231242, email cesareb@samart.co.th)
  Na Thon, Hat Lamai, Bo Phut and Hat Chaweng

Paddling

Blue Stars (☎/fax 077-230497, 01-835 9917) in Gallery Lafayette in Chaweng offers guided kayak trips in Ang Thong National Marine Park, to the west of Ko Samui, along with cave exploring, snorkelling and speedboat transfer.

Muay Thai

In Na Thon and Chaweng are Thai boxing rings with regularly scheduled matches. Admission is around 100B to most fights. The quality of the mostly local contestants isn't exactly top-drawer.

Buffalo Fighting

Local villagers love to bet on duelling water buffaloes, events arranged on a rotating basis at seven rustic fighting rings around the island in Na Thon, Na Muang, Saket, Hua Thanon, Chaweng and Bo Phut. Tourists are charged 100B to 200B entry.

Waterfalls

Besides the beaches and rustic, thatched-roof bungalows, Samui has a couple of waterfalls. Hin Lat Falls is a worthwhile visit if you're waiting in town for a boat back to the mainland. If you're up for a long walk, you can get there on foot – walk 3km or so south of town on the main road, turning left at the road by the hospital. Go straight along this road for about 2km to arrive at the entrance to the waterfall. From here, it's about a half hour walk along a trail to the top of the waterfall.

Na Muang Falls, in the centre of the island about 12km from Na Thon, is more scenic and somewhat less frequented. A songthaew from Na Thon should cost about 20B; get off at the marked turn-off, then walk 2km to the falls. Songthaews can also be hired at Chaweng and Lamai beaches.

Temples

For temple enthusiasts, at the southern end of the island, near the village of Bang Kao, Wat Laem Saw features an interesting and highly venerated old Srivijaya-style chedi. At Samui's northern end, on a small rocky island joined to Samui by a causeway, is the so-called **Temple of the Big Buddha**, or Wat Phra Yai. Erected in 1972, the modern image stands 15m high and makes a nice silhouette against the tropical sky and sea behind it. The image is surrounded by *kutis* (meditation huts), mostly unoccupied. The monks like receiving visitors there, though a sign in English requests that proper attire (no shorts or sleeveless shirts) be worn on temple premises. There is also an old semi-abandoned temple, **Wat Pang Ba**, near the northern end of Hat Chaweng where 10-day vipassana courses are occasionally held; the courses are led by foreign monks from Wat Suanmok in Chaiya.

Near the car park at the entrance to Hin Lat Falls is another trail left to **Suan Dharmapala**, a meditation temple. Another attraction is the ghostly **Mummified Monk** at Wat Khunaraam, which is south of Route 4169 between Ban Thurian and Ban Hua Thanon. At **Wat Samret** near Ban Hua Thanon you can see a typical Mandalay sitting Buddha carved from solid marble – a common sight in Northern Thailand but not so common in the south.

Ang Thong National Marine Park

This archipelago of around 40 small islands combines dense vegetation, sheer limestone cliffs, hidden lagoons and white sand beaches to provide a nearly postcard-perfect opportunity to enjoy Gulf islands at their best. The park itself encompasses 18 sq km of islands, plus 84 sq km of marine environments. From Ko Samui, a couple of tour operators run day trips out to the Ang Thong archipelago, 31km to the north-west. A typical tour costs 350B per person (some with faster boats cost up to 450B), leaves Na Thon at 8.30 am and returns at 5.30 pm. Lunch is included, along with snorkelling in a sort of lagoon formed by one of the islands (from which Ang Thong, meaning 'Golden Jar,' gets its name) and a climb to the top of a 240m hill to view the whole island group. Some tours also visit Tham Bua Bok, a cavern containing lotus-shaped cave formations. Tours depart daily in the high

season, less frequently in the rainy season. The tours are still getting mostly good reviews, though one reader complained that the tour was 'not informative'. Bring hiking shoes (the 400m climb on Ko Wua demands some kind of reasonable footwear), snorkelling gear and plenty of sunscreen and drinking water.

At least once a month there's also an overnight tour. At the park headquarters (077-400800) on Ko Wat Ta Lap you can rent eight to 10-person bungalows for 800B a night or tents for 50B. For reservations, call Ang Thong National Marine Park on ☎ 077-420225. You may be able to book a passage alone to the Ang Thong islands; inquire at Songserm Travel Service.

You can also arrange to join a more active but more expensive Ang Thong kayak trip through Blue Stars at Gallery La Fayette (☎ 077-230497) in Chaweng. The cost of 1890B per person includes several hours of paddling on stable open-top kayaks, lunch, nonalcoholic beverages and pickup anywhere on Samui.

Yet another alternative would be to get a group together, charter your own boat and design your own Ang Thong itinerary. This is what Richard, Françoise, Etienne and the rest of the fictional crew in the novel *The Beach* did.

Na Thon
• pop 4000

On the north-west side of Ko Samui, Na Thon (pronounced *nâa thâwn*) is the arrival point for express and night passenger ferries from the piers in Surat Thani. Car ferries from Don Sak and Khanom land at Thong Yang, about 10km south of Na Thon. If you're not travelling on a combination ticket you'll probably end up spending some time in Na Thon on your way in and/or out, waiting for the next ferry. Or if you're a long-term beach-comber, it makes a nice change to come into Na Thon once in a while for a little town life.

Although it's basically a tourist town now, Na Thon still sports a few old teak Chinese

Notes on *The Beach*

'There's no way you can keep it out of Lonely Planet, and once that happens it's countdown to doomsday.' So says one of the backpacking characters in *The Beach*, UK author Alex Garland's controversial novel set in Thailand. Published in 1997, the tale of a failed beach utopia slowly caught fire in the Gen X book market and in 1999 was transformed into a $40 million motion picture.

The story traces the fate of a small, loose-knit group of world travellers who decide to establish their own beach paradise on an island in Thailand's Ang Thong National Marine Park, not far from Ko Samui and Ko Pha-Ngan. The novel's selfish, Vietnam war-obsessed protagonist makes the mistake of passing on a map showing the beach's secret location to a pair of uninvited backpackers, whose island intrusion and subsequent confrontation with Thai dope growers brings the novel to its violent climax.

Although the consensus seems to be that the book makes a good beach or airport read, one could quibble about Garland's depiction of Thailand and the roving backpacker scene. Old Thai hands decried the attempts at Thai accents, which continually dropped the wrong consonants (resulting in an almost Cockney Thai, eg *le'er* for 'letter' and *Mis'er* for 'Mister', when something more like 'let-tah' and 'Misatah' would have been more realistic). Garland has Thais saying *gues'* for 'guest', when, as we all know, the Thai English pronunciation would be something like 'get'. And would a Thai ever say *banan'* for 'banana'? Never! Furthermore all the Thai characters seem rather dark and sinister. In interviews Garland has defended this criticism by pointing out that such portrayals were not intended to be realistic but were merely the perceptions of his characters. As Garland told *Asiaweek* magazine: 'I think it's fairly obvious this novel isn't about Thailand. It's about backpackers'.

More picky stuff: no Yank would say 'candy floss' but rather 'cotton candy', and it's common knowledge in Thailand, even among those who haven't tasted it themselves, that dog meat tastes like beef, not chicken. Also, given his supposed long history of South-East Asia travel, the protagonist, Richard, seems to be incredibly naive about the use of Asian squat toilets. The beach clubbers gladly eat plain rice for breakfast, but with the abundant fishing described in the novel there was no motivation for them to do so. Finally, why does Richard never wonder (as every reader must) where the money comes from to pay for The Beach's periodic supply runs to Ko Pha-Ngan?

The novel's strengths include good faràng dialogue and well narrated settings. Noting the resemblance between a dipterocarp's buttressed root system and a rocket's stabilising fins, Garland coins the delightful 'rocketship trees', for example. Intriguing video game references and a realistic travellers' conversation on Hat Rin regarding the use of 'Kampuchea' vs. 'Cambodia' also stood out. Although the novel's dip into backpacker culture and the Khao San Road scene hold up well enough (quote: 'You know, Richard, one of these days I'm going to find one of those Lonely Planet writers and I'm going to ask him, what's so fucking lonely about the Khao San Road?'), the novel really hits its stride once the story confines itself to the secret beach and lagoon. For more discussion of the book's literary merits, check out the lengthy reader reviews on amazon.com and the lively debate on Lonely Planet's Thorn Tree Web page.

Hollywood Invasion

Director Danny Boyle (of *Trainspotting* fame), teen idol Leonardo DiCaprio and a healthy 20th Century Fox crew turned up in Thailand in January 1999 to begin filming *The Beach* on the island of Ko Phi-Phi Leh. Almost immediately the film became embroiled in controversy when Bangkok protestors charged that the production's use of national park lands – with the express permission of the forestry ministry – was going to turn pristine Ao Maya (Maya Cove) into a wasteland.

The reality is that Ao Maya – like much of the rest of the Phi-Phi archipelago – has been under intense environmental pressure for many years now. First there were the dynamite and cyanide fishers, then came greedy resort developers and tour operators who over-ran Phi-Phi years ago and turned much of neighbouring Ko Phi-Phi Don into a trash heap. Ao Maya itself has received hundreds, perhaps thousands of group snorkelling tours over the last 10 years. Although some concession to the bay's park status had been observed – there are no bungalows or other permanent developments at Ao Maya (most likely because the licensed birdnest collectors on the island won't allow it) – improper anchoring and the dumping of trash had toppled this beach from any 'pristine' status it may once have enjoyed years before 20th Century Fox arrived on the scene.

Many local and international observers who visit Ao Maya on a regular basis and who were able to visit the production set here argue that Fox left the bay in better condition than it found it. During the crew's first week on Phi-Phi Leh, for example, they removed an estimated three to four tons of rubbish. Bangkok protestors, on the other hand, offered precious little evidence to support their claims of devastation.

Reef-World, an inependent non-profit, project that educates tourists and local tropical communities about coral reef ecology and coservation methods, has been supporting snorkelling programmes and UN-endorsed Reef Check surveys at Ao Maya and other areas in the Phi-Phi islands for several years. When Reef-World's Thailand coordinators, Robert Cogen and Anne Miller, visited the production site after filming was under way, they published the following on their Web site (www.ust.hk/~webrc/ReefCheck/):

We were surprised to find that all of the trash and debris were gone. Not just on the beach, but in the water, too. A boardwalk trail had been constructed and about one-fourth of the foliage removed. All of the bigger shrubs, the figs and wild hibiscus were still there. Tight lines along the boardwalk bore signs to stay on the walk and out of the brush. Further back, there was a wooden platform and stairs to a small deck at the hole in the rock. There were chemical toilets off to one side. There was not a baggie or a cigarette butt anywhere. All of the construction had been cleverly done so that it was completely removable. There would not be a nail hole or strap mark on a tree. All of the driftwood that had been far back of the beach was still there. I thought the area behind the beach looked better than it had in years. Brush and grasses that had been removed were being cared for in a nursery on the island.

During the last days of January, there were more stories of coral damage, sand removal and, most awful, the planting of coconut palms. My partner, Anne, and I went back. A large barge was anchored in Lo Sama. More than half a dozen lines led off in all directions to anchors. Two large catamarans were tied up alongside. The barge was connected by a floating wooden walkway to a wooden deck on shore which led through the rocks to the deck I had seen before. Anne and I checked every anchor. Each one was buried in the sand. None of the ropes touched any coral.

Notes on *The Beach*

No coral appeared to have been damaged in any way. In fact, the coral looked a bit healthier than it did in December. I inquired and was told that the catamarans, which came from Malaysia, did not pump any sewage into the water – all of it was retained, unlike the local boats. New mooring buoys with sand anchors had also replaced some that had been tied around coral heads.

I walked to the beach. The decks and stairs were all set above the landscape so as not to crush it. Lines and signs prevented access to the surrounding landscape. The deck had been expanded to approximately 7m sq. Again, the construction was exemplary by any standard. The area behind the beach was otherwise as I had seen it in December. The beach itself now had a forest of 60 coconut palms planted in the sand. Each was still in its burlap sack, watered by buried plastic lines, and could be easily removed. No new brush had been removed. Two areas of access from Ao Maya to this area had been widened, the sand pushed to one side, easily replaced. I wandered the water's edge, then back along the trail, double-checking my observations, wondering about the demonstrations in Bangkok, and why *The Beach* was the target of all this environmental ire.

For further information on reef ecology issues, contact Reef-World Center (☎ 76-383105, fax 76-383106, email indepth@loxinfo.co.th).

Joe Cummings

cafes along Th Ang Thong where descendants of the island's original Hainanese immigrants gather.

Na Thon Bookshop, near Coconuts, carries a good selection of used books, including maps and new and used guidebooks.

Places to Stay If you want or need to stay in Ko Samui's largest settlement there are seven places to choose from.

If you're looking for something inexpensive, check out the *Seaview Guest House* (☎ 077-420298) on Th Thawi Ratchaphakdi, which has good-sized singles/doubles with fan and shared bathroom for 200/250B, with fan and private bath for 280B, and air-con for 380B – none of the rooms actually have sea views.

Palace Hotel (Chai Thaleh; ☎ 077-421079, fax 421080)* has clean, spacious rooms starting at 350B with fan or 350B to 500B with air-con.

Win Hotel (☎ 077-421481), farther down Th Chonwithi, has all air-con rooms with TV and hot water for 550B, plus a nice coffee shop downstairs. Around the corner from the Win Hotel is the similar four storey *Seaview Hotel (☎ 077-421481)* with fan rooms for 300B, 450B with air-con, TV, phone and fridge.

On the main road north is *Dum Rong Town Hotel (☎ 077-421157)*, which charges 550B for rooms with air-con and private bath. *Chao Koh Bungalow (☎ 077-421214)*, just north of town nearer to the sea, is 300B for fan rooms with private bath. On the southern edge of town, the *Jinta Bungalows* has pretty basic rooms for 250B with fan and shared bathroom to 350B with private facilities. Bungalows are available for 4000B per month.

Places to Eat There are several good restaurants and watering holes in Na Thon.

On the road facing the harbour, the *Chao Koh Restaurant* is still serving good seafood and Thai standards at reasonable prices. *Ko Kaew* is a similar standby. A good place for breakfast is the *Roung Thong Bakery*, with home-made pastries and coffee.

Towards the Palace Hotel is a Thai rice and noodle place that's open all night, *Raan Khao Tom Toh Rung* (no roman-script sign) – the cheapest place to eat on this strip. During the high season, many of these restaurants fill up at night with travellers

waiting for the night ferry. After midnight the only places open are the Raan Khao Tom Toh Rung and the flashy Thai night-club *Pan On Cafe* on Th Na Amphoe, which is rather expensive, dark and well chilled.

On Th Ang Thong, the next street back from the harbour, are a few old Chinese coffee shops, and *Coconuts*, a tastefully decorated open-air restaurant/cafe serving pizza, pasta, Thai dishes, sandwiches, juices, coffee, wine and beer. A small vegetarian

KO SAMUI

See Hat Chaweng Map (Page 344)

See Hat Lamai Map (Page 348)

SOUTH-WESTERN GULF COAST

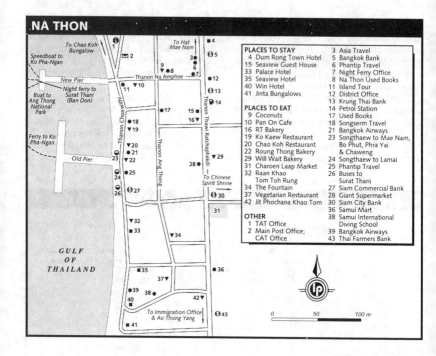

NA THON

PLACES TO STAY
4 Dum Rong Town Hotel
15 Seaview Guest House
33 Palace Hotel
35 Seaview Hotel
40 Win Hotel
41 Jinta Bungalows

PLACES TO EAT
9 Coconuts
10 Pan On Cafe
16 RT Bakery
19 Ko Kaew Restaurant
20 Chao Koh Restaurant
22 Roung Thong Bakery
29 Will Wait Bakery
31 Charoen Laap Market
32 Raan Khao
   Tom Toh Rung
34 The Fountain
37 Vegetarian Restaurant
42 Jit Phochana Khao Tom

OTHER
1 TAT Office
2 Main Post Office;
  CAT Office

3 Asia Travel
5 Bangkok Bank
6 Phantip Travel
7 Night Ferry Office
8 Na Thon Used Books
11 Island Tour
12 District Office
13 Krung Thai Bank
14 Petrol Station
17 Used Books
18 Songserm Travel
21 Bangkok Airways
23 Songthaew to Mae Nam,
   Bo Phut, Phra Yai
   & Chaweng
24 Songthaew to Lamai
25 Phantip Travel
26 Buses to
   Surat Thani
27 Siam Commercial Bank
28 Giant Supermarket
30 Siam City Bank
36 Samui Mart
38 Samui International
   Diving School
39 Bangkok Airways
43 Thai Farmers Bank

restaurant opens at night at the southern end of this street.

Th Thawi Ratchaphakdi, the third street back from the harbour, is mostly travel agencies, photo shops and other small businesses. Two small supermarkets, Samui Mart and Giant Supermarket are also back here. The *Charoen Laap day market* is still thriving on this street as well. The *RT Bakery* on the same street has an extensive Thai menu (dishes 35B and up) as well as fresh baked goods. *Will Wait Bakery* is diagonally across from Giant Supermarket. One of the few places in town still serving Thai (and Chinese) food on a large scale is *Jit Phochana Khao Tom*, also on Th Thawi Ratchaphakdi.

Ko Samui Beaches

Samui has plenty of beaches to choose from, although the proliferation of new places seems to have stabilised a bit over the past few years – at last count the TAT had registered over 250 places to stay on the island. Getting from beach to beach is usually no problem. The most crowded beaches for accommodation are Chaweng and Lamai, both on the eastern side of the island. Chaweng has more bungalow 'villages' – over 80 at last count – plus several recently built flashy tourist hotels. It is the longest beach, over twice the size of Lamai, and has the island of **Mat Lang** nearby. Both beaches have clear blue-green waters and OK coral reefs for snorkelling and underwater sightseeing. Both have open-air discos; Lamai has a higher concentration of bars.

There's a bit more to do around Hat Lamai because of its proximity to two villages – Ban Lamai and Ban Hua Thanon. At the wát in Ban Lamai is the **Ban Lamai Cultural Hall**, a sort of folk museum displaying local ceramics, household utensils, hunting weapons and musical instruments. The drawback to Lamai is the rather sleazy atmosphere of the strip of beer bars behind the beach; Chaweng's bar-and-disco strip is decidedly more sophisticated and more congenial for couples or single women.

Chaweng is the target of up-market development because of its long beach. Another factor is that only Hat Chaweng (and the northern part of Lamai) has water deep enough for swimming from October to April; most other beaches on the island become very shallow during these months.

For more peace and quiet, try the beaches along the north, south and west coasts. **Mae Nam, Bo Phut** and **Bang Rak (Phra Yai or Big Buddha)** are along the northern end; Bo Phut and Bang Rak are part of a bay that holds Ko Faan (the island with the 'big Buddha'), separated by a small headland. The water here is not quite as clear as at Chaweng or Lamai, but the feeling of seclusion is greater, and accommodation is cheaper.

Hat Thong Yang on the western side of the island is even more secluded (only a few sets of bungalows there), but the beach isn't very good by Samui standards. There is also **Hat Ang Thong**, just north of Na Thon, which is very rocky but with more local colour (eg, fishing boats) than the others. The southern end of the island now has many bungalows as well, set in little out-of-the-way coves that are worth seeking out. And then there's everywhere in-between right around the island – every bay, cove or cape with a strip of sand gets a bungalow nowadays.

Places to Stay & Eat Prices vary considerably according to the time of year and occupancy rates. Some of the bungalow operators on Samui have a nasty habit of tripling room rates when rooms are scarce, so a hut that's 100B in June could be 300B in August. Rates given in this section can only serve as a guide – they could go lower if you bargain or higher if space is tight.

Everyone has his or her own idea of what the perfect beach bungalow is. At Ko Samui, the search could take a month or two, with more than 250 licensed places to

choose from. Most offer roughly the same service and accommodation for 100B to 500B, though some cost quite a bit more. The best thing to do is to go to the beach you think you want to stay at and pick one you like – look inside the huts, check out the restaurant, the menu, the guests. You can always move if you're not satisfied.

Beach accommodation around Samui now falls into four basic categories chronicling the evolution of places to stay on the island. The first phase consisted of simple bungalows with thatched roofs and walls of local, easily replaceable materials; the next phase brought concrete bathrooms attached to the old-style huts; then came a transition to the third phase of cement walls and tile roofs – the predominant style now, with more advanced facilities like fans and sometimes air-con. The latest wave is luxury rooms and bungalows indistinguishable from mainland inns and hotels.

Generally, anything that costs less than 150B a night will mean a shared bathroom, which may be preferable when you remember that mosquitoes breed in standing water. For a pretty basic bungalow with private bath, 150B to 200B is the minimum on Ko Samui.

Food is touch and go at all the beaches – one meal can be great, the next at the very same place not so great. Fresh seafood is usually what they do best and the cheapest way to eat it is to catch it yourself and have the bungalow cooks prepare it for you, or buy it in one of the many fishing villages around the island, direct from the fisherfolk themselves, or in the village markets. Good places to buy are in the relatively large Muslim fishing villages of Mae Nam, Bo Phut and Hua Thanon.

The ownership and management of various lodgings around the island change so frequently that it's difficult to name favourites. Cooks come and go, bungalows flourish and go bankrupt, owners are assassinated by competitors – you never can tell from season to season. Prices have remained fairly stable in recent years, but they are creeping up. It's easy to get from one beach to another, so you can always change bungalows. With the establishment of several places charging well over 3000B per night, the jetset has discovered Samui. Finally, if Samui isn't to your liking, move islands! Think about Ko Pha-Ngan or Ko Tao.

What follows are some general comments on staying at Samui's various beaches, moving clockwise around the island from Na Thon.

Warning For several years now we have continued to receive reports of theft on Ko Samui. If you're staying in a beach bungalow, consider depositing your valuables with the management while off on excursions around the island or while you're swimming at the beach. Most of the theft reports have come from Chaweng, Lamai and Mae Nam beaches.

Ban Tai (Ao Bang Baw) Ban Tai is the first beach area north of Na Thon with accommodation; so far there are just a handful of places to stay here. The beach has fair snorkelling and swimming. The **Axolotl Village** (*☎/fax 077-420017, email axolotl@ loxinfo.co.th*), run by an Italian-German partnership, caters to Europeans (the staff speaks English, Italian, German and French) with tastefully designed, mid-range rooms for 450B or bungalows for 550B to 950B. Meditation and massage rooms are available – a massage costs 150B per hour. A very pleasant restaurant area overlooking the beach has an inventive menu featuring vegetarian, Italian and Thai dishes.

Next door is the similar-looking **Blue River**, under Thai management, with bungalows from 300B to 500B. Also at Ban Tai is **Sunbeam**, a set of bungalows in a very nice setting. Huts are 300B, all with private bath.

At the extreme new age end of the spectrum lies the **Healing Child Resort** (*☎ 077-420124, fax 420145, email conactus@ healingchild.com*), a set of brick buildings with rooms costing from 150B to 250B in the low season or up to 400B to 600B in the high. You may order health food from a menu or join the communal meals for 75B.

Among the many services offered are 'brain hemisphere tuning and balancing', 'small intestine cleaning' and 'vortex destiny astrology', along with pyramid-scheming invitations to become 'overseas reps, agents, distributors or business partners'.

Hat Mae Nam Hat Mae Nam is 14km from Na Thon and one of the main beaches for budget bungalow development – definitely still the cheapest area on the island.

At the headland (Laem Na Phra Lan) where Ban Tai ends and Mae Nam begins is the **Home Bay Bungalows** with basic huts for 150B and bungalows with bath for 400B. Next is **Coco Palm Village** (300B to 1200B), followed by **Plant Inn** *(Phalarn)*, with bungalows from 150B to 300B.

Also in this area are **Naplarn Villa**, **Harry's** (*☎ 077-425477*) and **OK Village** – all in the 120B to 450B range (OK Village has some 600B air-con rooms). The beach in front of Wat Na Phalaan is undeveloped and the locals hope it will stay that way – topless bathing is strongly discouraged here.

The next group of places east includes **Anong Villa**, **Shangrilah Bungalows** (we've received many bad reports on this one), **Palm Point Village** (nice ambience) and **Shady Shack Bungalows**, where prices start at 200B to 350B. **Maenam Resort** (*☎ 077-425116*) and **Sunrise Village** are upper budget places with spacious bungalows for 300B to 700B.

Cleopatra's Place (*☎ 077-425486*) in the middle of Hat Mae Nam has been recommended for its good seafood and bungalows right on the beach. Basic huts cost as little as 60B while doubles with fan and private shower are 160B.

Right on the beach in Hat Mae Nam are **Lolita Bungalows** with rooms ranging from 200B to 700B and **Friendly** (*☎ 077-425484*), which has clean, well kept huts for 150B to 300B, all with private bath. Also good are **New La Paz Villa** (*☎ 077-425296, fax 425402*), 300B with fan, or from 600B to 1800B with air-con, and **Near Sea Resort** for 200B to 400B with fan, 700B to 850B for nicer air-con cottages. Nearby, *Magic*

View and *Silent* must be among the cheapest places to stay on the entire island; 50B for a very small hut and 100B for bigger ones with toilet and private shower. They're old but quite acceptable.

Ban Mae Nam's huge **Santiburi Dusit Resort** (☎ 077-425038, Bangkok 02-238 4790) – complete with tennis courts, waterways, ponds, bakery and sports facilities – costs from 6000B a night in the low season, from 7800B in the high season. Another top-ender is **Paradise Beach Resort** (☎ 077-247227, fax 425290, 18/8 Hat Mae Nam), with deluxe singles for 2500B in the low season, up to 4000B high, plus Thai-style villas from 2700/4800B low/high season. There's a beachfront restaurant pool, jacuzzi and car rental service as well.

Moving towards Bo Phut you'll find a group of places all with old-style Samui huts ranging from 150B to 400B a night, or up to 700B with air-con. There are at least 10 or 15 other bungalow operations between Laem Na Phra Lan and Laem Sai, where Ao Mae Nam ends.

Hat Bo Phut This beach has a reputation for peace and quiet, and those who come here regularly hope it will stay that way; this is not the place to look for a party. The beach tends to be a little on the muddy side and the water can be too shallow for swimming during the dry season – a blessing wrapped in a curse which keeps development rather low-key and has preserved Bo Phut's village atmosphere.

Near Bo Phut village there's a string of bungalows in all price ranges, including the farthest north and budget-friendly **Sunny** (150B to 300B), followed by several others ranging from 200B to 1200B, and the long established, well run **Peace Bungalow** (☎ 077-425357), which charges 400B to 1500B. More money to spend? Go for semi-luxurious **Samui Palm Beach** (☎ 077-425494) at 2500B to 3900B or **Samui Euphoria** (☎ 077-425100, fax 425107, Bangkok ☎ 02-255 7901, fax 225 7903), a posh spot with rooms and bungalows for 3000B and up, including breakfast (from 2000B in the low season).

Proceeding east, a road off the main round-island road runs to the left and along the bay towards the village. One of the golden oldies here is **Ziggy Stardust** (☎ 077-425173), a clean, well landscaped and popular place with huts for 300B and a couple of nicer family bungalows with air-con for 1000B. Next to Ziggy's is the brightly coloured **Rasta Baby**, a small hotel with rooms for 250B with fan and hot water. Nearby, on the inland side (no sea view), **Smile House** starts at 250B and offers the bonus of a large swimming pool.

Up the street from Smile House and facing the ocean is a newer place, **The Lodge** (☎ 077-425337, fax 425336), which features a two storey design reminiscent of old Samui architecture. Rooms with air-con and TV cost 1000B to 1200B (200B less in the low season). Next door you'll find the original **Boon Bungalows**, still holding on with cheap, closely spaced huts from 100B a night.

If you continue through the village along the water, you'll find the isolated **Sand View** with huts for 200B to 450B. This area is sometimes called Hat Bang Rak. **Summer Night Resort** stretches over a fairly large area and offers fan rooms for 200B, air-con a bargain 500B.

The village has a couple of cheap local-style restaurants as well as French, German, Spanish and Italian restaurants. **Bird in the Hand,** next door to The Lodge serves good, reasonably priced Thai and western food in a rustic setting overlooking the water. A little farther east on Bo Phut's main street, **Ubon Waan Som Tam** serves cheap and tasty Isaan food.

Hat Bang Rak (Hat Phra Yai or Big Buddha Beach) This now has nearly 15 bungalow operations. The best is the moderately priced and well kept **Comfort Nara Garden Resort** (☎ 077-425364, fax 425292), with air-con rooms for 600B to 900B (more in the high season), nicely landscaped grounds, a seaside restaurant and a small swimming pool. It's just a 10 minute, 30B ride from the airport and is hence a favourite with Bangkok

Airways flight crews. This is also one of the cheapest places where you can make advance reservations. *MPS Resort (Samui Mermaid; ☎ 077-425282)* offers wooden bungalows for 600B with fan, 1200B with air-con and breakfast. The strangely castle-like *Pongpetch Servotel* has small rooms for 200B to 500B. The *Phayorm Park Resort* right next to the pier has two storey wood and concrete bungalows for 400B to 500B.

Next, heading south, is *Ocean View Resort* with basic cement bungalows for 300B, nothing special, and following that is the similar *Sunset Song 2 (☎ 077-425155)*. The pleasant *Secret Garden Bungalows (☎ 077-425419, fax 245253)* is a good choice, with A-frame bungalows starting at 300B, air-con 800B, all with nice sitting areas in front. They also have a beach pub and restaurant featuring live music. *Como's (☎ 077-425210)*, *Boonlerd House*, *Chalee Bungalows* and *Number One & Restaurant* are in the 150B to 300B range.

The French-managed *Chez Ban Ban Resort*, also the site of a bar/creperie, and *Nang Nual Resort* both have similar basic clean brick bungalows with wooden terraces from 300B. *Beach House* has a nice outdoor eating area where you can get Thai and western dishes. Concrete bungalows with attractive roofs go for 300B to 600B.

LA Resort is about the cheapest place here, with prices ranging from 100B for a small room close to the road to 300B for a big bungalow on the beach.

Ao Thong Son & Ao Thong Sai The big cape between Bang Rak and Chaweng is actually a series of four capes and coves, the first of which is Ao Thong Son. The road to Thong Son is a bit on the hellish side, but that keeps this area quiet and secluded. *Samui Thongson Resort* has its own cove and bungalows for 300B with fan, 850B to 1200B with air-con; knock off about 25% from May to November. *Thongson Bay Bungalows* next door has old-style bungalows for 150B to 200B.

The next cove along is as yet undeveloped and there isn't even a dirt road yet. The third,

Ao Thong Sai, has *The Tongsai Bay Cottages & Hotel (☎ 077-425015, fax 425462, Bangkok ☎ 02-254 0056, fax 254 0054, email tongsai@loxinfo.co.th)*, a heavily guarded resort with 72 suites (most with private jacuzzi) and a swimming pool, tennis courts and private beach. Rates start at 9000B.

Hat Choeng Mon The largest cove following Ao Thong Sai has several names, but the beach is generally known as Hat Choeng Mon. It's clean, quiet and recommended for families or for those who don't need night life and a variety of restaurants (these can be found at nearby Chaweng anyway). At Choeng Mon you'll find the well run, popular *PS Villa (☎ 077-425160)*, with rooms for 400B to 600B and the well-laid-out *Sun Sand Samui* (starting at 950B), which has sturdy thatched-roof bungalows connected by wooden walkways on a breezy hillside, along with several similarly priced places. Across from the beach is Ko Faan Yai, an island that can be reached on foot in low tide.

Between Choeng Mon Bungalow Village and PS Villa are two top-end places. The 216 room *Imperial Boat House Hotel (☎ 077-425041, Bangkok fax 02-261 9533, email imperial@ksc.net.th)* has a three storey hotel with rooms for 5445B and separate two storey bungalows made from authentic teak rice barges for 9025B. Just north is *The White House (☎ 077-245315, fax 425233, Bangkok ☎ 02-237 8734, email whitehouse@sawadee.com)*, a collection of deluxe bungalows for 3200B to 3700B (2500B to 3000B in the low season). The hotel motto is 'Where each guest is a president!'.

Next is a smaller bay called Ao Yai Noi, just before north Chaweng. This little bay is quite picturesque, with large boulders framing the white-sand beach. The secluded *IKK* bungalows are 300B to 500B while the long-running, eco-friendly *Coral Bay Resort (☎ 077-422223, fax 422392, email coralbay@samart.co.th)* has larger, well spaced bungalows with air-con, set on grassy grounds with a pool, for 2350B to 4500B (1900B to 3600B in the low season).

In Choeng Mon, friendly **Bongoes Bar** reputedly has good food. **Otto's Bar** is a nice place to have a drink and play a little pool. Otto's will rent motorcycles and change money.

Hat Chaweng Hat Chaweng, Samui's longest beach, also has the island's highest concentration of bungalows and hotels. Prices are moving up-market fast, and there is a commercial 'strip' behind the central beach jam-packed with restaurants, souvenir shops, bars and discos. The beach is beautiful here, and local developers are finally cleaning up some of the trashy areas behind the bungalows that were becoming a problem in the 1980s.

Chaweng has kilometre after kilometre of beach bungalows – perhaps 70 or more in all – so have a look around before deciding on a place. There are basically three sections: North Chaweng, Hat Chaweng proper and Hat Chaweng Noi.

North Chaweng Places here are mostly in the 100B to 800B range, with simple bungalows with private bath at the northern end. Besides being less expensive than lodgings farther south, the North Chaweng places are out of earshot of central Chaweng's throbbing discos. **Papillon Resort** (☎/fax 077-231169, 01-476 6169) and the northern-most, **Samui Island Resort** (☎ 077-422355), offer concrete bungalows starting at 400B, as well as more expensive air-con units for 800B to 1250B. The friendly **Matlang Resort** (☎ 077-422172) has better than average bungalows for 400B to 650B. **Venus Resort** (☎ 077-422406) and **Lazy Wave** cost 200B to 500B with fan only, while **Marine Bungalows** has fan units for 200B to 400B, plus air-con for 800B. In this same area, the most inexpensive place, **Lagoon Cottages** (☎ 01-979 4740, fax 077-230079) charges 100B to 400B and **JR Chalet** is receiving raves for its large, airy restaurant and clean rooms with modern bathroom facilities for 300B to 400B with fan, 600B with air-con.

The well designed and decorated, vaguely Mediterranean style **Corto Maltese** (☎/fax 077-230041, 01-477 9313) is a new, more up-scale place that seems very popular with the French. A single/double with air-con costs 1780B and rooms sleeping up to four are 2780B. All rooms have air-con, fan, mini-bar, hot water and TV. On the property are a pool and bar area as well. After that it's back to the lower end of the scale with **Chaweng Pearl Cabana** (☎ 077-422116) where prices range from 250B to 600B.

At the end nearest to central Chaweng is a small group of up-market places starting at 2000B or more: **Samui Villa Flora** (☎ 077-230048, fax 230942), **Chaweng Blue Lagoon Hotel** (☎ 077-422037, fax 422401), **Muang Kulaypan Hotel** (☎ 077-422305, 230031, Bangkok ☎ 02-713 0668, fax 713 0667, email kulaypan@sawadee .com) and **Amari Palm Reef Resort** (☎ 077-422015, fax 422394, Bangkok ☎ 02-267 9708, fax 267 9707). The Amari is the nicest of the four, with individual two storey, Thai-style cottages and two swimming pools; it's also the most environmentally conscious luxury resort on the island, using filtered sea water for most first uses and recycled grey water for landscaping. Rooms and bungalows start at US$136/145 for singles/doubles, up to US$203 for a terrace room or suite. There are also two mid-range places in the area, the **JR Palace** (400B to 1200B) and **The Island** (400B to 1500B); the latter has a very popular open-air restaurant.

Off the road that leads away from the beach towards the interior is **Coralia Mercure Resort** (formerly Novotel Ko Samui Resort; ☎ 077-230864, fax 230866, Bangkok ☎ 02-267 0810). The resort is built in stepped, two storey hotel wings on a slight slope with sea and lagoon views. Rates start at 3000B for deluxe doubles and continue up to 4200B for suites (about 400B less in the low season).

Chaweng Central The central area, Hat Chaweng proper, is the longest and has the most bungalows and hotels. This is also where the strip behind the hotels and huts is

HAT CHAWENG

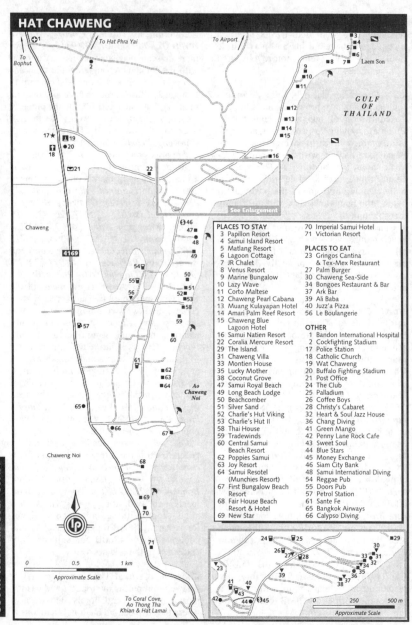

To Hat Phra Yai
To Airport
To Bophut
Laem Son

GULF OF THAILAND

Chaweng

4169

Ao Chaweng Noi

Chaweng Noi

See Enlargement

To Coral Cove,
Ao Thong Tha
Khian & Hat Lamai

0   0.5   1 km
Approximate Scale

0   250   500 m
Approximate Scale

PLACES TO STAY
3 Papillon Resort
4 Samui Island Resort
5 Matlang Resort
6 Lagoon Cottage
7 JR Chalet
8 Venus Resort
9 Marine Bungalow
10 Lazy Wave
11 Corto Maltese
12 Chaweng Pearl Cabana
13 Muang Kulayapan Hotel
14 Amari Palm Reef Resort
15 Chaweng Blue
   Lagoon Hotel
16 Samui Natien Resort
22 Coralia Mercure Resort
29 The Island
31 Chaweng Villa
33 Montien House
35 Lucky Mother
47 Samui Royal Beach
49 Long Beach Lodge
50 Beachcomber
51 Silver Sand
52 Charlie's Hut Viking
53 Charlie's Hut II
58 Thai House
59 Tradewinds
60 Central Samui
   Beach Resort
62 Poppies Samui
63 Joy Resort
64 Samui Resotel
   (Munchies Resort)
67 First Bungalow Beach
   Resort
68 Fair House Beach
   Resort & Hotel
69 New Star

70 Imperial Samui Hotel
71 Victorian Resort

PLACES TO EAT
23 Gringos Cantina
   & Tex-Mex Restaurant
27 Palm Burger
30 Chaweng Sea-Side
34 Bongoes Restaurant & Bar
37 Ark Bar
39 Ali Baba
40 Juzz'a Pizza
56 Le Boulangerie

OTHER
1 Bandon International Hospital
2 Cockfighting Stadium
17 Police Station
18 Catholic Church
19 Wat Chaweng
20 Buffalo Fighting Stadium
21 Post Office
24 The Club
25 Palladium
26 Coffee Boys
28 Christy's Cabaret
32 Heart & Soul Jazz House
36 Chang Diving
41 Green Mango
42 Penny Lane Rock Cafe
43 Sweet Soul
44 Blue Stars
45 Money Exchange
46 Siam City Bank
48 Samui International Diving
54 Reggae Pub
55 Doors Pub
57 Petrol Station
61 Sante Fe
65 Bangkok Airways
66 Calypso Diving

SOUTH-WESTERN GULF COAST

centred, with restaurants (most with videos), bars (yes, the girlie bar scene is sneaking in), discos, video parlours, pool halls, Tourist Police, TAT mini-office, post office, minimarts, one-hour film processing labs, tailors, souvenir shops and currency exchange booths.

Water sports are big here too, so you can hire sailboards, go diving, sail a catamaran, charter a junk and so on. Parasailing costs around 400B and water-skiing is 250B to 300B per hour. This area also has the island's highest average prices, not only because accommodation is more up-market but simply because this is (or was) the prettiest beach on the island. In general, the places get more expensive as you move south; many of these are owned by the same families who owned them under different names 10 or 15 years ago – some have just added the word 'Resort' to their name.

Samui Natien Resort (☎ 077-422405, fax 422309), formerly the Samui Cabana, starts off at the north end of central Chaweng with rustic fan bungalows set amongst dense palm and other natural vegetation for 700B, air-con 1100B to 1400B. *Chaweng Villa* (☎ 077-231123) offers simple air-con bungalows for 800B next to the Heart & Soul Jazz House, while *Coconut Grove* (☎ 077-422268) is a central Chaweng bargain at 250B to 400B for fan, 700B and up for air-con, plus some grass and flowers to look at from your small porch. In between these two, *Montien House* (☎ 077-422169, fax 421221) has a loyal following for its well equipped cottages on landscaped grounds for 700B fan or 1200B including air-con and breakfast. *Samui Royal Beach* (☎ 077-422154, fax 422155) is a bit cheaper at 600B fan, 800B air-con.

If you're on a budget, *Lucky Mother* and *Long Beach Lodge* (☎ 077-422162, fax 422372) much farther down are among the least expensive places along this strip, with decent fan bungalows from 300B to 600B.

If you're getting the idea that this isn't the beach for strict budget backpackers, you're right, but surprisingly a few popular cheapies have survived between the 1000B

Beachcomber (☎ 077-422041, fax 422388) and Central Samui Beach Resort (see later entry). From the northern end is *Silver Sand* (200B to 500B), followed by the least expensive, *Charlie's Hut Viking* (☎ 077-422343), with rustic huts for 120B to 200B and the similar *Charlie's Hut II* (☎ 077-422343) for 120B to 200B, followed by the *Thai House* (150B and up). In peak season these places fill early, so to save money it may be easier to go to another beach entirely – or try North Chaweng.

Tradewinds (☎/fax 077-231247, email tradewinds@sawadee.com) is a newer place where bungalows with air-con, hot water, refrigerators and large balconies face a pleasant garden area. A centre for the newly formed Ko Samui Hash House Harriers (and something of a yachtie hangout), the resort offers dive trips, kayaking, snorkelling and even lawn croquet.

A bit farther south, the queen of the central Chaweng properties is *Central Samui Beach Resort* (☎ 077-230500, fax 422385), a huge neo-colonial-style place with rooms starting at 5800B, plus two bars, a restaurant, a pool, tennis courts and health centre. Nearby *Poppies Samui* (☎ 077-422419, fax 422420, email poppies@samart.co.th), inspired by the original Poppies on Bali's Kuta Beach, offers Thai-style cottages containing everything from IDD phones to atrium baths, for US$124.

Finishing off central Chaweng are longtime *Joy Resort* (☎ 077-421376) with clean fan bungalows for 500B to 700B, or air-con for 800B to 1200B, and similar *Samui Resotel (Munchies Resort;* ☎ 077-422374, fax 422421, email resotel@loxinfo.co.th), 450B to 2400B.

Most bungalows and all the hotels on the beach provide food service of some kind. Back on the 'strip' are dozens of restaurants and cafes serving western cuisines, with Italian places outnumbering the rest as usual. Recommended spots include *Juzz'a Pizza* (pasta, pizza, recorded jazz, near the Green Mango), *Ali Baba* (Indian, north central Chaweng), *The Islander* (moderately priced seafood, up from the Green Mango),

Le Boulangerie (French bakery, on the main access road to the beach), *Ark Bar* (good 99B western breakfasts, on the beach), *Bongoes Restaurant & Bar* (everything form pseudo-Thai to burgers, on the beach), *Chaweng Sea-Side* (barbecued seafood, on the beach) and *Gringos Cantina & Mex-Tex Restaurant* (Mexican and Texan, plus vegetarian, behind the Green Mango and The Islander).

There is a range of entertainment options here. The *Reggae Pub* sports a huge zoo-like complex off the beach with several bars, an artificial waterfall and a huge open-air dance floor with high-tech equipment and trendy DJs who play music most of the night. Another popular dance place is the *Green Mango*, which stays open later. Newer clubs include *The Doors Pub*, a popular rock and roll place whose decor pays tribute to Jim Morrison et al; and the *Santa Fe*, a huge place with an American South-West theme, beach entrance and state-of-the-art sound and lighting. *Sweet Soul* is an another all-night dance place. A mellow alternative to the raging clubs is *The Club*. At another low-key spot, *Heart & Soul Jazz House*, next door to Montien House on the beach, patrons recline on mats and pillows while dining or drinking from low Northern Thai-style tables. *Penny Lane Rock Cafe* plays classic rock tracks from the 60s to the 90s, and also supplies satellite TV, darts, snooker, backgammon and other pub diversions.

The crowds tend to trek from bar to bar as the evening wears on, eg the Reggae Pub from midnight to 2 am, the Doors Pub or the Green Mango from 2 to 4 am and Santa Fe from 4 to 6 am. The order tends to shift around a bit, but don't be surprised if you find a place dead quiet at one time, and bursting at the seams just a few hours later.

Christy's Cabaret in Chaweng Center offers free transvestite cabaret nightly at 11 pm. There are also nightly drag shows at *Coffee Boys* (Centrepoint, 50m behind the Palmburger) and *Paladium* (across the plaza from Coffee Boys) – an area becoming known as 'boy's town'.

Hat Chaweng Noi This area is off by itself around a headland at the southern end of central Hat Chaweng. Straddling the headland on both bays is the aptly named *First Bungalow Beach Resort* (☎ 077-422327, fax 422243). This was the first built on this beach in 1970, and it's now gone way up-scale with a room in the main building costing 2000B and a bungalow on the beach 2500B. Likewise for *Fair House Beach Resort & Hotel* (☎ 077-422256, fax 422373), starting at 2400B and *New Star* (☎ 077-422405, fax 422346), from 950B. This is a pretty little area, however, and fairly insulated from the glitz and clatter of central Chaweng.

The plush, multi-storey *Imperial Samui Hotel* (☎ 077-422020, fax 422396) is built on a slope in the middle of Hat Chaweng Noi proper and costs 6380B to 7380B for air-con accommodation with telephone and TV – up to 40% less in the off-season. The Imperial's 56 cottages and 24 room hotel are built in a pseudo-Mediterranean style with two swimming pools and a terrace restaurant with a view. Finally there's the hotel-style *Victorian Resort* (☎ 077-422011, fax 422111) with all air-con rooms for 2900B to 4400B. Other amenities include a restaurant, swimming pool and sauna.

Coral Cove (Ao Thong Yang) Another series of capes and coves starts at the end of Hat Chaweng Noi, beginning with scenic Coral Cove. (The Thai name of this cove – Ao Thong Yang – is the same as another bay on the west coast of Samui; this one is more commonly known as Coral Cove and that's how we refer to it.) Somehow the Thais have managed to squeeze three places around the cove, plus one across the road. The only one with immediate beach access is *Coral Cove Resort*, where basic huts start at 200B and rise to 400B for a decent bungalow with fan, 600B to 900B with air-con.

Coral Mountain Chalets (☎ 077-231117), on the hill opposite the road, costs 200B to 500B for small, well-spaced huts in a wooded area. Almost directly opposite is the more up-scale *Coral Cove Chalet* (☎ *077-422173, 422496*) charges 2000/2200B single/double for nicely-furnished air-con rooms with TV. A restaurant on the property serves Thai, Chinese and western dishes. Other amenities include a pub, conference room and swimming pool. Farther south is the friendly *Blue Horizon Bungalows* (☎ *077-422426, fax 230293, email montien@samart.co.th*) with fan rooms for 500B, small air-con rooms for 600B and a larger bungalow for 800B.

Hi Coral Cove (☎ *077-422495*), on a lovely, remote spot above the bay, has rooms for 400B to 1000B – good value if you don't mind walking to the beach. The 12 bungalows at *Beverly Hills Resort & Restaurant* (☎ *077-422232*) sit atop a cliff overlooking Hat Chaweng. High season rates are 800B to 1000B, 200B less in low season. Even if you don't stay here, you should consider having a meal in the restaurant, if only for the incredible view.

On the lofty headlands between Ao Thong Yang and Ao Thong Ta Khian are a few more places taking advantage of the relative seclusion and views. The best of the bunch is *Bird's Eye View Bungalow*, with white wooden bungalows with little balconies overlooking Hat Chaweng. Rooms with air-con are 1200B, with fan 400B to 500B.

Ao Thong Ta Khian This is another small, steep-sided cove, similar to Coral Cove and banked by huge boulders. The *Samui Silver Beach Resort* has bungalows overlooking the bay for 400B to 700B with fan, or 800B to 1000B with air-con, and a pleasant restaurant with a beach view. Going south, *Thong Ta Kian Villa* (☎ *077-230978*) has white cement bungalows with red tin roofs for 400B with a fan, or 700B air-con. At the southern end of the cove is the *Samui Yacht Club* (☎/fax *077-422400*), with luxurious Thai-style bungalows for 2000B to 3000B (500B less in the low season). If you like to fish, this is a good area for shorecasting.

Jubilee Restaurant, an open-air place on the side of the road, has a nice view and serves everything from simple rice and noodle dishes to shark steak and curries. There are also a couple of other good *seafood restaurants* on the bay.

Hat Lamai After Chaweng, this is Samui's most popular beach for travellers. Rates for accommodation at Hat Lamai are just a bit lower than at Chaweng but it's without the larger places like the Central Samui or the Imperial (yet) and has fewer of the 500B-plus places. As at Chaweng, the bay has developed in sections. There is a long central beach flanked by hilly areas. There continue to be reports of burglaries and muggings at Lamai. Take care with valuables – have them locked away in a guesthouse or hotel office if possible. Muggings mostly occur in dark lanes and along unlit parts of the beach at night.

Northern Hat Lamai Accommodation at the north-eastern end of the beach is quieter and moderately priced, though the beach is a bit thin on sand. *Comfort Bungalow* (☎ *077-242110*) costs 350B for fan rooms to 1200B for all air-con rooms (with breakfast) plus there's a pool. The semi-secluded *Royal Blue Lagoon Beach Resort* (☎ *077-424086, fax 424195*) has garden-view rooms for 1000B, and sea-view rooms for 2500B. This is a bit overpriced for the area and the facilities, even though the resort has a pool and a good open-air seafood restaurant. Considerably less expensive are the simpler *Bay View Villa* (☎ *077-230769*) at 200B to 300B; *Lamai Garden*, 200B to 400B for fan, plus air-con for 1200B; *Island Resort*, 400B to 800B; and *Rose Garden*, 400B to 650B.

American-run *Spa Resort* (☎ *077-230855, fax 424126*) is a new-agey place that offers herbal sauna, massage, clay facials, natural foods, meditation and yes, even fasting and colon cleansing. At the moment simple bungalows here cost 200B to 500B, all with fan and private bath. The restaurant serves vegetarian and seafood dishes. Other activities include tai chi, qi gong, yoga and mountain biking. Fees for health services are extra.

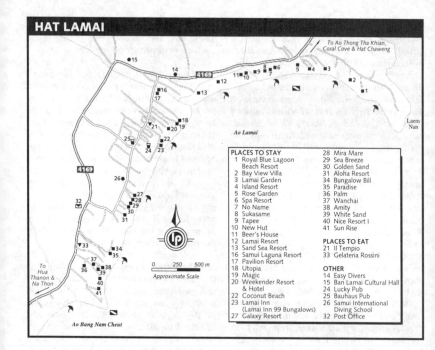

HAT LAMAI

To Ao Thong Tha Khian,
Coral Cove & Hat Chaweng

4169

Ao Lamai

Laem
Nan

4169

0   250   500 m
Approximate Scale

Ao Bang Nam Cheut

PLACES TO STAY
1 Royal Blue Lagoon
  Beach Resort
2 Bay View Villa
3 Lamai Garden
4 Island Resort
5 Rose Garden
6 Spa Resort
7 No Name
8 Sukasame
9 Tapee
10 New Hut
11 Beer's House
12 Lamai Resort
13 Sand Sea Resort
16 Samui Laguna Resort
17 Pavilion Resort
18 Utopia
19 Magic
20 Weekender Resort
   & Hotel
22 Coconut Beach
23 Lamai Inn
   (Lamai Inn 99 Bungalows)
27 Galaxy Resort

28 Mira Mare
29 Sea Breeze
30 Golden Sand
31 Aloha Resort
34 Bungalow Bill
35 Paradise
36 Palm
37 Wanchai
38 Amity
39 White Sand
40 Nice Resort I
41 Sun Rise

PLACES TO EAT
21 Il Tempio
33 Gelateria Rossini

OTHER
14 Easy Divers
15 Ban Lamai Cultural Hall
24 Lucky Pub
25 Bauhaus Pub
26 Samui International
   Diving School
32 Post Office

To
Hua
Thanon &
Na Thon

Several cheaper, more easy-going places in the 150B to 300B range follow to the south – *My Friend*, *No Name*, *Sukasame* and *Tapee* – before the strip of sand is interrupted by an estuary.

At the north-east end of the next section of beach is the inexpensive *New Hut*, with 150B to 200B huts which can accommodate two people. The proprietor here has been known to eject guests who don't eat in the restaurant, and we continue to get comments about rudeness and behaviour bordering on the violent. Connected with New Hut by a ramp that leads out to the road is the similar *Beer's House* (☎ 077-231088), with slightly nicer rooms for 200B to 250B. Farther south-east and almost as inexpensive is *Lamai Resort*, with huts for 150B to 350B. *Sand Sea Resort* is a more up-market place with air-con rooms for 1000B and fan rooms for 800B. In the low season

knock 300B off these rates. After another estuary, the *Samui Laguna Resort* (☎ 077-424215, fax 424371, Bangkok ☎ 02-252 5244, fax 254 5198) straddles a peninsula with closely spaced bungalows starting at 1600B, all with air-con, TV, phone, mini-bar and breakfast. There's a pool on the premises.

Pavilion Resort (☎ 077-424420, fax 424029) comes next, and enjoys a bit more thatched-roof Thai-style charm. All rooms, whether in the hotel wing (2000B) or cottages (3000B), come with air-con, porches, personal safe, hair dryer, mini-bar, TV and telephone. There are also a jacuzzi and swimming pool on the property.

Central Hat Lamai Down into the main section of Lamai is a string of places for 200B to 700B including *Mui*, *Utopia* and *Magic*. The 76 room *Weekender Resort &*

Hotel (☎ *077-424429, 424011, Bangkok* ☎ *02-466 2083*) has three types of accommodation: Thai-style houses (1820B); rooms in the main building (1050B); and bungalows (1330B). There's also a wide variety of activities to choose from, including miniature golf, swimming and a bit of nightlife. Moving into the centre of Hat Lamai, you'll come across *Coconut Beach* for 150B to 250B and *Lamai Inn (Lamai Inn 99 Bungalows;* ☎ *077-424427, fax 424211*) which charges 100B to 800B.

This is the part of the bay closest to Ban Lamai and the beginning of the Lamai 'scene'. Just about every kind of service is available here, including exchange offices, medical service units, supermarkets, one hour photo labs, clothing shops, bike and jeep rental places, travel agencies with postal and international telephone services, restaurants (many with videos), discos, bars and food stalls.

Next comes a string of slightly up-market 200B to 600B places, including among others *Mira Mare* which is good value and *Sea Breeze*, where air-con rooms are 700B. The *Aloha Resort* (☎ *077-424418, 424419, email aloha@loxinfo.co.th*) is a two storey up-market resort where bungalows start at 1550/1700B single/double, and suites go up to 3600B. All of these have fairly elaborate dining areas; the Aloha has a good restaurant with seafood, Thai and European food.

Also in this area are the *Galaxy Resort*, with fully equipped bungalows for 1000B to 2000B and a place right on the beach for 2200B. *Golden Sand* (☎ *077-424031/2, fax 424430*) is still looking good at 500B to 800B for fan-cooled bungalows, 1300B to 1650B for air-con.

Finishing up central Hat Lamai is a mixture of places costing anywhere from 80B to 600B. *Paradise* (☎ *077-424290*) has been here for over 20 years and is the second longest-running place on the beach, with fan rooms from 300B to 600B and air-con from 800B to 1000B. Standing apart in terms of providing high-quality and friendly service is *Bungalow Bill* (☎ *077-233054, fax 424286*), where bungalows are close

together but spacious inside and cost 300B to 400B with fan and private bath (for smaller bungalows up on the hill); 500B to 600B (for larger bungalows closer to the beach); and 1000B to 1200B (for air-con bungalows on the beach with hot shower and fridge). Email service is available here. *White Sand* is another Lamai original and rather ragged-looking huts are now 60B and up. Better are nearby *Amity* and *Wanchai*, both starting at 60B to 80B with communal facilities, 150B to 300B with private bath. A faràng flea market is held here on Sunday – many travellers sell handmade jewellery. The long-standing *Palm* has bungalows in the 250B to 500B price range, while *Nice Resort 1* has huts for 300B to 1500B, but they're really too close together. Just down the road, *Nice Resort 2* has cement huts for 150/200B single/double with fan, 600B with air-con. Finally, there's the *Sun Rise*, where acceptable huts go for 200B, new bungalows for 400B with fan or 700B with air-con.

Lamai doesn't have as wide a variety of places to eat as Chaweng. Most visitors appear to dine wherever they're staying. Once again Italian is well represented; *Il Tempio* does pizza, Italian and Thai, while *Gelateria Rossini* specialises in homemade Italian ice cream and cakes.

Chao Samui Restaurant, out on the main road, serves local Samui-style Thai cuisine at a reasonable 40B to 70B per dish. There are also several Thai *food stalls* in the central beach area.

Lamai has one large dance club, the long-running *Bauhaus Pub*, where DJ-ed music is interspersed with short drag shows and Thai boxing demos. Opposite Bauhaus Pub, *Lucky Pub* offers German beer, snacks and all the typical pub games. Several lanes are lined with Pattaya-style outdoor bars. By and large it's a faràng male-dominated scene, but unlike in Pattaya and other similar mainland places, where western males tend to take on Thai females as temporary appendages, you may see more than a few western women spending their holiday with Thai boys on Lamai.

Ao Bang Nam Cheut At this point a headland interrupts Ao Lamai and the bay beyond is known as Ao Bang Nam Cheut, named after the fresh water stream that runs into the bay here. During the dry months the sea is too shallow for swimming here, but in the late rainy season when the surf is too high elsewhere on the island's beaches, this can be a good area for swimming. Look for the well known, phallus-like 'Grandmother' and 'Grandfather' rock formations.

Closer to the road than the coast is the **Samui Park**, a concrete block with rooms and a few bungalows from 1600B (1200B low season) to 2000B. Down farther, **Noi** offers huts with shared bathroom starting at 100B and private bath from 200B. Next is **Chinda House**, with bungalows near the beach for 500B and air-con rooms in a hotel-like building for 1200B. The **Swiss Chalet** (☎ 077-424321, fax 232205) has large bungalows overlooking the sea for 300B (fan) to 900B (air-con) and the restaurant does Swiss as well as Thai food. Then comes the old-timer **Rocky**, with concrete bungalows with fan for 300B, air-con for 800B.

Ao Na Khai & Laem Set Just beyond the village of Ban Hua Thanon at the southern end of Ao Na Khai is an area sometimes called Hat Na Thian. As at Lamai, the places along the southern end of the island are pretty rocky, which means good snorkelling – there's also a long reef here – but perhaps not such good swimming. The inexpensive, natural bungalows that were still found here until recently have disappeared, replaced by the usual air-con architecture. It seems developers never stop and ask themselves, 'Who needs air-con on a tropical beach?' and as long as they keep making money, they probably never will.

Samui Maria Resort (formerly Royal Resort; ☎ 077-424023) has air-con bungalows with TV, phone and mini-bar for 800B to 2000B. The cheaper **Wanna Samui Resort** has bungalows with fan for 200B to 250B and air-con for 600B to 700B.

Sign-posted down a different road in the same area is the drab concrete **Samui Orchid Resort** (☎ 077-424017, fax 424019) which, with bungalows and hotel-like rooms over-priced at 950B (1100B with breakfast) and a swimming pool, makes an unsuccessful attempt to be up-market.

Turn right here, follow the coast to the foot of Khao Thaleh, and the secluded **Laem Set Inn** (☎ 077-424393, fax 424394, email inn@laemset.com) commands a pretty corner of the sand-and-boulder beach. Some of the buildings here are old Samui-style homes that have been salvaged by the English owner from other parts of the island. Rustic but charming bungalows start at US$50 with verandah, hot shower, fan and sea view. More contemporary air-con rooms facing the sea cost from US$100 to US$370. On the premises are a minor art gallery and a good **Thai restaurant** (pricey with small portions according to one reader). At Laem Set you pay for atmosphere and ecological sensitivity more than for amenities; some people will find this just what they're looking for, while others may feel they can find better value on the more popular beaches.

Beside Laem Set Inn, **Samui Butterfly Garden & Resort** (☎ 077-424020, fax 424022), features stylish modern wooden cottages linked by wooden walkways over a rocky landscape. Good landscaping, a pool and a mixed Thai and foreign clientele are pluses. Garden-view cottages cost 2800B, while those with sea views go for 3600B.

Ao Bang Kao This bay at the very south end of the island between Laem Set and Laem Saw has several inexpensive places to stay. You'll need to get off the round-island road onto winding sand roads for a couple of kilometres to find these places: **River Garden** (60B to 150B), **Diamond Villa** (100B to 300B) and **Waikiki** (300B to 400B).

Ao Thong Krut & Ko Taen Next to the village of Ban Thong Krut on Ao Thong Krut is, what else, **Thong Krut (TK Tour)**, where huts with private bath are 300B to 500B (less in low season). The beach here is not very private as it's a jumping-off point for boats to nearby islands as well as a mooring for local fishing boats.

Towards the south-west end of the bay, almost on Laem Hin Khom, the new and friendly *Coconut Villa* (*☎/fax 077-423151*) occupies a choice piece of property on its own small but clean and quiet beach with views of Ko Taen offshore. Well spaced bungalows start at 300B for a small one with fan and private shower, 400B for a slightly larger one, then 600B to 900B for yet larger bungalows with air-con and hot shower. Facilities include a pool on the beach, restaurant, motorcycle rental, money exchange, laundry service and mini-shop.

From Ban Thong Krut you can arrange boat trips to four offshore islands: **Ko Taen**, **Ko Raap**, **Ko Mat Daeng** (which has the best coral) and **Ko Mat Sum**. Ko Taen has three bungalow villages along the east coast beach at Ao Awk: *Tan Village*, *Ko Tan Resort* and *Coral Beach Bungalows* (*☎ 01-956 3076, 968 6096*), all in the range of 100B to 300B a night. A couple more in a sharply curving bay on the west side, *Dam Bungalows* and *BS Cove*, are similar. Ko Mat Sum has good beaches where travellers sometimes camp. Rubbish can be a problem.

Regular boats to Ko Taen cost 50B each way. If you want to have a good look at the islands, fishing boats carrying up to 10 people can be chartered in Thong Krut for 1000B to 1500B; try at one of the seafood restaurants, *Kung Kaew*, *Gingpagarang* or *Thong Krut Fishing Lodge* (*☎ 077-423257, fax 424013*) along the main beach. Seagull Coral Tour (*☎ 077-423091*) offers an 8 am to 3.30 pm boat tour to Ko Taen and Ko Mat Sum that costs 450B, including lunch, non-alcoholic beverages, snorkelling gear, boat transport and pickup anywhere on Samui.

West Coast Several bays along Samui's western side have places to stay, including Thong Yang, where the Don Sak and Khanom ferries dock. The beaches here turn to mudflats during low tide, however, so they're more or less for people wanting to get away from the east coast scene, not for beach fanatics.

Ao Phangkha Around Laem Hin Khom on the bottom of Samui's western side is this little bay, sometimes called Emerald Cove. The secluded *Emerald Cove* offers huts with rates from 80B to 300B, while at *Sea Gull* and *Pearl Bay* rooms range from 200B to 500B depending on the time of year. Both enjoy nice settings and are very quiet. The latter two offer boat trips to Ko Taen for 450B, including lunch, coffee, tea, snorkelling equipment and transportation. During the low season there are so few guests on this cove that the bungalow proprietors tend to let the rubbish pile up.

Ao Taling Ngam Dominating the north end of this shallow curving bay from its aerial perch atop a steep hill, *Le Royal Meridien Baan Taling Ngam* (*☎ 077-423019, fax 423220, ☎ 02-236 0400 in Bangkok*) is Samui's most ultra-exclusive resort at the moment. This resort boasts tennis courts, two swimming pools, a fitness centre and a full complement of equipment and instructors for kayaking, sailboarding and diving. As it's not right on the beach, a shuttle service transports guests back and forth. Luxuriously appointed guest accommodation containing custom-made Thai-style furnishings start at US$270 for a deluxe room up to US$500 for a cliff villa or deluxe suite, not including 20% tax and service.

Sharing the same bay just below Le Royal Meridian, *Wiesenthal* (*☎/fax 077-235165*) offers nine bungalows well spaced amid a coconut grove costing 200B to 400B for regular bungalow, 800B for a family-size bungalow. The Swiss-managed restaurant serves good Thai and European food. On the way to Wiesenthal, *Vastervik* has 300B fan rooms, but the staff seems quite hapless when it comes to any kind of service.

Ao Taling Ngam is a 15B to 20B songthaew ride from Na Thon or the vehicle ferry pier. Baan Taling Ngam of course provides airport/ferry transfers for all guests.

Ao Thong Yang The vehicle ferry jetty is here in Ao Thong Yang. Near the pier are several places ranging from 300B to 900B.

Coco Cabana Beach Club (☎ *077-423174*) is the best of the lot, with fan rooms for only 500B.

The vehicle ferry jetty may be moved to another location in the near future or this one may remain and a second one built elsewhere along the coast. Either way the local accommodation will be affected by the change, possibly winding down and eventually closing.

Ao Chon Khram On the way to Na Thon is sweeping Ao Chon Khram, with the *Lipa Lodge* and *International Bungalows & Big John Seafood Restaurant* (☎ *077-423025*). The Lipa Lodge is especially nice, with a good site on the bay. Most huts are 300B, with a few as high as 550B. There is a good restaurant and bar here. International Bungalows offers fan-equipped bungalows for 300B, (600B with hot water and sea view) and 800B air-con rooms. Between them is the up-market *Rajapruek Samui Resort* (☎ *077-423115*), where fan rooms are 500B and air-con rooms are 800B and up, and farther north, the isolated and slightly more expensive *The Siam Residence Resort* (☎ *077-420008*) for US$65 to US$70.

All four of these places will provide free transport to and from the Thong Yang pier for guests.

Getting There & Away

Air Bangkok Airways flies 14 times daily in the high season (11 times daily in the low season) to Ko Samui from Bangkok. There is an office in Na Thon near the old pier and another at the airport (☎ 077-425029). The fare is 3150B one way – no discount for a return ticket. Fares for children are half the adult fare. The flight duration is one hour and 20 minutes.

Bangkok Airways also offers twice daily flights to Samui from Phuket (1530B, 50 minutes). In June and September this is reduced to one departure per week. During the high season, flights may be completely booked out as much as six weeks in advance, so be sure to plan accordingly. An alternative is to fly to Surat Thani on THAI and then catch a THAI bus from the airport

directly to Ko Samui (via the Don Sak vehicle ferry) for 200B.

There are also daily Bangkok Airways flights to/from Singapore for 4000B each way.

The Samui airport departure tax is 100B. The attractive Samui airport is all open-air and has a nice bar, restaurant, money exchange and hotel reservations counter.

Bus The government bus/ferry combination fare from Bangkok's Northern bus terminal costs 427B. Most private buses from Bangkok charge around 400B for the same journey. From Th Khao San in Bangkok it's possible to get bus/ferry combination tickets for as low as 300B, but service is substandard and theft is more frequent than on the more expensive buses.

From Na Thon, Phantip Travel runs air-con buses to Krabi (191B), Phuket (193B) and Hat Yai (195), leaving the waterfront road in Na Thon daily at 7.30 am. These fares include the ferry ride.

To Surat Thani a bus/ferry combination ticket costs 70B ordinary (six times daily), 90B air-con (three times).

Train The SRT also does train/bus/ferry tickets straight through to Samui from Bangkok. These save you only 10B or 20B on 2nd class seats, otherwise for the other classes a combination ticket actually costs around 50B more than separate train, bus (from the train station to piers) and boat tickets but it may be worth it to avoid the hassles of separate bookings/connections.

Sample fares for joint tickets that include train, bus and ferry from Bangkok to Samui include:

speed/berth	fan	air-con
rapid upper	538B	658B
rapid lower	588B	708B
express upper	558B	708B
express lower	608B	778B

Departure times are 5.35, 6.20 and 7.15 pm daily.

See the Surat Thani Getting There & Away section for details on non-combination train travel.

Boat There are four ferry piers on the Surat Thani coast and two on Ko Samui (four if you count the two piers on the north coast that serve Ko Pha-Ngan). Songserm Travel runs express ferry boats from the Tha Thong pier, 6km north-east of central Surat, and slow night boats from the Ban Don pier in town. These take passengers only. The express boats used to leave from the same pier in Ban Don as the night ferry – when the river is unusually high they may use this pier again.

Vehicle ferries run from Don Sak, or from Khanom, around 15km south-west, at certain times of year. These are the lines that get most of the bus/boat and some of the train/bus/boat combination business.

Which boat you take will depend on what's next available when you arrive at the bus terminal in Surat or train station in Phun Phin – touts working for the ferry companies will lead you to one or the other.

During the low season (March to July and September to November), young Thais may throng the piers around departure time for the Ko Samui boats, inviting faràngs to stay at this or that bungalow. This same tactic is employed at the Na Thon and Thong Yang piers upon arrival at Ko Samui. During the high tourist season, however, this isn't necessary as every place is just about booked out. Some of the more out-of-the-way places to stay put touts on the boats to pass around photo albums advertising their establishments.

Tha Thong – Express Boat From November to May three express boats go to Samui (Na Thon) daily from Tha Thong and each takes two to 2½ hours to reach the island. The departure times are usually 7.30 am, noon and 2.30 pm, though these change from time to time. From June to October there are only two express boats a day, at 7.30 am and 1.30 pm – the seas are usually too high in the late afternoon for a third sailing in this direction during the rainy season.

The express ferry boats have two decks, one with seats below and an upper deck that is really just a big luggage rack – good for sunbathing. Passage is 130B one way, 240B return, but this fare seesaws from season to season; if any rivals to Songserm appear on the scene (as has happened twice in the last four years), Songserm tends to drop its fares immediately to as low as 50B one way to drive the competition out of business.

From Na Thon back to Surat, there are departures at 7.15 am, noon and 2.45 pm from November to May, or 7.30 am and 2.45 pm from June to October. The 7.15 am boat includes a bus ride to the train station in Phun Phin; the afternoon boats include a bus to the train station and to the Talaat Kaset bus stations in Ban Don.

Ban Don – Night Ferry There is also a slow boat for Samui that leaves the Ban Don pier each night at 11 pm, reaching Na Thon around 5 am. This one costs 80B for the upper deck (including pillows and mattresses), or 50B down below (straw mats only). The locals use this boat extensively and the craft itself is in better shape than some of the express boats. It's particularly recommended if you arrive in Surat Thani too late for the fast boat and don't want to stay in Ban Don. And it does give you more sun time on Samui, after all.

The night ferry back to Surat leaves Na Thon at 9 pm, arriving at 3 am; you can stay on the boat, catching some more sleep, until 8 am. Ignore the touts trying to herd passengers onto buses to Bangkok, as these won't leave till 8 am or later anyway.

Don't leave your bags unattended on the night ferry, as thefts can be a problem. The thefts usually occur after you drop your bags on the ferry well before departure and then go for a walk around the pier area. Most victims don't notice anything's missing until they unpack after arrival on Samui.

Vehicle Ferry Tour buses run directly from Bangkok to Ko Samui, via the vehicle ferry from Don Sak, north-east of Surat Thani, for around 400B. Check with the big tour bus companies or any travel agency. Nearby Khanom pier is also used by Songserm, which is now competing with the Don Sak company; so far Don Sak has the preponderance of the business but this could change as Songserm is a formidable business opponent.

From Th Talaat Mai in Surat Thani you can also get bus/ferry combination tickets straight through to Na Thon. These cost 80B for an ordinary bus, 100B for an aircon bus. Pedestrians or people in private vehicles can also take the ferry directly from Don Sak, which leaves roughly every two hours between 8 am and 5 pm, and takes one hour to reach the Thong Yang pier on Samui. In the opposite direction, ferries leave Thong Yang between 7 am and 4 pm; in this direction the trip takes around 1½ hours. During the rainy season the number of daily departures may decrease to as few as three, particularly in September.

Without bus fare included, the straight fare for pedestrians is 50B, for a motorcycle and driver 80B, and for a car and driver 200B. Passengers in private vehicles pay the pedestrian fare. The ferry trip takes about 1½ hours to reach Don Sak, which is 60km from Surat Thani.

Buses between the Surat Thani bus station and Don Sak cost 17B and take 45 minutes to an hour to arrive at the ferry terminal. If you're coming north from Nakhon Si Thammarat, this might be the ferry to take, though from Surat Thani the Tha Thong ferry is definitely more convenient.

From Ko Samui, air-con buses to Bangkok leave from near the old pier in Na Thon at 1.30 and 3.30 pm daily, both arriving in Bangkok around 5 am due to a stopover in Surat. Other through bus services from Na Thon include Hat Yai, Krabi and Phuket; all of these buses leave Na Thon around 7.30 am, arriving at their respective destinations around six hours later for around 200B each. Check with the several travel agencies in Na Thon for the latest routes.

Ko Pha-Ngan Two piers – one each in Bo Phut and Bang Rak – have boats to Hat Rin Nai on Ko Pha-Ngan's south coast. There are usually two departures daily for 60B (80B on full moon days); these boats take only 30 minutes to reach Hat Rin. See the later Laem Hat Rin section for more details.

Getting Around

To/From the Airport Samui Limousine operates an air-con van service between Samui airport and Hat Bang Rak (30B), Chaweng (120B), Lamai (100B), Mae Nam (100B) and Na Thon (100B). For other beaches you'll have to rely on songthaews or taxis. Chartered taxis from the airport cost 250B to anywhere on the island.

Public Transport Songthaew fares are 15B from Na Thon to Mae Nam or Bo Phut, 20B to Lamai or Bang Rak, 25B to 30B to Chaweng or Choeng Mon. From the carferry landing in Thong Yang, rates are 10B for Na Thon, 25B for Lamai, Mae Nam and Bo Phut/Big Buddha, 25B to 30B for Chaweng, 30B for Choeng Mon. A few years ago official fares were posted for these routes, but nowadays songthaew drivers like to overcharge newcomers, so take care. Songthaews run regularly during daylight hours only. A regular bus between Thong Yang and Na Thon costs 10B. Note that if you're arriving in Thong Yang on a bus (via the vehicle ferry), your bus/boat fare includes a ride into Na Thon, but not elsewhere.

Car & Motorcycle You can rent motorcycles from several places in Na Thon as well as at various bungalows around the island. The going rate is 150B per day for a 100cc bike, but for longer periods you can get the price down (say 280B for two days, 400B for three days etc). Rates are generally lower in Na Thon and it makes more sense to rent them there if you're going back that way. Take it easy on the bikes; several faràngs die or are seriously injured in motorcycle accidents every year on Samui, and, besides, the locals really don't like seeing their roads become race tracks.

Suzuki Caribian jeeps can be hired for around 800B per day from various Na Thon agencies as well as at Chaweng and Lamai. Aside from all the small independents doing rentals, Hertz has branches at Samui airport (☎ 077-425011) and at Le Royal Meridian and Chaweng Blue Lagoon Hotel. Avis Rent-A-Car has a branch at the Santiburi Dusit Resort (☎ 077-425031/38) and the Chaweng Regent (☎ 077-422389/90).

KO PHA-NGAN
• pop 10,300

Ko Pha-Ngan, about half hour's boat ride north of Ko Samui, has become the island of choice for those who find Samui too crowded or too expensive. It started out as a sort of 'back-door escape' from Samui but is well established now, with a regular boat service and over 156 places to stay around the 190 sq km island. It's definitely worth a visit for its remaining deserted beaches (they haven't all been developed) and, if you like snorkelling, for its live-coral formations.

Although hordes of backpackers have discovered Ko Pha-Ngan, the lack of an airport and relative lack of paved roads has so far spared it from tourist-hotel and package-tour development. Compared with Samui, Ko Pha-Ngan has a lower concentration of bungalows, less crowded beaches and coves, and an overall less 'modern' atmosphere. Pha-Ngan aficionados say the seafood is fresher and cheaper than on Samui's beaches, but it really varies from place to place. As Samui becomes more expensive for both travellers and investors, more and more people will be drawn to Pha-Ngan. But for the time being, overall living costs remain about half what you'd pay on Samui.

Except at the island's party capital, Hat Rin, the island hasn't yet been infested with blaring videos and stereos.

Dangers & Annoyances While many travellers may like to sample some of the local herb, it may be wise to think twice. There are constant reports of travellers being offered and sold marijuana or other drugs by restaurant or bungalow owners, and then being promptly busted by policemen who *somehow* know exactly who, when and where to check. Police roadblocks along the road between Thong Sala and Hat Rin are becomingly increasingly common, especially during the week leading up to the infamous full moon party on Hat Rin. These aren't cursory checks, either; if you're on a motorcycle the police look in the fuel tank, check the tires and search all your gear. One traveller reported the cops played 'a sort of pocket billiards' with his testicles looking for dope – not just pot, but ecstasy, acid, amphetamines and anything else an enterprising dealer might be shipping in for the big party. The result is often a steep fine (50,000B seems to be the standard fee) and in some cases, deportation. Not exactly the makings of a laid-back vacation.

Diving & Snorkelling
As at Ko Samui, coral reefs can be found intermittently at various points around the island. The better bay reef spots are at the island's north-western tip and are very suitable for snorkelling. There are also some rock reefs of interest on the eastern side of the island.

An outstanding site for scuba divers, a pinnacle called **Hin Bai**, lies about 13.5km north of the island. An abundance of corals and tropical fish can be seen at depths of 10 to 30m; conditions are best from April to October, when divers sometimes enjoy visibility up to 20m or more. Hin Bai can also be reached from Ko Tao, although the boating distance from the latter adds 4km to 5km to the trip.

Waterfalls
In the interior of this somewhat smaller island are four permanent waterfalls and a number of more seasonal ones. Boulders carved with the royal insignia of kings Rama V, Rama VII and Rama IX, all of whom have visited the falls, can be found at **Than Sadet Falls**, which cascades along Khlong Than Sadet in the north-eastern part of the island. **Phaeng Falls** is off the main road between Thong Sala and Chalok Lam, almost

in the centre of the island. A third falls, **Than Praphat Falls**, is near the eastern shore in an area that can be reached by road or boat, while **Than Prawet Falls** is in the north-east near Ao Thong Nai Pan.

Wat Khao Tham

This cave temple is beautifully situated on top of a hill near the little village of Ban Tai. An American monk lived here for over a decade and his ashes are interred on a cliff overlooking a field of palms below the wát.

Actually it's not a true wát since there are only a couple of monks and a nun in residence (among other requirements, a quorum of five monks is necessary for wát status), nor is it even a *sămnák sŏng* (monastic centre). It is rather, a retreat centre for foreigners interested in learning something about Theravada Buddhist meditation. An American-Australian couple lead 10-day meditation retreats here during the latter half of most months. The cost is 2500B; write in advance for information to Khao Tham, Ko Pha-Ngan, Surat Thani, or register in person. Anyone under 25 years of age must talk with the teachers before being accepted for the retreat. A bulletin board at the temple also has information.

If you arrive by motorcycle, it's best to leave the bike parked near the bottom of the narrow road that leads up the to the centre; the road is quite steep in places – too steep for many riders – and the engine noise could disturb the meditating residents.

Thong Sala

About half of Ko Pha-Ngan's population of 10,000 live in and around the small port of Thong Sala. This is where the ferry boats from Surat and Samui (Na Thon) dock, although there are also smaller boats from Mae Nam and Bo Phut on Samui that moor at Hat Rin.

The town sports several restaurants, travel agencies, banks, clothing shops and general stores.

Information Bovy Supermarket on the main street leading from the pier sells just about anything you might need – sunglasses, sunscreen, liquor, snorkelling gear, cereal, cosmetics, even frisbees.

The monthly *Phangan Newsletter* contains info on transport and activities on the island.

Money If you're continuing on to other areas of the island and need to do some banking, this is the place to do it. Krung Thai Bank, Siam City Bank and Siam Commercial Bank buy and sell travellers cheques and can arrange money transfers and credit card cash advances; Siam Commercial generally has the best service. Foreign exchange services at Hat Rin are comparable to those in Thong Sala, though you can't wire money there.

Post & Telephone The post office is at the southern end of town, in the direction of Hat Rin; it's open weekdays 8.30 am to noon and 1 to 4.30 pm, Saturday 9 am to noon. Cafe de la Poste, opposite the post office, sells stamps and offers a phone serviceas well as a parcel/packaging service. Phangan Travel Booking Center (☎ 077-377048, fax 377105) and Shine Travel (☎ 077-377240, fax 477028) can arrange long distance calls as well as faxes.

Email & Internet Access In Thong Sala, Phangan Batik (☎/fax 077-238401, email batik@surat.loxinfo) offers email services and Internet access.

Medical Services Ko Pha-Ngan hospital, about 2.5km north of Thong Sala, off the road to Chalok Lam, offers 24 hour emergency services. Anything that can wait until Bangkok should wait, as medical facilities there are of higher quality.

Places to Stay & Eat – Thong Sala At the *Pha-Ngan Chai Hotel* (☎ 077-377068, fax 377032), on the bay about 150m south of the pier, all rooms come with air-con, phone and TV and cost 1020B with a garden view (1260B with breakfast) or 1176B facing the sea (1380B with breakfast). *Bua Kao Inn*,

KO PHA-NGAN

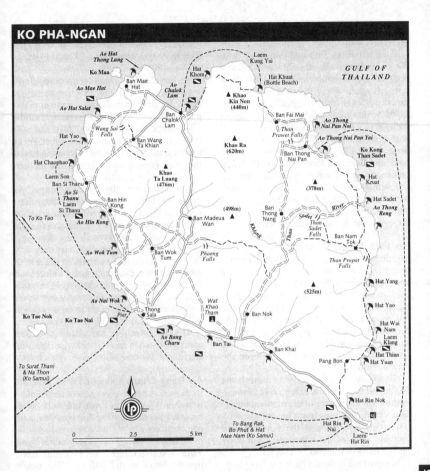

Ao Hat Thong Lang

Ko Maa

Ban Mae Hat

Ao Mae Hat

Ao Hat Salat

Hat Yao

Wang Sai Falls

Ban Wang Ta Khian

Hat Chaophao

Laem Son

Ban Si Thanu

Ao Si Thanu

Laem Si Thanu

Ban Hin Kong

Ao Hin Kong

To Ko Tao

Ao Wok Tum

Ban Wok Tum

Ao Nai Wok

Ko Tae Nok

Ko Tae Nai

Pier

Thong Sala

Ao Bang Charu

To Surat Thani & Na Thon (Ko Samui)

Laem Kung Yai

Hat Khom

Hat Khuat (Bottle Beach)

▲ Khao Kin Non (440m)

Ao Chalok Lam

Ban Chalok Lam

Ban Fai Mai

Than Prowet Falls

▲ Khao Ra (620m)

Ao Thong Nai Pan Noi

Ban Thong Nai Pan

Ao Thong Nai Pan Yai

Ko Kong Than Sadet

Hat Kruat

▲ Khao Ta Luang (476m)

Ban Madeua Wan

(498m) ▲

Ban Thong Nang

Khlong

Than

Sadet

River

Hat Sadet

Ao Thong Reng

Than Sadet Falls

Ban Nam Tok

▲ (378m)

Phaeng Falls

Than Prapat Falls

▲ (525m)

Hat Yang

Wat Khao Tham

Ban Nok

Ban Tai

Ban Khai

Pang Bon

Hat Yao

Hat Wai Nam

Hat Klang

Hat Thian

Hat Yuan

Hat Rin Nok

To Surat Thani & Na Thon (Ko Samui)

To Bang Rak, Bo Phut & Hat Mae Nam (Ko Samui)

Hat Rin Nai

Laem Hat Rin

GULF OF THAILAND

0   2.5   5 km

about 100m straight ahead from the pier, offers singles/doubles with private facilities in a guesthouse-like place for 250/350B, or 480B with air-con. In the low season rates drop to 200B to 400B. Similar *Kao Guest House* (☎ 077-238061, 210/9-10 Th Thong Sala – Chalok Lam), nearby, rents rooms with fan for 200B to 250B, air-con for 350B. This one also has a coffee shop.

Several cafes near the pier cater to faràng tastes and sell boat tickets. There are also a couple of karaoke bars in Thong Sala.

Places to Stay & Eat – Ao Nai Wok

There are a few beach bungalows within a couple of kilometres north of the pier. Although the beach here isn't spectacular, it's a fairly nice area to while away a few days if you need to be near Thong Sala for some reason. People waiting for an early boat back to Surat or on to Ko Tao may choose to stay here (or south of Thong Sala at Ao Bang Charu) since transport times from other parts of the island can be unpredictable. Swimming at this beach is best December to April when water levels are high. A reef offshore offers OK snorkelling.

Turn left at the first main crossing from the pier, then walk straight north till the road crosses a concrete bridge, and then turn left again where the road ends at a T-junction. Soon you'll come to *Phangan*, 100B with shared bathroom, up to 200B with private bath; *Charn*, 80B to 100B, all with private bath, high season up to 120B; *Siriphun*, 150B to 400B, all with private bath; and *Tranquil Resort*, 80B with shared bathroom, up to 200B with private bath. All are within about 2km of each other. Siriphun seems particularly good value and it still has the best kitchen locally, and some larger houses for long-term rentals.

Ko Pha-Ngan Beaches

Beach bungalows are still mostly concentrated north and south-east of Thong Sala and especially on the southern end of the island at Hat Rin, but there are many other places to stay around the island as well. The few paved roads on Pha-Ngan means transport can be a bit of a problem, though the situation is improving as enterprising Thais set up taxi and boat services between the various beaches.

Generally, beaches on the east coast don't tend to disappear at high tide as much as those on the west. For the moment the island's best road runs north to south, so visitors tend to cluster at the northern and southern ends of the island. Hat Rin is by far the most developed area so far.

Many of the huts on Pha-Ngan have been established by entrepreneurs from Ko Samui with several years experience in the bungalow business. Huts with shared bathing facilities go for 60B to 100B on average and as low as 40B between May and October; many of these do not have electricity or running water. Some have generators which are only on for limited hours in the evening – the lights dim when they make a fruit shake. For many people, of course, this adds to Pha-Ngan's appeal. Other places are moving into the 100B to 300B range, which almost always includes

a private bath, and a few scattered spots on the west and south-east coasts have resort-like amenities – including 24 hour electricity – for 500B and up.

As travel to Pha-Ngan seems particularly seasonal, you should be able to talk bungalow rates down by 30 to 40% when occupancy is low. During the peak months (December to February and July and August), there can be an acute shortage of rooms at the most popular beaches and even the boats coming to the island can be dangerously overcrowded.

Since many of the cheaper bungalows make the bulk of their profits from their restaurants rather than from renting huts, bungalow owners have been known to eject guests after a few days if they don't eat meals where they're staying. The only way to avoid this, besides patronising the restaurant, is to get a clear agreement beforehand on how many days you can stay. Even this may not be a 100% guarantee that you won't be kicked out. This seems to be a problem only at the cheaper (40B to 60B) places.

The following beach accommodation areas are listed in an anticlockwise direction starting at Thong Sala.

Ao Bang Charu South of Thong Sala, the shallow beach here is not one of the island's best, but it's close to town and so is popular with people waiting for boats or with bank business.

Sundance (☎ 077-283662), *Pha-Ngan Villa* and *Moonlight* have similar basic thatched huts in the 50B to 150B range, with a few wooden or concrete huts costing a bit more. *Petchr Cottage*, nearby, was closed for renovations when we visited, but will probably reopen in the 150B to 300B range. Following a coconut grove to the south are the distinctive high-pitched roofs of *Charm Beach Resort*, a nicely landscaped place starting in the same very low range and going up to 200B for a double with toilet; there's also one triple for 300B. *Chokana Resort* has big, solidly built hexagonal cottages in addition to more traditional huts, from 200B for fan to 1000B air-con. Charm Beach and Chokana resorts have decent restaurants.

First Villa (☎ 077-377225), farther southeast towards Ban Tai, past a school, offers cement-block, tiled-roof cottages for 400B (fan) to 800B (air-con), but lacks atmosphere.

Ban Tai & Ban Khai Between the villages of Ban Tai and Ban Khai is a series of sandy beaches with well-spaced bungalow operations, mostly in the 50B to 150B range (a few also have 200B bungalows). Not all bungalows here are signed from the paved road; to really survey the area you must walk along the beach. *Dewshore* can be reached from a road in the centre of Ban Tai, and offers well constructed huts in nicely landscaped grounds for 50B to 200B.

Starting at the southern outskirts of Ban Tai you'll find a cluster of places all around 300B to 600B. *Mac Bay Resort* stands out as one of the better choices.

In Ban Khai the locals also rent *rooms* to travellers, especially from December to February when just about everything is filled up. You can get a hut for a month at very low rates here. 'Dark moon parties' are held on the beach at Ban Khai on the day of the month when there's no moon as an alternative to Hat Rin's infamous 'full moon raves'.

Longtail boats to other parts of the island can be chartered from Ban Khai. At one time there was a regular boat service to and from Hat Rin, but with the paving of the road all the way to Hat Rin it has been discontinued.

Songthaews from Thong Sala to Ban Tai cost 20B per person, 30B to Ban Khai; a motorbike taxi is 30B to Ban Tai, 40B to Ban Khai.

Laem Hat Rin This long cape juts southeast and has beaches along both its western and eastern sides. The eastern side has the best beach, Hat Rin Nok, a long sandy strip lined with coconut palms. The snorkelling here is pretty good, but between October and March the surf can be a little hairy. The western side more or less acts as an overflow for people who can't find a place to stay on the eastern side, as the beach is

often too shallow for swimming. Together these beaches have become the most popular on the island.

The eastern beach, or Hat Rin Nok (Outer Rin Beach, often referred to as 'Sunrise Beach'), has gradually become a more or less self-contained town, complete with travel agencies, moneychangers, minimarts, restaurants, bars, tattoo shops and outdoor discos. A pier on Hat Rin Nai (Inner Rin Beach, often referred to as 'Sunset Beach') serves boats from the north-east coast of Ko Samui, half an hour away.

Hat Rin Nok is famous for its monthly 'full moon parties', featuring all-night beach dancing and the ingestion of various illicit substances – forget about sleeping on these nights unless you get a place off the beach. Even when the moon isn't full, several establishments blast dance music all night long – head for the western side if you prefer a quieter atmosphere.

Warning Suan Saranrom (Garden of Joys) psychiatric hospital in Surat Thani has to take on extra staff during full moon periods to handle the number of faràngs who freak out on magic mushrooms, acid or other abundantly available hallucinogens. There are plenty of other drugs available from the local drug mafia and drug-dependent visitors, and the police occasionally conduct raids. Travellers should be watchful of their personal safety at these parties, especially female travellers; assaults have occasionally been reported.

Money Siam City Bank has a foreign exchange kiosk near the Pha-Ngan Bayshore Resort.

Post & Telephone There's a licensed post office on the road between the two sides of the peninsula, and a public pay phone near the pier.

Diving Pha-Ngan Divers (☎ 01-958 4857), formerly Planet Scuba, on the cross-cape road and Chang Diving School (☎ 01-221 3127) at Anant Bungalows charge around

Full Mooning

It's 7 am, and the rhythm of the water pump behind the bungalow syncs perfectly with the techno mix down at the beach. Right, you're on Hat Rin, the morning after the monthly full moon rave, and a couple of thousand people are still hopping about in the sand. It's an updated version of an early 60s beach movie, only Frankie and Annette are staying up all night.

MICK WELDON

Ravers from around the globe have been gathering for the monthly party for at least 10 years now, and the crowd shows no sign of retreat. When I jumped ashore in 1990 for my first Hat Rin mooner it was a relatively small affair of perhaps 800 people tops. 'Shroom shakes, massive spliffs and glistening capsules of E were sold like sticks of barbecued *lûuk chin plaa* at a *ngaan wát*. The heart of the party pulsated in front of Paradise Bungalows, where Thai DJs longtailed over from Samui to do the knob-twisting.

Nowadays around 5,000 ravers – as many as 8,000 during the December-February peak season – turn up for the party, which has split among several beachfront venues: Paradise Bungalows, Bongo Club, Drop In, Vinyl Club, Cactus Club and Tommy's. On our most recent FM party the Cactus drew the steadiest crowd with a concoction of techno, house, drum 'n' bass, reggae, ambient and R&B. But Hat Rin's visiting DJs – who may hail from Belgium, the UK, Israel, Singapore and Thailand among others – are notoriously fickle, so by the time you reach Hat Rin somewhere else will probably be the 'in' house.

Dancers and groovers spill out of the open-air dance halls onto the beach and right up to the water's edge. Some people do their thing standing in the shallow breakers, but watch out where you plant yourself – by 2 am there's a chorus line of lads – well, mostly lads – releasing excess bodily fluids into the Gulf. In terms of party-goers, the numbers peak at around 5 or 6 am. The last of the DJs doesn't shut down till around 11 am. Some ravers take cat naps for an hour or three sometime between midnight and 5am, just so they can be up and at it for sunrise.

Drugs are still available but these days the more hardcore partakers have moved on to other beaches due to a pumped-up police presence (both uniformed and undercover) at Hat Rin's now-legendary full moon raves. Still, sober observers can amuse themselves trying to guess what's energising the folks hip-hopping in day-glo paint beneath black light tubes rigged to overhead nets. Mushrooms? Ecstasy? Saeng Thip? Red Bull?

Although the TAT once announced intentions to turn the Hat Rin FM into a family occasion complete with sporting events and beauty contests, authorities have yet to stop or co-opt the party and it's still very much in the original spirit of 'let's paint up and shake it'. The whole event is well organised by Thai residents who run the bungalows and bars along Hat Rin.

Public pay toilets are even available at Anant (Anan) Hotel. The proprietors also clean the beach of the substantial morning-after litter when the party's over.

Full Moon Party Tips

Safety Be watchful of your personal belongings and personal safety. Keep in mind that this is one night you can expect people who never otherwise take drugs or drink to excess to be

Full Mooning

on something and acting a little weird. Don't keep valuables in your bungalow – it's a big night for break-ins, especially at the cheaper bungalows. Ravers playing with fireworks add to the potential mayhem. If you're staying alone on the west side of the peninsula, think about having friends escort you home after dark.

Accommodation If you arrive on full moon day or even the day before, you can forget about finding a vacant room or bungalow on either Hat Rin Nawk (called 'Sunrise Beach' by tourists) or Hat Rin Nai (aka 'Sunset Beach'). Your best bet is to head over the rocky hills to the south end of the cape to places like Hua Laem Resort, Seaview Haadrin Resort, Sun Cliff Resort and especially Lighthouse Bungalow and Leela Beach Bungalows, which are farthest from the action and may have something available.

Many ravers travel to Hat Rin four or five days in advance to nail down a room, meet friends and 'warm up' for the party. Hat Rin and environs can house, at most, around 2,000 people, while the rave attracts 5,000 or more on a good full moon. Loads of party-goers, especially Thais, boat over from Samui during the afternoon, party all night, then boat back the next morning, thereby side-stepping the accommodation dilemma.

Food Beachfront barbecues offer fresh grilled seafood 'til around 11pm, after which the pickings are slim. Several beach bungalows shut down their restaurants the morning after so that staff can get some sleep. If you wake before noon you may have to wander into the village between inner and outer Hat Rin to find something to feed your abused stomach.

Transport If you're coming over from Ko Samui for the party, take one of the thrice-daily ferries from Big Buddha Pier or Bo Phut Pier on Samui for B80 per person, or hop on one of the frequent speedboats in operation the day and night of the full moon for B200 one way, B300 round-trip. The speedboats continue to depart from Bang Rak and Bo Phut until around 1 am, reaching a peak between 8pm and midnight.

A few places on Samui offer full moon package deals for B350 (these include mini-van transport to Big Buddha or Bo Phut piers), but these require that you leave Hat Rin at a specific time the next morning so you sacrifice flexibility.

Jet-setting full moon ravers can catch an early morning flight into Samui from Bangkok, get a mini-van direct from Samui airport to Big Buddha Beach (B30), and board the 10.30 am ferry to Hat Rin, hitting the sand by noon.

What to bring: If you're just a night tripper all you'll need is a change of clothes, swimsuit, sarong (for sitting/sleeping on the beach), ID (just in case) and money.

Drugs Thai police often set up inspection points on the road between Thong Sala and Hat Rin on days leading up to the full moon party. Every vehicle, including bicycles and motorcycles, is stopped and the passengers searched thoroughly. People go to jail, or pay through the nose. The going rate for escaping a small pot bust – or 'fine' if you wish – is B50,000.

Dates Check your lunar calendar for upcoming full moon party dates, or log onto www.googol.com/moon/.

Joe Cummings

SOUTH-WESTERN GULF COAST

650B for local dive trips, 2000B for a dive trip to Sail Rock or Ang Thong National Marine Park and 8000B for full certification. A snorkelling set can be rented for 80B to 100B.

Gym Jungle Gym, on the road between the two sides of the cape, near the pier on Hat Rin Nai, offers muay thai and other martial arts training, weight machines, Thai and western massage, sauna, aerobics, yoga and a full range of weight machines and free weights. Daily and monthly user fees are available, plus separate charges for instruction, massage or sauna.

Places to Stay The bungalows here are stacked rather close together and are among the most expensive on the island. Starting from the south, *Paradise Bungalows* (☎ *01-725 0662)* is one of the oldest establishments and offers a variety of cottages from near the beach to inland on the rocks, plus rooms in a motel-like structure perpendicular to the beach, from 250B to 350B. *Beach Blue* continues the trend of renting motel-like rows of rooms extending away from the beach for 80B to 150B a night. Next are the slightly more up-market *Anant Bungalows* and *Haadrin Resort* (☎ *01-229 6435)* with rooms in the 150B to 400B range. *Sea Garden Bungalows* is similar, with rooms for 200B to 300B, while *Phangan Orchid Resort* (☎ *01-229 3547)* is on the more expensive side with small fan rooms for 400B, or an air-con place on the beach for 1200B. *Sunrise Bungalows* (☎ *01-229 3884)*, more or less in the middle of the beach, is another long-runner; fan-cooled huts made of local materials are priced 120B to 300B (1000B for air-con) depending on position relative to the beach and the current occupancy rate.

Pha-Ngan Bayshore Resort (☎ *01-956 4367, fax 979 1312)*, Hat Rin's only semi-upscale establishment, occupies the middle section of the beach and charges around 450/650B for one-bed/two-bed rooms, up to 1500B for a large air-con bungalow on the beach. On the premises are an email/Internet centre and secondhand bookshop with lots of books in English and German. Next is

Tommy Resort (☎ *01-229 3327)*, a still popular old-timer; bungalows here cost from 150B with communal bathroom to 350B with private facilities. Similar *Palita Lodge* (☎ *077-377132, 01-822 1143)*, a large group of 30 wooden bungalows next door, costs 150B to 400B. Towards the north end of beach is the relatively quiet *Seaview Haadrin Resort*; well spaced bungalows with private bath cost 250B to 600B.

Built into the rocky headland at the north end of Hat Rin, *Mountain Sea Bungalows* shares a set of cement stairs (inundated by the surf at high tide) with *Serenity Hill Bungalows*. Each has huts with private facilities for 200B to 500B; an advantage of staying here is that it's relatively quieter here at night than at places right on the beach.

Behind the main row of beach lodgings a second row of bungalows has mushroomed, all in the 100B to 150B range.

Perched on the slopes of the hills in the centre of Hat Rin's southernmost point, overlooking the sea and catching sunset rays amid huge boulders and lots of vegetation, *Sun Cliff Resort* (☎ *077-299310, 01-970 3519)* offers 28 nicely appointed bungalows on stilts costing from 200B (for smaller ones) to 600B (for quite large ones). All come with fan and private shower and toilet; most have balconies with hammocks facing the sea. In a similar position on the opposite side of the highlands is the cheaper and less inspiring *Hua Laem Resort*. To find Sun Cliff and Hua Laem, follow signs posted along the cross-cape road.

A separate trail forks off the latter to the south-east and leads up and over the highlands to *Leela Beach Bungalows*, a set of widely separated bamboo thatch huts in a flat coconut grove with beds and mossie nets for 80B single/double. There's a thin strip of sand in front, and good breezes. The friendly Thai family who operate Leela Beach – which once belonged to the Rajneesh cult (a board bearing a large photo of 'Osho' still stands near the entrance) – prepare good meals. It's a 15 or 20 minute walk from Hat Rin. If you continue along the path through Leela till it meets a 100m raised walkway around a rocky headland you'll find *Lighthouse Bungalow*. At night – or when the surf is high – negotiating this walkway could be very tricky. Lighthouse's 18 simple and somewhat shabby bungalows, perched dramatically on boulders, cost 80B with outside bath, 150B inside. They have their own generator, with power from 6 to 11 pm only. It's a 30 minute walk here without luggage; you can hire a longtail at Hat Rin to shuttle you to Lighthouse's own pier for 100B. During monsoons the wind can be quite strong at this spot.

Across the ridge on the west side is Hat Rin Nai (Inner Rin Beach), which overall is much quieter than Hat Rin Nok. Here you'll find long-timers *Palm Beach* (80B to 150B) and *Sunset Bay Resort* (80B to 200B), plus a string of places in the 100B to 250B range: *Charung* is the best of the pack – quiet and well maintained. There are lots more, including *Family House* which also has aircon for 500B to 600B and *Neptune's Villa* at 120B to 400B. The *Rin Beach Resort* has a few larger huts with private bath and fan from 300B as well as concrete air-con bungalows for 800B.

At the northern end of Hat Rin Nai, around a small headland, is a bunch of places all in the 50B to 150B range. For 100B, the nicest thatched bungalows (all with private bath) are those at *Blue Hill*, situated on a hill above the beach.

Along the road that joins Hat Rin Nok and Hat Rin Nai, in the centre of the cape, you'll find the *Pooltrub (Phuntrap) Resort*, which charges 100B to 300B (80B to 100B in the low season) for solidly built bungalows on landscaped grounds. It's a short walk to Hat Rin Nai.

Places to Eat Restaurants here are still less expensive than on Samui, though prices are creeping well beyond 'local'. The seafood is good and fresh, particularly at *Sand* in the commercial zone on the Hat Rin Nok side. The *Rin Beach Kitchen & Bakery*, in the same area, offers a wide variety of cakes, rolls and other baked goods, including a 'magic bar' made from coconut and mushrooms. Nearby *Chicken Corner* (no sign) grills Thai-style chicken, then chops it up and makes tasty sandwiches.

Old Lamp, on the road immediately parallel to Hat Rin Nok, has become very popular for its well prepared stuffed baked potatoes, Thai food, sandwiches, salads and fruit shakes served in a rustic, dimly-lit atmosphere. *Oi's Kitchen* and *J Mon Thai Food* on the same road are two of the more traditionally Thai places in Hat Rin, and are not expensive. *Orchid Restaurant & Bar,* on the cross-cape road towards Hat Rin Nai, is popular for video dining. Near the pier, the relatively new *Om Ganesh* has good Indian food but service was painfully slow when we last visited. Off the road between the two beaches, long-running *Namaste Chai Shop* also serves decent Indian.

Getting There & Away Songthaew taxis go back and forth between Hat Rin and Thong Sala for 50B. This road was paved with concrete in 1996. The steeper, windier passages are more dangerous now than before the paving, since everyone drives faster and the smooth surface doesn't afford much braking traction. Motorcycles can be rented in Hat Rin Nok; take extra care when riding motorbikes on this road as lots of people wipe out on the steep downhill slopes; there is no shoulder on the road either, so watch out for passing vehicles.

There are also regular ferries a couple of times a day from two piers on northern Ko Samui, one each at Bo Phut and Hat Bang Rak. One leaves around 9 or 9.30 am, the other at around 1 pm; both cost 80B per person. During the monthly Hat Rin full moon party the number of departures increases and by midnight speedboats are leaving these piers every 15 or 30 minutes until around 3 or 4 am. The day boats are safer and less crowded.

East Coast Beaches Between Hat Rin and the village of Ban Nam Tok are several little coves. There you'll find the white-sand beaches of **Hat Yuan** (2.5km north of Hat Rin) and **Hat Wai Nam** (3.5km). The beach

SOUTH-WESTERN GULF COAST

at Hat Yuan has no places to stay but would be perfect for camping if you bring your own food; it's connected by an inland trail with Hat Rin. Around a smaller headland at the north-eastern end of Hat Yuan, there is accommodation at Hat Thian's *The Sanctuary*, a new age-oriented spot built into boulders overlooking the beach. Bungalows with shared facilities cost 60B to 100B, with private bathroom 100B to 300B; instruction in yoga, tai chi, meditation and massage is available. The Sanctuary can be reached on foot or boat (February to November only) from Hat Rin. Nearby, the *Haad Tien Resort* (☎ 01-229 3919) has 30 wood and bamboo bungalows with mosquito nets and private bath for 120B to 180B. Over the next headland at Hat Wai Nam is a *no-name place* that's only open from December to April. Haad Tien runs regular boat trips from Hat Rin Nok during high season – you can contact them via Yoghurt Home 3 in Hat Rin's commercial ghetto.

After that there is nothing else until **Hat Sadet**. A dirt track (traversable on foot but only partially by motorcycle) runs along the coast from Hat Rin before heading inland to Ban Nam Tok and Than Sadet Falls.

Hat Yao (5km north of Hat Rin) and **Hat Yang** (6km) are virtually deserted. After that, 2.5km north of Ban Nam Tok by dirt track, is the pretty double bay of **Ao Thong Reng**, where *No Name* bungalows are 50B. Above the beach on the headland, *Than Wung Thong Resort* offers huts for 100B to 250B. North of the headland, a pretty cove ringed by **Hat Sadet** features a string of places in the 80B to 200B range, including at last pass *Silver Cliff Bungalows*, *Mai Pen Rai*, *JS Hut* and *Nid's*.

The rough dirt track from Thong Sala to Hat Sadet is usable, subject to weather; a boat to/from Hat Rin (50B) and Thong Sala (70B) makes the trip every morning between September and April.

Ao Thong Nai Pan This bay is really made up of two bays, **Ao Thong Nai Pan Yai** and **Ao Thong Nai Pan Noi**. The latter is the best all-round swimming beach, although

Thong Nai Pan Yai is quieter. At the east end of Ao Thong Nai Pan Yai there's a good set of rocks for advanced climbers. Looking for used books? Try the Rainbow Shop, which carries both English and German titles.

On the beach at Thong Nai Pan Yai, south-east of Ban Thong Nai Pan village, are the *White Sand*, *AD View*, *Nice Beach* and *Central Cottage*, all with huts from 150B to 200B with shared bathroom, 300B to 600B for nicer ones with private bath. The other end of the beach features the similarly priced *Pen's*, *Pingjun Resort* and *Chanchit Dreamland*.

Up on Thong Nai Pan Noi *Panviman Resort* (☎/fax 077-377048, Bangkok ☎ 02-910 8660, email panviman@kohphangan.com) and *Thong Ta Pan Resort* are very nicely situated. Panviman sits on a cliff between two beaches and offers rooms in wooden bungalows or a two storey building for 1000B with fan up to 1800B with air-con, all with private bath. The much more basic but clean Thong Ta Pan Resort, at the north end of the smaller bay, costs 200B to 450B. Between them are the similarly priced *Rocky Blue* and *Big Yogurst*, both closed during the rainy season. Also in the middle is *Star Huts*, the biggest operation in the area, with huts for 120B with shared facilities, 180B to 250B with private toilet and shower. Behind Star Huts, away from the beach, the *Honey Bungalow* costs 100B with outside bath and 200B with private bath. Near the Honey and Star Huts, *Bio's Dynamic Kitchen* is a laid-back restaurant with several vegie dishes and a popular bar at night.

Songthaew taxis from Thong Sala to Thong Nai Pan cost 80B. During low season it can be difficult to find enough people to convince a songthaew driver to go at that price, hence you may have to charter a vehicle. Panviman runs its own taxi service from the Thong Sala pier. Take care if you're riding a motorcycle here, as this is probably the most dangerous road on the island – very steep in places, and mostly unsealed.

Hat Khuat & Hat Khom These are two pretty bays with beaches on the northern end of Pha-Ngan, still largely undeveloped because of the distances involved from major transport points to Samui and the mainland. Some of the island's least expensive accommodation is found here – hence it's popular with long-termers – but that means more likelihood of being evicted from your hut if you don't buy meals from the bungalow kitchens. Be sure to establish whether you'll be required to buy meals before taking a hut.

Hat Khuat (Bottle Beach) is the slightly larger of the two and currently has only two sets of bungalows, both in the 100B to 350B range – *Bottle Beach I* and *Bottle Beach II*. Boats leave twice a day during the dry season from Ban Chalok Lam for the 30B ride to Hat Khuat. West of Hat Khuat, 2.5km across Laem Kung Yai, is **Hat Khom**, where the *Coral Bay* rents standard huts for 50B to 100B. You can walk to Hat Khuat from Ban Chalok Lam via a steep trail, but no jeeps or motorcycles can reach it – all the better for quiet days and nights. It's also possible to walk to Hat Khuat from Ao Thong Nai Pan. We've been told Hat Khom may be reached by chartered songthaew from Ban Chalok Lam in the dry season, though we've never actually seen it done.

The fishing village of **Ban Chalok Lam**, at the centre of Ao Chalok Lam, features several small family run grocery stores, laundry services and lots of fish drying at the side of the main street. You can also rent bikes and diving equipment. Of the several restaurants, the best are *Seaside* and *Porn*. There are also a few inexpensive *noodle stands* around.

Chaloklum Diving School here offers scuba courses in English or German. There are also some places to stay along Hat Chalok Lam at the eastern and western edges of the bay. Starting from the northeastern corner of the village, *Fanta* has several rows of huts starting at 50B per person and a fair chunk of beach frontage.

Across Khlong Ok via a rickety footbridge, *Try Tong Resort* offers largish wooden cabins facing the bay and canal for 60B to 200B (closed during the rainy season). There's no beach at Try Thong save for a small chunk with boulders at the surf line. Farther on towards Hat Khom is *Thai Life*, with simple huts for 50B, and better bungalows with private facilities for up to 200B.

At the other end of long Hat Chalok Lam, west of the village, is the slightly nicer *Wattana,* with huts for 100B and bungalows with fan for 150B to 250B. The beach is better here, too. Still, we've received mixed reports on this place; some people loved it, others not.

The road between Thong Sala and Ban Chalok Lam is sealed all the way, and songthaews do the route regularly for 40B per person, or you can do the same trip by motorcycle for 60B.

Ao Chalok Lam is a good place to hire boats for explorations of the northern coast as many fishermen dock here (particularly from February to September). During this season boats run regularly from here to Hat Khuat twice a day for 30B per person. On some days the service may be cancelled due to high surf, so anyone electing to stay at Bottle Beach should leave a couple of extra days for planned departure from the island just in case.

Ao Hat Thong Lang & Ao Mae Hat As you move west on Pha-Ngan, as on Samui, the sand gets browner and coarser. The secluded beach and cove at Ao Hat Thong Lang has no accommodation at the moment.

An all-weather road leads west from Chalok Lam to Ban Mae Hat, a small fishing village with a few bungalow resorts. The beach at Ao Mae Hat isn't fantastic, but there is a bit of coral offshore. Close by, a little inland via a well-marked dirt track (200m off the road from Chalok Lam near Km 9), is **Wang Sai Falls**, also know as Paradise Falls. Towards the north-east end of the bay, *Maehaad Bungalows* has good, simple thatched huts for 50B plus wood and thatch huts with private bath for up to 100B, while the *Mae Hat Bay Resort* and *Crystal Island Garden* have small wooden huts in the same price range. Crystal Island has a good beach view. Moving south-westward, the *Island View Cabana* has good weather-board (clapboard) huts from 80B to as high as 250B for nicer ones. The Island View also has a good restaurant.

Wang Sai Resort, at the south-western end of Mae Hat, offers nice-sized bungalows built among boulders on a hillside; all have views of beach and bay. Rates run from 100B to 200B, depending on position on the slope. An open-air restaurant is situated well away from the huts, down on the beach. A dive operation here offers instruction and guided trips. Ko Maa, opposite the beach, sometimes has a few *bungalows* for rent; the bungalow owners provide transport.

The paved section of the road from Chalok Lam gives out at Km 10 (counting from Thong Sala), but a new road under construction will eventually link with Hat Yao to the south-west. Songthaew/motorcycle taxis from Thong Sala cost 25/30B.

Hat Salat & Hat Yao These coral-fringed beaches are fairly difficult to reach – the road from Ban Si Thanu to the south is very bad in spots, even for experienced dirt-bikers – come by boat if possible. Hat Yao (not to be confused with its namesake on the east coast) is a very long, pretty beach with a reasonable drop-off that makes it one of the island's best swimming beaches.

Hat Salat has *My Way* with huts for 80B to 150B. Down at Hat Yao are the basic *Benjawan*, *Dream Hill*, *Blue Coral Beach*, *Sandy Bay*, *Ibiza*, *Seaboard*, *Bayview* and *Hat Thian*; the latter two are isolated on a beach north of Hat Yao around the headland, and the road is very steep and rocky. All of these places offer basic huts starting at 60B to 100B, except for Benjawan and Bayview, which also have a few nicer cottages costing up to 600B. Along the best section of beach is *Haad Yao Bungalows*, which sensibly charges extra for basic accommodation if you don't eat there and has 200B to 500B bungalows; its tall security fence, however, lends a definite air of paranoia. At the end of this bay is the two story,

open-air *Eagle Pub*, a cool spot for a drink at night.

Around a small headland to the south of Hat Yao is *Rock Garden*, which lives up to its name with all manner of creative rock placements, including a steep rock path leading down to the bungalows from the road; tread carefully. Its isolation may appeal to those looking for a long-term hideaway. This one tends to close down in the rainy season.

Hat Chaophao & Ao Si Thanu Hat Chaophao is a rounded beach two headlands south of Hat Yao; then around a larger headland at the south end of Ao Chaophao is Ao Si Thanu. In these areas you begin to see the occasional mangrove along the coast; inland there's a pretty lagoon at the south end of Hat Chaophao near Laem Son.

There are four places to stay along the beach at Hat Chaophao. The popular *Jungle Huts*, *Sea Flower*, *Sri Thanu* and *Great Bay* all have bungalows with private bath for 100B to 250B. The Sea Flower (their card reads, 'no telephone numbers, no air condition') is especially well run. At the south end of the bay, past curving Laem Niat, *Bovy Resort* has standard huts with private bath for only 70B – when it's open. Ask at the Bovy Supermarket in Thong Sala to make sure.

On the rounded, pine-studded cape of Laem Son, at the north end of Ao Si Thanu proper, lies *Laem Son Bungalows*, with simple, quiet, shaded huts for 50B to 100B. Next door, *Laem Son Bay Bungalows* has nicer huts with private bath for 100B to 200B, depending on the season. South over a creek is *Seaview Rainbow* with very basic 60B to 80B huts. Down towards the south end of the bay, *Lada* offers 200B to 250B bungalows with fan and private bath. *Loy Fah* and *Chai*, both sitting high on a point at the southern end of the bay on Laem Si Thanu, offer good views and sturdy huts. Nicely landscaped Loy Fah, the better run of the two, offers good-sized wooden cottages for 150B, cement for 200B, all with fan, mosquito net, toilet and shower. Loy Fah also has two large, 400B cottages at the

367 South-Western Gulf Coast – Ko Pha-Ngan

bottom of the cliff on a private cove. In the low season you can knock 40% off these rates. Down at the southern base of the cliff is the similarly priced **Nantakarn**, but it's not as good value.

Ao Hin Kong & Ao Wok Tum This long bay – sometimes divided in two by a stream which feeds into the sea – is just a few kilometres north of Thong Sala but so far has hardly any development. At the centre of Hin Kong, not far from Ban Hin Kong, is the basic **Lipstick Cabana** with rooms for 60B to 180B. On the southern end of the village is the similarly priced **Hin Kong** (closed in low season). Down at the southern end of Ao Wok Tum on the cape between this bay and Ao Nai Wok is **Kiat**, in the 60B to 80B range. A little farther down around the same cape are **OK**, **Darin**, **Sea Scene**, **Porn Sawan**, **Cookies** and **Beach 99**, most with simple 60B to 80B huts – Darin and Sea Scene also have bungalows with private bath in the 120B to 150B range. Songthaews to this area cost 30B per person but you won't see them outside ferry departure and arrival times.

See the earlier Thong Sala section for accommodation just north of Thong Sala at Ao Nai Wok.

Getting There & Away
Ko Samui – Express Boat Songserm (☎ 077-377046) operates express boats between the Na Thon pier on Ko Samui and the Thong Sala pier on Ko Pha-Ngan two or three times daily, depending on the season. The trip takes 50 minutes and costs 80B each way.

Ko Samui – Other Boats Boats go direct from the pier at Samui's Hat Bang Rak to Hat Rin Nai on Ko Pha-Ngan for 60B (80B on full moon days). Depending on who's got the concession, the boat sometimes leaves from the pier at Bo Phut instead. This boat departs Bang Rak/Bo Phut just about every day at 10.30 am and 3.30 pm, depending on the weather and number of prospective passengers, and takes 40 to 45

minutes to reach the bay at Hat Rin. In the reverse direction it usually leaves at 9.30 am and 2.30 pm and takes 30 to 40 minutes.

From January to September there is also one boat a day from Hat Mae Nam on Samui to Ao Thong Nai Pan on Pha-Ngan, with a stop at Hat Rin. The fares are 120B and 60B respectively and the boat usually leaves Mae Nam around 1 pm. In the reverse direction the boat starts from Ao Thong Nai Pan around 8 am.

Faster, more powerful speedboats carrying 35 passengers go between Samui's Hat Mae Nam and Thong Sala for 150B; this boat runs twice daily from December to March, once a day the rest of the year and only takes about half an hour to reach Thong Sala.

Surat Thani – Night Ferry You can also take a slow night ferry direct to Pha-Ngan from the Ban Don pier in Surat. It leaves nightly at 11 pm, takes 6½ hours to arrive at Thong Sala, and costs 120B on the upper deck, 60B on the lower.

As with the night ferry to Samui, don't leave your bags unattended on the boat – there have been several reports of theft.

Ko Tao Subject to weather conditions, there are daily express boats between Thong Sala and Ko Tao, 47km north, at 2.30 pm. The trip takes 2½ hours and costs 150B one way.

Speedboats operate between Thong Sala and Ko Tao a couple of times a day for 350B per person; the crossing only takes about an hour.

Train/Bus/Boat Combination At Bangkok's Hualamphong station you can purchase train tickets that include a bus from the Surat Thani train station (Phun Phin) to the Ban Don pier and then a ferry to Ko Pha-Ngan. These generally cost around 30B to 50B more than buying each ticket separately yourself.

See the Ko Samui Getting There & Away section for sample joint fares; add 45B for through travel to Thong Sala.

Getting Around

A couple of roads branch out from Thong Sala, primarily to the north and the south. One road goes north-west from Thong Sala a few kilometres along the shoreline to the villages of Ban Hin Kong and Ban Si Thanu. From Ban Si Thanu the road travels north-east across the island to Ban Chalok Lam. Another road goes straight north from Thong Sala to Chalok Lam. There is also a very poor dirt road along the west coast from Ban Si Thanu to Ao Hat Yao and Ao Hat Salat.

Hat Khuat (Bottle Beach) can be reached on foot from Ban Fai Mai (2km) or Ban Chalok Lam (4km) or there are boats.

The road south from Thong Sala to Ban Khai passes an intersection where another road goes north to Ban Thong Nang and Ban Thong Nai Pan. The paved road to Hat Rin is now passable year-round, so there's regular transport between Thong Sala and Hat Rin. Even with the paving, only experienced motorbike riders should attempt the section between Ban Khai and Hat Rin. Steep grades, blind turns and a slippery road surface make it the second most dangerous piece of road on the island after the road to Thong Nai Pan (although there are more fatalities along the Hat Rin stretch due to greater speeds).

Songthaews and motorcycle taxis handle all the public transport along island roads. Some places can only be reached by motorcycle; some places only by boat or on foot.

You can rent motorcycles in Thong Sala for 150B to 250B a day.

Songthaew & Motorcycle Taxi From Thong Sala, songthaews to Hat Chaophao and Hat Yao, on the west coast, are 40B and 50B per person respectively, while motorcycle taxis cost 50B and 80B. To Ban Khai, it's 30B by songthaew, or 40B by motorcycle; if you're only going as far as Wat Khao Tham or Ban Tai the fare is 30B for motorcycles and drops to 20B for songthaews.

A songthaew from Thong Sala to Ban Chalok Lam is 25B, a motorcycle taxi 30B.

To get to Hat Rin from Thong Sala, a songthaew costs 50B one way while a motorbike is 70B. You can also get there by boat, see the following Boat section.

Thong Nai Pan can be reached from Thong Sala by songthaew (60B) or motorcycle (90B). See the following Boat entry for water transport to Thong Nai Pan.

Boat There are daily boats from Ao Chalok Lam to Hat Khuat at noon and 4 pm (returning at 9 am and 3.30 pm) for 30B per person. Boats run between Thong Sala and Hat Yao, on the west coast, daily at noon for 40B per person, but the service only operates from January to September, depending on the weather. Boats can also be chartered from beach to beach, price negotiable.

KO TAO

Ko Tao translates as 'Turtle Island', named for its shape. It's only about 21 sq km and the population of 750 are mostly involved in fishing, growing coconuts and catering to tourism. Snorkelling and diving are particularly good here due to the relative abundance of coral, though most of the beaches, except Ao Leuk (Deep Bay), are too shallow for swimming. is an exception to the latter.

Since it takes three to five hours to get there from the mainland (from either Chumphon or Surat Thani via Ko Pha-Ngan), Ko Tao doesn't get people coming over for day trips or for quick overnighters. Still, the island can become quite crowded during high season, when Mae Hat, Hat Sai Ri and Ao Chalok Ban Kao have people sleeping on the beach waiting for huts to vacate.

Ban Mae Hat, on the western side of the island, is where inter-island boats land. The only other villages on the island are **Ban Hat Sai Ri** in the centre of the northern part and **Ban Chalok Ban Kao** to the south. Just a kilometre off the north-west shore of the island is **Ko Nang Yuan**, which is really three islands joined by a sand bar.

The granite promontory of **Laem Tato** at the southern tip of Ko Tao makes a nice hike from Ban Chalok Ban Kao.

For Divers Only?

In the last five years or so the Ko Tao diving industry has come to dominate the island. If diving instruction is of interest, Ko Tao is one of the best places to learn in Thailand, as there are many good dive sites close by and prices are reasonable. In a very short time you may find yourself becoming a 'divemaster' (or as many who have gone through the procedure call it, 'dive slave'), a status that allows you to help teach diving courses without pay. It's a great system for the dive centre owners, who recruit instructors from their students and then get away with paying them little or nothing as they move through the instructor hierarchy.

On the other hand, if you don't intend to don scuba gear on Ko Tao you may be annoyed by the constant come-ons from dive staff in residence at the various bungalows – it's become a bit like the trekking guide culture in Chiang Mai. You also may find it very difficult to find a bungalow that will accept guests who don't sign up for dive instruction or for some sort of dive trip. Almost all the bungalows on the island now have some sort of partnership with a dive operation and during high season few will allow non-divers to spend the night.

Joe Cummings

Information

Ban Mae Hat, a one-street town with a busy pier, is the only commercial centre on the island. Here you'll find a police station, post and telephone office, travel agencies, dive shops, restaurants and general stores. Boat tickets can be purchased at a booking office by the harbour as well as from travel agencies.

Money

Krung Thai Bank has a money exchange window near the pier, and several money-changers also offer exchange services.

Post & Telephone

The post and phone office in Ban Mae Hat is open daily from 8.30 am to 4 pm. Watch out for private phone offices, which charge exorbitant rates.

Diving & Snorkelling

Relative to its size, Ko Tao has a large number of dive centres, with some of Thailand's lowest prices for training and/or excursions. Underwater visibility is high and the water is cleaner than around most other inhabited

islands in the Gulf. Because of the faràng presence, the best diving spots have English names, such as White Rock, Shark Island, Chumphon Pinnacle, Green Rock and South-West Pinnacles.

At the time of writing there were more than 20 dive operations on the island, most charging basically the same rates. To support the many dive instructors, dive operations have to solicit nearly every tourist who visits Ko Tao; most are directly affiliated with accommodation on the island for just this purpose. During high season you may have to sign up for diving or be refused accommodation. (See the 'For Divers Only?' boxed text.)

Rates typically run from 800B per dive, up to 5400B for a 10 dive package (including gear, boat, guide, food and beverages) or 550B per dive if you bring your own gear. An all-inclusive introductory dive lesson costs 1500B while a four day, open-water PADI certificate course goes for around 8000B – these rates include gear, boat, instructor, food and beverages. A snorkel, mask and fins typically rent for 80B to 100B (or 50B separately) per day.

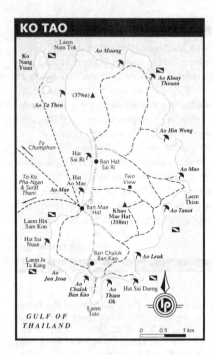

KO TAO

Laem
Nam Tok

Ao Muang

Ko
Nang
Yuan

Ao Kluay
Theuan

(379m) ▲

Ao Ta Then

Ao Hin Wong

To
Chumphon

Hat
Sai Ri   Ban Hat
                Sai Ri

To Ko   Hat   Two
Pha-Ngan &   Ao Mae   View
Surat Thani   Ao Mae   Ao Mao

                                          Laem
                                          Thian
              Ban Mae   Khao   Ao Tanot
              Hat   Mae Hat
Laem Hin   (310m)
Sam Kon

Hat Sai
Nuan

Laem Je   Ban Chalok   Ao Leuk
Ta Kang   Ban Kao

              Ao
              Jun Jeua
                    Ao   Ao   Hat Sai Daeng
                    Chalok   Thian
                    Ban Kao   Ok
GULF OF   Laem
THAILAND   Tato

0   0.5   1 km

Places to Stay

With the steady transformation of Ko Tao into a diving resort, huts have moved up-market relative to Ko Pha-Ngan, standing approximately between Samui and Pha-Ngan in terms of cost and amenities. Few bungalows are made with local materials any more, perhaps a boon to the environment. At last count there were about 650 huts in 48 locations around the island. At most places electricity is provided by generators from 6 pm to midnight. Simple thatched or wooden huts typically cost 80B to 150B per night, while larger wooden, brick or concrete bungalows with private bath range from 200B to 600B.

During the peak season – December to March – it can be difficult to find accommodation anywhere on the island – no matter what the time of day – and people end up sleeping on the beach or in restaurants for one or two nights until a hut becomes available. What is more common is that all the cheaper huts are occupied and only the places costing 250B or more are available. On arrival at Ban Mae Hat it may be best to follow a tout who can find vacant huts, otherwise your chances of finding a place on your own might be very slim.

Some bungalows with associated diving operations will refuse accommodation to visitors who don't sign up for a dive trip or instruction. Some of the cheaper operations – especially those at the north end of Hat Sai Ri and at Ao Ta Then – will give you the boot if you don't buy food at their restaurant; we still receive reports of visitors being locked out of their bungalows or violently ejected. In the off season it can be a problem finding a bungalow operation that hasn't closed down till next high season.

Ao Mae At Hat Ao Mae, just north of Ban Mae Hat, the shallow bay has plenty of coral but the south end receives a lot of rubbish from the pier area at Ban Mae Hat. *Crystal* (☎ 01-229 4643, fax 229 3828) offers small, basic plywood huts for 100B and more spacious concrete and wood bungalows with private bath for 500B. *Beach Club* (☎ 01-213 4646) has small thatched huts with shared facilities (no fans) and small verandahs with hammocks for 200B; larger huts with fan are a steep 800B, 1500B with air-con. On the headland overlooking the bay are *Queen Resort* (150B to 300B for standard bungalows with shared bathroom) and *Tommy's* (50B to 80B for a very small room over the restaurant/office, and from 250B to 1300B for a nicer bungalow). Just beyond Tommy's, the *View Cliff Restaurant & Bungalows* offers basic huts with fan for 250B, larger air-con huts for 1000B to 1900B depending on the season.

Hat Sai Ri Around the headland to the north is the longest beach on the island, with a string of bungalow and dive operations starting with *In Touch*, a friendly spot where bungalows with private bath cost just 120B. Next is the larger *AC Resort II*, which has sturdy bungalows with private bath and nice landscaping in the 200B to 350B range. *AC Resort I* and *Haad Sai Ree Resort* are both affiliated with Ban's Diving Resort, and will only rent rooms to people who agree in advance to sign up for their dives. Rooms at AC I with private bath and fan are 150B to 400B, while those at Haad Sai Ree are 200B. *Ko Tao Marina Resort* has similar rooms ranging from 250B to 400B, depending on location. Up next, *SB Cabana* has clean wooden bungalows with fan, mosquito net, private toilet and shower for 250B to 300B. *Bing Bungalow*, on the other side of the road, has cheaper huts for 150B with shared bathroom, 200B with private bath. *Ban's Diving Resort* (☎ 01-725 0181) offers sturdy bungalows ranging from 50B to 400B.

The air-con stucco cottages at *Sunset Bari Resort* go for a Mediterranean look, start at 750B for fan rooms and are the poshest digs on the island; there's a swimming pool on the premises. Farther north along Hat Sai Ri are four places in the 200B to 400B range: *Sai Ree Cottage*, *New Way*, *Sai Ree Hut*, *O-Chai*, *Simple Life Villa* and *Blue Wind*. Owned by a friendly English-speaking Thai woman from Ko Samui, *Seashell Bungalows* (☎ 01-229 4621) is one of the only places along this beach not directly affiliated with a dive op. Huts with fan, private toilet and shower cost 350B to 500B (down to 250B in off-season months), a little high for this beach but cheaper than taking a dive course. *Pranee's* is on a large property and boasts electric power all night; a nice bungalow with fan and private bath costs 300B.

North of the beach, in an area sometimes called Ao Ta Then, there are several inexpensive bungalow operations with very basic huts – most off the beach and built high on the rocks – in the 50B to 250B range. *Silver Cliff* is the best choice – some huts have great bay views – while *Golden Cape* is definitely deteriorating. Farther north, the lone *CFT* has basic huts for 70B and bungalows with private bath for up to 300B.

Ao Muang & Ao Kluay Theuan On the northern and north-eastern tip of the island, accessible only by boat or on foot, are two coral-fringed coves without bungalow accommodation. As the pressure for places to stay increases, new operations should start appearing at both.

Ao Hin Wong South of Ao Kluay Theuan by sea, or 2km north-east of Ban Hat Sai Ri by trail, tranquil Ao Hin Wong has a handful of huts called *Hin Wong Bungalows* and another called *Green Tree* for 80B to 100B with shared bathroom.

Ao Mao, Laem Thian & Ao Tanot Continuing clockwise around the island, Ao Mao, connected by a 2km dirt trail with Ban Hat Sai Ri, is another cove with no beach accommodation so far. On the cape which juts out over the north end of Ao Tanot, *Laem Thian* has huts built among the rocks from 80B to 150B with shared bathroom; the owners have plans to build additional bungalows with private facilities in the near future.

Ao Tanot proper, to the south, is one of the island's best spots for snorkelling and features a good set of bungalow operations, the proprietors of which so far cooperate to keep the beach clean. The well landscaped *Tanote Bay Resort* (☎ 01-970 4703) charges 200B to 500B for simple but well maintained huts, all with private bath, while *Poseidon* has very simple huts for 60B to 120B. *Mountain Deep* has basic bungalows with outside bath for 80B to 150B, or 120B to 500B with private bath. The friendly *Diamond Beach* offers huts from 80B to 150B. *Bamboo Hut* has 11 decked bungalows (with more under construction) for 150B to 450B; the kitchen specialises in spicy southern Thai-style food.

From May to August it is difficult to get to Ao Tanot by boat as the water is very shallow and the taxi boats may become stranded and/or damage coral if they attempt it. Some years are better than others depending on tidal cycles.

Khao Mae Hat On the way to Ao Tanot from Ban Mae Hat, a path forks off the main track and leads up the slopes of 310m Khao Mae Hat in the centre of the island to *Two View*, so named because it affords sunrise and sunset views of both sides of the island. It's a 30 minute walk up the path from Ao Tanot. There are only six bungalows, ranging from 50B to 85B. Vegetarian food and herbal teas are available in the restaurant. Two View advertises three-day meditation retreats and five-day massage courses (but not Thai massage as advertised).

Another place farther along the same trail atop the ridge in the centre of the island is *Mountain*, where rooms are 50B to 100B. Mountain is more easily accessed from a trail that leads from near Tommy's on Hat Ao Mae.

Ao Leuk & Hat Sai Daeng Ao Leuk, connected by a 2.2km track with Ban Mae Hat, has the lone *Ao Leuk Resort*, with seven huts for 150B with shared facilities, 200B en suite. Nearby *Nice Moon* has only four simple bungalows, bath outside, starting at 200B – probably negotiable except in high season. Another kilometre or so south is Hat Sai Daeng, where *Kiet* offers simple huts from 80B or nicer ones with private bath for up to 400B. After Kiet comes a new place called *Coral View Resort* (☎ 01-970 0378) with 10 bungalows, all with private bath, starting at 300B in the high season, a bit less in the low season. If you call in advance, Coral View will pick you up in a taxi boat at the Thong Sala pier.

Ao Thian Ok & Laem Tato Farther west on the side of the impressive Laem Tato is pretty Ao Thian Ok with *Rocky* at 150B to 350B. The food is reputedly good at *New Heaven*, a restaurant atop the cliff overlooking the bay and resort.

Ao Chalok Ban Kao This nicely situated coral beach, about 1.7km south of Ban Mae Hat by road, has become quite crowded. In peak season it can be very difficult to find a vacant hut here, and travellers end up sleeping on the floor of a restaurant for a night or two until something becomes available.

On the hill overlooking the western part of the bay you'll find *Laem Khlong*, 150B to 250B and no beach; and *Viewpoint*, with lots of bungalows for 100B to 250B. Next is *Sunshine*, with basic but clean bungalows for 100B to 400B, all with fan and private bath. *Buddha View Dive Resort* (☎ 01-229 4693, 229 3948, email buddha@samart.co.th) next door has similar bungalows for 100B if you book a dive trip, 300B to 400B if you don't (their open-water dive course is 7800B). The restaurant is one of the better ones outside of Hat Sai Ri. Next is the well run *Carabao* (☎ 01-229 3602, fax 077-337196) where huts are 50B for divers, 100B for non-divers. *Big Fish* is another bungalow-cum-dive-centre with huts from 50B to 200B depending on proximity to the beach. Normally all huts are reserved for divers. The friendly *Ko Tao Cottages* (☎/fax 01-229 3751, 229 3662, email ktcdive@samart.co.th), towards the eastern end of the bay, has some of the island's most luxurious bungalows for 550B to 780B; it's popular with package tour groups. Naturally there's a dive centre here, too.

Around a couple of small points to the south along Laem Tato is a beach which can only be reached on foot and at low tide. Here *Taa Toh Lagoon* offers 18 screened huts with private bath for 250B to 350B. Nearby *Freedom Beach* has a few basic bungalows for 80B with private bath, better ones for 150B and a furnished wooden bungalow with a view for 500B. Connected by a network of bridges and walkways, bungalows at the *Pond Resort* perch on rocks overlooking the bay and start at 300B. Also on the hillside is the rather shabby *Aud Bungalow* for 250B to 350B.

South-West of Mae Hat As might be expected, beaches just south of town get better the farther south you go. A few hundred metres south-west of Mae Hat, across a stream and down a footpath, is the upmarket *Sensi Paradise Resort* (☎ 01-229 3645, fax 077-377196), with solid cottages made from local materials for 200B to 800B depending on size and quality, as well as a few larger places with sleeping lofts suitable for families for 1500B to 2500B. Another semi-upscale one, *Ko Tao Royal Resort*, offers bungalows for 600B with fan and toilet or 2500B for air-con. Basic *CL Bungalows* has huts for 80B to 250B. *Sai Thong*, owned by the Jansom Thara hotel group, is currently undergoing renovation and expansion from 26 to 46 bungalows; when finished, rates are likely to be around 500B per night. Sai Thong has its own pier.

A couple of kilometres farther south is a series of small beaches collectively known as Hat Sai Nuan, where you'll find the popular *Siam Cookie* and *Char Bungalows*, both 60B to 150B.

At Laem Je Ta Kang (about 1.2km west of Ao Chalok Ban Kao), on a difficult-to-reach rocky area between two beaches, you'll find *Tao Thong Villa* (80B to 150B). South of Laem Je Ta Kang, by itself on Ao Jun Jeua, is *Sunset* (100B to 150B). The latter commands a beautiful point that juts out into the sea. The only way to get to these is to walk along the dirt track from Mae Hat or take a longtail boat.

Ko Nang Yuan This pretty little tripartite island is occupied by *Ko Nangyuan Dive Resort* (☎/fax 01-276 0212, ☎ 01-229 5085) where, as the name suggests, the emphasis is on diving. Accommodation starts at 400B for standard bungalows and goes up to 2500B for air-con villas. Regular boats to Nang Yuan leave from the Ban Mae Hat pier daily at 10 am and return at 4 pm, for 50B round trip. You can easily charter a ride there for 50B. Note that the management does not allow any plastic bottles on the island – these will be confiscated on arrival.

Places to Eat
In Ban Mae Hat there's a string of simple seafood restaurants south of pier – *Mae Haad, Lucky, Neptune* and *Baan Yaay* – all with dining platforms built over the water's edge. The *Swiss Bakery* on the road that leads to the pier sells very good breads

and pastries; it's open from 7 am to 6 pm. There are also several restaurants on Hat Sai Ri, most associated with bungalows.

Getting There & Away
Bangkok Bus/boat combination tickets from Bangkok cost 750B to 850B and are available from travel agencies on Th Khao San.

Beware of travel agencies on Ko Tao selling boat/train combinations. Usually this involves receiving a 'voucher' that you're supposed to be able to exchange for a train ticket in Surat Thani or Chumphon; more than a few travellers have found the vouchers to be worthless. If you book train reservations a few days (or more) in advance, any legitimate agency on Ko Tao should be able to deliver the train tickets themselves. It's same-day or day-before reservations that usually involve voucher problems.

Chumphon At least three boats run daily from Chumphon on the mainland to Ko Tao. Departures may be fewer if the swells are high. The slow boat leaves Chumphon at midnight, takes five or six hours or so to reach Ko Tao and costs 200B one way. In the opposite direction it departs from Ko Tao at 10 am. See the Chumphon section for more details.

A speedboat departs Chumphon at 7.30 am (from Ban Mae Hat at 1.30 pm) and takes about one hour and 40 minutes, for 400B per person. Jansom Thara also operates a speedboat to Chumphon daily at 3 pm for 400B.

Surat Thani Every night, depending on the weather, a boat runs between Surat Thani (Tha Thong) and Ko Tao, a seven to eight hour trip for 300B one way. Boats depart from Surat at 11 pm and from Ban Mae Hat at 9 am.

Ko Pha-Ngan Depending on weather conditions, boats run daily between the Thong Sala pier on Ko Pha-Ngan and Ban Mae Hat on Ko Tao. The trip takes anywhere from 2½ to three hours and costs 150B per person. Boats leave Thong Sala around noon and return from Ko Tao at 9 am the next day.

Songserm also runs an express boat to Thong Sala daily at 10.30 am that takes 1½ hours and costs 250B. Need faster service? Twice a day – again depending on marine conditions – an 800hp, 35 passenger speedboat does the trip in an hour and costs 350B per person.

Ko Samui A slow boat leaves Ko Tao daily at 9.30 am and arrives at Na Thon at 1 pm for 250B. Speedboats leave at 9.30 am and 3 pm, arriving an hour and 20 minutes later at Na Thon for 450B.

Getting Around
Songthaews cost 30B per person from the pier to Hat Sai Ri and Ao Chalok Ban Kao. To bays on the other side of the island, like Ao Tanot, expect to pay about 50B (less if the songthaew is full). At night it may take up to 100B to motivate a driver. Longtail boats can also be chartered for up to 2000B a day depending on the number of passengers carried.

Between 9 and 10 am each morning (weather permitting), a round-the-island boat tour takes off from Hat Sai Ri and stops off in four or five places, including Ko Nang Yuan, while people snorkel and swim, returning to Hat Sai Ri around 4 pm. The cost is 250B per person.

Walking is an easy way to get around the island, but some trails aren't clearly marked and can be difficult to follow. You can walk around the whole island in a day, though the up-and-down, rocky paths make it a challenging proposition.

NAKHON SI THAMMARAT
• pop 71,500

Centuries before the 8th century Srivijaya Empire subjugated the peninsula, there was a city-state here called Ligor or Lagor, capital of the Tambralinga kingdom, which was well known throughout Oceania. Later, when Sri Lankan-ordained Buddhist monks established a cloister at the city, the name was changed to the Pali-Sanskrit *Nagara*

Sri Dhammaraja (City of the Sacred Dharma-King), rendered in Thai phonetics as Nakhon Si Thammarat. An overland route between the western port of Trang and eastern port of Nakhon Si Thammarat functioned as a major trade link between Thailand and the rest of the world, and between the western and eastern worlds.

During the early development of the various Thai kingdoms, Nakhon Si Thammarat also became a very important centre of religion and culture. Thai shadow play (*năng thalung*) and classical dance-drama (*lákhon* – Thai pronunciation of 'Lagor') were developed in Nakhon Si Thammarat; buffalo-hide shadow puppets and dance masks are still made here.

Today Nakhon Si Thammarat is also known for its nielloware (*khrêuang thŏm*), a silver and black alloy/enamel jewellery technique borrowed from China many centuries ago. Another indigenous handicraft is *yaan lipao*, basketry woven from a hardy local grass into intricate contrasting designs. Yaan lipao handbags are a fashion staple among Thai women, so you should see lots for sale around town.

Much of the surrounding province is covered with rugged mountains and forests, which were, until relatively recently, the last refuge of Thailand's Communist insurgents. The province's eastern border is formed by the Gulf of Thailand and much of the provincial economy is dependent on fishing and shrimp farming. Besides fishing, rural Nakhon residents earn a living by growing coffee, rice, rubber and fruit (especially *mongkhút*, or mangosteen).

Along the north coast are several nice beaches: **Ao Khanom, Nai Phlao, Sichon, Thong Yi** and **Hin Ngam** – see Around Nakhon Si Thammarat further on for details.

Orientation

Nakhon Si Thammarat can be divided into two sections, the historic half, south of the clock tower, and the new city centre, north of the clock tower and Khlong Na Meuang. The new city has all the hotels and most of the restaurants, as well as more movie theatres per square kilometre than any other city in Thailand.

Information

Tourist Office A TAT office (π 075-346516) is housed in a 70-year-old building in the north-west corner of the Sanaam Naa Meuang (City Field) off Th Ratchadamnoen, near the police station. They distribute the usual helpful information printed in English, and can also assist with any tourism-related problems.

Post & Telephone The main post office is also on Th Ratchadamnoen and is open from 8.30 am to 4.30 pm Monday to Friday. An upstairs telephone office with international service is open daily from 8 am to 11 pm.

Suan Nang Seu Nakhon Bowonrat

The Suan Nang Seu, or Book Garden, at 116 Th Ratchadamnoen next to Bovorn Bazaar and Siam Commercial Bank, is Nakhon's intellectual centre (look for the traditional water jar on a platform in front). Housed in an 80-year-old building that once served variously as a *sinsae* (Chinese doctor) clinic, opium den and hotel, this nonprofit bookshop specialises in books (mostly in Thai) on local history as well as national politics and religion. It also coordinates Dhamma lectures and sponsors local art and craft exhibits.

Nakhon Si Thammarat National Museum

Since the Tampaling (or Tambralinga) kingdom traded with Indian, Arabic, Dvaravati and Champa states, much art from these places found its way to the Nakhon Si Thammarat area, and some is now on display in the national museum. Notable are Dong-Son bronze drums, Dvaravati Buddha images and Pallava (south Indian) Hindu sculpture. Locally produced art is also on display.

If you've already had your fill of the usual Thai art history surveys from Ban Chiang to Ayuthaya, go straight to the 'Art of Southern Thailand' exhibit in a room to the left of the foyer. Here you'll find many fine images of Nakhon Si Thammarat provenance, including Phutthasihing, U Thong and late Ayuthaya styles.

Admission to the museum is 30B and hours are Wednesday to Sunday from 9 am to 4 pm. The museum is well south of the principal wáts on Th Ratchadamnoen, across from Wat Thao Khot and Wat Phet Jarik, on the left – 5B by songthaew.

Wat Phra Mahathat

This is the biggest wát in the south, comparable to Wat Pho and other large Bangkok wáts. If you like wáts, this one is well worth a trip. Reputed to have been founded by Queen Hem Chala over a thousand years ago, and reconstructed in the mid-13th century, the huge complex features a 78m chedi, crowned by a solid gold spire weighing several hundred kilograms. Numerous smaller grey-black chedis surround the main chedi.

Besides the distinctive bòt and chedi there are many intricately designed *wihǎans* surrounding the chedi, several of which contain crowned Nakhon Si Thammarat/Ayuthaya-style Buddhas in glass cabinets. One wihǎan houses a funky museum with carved wooden *kruts* (garudas, Vishnu's mythical bird-mount), old Siwichai votive tablets, Buddha figures of every description including a standing Dvaravati figure and a Siwichai naga Buddha, inlaid-pearl alms bowls and other oddities. A 12m whale skeleton lies in the back of the complex under the northern cloister.

Wat Phra Mahathat's full name, Wat Phra Mahathat Woramahawihaan, is sometimes abbreviated as Wat Phra Boromathat. It's about 2km from the new town centre – hop on any bus or songthaew going down Th Ratchadamnoen.

Wat Na Phra Boromathat

Across the road from Wat Phra Mahathat, this is the residence for monks serving at Mahathat. There is a nice Gandhara-style fasting Buddha in front of the bòt here.

Phra Phuttha Sihing Chapel (Haw Phra Phuttha Sihing)

This hall next to the provincial offices contains one of Thailand's three identical Phra Singh Buddhas, one of which is supposed to have been originally cast in Sri Lanka before being brought to Sukhothai (through Nakhon Si Thammarat), Chiang Mai and later, Ayuthaya. The other images are at Wat Phra Singh in Chiang Mai and the National Museum in Bangkok – each is claimed to be the original.

Shadow Puppet Workshops

Traditionally, there are two styles of shadow puppets, *năng thalung* and *năng yài*; the former are similar in size to the typical Malay-Indonesian style puppets while the latter are nearly life-size and unique to Thailand. Both are intricately carved from buffalo-hide. Performances of Thai shadow theatre are rare nowadays (usually only during festivals), but there are two places in town where you can see the puppets being made.

The acknowledged master of shadow puppet craft – both manufacture and performance – is Suchart Subsin (Suchaat Sapsin, ☎ 075-346394) a Nakhon resident

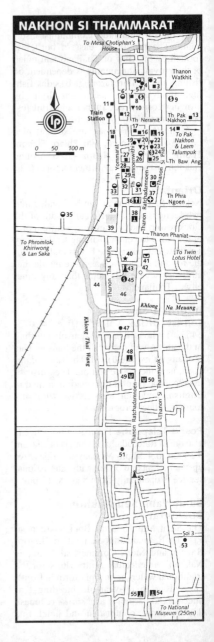

NAKHON SI THAMMARAT

SOUTH-WESTERN GULF COAST

NAKHON SI THAMMARAT

PLACES TO STAY
3 Taksin Hotel
7 Thai Fa Hotel
11 Phetpailin Hotel
12 Si Thong Hotel
13 Nakorn Garden Inn
14 Grand Park Hotel
16 Thai Hotel
17 Siam Hotel
18 Montien Hotel
25 Thai Lee Hotel
27 Muang Thong Hotel
28 Nakhon Hotel
29 Bue Loung (Bua Luang) Hotel
34 Laem Thong Hotel

PLACES TO EAT
5 Dam Kan Aeng
10 Yong Seng
20 Sin Ocha Bakery
21 Kuang Meng
22 Bovorn Bazaar; Hao Coffee;
   Khrua Nakhon; Ban Nakhon

OTHER
1 Share Taxis to Surat Thani,
   Chumphon & Ranong
2 THAI Office
4 Crystal Palace
6 Minivans to Sichon
   & Khanom
8 Bangkok Bank
9 Thai Farmers Bank
15 Wat Buranaram
19 Muang Thai Tours
23 Suan Nang Seu Nakhon
   Bowonrat
24 Siam Commercial Bank
26 Minivans to Surat
   Thani
30 Matsayit Yamia (Friday
   Mosque)
31 Minivans to Phuket
   & Krabi
32 Minivan to Hat Yai
33 Share-Taxi Terminal
35 Bus Station

36 Bethlehem Church
37 Christian Hospital
38 Wat Maheyong
39 Market
40 Police Station
41 Main Post Office;
   Telephone Office
42 Circle
43 Lak Meuang (City Pillar)
44 Handicraft Shops
45 TAT Office
46 Sanaam Naa Meuang (City
   Field)
47 Prison
48 Wat Sema Muang
49 Shiva Shrine
50 Vishnu Shrine
51 Provincial Offices; Phra
   Phuttha Sihing Chapel
52 Clock Tower
53 Suchart's Workshop
54 Wat Na Phra Boromathat
55 Wat Phra Mahathat

with a workshop at 110/18 Soi 3, Th Si Thammasok, not far from Wat Phra Mahathat. Khun Suchart has received several awards for his mastery and preservation of the craft and has performed for the king. His workshop is open to the public; if enough people are assembled he may even be talked into providing a performance at his small outdoor studio. Puppets can be purchased here at reasonable prices – and here only, as he refuses to sell them through distributors. On some puppets the fur is left on the hide for additional effect – these cost a bit more as special care must be taken in tanning them.

Another craftsperson, Mesa Chotiphan, has a workshop in the northern part of town where visitors are welcome. Mesa's house is at 558/4 Soi Rong Jeh, Th Ratchadamnoen (☎ 075-343979). Call if you would like to be picked up from anywhere in the city. To get there on your own, go north from the city centre on Th Ratchadamnoen and about 500m north of the sports field, take the soi opposite the Chinese cemetery (before reaching the golf course and military base).

Places to Stay

Most of Nakhon Si Thammarat's hotels are near the train and bus stations. The best budget value in town is the friendly *Thai Lee Hotel* (☎ 075-356948, 1130 Th Ratchadamnoen), where spacious clean rooms with ceiling fan, shower and toilet cost 120B with one bed, 200B with two.

On Th Yommarat (spelt 'Yammaraj' on some signs), almost across from the train station, is the *Si Thong Hotel* (☎ 075-356357), with adequate rooms with fan and private bath for 140B to 200B. Also on Th Yommarat is the *Nakhon Hotel* (☎ 075-356318), with similar rates and facilities to the Si Thong. An air-con room with two beds is 350B.

On Th Jamroenwithi (walk straight down Th Neramit opposite the train station two blocks and turn right into Th Jamroenwithi) is the large *Siam Hotel* (☎ 075-356090); rooms with fan and bath cost from 150B. Farther south on this street is the *Muang Thong Hotel*, where 150/200B will get you a clean single/double with fan and bath, 350B for air-con. A block north of the Siam, on the same side of the street, is the

Thai Fa Hotel (☎ *075-356727*), a small, two storey place with adequate rooms for 120B to 180B.

Once Nakhon Si Thammarat's flashiest, *Thai Hotel* (☎ *075-341509, fax 344858*) on Th Ratchadamnoen, two blocks from the train station, now seems rather ordinary with fan-cooled singles/doubles for 245/350B, and regular air-con rooms for 440/600B. Special 650B air-con rooms are larger, better furnished and have a refrigerator stocked with snacks. All rooms have cable TV.

The six storey *Taksin Hotel* (☎ *075-342790, fax 342794*) stands off Th Si Prat amid a string of massage places and costs 490B for air-con rooms with hot showers and TV, 590B with phone.

The *Bue Loung (Bua Luang) Hotel* (☎ *075-341518, fax 343418*), on Soi Luang Meuang off Th Jamroenwithi, has large, clean singles and doubles with fan and bath for 170B (240B with TV), with air-con for 270B (350B with TV and fridge). On Th Yommarat the fading, eight storey *Montien Hotel* (☎/fax *075-341908*), next to the train station, has large rooms with fan and private bath from 240B and air-con for 380B – a bit overpriced considering the low upkeep. The nearby *Phetpailin* (☎ *075-341896, fax 343943*), a block north, is similar but costs 180/220B with fan, 380B with air-con.

The quiet *Nakorn Garden Inn* (☎ *075-344831, fax 342926, 1/4 Th Pak Nakhon*), east of the centre, is more mid-range than top-end. It has rooms with air-con and TV for 500B to 600B.

The new *Grand Park Hotel* (☎ *075-317666/73, fax 317674, 1204/79 Th Pak Nakhon*) offers nicely furnished spacious carpeted rooms with fridge and TV for 750B and suites for 1400B (discounted to 700B and 1000B respectively). Parking is available.

Nakhon's top spot now is on Th Pattanakan Kukwang in the extreme south-eastern corner of town, opposite the Lotus Super Center. The 16 storey, 413 room *Twin Lotus Hotel* (075-323777, fax 323821, Bangkok ☎ 02-711 0360, fax 381 0930, 97/8 Th Pattanakan Kukwang) has all the amenities expected by Bangkok business travellers, such as IDD phones, minibars, satellite TV, restaurants, cocktail lounge, coffee shop, karaoke, massage, a swimming pool, saunas, and a fully equipped gym. Non-smoking rooms are available. Rates are 1200B for a standard single/double room, 1400B for a superior room, 1600B for a deluxe room and 2400B for a suite, though 50% discounts are easily obtained.

Places to Eat

There are lots of funky old Chinese restaurants along Th Yommarat and Th Jamroenwithi. The latter street is the city's main culinary centre. At night the entire block running south from the Siam Hotel is lined with cheap *food vendors* – Muslim stands opposite the hotel sell delicious *roti klûay* (banana pancake), *khâo mók* (chicken biryani) and *mátàbà* (pancakes stuffed with chicken or vegetables) in the evening and by day there are plenty of rice and noodle shops. *Yong Seng* (no roman-script sign) is a good, inexpensive Chinese restaurant on Th Jamroenwithi.

To try some of Nakhon's excellent Thai coffee, stop by *Hao Coffee* at Bovorn Bazaar. Basically an updated version of an original Hokkien-style coffee shop once run by the owner's family in Nakhon, Hao Coffee serves international coffees as well as southern-Thai Hokkien-style coffee (listed as 'Hao coffee' on the menu) served with a tea chaser. Ask for fresh milk (nom sòt) if you abhor powdered non-dairy creamer.

Bovorn Bazaar offers several other culinary delights. Adjacent to Hao Coffee is *Khrua Nakhon*, a large open-air restaurant serving real Nakhon cuisine, including *khâo yam* (southern-style rice salad), *kaeng tai plaa* (spicy fish curry), *khanŏm jiin* (curry noodles served with a huge tray of vegies) and seafood. The restaurant also has egg-and-toast breakfasts and you can order Hao coffee from next door if you'd like. With a banyan tree in front and a modest display of southern-Thai folk art, the atmosphere is hard to beat. Get there early as it's only open from 7 am to 3 pm. Behind Khrua Nakhon is *Ban Lakhon*, in an old house, which is also very good for Thai food and is open for dinner.

On the corner of the alley leading into Bovorn Bazaar, *Ligor Home Bakery* bakes fresh European-style pastries daily. At night the bakery closes and Nakhon's most famous *roti vendors* set up along the alley. In Nakhon, roti klûay (banana roti or pancake) is a tradition – the vendors here use only fresh mashed bananas. Other offerings here include roti with curry *(roti kaeng)*, with egg *(roti khài)* or as mátàbà (stuffed with meat and vegetables). They also do great *khanŏm jìip* (dumplings), stuffed with a chicken-shrimp mixture, along with Nakhon coffee and better-than-average milk tea.

On the north-western corner of Th Ratchadamnoen and Th Watkhit, the popular Thai-Chinese *Dam Kan Aeng* is packed with hungry customers every night. *Kuang Meng* (no roman-script sign) at 1343/12 Th Ratchadamnoen, opposite the Siam Commercial Bank, is a very small Hokkien coffee shop with marble-top tables and very nice pastries. *Sin Ocha Bakery,* opposite the entrance to the Thai Hotel, is a slightly updated Hokkien coffee shop with *tim cham* (dim sum).

Entertainment

Beyond the cinemas in town, there's not a lot of night life. *Rock 99% Bar & Grill*, an American roadhouse-style pub inside the Bovorn Bazaar, offers draught beer, cocktails and western pop music, as well as pizza, baked potatoes, sandwiches and a few Thai dishes; this is where the few expats that live in NST hang out. It's open 6 pm to 2 am.

On Th Phattanakan Khukhwang, on the north-west corner of the intersection with Th Neramit, stands a 'music hall' called *Martini* where live bands cover Thai pop songs. Similar is *Crystal Palace*, 50m down the soi which is opposite the THAI office.

Shopping

Several shops along Th Tha Chang, just behind the TAT office and Sanaam Naa Meuang, sell Nakhon's famous line of nielloware *(thŏm)*, silver and basketry. Den Nakhon, on the grounds of Wat Mahathat, sells thŏm, silver and other local crafts at good prices.

Getting There & Away

Air THAI has daily flights to/from Bangkok (two hours, 1770B). The THAI office (☎ 075-342491) in Nakhon is at 1612 Th Ratchadamnoen. The airport is a few kilometres north of town on Route 408.

Bus & Minivan Air-con buses bound for Nakhon Si Thammarat leave Bangkok's Southern bus terminal daily every 30 minutes or so from 5 to 8 pm, arriving 12 hours later, for 414B. Air-con buses in the reverse direction leave at about the same times from the bus station just off Th Phaniat west of the river. There are also two 2nd class air-con departures (322B) and one VIP departure (640B) nightly in both directions. Ordinary buses leave Bangkok at 6.40, 7 and 8.30 am, and 4.30, 5.30 and 6.30 pm for 230B.

Ordinary buses from Surat cost 37B and leave four times a day, while air-con departures are slightly less frequent and cost 53B. Direct buses run from Songkhla via a bridge over the entrance to Thaleh Noi (the inland sea). Check with one of the tour-bus companies on Th Niphat Uthit 2 in Hat Yai. Muang Tai Tours, on Th Jamroenwithi in Nakhon Si Thammarat, does a 70B trip to Surat that includes a good meal and a video movie. There are a couple of other private bus companies on Th Jamroenwithi near the Siam Hotel.

Hourly buses between Nakhon Si Thammarat and Krabi cost 64B per person (70B air-con) and take about three hours. Other routes include Trang (35B ordinary, 50B air-con), Phattalung (35B ordinary, 50B air-con), Phuket (93B ordinary, 125B air-con) and Hat Yai (64B ordinary, 90B air-con).

Minivans to Krabi leave from in front of the municipality office every half hour from 7 am to 3 pm for 100B; the trip takes 2½ hours; you can also catch minivans to Phuket (130B, five hours) and Hat Yai (100B, four hours). To Ko Samui (via Don Sak vehicle ferry) there's one air-con bus per day from the bus station at 11.20 am (110B, four hours).

Share Taxi This seems to be the most popular form of intercity travel out of Nakhon. The huge share-taxi terminal on Th Yommarat has taxis to Yala (130B), Thung Song (30B), Khanom (50B), Sichon (30B), Krabi (100B), Hat Yai (80B), Trang (70B) and Phattalung (60B). A second, smaller stand on Th Thewarat has taxis to Surat (70B), Chumphon (140B) and Ranong (180B).

Train Most southbound trains stop at the junction of Thung Song, about 40km west of Nakhon Si Thammarat, from where you must take a bus or taxi to the coast. However, two trains actually go all the way to Nakhon Si Thammarat (there is a branch line from Khao Chum Thong to Nakhon Si Thammarat): the rapid No 173, which leaves Bangkok's Hualamphong station at 5.35 pm, arriving in Nakhon Si Thammarat at 8.55 am; and the express No 85, which leaves Bangkok at 7.15 pm and arrives in Nakhon Si Thammarat at 9.55 am. Most travellers will not be booking a train directly to Nakhon Si Thammarat, but if you want to, 1st class costs 652B, 2nd class 308B and 3rd class 133B, not including surcharges for rapid/express service or sleeping berths.

Getting Around
Blue songthaews run north-south along Th Ratchadamnoen and Th Si Thammasok for 5B, a bit more at night. Motorbike taxis start at 10B, up to 50B for longer distances. THAI runs vans between its office and the airport for 40B.

AROUND NAKHON SI THAMMARAT
Laem Talumpuk
This is a small scenic cape about 50km north-east of Nakhon Si Thammarat by road

and only about 30km by ferry. Take a bus from Th Neramit going east to Pak Nakhon for 10B, then cross the inlet by ferry to Laem Talumpuk for 20B.

Hat Sa Bua
Twenty-five kilometres north of Nakhon Si Thammarat in the Tha Sala district, off Route 401 (at Km 12) to Surat and about 15B by songthaew, this somewhat muddy beach, lined with casuarinas (a type of sea pine) a few coco palms and a bit of dune vegetation, is a favourite local picnic spot on weekends but virtually deserted during the week. Shabby accommodation is available at *Sala Manum*, a place with individual carports which suggest the sex trade. There are some very reasonably priced *restaurants* here.

Hat Sichon & Hat Hin Ngam
Even the locals have a difficult time separating Hat Sichon from Hat Hin Ngam, two beaches side-by-side along a small curving bay about 65km north of Nakhon Si Thammarat in Sichon district. Hat Sichon ends at a pier in the small fishing hamlet of Sichon, while Hin Ngam to the immediate south is marked by a cluster of boulders at its north end. Hat Sichon has the advantage of a ban on beach vendors, though you can rent sling chairs and beach umbrellas at one end of the beach. Coconut is a major local product, so there are plenty of coco palms to set the tone. Very few foreigners seem to turn up here. Anyone who likes a low-key, local scene will like this beach and the fact that you can easily walk to the town of Sichon for a meal or to peruse the market. The harbour in front of the picturesque town is often filled with large, colourful fishing boats lined along spindly wooden piers – it looks very much the way Hua Hin once did. Near the waterfront are a lot of old one storey wooden shophouses.

South of Hin Ngam and Sichon are the lesser known beaches of **Hat Piti** and **Hat Saophao**. Hat Piti is quite a pretty stretch of white sand with one medium-scale resort. Hat Saophao stretches for 5km and could be the most beautiful beach in the area if it weren't for the disastrous shrimp farms just inland, which use the most environmentally unfriendly techniques for raising the pink crustaceans the world loves to nibble on. There are some nice sand dunes in the area, but it can be hard to reach them because there are so many artificial shrimp breeding lagoons dug into the beach.

Places to Stay & Eat On Sichon, *Prasarnsuk Villa* (☎ 075-536299) is a choice place because it's right at the end of the sandy part of the beach, so you have easy beach access while at the same time you're near the rocky headland (with fair snorkelling) that starts Hat Hin Ngam. Thirty solid-looking bungalows go for 280B to 420B and there's a simple open-air seafood restaurant out the front.

On Hat Hin Ngam *Hin Ngam Bungalow* (☎ 075-536204) has six bungalows of wood and thatch with metal roofs, rather close together, for 120B. A restaurant overlooks the bay. The clientele at these places is almost entirely Thai.

Hat Piti Beach Resort on lengthy, unspoiled Hat Piti almost looks lost here with its American South-Western designs, but it's a very well run place with a good open-air restaurant and large, fully equipped bungalows for 600B out the back, 800B on the beach. A single-building, hotel style unit is going up next on the property and may offer less expensive rooms.

Best of the local restaurants is clean, simple *Hat Sichon Seafood*, which overlooks the beach and is open from 7 am to 10 pm. A couple of other OK spots at or near Hat Sichon are *Phloi Seafood* and *Khrua Pawy*. Don't look for English signs, you won't find any, though the staff at Hat Sichon Seafood can speak a little English and these places are easy to find.

Getting There & Away Get a bus for Sichon from the Nakhon Si Thammarat bus station for 20B or take a share taxi for 50B. From Sichon, you can take a motorcycle taxi to Hat Sichon, Hat Hin Ngam or Hat Piti for around 20B per person.

If you have your own vehicle, it's easy to find Sichon District via Route 401 from Nakhon Si Thammarat (or from Surat Thani, 73km to the north). From Sichon you have to take either Route 4161 (through the town of Sichon) or Route 4105, 4km south of town at Ban Chom Phibun, then start heading for the coast. Just remember that the beaches are all south of Sichon; you may have to stop and ask directions. If you're coming north along Route 401 and turn right onto 4105, you'll end up almost immediately at Hat Saophao. Turn left on the road parallel to the beach and you'll get to the other three beaches mentioned earlier.

Ao Khanom

About 25km from Sichon, 70km from Surat Thani and 80km from Nakhon Si Thammarat is the bay of Ao Khanom. Not far from the vehicle-ferry landing for Ko Samui in Khanom is a string of four white-sand beaches – Hat Nai Praet, Hat Nai Phlao, Hat Na Dan and Hat Pak Nam. In some areas they're starting to develop shrimp farms with great potential for damage to the environment and to local tourism, but so far they haven't multiplied to the point where they appear bothersome. At the northern end of Ao Khanom is a major quarry site, also worrisome.

In Nai Phlao, the best beach (8.4km south of the town of Khanom), the thousands of coconut palms give the impression that a chunk of Ko Samui somehow cut loose and drifted ashore. Two kilometres south of Nai Phlao is scenic **Hin Lat Falls** – another Samui echo. Around a tall headland south of Hat Nai Phlao is the deserted **Hat Thong Yi**. A road was recently built around the headland to the beach but at the time of writing, it was barricaded off for no apparent reason, so the best way to get here may still be by boat.

Most places to stay are concentrated along the southern half of Hat Nai Phlao, the prettiest part, and offer five to 10 solid, plain bungalows with private bath for 500B to 800B a night; the lower end of this range may have fan only, while the upper end offers air-con. Among the better places to stay along Hat Nai Phlao is the friendly *Khanom Hill Resort* (☎ 075-529403), which features red-roofed bungalows on stilts overlooking the sea, with large areas of decking for sitting outside and enjoying the view. Rates start at 500B and top out at 1600B. *Supa Villa* (☎ 075-528522, fax 528553) offers solid-looking brick bungalows with tile roofs, right on the beach for 400B to 600B, or 1200B VIP. The new six storey *Supar Royal Beach* (☎ 075-529237, fax 528553) opposite Supa Villa and with the same owners has air-con rooms ranging from 1430B to 5000B. It's not on the beach, but does have a swimming pool. Next south comes *White Beach Resort* (no English sign; ☎ 075-529419) which is just a couple of cement bungalows and a couple of motel-like structures with the lowest rates on the beach – 300B a night.

Nai Phlao Bay Resort (☎ 075-539039, fax 529425) follows immediately with stone and cement bungalows on spacious grounds towards the south end of the bay for 750B to 1500B. To reach *GB Resort* (☎ 075-529253), you have to take a narrow sand road off the main road just south of Nai Phlao Resort. A-frame bungalows with sloping red roofs and small terraces out front cost 400B to 600B. Casuarina, pandanus and mango trees provide shade on the property, and there are lots of tables on the beach.

High on a rocky cliff at the southern end of the bay, the *Khanab Nam Diamond Cliff Resort* (☎ 075-529147, 529144, fax 529111) handles the top end with octagonal bamboo and thatch bungalows for 500B to 2500B. A free-form pool overlooks the sea, as does the resort's *Khanap Nam* restaurant – a nice place to eat even if you're not staying here.

At Hat Na Dan the *Watanyoo Villa* (☎ 075-528582) has fan-cooled bungalows for 120B to 400B.

Up towards Khanom are four or five more places, none of them recommended over Nai Phlao unless everything else is full. The only standout in this group is *Wanita Resort* (☎ 075-528186), a small collection of new red-tile-roofed bungalows

of brick or cement, some with air-con, for 400B to 500B a night. There are thatched beach umbrellas along the beach, and a restaurant at the end of the narrow property overlooking the beach.

Getting There & Away You can get a share taxi from Nakhon Si Thammarat's share taxi terminal to Khanom for 50B. From Khanom you can hire motorcycle taxis on to the beaches for 30B to 50B. If you're driving, pedalling or riding, get off Route 401 at the junction marked for Route 4014, and follow the latter to Route 4232, which runs parallel to the coast all along Ao Khanom (and as far south as Sichon).

Since one of the terminals for the vehicle ferry to Ko Samui is in Khanom, there are also frequent buses from Surat Thani.

SONGKHLA
• pop 85,000

Songkhla, 950km from Bangkok, is another former Srivijaya satellite on the east coast. Not much is known about the pre-8th-century history of Songkhla, a name derived from the Yawi 'Singora' – a mutilated Sanskrit reference to a lion-shaped mountain (today called Khao Daeng) opposite the harbour. Originally the settlement lay at the foot of Khao Daeng, on the other side of Thaleh Sap Songkhla, where two cemeteries and the ruins of a fort are among the oldest structural remains.

About 3km north of Khao Daeng village, off the road to Nakhon Si Thammarat, is the tomb of Suleiman (1592-1668), a Muslim trader who was largely responsible for Songkhla's commercial eminence during the 17th century. Just south of Suleiman's tomb, a Dutch graveyard testifies to a 17th century Dutch presence as well (look for large granite slabs in an overgrown area next to a Total warehouse). Suleiman's son Mustapha subsequently fell out of grace with Ayuthaya's King Narai, who burned the settlement to the ground in the following century.

Songkhla later moved across the harbour to its present site on a peninsula between the Thaleh Sap Songkhla (an inland sea) and the South China Sea (or Gulf of Thailand, depending on how you look at it). Today's inhabitants are a colourful mixture of Thais, Chinese and ethnic Malays, and the local architecture and cuisine reflect the combination. Older southern Thais still refer to the city as Singora or Singkhon.

The seafood served along the white Hat Samila is excellent, though the beach itself is not that great for swimming, especially if you've just come from the Ko Samui archipelago. Beaches are not Songkhla's main attraction, even if the TAT promotes them as such, though the sand-and-casuarina scenery along Hat Samila can be visually striking and the city is keeping the quiet, low-key beach cleaner than ever before.

Offshore petroleum exploration projects commissioned through Unocal and Total – and the resultant influx of multi-national oil company employees (particularly British and American) – have created a strong western presence in Songkhla. This, along with a strong Thai naval presence, has created a wealthier than average Thai city.

Orientation
The town has a split personality, with the charming older town west of Th Ramwithi towards the waterfront, and the new town to the east of – a modern mix of business and suburbia.

Information
Foreign Consulates A Malaysian consulate (☎ 074-311062, 311104) stands next to Khao Noi temple at Th 4 Sukhum, near Hat Samila. There is also a Chinese consulate (☎ 074-311494) on Th Sadao, not far from the Royal Crown Hotel, and an Indonesian consulate (☎ 074-311544) on the western end of Th Sadao, near the junction with Th Ramwithi.

Money Songkhla is well supplied with banks, and you'll find ATMs at Bangkok Bank (Th Nakhon Nai), Thai Farmers Bank (Th Nakhon Nawk) and Siam Commercial Bank (Th Saiburi), all in the old town area.

Post & Telephone The post office is opposite the department store/market on Th Vichianchom, open Monday to Friday 8.30 am to 3.30 pm; international calls can be made upstairs daily from 8 am to 6 pm.

Thaleh Sap Songkhla
Stretching north-west of the city is the huge brackish lake or 'inland sea' of Thaleh Sap Songkhla. Parts of the Thaleh Sap are heavily fished, the most sought-after catch being the famous black tiger prawn. Illegal gill-net trawling for the prawn is now threatening the overall fish population; legal fishermen have begun organising against gill-net use and the situation has improved slightly in recent years (an improvement supported by the increase of shrimp farming, which of course carries its own environmental baggage).

The city's waterfront on the inland sea buzzes with activity: ice is loaded onto fishing boats on their way out to sea, baskets of fish are unloaded onto the pier from boats just arrived, fish markets are set up and disassembled, longtail boats doing taxi business between the islands and mainland tool about. The fish smell along the piers is pretty powerful.

National Museum
Contained in a 100-year-old building of southern Sino-Portuguese architecture, between Th Rong Meuang and Th Jana (off Th Wichianchom), this is easily the most picturesque national museum in Thailand. Along with the innate architectural charms of its curved rooflines and thick walls (in bad need of a paint job at the moment), it's a quiet, breezy building with a tranquil garden in front. The museum contains exhibits from all national art-style periods, particularly the Srivijaya, including a 7th to 9th century Shivalingam found in Pattani. Also on display are Thai and Chinese ceramics and sumptuous Chinese furniture owned by the local Chinese aristocracy. The museum is open Wednesday to Sunday (closed national holidays), 9 am to 4 pm; admission is 30B.

SONGKHLA

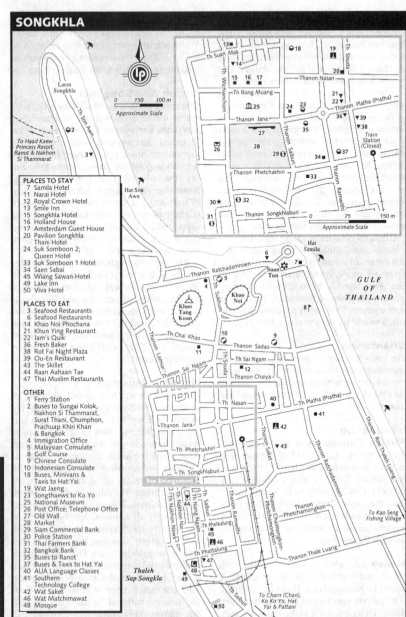

Laem Songkhla

To Haad Kaew
Princess Resort,
Ranot & Nakhon
Si Thammarat

Hat Son Awn

Th Son Awn

0   150   300 m
Approximate Scale

Th Suan Mak

Th Wichianchom

Th Rong Muang

Thanon Jana

Thanon Nasan

Th Sisuda

Thanon Platha (Pratha)

Train
Station
(Closed)

Thanon Saiburi

Thanon Phetchakhiri

Thanon Ramwithi

Thanon Songkhlaburi

0   75   150 m
Approximate Scale

Hat Samila

Suan Tun

GULF
OF
THAILAND

Thanon Ratchadamnoen

Khao Tang Kuan

Khao Noi

Th Sukhon

Th Chai Khao

Thanon Sadao

Th Sai Ngam

Th Sisuda

Thanon Chaiya

Thanon Sai Ngam

Thanon Lamai

Th Nasan

Th Platha (Pratha)

Thanon Jana

Thanon Saket

Th Phetchakhiri

Thanon Ramwithi

Th Songkhlaburi

See Enlargement

Thanon Ratchadamnoen

Thanon Rim Thaleh Luang

To Kao Seng
Fishing Village

Th Nakhon Nai

Th Rang Ngam

Th Saiburi

Th Phetkalung

Thanon Chaimongkon-
Phetchamongkon

Thanon
Phetchamongkon

Thanon Thale Luang

Thaleh
Sap Songkla

Th Phattalung

Th Saiburi

To Charn (Chan),
Ko Ko Yo, Hat
Yai & Pattani

PLACES TO STAY
7 Samila Hotel
11 Narai Hotel
12 Royal Crown Hotel
13 Smile Inn
15 Songkhla Hotel
16 Holland House
17 Amsterdam Guest House
20 Pavilion Songkhla
   Thani Hotel
24 Suk Somboon 2;
   Queen Hotel
33 Suk Somboon 1 Hotel
34 Saen Sabai
45 Wiang Sawan Hotel
49 Lake Inn
50 Viva Hotel

PLACES TO EAT
3 Seafood Restaurants
6 Seafood Restaurants
14 Khao Noi Phochana
21 Khun Ying Restaurant
22 Jam's Quik
36 Fresh Baker
38 Rot Fai Night Plaza
39 Ou-En Restaurant
43 The Skillet
44 Raan Aahaan Tae
47 Thai Muslim Restaurants

OTHER
1 Ferry Station
2 Buses to Sungai Kolok,
   Nakhon Si Thammarat,
   Surat Thani, Chumphon,
   Prachuap Khiri Khan
   & Bangkok
4 Immigration Office
5 Malaysian Consulate
8 Golf Course
9 Chinese Consulate
10 Indonesian Consulate
18 Buses, Minivans &
   Taxis to Hat Yai
19 Wat Jaeng
23 Songthaews to Ko Yo
25 National Museum
26 Post Office; Telephone Office
27 Old Wall
28 Market
29 Siam Commercial Bank
30 Police Station
31 Thai Farmers Bank
32 Bangkok Bank
35 Buses to Ranot
37 Buses & Taxis to Hat Yai
40 AUA Language Classes
41 Southern
   Technology College
42 Wat Saket
46 Wat Matchimawat
48 Mosque

Temples & Chedis

On Th Saiburi towards Hat Yai, **Wat Matchimawat** typifies the Sino-Thai temple architecture of 17th century Songkhla. One wihãan contains an old marble Buddha image and a small museum. Another temple with similar characteristics, **Wat Jaeng** on Th Ramwithi, is currently under renovation.

There is a Sinhalese-style chedi and royal pavilion atop **Khao Tang Kuan**, a hill rising up at the northern end of the peninsula; to reach the top you'll have to climb 305 steps.

Beaches

Besides the strip of white sand along **Hat Samila**, there's the less frequented **Hat Son Awn** on a slender cape jutting out between the Gulf of Thailand and Thaleh Sap, north of Samila. Both beaches are lined with casuarina trees rather than the usual palms. The water is clearest and calmest from April to October. At Samila, beach umbrellas and sling chairs can be used at no charge as long as you order something from one of the many food vendors.

Other Attractions

Songkhla is Southern Thailand's educational centre: a university, a nursing college, a military training camp and several colleges, technical schools and research institutes are all situated in or near town.

Suan Tun, a **topiary park** across from the Samila Hotel, has yew hedges trimmed into animal shapes.

If you are interested in seeing some traditional **Songkhla architecture**, walk along the back streets parallel to the inland sea waterfront – Th Nang Ngam, Th Nakhon Nai and Th Nakhon Nawk all have some older Songkhla architecture showing Chinese, Portuguese and Malay influence. Much of it disappeared during Thailand's economic boom, but a few have been restored and one hopes the city will support some sort of historical architectural legacy.

A few kilometres south of Hat Samila is **Kao Seng**, a quaint Muslim fishing village – this is where the tourist photos of gaily painted fishing vessels are taken. Songthaews run regularly between Songkhla and Kao Seng for 8B per person.

With all the expats living in Songkhla, there would have to be a **Hash House Harriers** chapter. Songkhla's HHH, founded in 1981, meet every Saturday at 3.30 pm at the Pa Lang restaurant opposite the Royal Crown Hotel – the runs begin at about 4.30 at different locations around the city. Information is available in the lobbies of the Pavilion and Royal Crown hotels.

Language Courses

A branch of AUA (☎ 074-311258, 01-969 1227), a block east of the Pavilion Songkhla Thani Hotel on the campus of Woranari Chaloem School on Th Platha, offers small group classes in Thai language.

Places to Stay – Budget

The popular and clean *Amsterdam Guest House (☎ 074-314890, 15/3 Th Rong Meuang)* is a homey place with plenty of cushions and wandering pet dogs and cats. Basic rooms with shared bathroom cost 180B. It is run by a friendly Dutch woman. On the same street, near the corner of Th Wichianchom, *Holland House* has clean rooms with shared facilities for 250B and an apartment for 400B; Dutch breakfasts are available.

One of the best deals in Songkhla is the friendly *Narai Hotel (☎ 074-311078, 14 Th Chai Khao)*, near the foot of Khao Tang Kuan. It's an older wooden hotel with clean, quiet singles/doubles with fan and shared bathroom (though each room has a washbasin) for 120/150B. A huge double room with bath is 200B.

The refurbished *Songkhla Hotel (☎ 074-313505)*, on Th Wichianchom across from the Fishing Station, has well scrubbed 150B rooms with shared bathroom, 180B with private shower and Thai-style toilet. Just up the street from the Songkhla Hotel, *Smile Inn (☎ 074-311258)*, which old Thai hands may remember as the Choke Dee, is a clean place with medium-size rooms with ceiling fan and private cold shower for 200B, or identical rooms with air-con for 300B (350B with TV). The attached restaurant opens at 5 am.

Suk Somboon 1 Hotel (☎ 074-311049, 40 Th Phetchakhiri) is not bad for 160/240B single/double, although they're just wooden rooms off a large central area, and you have to ask for that price – posted rates start at 180B. Rooms in the air-con wing next door are 280B.

Wiang Sawan Hotel (☎ 074-311607) on Th Saiburi, not far from Wat Matchimawat, has small musty rooms from 200B, definitely not a bargain.

Saen Sabai (☎ 074-311090, 1 Th Phetchakhiri) is well located and has clean, if small, rooms in an early Bangkok-style building for 150B with fan and shared bathroom, 220B with private bath, or 270B with air-con. Nearby is *Suk Somboon 2 (☎ 074-311149, 18 Th Saiburi)*, with fan-cooled singles/doubles with private bath for 180/300B, along with a few shared-bath rooms for only 100B. Next door is an all air-con wing with rooms for 350B with TV, bath and fridge.

The *Queen (☎ 074-313072, 20 Th Saiburi)*, next door to Suk Somboon 2, has decent but nothing-special air-con rooms from 300/400B. The similarly priced *Charn (Chan; ☎ 074-322347)* is on the same road but on the outskirts of the central area on the way to Hat Yai. Air-con rooms in this six storey hotel go for 240B.

Places to Stay – Mid-Range

The five storey *Viva Hotel (☎ 074-321033/7, fax 312608, 547/2 Th Nakhon Nawk)* has modern, clean air-con rooms for 596B single, 696B double. The staff speak English and are friendly and helpful. The attached coffee shop has live music nightly.

Catering mostly to visiting oil company employees and their families, the five storey *Royal Crown Hotel (☎ 074-312174, fax 321027, 38 Th Sai Ngam)* costs 625B to 650B for rooms with air-con, TV with in-house video, fridge and carpet; the tariff includes continental breakfast.

Popular with Thais, *Lake Inn (☎ 074-314240)* is a rambling multi-storey place with great views right on the Thaleh Sap. Rooms are 450B with air-con, carpet, hot water, TV and mini-bar, 525B with the same plus a bath, or 600B with a balcony and lake view.

Places to Stay – Top End

The poshest place to stay in Songkhla is the nine storey *Pavilion Songkhla Thani Hotel (☎ 074-441850, fax 323716, 17 Th Platha)*, one block east of Th Ramwithi at the intersection of Th Nasan and Th Sisuda. Large, luxurious rooms with wood panelling, air-con, IDD phones, satellite TV, carpeting and so on cost 1089B single, 1307B double. The lobby is very swanky compared to the Royal Crown's.

Samila Hotel on the beachfront is being rebuilt as a new luxury hotel to open in 2000.

Haad Kaew Princess Resort (☎ 074-331059, fax 331220), on the other side of the Thaleh Sap on the road to Ranot, has its own beachfront and a swimming pool (available to non-guests for 50B a day). The landscaped grounds are a plus. Nice air-con rooms with all the amenities cost from 771B to 899B.

Places to Eat

There are lots of good restaurants in Songkhla but a few tend to overcharge foreign tourists. The best seafood place according to locals is the *Raan Aahaan Tae* at 85 Th Nang Ngam (off Th Songkhlaburi and parallel to Th Saiburi). Look for a brightly lit place just south of the cinema. The *seafood restaurants* on Hat Samila are pretty good too – try the curried crab claws or spicy fried squid. Hours are 11.30 am to 2 pm and 5 to 8 pm. Prices are low to moderate.

Fancier seafood places are found along Th Son Awn near the beach – *Seven Sisters, Mark, Suda, Ying Muk, Smile Beach, Son Awn* – but these also tend to have hordes of young Thai hostesses kept on to satisfy the Thai male penchant for chatting up *áw-áw* (young girls).

Along Th Nang Ngam north of Th Phattalung in the Chinese section are several cheap *Chinese noodle and congee shops*. At the end of Th Nang Ngam along Th Phattalung (near the mosque) are some modest Thai Muslim restaurants, including *Sharif*, *Suda* and *Dawan*; Sharif and Dawan open at 8 am and stay open till 9 pm. *Khao Noi Phochana*, on Th Wichianchom near the Songkhla Hotel, has a very good lunchtime selection of Thai and Chinese rice dishes and is open 8 am to 10 pm.

There are several fast-food spots at the intersection of Th Sisuda and Th Platha, including *Jam's Quik* and *Fresh Baker*, both with burgers, ice cream and western breakfasts; there are also a few popular Thai and Chinese restaurants. The *kíaw náam (wonton soup) place* next to Fresh Baker is cheap and quite good.

Farther south along Th Sisuda near the Chalerm Thong cinema and the old train station is a hawkers' centre and night market called *Rot Fai Night Plaza*. In this section *Ou-en Restaurant* is a very popular Chinese place with outdoor tables; the house speciality is Peking duck. Open 4 pm to 3 am. The very clean *Khun Ying* on Th Sisuda near the Th Platha intersection, has inexpensive curries and khanŏm jiin during the day only.

Of the several expat pubs around town, *The Skillet* on Th Saket has the cleanest kitchen and best food, including sandwiches, pizza, chili, breakfast and steaks.

Entertainment

The *Sugar*, *Lipstick*, *Cheeky* and *The Skillet* on Th Saket next to Wat Saket cater to oil company employees and other expats in town with imported liquors, air-con and cable TV offering a mix of music videos and sports. The *Offshore*, *Anytime* and *Casanova* are similar.

Thais tend to congregate at bars with live music in the vicinity of the Th Sisuda and Th Platha intersection.

Getting There & Away

Air THAI operates several daily flights to/from nearby Hat Yai; see the Hat Yai Getting There & Away section later in this chapter for details. A taxi from Hat Yai airport to Songkhla costs 340B; in the reverse direction you should be able to find a car or songthaew to the airport for 150B to 200B from the stop on Th Saiburi.

Bus, Minivan & Share Taxi Two air-con public buses leave Bangkok's Southern bus terminal daily between 5 and 8 pm, arriving in Songkhla 13 hours later, for 470B. Ordinary buses are 260B from Bangkok, but there are only a couple of departures a day and the trip lasts at least 16 hours. The privately owned tour buses out of Bangkok (there are several available) are quicker but cost around 385B. VIP buses are available for 550B to 680B depending on the number of seats.

Air-con buses from Surat Thani to Songkhla and Hat Yai cost 135B one way. From Songkhla to Hat Yai, big green buses leave every 15 minutes (12B) from Th Saiburi, around the corner from the Songkhla Hotel, or they can be flagged down anywhere along Th Wichianchom or Th Saiburi towards Hat Yai. Directly opposite the ferry station on Laem Songkhla is a small Baw Khaw Saw terminal for buses going to Sungai Kolok, Nakhon Si Thammarat, Surat Thani, Chumphon, Prachuap Khiri Khan and Bangkok.

Air-con minivans to Hat Yai are 20B: these arrive and depart from a parking area in front of Wat Jaeng. Share taxis are 20B to Hat Yai if there are five other passengers, 100B if chartered; after 8 pm the rates go up to 25B and 125B respectively. Share taxis cost 55B to Pattani and 50B to Yala.

See the Hat Yai Getting There & Away section later in this chapter for more options, as Hat Yai is the main transport hub for Songkhla Province.

Train The old train spur to Songkhla no longer has a passenger service. See the Hat Yai Getting There & Away section later in this chapter for trains to/from nearby Hat Yai.

Ferry A government-run car ferry at the head of Laem Songkhla plies the short distance across the channel where the Thaleh Sap meets the Gulf of Thailand. The barge-like ferry holds about 15 cars, plus assorted motorcycles and pedestrians. The fare for the seven minute ride is 12B per car, plus 3B per person; it operates 6 am to 6 pm daily. The ferry stop on the other side is a semi-floating village called Ban Hua Khao. From this point Sathing Phra is 36km north via Route 408, which terminates in Nakhon Si Thammarat.

Getting Around

Small red songthaews circulate around Songkhla and take passengers, for 7B, to any point on their route. Motorcycle taxis anywhere in town cost 10B, double that after 10 pm or so.

KO YO

An island on the inland sea, Ko Yo (pronounced *kaw yaw*) is worth visiting just to see the cotton-weaving cottage industry there. The good-quality, distinctive *phâa kàw yaw* is hand-woven on rustic looms and available on the spot at 'wholesale' prices – meaning you still have to bargain but have a chance of undercutting the usual city price.

Cotton-weaving is a major household activity around this forested, sultry island, and there is a central market off the highway so you don't have to go from place to place comparing prices and fabric quality. At the market, prices for cloth and ready-made clothes are excellent if you bargain, and especially if you speak Thai. If you're more interested in observing the weaving process, take a walk down the road behind the market where virtually every other house has a loom or two – listen for the clacking sound made by the hand-operated wooden looms. As condo and vacation home developments gradually take over the island, the weaving villages may fade away.

There are also a couple of wáts, Khao Bo and Thai Yaw, that are semi-interesting to visit. Along the main road through Ko Yo

are several large seafood restaurants overlooking Thaleh Sap. *Pornthip* (about 500m before the market) is reputedly the best.

Folklore Museum

At the northern end of the island at Ban Ao Sai, about 2km past the Ko Yo cloth market, is a large folklore museum run by the Institute of Southern Thai Studies, a division of Si Nakharinwirot University. Opened in 1991, the complex of Thai-style pavilions overlooking the Thaleh Sap Songkhla contain well curated collections (about 75% with English labels) of folk art as well as a library and souvenir shop. Displays include pottery, beads, shadow puppets, basketry, textiles, musical instruments, boats, religious art, weapons and various household, agricultural and fishing implements. Among these is a superb collection of coconut-grater seats carved into various animal and human shapes.

On the institute grounds are a series of small gardens, including one occasionally used for traditional shadow theatre performances, a medicinal herb garden and a bamboo culture garden.

Admission to the museum is 50B for foreigners, 30B for Thais, open 8.30 am to 5 pm daily.

Getting There & Away

From Hat Yai, direct Ko Yo buses – actually large wooden songthaews – leave from near the clock tower on Th Jana frequently throughout the day. The fare to Ko Yo is 10B; although the bus terminates on farther on, it will stop in front of the cloth market on Ko Yo (ask for *nâa talàat*, 'in front of the market'). To get off at the museum, about 2km past the market, ask for *phíphítaphan*; it takes about 30 minutes to reach the museum from Songkhla. Buses to Ranot pass through Ko Yo for the same fare.

Nakhon Si Thammarat or Ranot-bound buses from Hat Yai also pass through Ko Yo via the new bridge system (part of Route 4146) and will stop at the market or museum. Another way to get there is to take a Hat Yai-Songkhla bus to the junction for Ko Yo (7B), then catch the Songkhla-Ranot bus for 5B to the market or museum.

HAT YAI
• pop 139,400

Hat Yai, 933km from Bangkok, is southern Thailand's commercial centre and one of the kingdom's largest cities, much larger in fact than the namesake capital of Songkhla Province. A steady stream of Malaysian customers keeps Hat Yai's central business district booming, but South-East Asia's current economic doldrums and the Malaysian government's ban on the exchange of Malaysian currency anywhere outside Malaysia, have slowed things down considerably. Still it's very much an international market town, and everything from dried fruit to stereos are sold in the shops along Th Niphat Uthit Nos 1, 2 and 3, near the train station.

Hat Yai is also a major transport hub for travel around Southern Thailand and between Thailand and Malaysia. Many travellers stop over in the city on their way to and from Malaysia.

Culturally, Hat Yai is very much a Chinese town at its centre, with loads of gold shops and Chinese restaurants. A substantial Muslim minority is concentrated in certain sections of the city, eg near the mosque off Th Niphat Songkhrao.

Information

Tourist Office The TAT Office (☎ 074-243747, 238518) is at 1/1 Soi 2, Th Niphat Uthit 3 and is open daily from 8.30 am to 4.30 pm. The Tourist Police (☎ 1699 or 074-246733) can be found opposite the Florida Hotel.

Immigration The immigration office (☎ 074-243019, 233760) is on Th Phetkasem near the railway bridge. The nearest Malaysian consulate is in Songkhla.

Money Hat Yai is loaded with banks. Several after-hours exchange windows can be found along Th Niphat Uthit Nos 2 and 3 near the Th Thamnoonvithi (pronounced *thammanun-withi*) intersection.

Post & Telephone Hat Yai's main post office is on Th Niphat Songkhrao 1 just south of the stadium and is open from 8.30 am to 4.30 pm weekdays, 9 am to noon weekends. The adjacent telephone office is open from 7 am to 11 pm daily. For visitors staying in the centre, there is a more convenient branch post office on Th Rattakan, just north of the train station. A private packing service is available next door to this post office.

Email & Internet Access Taksin Cybernet (☎ 074-367456), at 72/20 Th Niphat Songkhrao 3, has a few terminals for hire by the hour.

Film & Photography The Chia Colour Lab at 58-60 Th Suphasan Rangsan, next to the Singapore Hotel, offers a good selection of films and quality processing. There are many other photo shops in the city's centre.

Bullfighting

Bullfighting, involving two bulls in opposition rather than a person and a bull, takes place as a spectator sport twice monthly in Hat Yai. Fights take place on the first Saturday of each month, or on the second Saturday if the first Saturday is a *wan phrá* or Buddhist worship day (full or new moon). The venue changes from time to time, but lately they've been held at Noen Khum Thong Stadium, west of the city on the way to airport (50B by tuk-tuk). On the first Sunday of each month another round is held in Klonggit district (between Hat Yai and Sadao). Matches take place continuously from 9 am until 4 pm and admission is 500B to 800B all day or 100B to 200B per round – although many hundred times that amount changes hands during the constant betting by Thai spectators.

Because the times and venues for these bullfights tend to change every other year or

HAT YAI

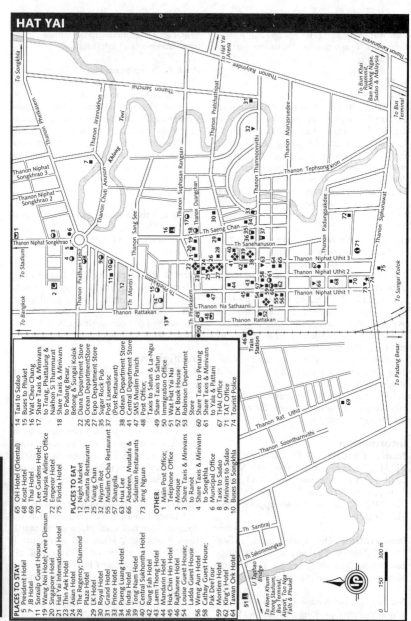

PLACES TO STAY
5 President Hotel
7 JB Hotel
11 Sorasilp Guest House
19 Wang Noi Hotel; Aree Dimsum
20 Singapore Hotel
21 Hat Yai International Hotel
23 Thin Aek Hotel
24 Asian Hotel
28 The Regency; Diamond
   Plaza Hotel
29 LK Hotel
30 Royal Hotel
31 Grand Hotel
33 Prince Hotel
34 Pueng Luang Hotel
36 Indra Hotel
39 Tong Nam Hotel
40 Central Sukhontha Hotel
42 Rung Fah Hotel
43 Laem Thong Hotel
44 Mandarin Hotel
45 Hok Chin Hin Hotel
46 Rajthanee Hotel
54 Louise Guest House;
   Ladda Guest House
56 Weng Aun Hotel
58 Cathay Guest House;
   Pak DeeTour
59 Montien Hotel
62 King's Hotel
64 Tawan Ok Hotel
65 OH Hotel (Oriental)
68 Kosit Hotel
69 Thai Hotel
70 Lee Gardens Hotel;
   Malaysia Airlines Office
72 Emperor Hotel
75 Florida Hotel

PLACES TO EAT
12 Night Market
13 Sumatra Restaurant
25 Viang Chan
32 Niyom Rot
55 Muslim Ocha Restaurant
57 Shangrila
63 Hua Lee
66 Abedeen, Mustafa &
   Sulaiman Restaurants
73 Jeng Nguan

OTHER
1 Main Post Office;
   Telephone Office
2 Mosque
3 Share Taxis & Minivans
   to Ranot
4 Share Taxis & Minivans
   to Songkhla
6 Municipal Office
8 Taxis to Sadao
9 Minivans to Sadao
10 Buses to Songkhla
14 Taxi to Sadao
15 Buses to Phuket
16 Wat Cheu Chang
17 Share Taxis & Minivans
   to Trang, Phattalung &
   Nakhon Si Thammarat
18 Share Taxis & Minivans
   to Padang Besar,
   Betong & Sungai Kolok
22 Diana Department Store
26 Ocean Department Store
27 Expo Department Store
35 Sugar Rock Pub
37 Post Laserdisc
   (Post Restaurant)
38 Odean Department Store
41 Central Department Store
47 SMS Muslim Panich
48 Post Office;
   Taxis to Satun & La-Ngu
49 Share Taxis to Satun
50 Immigration Office
51 Wat Hat Yai Nai
52 DK Book House
53 Robinson Department
   Store
60 Share Taxis to Penang
61 Share Taxis & Minivans
   to Yala & Pattani
67 THAI Office
71 TAT Office
74 Tourist Police

so, check with the TAT office (☎ 074-243747, 238518) for the latest.

Muay Thai

Thai boxing matches are held at Noen Khum Thong Stadium on the way to the airport the first Saturday evening of the month. Admission is 180B for all foreigners and Thai men, 50B for Thai women. Another set of matches takes place the first Sunday of the month at Ban Khlong Ngae, about 50km south-west of Hat Yai off Hwy 4. Check with TAT to confirm the schedule.

Places to Stay – Budget

Hat Yai has dozens of hotels within walking distance of the train station. During Chinese New Year, prices double for most lower-end rooms.

Cheaper places near the station include the 30-year-old *Cathay Guest House* (☎ 074-243815), on the corner of Th Thamnoonvithi and Th Niphat Uthit 2 three blocks from the station, with rooms ranging from 160B to 240B; there is also a 90B dorm. The Cathay has become a travellers' centre in Hat Yai because of its good location, helpful staff and plentiful of information about onward travel, including tips on travel in Malaysia. It has a laundry service and serves inexpensive breakfasts as well as other meals (and the staff don't mind if you bring in takeaways and eat in the lounge). There is a reliable bus ticket agency downstairs with irregular hours.

Cheaper still are some of the older Chinese hotels in the central area. Rooms are very basic but they're usually secure and service is quite OK – you can get towels and soap on request. The *Weng Aun* is an old Chinese hotel across from King's Hotel on Th Niphat Uthit 1, four doors down from the Muslim Ocha restaurant. Very basic singles start at 120B. Another good deal is the *Hok Chin Hin Hotel* (☎ 074-243258) on Th Niphat Uthit 1, a couple of blocks from the train station. Small but very clean rooms with TV, bath and fan cost 150B single, 240B double; there's a

good coffee shop downstairs. *Tong Nam Hotel (118-120 Th Niphat Uthit 3)* is a basic Chinese hotel; rooms on the top floor start at 150B with fan and shared facilities, rooms on the lower floors have private baths for 200B. Hat Yai used to have more hotels like this, but they're closing down one by one.

On Th Niphat Uthit 1 is *Mandarin Hotel*, with small dark rooms for 210B a double with fan and bath, 270B with air-con, 250B triple. The *Grand Hotel* (☎ 074-233669, 257-9 Th Thamnoonvithi) is better, with 24 fairly clean rooms with fan and bath for 180B, air-con for 250B. *Prince Hotel* (☎ 074-243160, fax 232496, 138/2-3 Th Thamnoonvithi) offers small, musty rooms with fan and cold water for 250B, air-con rooms are 350B.

Rung Fah Hotel (☎ 074-244808, 117/5-6 Th Niphat Uthit 3) is a slightly upgraded old Chinese place. Rooms cost 190B with fan and bath or 290B with air-con – a bargain for air-con, although the rooms are nothing great. *Thai Hotel* (☎ 074-253080, 9 Soi 3, Th Rat Uthit), rather out of the way south-west of the train station, features fan rooms from 150B and up to 320B for air-con rooms.

There's a rash of places in town calling themselves 'guesthouses' that are really small budget hotels. *Louise Guest House* (☎ 074-220966, 21-23 Th Thamnoonvithi) is an apartment-style place with clean rooms for 300B with fan, 320B with air-con; all have hot water – not a bad bargain compared with some of the previously described places. At *Ladda Guest House* (☎ 074-220233), next to the Robinson department store complex near the train station, narrow stairs lead to tiny rooms with fan from 200B and air-con from 290B; this is good value for air-con if the lack of fire exits doesn't frighten you away. Near the Songkhla bus stand off Th Phetkasem is *Sorasilp Guest House* (☎ 074-232635), where clean rooms with fan and cold bath are 160/200B single/double, 250/350B for air-con. One extra large room is available for 450B.

Places to Stay – Mid-Range

For some reason hotels in Hat Yai take a disproportionate leap upward in quality once you move up another 100B to 200B a night.

Very popular with Malaysian visitors as well as travellers is the *King's Hotel* (☎ *074-234140, fax 236103, 126 Th Niphat Uthit 1*). Rooms start at 500B with satellite TV, air-con and hot water. Not far from the train station on Th Thamnoonvithi is *Laem Thong Hotel* (☎ *074-352301, fax 237574*). Singles/doubles here for 250B with fan and cold bath, or 350B to 600B with air-con are fairly noisy but comfortable. The hotel restaurant serves imported coffee, faràng breakfast and Thai dishes. *OH Hotel (Oriental; ☎ 074-230142, fax 354824, 135 Th Niphat Uthit 3*) has very good fan-cooled singles/doubles in the old wing for 250B. In the new wing it's 650/750B for singles/doubles with air-con, TV, phone and hot water. Unusually for Thailand all areas of the OH Hotel are non-smoking. Beside the OH, *Tawan Ork Hotel* (☎ *074-243071, 131/1-3 Th Niphat Uthit 3*) offers overpriced, dark and shabby rooms for an 360B with fan, 460B with air-con.

At the friendly, security-conscious *Singapore Hotel* (☎ *074-237478, 62-66 Th Suphasan Rangsan*) good clean singles/doubles with fan and bath are 270/280B, air-con 350B, and air-con rooms with two beds, satellite TV and hot water for 400B. The friendly *Pueng Luang (Pheung Luang) Hotel* (☎ *074-244548, 241-5 Th Saeng Chan*) has huge fan rooms with private bath for 250B plus a few smaller ones for 200B. *Wang Noi Hotel* (☎ *074-231024, 114/1 Th Saeng Chan*) has better rooms for 220B with fan or 390B with air-con; it seems to be a relatively quiet location.

Indra Hotel (☎ *074-245886, fax 232464, 94 Th Thamnoonvithi*) is an older tourist hotel with decent air-con rooms for 480B. On the premises are a Chinese restaurant, coffee shop, snooker centre and traditional Thai massage centre.

Rajthanee (☎ *074-354446*), at the Hat Yai train station, couldn't be more convenient if you have an early morning train to catch or just like to be near the rails; good standard rooms with air-con, hot water, TV and phone cost 500B.

At the high mid-range end, *Montien Hotel* (☎ *074-234386, fax 230043*) on Th Niphat Uthit 1 is a large place that caters most specifically to Chinese visitors; decent air-con doubles cost 750B, including breakfast.

Places to Stay – Top End

The top end in Hat Yai is mainly geared towards Malaysian Chinese weekenders, which keeps rates considerably lower than in Bangkok or Chiang Mai. *Hat Yai International Hotel* (☎ *074-231022, fax 232539, 42-44 Th Niphat Uthit 3*) offers a variety of comfortable rooms with all the amenities costing from 550B to 910B; the hotel features a coffee house and restaurant with Thai, Chinese and European food, a disco and a traditional massage centre. Also at the lower end of the top-enders is *Lee Gardens Hotel* (☎ *074-234422, fax 231888*) on Th Lee Pattana, where 690B buys a room with satellite TV, phone, bath and refrigerator.

The modern *President Hotel* (☎ *074-349500, fax 230609, 420 Th Phetkasam*) is a white cement monolith near the Songkhla share taxi stand with 110 rooms for 600B. It's still under construction, so prices may rise when both wings are completed. Standing alone at the southern edge of the city centre, 10-year-old *Florida Hotel* (☎ *074-234555, fax 234553*) is another tall white hotel with modern but well worn rooms for around 800B, along with the usual Chinese restaurant and massage centre. Also in this category is *LK Hotel* (☎ *074-230120, fax 238112, 150 Th Saeng Chan*), where decent doubles with most of the trimmings cost 850B.

The Royal Hotel (☎ *074-351451, 106 Th Prachathipat*) has rooms starting at 750B and some less than friendly staff. Catering primarily to Chinese visitors, the older *Kosit Hotel* (☎ *074-234366, fax 232365*) on Th Niphat Uthit 2 has air-con rooms for 690B, plus a restaurant, karaoke facilities and massage centre. *Park Hotel* (☎ *074-233351, fax 232259, 81 Th Niphat Uthit 2),* connected to a shopping mall, is similar.

Slightly more upscale are *Asian Hotel (☎ 074-353400, fax 234890, 55 Th Niphat Uthit 3)* and *Diamond Plaza Hotel (☎ 074-230130, fax 239824, 62 Th Niphat Uthit 3),* both of which offer comfortable, modern rooms for 800B to 990B.

Twenty-eight storey *The Regency (☎ 074-353333, fax 234102, 23 Th Prachathipat)* offers 438 rooms and suites stuffed with modern amenities for 1398B double and up. Facilities include a lobby lounge, coffee shop, dim sum restaurant, huge swimming pool with bar and a gym. Also close to the top of the scale is the well managed *JB Hotel (☎ 074-234300/8, fax 243499, 99 Th Chuti Anuson),* with rooms for 1400B to 1800B. The JB contains a popular disco.

The nicest hotel in town is *Central Sukhontha Hotel (☎ 074-352222, fax 352223, 3 Th Sanehanuson),* where spacious, fully outfitted rooms and suites cost 3148B and up; facilities include a swimming pool with snack bar, sauna, Chinese restaurant, 24-hour cafe, lobby lounge, fitness centre, business centre and shopping mall (with a branch of Central department store).

Places to Eat

Hat Yai is Southern Thailand's gourmet Mecca, offering fresh seafood from both the Gulf of Thailand and the Andaman Sea, bird's nest soup, shark fins, Muslim roti and curries, Chinese noodles and dim sum. Lots of good, cheap restaurants can be found along the three Niphat Uthit roads, in the markets off side streets between them, and near the train station. Many Hat Yai restaurants, particularly the Chinese ones, close in the afternoon between 2 and 6 pm – unusual for Thailand.

Chinese Start the day with inexpensive dim sum at *Shangrila* on Th Thamnoonvithi near the Cathay Guest House. Specialities include khanŏm jìip, *salabao* (Chinese buns) and *khâo nâa pèt* (roast duck on rice); open 5 am to 3 pm. In the evenings the Chinese-food action moves to

Hua Lee on the corner of Th Niphat Uthit 3 and Th Thamnoonvithi; it's open till the wee hours. Another excellent dim sum place is *Aree Dimsum (116-118 Th Saeng Chan),* next door to the Wang Noi Hotel. Dim sum here costs about 10B to 15B per dish and the restaurant is open daily from 6 to 11 am and 6.30 to 10 pm.

Jeng Nguan is an old feasting stand-by near the end of Th Niphat Uthit 1. Try the *tâo hûu thâwt kràwp* (fried bean curd), *hŭu chalãam* (shark-fin soup), *bàmìi plaa phàt* (fried noodles with fish), or *kíaw plaa* (fish wonton). It's open from 11 am to 2 pm and 5 to 9 pm.

Several hotels in town also have good splurge-style Chinese restaurants, including JB Hotel's well regarded *Dynasty*.

Malay & Indian The *Muslim-O-Cha (Muslim Ocha),* opposite King's Hotel, is still going strong, with roti kaeng (roti chanai in Malay) in the mornings and curries all day. This is one of the few Muslim cafes in town where women – even non-Muslim – seem welcome. There are a couple of other Muslim restaurants nearby. *Makanan Muslim* at the corner of Th Saeng Chan and Th Prachathipat is a clean open-air place with roti and mátàbà.

On Th Niyomrat between Niphat Uthit 1 and 2 are *Abedeen*, *Sulaiman* and *Mustafa*, all specialising in Muslim food. Sulaiman has the best selection of dishes, including Indian *paratha, dal, chapati, biryani,* and various mutton, chicken, fish and vegie dishes. Abedeen is good for *tôm yam kûng* (spicy shrimp lemon-grass soup), a Thai speciality here rendered in a slightly different way.

Sumatra Restaurant, next to the Pakistan Mosque on Th Rattakan, does Malay dishes like *rojak* (peanut-sauce salad) and *nasi biryani* (spiced rice plate).

Thai Although Chinese and Malay food rules in Hat Yai, there are a few Thai places as well. An old, established Thai restaurant is *Niyom Rot (the roman-script sign says 'Niyomrosh' 219-21 Th Thamnoonvithi).* The *plaa krabàwk thâwt,* whole sea mullet fried with eggs intact, is particularly prized here. Hours are 10.30 am to 2 pm and 5 to 9.30 pm.

Although the name is Lao, the *Viang Chan* (*no roman-script sign; 12 Th Niphat Uthit 2*) serves Thai and north-eastern Thai dishes along with Chinese; it opens at 5 pm. The *food centre* below the Tong Nam Hotel has both Thai and Chinese dishes.

Night Markets The extensive night market along Th Montri 1 specialises in fresh seafood; you can dine on two seafood dishes and one vegetable dish for less than 200B here if you speak Thai. There are smaller night markets along Th Suphasan Rangsan and Th Siphunawanat.

Other Options Adjacent to Robinson department store on Th Thamnoonvithi are *KFC*, *Mister Donut* and *Burger King*.

Or for something very different, cruise down Th Nguu (Snake Street – Soi 2, Th Channiwet), Hat Yai's most popular spot for snake fetishists. After a live snake is slit lengthwise with a scalpel, the blood is drained and drunk with honey, Chinese rice wine or herbal liquor. Besides the blood, the heart, gall bladder and penis are also highly regarded. Skins are sold to manufacturers of wallets, belts and other accessories, while the meat is given away to customers for soup. Rates range from 150B for the evisceration of a small-to-medium cobra to 2300B for a king cobra 3 or 4m in length.

Entertainment

Most of the many clubs and coffee shops in town cater to Malaysian clientele. The bigger hotels have discos: among the most popular are the *Disco Palace* (Emperor Hotel), the *Metro* (JB Hotel), the *Diana Club* (Lee Gardens Hotel) and the *Inter* (Hat Yai International Hotel). Cover charges are only 100B to 150B.

The *Post Laserdisc (Post Restaurant)* on Th Thamnoonvithi, a block east of the Cathay Guest House, is a music video/laserdisc restaurant/bar with an excellent sound system and well placed monitors. It shows mostly western movies,

and programmes change nightly – the fairly up-to-date music videos are fillers between the films. The daily schedule starts at 10 am and goes until 1 am – mostly Thais and faràngs come here. There's a 20B charge to view movies upstairs and drink prices are only a little higher than at the average bar. Meals, including breakfast, are served as well.

Opposite the Post Laserdisc, *Sugar Rock* is one of the more durable Hat Yai pubs, with good food, good prices and a low-key atmosphere. Open from 8 pm to 1 or 2 am.

Shopping

Shopping is Hat Yai's No 1 draw, with most of the market action taking place along Th Niphat Uthit 2 and 3. Here you'll find Thai and Malaysian batik, cheap electronics and inexpensive clothing.

SMS Muslim Panich, 17 Niphat Uthit 1, has an excellent selection of south Indian sarongs, plus Thai, Malay and Indonesian batiks; although the markets are cheaper they can't compare with SMS in terms of quality and selection.

Hat Yai has three major department stores on Th Niphat Uthit 3 (Diana, Ocean and Expo) and two on Th Thamnoonvithi (Odean and Robinson), plus the newer Central department store next to the Central Sukhontha Hotel.

DK Book House, about 50m from the train station on Thamnoonvithi, carries English-language books and maps. On the 4th floor of Central department store is a selection of English books and magazines.

Getting There & Away – Within Thailand

Air THAI operates flights between Hat Yai and Bangkok five times daily. Flights take 1½ hours; the fare is 2280B one way. There are also THAI flights to Hat Yai from Phuket daily for 780B. THAI's office (☎ 074-233433) is at 166/4 Th Niphat Uthit 2.

Bus To Songkhla the green buses leave from outside the small clock tower on Th

Phetkasem. Share taxis leave from around the corner near the President Hotel.

Air-con buses from Bangkok are 428B (VIP 500B) and leave the Southern bus terminal at 7 am and 4, 5.30, 6, 6.15, 6.30, 7, 8 and 8.20 pm. The trip takes 14 hours. Private companies sometimes have fares as low as 300B. Ordinary government buses cost 227B and leave Bangkok at 9.45 and 10.50 pm. Buses to Bangkok leave from the main bus terminal on Th Phetkasem (Hwy 4).

There are lots of buses running between Phuket and Hat Yai; ordinary buses are 135B (eight hours) and air-con 243B (six hours). Three daily buses go to Pak Bara (for Ko Tarutao) for 35B (three hours). In hat Yai they stop at the main bus station on Th Phetkasem (Hwy 4).

Pak DeeTour (☎ 074-234535), a travel agency downstairs from the Cathay Guest House, runs express air-con buses and minivans to Phuket (200B), Krabi (130B), Ko Samui (250B) and Surat Thani (130B). Other buses from Hat Yai include:

destination	fare (B)	hours
Ko Samui	195	7
(air-con only)		
Krabi	150	4
(air-con only)		
Narathiwat	55	3
(air-con)	72	3
Padang Besar	23	1½
Pattani	38	2
(air-con)	55	1½
Phattalung	35	2
Satun	35	2
(air-con)	40	1
Sungai Kolok	123	4
(air-con only)		
Surat Thani	100	6½
(air-con)	160	5½
Trang	50	2
Yala	50	2½
(air-con)	60	2

Travel agencies that arrange private buses include:

Golden Way Travel
  (☎ 074-233917) 132 Th Niphat Uthit 3
Hat Yai Swanthai Tours
  (☎/fax 074-246706) 108 Th Thamnoonvithi
Pak DeeTour
  (☎ 074-234535) ground floor, Cathay Guest House
Pan Siam
  (☎ 074-237440) 99 Th Niphat Uthit 2
Sunny Tour
  (☎ 074-231258) Th Niphat Uthit 2
Universal On-Time Co
  (☎ 074-231609) 147 Th Niphat Uthit 1

Beware of a company called Chaw Weng Tours, about which we have had several reports of bad service and bait-and-switch tactics with buses, particularly between Ko Samui and Hat Yai and between Hat Yai and Malaysia.

Share Taxi Share taxis are a good way of getting from one province to another quickly in the South. There are seven share-taxi stands in Hat Yai, each specialising in certain destinations (see the Share Taxi table).

In general, share-taxi fares cost about the same as an air-con bus, but the taxis are about 30% faster. Share taxis also offer door-to-door drop-offs at the destination. The downside is that the drivers wait around for enough passengers (usually five minimum) for a departure. If you hit it right the taxi may leave immediately; otherwise you may have to wait for half an hour or more. The drivers also drive at hair-raising speeds – not a pleasant experience for highly-strung passengers.

According to the TAT, the city may soon be establishing a single share-taxi stand on Th Siphunawanat. Whether or not it will work (each of the current share-taxi stands takes advantage of the quickest route out of the city towards its respective destination) remains to be seen; they've been promising this for at least four years.

Train Trains from Bangkok to Hat Yai leave Hualamphong station daily at 1.15 pm (rapid No 45), 2.35 pm (special express No 19), 3.15 pm (special express No 11, 1st and 2nd class only), 3.50 pm (rapid No 43) and

10.30 pm (express No 983, 2nd class only), arriving in Hat Yai at 5.48, 6.33, 6.53, 8.25 and 11.14 am. The basic fares are 734B 1st class (express only), 345B 2nd class and 149B 3rd class. Going to Bangkok, you can take the 3.35 pm (rapid No 46), 4.56 pm (rapid No 44), 5.25 pm (express No 984), 6.10 pm (special express No 12) and 6.40 pm (special express No 20), arriving in Bangkok at 6.30, 8.35, 9.30, 10 and 10.35 am.

There are four ordinary 3rd class trains per day between Hat Yai and Sungai Kolok (31B) and one per day to/from Padang Besar (10B).

The advance booking office at Hat Yai station is open from 7 am to 5 pm daily. The station's Rajthanee Restaurant in the Rajthanee Hotel is good and not that expensive; there's a cheaper eating area on the platform. A left-luggage office (the sign reads 'Cloak Room') is open daily from 6 am to noon and 1 to 5 pm.

Getting There & Away – International

Hat Yai is a very important travel junction – almost any Thailand-Malaysia overland trip involves a stop here.

Air Both THAI and Malaysia Airlines fly from Penang; there are also Silk Air flights from Singapore.

THAI (☎ 074-233433 reservations) has an office in the centre of town at 166/4 Th Niphat Uthit 2. Malaysia Airlines (☎ 074-245443) has its office in the Lee Gardens Hotel, with a separate entrance on Th Niphat Uthit 1.

Hat Yai international airport has a post office with an IDD telephone in the arrival area; it's open from 8.30 am to 4.30 pm weekdays, 9 am to noon Saturday, closed Sunday. Other airport facilities include the Sky Lounge Cafe & Restaurant on the ground floor near the domestic check-in, a less expensive coffee shop on the 2nd floor departure level and foreign-exchange kiosks.

Bus From Padang Besar at the Malaysian border, buses are 18B and take an hour and a

half to reach Hat Yai. Bus services operate every 10 minutes between 6 am and 7.20 pm.

Pak DeeTour (formerly Magic Tour; ☎ 074-234535), downstairs from the Cathay Guest House, runs express air-con buses and minivans to Penang (320B, four hours), Kuala Lumpur 300B to 400B, 12 hours), Singapore (450B to 550B, 15 hours), and destinations within Thailand. Golden Way Travel (☎ 074-233917, fax 235083), 132 Th Niphat Uthit 3, runs VIP buses (30 reclining seats) to Singapore for 450B including all meals; super VIP (24 seats) costs 550B.

Warning Care should be taken in selecting travel agencies for bus trips into Malaysia. There are still reports of bus companies demanding 'visa fees' before crossing the border – since visas aren't required for most nationalities, this is a blatant rip-off. The offending company collects your passport on the bus and then asks for the fee – holding your passport hostage. Refuse all requests for visa or border-crossing fees – all services are supposed to be included in the ticket price. Chaw Weng Tours is allegedly one agency to be careful of.

Private Car Several travel agencies in town specialise in arranging a private car and driver for a quick trip to the border and back for those who need to cross the border to renew their visas automatically. The going rate for this service is 500B to 600B.

Share Taxi Share taxis are a popular way of travelling between Hat Yai and Penang in Malaysia. They're faster and less expensive (200B) than the tour buses, although less comfortable and more expensive. Big old Thai-registered Chevys or Mercedes depart from Hat Yai around 9 am every morning. You'll find them at the train station or along Niphat Uthit 1 near the King's Hotel. In Penang you can find them around the cheap travellers' hotels in Georgetown. The cost is about 200B/M$20 – this is probably the fastest way of travelling between the two countries, and you cross the border with a minimum of fuss.

Share Taxi & Minivan Fares From Hat Yai

destination	fare (B)	hours	taxi/minivan stand
Betong	100	3½	Th Suphasan Rangsan, near Wat Cheu Chang
La-Ngu	60	1½	Th Rattakan, near the post office
Nakhon Si Thammarat	80	2½	Th Suphasan Rangsan, near Wat Cheu Chang
Narathiwat	80	3	Th Niphat Uthit 1
Padang Besar	50	1	Th Duangchan, near Wang Noi Hotel
Phattalung	60	1¼	Th Suphasan Rangsan, near Wat Cheu Chang
Ranot	50	2	Soi 2, Th Niphat Songkhrao 1
Sadao	25	1	Th Pratham Uthit, near the President Hotel
Satun	50	1½	Th Rattakan, near the post office
Songkhla	15	½	off Th Phetkasem, near the President Hotel
Sungai Kolok	120	3½	Th Duangchan, near Wang Noi Hotel
Surat Thani	150	5	Th Duangchan
Trang	70	2½	Th Suphasan Rangsan, near Wat Cheu Chang
Yala	60	2	Th Niphat Uthit 2, near Cathay Guest House

From Hat Yai the fare to Padang Besar is 25B for the one hour trip; taxis are on Th Duangchan.

Getting Around

To/From the Airport The THAI van costs 50B per person for transport to or from the city; there's also a private 150B THAI limo service. A regular taxi costs 150B from the airport to the city, about 100B in the reverse direction.

Car Hertz (☎ 074-751007) has an office at Hat Yai international airport, while Avis Rent-A-Car (☎ 074-234300/28) maintains an office at the JB Hotel. You may also be able to arrange car rental through travel agencies in town.

Local Transport The innumerable songthaews around Hat Yai cost 7B per person (10B at night). Watch out when you cross the street or they'll mow you down.

AROUND HAT YAI
Ton Nga Chang Falls

'Elephant Tusk' Falls, 24km south-west of Hat Yai via Hwy 4 in Rattaphum district, is a 1200m, seven-tier cascade that falls in two streams (thus resembling two tusks). If you're staying over in Hat Yai, the falls make a nice break from the hustle and bustle of the city. The waterfall looks its best at the end of the rainy season, October to December.

To get to the falls take a Rattaphum-bound songthaew (about 25B) from anywhere along Th Phetkasem and ask to get off at the *náam tòk* (waterfall).

Ban Khai Ruammit

About 62km south-east of Hat Yai on Hwy 42, this village is famous for the crafting of grass brooms, baskets, fish traps and thatched bamboo wall panels. Woven into clever green and tan checkerboard patterns by alternately exposing the outside and inside of sliced bamboo, the panels come in segments measuring 4 sq m and can be purchased for 180B each. Vendors line both sides of the road near Km 45 selling all of these items. If you had a truck to carry them, you could buy a few of the bamboo wall panels to take to the beach and build your own bungalow.

PATTANI
• pop 41,000

Unlike most provincial capitals in the deep south, which tend to function as trading posts operated by the Chinese for the benefit (or exploitation, depending on your perspective) of

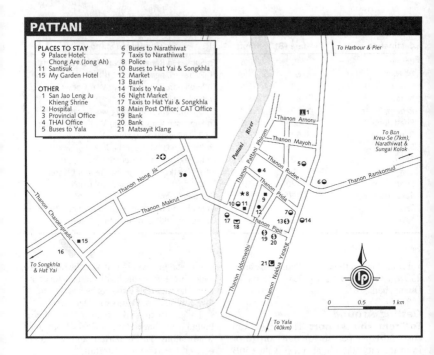

PATTANI

PLACES TO STAY
9 Palace Hotel;
   Chong Are (Jong Ah)
11 Santisuk
15 My Garden Hotel

OTHER
1 San Jao Leng Ju
   Khieng Shrine
2 Hospital
3 Provincial Office
4 THAI Office
5 Buses to Yala

6 Buses to Narathiwat
7 Taxis to Narathiwat
8 Police
10 Buses to Hat Yai & Songkhla
12 Market
13 Bank
14 Taxis to Yala
16 Night Market
17 Taxis to Hat Yai & Songkhla
18 Main Post Office; CAT Office
19 Bank
20 Bank
21 Matsayit Klang

the surrounding Muslim villages, Pattani has more of a Muslim character. In the streets, you are more likely to hear Yawi, the traditional language of Java, Sumatra and the Malay peninsula (the written form uses classic Arabic script plus five more letters), than any Thai dialect. The markets are visually similar to those in Kota Bharu in Malaysia.

Until the start of the 20th century Pattani was the centre of an independent principality that included Yala and Narathiwat. It was also one of the earliest kingdoms in Thailand to host international trade; the Portuguese established a trading post here in 1516, the Japanese in 1605, the Dutch in 1609 and the British in 1612. During WWII, Japanese troops landed in Pattani to launch attacks on Malaya and Singapore.

Although they can be somewhat difficult to reach, Pattani's beaches are among the most pristine in Thailand.

Orientation & Information

The centre of this mostly concrete town is at the intersection of Th Naklua Yarang, the road that runs north-south between Yala and Pattani harbour, and Th Ramkomud, which runs east-west between Songkhla and Narathiwat. Intercity buses and taxis stop at this intersection. Th Ramkomud crosses Th Yarang and then becomes Th Rudee, and it is along Th Rudee that you can see what is left of old Pattani architecture – the Sino-Portuguese style that was once so prevalent in this part of southern Thailand.

Pattani's main post office is on Th Pipit, near the bridge. The attached CAT office provides overseas telephone service daily between 7 am and 10 pm.

Several banks are found along the southeastern end of Th Popot, near the intersection with Th Naklua Yarang.

Mosques & Shrines

Thailand's second-largest mosque is the **Matsayit Klang**, a traditional structure with a green hue, probably still the south's most important mosque. It was built in the early 1960s.

The oldest mosque in Pattani Province is the **Matsayit Kreu-Se**, built in 1578 by an immigrant Chinese named Lim To Khieng who had married a Pattani woman and converted to Islam. Actually, neither To Khieng, nor anyone else, ever completed the structure.

The story goes that To Khieng's sister, Lim Ko Niaw, sailed from China on a sampan to try and persuade her brother to abandon Islam and return to his homeland. To demonstrate the strength of his faith, he began building the Matsayit Kreu-Se. His sister then put a Chinese curse on the mosque, saying it would never be completed. Then, in a final attempt to dissuade To Khieng, she hanged herself from a nearby cashew-nut tree. In his grief, Khieng was unable to complete the mosque, and to this day it remains unfinished – supposedly every time someone tries to work on it, lightning strikes.

The brick, Arab-style building has been left in its original semi-completed form, but the faithful keep up the surrounding grounds. The mosque is in the village of Ban Kreu-Se, about 7km east of Pattani next to Hwy 42 at Km 10; a gaudy Tiger Balm Gardens-style Chinese temple has been built next to it.

The tree that Lim Ko Niaw hanged herself from has been enshrined at the **San Jao Leng Ju Kieng** (or San Jao Lim Ko Niaw), the site of an important Chinese-Muslim festival in late February or early March. During the festival a wooden image of Lim Ko Niaw is carried through the streets; additional rites include fire-walking and seven days of vegetarianism. The shrine is in the northern part of Pattani towards the harbour.

Another festival fervently celebrated in Pattani is Hari Rayo, the Muslim month of fasting during the 10th lunar month.

Beaches

Pattani has some of the prettiest beaches in peninsular Southern Thailand. Because of the local Muslim culture, women visitors should wear T-shirts over their swimsuits when at the beach or swimming. Otherwise be prepared for a crowd of oglers.

The only beach near town is at **Laem Tachi**, a cape that juts out over the northern end of Ao Pattani. You must take a boat taxi to get there, either from the Pattani pier or from Yaring district. This white-sand beach is about 11km long, but is sometimes marred by refuse from Ao Pattani, depending on the time of year and the tides.

About 15km west of Pattani, **Hat Ratchadaphisek** (or Hat Sai Maw) is a relaxing spot, with lots of casuarinas for shade, but the water is a bit on the murky side. Then there's **Hat Talo Kapo**, 14km east of Pattani, near Yaring district, a pretty beach that's also a harbour for *kaw-lae*, the traditional fishing boats of southern Thailand. A string of vendors at Talo Kapo sell fresh seafood; during the week it's practically deserted.

About 50km north-west of Pattani is **Hat Thepha**, near Khlong Pratu village at Km 96 near the junction of Hwy 43 and Route 4085. Hwy 43 has replaced Route 4086 along this stretch and parallels the beach. Vendors with beach umbrellas set up here on weekends. Places to stay at Hat Thepha are oriented towards middle-class Thais and include *Club Pacific (☎ 01-230 4020)* with rooms from 600B to 1500B, *Leela Resort (☎ 01-230 3144)* starting at 400B, *Sakom Bay Resort (☎ 073-238966)*, 200B for fan rooms or up to 600B with air-con and *Sakom Cabana (☎ 01-213 0590)* with air-con cabins for 700B to 1000B. Any Songkhla-bound bus from Pattani can drop you off at Km 96 for around 24B. From here its less than a kilometre to the beach.

Other beaches can be found south-east of Pattani on the way to Narathiwat, especially in the Panare and Saiburi districts, where there are kilometres of virtually deserted beach. **Hat Chala Lai** is a broad white-sand beach 43km south-east of Pattani, near Panare. Eight kilometres farther on towards Narathiwat is **Hat Khae Khae**, a pretty beach studded with boulders. Three kilometres

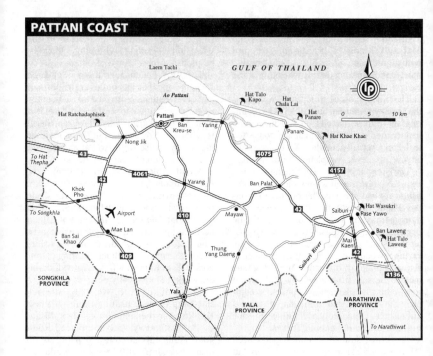

PATTANI COAST

north of Panare is **Hat Panare**, which is another colourful kaw-lae harbour.

If you have your own wheels, follow Route 4136 along the coast south of where the broad Saiburi River empties into the Gulf. Near Saiburi is **Hat Wasukri**, also called Chaihat Ban Patatimaw, a beautiful white-sand beach with shade. It's 53km from Pattani. You'll find miles of deserted beach starting at around Km 22, a few kilometres before you reach the Narathiwat provincial border. The cleanest and prettiest stretch, **Hat Talo Laweng**, is found near a Muslim cemetery just south of the tidy Muslim village of Laweng, where you could probably rent rooms from local villagers. The people here make their living from fishing and coconuts. Route 4136 veers off to Mai Kaen just before Laweng if you're heading north to Pattani. None of these beaches are signposted but you can't miss them if you're on Route 4136.

A good place to watch the building of kaw-lae is in the village of Pase Yawo (Ya-Waw), near the mouth of the Saiburi River. It's a tradition that is slowly dying out as the kaw-lae is replaced by flat-sterned boats painted in the same style.

Places to Stay & Eat
Palace Hotel (☎ 073-349173, 38 Soi Talaat Tetiwat), off Th Prida, is a decent place with fairly clean rooms with cold baths for 160B with fan, 210B with two beds or aircon, plus another 50B if you want TV.

Santisuk (☎ 073-349122, 29 Th Pipit) has OK rooms for 200B with private bath and fan, 400B with air-con.

A favourite with travelling business-people, the four storey *My Garden Hotel* (☎ 073-331055, fax 348200, 8/28 Th Chareonpradit), about a kilometre outside town, is good mid-range value – 350B for a large two-bed room with fan and bath, 550B with air-con, bath, hot shower, phone, cable TV and mini-bar. The disco is very popular on weekends. Samlor or songthaew drivers may know it by its former name, the Dina.

The *Chong Are (Jong Ah)* restaurant, next to the Palace Hotel on Th Prida, serves decent Thai and Chinese food. A *night market* with plenty of food vendors convenes opposite My Garden Hotel each evening.

Shopping
Thai Muslims in southern Thailand have their own traditional batik methods that are similar but not identical to the batik of north-east Malaysia. The best place to shop for local batik is at the Palat Market *(talàat nát paalát)*, which is off Hwy 42 south-east of Pattani on the way to Saiburi in Ban Palat. The market is held all day Wednesday and Sunday only. If you can't make it to this market, the shops of Muslim Phanit and Nadi Brothers on Th Rudee in Pattani sell local and Malaysian batik at perhaps slightly higher prices.

Getting There & Away
Air Pattani has an airport, but since mid-1994 no flights have been available. However, Pattani's THAI office (☎ 073-349149) at 9 Th Prida will check you in and take you to Hat Yai airport (110km away) as part of their service for no additional charge.

Bus & Share Taxi Pattani is only 40km from Yala. Share taxis cost 30B and take about half an hour; buses, which depart from Th Naklua Yarang near Th Ramkomud, cost only 20B but take around an hour. From Narathiwat, a share taxi is 50B, minivan 60B, bus 30B. From Hat Yai ordinary buses cost 38B and air-con 55B. Buses to Narathiwat depart form Th Ramkomud at the intersection with Th Naklua Yarang.

From Bangkok there is only one ordinary bus departure at 6.30 pm; the fare for the 17 hour trip is 285B. A 1st class air-con bus departs at 10 am for 560B.

In the reverse direction these buses depart Pattani at 6.30 pm and 2.30 pm respectively.

Boat Certain boats between Songkhla and Pattani will reputedly take paying passengers – the fare depends on boat size.

Getting Around
Songthaews go anywhere in town for 7B per person.

NARATHIWAT
• pop 40,500
Narathiwat is a pleasant, even-tempered little town, one of Thailand's smallest provincial capitals, with a character all of its own. Many of the wooden buildings are a hundred years old or more. The local businesses seem to be owned by both Muslims and Chinese, and nights are particularly peaceful because of the relative absence of male drinking sessions typical of most provincial towns in Thailand. The town is right on the sea, and some of the prettiest beaches on southern Thailand's east coast are just outside town. A new promenade has been built along the waterfront at the south end of town.

Local radio stations broadcast in a mix of the Yawi, Thai and Malay languages, with musical selections to match – everything ranging from north-eastern *lûuk thûng* to Arabic-melodied *dangdut*. Many signs around town appear in Yawi as well as Thai, Chinese and English.

Information
The main post office is at the southern end of Th Pichitbamrung. An attached international phone office is open daily from 7 am to 10 pm.

Beaches
Just north of town is a small Thai-Muslim fishing village at the mouth of the Bang Nara River, lined with the large painted fishing boats called *reua kaw-lae* which are peculiar to Narathiwat and Pattani. Near the fishing village is **Hat Narathat**, a sandy beach 4 to 5km long, which serves as a kind

of public park for locals, with outdoor seafood restaurants, tables and umbrellas etc. The constant breeze here is excellent for sailboarding, though only the occasional visiting Malaysian seems to take advantage of this. Shade is provided by a mixture of casuarinas and coconut palms.

The beach is only 2km north of the town centre – you can easily walk there or take a samlor. This beach extends all the way north to Pattani, interrupted only by the occasional stream or river mouth; the farther north you go the cleaner and prettier the beach becomes.

JENNY BOWMAN

Golden-tiled Buddha on Khao Kong, Narathiwat

Seven kilometres south of town, **Ao Manao**, is a pretty, curved bay lined with casuarinas. Vendors on the beach offer food and drinks, along with umbrellas and sling chairs. The locals believe Ao Manao to be the province's prettiest bay, but it's not as nice as some stretches of sand farther north or south.

Almost the entire coastal stretch between Narathiwat and Malaysia, 40km south, is sandy beach as well – so remote that the beaches don't even have names yet. Unfortunately there is no direct public transport to any of them. Either you must have your own transport or you'll have to try your luck getting off along the highway on the way to Sungai Kolok, then walk to the coast – which is often no more than a couple of kilometres away.

Matsayit Klang (Central Mosque)

Toward the south end of Th Pichitbamrung stands an old wooden mosque built in the Sumatran style. It was reputedly built by a prince of the former kingdom of Pattani, over a hundred years ago. Today it's of secondary importance relative to the newer Arabian modernist-style provincial mosque at the north end of town but is architecturally more interesting.

Taksin Palace

About 7km south of town, at the end of Ao Manao, is Tanyongmat Hill, where Taksin Palace (Phra Taksin Ratchaniwet) is located. The royal couple stay here for about two months between August and October every year. When they're not in residence, the palace is open to the public daily from 8.30 am to noon and 1 to 4.30 pm. The buildings themselves are not that special, but there are gardens with the Bangsuriya palm, a rare fan-like palm named after the embroidered sunshades used by monks and royalty as a sign of rank. There is also a small zoo and a ceramics workshop on the grounds.

A songthaew from the town to the palace area is 5B.

Wat Khao Kong

The tallest seated-Buddha image in Thailand is at Wat Khao Kong, 6km south-west on the way to the train station in Tanyongmat. Called Phra Phuttha Taksin Mingmongkon, the image is 25m high and made of bronze. The wát itself isn't much to see. A songthaew to Wat Khao Kong is 5B from Narathiwat Hotel.

Narathiwat Fair

Every year during the third week of September, the Narathiwat Fair features kawlae boat racing, a singing dove contest judged by the queen, handicraft displays and *silat* martial arts exhibitions. Other highlights include performances of the local dance forms, *ram sam pen* and *ram ngeng*.

Places to Stay

The cheapest places to stay are all on Th Puphapugdee (Phupha Phakdi) along the Bang Nara River. The best deal is ***Narathiwat Hotel*** (☎ 073-511063), a funky wooden building that's quiet, breezy, clean and comfortable. Rooms on the waterfront cost

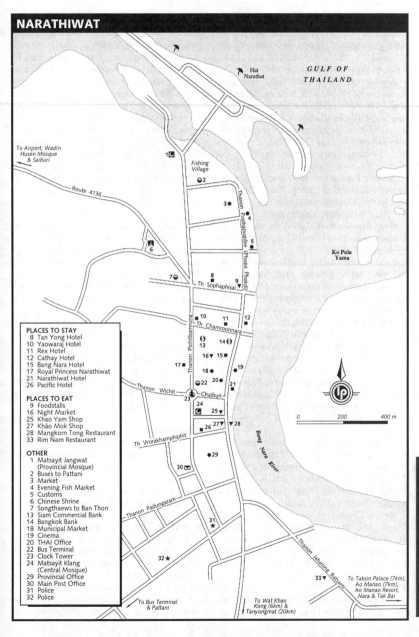

NARATHIWAT

PLACES TO STAY
8 Tan Yong Hotel
10 Yaowaraj Hotel
11 Rex Hotel
12 Cathay Hotel
15 Bang Nara Hotel
17 Royal Princess Narathiwat
21 Narathiwat Hotel
26 Pacific Hotel

PLACES TO EAT
9 Foodstalls
16 Night Market
25 Khao Yam Shop
27 Khâo Mok Shop
28 Mangkorn Tong Restaurant
33 Rim Nam Restaurant

OTHER
1 Matsayit Jangwat
   (Provincial Mosque)
2 Buses to Pattani
3 Market
4 Evening Fish Market
5 Customs
6 Chinese Shrine
7 Songthaews to Ban Thon
13 Siam Commercial Bank
14 Bangkok Bank
18 Municipal Market
19 Cinema
20 THAI Office
22 Bus Terminal
23 Clock Tower
24 Matsayit Klang
   (Central Mosque)
29 Provincial Office
30 Main Post Office
31 Police
32 Police

GULF OF
THAILAND

Hat
Narathat

To Airport, Wadin
Husen Mosque
& Saiburi

Route 4136

Fishing
Village

Thanon Puphapugdee (Phupa Phadi)

Ko Pula
Yama

Th Sophaphisai

Th Chamroonnara

Thanon Pichitbamrung

Thanon Wichit

Chaibun-

Th Worakhamphiphit

Bang Nara River

Thanon Padungaram

Thanon Jaturong Ratsami

To Bus Terminal
& Pattani

To Wat Khao
Kong (6km) &
Tanyongmat (20km)

To Taksin Palace (7km),
Ao Manao (7km),
Ao Manao Resort,
Nara & Tak Bai

0   200   400 m

110B with shared bathroom; the downstairs rooms can sometimes get a bit noisy from the night trade – try to get an upstairs room. Mosquitos could be a problem – don't forget your repellent or mozzie coils.

Another OK place, a bit farther north on the same side of the street, is the quiet *Cathay Hotel* (☎ 073-511014) – signed in Yawi, English, Thai and Chinese – where spacious, clean, if somewhat cheerless, rooms with private bath and fan cost 120B. The elderly Chinese owner speaks good English. There's a view of the river from the roof.

Across the street and next to the Si Ayuthaya Bank is *Bang Nara Hotel*, a barely disguised brothel with large rooms for 100B with shared bathroom.

Rex Hotel (☎ 073-511134, 6/1-3 Th Chamroonnara) is a fair place costing 170B for rooms with fan, 320B for air-con. Similar rooms with fan for 120B to 160B, 280B to 300B with air-con, are available at *Yaowaraj Hotel* on the corner of Th Chamroonnara and Th Pichitbamrung. Because of its busy location, it's not as quiet as the previously mentioned places.

The renovated *Pacific Hotel* (☎ 073-511076), on Th Worakhamphiphit, costs 300B for large, clean rooms with fan and private bath plus air-con for 330B to 410B.

The top end for the moment is *Tan Yong Hotel* (☎ 073-511477), on Th Sophaphisai, with air-con rooms from 500B. Most of the guests are Malaysians and Thai government officials.

A new upscale place is under construction off the west side of Th Pichitbamrung, the *Royal Princess Narathiwat* (☎ 073-511027). When completed it will offer 126 rooms in an eight storey building somewhere in the 1500B to 2000B range.

Seven kilometres south of town at Ao Manao, *Ao Manao Resort* features large but closely spaced cement cottages with fan and private bath for 400B to 600B a night. It's about 400m from the beach.

Places to Eat

The *night market* off Th Chamroonnara behind the Bang Nara Hotel is good. There are also several inexpensive places along Th Chamroonnara, especially the *khâo kaeng place* next to the Yaowaraj Hotel, for curries. A cluster of *food stalls* on Th Sophaphisai at Th Puphapugdee serve inexpensive noodle dishes.

On Th Puphapugdee at the north-west corner of a soi leading to the back of the Central Mosque, an elderly couple operate a *small shop* (in a wooden building with a tile roof) selling delicious and inexpensive khâo yam. Malay-style fried rice noodles are served on the side with each order. Curries and rice are also available at this shop. Other places in town have khâo yam in the morning, but this one's best so go early before they run out. Farther south on the same side of the street is a *Muslim shop* with khâo mók and duck over rice. Along Th Wichit Chaibun west of Th Puphapugdee are several inexpensive Muslim food shops.

Mangkorn Tong Restaurant is a small seafood place on Th Puphapugdee that has a floating dining section out back. The food's quite good and prices are reasonable.

The outdoor *Rim Nam* restaurant, on Th Jaturong Ratsami a couple of kilometres south of town, has good medium-priced seafood and curries. South of Rim Nam is the similar but larger *Bang Nara*; both restaurants are popular with Malaysian tour groups these days.

Shopping

Two batik factories near town, M Famabatik (☎ 073-512452) and Saenghirun Batik (☎ 073-513151) will sell batik direct to visitors at decent prices. They're not easy to find but any taxi or songthaew driver should be able to take you to them.

Getting There & Away

Air THAI has daily flights between Narathiwat and Bangkok, via Phuket. The fare to Phuket is 990B, to Bangkok it's 2575B. The THAI office (☎ 073-511161, 513090/2) is at 322-5 Th Puphapugdee (Phupha Phakdi); A THAI van between here and the airport, 12km north via Route 4136, costs 30B per person.

Bus & Share Taxi Share taxis between Yala and Narathiwat are 45B, buses 35B (with a change in Pattani). Buses cost 28B from Pattani. From Sungai Kolok, buses are 18B, share taxis and minivans 40B. To Hat Yai it's 120B by share taxi or 100B by air-con minivan; the latter leave several times a day from opposite the Rex Hotel.

To/from Tak Bai, the other border crossing, it is 10B by songthaew (catch one in front of the Narathiwat Hotel), 20B by taxi.

Train The train from Yala costs 13B for 3rd class seats to Tanyongmat, 20km west of Narathiwat, then it's either a 15B taxi to Narathiwat or 10B by songthaew.

Getting Around

A THAI van between Nara airport (12km north via Route 4136) and the THAI office costs 30B per person.

Motorcycle taxis around town cost 10B. Wicker-chair samlors from Malaysia are mainly used for carrying goods back and forth to market; these cost from 10B to 25B depending on the distance and load.

AROUND NARATHIWAT
Wadin Husen Mosque

One of the most interesting mosques in Thailand, the Wadin Husen was built in 1769 and mixes Thai, Chinese and Malay architectural styles to good effect. It's in the village of Lubosawo in Bajo (Ba-Jaw) district, about 15km north-west of Narathiwat off Hwy 42, about 8B by songthaew.

Wat Chonthara Sing-He

During the British colonisation of Malaysia (then called Malaya), the Brits tried to claim Narathiwat as part of their Malayan empire. The Thais constructed Wat Chonthara Sing-He (also known as Wat Phitak Phaendin Thai) in Tak Bai district near the border to prove that Narathiwat was indeed part of Siam. As a result the British relinquished their claim.

Today it's most notable because of the genuine southern-Thai architecture, rarely seen in a Buddhist temple – sort of the Thai-

Buddhist equivalent of the Wadin Husen Mosque. A wooden wihãan here resembles a Sumatran-style mosque. An 1873 wihãan on the grounds contains a reclining Buddha decorated with Chinese ceramics from the Song Dynasty. Another wihãan contains murals painted by a famous Songkhla monk during the reign of King Mongkut. The murals are religious in message but also depict traditional southern-Thai life. There is also a larger, typical Thai wihãan.

Wat Chon is 34km south-east of Narathiwat in Tak Bai. It's probably not worth a trip from Narathiwat just to see this 100-year-old temple unless you're a real temple freak, but if you're killing time in Tak Bai or Sungai Kolok this is one of the prime local sights. It's next to the river and the quiet, expansive grounds provide a retreat from the busy border atmosphere.

To get there from Narathiwat, take a bus or songthaew bound for Ban Taba and get off in Tak Bai. The wát is on the river about 500m from the main Tak Bai intersection.

Ko Losin

This recently 'discovered' dive site, a rocky islet around 100km north-east of Narathiwat, boasts more marine species than anyother island in the Gulf of Thailand. Because of the island's distance from the mainland and relative isolation from major shipping lanes, the surrounding waters also feature superior visibility – up to 25m in May.

The reef surrounding the islet varies in depth from just below the water's surface to 40m; most of the coral garden (containing around 60 species of hard and soft corals) can be viewed within a range of 5m to 20m. Although trap fishing has had an adverse effect on the coral at Ko Losin, there are plans afoot to make it a marine sanctuary. Whether or not such protection will be enforced is, of course, another story altogether, but if the Thai navy takes a serious interest in enforcement – as it has in the Similan and Surin islands, for example – then Ko Losin may benefit immensely.

In addition to myriad reef shark and smaller tropical fish varieties, divers may commonly encounter manta rays, hammerhead sharks and whale sharks.

Unless you have your own boat, the only feasible way to visit Ko Losin is by joining a live-aboard dive excursion. It takes around five hours to reach the island from Narathiwat, so at least one night's stay is recommended. Only one dive operator in Thailand arranges live-aboard trips to Ko Losin at the moment: Dive Master (☎ 02-938 4216, fax 938 4218, email divemaster@divemaster .net), 110/63 Soi 18, Th Lat Phrao, Bangkok, or 16 Asoke Court, Soi 21, Th Sukhumvit. Divemaster charges US$375 and only schedules Losin trips from May to October.

SUNGAI KOLOK & BAN TABA

These small towns in the south-east of Narathiwat Province are departure points for the east coast of Malaysia. There is a fair batik *(paa-té)* cottage industry in this district.

Be prepared for linguistic shock if you're coming from Malaysia. Not only are most signs in Thai script, but fewer people speak English in Thailand than in Malaysia.

Sungai Kolok

The Thai government once planned to move the border crossing from Sungai Kolok to Ban Taba in Tak Bai district, on the coast 32km north-east. The Taba crossing is now open and is a shorter and quicker route to Kota Bharu, the first Malaysian town of any size, but it looks like Sungai Kolok will remain open as well for a long time. The Thais even maintain a TAT office next to the immigration post.

As a town it's a bit of a mess; prostitution is the second biggest industry. The rest of the economy is dedicated to Thai-Malaysia shipping; in the north-eastern part of town there's an entire district of warehouses which store goods moving between the countries.

The border is open from 5 am to 5 pm (6 am to 6 pm Malaysian time). On slow days they may close the border as early as 4.30 pm.

Information The TAT office (☎ 073-612126), next to the immigration post, is open daily from 8.30 am to 5 pm. The post and telephone office is on Th Thetpathom, while immigration is near the Merlin Hotel on Th Charoenkhet.

Places to Stay & Eat According to the TAT there are over 45 hotels in Sungai Kolok, most in operation to accommodate the weekend trips of Malaysian males and bearing names like *Marry*, *Come In*, *Honey*, *My Love* and *Hawaii*. Of the cheaper hotels, only a handful are under 200B and they're mainly for those only crossing for a couple of hours. So if you have to spend the night here it's best to pay a little more and get away from the short-time trade.

Most places in Sungai Kolok will take Malaysian ringgit as well as Thai baht for food or accommodation.

The cheapest places are along Th Charoenkhet. The fairly clean *Thailang Hotel* (☎ 073-611132) at No 12 costs 160B. *Pimarn Hotel* (☎ 073- 611464) at No 76-4 is good value at 150B with fan and private bath.

On the corner of Th Thetpathom and Th Waman Amnoey is the pleasant *Valentine Hotel* (☎ 073-611229), with rooms for 180B with fan, 280B to 350B with air-con. There's a coffee shop downstairs.

Other reasonably decent hotels in the 100B to 200B range include *An An Hotel* (☎ 073-611058, 183/1-2 Th Prachawiwat), *Taksin 2* (☎ 073-611088, 4 Th Prachasamran) and the cheaper *San Sabai 1* (☎ 073-612157, 32/34 Th Bussayapan). Some of these offer air-con rooms for 200B to 380B.

Mid-range and top-end hotels in Sungai Kolok include *Genting Hotel* (☎ 073-613231, fax 611259, Asia Hwy 18), from 600B; *Merlin Hotel* (☎ 073-611003, fax 611431, 40 Th Charoenkhet), from 440B; and *Tara Regent Hotel* (☎ 073-611401, fax 611801, Soi Phuthon, Th Charoenkhet), from 400B.

The town has plenty of food stalls selling Thai, Chinese and Malaysian food. There's a good Chinese *vegetarian restaurant* between the Asia and Savoy hotels that's open daily 7 am to 6 pm. A cluster of reliable *Malay food vendors* can be found at the market and in front of the train station.

Getting There & Away Air-con buses to/from Bangkok cost 580B, take 18 hours and depart from Bangkok between 6 and 7 pm (from Sungai Kolok around noon). Standard bus fares are 320B, departing from Bangkok at 9 or 10 pm or from Sungai Kolok at 8 or 9 am – but you would have to be a dyed-in-the-wool masochist to ride this entire 20 hour trip by ordinary bus. To Surat Thani, standard buses cost 155B (taking 10 hours), air-con 285B (nine hours). The bus station is in the south of town, just off Th Pratchawiwat, near An An Hotel.

Share taxis from Yala to Sungai Kolok costs 70B, from Narathiwat 40B; in Sungai Kolok the taxi stand is at the west end of Th Thetpathom. There are also buses from Narathiwat for 25B (35B air-con). From Sungai Kolok taxis to Narathiwat leave from in front of An An Hotel.

Air-con buses to Hat Yai cost 120B and leave from the Valentine Hotel twice in morning, twice in the afternoon. From Hat Yai, departure times are similar. The trip takes about four hours. Share taxis to Hat Yai cost 130B and leave from next to the Thailiang Hotel.

The rapid No 171 leaves Bangkok at 12.20 pm and arrives at 10 am the next day, while the daily special express No 37 to Sungai Kolok departs Bangkok at 2.35 pm and arrives at 10.40 am. These trains have 1st (893B), 2nd (417B) and 3rd (180B) class fares, not including the special-express or rapid surcharges of 80B or 40B (and 1st or 2nd class sleeping berths if you so choose).

You can also get trains to Sungai Kolok from Yala and Tanyongmat (for Narathiwat), but buses are really faster and more convenient along these routes.

From Sungai Kolok to points farther north (via Yala), however, the train is a reasonable alternative. A train to Hat Yai takes about 4½ hours and costs 31B for a 3rd class seat, 75B for 2nd class. Local train Nos 124 and 132 leave Sungai Kolok at 6.30 and 8.50 am, arriving in Hat Yai at 11.17 am and 1.34 pm. You won't find these trains listed on your English train timetable.

Special express No 20 leaves Sungai Kolok at 3 pm and arrives in Bangkok at 10.35 am the next day, with stops in Hat Yai (6.40 pm), Surat Thani (11.26 pm) and Hua Hin (6.07 am) among other towns along the way.

Getting Around The border is about a kilometre from the centre of Sungai Kolok or the train station. Transport around town is by motorcycle taxi – it's 15B for a ride to the border. Coming from Malaysia, just follow the old train tracks to your right, or, for the town, turn left at the first junction and head for the high-rises.

From Rantau Panjang (Malaysian side), a share taxi to Kota Bharu costs M$5 per person (M$20 to charter the whole car) and takes about an hour. The regular yellow-and-orange bus to Kota Bharu costs M$3.50.

Ban Taba

Ban Taba, 5km south of bustling Tak Bai, is a blip of a town with a large market and a few hotels. Takbai Border House, a large customs complex built in the hope of diverting traffic from Sungai Kolok, is under-used and neglected. From the Customs and market area you can see Malaysia across the Kolok River.

A few hundred metres north of the complex, **Hat Taba** is a beach park of sorts planted with casuarinas and bearing a few open-air shelters. You can change money at street vendors by the ferry on the Thai side.

A ferry across the river into Malaysia is 8B. The border crossing here is open the same hours as in Sungai Kolok. From the Malaysian side you can get buses direct to Kota for M$2.50.

Places to Stay *Masaya Resort* (☎ 073-581125) has good rooms for 200B to 300B with fan and private bath, 350B with air-con or 400B with air-con and TV. It's set back off the road leading to the Malaysian border and a bit difficult to find; take a motorcycle taxi there for 10B. The *Pornphet* (☎ 073-581331), a motel-like place near the beach north of Taba, isn't bad for 280B to 400B, all air-con.

Northern Andaman Coast (Ranong to Phuket)

Stretching from the Isthmus of Kra south to Ko Phuket and Ao Phang-Nga, Thailand's Northern Andaman Coast probably offers more geographic variety than any other coastal reach in the country. Pristine, little-visited mangrove forests in Ranong Province, the remote oceanic island groups of Surin and Similan, the quiet beaches around Khao Lak and the international jet-set destination of Phuket are all encompassed within this relatively compact area.

RANONG
• pop 18,500

The small capital and port of Ranong is only separated from Myanmar by Pak Chan, the estuary of the Chan River. Burmese residents from nearby Kawthoung (Victoria Point) hop across to trade in Thailand or to work on fishing boats. Many Burmese now reside in Ranong as well, and you'll see lots of men wearing the Burmese *longyi*, a long plaid cotton sarong. Although there are no great cultural attractions in town, the buildings are architecturally interesting since this area was originally settled by Hokkien Chinese. Ranong also has a lively, friendly appeal that makes it easy to while away a day or two just strolling about, poking around the market and visiting a Hokkien coffee shop or two.

Beaches with tourist facilities include nearby Hat Chandamri and the coastal islands of Ko Chang and Ko Phayam; see the Around Ranong and Laem Son National Park sections for details.

Tourists, mostly of Asian origin, are beginning to use Ranong as a gateway to Kawthoung and Thahtay Island. Several Phuket-based dive tour operators arrange live-aboard dive excursions to various islands and reefs off the southern tip of Myanmar, using Ranong as a launching point.

HIGHLIGHTS

• The Similan and Surin Islands National Marine Parks have Thailand's best coral colonies and are world-famous for their magnificent diving and snorkelling.

• The sea cliffs, beaches, estuaries and forested valleys of Khao Lak/Lam Ru National Park contain an exotic array of wildlife, including the Asiatic black bear, drongo and tapir.

• Phuket, one of Thailand's most popular beach destinations, also has world-class diving and yachting, a tantalising unique cuisine, lively markets and cosmopolitan nightlife.

• Friendly Ranong town boasts hot springs at Wat Tapotaram, where you can bathe in rustic rooms Thai style.

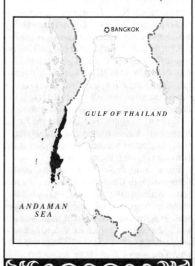

Information

Ranong is about 600km south of Bangkok and 300km north of Phuket. Most of Ranong's banks are on Thanon (Th) Tha Meuang (the road to the fishing pier), near the intersection with Th Ruangrat. The main post office is on Th Dap Khadi, while the CAT telephone office is off Th Phoem Phon in the south of town. There is also a TOT office in Th Ruangrat at the north end of town.

Chaon Thong Food & Drinks, 8-10 Th Ruangrat, dispenses good travel info. The proprietor, Khun Nuansri, is quite knowledgeable and speaks good English.

Immigration The main Thai immigration office can be found on the road to Saphaan Plaa, about halfway between town and the main piers, across from a branch of Thai Farmer's Bank. There is also a smaller immigration post in the vicinity of the Saphaan Plaa pier. If you're just going in and out of Kawthoung, Myanmar, for the day, a visit to the small post will suffice. However if you're entering Thailand from Myanmar via Kawthoung, you'll have to visit the larger office to get your passport stamped with a visa on arrival.

Bookshops Chaun Aksarn, a few doors south of Asia Hotel on Th Ruangrat, carries a fair selection of English-language titles, including travel guides and maps.

Nai Khai Ranong

During the reign of King Rama V, a Hokkien named Koh Su Chiang became governor of Ranong (thus gaining the new name Phraya Damrong Na Ranong) and his former residence, Nai Khai Ranong, has become a combination clan house and shrine. It's on the northern edge of town and is worth a visit.

Of the three original buildings, one still stands and is filled with mementoes of the Koh family glory days. The main gate and part of the original wall also remain. Koh Su Chiang's great-grandson Koh Sim Kong is the caretaker and he speaks some English. Several shophouses on Th Ruangrat preserve the old Hokkien style, too. Koh Su

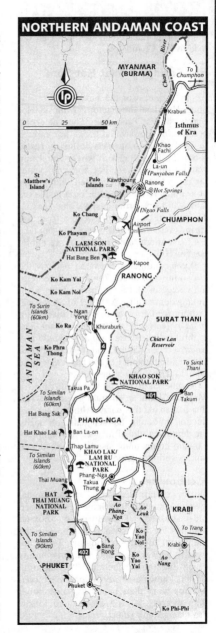

NORTHERN ANDAMAN COAST

Chiang's mausoleum is set into the side of a hill a few hundred metres north on the road to Hat Chandamri.

Hot Springs & Wat Hat Som Paen

About 1km east of the Jansom Thara Ranong Hotel is the Ranong Mineral Hot Springs at Wat Tapotaram. The water temperature hovers around 65°C, hot enough to boil eggs. You can bathe in rustic rooms (10B per person) where you scoop water from separate hot and cool water tanks and sluice the mixed water over your body Thai style. Don't get inside the tanks and spoil the water. The Jansom Thara Hotel also pipes water from the springs into the hotel, where you can take a 42°C mineral bath in their large public spa for 100B.

If you continue on the same road past the hot springs for about 7km, you'll come to the village of Hat Som Paen, a former tin-mining community. At Wat Hat Som Paen, visitors feed fruit to the huge black carp (plaa phluang) in the temple stream. The faithful believe these carp are actually the-wada, a type of angel, and it's forbidden to catch and eat them. Legend has it that those who do will contract leprosy.

Another 3km down a bumpy dirt road is **Morakot Thara**, an emerald-green reservoir that fills an old tin quarry. Although tin production in Ranong has slackened off due to the depressed global market, the mining of calcium compounds, used to make porcelain, is still profitable.

Kickboxing

During certain festivals, eg the annual Vegetarian Festival in September/October, old-fashioned Thai-Burmese boxing matches are held in a field opposite the municipal offices in Ranong. There are usually between six and 12 bouts on any given evening's schedule. This fighting style is known as *muay khàat che ak*; contestants wrap their hands in hemp rather than wearing boxing gloves and follow pre-Queensbury rules.

Places to Stay

Asia Hotel (☎ 077-811113, 39/9 Th Ruangrat), near the market, has spacious clean rooms with fan and private bath for 240B to 300B and air-con rooms for 620B. Information on local islands is posted in the lobby.

Across from the market is the not very friendly *Sin Ranong Hotel* (☎ 077-811454, 24/24 Th Ruangrat) with adequate singles/doubles with fan for 180/200B, air-con for 320/400B. North a bit, *Sin Tavee (Thawi) Hotel* (☎ 077-811213, 81/1 Th Ruangrat) offers somewhat inferior rooms for 160B to 200B single, 300B double, plus air-con singles/doubles for 280/500B. The *Boat Restaurant* (☎ 077-823996), next to Suriyanan Hotel, also rents out a few rooms for 300B to 350B with fan and private bath, 400B with air-con.

Farther up Th Ruangrat are the multi-storey *Rattanasin Hotel* (no sign; look for a green building) on the right and *Suriyanan Hotel*. Despite a 'renovation' the Rattanasin is a typical Thai-Chinese place that looks worse for wear. Singles/doubles with fan and private bath cost 100/170B. The Suriyanan is dark and decaying, but the staff are friendly and claim they don't allow any prostitutes in the hotel. A basic room is 100B with a fan, and 120B with fan and private bath.

Ranong Inn Hotel (☎ 077-822777, fax 821527, 29/9 Th Phetkasem), a few kilometres south of the town centre on the highway to Kapoe, has ill kept rooms for 240B with fan and private bath, 430B with air-con and TV. In the same direction, the *Eiffel Inn* (☎ 077-823271) – you can't miss it, there's a 15m-high Eiffel Tower model in the parking lot – offers fancy bungalows with TV, fridge, phone and hot showers for 1500B (discounted rates of 600B are readily dispensed).

Back towards town, just south of the river and road to the hot springs, is *Jansom Thara Ranong Hotel* (☎ 077-823350, Bangkok ☎ 02-946 3639, 2/10 Th Phetkasem), which offers just about everything you could possibly want in a hotel. Standard rooms come with air-con and colour TV and there's in-house video, hot bath with spa (piped in from

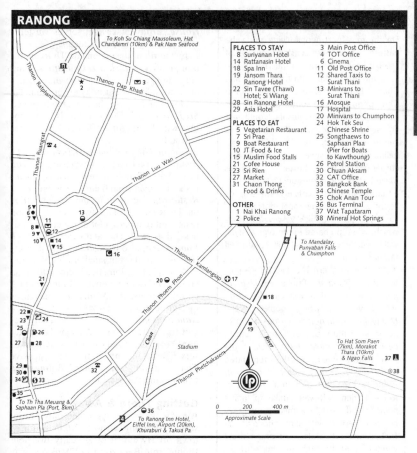

RANONG

To Koh Su Chiang Mausoleum, Hat
Chandamri (10km) & Pak Nam Seafood

Thanon Ratphant

Thanon Dap Khadi

Thanon Ruangrat

Thanon Luu Wan

Thanon Kamlangsap

Thanon Phoem Phon

Chan

Thanon Phetchakasem

River

Stadium

PLACES TO STAY
8 Suriyanan Hotel
14 Rattanasin Hotel
18 Spa Inn
19 Jansom Thara
   Ranong Hotel
22 Sin Tavee (Thawi)
   Hotel; Si Wiang
28 Sin Ranong Hotel
29 Asia Hotel

PLACES TO EAT
5 Vegetarian Restaurant
7 Sri Prae
9 Boat Restaurant
10 JT Food & Ice
15 Muslim Food Stalls
21 Coffee House
23 Sri Rien
27 Market
31 Chaon Thong
   Food & Drinks

OTHER
1 Nai Khai Ranong
2 Police

3 Main Post Office
4 TOT Office
6 Cinema
11 Old Post Office
12 Shared Taxis to
   Surat Thani
13 Minivans to
   Surat Thani
16 Mosque
17 Hospital
20 Minivans to Chumphon
24 Hok Tek Seu
   Chinese Shrine
25 Songthaews to
   Saphaan Plaa
   (Pier for Boats
   to Kawthoung)
26 Petrol Station
30 Chuan Aksam
32 CAT Office
33 Bangkok Bank
34 Chinese Temple
35 Chok Anan Tour
36 Bus Terminal
37 Wat Tapataram
38 Mineral Hot Springs

To Mandalay,
Punyaban Falls
& Chumphon

To Hat Som Paen
(7km), Morakot
Thara (10km)
& Ngao Falls

To Th Tha Meuang &
Saphaan Pla (Port, 8km)

To Ranong Inn Hotel,
Eiffel Inn, Airport (20km),
Khuraburi & Takua Pa

0   200   400 m
Approximate Scale

the hot springs), and a refrigerator stocked with booze. There are also two restaurants, one of which specialises in Chinese dim sum and noodles, two large mineral spas, a fitness centre, a disco, a coffee house/cocktail lounge, a swimming pool and a travel agency. Rates start at 968B, but sometimes they offer discounted rooms for as low as 770B.

On the opposite side of the river from Jansom Thara Hotel, on Hwy 4, *Spa Inn* (☎ 077-811715) charges 200B per fan room, 380B to 420B per air-con room.

Places to Eat

For inexpensive Thai and Burmese breakfasts, try the *market* on Th Ruangrat. Also along Th Ruangrat are several traditional *Hokkien coffee shops* with marble-topped tables and enamelled metal teapots. A good example of the genre is the *Si Wiang,* next to the Sin Tavee Hotel. Between the Rattanasin and Sin Tavee hotels (same side of Th Ruangrat as the Rattanasin) are three modest *Muslim food stalls* where you can get Malaysian-style curry, rice and *roti.*

Regional Food Differences

For the most part people living along the eastern and northern coasts of the Gulf of Thailand eat standard, central Thai cuisine as found in Bangkok and the surrounding Chao Phraya River Valley. From Chumphon Province south, on both sides of the Thai-Malay peninsula, you'll find yourself in the domain of southern Thai cuisine – *aahǎan pàk tâi*. One of the major hallmarks of this style of cooking is that curries are generally hotter – sometimes much hotter, sometimes only a little hotter – than their counterparts elsewhere in the country. One of the most notorious is *kaeng tai plaa*, a thick yellow fish curry which, when prepared in the typical style, will leave all but the most chilli-habituated *faràngs* weeping.

Another southern Thai speciality – particularly in Trang and Phuket – is *khǎnom jiin náam yaa*, a thin, yellowish fish curry served over white wheat noodles. Several Malay and Indian-style curries are also available in the south, and these tend to be milder than most Thai curries. In the four southernmost, Muslim-dominated provinces you may come across *roti kaeng*, a breakfast dish that consists of *roti* – a fried flatbread similar to India's *paratha* – dipped in a mild curry gravy *(kaeng)*. Served with jam, chocolate or fruit fillings, roti is also a common street vendor food throughout the south – Nakhon Si Thammarat is known to have the best sweet roti.

For breakfast the most typical southern Thai dish is *khâo yam*, a delicious concoction of room-temperature rice, chopped lemongrass and lime leaves, bean sprouts, dried shrimp, toasted coconut and powdered red chilli served with a salty-sour-sweet tamarind sauce – sort of a southern-style rice salad.

Joe Cummings

Around here also is the friendly *Coffee House*, a tiny place that serves western-style breakfasts and light meals.

Just north of the cinema on Th Ruangrat is a small *vegetarian restaurant* serving very inexpensive Thai vegie dishes; it's open Monday to Saturday from around 7 am to 6 pm. Nearby, the moderately priced *Sri Prae (313/2 Th Ruangrat)* is very popular with locals for stuffed crab and other seafood.

Chaon Thong Food & Drinks (8-10 Th Ruangrat) is a clean, inexpensive air-con place with Thai food and western breakfasts. It's open from 6 am to 9.30 pm. *Boat Restaurant*, across from the old post office on Th Ruangrat, is a two storey air-con restaurant that does a lot of ice cream business, along with Thai and western food. *JT Food & Ice*, also opposite the old post office, is a similar but smaller air-con place.

A couple of kilometres north of town on Highway (Hwy) 4, between Caltex and PT petrol stations, the *Mandalay* specialises in Burmese and Thai-style seafood. *Pak Nam Seafood*, out past Jansom Thara Resort (the sister hotel to Jansom Thara Ranong) on the road to Hat Chandamri, serves delicious and relatively inexpensive Thai seafood in a terraced dining area overlooking the seaside.

Getting There & Away

Air Bangkok Airways is the only carrier serving Ranong airport, 20km south of town off Hwy 4. It offers daily two-hour flights from Bangkok for 2280B one way (half that for children). Bangkok Airways' Ranong office (☎ 077-835096) is at 50/18 Muu 1, Th Phetkasem, about 5km south of town on Hwy 4, near Km 616. You can also purchase Bangkok Airways tickets at a desk inside Chaon Thong Food & Drinks in town.

Bus You can get to Ranong via Chumphon (40B, 60B air-con), Surat Thani (70B, 91B air-con), Takua Pa (54B, 80B air-con) and Phuket (91B, 130B air-con). The bus terminal in Ranong is out of town on Hwy 4 near the Jansom Thara Hotel, but buses stop in town all along Th Ruangrat, picking up passengers that flag them down along the way, before proceeding on to the terminal. Songthaew No 2 passes the bus terminal.

To and from Bangkok, ordinary buses cost 160B, 2nd class air-con 230B, 1st class air-con 302B, VIP 470B. Air-con buses don't depart that frequently, usually twice in the morning and three or four times in the afternoon/evening. From Ranong, Chok Anan Tour (☎ 077-811337) on Th Phoem Phon, operates air-con buses to Bangkok at 8 am and 8 pm daily for 302B.

Air-con minivans run between Surat Thani and Ranong for 120B. They depart from Ranong's Th Luu Wan (near the Rattanasin Hotel) around 8 am, arriving in Surat Thani around noon. From Surat Thani the van leaves at around 1 pm and returns to Ranong at 4 pm. You can also catch share taxis to Surat for the same fare at the northeast corner of the intersection of Th Luu Wan and Th Ruangrat.

Daily air-con minibuses to Chumphon cost 80B and depart hourly between 7 am and 5.30 pm from Th Phoem Phon near the provincial hospital. Vans to Chumphon have the letters 'CTR' printed on the back end.

Buses to Khuraburi cost 37B and take one hour and 20 minutes. Other routes include Khao Lak (35B ordinary, 60B aircon) and Phang-Nga (70B ordinary, 120B air-con).

Getting Around

Songthaews ply the roads around Ranong and out to the hot springs and Hat Som Paen (No 2), Hat Chandamri (No 3) and Saphaan Plaa (No 2). The fare is 6B to any of these places. See the Around Ranong section for details. Motorcycle taxis (look for the drivers wearing orange vests) will take you anywhere in town for 15B, or to the area around the Jansom Thara for 20B.

Mayline, a minimart next to the Jansom Thara, rents Honda Dreams for 200B per day. Ranong Travel, inside Chaon Thong Food & Drinks, can assist with motorcycle and car rentals.

AROUND RANONG
Hat Chandamri

Touted as the nearest beach to Ranong, Hat Chandamri is really more of a mud flat. A sister hotel to the Jansom Thara in Ranong, the *Jansom Thara Resort (☎ 077-821611, fax 821821)* has similarly equipped bungalows (but no spas) for 1400B (discounts to 935B frequently available). From the dining terrace overlooking the bay you can eat seafood and watch the sun set over Kawthoung.

Hat Chandamri is 10km north-west of Ranong, about 50B by motorcycle taxi or 10B by songthaew.

Saphaan Plaa (Fishing Pier)

The provincial fishing port, Tha Thiap Reua Pramong, is 8km south-west of Ranong. It's called **Saphaan Plaa** (Fishing Pier) for short and is always bustling with activity as fishing boats are loaded and unloaded with great cargoes of flapping fish. The fish traders buy from anyone who lands fish here, and about half the boats are Burmese. Boats can be chartered here for day trips to nearby islands. Unless you want to see heaps of fish or charter a fishing boat (or visit Kawthoung, see the appropriate section), there's really no reason to go out to the port. Songthaew No 2 – some of which are labelled 'Sa Phan Pla' – ply between central Ranong and the port frequently during daylight hours for 6B per person.

Kawthoung (Victoria Point)

This lively, dusty port at the southern-most tip of mainland Myanmar (Burma) is only separated from Thailand by a broad estuary of the Chan River. To the British it was Victoria Point and to the Thais it's Ko Sawng, which means Second Island. The Burmese name, Kawthoung, is probably a variation on the latter.

The main business here is trade with Thailand, followed by fishing. Among the Burmese, Kawthoung is perhaps best known for producing some of the country's best kickboxers. Most residents are bilingual, speaking Thai and Burmese. Many people born and raised around Kawthoung, especially Muslims, also speak Pashu, a dialect that mixes Thai, Malay and Burmese. Nearby islands are inhabited by bands of nomadic Moken or sea gypsies.

At the moment Kawthoung is only accessible to foreigners by boat from Ranong, Thailand. It's probably not worth making a special trip to Ranong just to visit Kawthoung, but if you're in the area and decide to cross over, you'll find it's similar to Southern Thailand except that many more men wear the *longyi* (the Burmese sarong). It is now legal to travel from Kawthoung into the interior of Myanmar – eg Dawei (Tavoy), Myeik (Mergui) or Yangon – by plane or ship. Road travel north of Kawthoung, however, is forbidden by the Myanmar government due to security concerns – this is an area plagued by Mon insurgency.

Boats to Kawthoung leave the Saphaan Plaa pier in Ranong regularly from around 7 am till 6 pm for 40B per person. Take the No 2 songthaew from Ranong and when the vehicle stops to pay a toll at the entrance to the pier area, get off and walk down a soi to the right (you'll see a petrol station on your left). At the end of the soi are boats to Kawthoung. If you want you can charter a boat holding six to seven people for 400B roundtrip.

Once the boat is underway, there's an initial stop at Thai immigration, where your passport is stamped. Then upon arrival at the Kawthoung jetty, again before leaving the boat, there's a stop at Myanmar immigration. At this point you must inform immigration authorities whether you're a day visitor – in which case you must pay a fee of US$5 or 500B for a day permit. If you have a valid Myanmar visa in your passport, you'll be permitted to stay up to 28 days, but are required to buy US$300 worth of foreign exchange certificates (FECs).

Yangon Airways flies an ATR-72 several times a week Kawthoung to Yangon for US$120. By ship it's two nights (via Dawei and Myeik) – 36 hours total – to Yangon.

Organised Tours Jansom Thara Hotel in Ranong offers Kawthoung and island tours aboard four boats with capacities ranging from 15 to 200 people. A 'half-day tour' costing 750B per person sails from Ranong, visits a couple of pagodas in Kawthoung and returns to Ranong around 11 am. The 'full day tour' costing 1000B goes to Pulau Besin for beach swimming and lunch and returns at 2 pm. Rates include immigration procedures on both sides, guide and boat; lunch costs extra.

Places to Stay So far there are two places in Kawthoung itself that are approved to accept foreigners. Closest to the pier is the modern and friendly *Honey Bear Hotel (☎ 01-229 6190)*, which offers 24 hour power and clean air-con rooms with satellite TV and cold shower for 700B: not a great deal by Thai standards but it's a comfortable hotel. The other option is the shabby *Kawthoung Motel (☎ 09-22611, 01-272723)*, located about 300m beyond the main immigration office and about 500m from the pier. For simple double rooms with private cold bath, foreigners pay US$25 single/double or 1000B, breakfast included.

On nearby Thahtay Island (Thahtay Kyun in Burmese, literally 'Rich Man's Island', also spelt Thahte or Thade), well-heeled Thai and Singaporean gamblers stay at the *Andaman Club Resort (☎ 01-956 4354, Bangkok ☎ 02-856 4047, fax 285 6408)*, a huge five-star hotel complex sporting a casino and a Jack Nicklaus-designed, 18 hole golf course. All rooms have sea views and prices start at US$200 – unless you happen to be a regular high roller, in which case the casino will pick up your room tab. Guests with bookings are able to take a 250B boat direct from Jansom Thara Resort on Hat Chandamri, about 10km north-west of Ranong. If you're already in Kawthoung, you can catch a five minute boat ride out to the island from the Kawthoung jetty for 100B.

Waterfalls

Of the several well-known waterfalls in Ranong Province, **Ngao Falls** and **Punyaban Falls** are within walking distance of Hwy 4. Ngao is 13km south of Ranong while Punyaban is 15km north. Just take a songthaew in either direction and ask to be let off at the *náam tòk* (waterfall).

Isthmus of Kra

About 60km north of Ranong, in Kraburi district, is the Isthmus of Kra, the narrowest strip of land in Thailand, where barely 50km separates the Gulf of Thailand from the Andaman Sea. Just off Hwy 4 is a monument commemorating this geographical wonder. At one time the Thai government had plans to construct the so-called Kra Canal here, but the latest word is that the canal – if it's built – will run east from Satun Province through Songkhla, about 500km farther south.

Ko Chang

Don't confuse this island off the coast of Ranong with the much larger Ko Chang in Trat Province. As with many of the islands in this area, estuarial effluent from the Chan River inhibits clarity in the surrounding Andaman waters, but natural mangrove on the east coast and a hilly, forested interior are attractions enough for some. Birdlife includes hornbills, sea eagles and Andaman kites.

A couple of trails meander around the island and so far there are no motor vehicles. Nor is there electricity – the few resorts on the island either do without or generate their own. Beaches are found along the western shore, and though they're not classic white-sand strands, regular visitors enjoy the laid-back atmosphere.

Bungalow operations on the island can arrange boat trips to Ko Phayam and other nearby islands for around 150B per person (including lunch) for groups of six or more.

Places to Stay & Eat Several beach places have opened up over the last few years, though for the most part they're only open from November to April. Starting at the northern end of the island, *Rasta Baby (Ranong ☎ 077-833077)*, established by a dreadlocked Thai and his American wife, has eight bungalows. They recently left the island and it's unsure whether someone else

will take over. Sharing the same small beach, *Ko Chang Contex (Ranong ☎ 077-812730)* is run by a Thai family with huts for 100B to 200B a night, along with an à la carte restaurant menu.

Next south and west, the *Eden Bistro Café* offers two small bungalows with shared bathroom for 100B each, and one large bungalow with attached shower for 150B. Just down the beach from Eden, *Ko Chang Sunset Bungalow (☎ 01-229 4681)* offers nicely built bungalows in a shady, breezy spot for 100B to 250B each.

Cashew Resort (☎ 077-824741), the oldest and largest place on the island, charges 100B for simple huts with shared facilities. Service has slipped over the years, perhaps because the proprietors were the only game on the island for so long. Both Cashew and Ko Chang Sunset will pick prospective guests up at JT Food & Ice in Ranong.

A few hundred metres past the pier for boats from the mainland are the friendly *Chang Thong Bungalows (☎ 077-833820)* and *Pheung Thong*, side-by-side operations run by a brother and sister. Bamboo or plasterboard huts here cost 100B, 150B with private bath; Chang Thong's restaurant serves decent Thai food. Chang Thong often picks visitors up at Chaon Thong Food & Drinks in Ranong. *Suphan Nee Paradise* is much the same.

Ko Chang Resort sits on a section of rocky headland and offers huts with shared bathroom for 100B, with private bath 150B.

At the southern end of the island at Ao Lek (Small Bay), *N & X Bungalows* offers more of the same thatched huts for 100B each.

Getting There & Away From Ranong take a songthaew (red No 2, 6B) to Saphaan Plaa, getting off by the petrol station towards the main pier. Look for signs advertising Ko Chang bungalows and follow them down a zigzag soi a couple of hundred metres, where you'll find longtail boats that run to Ko Chang. If you have a heavy bag, a motorcycle taxi can bring you to this landing for 20B.

Depending on the tide, two or three boats leave every morning from November to April; turn up around 9 am to see when they're going as they don't usually leave before this hour. During the high season – December to March – there's a consistent 11 am departure daily. Boats return to Ranong at 8 am the next day. The cost is negotiable depending on how many passengers board; if you book a bungalow through Ranong Travel in town, you may get a free boat ride along with a ride down to Saphaan Plaa. Otherwise count on paying up to 100B per person.

LAEM SON NATIONAL PARK

The Laem Son (Pine Cape) Wildlife & Forest Preserve stretches 315 sq km over the Kapoe district of Ranong and Khuraburi district in Phang-Nga. This area includes about 100km of Andaman Sea coastline – the longest protected shore in the country – as well as over 20 islands. Much of the coast here is covered with mangrove swamps, home to various species of birds, fish, deer and monkeys, including crab-eating macaques, often seen while driving along the road to the park headquarters. Sea turtles lay eggs on Hat Praphat.

The best known and most accessible beach is **Hat Bang Ben**, where the main park offices, restaurant and bungalows are. This is a long, sandy beach backed by shady casuarina trees and is said to be safe for swimming year-round. From Hat Bang Ben you can see several islands, including the nearby Ko Kam Yai, Ko Kam Noi, Mu Ko Yipun, Ko Kang Kao and, to the north, Ko Phayam. The park staff can arrange boat trips out to any of these islands for 800B per boat per day. During low tide you can walk to an island just a couple of hundred metres away from Hat Bang Ben.

Ko Phayam is inhabited by around 100 Thais, who mostly make their living fishing or growing cashews. There are good swimming beaches on Phayam and on the western side of some of the Kam islands, as well as some live coral. Although underwater visibility isn't great, it's a little better here than on Ko Chang as it's farther from the mouth

of the Chan River. The beach on **Ko Kam Noi** has relatively clear water for swimming and snorkelling (April is the best month) plus the added bonus of fresh water year-round and plenty of grassy areas for camping. One island on the other side of Ko Kam Yai that can't be seen from the beach is **Ko Kam Tok** (also called Ko Ao Khao Khwai). It's only about 200m from Ko Kam Yai, and, like Ko Kam Noi, has a good beach, coral, fresh water and a camping area. **Ko Kam Yai** is 14km south-west of Hat Bang Ben.

About 3km north of Hat Bang Ben, across the canal, is another beach, **Hat Laem Son**, which is almost always deserted. The only way to get there is to hike from Bang Ben. In the opposite direction, about 50km south of Hat Bang Ben, is **Hat Praphat**, very similar to Bang Ben with casuarina trees and a long beach. There is a second park office here which can be reached by road via the Phetkasem Hwy (Hwy 4).

In the canals you ford coming into the park, you may notice large wooden racks which are used for raising oysters.

Places to Stay & Eat

Camping is allowed anywhere among the casuarina trees for 10B per person (pay at the park unit just inside the park entrance). National park *bungalows* have dorm-like 10-person and 16-person wooden houses – 700B and 900B respectively – but will allow individuals to stay for 100B per night. Similar park accommodation is also available on Ko Kam Yai but should be arranged in advance; call ☎ 077-823255 in Ranong or ☎ 02-579 0529 in Bangkok for information.

A few hundred metres before the park entrance (9.5km from the Hwy 4 junction) is the private *Wasana Resort*, run by a Thai-Dutch couple. Clean bamboo bungalows with mosquito nets, fan and private bath cost 300B, larger concrete bungalows with verandahs as much as 600B; discounts for long-term stays are available. The nearby *Andaman Peace Resort (☎ 077-821796)* offers five different styles of concrete bungalows for 700B to 1500B. Just outside the park entrance, the lacklustre Burmese-owned

Komain Villa offers small bungalows with fan and bath for 250B per night.

The food at the *park canteen* is quite reasonable, although *Wasana Resort* is the better choice.

Ko Phayam There are only a few places to stay on Ko Phayam. On the south-west side of the island is a curving beach with *Aow Yai Bungalow* (☎ 01-464 5127) for 150B per day for the first week and 100B a day after that. If you stay more than two weeks the price drops to 80B a day. On a larger north-western beach, *Vijit Bungalow* (☎ 01-476 0753, 077-834082) has huts for 100B and 150B with private facilities.

On the eastern side is the more expensive *Payam Island Resort* (☎ 077-812297, Bangkok ☎ 02-390 2681) with bungalows from 400B to 2500B.

On Ko Chang to the immediate north there are also several places to stay – see the earlier entry under Around Ranong.

Getting There & Away
The turn-off for Laem Son National Park is about 58km down the Phetkasem Hwy (Hwy 4) from Ranong, between Km 657 and 658. Any bus heading south from Ranong can drop you off here (ask for Hat Bang Ben) or you could hitch fairly easily – there is plenty of traffic along Hwy 4. Once you're off the highway, however, you'll have to wait a bit to flag down pickup trucks going towards the park. If you can't get a ride all the way, it's a 10km walk from Hwy 4 to the park entrance. At the police box at the junction you may be able to hire a motorcycle taxi for 30B. The road is now paved all the way to the park, so if you're driving, it's a breeze.

Ferries to Ko Phayam leave Ranong's Saphaan Plaa for Ko Phayam at 2 pm and arrive on the east coast at 4 pm and on the west coast at 4.30 pm. In the reverse direction they leave from Phayam's west coast at 7 am and the east coast at 8 am, arriving in Ranong around 10 am. The ferry fare is 50B per person. Longtail boats also make this route for 200B per person or 2000B for a

charter. Sometimes the Ko Chang boats continue to Ko Phayam – inquire at Ranong's Jansom Thara Hotel, Ranong Travel or at Saphaan Plaa.

Boats out to the various islands can be chartered from the park's visitors centre; the general cost is 800B per day. You can arrange to go as far as the Similan or Surin islands (see in the following Phang-Nga Province section for descriptions) for 900B and 1200B per person respectively.

KHURABURI, TAKUA PA & THAI MUANG
These districts of Phang-Nga Province are of minor interest in themselves but are departure points for other destinations. From **Khuraburi** you can reach the remote Surin and Similan islands, or from Takua Pa you can head east to Khao Sok National Park and Surat Thani. (See the South-Western Gulf Coast chapter for details.)

Takua Pa is also about halfway between Ranong and Phuket so buses often make rest stops here. Just off the highway is the *Extra Hotel* (☎ 076-421412) with rooms from 220B.

In the district of Thai Muang is **Hat Thai Muang National Park**, where sea turtles come to lay eggs between November and February. **Thap Lamu**, about 23km north of Thai Muang, has a pier with boats to the Similan Islands.

SURIN ISLANDS (MUU KO SURIN) NATIONAL MARINE PARK
A national park since 1981, the Surin Islands are famous for excellent diving and snorkelling. The two main islands (there are five in all) of Ko Surin Neua and Ko Surin Tai (North Surin Island and South Surin Island) lie about 70km north-west of Khuraburi and less than 5km from Thailand's marine border with Myanmar. The park office and visitor centre are on the south-western side of the northern island at Ao Mae Yai, where boats anchor. Admission to the park is 40B. Some of the best diving is said to be in the channel between the two islands.

On the southern island is a village of *chao náam* (*chao leh* or sea gypsies). In April the chao náam hold a major ancestral worship ceremony, called Loi Reua, on Ko Surin Tai. The island may be off limits during that time, so check first at the park office. Longtail boats can be hired at Ao Mae Yai to take you to the southern island for around 150B to 200B per person for the day.

Compared with the Similan Islands to the south, Surin is more suited to visitors who are interested in hiking and exploring rather than diving. There are several hiking trails, especially on the northern island. Also, getting to some of the best reefs doesn't require scuba gear, another plus for non-divers. Snorkelling gear can be rented at the park office for 150B per day.

Most visitors to the islands are Thai tourists, who tend to arrive in large numbers on national holidays. There also seems to be a fairly steady flow of tour groups, again mostly Thai, visiting from December to March, though most only stay a night or two. The main advantage of going at this time, especially if you're not a diver, is that you can probably catch a ride on one of the tour boats for 1000B return: at other times the only way out to the islands is chartering your own boat (which is costly) or joining a diving trip. The disadvantage of course is that accommodation can easily get booked up.

Surrounding the Surin Islands are the most well-developed coral colonies in Thai seas, according to Piprell & Boyd's *Diving in Thailand*, though the Similans boast a richer variety of fish species. There are seven major dive sites in the immediate vicinity of the Surin Islands, of which the best are found extending south-east from **HQ Bay** on Surin Neua; at **Ko Chi**, a small island off the north-eastern shore of Surin Neua; and at **Richelieu Rock**, a seamount about 14km south-east of Surin Tai. Whale sharks – the largest fish in the world – are reportedly spotted near Richelieu on 50% of dive trips, most commonly during the months of March and April. Snorkelling is excellent in many areas due to relatively shallow reef depths of 5 to 6m.

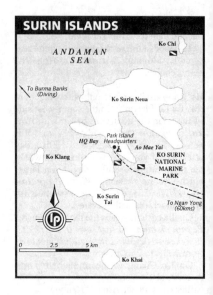

SURIN ISLANDS

ANDAMAN SEA
Ko Chi
To Burma Banks (Diving)
Ko Surin Neua
Park Island HQ Bay   Headquarters
Ao Mae Yai
Ko Klang
KO SURIN NATIONAL MARINE PARK
Ko Surin Tai
To Ngan Yong (60kms)
0   2.5   5 km
Ko Khai

The little-explored **Burma Banks**, a system of submerged seamounts around 60km north-west of Muu Ko Surin, are so prized by Thai dive operations that the GPS (Global Positioning System) co-ordinates are kept virtually secret. The only way to visit the Burma Banks – unless you have your own boat – is by way of seven to 10 day live-aboard dive trips out of Phuket. The three major banks – Roe, Silvertip and Rainbow – provide four to five-star class diving experiences, with fields of psychedelic coral laid over flat, underwater plateaux and loads of large oceanic as well as smaller reef marine species. Sharks – silvertip, reef, nurse, leopard and at least a half dozen other species – abound.

Many of the dive ops in Phuket have live-aboard diving excursions to the Surin Islands. Because of the distances involved, Surin is the most expensive dive destination in Thailand; rates start at around 9000B to 10,000B for a minimum two night, three day trip.

Ko Surin National Marine Park closes in early to mid May every year and doesn't reopen till mid November. The exact dates appear to vary from year to year, perhaps influenced by perceived weather patterns.

Places to Stay & Eat

Accommodation at the park *longhouses* is 100B per person or you can rent six and eight-person bungalows for 1200B. At the campground, two-person tents cost 100B a night or you can use your own (or camp without a tent) for 20B per night per person. The park also offers three good meals a day (mostly seafood) for 300B or you can order meals separately. Electricity is generated from 6 to 11 pm. It's strongly recommended that you make bookings in advance by calling the park's mainland office (☎ 076-491378).

Should you get stuck in Khuraburi, the *Rungtawan* next to the bus stop has adequate rooms for 220B. If the attached singsong cafe is too noisy, the only other possibility is *Tararain Resort*, 2km south of town, with three-person bungalows for 300B to 500B.

At the park office in Ngan Yong is a good *outdoor restaurant* serving Thai seafood daily from 7 am to 8 pm.

Getting There & Away

The mainland office of Ko Surin National Park is in the messy fishing village of Ngan Yong, from where boats to the islands depart. The road to Ngan Yong turns off Hwy 4 at Km 720, 6km north of Khuraburi and 109km south of Ranong. The park office, which is also at the pier, is about 2km down the road on the right hand side: from Hwy 4, a motorcycle taxi will take you there for about 10B.

Buses between Khuraburi and Ranong cost 37B and take about an hour and 20 minutes; ask to be let off at Ngan Yong (saying Ko Surin should also work). To and from Phuket, buses cost 55B and take about three hours. From Khuraburi to Ngan Yong costs 35B by motorcycle taxi.

The cheapest way out to the island is to latch on to one of the tour group boats heading out there. To do this you'll need to call the Surin mainland office (☎ 076-491378)

to find out when and if any boats are making the trip. If so, park staff will try and book you seats: the price is usually 1000B per person return. Tour boats run from December to April, and the busiest time is between February and April.

You can charter a boat out to the Surin Islands from Ngan Yong through the park officers, who will serve as brokers/interpreters. A boat that takes up to 30 people can be chartered for 6000B return – it takes four to five hours each way. Ordinarily, boat travel is only considered safe between December and early May, ie between the two monsoons. The park itself is closed mid May to mid November.

HAT BANG SAK

About 14km south of Takua Pa municipality, this beach stretches for several kilometres, and is mainly a destination for locals out for a picnic or drinks and seafood at one of the little open-air places that line the shore. The beach itself is nice, offers good views of the coast to the south, and is lined with casuarinas. But it's not regularly cleaned, so there's more litter here than farther south at Hat Khao Lak. The areas inland are also cluttered with shrimp farms and are not too inviting. Still, if you have time on your hands, it might be fun to do like the locals and come for a sunset meal or a drink.

If you do decide it's worth more than that, there are two places to stay. *Bang Sak Resort* (☎ 076-421380) is a modest place that has 16 bungalows and motel-style rooms for 200B to 500B with fan and bath. From the 'Bang Sak beach' turn-off from Hwy 4 (near Km 77), it's about 2km north on the road running along the beach. *Sun Splendor Lodge* (☎ 076-446025, 421350, 01-929 7047), 1.2km farther north from the Bang Sak turnoff, is a group of long one-storey, green-roofed buildings with terraces out front – it almost looks like a coastal Mississippi motel. It caters mostly to Thais. Facilities include a large covered restaurant area and a tiny pool. The 19 units cost 500B fan, 1000B air-con. The village next to the lodge is called **Ban Chai Thaleh**.

Hat Bang Sak has several good, relatively inexpensive seafood restaurants, including *Nit Noi, Rim Nam, Nawng Awn* and *Khrua Bang Sak*.

Buses running between Takua Pa and Phuket will get you here; just ask to be let off at Hat Bang Sak.

HAT KHAO LAK

Though still pretty sleepy, this scenic beach is becoming increasingly popular, mainly with European visitors. It's easy to reach, quiet and, as yet, not overdeveloped: the kind of place you can imagine Phuket to have been 20 years ago. The beach is a pretty stretch of sand studded with smooth granite boulders. You can easily walk northward along the sand for many kilometres, almost as far as Hat Bang Sak. A coral reef suitable for snorkelling lies 45 minutes offshore by longtail boat, and some of the bungalow resorts here offer dive excursions to this reef, as well as to the Similan and Surin Islands groups.

Hat Khao Lak is located about 25km south of Takua Pa municipality. It's actually located in a town called Ban La-on, but developers decided associating the beach with the nearby national park would sound more appealing.

The area immediately south of Hat Khao Lak is encompassed by the 125 sq km **Khao Lak/Lam Ru National Park**, a beautiful collection of sea cliffs, 1000m hills, beaches, estuaries, forested valleys and mangroves. Wildlife seen in the park includes hornbills, drongos, tapirs, gibbons, monkeys and Asiatic black bears. The visitors centre, just off Hwy 4 between Km 56 and 57, has little in the way of maps or printed info, but there's a very nice open-air restaurant perched on a shady slope overlooking the sea.

Activities

Park ranger-guided treks along the coast or inland can be arranged through Poseidon Bungalows (π/fax 076-443248), as can longtail boat trips up the scenic Khlong Thap Liang estuary. The latter afford opportunities to view mangrove communities of crab-eating macaques.

Live coral formations can be found just off Hat Khao Lak and along the west tip of the bay near Poseidon. Sea Dragon Dive Service (π/fax 01-229 2418), on Hwy 4 opposite the main entrance to Hat Khao Lak, is the main diving operation in the area. In addition to selling and renting diving and snorkelling equipment, it offers PADI-certified scuba instruction and dive trips to the Similan Islands. Sea Dragon's four day, four night Similan and Surin excursion costs 13,800B for divers, including food, transport, accommodation and all equipment, or 6900B for non-divers. These are among the lowest rates available for dive excursions to the Similans; companies working out of Phuket typically charge more to cover the costs of the lengthy boat journey from Phuket. Local dive trips to nearby coral reefs cost 1200B per day including equipment and two tanks.

Poseidon Bungalows offers three day, two night snorkelling-only trips to the Similan Islands for 3700B per person. These depart twice a week during the November to April dive season. For both Poseidon and Sea Dragon, count on five hours one way to reach the islands; such trips operate only from November and April due to climatic conditions. For further information on getting to the Similans, see the Similan National Marine Park section farther on in this chapter.

Between Khao Lak and Bang Sak is a network of sandy beach trails – some of which lead to deserted beaches – that are fun to explore on foot or by rented motorcycle.

Places to Stay & Eat

Hat Khao Lak There is some reasonably priced accommodation at Hat Khao Lak, although the area seems to be moving steadily up-market. The two most recent additions, Khao Lak Laguna Resort and Khao Lak Sunset Resort, are both in the top-end bracket, and there's talk of two more such operations targeting this area.

At the northern end of Hat Khao Lak is *Gerd & Noi Khao Lak Bungalow* (π/fax 01-229 2197), which has basic huts with mosquito nets and shared bathroom for 150B, and nicely designed Thai-style cottages with private bath and fan for 600B. There are also air-con rooms for 800B and up. The entire operation is set in a pleasant landscaped courtyard.

Next door is *Garden Beach Resort* (☎ 01-229 1179) which has clean, small huts with bath and fan for 200B. More spacious bungalows cost 300B or 400B depending on proximity to the beach. It has a relaxed atmosphere and the restaurant is good. This place also rents motorbikes (200B per day) and Suzuki jeeps (900B).

Towards the centre of Hat Khao is *Nang Thong Bay Resort* (☎ 01-229 1181). This place is similar in style to the Garden Beach Resort, with smaller bungalows (private bath) away from the beach for 200B, larger ones for 300B and 550B for those closest to the beach. This is the only place in Khao Lak where you can change money (cash or travellers cheques). Motorbikes and jeeps are also available for rent here. Towards the southern end of the beach, *Nang Thong Bay II Bungalows* (☎ 01-229 2727) has larger, more attractive cottages with bath and fan for 500B.

Dwarfed by Nang Thong Bay II is *Tukta Bungalow*, a tiny place owned by an affable European gentleman. There are three small but clean rooms with bath and fan for 250B, as well as more spacious apartments for longer-term stays. Tukta also has a very nice little restaurant right on the beach. During the rainy season it closes down.

Farther south *Khao Lak Laguna Resort* (☎ 01-229 2274, fax 076-431297) features 56 Thai-style cottages, 24 with fan for around 1800B and 32 with air-con for 2200B. It's very popular, and commands a nice section of beach, but the grounds could be better kept. About half a kilometre farther south again along Hwy 4, *Khao Lak Sunset Resort* (☎ 076-421807) has upscale air-con hotel rooms stacked against a cliff with balcony and sea views for 1200B to 1500B.

A cluster of simple thatched-roof *beach restaurants* towards the centre of the beach (just north of Nang Thong Bay Resort) offer reasonably priced Thai dishes and tasty seafood, as well as a fine view of the sea and sunset.

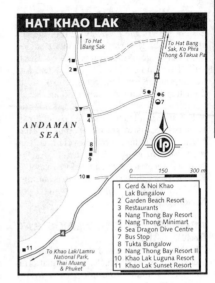

HAT KHAO LAK

1 Gerd & Noi Khao Lak Bungalow
2 Garden Beach Resort
3 Restaurants
4 Nang Thong Bay Resort
5 Nang Thong Minimart
6 Sea Dragon Dive Centre
7 Bus Stop
8 Tukta Bungalow
9 Nang Thong Bay Resort II
10 Khao Lak Luguna Resort
11 Khao Lak Sunset Resort

National Park Environs Khao Lak/Lam Ru National Park has four simple *bungalows* for 200B at its headquarters, located 2km south of Hat Khao Lak. The restaurant nearby, in addition to its wonderful setting, has good food for pretty reasonable prices.

On the other side of the headland of Khao Lak/Lam Ru National Park, 5.5km south of Hat Khao Lak, is *Poseidon Bungalows* (☎ 076-443258), in a sheltered bay south of Hat Khao Lak, where basic thatched huts are 150B single/double with shared bathroom, larger huts with private bath for 400B or 500B for three people. The huts are discretely dispersed among huge boulders and coastal forest, affording quiet and privacy. The proprietors dispense information on the area and organise boat excursions and dive trips to the local reef and to the Similan Islands. A pleasant restaurant built on stilts over the sea serves Thai and European food.

Getting There & Away

Any bus running along Hwy 4 between Takua Pa and Phuket or Thai Muang will stop at Hat Khao Lak if asked (for the latter, look for Sea Dragon Dive Service on the eastern side of the highway). From the bus stop it's about 400m to the dirt road on which the accommodation is located. Buses will also stop near Hat Chongfa, Khao Lak Laguna and Khao Lak Sunset resorts and the Khao Lak/Lam Ru National Park Headquarters.

If you're headed to Poseidon Bungalows, your best bet is to get off the bus at Thap Lamu and then take a motorcycle taxi from there for 30B to 40B. The turn-off for Poseidon is located between the 53 Km and 54 Km markers, but from there it's another 1.2km; a pretty hot and dusty walk if you have bags to carry.

AROUND HAT KHAO LAK & HAT BANG SAK

Along the beach north of the Hat Khao Lak area are a couple of places to stay that offer still more solitude. *Chongfa Beach Resort* (☎ 01-229 1253) has rooms in two-storey, four-unit blocks for 400B to 500B: they're not the most architecturally appealing, but are relatively new and quite clean. Considering the nearly private beach, which doesn't have the boulders of Khao Lak, and the pleasant restaurant overlooking the sea, this is one of the best deals in the area. Turn off Hwy 4 between Km 62 and 63 Km to reach it.

If you're looking for a luxurious, aesthetic get-away, the only real choice in the whole Khao Lak/Bang Sak area is *Similana Resort* (☎/fax 01-211 2564, 076-229 2337, Bangkok ☎ 02-677 6240, fax 677 6246, email sandler@mozart.inet.co.th). Sitting atop a headland 20km south of Takua Pa, it's a beautifully designed and landscaped group of all-wood Thai-style bungalows with tiled roofs and hotel rooms, artfully hidden among pandanus trees and coco palms. Amenities include a swimming pool, although the beach around here looks so clean and secluded you may never touch the diving board. All units come with refrigerators and hot showers. Of course none of this comes cheap: during the high-season (November to April) hotel rooms cost 2300B, and fan/air-con bungalows 2500/3600B,

breakfast is included in the rates. However, management will usually offer a discount of 25% except between 15 December and 10 January and major public holidays when rates are non-negotiable and there's a peak season surcharge of 500B per room. In the low season, rates drop by around 50%. Food at the restaurant (your only eating option within 10km) is good, but quite expensive. The resort has a pickup and dropoff service to Phuket for 1200B, and jeeps and motorcycles are available for rent. Staff will also pick you up from Takua Pa free of charge if you ring them up.

Ko Phra Thong

The group that manages the Similana Resort also has the *Golden Buddha Beach Resort* (☎ 01-230 4744, Bangkok ☎ 02-863 3180 fax 02-863 1301, email sandler@mozart.inet.co.th), set on a sandy peninsula between two pristine beaches on the large island of Ko Phra Thong (Golden Buddha Island). The only resort on the island, Golden Buddha offers 29 rooms, including one-bedroom thatched-roof cottages and two-bedroom family houses, made of tropical hardwoods and other natural materials. All have open-air bathrooms with views of the sea and surrounding forest. Rates run at 1200B per day, with a peak season surcharge (22 December to 5 January) of 200B. Full board costs an extra 550B per person per day.

For Ko Phra Thong you should call Golden Buddha Beach Resort in advance and arrange for transport. The turnoff for the Golden Buddha pier is near Km 722 on Hwy 4.

SIMILAN ISLANDS (MUU KO SIMILAN) NATIONAL MARINE PARK

The Similan Islands are world-renowned among diving enthusiasts for incredible underwater sightseeing at depths ranging from 2 to 30m. Besides attractive sandy beaches, huge, smooth granite rock formations plunge into the sea and form seamounts, rock reefs and dive-throughs.

As elsewhere in the Andaman Sea, the best diving months are December to May when the weather is good and the sea is at its clearest (and boat trips are much safer).

The Thais sometimes refer to the Similans as Ko Kao, or Nine Islands, because there are nine of them – each has a number as well as a name. The word 'Similan' in fact comes from the Malay word *sembilan* meaning 'nine'. Counting in order from the north, they are Ko Bon, Ko Ba-Ngu, Ko Similan, Ko Payu, Ko Miang (which is ac-

tually two islands close together), Ko Payan, Ko Payang and Ko Hu Yong. They're relatively small islands and uninhabited except for park officials and occasional tourist groups from Phuket.

Princess Chulabhorn, the present Thai monarch's youngest daughter, has a cottage on Ko Miang, a royal association that adds an extra layer of protection to the islands' national park status. The Thai navy operates a sea turtle preserve on Ko Ba-Ngu, yet another bonus for enforcement of park preservation.

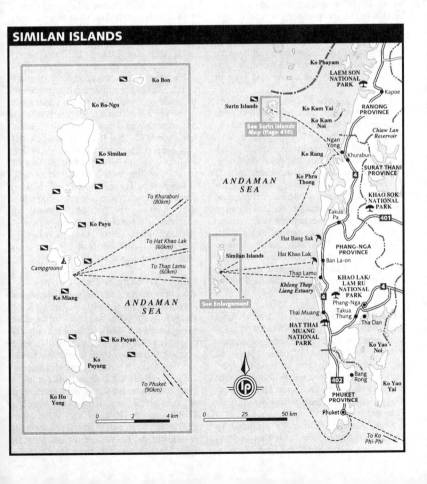

SIMILAN ISLANDS

Also on Ko Miang, which is second in size to Ko Similan, you'll find the park headquarters, a visitors centre and accommodation. Venturing inland from the beach, you should easily be able to catch glimpses of the Nicobar pigeon or the hairy-legged mountain land crab. If you're not into aqualungs, the beaches on this island are good for snorkelling (as opposed to scuba diving), as is the channel between Ko Miang and Ko Payu. Ko Similan is also good for hiking and snorkelling. In a small bay on the Similan's western side you may be able to see spiny lobsters resting in rock crevices, along with sea fans, plume worms and soft corals swaying in the current. The largest granite outcrop in the Similan archipelago is also found on Ko Similan; scramble to the top to enjoy a sweeping view of the sea.

Thirty-two species of birds can be seen on the nine islands, including resident birds such as the Brahminy kite and the white-breasted waterhen. Migratory species of note include the pintail snipe, grey wagtail, cattle egret, watercock and the roseate tern. Fairly common mammal residents include the bush-tailed porcupine, common palm civet, flying lemur and bottlenosed dolphin. Species of reptiles and amphibians found in the park include the banded krait, reticulated python, white-lipped pit viper, common pit viper, hawksbill turtle, leather turtle, Bengal monitor lizard, common water monitor lizard and ornate froglet.

Admission to the park – collected on Ko Miang – is 40B.

Ko Bon & Ko Kachai

These small islands lie approximately midway between the Similan and Surin archipelagos. Profuse hard corals appear at depths of 18 to 35m and, in good weather, visibility extends to 25m. Without a doubt these are two of the area's top dive sites, although they are hardly known outside Thailand.

Both islands are usually included in longer live-aboard dive trips that run between the Similan and Surin Islands.

Organised Tours

Khao Lak Sea Dragon at Hat Khao Lak does three-day/two-night dive trips to the Similans for 10,800B, four-day/four-night Similan and Surin trips for 13,800B. Poseidon Bungalows next to Khao Lak/Lam Ru National Park does a Similan snorkelling trip for a bargain 3700B. Their boats depart from Thap Lamu; see the earlier Hat Khao Lak section for more details.

Phuket Overnight diving excursions from Phuket are fairly reasonably priced – about 5000B a day including food, accommodation, diving equipment and underwater guides. Non-divers may be able to join these trips for around half the cost – snorkellers are welcome.

Package deals out of Phuket typically start at 9000B for a three day/two night dive trip, and go up to 40,000B for a seven day, seven night Similan and Burma Banks trip on Siam Diving Center's (☎ 076-330608) live-aboard MV *Sai Mai*. The latter also offers longer, more exotic dive excursions such as a 10 day/10 night whale shark expedition costing over 50,000B per person.

Songserm Travel (☎ 076-222570) in Phuket operates a one day excursion trip to the Similans every Tuesday, Thursday and Saturday at 8 am for 1800B per person including lunch. Considering it takes 3½ hours each way, this doesn't leave a lot of time for island exploration.

Places to Stay & Eat

Accommodation, including camping, is only allowed on Ko Miang. The park has *bungalows* for 600B and four-bed rooms in a *longhouse* for 400B. If there are only one or two in your party, you may be able to get a per-person rate of 100B for the longhouse, but don't count on it. Tent rental costs 150B, and there's a 20B tent site fee if you bring your own. Bookings must be made in advance at the park's mainland office in Thap Lamu (☎ 076-411914).

The only source of food is a privately run *restaurant* on Ko Miang. Prices here are ridiculously high (40B for a fried egg, for instance), and even then you need to let park staff know you're coming in advance if you want food to be there for you. Bringing your own food is strongly recommended, though occasional restrictions on open fires may force you to the restaurant at least a few times.

Getting There & Away
You can get boats to the Similans from the port at Thap Lamu (39km south of Takua Pa off Hwy 4, or 20km north of Thai Muang) and from Phuket. The park mainland office is also in Thap Lamu, about 1km from the pier.

The islands are 60km from Thap Lamu, about three hours by boat. Met Sine Tours (☎ 01-229 0280), located near the pier, is the place to go for boat bookings. When we last checked, boats ran Wednesday, Friday and Sunday, departing Thap Lamu at 9 am and heading back from Ko Miang at 3.30 pm the same day. The return (round trip) fare is 1600B. It would be best to call ahead just to make sure what's going on, as the situation seems rather fluid (there is at least one English speaker at Met Sine). Boats run to the Similans from November to May only; during the remainder of the year the seas are too rough. If the weather looks rough when you arrive give some thought as to how badly you want to go: there have been several incidents in recent years of boats operating out of Thap Lamu having foundered or becoming stranded, though no casualties have resulted.

AO PHANG-NGA & PHANG-NGA
Over 95km north-east of Phuket, this expansive, turquoise extension of the Andaman Sea is dotted with hundreds of islands, many are mere limestone outcrops that protrude from the sea. At some islands, partially submerged grottoes can be entered by small boats during low tide. Other islands are encircled by sandy coves where the only visible inhabitants are swiftlets which build their nests on high cliffs. Itinerant collectors farm the highly prized nests for use in the Chinese delicacy 'bird's nest

soup', a broth made from the hardened bird saliva holding the nests together. Many of the islands are part of **Ao Phang-Nga National Marine Park** and can be explored by boat or canoe.

Very few of these islands receive overnight visitors. Ko Phi-Phi, the most famous, is a dumbbell-shaped island ringed by coral reefs, caves and white-sand beaches; in this book it is covered in the Southern Andaman Coast chapter under Krabi Province.

Information
The TAT distributes a map of Phang-Nga Province that includes a separate map of Phang-Nga town, as well as pamphlets listing sights, accommodation and restaurants. The most complete information is at the regional office in Phuket town, and you may be able to get some material in Bangkok. The Books, 265/1 Th Phetkasem, Phang-Nga, carries a small selection of English language books and magazines.

Money
In the centre of Phang-Nga town along Hwy 4 are several banks open during regular banking hours.

Post & Telephone
The post and telephone office is about 2km south-west of the bus station. Air-con phone booths in front of the telephone office accept coins and Thai phonecards.

Things to See & Do
Along the northern shore of the bay is **Phang-Nga**, a small provincial capital wedged between verdant limestone cliffs. Phang-Nga is the best – and least expensive – place to hire boats for exploring the northern half of the bay. The southern half of the bay is best approached from Phuket or Krabi.

In Phang-Nga itself there's little to see or do that isn't beachy unless you happen to be there during the annual Vegetarian Festival in October (see the 'Vegetarian Festival' boxed text in the Phuket section for information on this unusual event). Nearby Suan

Somdet Phra Sinakharin Park and Sa Nang Manora Forest Park are good places for hiking and picnicking (see Around Phang-Nga further on).

On the way to Phang-Nga, turn left off Hwy 4 at Km 31. Just 5km past the small town of Takua Thung is **Wat Tham Suwankhuha** (Heaven Grotto Temple), a cave shrine full of Buddha images. The shrine consists of two main caverns: a larger one containing a 15m reclining Buddha and tiled with *laikhram* and *benjarong*, two coloured patterns more common in pottery, and a smaller cavern displaying spirit flags and a *rishi* (hermit-sage) statue. Royal seals of several kings, including Rama V, Rama VII and Rama IX – as well those of lesser royalty – are inscribed on one wall of the latter cave.

Other nearby caves in the province include **Tham Reusisawan** ('Hermit Heaven'; 3km south of Phang-Nga) and **Tham Phung Chang** ('Elephant Belly Cave'; also 3km south).

Phang-Nga Province's best beach areas are on the west coast facing the Andaman Sea. Between Thai Muang in the south and Takua Pa in the north are the beaches of Hat Thai Muang and Hat Bang Sak – see the Khuraburi, Takua Pa & Thai Muang and the Hat Bang Sak sections for more details.

Organised Tours

Boat Trips Between Takua Thung and Phang-Nga is the road to **Tha Dan**, where you can find the Phang-Nga Customs pier. At an adjacent pier, boats can be hired to tour Ao Phang-Nga National Park, with visits to a Muslim fishing village on stilts, half-submerged caves, and strangely shaped islands, including several which were used in the 1970s James Bond film *The Man with the Golden Gun*.

Posted boat charter rates are as follows: 650B for a longtail boat carrying up to eight people; 750B for a longtail carrying up to 10; 1500B for a larger longtail holding up to 20; and 3000B to 3500B for a cruise boat carrying 40 to 70. The standard boat tour goes to Ko Panyi, Khao Ping

Kan, Tham Lawt, Khao Maju, Ko Khao Tapu and Khao Khian.

An alternative to chartering a whole boat is to go with a local tour arranged through one of the two small agencies next to the bus terminal in Phang-Nga town. Sayan Tours (☎ 076-430348) has been doing overnight tours of Ao Phang-Nga for many years now, and these continue to receive good reviews from some travellers, although it's all pretty formalised nowadays. The overnight tour costs 400B per person and includes a boat tour of **Tham Lawt** (Tunnel Cave, a large water cave), **Ko Phing Kan** (Leaning Island, aka 'James Bond Island'), **Ko Khao Tapu** (Nail Mountain Island), **Khao Maju** (Poodle Mountain), **Tham Naak** (Dragon Cave), **Khao Khian** (Drawing Mountain; rock wall murals), a former mangrove charcoal factory, plus dinner, breakfast and very rustic accommodation in a Muslim fishing village on **Ko Panyi**. Sayan also leads morning (rainy season) and afternoon (dry season) trips for 200B, as well as a full day tour for 450B. Both include a seafood lunch and return in the afternoon. The overnight trip is recommended over either day trip; the latter tend to be a bit rushed. Sayan Tours can also arrange trips to nearby sites on land, including Sa Nang Manora Forest Park and the various caves near town.

The other tour agency at the bus terminal, Kean Tours (☎ 076-411247), charges exactly the same rates for similar half day, full day and overnight tours.

These same tours are available out of Phuket, but cost at least 200B to 400B per person more. Whatever you do, try to avoid touring the bay in the middle of the day (10 am to 4 pm) when hundreds of package tourists crowd the islands.

Alternatively, you could do a canoe tour from Phuket. See the following Paddling entry.

See the Around Phang-Nga section for more extensive descriptions and information about Ao Phang-Nga National Park.

Paddling Several companies based in Phuket offer inflatable canoe tours of scenic

Ao Phang-Nga .The first and still the most famous is a company based in Phuket, Sea-Canoe Thailand (☎ 076-212252, fax 212172, email webinfo@seacanoe.com), at 367/4 Th Yaowarat. The kayaks are able to enter semi-submerged caves, which Thai fishermen call *hâwng* (room), inaccessible by the longtail boats. A day paddle costs 3495B per person and includes meals, beverages and equipment, while all-inclusive, three or six-day camping trips are 22,000B and 39,600B per person, respectively. Sea-Canoe prefers to quote prices in US dollars; the latter baht prices were determined by multiplying their published dollar prices by the exchange rate that was current at the time of writing (41B to the dollar). The multi-day trips leave on Wednesday and Sunday. The day trips can also be booked from Ao Nang in Krabi for 1700B.

Several other companies in the area offer similar inflatable canoe trips for less than half these prices, but SeaCanoe Thailand claim they are still the most ecologically conscious in terms of the way in which they organise and operate their tours. Other companies with experience navigating the hongs (hâwng) and for which we've received good feedback from readers are Andaman Sea Kayak (☎ 076-235353) and Andaman Trails (☎/fax 076-235353, email seakayak@loxinfo.co.th). Just about any travel agency on the island can book trips with any of these three outfits.

Places to Stay – Budget

Phang-Nga Phang-Nga has several small hotels. *Thawisuk* (☎ 076-412100, 77-79 Th Phetkasem) is right in the middle of town, a bright blue building with the English sign 'Hotel'. Simple but usually clean rooms upstairs go for 150B/200B for one/two beds with fan and private bath, plus towel and soap on request. You can sit and have a beer on the roof of Thawisuk while watching the sun set over Phang-Nga's rooftops and the limestone cliffs surrounding the town.

Lak Meuang Hotel (☎ 076-412486, fax 411512), on Th Phetkasem, just outside town towards Krabi, has rooms for 200B with fan and bath, 480B air-con, plus an OK restaurant downstairs. On the same side of the street farther south-west is *Ratanapong Hotel* (☎ 076-411247), which offers decent one-bed rooms for 150B, two-bed rooms for 230B, three beds for 280B and 350B for four beds; air-con rooms are also available at 300/430B for one/two beds.

Farther down the road towards Phuket is *Muang Thong* (☎ 076-412132, 128 Th Phetkasem), where clean, quiet singles/doubles are 120/180B with fan, 250B to 320B with air-con.

Places to Stay – Mid-Range

On the outskirts of town in the direction of Phuket is *New Lak Meuang II* (☎ 076-411500, fax 411501, 540 Th Phetkasem), with all air-con rooms from 480B to 780B. It's a convenient location for exploring the central area.

Hotel Summit (Sunimitr; ☎ 076-411422, ☎/fax 411130, 21/1 Th Sirirat) is a 20 room, four storey hotel off the main drag in the centre of town with rates of 350B (air-con), 400B (air-con, mid-sized refrigerator, TV) and 600B (same in a larger suite). Bread and coffee or Ovaltine are complimentary from 7 to 10 am.

Phang-Nga Valley Resort (☎ 076-412201, 411353, fax 411393, 5/5 Th Phetkasem) is on the southern outskirts of town before you reach the highway to Krabi. Rooms in large tile-roofed bungalows range from 300B to 2500B.

Tha Dan On Route 4144 towards the customs pier, the fading *Phang-Nga Bay Resort Hotel* (☎ 076-412067/70, fax 412057) costs 850B in the low season, up to 1500B during holidays. Facilities include a swimming pool and a decent restaurant. All rooms come with TV, telephone and fridge. Hardly anyone ever seems to stay here except the occasional surprised tour group.

Places to Eat

Duang Restaurant, next to Bangkok Bank on the main road, has a bilingual menu and a good selection of Thai and Chinese dishes, including Southern Thai specialities. Prices have crept up a little higher than the standard of the food would indicate. *Suan Aahaan Islam* (no roman-script sign), on the left just north-east of Soi Langkai, serves simple Thai Muslim food, including *roti kaeng* (flatbread and curry) in the morning. On the other side of Soi Langkai is a cafe called *Chai Thai* (no roman-script sign) that's open early and specialises in *paa-thông-kŏh*.

South-west of the market, a little way past the bus terminal, the tidy *Bismilla* also does Thai Muslim food.

Several *food stalls* on the main street of Phang-Nga sell cheap and delicious *khanŏm jiin* (thin wheat noodles) with chicken curry, *náam yaa* (spicy ground-fish curry) or *náam phrík* (sweet and spicy peanut sauce). One vendor in front of the market (opposite Bangkok Bank) serves khanŏm jiin with an amazing 12 varieties of free vegetable accompaniments – but only from 1 to 8 pm Tuesday to Sunday; an adjacent vendor does *khâo mòk kài* (chicken biryani) from 6 am to noon. Roti kaeng is available in the *morning market* from around 5 to 10 am. There are also the usual Chinese *khâo man kài* places around town.

Lak Muang Hotel has a decent, moderately priced open-air restaurant downstairs.

Getting There & Away

Buses for Phang-Nga leave from the Phuket bus terminal on Th Phang-Nga, near the Th Thepkasatri intersection, at 10.10 am, noon and 1.40, 3.30 and 4.30 pm. The trip to Phang-Nga takes 2½ hours and the one way fare is 37B non-air-con. Alternatively you could rent a motorcycle in Phuket and navigate here on your own.

Buses to and from Krabi leave every half hour, cost 36B and take 1½ hours; air-con buses leave hourly and cost 52B. To and from Surat Thani ordinary buses cost 55B and take 3½ hours. Other air-con departures to and from destinations around Southern Thailand include Ranong (120B, two or three times daily), Hat Yai (196B, six times), Trang (121B, 11 times) and Satun (198B, two departures per day).

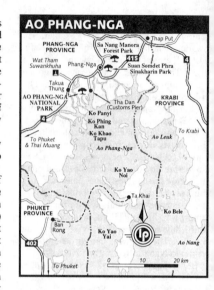

Ordinary buses to and from Bangkok cost 192B and take a long 14 hours, while air-con is 350B and VIP is 403B, both taking 13 hours. All buses depart from the main bus terminal in the centre of town, but they can also be flagged down along Th Phetkasem (Hwy 4), the main road through Phang-Nga.

Getting Around

Most of the town is easily accessible on foot. Sayan Tour at the bus terminal can assist with motorcycle rental.

Songthaews between Phang-Nga and Tha Dan (the Phang-Nga Customs pier) cost 15B.

AROUND PHANG-NGA
Suan Somdet Phra Sinakharin Park

This public park has two entrances. The most dramatic entry is via a huge hole through a limestone cliff near Phang-Nga Bay Resort Hotel. A road goes through the cliff, so if you have a vehicle you can drive through it and into the park. The second, main entrance is off Phang-Nga's principal street towards the southern end of town, opposite the provincial transport department. Nearly the entire park is surrounded by limestone cliffs and buffs, into which nature has carved a scenic network of caves and tunnels, some containing ponds. Wooden walkways link the water-filled caverns so that visitors can admire the ponds and amazing limestone formations. One of the larger caves, **Tham Reusi**, is marked by a gilded statue of a Hindu-Buddhist hermit sage – complete with tiger skins and staff – outside the entrance. Entry is free.

Sa Nang Manora Forest Park

North of town via Hwy 4 (turnoff 3.4km from the Shell station and the Lak Muang II Hotel, then 4.5km down a winding road through rubber plantations), this recently established park features lots of dense rainforest and a set of cool green cascades. The setting is truly impressive, with plenty of rattan vines, moss-encrusted roots and rocks. The many-levelled cascade has several pools suitable for swimming. The overall impression is similar to that of Krabi's Than Bokkharani National Park but it receives many fewer visitors, whether Thai or foreign. As a result it's much cleaner. Primitive trails follow the falls level after level and beyond – you could easily get a full day's hiking in without retracing your track. Bring plenty of drinking water – although the shade and the falls moderate the temperature, the humidity in the park is quite high.

The park's name comes from a local folk belief that the mythical Princess Manora bathes in the pools of the park when no one else is around.

Facilities include some tables and chairs here and there, plus a small restaurant next to the car park. Entry is free.

Ao Phang-Nga National Park

Established in 1981 and covering an area of 400 sq km, Ao Phang-Nga National Park is noted for its classic karst scenery, created by fault movement on the mainland which pushed massive limestone blocks into geometric patterns. As these blocks extend southward into Ao Phang-Nga, they form over 40 islands with huge vertical cliffs. Over 80% of the area within the park boundaries is covered by the Andaman Sea. The bay itself is composed of large and small tidal channels which originally connected with the mainland river system. The main tidal channels – Khlong Ko Panyi, Khlong Phang-Nga, Khlong Bang Toi and Khlong Bo Saen – run through vast mangroves in a north-south direction and today are used by fisherfolk and island inhabitants as aquatic highways. This is the largest remaining primary mangrove forest in Thailand.

The biggest tourist destination in the park is so-called 'James Bond Island', known to the Thais as **Ko Phing Kan** (Leaning on Itself Island). Once used as a location setting for the James Bond flick *The Man with the Golden Gun*, the island is now given over to souvenir vendors hawking all manner of coral and shells that should have stayed in the sea, along with butterflies, scorpions and spiders encased in plastic – not exactly the stuff to inspire confidence in Thailand's national park system. The Thai name for the island refers to a flat limestone cliff that appears to have tumbled sideways to lean on a similar rock face in the centre of the island. Off one side of the island in a shallow bay stands a tall slender limestone formation that looks like a big rock spike that fell from the sky. There are a couple of caves you can walk through on the island, and a couple of small sand beaches, often littered with rubbish from tourist boats. About the only positive development recently has been the addition of a concrete pier so that tourist boats don't have to moor directly on the island's beaches. Of course that hasn't stopped the boat operators from doing so when the water level is high and the pier is crowded with other boats.

Flora & Fauna Two types of forest, limestone scrub and true evergreen forest, predominate in the park. The marine limestone environment favours a long list of reptiles including the Bengal monitor, flying lizard, banded sea snake, dogface water snake, shore pit viper and Malayan pit viper. Keep an eye out for the two-banded or water monitor *(Varanus salvator)*, which looks like a crocodile when seen swimming in the mangrove swamp and can measure up to 2.2m in length (only slightly smaller than the Komodo dragon, the largest lizard in the Varanidae family). Like its Komodo cousin, the water monitor (called *hîa* by the Thais, who generally fear or hate the lizard) is a carnivore that prefers to feed on carrion but occasionally preys on live animals. Amphibians in the Ao Phang-Nga area include marsh frog, common bush frog and crab-eating frog. Avian residents of note are the helmeted hornbill (the largest of Thailand's 12 hornbill species, with a body length of up to 127cm), the edible-nest swiftlet *(Aerodramus fuciphagus)*, white-bellied sea eagle, osprey and Pacific reef egret.

Over 200 species of mammals reside in the mangrove forests and on some of the larger islands, including the white-handed gibbon, crab-eating macaque, serow and dusky langur.

Rock Art Many of the limestone islands in Ao Phang-Nga feature prehistoric rock art painted or carved onto the walls and ceilings of caves, rock shelters, cliffs and rock massifs. In particular you can see rock art on Khao Khian, Ko Panyi, Ko Raya, Tham Nak and Ko Phra At Thao. The images contain scenes of human figures, fish, crab, shrimp, bats, birds and elephants, as well as boats and fishing equipment – it's obvious this was some sort of communal effort tied to the all-important harvesting of sustenance from the sea. Some drawings also contain rows of lines thought to be some sort of cabbalistic writing. The rock paintings don't fall on any one plane of reference, ie may be placed right-side up, upside-down or sideways. Most of the paintings are monocoloured, while some have been repeatedly traced over in orange-yellow, blue, grey and black.

Places to Stay & Eat National park *bungalows (☎ 076-412188)* are available for

rent next to the visitors centre parking lot for 400B to 750B a night but almost no one other than visiting park officers ever rents them. Camping is permitted in certain areas within park boundaries but you should ask permission at the visitors centre first.

There's a small, clean restaurant in front of the visitors centre.

Getting There & Around To reach the park headquarters and pier for Ao Phang-Nga trips, take a songthaew going from Phang-Nga to Tha Dan (customs pier). If you're driving yourself, proceed 8km south-east of Phang-Nga on Hwy 4, then turn left onto Route 4144; you'll reach park headquarters after an additional 2km.

Boats can be hired to explore the bay from the *thâa reua naam thîaw* (tourist pier) opposite the visitors centre in Tha Dan. See Organised Tours for details.

Ko Panyi & Muslim Stilt Villages
This small island in the north-western part of Ao Phang-Nga is well known for its Muslim fishing village built almost entirely on stilts and nestled against a towering limestone cliff. The village appears very commercialised during the day when hordes of tourist boats invade to eat lunch at the village's many overpriced seafood restaurants and buy tacky souvenirs at the many stalls. Yet once the tourist boats depart, the village returns to its normal self.

The 200 households here – supporting perhaps a total of 2000 inhabitants – are said to descend from two seafaring Muslim families who arrived here from Java around 200 years ago. Ko Panyi's primary livelihood remains fishing, since only during the dry season do a significant number of tourists visit. In addition to a big green mosque, a health clinic and a school, you'll find a market filled with small shops selling clothes, toiletries, medicines and all the other usual staples seen in markets all over Thailand – except for beer, liquor or any other type of alcoholic beverage. Besides alcohol, two other things forbidden on the island are dogs and pigs. Houses mixed in with the shops vary from grubby little shacks to houses with fancy tile fronts and curtained windows. The people are generally quite friendly, especially if you can speak a little Thai. Village men often gather to gossip and watch the sunset on the west side of the village near the mosque.

There's a pay phone at the island's northern pier.

If you fancy a look at similar but less well known Muslim stilt villages in Ao Phang-Nga, take a boat to one of these villages in the huge mangrove forests at the north end of the bay: **Ban Ling** (Monkey village), **Ban Mai Phai** (Bamboo village) or **Ban Sam Chong** (Three Channels Island). All are smaller and less touristed than Ko Panyi.

Places to Stay & Eat Very *basic accommodation* with shared toilet and scoop shower is available at a tattered set of thin-walled rooms near the village's northern pier. Figure on 100B per night for two. Although the rooms aren't much, they do have windows that catch sea breezes. Some of the overnight tours from Phang-Nga use these rooms; if they're full you should be able to find a room in a village home for about the same price, or less. Ask at one of the restaurants.

Along with the more expensive seafood restaurants built out over the sea in front of the village (which are generally open for lunch only), there are some smaller *cafes* and *restaurants* along the interior alleys where locals eat. *Khâo yam* (southern Thai rice salad) and *roti* are available in the morning. The villagers raise grouper in floating cages next to the island, selling them to the island restaurants and on the mainland. A local culinary speciality is *khanōm pâo lâng*, a savoury made with black sticky rice, shrimp, coconut, black pepper and chilli steamed in a banana leaf – a breakfast favourite.

Getting There & Away Most visitors to the island arrive on tour boats, whether for brief day visits or overnight stays. You can also take a regular ferry from Tha Dan for

just 20B per person. These leave frequently from dawn to dusk, arriving and departing from the village's northern pier (the southern pier is mostly reserved for tourist boats). Or you can charter a longtail boat from the pier opposite Phang-Nga National Park Headquarters in Tha Dan direct to the island for 300B. During heavy monsoon weather boat service may be cancelled.

Ko Yao

Ko Yao Yai and Ko Yao Noi ('Big Long Island' and 'Little Long Island'), directly south of the provincial capital, in the middle of the bay between the provinces of Phuket and Krabi, together encompass 137 sq km of forest, beaches and rocky headlands with views of surrounding karst formations characteristic of Ao Phang-Nga. In spite of being smaller, Ko Yao Noi is the main population centre of the two, although even there fishing, coconuts and a little tourism sustains a relatively small group of year-rounders. **Hat Paa Sai** and **Hat Tha Khao**, both on Yao Noi, are the best beaches. Bring along a mountain bike if you want to explore the island's numerous dirt trails.

Ta Khai, the largest settlement on the island, is a subdistrict government seat and the source of minimal supplies. Boat trips to neighbouring islands, bird-nest caves and sea gypsy funeral caves are possible. **Ko Bele**, a small island east of the twin Ko Yao, features a large tidal lagoon, three white-sand beaches, and easily accessible caves and coral reefs around the entire island. A longtail boat from Ko Yao Noi or from Ao Nang in Krabi can be chartered for around 600B to 1000B per day depending on the size of the boat.

Places to Stay On Ko Yao Noi, the only island with regular visitor lodgings, *Sabai Corner* is an environmentally sensitive resort associated with SeaCanoe Thailand (see the earlier Ao Phang-Nga Paddling section for contact details), which arranges kayak trips here – self-paddles or guided trips – from November to August. Thatch-and-wood bungalows cost 300B to 700B a night.

Long Beach Village (☎/*fax 01-211 8647, Phuket 076-381623*) has large wood-and-thatch bungalows for 500B to 1500B a night.

Getting There & Away Although both islands fall within the Phang-Nga Province boundaries, the easiest places to find boat transport to Ko Yao Noi are Phuket (Phuket Province), Ao Leuk and Ao Nang (both in Krabi Province).

In Phuket city, catch a songthaew from in front of the Th Ranong market to Bang Rong on Ao Paw for 25B. From the public pier at Ao Paw there are usually two mail boats a day to Ko Yao Noi, one between 8 and 9 am and another around noon. The fare is 45B per passenger and the trip takes about one hour. Between departures or after hours you can charter a longtail boat out to the island for 600B one way. Coming back to Phuket from Yao Noi, there's one boat that leaves between 6 and 7 am.

You can also get boats from Ko Yao Noi north-east across Ao Phang-Nga to Tha Laem Sak at Ao Leuk, Krabi. These cost around 40B on regular ferries, or 600B to charter. From Krabi's Ao Nang you can charter a boat for about 600B to 1000B each way. Shared with five or six friends, this doesn't have to dent your budget much.

If you want to take a look around Ko Yao Yai, which is similar to Ko Yao Noi though more sparsely populated, catch a shuttle boat from Ko Yao Noi's Tha Manaw pier (20B each way), or charter a longtail boat or kayak from Sabai Corner.

Phuket Province

Dubbed 'Pearl of the South' by the tourist industry, Phuket (pronounced 'Poo-get') is the country's largest, most populous and most visited island, a whirl of colour and cosmopolitanism that's a province unto itself. The coastal terrain of the 810 sq km island encompasses broad, sandy bays, rocky peninsulas, limestone cliffs, forested hills and tropical vegetation while the interior

has rice paddies, rubber, cashew nut, cacao, pineapple and coconut plantations, as well as Phuket's last bit of island rainforest. Although Phuket is connected to Phang-Nga Province by a causeway, most visitors arrive via the island's international airport located near its northern tip.

Formerly called Ko Thalang and before that Junk Ceylon (an English corruption of the Malay 'Tanjung Salang' or Cape Salang), Phuket has a culture all of its own, combining Chinese and Portuguese influences with that of the southern Thais, and the chao náam, a seafaring, semi-nomadic group that depend on fishing and boat building for their livelihood. Only about 35% of the island's population are Thai Muslims; even so, mosques slightly outnumber Buddhist wáts, 38 to 37. This is Thailand's wealthiest province, and since the late 80s tourism has eclipsed tin mining as the island's largest source of income.

There is a lot to do in Phuket, and consequently, a lot to spend your money on. There are also more tourists in Phuket than on any other Thai island, though most flock to three beaches on the south-west side – Patong, Karon and Kata. The beach towns themselves are quite built up, and have all the amenities and entertainment one could wish for. This is the area to visit if you're looking for a lively, action-filled vacation.

Beaches like Nai Han, near the southern tip, and Kamala, on the western coast, are relatively quiet, in spite of major tourist development at both, while Nai Thon, Nai Yang and Mai Khao to the north remain mostly untouched. In general the northern half of the island, both along the shore and in the interior, has not been swept up in the development wave, and thus offers quiet beach retreats and chances to explore rural inland areas.

Development on Phuket has been influenced by the fact that it is connected to the mainland by a bridge, and hence it receives much more vehicular traffic than any other island in the country. Phuket's high per-capita wealth also means there's plenty of money available for investment. A turning

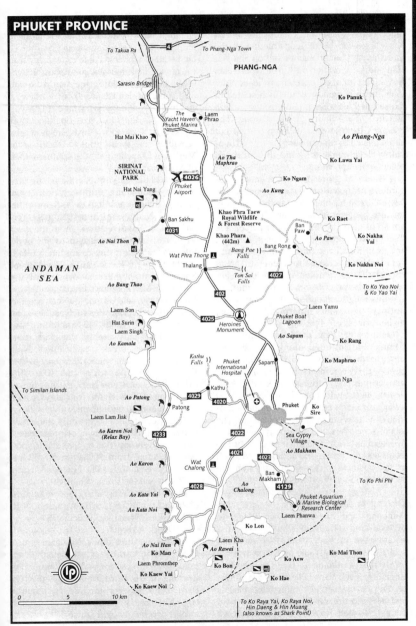

PHUKET PROVINCE

To Takua Pa

To Phang-Nga Town

PHANG-NGA

Sarasin Bridge

Ko Panuk

The Yacht Haven
Phuket Marina

Laem Phrao

Ao Phang-Nga

Hat Mai Khao

Ko Lawa Yai

Ao Tha Maphrao

SIRINAT NATIONAL PARK

Ko Ngam

Ao Kung

4026

Phuket Airport

Hat Nai Yang

Khao Phra Taew Royal Wildlife & Forest Reserve

Ko Raet

Ban Paw

Ko Nakha Yai

Ban Sakhu

4031

Khao Phara (442m) ▲

Ao Paw

Ao Nai Thon

Bang Pae Falls

Bang Rong

Ko Nakha Noi

ANDAMAN SEA

Wat Phra Thong

Thalang

Ton Sai Falls

4027

To Ko Yao Noi & Ko Yao Yai

402

Ao Bang Thao

Laem Yamu

Laem Son

4025

Heroines Monument

Phuket Boat Lagoon

Hat Surin

Laem Singh

Ao Sapam

Ao Kamala

Ko Rang

Kathu Falls

Phuket International Hospital

Ko Maphrao

Laem Nga

Ao Patong

4029

4020

Sapam

Kathu

Patong

Laem Lam Jiak

Ao Karon Noi (Relax Bay)

4233

Phuket

Ko Sire

To Similan Islands

4022

Ao Karon

4021

Sea Gypsy Village

Ao Makham

Wat Chalong

4023

Ao Kata Yai

4028

Ban Makham

4129

To Ko Phi Phi

Ao Chalong

Ao Kata Noi

Phuket Aquarium & Marine Biological Research Center

Laem Phanwa

Ao Nai Han

Ko Lon

Ko Man

Laem Kha

Ao Rawai

Laem Phromthep

Ko Bon

Ko Mai Thon

Ko Kaew Yai

Ko Aew

Ko Kaew Noi

Ko Hae

0   5   10 km

To Ko Raya Yai, Ko Raya Noi, Hin Daeng & Hin Muang (also known as Shark Point)

point was reached when a Club Méditer-ranée (Club Med) was established at Hat Kata, followed by the construction of the more lavish Phuket Yacht Club on Hat Nai Han and Le Meridien on Karon Noi (Relax Bay). This marked an end to the decade-long cheap bungalow era, which started in the early 1970s when a 10B guesthouse was attached to a laundry on Hat Patong. The cheapies have long since been bought out and replaced by all manner of hotel and bun-galow developments, some ill-conceived, others quite appealing.

The era of going for quick money re-gardless of the cost to the environment has passed. Most beach resorts are now looking towards long-term, sustainable practices – not all of them, but a far greater percentage than on Ko Samui, Ko Pha-Ngan, Ko Tao, and even Ko Chang (though the total num-ber of beach places on the latter is still small enough that the total impact of negative en-vironmental practices is so far minimal). For this long-term outlook, the Phuket vis-itor pays a premium in terms of somewhat higher prices.

On the other hand the general growth of commercialism seen along the island's main roads detracts from the island's ap-peal – there seems to be a snake farm, bungee-jumping operation, gaudy bill-board, half-built condo project, travel agency or tacky craft shop every half kilo-metre in the southern half of the island. The island's beaches and relatively unspoiled northern interior remain its main attrac-tions, and the provincial authorities as well as the business sector should do more to recognise and support this.

Diving & Snorkelling

Although there are many, many places to dive around Thailand, Phuket is indis-putably the primary centre for the Thai scuba-diving industry and one of the world's top 10 dive destinations. The island itself is ringed by good to excellent dive sites, in-cluding several small, uninhabited islands and islets to the south and east with hard corals – Ko Hae, Ko Raya (Noi and Yai), Ko Yao (Noi and Yai), Hin Daeng and Hin Muang (Shark Point; a habitat for harmless leopard sharks) at the southern tip of the is-land – all of which make favourite day trips for novice and intermediate divers. Excur-sions farther afield to the world-famous Surin and Similan Islands to the north-west, and to the Ao Phang-Nga islands to the east are also for the most part operated from Phuket. At least four outfits are now also providing live-aboard trips to islands in the Mergui Archipelago off the southern coast of Myanmar.

Most Phuket diving operations are cen-tred at Hat Patong, with a sprinkling of branch offices in Phuket and on other beaches. Many companies stagger regu-larly scheduled dives throughout the week so that different dive groups don't bump into one another; for example, Santana might go to Ko Raya Yai on Monday and Shark Point on Tuesday while Calypso might do Shark Point Monday and Raya Yai Tuesday, and so on. Typical one day dive trips to nearby sites such as these cost around 1500B to 1750B, including two dives, tanks and weights, transport, dive-master service, breakfast and lunch. Non-divers – including snorkellers – can often join such dive trips for around 30 to 50% off. PADI open-water certification courses cost around 8500B for four days of in-struction and all equipment.

A few companies – generally the larger, better established ones – offer extended three to seven-day trips on live-aboard dive boats, ranging from 3000B to 5000B per day per person, to Ko Phi-Phi, Ko Similan, Ko Surin and the Burma Banks.

Most dive shops also rent regulators (250B a day), BCDs (250B), wetsuits (150B) and masks, fins and snorkels (200B).

In Depth Adventures (see list below) of-fers a unique three-day certificated course (US$450) in coral reef ecology that ap-proaches reef systems as living communi-ties based on town or village models. Participants may enrol in one-day modules (US$150 per day) or take all three modules as part of a live-aboard cruise.

Phuket boasts 46 dive companies. Some of the more reputable ones are:

Aqua Divers
  (☎ 076-327006, fax 327338)
  Pearl Village Resort
Calypso Divers
  (☎/fax 076-330869)
  Hat Kata-Karon
Dive Inn
  (☎ 076-341927, fax 342453, email
  dive@phuket.com)
  Hat Patong
Fantasea Divers
  (☎ 076-340088, fax 340309, email info@
  fantasea.net)
  Hat Patong
In Depth Adventures
  (☎ 076-383105, fax 383106, email
  indepth@loxinfo.co.th)
  Ao Chalong
Neptune Diving
  (☎/fax 076-340585, email
  neptun@loxinfo.co.th)
  Hat Patong
Santana
  (☎ 076-294220, fax 340360, email
  diving@santanaphuket.com)
  Hat Patong
Sea Bees Diving Club
  (☎/fax 076-381765, email
  seabees@loxinfo.co.th)
  Ao Chalong
Siam Diving Center
  (☎/fax 076-330608)
  Hat Karon
South East Asia Liveaboards
  (☎ 076-340406, fax 340586)
  Hat Patong

There are many others in Phuket that are equally good, but it's a good idea to make sure that the dive shop you pick is affiliated with Dive Safe Asia's Sub-aquatic Safety Service (SSS; ☎ 076-342518, 01-606 1869, fax 342519) which operates a hyperbaric (decompression) chamber in Patong. This means the dive shop is insured should one of their customers need to use the chamber in an emergency. If the operation that you choose is not a member, and should you need Dive Safe Asia's services, you may end up footing the bill (around US$3000).

Snorkelling is best along Phuket's west coast, particularly at rock headlands between beaches. Mask, snorkel and fins can be rented for around 250B a day. As with scuba diving, you'll find better snorkelling – greater visibility and variety of marine life – along the shores of small outlying islands like Ko Hae, Ko Yao and Ko Raya.

As elsewhere in the Andaman Sea, the best diving months are December to May when the weather is good and the sea is at its clearest (and boat trips are much safer).

Diving Supplies Sea Sports (☎ 076-381065) at 1/11-12 Th Chao Fa, Phuket, carries all manner of water-sport equipment and supplies, along with canoes and kayaks. Dive Supply (☎ 076-286998, email dsupply@loxinfo.co.th) at 33/92 Th Patak on Hat Karon claims to stock the largest variety of dive supplies and equipment in Phuket. Hotwave (☎ 076-280787, fax 280788, email info@hotwavephuket.com) specialises in making custom neoprene wetsuits in 24 hours.

Yachting

Phuket is one of South-East Asia's main yacht destinations and you'll find all manner of craft anchored along its shores, from 80-year-old wooden sloops that look like they can barely stay afloat, to the latest in high-tech world motor cruisers. Marina-style facilities with year-round anchorage are available at two locations on the protected east side of the island: Phuket Boat Lagoon (☎ 076-239055, fax 239056) at Ao Sapam, about 20km north of Phuket town on the east shore; and The Yacht Haven Phuket Marina (☎ 076-206022/5, fax 206026) at Laem Phrao on the eastern side of the northern tip.

Phuket Boat Lagoon offers an enclosed marina with tidal channel access, serviced pontoon berths, 60 and 120-tonne travel lifts, hard-stand area, plus a resort hotel, laundry, coffee shop, fuel, water, repairs and maintenance services. The Yacht Haven boasts 130 berths, condominiums, immigration facilities, restaurants and a health spa.

In season (December to April) Ao Nai Han and Ao Chalong are popular anchorages with more limited services. At the latter, berthing fees run 164B to 272B per metre paid weekly, or 590B to 1000B per metre per month.

Port clearance is rather complicated; both marinas will take care of the paperwork (for a fee of course), if notified of your arrival in advance.

You may be able to travel by yacht between Phuket and Penang (Malaysia) as a paying passenger or as crew. Ask around at these marinas or at Hat Patong to see what's available. You may also find yachts going farther afield, particularly to Sri Lanka. December and early January are the best months to look for them. The crossing takes about 10 to 15 days.

Ao Chalong Yacht Club (☎ 076-381914, fax 381934) holds monthly races for members. Other Phuket residents and visitors to Phuket are also welcome to participate; call for details.

Parts & Service The Yacht Haven and Phuket Boat Lagoon offer routine repair and maintenance services, along with limited parts and supplies. In Ao Chalong there are several smaller marine repair/supply shops. If you need sails, Rolly Tasker Sailmakers (☎ 076-280347, fax 280348, email rolly@sun.phuket.ksc.co.th) claims to have the lowest sail prices in Asia; riggings, spars and hardware are also available.

Charters For information on yacht charters – both bareboat and crewed – yacht sales and yacht deliveries, contact the following:

Asia Yachting
  (☎ 076-381615, 01-941 5660)
  Ao Chalong
Big A Yachting Swann 55
  (☎ 076-381934, fax 381934)
  Ao Chalong
Phuket Boating Association
  (☎/fax 076-381322)
  Phuket Boat Lagoon
South East Asia Liveaboards
  (☎ 076-340406, fax 340586)
  Hat Patong

Sunsail Yacht Charters
  (☎ 076-239057, fax 238940, email sunthai@ phuket.loxinfo.co.th)
  Phuket Boat Lagoon
Thai Marine Leisure
  (☎ 076-239111, fax 238974, email tml@ loxinfo.co.th)
  Hat Patong

Charters aboard 32 to 44-foot yachts start at 900B a day, while larger ones (39 to 85-foot yachts) start at 14,000B a day. Discounts of around 33% are available June to October. Day trips usually include boat, crew, lunch and soft drinks, plus snorkelling and fishing gear.

Paddling

Several companies based in Phuket offer inflatable canoe tours of scenic Ao Phang-Nga; see the Ao Phang-Nga section earlier in this chapter for details.

Cycling

Tropical Trails (☎/fax 076-263239) offers fully supported half-day and full-day 'cycle safaris' around Phuket as well as on neighbouring Ko Yao Noi. Half-day trips range from 975B to 1350B; the latter including elephant and walking treks as well. Full-day rides cost 1650B. Discounts of around 30% are available for children under 12. Rates include hotel pickup (plus boat transport for Ko Yao), van support, mountain bike and equipment, a guided hike, snorkelling, 'cultural break stops', lunch, insurance and a Thai massage. The owners are also looking at developing multi-day cycling tours of neighbouring areas like Phang-Nga and Krabi.

Phuket Mountain Bike Club (☎ 076-280116) does mountain bike tours and rentals for half and full-day trips at similar rates.

Soft Adventure Treks

Siam Safari (☎ 076-280116) and Adventure Safaris (☎ 076-340800) combine 4WD tours of the island's interior with short elephant rides and short hikes for around

1850B a day. Half-day trips are also available, although the difference in price is not that great.

PHUKET
• pop 61,800

Centuries before Phuket began attracting sand-and-sea hedonists it was an important trade centre for Arab, Indian, Malay, Chinese and Portuguese traders who exchanged goods from the world at large for tin and rubber. Francis Light, the British colonialist who made Penang the first of the British Straits Settlements, married a native of Phuket and tried unsuccessfully to pull this island into the colonial fold as well. Although this polyglot, multicultural heritage has all but disappeared from most of the island, a few vestiges can be seen and experienced in the province's *amphoe meuang* (provincial capital), Phuket.

In the older town centre you'll see plenty of Sino-Portuguese architecture, characterised by ornate two storey Chinese *haang tháew* or 'row companies' fronted by Romanesque arched porticoes with 'five-foot ways' that were a 19th century tradition in Malaysia, Singapore, Macau and Hainan Island (China). For a time it seemed this wonderful old architecture was all being torn down and replaced with modern structures but in recent years a preservation ethic has taken hold.

Information

Tourist Office & Tourist Police The TAT office (☎ 076-212213, 211036) at 73-75 Th Phuket has maps, information brochures, a list of standard songthaew fares out to the various beaches, and also the recommended charter costs for a vehicle. The TAT office is open daily from 8.30 am to 4.30 pm. The Tourist Police can be reached at ☎ 1699.

Maps Although it might not look like it at first glance, the advertisement-plastered A-O-A Phuket Map is probably the best one to have if you're going to do any driving around. It's more accurate than the other freebies available, and it has all the route numbers on it. The free Thaiways map isn't very good for island navigation, though the inset maps for Patong and Karon-Kata are better than the A-O-A's. You can pick up both maps at the TAT office as well as other locations around the island.

Periplus Editions also puts out a good map of the island, capital and beaches.

Money Several banks along Th Takua Pa, Th Phang-Nga and Th Phuket offer exchange services and ATMs. Bank of Asia, opposite the TAT office on Th Phuket, has an exchange window open from 8.30 am until 8 pm daily.

Post The main post office, housed in a new building next to the smaller, older architectural gem on Th Montri, is open Monday to Friday from 8.30 am to 4.30 pm, Saturday, Sunday and holidays 9 am to noon.

Mail Boxes Etc (☎ 076-256409, fax 256411) has a branch at 168/2 Th Phuket, almost opposite The Books. MBE rents private mail boxes, sells packaging and mailing materials and offers laminating, binding, passport photo and business card services.

Two courier services in town are DHL World Wide Express (☎ 076-220250) at the Phuket Merlin Hotel and UPS (☎ 076-218719) at 9/44 Th Chao Fa.

Telephone The Phuket Telecommunications Centre, on Th Phang-Nga, offers Home Direct service and is open daily 8 am to midnight.

Email & Internet Access To get online in Phuket, try The Tavern (☎ 076-223569, email creative@phuket.ksc.co.th) at 64/3-4 Th Rasada.

Internet Resources Phuket Island Access (www.phuket.com) offers a sophisticated compendium of many kinds of information, including accommodation on the island. Phuket Net is an Internet service (email info@phuket.net or www.phuket.net) that provides forums for tourism and business-oriented exchange, with limited listings.

The *Phuket Gazette* (see Newspapers & Magazines elsewhere in this section) posts articles and updated info along with its searchable *Gazette Guide* on Phuket Gazette Online (www.phuketgazette.net). Phuket Travellers Net (www.trv.net) also carries info on Phuket, though not very much.

Bookshops Phuket has one very good bookshop, The Books at 53-55 Th Phuket, near the TAT office. The selection includes English-language magazines, guidebooks and novels. There's also a branch at 198/2 Th Rat Uthit in Patong.

Newspapers & Magazines The daily English-language *Phuket Gazette* publishes lots of info on activities, events, dining and entertainment in town as well as around the island. The same publisher issues *Gazette Guide*, a 244-page listing of services and businesses on the island. A weekly English language newspaper called *Siangtai Times* is also available. There are also the usual tourist freebies around, such as *South*. *Phuket* magazine, published nine times yearly, is an in-flight-style magazine that relies heavily on advertising but still manages to publish an interesting article about Phuket once in awhile.

Although the name may be off-putting, the small-format *Heritage Phuket Holiday Guide* (120B) contains lots of solid info and insider's tips on accommodation, transport and other travel practicalities on the island. It also contains the most unbiased sightseeing information of any of the glossies available, probably because it relies less on advertising.

Medical Services Western doctors rate the Phuket International Hospital (☎ 076-249400, emergency 210935), Airport Bypass Rd, north west of the city, as the best on the island. Bangkok Phuket Hospital (☎ 076-254421), Th Yongyok Uthit, is reportedly the favourite with the locals, and is

run by Bangkok General Hospital. Both hospitals are equipped with modern facilities, emergency rooms and outpatient clinics.

Feedback we've received about these hospitals indicates that, although they're well equipped, better treatment is available in Bangkok.

Other hospitals on the island include:

Patong/Kathu Hospital
  (☎ 076-340444) Th Sawatdirak, Patong
Phya Thai Phuket Hospital
  (☎ 076-252603) 28/36-37 Th Si Sena, Phuket
Wachira Hospital
  (☎ 076-211114) Th Yaowarat, Phuket

Things to See & Do

If you want to see historic **Sino-Portuguese architecture**, your best bets are along Thalang, Deebuk, Yaowarat, Ranong, Phang-Nga, Rasada and Krabi streets. The most magnificent examples in town are the Standard Chartered Bank – Thailand's oldest foreign bank – on Th Phang-Nga and the THAI office on Th Ranong, but there are lots of more modest buildings of interest along these streets. The best restored residences are found along Th Deebuk and Th Thalang.

Phuket's main **market** on Th Ranong is fun to wander through and is a good place to buy Thai and Malay sarongs as well baggy fisherman pants. A few old **Chinese temples** can be found in this area. Most are standard issue. One that's a little bit different is the **Shrine of the Serene Light**, or as it's known in Thai Saan Jao Sang Tham ('shrine of dharmic light'), which is tucked away at the end of a 50m alley right next to the Bangkok Bank of Commerce on Th Phang-Nga. There's a little garden in front of the shrine, which is a very calm and peaceful spot with some interesting pieces of temple art. Said to be 100 to 200 years old, the shrine was only restored three years ago. It's open 8.30 am to noon and 1.30 to 5.30 pm daily.

Walk up **Khao Rang**, sometimes called Phuket Hill, north-west of town, for a nice view of the city, jungle and sea. If, as many people say, Phuket is a corruption of the

Malay word *bukit* (hill), then this is probably its namesake.

Language Courses
A branch of AUA (☎ 076-217756) at Phuket Community College, Th Phuket, Saphan Hin, near the waterfront, offers Thai-language instruction.

Vegetarian Festival
The Vegetarian Festival, Phuket's most important festival, usually takes place during late September or October.

The TAT office in Phuket prints a helpful schedule of events for the Vegetarian Festival. If you plan to attend the street processions, consider bringing earplugs to make the noise of the firecrackers more tolerable. See the 'Vegetarian Festival' boxed text for more information.

Places to Stay – Budget
Near the centre of town, and close to the songthaew terminal for most outlying beaches, is *On On Hotel (☎ 076-211154, 19 Th Phang-Nga)*. This hotel has real character with its old Sino-Portuguese architecture (established 1929), though the rooms are basically just four walls and a bed. Rates are 100B for a single with ceiling fan and shared facilities, 150/220B single/double with fan and private bath, 250/360B with air-con. The simple *Pengman (☎ 076-211486, ext 169, 69 Th Phang-Nga)*, above a Chinese restaurant nearby, costs 100B for basic but quite clean singles/doubles with ceiling fan and shared bathroom.

On Soi Rommani, in a row of old unrestored Sino-Portuguese shophouses, two storey *Wibunsin Hotel* (no English sign) charges 100B per night for very basic rooms. Unless you really want to stay on Soi Rommani, the Pengman is a better deal.

Thara Hotel (☎ 076-216208) on Th Thepkasatri costs 140B with fan and bath. The nearby *Suksabai Hotel (☎ 076-212287)*, on Soi Nam Pheung is a bit better at 150B to 200B for similar but cleaner rooms. The dark *Siam Hotel (☎ 076-224543, 13-15 Th Phuket)* is basically a

brothel with adequate rooms with fan and bath for 150/200B one bed/two beds.

Three storey *Talang Guest House (☎ 076-214225, 37 Th Thalang)*, in a classic, tidy shophouse in the old city centre, rents large rooms with one bed and fan for 250B, two beds for 300B. Air-con rooms with three or four beds cost 400B. From May to October a discount of 30% is available. If you want a good street view, ask for No 31, a fan room on the third floor.

Wasana Guest House (☎ 076-211754, 213385, 159 Th Ranong), next to the Th Ranong market, has clean rooms for 180B with fan and bath or 280B with air-con.

Montri Hotel (☎ 076-212936, fax 232097, 12/6 Th Montri), once one of Phuket's nicer hotels, has descended into a zone somewhere between budget and midrange, with rather ordinary rooms costing 210B with fan, 330B to 490B with air-con.

Thai Inter Hotel (☎ 076-220275, 22 Th Phunphon) is convenient to the airport shuttle drop-off in town if you've just flown into Phuket or are trying to catch an early morning flight. Fan rooms cost 280B, air-con 390B, both with private bath.

Places to Stay – Mid-Range
Thavorn (Thawon) Hotel (☎ 076-211333, 74 Th Rasada) is a huge place consisting of an original, less expensive wing at the back and a flashier place up front. In the back wing, large rooms with ceiling fan and private bath cost 230/280B single/double, while in the front building, larger rooms come with TV, air-con, hot water and carpet and cost 550B to 650B. The best thing about the Thavorn is the lobby, which is filled with antiques and historic photos of Phuket.

City Hotel (☎ 076-216910), at the corner of Th Thepkasatri and Th Deebuk, offers decent rooms with air-con, TV, phone, bath and carpet for 545/605B single/double, up to 908B for a suite.

The friendly, recently refurbished and well located *Imperial Hotel (☎ 076-212311, fax 212894, 51 Th Phuket)* has clean, comfortable rooms for 650B with air-con, TV, hair dryer and other amenities.

Vegetarian Festival

The Vegetarian Festival, Phuket's most important festival, takes place during the first nine days of the ninth lunar month of the Chinese calendar – usually late September or October.

Basically, the festival celebrates the beginning of the month of 'Taoist Lent', when devout Chinese abstain from eating all meat and meat products. In Phuket, the festival activities are centred around five Chinese temples, with the Jui Tui temple on Th Ranong the most important, followed by Bang Niaw and Sui Boon Tong temples. Events are also celebrated at temples in the nearby towns of Kathu (where the festival originated) and Ban Tha Reua.

The TAT office in Phuket prints a helpful schedule of events for the Vegetarian Festival each year. The festival also takes place in Trang, Krabi and other Southern Thai towns.

Besides abstention from meat, the Vegetarian Festival involves various processions, temple offerings and cultural performances, and culminates with incredible acts of self-mortification – walking on hot coals, climbing knife-blade ladders, piercing the skin with sharp objects and so on. Shop owners along Phuket's central streets set up altars in front of their shopfronts offering nine tiny cups of tea, incense, fruit, candles and flowers to the nine emperor gods invoked by the festival. Those participating as mediums bring the nine deities to earth for the festival by entering into a trance state and piercing their cheeks with all manner of objects – sharpened tree branches (with leaves still attached), spears, slide trombones, daggers; some even hack their tongues continuously with saw or axe blades. During the street processions these mediums stop at the shopfront altars, where they pick up the offered fruit and either add it to the objects piercing their cheeks or pass it on to bystanders as a blessing. They also drink one of the nine cups of tea and grab some flowers to stick in their waistbands. The shop owners and their families stand by with their hands together in a *wâi* gesture, out of respect for the mediums and the deities by whom they are temporarily possessed.

The entire atmosphere is one of religious frenzy, with deafening firecrackers, ritual dancing, and bloody shirt fronts. Oddly enough, there is no record of this kind of activity associated with Taoist Lent in China. Some historians assume that the Chinese here were somehow influenced by the Hindu festival of Thaipusam in nearby Malaysia, which features similar acts of self-mortification. The local Chinese claim, however, that the festival was started by a theatre troupe from China that stopped off in nearby Kathu around 150 years ago. The story goes that the troupe was struck seriously ill because the members had failed to propitiate the nine emperor gods of Taoism. The nine day penance they performed included self-piercing, meditation and a strict vegetarian diet.

Joe Cummings

Sinthavee Hotel (☎ 076-211186, fax 211400, 85-91 Th Phang-Nga) offers reasonable air-conditioned singles/doubles for 471/589B or 850/950B for deluxe rooms. All the rooms here come with carpet, hot bath and refrigerator (deluxe rooms also have TV and video); other facilities include a 24 hour coffee shop, business centre, spa and disco.

Places to Stay – Top End
Phuket Garden Hotel (☎ 076-216900/8) on Th Krung Thep charges 650B to 1200B for rooms with all the usual amenities, though it's location west of the town centre isn't a big recommendation.

Pearl Hotel (☎ 076-211044, 212911, 42 Th Montri) has rooms from 1600B, a rooftop restaurant, fitness centre, swimming pool

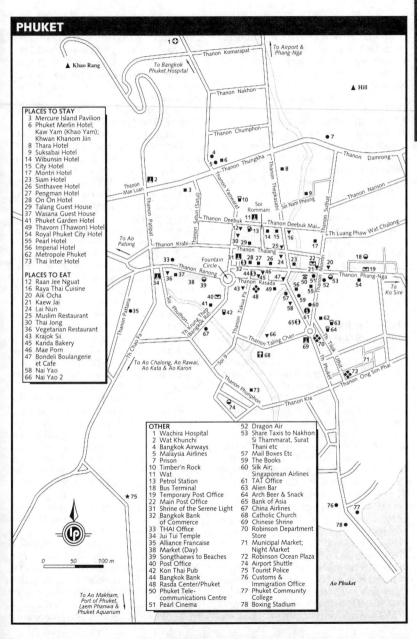

PHUKET

▲ Khao Rang

To Bangkok
Phuket Hospital

Thanon Komarapat

To Airport &
Phang-Nga

Thanon Nakhon

▲ Hill

Thanon Chumphon

PLACES TO STAY
3 Mercure Island Pavilion
6 Phuket Merlin Hotel;
   Kaw Yam (Khao Yam);
   Khwan Khanom Jiin
8 Thara Hotel
9 Suksabai Hotel
14 Wibunsin Hotel
15 City Hotel
17 Montri Hotel
23 Siam Hotel
26 Sinthavee Hotel
27 Pengman Hotel
28 On On Hotel
29 Talang Guest House
37 Wasana Guest House
41 Phuket Garden Hotel
49 Thavorn (Thawon) Hotel
54 Royal Phuket City Hotel
55 Pearl Hotel
56 Imperial Hotel
62 Metropole Phuket
73 Thai Inter Hotel

PLACES TO EAT
12 Raan Jee Nguat
16 Raya Thai Cuisine
21 Aik Ocha
21 Kaew Jai
24 Lai Nun
25 Muslim Restaurant
30 Thai Jong
36 Vegetarian Restaurant
43 Krajok Sii
45 Kanda Bakery
46 Mae Porn
47 Bondeli Boulangerie
   et Cafe
58 Nai Yao
66 Nai Yao 2

OTHER
1 Wachira Hospital
2 Wat Khunchi
4 Bangkok Airways
5 Malaysia Airlines
7 Prison
10 Timber'n Rock
11 Wat
13 Petrol Station
18 Bus Terminal
19 Temporary Post Office
22 Main Post Office
31 Shrine of the Serene Light
32 Bangkok Bank
   of Commerce
33 THAI Office
34 Jui Tui Temple
35 Alliance Francaise
38 Market (Day)
39 Songthaews to Beaches
40 Post Office
42 Kon Thai Pub
44 Bangkok Bank
48 Rasda Center/Phuket
50 Phuket Tele-
   communications Centre
51 Pearl Cinema
52 Dragon Air
53 Share Taxis to Nakhon
   Si Thammarat, Surat
   Thani etc
57 Mail Boxes Etc
59 The Books
60 Silk Air;
   Singaporean Airlines
61 TAT Office
63 Alien Bar
64 Arch Beer & Snack
65 Bank of Asia
67 China Airlines
68 Catholic Church
69 Chinese Shrine
70 Robinson Department
   Store
71 Municipal Market;
   Night Market
72 Robinson Ocean Plaza
74 Airport Shuttle
75 Tourist Police
76 Customs &
   Immigration Office
77 Phuket Community
   College
78 Boxing Stadium

Thanon Thungkha
Thanon Thepkasatti
Thanon Damrong
Thanon Narison
Thanon Suthat
Th Luang Phaw Wat Chalong

Thanon Mae Luan
Thanon Patipat
Thanon Yaowarat
Soi Rommani
Thanon Deebuk
Thanon Deebuk Mai
Thanon Satun (Satul)
Thanon Krabi
Thanon Thalang
To Ao Patong
Soi Nam Pheung

Fountain Circle
Thanon Ranong
Thanon Rasada
Thanon Phang-Nga
Thanon Takua Pa
Soi Phuthon Thep (Bangkok Rd)
Th Krung Thep (Bangkok Rd)
Th Chao Fa
Thanon Pattana
Thanon Taling Chan
Thanon Phunphon
Thanon Kra
Thanon Ong Sim Phai
Th Phuket
Th Tilok
Uthit
Th Montri

To Ao Chalong, Ao Rawai,
Ao Kata & Ao Karon

To Ao Makham,
Port of Phuket,
Laem Phanwa &
Phuket Aquarium

To Ko Sire

Ao Phuket

★ 75

0 50 100 m

LP

and so on. *Phuket Merlin Hotel (☎ 076-212866, fax 216429, 158/1 Th Yaowarat)* has rooms for 1452B and more, and again there's a swimming pool and fitness centre.

One of the best located top-enders is the plush *Metropole Phuket (☎ 076-215050, fax 215990)*, right in the centre of things on Th Montri. 'Superior' rooms start at 2000B, deluxe from 3000B, American breakfast included. Facilities include two Chinese restaurants, a coffee shop, three bars, swimming pool, fitness centre, business centre and airport shuttle service. Another well located spot is *Mercure Island Pavilion (☎ 076-210444, fax 210458, 133 Th Satun)*, where spacious, well appointed rooms go for 824B to 1648B.

A short walk east of the Phuket Telecommunications Centre is the towering *Royal Phuket City Hotel (☎ 076-233333, fax 233335, email pktcity@ksc.co.th, 154 Th Phang-Nga)*, where state-of-the-art rooms start at 3509B, though discounts to 2106B are readily available.

Places to Eat

Town Centre If there's one thing the town of Phuket is known for, it's good food – even if you're staying at the beach it's worth a trip into the city to sample authentic, Phuket-style cooking (a blend of Thai, Malay and Straits Chinese influences). Meals in the city tend to cost at least 50% less (often many times less) than meals at the beach.

One long-running local institution is *Raan Jee Nguat*, a very humble, Phuket-style restaurant run by Hokkien Chinese, across the street from the now defunct Siam Cinema, on the corner of historic Th Yaowarat and Th Deebuk. Jee Nguat serves Phuket's most famous dish, delicious *khanŏm jiin náam yaa phukèt* – Chinese noodles in a pureed fish and curry sauce, Phuket style, with fresh cucumbers, long green beans and other fresh vegetables on the side – for under 20B. Also good are *khài plaa mòk*, a Phuket version of *hàw mòk* (eggs, fish and curry paste steamed in banana leaves), and the *kari mai fan*, similar to Malaysian laksa, but using rice noodles.

The curries are highly esteemed as well. Don't leave it too late, though; they open early in the morning but close around 2 pm. A few doors south of Jee Nguat on Th Yaowarat, *Thai Jong* (no roman-script sign) is a small Hokkien coffee shop serving Southern Thai food.

The inexpensive *coffee shop* below the Pengman Hotel specialises in seafood noodles and is very popular at lunchtime. *On On Cafe* beside the On On Hotel serves all kinds of rice dishes and curries at reasonable prices; it's open 7 am to 8 pm. Adjacent to the hotel's other side – all part of the same building – is *On On Ice Cream*, an air-con ice cream parlour.

Very popular with Thais and faràngs alike, and deservedly so, is the *Mae Porn*, a restaurant on the corner of Th Phang-Nga and Soi Pradit, close to the On On and Sinthavee hotels. There's an air-con room as well as outdoor tables. They sell curries, seafood, fruit shakes – you name it and Mae Porn has it – all at very reasonable prices.

Another popular spot in town is *Kanda Bakery* on Th Rasada, just south of the Bangkok Bank. It's open early in the morning with fresh-baked whole-wheat bread, baguettes, croissants, cakes and real brewed coffee; they also serve a variety of khâo tôm specialities any time of day.

The simple *Muslim restaurant* on the corner of Th Thepkasatri and Th Thalang is another good local discovery – look for the star and crescent. This friendly family-run place serves delicious and inexpensive *mát-saman kài* (chicken-potato curry), roti kaeng (flatbread and curry – in the morning only) and khâo mòk kài (usually gone by 1 pm). *Lai Nun* (no roman-script sign, look for sign with a red star) is a similar Muslim restaurant on the opposite side of Th Thalang, west of the intersection.

Fried rice and Thai pastry fans shouldn't miss *Kaew Jai (no roman-script sign; 151 Th Phang-Nga)* between Th Phuket and Th Montri. More basic than Kanda Bakery, this is the Thai idea of pastry heaven – especially the custard cake and cashew cake – even if the service is a bit surly. Among the highly varied fried rice dishes on hand are *khâo phàt náam phrík phăo* (fried rice with roasted chilli paste), *khâo phàt khreûang kaeng* (rice fried in curry paste) and *khâo phàt bai kà-phrao* (with holy basil), each with a choice of chicken, pork, crab, shrimp or squid. In the same vicinity on Th Phang-Nga are two or three other inexpensive Phuket-style *ráan khâo kaeng* (rice-and-curry shops), including the **Aik Ocha**; try the tasty cashew-nut curry.

Venerable *Nai Yao* is still hanging on in an old wooden building with a tin roof near the Honda dealer on Th Phuket. It features an excellent, inexpensive seafood menu (bilingual), cold beer and, at night, tables on the sidewalk. The house speciality is the unique and highly recommended *tôm yam hâeng* (dry tôm yam), which can be ordered with chicken, shrimp or squid. Open evenings only. *Nai Yao 2*, a second and larger branch, can be found on Th Taling Chan, opposite a Catholic church. Besides fresh seafood, Nai Yao 2 also offers Isaan dishes and khâo tôm; the place keeps *tôh rûng* (till dawn) hours, 5.30 pm to 5.30 am.

Another Phuket institution, perfect for an intimate night out, is *Krajok Sii* (☎ 076-217903), in an old shophouse on the western side of Th Takua Pa, just south of Th Phang-Nga on the west side of street. It's hard to spot as there's no roman-script sign; look for the coloured glass transom (the restaurant's name means 'coloured glass') over the door. There aren't more than a dozen tables in the tastefully decorated dining room, but it's worth waiting for a table as the kitchen specialises in home-made Phuket cuisine, including delicious *hàw mòk tháleh* (steamed seafood curry), green mango salad, shrimp toast and other delights. Krajok Sii recently raised its prices substantially, which has effectively turned away most of its Thai clientele and made it a nearly all-faràng restaurant. It remains to be seen whether this will gradually ruin the cuisine, which is often the case when a chef prepares food for faràng palates. It's open Tuesday to Sunday, form 6 pm to midnight only.

The tourist-oriented *Raya Thai Cuisine* (☎ 076-218155, 48/1 Th Deebuk Mai), on the corner of Th Thepkasatri, is yet another place that takes advantage of old Phuket architecture. Housed in a two storey Sino-Portuguese mansion, the high ceilings and tall windows provide lots of air flow and offer glimpses of the surrounding garden. The food is good, if a bit expensive by local standards.

A *vegetarian restaurant* on Th Ranong east of the garish Jui Tui Chinese temple serves good Chinese vegetarian food during daylight hours.

Kaw Yam (Khao Yam), on Th Thungkha in front of the Phuket Merlin, has a clean, middle-class, indoor-outdoor atmosphere enjoyed by local office workers for breakfast and lunch. The kitchen serves very well prepared khâo yam, the Southern Thai rice salad, as well as khanŏm jiin and many other Phuket specialities. Prices are low to moderate. Just as good for khanŏm jiin, but cheaper, is *Khwan Khanom Jiin* (no roman-script sign) next door.

There's a *KFC* in the Robinson Ocean Plaza off Th Ong Sim Phai towards the south end of town. Next door to the shopping complex is Phuket's municipal market. Around three sides of this market you'll find an inexpensive *night market*.

Khao Rang (Phuket Hill) *Thungkha Kafae* is an outdoor restaurant at the top of the hill with a very pleasant atmosphere and good food. Try the *tôm khàa kài* (chicken coconut soup) or *khài jiaw hãwy naang rom* (oyster omelette).

Ao Chalong Just past Wat Chalong (on the left past the five-road intersection) is *Kan Eang 1* (☎ 076-381212), a good fresh seafood place that used to sit on a pier over the bay itself. Now housed in an enclosed air-con restaurant (open-air dining is still available as well), it still sets a standard for Phuket seafood though prices have risen considerably. You order by weight, choosing from squid, oysters, cockles, crab, mussels and several kinds of fish, and then specify the method of cooking, whether grilled *(phão)*, steamed *(nêung)*, fried *(thâwt)*, par-boiled *(lûak* – for squid), or in soup *(tôm yam)*. They also offer a decent wine list. At the other end of Ao Chalong is a second location, **Kan Eang 2** *(☎ 076-381323).*

Entertainment

The **Pearl Cinema**, on the corner of Th Phang-Nga and Th Montri near the Pearl Hotel, occasionally shows films in English. **Alliance Française** *(☎ 076-222988, 3 Soi 1, Th Phattana)*, shows French films (subtitled in English) weekly. They also have a TV with up-to-date news broadcasts and a library.

The major hotels have discos and/or karaoke clubs. The **Timber 'n Rock**, on the eastern side of Th Yaowarat just south of Th Thungkha, is a well run pub with attractive rustic decor, lots of Phuket and Thai food and live music after 9 pm. Along the same lines is the **Kon Thai Pub**, on Th Krung Thep, which has a Thai band playing rock, folk and Thai pop tunes from 9.30 pm nightly.

Shopping

Although there are loads of souvenir shops and clothing boutiques surrounding the beach resorts of Patong, Kata and Karon, the best bargains on the island are found in the provincial capital. There are two main markets, one off the south side of Th Ranong near the centre of town, and a second off the north side of Th Ong Sim Phai a bit south-east of the town centre. The Th Ranong market traces its history back to the days when pirates, Indians, Chinese, Malays and Europeans traded in Phuket and offers a wide variety of sarongs and fabrics from Thailand, Malaysia, Indonesia and India. You'll also find inexpensive clothing and crafts here.

At the newer Th Ong Sim Phai market the focus is on fresh produce. Adjacent to the market is the large Robinson Ocean Plaza, which contains a branch of the Robinson department store, as well as smaller shops with moderately priced clothing and housewares.

Along Th Yaowarat between Th Phang-Nga and Th Thalang are a number of Indian-run tailor and fabric shops, while Chinese gold shops line Th Ranong opposite the market. Another shopping venue is the small Rasda Center/Phuket shopping centre on Th Rasada.

The Loft (☎ 076-258160), in a well restored shophouse at 36 Th Thalang, sells Asian antiques, Nepalese-Tibetan carpets and *objets d'art* downstairs, contemporary art upstairs. Other antique shops in central Phuket town include 88 Ancient Art, (☎ 076-258043) and Ban Boran Antiques (☎ 076-212473), both on Th Yaowarat. Tailors in Phuket with names like Taj Mahal and Maharaja can also be found along Th Yaowarat.

Phuket Unique Home (☎ 076-212093), 186 Th Phuket, opposite The Books and the Imperial Hotel, carries lots of original designs in silverware, dishware, home decor accessories and furniture, much of it a blend of old and new influences. Out of town on the way to Ao Chalong, Island Furniture (☎ 076-253707), Th Chao Fa, sells lounge and patio furniture made from farmed Indonesian teak, along with deluxe bamboo furniture and imported wood block flooring.

Getting There & Away

Air THAI operates nearly a dozen daily flights from Bangkok for 2000B one way. The direct flight takes an hour and 25 minutes, but some flights stop in Hat Yai for half an hour. There are also regular flights to and from Hat Yai for 780B. The THAI office (☎ 076-211195) is at 78/1 Th Ranong.

Bangkok Airways (☎ 076-225033) flies between Ko Samui and Phuket twice daily (once a week in June and September) for 1530B each way. The office is 158/2-3 Th Yaowarat. Angel Airlines (☎ 076-351337) recently introduced flights to Phuket from Bangkok (1890B one way) and Singapore (2990B one way). Angel's office is at Phuket international airport.

THAI flies between Phuket and several international destinations, including Penang, Langkawi, Kuala Lumpur, Singapore, Hong Kong, Taipei and Sydney. Other international airlines with offices in Phuket are: Malaysia Airlines (☎ 076-216675), 1/8-9 Th Thungkha; Silk Air (☎ 076-213891), 95/20 Th Montri; Singapore Airlines (same offices and phone number as Silk Air); Dragonair (☎ 076-217300), 37/52 Th Montri; and China Airlines (☎ 076-223939), Th Krung Thep.

Southern Helicopter Service (☎ 076-216398) at the airport charters a seven-passenger helicopter for 48,000B per hour. The service covers all of Phuket and Ao Phang-Nga, including Ko Phi-Phi. Southern Flying Group (☎ 076-247237) does small aeroplane charters.

Bus From Bangkok, one government 1st class air-con bus leaves the Southern bus terminal at 7 pm for 446B. Buses leave Phuket for the return journey at 5.30 pm. Two VIP buses (690B) run daily from Bangkok (Southern bus terminal) at 5.30 pm and 6 pm. Departure times from Phuket are 4 and 5 pm. The trip takes 14 hours. The ride along winding Hwy 4 between Ranong and Phuket can be hair-raising if you are awake. Only ordinary buses travel during the day; these leave six times a day from 6 am until 6.30 pm for 254B, and take a gruelling 15 or 16 hours.

A couple of private tour buses run from Bangkok's Southern terminal to Phuket in the early evening with fares of 452B one way or 800B return. From Phuket, tour buses to Bangkok leave between 3 and 5 pm. Several agencies have offices on Th Rasada and Th Phang-Nga in the city's centre.

The main bus terminal for government buses is off the north side of Th Phang-Nga, a little to the north of Royal Phuket City Hotel. Fares and durations for bus trips to and from Phuket's government terminal include:

destination	fare (B)	hours
Hat Yai	135	8
(air-con)	233 to 243	7
Krabi	56	4½
(air-con)	101	4
Nakhon Si Thammarat	85 to 93	8
(air-con)	150 to 180	7
Phang-Nga	37	2½
Surat Thani	90	6
(air-con)	150	5½
Takua Pa	45	3
Trang	94	6
(air-con)	132 to 169	5

Taxi & Mini-van There are also share taxis between Phuket and other provincial capitals in the south; taxi fares are generally double the fare of an ordinary bus. The taxi stand for Nakhon Si Thammarat, Surat Thani, Krabi, Trang and Hat Yai is on Th Phang-Nga, near the Pearl Cinema.

Some companies sell air-con minivan (*rot tûu*) tickets to Ko Samui; the fare includes ferry transport. Air-con minivan services to Surat, Krabi and Ranong are also available. As with share taxis, fares are about double the public bus fares. You can also get vans to Hat Yai (260B), Krabi (180B), Penang (650B), Kuala Lumpur (750B) and Singapore (850B). Vans can be booked at a stand at the same intersection as the share taxis.

Getting Around
Phuket is a big island, and while there is public transport, it's only available during the daytime. In many cases you'll still need to take a taxi or tuk-tuk to get to some of the more out-of-the-way destinations, which will often cost 200B or more. Unless you're happy to stay rooted to one area of the island, you should seriously consider renting either a motorcycle or jeep, especially if there are several of you to share the cost.

To/From the Airport There is a minibus service at the airport that will theoretically take you into town for 80B per person. However, if there aren't enough of you to fill the van, you'll most likely be directed towards a taxi. If you do get the shuttle bus, the dropoff point in town is a bit out of the way on a soi off Th Phunphon. There's a similar service to Patong, Kata or Karon beaches for 120B, but again unless there are enough of you, you're probably out of luck.

Taxis ask 360B for the trip from the airport to the city, 480B to 540B to the beaches; in the reverse direction you should be able to negotiate a fare of 200B.

You can also rent cars at the airport; see the Car entry farther on.

Songthaew & Tuk-tuk Large bus-size songthaews run regularly from Th Ranong near the market to the various Phuket beaches for 10B to 30B per person – see the following Phuket Beaches & Nearby Islands section for details. Beware of tales about the tourist office being 5km away, or that the only way to reach the beaches is by taxi, or even that you'll need a taxi to get from the bus station to the town centre (the bus station is more or less *in* the town centre). Officially, beach songthaews run from 7 am to 5 pm; after that time you must charter a tuk-tuk to the beaches. The latter cost from 150B for Karon, Kata, Nai Han and Patong to 250B for Hat Kamala.

Smaller songthaews around town cost a standard 10B, tuk-tuks 20B.

Car Several agencies in town rent Suzuki jeeps for 900B per day, including insurance. If you rent for a week or more you can get the price down to 800B per day. Your best choice in the town centre is Pure Car Rent (☎ 076-211002) at 75 Th Rasada. Avis Rent-A-Car (airport ☎ 076-327358) charges a bit more (around 1100B a day) but has outlets around the island at Le Meridien, on Hat Karon; Dusit Laguna, Laguna Beach Club, Sheraton Grande Laguna Beach all at Ao Bang Thao; and at the airport. Hertz is similar and has branches at the airport, Banyan Tree Resort (Ao Bang Thao) and Holiday Inn (Hat Patong).

In the bigger beach towns there are numerous shops, hotels and bungalows where you can rent jeeps and motorcycles.

Motorcycle Motorcycle taxis around town are 10B. You can hire motorcycles (usually 100cc Japanese bikes) along Th Rasada

between Th Phuket and Th Yaowarat or from various places at the beaches. Costs are around 200B to 300B per day. Bigger bikes (over 125cc) can be rented at a couple of shops at Patong and Karon.

Take care when riding a bike, and use common sense. People who ride around in shorts, T-shirt, a pair of thongs and no helmet are asking for trouble – a minor spill while wearing reasonable clothes would leave you bruised and shaken, but for somebody clad in shorts it could result in enough skin loss to end your travels right there. If you do have an accident you're unlikely to find that medical attention is up to international standards.

Phuket has the highest injury and death rate for faràngs in the country. In the high season 50 to 100 faràngs are seen by Kathu Hospital staff each week. Even for experienced riders some of the winding roads through the mountain can be downright dangerous, especially if you are caught out by the rain.

Matt King

Phuket now has a helmet law that police claim will be enforced without exception: those caught not wearing one will be fined 500B. When we last visited there still seemed to be plenty of 'exceptions', but then again, it's just stupid to ride without a helmet.

AROUND THE ISLAND
Ko Sire

This tiny island, 4km east of the capital and connected to the main island by a bridge over a canal, is known for its chao náam (sea gypsy) village and a hilltop reclining Buddha. There's a loop road that goes around the island, passing a few residences, shrimp farms, lots of rubber plantations and a bit of untouched forest. On the east side of the island is a public beach called **Hat Teum Suk** with a few chairs and thatched roof shelters; it's nothing special, rather a local hangout.

This village, the largest settlement of Urak Lawoi sea gypsies in Thailand, is little more than a poverty stricken cluster of tin shacks on stilts, plus one seafood restaurant called *Gypsy World*. The Urak Lawoi, the most sedentary of the three sea gypsy groups, are found only between the Mergui Archipelago and the Tarutao-Langkawi Archipelago and speak a creolised mixture of Malay and Mon-Khmer.

Laem Phanwa

South of Phuket town Route 4023 splits off Route 4021, then connects with Route 4129 to lead south-east from Phuket town to Laem Phanwa, a large cape which juts out into the Sea of Phuket. Just past the junction of Routes 4023 and 4129 you'll pass **Ao Makham**, a large mudflat bay where the Petroleum Authority of Thailand maintains a large oil depot. Most of the cape is inhabited by Thai Muslims; you'll see lots of goats wandering around and, in the village of **Ban Makham**, facing Route 4129, stands a very large and beautiful mosque. Past the oil facility is the **Port of Phuket**, near the entrance to which are several little roadside restaurants serving khâo mòk kài and other Muslim food.

Rubber, coconut and tamarind are farmed heavily in the interior of the cape. A winding, unnumbered road leads up the west side of the cape through the plantations, should you care to see them and have your own wheels.

At the end of Route 4129, at the tip of the cape, **Phuket Aquarium & Marine Biological Research Center** (☎ 076-391128) displays a varied collection of tropical fish and other marine life. Some are alive in tanks, others stuffed and displayed. The sea turtle exhibit is the most impressive and informative. Open daily 8.30 am to 4 pm; admission is 20B.

The seafood restaurants along the Laem Phanwa waterfront are a great place to hang out for a while, checking out the pleasure skiffs and painted fishing boats passing by.

Places to Stay & Eat *Cape Phanwa Hotel* (☎ 076-391123, fax 391177, Bangkok ☎ 02-233 3433, email capepanwa@phuket.com) offers semi-luxury digs spread out over a ridge starting at 3500B, about half that from

April to November. **Phanwa House**, a classic Sino-Portuguese mansion, on the grounds of the hotel, is open to the public. The mansion has a library and a collection of antique furniture and art; high tea and cocktails are served daily on the verandah, as well as Thai cuisine in the original dining room. A lighthouse on the grounds has also been turned into a lounge.

Not far from the aquarium are several old-fashioned Thai seafood restaurants. *Yam Yen Seafood* offers excellent and moderately priced outdoor dining under thatched shelters facing the bay.

Khao Phra Taew Royal Wildlife & Forest Reserve

This mountain range in the northern interior of the island protects 2333 hectares of virgin island rainforest (evergreen monsoon forest). There are some nice jungle hikes in this reserve, along with a couple of waterfalls, **Ton Sai** and **Bang Pae**. The falls are best seen in the rainy season between June and November; in the dry months they slow to a trickle. Because of its royal status, the reserve is better protected than the average Thai national park.

A German botanist discovered a rare and unique species of palm in Khao Phra Taew about 50 years ago. Called the white-backed palm or langkow palm, the fan-shaped plant stands 3 to 5m tall and is found only here and in Khao Sok National Park. The highest point in the park is the 442m **Khao Phara**.

Tigers, Malayan sun bears, rhinos and elephants once roamed the forest here, but nowadays resident mammals are limited to humans, gibbons, monkeys, slow loris, langur, civets, flying foxes, squirrels, mousedeer and other smaller animals. Watch out for cobras and wild pigs.

The **Phuket Gibbon Rehabilitation Centre** (☎ 076-381065, 260492, 01-212 7824), in the park near Bang Pae Falls, is open to the public daily 10 am to noon and 1 to 4 pm. Financed by donations (1000B will care for a gibbon for a year), the centre adopts gibbons which have been kept in captivity and re-introduces them to the wild.

Park rangers may act as guides for hikes in the park on request; call ☎ 01-676 7864. Payment is by donation.

To get to Khao Phra Taew from the provincial capital, take Th Thepkasatri north about 20km to the district of Thalang, and turn right at the intersection for Ton Sai Falls 3km down the road.

Thalang District

A few hundred metres north-east of the famous Heroines Monument in Thalang District on Route 4027, about 11km north of Phuket town or about 4km south-east of Thalang town is **Phuket National Museum** (☎ 076- 311426), which, at the time of writing was undergoing a facelift that was due to be completed at the end of 1999. Altogether the museum will contain five exhibit halls; the first two are now open to the public and chronicle southern themes such as the history of Thalang-Phuket and the colonisation of the Andaman coast, as well as descriptions of the various ethnicities found in Southern Thailand. The focal point of one hall is the impressive 2.3m-tall statue of Vishnu, which dates to the 9th century and was found in Takua Pa early in the 20th century. When finished the museum will sport back-lit display panels, touch-screen electronic presentations and CD video mini-theatres. It's open daily except holidays from 9 am to 4 pm. Admission is 10B for Thais, 30B for foreigners.

Also in Thalang district, just north of the crossroads near Thalang town, is **Wat Phra Thong**, Phuket's 'Temple of the Gold Buddha'. The image is half buried so that only the head and shoulders are visible above ground. According to local legend, those who have tried to excavate the image have become very ill or encountered serious accidents soon after failing to move the image.

The temple is particularly revered by Thai Chinese, many of whom believe the image hails from China. During Chinese New Year the temple is an important focus for pilgrims from Phang-Nga, Takua Pa and Krabi. In addition to the 4m Phra Thong (2m above ground, 2m below) there are several other

Buddha images, including seven representing the different days of the week, plus a Phra Praket (an unusual pose in which the Buddha is touching his own head with his right hand) and a Phra Palelai (sitting in 'European pose').

Parts of the movie *Good Morning Vietnam* were filmed in Thalang.

PHUKET BEACHES & NEARBY ISLANDS

Phuket beach accommodation has come a long way since 1977 when we first visited Kata and Nai Han and found thatched-roof huts for 10B a night. Nowadays 150B is rock-bottom. Any remaining accommodation costing under 300B will probably be upgraded within the next couple of years to a minimum of 500B as Phuket completes the final stages of moving from rustic beach hideaway to full-fledged international resort.

Warning

All of the western Phuket beaches, including Surin, Laem Singh and Kamala, have strong riptides during the monsoons. Take care when swimming, or don't go in the water at all if you're not a strong swimmer.

Keep an eye out for jet skis when you're in the water. Although the Phuket governor declared jet skis illegal in 1997, the ban has so far had little visible effect on these noisy and dangerous craft. Many rental units are reputedly owned by local police. Lately we've heard stories of police fining foreigners for renting jet skis; obviously they've discovered they can make more money fining tourists than they can renting the jet skis out.

Hat Patong

Fifteen kilometres west of Phuket by road, this large curved beach is the epicentre of the tourist earthquake that rattles Phuket throughout the high season (December to March). Over the last 10 years, Hat Patong has been rapidly turning into another Pattaya in all respects. It is now a strip of hotels, up-market bungalows, German and Italian restaurants, expensive seafood places, beer bars, nightclubs and coffee

Ko Khao Tapu and Ko Phing Kan, Ao Phang-Nga.

Ko Phing Kan, Ao Phang-Nga.

Canoeing around limestone formations in Phang-Nga National Park, Northern Andaman Coast.

Tham Lawt, Ao Phang-Nga.

Moken (sea gypsies) on Ko Surin, Northern Andaman Coast.

JOE CUMMINGS

JOE CUMMINGS

HERMANN MOLL

JOE CUMMINGS

HERMANN MOLL

Colourful beach umberellas on Hat Patong, Phuket Province.

Ko Panyi muslim village, Ao Phang-Nga.

Leaving Saphan Pla, Ranong, for Myanmar.

The bustling main street of Hat Patong, Phuket.

houses. It's also a major party scene; anyone looking for peace and quiet will be disappointed, while those looking for maximum nightlife need look no farther. Ironically, though this began as Phuket's most expensive beach, the prices are stabilising as the local accommodation market has become saturated with over 80 places to stay. As it becomes funkier and rowdier, Patong is rapidly becoming the cheapest beach on the island for accommodation.

If you spend some time in Patong and need to get away from the glass and concrete, take the dirt road to the left just before the Amari Coral Beach Resort, past the Kubu Restaurant. Here you can hike into the hills overlooking the bay's southern end, among secondary forest of Indian almond, passion fruit and rubber.

Information Patong has many foreign exchange booths, plus a post and telephone office on the corner of Soi Phoemphong (Soi Post Office) and Th Thawiwong.

For information about Phuket's chapter of the Hash House Harriers call ☎ 076-342143 (or email hhh@phuket.com).

Email & Internet Access Several places in Patong offer terminals, including Megabyte Cafe on the 3rd floor of Patong shopping centre on Th Thawiwong.

Dive Shops Patong is the diving centre of the island. See Diving & Snorkelling at the beginning of the Phuket Province section for a list of established dive shops.

Boat Trips Several companies on Patong do one-day cruises to nearby islands. For excursions to the Similan and Surin Islands off the Andaman coast of Phang-Nga Province, see the sections on those islands earlier in this chapter.

Boat Charter Motor yachts, sailboats and catamarans can sometimes be chartered with or without crew. Read the earlier Yachting section or check with dive shops around Patong to find out who has what.

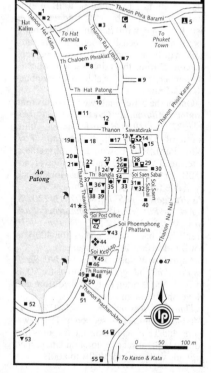

PATONG

PLACES TO STAY
1 Patong Lodge Hotel
2 Diamond Cliff Resort
3 PS Bungalow (PS II)
6 Eden Bungalow
7 Shamrock Park Inn
8 Swiss Palm Beach
9 Patong Grand Condotel; Sky Inn
10 Club Andaman
11 Casuarina Patong Garden Resort
12 The Living Place
17 Chanathip Guest House
18 Thara Patong
19 Phuket Cabana Resort
20 Patong Beach Bungalow
21 Patong Bay Garden Resort
22 Safari Beach Hotel
25 Capricorn Village; Savoey
26 K Hotel
28 PS Hotel (PS I)
30 Expat Hotel
31 Andaman Resortel; Casa Summer Breeze
33 Baan Sukhothai
37 Tropica Bungalow
39 Patong Beach Hotel
40 Sansabai Bungalows
46 Holiday Inn Resort Phuket
48 Comfort Resort Patong
49 Patong Merlin Hotel
51 Duangjit Resort
52 Amari Coral Beach Resort

PLACES TO EAT
13 Ngoen Laan
23 Restaurant 4
24 Bangla Seafood Restaurant
32 Pizzeria Hut
34 Le Croissant
36 Noodle and Rice Stalls
43 Viva Mexico; Saloniki Greek; Europa Frank's
45 Tandoor; Shalimar; Kwality
53 Kubu Restaurant

OTHER
4 Mosque
5 Wat Suwan Khiri Wong
14 Kathu Hospital
15 Paradise Complex
16 Pow Wow Pub
27 Rock Hard a Go Go
29 Soi Sunset Bars
35 Songserm Travel
38 Banana Discotheque & Pub
41 Police
42 Post & Telephone Office
44 Patong Shopping Centre
47 The Hideaway
50 Buses to Phuket
54 Phuket Simon Cabaret
55 Safari Disco

Massage & Herbal Sauna The Hideaway (☎ 076-340591), on Th Na Nai in the foothills of east Patong, is an excellent sauna and massage centre. A Thai herbal massage costs 300B an hour, sauna 100B. Other treatments are available, including facials and aromatherapy. Open noon to 9 pm daily.

Places to Stay – Budget Rates on Patong vary according to season. In the high season (December to March, and August) you'll be doing very well to find something under 300B a night. On the beach there is nothing under 600B, but on and off Th Rat Uthit, especially in the Paradise Complex and along Soi Saen Sabai, there are several nondescript guesthouses with rooms for 200B to 300B.

During off months some of the 600B places will drop to as low as 400B or even 300B, but that's about it. Budget places usually come with fan and shared bathroom; more expensive rooms in this category will have a private bath and perhaps air-con. During the rainy season, May to November, you may be able to knock about 100B off rates.

One of the better deals we found this time around is *Chanathip Guest House* (☎ 076-294087, fax 294088), off Th Rat Uthit, south of Th Sawatdirak (opposite Pow Wow Pub). Rooms with fan, refrigerator, satellite TV, phone and hot shower are 350B, air-con for 700B. Private lockers are available for guests in the lobby.

PS Bungalow (PS II; ☎ 076-342207/8, 78/54 Th Rat Uthit) and *Shamrock Park Inn* (☎ 076-340991, 17/2 Th Rat Uthit) aren't bad back-street places for 400B to 650B (add 100B in December).

Capricorn Village (☎ 076-340390, 82/29 Th Rat Uthit) has good bungalows for 500B to 700B and is often fully booked from mid November through January.

Duangjit Resort (☎ 076-340778, fax 340288), near the intersection of Th Thawiwong and Th Prachanukhro, has rooms in a solidly built, attractive hotel on landscaped grounds with pool for 400B to 800B.

Places to Stay – Mid-Range A large number of places in Patong fall into the 700B to 1800B range, which always includes air-con and private bath; the more expensive ones will have hot showers, lower priced ones cold water only. Prices in this category can usually be negotiated downwards at least 100B to 200B during the rainy season.

At the friendly, quiet and efficient *Sansabai Bungalows* (☎ 076-342948/9, fax 344888), at the end of Soi Saen Sabai off Th Rat Uthit, all rooms have hot water, mini-bar and TV. High season prices are 850B for rooms with fan, 1150B for deluxe rooms with air-con, 1300B to 1400B for superior rooms and 1800B for bungalows with air-con and kitchen. During low season these drop to 700B fan, 850B deluxe, 1000B to 1100B superior and 1400B bungalow. These rates include breakfast but not 10% tax. On the premises is a restaurant serving Italian and Thai dishes. Also on this soi is the less interesting but OK *Andaman Resortel* (☎ 076-341516, fax 340847, 65/21 Soi Saen Sabai), costing 800B to 1200B and the clean and friendly *Casa Summer Breeze* (☎ 076-340464, fax 340493, 171/12 Muu 4, Soi Saen Sabai), from 500B to 1150B.

Nearby, off Th Rat Uthit, *Expat Hotel* (☎ 076-342143, fax 340300, email expat@ loxinfo.co.th) offers spacious but shabby and somewhat musty rooms for 790B to 840B (440B to 490B low season). *PS Hotel (PS I;* ☎ 076-340184, fax 341097, 50/2 Th Rat Uthit) near the Paradise Complex has decent if characterless air-con rooms with satellite TV for 950B to 1050B.

Considering its central location facing the beach on Th Thawiwong, rooms at the friendly *Safari Beach Hotel* (☎ 076-341170, fax 340231) are a bargain at 800B low season, 1400B high. On the premises are a small but pleasant pool and a good seafood restaurant.

Just a little farther south on the same stretch of Th Thawiwong, *Tropica Bungalow* (☎ 076-340204, fax 340206) offers similar rooms for 1600B to 1800B in high season, somewhat lower in the off season. The Banana Disco is right next door.

K Hotel (☎ 076-340833, fax 340124, 82/47 Th Rat Uthit), a one storey place in a pleasant garden setting, deals mostly with Germans booked through the Kuoni tour company, but when there's space you can get a decent room for 900B to 1500B. **The Living Place** (☎/fax 076-340121, fax 341757, 38/6 Th Sawatdirak) has a quiet spot in north Patong with small bungalows (all with air-con, hot water and refrigerator) for 600B to 1000B depending on the season. On an even quieter road, Th Chaloem Phrakiat, are two similar places, **Swiss Palm Beach** (☎ 076-342381, fax 342698) where rooms are 1600B, and **Eden Bungalow** (☎/fax 076-340944), 1230B to 1690B.

The **Sky Inn** (☎ 076-342486, fax 340576) on the 9th floor of the Patong Grand Condotel, caters to a primarily gay clientele and costs 600B with fan to 900B with air-con in high season, as low as 500B during the rainy season.

Patong Lodge Hotel (☎ 076-341020/4, fax 340287), just north of Hat Patong in a more secluded and rocky area known as Hat Kalim, has well kept rooms with all the amenities for 1000B to 1800B depending on the season.

Places to Stay – Top End At the lower end of the top price range, roughly around 1800B to 3000B, you'll find a number of all air-con places with swimming pools, modest room service, phones and most of the other amenities desired by the average mainstream visitor and package tourist.

Towards the north end of Th Thawiwong facing the beach, long-established **Casuarina Patong Garden Resort** (☎/fax 340123, 77/1 Th Thawiwong) has transformed itself bit by bit from a small collection of bungalows to a top-ender costing 1800B to 3000B, depending on the season. **Thara Patong** (☎ 076-340135, fax 340446, email thara@sun.phuket.ksc.co.th), between Th Sawatdirak and Th Bangla on the beachfront road, is a similar place with rates running 1609B to 2800B in the high season,

but with discounts to as low as 700B in June and September.

Only a few hotels in central Hat Patong actually sit right on the beach side of Th Thawiwong. One is **Patong Bay Garden Resort** (☎ 076-340297/8, fax 340560), a luxury place with rooms for 2400B in the high season, a bit lower in the rainy season. Adjacent **Patong Beach Bungalow** (☎ 076-340117, fax 340213) has separate deluxe bungalows starting at 2400B.

At the American style **Comfort Resort Patong** (☎ 076-294130/4, fax 294143, 18/110 Th Ruamjai) singles/doubles with all the amenities are 2600/3000B. On the premises are a pool and restaurant. Rates at the nearby long-running **Patong Merlin Hotel** (☎ 076-340037, fax 340394) vary wildly from 1500B to 4336B according to the season.

Moving up a couple of notches to places with true world-class standards, rates start at 3000B and reach epic proportions for large suites with the best bay views. Many top-end places add a 500B to 1000B peak season surcharge between late December and mid-January.

Another place right on the beach, **Phuket Cabana Resort** (☎ 076-340138, fax 340178, 41 Th Thawiwong) has luxuriously appointed bungalows for 4512B (40% off in the low season), including breakfast. The independently owned and managed **Patong Beach Hotel** (☎ 076-340301, fax 340541, email patong-sun@phuket.ksc.co.th), which actually isn't on the beach, but back off Th Thawiwong south of Th Bangla, starts at 3267B for large, luxurious rooms on landscaped grounds.

The much more private, five-star **Amari Coral Beach Resort** (☎ 076-340106, fax 340115, email coralbea@phuket.loxinfo.co.th), the southern-most property in Hat Patong, on a cliff overlooking the bay; charges 6336B to 7412B from 1 November to 31 March, from 4390B the remainder of the year.

If you're looking for Thai ambience, **Baan Sukhothai Hotel** (☎ 076-314394, fax 340197) off Th Bangla may be your best choice. Set on spacious grounds, the hotel uses lots of teak assembled in semi-open, central Thai architectural motifs – a bit out of place in Phuket perhaps, but a favourite with tour groups. Rack rates are 3025B but discounts are available in the low season.

Club Andaman (☎ *076-340530, 340361, fax 340527, email clubandaman@resort-hotels.com),* up towards the north end of the beach on Th Hat Patong, charges 3049B to 4444B for rich bungalows in a relatively quiet setting.

Holiday Inn Resort Phuket (☎ *076-340608, fax 340435, email holidayinn@phuket.com),* at the south end of Th Thawiwong near the Merlin, ranges from 3400B in low season to 5082B in the high, including breakfast.

Back off Th Rat Uthit, the *Patong Grand Condotel* (☎ *076-341043, fax 342205, 63 Th Rat Uthit)* offers sizeable one to three-bedroom units with kitchens for 6500B to 10,000B.

Up on Hat Kalim, the *Diamond Cliff Resort* (☎ *076-340501, fax 340507)* has units in spacious grounds with good sea views from 4235B.

Places to Eat Patong has stacks of restaurants, some of them quite good. The seafood restaurants are concentrated along Th Bangla. Most are expensive; lobster in Patong is going for about 1000B per kilogram these days. *Restaurant 4*, in a no-nonsense, fluorescent-lit shed, off Th Bangla, is the best priced of the seafood places; add your name to the graffiti on the walls when you're finished dining. Around the corner, on Th Bangla itself, *Bangla Seafood Restaurant* is a decent open air seafood place with medium prices and a low-key staff. If you can spend a little more, *Savoey* is a big open-air place in front of the Safari Beach Hotel on Th Thawiwong with atmosphere and a good 'slay 'em and weigh 'em' style setup.

Around the intersection of Th Rat Uthit and Th Bangla are a few inexpensive Thai and faràng cafes worth trying. *Le Croissant* (☎ *076-342743),* on Th Bangla, carries

French pastries, French wines, sandwiches, salads, baguettes and imported cheeses. A couple of sois south, Soi Phoemphong Phattana offers a string of international eateries, including *Viva Mexico, Saloniki Greek* and *Europa Frank's.*

Pizzeria Hut, a little south of Soi Saen Sabai on Th Rat Uthit, bakes good, reasonably priced pizza in a wood-fired oven; take away and delivery are available. There's another location on Th Bangla opposite the Shark Club.

Three OK Indian restaurants, the *Tandoor, Shalimar* and *Kwality* can be found on Soi Kepsap.

For inexpensive noodle and rice vendors, check Th Sawatdirak. *Ngoen Laan* (no roman-script sign), on the south-east corner of Th Sawatdirak and Th Rat Uthit, is an all night *khâo tôm* (rice soup) place that's both good and inexpensive.

For a special Thai meal, call or visit *Kubu Restaurant* (☎ *076-292191)* to order a set Thai meal 24 hours in advance. In this way the cooks can prepare everything from scratch, using fresh ingredients purchased in the exact quantity needed. Show up the next evening and enjoy a fine multi-course Thai dinner at a cost of 600B for two. Kubu is on an unsealed road, off Th Thawiwong, just before you arrive at Amari Coral Beach Resort travelling south-west.

Entertainment Dancing has become the main night-time activity in Patong as a new generation of tourists interested in more than just sitting on their bums in a bar has taken over the scene. *Banana Discotheque* (☎ *076-340301, 96 Th Thawiwong)* is still one of the more popular dance clubs. The attached *Banana Pub* is very in with Thais at the moment, and offers a non-threatening coffee house-like atmosphere where most western women and couples should feel comfortable. Two other popular dance clubs are the high-tech *Shark Club* on Th Bangla and the jungle-decor *Safari Disco Pub* on the road to Karon/Kata south of town. Banana, Shark and Safari all collect cover charges of

100B to 200B, which includes a drink coupon or two.

Pow Wow Pub on Th Rat Uthit near the Paradise Complex is a typical old west Thai bar with live country and western mixed with Thai folk rock.

There are dozens of simple *bars* around town, many of them little more than a collection of stools around a rectangular bar and a handful of female touts whose objective is to hook passers-by and keep them drinking long enough to pay the rent. Th Bangla is the main 'zone' but they're also found all along Th Thawiwong and Th Rat Uthit – anywhere there isn't a hotel, restaurant or souvenir shop. *Rock Hard a Go Go* (☎ 076-340409) on the corner of Th Bangla and Th Rat Uthit is one of the larger and more popular go-go bars. Also on Th Bangla, *Kangaroo Bar, Gonzo Bar* and *U2 Bar* get started late and go into the morning hours.

A string of bars located on Soi Sunset (near the PS Hotel and the intersection of Rat Uthit and Th Bangla) doesn't get started until around midnight, and rocks until about 6 am. The crowd consists mainly of western men and Thai women (many of whom will have just got off work), but it's still enough of a social scene that couples and female travellers can join in the partying with no problem. There's a strip of gay bars on the sois leading into the Paradise Complex, including *Black & White Music Factory, Heaven, Cupid Bar, Passport, Go Go Boys* and *Gay World*.

If you like transvestite shows, check out the well done *Phuket Simon Cabaret* (☎ 076-342011) south of town on the way to Karon/Kata. Performances occur at 7.30 pm and 9.30 pm nightly.

Shopping A string of shops and stalls along the central part of Th Thawiwong sell clothing, silk, jewellery and souvenirs from all over Thailand. Prices are higher than average.

Getting There & Away Songthaews to Patong from Phuket leave from Th Ranong, near the day market and fountain circle; the fare is 20B. The after-hours charter fare is 150B. From Patong you can find songthaews to Phuket anywhere along Th Rat Uthit and Th Thawiwong.

Getting Around Tuk-tuks circulate Patong for 10B per ride. There are numerous places to rent 125cc motorcycles and jeeps. Patong Big Bike on Th Rat Uthit rents 250 to 750cc bikes.

Hat Karon
Karon is a long, gently curving beach with small sand dunes and a few palms and casuarina trees. Sometimes it is referred to as two beaches: Karon Yai and Karon Noi. Karon Noi, also known as Relax Bay, can only be reached from Hat Patong and is completely monopolised by Le Meridien Hotel. The main section of Karon now has a paved promenade with streetlights, and the entire area has blended with Hat Kata to the south to produce a self-contained village inhabited by a mixture of tourists, seasonal residents and year-rounders. It is still a fairly peaceful beach where a few fisherfolk cast nets, and where you can occasionally buy fresh seafood from their boats, though the rice fields between the beach and the surrounding hills have been abandoned or filled with high-rise hotels. Karon's worst feature are the canals that feed into the sea; they badly need cleaning, not so much from the effluent they contains as the rubbish which is allowed to collect in them year round. Developers in Karon like to boast that this is one of Phuket's 'high end' beaches with an 'ecological' consciousness; the canal situation proves them dead wrong.

Dino Park (☎ 076-330625), next to Marina Cottage, features an 18 hole minigolf course with a Fred Flintstone-looking environment, along with a fake waterfall. There is also food (eg Bronto Burgers) and music in the Rock Garden and drinks at the Dino Bar. It's open all day and late into the night.

Internet & Email Access Karon Beach Internet Center (☎ 076-286086, email karoncenter@usa.net) at 36/31 Th Patak has a few terminals hooked to the Net for use by the general public at rates of around 3B to 4B per minute.

Places to Stay Karon is lined with multi-storey inns and deluxe bungalows, along with a number of places with rooms or huts for under 400B. During the low season – May to November – you can often get a 400B room for as low as 150B to 250B, a 1000B room for 600B, and a 2000B room for 1000B.

Most of the places under 700B are located well off the beach, often on small hillocks to the east of the main road. At the northern end of the beach, *Ann House* (no phone) has a row of 14 very basic fan rooms with private bath for 100B to 300B. Next door *Lume & Yai Bungalow* (☎/fax 076-396096) has the advantage of a hillside location for 19 huts costing 300B to 500B. One advantage to both of these places is that beach songthaews usually pass right in front.

In the commercial centre of Karon, near the roundabout, quiet *Karon Seaview Bungalow* (☎ 076-396798/9) offers OK concrete duplexes and row houses for 300B to 500B, less in the low season. On the main road away from the beach is the *Crystal Beach Hotel* (☎ 076-396580/5, fax 336584); it's good value at 300B to 400B for air-con rooms. Farther south and nearer the beach is the popular and friendly *My Friend Bungalow* (☎ 076-396344), with rooms for 200B to 500B; the cafe out front is a plus. *Fantasy Hill Bungalow* (☎ 076-330106), farther south still on a small hill off the main road, has good budget bungalows for 300B to 500B, or as low as 150B to 250B in the rainy season. All rooms have fans and small refrigerators.

On the north of the headland straddling Karon and Kata is the friendly *Kata Tropicana* (☎ 076-330141, fax 330408), with well maintained bungalows for 500B (250B in the low season) to 1500B.

In the mid-range (averaging 500B and up) are the *Karon Village* (☎ 076-396431), 600B to 800B; *Karon Guest House* (☎ 076-396860), 500B to 800B; *Phuket Ocean Resort* (☎ 076-396176), 1200B to

1400B; and *Ruam Thep Inn* (☎ 076-330281), 400B to 900B.

The remaining places on Karon are newer resort-type hotels with rooms starting at 1000B or above, with air-con, swimming pools, multiple restaurants, etc. Prices at most places have come down a bit over the last two years due to competition, though a few places have raised their rates. Bargaining at the larger ones is worthwhile; as a rule of thumb the more rooms they have, the more they'll drop the price, especially during the south-west monsoon season, May to October. Among the more reliable are vaguely American South-Western style *Felix Karon Phuket* (☎ 076-396666, fax 396853), 81 rooms, from 3800B; *The Islandia Travelodge Resort* (☎ 076-396604, fax 396139), 128 rooms, 1000B to 3000B; *Phuket Arcadia Hotel* (☎ 076-396038, fax 396136, email arcadia@phuket.ksc.co.th), 468 rooms, from 4000B; *Thavorn Palm Beach Hotel* (☎ 076-396090, fax 396555, email palm@phuket.com), 210 rooms, from 5400B.

Up at Karon Noi ('Relax Bay'), the small bay around the northern headland of Karon, the top-end *Le Meridien Phuket* (☎ 076-340480, fax 340479, email meridien@phuket.ksc.co.th) has 470 well appointed rooms from 3800B. Above Le Meridien on a hillside, a bit of a hike from the beach, the *Karon Hill* (☎/fax 076-341343) has simple but adequate rooms with private bath for 300B to 500B depending on the season or your bargaining power.

Places to Eat As usual, almost every place to stay provides some food. The cheapest *Thai and seafood places* are off the roundabout near the commercial centre.

The Little Mermaid, 100m south-east of the traffic circle, has a long, inexpensive, mostly Scandinavian menu written in 12 languages; it's open 24 hours.

Old Siam Authentic Thai Restaurant, part of Thavorn Palm Beach, is a large open-air place, designed in central Thai style, and producing Thai dishes for the tourist palate for 100B to 300B.

Better eating value can be found at the string of open-air *seafood places* along the main beach road between Karon Villa/Karon Royal Wing and Karon Seaview. Two of the better ones here are *Family Seafood* and *On-Lee Seafood*.

Getting There & Away See the Kata Getting There & Away section for details on transport to Karon.

Hat Kata

Just around a headland south from Karon, Kata is a more interesting beach and is divided into two – Ao Kata Yai (Big Kata Bay) and Ao Kata Noi (Little Kata Bay). The small island of Ko Pu is within swimming distance of the shore and on the way are some OK coral reefs. Snorkelling gear can be rented from several of the bungalow groups. Although it has around 30 hotels and bungalow resorts and a slightly urban feel, it is much less crowded than Patong. Concrete walls, protecting up-market resorts from the riff-raff, are a detraction.

Contrary to persistent rumour, the beach in front of Club Med is open to the public.

Information Along Th Thai Na in Kata Yai, near the Rose Inn, is a Thai Farmers Bank (with exchange services) and a post office.

Activities & Events The Chao Phraya River Club (**CPRC Literary Society**), an informal group of local writers and readers, meets regularly at The Boathouse at the southern end of Kata Yai. On occasion the CPRC meetings will host a travelling author, or an author from Bangkok. For information call ☎ 076-330015.

The Boathouse offers a two day Thai **cooking class** each Saturday and Sunday from 10 am to 2 pm for a reasonable 1800B per person including two lunches, Boathouse recipes and a certificate.

A more sophisticated **culinary school** has recently opened in connection with the Gallery Grill (☎ 076-330975, 330482), around the headland overlooking the north

---

KARON & KATA

PLACES TO STAY	
1	Felix Karon Phuket
2	Ann House
3	Lume & Yai Bungalows
4	Phuket Ocean Resort
6	The Islandia Travelodge Resort
7	Karon Guest House
8	Crystal Beach Hotel
9	My Friend Bungalow
10	South Sea Resort
11	Karon Villa; Karon Royal Wing
13	Karon Seaview Bungalow
14	Karon Village
15	Phuket Arcadia Hotel
16	Thavorn Palm Beach Hotel
18	Karon Inn
20	Ruam Thep Inn
22	Karon Beach Resort
23	Marina Cottage
24	Kata Garden Resort
25	Kata Tropicana
28	Lucky Guest House; Charlie's Guest House
31	Kata On Sea
32	Rose Inn
34	Fantasy Hill Bungalow
35	Peach Hill Hotel
36	Smile Inn
38	Dome Bungalow; Sumitra Thai House
39	Club Med
40	Kata View Point Resort
41	Bell's Bungalow
42	Sea Bees Bungalow
45	Kata Beach Resort
46	The Boathouse
47	Friendship Bungalow
48	Cool Breeze
49	Pop Cottage
51	Kata Thani Resort
52	Katanoi Riviera
53	Mountain Beach Resort
54	Kata Thani Resort (Kata Buri Wing)
55	C Tabkew (Chor Tabkaew) Bungalow
56	Katanoi Club Hotel

PLACES TO EAT	
5	Seafood Restaurants
12	Family Seafood; On-Lee Seafood
17	Old Siam Authentic Thai Restaurant
26	Raan Khao Kaeng
27	Bluefin Tavern
30	Bondeli Kata
33	Kampong-Kata Hill Restaurant & Galleria
37	Seafood Restaurants
44	Islander's
50	Gallery Grill; Baan Kata

OTHER	
19	Maxim Supermarket
21	Dino Park
29	Post Office
43	Songthaews to Phuket

To Le Meridien Phuket Karon Hill & Patong

ANDAMAN SEA

Thanon Patak (West)

Thanon Patak

Karon

Laem Sai

Ko Pu

Ao Karon

Hat Kata Yai

Ao Kata Yai

Kata

Thanon Thai Na

To Phuket Town

Thanon Kata–Soi Yuan

0   0.5   1 km
Approximate Scale

Hat Kata Noi

Ao Kata Noi

To Hat Nai Han

end of Kata Noi. The staff present two series of three-hour cooking classes per month, each one a different menu, all of it Asian fusion cooking, for 700B per person. Classes are held in the Gallery Grill kitchen and often feature guest chefs. See Places to Eat for further information on the Gallery Grill.

Next door to the Gallery Grill, Baan Kata, the cliffside home of noted Thai architect ML Tri Devakul (who built The Boathouse), contains an **art gallery** featuring the work of local and international artists. The **Baan Kata Arts Fest** is held here annually in mid to late February.

Places to Stay – Budget The crowd of 34 places to stay ranges from 100B to 300B at *Bell's Bungalow*, quite a distance back from the beach towards the southern end of Kata Yai, to 8500B for a suite at the classy *The Boathouse*, a step above Club Med on Kata Yai. In general the less expensive places tend to be off the beach between Kata Yai (to the north) and Kata Noi (to the south) or well off the beach on the road to the island interior.

Kata View Point Resort (☎ 076-330815), just north-east of Bell's Bungalow, has adequate units with fan and private bath costing 200B to 300B. *Friendship Bungalow (☎ 076-330499)*, a popular place off the beach at the headland between Kata Yai and Kata Noi, is 370B to 700B. *Kata On Sea (☎ 076-330594)*, on a ridge off Th Thai Na east of Kata Yai, offers simple huts with ceiling fans, mosquito nets and private bath for 200B to 300B depending on the season. Two budget apartment-style places worth checking out – both basic but clean and friendly – are *Lucky Guest House* at 200B to 800B and *Charlie's Guest House (☎ 076-330855)* at 250B to 350B; both are found towards the back road that parallels the beach, north-east of Rose Inn and Bondeli Kata restaurant.

Rooms at the *Cool Breeze (☎ 076-330484, fax 330173)* in Kata Noi start at 200B and go up to 750B. *Katanoi Club Hotel (☎ 076-330194, 284025)* at the end of the road and at the southern end of Kata

Noi, behind the more expensive C Tabkew, costs just 200B to 500B for simple rooms in slightly ramshackle buildings against the side of a rocky cliff. The beach is only 50m away.

A sprinkling of other spots starting under 500B include *Dome Bungalow (☎ 076-330620, fax 330269)*, 400B to 750B; the nearby *Sumitra Thai House (☎ 076-330515)*, 400B and up; *Sea Bees Bungalow (☎/fax 076-330090)*, 250B to 350B; and the hotel-like *Rose Inn (☎ 076-396519, fax 396526)*, 250B to 500B. All will give discounts during the low season from May to October.

Places to Stay – Mid-Range Recommended medium-range places (all air-con) in Kata are *Peach Hill Hotel (☎ 076-330603, fax 330895)*, in a nice setting with a pool from 500B to 1500B and *Smile Inn (☎ 076-330926, fax 330925)*, a clean, friendly place with a nice open-air cafe and air-con rooms with hot showers, TV and fridge for 700B (800B including breakfast). One of the best places in this area is *C Tabkew (Chor Tabkaew) Bungalow (☎ 076-330433, fax 330435)*, down at the south end of Kata Noi beach. At 900B low season, 1200B high, it's one of the few mid-range spots that's right on the beach, and the balconied bungalows are spacious and well maintained. Some are high on a steep hillside among large boulders, so you may have to climb stairs. You'll be rewarded by incredible sunset views over the bay.

Other mid-priced lodgings are available at *Pop Cottage (☎ 076-330181, fax 330794, email popcott@loxinfo.co.tha)*, which has units high on a hill opposite the south end of Kata Yai costing from 500B to 1000B. *Kata Garden Resort (☎ 076-330627, fax 330446)*, opposite the well laid-out Marina Cottage, charges 500B fan, and up to 1500B air-con, for 50 stilted bungalows and lots of trees.

Across the road from the beach at Kata Noi, *Katanoi Riviera (☎ 076-330726, fax 330294)* is a cluster of row houses and bungalows, with a little bit of landscaping, costing 300B to 1200B. Much of its beach view is blocked by the Kata Thani, and what's left will be obliterated when construction of the *Mountain Beach Resort* is completed. The latter will probably straddle the gap between mid-range and top end accommodation.

Places to Stay – Top End Moving up in price, one of the more exemplary of the less-extravagant top end places is *Marina Cottage* (☎ 076-330625, fax 330516, email info@marina-cottage.com), a long-running, medium-scale, low-rise, low-density place on shady, palm-studded grounds near the beach. Marina Cottage doesn't accept tour groups and takes reservations only through selected travel agents, yet manages to keep rates for its comfortable, well designed Thai-style bungalows in the 1000B to 3000B range.

The Boathouse (☎ 076-330015, fax 330561, Bangkok ☎ 02-438 1123, email the.boathouse@phuket.com), the brainchild of architect and Phuket resident ML Tri Devakul, is a 36 room boutique resort that manages to stay full year-round without resorting to off-season rates. In spite of rather ordinary-looking if capacious rooms, the hotel hosts a steady influx of Thai politicos, pop stars, artists, celebrity authors (the hotel hosts periodic poetry and fiction readings) and the ordinary rich on the strength of its stellar service and acclaimed restaurant, and because it commands a scenic spot at the south end of Kata Yai. Rooms start at 6200B, plus tax and service.

The palatial *Kata Thani Resort* (☎ 076-330417, 330124/6, fax 330426, email katathani@phuket.com) commands most of the beach at Kata Noi and is one of the choicest spots anywhere along Karon or Kata. Up-market, well appointed rooms go for 2500B to 4200B. There are two pools at the main resort, and another across the road and south a bit at the Kata Buri Wing (formerly under separate management).

Close to Kata Yai and near Club Med, the *Kata Beach Resort* (☎ 076-330530, fax 330128, email katagrp@loxinfo.co.th) is a three storey concrete hotel that's on the access road to the beach, with rooms from 3200B to 3800B – not all have beach views. *Club Med* (☎ 076-330455/9, fax 330461) occupies a large chunk of land near Kata Yai, as well as a fair swathe of beachfront. Rates range from around 3400B to 6000B per person.

Places to Eat Most of the restaurants in Kata offer standard tourist food and service. The two best restaurants in the entire area, including Karon and Patong to the north, are both owned by ML Tri, the architect who is attempting to bring high culture, art and cuisine to Phuket. *The Boathouse Wine & Grill* started as an indoor/outdoor restaurant only, but now has 36 rooms attached to its original location at the south end of Kata Yai. It boasts a wine collection that so far is the only one in Thailand to have been cited for excellence by *Wine Spectator* magazine. The nightly seafood buffet is excellent. It's a pricey place but the atmosphere is casual and service is tops. Slightly more formal is the *Gallery Grill* (☎ 076-330975) at Baan Kata, overlooking the north end of Kata Noi. The very creative menu features California wine country and Asian fusion cuisine, presided over by noted Napa Valley chef Sue Farley. It's open 6 to 10 pm and expensive by any standards (but worth it if you have expensive tastes); reservations are requested.

Another standout, though considerably less expensive, is the *Kampong-Kata Hill Restaurant & Galleria*, a Thai-style place decorated with antiques and situated on a hill a bit inland from the beach. It's open only for dinner, from 5 pm till midnight. Just up the street the *Dive Café* serves a multi-course Thai dinner for two 200B per person. *Bondeli Kata* (☎ 076-396482) on the same road serves fresh pastries, four kinds of coffee and nine teas, while *Bluefin Tavern* features Tex-Mex, pizza, burgers and Thai food.

The very large and medium-priced *Islander's* (☎ 076-330740) strives to provide something for everyone, including seafood, Italian, barbecue and fresh baked goods; if you call they'll provide free transport to and from your hotel.

Towards the east end of Th Thai Na, well past the Kampong-Kata Hill Restaurant and Rose Inn, **Raan Khao Kaeng** (no roman-script sign) is one of the few restaurants in Kata that an ordinary Thai person can afford to eat at. As the name suggests, it specialises in Thai curries over rice.

Getting There & Away Songthaews to both Kata and Karon leave frequently from the Th Ranong market in Phuket from 7 am to 5 pm for 20B per person. After-hour charters cost 150B to 200B. The main songthaew stop is in front of Kata Beach Resort.

Hat Nai Han

A few kilometres south of Kata, this beach set around a picturesque bay is similar to Kata and Karon but, in spite of the 1986 construction of the Phuket Yacht Club, not as developed – thanks to the presence of Samnak Song Nai Han, a monastic centre in the middle of the beach that claims most of the beachfront land. To make up for the loss of saleable beachfront, developers started cutting away the forests on the hillsides overlooking the beach. Recently, however, the development seems to have reached a halt. This means that Nai Han is usually one of the least crowded beaches on the southern part of the island.

Nai Harn Herbal Sauna, off Route 4233 past the Nai Han Beach Resort, offers Thai-style steam saunas for 50B, plus massage for 150B an hour.

The TAT says Nai Han beach is a dangerous place to swim during the monsoon season (May to October), but it really varies depending on the weather – look for the red flag, which means dangerous swimming conditions.

Places to Stay Except for the Yacht Club, there's really not much accommodation available on or even near the beach. If you follow the road about 1km through the Yacht Club and continue west beyond the next cape, you'll come to the simple *Ao*

Sane Bungalows (☎ 076-288306), which cost 80B to 200B depending on the season and condition of the huts.

Farther on at the end of this road is the secluded **Jungle Beach Resort** (☎ 076-381108, fax 381542). The cottages are well spaced along a naturally wooded slope with a small beach below. Low-season rates start at 400B for a sturdy hut without bath; high-season rates peak at 5000B for a large terraced cottage with private bath. The cottages could use some renovation, especially considering the pricing; while they're at it, management should repair the dangerously decaying wooden bridges. We've also received complaints about the food service.

Well back from the beach, near the road into Nai Han and behind a small lagoon is the motel-like *Nai Han Beach Resort* (☎ 076-381810), with decent rooms for 500B with fan, 800B for air-con; add 200B in peak season (December to February). On the other side of the reservoir *Romzai Bungalows* (☎ 076-381338) has simple huts for around 300B in the December to April high season, and as low as 150B the remainder of the year. About a kilometre farther along there's a road branching off to the left (north). It leads to *Orchid Bungalows* (☎ 076-381396) which offers more motel-like rooms next to an orchid nursery for around 300B.

The *Le Royal Meridien Phuket Yacht Club* (☎ 076-381156, fax 381164, email info@phuket-yachtclub.com) sits on the western end of Nai Han. Originally built at the astronomical cost of 145 million baht, the hotel has given up on the idea of becoming a true yacht club (apparently the bay currents aren't right for such an endeavour) with a mobile pier. The pier has gone but luxurious 'state rooms' are still available for US$280 to US$900 a night.

On the other end of the bay from the Yacht Club, off the road to Rawai, the *Yahnui (Yanoi) Beach Bungalows* (☎/fax 076-238180) features a set of plain cottages on the opposite side of the road from the beach with ceiling fans and private shower. Smaller bungalows cost 350B a night, some-

Phuket Province – Phuket Beaches & Nearby Islands 459

NORTHERN ANDAMAN COAST

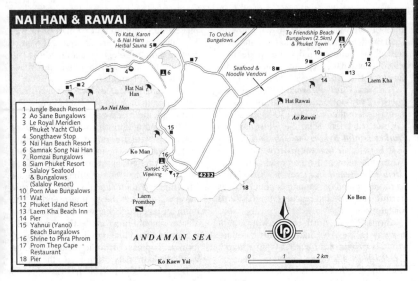

NAI HAN & RAWAI

1 Jungle Beach Resort
2 Ao Sane Bungalows
3 Le Royal Meridien
  Phuket Yacht Club
4 Songthaew Stop
5 Nai Han Beach Resort
6 Samnak Song Nai Han
7 Romzai Bungalows
8 Siam Phuket Resort
9 Salaloy Seafood
  & Bungalows
  (Salaloy Resort)
10 Porn Mae Bungalows
11 Wat
12 Phuket Island Resort
13 Laem Kha Beach Inn
14 Pier
15 Yahnui (Yanoi)
   Beach Bungalows
16 Shrine to Phra Phrom
17 Prom Thep Cape
   Restaurant
18 Pier

what nicer ones 500B. A rustic restaurant enjoys a beautiful location on its own small sandy cove opposite the bungalows. It's a very quiet and peaceful spot among coconut palms, mangroves and casuarina trees; the cape and grassy hills nearby have lots of hiking potential. You'll need your own transport to get here.

Getting There & Away Nai Han is 18km from Phuket and a songthaew (leaving from the intersection of Th Krung Thep and the fountain circle) costs 25B per person. Tuk-tuk charters are, as usual, 150B to 200B one way.

Hat Rawai & Laem Kha

Rawai was one of the first coastal areas on Phuket to be developed, simply because it was near Phuket and there was already a rather large fishing community there. Once other nicer beach areas like Patong and Karon were 'discovered', Rawai gradually began to lose popularity and today it is a rather spiritless place – but at least it's not crowded.

The beach is not great, but there is a lot

happening in or near Rawai: there is a local sea gypsy village; Hat Laem Kha (better than Rawai) is to the north-east; boats to the nearby islands of Ko Lon, Ko Hae, Ko Aew, Ko Phi and others; and good snorkelling off **Laem Phromthep** at the southern tip of Phuket island, easy to approach from Rawai. In fact, most of the visitors who stay at Rawai these days are divers who want to be near Phromthep and/or boat facilities for offshore diving trips.

Laem Phromthep is also a popular viewing point at sunset, when lots of shutterbugs gather to take the famous Phromthep shot. On a hill next to the viewpoint is a shrine to Phra Phrom (Brahma).

The diving around the offshore islands is not bad, especially at Kaew Yai and Kaew Noi, off Phromthep and at Ko Hae. It's a good idea to shop around for boat trips to these islands to find the least expensive passage – the larger the group, the lower the cost per person.

Places to Stay The long-running *Salaloy Seafood & Bungalows (Salaloy Resort;*

☎ 076-381370, 52/2 Th Wiset) has bungalows for 300B with fan, up to 800B with air-con. Their well patronised seafood restaurant is one of the better – and more moderately priced – ones in the area. Adjacent is the similar **Porn Mae Bungalows** (☎/fax 381300).

The **Siam Phuket Resort** (☎ 076-381346, fax 3812347) offers quite sturdy-looking bungalows in the 750B to 1300B range.

Round at Laem Kha, the well-managed **Phuket Island Resort** (☎ 076-381010, fax 381018) has air-con rooms from 2000B, a swimming pool and other mod-cons. The **Laem Kha Beach Inn** (☎ 076-381305) has 20 rooms spread out among coconut groves starting at 450B, and reaching up to 1200B for larger ones.

About 2.5km north of Rawai, about halfway to the Ao Chalong traffic roundabout, is **Friendship Beach** (☎ 076-381281, fax 381034), a little self-contained bungalow complex that seems to cater to longer-term visitors. The nine units cost 300B to 500B. Aside from its own modest little beach, this place has a pool table, a useful bulletin board, universal gym, a video library, and second-hand shops for books, clothing and marine equipment. Perhaps most interesting, it hosts live music jam sessions every weekend (rock, R&B and blues on Saturday, jazz on Sunday).

Places to Eat Aside from the restaurants attached to the resorts in Rawai (Salaloy is the best), the only places to eat are the **seafood and noodle vendors** set up along the roadside near the beach. Just below the viewpoint for Laem Phromthep, **Prom Thep Cape Restaurant** offers simple Thai meals.

Getting There & Away Rawai is about 16km from Phuket and getting there costs 15B by songthaew from the circle at Th Krung Thep. Tuk-tuk charters cost at least 110B from Phuket.

Laem Singh & Hat Kamala

North of Ao Patong, 24km from Phuket, Laem Singh (Cape Singh) is a beautiful little rock-dominated beach. You could camp

here and eat at the rustic roadside seafood places at the north end of Singh or in Ban Kamala, a village farther south. If you're renting a motorbike, this is a nice little trip down Route 4025 and then over dirt roads from Surin to Kamala.

Hat Kamala is a lovely stretch of sand and sea south of Surin and Laem Singh. The north end, the nicest area, is shaded by casuarinas and features a small thatched-roof snack bar with free sling chairs and umbrellas available. The middle of the beach is now dominated by resorts and seafood restaurants. Most of the villagers here are Muslim, and there are a couple of rustic mosques towards the southern end of the main village, also known as Bang Wan. Visitors should dress modestly when walking around the village in deference to local mores. Topless or nude beach bathing would be extremely offensive to the locals.

Bangkok's Safari World has leased a 160 acre plot near the beach for the construction of a US$60 million entertainment park called Phuket Fantasea. The sagging Thai economy has delayed the project but the developers claim it will eventually be completed.

Places to Stay The up-market **Phuket Kamala Resort** (☎ 076-324396, fax 324399) dominates the centre of the beach and costs 1650B to 1950B. The bungalows have private balconies, air-con and TV; the coffee shop serves Thai and western food.

Also on the other side of the road from the beach are several less expensive options. Many eschew air-con, which is eminently sensible as Kamala hasn't become 'concrete-ised' enough yet to demand it. The quiet **Bird Beach Bungalows** (☎/fax 076-270669) offers small, clean cottages with fan and cold water for 500B. In this same area are several laundry services and minimarts, evidence that Kamala is attracting long-termers. Other modest places to stay include the nearby **Malinee House** (☎ 076-271355), which offers five fan rooms for 350B to 440B each, **Kamala Seafood** (☎ 076-324426), with four rooms for 400B, and **Pa Pa Crab** (☎ 076-324315), where a room in a house costs 300B and a bungalow on the beach is 500B. Towards the north end of the beach near the police station, *Nanork Seafood & Buffalo Bar* (☎ 076-270668) has clean, new fan rooms for rent for 500B. Most of these places don't take guests from May to October.

At the southern end of the bay, overlooking but not on the beach, is *Kamala Beach Estate* (☎ 076- 270756, fax 324115, email kamala.beach@phuket.com), where fully equipped, high-security, modern time-share apartments go for US$100 to US$312 a night. Around the headland farther south, the similar *Kamala Bay Terrace* (☎ 076-270801, fax 270818, email kamala@samart.co.th) has more luxurious apartments and time-shares for 3400B to 7000B per night (low season), 4150B to 13,300B (high season). Between 20 December and 5 January there is a five-night minimum stay; peak season surcharges apply.

Places to Eat The best value for eating is the friendly and moderately priced *thatched-roof restaurant* at the north end of the beach. Near Bird Beach Bungalow are the decent *Kamala Seafood* and *Jaroen Seafood*, both family-run Thai seafood places that cater to faràngs. *Paul's Place Pub & Kitchen* (☎ 076-270756), next to Kamala Beach Estate at the south end of the bay, is the most up-market place to eat; it offers good views of the bay and reliable Thai and western food.

For something more local, try one of the several *kopíi shops* (with strong coffee or kopíi) in the village.

Getting There & Away A regular songthaew to Kamala costs 25B per person 7 am to 5 pm, while a charter reaches 250B.

Hat Surin

North of Hat Kamala and a little north of Laem Singh, Hat Surin has a long beach and sometimes fairly heavy surf. When the water is calm, there's fair snorkelling here. The beach has long been a popular place for local Thais to come and nibble at seafood snacks sold by vendors along the beach. Just before Surin, in Bang Thao Village No 2, is one of Southern Thailand's most beautiful mosques, **Matsayit Mukaram**, a large, whitewashed, immaculate structure with lacquered wooden doors.

Places to Stay Surin's northern end has been dubbed 'Pansea Beach' by developers and is claimed by the exclusive Amanpuri and The Chedi resorts. The former Pansea has been re-christened *The Chedi Phuket* (☎ 076-324017, fax 324252, email info@chedi-phuket.com) and now offers 89 rooms and 21 two-bedroom cottages with teak floors and private verandahs starting from US$140 to US$840, depending on the season and type of accommodation. The Chedi has its own golf course.

Amanpuri Resort (☎ 076-324333, fax 324100, email amanpuri@phuket.com) plays host to Thailand's celebrity traffic, each of whom gets a 133 sq metre pavilion or private two to six-bedroom villa home and a personal attendant; the staff to guest ratio is 3½ to one. It's owned by Indonesian Adrian Zecha and designed by the architect who designed the former Shah of Iran's Winter Palace. Depending on the season, you can expect to pay US$380 to US$860 for a pavilion, US$1220 to US$3276 for a villa. The resort offers about 20 cruisers for sailing, diving and overnight charters, six tennis courts, a gym, and Thai and Italian restaurants. The Amanpuri was once censured by the local community for the improper display of Buddha images.

Towards the southern end of Hat Surin, *Surin Sweet Apartment* (☎ 076-270863, fax 270865), *Sabai Corner Apartment* (☎ 076-2711467, 01-956 4795) and *Tangthai Guesthouse & Restaurant* (☎ 076-270259) offer simple but modern rooms in the 400B to 800B range.

Getting There & Away A regular songthaew from Phuket's Th Ranong to Hat Surin costs 20B per person and tuk-tuk or songthaew charter 250B to 300B.

HAT KAMALA, HAT SURIN & AO BANG THAO

1 Banyan Tree Phuket
2 The Allamanda .
3 Sheraton Grande Laguna
   Beach
4 Dusit Laguna Resort
5 Tatonka
6 Laguna Beach Club
7 Royal Park Travelodge
   Resort
8 Bangtao Lagoon
   Bungalow
9 Amanpuri Resort

Ao Bang Thao

Choeng Thaleh

To Matsayit
Mukaram
& Heroines
Monument

0   1   2 km

Approximate Scale

ANDAMAN
SEA

Laem Son
Laem Singh
Hat Surin
Hat Kamala

To
Patong

Kamala

10 The Chedi Phuket
11 Surin Sweet Apartment
12 Tangthai Guesthouse
   & Restaurant
13 Nanork Seafood
   & Buffalo Bar
14 Malinee House
15 Bird Beach Bungalows;
   Kamala Seafood;
   Javoen Seafood
16 Phuket Kamala Resort
17 Mosque
18 Kamala Beach Estate;
   Paul's Place Pub
   & Kitchen
19 Kamala Bay Terrace

Ao Bang Thao

North of Surin around Laem Son lies Ao Bang Thao, an 8km sand-rimmed bay and beach with an 18 hole golf course that has attracted much upscale development. A steady breeze makes it a haven for sailboarders; since 1992 the annual Siam World Cup windsurfing championships have been held here (formerly at Pattaya's Hat Jomtien). A system of lagoons inland from the beach has been incorporated into the resorts and golf course, hence this is sometimes referred to as 'Laguna Beach'.

Places to Stay With one exception, Bang Thao is strictly for the well-to-do nowadays. All the hotels in Bang Thao (except for Royal Park Travelodge Resort) are part of an integrated resort system so if you stay at one of the hotels you can use any of the

facilities of the other hotels. A shuttle operates between all of the properties.

Least expensive is the quiet and secluded *Bangtao Lagoon Bungalow* (☎ 076-324260, fax 324168) at the south end of the bay, with 50 private bungalows ranging from 500B to 1600B. Newer bungalows are 1300B. Rates are 30% less in the low season. The restaurant on the premises serves Thai and European dishes.

The plush *Dusit Laguna Resort* (☎ 076-324320, fax 324174, Bangkok ☎ 02-238 4790, email dusit@lagunaphuket.com) has 226 guest rooms and suites starting at US$303, with suites costing up to US$847, not including tax. From 20 December to 20 February peak-season surcharges apply. Another top-end place towards the centre of the beach is *Royal Park Travelodge Resort* (☎ 076-324021, fax 324243), where rooms start at 3250B in the low season, up to 3800B in the high.

Bringing yet more beachside luxury to the bay are *Sheraton Grande Laguna Beach* (☎ 076-324101, fax 324108, email sheraton@phuket.com) and *Banyan Tree Phuket* (☎ 076-324374, fax 324375, email banyan@phuket.com). The Sheraton features a sprawling 240 guest rooms (US$220 to US$290) and 84 'grande villas' (US$375 to US$635) in the high season (US$20 less in the low season), while the more exclusive Banyan Tree has 98 villas (all with open-air sunken bathtubs, 34 with private pool and jacuzzi) from US$400 to US$780. The hotel boasts a golf course, full-service spa, three tennis courts, a lap pool and free-form swimming pool. The Sheraton is the only place on this beach with a fitness centre. The Banyan Tree specialises in spiritual and physical spa treatments, including massage, seaweed packs and meditation; in 1998 it was voted the world's best spa by readers of *Condé Nast Traveler*.

The Allamanda (☎ 076-324359, fax 324360, email allamanda@lagunaphuket .com) offers 94 units starting at US$145 for a junior suite in the low season to US$380 for a duplex villa in the high season; all suites come with kitchenette and satellite TV. The

Laguna Beach Club (☎ *076-324352, fax 324353 or 270993 reservation fax only, email beachclub@lagunaphuket.com*) rivals the Sheraton and Dusit in providing 252 rooms for US$185 to US$215 plus tax and service. Set on 20 acres, the resort features a four-acre water park that incorporates waterfalls, water slides, whirlpool swimming pools and a scuba pool.

Places to Eat The Sheraton boasts four restaurants, including the *Tea House*, an upscale recreation of an old traditional Hong Kong tea house, specialising in Chinese cuisine, as well as private dinner boats on the lagoons.

Tatonka (☎ *076-324349*), near the entrance to the Dusit Laguna Resort, features 'globetrotter' cuisine, which owner-chef Harold Schwarz developed by taking fresh local products and combining them with cooking and presentation techniques learned from his kitchen training in Europe and his experiences with the foods of Hawaii and the American South-West ('tatonka' is the Sioux word for American buffalo). It's expensive and open for dinner only; reservations suggested.

Getting There & Away A songthaew from Phuket's Th Ranong to Surin, Kamala or Bang Thao costs 20B per person. Tuk-tuk charters are 200B.

Nai Thon

Improved roads to Hat Nai Thon have brought only a small amount of development to this broad expanse of pristine sand backed by casuarina and pandanus trees. Down on the beach, umbrellas and sling chairs are available from Thai vendors. Swimming is quite good here except at the height of the monsoon, and there is some coral near the headlands at either end of the bay. The submerged remains of a wrecked 50m-long tin dredger lie farther off the coast near tiny **Ko Waew** at a depth of 16m. Naithon Beach Resort can arrange dive trips in the vicinity.

North of Naithon Beach Resort on the beach side of the road stands a **spirit shrine**

erected by local Muslim fishermen to appease the sea deities of their chao náam forebears. The road up over the headland of Laem Son (Pine Cape) to the south was completed in 1995 but has already suffered bridge washouts and potholing. This road passes two smaller coves, **Nai Thon Noi** and **Hin Khruai** with deserted strips of sand. Hin Khruai usually has a seafood vendor or two during the dry months. The tiny settlement of **Ban Sakhu**, inland to the north-east of Hat Nai Thon, is awash with flowers and fruit orchards.

Plenty of construction seems to be going on behind the beach, most of it residential.

Places to Stay & Eat American-managed *Naithon Beach Resort* (☎ *076-205379, fax 205381*) starts at 1000B a night for large, tastefully designed wooden cottages on the opposite side of the access road from the beach. Air-con cottages start at 1400B. Rates fall to 800B and 1000B respectively if you stay three days or more. A small restaurant serves sandwiches and Thai food. The resort closes down in the rainy season.

Down the beach a short distance, *Tien Seng* serves Thai and Chinese dishes. A few food vendors can usually be found beneath the trees along the back edge of the beach as well. Tien Seng's proprietors plan to add a few 500B to 800B guest rooms to the restaurant in the near future.

Getting There & Away Songthaews from Phuket cost 30B per person and run between 7 am and 5 pm only. A charter costs 300B; if you're coming straight from the airport it would be less trouble, less expensive and quicker to hire a taxi for 200B.

Hat Nai Yang & Hat Mai Khao

Both of these beaches are near Phuket international airport, about 30km from Phuket town. Nai Yang, a fairly secluded beach favoured by Thais, belongs to **Sirinat National Park**, a relatively new protected area that combines former Nai Yang National Park with a wildlife reserve at Mai Khao. The park encompasses 22 sq km of coastline, plus

68 sq km of sea, from the western Phang-Nga provincial border south to the headland that separates Nai Yang from Nai Thon.

About 5km north of Nai Yang is Hat Mai Khao, Phuket's longest beach. Sea turtles lay their eggs on the beach here between November and February each year. A visitors centre with toilets, showers and picnic tables can be found at Mai Khao (replacing the old headquarters at the northern end of Nai Yang), from which there are some short trails through the casuarinas to a steep beach. Take care when swimming at Mai Khao, as there's a strong year-round undertow. Except on weekends and holidays you'll have this place almost entirely to yourself; even during peak periods, peace and solitude are usually only a few steps away, as there's so much space here.

On the other side of the road from the visitors centre, a network of raised wooden walkways takes visitors on a self-guided tour of natural mangrove forest.

About a kilometre off Nai Yang is a large reef at a depth of 10 to 20m. Snorkelling and scuba equipment can be hired at the Pearl Village Resort. Judging from the lie of the reef, there could be a surfable reef break here during the south-west monsoon.

The area between Nai Yang and Mai Khao is largely given over to shrimp farming. Fortunately shrimp farmers here don't dig artificial lagoons into the beach or mangrove (as at Ko Chang or Khao Sam Roi Yot) but rather they raise the spawn in self-contained concrete tanks, a practice significantly less harmful to the environment.

Places to Stay & Eat Camping is allowed on both Nai Yang and Mai Khao beaches without any permit. *Sirinat National Park* (☎ 076-327407) rents six-bed bungalows at Nai Yang for 400B and a 12 bed bungalow for 800B. Check at the building opposite the visitor centre. Two-person tents can be rented for 60B a night.

Privately operated *Phuket Campground* (☎ 01-676 4318, email camp-ground@ phuket-mall.com) on Ao Mai Khao charges 100B per person to rent tents very near the beach, each with rice mats, pillows, blankets and a torch (flashlight). A light mangrove thicket separates the campground from the beach, but the proprietors don't mind if you move their tents onto the beach crest. A small outdoor restaurant/bar provides sustenance. Other amenities include a shower and toilet, hammocks, sling chairs and beach umbrellas, and a fireplace.

Commercial hotel development has been permitted towards the southern end of Hat Nai Yang, well back from the beach itself. *Garden Cottage* (☎/fax 076-327293) is actually on Route 4026, back from the southern end of Hat Nai Yang, 1.5km from the airport, but still within a five minute walk of the beach. Tidy cottages with fan, fridge and private bath start at around 800B; 400B more for air-con (less in low season).

The fancy *Pearl Village Resort* (☎ 076-327006, fax 327338, email pearlvil@loxinfo .co.th) commands 8.1 hectares at the southern end of Nai Yang. The resort has three pricey restaurants and a German-operated dive centre. Air-con rooms start at 2800B, cottages are 3200B to 4000B. Suites are available for up to 16,000B. Also at this end is the *Crown Nai Yang Suite Hotel* (☎ 076-327420, fax 327323, email crown@phuket .com), a rather unsightly multi-storey place that rents modern boxes (some without windows) for 1815B and up, around 300B less in low season. Airline crews stopping over between flights in and out of Phuket often use this hotel.

Along the dirt road at the very southern end of the beach is a seemingly endless strip of *seafood restaurants* and, oddly enough, tailor shops. There is also a small minimart near the entrance to the Pearl Village Resort.

Getting There & Away A songthaew from Phuket to Nai Yang costs 20B, while a tuk-tuk charter is 250B to 300B. There is no regular songthaew stop for Mai Khao but a tuk-tuk charter costs the same as for Nai Yang.

Nearby Islands

On **Ko Hae**, an island a few kilometres south-south-east of Ao Chalong, the **Coral Island Resort** (☎ 076-281060, fax 381957, email coral_island@phuket.com) has up-market bungalows from 2300B with air-con. Ko Hae is also referred to as Coral Island. It's a good spot for diving and snorkelling if you don't plan on going farther out to sea, although jet skis and other pleasure craft can be an annoyance. The island gets lots of day-trippers from Phuket, but at night it's pretty quiet.

Ko Mai Thon, south-east of Laem Phanwa, is similar but slightly smaller. On this island **Maiton Resort** (☎ 076-214954, fax 214959) rents luxurious hillside bungalows for 9075B, beachside for 10,890 (low season from 7500B).

Two islands about 1½ hours by boat south of Phuket, **Ko Raya Yai** and **Ko Raya Noi** (also known as Ko Racha Yai/Noi), are highly favoured by divers and snorkellers for their hard coral reefs. Because the coral is found in both shallow and deep waters, it's a good area for novice scuba divers and snorkellers as well as accomplished divers. Visibility can reach 15 to 30m during dry, post-monsoon months. Most tourist activity focuses on Ao Nam Ta Tok (Falling Teardrops Bay), a broad sandy beach on Ko Raya Yai with very calm surf November to May and several types of accommodation. A footpath leads over a central ridge from Ao Nam Ta Tok to a pretty and as yet un-developed white sand beach on the other side of the island.

At Ao Nam Ta Tok on Ko Raya Yai, accommodation is available at **Jungle Bungalow** (☎ 076-228550, 01-229 1913), with 300B to 500B rooms; **Raya Resort** (☎ 076-327803) with simple palm-thatch bungalows for 300B to 500B; the identically named **Raya Resort** with 700B fan rooms; and **Raya Andaman Resort** (☎ 076-381710, fax 381713) with air-con digs from 700B. All accommodations close down during the south-west monsoon, May to November.

For information on attractions and accommodation on the island of Ko Yao Noi and Ko Yao Yai, off Phuket's north-eastern shore, see the Around Phang-Nga section earlier in this chapter.

Getting There & Away Boats leave Ao Chalong for Ko Hae once daily at 9.30 am, take 30 minutes and cost 60B.

Songserm Travel (☎ 076-222570) runs passenger boats to Ko Raya Yai from Phuket town port daily at 8.30 am. The trip takes 1¼ hours and costs 300B one way or 550B return. Pal Travel Service (☎ 076-344920) runs a similar service, while Seatran (☎ 076-211809) has an express boat that leaves Phuket daily at 7 pm and reaches Ko Raya Yai in just 45 minutes, then returns the next day around noon. You can also charter a longtail boat from Ao Chalong for 1500B.

Southern Andaman Coast (Krabi to Satun)

South-east of Phuket, the southern reach of island-studded Ao Phang-Nga opens into the Andaman Sea, and Thailand's greatest concentration of national marine parks begins to unfold, one after another all the way to the Malaysian border. The coastal provinces of Krabi, Trang and Satun represent the country's new frontier in terms of marine tourism. Aside from intensive developments on Ko Phi-Phi and along one small area of the mainland coast near Krabi's provincial capital, most of this stretch remains relatively undiscovered by international visitors.

Krabi Province

The coastal province of Krabi, 60km due east of Phuket, continues the scenic marine karst topography typical of Ao Phang-Nga. More than 200 islands offer excellent recreational opportunities; many of the islands belong to **Hat Nopparat Thara/Ko Phi-Phi National Marine Park** or **Ko Lanta National Marine Park**. Many of Krabi's beaches feature shimmering stretches of sand lapped by calm, clear seas and backed by vine-choked limestone cliffs. Such cliffs have turned into a world-class rock-climbing mecca, and good reef diving is available at several offshore islets nearby. Intact mangrove forests can be seen in several estuarial areas. Krabi is also a jumping off point for Ko Phi-Phi, Ko Lanta and other islands in the area.

Hundreds of years ago, Krabi's waters were a favourite hideout for Asian pirates because of the abundance of islands and water caves. Latter-day pirates now steal islands or parts of islands for development: targets thus far include Phi-Phi Don, Poda, Bubu, Jam (Pu), Po, Bilek (Hong), Kamyai and Kluang. About 40% of the provincial population is Muslim.

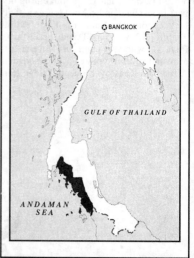

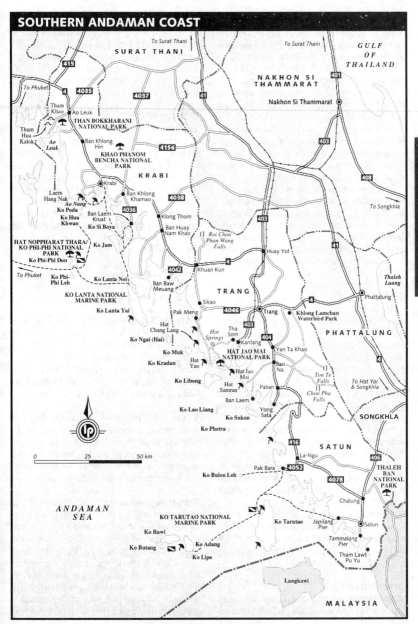

SOUTHERN ANDAMAN COAST

To Surat Thani

To Surat Thani

GULF OF THAILAND

SURAT THANI

415

To Phuket

4

4035

4037

41

401

NAKHON SI THAMMARAT

Nakhon Si Thammarat

Tham Khao

Ao Leuk

THAN BOKKHARANI NATIONAL PARK

Tham Hua Kalok

Ao Leuk

403

Ban Khlong Hin

KHAO PHANOM BENCHA NATIONAL PARK

4156

408

KRABI

Krabi

Ban Khlong Khamao

4038

To Songkhla

Laem Hang Nak

Ao Nang

Ko Poda

Ko Hua Khwan

Ban Laem Kruat

Ko Si Boya

4036

Klong Thom

403

Ban Huay Nam Khao

Roi Chan Phan Wang Falls

Huay Yot

41

HAT NOPPHARAT THARA/ KO PHI-PHI NATIONAL PARK

Ko Phi-Phi Don

Ko Jam

4042

Khuan Kun

Thaleh Luang

To Phuket

Ko Phi-Phi Leh

Ko Lanta Noi

Ban Baw Meuang

TRANG

KO LANTA NATIONAL MARINE PARK

Ko Lanta Yai

Sikao

4046

Trang

Khlong Lamchan Waterbird Park

Phattalung

4

PHATTALUNG

Pak Meng

403

Hat Chang Lang

Tha Som

Hot Springs

Kantang

404

Yan Ta Khao

Ko Ngai (Hai)

Ko Muk

Ko Kradan

Hat Yao

HAT JAO MAI NATIONAL PARK

Hat Jao Mai

Ban Na

Ton Te Falls

To Hat Yai & Songkhla

Ko Libong

Hat Samran

Palian

Choo Pha Falls

SONGKHLA

Ban Laem

Ko Lao Liang

Yong Sata

Ko Sukon

Ko Phetra

SATUN

416

La-Ngu

405

THALEH BAN NATIONAL PARK

Pak Bara

4052

Ko Bulon Leh

4078

Chalung

ANDAMAN SEA

KO TARUTAO NATIONAL MARINE PARK

Ko Tarutao

Jepilang Pier

Satun

Ko Rawi

Tammalang Pier

Ko Butang

Ko Adang

Tham Lawt Pu Yu

Ko Lipe

Langkawi

MALAYSIA

0   25   50 km

LP

The interior of the province, noted for its tropical forests and the Phanom Bencha mountain range, has barely been explored. Birdwatchers come from far and wide to view Gurney's pitta (formerly thought to be extinct) and Nordmann's greenshank.

Krabi has a seldom used deep-sea port financed by local speculators in tin, rubber and palm oil, Krabi's most important sources of income. The port's full potential has never been realised and there's now talk of developing a new, substitute deep-sea port farther south in Satun to spare Krabi's natural tourist attractions from shipping pollution.

Beach accommodation is relatively inexpensive (though not as cheap as, for example, Ko Pha-Ngan) and there are regular boats to Ko Phi-Phi, 42km south-west. While nearly deserted in the rainy season (a good time to go if you're seeking solitude or low rates), the hotels and bungalows along Krabi's beaches can fill up from December to March.

KRABI
• pop 18,500

Nearly 1000km from Bangkok and 180km from Phuket, this fast-developing provincial capital has friendly people, good food and some good beaches nearby. The capital sits on the banks of the Krabi River right before it empties into the Andaman Sea. Across from town you can see Bird, Cat and Mouse islands, limestone isles named for their shapes.

Most travellers breeze through town on their way to Ko Lanta to the south, Ko Phi-Phi to the south-west or the beaches near Ao Nang to the west. But Krabi, with its pleasant riverside setting and good selection of restaurants, is also not a bad place to kick back for a day or two.

Although Krabi is essentially more Taoist-Confucianist and Muslim than Theravada Buddhist, **Wat Kaew** contains some older late 19th and 20th century buildings and lots of large old trees.

Orientation
Maps Bangkok Guide publishes the handy *Guide Map of Krabi* (50B) which contains several minimaps of areas of interest throughout the province. If it's kept up to date it should prove to be very useful for travel in the area. *Krabi Holiday Guide*, a locally produced, undated pamphlet costing 100B, is also very informative, though somewhat biased towards advertisers.

Information
Tourist Offices TAT (☎ 075-612740) maintains a small office on Thanon (Th) Utarakit near the waterfront. They have lots of useful printed information, including a few maps that depict the province, the capital and the islands of Ko Phi-Phi and Ko Lanta, along with accommodation lists.

Another 'tourist information booth' can be found near the night market on the waterfront; it's actually a ticket agency for buses and boats run by PP Family Co.

Immigration Visas can easily be extended at the immigration office, south of the post office on Th Chamai Anuson.

Post & Telephone The post and telephone office is on Th Utarakit south of the turn-off for the Saphaan Jao Fah (Jao Fah pier); there's a separate poste restante entrance at the side. Home Direct international phone service is available here daily, 7 am to midnight.

Email & Internet Access Paknam Restaurant, towards the south end of Th Khongkha on the waterfront, offers email and Internet services. No doubt several more places will open up as the Net continues to tighten its grip on the masses.

Travel Agencies Krabi has dozens of fly-by-night travel agencies that will book accommodation at beaches and islands as well as tour-bus and boat tickets. Use these places with caution: few travellers have given any of these places glowing reports. Chan Phen Travel and Jungle Book, both on Th Utarakit, are still the most reliable. Jam Travel, between the two aforementioned places, is also good.

Bookshops Phuket-based The Books has the an outlet at 78-80 Th Maharat. The selection of English language books and magazines is rather slim, although they do carry same-day issues of the *Bangkok Post*.

Eco-Trips

Chan Phen Travel runs half-day boat tours to nearby estuaries for a look at mangrove ecology (300B to 350B per person), or you can simply hire a boat at Saphaan Jao Fah for 200B per hour. Bird species that frequent mangrove areas include the sea eagle and ruddy kingfisher. In mud and shallow waters, keep an eye out for fiddler crabs and mudskippers.

At the Khao Nor Chuchi (Naw Juu-Jii) Lowland Forest Project, visitors can follow trails through lowland rainforest, swim in clear forest pools and observe or participate in local village activities like rubber-tapping. A daily fee of 250B includes these activities along with meals and lodging in thatched huts – proceeds go towards reforestation, rural development, nature education and wildlife research. The project is 56km south of Krabi, but arrangements can be made through Chan Phen Travel; you'll need a minimum of four people to arrange this trip.

Chan Phen and other travel agencies in Krabi do day trips to Khao Nor Chuchi for 450B per person with visits to a hot springs near Khlong Thom, a rubber plantation, lunch at Sa Thung Tiaw and a visit to the museum at Wat Khlong Thom. The fee includes air-con transport, lunch and beverages; bring a swimsuit and good walking shoes.

Travel agencies in Krabi (as well as at Ao Nang or Ao Phra Nang farther north) can also arrange trips to idyllic uninhabited isles nearby, all with coral reefs and luscious beaches set in tranquil sandy coves. Rates for such trips run from 250B to 280B.

SeaCanoe Thailand and Krabi Canoe Tour operate sea canoe/kayak trips along the coast; both companies can be contacted on Ao Nang (see the later Ao Nang & Laem Phra Nang section).

Places to Stay

Guesthouses The cheapest places to stay in Krabi are the many guesthouses, which seem to be everywhere. Some stay around only a season or two, others seem fairly stable. The ones situated in the business district feature closet-like rooms above modern shop buildings, often with faulty plumbing – OK for one night before heading to a nearby beach or island but not great for longer stays.

The small *Riverside Guest House* (☎ 075-612536) on Th Khongkha near Saphaan Jao Fah and Customs House has decent 80B and 100B rooms with shared facilities and a restaurant with good vegetarian food. The local Rotary Club meets here on Thursday afternoons. Next door to the Riverside, *S&R Guest House* (☎ 075-611930) has similar rooms for 100B.

Swallow Guest House (☎ 075-611645), on Th Prachacheun, is a popular place with fairly clean and comfortable rooms for 100B (no window) and 120B (with window).

On Th Ruen Rudee are several other places with the usual upstairs rooms and slow plumbing, including the *KL Guest House* (☎ 075-612511) with rooms for 100B single/double with shared bathroom. Around the corner on Th Maharat is the similar *Seaside Guest House* (☎ 075-612801), with rooms for 100B to 150B.

Better than either of these are the large, fairly clean rooms with private bath at *Grand Tower Hotel & Guest House* (☎ 075-621456/7), over Grand Travel Center on Th Utarakit. Rates here are 250/300B for singles/doubles with fan, phone and private bath; despite its name it has none of the facilities of a hotel and is run like a guesthouse. There are also a few rooms with shared bathroom for 130/150B. Just down Th Utarakit from here, *PS Guest House* has a few well maintained 80/100B rooms behind a travel agency.

Quieter and more comfortable are a few guesthouses just south-west of town near the courthouse. At *Chao Fa Valley Guesthouse & Resort* (☎ 075-612499, 50 Th Jao Fah) has good-sized bamboo bungalows with fan for 200B to 400B. Next, on the same side of Th Jao Fah, **KR Mansion & Guest House** (☎ 075-612761) offers 40 hotel-style rooms for 150B with fan and shared bathroom, 200B with private bath. The KR will also rent rooms by the month. The rooftop beer garden provides a 360° view of Krabi – great for sunsets. The staff can arrange motorcycle rentals, local tours and boat tickets as well.

Along Th Utarakit, near the post office, **Cha Guest House** is a plain wooden building

atop shophouses, with shared facilities for 60/80B. Even cheaper are the rooms behind **Jungle Book Tour & Guest House** (☎ 075-611148, ☎/fax 621186, 141 Th Utarakit), where tiny, older cubicles cost 50B while slightly bigger cubicles are 80B. All come with fans, and mattresses in both kinds of room are surprisingly good; bath/toilet facilities are shared.

Hotels In the centre of town, **City Hotel** (☎ 075-621280, fax 621301, 15/2-3 Th

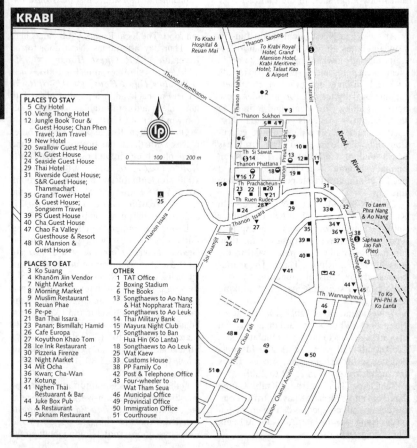

KRABI

PLACES TO STAY
5 City Hotel
10 Vieng Thong Hotel
12 Jungle Book Tour & Guest House; Chan Phen Travel; Jam Travel
19 New Hotel
20 Swallow Guest House
22 KL Guest House
24 Seaside Guest House
29 Thai Hotel
31 Riverside Guest House; S&R Guest House; Thammachart
35 Grand Tower Hotel & Guest House; Songserm Travel
39 PS Guest House
40 Cha Guest House
47 Chao Fa Valley Guesthouse & Resort
48 KR Mansion & Guest House

PLACES TO EAT
3 Ko Suang
4 Khanŏm Jiin Vendor
7 Night Market
8 Morning Market
9 Muslim Restaurant
11 Reuan Phae
16 Pe-pe
21 Ban Thai Issara
23 Panan; Bismillah; Hamid
26 Cafe Europa
27 Koyuthon Khao Tom
28 Ice Ink Restaurant
30 Pizzeria Firenze
32 Night Market
34 Mit Ocha
36 Kwan; Cha-Wan
37 Kotung
41 Nghen Thai Restuarant & Bar
44 Juke Box Pub & Restaurant
45 Paknam Restaurant

OTHER
1 TAT Office
2 Boxing Stadium
6 The Books
13 Songthaews to Ao Nang & Hat Nopparat Thara; Songthaews to Ao Leuk
14 Thai Military Bank
15 Mayura Night Club
17 Songthaews to Ban Hua Hin (Ko Lanta)
18 Songthaews to Ao Leuk
25 Wat Kaew
33 Customs House
38 PP Family Co
42 Post & Telephone Office
43 Four-wheeler to Wat Tham Seua
46 Municipal Office
49 Provincial Office
50 Immigration Office
51 Courthouse

Sukhon) also has pretty clean rooms at 300/480B for fan/air-con. Larger rooms with better TVs and air-conditioners cost 550B to 750B; parking is available in a small lot next to the hotel.

Among the town's older hotels, *New Hotel* (☎ 075-611541) on Th Phattana has somewhat seedy rooms for 150B to 200B with fan and bath, 400B with air-con. *Thai Hotel* (☎ 075-611474, fax 620564, 3-7 Th Issara) used to be good value, but they continue to raise the rates and lower the standards (stained carpets, cigarette-burned blankets). Overpriced single/double rooms with fan cost 300/330B, air-con 440/520B. *Vieng Thong Hotel* (☎ 075-620020, fax 612525, 155 Th Utarakit) has small OK rooms for 300B with fan, 600B with air-con; all rooms have phones and there's a parking lot attached.

The well run *Grand Mansion Hotel* (☎ 075-620833, fax 611372, 289/1 Th Utarakit) offers plain but comfortable fan-cooled rooms with hot shower for 300B, with air-con 480B to 900B.

The relatively new *Krabi Royal Hotel* (☎ 075-611582, fax 611581, 403 Th Utarakit), near the more expensive Krabi Meritime at the northern edge of town, charges 900B for a comfortable air-con room with TV, minifridge, phone and hot shower with tub, including breakfast for two. Discounts are available for stays of more than one night.

The swanky *Krabi Meritime Hotel* (☎ 075-620028/46, fax 612992, Bangkok ☎ 02-719 0034, fax 318 7687) is near the river on the way to Talaat Kao, about 2km from downtown Krabi. Rates for well decorated rooms with balconies and impressive views of the river and mountains start at 2200B. Facilities include a nightclub, a great swimming pool, walking path, a lake with swan-shaped paddleboats and canoes, a fitness centre, sauna and convention facilities. The pool is open to the public for a daily fee of 60B for adults, 40B children.

Places to Eat

What Krabi lacks in good guesthouses it more than makes up for in good eating

places. Along Th Khongkha is a *night market* near Saphaan Jao Fah, with great seafood at low prices and a host of Thai dessert vendors. There's also another *night market* near the intersection of Th Maharat and Maharat Soi 8 (Th Si Sawat).

One of the better and most reasonably priced restaurants in town for standard Thai dishes and local cuisine is the *Kotung*, also near Saphaan Jao Fah. The *tôm yam kûng* (spicy shrimp lemon-grass soup) is especially good, as is anything else made with fresh seafood.

Reuan Phae, an old floating restaurant on the river in front of town, is fine for a beer or rice whisky while watching the river rise and fall with the tide. Although the food at Reuan Phae is not that great overall, certain dishes, including the fried shrimp cakes *(thâwt man kûng)* and spicy steamed curried fish *(hàw mòk thâleh)*, are well worth trying and prices are low to moderate.

Pe-pe, on the corner of Th Maharat and Th Prachacheun, is a clean place that serves good, inexpensive noodles and *khâo man kài* (Hainanese-style chicken and rice); it's very popular at lunchtime. Another good area for lunches is the three-way intersection at Th Preuksa Uthit and Th Sukhon (aka Soi 10, Th Maharat). Along with the *roti kaeng* place mentioned in the following Southern Thai & Muslim entry, you'll find several inexpensive noodle and rice shops. *Ko Suang* (no roman-script sign), on Th Sukhon opposite the north end of Th Preuksa Uthit, serves good, inexpensive khâo man kài, *khâo mūu dàeng* ('red' pork with rice), *kūaytīaw* (wide rice noodles) and *bà-mìi* (wheat noodles). At the south-western corner of this intersection is a good *khanŏm jiin* (Chinese noodles with curry) *vendor*.

For cheap Thai breakfasts, the *morning market* off Th Si Sawat in the middle of town is good. Another cheap and tasty breakfast spot is *Mit Ocha*, a funky coffee shop on the corner of Th Khongkha and Th Jao Fah, opposite the customs house. Besides Thai-style coffee and tea, the old Chinese couple here serve khanŏm jiin (served with chunks of pineapple as well as the

SOUTHERN ANDAMAN COAST

usual assorted vegies), and custard and sticky rice wrapped in banana leaves *(khâo nĭaw săngkha-yaa)* – help yourself from the plates on the tables. It's a good place to hang out if you're waiting for the morning boat to Phi-Phi.

The nicely decorated *Ban Thai Issara* on Th Ruen Rudee, run by a New Zealand woman and her Thai husband, specialises in western breakfasts and a mixed menu of decent Thai and faràng food; the selection of home-baked breads and imported cheeses is particularly good. It's only open 8 am to late afternoon, and is closed throughout the rainy season. *Pizzeria Firenze (10 Th Khongkha)*, does good pizza, pasta, wine, gelato and Italian breads. Around the bend on Th Khongkha, near Saphaan Jao Fah, are a couple of other faràng-oriented eateries, including *Kwan* and *Cha-Wan*, both of which specialise in Thai food designed for timid western palates. Nicely decorated with modern art, both restaurants also serve pasta, salads, burgers, sandwiches and breakfasts; there are a few tables out the front.

Farther south along Th Khongkha are the less frequented *Juke Box Pub & Restaurant* and *Paknam Restaurant*, both small bar/restaurants with limited food service. The Paknam offers email and Internet service downstairs and is open 8 am to 11 pm.

Thammachart, below the Riverside Guest House, serves good vegetarian food. *Ice Ink Restaurant*, opposite Ban Thai Issara, is a Thai curry place with lots of vegetarian dishes, especially tofu. Over on Th Jao Fa, *Nghen Thai Restaurant & Bar* features indoor and outdoor sections in a wooden house, and a menu of the same kind of food all the other tourist restaurants in town have – sandwiches, breakfast, milkshakes, spaghetti, Thai food, rice and noodles.

More substantial western meals are available at *Cafe Europa* (☎/fax 075-620407, 1/9 Soi Ruamjit) off Th Issara, a Scandinavian-style restaurant with imported Danish cheeses, steaks, Danish roast pork, baked potatoes, sandwiches and imported wines.

Reuan Mai is a very good Thai-style *sŭan aahăan* (garden restaurant) on Th Maharat near Krabi Hospital about 1.6km north-north-east from the intersection of Th Maharat and Th Sukhon, 400m past the big Chinese temple on the left. It's mostly a locals' place but well worth seeking out for the high-quality Thai food.

If you're out late – many restaurants in town close by 9 pm – *Koyuthon Khao Tom* (no roman-script sign) is an all night *khâo tôm/aahăan taam sàng* place on Th Issara near Th Maharat.

Southern Thai & Muslim Places for spicy Thai-Malay Muslim cuisine continue to multiply as the earnings of the local populace rise with tourism development. *Panan*, on the corner of Th Ruen Rudee and Th Maharat, has *khâo mòk kài* (chicken biryani) in the mornings, inexpensive curries and kŭaytĭaw the rest of day. The roman-script sign reads 'Makanan Islam' (Malay for 'Muslim food'). Next door are two other decent Muslim places, *Bismillah* and *Hamid*, with signs in Thai/Yawi only.

Not far from the morning market, on Th Preuksa Uthit, the *Muslim Restaurant* serves *roti kaeng* (known as roti chanai in Malay), the Malaysian-style breakfast of flatbread and curry. Look for a sign that says 'Hot Roti Curry Service'. They have other Thai-Malay dishes as well.

Getting There & Away

Air The airport is 24km south-east of Krabi, on the northern side of Hwy 4. THAI flies between Bangkok and Krabi three times a week, at the time of writing, but is expected to increase to daily flights by the time you read this. A one-way fare is 2150B and the flight is 1¼ hours each way. Bangkok Airways flies between Ko Samui and Krabi daily for 1770B one way. This flight takes around 40 minutes.

Travel agencies in Krabi offer minivan transport to and from the airport for 50B.

Bus & Minivan Grumpy agents at Songserm Travel (in the Grand Tower Hotel) and PP Family Co scoop up much of the naive tourist business in the city centre.

It's easy buying tickets here but departure times and bus conditions are unreliable and at times unpredictable. If you use the government (Baw Khaw Saw) terminal in nearby Talaat Kao you'll save yourself the trouble of worrying about whether private buses booked in town really turn out to be what was advertised or whether they will leave at the scheduled time. This well organised government bus terminal features separate ticket booths for each line (printed in English), a clean little restaurant, snacks and drinks for sale and clean toilets. The terminal is at Talaat Kao, about 4km north of Krabi on the highway between Phang-Nga and Trang. To get to the centre of Krabi, catch a songthaew for 7B or motorcycle taxi for 20B.

Government buses to/from Bangkok cost 240B ordinary, 328B to 347B 2nd class air-con, 446B 1st class air-con or 550B VIP (655B for super VIP – 24 seats). Air-con buses leave Bangkok's Southern bus terminal between 6 and 8 pm; in the reverse direction they leave Krabi (Talaat Kao) between 4 and 5 pm. Songserm and PP Family arrange air-con buses (or vans, you never know for sure) to Th Khao San (Khao San Rd) in Bangkok for 350B.

Buses to/from Phuket leave hourly during daylight hours, cost 56B (101B with air-con) and take three to four hours. Air-con minivans from PP Family cost 180B to Phuket airport or Phuket town, 250B to Patong, Karon or Kata beaches.

Buses for Krabi leave Phang-Nga hourly throughout the day for 36B ordinary, 52B air-con. Most of these buses originate in Phuket and have Trang as their final destination. Government buses to/from Hat Yai cost 150B air-con and take five hours; from Trang it's 43B (77B air-con) and 2½ hours. There are also share taxis to/from Trang, Hat Yai and Satun; fares are roughly twice the ordinary bus fare.

Ordinary buses between Surat Thani and Krabi make the four hour trip 13 times daily between 5 am and 2.30 pm for 70B. Air-con buses depart from Krabi three times a day between 7 am and 3.30 pm for 160B and

take around three hours (it's the same price if you get out at Khao Sok National Park). Through various agencies in town, you can pay 150B for a private air-con bus or minivan to Surat. These agencies also arrange minivans to Hat Yai, Trang or Phattalung, each for the same fare of 180B. There are no minivans from the Baw Khaw Saw station, so if you want to go by this method, you'll have to book through one of the many private agencies in town.

Songthaews to Ban Hua Hin (for Ko Lanta) leave from Th Phattana in town, with a second stop in Talaat Kao, for 30B. They leave about every half hour from 10 am to 2 pm and take 40 minutes to reach Ban Hua Hin. There are also air-con minivans available from Krabi travel agencies straight through to Ko Lanta for 150B.

Boat Krabi can be reached by sea from Ko Phi-Phi and Ko Lanta. See the respective Ko Phi-Phi and Ko Lanta sections for details.

Getting Around

Any place in town can easily be reached on foot, but if you plan to do a lot of exploring out of town, renting a motorcycle might be a good idea. Several travel agencies and guesthouses can arrange motorcycle rentals for 150B to 250B a day, with discounts for multiday rentals. Jeep rentals range from 800B (open-top) to 1200B (air-con) per day.

Most buses into Krabi terminate at Talaat Kao, about 4km north of Krabi on the highway between Phang-Nga and Trang. You can catch a songthaew between Talaat Kao and the centre of Krabi for 7B, or a motorcycle taxi for 20B.

Songthaews to Ao Leuk (for Than Bokkharani National Park) leave from the intersection of Th Phattana and Th Preuksa Uthit for 30B. To Ao Nang (30B) they leave from Th Phattana near the New Hotel – departures are about every 15 minutes from 7 am to 6 pm during the high season (December to March), till 4 or 4.30 pm the remainder of the year. Boats to the islands and beaches mostly leave from Saphaan Jao Fah. See the Getting There & Away entry under Ao Nang & Laem Phra Nang for boat details.

AROUND KRABI

You can hire boats at Saphaan Jao Fah for 150B to 250B per hour for a look at **mangrove swamps** just across the river. Two bird species that frequent mangrove areas include the sea eagle and ruddy kingfisher. In mud and shallow waters, keep an eye out for fiddler crabs and mudskippers.

Nineteen kilometres west of Krabi, on Laem Pho, is the so-called **Shell Fossil Cemetery**, a shell 'graveyard' where 75-million-year-old shell fossils have formed giant slabs jutting into the sea.

To get there, take a songthaew from the Krabi waterfront for 20B – ask for 'Su-Saan Hawy'.

Wat Tham Seua

In the other direction, about 5km north and 2km east of town, is Wat Tham Seua (Tiger Cave Temple), one of Southern Thailand's most famous forest wáts. The main *wihǎan* is built into a long, shallow limestone cave, on either side of which dozens of *kutis* (monastic cells) are built into the cliffs and caves.

Wat Tham Seua's abbot is Ajaan Jamnien Silasettho, a Thai monk in his 50s who has allowed a rather obvious personality cult to develop around him. In the large, main cave the usual pictures of split cadavers and decaying corpses on the walls (useful meditation objects for countering lust) are interspersed with large portraits of Ajaan Jamnien, who is well known as a teacher of vipassana and *metta* (loving-kindness). It is said that he was apprenticed at an early age to a blind lay priest and astrologer who practised folk medicine and that he has been celibate his entire life. On the inside of his outer robe, and on an inner vest, hang scores of talismans presented to him by his followers – altogether they must weigh several kilograms, a weight Ajaan Jamnien bears to take on his followers' karma. Many young women come to Wat Tham Seua to practise as eight-precept nuns.

A Reminder

If you decide to visit Wat Tham Seua, please try to remember the dress protocol for Thai monasteries. On my last visit every single faràng visitor I saw here was dressed impolitely in spite of an English sign at the cave entrance asking visitors not to enter wearing shorts, sleeveless tops, tank tops and so on. Every western visitor – male and female – I encountered over two hours of wandering the grounds was wearing very abbreviated shorts. Two western male visitors arrived wearing only shorts, and no shirts. It is absolutely insulting to dress like this in a Thai temple compound, as was obvious from looking at the faces of all the Thais visiting or residing at the temple. If the Southern Thai climate is too hot for you and you simply can't suffer the pain of wearing long pants/skirts, and shirts with short sleeves, then consider crossing Wat Tham Seua off your itinerary.

Joe Cummings

In the back of the main cave a set of marble stairs behind the altar leads up to a smaller cavern (watch your head when you go up the steps) known as the 'tiger cave', behind which a Buddha footprint symbol sits on a gilded platform, locked behind a gate. Near one of the main cave entrances a life-size wax figure of Ajaan Jamnian sits in a glass case. A sign on the case in English and Thai says 'Not real man', though the more you look at the figure the more real it appears.

The best part of the temple grounds can be found in a little valley behind the ridge where the *bòt* is located. Follow the path past the main wát buildings, through a little village with nuns' quarters, until you come to a pair of steep stairways on the left. The first stairway leads to an arduous climb of 1272 steps to the top of a karst hill with another Buddha footprint shrine and a good view of the area.

The second stairway, next to a large statue of Kuan Yin, leads over a gap in the ridge and into a valley of tall trees and limestone caves, 10 of which are named. Enter the caves on your left and look for light switches on the walls – the network of caves is wired so that you can light your way chamber by chamber through the labyrinth until you rejoin the path on the other side. There are several kutis in and around the caves, and it's interesting to see the differences in interior decorating – some are very spartan and others are outfitted like oriental bachelor pads.

A path winds through a grove of 1000-year-old dipterocarps surrounded by tall limestone cliffs covered with a patchwork of foliage. If you continue to follow the path you'll eventually end up where you started, at the bottom of the staircase.

Places to Stay The friendly new *Tiger House* (☎ 075-631625), on the access road, just outside the entrance to the temple grounds, offers 13 rooms for 200B with fan, 300B with air-con, all with private cold shower. Rooms surround a shaded parking area. Spotlessly clean and nicely landscaped with potted plants, this might be a good place to stay if you wanted to explore Wat Tham Seua thoroughly.

Getting There & Away To get to Wat Tham Seua, take a songthaew from Th Utarakit to the Talaat Kao junction for 7B, then catch any bus or songthaew east on Hwy 4 towards Trang and Hat Yai and get off at the road on the left just after Km 108 – if you tell the bus operators 'Wat Tham Seua', they'll let you off at the right place. It's a 2km walk straight up this road to the wát.

In the mornings there are a few songthaews from Maharat Soi 6 in town that pass the turn-off for Wat Tham Seua (12B) on their way to Ban Hua Hin. Also in the morning there is usually a songthaew or two going direct to Wat Tham Seua from Talaat Kao for around 10B. Blue-and-yellow four-wheelers parked in front of Saphaan Jao Fah on the waterfront in Krabi also go to Wat Tham Seua – once they're full you can expect to pay no more than 15B.

Wat Sai Thai

A 15m reclining Buddha can be seen in a long rock shelter under an immense limestone cliff on the way to Ao Nang, about 7km from Krabi beside Route 4034. Though a wát in name only (there aren't sufficient monks in residence for official wát status, although a few monks look after the place), you can see an old bell-less bell tower, some *thâat kradùuk* (bone reliquaries; small stupas where devotees' ashes are interred) and the foundation for a former cremation hall remaining from the time it was an active monastery.

Hat Noppharat Thara

Eighteen kilometres north-west of Krabi, this beach used to be called Hat Khlong Haeng (Dry Canal Beach) because the canal that flows into the Andaman Sea here is dry except during, and just after, the monsoon season. Field Marshal Sarit gave the beach its current Pali-Sanskrit name, which means Beach of the Nine-Gemmed Stream, as a tribute to its beauty. The Thai navy has cleared the forest backing the beach to make way for a new royal residence.

The 2km-long beach, part of Hat Noppharat Thara/Ko Phi-Phi National Marine Park, is a favourite spot for Thai picnickers. There are some government bungalows for rent and a recently upgraded visitors centre with wall maps of the marine park and displays on coral reefs and ecotourism, most labelled in Thai only, a few in English.

Places to Stay *Government bungalows* at the park headquarters are available for 300B (three-person bungalow), 400B (four persons) and 900B (nine persons); they're quite OK, though on weekends the beach and visitors centre throngs with local visitors. You can also rent tents for 100B (two persons) to 150B (three persons). A row of open-air restaurants and vendors strung out along the parking lot sell snacks and simple meals.

The park pier, at the eastern end of Nop-pharat Thara, has boats across the canal to Hat Ton Sai, where the *Andaman Inn* (☎ 075-612728) has small huts with shared facilities for 70B, small huts with private bath for 150B and larger huts with private bath for 350B. Huts are well spaced and the grounds are well maintained. Down the beach are the similar but even more secluded *Emerald Bungalows* (200B shared bath-room, 400B to 500B private bath), *Bamboo Bungalows* (100B with private bath) and *Sara Cove* (☎ 01-677 1763, 676 8877) (100B with shared bathroom, 250B with pri-vate bath). Sara Cove can arrange inexpen-sive boating, fishing and oystering trips.

Farther west, around Laem Hang Nak (Dragon Tail Cape), *Pine Bungalow* (☎ 075-644332, 01-464 4298) on Ao Siaw is similarly priced but even more secluded. It's best approached by road via Route 4034.

Longtail boats ferry passengers across Khlong Haeng from Hat Noppharat Thara to the Andaman Inn for free.

Getting There & Away Hat Noppharat Thara can be reached by songthaews that leave about every 15 minutes from 7 am to 6 pm (high season) or 4 pm (low season) from Th Phattana (Soi 6, Th Maharat) in Krabi town.

Boats from the tourist pier in Krabi also do the half-hour run to Hat Noppharat Thara frequently between 7 am and 4 pm for 20B per person. There are also occa-sional boats between Hat Noppharat Thara and Ao Nang, mainly in the high season, during the same hours (10B, 10 minutes).

Ao Nang & Laem Phra Nang

South of Noppharat Thara is a series of bays where limestone cliffs and caves drop right into the sea. The water is quite clear and there are some coral reefs in the shallows. The longest beach runs along Ao Nang, a lovely but fast developing strand easily reached by road from Krabi.

Over the headlands to the south are the beaches of **Phai Phlong**, **Ton Sai** and **West Rai Leh**, and then the cape of Laem Phra

Nang, which encompasses **Hat Tham Phra Nang** (Princess Cave Beach) on the western side, a mangrove-rimmed beach facing east usually called **East Rai Leh**, but also known as Hat Nam Mao, and finally **Hat Nam Mao** proper.

All these beaches are accessible either by hiking over the headland cliffs or by taking a boat from Ao Nang or Krabi – although for several years now there have been ru-mours that a tunnel road will be built to Hat Phai Phlong to provide access for a new re-sort hotel being constructed there. So far nothing has happened, and with local con-servation groups growing stronger it's un-likely any such tunnel will be built in the near future.

Highway signs are beginning to refer to Ao Nang as 'Ao Phra Nang', which was it's original full name (in typical Southern Thai fashion, the locals shortened it to Ao Nang), but it leads some people to confuse Ao Nang/Ao Phra Nang with Laem Phra Nang, the cape with the famous cave for which the bay was named, or Hat Tham Phra Nang, the beach near this cave.

Hat Tham Phra Nang This is perhaps the most beautiful beach in the area. At one end is a tall limestone cliff that contains **Tham Phra Nang Nok** (Outer Princess Cave), a cave that is said to be the home of a myth-ical sea princess. Local legend says that during the 3rd century BC a passing royal barque carrying a charismatic Indian princess named Sri Guladevi foundered in a storm. The princess' spirit came to inhabit a large cave near the wreck, using power gained through many past lives to grant favours to all who came to pay respect. Local fisherfolk place carved wooden phalli in the cave as offerings to the Phra Nang (Holy Princess) so that she will provide plenty of fish for them. Inside the cliff is a hidden 'lagoon' called **Sa Phra Nang** (Holy Princess Pool) that can be reached by fol-lowing a sometimes slippery cave trail into the side of the mountain. A rope guides hik-ers along the way and it takes about 45 min-utes to reach the pool – guides are available

AROUND KRABI

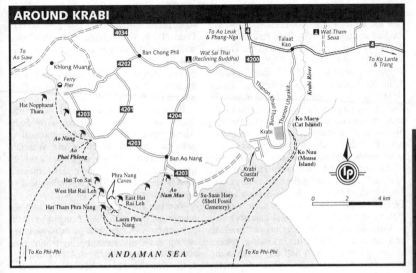

from local guesthouses. If you turn left off the trail after 50m from the start, you can reach a 'window' in the cliff that affords a view of Rai Leh West and East beaches. It's also possible to climb to the top of the mountain from here (some rock-climbing is involved) and get an aerial view of the entire cape and the islands of **Ko Poda** and **Ko Hua Khwan** (also known as Chicken Island) in the distance.

A second, larger cave on Laem Phra Nang was discovered only a few years ago. The entrance is in the middle of the peninsula near a batch of beach huts on East Rai Leh. This one is called **Tham Phra Nang Nai** (Inner Princess Cave) and consists of three caverns. All three contain some of the most beautiful limestone formations in the country, including a golden 'stone waterfall' of sparkling quartz. Local mythology says that this cave is the grand palace of the sea princess while Tham Phra Nang on the beach is her summer palace. The cliffs around Ao Phra Nang have become a world-wide mecca for rock-climbers and it's easy to arrange equipment, maps and instruction

from beach bungalows on (both East and West) Hat Rai Leh.

The islands off Laem Phra Nang are good for snorkelling. Besides Ko Poda and Ko Hua Khwan there is the nearer island of **Ko Rang Nok** (Bird Nest Island) and, next to that, a larger, unnamed island (possibly part of the same island at low tide) with an undersea cave. Some of the bungalows do reasonably priced day trips to these and other islands in the area.

Ao Phai Phlong This peaceful, palm-studded cove is worth boating to for the day. At the moment there is no accommodation here. It's been rumoured for years that a hotel conglomerate had purchased the land, but so far there are no signs of construction.

Rock Climbing Practically endless rock-climbing opportunities are provided by limestone cliffs on the huge headland between Hat Tham Phra Nang and Hat Rai Leh East, and on nearby islands. Most surfaces provide high-quality limestone with steep, pocketed walls, overhangs and the occasional hanging stalactite. Over 460 routes have been identified and bolted by zealous climbers, most in the mid to high difficulty level (grades 16 to 25). They bear names like Lord of the Thais, The King and I, Andaman Wall, One-Two-Three, Sleeping Indian Cliffs and Thaiwan Wall. Novices often begin with Muay Thai, a 50m wall with around 20 climbs in the 17 to 21 grade range at the south end of East Rai Leh. According to King Climbers, during high season as many as 300 visitors a day will climb up and down this rock face. Certain areas are off limits because they're part of Hat Noppharat Thara/Ko Phi-Phi National Marine Park, including the cliff next to the Dusit Premier Resort and cliffs outside Tham Phra Nang Nai (Inner Princess Cave, called 'Diamond Cave' by the tourist industry).

Virtually any of the lodgings in this area can arrange guided climbs and/or rock-climbing instruction. A half-day climb with instruction and guidance generally costs around 500B, while all-day starts at 1000B, three days 3000B; all equipment and insurance is included. Equipment rental rates for a two person lead set are around 400B for a half-day, 800B for a full day. King Climbers Rock Climbing School (fax 075-612914, email kingclimbers@iname.com) at Ya Ya Resort, Tex Rock Climbing at Railay Bay Bungalows, Krabi Climbers (with the only female Thai teacher, Pung) near Ya Ya reception and Phra Nang Rock Climbers near the Viewpoint Resort are the four main local outfits. King Climbers sells a book with details on climbing routes in the area for 450B.

Diving & Snorkelling Phra Nang Divers at Railay Village, Coral Diving at Krabi Resort and Aqua Vision Dive Center on Ao Nang arrange day dives to local islands and live-aboard trips as far afield as the Burma Banks, Ko Bida Nok/Ko Bida Nai (in Ko Lanta National Park), the Maya Wall (on Ko Phi-Phi Leh), Hin Daeng, Hin Muang, and the Surin and Similan archipelagos. Going rates are 1000B to 1800B for a day trip to nearby islands, while three to four-day certification courses cost 8000B to 9000B. The most convenient local dive

spots are Ko Poda Nai and Ko Poda Nawk. At nearby Ko Mae Urai, a kilometre west of Poda Nawk, two submarine tunnels lined with soft and hard corals offer lots of tropical fish and are suitable for all levels of divers. Another fairly interesting dive site is the sunken boat just south of Ko Rang Nok, a favoured fish habitat.

Barracuda's Tour & Travel (☎ 01-958 2756) on Ao Nang operates daily four-island trips for 230B, including snorkelling gear and a basic lunch, while Wanna's Place, also on Ao Nang, organises a similar tour which costs 200B and offers some customers the flexibility of spending less or more time at each of the islands.

You can also negotiate directly with the boat operators along Ao Nang. For 150B per person you can arrange to be dropped off on Ko Poda around 8 or 9 am, then scooped up again at 5 pm. You can buy seafood and beer at the island's own restaurant; rent snorkelling gear in Ao Nang to take along. Fun three-day snorkelling/camping trips – sometimes led by *chao náam* (sea gypsies) – can be arranged for 1000B to 1500B per person.

Paddling Tours of the coast, islands and semi-submerged caves by inflatable canoe or kayak can be arranged through SeaCanoe Thailand (☎ 075-637170) near Wanna's Place at Ao Nang or through Sea, Land & Trek (formerly Krabi Canoe, ☎ 075-637359) based in front of Gift's Bungalows on the Ao Nang beach road. One of the best local paddles is the canyon river cruise, an estuary trip that cuts through 200m foliaged limestone cliffs, mangrove channels and tidal lagoon tunnels or *hongs* (from the Thai word for 'room'). Birds frequently sighted in the mangroves include brown-winged kingfishers, Pacific reef egrets, Asian dowitchers and white-bellied sea eagles, while the most commonly seen mammals and reptiles are otters, macaques, gibbons and two-banded monitor lizards. Mudskippers and fiddler crabs abound.

SeaCanoe Thailand charges 1700B for a full day excursion. Sea, Land & Trek does a shorter sunset paddle from Ao Nang to Rai Leh, Phra Nang and back for 700B per person, cavern explorations for 1500B or a Ban Talen estuary/mangrove paddle for 1200B.

Sailing Look for information on yachts sailing in and out of Ao Nang waters at the bulletin boards found at Gift's Bungalow and The Last Cafe in Ao Nang and Sunset Bar on Hat Rai Leh. One vessel that's made a long tradition of sailing back and forth between Krabi, Phuket, Penang and Bali is *Syzygie*, a 14m steel-hulled, French-built ketch with eight berths in three sleeping areas, two cabins and a saloon. In Penang reservations can be made through Maju Travel (☎ 60-4-261 5170, fax 262 0739), or in Krabi through Gift's Bungalow (☎ 01-229 2128, fax 075-637193, email syzygie@hotmail.com).

A squared-rigged Chinese junk called *Dauw Talae II* sails between Ao Nang, Ko Phi-Phi and Ko Hong for a two day, one night voyage around twice a week in high season. The junk can take 14 passengers at a cost of 3960B per person, including all meals, soft drinks, accommodation in two-bed cabins, the use of snorkelling equipment and dinghy excursions to lagoons, beaches and coves along the way. For reservations or information, contact Nosey Parker on (☎ 075-637464).

Places to Stay & Eat A large and growing number of bungalows and inns can be found along Ao Nang and nearby beaches. Most of the cheap places are being edged out, but there are still a few to be found in the 100B to 200B range. Also, when picking a place, scan around for an open-air bars in the area: these often go rather late and sound carries pretty easily: light sleepers take heed.

Ao Nang Because it's easily accessible by road, this beach has become fairly developed of late. The more expensive places usually have booking offices in Krabi town. The oldest resort in the area, *Krabi Resort* (☎ 075-612160, Bangkok ☎ 02-208 9165), at the northern end of Ao Nang, has luxury

bungalows that cost 1626B to 5476B depending on proximity to the beach and whether you stay in a bungalow or in the hotel wing. Most of the guests are with package tours or conferences. There are the usual resort amenities, including a swimming pool, bar and restaurant. Bookings can be made at the Krabi Resort office on Th Phattana in Krabi and guests receive free transport out to the resort. We've received complaints that Krabi Resort bookings are not always honoured, however.

Off Route 4203, the road leading to the beach's north end, *Beach Terrace* (☎ 075-637180, fax 637184) is a modern apartment-style hotel where rooms cost 1340B with air-con, hot water, TV and fridge, 40% less in the rainy season. *Ao Nang Ban Lae* (☎ 075-637078), about 150m south-west on the same side of Route 4203, has a cluster of simple but well maintained bungalows for 200B. On the opposite side of the road, *Ban Ao Nang* (☎ 075-637071) is a modern hotel with rooms for 1200B to 1600B, less in the rainy season. About half a kilometre from the beach, on the north side of Route 4203, just opposite the Krabi Resort, is the quiet *Ao Nang Thara Lodge* (☎ 075-637087) with mid-range cottages with fans on nicely landscaped grounds for 350B to 700B, depending on the season.

Down on the beach, heading south you'll come to *Wanna's Place* (☎ 01-476 7507) with simple fan huts for 200B (150B low season), air-con up to 800B for fairly simple huts. There's a restaurant in front. Farther south-east down the road, *Gift's* (☎ 075-637193, 01-229 2128) has larger bamboo thatch bungalows with private bath for 350B, down to 250B in low season. A bulletin board posts information on yachts coming and going. Both Wanna's and Gift's tend to be full from November to April. Next comes *Ban Ao Nang Resort*, a new pseudo Thai-style hotel painted all pink and over-priced at 700B a night.

The beach road intersects Route 4203 to Krabi just before you arrive at *Phra Nang Inn* (☎ 075-637130, fax 637134), a tastefully designed 'tropical hotel' with partial views of the bay and a small pool; street-side rooms can be noisy. Large air-con rooms start at 1766B a night in the high season (usually December to February), or 1300B the remainder of the year. It has a good restaurant. A second, similarly designed branch stands just across the road from the original.

Next door is *Ao Nang Villa Resort* (☎ 075-637270), with upgraded cottages for 450B to 2000B depending on amenities. Right around the corner on Route 4203, the newer *Ao Nang Royal Resort* (☎ 075-637188) has concrete bungalows, rather close to the road, for 700B with fan and private bath, up to 1200B with air-con.

Just around the corner from the beach on the left side of Route 4203, *Jinda Guest House* and *Sea World Guest House* offer apartment-like rooms upstairs in two modern shophouses for 200B double. A little farther up Route 4203, *Barracuda's Tour & Travel* is a dive shop with six clean rooms above the office for 150B to 200B, with shared facilities. Next, about 100m or so from the beach, is the small *BB Bungalow*

(☎ 075-637147) with simple but solid fan-equipped bungalows for 150B to 400B depending on the season, plus upscale air-con hotel accommodation for 1200B. *Ya Ya* (☎ 075-637176, 01-476 0270) next door (not to be confused with Ya-Ya on East Hat Rai Leh) has nicer bungalows with terraces for around 400B. Farther up the road, about 200m from the beach, *Green Park* (☎ 075-637300) is one of the better cheapies with well maintained huts for 100B with shared bathroom, 150B with private bath – as low as 50B in the low season.

Moving farther away from the beach along Route 4203 is *Krabi Seaview Resort* (☎ 075-637242), with modern air-con A-frames for 500B with fan and up to 1700B double with air-con, followed by *Jungle Hut* (☎ 075-637301), with adequate bungalows for 100B with shared bathroom, 120B to 200B with private bath – down to 50B in the low season.

On the opposite side of Route 4203, set well back from the road next to a pond, *Peace Laguna Resort* (☎ 075-637345) is more up-market with bungalows for 450B

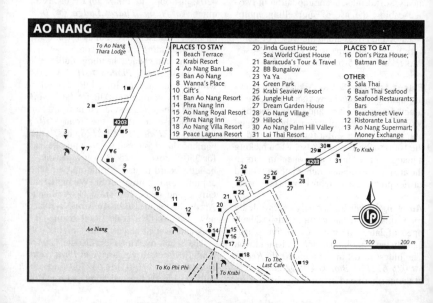

Marine karst topography of Ao Phang-Nga, Krabi Province, Southern Andaman Coast.

Hat Tham Phra Nang, Krabi Province.

oats come direct to Hat Phra Nang from Krabi.

Wat Tham Seua, a famous forest wát near Krabi.

PAUL BEINSSEN

Princess Cave, home of a mythical sea princess, Hat Tham Phra Nang, Krabi.

PAUL BEINSSEN

Rock climbing is another attraction of Hat Tham Phra Nang, near Krabi.

with fan and private bath, 600B to 1200B with air-con. A trail leads directly to the beach from Peace Laguna so that it's not necessary to walk out to the main road.

Farther east along Route 4203 is the simple *Ao Nang Village* (☎ *075-637109*), with plain but serviceable huts for 100B to 200B. The adjacent *Dream Garden House* (☎ *075-637338*) offers more up-market rooms for 700B to 1200B. Farther on yet, *Hillock* offers dreary thatched huts for around 100B. *Lai Thai Resort* on the opposite side of the road (☎ *075-637281, fax 075-637283*) is a collection of upscale Northern Thai-style pavilions around a pool. All rooms come with air-con, satellite TV and marbled bathrooms for 2000B to 2500B, or about 40% less in the rainy season. The latest place to appear at this end of the road is *Ao Nang Palm Hill Valley* (☎ *075-637207*), where comfortable green-roofed bungalows with air-con cost 900B to 1200B. It's a long walk to the beach.

At the north end of the beach, past where Hwy 4203 turns inland, is a short string of thatched-roof bars and seafood restaurants. *Sala Thai*, the last in the series, has the best Thai-style seafood, while most of the other restaurants serve pale cuisine. The seafood at *Beachstreet View*, a small outdoor cafe with bamboo tables near Wanna's Place, isn't bad. A short distance north along Route 4203, around the corner from Wanna's Place, *Baan Thai Seafood* features a nice outdoor bar and decent barbecued seafood. Out on the Ao Nang 'strip', *Ristorante La Luna* does pizza and pasta, as does friendly *Don's Pizza House*, a vendor-style place around the corner towards Ao Nang Royal Resort. Nearby *Batman Bar* has a pool table and dart board.

If you follow the road parallel to the beach south-east past Phra Nang Inn and Ao Nang Villa until the road ends, you'll find *The Last Cafe*, a shady open-air spot with simple food and drink, a pleasantly laid-back ambience and even a few chairs on the beach. A corner out the back holds a paperback exchange library and bulletin board.

Hat Ton Sai This beach can only be reached by boat from Ao Nang, Ao Nam Mao or Krabi. On-again, off-again *Ton Sai Huts* may provide accommodation for 80B to 350B per night.

West Hat Rai Leh At the centre of this pretty bay, *Railay Bay Bungalows* (☎ *01-228 4112*) packs in nearly a hundred huts right across the peninsula to East Hat Rai Leh. Rates range from 500B to 1000B depending on the size of the hut, number of beds and whether it has air-conditioning; rates can be negotiated down to 250B in the off season. *Sand Sea* (☎ *01-228-4114*), next door, features two rows of cottages facing each other, some thatched, some with hard walls, for 600B to 900B for standard to deluxe fan-equipped cold-water bungalows. Air-con will cost you 1200B to 1400B, though all these rates should be lower in the off season. The similar *Railay Village* (☎*/fax 01-228 4366, ☎ 01-464 6484*) has small cottages with glass fronts in two facing rows for about 600B to 700B (fan) and 1400B to 2000B (air-con), 30 to 40% less in the low season. All three have pleasant dining areas, but as Railay Village and Sand Sea are owned and operated by Muslim families, only Railay Bay serves alcohol. Railay Village cooks the best food and has the best atmosphere (all bamboo, no plastic).

At the northern end of the beach is *Railei Beach Club* (☎*/fax 01-464 4338, fax 075-612914, email rbclub@phuket.ksc.co.th*), also known as Langkha Daeng (Thai for 'red roof'), a private home development where it's possible to rent 20 vacant one to three-bedroom beach homes from the caretakers for 2000B to 7000B a night; a daily light housekeeping service is included. It's necessary to book several months in advance (several years in advance if you want to book in December).

West Rai Leh can be reached by longtail boat from Ao Nang, Ao Nam Mao or Krabi, or on foot from Hat Tham Phra Nang and East Hat Rai Leh (but these must be approached by boat as well).

SOUTHERN ANDAMAN COAST

The only place to eat not associated with overnight accommodation is *BoBo Bar & Restaurant* next to Railay Village going north. Here you'll find a stand selling real coffee and a good assortment of herbal teas, plus a little bar. The restaurant, alas, is not very good and the service – provided by ganja-smoking young Thais – is excruciatingly slow. During the high season the restaurant allows people to camp out the back for a modest fee. The *Sunset Bar* at Railay Bay Bungalows is still the most popular night-time scene.

Hat Tham Phra Nang The only place to stay at this beautiful beach is *Dusit Premier Resort* (☎ 075-620740, Bangkok ☎ 02-238 0032), a tastefully designed and fairly unobtrusive resort with 179 luxurious rooms in domed cement-and-stucco or wooden cottages starting at 9000B.

The beach is not Dusit's exclusive domain – a wooden walkway has been left around the perimeter of the limestone bluff so that you can walk to Hat Tham Phra Nang from East Rai Leh. From West Rai Leh a footpath leads through the forest around to the beach.

Hat Tham Phra Nang is accessible by boat or foot only.

East Hat Rai Leh Often referred to as Hat Nam Mao, even though another beach substantially farther east had the name first, the beach along here tends towards mud flats during low tide. The north-east end of the bay is vegetated with mangrove, so between the mangrove and the mudflats there's not much traditional beach scenery. Most people who stay here walk over to Hat Tham Phra Nang for beach activities.

Railay Bay Bungalows has another entrance on this side (see West Hat Rai Leh). Right next door, the relatively small *Sunrise Bay Bungalows* (☎ 01-228 4236) has 15 fairly solid looking cottages for 250B to 450B, 50B less in the low season. Videos are played nightly in Sunrise Bay's large, featureless, tin-roofed restaurant.

Ya-Ya has some interesting bungalow designs, mostly two and three-storey structures with brick downstairs, wood upstairs, the designs integrated with pre-existing coconut palms and such. A very few five storey 'tree house' units remain; these are usually reserved for staff but you may be able to get in during the low season. Rates range from 300B to 600B, all rooms come with private bath. *Coco Bungalows* (☎ 075-612730), farther north-east towards the mangrove area, is set back from the shoreline and offers quiet but very tattered thatched or concrete bungalows for 150B (100B low season) and one of the better restaurants in the area.

A bit farther along, near the Phra Nang Nai caves, *Diamond Cave Bungalows* (☎ 01-477 0933) enjoys a beautiful setting and has simple thatch bungalows for 200B to 250B and nicely done cottages farther back towards the caves for 400B: the latter seem the better deal for the money. The proprietors say they plan to tear down the thatch bungalows and replace them with the more enduring, and more expensive, concrete. When we visited, a huge pile of rubbish in front of the bungalows was a definite turnoff.

On a hill overlooking Rai Leh East and the mangrove, *Viewpoint Resort* (☎ 01-228 4115) offers clean, well maintained two-storey cottages for 800B with fan, 1600B air-con, negotiable to 500B and 1300B in the off season.

Ao Nam Mao This large bay, around a headland to the north-east of East Rai Leh, about 1.5km from the Shell Fossil Cemetery, has a coastal environment similar to that of East Rai Leh – mangroves and shallow, muddy beaches.

The beach is sandier towards the bay's east end, where you'll find the environmentally friendly *Dawn of Happiness Beach Resort* (☎ 075-612730, ext 207, 01-464 4362, fax 075-612914). Natural, renewable, locally available building materials are used wherever possible and no sewage or rubbish ends up in the bay. Thatched bungalows with private baths and mosquito nets cost 750B with a garden view, 950B with a sea view and 850B for 'family rooms' which can accommodate three to four people; low season rates are 500/750/500B. The staff can arrange trips to nearby natural attractions. Among many local excursions offered by staff is an overnight camping safari to Khao Phanom Bencha National Park – a rare opportunity to see primary rainforest up close.

Ao Nam Mao is accessible by road via Route 4204. The turnoff for Dawn of Happiness Resort is exactly 4.2km south-east of the Km 0 marker on Route 4203, the road to Su-saan Hawy (the Shell Fossil Cemetery), where it splits from Route 4204 on its way to Ao Nang. It's about 6km from Ao Nang. If you phone from Krabi, the Dawn of Happiness will arrange free transport.

Getting There & Away Hat Noppharat Thara and Ao Nang can be reached by songthaews that leave about every 15 minutes from 7 am to 6 pm (high season) or 4 pm (low season) from Th Phattana in Krabi town, near the New Hotel. The fare is 30B and the trip takes 30 to 40 minutes.

You can get boats to Ton Sai, West Rai Leh and Laem Phra Nang at several places. For Ton Sai, the best thing to do is get a songthaew out to Ao Nang, then a boat from Ao Nang to Ton Sai. It's 20B per person for two people or more, 40B if you don't want to wait for a second passenger to show up. You may have to bargain to get this fare. Boats also go between Ao Nang and Ko Phi-Phi for 150B, October to April only.

For West Rai Leh or anywhere on Laem Phra Nang, you can get a boat direct from Krabi's Saphaan Jao Fah for 50B. It takes about 45 minutes to reach Phra Nang. However, boats will only go all the way round the cape to West Rai Leh and Hat Tham Phra Nang from October to April when the sea is tame enough. During the other half of the year they only go as far as East Rai Leh, but you can easily walk from here to West Rai Leh or Hat Phra Nang. You can also get boats from Ao Nang for 30B all year round, but in this case they only go as far as West

Rai Leh and Hat Phra Nang (again, you can walk to East Rai Leh from there). From Ao Nang you'll have to pay 30B per person for two or more passengers, 60B for one.

Another alternative is to take a songthaew as far as Ao Nam Mao, to the small fishing bay near the Shell Fossil Cemetery, for 15B and then a boat to Laem Phra Nang for 25B (three or more people required).

Some of the beach bungalows have agents in Krabi who can help arrange boats – but there's still a charge.

Than Bokkharani National Park

In Ao Leuk district in northern Krabi Province, Than Bokkharani National Park encompasses nine caves, as well as the former botanical gardens for which the park was named.

The park is best visited just after the monsoons – when it has been dry a long time the water levels go down and in the midst of the rains it can be a bit murky. In December Than Bokkharani looks like something cooked up by Walt Disney, but it's real and entirely natural. Emerald-green waters flow out of a narrow cave in a tall cliff and into a large lotus pool, which overflows steadily into a wide stream, itself dividing into many smaller streams in several stages. At each stage there's a pool and a little waterfall. Tall trees spread over 40 *râi* (6.4 sq km) provide plenty of cool shade. Thais from Ao Leuk come to bathe here on weekends and at that time it's full of laughing people playing in the streams and pools. During the week there are only a few people about, mostly kids doing a little fishing. Vendors sell noodles, roast chicken, delicious batter-fried squid and *sôm-tam* (green papaya salad) under a roofed area to one side.

Watch out for aggressive monkeys in the park.

Entry to the park is free.

Caves

Among the protected caves scattered around Ao Leuk district, one of the most interesting is **Tham Hua Kalok**, set in a limestone hill in a seldom-visited bend of

SOUTHERN ANDAMAN COAST

mangrove-lined Khlong Baw Thaw. Besides impressive stalactite formations, the high-ceilinged cave features 2000 to 3000-year-old cave paintings of human and animal figures and geometric designs.

Nearby **Tham Lawt** (literally, 'Tube Cave') is distinguished by a navigable stream flowing through it – it's longer than Phang-Nga's Tham Lawt but shorter than Mae Hong Son's.

There are seven other similar limestone caves in Ao Leuk district – Tham Chao Leh, Tham Khao Phra Khao Rang, Tham Phet, Tham Sa Yuan Thong, Tham Thalu Fah, Tham To Luang and Tham Waririn. To find them will require the services of a guide; further information is available at the Than Bok visitors centre.

Places to Stay *Ao Leuk Resort* (☎ 075-681369), on the highway about 300m northeast of Than Bok, as the locals call Than Bokkharani, offers OK cottages for 200B with private bath.

Getting There & Away Than Bok, is off Hwy 4 between Krabi and Phang-Nga, 1.3km south-west of the town of Ao Leuk, on Route 4039 towards Laem Sak. To get there, take a songthaew from the intersection of Th Phattana and Th Preuksa Uthit in Krabi to Ao Leuk for 30B; get off just before town and it's an easy walk to the park entrance on the left.

To visit Tham Lawt and Tham Hua Kalok you must charter a boat from Tha Baw Thaw, around 6.5km west of Than Bok. The tours are run exclusively by Ao Leuk native Uma Kumat and his son Bunma. They'll take one or two people for 100B; up to 10 can charter a boat for 300B. The boats run along secluded Khlong Baw Thaw and through Tham Lawt before stopping at Tham Hua Kalok. The pier at Tha Baw Thaw is 4.3km from Than Bok via Route 4039, then 2km by dirt road through an oil palm plantation. You must find your own transport to Tha Baw Thaw. Most people go by rented motorcycle or car (you could also charter a songthaew from Ao

Leuk for around 200B one way, but you'd have to hitchhike back afterwards).

Khao Phanom Bencha National Park

This 50 sq km park is in the middle of virgin rainforest along the Phanom Bencha mountain range. The main scenic attractions are the three-level **Huay To Falls**, **Tham Khao Pheung** and **Huay Sadeh Falls**, all within 3km of the park office. Other less well known streams and waterfalls can be discovered as well. Clouded leopard, black panther, tiger, Asiatic black bear, barking deer, serow, Malayan tapir, leaf monkey, gibbon and various tropical birds – including the helmeted hornbill, argus pheasant and extremely rare Gurney's pitta make their home here. At 1350m, Khao Phanom Bencha is the highest point in Krabi Province. The name means 'Five-Point Prostration Mountain', a reference to the mountain's resemblance, in profile, to a man prostrating so that is knees, hands and head all touch the ground.

The park has a campground where you are welcome to pitch your own tent for 5B per person per night.

Getting There & Away Public transport direct to Khao Phanom Bencha National Park from Krabi or Talaat Kao is rare. Two roads run to the park off Hwy 4. One is only about half a kilometre from Talaat Kao – you could walk to this junction and hitch, or hire a truck in Talaat Kao all the way for 100B or so. The other road is about 10km north of Krabi off Hwy 4. You could get to this junction via a songthaew or a bus heading north to Ao Leuk.

It would be cheaper to rent a motorcycle in Krabi for a day trip to Phanom Bencha than to charter a pickup. Try to have someone at the park watch your bike while hiking to nearby falls – motorcycle theft at Phanom Bencha has been a problem in the past.

KO PHI-PHI

Ko Phi-Phi consists of two islands situated about 40km from Krabi, Phi-Phi Leh and

Phi-Phi Don. Both are part of Hat Nop-pharat Thara/Ko Phi-Phi National Marine Park, though this means little in the face of the blatant land encroachment now taking place on Phi-Phi Don.

Only parts of Phi-Phi Don are actually under the administration of the National Parks Division of the Forestry Department. Phi-Phi Leh and the western cliffs of Phi-Phi Don are left to the nest collectors, and the parts of Phi-Phi Don where the chao náam live are also not included in the park.

After Phuket this is probably the most popular tourist destination along the Andaman Coast, especially during the peak months from December to March, when hordes descend on the island and snatch up every room and bungalow on Phi-Phi Don. Even so, the island still retains some of its original beauty, though to truly appreciate it usually means a fair hike to escape the crowds.

Ko Phi-Phi Don

Phi-Phi Don is the larger of the two islands, a sort of dumbbell-shaped island with scenic hills, awesome cliffs, long beaches, emerald waters and remarkable bird and sea life. The 'handle' in the middle has long, white-sand beaches on either side, only a few hundred metres apart. The beach on the southern side curves around **Ao Ton Sai**, where boats from Phuket and Krabi dock. There is also a very untidy Thai-Muslim village here. On the northern side of the handle is **Ao Lo Dalam**.

The uninhabited (except for beach huts) western section of the island is called Ko Nawk (Outer Island), and the eastern section, which is much larger, is Ko Nai (Inner Island). At the north of the eastern end is Laem Tong, where the island's chao náam population lives. The number of chao náam living here varies from time to time, as they are still a somewhat nomadic people, but there are generally about 100. With stones tied to their waists as ballast, chao náam divers can reportedly descend to 60m while breathing through an air hose held above the water surface. Like Pacific islanders of around 100

years ago, they tend to be very warm and friendly horizon-gazers.

Hat Yao (Long Beach), facing south at the south-eastern tip of the island, has some of Phi-Phi Don's best coral reefs. Ton Sai, Ao Lo Dalam and Hat Yao all have beach bungalows. Over a ridge north from Hat Yao is another very beautiful beach, **Hat Lanti**, with good surf. For several years the locals wouldn't allow any bungalows to be built here out of respect for the large village mosque in a coconut grove above the beach – but money talked, and the chao náam walked. Farther north is the sizeable bay of **Ao Lo Bakao**, where there is a small resort, and near the tip of Laem Tong are three luxury resorts.

Park administrators have allowed development on Phi-Phi Don to continue unchecked, though it's doubtful they ever had the power or influence to stop the building. Rumour has it that many park officials won't dare even set foot on Ko Phi-Phi for fear of being attacked by village chiefs and bungalow developers profiting from tourism. Beautiful Ao Ton Sai is more of a boat basin than a beach, and more and more bungalows have crowded onto this section of the island. For solitude and scenery, this place falls shorts. On the other hand, those in search of a more lively social scene will be rewarded by a wide choice of restaurants, beachfront bars and up-market accommodation.

Other parts of Phi-Phi Don aren't so bad, though the once-brilliant coral reefs around the island are suffering from anchor drag and run-off from large beach developments. The least disturbed parts of the island at present are those still belonging to the few chao náam who haven't cashed in.

Development on Ko Phi-Phi Don has stabilised to a significant degree over the last four years and it seems a near-truce between park authorities and greedy developers has come about. Still, there's much room for improvement in terms of rubbish collection and waste disposal.

A small power plant has been built in the centre of the island, but it doesn't have sufficient capacity to power all the resorts even in Ao Lo Dalam and Ton Sai. Many on this part of the island are forced to use generators on certain calendar days (odd or even depending on their location). Likewise the single brackish reservoir on this island usually can't supply enough water, so some resorts have to turn their water supply off completely during certain hours of the day. In 1997 and 1998 there was an extreme water shortage on the island due to general lack of rain in the south, and all tap water was brackish.

If you go to the island and want to air your opinion on the what's going on there with regard to the environment, please contact one of the organisations listed under Ecology & Environment in the Facts about Thailand chapter with your assessments, whether good or bad.

Money Near Ton Sai pier, Krung Thai Bank has an exchange booth open daily from 8.30 am to 3.30 pm. There's another Krung Thai booth farther on in the village

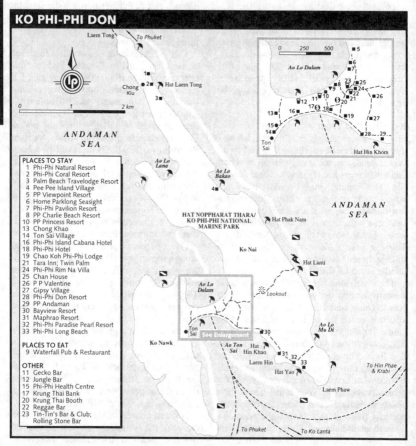

KO PHI-PHI DON

PLACES TO STAY
1 Phi-Phi Natural Resort
2 Phi-Phi Coral Resort
3 Palm Beach Travelodge Resort
4 Pee Pee Island Village
5 PP Viewpoint Resort
6 Home Parklong Seasight
7 Phi-Phi Pavilion Resort
8 PP Charlie Beach Resort
10 PP Princess Resort
13 Chong Khao
14 Ton Sai Village
16 Phi-Phi Island Cabana Hotel
18 Phi-Phi Hotel
19 Chao Koh Phi-Phi Lodge
21 Tara Inn; Twin Palm
24 Phi-Phi Rim Na Villa
25 Chan House
26 P P Valentine
27 Gipsy Village
28 Phi-Phi Don Resort
29 PP Andaman
30 Bayview Resort
31 Maphrao Resort
32 Phi-Phi Paradise Pearl Resort
33 Phi-Phi Long Beach

PLACES TO EAT
9 Waterfall Pub & Restaurant

OTHER
11 Gecko Bar
12 Jungle Bar
15 Phi-Phi Health Centre
17 Krung Thai Bank
20 Krung Thai Booth
22 Reggae Bar
23 Tin-Tin's Bar & Club; Rolling Stone Bar

next to Andaman Seafood and Reggae Bar with the same hours, and many of the travel agents will also change money, though at predictably poor rates.

Medical Facilities Phi-Phi Health Centre, east of the harbour near Ton Sai Village, can handle minor emergencies and is open 24 hours.

Diving & Snorkelling

Several places in Ton Sai village – around a dozen at last count – can arrange diving and snorkelling trips around the island or to nearby islands. Several dive centres maintain small offices along the brick walkway east of the Ton Sai harbour. The typical all day snorkelling trip includes lunch, water, fruit and equipment for 360B to 400B. These usually stop at Ko Yung (Mosquito Island), Ko Mai Phai (Bamboo Island), Hin Pae (Goat Rock) and Ko Phi-Phi Leh.

Guided dive trips start at 500B for one dive. An open-water certification course costs 8000B to 9000B. The best months for diving are December to April.

Mask, fins and snorkel can be rented for 50B a day.

Paddling

You can rent kayaks on the beach along Ao Lo Dalam for 300B per hour, or 600B per half day (700B for a double seater), all day 800B (1000B double).

Fishing

All day (9 am to 5 pm) fishing trips for marlin, sailfish, barracuda and other gamefish in nearby waters are available aboard longtail boats for 1800B for two people, including soft drinks, lunch and fishing tackle. A half day (9 am to 1 pm or 1 to 5 pm) costs only 400B less. Look for signboards along the brick walkway in Ton Sai.

Rock-Climbing

Between 150 and 200 routes have been bolted into the sheer limestone cliffs on Phi-Phi Don. Ask at Mama Resto for guides. (See Places to Eat later.)

Organised Tours & Boat Charters

From Ko Phi-Phi Don, boats to Ko Phi-Phi Leh can be chartered for 200B per trip. A half day trip to Phi-Phi Leh or Bamboo Island costs 500B, a full day 800B.

Places to Stay

During the high tourist months of December to February, July and August, nearly all the accommodation on Phi-Phi Don is booked out. As elsewhere during these months, it's best to arrive early in the morning to stake out a room or bungalow. Latecomers sometimes wind up sleeping on the beach. At this time, prices are at their peak, but during the off season rooms free up and rates are negotiable.

Ao Ton Sai *Ton Sai Village* (☎ 075-612434, fax 612196), towards the west end of the bay, offers comfortable wooden bungalows with air-con (but no fans), hot water, TV and minibar for 1800B including breakfast; it's also a little removed from others on this beach so is a bit quieter. Many Korean and Taiwanese tour groups make a stop at the beach chairs in front of this hotel. *Phi Phi Island Cabana Hotel* (☎ 075-620634, fax 612132), the oldest resort on the island, stretches across from the centre of Ton Sai to the beach at Ao Lo Dalam. Bungalows with fan start at 1200B while a standard room in the three-storey hotel building are 2600B and up to 9300B for the Andaman Suite. Amenities include a restaurant, coffee shop, snooker club, nightclub, tennis court, basketball court and a swimming pool overlooking the beach and surrounded by pseudo-Greek statues and a large fountain that looks like it's been brought in from Las Vegas. Non-guests may use the pool for a steep 300B.

Behind the main restaurant-bar-diveshop strip, *Phi Phi Hotel* (☎ 01-230 3138, 01-985 2667, Bangkok ☎ 02-941 7184, fax 02-579 5764, email phiphi@samart.co.th) features 64 well appointed rooms in a four storey building. These rooms, which are probably the best on the island in terms of amenities (air-con, hot showers, satellite

TV, mini-bars), cost 1800B (1500B in low season) including breakfast.

Chao Koh Phi-Phi Lodge (☎ 075-611313) consists of fairly basic but clean concrete bungalows with bath and fan for 300B to 500B, a bit off the beach on the way to Hat Hin Khom.

Ao Lo Dalam *Chong Khao* is set inland along a path between Ao Lo Dalam and Ton Sai beaches. Fairly quiet rooms in a row house or bungalow situated among coconut palms range from 100B to 300B all with fan and private bath. This is one of the best deals on the island as long as you don't need to be on the beach.

PP Princess Resort (☎/fax 075-620615) has large, well spaced upscale wooden bungalows with glass doors and windows for 1390B to 2990B. The bungalows feature nice deck areas and are connected by wooden walkways. Discounts to 1000B are available from May to October.

PP Charlie Beach Resort (☎ 01-229 0495) has simple, clean thatched-roof bungalows, a pleasant restaurant and a beach bar in an atmospheric setting. Rooms cost 250B to 650B, all with private bath and fan, depending on size and position on the beach. The 250B rooms are quite far back and near a generator.

Phi Phi Pavilion Resort (☎ 075-620633) is another thatched-roof place nicely situated in a coconut grove with high-ceilinged fan bungalows for 900B, air-con for 1400B; 650/1000B in the low season.

Home Parklong Seasight consists of five rooms in the home of a local entrepreneur on the beach just before you get to the end of Ao Lo Dalam and PP Viewpoint Resort. Small but clean rooms with fan and private cold bath are 800B in the high season, while a much larger room with two double beds, two fans and a large bathroom is 1200B; prices drop to 550/800B in the low season. All rooms share a spacious covered wooden sitting area in front.

PP Viewpoint Resort (☎ 01-228 4111) is situated on a hillside approached by a small bridge over a canal. Units in front overlook

Ao Lo Dalam while those at the back have no view. Rates range from 500B for a room to 600B to 750B for a bungalow, depending on size and location. The bungalows are a bit rickety, but the ones with good views make a great spot for a sunset cocktail. During the hot dry season, March to June, this hillside is hotter than most other locations.

Hat Hin Khom This beach, a little southeast of Ton Sai, has gone way downhill of late, with lots of rubbish floating on the water and collecting on land. Bungalow owners here don't seem to give a toss about keeping the area clean. *Phi-Phi Don Resort* (☎ 01-228 4083) is overpriced at 500B to 700B for precipitously decaying cement and stucco bungalows with fan and bath, 800B to 900B with air-con. Service is indifferent. *PP Andaman* has thatched huts – some in need of repair – for 200B to 250B, plus sturdier cement and stucco ones for 350B. No great shakes, either, but better than Phi-Phi Don Resort.

Behind the Andaman, well away from the beach, well kept *Gipsy Village* (☎ 01-229 0674) is a collection of solid bungalows arranged in a large U shape amid coconut palms. They come with private toilet and shower for 400B (200B low season). A second group of huts under the same name, farther back towards the interior of the island, costs about the same but is far inferior.

Bayview Resort (☎ 01-229 1134) is an upmarket place with modern-looking cottages geared to the Thai market, though plenty of foreigners stay here as well. Clean, spacious, wood-floored cottages sit on a hillside and feature large decks overlooking the sea. With fan, minifridge and cold shower a cottage costs 1200B, while one with air-con and hot water costs 1500B to 1800B. When the manager is present, the Thai cuisine at the restaurant can be quite good.

Hat Hin Khao Off by itself on a little cove that must be reached via a path over a headland to the south of Hin Khom, *Maphrao Resort* offers thatched huts in a natural setting for 150B to 350B. Showers are shared for the 150B bungalows, while 250B and 350B huts have private ones. The huts are in dire need of repair, however. The resort closes in the rainy season.

Hat Yao Bungalows on this beach are practically piled onto one another, with very little space in between. A shortage of fresh water means most showers employ salt water. The beach, however, is long and pretty. You can follow a trail over to a secluded beach at Ao Lo Mu Di.

Phi-Phi Paradise Pearl Resort (☎ 01-229 0484, fax 722 0370) is the most substantial place on the beach, and consists of nearly 80 solid, well kept bungalows in all shapes and sizes, ranging from 400B to 1300B in the high season; prices drop by half in low season. All come with toilet, shower and fan. This one's a little tidier and better spaced than others on Hat Yao.

Phi-Phi Long Beach (☎ 075-612410) has closely spaced huts starting at 100B on the hillside, 120B for better locations, 150B for newer huts, all with shared shower. For 200B to 300B you can get a hut with private bath and fan.

Hat Lanti A Muslim family living on this beach offers seven to 10 thatched *huts* with beds and mosquito nets on stilts on a hillside overlooking the beach for 120B year round – no dickering between high and low seasons. The huts are in varying condition, so have a look around before choosing one, but basically it's a clean place. Toilets and showers are in separate huts. It can be hard to get boat operators from Ao Ton Sai to bring you to Hat Lanti, since the family there refuses to pay commissions. You can walk there via the viewpoint trail, however, and once you're on Hat Lanti the family can arrange boat trips anywhere around the island, and more cheaply than in Ton Sai. Note that the management at Phi-Phi Paradise Resort and other places on Hat Yao may tell you that there are no bungalows on Hat Lanti, or that they've been torn down. Come see for yourself.

The family patriarch does a little farming and a little fishing, and one almost gets

the impression he builds and lets these bungalows as much for company as for extra income. A nice little rustic restaurant overlooks the bay. The family cooks Thai Muslim food only and not much English is spoken; if you speak a little Thai you could very well learn a lot more here. There's decent snorkelling right off the beach.

Ao Lo Bakao *Pee Pee Island Village* (*Bangkok* ☎ 02-276 6056, fax 277 3990) is the only resort on this beautiful, secluded stretch of sand on the island's east coast. Limestone outcrops add a dramatic background, along with rock-climbing and hiking potential. From November to April, rooms start at 1400B and reach as high as 3000B. The remainder of the year they cost 1000B to 2000B; air-con is available at the upper end of the price bracket.

Hat Laem Tong This is another nice beach, with pricey resorts and its own pier. At the southern-most point, European-managed *Palm Beach Travelodge Resort* (☎ 076-214654, fax 215090) consists of large Thai/Malay-style cottages on 2m stilts spread over spacious, landscaped grounds with lots of coco palms. Ocean-front units have air-con, hot water and small refrigerators along with big two-level decks, while the mere deluxe ones have smaller decks, fan and cold water. High season rates run 5000/5200B single/double in a 'deluxe' duplex, 7300B for separate ocean-front units or 9900B for a family cottage (two connecting rooms, two bathrooms, up to six persons maximum); low season rates start at 3700/3900B. High season surcharges of 400B per room apply 20 December to 31 January. On the grounds are a medium-sized free form swimming pool and a well-equipped watersports centre.

Phi-Phi Coral Resort (☎/fax 01-676 7795, Bangkok ☎ 02-270 1520, fax 271 4374) offers octagonal wood and bamboo cottages on the beach for 2300B high season, 1800B low season. One major drawback is that the resort caters to huge tour groups which visit the beach daily, and the beach is not very well maintained.

At the northern end of the beach, with views over the rocky cape, *Phi-Phi Natural Resort* (☎ 076-223636, 01-229 2250, fax 076-214301, Bangkok ☎ 02-984 5600, fax 573 0376) offers very spacious grounds, a restaurant area overlooking the sea, and large split-level rooms with air-con and hot water. Although the rooms are very well maintained, maintenance in the public areas could be better. Mountain-view rooms cost 900B single/double, garden view 1500B and sea view 2500B. A surcharge of 1000B is added 20 December to 10 January.

Between Phi-Phi Coral Resort and the Palm Beach Travelodge Resort is an area with beach chairs, a restaurant and small dive centre with inexpensive snorkelling equipment for hire. A sea gypsy settlement at the end of that beach, signed 'Yipsae Village' in English, 'Muu Baan Thai Mai Pattana' (New Thai Development Village) in Thai, consists of 17 households living in corrugated metal shacks.

Interior A little village of sorts has developed in the interior of the island near Ao Ton Sai and Hat Hin Khom. Amid the gift shops, scuba shops and cafes there are several budget-oriented places to stay that most people choose only as a last resort, as none of them can be recommended as a first choice even if you're on a tight budget since there are better alternatives elsewhere on the island. *Tara Inn* (☎ 01-476 4830) has very basic rooms in a two storey wooden building for 350/400B single/double with private bath, as low as 150B in low season. *Twin Palm* (☎ 01-477 9251) is a more interesting place that looks vaguely like a Pacific colonial lodge, containing several rooms for 200B to 400B, shared bathroom. There's some minor landscaping and a little sitting area in front with built-in wood benches. Bungalows across from the guesthouse have private baths and cost 350B to 400B. In the low season you may be able to bargain these rates down. *Chan House,* nearby in the slummiest part of the village (lots of rubbish

lying around), offers bare cubicles for 200B to 300B. Rates for all of the these may drop to as low as 50B to 100B a night between May and November, except in August.

Out of the centre of the village towards the hills in the middle of the island, *PP Valentine* is a collection of thatched-roof huts with flowers growing around them for 250B to 350B. Friendly *Phi-Phi Rim Na Villa* costs 350/550B for singles/doubles, fan and private bath; the view of the reservoir isn't particularly inspiring.

Places to Eat

Most of the resorts, hotels and bungalows around the island have their own restaurants. Cheaper and sometimes better food is available at the restaurants and cafes in Ton Sai village. However virtually all of it is prepared for faràng, not Thai, palates so the Thai dishes usually aren't very authentic.

In the centre of the tourist village at Ao Ton Sai, *Mama Resto* has the most reliable kitchen and best service, and is one of the few places open on two sides, so it gets a breeze. Fresh seafood, pizza, Thai dishes, salads, wine and desserts are all on the menu, which is printed in English, French, Japanese and Thai. The recorded music selection is another plus. *Twin Palm Pizza Place* is a clean little spot with decent pizza and a much better atmosphere than the popular *PP Pizza*. *Garlic 1992* isn't bad for seafood, Thai and Italian and it's open 7 am to 10 pm. Nearby *Andaman Seafood*, across from the Reggae Bar, is a rustic setup with OK food, though it varies from meal to meal.

On the beach at Ao Lo Dalam, *Waterfall Pub & Restaurant* features a collection of wood tables and chairs under shade cloth, and serves sandwiches, spaghetti, Thai food, salads, good fruit shakes and a long list of cocktails. It's one of the few independent places where you can get a bite to eat with a sea breeze.

Entertainment

The most popular late night spots are *Tin-Tin's Bar & Club* and the large *Reggae Bar*, both in the tourist village in the island centre. *Rolling Stone Bar* is a laid-back place with Thai cushions to lie around on and occasional live music. On Ao Lo Dalam next to the beach, *Gecko Bar* is a fairly small place with some tables outside on the sand, while *Jungle Bar* is a larger beach club in front of Phi-Phi Island Cabana and open only November to May.

Over towards Hat Hin Khom, *Columbus Cocktails* has tables and chairs on the beach, where you can order food as well as drinks.

Getting There & Away

Ko Phi-Phi is equidistant from Phuket and Krabi, though the latter is the most economical point of departure. Boats used to travel only during the dry season, from late October to May, as the seas are often too rough during the monsoons for safe navigation.

Nowadays the boat operators risk sending boats out all year round – we've received several reports of boats losing power and drifting in heavy swells during the monsoons. It all depends on the weather – some rainy season departures are quite safe, others are risky. If the weather looks chancy, keep in mind that there usually aren't enough life jackets to go around on these boats.

Boats moor at the pier at Ao Ton Sai, except for a few from Phuket which go to the pier at Laem Tong.

Krabi From Krabi's Saphaan Jao Fah, PP Family Co has the monopoly on boats to Ko Phi-Phi at the moment. There are two departures daily, one at 10 am and another at 2.30 pm (in the reverse direction the times are 9 am and 1 pm). The one-way fare is 150B and the trip takes 1½ hours. These fares are sometimes discounted by agents in town to as low as 100B. Departures are sometimes delayed because boats often wait for buses from Bangkok to arrive at the Krabi pier.

Ao Nang You can also get boats from Ao Nang on the Krabi Province coast for 150B per person between October and April; there's usually only one departure a day, at

around 9 am. The trip lasts an hour and 20 minutes. The boat from Ko Phi-Phi back to Ao Nang usually leaves between 3 and 4 pm.

Phuket A dozen different companies operate boats from various piers on Phuket, ranging from 250B to 450B depending on the speed of the boat – from an hour and 40 minutes to two hours. Any guesthouse or hotel on Phuket can arrange tickets; the more expensive fares include bus or van pickup from your hotel. Boats leave frequently between 8 am and 3.30 pm from May to September.

Songserm Travel (☎ 076-222570) runs the *Jet Cruise*, which leaves Phuket at 8.30 am (returning from Laem Tong at 2.30 pm) and takes 40 minutes.

Various tour companies in Phuket offer day trips to Phi-Phi for 500B to 950B per person, including return transport, lunch and a tour. If you want to stay overnight and catch another tour boat back, you have to pay another 100B. Of course it's cheaper to book one way passage on the regular ferry service.

Other Islands As Ko Lanta is becoming more touristed, there are now fairly regular boats between that island and Ko Phi-Phi from October to April. Boats generally leave from the pier on Lanta Yai around 8 am, arriving at Phi-Phi Don around 9.30 am. In the reverse direction the departure is usually at 2 pm. Passage is 170B per person. It's also possible to get boats between Ko Phi-Phi and Ko Jam; the same approximate departure time, fare and trip duration applies.

Getting Around

Transport on the island is mostly on foot, although fishing boats can be chartered at Ao Ton Sai for short hops around Phi-Phi Don and Phi-Phi Leh. Touts meet boats from the mainland to load people onto to longtail boats going to Hat Yao (Long Beach) for 30B per person. Other boat charters around the island from the pier at Ton Sai include Laem Tong (300B), Ao Lo Bakao (200B) and Viking Cave on Ko Phi-Phi Leh (200B).

Ko Phi-Phi Leh

Phi-Phi Leh is almost all sheer cliffs, with a few caves and a sea lake formed by a cleft between two cliffs that allows water to enter into a bowl-shaped canyon. The so-called **Viking Cave** (officially called Tham Phaya Naak or Revered Naga Cave) on Phi-Phi Leh's north-east shore contains prehistoric paintings of stylised human and animal figures alongside later paintings of ships (Asian junks) no more than 100 years old.

The cave is also a collection point for swiftlet nests. The swiftlets like to build their nests high up in the caves in rocky hollows which can be very difficult to reach. (See the 'White Gold' boxed text for more about bird's nests.)

Ao Maya and Lo Sama, scenic coves on the island's western and south-eastern shores, are favourite stops for day-tripping snorkellers. Although once very pristine, the corals at these coves have been marred by bad anchoring and the beaches littered with rubbish jettisoned by tour boats. In 1999 a Hollywood film company spent about two months shooting scenes for the motion picture *The Beach*, based on UK author Alex Garland's novel of the same name. See the 'Notes on *The Beach*' boxed text in the South-Western Gulf chapter for more on the controversy that surrounded the filming here.

KO JAM (KO PU) & KO SI BOYA

These large islands between Krabi and Ko Lanta (see the Ko Lanta map) are inhabited by a small number of fishing families and are perfect for those seeking complete escape from the videos, faràng restaurants, beach bars and so on. About the only entertainment is watching the local fishermen load or unload their boats or collect cashews and coconuts; swimming or taking long walks on the beach.

Joy Resort (☎ *01-229 1502*) on the south-western coast of Ko Jam offers spacious bungalows from 150B (bamboo) to 450B (wood). A bit farther south along the coast is *New Bungalow* (☎ *01-464 4230*), where rates range from 120B for more basic

---

White Gold

On either side of the Thai-Malay peninsula – in Ao Phang-Nga, parts of the Andaman Sea near Phuket and the Gulf of Thailand near Chumphon – limestone caves and cliffs are often home to birds whose nests are a highly valued ingredient in 'bird's nest soup'. Sea swallows (*Collocalia esculenta*, also known as 'edible-nest swiftlets') like to build their nests high up in rocky limestone hollows which can be very difficult to reach. Agile collectors build vine-and-bamboo scaffolding to get at the nests but are occasionally injured or killed in falls. Before ascending the scaffolds, the collectors pray and make offerings of tobacco, incense and liquor to the cavern *phĩi* (spirits). The collectors sell the nests to intermediaries who then sell them to Chinese restaurants abroad. Known as 'white gold', premium teacup-sized bird nests sell for US$2000 per kilo – Hong Kong alone imports US$25 million worth every year.

The translucent nests are made of saliva which the birds secrete – the saliva hardens when exposed to the air. Cooked in chicken broth, the bird's nests soften and separate and look like bean thread noodles. The Chinese value the expensive bird secretions highly, believing them to be a medicinal food that imparts vigour.

Joe Cummings

---

huts to 400B for nicer ones – including a couple of tree houses. During the rainy season either place will drop rates to as low as 50B to 150B.

On nearby Ko Si Boya, *Siboya Bungalow* (☎ *01-229 1415*) offers 20 simple huts for 100B to 200B.

Getting There & Away

Boats to both islands leave once or twice a day from Ban Laem Kruat, a village about

30km from Krabi, at the end of Route 4036, off Hwy 4. Passage is 25B to Si Boya, 30B to Ban Ko Jam.

You can also take boats bound for Ko Lanta from Krabi's Saphaan Jao Fah and ask to be let off at Ko Jam. There are generally two boats daily which leave around 11 am and 2 pm; the fare is supposed to be 150B as far as Ko Jam, though some boat operators will charge the full Ko Lanta fare of 170B.

KO LANTA
• pop 18,540

Ko Lanta is a district of Krabi Province that consists of 52 islands. The geography here is typified by stretches of mangrove interrupted by coral-rimmed beaches, rugged hills and huge umbrella trees. Twelve of the islands are inhabited and, of these, three are easily accessible: Ko Klang, Ko Lanta Noi and Ko Lanta Yai. You can reach the latter by ferry and road from Ban Hua Hin on the mainland across from Ko Lanta Noi, from Ban Baw Meuang, farther south, and by ferry from Ko Phi-Phi, Ko Jam and Krabi.

Modest beach accommodation is available on the group's largest island, Ko Lanta Yai, a long, slender portion of sand and coral with low, forested hills down the middle; room and transport reservations are available through travel agencies in Krabi or Phuket. You can camp on any of the other islands – all have fresh water. Ban Sala Dan, at the northern tip of the island, is the largest settlement on the island and has a couple of ferry piers, tour outfits, dive shops and a Siam City Bank with exchange services. It's connected to the mainland by power lines. The district capital Ban Ko Lanta, on the southern section of the east coast, boasts a post office and long pier; there's not much to the town but the buildings are more solid-looking than those in Sala Dan. A vehicle ferry service to Ban Ko Lanta was recently discontinued. The village of Ban Sangkha-U on Lanta Yai's southern tip is a traditional Muslim fishing village and the people are friendly.

The people in this district are a mixture of Muslim Thais and chao náam who settled

here long ago. Their main livelihood is the cultivation of rubber, cashew and bananas, along with a little fishing. There is now a long string of inexpensive and moderately priced bungalow operations on Lanta Yai.

An unpaved road nearly encircles the island; only the south-eastern tip around Ban Sangkha-U is devoid of vehicles. In the centre of the island is Tham Khao Mai Kaew, a five or six cavern limestone cave complex. A narrow, 1.5km dirt track through a rubber plantation leads to the cave from the more southerly of the two cross-island roads.

Ko Lanta National Marine Park

In 1990, 15 islands in the Lanta group (covering an area of 134 sq km) were declared part of Ko Lanta National Marine Park in an effort to protect the fragile coastal environment. Ko Rok Nawk is especially beautiful, with a crescent-shaped bay featuring cliffs and a white-sand beach and a stand of banyan trees in the interior. The intact coral at Ko Rok Nai and limestone caves of Ko Talang are also worth seeing. Dive shops in Ban Sala Dan can arrange dives to these islands as well as to coral-encrusted Ko Ha, Ko Bida, Hin Bida and Hin Muang. Camping is permitted on Ko Rok Nawk.

Ko Lanta Yai itself is only partially protected since most of the island belongs to chao náam. As on Ko Phi-Phi, many bungalows have been built on shore-lands under the nominal protection of the Forestry Department. The interior of the island consists of rubber, cashew and fruit plantations, with a few stands of original forest here and there, mostly in the hilly southern section of the island. The park headquarters is situated at the southern tip of Ko Lanta Yai.

Tham Khao Mai Kaew

A great break from the beach is a trip to this complex of caves in the centre of Ko Lanta Yai. Even the hike in, through original forest, is quite pleasant. But the real fun begins when you descend in through a small, indistinct hole in the rocks and enter the series of diverse caverns. Some sections are as large as church halls, others require you to squeeze through on hands and knees. Sights en route include impressive stalactites and stalagmites, bats and even a cavern pool which you can swim in. The latter is not recommended for the faint-hearted, as access to the pool is via a long, slippery slope and a knotted rope that's almost as slimy: a bit of a challenge on the way back up.

A Muslim family that lives near the trailhead to the caves offers a guide service for 50B per person. You really need a guide to find your way around, particularly inside the caves, and the service is definitely worth it. The family also runs a very basic restaurant where you can get snacks and drinks.

The caves are off the more southerly of the two cross-island roads, down a narrow, 1.5km dirt track through a rubber plantation which ends up at the Muslim home. The best way to get there is by renting a motorcycle, though your bungalow may be willing to arrange transport.

Beaches

The western sides of all the islands have beaches, though in overall quality Lanta's beaches don't quite measure up to those found in Phuket or along Krabi's Hat Tham Phra Nang. The best are at either end of Lanta Yai's west coast, with middle sections given over more to rocky shores and reefs. There are coral reefs along parts of the western side of Lanta Yai and along Laem Khaw Kwang (Deer Neck Cape) at the north-western tip. A hill atop the cape gives a good aerial view of the island.

The little island to the south-east of Ko Klang has a nice beach called **Hat Thung Thaleh** – hire a boat from Ko Klang. Also worth exploring is Ko Ngai (Hai), southeast of Ko Lanta – see the Around Trang section farther on for more details, as Ko Ngai is more accessible from that province.

Diving & Snorkelling

The uninhabited islands of **Ko Rok Nai**, **Ko Rok Yai** and **Ko Ha**, south of Ko Lanta Yai, offer plenty of coral along their western and south-western shores. According to Ko Lanta Dive Centre in Sala Dan, the undersea

pinnacles of **Hin Muang** and **Hin Daeng** farther south-west are even better, with good-weather visibility of up to 30m, hard and soft corals, and plenty of large schooling fish such as shark, tuna and manta ray. Whale sharks have also been spotted in the area.

In any given season there may be as many as four dive operations on Ko Lanta, all working out of Sala Dan but often bookable at beach bungalows. Atlantis Dive Centre (☎ 01-228 4106, 075-612914) charges 2400B for a one-day dive trip, including equipment hire. Two-day trips with five dives start at 5000B. Atlantis also rents MX 10 underwater cameras for 480B per day. Aquarius Diving (☎ 076-234201) has received some good reviews from travellers, and Dive Zone also appears to be well equipped. November to April is the best season for diving in these areas.

Places to Stay

Ko Lanta Yai now has power lines extending from Ban Sala Dan as far south as Miami Bungalows, although Deer Neck and Kaw Kwang at the north-west end of the island aren't yet on the grid. This means air-con bungalows are on their way; videos and discos can't be far behind if we can judge by lines of development followed in Phuket, Ko Samui and Ko Phi-Phi.

Ko Lanta has the opportunity of becoming a model for environmentally conscious island tourism if the beach developers here will co-operate to keep the island clean and noise-free. Deforestation has become a problem as unscrupulous developers cut down trees to build up-market bungalows with hectares of decks. The simple places catering to backpackers still use renewable bamboo. As seems obvious elsewhere in Thailand, the national park system cannot be relied upon to protect the lands, so it's really up to the local private sector as to how they want to handle tourism.

So far they seem to be making all the wrong choices. At the northern end of the west coast, hotel proprietors are building ugly, broken-glass topped walls to divide the properties, thus blocking air circulation

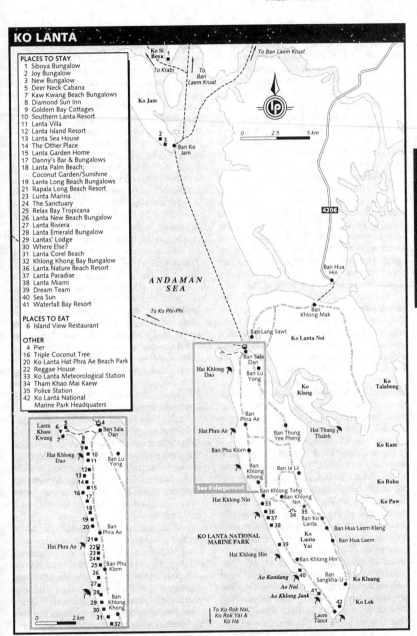

KO LANTA

PLACES TO STAY
1 Siboya Bungalow
2 Joy Bungalow
3 New Bungalow
5 Deer Neck Cabana
7 Kaw Kwang Beach Bungalows
8 Diamond Sun Inn
9 Goldern Bay Cottages
10 Southern Lanta Resort
11 Lanta Villa
12 Lanta Island Resort
13 Lanta Sea House
14 The Other Place
15 Lanta Garden Home
17 Danny's Bar & Bungalows
18 Lanta Palm Beach;
 Coconut Garden/Sunshine
19 Lanta Long Beach Bungalows
21 Rapala Long Beach Resort
23 Lunta Marina
24 The Sanctuary
25 Relax Bay Tropicana
26 Lanta New Beach Bungalow
27 Lanta Riviera
28 Lanta Emerald Bungalow
29 Lantas' Lodge
30 Where Else?
31 Lanta Corel Beach
32 Khlong Khong Bay Bungalow
36 Lanta Nature Beach Resort
37 Lanta Paradise
38 Lanta Miami
39 Dream Team
40 Sea Sun
41 Waterfall Bay Resort

PLACES TO EAT
6 Island View Restaurant

OTHER
4 Pier
16 Triple Coconut Tree
20 Ko Lanta Hat Phra Ae Beach Park
22 Reggae House
33 Ko Lanta Meteorological Station
34 Tham Khao Mai Kaew
35 Police Station
42 Ko Lanta National
 Marine Park Headquaters

SOUTHERN ANDAMAN COAST

and pushing everything more quickly in the direction of air conditioning, an absolute non-necessity on any island beach in Thailand. When it comes to that most precious island commodity – peaceful, natural solitude – the northern end of Ko Lanta is quickly using up its legacy.

The prettiest beach areas are found along the north-west side of the island just south of Ban Sala Dan, and this is where all the development is concentrated. Because it's long, wide and flat, this is a perfect beach for walking and jogging. Few places on this end costs less than 400B a night during high season (November to May). During low season prices plummet to 80B a night but the road along the west coast of the island becomes nearly impassable during the south-west monsoon; only a handful of beach bungalow operations actually stay open during low season. At this time proprietors make little effort to clean the beach of accumulating refuse and hence it becomes rather unappealing.

At the northern-most section of the beach near Ban Sala Dan is *Deer Neck Cabana*, a semi-circle of solid-looking bungalows with roofs of corrugated fibre or tin, facing the western side of the small Laem Khaw Kwang that juts west from the island, on its own shallow beach – a particularly safe one for children. When the tide is in you can see trees seemingly growing out of the sea (rooted in submerged sand banks). Rates are low, around 150B to 250B.

The locally owned *Kaw Kwang Beach Bungalows* (☎ 01-228 4106) is the oldest of the beach places and still commands one of the best stretches of beach; it's also close to snorkelling areas on the south-eastern side of this tiny cape. Nicely separated thatched huts with private bath, fan and good cross ventilation cost 80B to 800B depending on size, time of year and proximity to the beach. Hammocks are strung from casuarina trees along the beach and snorkelling gear is available for rent. The proprietors offer fishing and snorkelling trips to nearby islands. The Kaw Kwang owner is struggling with whether to add

air-con bungalows. He doesn't regard it as 'the natural way' but feels pressure from tourists to follow the lead of his neighbours.

Starting about 2.5km south of Ban Sala Dan along the western side of the island are a cluster of places in higher price ranges along a wide stretch of sand known as Hat Khlong Dao. *Diamond Sand Inn* (☎ 01-228 4473) comes up first, with new, large cottages with air-con and cold showers for 1500B. The restaurant has very good Thai food, and unlike the bungalows, it's not overpriced. *Golden Bay Cottages* (☎ 01-229 0879) is a very pleasant spot, with clean, sturdy bungalows with private bath for 100B to 450B. Next comes another newbie, *Southern Lanta Resort* (☎ 075-218947, fax 218242, 01-228 3083) which has a pool and 65 air-con rooms costing 1500B to 2000B. *Lanta Villa* (☎ 075-620629) offers bungalows with distinctive high-pitched roofs for 400B to 600B with fan, 800B with air-con; it's open year-round. Next is the *Lanta Island Resort* (☎ 01-212 4183) where bungalows with faux thatch walls and red corrugated roofs are 350B with fan, up to 980B air-con. It's popular with tour groups. This is followed by the slightly more up-market *Lanta Sea House* (☎ 01-228 4160) with vaguely Malay-style bungalows for 600B to 800B with fan, 1500B with air-con; open year-round.

From here south, accommodation becomes simpler and less expensive. *The Other Place* consists of just a few fan units, thatched and natural, for 100B to 200B or perhaps a bit more in the December to February peak season. *Lanta Garden Home*, next door, has similarly basic huts with shared bathroom for 150B, up to 400B with private bath.

Just around a headland famous for a triple-trunked coconut palm begins Hat Phra Ae, where *Danny's Bar & Bungalows* offers five old-style thatched bungalows and four outside bathrooms for 80B low season, 120B high season. The friendly *Lanta Palm Beach* has both wood and concrete huts of widely varying quality for 80B to 150B. Close by, down the beach, is a new place under construction in front of the house of the local kamnan (precinct officer) – a good distance from the road (good for quiet nights). These simple huts of simple bamboo and palm thatch, containing fan and scoop baths, may be called either *Coconut Garden* or *Sunshine*; the owners hadn't quite made their minds up (when asked our opinion, we voted for Coconut Garden since the place is surrounded by slender coco palms). The predicted rates are only 80B to 100B.

Just before Ko Lanta Hat Phra Ae Beach Park, an access road, signed for the Flintstone Pub, leads 400m to *Lanta Long Beach Bungalows*, a group of rustic thatched bungalows on cement stilts with private bath and nice decks. The huts are rather close together, but the open-air restaurant offers good beach views. Rates are 200B a night, less in off-peak months (October to November and March to May; it's closed June to September like most places on Ko Lanta).

Just beyond the small village of Ban Phra Ae is the up-market *Rapala Long Beach Resort* (☎ 01-228 4286), with 22 hexagonal units for 150B to 500B. The accommodation is actually quite nice, but you'll have to contend with barbed wire fencing and uneven service. The same access road leads to *Lunta Marina*, where wood and bamboo bungalows use an interesting elevated A-frame design with a ladder up to each unit, and a deck underneath with a built-in bench. They're back away from the beach, near the bars, Reggae House and Blue Marlin, and cost 150B to 300B. In this same area *The Sanctuary* offers six rustic huts and good vegetarian food; it's a nice place but is almost always full (closed during the rainy season).

The nearby *Relax Bay Tropicana* features spacious bungalows with large decks for 200B to 600B; huts are perched around a rocky hillside overlooking the sea. The beach along this stretch – and for the next 2km – is nothing special. It's followed by a little farther south, near Ban Phu Klom, by *Lanta New Beach Bungalow*, two rows of

cement bungalows painted white on the front but unpainted on the other three sides, topped by red corrugated roofs and renting for 200B to 300B a night, and the *Lanta Riviera*, very small but well kept concrete cottages with wooden cladding on the front walls, corrugated green roofs and private bath for 200B in a nice coconut grove. There's a basic open-air restaurant at the latter. This theme continues at similarly priced *Lanta Emerald Bungalow*, only this time the front walls feature thatch instead of wood or white paint – and the corrugated roofs are red.

Next south towards Ban Khlong Khong (the beach here is also sometimes referred to as Hat Khlong Khong), *Lantas' Lodge* (formerly Blue Lanta) has thatched huts in a coconut grove for 500B to 700B in high season, 200B to 300B in the low season; a little overpriced, but it's quiet and has a pleasant outdoor restaurant. Next comes *Where Else?* with basic thatched huts on stilts for 150B to 200B, followed by *Lanta Coral Beach*, down a sandy road which winds through coconut trees. The tidy thatched huts have cement foundations and small verandahs. All have private baths and go for 200B to 300B. There's a restaurant on the beach in front. Closed during the rainy season.

To reach the next one down, *Khlong Khong Bay Bungalow*, take a dirt road to the right through a village and past a mosque, then through a wooden gateway past some private homes. The nine traditional thatch huts here all come with private bath for 200B to 300B in season. A simple open-air restaurant offers food. This is a good place to stay if you desire to get involved in village life at Ban Khlong Khong.

Another kilometre or so farther south the beach changes name again, to Hat Khlong Nin, and the accommodation becomes yet cheaper. *Lanta Nature Beach Resort* offers what's becoming the Lanta stereotype, cement bungalows with corrugated roofs and small terraces for 150B to 300B depending on the month. Next, *Lanta Paradise* offers OK wood and concrete bungalows with good beach frontage for 150B to 400B, while *Lanta Miami* (☎ *01-228 4506),* immediately south, costs 300B to 400B.

Sitting by itself on a little headland with a rocky stretch of beach called Hat Khlong Hin is the well landscaped *Dream Team* (☎ *01-477 1626),* where well kept, large, screened bungalows go for 100B to 600B depending on proximity to the shoreline. A better sand beach at Ao Kantiang is only about 10 minutes away on foot. At the north end of Ao Kantiang is the secluded *Sea Sun* with 80B to 120B cement bungalows. One of the huts has a particularly good view.

The next cove down, Ao Nui, is one of the most beautiful on the island and as yet has no bungalows – probably because it's a steep walk down to the beach.

At this point the road begins climbing and winding steeply as it approaches the southern tip of the island. Near the end of the road, on Ao Khlong Jaak, the well designed, eco-oriented *Waterfall Bay Resort* (☎ *01-228 4014, Krabi ☎ 075-612084)* offers 18 well spaced wooden bungalows with thatched roofs overlooking a secluded bay. The bungalows cost 300B to 800B depending on their position relative to the beach. All have two rooms, one below and one above as a loft, making it very suitable for family stays. The namesake waterfall is a 30 to 40 minute walk, and boat trips to Ko Rok Nai and Ko Rok Nawk can be arranged. The restaurant serves Indian, Thai and faràng food. As Waterfall is often booked out when open (October to mid-June only), it's best to book in advance through its office in Krabi. A 4WD vehicle picks guests up from the pier in Sala Dan. From the resort a dirt track continues to the park headquarters and Ban Sangkha-U. This is a good spot to stay if you're interested in hiking into the park interior.

In Ban Ko Lanta, on the island's southeast coast, near the pier, *No Name* provides very basic accommodation for 50B a night.

Places to Eat

If you get tired of bungalow food there are a couple of basic places to eat in Ban Sala Dan at the northern end of Lanta Yai.

Seaview and *Seaside* are two small moderately priced restaurants over the water with Thai food and seafood. The *Swiss Bakery* next to the pier has good coffee and pastries; they close in the rainy season. Restaurants on the beach near Lanta Garden Home come and go with the seasons, usually offering Swiss, French or Italian food.

Island View Restaurant sits on the crest of the hill between the two bungalow operations on either side of Laem Khaw Khwang and is only open during high season. The food is standard but the view and surrounding cashew trees add novelty to the dining experience.

At the *Diamond Sand Inn*, try the excellent *kûng phàt náam má khāam* (shrimp stir-fried in tamarind sauce). *Danny's Bar & Bungalows* serves good, inexpensive to moderately priced Thai and western dishes, and even Mexican food. Danny is a Thai who once worked as a chef in Europe. Every month during high season the restaurant hosts a small full moon party with Thai boxing, music, dancing and a seafood barbecue. *The Sanctuary* makes good vegetarian food, including a few Indian dishes.

Getting There & Away

Krabi The slow way to get to Ko Lanta is to take a songthaew (30B) from Th Phattana in Krabi all the way to Ban Hua Hin, and then a vehicle ferry across the narrow channel to Ban Khlong Mak on Ko Lanta Noi. From there, get a motorcycle taxi (20B) across to another pier on the other side, then another vehicle ferry to Ban Sala Dan on Ko Lanta Yai. Both ferries cost 3B for pedestrians, 5B for a bicycle and one rider, 10B per motorcycle and 50B in a car or truck (plus a 3B per passenger fee for the crossing between Ban Hua Hin and Ban Khlong Mak). There are now two ferries at Ban Sala Dan, a larger new one a little south of Ban Sala Dan and the older, smaller one (two cars at a time only) that goes directly to the village. Both ferries run frequently 6 am to 6 pm except on Friday when they close at noon so that the Muslim operators can visit local mosques. There is talk of building a bridge somewhere along here to supplant the ferry services.

Ban Hua Hin is 26km down Route 4206 from Ban Huay Nam Khao, which is about 44km from Krabi along Hwy 4. Direct songthaews from Krabi (Talaat Kao junction) to Ban Hua Hin run regularly until about 3 pm. Count on two hours to complete the trip, including ferry crossing. If you're travelling by private car or motorcycle, the turn-off for Route 4206 is near the village of Ban Huay Nam Khao (Km 64) on Hwy 4.

If you're coming from Trang, there's no direct public transport to Ban Hua Hin, but you can take a bus from Trang to Ban Huay Nam Khao (25B), then transfer to a songthaew going south-west to the Ban Hua Hin pier.

The quickest way to reach Ko Lanta from Krabi is to take a boat from Krabi's Saphaan Jao Fah, only available November to April. Boats usually depart at 10.30 am and 1.30 pm and take one to 1½ hours to reach Ban Sala Dan; the fare is 150B. In the reverse direction boats leave at 8 am and 1 pm.

Ko Phi-Phi During the dry season, October to April, there are two boats a day from Ko Phi-Phi; at 11 am and 1 pm for 150B per person. They take about an hour and 20 minutes to reach Ban Sala Dan; in the opposite direction boats leave around 8 am and 2 pm. There are also occasional boats to Lanta from Ko Jam.

Getting Around

Most of the bungalows on Ko Lanta will provide free transport to and from Ban Sala Dan. Motorcycle taxis are available from Ban Sala Dan to almost anywhere along the beaches for 10B to 40B depending on the distance.

Motorcycles can be rented in Ban Sala Dan for a steep 250B a day.

Trang Province

The province of Trang, as well as its southern neighbour Satun Province, bears a geography similar to that of Krabi and Phang-Nga,

with islands and beaches along the coast and limestone-buttressed mountains inland. The area is much less frequented by tourists though. Caves and waterfalls are the major attractions in the interior.

Twenty kilometres north of Trang's provincial capital is a 3500 râi (5.6 sq km) provincial park, which preserves a tropical forest in its original state. In the park there are three waterfalls and government resthouses. About 50km north-west of Trang is **Thaleh Song Hong** (Sea of Two Rooms), a large lake surrounded by limestone hills. Hills in the middle of the lake nearly split it in half, hence the name. There's no accommodation here but there is swimming, fishing and waterfowl.

Music & Dance

As in other southern provinces, public holidays and temple fairs feature performances of *Manohra*, the classical Southern Thai dance-drama, and *nãng thalung* (shadow play). But because of its early role as a trade centre, Trang has a unique Indian-influenced music and dance tradition as well as *lí-khe pàa* (also called *lí-khe bòk* and *lí-khe ram ma-naa*), a local folk opera with a storyline that depicts Indian merchants taking their Thai wives back to India for a visit. It's part farce, part drama, with Thais costumed as Indians with long beards and turbans.

Traditional funerals and Buddhist ordinations often feature a musical ensemble called *kaa-law*, which consists of four or five players sitting on a small stage under a temporary coconut-leaf roof or awning. The instruments include two long Indian drums, a *pii haw* (a large oboe similar to the Indian *shahnai*) and two gongs.

TRANG
* pop 50,900

Historically, Trang has played an important role as a centre of trade since at least the 1st century AD; it was especially important between the 7th and 12th centuries, when it was a seaport for ocean-going sampans sailing between Trang and the Straits of Malacca. Nakhon Si Thammarat and Surat

Thani were major commercial and cultural centres for the Srivijaya empire at this time, and Trang served as a relay point for communications and shipping between the east coast of the Thai peninsula and Palembang, Sumatra. Trang was then known as Krung Thani and later as Trangkhapura (City of Waves) until the name was shortened during the early years of the Ratanakosin period.

During the Ayuthaya period, Trang was a common port of entry for seafaring western visitors, who continued by land to Nakhon Si Thammarat or Ayuthaya. The town was then located at the mouth of the Trang River, but King Mongkut later gave orders to move the city to its present location inland because of frequent flooding. Today Trang is still an important point of exit for rubber from the province's many plantations.

Trang's main attractions are the nearby beaches and islands, plus the fact that it can be reached by train. Among Thais, one of Trang's claims to fame is that it often wins awards for 'Cleanest City in Thailand' – its main rival in this regard is Yala. It may not seem that sparkling to the average visitor, but Trang does have a lively, trading town appeal that merits a stroll if you find yourself here overnight.

Orientation

Maps Outdated but useful maps of Trang, as well as English-language newspapers, are available at Mittasason Bookshop at the intersection of Th Visetkul (Wisetkun) and Th Phra Ram VI.

Information

Tourist Offices Trang Tourism Business Association (☎/fax 075-215580), on Th Phra Ram VI around the corner from the Trang Hotel, distributes printed information on the province and can answer most tourist questions. TAT had plans to open a branch office on Th Ratchadamnoen, but budget cuts have caused a temporary delay.

Money Bangkok Bank, Thai Farmers Bank and Siam Commercial Bank all have

branches along Th Phra Ram VI in the centre of town. Bangkok Bank and Thai Farmers Bank have ATMs, as does the Thai Military Bank on Th Visetkul.

Post & Telephone The post and telephone office is on the corner of Th Phra Ram VI and Th Kantang.

Bookshops Mittasason Bookshop, right across from the municipal office near the clock tower, carries the *Bangkok Post*, *The Nation* and a few English magazines.

Things to See

One odd aspect of Trang is the seeming lack of Thai Buddhist temples. Most of those living in the central business district are Chinese, so you do see a few joss houses but that's about it. Meun Ram, a Chinese temple between sois 1 and 2, Th Visetkul, sometimes sponsors performances of southern Thai shadow theatre.

Places to Stay

A number of hotels are found along the city's two main thoroughfares, Th Phra Ram VI and Th Visetkul (Wisetkun), which run in four directions from the clock tower. The long-running **Ko Teng** (☎ 075-218148) on Th Phra Ram VI has large singles/doubles for a reasonable 180/300B, and a good restaurant downstairs. The front doors of the hotel are closed at 7 pm every day; there's another entrance around the back. The **Wattana Hotel** (☎ 075-218184), on the same street, offers rooms for 180B with fan and bath, 260B with TV and phone or 450B with air-con. This is one of those hotels with lots of smoking men and painted ladies in the lobby.

Rock bottom is the three storey **Si Trang Hotel**, just north-east of the train station on Th Sathani (the south-western-most extension of Th Phra Ram VI). The 1st and 2nd stories have cement walls, while the 3rd storey is wooden. All rooms cost 120B whether with private toilet and shower or communal facilities, and all are dark and dingy. The hotel gets a lot of transients who

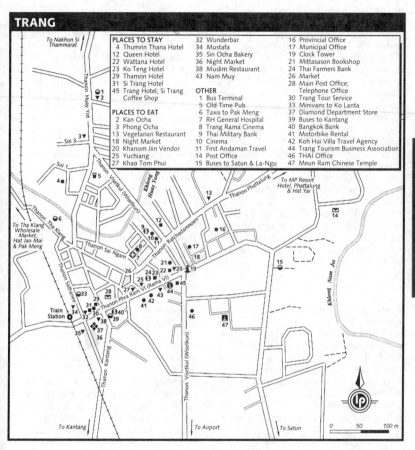

TRANG

PLACES TO STAY
4 Thumrin Thana Hotel
12 Queen Hotel
22 Wattana Hotel
23 Ko Teng Hotel
29 Thamrin Hotel
31 Si Trang Hotel
45 Trang Hotel; Si Trang Coffee Shop

PLACES TO EAT
2 Kan Ocha
3 Phong Ocha
13 Vegetarian Restaurant
18 Night Market
20 Khanom Jiin Vendor
25 Yuchiang
27 Khao Tom Phui

32 Wunderbar
34 Mustafa
35 Sin Ocha Bakery
36 Night Market
38 Muslim Restaurant
43 Nam Muy

OTHER
1 Bus Terminal
5 Old Time Pub
6 Taxis to Pak Meng
7 RH General Hospital
8 Trang Rama Cinema
9 Thai Military Bank
10 Cinema
11 First Andaman Travel
14 Post Office
15 Buses to Satun & La-Ngu

16 Provincial Office
17 Municipal Office
19 Clock Tower
21 Mittasason Bookshop
24 Thai Farmers Bank
26 Market
28 Main Post Office; Telephone Office
30 Trang Tour Service
33 Minivans to Ko Lanta
37 Diamond Department Store
39 Buses to Kantang
40 Bangkok Bank
41 Motorbike Rental
42 Koh Hai Villa Travel Agency
44 Trang Tourism Business Association
46 THAI Office
47 Meun Ram Chinese Temple

SOUTHERN ANDAMAN COAST

have disembarked from the Bangkok to Singapore rail line. When we checked a room out, two recent arrivals were cooking on a charcoal firepot right in the hallway; you won't find any fire exits.

On Th Visetkul are the *Queen Hotel* (☎ 075-218522), with large clean rooms with fan for 230B, or 360B with air-con, and the business-like *Trang Hotel* (☎ 075-218944), near the clock tower, with expansive air-con rooms with TV, hot water, fan and phone, some with balconies, for 500B,

with bath for 550B. The downstairs coffee shop at the latter is quite popular.

The 10 storey *Thamrin Hotel* (☎ 075-211011, fax 218057) is an up-market place on Th Kantang near the train station. Modern air-con rooms cost 580B standard, 880B deluxe, not including tax and service. The Trang Hotel is better value.

Uppermost on the local scale is the relatively new *Thumrin Thana Hotel* (☎ 075-211211, fax 223288, 69/8 Th Trang Thana) a big fancy place, not far from the bus terminal, with a gleaming marbled lobby and 289 spacious rooms, each with two beds, IDD phones with voice mail, minibar/fridge, TV and smoke detector, all for 1200B to 1500B. Other facilities include a small bakery, three restaurants, a coffee shop, attached shopping centre, business centre, safety deposit boxes, pool, fitness centre, sauna room and jacuzzi.

Looking like a beached Titanic on the north-eastern outskirts of town, *MP Resort Hotel (☎ 075-214230, fax 211177, 184 Th Phattalung)* is a huge sky-blue building designed to resemble a cruise ship from a distance. Despite the strange, kitsch exterior, the hotel has a classy lobby and the rates of 1150B to 1440B (from 2230B for suites) are pretty good considering the luxuries: pool, poolside bar, sauna, jacuzzi, snooker, tennis court, golf driving range, games room, fitness centre, karaoke, restaurants and business centre. However it's a bit far from town compared with the Thumrin Thara and lacks the polish of the latter.

Kantang If you happen to become stranded in nearby Kantang waiting for a boat to Hat Jao Mai or the islands, there are a couple of inexpensive places to stay. The *Siri Chai Hotel (☎ 075-251172)*, on the main road leading to the port from the train station, has small but fairly clean singles for 140B, doubles for 240B – or you can have a room for two hours for 100B!

Near the main market near the waterfront, *JT Hotel (☎ 075-251755)* has fan rooms for 200B, air-con for 300B.

Places to Eat

Plenty of good restaurants can be found near the hotels. The *Ko Teng Hotel* still serves some of the best *kaeng kari kài* (chicken curry) in the city. The English tourist menu prices it at 60B, which means a bowl of the stuff, while the Thai menu lists 25B – served *râat khâo* or over rice. The air-con *Si Trang Coffee Shop* in the Trang Hotel (not to be confused with the smaller Si Trang Hotel, which has no restaurant other than the guests cooking in the hallway!) serves very good Thai, Chinese and western food at moderate

prices. *Nam Muy* is a large Chinese restaurant opposite the Ko Teng Hotel; although it looks fancy, the menu is medium-priced.

Khao Tom Phui (no roman-script sign; look for a red sign with chopsticks) on Th Phra Ram VI serves all manner of Thai and Chinese standards in the evenings till 2 am, and has been honoured with the Shell Chuan Chim designation for its *tôm yam* (available with shrimp, fish or squid), *plaa kraphõng náam daeng* (sea bass in red sauce) and *yâwt phàk kha-náa pûm pûy* (greens stir-fried in red bean sauce with chunks of smoked mackerel).

If you're longing for a fix of western food or beer, *Wunderbar*, next door to Trang Tour Service near the train station, serves good sandwiches, cheeses, salads, Thai dishes, fruit shakes, milkshakes and icy cold beer. They have a good selection of German magazines, paperbacks and the Bangkok Post on hand – not a bad place to wait in air-con comfort for the next train. Open 11 am to 11.30 pm.

Diamond department store on Th Phra Ram VI has a small hawkers' centre on the 3rd floor. Around the corner from the department store along Th Sathani, a *night market* convenes in the evening.

Khanõm Jiin Trang is famous for khanõm jiin. One of the of the best places to try it is at the *tables* set up on the corner of Th Visetkul and Th Phra Ram VI. You have a choice of dousing your noodles in *náam yaa* (a spicy ground fish curry), *náam phrík* (a sweet and slightly spicy peanut sauce) or *kaeng tai plaa* (a very spicy mixture of green beans, fish, bamboo shoots and potato). To this you can add your choice of fresh grated papaya, pickled vegies, cucumber and bean sprouts – all for just 8B per bowl.

Across the street from this vendor, in front of the municipal offices, is a small night market that usually includes a couple of *khanõm jiin vendors*.

Muslim The Malay culinary influence is strong in Trang. The *Muslim Restaurant* opposite the Thamrin Hotel on Phra Ram

VI serves inexpensive roti kaeng, curries and rice. *Mustafa* (no roman-script sign – look for a large, brightly lit tiled place with curries in a glass cabinet at the front) near the train station serves inexpensive Malay style curries, roti kaeng, *roti khài* (roti with egg) and *màtàbà* (martabak) in relatively clean surroundings. Nearby are several smaller *food stalls* serving Muslim cuisine.

Ko-píi Shops Trang is even more famous for its coffee and *ráan kafae* or *ráan ko-píi* (coffee shops), which are easily identified by the charcoal-fired aluminium boilers with stubby smokestacks seen somewhere in the middle or back of the open-sided shops. Usually run by Hokkien Chinese, these shops serve real filtered coffee (called *kafae thŭng* in the rest of the country) along with a variety of snacks, typically *paa-thông-kō* (fried sweet pastry), *salabao* (Chinese buns), *khanŏm jìip* (dumplings), Trang-style sweets, *mŭu yâang* (barbecued pork) and sometimes noodles and *jók* (thick rice soup).

When you order coffee in these places, be sure to use the Hokkien word *ko-píi* rather than the Thai *kafae*, otherwise you may end up with Nescafé or instant Khao Chong coffee – the proprietors often think this is what faràngs want. Coffee is usually served with milk and sugar – ask for *ko-píi dam* for sweetened black coffee or *ko-píi dam, mâi sài náam-taan* for black coffee without sugar.

The most convenient ráan ko-píi for most visitors staying in the town centre is the *Sin Ocha Bakery*, on Th Sathani near the train station. Once the queen of Trang coffee shops (under its old name, Sin Jiaw), it was completely renovated a few years ago and made into a modern cafe. Ko-píi is still available here, along with international pastries and egg-and-toast breakfasts.

If you're more hard core, try *Yuchiang* (sign in Thai and Chinese only) at the corner of Soi 1, Th Phra Ram VI and Soi 6, Th Phra Ram VI (opposite Khao Tom Phui). This is a real classic Hokkien coffee house with marble-topped round tables in an old wooden building. It's open early morning to mid afternoon only. On Th Huay Yot between the

Thumrin Thana Hotel and the turnoff for the bus terminal, *Phong Ocha* (☎ 075-219918) does traditional ko-píi along with jók and *mìi sŭa kài tŭun*, super thin rice noodles with herb-steamed chicken. Open 7 am to 10 pm but most active in the morning hours. Farther north along Th Huay Yot on the right, closer to the bus terminal, *Kan Ocha* catches the evening ko-píi shift.

Entertainment
Old Time Pub, off Th Huay Yot a bit north of the town centre, is a cosy, air-con place with good service and no hassling from *jii-khōh* (Thailand's 'hoodlums'), who sometimes harass unaccompanied women at night spots elsewhere in Thailand.

Shopping
Trang is known for its wickerwork and, especially, mats woven of *bai toei* (pandanus leaves), which are called *sèua paa-nan*, or Panan mats. Panan mats are important bridal gifts in rural Trang, and are a common feature of rural households. The process of softening and drying the pandanus leaves before weaving takes many days. They can be purchased in Trang for about 100B to 200B.

The province also has its own distinctive cotton-weaving styles. The villages of Na Paw and Na Meun Si are the most highly regarded sources for these fabrics, especially the intricate diamond-shaped *lai lûuk kâew* pattern, once reserved for nobility.

The best place in town for good buys is the Tha Klang wholesale market along Th Tha Klang.

Getting There & Away
Air THAI operates daily flights from Bangkok to Trang (2005B). The Trang THAI office (☎ 075-218066) is at 199/2 Th Visetkul. The airport is 4km south of Trang; THAI runs shuttle vans back and forth for 50B per person.

Bus & Share Taxi Ordinary buses from Satun or Krabi to Trang cost 43B. A share taxi from the same cities is around 80B.

Aircon buses from Satun cost 86B and take three hours. From Phattalung it's 20B (two hours) by bus, 40B by share taxi. You can get an air-con minivan to Hat Yai from the Trang bus terminal for 65B (two hours); they leave frequently 5.30 am to 5.30 pm. Otherwise an ordinary bus to/from Hat Yai is 50B.

Air-con 1st class buses to/from Bangkok are 443B (344 for 2nd class air-con) or 685B for a VIP bus. The air-con buses take about 12 hours.

Trang's open-air bus terminal is on a back street off Th Huay Yot.

If you're coming from Ko Lanta, you can catch any north-bound vehicle and get off at Ban Huay Nam Khao, the junction for Hwy 4 and the road to Ko Lanta, then catch a bus south to Trang for 30B.

Minivans to Kantang leave from behind the train station in Trang several times a day for 35B.

Train Only two trains go all the way from Bangkok to Trang: the express No 83, which leaves Bangkok's Hualamphong station at 5.05 pm and arrives in Trang at 7.55 am the next day; and the rapid No 167, which leaves Hualamphong station at 6.20 pm, arriving in Trang at 9.57 am. Both trains offer all three classes of travel. The fare is 660B 1st class, 311B 2nd class and 135B 3rd class, not including rapid or express surcharges. From Thung Song in Nakhon Si Thammarat Province there are two trains daily to Trang, leaving at 6.27 and 8.25 am, arriving an hour and 45 minutes later.

If you want to continue to Kantang on the coast, there is one daily rapid train out of Trang at 9.23 am which arrives in Kantang at 10.35 am. The fare from Trang to Kantang is 45B in 3rd class (including rapid surcharge).

Boat From the harbour at nearby Kantang, ferries used to operate back and forth to Pulau Langkawi, just across the border in Malaysia; at times the service has gone as far afield as Medan (Indonesia) and Singapore, but for the moment the only boat option is the ferry across the Trang River estuary to Tha Som for Hat Jao Mai and Ko Libong. See the Trang Beaches section for details.

Getting Around

Samlors and tuk-tuks around town cost 10B to 20B per trip.

Suzuki 110cc motorbikes can be rented from the motorcycle dealer opposite the Ko Teng Hotel at 44A Th Phra Ram VI for 200B per day.

Big orange buses to the harbour at Kantang leave frequently from Th Kantang near the train station for 10B. There are also air-con minivans which do the same trip every hour or so for 20B each; a motorcycle taxi will cost 60B to 70B, but this is really too long a jaunt for a comfortable pillion ride.

TRANG BEACHES & ISLANDS

Trang Province has several sandy beaches and coves along the coast, especially in the Sikao and Kantang districts. On Route 403 between Trang and Kantang is a turn-off west onto a paved road that leads down to the coast through some interesting Thai-Muslim villages. At the end, it splits north and south. The road south leads to Hat Yao, Hat Yong Ling and Hat Jao Mai. The road north leads to Hat Chang Lang and Hat Pak Meng. A more direct way to Hat Pak Meng from Trang is to take Route 4046 via Sikao.

Ban Tung Laem Sai

At Ban Tung Laem Sai in Sikao district is an alternative homestay for visitors interested in ecotourism. Operated by Yat Fon, a local nonprofit organisation that promotes community development and environmental conservation, the staff educate visitors about local mangroves, coral reefs, coastal resources and the Thai-Muslim way of life.

Very little English is spoken so this is an endeavour best undertaken by those who already speak Thai or who will be accompanied by a Thai-speaking companion. It is offered mostly for the benefit of other practitioners of community environmental stewardship programmes. No sunbathing or drinking is allowed in the vicinity. Contact

Khun Suwit at Yat Fon ☎ 075-219737, for reservations and transport.

Hat Pak Meng

Thirty-nine kilometres from Trang in Sikao district, north of Hat Jao Mai, Yao and Chang Lang, is another long, broad, sandy beach near the village of Ban Pak Meng. The waters are usually shallow and calm, even in the rainy season. A couple of hundred metres offshore are several limestone rock formations, including a very large one with caves. Several vendors and a couple of restaurants offer fresh seafood. You can use the sling chairs and umbrellas on the beach as long as you order something. A long promenade/sea wall runs along the middle and southern sections of the beach.

Around the beginning of November, locals flock to Hat Pak Meng to collect *hãwy taphao*, a delicious type of sea mussel. The tide reaches its lowest this time of year, so it's relatively easy to pick up the shells.

About halfway between Pak Meng and Trang, off Route 4046, is the 20m-high **Ang Thong Falls**.

At Hat Pak Meng there are unnamed brick *bungalows* for rent at 200B to 300B a night, plus the *Pakmeng Resort* (☎ 075-218940) with sturdier bungalows with fan and bath for 300B to 500B.

Pakmeng Resort operates one day boat tours of Ko Cheuak, Ko Muk and Ko Kradan for 350B including lunch and beverages.

Getting There & Away Take a van (20B) or songthaew (15B) to Sikao from Trang, and then a songthaew (10B) to Hat Pak Meng. There are also one or two direct vans daily to Pak Meng from Trang for 30B.

If you're coming by your own transport from Trang, make a left before you get to the clock circle in Sikao, following a blue sign for Route 2021. You'll come to a forked junction after 3.5km, where you should continue straight to get to Pak Meng, 6km farther.

A paved road now connects Pak Meng with the other beaches south, so if you have your own wheels there's no need to backtrack through Sikao.

Ko Ngai (Hai)

This island is actually part of Krabi Province to the north, but is most accessible from Trang. It's a fairly small island, covering about 3000 rãi (4.8 sq km), but the beaches are fine white sand and the water is clear and virtually the entire island is ringed by coral. The resorts on the island operate half-day boat tours of nearby islands, including Morakot Cave on Ko Muk, for around 200B per person.

Places to Stay Along the eastern shore of Ko Ngai are two 'resorts'. Towards the middle of the island is *Koh Hai Villa* (☎ 075-218029, Bangkok ☎ 02-318 3107), with fan-cooled bungalows for 300B double, 600B to 800B for four people and tents for 150B. The vapid food here is overpriced, and the staff can be surly.

At the southern end is *Ko Ngai Resort* (☎ 075-210496, 210317, Bangkok ☎ 02-246-4399), where one bed seaside huts cost 300B, two-bed rooms in large bungalows are 600B to 900B and a six bed bungalow is 1200B. Tents are also available for 150B.

You can book any of these through the Koh Hai Villa Travel Agency in Trang (☎ 075-210496, Bangkok ☎ 02-246 4399) at 112 Th Phra Ram VI. Each resort has its own office in the city, but this one is the most conveniently located if you're staying in the central business district. Trang Tour Service (☎ 075-214564, fax 219280) next to Wunderbar near the train station in Trang also handles booking for Koh Hai Villa.

Getting There & Away Boats leave from the jetty at Pak Meng for Ko Ngai daily at 10 am and 2 pm for 80B per person. You can also charter a longtail for 400B to 500B.

Hat Chang Lang

Hat Chang Lang is part of the Hat Jao Mai National Park, and this is where the park office is located. The beach is about 2km long and very flat and shallow. At the northern end is a stream, Khlong Chang Lang. On a cliff near the office is a series of ancient rock art sketched in ochre. There's also a fresh water spring and a grassy campsite beneath casuarinas.

Ko Muk & Ko Kradan

Ko Muk is nearly opposite Hat Chang Lang and can be reached by boat from Kantang or Pak Meng. The coral around Ko Muk is lively, and there are several small beaches on the island suitable for camping and swimming. The best beach, Hat Sai Yao, is on the opposite side of the island from the mainland and is nicknamed Hat Farang because it's 'owned' by a faràng from Phuket.

Near the northern end is **Tham Morakot** (Emerald Cave), a beautiful limestone tunnel that can be entered by boat during low tide. The tunnel stretches for 80m to emerge in an open pool of a beautiful emerald hue, hence the cave's name. At the southern end of the island is pretty Phangka Cove and the fishing village of Hua Laem.

Ko Kradan is the most beautiful of the islands that belong to Hat Jao Mai National Park. Actually, only five of six precincts on the island belong to the park: one is devoted to coconut and rubber plantations. At both islands the water is so clear in places that the bottom is clearly visible from the surface. This clear water permits the growth of corals and good healthy reefs along the north side of the islands, and the water is often shallow enough for snorkelling. There are fewer white-sand beaches on Ko Kradan than on Ko Muk, but the coral reef on the side facing Ko Muk is quite good for diving. **Ko Cheuak** and **Ko Waen** are small islands between Ko Muk, Ko Kradan and the Trang coast. Both feature sand beaches and coral reefs. Ko Cheuak has a small cave which can be entered by boats at low tide.

Places to Stay & Eat *Ko Muk Resort* (☎ 075-212613 Trang office, 25/36 Th Sathani) on Ko Muk facing the mainland next to the Muslim fishing village of Hua Laem, has simple but nicely designed bungalows for 200B with shared bathroom, 250B to 300B with private bath. The beach in front tends towards mud flats during low tide; the beach in front of the nearby village

is slightly better but modest dress is called for. The resort organises boats to nearby islands like Ko Ngai (Hai), Waen, Kradan and Lanta. The newer ***Morning Calm Resort*** (☎ 01-979 1543) on the opposite side of the island offers 50 bungalows, all with fan and private bath, for 200B to 800B depending on size.

Ko Kradan Resort (☎ 075-211391, Bangkok ☎ 02-392 0635) has OK bungalows and ugly cement shophouse-style rooms with fans and private bath for 700B to 900B a night and up. The beach isn't bad, but this resort still gets low marks for serving lousy, expensive food and for littering the area – a perfect example of the worst kind of beach resort development.

Getting There & Away The easiest place to get a boat to either Ko Muk or Ko Kradan is from Kantang. Songthaews from Trang to Kantang leave regularly and cost 20B; aircon minivans (35B) are also available. Once in Kantang you must charter another songthaew to the ferry pier for 20B, where you can get a regular longtail boat to Ko Muk for 50B (or charter for 300B), to Ko Kradan for 100B or to Ko Libong for 25B (noon daily).

You can also get to the islands from Hat Pak Meng. There are two piers, one at the northern end of the beach and one at the southern end. Boats are more frequent from the southern pier, especially during the rainy season. Boats cost 30B to 60B per person to Ko Muk (depending on the number of passengers), 120B to Ko Kradan.

Hat Yong Ling & Hat Yao

A few kilometres north of Hat Jao Mai are these two white-sand beaches separated by limestone cliffs. Hat Yong Ling is a short walk from the Hat Yong Ling park unit parking lot. It's a pretty bay and there are snack stands on weekends. There are some tidal pools off the beach at the base of the limestone cliffs, and you can camp nearby if you check in with the park officers first. Another curving beach nearby, **Hat San** can only be approached via a large cave which connects the two beaches. The access road into the Yong Ling unit is 2km long.

Hat Jao Mai & Ko Libong

Hat Jao Mai and Ko Libong are in Kantang district, about 35km from Trang. The wide white-sand beach of Hat Jao Mai is 5km long and gets some of Thailand's biggest surf (probably the source of the Trang's original unshortened name, City of Waves). Hat Jao Mai is backed by casuarina trees and limestone hills with caves, some of which reputedly contain prehistoric human skeletal remains. Two large caves nearby can be reached by boat. You can charter a fisherman's longtail for 100B an hour from Ban Jao Mai Hat Yao. Two hours is enough. **Tham Jao Mai** is big enough to enter by boat, and contains at least three levels and many side caverns with extensive stalactites, stalagmites, crystal curtains and fossils. In a small chamber at the top level is a beautiful small spring.

This beach is part of the 231,000 sq km **Hat Jao Mai National Park**, which includes Hat Chang Lang farther north and the islands of Ko Muk, Ko Kradan, Ko Jao Mai, Ko Waen, Ko Cheuak, Ko Pling and Ko Meng. In this area the endangered dugong (also called manatees or sea cows) can sometimes be spotted. In their only known appearance on the Thai-Malay peninsula, rare black-necked storks frequent Jao Mai to feed on molluscs and crustaceans. More common wildlife that visitors may actually spot include sea otters, macaques, langurs, wild pigs, pangolins, little herons, Pacific reef-egrets, white-bellied sea eagles, monitor lizards and water monitors. The park is also rich in evergreen forest, mangrove forest, beach forest and limestone crag forest.

Ko Libong, Trang's largest island, lies opposite Hat Jao Mai. There are three fishing villages on the island, so boats from Kantang port are easy to get for the one hour trip, or from Ban Jao Mai Hat Yao near Hat Jao Mai it's about 15 minutes.

Places to Stay A number of *bungalows* are available for rent at Hat Jao Mai National

Trang Festivals

At Hat Jao Mai, a unique sailboat regatta is held on the first weekend of May. This one differs from the usual Phuket affair in that only wooden sailboats of the traditional Andaman Sea type may enter. These boats feature square or triangular sails dyed with natural pigments from the *samèt* or cajeput tree. In addition to the races, events include live musical and theatrical performances, including *lí-khe pàa* and *nãng thálung*.

The Vegetarian Festival is also celebrated fervently in Trang in September or October (see the Phuket section for details on this festival).

Joe Cummings

Park. For reservations, contact the National Park Division, Royal Forest Department (☎ 02-579 0529, 579 4842, 579 5269). *Camping* is permitted on Jao Mai and there are a few *bungalows* for rent as well. *Sinchai's Chaomai Resort (☎ 01-464 4140)* offers a couple of two room wooden cottages with shared facilities for 200B and two, more substantial, bungalows with private bath for 300B. Cheaper but no bargain are three 100B dilapidated huts. Bathing is done at a well. When full, tents are available for rent for 50B. Sinchai's wife is a good Thai cook and meals are inexpensive. The family can arrange boat trips to nearby caves and islands and it's a short walk from here to the village of Ban Jao Mai Hat Yao, where there's a local *coffee shop* and a *seafood restaurant* built on one of the village piers. There are also a few wood *bungalows* on the pier for rent for an overpriced 200B.

The turnoff for Sinchai's is 3.6km past the turnoff for the Hat Yong Ling park unit (or 9km from Pak Meng). There's no sign for the resort, so look for a shrimp farm sign, hand-painted in Thai with red letters on a blue background and pictures of shrimp. After you're on this access road, the road forks; the right fork goes to the 'resort', the left to the Chok Chai Shrimp Farm. It's the only dirt road between Ban Jao Mai Hat Yao and the limestone cliff which you see about a half kilometre from the village.

Boats bound for Ko Libong leave Ban Jao Mai Hat Yao every half hour during daylight hours for 20B per person, or you can charter to Ko Libong Resort for 200B. The Botanical Department maintains free *shelters* on Laem Ju-Hoi, a cape on the western tip of Ko Libong. On the south-western side of the island is a beach where camping is permitted. *Libong Beach Resort (☎ Trang 075-214676)* has A-frame thatched bungalows for 350B to 500B. About 1km from the pier on Libong is *Tongkran Bungalow* with basic huts for 50B.

Getting There & Away The quickest way to reach Hat Jao Mai by public transport is via vans from the Trang market, which leave every hour in the high season, less frequently in the low season, for 50B per person. You can also catch a bus, train or taxi from Trang to Kantang harbour, then hop on one of the frequent ferries across to Tha Som on the opposite shore of the Trang River estuary. Tickets cost 2B for pedestrians, 5B for motorcycles, 15B per car and 20B per pickup; the ferry operates daily from 6 am to 8 pm. From Tha Som there are frequent songthaews to Hat Jao Mai. A longtail boat from the pier at Hat Jao Mai to Ko Libong costs just 20B.

Hat Samran & Ko Sukon

Hat Samran is a beautiful and shady whitesand beach in Palian district, about 40km south-west of Trang city. From the Customs pier at nearby Yong Sata you should be able to get a boat to **Ko Sukon** (also called Ko Muu), an island populated by Thai Muslims, where there are more beaches.

Sukon Island Resort (☎ 075-211460, Trang ☎ 219679) has bungalow accommodation for 200B to 500B a night. The resort

maintains a small kiosk at the Trang bus terminal for advance bookings and transport.

WATERFALLS

A lightly trafficked, paved road runs south from Hwy 4 near the Trang-Phattalung border past a number of scenic waterfalls where the Trang and Palian rivers (or their tributaries) meet the Khao Banthat Mountains. **Ton Te Falls**, 46km from Trang, is the loftiest. It's best seen during or just after the rainy season, say from September to November, when the 320m vertical waterfall is fullest.

Chao Pha Falls in the Palian district near Laem Som has about 25 stepped falls of 5 to 10m each, with pools at every level. The semi-nomadic Sakai tribe are sometimes seen in this area.

Perhaps the most unusual waterfall in the province is **Roi Chan Phan Wang** (literally, 'Hundred Levels – Thousand Palaces'), about 70km north-west of Trang in Wang Wiset district, a little-explored corner of the province. Surrounded by rubber groves, dozens of thin cascades of water tumble down limestone rock formations into pools below. The entire area is well shaded and a good spot for picnics. There is no public transport to the falls, however, and the road is none too good – motorcycle or jeep would be the best choice of transport.

CAVES

A limestone cave in the north-eastern district of Huay Yot, **Tham Phra Phut**, contains a large Ayuthaya-period reclining Buddha. When the cave was re-discovered early in the 20th century, a cache of royal-class silverwork, nielloware, pottery and lacquerware was found hidden behind the image – probably stashed there during the mid-18th century Burmese invasion.

Also in this district, near the village of Ban Huay Nang, is **Tham Tra** (Seal Cave), with mysterious red seals carved into the cave walls which have yet to be explained by archaeologists. Similar symbols have been found in the nearby cave temple of **Wat Khao Phra**.

More easily visited is **Tham Khao Pina**, off Hwy 4 between Krabi and Trang at Km 43, which contains a large, multilevel Buddhist shrine popular with Thai tourists. Another famous cave, **Tham Khao Chang Hai** near Na Meun Si village, in Nayong district, contains large caverns with impressive interior formations.

There is no public transport available to any of these.

KHLONG LAMCHAN WATERBIRD PARK

This large swampy area in the Nayong district, east of Trang, is an important habitat for several waterbird species – similar to Thaleh Noi or Khukhut in Songkhla Province. Accommodation is available.

Satun Province

Bordering Malaysia, Satun (or Satul) is the Andaman Coast's southern-most province. Besides offering a convenient crossing to Malaysia by land or sea, Satun is also home to the stunningly beautiful Ko Tarutao National Marine Park.

Before 1813 Satun was a district of the Malay state of Kedah: the name 'Satun' comes from the Malay *setul*, a type of tree common in this area. At the time Kedah, along with Kelantan, Terengganu and Perlis, paid tribute to Siam. The Anglo-Siamese Treaty of 1909 released parts of these states to Britain and they later became part of independent Malaysia. Satun didn't become a province of Siam until 1925. Today an estimated 66% of the population is Muslim, most of who speak Yawi or Malay as a first language, and there are 14 mosques for every wát in the province.

SATUN

• pop 22,700

Although the provincial capital of Satun itself is not that interesting, a trickle of visitors enter or leave Thailand here by boat via Kuala Perlis in Malaysia. Sixty kilometres north-west of Satun is the small port of Pak Bara, the departure point for boats to Ko Tarutao.

As in Thailand's other three predominantly Muslim provinces (Yala, Pattani and Narathiwat), the Thai government has installed a loudspeaker system in the streets which broadcasts government programs at 6 am and 6 pm (beginning with a wake-up call to work and ending with the Thai national anthem, for which everyone must stop and stand in the streets), either to instil a sense of nationalism in the typically rebellious Southern Thais, or perhaps to try and drown out the prayer calls and amplified sermons from local mosques. As in Pattani and Narathiwat, one hears a lot of Yawi spoken in the streets.

A very few old Sino-Portuguese shophouses, some said to date back as far as 1839, can be seen along Th Buriwanit. The modern, parachute-domed Bambang Mosque nearby was constructed in 1979.

Information

Immigration The Wang Prachan Customs complex at the Tammalang pier south of town contains an immigration office where anyone departing or arriving to/from Malaysia by boat will have their papers processed. You can also use this office for visa extensions. There's an immigration office in town as well, but compared to the Wang Prachan Customs complex it's understaffed and if you try to extend your visa there you will probably be sent to Tammalang.

Money You can change money at Thai Farmers Bank, Bangkok Bank or Siam Commercial Bank, all of which have branches, the latter two with ATMs, in the town centre either on Th Buriwanit or Th Satun Thani.

If you are going to Kuala Perlis in Malaysia, remember that banks on the east coast of Malaysia are not open on Thursday afternoon or Friday, due to the observance of Islam. If you don't already have Malaysian ringgit you'd best postpone your crossing till another day, unless the

Malaysian government's ban on Malaysian currency trading outside Malaysia has been rescinded. You won't be able to buy ringgit on the Thai side legally as long as the ban is in place.

Post & Telephone The main post and telephone office is on the corner of Th Samanta Prasit and Th Satun Thani.

Khao Phaya Wang

If you find yourself with time to kill in Satun, you might consider a visit to the park along the western side of Khao Phaya Wang, a limestone outcrop next to Khlong Bambang (sometimes referred to as Khlong Mambang). Steps lead up the vine-choked cliff on the khlong side of Khao Phaya Wang and at the top there are views of the winding green khlong, rice fields and coconut plantations. Pandan mats are available at the cool, bamboo-shaded picnic area next to the canal below. Vendors sell sôm-tam, *khâo niăw* (sticky rice), *kài thâwt* (fried chicken), *kûng thâwt* (fried prawns) and *mîang kham* (pieces of ginger, onion, dried shrimp, toasted coconut, chilli, peanuts and lime placed into a wild tea leaf with a thick, sweet and salty tamarind sauce).

Places to Stay

Rain Tong (Rian Thong) Hotel is a three-storey cube at the end of Th Samanta Prasit, next to the Rian Thong pier, an embarkation point for boats to and from Malaysia. Large, clean rooms with ceiling fan and attached shower and toilet cost 120B. Near the municipal offices on Th Hatthakam Seuksa is the two storey *Udomsuk Hotel* (☎ 074-711006), with reasonably clean singles/doubles with ceiling fan and private bath for 120B/130B.

The four storey *Satul Tanee (Satun Thani) Hotel*, near the centre of town, is OK but noisy, with single/double fan rooms for 190B/250B, air-con rooms for 290/390B.

At the up-market *Wang Mai Hotel* (☎ 074-711607/8), near the northern end of town off Th Satun Thani, all rooms come

with air-con, carpet, hot water and TV for 550/590B single/double, 650B for deluxe, or 1300B VIP.

Sinkiat Thani Hotel (☎ 074-721055, fax 721059) in the centre of town on Th Buriwanit has comfortable rooms similar to those at the Wang Mai but in better condition for 680B single/double.

Places to Eat

Near the gold-domed Bambang Mosque in the centre of town are several cheap Muslim food shops, including the reliable *Suhana Restaurant,* almost opposite the mosque on Th Buriwanit. Two doors south of Suhana, a *roti food stall* with bright green walls serves light and fluffy roti with curry. A cluster of cheap **Chinese food stalls** can be found on Th Samanta Prasit near the intersection with Th Buriwanit. Lots of places serve khâo man kài and kŭaytĭaw around town, though none of them stand out.

Hok Heng Yong, across from Siam Commercial Bank on Th Satun Thani, is a traditional Hokkien coffee shop with round marble-topped tables and a few snacks where older Chinese men sit around and chat. *Raya*, the coffee shop behind Sinkiat Thani Hotel, has more Thai dishes than anywhere else in town.

A no-name *coffee shop* next to the Udomsuk Hotel is a good spot for Thai and western breakfasts. For Chinese food, wander about the little Chinese district near the Rain Tong Hotel. There's nothing fancy, just a few *noodle shops* and small *seafood places*.

North of the Satul Tanee Hotel, along a short street running west off Th Satun Thani, a very good *night market* convenes every evening beginning around 5 pm. Many of the vendors sell Thai Muslim food and the prices are quite low. Considering the overall quality of food in Satun, this is one of the best places to eat in town.

Getting There & Away

Bus & Share Taxi A share taxi to Hat Yai costs 50B per person, while an air-con bus

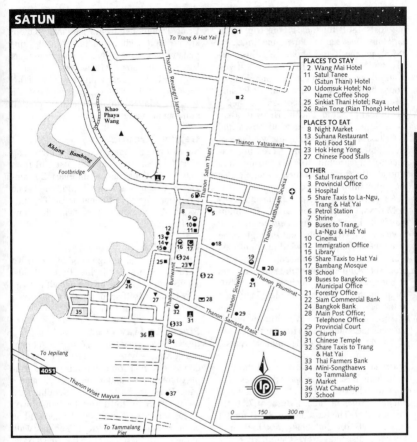

costs 40B. Buses to Trang are 43B (86B air-con), share taxis 80B.

Share taxis to Hat Yai park in at least three places in Satun: near the Satul Tanee Hotel; near the mosque; and on the corner of Th Samanta Prasit and Th Buriwanit. The stand near the Satul Tanee Hotel also has taxis to La-Ngu (30B) and to Trang. You can hire a whole taxi straight to Pak Bara for 250B.

Satul Transport Co (☎ 074-711049), about half a kilometre north of the Wang

Mai Hotel on the same side of the road, sells THAI tickets (for flights out of Trang or Hat Yai), and also operates buses to Trang (43B) and Hat Yai (35B, 40B air-con) frequently from 6 am to 4.30 pm. With two days advance booking, the agency can also arrange rail tickets for the Hat Yai to Bangkok route. Buses to Hat Yai also stop in front of the no-name, green-walled roti kaeng place on Th Buriwanit.

An air-con bus leaves Bangkok's Southern bus terminal once a day for Satun around 7 pm (2 pm in the reverse direction) and costs 480B for the 15 hour trip. Ordinary buses leave around the same time, cost 284B and take 16 to 17 hours. But this is really too long a bus trip for comfort – if you want to get to Satun from Bangkok, it would be better to take a train to Padang Besar on the Malaysian border and then a bus or taxi to Satun. Padang Besar is 60km from Satun and you can find buses and share taxis heading north on the west side of the highway near the border crossing; expect to pay around 30B on the bus and around 50B for a share taxi to Satun. See the following Train section.

A new highway between Satun and Perlis in Malaysia has been proposed. The highway would cut travel time between the two towns, but it would also cut through some of southern Thailand's dwindling rainforest – many Thais have organised to protest the proposal. For the moment the empty coffers of both governments preclude the possibility the highway will be completed anytime in the near future.

Buses to Bangkok leave from the terminal near the municipal office on the corner of Th Phuminat and Th Hatthakam Suksa.

Train The only train that goes all the way to Padang Besar is the special express No 35, which leaves Hualamphong station at 2 pm and arrives in Padang Besar at 7.50 am the next day. The basic fare is 843B for 1st class, 390B for 2nd class, not including sleeper and special express surcharges.

Boat From Kuala Perlis in Malaysia, boats are M$5. All boats dock at the Wang Prachan Customs complex in Tammalang, the estuary 7.5km south of Satun. In the reverse direction the fare is 50B. Boats leave frequently in either direction between 9 am and 1 pm, then less frequently to around 4 pm, depending on marine conditions. You can charter a boat to Perlis holding up to 20 people for 1000B.

From Langkawi Island in Malaysia boats for Tammalang leave daily at 9.30 and 11 am and 1.30 and 4 pm. The crossing takes

1½ to two hours and costs M$18 one way. Bring Thai money from Langkawi, as there are no money-changing facilities at Tammalang pier. In the reverse direction boats leave Tammalang for Langkawi at 9 and 11 am and 1, 1.30 and 4 pm and cost 180B. Tickets for the Satun-Langkawi boat are sold at booths outside the immigration building at Wang Prachan.

Getting Around
Small orange songthaews to Tammalang pier (for boats to Malaysia) cost 10B from Satun. The songthaews run every 20 minutes between 8 am and 5 pm; catch one from opposite Wat Chanathip on Th Buriwanit. A motorcycle taxi from the same area costs 30B.

PAK BARA
Pak Bara is the jumping-off point for the Ko Tarutao National Marine Park islands. There is not much to the town itself but you may find yourself spending the night if you miss the boat to the islands.

Places to Stay & Eat
In Pak Bara, *Bara Guest House* (no phone) is a new place with a travel agency and cafe downstairs, five rooms upstairs and a couple of bungalows under construction out the back. Rates are 80/150B single/double for a room, 200B to 250B for the bungalows. There was a very unhappy chained gibbon downstairs when we visited. You can walk to the Ko Tarutao pier from the guesthouse.

Just over a kilometre before the pier in Pak Bara, along the shore among the casuarina trees, are the *Diamond Beach Bungalows*, *Saengthien Bungalows*, *Krachomsai Bungalows*, *Pornaree Bungalows*, *Sai Kaew Resort* and *Koh Klang Bungalows*, all with huts for around 150B to 300B a night. None are that special; Diamond Beach is the top pick only because it's newer and nearest to town.

On rocky, palm-fringed Ko Baw Jet Luk (often referred to as Ko Kabeng, though that's an adjacent island), a 10 minute drive north of Pak Bara over a new bridge, the quiet *Paknam Resort* (☎ *074-781129*) of-fers beds (mattresses on the floor) in a long-house for 100B per person and thatched A-frame bungalows for 180B to 260B.

You can also stay in nicely designed and relatively new *park bungalows* at the main-land headquarters for Ko Phetra National Marine Park, which are near Ban Talo Sai, about 4km before you reach Pak Bara off Route 4052. The turnoff is between Km 5 and 6 on this highway; from here it's about 1.5km to the park HQ. When asked the bun-galow rates, park officials said it was up to the individual how much they wanted to pay, ie it's done by donation. This may change as park staff tire of visitors taking advantage of such policies.

There are several *food stalls* near the Pak Bara pier that do fruit shakes and seafood.

Getting There & Away

From Hat Yai, there are three daily buses to La-Ngu and Pak Bara which cost 38B and take 2½ hours. If you miss one of the direct La-Ngu buses, you can also hop on any Satun-bound bus to the junction town of Chalung (28B, 1½ hours), which is about 15km short of Satun, then get a songthaew north on Route 4078 for the 12B, 45 minute trip to La-Ngu. Or take a share taxi from Hat Yai to La-Ngu for 50B; there is also a mini-van service from Hat Yai for 50B, a better deal since it goes all the way to Pak Bara.

To get to Pak Bara from Satun, you must take a share taxi or bus to La-Ngu, then a songthaew on to Pak Bara. Taxis to La-Ngu leave from a stand diagonally opposite a petrol station on Th Satun Thani, about a hun-dred metres north of the Satul Tanee Hotel, when there are enough people to fill a taxi for 30B per person. Buses leave frequently from a spot on the opposite side of the road, a lit-tle south towards the hotel, and cost 18B. From La-Ngu, songthaew rides to Pak Bara are 8B and terminate right at the harbour; you can take a motorcycle taxi this same distance for 20B. You can also charter a whole taxi to Pak Bara from Satun for 250B.

You can travel to La-Ngu from Trang by songthaew for 30B, or by share taxi for 50B.

For getting to the Ko Tarutao National Marine Park see that section's Getting There and Away information.

KO TARUTAO NATIONAL MARINE PARK

This park protects a sizeable archipelago of 51 islands, approximately 30km from Pak Bara in La-Ngu district, which is 60km north-west of Satun. Ko Tarutao, the biggest of the group, is only 5km from Langkawi Island in Malaysia. Only five of the islands (Tarutao, Adang, Lipe, Rawi and Klang) have any kind of regular boat service to them, and of these, only the first three are generally visited by tourists. Ac-cess to the other islands, which offer excel-lent beaches and coral reefs, can only be arranged by chartering longtail boats.

This park remains one of the most pristine and beautiful coastal areas in Thailand, in part because it requires a bit more effort to get there. Accommodation is fairly basic and transport slow and sometimes inconvenient.

The Forestry Department has been con-sidering requests from private firms to build hotels and bungalows in Tarutao National Park. This would be a very unfortunate event if it means Ko Tarutao is going to be-come like Ko Phi-Phi or Ko Samet, both of which are national parks that have permit-ted private development with disastrous re-sults. So far nothing has transpired.

Ko Tarutao

The park's namesake covers around 151 sq km and features waterfalls, inland streams, beaches, caves and protected wildlife. No-body lives on this island except for the em-ployees of the Forestry Department. It was a place of exile for political prisoners be-tween 1939 and 1947, and remains of the prisons can be seen near Ao Talo Udang, on the southern tip of the island, and at Ao Talo Wao, on the middle of the east coast. There is also a graveyard, charcoal furnaces and even fermentation tanks for making fish sauce. Wildlife on the island includes the dusky langur, mousedeer, wild pig, fishing cat and crab-eating macaque; dolphins and

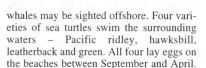

Treading Lightly on Tarutao

A remote location, small population and, more recently, near heroic efforts by Thailand's park service have kept Ko Tarutao National Marine Park one of the country's most pristine and beautiful areas. Not surprisingly it is drawing increasing numbers of tourists, both Thai and foreign, which poses a threat to the park's delicate environment. How you decide to visit it, therefore, may help stop it from going the way of Ko Phi Phi or Ko Samet.

While the park officials and staff are quite hospitable, they have limited time and resources to cater to foreign tourists. This is particularly true of Ko Adang, which has only basic facilities and accommodation (Ko Tarutao is better equipped and staffed). If the number of visitors demanding modern services grows too quickly, the National Parks Division of the Royal Thai Forestry Department may consider requests from private firms to build bungalows and hotels on park land to handle the load. If past history is any guide, this could ruin the park.

If you want to stay on Ko Adang, try to be fairly self-sufficient: bring a tent and your own food. Kitchen staff will happily prepare meals using visitors' food: it's a way for the cash strapped operation to bring in a little extra revenue. But the restaurant's own food stocks are usually inadequate. The more visitors that show up prepared to look after themselves, the more confident park staff will be that the current setup can do the job. And the greater the chance that Ko Tarutao's gorgeous coral formations, pearl white beach and lush islands will remain intact.

Joe Cummings

whales may be sighted offshore. Four varieties of sea turtles swim the surrounding waters – Pacific ridley, hawksbill, leatherback and green. All four lay eggs on the beaches between September and April.

Tarutao's largest stream, Khlong Phante Malaka, enters the sea at the north-west tip of the island at Ao Phante Malaka; the brackish waters flow out of **Tham Jara-Khe** (Crocodile Cave – the stream was once inhabited by ferocious crocodiles, which seem to have disappeared) on the eastern side of the island. The cave extends for at least 1km under a limestone mountain – no one has yet followed the stream to the cave's end. The mangrove-lined watercourse should not be navigated at high tide, when the mouth of the cave fills.

The park pier, headquarters and bungalows are also here at Ao Phante Malaka. A 50B park fee is payable on arrival. For a view of the bays, climb Topu Hill, 500m north of the park office.

The best camping is at the beaches of **Ao Jak** and **Ao San**, two bays south of park headquarters on the west coast. There is also camping at Ao Makham (Tamarind Bay), at the south-west end of the island, about 2.5km from another park office at Ao Talo Udang. Except for Ao Jak, these beaches are a long walk from park headquarters so you may want to consider hiring a longtail to take you there: there are usually one or two boat operators snoozing in the shade near the information booth.

There is a road between Ao Phante Malaka, in the north, and Ao Talo Udang, in the south, of which 11km was constructed by political prisoners in the 1940s and 12km has since been constructed by the park division. The road is, for the most part, overgrown, but park personnel have kept a path open to make it easier to get from north to south without having to climb over rocky headlands along the shore. The entire trek takes about eight hours, and while there are ranger stations to Talo Wao and Talo Udang, you'll need to bring a tent and your own supplies if you want to head down there.

Ko Rang Nok (Bird Nest Island), off Ao Talo Udang, is another treasure trove of the valuable swiftlet nests craved by Chinese throughout the world. Good coral reefs are at the north-west part of Ko Tarutao at **Pha Papinyong** (Papillon Cliffs), at Ao San and in the channel between Ko Tarutao and Ko Takiang (Ko Lela) off the north-east shore.

At the park headquarters, for 20B, you can pick up *Tarutao National Park: a Travellers Adventure Handbook*, a paper booklet that details the park's facilities, flora and fauna and hiking options. It's quite informative, and the history section in particular makes for interesting reading, complete with tales from the prison camps and accounts of gun battles between early park officials and angry locals opposed to having their home turf turned into protected parkland.

Ko Khai & Ko Klang

Between Ko Tarutao and Ko Adang and Rawi is a small cluster of three islands called **Muu Ko Klang** (Middle Island Group), where there is good snorkelling. One of the islands, Ko Khai, also has a good white-sand beach. Boats from Ko Tarutao take about 40 minutes to reach Ko Khai. You can also charter longtails from Ko Lipe out to here: a full day's hire will cost around 600B to 700B.

Ko Adang & Ko Rawi

Ko Adang is 43km west of Tarutao, and about 80km from Pak Bara on the mainland. Ko Adang's 30 sq km are covered with forests and freshwater streams, which fortunately supply water year-round. Green sea turtles lay their eggs here between September and December. At the south-eastern corner of the island where the pier and park office are located, visitors can stay in a thatched longhouse. Camping is also allowed. The restaurant is a little expensive considering the basic fare served – but then considering the transport problems, perhaps

not. As on Tarutao, it's a good idea to bring some food from the mainland.

An interesting hike can be undertaken along the island's east coast to a pretty beach 2km from the park station. Inland a little way from the beach is a waterfall once – perhaps still – used by passing pirate ships as a fresh water source. Around on the west coast, 3km from Laem Son, is another waterfall and the chao náam village of Talo Puya.

Ko Rawi is just east of Ko Adang, and a bit smaller. There are no facilities there at all. Off the west coast of Ko Adang, and the south-east coast of Ko Rawi, are coral reefs with many live species of coral and tropical fish. Other excellent snorkelling spots include the north side of **Ko Yang** and tiny **Ko Hin Ngam**. The latter is known for its beautiful smooth stones. However, you may not want to take one as a souvenir. Doing so is said to bring bad luck, and the visitor centre on Ko Tarutao has a basket of stones sent back by people who blamed the rocks for their subsequent misfortunes.

Through the efforts of park officials, many of these reefs have been spared degradation caused by dynamite fishing and other human activities. The park service has also set up around 40 mooring buoys in this area (used mainly by longtails bringing snorkellers to the area) so that boat operators need not drop anchor in this ecologically delicate area. Try to make sure your boat uses one of the moorings. Longtail boat operators on Ko Lipe generally charge around 600B to 700B to take groups out for a full day of snorkelling.

Ko Lipe

Ko Lipe is immediately south of Ko Adang and is inhabited by about 500 chao náam (*orang rawot* or *orang laut* in Malay), who are said to have originated on the Lanta islands in Krabi Province. They subsist on fishing and some cultivation of vegetables and rice on the flatter parts of the island. One can camp here, or rent a hut from the chao náam for 150B to 300B a night at any of several bungalow operations in or near the main village along the east coast. There is a coral reef along the southern side of the small island and several small beachy coves. The chao náam can provide boat hire to nearby islets ringed by coral reefs. For some reason the sea gypsies on this island prefer to be called 'chao leh' – a term despised by other sea gypsies on islands to the north, who prefer the term chao náam. In their own tongue, they refer to themselves as 'iraklahoi'. They also go by the term Thai Mai (New Thai), nomenclature favoured by the Thai government.

The chao leh village is in the island's north-east.

Ko Lipe is not under park control, and has thus become the main place to stay, given the limited facilities on Ko Adang. Several bungalow operations have been set up in the main village along the east coast and on Hat Pattaya, on the southern side of this island. There are also one or two simple restaurants and shops in the main village. You can walk overland between the village and Hat Pattaya in around 20 to 30 minutes, or take a longtail for 20B.

Pattaya is the nicest of the two main beaches, as the one in front of the chao leh village is partially covered with boat moorings and some litter. However, the little island just opposite the village, **Ko Kra**, has some well preserved coral and makes for fine snorkelling. You can easily swim there from the village beach.

Places to Stay & Eat

Officially, Ko Tarutao National Park is only open from November to May. Visitors who show up on the islands during the monsoon season can stay in *park accommodation*, but they must bring their own food from the mainland unless staying with the chao náam on Ko Lipe.

Bungalows may be booked in advance at the park office in Pak Bara (☎ 074-711383, no English spoken) or through the Forestry Department (☎ 02-579 0529) in Bangkok. For Ko Tarutao and/or Ko Adang, you may want to bring some food of your own from Satun or Pak Bara – the

park restaurants are a bit expensive and nothing to write home about.

Ko Tarutao Park accommodation on Ko Tarutao, near park headquarters, costs 500B for a large 'deluxe' two room bungalow sleeping four, or 600B for cottages that sleep up to six people. A four bed room in a longhouse goes for 320B, or 80B per person. Full rates must be paid for the bungalows and cottages, regardless of how many of you there are. Tents can be rented for 100B. If you have your own, the fee is 10B.

Staying at the park feels a bit like going back to youth camp: lights off at 10.30 pm, running water from 6 to 8 am and 6 to 10 pm only. But the buildings are clean and well maintained. One point worth noting: the longhouses have no screens or mosquito nets, so you may want to bring your own net, or at the very least some effective insect repellent.

Ko Adang Laem Son has *longhouse accommodation* similar to that on Ko Tarutao, and for the same rates. A small *restaurant* provides basic meals and sundries; it's closed in the rainy season. You can pitch your own tent for 10B.

Ko Lipe There are basically five places to stay on the island. Two are in the chao leh village, on the north-east side of the island. At the northern side of the village *Andaman Resort (☎ 074-711313 in Satun)* has good bungalows with private bath for 300B and tents for 100B. You can also pitch your own tent here for 20B. At the other end of the village, *Chao Leh Resort* has some pretty shaky thatch huts for 150B, more solid ones for 250B with private bath, and wooden and thatch versions with glass windows that overlook the village backstreets for 300B. The beach is nicer in front of Andaman Resort than near Chao Leh Resort.

On Hat Pattaya, the biggest operation is *Lee Pae (Lipe) Resort*, which has spacious thatch bungalows for 300B with private bath and shower. Though it has more amenities than its competitors, this place

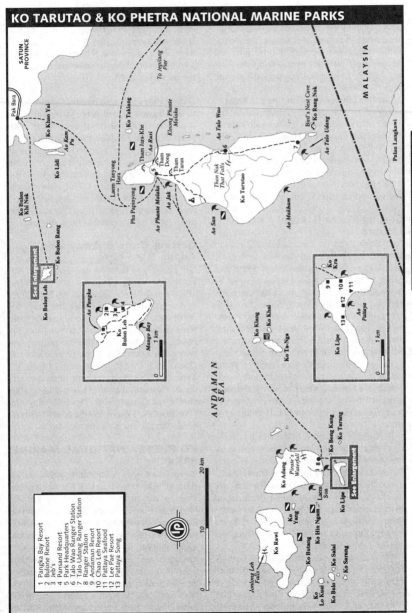

KO TARUTAO & KO PHETRA NATIONAL MARINE PARKS

SOUTHERN ANDAMAN COAST

1 Pangka Bay Resort
2 Bulone Resort
3 Jeb's
4 Pansand Resort
5 Park Headquarters
6 Talo Wao Ranger Station
7 Talo Udang Ranger Station
8 Ranger Station
9 Andaman Resort
10 Chao Leh Resort
11 Pattaya Seafood
12 Lee Pae Resort
13 Pattaya Song

also wins the prize for the least personality. Down at the western end of the beach *Pattaya Song* has simple huts on the beach with shared bathroom for 100B to 150B. On the adjacent hillside, overlooking the bay, are slightly fancier bungalows with private bath for 200B.

On the other end of the beach *Pattaya Seafood* is mainly a restaurant, but the owner also has three decent bungalows with private bath for 100B. This seems to be the only operation on the island that's actually run by an islander. Even if you don't stay, stop by for dinner: the food is excellent.

See the previous section for places to stay and eat in Pak Bara if you miss the boat.

Getting There & Away – Ko Tarutao

Pak Bara Boats to Tarutao leave regularly between November and April from the pier in Pak Bara, 60km north-west of Satun and 22km from Ko Tarutao. During the rest of the year boat service is irregular, since the park is supposedly closed. Satun Province officials have discussed constructing a new pier in Tan Yong Po district, nearer Satun, that will serve tourist boats to Tarutao and other islands, possibly on a year-round basis.

For now, boats leave Pak Bara for Tarutao in season daily at 10.30 am and 3 pm. The return fare is 200B, one way 100B, and it takes 1½ to two hours, depending on the boat. Departures back to Pak Bara are at 9 am and 2 pm.

If possible, it would be best to buy one-way tickets for each leg of your journey, as this would allow a choice of routes back (say direct from Ko Lipe to Pak Bara). Also, if the boat you have a ticket for doesn't make it to the islands due to bad weather or an engine mishap, you won't have to worry about getting a refund for both tickets. Some companies will refuse to refund an unused return ticket.

There are also occasional tour boats out to Tarutao, but these usually cost several hundred baht per person, as they include a guided tour, meals etc. Your final alternative is to charter a boat with a group of people.

The cheapest are the longtail boats, which can take eight to 10 people out from Pak Bara's commercial pier for 800B. On holidays, boats may travel back and forth to Tarutao every hour or so to accommodate the increased traffic.

Other Piers It is also possible to hire boats to Ko Tarutao from three different piers *(thâa reua)* on the coast near Satun. The nearest is the Ko Nok pier, 4km south of Satun (40km from Tarutao). Then there is the Tammalang pier, 9km from Satun, on the opposite side of the estuary from Ko Nok pier. Tammalang is 35km from Tarutao. Finally there's the Jepilang pier, 13km west of Satun (30km from Tarutao); this one seems most geared to boat charters.

Getting There & Away – Ko Adang & Ko Lipe

On Tuesday, Thursday and Saturday (November to May), a boat leaves Pak Bara at 10.30 am for Ko Adang and Ko Lipe, with a stop at Ko Tarutao along the way, for 300B each way. The boat continues on from Ko Tarutao to Adang and Lipe at 1 pm, arriving at a point more or less midway between Ko Adang and Ko Lipe around 4 pm (180B each way if you're starting from Ko Tarutao). The boat anchors here and you choose a longtail boat to the island of your choice for another 30B. The following day (Wednesday, Friday and Sunday) the boat heads back from Ko Lipe at 9 am.

KO PHETRA NATIONAL MARINE PARK

Twenty-two islands stretching between Pak Bara and the boundaries of Ko Tarutao belong to the little-visited, 495 sq km Ko Phetra National Marine Park. Uninhabited **Ko Khao Yai**, the largest in the group, boasts several pristine beaches suitable for swimming, snorkelling and camping. Crab-eating macaques are plentiful here as local Muslims don't hunt them. There's a castle-shaped rock formation on one shore; during low tide boats can pass beneath a natural arch in the formation. A park unit is on nearby **Ko Lidi** (sometime spelt 'Lide'), which features a number of picturesque and unspoiled caves, coves, cliffs and beaches. Camping facilities are available here. Between Ko Lidi and Ko Khao Yai is a channel bay known as **Ao Kam Pu**, a tranquil passage with cascading waters during certain tidal changes and some coral at shallow depths.

A new park headquarters, visitors centre and pier for Ko Phetra National Marine Park recently opened on the mainland at Ban Talo Sai, about 4km south-east of Pak Bara off Route 4052. You can arrange boat transport to Ko Lidi and Ko Khao Yai here. Trees and plants on the park grounds are labelled in English, and staff are busy constructing a 300m nature trail through intact lowland evergreen forest just behind the park bungalows.

Ko Bulon Leh

This is a beautiful, laid-back island approximately 20km west of Pak Bara, and is the largest of the Ko Bulon island group. Though considerably smaller than the major islands of Ko Tarutao, Bulon Leh shares many of the same geographical characteristics, including sandy beaches and coral reefs. A fine white sand beach runs along the east and north shores of the island, and offshore are some fine coral sites that make for good snorkelling. There are a few tiny villages in the northern part of the island near Ao Pangka. Nearby Ko Bulon Don sports a chao leh village and some nice beaches, but no accommodation so far. Ko Bulon Mai Phai farther out is uninhabited and pristine. Officially all of the Bulon group belongs to Ko Phetra National Marine Park, a fact conveniently forgotten by people living on these islands.

Boat trips around the island and to nearby snorkelling sites can be easily arranged. The best place to check is at Bulone Resort, which has good contacts with some of the longtail operators. You can also arrange passage direct between Bulon Leh and Ko Lipe in Ko Tarutao National Marine Park for around 300B to 400B per person if you can get a group of five or six together. Four

to five-day island hopping trips out to Ko Tarutao are also available. Rates vary depending on the specific itinerary, but range between 2200B and 3000B and include accommodation, snorkelling and fishing gear, lunch and one barbecue dinner.

Places to Stay & Eat Ko Bulon Leh has four accommodation options. The most upmarket is the nicely designed *Pansand Resort* (☎ 01-228 4279), which has basic, somewhat rickety huts with shared bathroom for 100B, A-frame fan-equipped bungalows for 200 and 250B, and solid brick and thatch cottages with deck and private bath for 650B to 800B. Two-person tents can be hired for 70B or you can pitch your own for 10B. For more information and reservations you can also contact First Andaman Travel in Trang (☎ 075-218035, fax 211010), 82-84 Th Visetkul, opposite the Queen Hotel.

Bulone Resort, on the north-east shore close to Pansand, has simple bungalows with shared bathroom for 100B to 200B, and dorm beds in a longhouse for 70B. The huts are well spread out, giving guests a sense of privacy. Bulone Resort has no phone, but bookings can be made by writing to the Ongsara Family, Bulone Resort, 23 Muu 4, Tambon Paknam, Amphoe La-Ngu, Satun, Thailand 91110. Both Pansand and Bulone enjoy nice locations overlooking the island's best beach.

In between Pansand and Bulone is *Jeb's*, a small shop with basic necessities. The owner, Jeb, is in charge of renting out two government-owned *bungalows* with private bath for 400B per night.

On the north side of the island, set near a rocky cove, is *Pangka Bay Resort*, which has fairly primitive bungalows for 150B. It's not really possible to go swimming around here; you'll need to hike about 15 minutes back to the main beach.

Although Ko Bulon Leh is still a sleepy place, it is getting increasingly popular, and in the high season both Pansand and Bulone resorts are often booked solid, though you can usually get a tent at Pansand.

SOUTHERN ANDAMAN COAST

Reservations are highly recommended. You probably won't have trouble finding a free bungalow at Pangka Bay Resort due to its more remote location.

Bulone Resort probably has the best food of the three places, though Pansand's fare is good too. Jeb's also has a little side *restaurant*, where they serve dinners.

Getting There & Away Longtail boats to Ko Bulon Leh depart from the Pak Bara pier at 2 pm and cost 100B per person one way. The trip takes 1½ hours each way. On the return, boats usually leave Bulon Leh at 9 am.

Other Islands

Ko Kabeng and **Ko Baw Jet Luk**, accessible by boat and bridge from Pak Bara, are of mild interest. The beaches here are often littered and murky, so it's basically just a convenient place to stay in Pak Bara, but if you have time to kill visit the charcoal factory at Khlong La-Ngu or check out the cashew plantations. Paknam Resort on Ko Baw Jet Luk can also arrange boat trips to other, more pristine islands in the area, or if you speak enough Thai you could hire a fishing boat directly from Ko Kabeng's little harbour at the fishing village of Ban Jet Luk.

Language

Learning some Thai is indispensable for travelling in the kingdom; naturally, the more language you pick up, the closer you get to Thailand's culture and people. Foreigners who speak Thai are so rare in Thailand that it doesn't take much to impress most Thais with a few words in their own language.

Your first attempts to speak the language will probably meet with mixed success, but keep trying. When learning new words or phrases, listen closely to the way the Thais themselves use the various tones – you'll catch on quickly. Don't let laughter at your linguistic forays discourage you; this apparent amusement is an expression of appreciation. Thais are among the most supportive people in the world when it comes to foreigners learning their language.

Travellers, both young and old, are particularly urged to make the effort to meet Thai college and university students. Thai students are, by and large, eager to meet visitors from other countries. They'll often know some English, and are generally willing to teach you useful Thai words and phrases.

For a handy pocket-size guide to Thai, get a copy of Lonely Planet's fully updated and expanded 3rd edition *Thai phrasebook*; it contains a section on basic grammar and a broad selection of useful words and phrases for travel in Thailand.

Many people have reported modest success with *Robertson's Practical English-Thai Dictionary* (Charles E Tuttle Co, Tokyo), which has a phonetic guide to pronunciation with tones and is compact in size. If you have difficulty finding it, write to the publisher at 2-6 Suido 1-chome, Bunkyo-ku, Tokyo, Japan.

More serious learners of the language should get Mary Haas' *Thai-English Student's Dictionary* (Stanford University Press, Stanford, California) and George McFarland's *Thai-English Dictionary* (also Stanford University Press) – the cream of the crop. Both of these require that you know the Thai script. The US State Department's *Thai Reference Grammar* by RB Noss (Foreign Service Institute, Washington, DC, 1964) is good for an in-depth look at Thai syntax.

Other learning texts worth seeking out include:

AUA Language Center Thai Course: Reading & Writing (two volumes) – AUA Language Center (Bangkok), 1979

AUA Language Center Thai Course (three volumes) – AUA Language Center (Bangkok), 1969

Foundations of Thai (two volumes) – by EM Anthony, University of Michigan Press, 1973

A Programmed Course in Reading Thai Syllables – by EM Anthony, University of Hawaii, 1979

Teaching Grammar of Thai – by William Kuo, University of California at Berkeley, 1982

Thai Basic Reader – by Gething & Bilmes, University of Hawaii, 1977

Thai Cultural Reader (two volumes) – by RB Jones, Cornell University, 1969

Thai Reader – by Mary Haas, American Council of Learned Societies, Program in Oriental Languages, 1954

The Thai System of Writing – by Mary Haas, American Council of Learned Societies, Program in Oriental Languages, 1954

A Workbook for Writing Thai – by William Kuo, University of California at Berkeley, 1979

Dialects

Thailand's official language is Thai as spoken and written in Central Thailand. This dialect has successfully become the lingua franca of all Thai and non-Thai ethnic groups in the kingdom. Of course, native Thai is spoken with differing tonal accents and with slightly differing vocabularies as you move from one part of the country to the next, especially from north to south. The Central Thai dialect is the most widely understood.

All Thai dialects are members of the Thai half of the Thai-Kadai family of languages and are closely related to languages spoken in Laos (Lao, Northern Thai, Thai Lü), northern Myanmar (Shan, Northern Thai), north-western Vietnam (Nung, Tho), Assam (Ahom) and pockets of south China (Zhuang, Thai Lü). Modern Thai linguists recognise four basic dialects within Thailand: Central Thai (spoken as a first dialect through Central Thailand and throughout the country as a second dialect); Northern Thai (spoken from Tak Province north to the Myanmar border); North-Eastern Thai (north-eastern provinces towards the Lao and Cambodian borders); and Southern Thai (from Chumphon Province south to the Malaysian border). Each of these can be further divided into subdialects; North-Eastern Thai, for example, has nine regional variations easily distinguished by those who know Thai well. There are also a number of Thai minority dialects such as those spoken by the Phu Thai, Thai Dam, Thai Daeng, Phu Noi, Phuan and other tribal Thai groups, most of whom reside in the North and North-East.

Vocabulary Differences

Like most languages, Thai distinguishes between 'informal' and 'polite' vocabulary, so that *thaan*, for example, is a more polite everyday word for 'eat' than *kin*, and *sīi-sà* for 'head' is more polite than *hūa*. When given a choice, foreigners are better off learning and using the polite terms since these are less likely to lead to unconscious offence.

A special set of words, collectively called *kham râatchaasàp* (royal vocabulary), is set aside for use with Thai royalty within the semantic fields of kinship, body parts, physical and mental actions, clothing and housing. For example, in everyday language Thais use the word *kin* or *thaan* for 'eat', while with reference to the royal family they say *ráppràthaan*. For the most part these terms are used only when speaking to or referring to the king, queen and their children, hence as a foreigner you'll have little need to learn them.

Script

The Thai script, a fairly recent development in comparison with the spoken language, consists of 44 consonants (but only 21 separate sounds) and 48 vowel and diphthong possibilities (32 separate signs). Experts disagree as to the exact origins of the script, but it was apparently developed around 800 years ago using Mon and possibly Khmer models, both of which were in turn inspired by south Indian scripts. Like these languages, written Thai proceeds from left to right, though vowel signs may be written before, after, above, below, *or* 'around' (before, after *and* above) consonants, depending on the sign.

Though learning the alphabet is not difficult, the writing system itself is fairly complex, so unless you are planning a lengthy stay in Thailand it should perhaps be foregone in favour of actually learning to speak the language. The place names included in the Gazetteer at the back of this chapter are given in both Thai and roman script, so that you can at least 'read' the names of destinations at a pinch, or point to them if necessary.

Tones & Pronunciation

In Thai the meaning of a single syllable may be altered by means of different tones – in standard Central Thai there are five: low tone, level or mid tone, falling tone, high tone and rising tone. For example, depending on the tone, the syllable *mai* can mean 'new', 'burn', 'wood', 'not?' or 'not'; ponder the phrase *mái mài mâi mâi mãi* (New wood doesn't burn, does it?) and you begin to appreciate the importance of tones in spoken Thai. This makes it a rather tricky language to learn at first, especially for those of us unaccustomed to the concept of tones. Even when we 'know' what the correct tone in Thai should be, our tendency to denote emotion, verbal stress, the interrogative etc,

Thai Tones

If the tones were to be represented on a visual curve they might look like this:

Low	Mid	Falling	High	Rising

through tone modulation, often interferes with producing the correct tone. Therefore the first rule in learning to speak Thai is to divorce emotions from your speech, at least until you have learned the Thai way to express them without changing essential tone value.

The following is a brief attempt to explain the tones. The only way to really understand the differences is by listening to a native speaker (or a fluent non-native speaker). The range of all five tones is relative to each speaker's vocal range so there is no fixed 'pitch' intrinsic to the language.

1 The low tone is 'flat' like the mid tone, but pronounced at the relative bottom of one's vocal range. It is low, level and with no inflection, eg *bàat* (baht – the Thai currency).

2 The level or mid tone is pronounced 'flat', at the relative middle of the speaker's vocal range, eg *dii* (good); no tone mark used.

3 The falling tone is pronounced as if you were emphasising a word, or calling someone's name from afar, eg *mâi* (no/not).

4 The high tone is usually the most difficult for westerners. It is pronounced near the relative top of the vocal range, as level as possible, eg *níi* (this).

5 The rising tone sounds like the inflection used by English speakers to imply a question – 'Yes?', eg *sǎam* (three).

Words in Thai that appear to have more than one syllable are usually compounds made up of two or more word units, each with its own tone. They may be words taken directly from Sanskrit, Pali or English, in which case each syllable must still have its own tone. Sometimes the tone of a first syllable is not as important as that of a final one, so in this book first syllable tones are not shown.

The following is a guide to the phonetic system that has been used for the words and phrases included in this chapter (and throughout the rest of the book when transcribing directly from Thai). It's based on the Royal Thai General System (RTGS), except that it distinguishes: between short and long vowels (eg 'i' and 'ii'; 'a' and 'aa'; 'e' and 'eh'; 'o' and 'oh'); between 'o' and 'aw' (both would be 'o' in the RTGS); between 'u' and 'eu' (both would be 'u' in the RTGS); and between 'ch' and 'j' (both would be 'ch' in the RTGS).

Consonants

The majority of consonants correspond closely to their English counterparts. Here are a few exceptions:

k	as the 'k' in 'skin'; similar to 'g' in 'good', but unaspirated (no accompanying puff of air) and unvoiced
p	as the 'p' in 'stopper', unvoiced and unaspirated (not like the 'p' in 'put')
t	as the 't' in 'forty', unaspirated; similar to 'd' but unvoiced
kh	as the 'k' in 'kite'
ph	as the 'p' in 'put' (never as the 'ph' in 'phone')
th	as the 't' in 'tea'
ng	as the 'ng' in 'sing'; can occur as an initial consonant in Thai (practise by saying 'sing' without the 'si')
r	similar to the 'r' in 'run' but flapped (tongue touches palate); in everyday speech often pronounced like 'l'

Vowels

i	as the 'i' in 'it'
ii	as the 'ee' in 'feet'
ai	as the 'i' in 'pipe'
aa	as the 'a' in 'father'
a	half as long as aa

ae	as the 'a' in 'bat' or 'tab'
e	as the 'e' in 'hen'
eh	as the 'a' in 'hate'
oe	as the 'u' in 'hut' but more closed
u	as the 'u' in 'flute'
uu	as the 'oo' in 'food', longer than **u**
eu	as the 'u' in 'fur'
ao	as the 'ow' in 'now'
aw	as the 'aw' in 'jaw' or 'prawn'
o	as the 'o' in 'bone'
oh	as the 'o' in 'toe'
eua	a combination of **eu** and **a**
ia	as 'ee-ya', or as the 'ie' in French *rien*
ua	as the 'ou' in 'tour'
uay	as the 'ewy' in 'dewy'
iu	as the 'ew' in 'yew'
iaw	as the 'io' in 'Rio' or Italian *mio*

Here are a few extra hints to help you with the alphabetic tangle:

- **ph** is never pronounced as the 'ph' in phone but like the 'p' in 'pound' (the 'h' is added to distinguish this consonant sound from the Thai 'p' which is closer to the English 'b'). This can be seen written as **p**, **ph**, and even **bh**.
- to some people, the Thai **k** sounds closer to the English 'g' than the English 'k'. The standard RTGS chooses to use 'k' to represent this sound to emphasise that it is not a 'voiced' sound, but more a glottal stop; **p** also sounds closer to an English 'b', its voiced equivalent.
- there is no 'v' sound in Thai; *Sukhumvit* is pronounced Sukhumwit and *Viang* is really Wiang
- **l** and **r** are always pronounced as an 'n' when word-final, eg *Satul* is pronounced as Satun, *Wihar* as Wihan. The exception to this is when 'er' or 'ur' are used to indicate the sound 'oe', as in 'ampher' *(amphoe)*. In the same way, 'or' is sometimes used for the sound 'aw', as in 'Porn' *(phawn)*.
- **l** and **r** are often interchanged in speech and this shows up in some transliterations. For example, *naliga* (clock) may appear as 'nariga' and *râat nâa* (a type of noodle dish) might be rendered 'laat naa' or 'lat na'.

- **u** is often used to represent the short 'a' sound, as in *tam* or *nam*, which may appear as 'tum' and 'num'. It is also used to represent the 'eu' sound, as when *beung* (swamp) is spelt 'bung'.
- phonetically, all Thai words end in a vowel (**a**, **e**, **i**, **o**, **u**), semi-vowel (**w**, **y**), nasal (**m**, **n**, **ng**) or one of three stops (**p**, **t**, **k**). That's it. Words transcribed with 'ch', 'j', 's' or 'd' endings – like Panich, Raj, Chuanpis and Had – should be pronounced as if they end in 't', as in Panit, Rat, Chuanpit and Hat. Likewise 'g' becomes 'k' (Ralug is actually Raluk) and 'b' becomes 'p' (Thab becomes Thap).
- the 'r' in *sri* is always silent, so the word should be pronounced 'sii' (extended 'i' sound, too). Hence 'Sri Racha' really comes out 'Si Racha'.

Transliteration

Writing Thai in roman script is a perennial problem – no wholly satisfactory system has yet been devised to assure both consistency and readability. The Thai government uses the Royal Thai General System of transcription for official government documents in English and for most highway signs. However, local variations crop up on hotel signs, city street signs, menus, and so on in such a way that visitors often become confused. Add to this the fact that even the government system has its flaws. For example, 'o' is used for two very different sounds (see **o** and the **aw** in the preceding Vowels section), as is 'u' (for 'u' and 'eu' above). Likewise for 'ch', which is used to represent two different consonant sounds ('ch' and 'j'). The government transcription system also does not distinguish between short and long vowel sounds, which affect the tonal value of every word.

To top it off, many Thai words (especially names of people and places) have Sanskrit and Pali spellings but their actual pronunciation bears little relation to that spelling if Romanised strictly according to the original Sanskrit/Pali. Thus Nakhon Si Thammarat, if transliterated literally, becomes 'Nagara Sri Dhammaraja'. If you tried to pronounce it using this Pali transcription, very few Thais would be able to understand you.

Generally, names in this book follow the most common practice or, in the case of hotels for example, simply copy their roman script name, no matter what devious process was used in its transliteration! When this transliteration is markedly different from actual pronunciation, the pronunciation is included (according to the system outlined in this section) in parentheses after the transliteration. Where no roman model was available, names have been transliterated phonetically, directly from Thai. Of course, this will only be helpful to readers who bother to acquaint themselves with the language – and it's surprising how many people manage to stay for great lengths of time in Thailand without learning a word of Thai.

Problems often arise when a name is transliterated differently, even at the same location. 'Thawi', for example, can be seen as Tavi, Thawee, Thavi, Tavee or various other versions. Other than employing the International Phonetic Alphabet, there is no ideal way to transliterate Thai – only wrong ways. The Thais themselves are incredibly inconsistent in this matter, often using English letters that have no equivalent sound in Thai: Faisal for Phaisan, Bhumibol for Phumiphon, Vanich for Wanit, Vibhavadi for Wiphawadi. Sometimes they even mix literal Sanskrit transcription with Thai pronunciation, as in King Bhumibol (which is pronounced Phumiphon but if transliterated according to the Sanskrit would be Bhumibala).

Here are a few words that are often spelt in a way that encourages native English speakers to mispronounce them:

common spelling	pronunciation	meaning
bung	beung	pond or swamp
ko or koh	kàw	island
muang	meuang	city
nakhon or nakorn	nákhawn	large city

raja	usually râatchá if at the beginning of a word, râat at the end of a word	royal

Greetings & Civilities

When being polite, the speaker ends his or her sentence with *khráp* (for men) or *khâ* (for women). It is the gender of the speaker that is being expressed here; it is also the common way to answer 'yes' to a question or show agreement.

Greetings/Hello.
   sawàt-dii   สวัสดี
   (khráp/khâ)   (ครับ/ค่ะ)
How are you?
   sàbaai dii rēu?   สบายดีหรือ?
I'm fine.
   sabàay dii   สบายดี
Thank you.
   khàwp khun   ขอบคุณ
Excuse me.
   khāw thôht   ขอโทษ

you
   phōm   ผม(ผู้ชาย)
   (for men)
   dii chán   ดิฉัน(ผู้หญิง)
   (for women)
   khun   คุณ
   (for peers)
   thâan   ท่าน
   (for elders and
   people in authority)
What's your name?
   khun chêu arai?   คุณชื่ออะไร?
My name is ...
   phōm chêu ...   ผมชื่อ...
   (men)
   dii chán chêu ...   ดิฉันชื่อ...
   (women)
Do you have ...?
   mii ... mãi?/   มี...ไหม/
   ... mii mãi?   ...มีไหม?
No.
   mâi châi   ไม่ใช่
No?
   mãi?/châi mãi?   ไหม?/ใช่ไหม?
(I) like ...
   châwp ...   ชอบ...

LANGUAGE

(I) don't like ...
mâi châwp ... ไม่ชอบ...

(I) would like ...
(+ verb)
yàak jà ... อยากจะ...

(I) would like ...
(+ noun)
yàak dâi ... อยากได้...

When?
mêu-arai? เมื่อไร?

It doesn't matter.
mâi pen rai ไม่เป็นไร

What is this?
nîi arai? นี่อะไร?

go
pai ไป

come
maa มา

Language Difficulties

I understand.
khâo jai เข้าใจ

I don't understand.
mâi khâo jai ไม่เข้าใจ

Do you understand?
khâo jai mãi? เข้าใจไหม?

A little.
nít nàwy นิดหน่อย

What do you call
this in Thai?
nîi phaasãa thai นี่ภาษาไทย
rîak wâa arai? เรียกว่าอะไร?

Getting Around

I'd like to go ...
yàak jà pai ... อยากจะไป...

Where is (the) ...?
... yùu thîi nãi? ...อยู่ที่ไหน?

airport
sanãam bin สนามบิน

bus station
sathãanii khõn sòng สถานีขนส่ง

bus stop
thîi jàwt rót pràjam ที่จอดรถประจำ

train station
sathãanii rót fai สถานีรถไฟ

taxi stand
thîi jàwt rót ที่จอดรถแท็กซี่
tháek-sîi

I'd like a ticket.
yàak dâi tũa อยากได้ตั๋ว

What time will the
train leave?
kìi mohng rót กี่โมงรถจ
jà àwk? ะออก?

bus
rót meh/rót bát รถเมล์/รถบัส

car
rót yon รถยนต์

motorcycle
rót maw-toe-sai รถมอเตอร์ไซค์

train
rót fai รถไฟ

straight ahead
trong pai ตรงไป

left
sáai ซ้าย

right
khwãa ขวา

far/not far
klai/mâi klai ใกล/ไม่ใกล

Accommodation

hotel
rohng raem โรงแรม

guesthouse
bâan phák บ้านพัก
(kèt háo) (เกสต์เฮาส์)

Do you have a
room available?
mii hâwng mãi? มีห้องว่างไหม?

How much is it
per night?
kheun-lá thâo rai? คืนละเท่าไร?

bathroom
hâwng náam ห้องน้ำ

toilet
hâwng sûam ห้องส้วม

room
hâwng ห้อง

hot
ráwn ร้อน

cold
não หนาว

bath/shower
àap náam อาบน้ำ

towel
phâa chét tua ผ้าเช็ดตัว

Around Town

bank
thanaakhaan ธนาคาร

beach
hàat หาด

chemist/pharmacy
ráan khāai yaa ร้านขายยา

hospital
rohng phayaabaan โรงพยาบาล

market
talàat ตลาด

museum
phíphítháphan พิพิธภัณฑ์

post office
praisanii ไปรษณีย์

restaurant
ráan aahāan ร้านอาหาร

tourist office
sāmnák-ngaan สำนักงาน
thâwng thîaw ท่องเที่ยว

Can (I/we) change money here?
lâek ngoen thîi nîi dâi māi?
แลกเงินที่นี่ได้ไหม?

What time does it open?
ráan pòet mêua rai?
ร้านเปิดเมื่อไร?

What time does it close?
ráan pìt mêua rai?
ร้านปิดเมื่อไร?

Shopping

How much?
thâo raí? เท่าไร?

too expensive
phaeng pai แพงไป

How much is this?
níi thâo rai?/ นี้เท่าไร?/กี่บาท?
kìi bàat?

cheap, inexpensive
thùuk ถูก

Time, Days & Numbers

What's the time?
kìi mohng láew? กี่โมงแล้ว?

today
wan níi วันนี้

tomorrow
phrûng níi พรุ่งนี้

yesterday
mêua waan เมื่อวาน

Emergencies

(I) need a doctor.
tâwng-kaan māw ต้องการหมอ

Help!
chûay dûay! ช่วยด้วย

Stop!
yùt! หยุด

Go away!
bai sí! ไปซิ

I'm lost.
chān lōng thaang ฉันหลงทาง

Sunday
wan aathít วันอาทิตย์

Monday
wan jan วันจันทร์

Tuesday
wan angkhaan วันอังคาร

Wednesday
wan phút วันพุธ

Thursday
wan phréuhàt วันพฤหัสฯ

Friday
wan sùk วันศุกร์

Saturday
wan sāo วันเสาร์

0	*sūun*	ศูนย์
1	*nèung*	หนึ่ง
2	*sāwng*	สอง
3	*sāam*	สาม
4	*sìi*	สี่
5	*hâa*	ห้า
6	*hòk*	หก
7	*jèt*	เจ็ด
8	*pàet*	แปด
9	*kâo*	เก้า
10	*sìp*	สิบ
11	*sìp-èt*	สิบเอ็ด

12	*sìp-sāwng*	สิบสอง
13	*sìp-sāam*	สิบสาม
20	*yîi-sìp*	ยี่สิบ
21	*yîi-sìp-èt*	ยี่สิบเอ็ด
22	*yîi-sìp-sāwng*	ยี่สิบสอง
30	*sāam-sìp*	สามสิบ
40	*sìi-sìp*	สี่สิบ
50	*hâa-sìp*	ห้าสิบ
100	*ráwy*	ร้อย
200	*sāwng ráwy*	สองร้อย
300	*sāam ráwy*	สามร้อย
1000	*phan*	พัน
10,000	*mèun*	หมื่น
100,000	*sāen*	แสน
one million	*láan*	ล้าน
one billion	*phan láan*	พันล้าน

FOOD
Ordering
(For 'I' men use *phōm*; women use *dii-chān*)

I eat only vegetarian food.
phōm/dii-chān kin jeh
ผม/ดิฉันกินเจ

I can't eat pork.
phōm/dii-chān kin mūu mâi dâi
ผม/ดิฉันกินหมูไม่ได้

I can't eat beef.
phōm/dii-chān kin néua mâi dâi
ผม/ดิฉันกินเนื้อไม่ได้

(I) don't like it hot & spicy.
mâi châwp phèt
ไม่ชอบเผ็ด

(I) like it hot & spicy.
châwp phèt
ชอบเผ็ด

(I) can eat Thai food.
kin aahāan thai pen
กินอาหารไทยเป็น

What do you have that's special?
mii a-rai phí-sèt?
มีอะไรพิเศษ?

I didn't order this.
nîi phōm/dii-chān mâi dâi sàng
นี่ผม/ดิฉันไม่ได้สั่ง

Do you have ...?
mii ... mãi?
มี ... ไหม?

Food Glossary
The following list gives standard dishes in Thai script with a transliterated pronunciation guide, using the system outlined at the beginning of this chapter.

Soups   *(súp)*   ซุป

mild soup with vegetables & pork
kaeng jèut
แกงจืด

mild soup with vegetables, pork & bean curd
kaeng jèut tâo-hûu
แกงจืดเต้าหู้

soup with chicken, galanga root & coconut
tôm khàa kài
ต้มข่าไก่

prawn & lemon grass soup with mushrooms
tôm yam kûng
ต้มยำกุ้ง

fish-ball soup
kaeng jèut lûuk chín
แกงจืดลูกชิ้น

rice soup with fish/chicken/ shrimp
khâo tôm plaa/kài/kûng
ข้าวต้มปลา/ไก่/กุ้ง

Egg   *(khài)*   ไข่

hard-boiled egg
khài tôm
ไข่ต้ม

fried egg
khài dao
ไข่ดาว

plain omelette
  khà i jiaw
  ไข่เจียว

omelette with vegetables & pork
  khài yát sài
  ไข่ยัดไส้

scrambled egg
  khài kuan
  ไข่กวน

Noodles *(kŭaytĭaw/*   ก๋วยเตี๋ยว/
                bà-mii)   บะหมี่

rice noodle soup with vegetables & meat
  kŭaytĭaw náam
  ก๋วยเตี๋ยวน้ำ

rice noodles with vegetables & meat
  kŭaytĭaw hâeng
  ก๋วยเตี๋ยวแห้ง

rice noodles with gravy
  râat nâa
  ราดหน้า

thin rice noodles fried with tofu, vegetables
egg & peanuts
  phàt thai
  ผัดไทย

fried noodles with soy sauce
  phàt sii-yíw
  ผัดซีอิ๊ว

wheat noodles in broth with vegetables &
meat
  bà-mii náam
  บะหมี่น้ำ

wheat noodles with vegetables & meat
  bà-mii hâeng
  บะหมี่แห้ง

Rice *(khâo)*   ข้าว

fried rice with pork/chicken/ shrimp
  khâo phàt mŭu/kài/kûng
  ข้าวผัดหมู/ไก่/กุ้ง

boned, sliced Hainan-style chicken with
marinated rice
  khâo man kài
  ข้าวมันไก่

chicken with sauce over rice
  khâo nâa kài
  ข้าวหน้าไก่

roast duck over rice
  khâo nâa pèt
  ข้าวหน้าเป็ด

'red' pork with rice
  khâo mŭu daeng
  ข้าวหมูแดง

curry over rice
  khâo kaeng
  ข้าวแกง

Curries *(kaeng)*   แกง

hot Thai curry with chicken/beef/ pork
  kaeng phèt kài/néua/mŭu
  แกงเผ็ดไก่/เนื้อ/หมู

rich & spicy, Muslim-style curry with
chicken/beef & potatoes
  kaeng mátsàman kài/néua
  แกงมัสมั่นไก่/เนื้อ

mild, Indian-style curry with chicken
  kaeng karìi kài
  แกงกะหรี่ไก่

hot & sour, fish & vegetable ragout
  kaeng sôm
  แกงส้ม

'green' curry with fish/chicken/beef
  kaeng khĭaw-wăan plaa/kài/néua
  แกงเขียวหวานปลา/
  ไก่/เนื้อ

savoury curry with chicken/beef
  kaeng phánaeng kài/néua
  แกงพะแนงไก่/เนื้อ

chicken curry with bamboo shoots
  kaeng kài nàw mái
  แกงหน่อไม้ไก่

catfish curry
  kaeng plaa dùk
  แกงปลาดุก

Seafood (*aahǎan tháleh*) อาหารทะเล

steamed crab
puu nêung
ปูนึ่ง

steamed crab claws
kâam puu nêung
ก้ามปูนึ่ง

shark-fin soup
hǔu chalǎam
หูฉลาม

crisp-fried fish
plaa thâwt
ปลาทอด

fried prawns
kûng thâwt
กุ้งทอด

batter-fried prawns
kûng chúp pâeng thâwt
กุ้งชุบแป้งทอด

grilled prawns
kûng phǎo
กุ้งเผา

steamed fish
plaa nêung
ปลานึ่ง

grilled fish
plaa phǎo
ปลาเผา

whole fish cooked in ginger,
onions & soy sauce
plaa jǐan
ปลาเจี่ยน

sweet & sour fish
plaa prîaw wǎan
ปลาเปรี้ยวหวาน

cellophane noodles baked with crab
puu òp wûn-sên
ปูอบวุ้นเส้น

spicy fried squid
plaa mèuk phàt phèt
ปลาหมึกผัดเผ็ด

roast squid
plaa mèuk yâang
ปลาหมึกย่าง

Seafood the Way You Like It

The most common forms of seafood preparation include:

dìp – raw; usually served with a variety of dipping sauces
nêung – steamed
phǎo – grilled
phàt – sliced, filleted and fried
râat phrík – smothered in garlic and chillies
thâwt – fried whole; the Thai style is to make the edges of the fish very crisp
chúp pâeng thâwt – batter-fried, a popular way to prepare shrimp
tôm yam – in a hot and tangy broth made with lemon grass and chillies
yâang – roast (squid only)

oysters fried in egg batter
hǎwy thâwt
หอยทอด

squid
plaa mèuk
ปลาหมึก

shrimp
kûng
กุ้ง

fish
plaa
ปลา

saltwater eel
plaa lòt
ปลาหลด

spiny lobster
kûng mangkawn
กุ้งมังกร

green mussel
hǎwy malaeng phùu
หอยแมลงภู่

scallop
hǎwy phát
หอยพัด

oyster
hǎwy naang rom
หอยนางรม

Miscellaneous

stir-fried mixed vegetables
  phàt phàk ruam
  ผัดผักรวม

spring rolls
  pàw-pía
  เปาะเปี๊ยะ

beef in oyster sauce
  néua phàt náam-man hǎwy
  เนื้อผัดน้ำมันหอย

duck soup
  pèt tǔn
  เป็ดตุ๋น

roast duck
  pèt yâang
  เป็ดย่าง

fried chicken
  kài thâwt
  ไก่ทอด

chicken fried in holy basil
  kài phàt bai kà-phrao
  ไก่ผัดใบกะเพรา

grilled chicken
  kài yâang
  ไก่ย่าง

chicken fried with chillies
  kài phàt phrík
  ไก่ผัดพริก

chicken fried with cashews
  kài phàt mét má-mûang
  ไก่ผัดเม็ดมะม่วง

morning-glory vine fried in garlic, chilli &
bean sauce
  phàk bûng fai daeng
  ผักบุ้งไฟแดง

skewers of barbecued meat (satay)
  sà-té
  สะเต๊ะ

spicy green papaya salad
(North-Eastern speciality)
  sôm-tam
  ส้มตำ

noodles with fish curry
  khǎnom jiin náam yaa
  ขนมจีนน้ำยา

prawns fried with chillies
  kûng phàt phrík phǎo
  กุ้งผัดพริกเผา

chicken fried with ginger
  kài phàt khǐng
  ไก่ผัดขิง

fried wonton
  kíaw kràwp
  เกี๊ยวกรอบ

cellophane noodle salad
  yam wún sên
  ยำวุ้นเส้น

spicy chicken or beef salad
  lâap kài/néua
  ลาบไก่/เนื้อ

hot & sour, grilled beef salad
  yam néua
  ยำเนื้อ

fried chicken with bean sprouts
  kài phat thùa ngâwk
  ไก่ผัดถั่วงอก

fried fish cakes with cucumber sauce
  thâwt man plaa
  ทอดมันปลา

Southern Thailand Specialities

flat bread (roti)
  roh-tii
  โรตี

roti with bananas
  roh-tii klûay
  โรตีกล้วย

roti with curry dip
  roh-tii kaeng
  โรตีแกง

strong Hokkien-style coffee
  koh-píi
  โกปี๊

chicken briyani
  khâo mòk kài
  ข้าวหมกไก่

rice salad (with toasted coconut, dried
shrimp, lime leaves)
  khâo yam
  ข้าวยำ

southern fish curry (very hot)
kaeng tai plaa
แกงใต้ปลา

noodles with mild fish curry
khanŏm jiin náam yaa
ขนมจีนน้ำยา

Vegetables *(phàk)* ผัก

bitter melon
márá-jiin
มะระจีน

brinjal (round eggplant)
mákhĕua pràw
มะเขือเปราะ

cabbage
phàk kà-làm (or kà-làm plii)
ผักกะหล่ำ(กะหล่ำปลี)

cauliflower
dàwk kà-làm
ดอกกะหล่ำ

Chinese radish
phàk kàat hŭa
ผักกาดหัว

corn
khâo phôht
ข้าวโพด

cucumber
taeng kwaa
แตงกวา

eggplant
mákhĕua mûang
มะเขือม่วง

garlic
kràthiam
กระเทียม

lettuce
phàk kàat
ผักกาด

long bean
thùa fák yao
ถั่วฝักยาว

okra ('ladyfingers')
krà-jíap
กระเจี๊ยบ

onion (bulb)
hŭa hăwm
หัวหอม

onion (green, 'scallions')
tôn hăwm
ต้นหอม

peanuts (ground nuts)
tùa lísŏng
ถั่วลิสง

potato
man faràng
มันฝรั่ง

pumpkin
fák thawng
ฟักทอง

taro
pheùak
เผือก

tomato
mákhĕua thêt
มะเขือเทศ

Fruit *(phŏn-lá-mái)* ผลไม้

banana – over 20 varieties (year-round)
klûay
กล้วย

coconut (year-round)
máphráo
มะพร้าว

Patate

Ananas

LANGUAGE

custard-apple
  náwy naa
  น้อยหน่า

durian
  thúrian
  ทุเรียน

guava (year-round)
  fa-ràng
  ฝรั่ง

jackfruit
  kha-nŭn
  ขนุน

lime (year-round)
  má-nao
  มะนาว

longan – 'dragon's eyes'; similar to
rambutan (July to October)
  lam yài
  ลำใย

mandarin orange (year-round)
  sôm
  ส้ม

mango – several varieties & seasons
  má-mûang
  มะม่วง

mangosteen
  mang-khút
  มังคุด

papaya (year-round)
  málákaw
  มะละกอ

pineapple (year-round)
  sàp-pàrót
  สับปะรด

pomelo
  sôm oh
  ส้มโอ

rambeh – small, reddish-brown and apricot-
like (April to May)
  máfai
  มะไฟ

rambutan
  ngáw
  เงาะ

FROM DU ROYAUME DE SIAM, BY SIMON DE LA LOUBÈRE

rose-apple – apple-like texture; very fragrant
(April to July)
  chom-phûu
  ชมพู่

tamarind – sweet and tart varieties
  mákhăam
  มะขาม

sapodilla – small and oval; sweet but
pungent (July to September)
  lámút
  ละมุด

watermelon (year-round)
  taeng moh
  แตงโม

Sweets *(khăwng wăan)*   ของหวาน

Thai custard
  săngkha-yaa
  สังขยา

coconut custard
  săngkha-yaa ma-phráo
  สังขยามะพร้าว

sweet shredded egg yolk
  făwy thawng
  ฝอยทอง

egg custard
  mâw kaeng
  หม้อแกง

banana in coconut milk
klûay bùat chii
กล้วยบวดชี

fried, Indian-style banana
klûay khàek
กล้วยแขก

sweet palm kernels
lûuk taan chêuam
ลูกตาลเชื่อม

Thai jelly with coconut cream
ta-kôh
ตะโก้

sticky rice with coconut cream
khâo nĭaw daeng
ข้าวเหนียวแดง

sticky rice in coconut cream with ripe mango
khâo nĭaw má-mûang
ข้าวเหนียวมะม่วง

DRINKS
Beverages *(khreûang dèum)*
เครื่องดื่ม

plain water
náam plào
น้ำเปล่า

hot water
náam ráwn
น้ำร้อน

boiled water
náam tôm
น้ำต้ม

bottled drinking water
náam dèum khùat
น้ำดื่มขวด

cold water
náam yen
น้ำเย็น

ice
náam khǎeng
น้ำแข็ง

soda water
náam sōh-daa
น้ำโซดา

orange soda
náam sôm
น้ำส้ม

iced lime juice with sugar
(usually with salt too)
náam manao
น้ำมะนาว

no salt (command)
mâi sài kleua
ไม่ใส่เกลือ

plain milk
nom jèut
นมจืด

Chinese tea
chaa jiin
ชาจีน

weak Chinese tea
náam chaa
น้ำชา

iced Thai tea with milk & sugar
chaa yen
ชาเย็น

iced Thai tea with sugar only
chaa dam yen
ชาดำเย็น

no sugar (command)
mâi sài náam-taan
ไม่ใส่น้ำตาล

hot Thai tea with sugar
chaa dam ráwn
ชาดำร้อน

hot Thai tea with milk & sugar
chaa ráwn
ชาร้อน

hot coffee with milk & sugar
kafae ráwn
กาแฟร้อน

traditional filtered coffee
with milk & sugar
kafae thũng (*ko-píi* in the South)
กาแฟถุง/ ภาคใต้เรียกโกพี้

iced coffee with sugar, no milk
oh-líang
โอเลี้ยง

Ovaltine
oh-wantin
โอวันติน

bottle
khùat
ขวด

glass
kâew
แก้ว

GAZETTEER
Bangkok

Abhisek Dusit Throne Hall
(Phra Thii Nang Aphisek Dusit)
พระที่นั่งอภิเศกดุสิต

Chinatown (Sampeng)
เยาวราช(สำเพ็ง)

Dusit Zoo
สวนสัตว์ดุสิต(เขาดิน)

Floating Markets
ตลาดน้ำ

Jim Thompson's House
บ้านจิมทอมป์สัน

Lak Meuang (City Pillar)
ศาลหลักเมือง

Lumphini Park
สวนลุมพินี

Maha Uma Devi Temple
วัดมหาอุมาเทวี(วัดแขกสีลม)

National Museum
พิพิธภัณฑ์สถานแห่งชาติ

Pahurat
พาหุรัด

Queen Saovabha Memorial Institute
(Snake Farm)
สถานเสาวภา

Rama IX Royal Park
สวนหลวงร.9

Royal Barges
เรือพระที่นั่ง

Royal Elephant Museum
พิพิธภัณฑ์ช้างต้น

Sanam Luang
สนามหลวง

Vimanmek Teak Mansion
(Phra Thii Nang Wimanmek)
พระที่นั่งวิมานเมม

Wat Arun
วัดอรุณฯ

Wat Benchamabophit
วัดเบญจมบพิตร

Wat Bovornives (Bowonniwet)
วัดบวรนิเวศ

Wat Pho (Wat Phra Chetuphon)
วัดโพธิ์(วัดพระเชตุพน)

Wat Phra Kaew & Grand Palace
วัดพระแก้ว/พระบรมมหาราชวัง

Wat Saket
วัดสระเกศ

Wat Traimit
วัดไตรมิตร

Eastern Gulf Coast

Chachoengsao
อ.เมืองฉะเชิงเทรา

Chanthaburi
จันทบุรี

Ko Chang
เกาะช้าง

Ko Samet
เกาะเสม็ด

Ko Si Chang
เกาะสีชัง

National Museums
พิพิธภัณฑ์เจ้าสามพระยา

Pattaya
พัทยา

Rayong
อ.เมืองระยอง

Si Racha
ศรีราชา

Si Racha Tiger Farm
สวนเสือศรีราชา

Trat
ตราด

North-Western Gulf Coast

Cha-Am
ชะอำ

Chumphon
อ.เมืองชุมพร

Hua Hin
หัวหิน

Khao Luang Caves
ถ้ำเขาหลวง

Khao Wang & Phra Nakhon Khiri
Historical Park
เขาวัง/อุทยานประวัติศาสต-
ร์พระนครคีรี

Ko Chang
เกาะช้าง

Nakhon Pathom
อ.เมืองนครปฐม

Petchaburi
เพชรบุรี

Prachuap Khiri Khan
อ.เมืองประจวบคีรีขันธ์

Ratchaburi
ราชบุรี

Thap Sakae & Bang Saphan
ทับสะแก/บางสะพาน

Wat Borom & Wat Trailok
วัดบรมและวัดไตรโลก

Wat Kamphaeng Leng
วัดกำแพงแลง

Wat Ko Kaew Sutharam
วัดเกาะแก้วสุทธาราม

Wat Mahathat
วัดมหาธาตุ

Wat Phra Suang & Wat Lat
วัดพระสวงและวัดลาด

Wat Yai Suwannaram
วัดใหญ่สุวรรณาราม

South-Western Gulf Coast

Ang Thong National Marine Park
อุทยานแห่งชาติหมู่เกาะอ่างทอง

Ao Bang Kao
อ่าวบางเก่า

Ao Khanom
อ่าวขนอม

Ao Nai Wok
อ่าวในว่าว

Ao Na Khai & Laem Set
อ่าวหน้าค่าย/แหลมเส็ด

Ao Thong Krut & Ko Taen
อ่าวท้องกรุด/เกาะแตน

Ao Thong Son & Ao Thong Sai
อ่าวท้องสน/อ่าวท้องทราย

Ao Thong Ta Khian
อ่าวท้องตะเคียน

Ban Taba
บ้านตาบา

Ban Tai (Ao Bang Baw)
บ้านใต้(อ่าวบางบ่อ)

Big Buddha Beach (Hat Phra Yai)
หาดพระใหญ่

Chaiya
ไชยา

Coral Cove (Ao Thong Yang)
อ่าวท้องยาง

Folklore Museum
สถาบันทักษิณคดีศึกษา

Hat Bo Phut
หาดบ่อผุด

Hat Chaweng
หาดเฉวง

Hat Choeng Mon
หาดเชิงมน

Hat Lamai
หาดละไม

Hat Mae Nam
หาดแม่น้ำ

Hat Narathat
หาดนราทัศน์

Hat Sa Bua
หาดสระบัว

Hat Sichon & Hat Hin Ngam
หาดสิชล/หาดหินงาม

Hat Yai
หาดใหญ่

Khao Sok National Park
อุทยานแห่งชาติเขาสก

Ko Pha-Ngan
เกาะพงัน

Ko Samui
เกาะสมุย

Ko Tao
เกาะเต่า

Ko Yo
เกาะยอ

Laem Hat Rin
แหลมหาดริน

Laem Talumpuk
แหลมตะลุมพุก

Matsayit Klang (Central Mosque)
มัสยิดกลาง

Nakhon Si Thammarat
อ.เมืองนครศรีธรรมราช

Nakhon Si Thammarat National Museum
พิพิธภัณฑ์สถานแห่งชาติ
นครศรีธรรมราช

Narathiwat
อ.เมืองนราธิวาส

Na Thon
หน้าทอน

National Museum
พิพิธภัณฑ์สถานแห่งชาติสงขลา

Pattani
อ.เมืองปัตตานี

Phattalung
อ.เมืองพัทลุง

Songkhla
สงขลา

Suan Nang Seu Nakhon Bowonrat
สวนหนังสือนครบวรรัตน์

Sungai Kolok
สุไหงโกลก

Surat Thani/Ban Don
อ.เมืองสุราษฎร์ธานี/บ้านดอน

Taksin Palace
พระตำหนักทักษิณราชนิเวศน์

Thaleh Sap Songkhla
ทะเลสาบสงขลา

Thong Sala
ท้องศาลา

Ton Nga Chang Falls
น้ำตกโตนงาช้าง

Wat Chonthara Sing-He
วัดชลธาราสิงเห

Wat Khao Kong
วัดเขากง

Wat Khao Tham
วัดเขาถ้ำ

Wat Na Phra Boromathat
วัดหน้าพระบรมธาตุ

Wat Phra Boromathat, Wat Kaew & Chaiya National Museum
วัดพระบรมธาตุไชยา,วัดแก้ว,
พิพิธภัณฑ์สถานแห่งชาติไชยา

Wat Phra Mahathat
วัดพระมหาธาตุ

Wat Suan Mokkhaphalaram
วัดสวนโมกข์พลาราม

Yala
อ.เมืองยะลา

Northern Andaman Coast

Ao Bang Tao
อ่าวบางเทา

Ao Phang-Nga & Phang-Nga
อ่าวพังงา/อ.เมืองพังงา

Ao Phang-Nga National Park
อุทยานแห่งชาติอ่าวพังงา

Hat Bang Sak & Hat Khao Lak
หาดบางสัก/หาดเขาหลัก

Hat Chandamri
หาดชาญดำริ

Hot Springs & Wat Hat Som Paen
บ่อน้ำร้อน/วัดหาดส้มแป้น

Isthmus of Kra
คอคอดกระ

Karon
กะรน

Kata
กะตะ

Khao Phra Taew Royal Wildlife & Forest Reserve
อุทยานสัตว์ปาเขาพระแทว

Khuraburi, Takua Pa & Thai Muang
คุระบุรี,ตะกั่วปาและท้ายเหมือง

Ko Panyi
เกาะปันหยี

Ko Similan National Marine Park
อุทยานแห่งชาติหมู่เกาะสิมิลัน

Ko Sire
เกาะสิเหร่

Ko Surin National Marine Park
อุทยานแห่งชาติหมู่เกาะสุรินทร์

Ko Yao
เกาะยาว

Laem Phanwa
แหลมพันวา

Laem Singh & Kamala
แหลมสิงห์/หาดกมลา

Laem Son National Park
อุทยานแห่งชาติแหลมสน

Nai Han
ในหาน

Nai Khai Ranong
ในค่ายระนอง

Nai Thon
ในทอน

Nai Yang & Mai Khao
ในยาง/ไม้ขาว

Patong
ปาตอง

Phuket
อ.เมืองภูเก็ต

Ranong
อ.เมืองระนอง

Rawai
ราไวย์

Sa Nang Manora Forest Park
สวนป่าสระนางมโนราห์

Saphaan Plaa (Fishing Pier)
สะพานปลา

Surin
หาดสุรินทร์

Victoria Point (Kawthoung)
วิคตอเรียพอยท์(เกาะสอง)

Southern Andaman Coast

Ao Nang Area
อ่าวนาง

Ban Tung Laem Sai
บ้านทุ่งแหลมทราย

Hat Chang Lang
หาดฉางหลาง

Hat Jao Mai & Ko Libong
หาดเจ้าไหมและเกาะลิบง

Hat Noppharat Thara
หาดนพรัตน์ธารา

Hat Pak Meng
หาดปากเมง

Hat Samran & Ko Sukon
หาดสำราญและเกาะสุกร

Hat Yong Ling & Hat Yao
หาดหยงหลิ/หาดยาว

Khao Phanom Bencha National Park
อุทยานแห่งชาติเขาพนมเบ็ญจา

Khao Phaya Wang
เขาพญาวัง

Khlong Lamchan Waterbird Park
อุทยานนกน้ำลำฉาน

Ko Adang
เกาะอาดัง

Ko Bulon Leh
เกาะบุโล้นแล

Ko Jam (Ko Pu) & Ko Si Boya
เกาะจำ(ปู)/เกาะศรีบอยา

Ko Lanta
เกาะลันตา

Ko Lanta National Marine Park
อุทยานแห่งชาติเกาะลันตา

Ko Muk & Ko Kradan
เกาะมุก/เกาะกระดาน

Ko Ngai (Hai)
เกาะไหง(ไห)

Ko Phi-Phi
เกาะพีพี

Ko Phi-Phi Don
เกาะพีพีดอน

Ko Phi-Phi Leh
พีพีเล

Ko Rawi & Ko Lipe
เกาะราวี/เกาะลิเป๊ะ

Ko Tarutao
เกาะตะรุเตา

Ko Tarutao National Marine Park
อุทยานแห่งชาติหมู่เกาะตะรุเตา

Krabi
กระบี่

Satun
อ.เมืองสตูล

Su-Saan Hawy (Shell Cemetery)
สุสานหอย

Than Bokkharani National Park
อุทยานแห่งชาติธารโบกขรณี

Trang
อ.เมืองตรัง

Wat Tham Seua
วัดถ้ำเสือ

Glossary

aahãan – food

aahãan pàa – 'jungle food', usually referring to dishes made with wild game

aahãan taam sàng – 'food according to order'; a type of restaurant where cooks will attempt to prepare any Thai dish you name, including one-plate rice and noodle dishes as well as more complex multi-dish meals

ajaan – respectful title for teacher

amphoe – district; next subdivision down from province; sometimes spelt *amphur*

amphoe meuang – provincial capital

ao – bay or gulf

bâan – house or village; often spelt *ban*

bai toey – pandanus leaf

bàw náam ráwn – hot springs

bhikkhu – Pali term for Buddhist monk; Thai pronunciation: 'phík-khù'

bòt – central sanctuary or chapel in a Thai temple; from the Pali *uposatha*

chaa – tea

chaihàat – beach; also hat and *hàat*

chao náam (chao leh) – sea gypsies; also known as Moken

chedi – stupa; monument erected to house a Buddha relic

dhammachakka – Buddhist wheel of law

doi – mountain peak

faràng – foreigner of European descent

hàat – beach; short for *chaihaat*; also hat

hâwng thaéw – Chinese shophouse

hãw trai – a *tripitaka* (Buddhist scripture) library

hong – room; in southern Thailand this word may refer to the island caves semi-submerged in the sea; pronounced 'hâwng'

isãan – general term for north-eastern Thailand, from the Sanskrit name for the medieval kingdom Isana, which also encompassed parts of Cambodia

jataka – life-stories of the Buddha

jiin – Chinese

jók – broken-rice soup

kâew – crystal, jewel, glass, or gem; also spelt *keo*

kafae thũng – filtered coffee, called *ko-píi* in southern Thailand

ka-toey – Thai transvestite

kaw-lae – traditional fishing boats of southern Thailand

khão – hill or mountain

khâo tôm – boiled rice soup

khlong – canal

khõn – masked dance-drama based on stories from the *Ramakian*

ko – island; also spelt *koh*; pronounced *kàw*

ko-píi – southern-style filtered coffee, particularly famous in Trang Province on the Southern Andaman Coast

kúay hâeng – Chinese-style work shirt

kuti – meditation hut

lâap – spicy meat or fish salad with mint leaves

lãem – cape (in the geographical sense)

lákhon – classical Thai dance-drama

làk meuang – city pillar/phallus

lâo khão – white liquor

lâo thèuan – contraband liquor

lí-khe – Thai folk dance-drama

lûuk thûng – a rhythmic style of popular music from north-east Thailand

mâe chii – Thai Buddhist nun

mâe náam – river; literally 'mother water'

maha that – literally 'great element', from the Sanskrit-Pali *mahadhatu*; common name for temples that contain Buddha relics

mánohra – southern Thailand's most popular traditional dance drama

mát-mii – a technique of tie-dying silk or cotton threads, and then weaving them into complex patterns, similar to Indonesian ikat; also refers to the patterns themselves

mâw hâwm – Thai work shirt
meuang/muang – city; pronounced *meu-ang*
mondòp – small square building in a *wát* complex generally used by laypeople, as opposed to monks; from the Sanskrit *mandapa*
muay thai – Thai boxing
mùu-bâan – village

náam – water
náam phrík – chilli sauce
náam plaa – fish sauce
náam tòk – waterfall
naga – dragon-headed serpent
nakhon – city; from the Sanskrit-Pali *nagara*; also spelt *nakhorn*
năng thalung/năng yài – Thai shadow play
ngaan wát – temple fair
ngôp – traditional Khmer rice farmer's hat

pàak náam – estuary
paa-té – batik
pàk tâi – southern Thai
Pali – language derived from Sanskrit in which the Buddhist scriptures are written
phâakhamãa – cotton cloth worn as a wraparound by men
phâasîn – same as above for women
phrá – monk or Buddha image; an honorific term from the Pali *vara*, 'excellent'
phrá phum – earth spirits
pìi-phâat – classical Thai orchestra
prang – Khmer-style tower on temples
prasat – small ornate building with a cruciform ground plan and needle-like spire, used for religious purposes, located on *wát* grounds; from the Sanskrit term *prasada;* pronounced *pràasàat*

rai – one *rai* is equal to 1600 sq metres
reua haang yao – long-tail taxi boat
reua kaw-lae – traditional painted fishing boats of southern Thailand
reuan tháew – longhouse
reu-sǐi – a Hindu *rishi* or 'sage'
rishi – hermit sage, a popular figure in the Hindu-Buddhist tradition
rót fai – train

rót thamadaa – ordinary bus (non air-con) or ordinary train (not rapid or express)
roti – round flatbread, common street food, particularly in the south

sãalaa (sala) – an open-sided, covered meeting hall or resting place; from the Portuguese *sala* or 'room'
sala klang – provincial office; pronounced *sãalaa klaang*
samlor – three-wheeled pedicab; pronounced *sãam-láw*
sanùk – fun
sêua mâw hâwm – blue cotton farmer's shirt
Shivalingum – sculpture representing the phallus of Shiva, an object of veneration in the Hindu-Buddhist world
sinsae – Chinese doctor
soi – lane or small street
sõngkhran – Thai New Year, held in mid-April
songthaew – literally 'two rows'; common name for small pickup trucks with two benches in the back, used as buses/taxis
sũan aahãan – garden restaurant
sùsãan – cemetery
suttas – discourses of the Buddha

tâi – south
talàat náam – floating market
tambon – 'precinct', next subdivision below *amphoe*; also spelled *tambol*
tha – pier, pronounced *thâa*
thaleh sàap – inland sea or large lake
thâm – cave
thanõn – street/road/avenue
thêp – angel or divine being; from the Sanskrit *deva*
thewada – a kind of angel
tripitaka – Theravada Buddhist scriptures; see also *hãw trai*
túk-túk – motorised *samlor*

vipassana – Buddhist insight meditation

wâi – palms-together Thai greeting
wang – palace
wan phrá – Buddhist holy days (the full and new moons every fortnight)

wát – temple-monastery; from the Pali *avasa*, monk's dwelling

wihãan – counterpart to *bòt* in Thai temple, containing Buddha images but not circumscribed by *sema* stones. Also spelt *wihan* or *viharn*; from the Sanskrit *vihara*

yàa dong – herbal liquor; also the herbs inserted in *lâo khão*

yam – Thai-style salad; usually made with meat or seafood

yoni – uterus-shaped pedestal that holds the *Shivalingum*

LONELY PLANET

Phrasebooks

Lonely Planet phrasebooks are packed with essential words and phrases to help travellers communicate with the locals. With colour tabs for quick reference, an extensive vocabulary and use of script, these handy pocket-sized language guides cover day-to-day travel situations.

- handy pocket-sized books
- easy to understand Pronunciation chapter
- clear & comprehensive Grammar chapter
- romanisation alongside script to allow ease of pronunciation
- script throughout so users can point to phrases for every situation
- full of cultural information and tips for the traveller

'... vital for a real DIY spirit and attitude in language learning'
— *Backpacker*

'the phrasebooks have good cultural backgrounders and offer solid advice for challenging situations in remote locations'
— *San Francisco Examiner*

Arabic (Egyptian) • Arabic (Moroccan) • Australian *(Australian English, Aboriginal and Torres Strait languages)* • Baltic States *(Estonian, Latvian, Lithuanian)* • Bengali • Brazilian • British • Burmese • Cantonese • Central Asia (Uyghur, Uzbek, Kyrghiz, Kazak, Pashto, Tadjik • Central Europe *(Czech, French, German, Hungarian, Italian, Slovak)* • Eastern Europe *(Bulgarian, Czech, Hungarian, Polish, Romanian, Slovak)* • Ethiopian (Amharic) • Fijian • French • German • Greek • Hebrew • Hill Tribes • Hindi & Urdu • Indonesian • Italian • Japanese • Korean • Lao • Latin American Spanish • Malay • Mandarin • Mediterranean Europe *(Albanian, Croatian, Greek, Italian, Macedonian, Maltese, Serbian, Slovene)* • Mongolian • Nepali • Pidgin • Pilipino (Tagalog) • Quechua • Russian • Scandinavian Europe *(Danish, Finnish, Icelandic, Norwegian, Swedish)* • South-East Asia *(Burmese, Indonesian, Khmer, Lao, Malay, Tagalog Pilipino, Thai, Vietnamese)* • South Pacific Languages • Spanish (Castilian) *(also includes Catalan, Galician and Basque)* • Sri Lanka • Swahili • Thai • Tibetan • Turkish • Ukrainian • USA *(US English, Vernacular, Native American languages, Hawaiian)* • Vietnamese • Western Europe *(Basque, Catalan, Dutch, French, German, Greek, Irish, Italian, Portuguese, Scottish Gaelic, Spanish (Castilian), Welsh)*

LONELY PLANET

Lonely Planet Journeys

JOURNEYS is a unique collection of travel writing – published by the company that understands travel better than anyone else. It is a series for anyone who has ever experienced – or dreamed of – the magical moment when they encountered a strange culture or saw a place for the first time. They are tales to read while you're planning a trip, while you're on the road or while you're in an armchair in front of a fire.

These outstanding titles explore our planet through the eyes of a diverse group of international writers. JOURNEYS books catch the spirit of a place, illuminate a culture, recount a crazy adventure or introduce a fascinating way of life. They always entertain, and always enrich the experience of travel.

IN RAJASTHAN
Royina Grewal

As she writes of her travels through Rajasthan, Indian writer Royina Grewal takes us behind the exotic facade of this fabled destination: here is an insider's perceptive account of India's most colourful state, conveying the excitement and challenges of a region in transition.

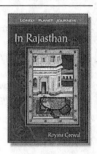

SHOPPING FOR BUDDHAS
Jeff Greenwald

In his obsessive search for the perfect Buddha statue in the backstreets of Kathmandu, Jeff Greenwald discovers more than he bargained for ... and his souvenir-hunting turns into an ironic metaphor for the clash between spiritual riches and material greed. Politics, religion and serious shopping collide in this witty account of an enlightening visit to Nepal.

BRIEF ENCOUNTERS
Stories of Love, Sex & Travel
edited by Michelle de Kretser

Love affairs on the road, passionate holiday flings, disastrous pick-ups, erotic encounters ... In this seductive collection of stories, 22 authors from around the world write about travel romances. A tourist in Peru falls for her handsome guide; a writer explores the ambiguities of his relationship with a Japanese woman; a beautiful young man on a train proposes marriage ... Combining fiction and reportage, *Brief Encounters* is must-have reading – for everyone who has dreamt of escape with that perfect stranger.

Includes stories by Pico Iyer, Mary Morris, Emily Perkins, Mona Simpson, Lisa St Aubin de Terán, Paul Theroux and Sara Wheeler.

Lonely Planet Travel Atlases

L onely Planet has long been famous for the number and quality of its guidebook maps. Now we've gone one step further and produced a handy companion series: Lonely Planet travel atlases – maps of a country produced in book form.

Unlike other maps, which look good but lead travellers astray, our travel atlases have been researched on the road by Lonely Planet's experienced team of writers. All details are carefully checked to ensure the atlas corresponds with the equivalent Lonely Planet guidebook.

- full-colour throughout
- maps researched and checked by Lonely Planet authors
- place names correspond with Lonely Planet guidebooks
- no confusing spelling differences
- legend and travelling information in English, French, German, Japanese and Spanish
- size: 230 x 160 mm

Available now: Chile & Easter Island ● Egypt ● India & Bangladesh ● Israel & the Palestinian Territories ● Jordan, Syria & Lebanon ● Kenya ● Laos ● Portugal ● South Africa, Lesotho & Swaziland ● Thailand ● Turkey ● Vietnam ● Zimbabwe, Botswana & Namibia

Lonely Planet TV Series & Videos

L onely Planet travel guides have been brought to life on television screens around the world. Like our guides, the programs are based on the joy of independent travel and look honestly at some of the most exciting, picturesque and frustrating places in the world. Each show is presented by one of three travellers from Australia, England or the USA and combines an innovative mixture of video, Super-8 film, atmospheric soundscapes and original music.

Videos of each episode – containing additional footage not shown on television – are available from good book and video shops, but the availability of individual videos varies with regional screening schedules.

Video destinations include: Alaska ● American Rockies ● Argentina ● Australia – The South-East ● Baja California & the Copper Canyon ● Brazil ● Central Asia ● Chile & Easter Island ● Corsica, Sicily & Sardinia – The Mediterranean Islands ● East Africa (Tanzania & Zanzibar) ● Cuba ● Ecuador & the Galapagos Islands ● Ethiopia ● Greenland & Iceland ● Hungary & Romania ● Indonesia ● Israel & the Sinai Desert ● Jamaica ● Japan ● La Ruta Maya ● London ● The Middle East (Syria, Jordan & Lebanon ● Morocco ● New York City ● Northern Spain ● North India ● Outback Australia ● Pacific Islands (Fiji, Solomon Islands & Vanuatu) ● Pakistan ● Peru ● The Philippines ● South Africa & Lesotho ● South India ● South West China ● South West USA ● Trekking in Uganda & Congo ● Turkey ● Vietnam ● West Africa ● Zimbabwe, Botswana & Namibia

The Lonely Planet TV series is produced by: Pilot Productions
The Old Studio
18 Middle Row
London W10 5AT, UK

Lonely Planet Online

Whether you've just begun planning your next trip, or you're chasing down specific info on currency regulations or visa requirements, check out Lonely Planet Online for up-to-the-minute travel information.

As well as miniguides to more than 250 destinations, you'll find maps, photos, travel news, health and visa updates, travel advisories and discussion of the ecological and political issues you need to be aware of as you travel. You'll also find timely upgrades to popular guidebooks that you can print out and stick in the back of your book.

There's an online travellers' forum (The Thorn Tree) where you can share your experience of life on the road, meet travel companions and ask other travellers for their recommendations and advice.

There's also a complete and up-to-date list of all Lonely Planet travel products including travel guides, diving and snorkeling guides, phrasebooks, atlases, travel literature and videos, and a simple online ordering facility if you can't find the book you want elsewhere.

Lonely Planet Diving & Snorkeling Guides

Beautifully illustrated with full-colour photos throughout, Lonely Planet's Pisces books explore the world's best diving and snorkeling areas and prepare divers for what to expect when they get there, both topside and underwater.

Dive sites are described in detail with specifics on depths, visibility, level of difficulty, special conditions, underwater photography tips and common and unusual marine life present. You'll also find practical logistical information and coverage on topside activities and attractions, sections on diving health and safety, plus listings for diving services, live-aboards, dive resorts and tourist offices.

FREE Lonely Planet Newsletters

We love hearing from you and think you'd like to hear from us.

Planet Talk

Our FREE quarterly printed newsletter is full of tips from travellers and anecdotes from Lonely Planet guidebook authors. Every issue is packed with up-to-date travel news and advice, and includes:

- a postcard from Lonely Planet co-founder Tony Wheeler
- a swag of mail from travellers
- a look at life on the road through the eyes of a Lonely Planet author
- topical health advice
- prizes for the best travel yarn
- news about forthcoming Lonely Planet events
- a complete list of Lonely Planet books and other titles

To join our mailing list, residents of the UK, Europe and Africa can email us at go@lonelyplanet.co.uk; residents of North and South America can email us at info@lonelyplanet.com; the rest of the world can email us at talk2us@lonelyplanet.com.au, or contact any Lonely Planet office.

Comet

Our FREE monthly email newsletter brings you all the latest travel news, features, interviews, competitions, destination ideas, travellers' tips & tales, Q&As, raging debates and related links. Find out what's new on the Lonely Planet Web site and which books are about to hit the shelves.

Subscribe from your desktop: www.lonelyplanet.com/comet

LONELY PLANET

Guides by Region

Lonely Planet is known worldwide for publishing practical, reliable and no-nonsense travel information in our guides and on our Web site. The Lonely Planet list covers just about every accessible part of the world. Currently there are thirteen series: travel guides, shoestring guides, walking guides, city guides, phrasebooks, audio packs, city maps, travel atlases, diving & snorkeling guides, restaurant guides, first-time travel guides, healthy travel and travel literature.

AFRICA Africa on a shoestring • Africa – the South • Arabic (Egyptian) phrasebook • Arabic (Moroccan) phrasebook • Cairo • Cape Town • Cape Town city map • Central Africa • East Africa • Egypt • Egypt travel atlas • Ethiopian (Amharic) phrasebook • The Gambia & Senegal • Healthy Travel Africa • Kenya • Kenya travel atlas • Malawi, Mozambique & Zambia • Morocco • North Africa • South Africa, Lesotho & Swaziland • South Africa, Lesotho & Swaziland travel atlas • Swahili phrasebook • Tanzania, Zanzibar & Pemba • Trekking in East Africa • Tunisia • West Africa • Zimbabwe, Botswana & Namibia • Zimbabwe, Botswana & Namibia travel atlas
Travel Literature: The Rainbird: A Central African Journey • Songs to an African Sunset: A Zimbabwean Story • Mali Blues: Traveling to an African Beat

AUSTRALIA & THE PACIFIC Auckland • Australia • Australian phrasebook • Bushwalking in Australia • Bushwalking in Papua New Guinea • Fiji • Fijian phrasebook • Islands of Australia's Great Barrier Reef • Melbourne • Melbourne city map • Micronesia • New Caledonia • New South Wales & the ACT • New Zealand • Northern Territory • Outback Australia • Out To Eat – Melbourne • Papua New Guinea • Pidgin phrasebook • Queensland • Rarotonga & the Cook Islands • Samoa • Solomon Islands • South Australia • South Pacific Languages phrasebook • Sydney • Sydney city map • Tahiti & French Polynesia • Tasmania • Tonga • Tramping in New Zealand • Vanuatu • Victoria • Western Australia
Travel Literature: Islands in the Clouds • Kiwi Tracks: A New Zealand Journey • Sean & David's Long Drive

CENTRAL AMERICA & THE CARIBBEAN Bahamas, Turks & Caicos • Bermuda • Central America on a shoestring • Costa Rica • Cuba • Dominican Republic & Haiti • Eastern Caribbean • Guatemala, Belize & Yucatán: La Ruta Maya • Jamaica • Mexico • Mexico City • Panama • Puerto Rico
Travel Literature: Green Dreams: Travels in Central America

EUROPE Amsterdam • Amsterdam city map • Andalucía • Austria • Baltic States phrasebook • Barcelona • Berlin • Berlin city map • Britain • British phrasebook • Brussels, Bruges & Antwerp • Budapest city map • Canary Islands • Central Europe • Central Europe phrasebook • Corsica • Croatia • Czech & Slovak Republics • Denmark • Dublin • Eastern Europe • Eastern Europe phrasebook • Edinburgh • Estonia, Latvia & Lithuania • Europe on a shoestring • Finland • France • French phrasebook • Germany • German phrasebook • Greece • Greek phrasebook • Hungary • Iceland, Greenland & the Faroe Islands • Ireland • Italian phrasebook • Italy • Lisbon • London • London city map • Mediterranean Europe • Mediterranean Europe phrasebook • Norway • Paris • Paris city map • Poland • Portugal • Portugal travel atlas • Prague • Prague city map • Provence & the Côte d'Azur • Romania & Moldova • Rome • Russia, Ukraine & Belarus • Russian phrasebook • Scandinavian & Baltic Europe • Scandinavian Europe phrasebook • Scotland • Slovenia • Spain • Spanish phrasebook • St Petersburg • Switzerland • Trekking in Spain • Ukrainian phrasebook • Vienna • Walking in Britain • Walking in Ireland • Walking in Italy • Walking in Spain • Walking in Switzerland • Western Europe • Western Europe phrasebook
Travel Literature: The Olive Grove: Travels in Greece

INDIAN SUBCONTINENT Bangladesh • Bengali phrasebook • Bhutan • Delhi • Goa • Hindi & Urdu phrasebook • India • India & Bangladesh travel atlas • Indian Himalaya • Karakoram Highway • Kerala • Mumbai (Bombay) • Nepal • Nepali phrasebook • Pakistan • Rajasthan • Read This First: Asia & India • South India • Sri Lanka • Sri Lanka phrasebook • Trekking in the Indian Himalaya • Trekking in the Karakoram & Hindukush • Trekking in the Nepal Himalaya
Travel Literature: In Rajasthan • Shopping for Buddhas

LONELY PLANET

Mail Order

Lonely Planet products are distributed worldwide. They are also available by mail order from Lonely Planet, so if you have difficulty finding a title please write to us. North and South American residents should write to 150 Linden St, Oakland, CA 94607, USA; European and African residents should write to 10a Spring Place, London NW5 3BH, UK; and residents of other countries to PO Box 617, Hawthorn, Victoria 3122, Australia.

ISLANDS OF THE INDIAN OCEAN Madagascar & Comoros • Maldives • Mauritius, Réunion & Seychelles

MIDDLE EAST & CENTRAL ASIA Arab Gulf States • Central Asia • Central Asia phrasebook • Hebrew phrasebook • Iran • Israel & the Palestinian Territories • Israel & the Palestinian Territories travel atlas • Istanbul • Istanbul to Cairo • Jerusalem • Jordan & Syria • Jordan, Syria & Lebanon travel atlas • Lebanon • Middle East on a shoestring • Syria • Turkey • Turkey travel atlas • Turkish phrasebook • Yemen
Travel Literature: The Gates of Damascus • Kingdom of the Film Stars: Journey into Jordan

NORTH AMERICA Alaska • Backpacking in Alaska • Baja California • California & Nevada • Canada • Chicago • Chicago city map • Deep South • Florida • Hawaii • Honolulu • Las Vegas • Los Angeles • Miami • New England • New Orleans • New York City • New York city map • New York, New Jersey & Pennsylvania • Pacific Northwest USA • Puerto Rico • Rocky Mountain • San Francisco • San Francisco city map • Seattle • Southwest USA • Texas • USA • USA phrasebook • Vancouver • Washington, DC & the Capital Region • Washington DC city map
Travel Literature: Drive Thru America

NORTH-EAST ASIA Beijing • Cantonese phrasebook • China • Hong Kong • Hong Kong city map • Hong Kong, Macau & Guangzhou • Japan • Japanese phrasebook • Japanese audio pack • Korea • Korean phrasebook • Kyoto • Mandarin phrasebook • Mongolia • Mongolian phrasebook • North-East Asia on a shoestring • Seoul • South-West China • Taiwan • Tibet • Tibetan phrasebook • Tokyo
Travel Literature: Lost Japan

SOUTH AMERICA Argentina, Uruguay & Paraguay • Bolivia • Brazil • Brazilian phrasebook • Buenos Aires • Chile & Easter Island • Chile & Easter Island travel atlas • Colombia • Ecuador & the Galapagos Islands • Latin American Spanish phrasebook • Peru • Quechua phrasebook • Rio de Janeiro • Rio de Janeiro city map • South America on a shoestring • Trekking in the Patagonian Andes • Venezuela
Travel Literature: Full Circle: A South American Journey

SOUTH-EAST ASIA Bali & Lombok • Bangkok • Bangkok city map • Burmese phrasebook • Cambodia • Hanoi • Healthy Travel Asia & India • Hill Tribes phrasebook • Ho Chi Minh City • Indonesia • Indonesia's Eastern Islands • Indonesian phrasebook • Indonesian audio pack • Jakarta • Java • Laos • Lao phrasebook • Laos travel atlas • Malay phrasebook • Malaysia, Singapore & Brunei • Myanmar (Burma) • Philippines • Pilipino (Tagalog) phrasebook • Singapore • South-East Asia on a shoestring • South-East Asia phrasebook • Thailand • Thailand's Islands & Beaches • Thailand travel atlas • Thai phrasebook • Thai audio pack • Vietnam • Vietnamese phrasebook • Vietnam travel atlas

ALSO AVAILABLE: Antarctica • The Arctic • Brief Encounters: Stories of Love, Sex & Travel • Chasing Rickshaws • Lonely Planet Unpacked • Not the Only Planet: Travel Stories from Science Fiction • Sacred India • Travel with Children • Traveller's Tales

Index

Abbreviations

NMP – National Marine Park   NP – National Park

Text

Bold indicates maps.

Bold indicates maps.

Boxed Text

MAP LEGEND

BOUNDARIES

─ ─ ─ ─ ─ International
─ ─ ─ ─ ─ Province
─ ─ ─ ─ ─ Disputed

HYDROGRAPHY

Coastline
River, Creek
Lake
Intermittent Lake
Salt Lake
Canal
Spring, Rapids
Waterfalls
Swamp

○ **CAPITAL** National Capital
◉ **CAPITAL** Provincial Capital
● **CITY** City
● Town Town
● Village Village
○ Point of Interest

■ Place to Stay
Å Camping Ground
⊞ Caravan Park
⌂ Hut or Chalet

▼ Place to Eat
▽ Pub or Bar

ROUTES & TRANSPORT

Freeway
Highway
Major Road
Minor Road
Unsealed Road
City Freeway
City Highway
City Road
City Street, Lane

Pedestrian Mall
Tunnel
Train Route & Station
Skytrain
Tramway
Cable Car or Chairlift
Walking Track
Walking Tour
Ferry Route

AREA FEATURES

Building
✿ Park, Gardens
Cemetery
Market
Beach, Desert
Urban Area

MAP SYMBOLS

✈ Airport
Ancient or City Wall
θ Bank
Beach
Bird Sanctuary, Zoo
Cathedral, Church
Cave
Dive Site, Snorkelling
Embassy, Hospital
Fort, Monument
Golf Course, Picnic Area
Mosque, Pagoda
▲ Mountain or Hill
🏛 Museum, Stately Home

National Park
)(Pass
★ Police Station
Post Office, Telephone
Shopping Centre
Stupa or Chedi
Surf Beach
Temple
Temple (Hindu)
Temple (Sikh)
Temple (Taoist)
Tourist Information
Trail Head, Lookout
Transport, Petrol Station

Note: not all symbols displayed above appear in this book

LONELY PLANET OFFICES

Australia
PO Box 617, Hawthorn, Victoria 3122
☎ 03 9819 1877 fax 03 9819 6459
email: talk2us@lonelyplanet.com.au

USA
150 Linden St, Oakland, CA 94607
☎ 510 893 8555 TOLL FREE: 800 275 8555
fax 510 893 8572
email: info@lonelyplanet.com

UK
10a Spring Place, London NW5 3BH
☎ 020 7428 4800 fax 020 7428 4828
email: go@lonelyplanet.co.uk

France
1 rue du Dahomey, 75011 Paris
☎ 01 55 25 33 00 fax 01 55 25 33 01
email: bip@lonelyplanet.fr
www.lonelyplanet.fr

World Wide Web: www.lonelyplanet.com _or_ AOL keyword: lp
Lonely Planet Images: lpi@lonelyplanet.com.au